Texas Estate Planning Statutes

Texas Estate Planning Statutes

Student Edition

Gerry W. Beyer
St. Mary's University School of Law

1185 Avenue of the Americas, New York, NY 10036
www.aspenpublishers.com

A Wolters Kluwer Company
www.aspenpublishers.com

Printed in the United States of America

1 2 3 4 5 6 7 8 9 0

ISBN 0-7355-4138-8

ISSN 1545-6447

About Aspen Publishers

Aspen Publishers, headquartered in New York City, is a leading information provider for attorneys, business professionals, and law students. Written by preeminent authorities, our products consist of analytical and practical information covering both U.S. and international topics. We publish in the full range of formats, including updated manuals, books, periodicals, CDs, and online products.

Our proprietary content is complemented by 2,500 legal databases, containing over 11 million documents, available through our Loislaw division. Aspen Publishers also offers a wide range of topical legal and business databases linked to Loislaw's primary material. Our mission is to provide accurate, timely, and authoritative content in easily accessible formats, supported by unmatched customer care.

To order any Aspen Publishers title, go to *www.aspenpublishers.com* or call 1-800-638-8437.

To reinstate your manual update service, call 1-800-638-8437.

For more information on Loislaw products, go to *www.loislaw.com* or call 1-800-364-2512.

For Customer Care issues, email *CustomerCare@aspenpublishers.com,* call 1-800-234-1660, or fax 1-800-901-9075.

Aspen Publishers
A Wolters Kluwer Company

SUMMARY OF CONTENTS

CONTENTS

CONTENTS

CONTENTS

CONTENTS

CONTENTS

CONTENTS

CONTENTS

CONTENTS

CONTENTS

PREFACE

Texas Estate Planning Statutes: Student Edition is a compilation of Texas statutes that are significant to courses related to estate planning such as Wills & Estates, Trusts, Estate Planning, Elder Law, and Guardianship. I have included commentary entitled *Statutes in Context* in many sections. These annotations provide background information, explanations, and citations to key cases and should assist you in identifying the significance of the statutes and how they operate.

Despite my best efforts and those of the publisher, errors may have crept into the text or the *Statutes in Context.* In addition, new cases and legislation make important changes to the law. You may access a list of updates to this work at *http://www.ProfessorBeyer.com*.

I invite you to assist me in making the next edition of this book even more useful. Please let me know if you detect any problems with this book or have suggestions for future editions. I am especially interested in recommendations regarding other statutes that should be included and areas in which additional commentary would be helpful. You may contact me via e-mail at gwb@ProfessorBeyer.com.

Good luck in your course and in your legal career.

The author wishes to thank the following individuals for their assistance in the preparation of this book.

Aspen Publishers Personnel: Lynn Churchill, Suzanne Rapcavage, and Kathy Yoon.

Student Assistants: Erik C. Greiner, Jennifer A. Owens, and Katharine L. Smith.

Gerry W. Beyer
St. Mary's University
November 2003

Texas Estate Planning Statutes

I.

Business and Commerce Code

Title 3. Insolvency, Fraudulent Transfers, and Fraud

Chapter 24. Uniform Fraudulent Transfer Act

Statutes in Context

A creditor may set aside a transfer if that transfer meets the requirements set forth in the Texas version of the Uniform Fraudulent Transfer Act. This Act frequently comes into play when a donor makes an outright gift or creates a trust which would otherwise restrict the ability of an existing or future creditor to get paid from the transferred property. Note that a disclaimer under Probate Code § 37A or Property Code § 112.010 will not be considered as fraudulent even if the disclaiming beneficiary's intent is to keep the property away from the beneficiary's creditors (definition of "transfer" in § 24.002(12)).

§ 24.001. Short Title

This chapter may be cited as the Uniform Fraudulent Transfer Act.

Amended by Acts 1987, 70th Leg., ch. 1004, § 1, eff. Sept. 1, 1987.

§ 24.002. Definitions

In this chapter:

(1) "Affiliate" means:

(A) a person who directly or indirectly owns, controls, or holds with power to vote, 20 percent or more of the outstanding voting securities of the debtor, other than a person who holds the securities:

(i) as a fiduciary or agent without sole discretionary power to vote the securities; or

(ii) solely to secure a debt, if the person has not exercised the power to vote;

(B) a corporation 20 percent or more of whose outstanding voting securities are directly or indirectly owned, controlled, or held with power to vote, by the debtor or a person who directly or indirectly owns, controls, or holds, with power to vote, 20 percent or more of the outstanding voting securities of the debtor, other than a person who holds the securities:

(i) as a fiduciary or agent without sole power to vote the securities; or

(ii) solely to secure a debt, if the person has not in fact exercised the power to vote;

(C) a person whose business is operated by the debtor under a lease or other agreement, or a person substantially all of whose assets are controlled by the debtor; or

(D) a person who operates the debtor's business under a lease or other agreement or controls substantially all of the debtor's assets.

(2) "Asset" means property of a debtor, but the term does not include:

(A) property to the extent it is encumbered by a valid lien;

(B) property to the extent it is generally exempt under nonbankruptcy law; or

(C) an interest in property held in tenancy by the entireties to the extent it is not subject to process by a creditor holding a claim against only one tenant, under the law of another jurisdiction.

(3) "Claim" means a right to payment or property, whether or not the right is reduced to judgment, liquidated, unliquidated, fixed, contingent, matured, unmatured, disputed, undisputed, legal, equitable, secured, or unsecured.

(4) "Creditor" means a person, including a spouse, minor, person entitled to receive court or administratively ordered child support for the benefit of a child, or ward, who has a claim.

(5) "Debt" means a liability on a claim.

(6) "Debtor" means a person who is liable on a claim.

(7) "Insider" includes:

(A) if the debtor is an individual:

(i) a relative of the debtor or of a general partner of the debtor;

(ii) a partnership in which the debtor is a general partner;

(iii) a general partner in a partnership described in Subparagraph (ii) of this paragraph; or

(iv) a corporation of which the debtor is a director, officer, or person in control;

(B) if the debtor is a corporation:

(i) a director of the debtor;

(ii) an officer of the debtor;

(iii) a person in control of the debtor;

(iv) a partnership in which the debtor is a general partner;

(v) a general partner in a partnership described in Subparagraph (iv) of this paragraph; or

(vi) a relative of a general partner, director, officer, or person in control of the debtor;

(C) if the debtor is a partnership:

(i) a general partner in the debtor;

(ii) a relative of a general partner in, a general partner of, or a person in control of the debtor;

(iii) another partnership in which the debtor is a general partner;

(iv) a general partner in a partnership described in Subparagraph (iii) of this paragraph; or

(v) a person in control of the debtor;

(D) an affiliate, or an insider of an affiliate as if the affiliate were the debtor; and

(E) a managing agent of the debtor.

(8) "Lien" means a charge against or an interest in property to secure payment of a debt or performance of an obligation, and includes a security interest created by agreement, a judicial lien obtained by legal or equitable process or proceedings, a common-law lien, or a statutory lien.

(9) "Person" means an individual, partnership, corporation, association, organization, government or governmental subdivision or agency, business trust, estate, trust, or any other legal or commercial entity.

(10) "Property" means anything that may be the subject of ownership.

(11) "Relative" means an individual related by consanguinity within the third degree as determined by the common law, a spouse, or an individual related to a spouse within the third degree as so determined, and includes an individual in an adoptive relationship

within the third degree.

(12) "Transfer" means every mode, direct or indirect, absolute or conditional, voluntary or involuntary, of disposing of or parting with an asset or an interest in an asset, and includes payment of money, release, lease, and creation of a lien or other encumbrance. The term does not include a transfer under a disclaimer filed under Section 37A, Texas Probate Code, or Section 112.010, Property Code.

(13) "Valid lien" means a lien that is effective against the holder of a judicial lien subsequently obtained by legal or equitable process or proceedings.

Amended by Acts 1987, 70th Leg., ch. 1004, § 1, eff. Sept. 1, 1987. Amended by Acts 1993, 73rd Leg., ch. 846, § 2, eff. Sept. 1, 1993; Acts 1997, 75th Leg., ch. 911, § 95, eff. Sept. 1, 1997.

§ 24.003. Insolvency

(a) A debtor is insolvent if the sum of the debtor's debts is greater than all of the debtor's assets at a fair valuation.

(b) A debtor who is generally not paying the debtor's debts as they become due is presumed to be insolvent.

(c) A partnership is insolvent under Subsection (a) of this section if the sum of the partnership's debts is greater than the aggregate, at a fair valuation, of all of the partnership's assets and the sum of the excess of the value of each general partner's nonpartnership assets over the partner's nonpartnership debts.

(d) Assets under this section do not include property that has been transferred, concealed, or removed with intent to hinder, delay, or defraud creditors or that has been transferred in a manner making the transfer voidable under this chapter.

(e) Debts under this section do not include an obligation to the extent it is secured by a valid lien on property of the debtor not included as an asset.

Amended by Acts 1987, 70th Leg., ch. 1004, § 1, eff. Sept. 1, 1987. Amended by Acts 1993, 73rd Leg., ch. 570, § 8, eff. Sept. 1, 1993.

§ 24.004. Value

(a) Value is given for a transfer or an obligation if, in exchange for the transfer or obligation, property is transferred or an antecedent debt is secured or satisfied, but value does not include an unperformed promise made otherwise than in the ordinary course of the promisor's business to furnish support to the debtor or another person.

(b) For the purposes of Sections 24.005 (a)(2) and 24.006 of this code, a person gives a reasonably equivalent value if the person acquires an interest of the debtor in an asset pursuant to a regularly conducted, noncollusive foreclosure sale or execution of a power of sale for the acquisition or disposition of the interest of the debtor upon default under a mortgage, deed of trust, or security agreement.

(c) A transfer is made for present value if the exchange between the debtor and the transferee is intended by them to be contemporaneous and is in fact substantially contemporaneous.

(d) "Reasonably equivalent value" includes without limitation, a transfer or obligation that is within the range of values for which the transferor would have sold the assets in an arm's length transaction.

Amended by Acts 1987, 70th Leg., ch. 1004, § 1, eff. Sept. 1, 1987. Amended by Acts 1993, 73rd Leg., ch. 570, § 9, eff. Sept. 1, 1993.

§ 24.005. Transfers Fraudulent as to Present and Future Creditors

(a) A transfer made or obligation incurred by a debtor is fraudulent as to a creditor, whether the creditor's claim arose before or within a reasonable time after the transfer was made or the obligation was incurred, if the debtor made the transfer or incurred the obligation:

(1) with actual intent to hinder, delay, or defraud any creditor of the debtor; or

(2) without receiving a reasonably equivalent value in exchange for the transfer or obligation, and the debtor:

(A) was engaged or was about to engage in a business or a transaction for which the remaining assets of the debtor were unreasonably small in relation to the business or transaction; or

(B) intended to incur, or believed or reasonably should have believed that the debtor would incur, debts beyond the debtor's ability to pay as they became due.

(b) In determining actual intent under Subsection (a)(1) of this section, consideration may be given, among other factors, to whether:

(1) the transfer or obligation was to an insider;

(2) the debtor retained possession or control of the property transferred after the transfer;

(3) the transfer or obligation was concealed;

(4) before the transfer was made or obligation was incurred, the debtor had been sued or threatened with suit;

(5) the transfer was of substantially all the debtor's assets;

(6) the debtor absconded;

(7) the debtor removed or concealed assets;

(8) the value of the consideration received by the debtor was reasonably equivalent to the value of the asset transferred or the amount of the obligation incurred;

(9) the debtor was insolvent or became insolvent shortly after the transfer was made or the obligation was incurred;

(10) the transfer occurred shortly before or shortly after a substantial debt was incurred; and

(11) the debtor transferred the essential assets of the business to a lienor who transferred the assets to an insider of the debtor.

Amended by Acts 1987, 70th Leg., ch. 1004, § 1, eff. Sept. 1, 1987. Amended by Acts 1993, 73rd Leg., ch. 570, § 10, eff. Sept. 1, 1993.

§ 24.006. Transfers Fraudulent as to Present Creditors

(a) A transfer made or obligation incurred by a debtor is fraudulent as to a creditor whose claim arose before the transfer was made or the obligation was incurred if the debtor made the transfer or incurred the obligation without receiving a reasonably equivalent value in exchange for the transfer or obligation and the debtor was insolvent at that time or the debtor became insolvent as a result of the transfer or obligation.

(b) A transfer made by a debtor is fraudulent as to a creditor whose claim arose before the transfer was made if the transfer was made to an insider for an antecedent debt, the debtor was insolvent at that time, and the insider had reasonable cause to believe that the debtor was insolvent.

Amended by Acts 1987, 70th Leg., ch. 1004, § 1, eff. Sept. 1, 1987.

§ 24.007. When Transfer is Made or Obligation is Incurred

For the purposes of this chapter:

(1) a transfer is made:

(A) with respect to an asset that is real property other than a fixture, but including the interest of a seller or purchaser under a contract for the sale of the asset, when the transfer is so far perfected that a good faith purchaser of the asset from the debtor against whom applicable law permits the transfer to be perfected cannot acquire an interest in the asset that is superior to the interest of the transferee; and

(B) with respect to an asset that is not real property or that is a fixture, when the transfer is so far perfected that a creditor on a simple contract cannot acquire a judicial lien otherwise than under this chapter that is superior to the interest of the transferee;

(2) if applicable law permits the transfer to be perfected as provided in Subdivision (1) of this section and the transfer is not so perfected before the commencement of an action for relief under this chapter, the transfer is deemed made immediately before the commencement of the action;

(3) if applicable law does not permit the transfer to be perfected as provided in Subdivision (1) of this section, the transfer is made when it becomes effective between the debtor and the transferee;

(4) a transfer is not made until the debtor has acquired rights in the asset transferred; and

(5) an obligation is incurred:

(A) if oral, when it becomes effective between the parties; or

(B) if evidenced by a writing, when the writing executed by the obligor is delivered to or for the benefit of the obligee.

Amended by Acts 1987, 70th Leg., ch. 1004, § 1, eff. Sept. 1, 1987.

§ 24.008. Remedies of Creditors

(a) In an action for relief against a transfer or obligation under this chapter, a creditor, subject to the limitations in Section 24.009 of this code, may obtain:

(1) avoidance of the transfer or obligation to the extent necessary to satisfy the creditor's claim;

(2) an attachment or other provisional remedy against the asset transferred or other property of the transferee in accordance with the applicable Texas Rules of Civil Procedure and the Civil Practice and Remedies Code relating to ancillary proceedings; or

(3) subject to applicable principles of equity and in accordance with applicable rules of civil procedure:

(A) an injunction against further disposition by the debtor or a transferee, or both, of the asset transferred or of other property;

(B) appointment of a receiver to take charge of the asset transferred or of other property of the transferee; or

(C) any other relief the circumstances may require.

(b) If a creditor has obtained a judgment on a claim against the debtor, the creditor, if the court so orders, may levy execution on the asset transferred or its proceeds.

Amended by Acts 1987, 70th Leg., ch. 1004, § 1, eff. Sept. 1, 1987.

§ 24.009. Defenses, Liability, and Protection of Transferee

(a) A transfer or obligation is not voidable under Section 24.005 (a)(1) of this code against a person who took in good faith and for a reasonably equivalent value or against any subsequent transferee or obligee.

(b) Except as otherwise provided in this section, to the extent a transfer is voidable in an action by a creditor under Section 24.008 (a)(1) of this code, the creditor may recover judgment for the value of the asset transferred, as adjusted under Subsection (c) of this section, or the amount necessary to satisfy the creditor's claim, whichever is less. The judgment may be entered against:

(1) the first transferee of the asset or the person for whose benefit the transfer was made; or

(2) any subsequent transferee other than a good faith transferee who took for value or from any subsequent transferee.

(c)(1) Except as provided by Subdivision (2) of this subsection, if the judgment under Subsection (b) of this section is based upon the value of the asset transferred, the judgment must be for an amount equal to the value of the asset at the time of the transfer, subject to adjustment as the equities may require.

(2) The value of the asset transferred is not to be adjusted to include the value of improvements made by a good faith transferee, including:

(A) physical additions or changes to the asset transferred;

(B) repairs to the asset;

(C) payment of any tax on the asset;

(D) payment of any debt secured by a lien on the asset that is superior or equal to the rights of a voiding creditor under this chapter; and

(E) preservation of the asset.

(d)(1) Notwithstanding voidability of a transfer or an obligation under this chapter, a good faith transferee or obligee is entitled, at the transferee's or obligee's election, to the extent of the value given the debtor for the transfer or obligation, to:

(A) a lien, prior to the rights of a voiding creditor under this chapter, or a right to retain any interest in the asset transferred;

(B) enforcement of any obligation incurred; or

(C) a reduction in the amount of the liability on the judgment.

(2) Notwithstanding voidability of a transfer under this chapter, to the extent of the value of any improvements made by a good faith transferee, the good faith transferee is entitled to a lien on the asset transferred prior to the rights of a voiding creditor under this chapter

(e) A transfer is not voidable under Section 24.005(a)(2) or Section 24.006 of this code if the transfer results from:

(1) termination of a lease upon default by the debtor when the termination is pursuant to the lease and applicable law; or

(2) enforcement of a security interest in compliance with Chapter 9 of this code.[1]

(f) A transfer is not voidable under Section 24.006 (b) of this code:

(1) to the extent the insider gave new value to or for the benefit of the debtor after the transfer was made unless the new value was secured by a valid lien;

(2) if made in the ordinary course of business or financial affairs of the debtor and the insider; or

(3) if made pursuant to a good-faith effort to rehabilitate the debtor and the transfer secured present value given for that purpose as well as an antecedent debt of the debtor.

Amended by Acts 1987, 70th Leg., ch. 1004, § 1, eff. Sept. 1, 1987. Amended by Acts 1993, 73rd Leg., ch. 570, § 11, eff. Sept. 1, 1993.

§ 24.010. Extinguishment of Cause of Action

(a) Except as provided by Subsection (b) of this section, a cause of action with respect to a fraudulent transfer or obligation under this chapter is extinguished unless action is brought:

(1) under Section 24.005 (a)(1) of this code, within four years after the transfer was made or the obligation was incurred or, if later, within one year after the transfer or obligation was or could reasonably have been discovered by the claimant;

(2) under Section 24.005 (a)(2) or 24.006 (a) of this code, within four years after the transfer was made or the obligation was incurred; or

(3) under Section 24.006 (b) of this code, within one year after the transfer was made.

(b) A cause of action on behalf of a spouse, minor, or ward with respect to a fraudulent transfer or obligation under this chapter is extinguished unless the action is brought:

(1) under Section 24.005 (a) or 24.006 (a) of this code, within two years after the cause of action accrues, or if later, within one year after the transfer

[1] V.T.C.A., Bus. & C. § 9.101 et seq.

or obligation was or could reasonably have been discovered by the claimant; or

(2) under Section 24.006 (b) of this code within one year after the date the transfer was made.

(c) If a creditor entitled to bring an action under this chapter is under a legal disability when a time period prescribed by this section starts, the time of the disability is not included in the period. A disability that arises after the period starts does not suspend the running of the period. A creditor may not tack one legal disability to another to extend the period. For the purposes of this subsection, a creditor is under a legal disability if the creditor is:

(1) younger than 18 years of age, regardless of whether the person is married; or

(2) of unsound mind.

Amended by Acts 1987, 70th Leg., ch. 1004, § 1, eff. Sept. 1, 1987. Amended by Acts 1993, 73rd Leg., ch. 570, § 12, eff. Sept. 1, 1993.

§ 24.011. Supplementary Provisions

Unless displaced by the provisions of this chapter, the principles of law and equity, including the law merchant and the law relating to principal and agent, estoppel, laches, fraud, misrepresentation, duress, coercion, mistake, insolvency, or other validating or invalidating cause, supplement its provisions.

Amended by Acts 1987, 70th Leg., ch. 1004, § 1, eff. Sept. 1, 1987.

§ 24.012. Uniformity of Application and Construction

This chapter shall be applied and construed to effectuate its general purpose to make uniform the law with respect to the subject of this chapter among states enacting it.

Amended by Acts 1987, 70th Leg., ch. 1004, § 1, eff. Sept. 1, 1987.

§ 24.013. Costs.

In any proceeding under this chapter, the court may award costs and reasonable attorney's fees as are equitable and just.

Added by Acts 2003, 78th Leg., ch. 420, § 1, eff. Sept. 1, 2003.

II.
Civil Practice and Remedies Code

Title 2. Trial, Judgment, and Appeal

Subtitle B. Trial Matters

Chapter 15. Venue

Subchapter A. Definitions; General Rules

Statutes in Context

The venue provisions of the Probate Code trump many of the normal venue provisions contained in the Civil Practice and Remedies Code.

§ 15.007. Conflict With Certain Provisions

Notwithstanding Sections 15.004, 15.005, and 15.031, to the extent that venue under this chapter for a suit by or against an executor, administrator, or guardian as such, for personal injury, death, or property damage conflicts with venue provisions under the Texas Probate Code, this chapter controls.

Acts 1995, 74th Leg., ch. 138, § 1, eff. Aug. 28, 1995.

Subchapter B. Mandatory Venue

Statutes in Context

Civil Practice and Remedies Code §§ 15.011 and 15.031 contain venue provisions that may impact the proper location in which to bring a suit involving estates and trusts.

§ 15.011. Land

Actions for recovery of real property or an estate or interest in real property, for partition of real property, to remove encumbrances from the title to real property, for recovery of damages to real property, or to quiet title to real property shall be brought in the county in which all or a part of the property is located.

Acts 1985, 69th Leg., ch. 959, § 1, eff. Sept. 1, 1985. Amended by Acts 1995, 74th Leg., ch. 138, § 2, eff. Aug. 28, 1995.

Subchapter C. Permissive Venue

§ 15.031. Executor; Administrator; Guardian

If the suit is against an executor, administrator, or guardian, as such, to establish a money demand against the estate which he represents, the suit may be brought in the county in which the estate is administered, or if the suit is against an executor, administrator, or guardian growing out of a negligent act or omission of the person whose estate the executor, administrator, or guardian represents, the suit may be brought in the county in which the negligent act or omission of the person whose estate the executor, administrator, or guardian represents occurred.

Acts 1985, 69th Leg., ch. 959, § 1, eff. Sept. 1, 1985.

Chapter 16. Limitations

Subchapter A. Limitations of Personal Actions

Statutes in Context

The comprehensive provisions of Chapter 16 provide statutes of limitations for a variety of causes of action. Section 16.062 is of particular importance because it extends the running of a limitations period for 12 months after the decedent's death, unless a personal representative is appointed sooner in which case the limitations period resumes running at the time the personal representative qualifies.

§ 16.001. Effect of Disability

(a) For the purposes of this subchapter, a person is under a legal disability if the person is:

(1) younger than 18 years of age, regardless of whether the person is married; or

(2) of unsound mind.

(b) If a person entitled to bring a personal action is under a legal disability when the cause of action ion accrues, the time of the disability is not included in a limitations period.

(c) A person may not tack one legal disability to another to extend a limitations period.

(d) A disability that arises after a limitations period starts does not suspend the running of the period.

Acts 1985, 69th Leg., ch. 959, § 1, eff. Sept. 1, 1985. Amended by Acts 1987, 70th Leg., ch. 1049, § 56, eff. Sept. 1, 1987.

§ 16.002. One-Year Limitations Period

(a) A person must bring suit for malicious prosecution, libel, slander, or breach of promise of marriage not later than one year after the day the cause of action accrues.

(b) A person must bring suit to set aside a sale of property seized under Subchapter E, Chapter 33, Tax Code,[1] not later than one year after the date the property is sold.

Acts 1985, 69th Leg., ch. 959, § 1, eff. Sept. 1, 1985. Amended by Acts 1995, 74th Leg., ch. 1017, § 3, eff. Aug. 28, 1995.

§ 16.003. Two-Year Limitations Period

(a) Except as provided by Sections 16.010 and 16.0045, a person must bring suit for trespass for injury to the estate or to the property of another, conversion of personal property, taking or detaining the personal property of another, personal injury, forcible entry and detainer, and forcible detainer not later than two years after the day the cause of action accrues.

(b) A person must bring suit not later than two years after the day the cause of action accrues in an action for injury resulting in death. The cause of action accrues on the death of the injured person.

Acts 1985, 69th Leg., ch. 959, § 1, eff. Sept. 1, 1985. Amended by Acts 1995, 74th Leg., ch. 739, § 2, eff. June 15, 1995; Acts 1997, 75th Leg., ch. 26, § 2, eff. May 1, 1997.

§ 16.004. Four-Year Limitations Period

(a) A person must bring suit on the following actions not later than four years after the day the cause of action accrues:

(1) specific performance of a contract for the conveyance of real property;

(2) penalty or damages on the penal clause of a bond to convey real property;

(3) debt;

(4) fraud; or

(5) breach of fiduciary duty.

(b) A person must bring suit on the bond of an executor, administrator, or guardian not later than four years after the day of the death, resignation, removal, or discharge of the executor, administrator, or guardian.

(c) A person must bring suit against his partner for a settlement of partnership accounts, and must bring an action on an open or stated account, or on a mutual and current account concerning the trade of merchandise between merchants or their agents or factors, not later than four years after the day that the cause of action accrues. For purposes of this subsection, the cause of action accrues on the day that the dealings in which the parties were interested together cease.

Acts 1985, 69th Leg., ch. 959, § 1, eff. Sept. 1, 1985. Amended by Acts 1999, 76th Leg., ch. 950, § 1, eff. Aug. 30, 1999.

[1] V.T.C.A., Tax Code § 33.91 et seq.

§ 16.0045. Five-Year Limitations Period

(a) A Person must bring suit for personal injury not later than five years after the day the cause of action accrues if the injury arises as a result of conduct that violates:

(1) Section 22.011, Penal Code (sexual assault); or

(2) Section 22.021, Penal Code (aggravated sexual assault).

(b) In an action for injury resulting in death arising as a result of conduct described by Subsection (a), the cause of action accrues on the death of the injured person.

(c) The limitations period under this section is tolled for a suit on the filing of a petition by any person in an appropriate court alleging that the identity of the defendant in the suit is unknown and designating the unknown defendant as "John or Jane Doe." The person filing the petition shall proceed with due diligence to discover the identity of the defendant and amend the petition by substituting the real name of the defendant for "John or Jane Doe" not later than the 30th day after the date that the defendant is identified to the plaintiff. The limitations period begins running again on the date that the petition is amended.

Added by Acts 1995, 74th Leg., ch. 739, § 1, eff. June 15, 1995.

§ 16.005. Action for Closing Street or Road

(a) A person must bring suit for any relief from the following acts not later than two years after the day the cause of action accrues:

(1) the passage by a governing body of an incorporated city or town of an ordinance closing and abandoning, or attempting to close and abandon, all or any part of a public street or alley in the city or town, other than a state highway; or

(2) the adoption by a commissioners court of an order closing and abandoning, or attempting to close and abandon, all or any part of a public road or thoroughfare in the county, other than a state highway.

(b) The cause of action accrues when the order or ordinance is passed or adopted.

(c) If suit is not brought within the period provided by this section, the person in possession of the real property receives complete title to the property by limitations and the right of the city or county to revoke or rescind the order or ordinance is barred.

Acts 1985, 69th Leg., ch. 959, § 1, eff. Sept. 1, 1985.

§ 16.006. Carriers of Property

(a) A carrier of property for compensation or hire must bring suit for the recovery of charges not later than three years after the day on which the cause of action accrues.

(b) Except as provided by Subsections (c) and (d), a person must bring suit for overcharges against a carrier of property for compensation or hire not later than three years after the cause of action accrues.

(c) If the person has presented a written claim for the overcharges within the three-year period, the limitations period is extended for six months from the date written notice is given by the carrier to the claimant of disallowance of the claim in whole or in part, as specified in the carrier's notice.

(d) If on or before the expiration of the three-year period, the carrier brings an action under Subsection (a) to recover charges relating to the service or, without beginning an action, collects charges relating to that service, the limitations period is extended for 90 days from the day on which the action is begun or the charges are collected.

(e) A cause of action regarding a shipment of property accrues on the delivery or tender of the property by the carrier.

(f) In this section, "overcharge" means a charge for transportation services in excess of the lawfully applicable amount.

Acts 1985, 69th Leg., ch. 959, § 1, eff. Sept. 1, 1985.

§ 16.007. Return of Execution

A person must bring suit against a sheriff or other officer or the surety of the sheriff or officer for failure to return an execution issued in the person's favor, not later than five years after the date on which the execution was returnable.

Acts 1985, 69th Leg., ch. 959, § 1, eff. Sept. 1, 1985.

§ 16.008. Architects, Engineers, Interior Designers, and Landscape Architects Furnishing Design, Planning, or Inspection of Construction of Improvements

(a) A person must bring suit for damages for a claim listed in Subsection (b) against a registered or licensed architect, engineer, interior designer, or landscape architect in this state, who designs, plans, or inspects the construction of an improvement to real property or equipment attached to real property, not later than 10 years after the substantial completion of the improvement or the beginning of operation of the equipment in an action arising out of a defective or unsafe condition of the real property, the improvement, or the equipment.

(b) This section applies to suit for:

(1) injury, damage, or loss to real or personal property;

(2) personal injury;

(3) wrongful death;

(4) contribution; or

(5) indemnity.

(c) If the claimant presents a written claim for damages, contribution, or indemnity to the architect, engineer, interior designer, or landscape architect within the 10-year limitations period, the period is extended for two years from the day the claim is presented.

Acts 1985, 69th Leg., ch. 959, § 1, eff. Sept. 1, 1985. Amended by Acts 1997, 75th Leg., ch. 860, § 1, eff. Sept. 1, 1997.

§ 16.009. Persons Furnishing Construction or Repair of Improvements

(a) A claimant must bring suit for damages for a claim listed in Subsection (b) against a person who constructs or repairs an improvement to real property not later than 10 years after the substantial completion of the improvement in an action arising out of a defective or unsafe condition of the real property or a deficiency in the construction or repair of the improvement.

(b) This section applies to suit for:

(1) injury, damage, or loss to real or personal property;

(2) personal injury;

(3) wrongful death;

(4) contribution; or

(5) indemnity.

(c) If the claimant presents a written claim for damages, contribution, or indemnity to the person performing or furnishing the construction or repair work during the 10-year limitations period, the period is extended for two years from the date the claim is presented.

(d) If the damage, injury, or death occurs during the 10th year of the limitations period, the claimant may bring suit not later than two years after the day the cause of action accrues.

(e) This section does not bar an action:

(1) on a written warranty, guaranty, or other contract that expressly provides for a longer effective period;

(2) against a person in actual possession or control of the real property at the time that the damage, injury, or death occurs; or

(3) based on wilful misconduct or fraudulent concealment in connection with the performance of the construction or repair.

(f) This section does not extend or affect a period prescribed for bringing an action under any other law of this state.

Acts 1985, 69th Leg., ch. 959, § 1, eff. Sept. 1, 1985.

§ 16.010. Misappropriation of Trade Secrets

(a) A person must bring suit for misappropriation of trade secrets not later than three years after the misappropriation is discovered or by the exercise of reasonable diligence should have been discovered.

(b) A misappropriation of trade secrets that continues over time is a single cause of action and the limitations period described by Subsection (a) begins running without regard to whether the misappropriation is a single or continuing act.

Added by Acts 1997, 75th Leg., ch. 26, § 1, eff. May 1, 1997.

§ 16.011. Surveyors

(a) A person must bring suit for damages arising from an injury or loss caused by an error in a survey conducted by a registered public surveyor or a licensed state land surveyor:

(1) not later than 10 years after the date the survey is completed if the survey is completed on or after September 1, 1989; or

(2) not later than September 1, 1991, or 10 years after the date the survey was completed, whichever is later, if the survey was completed before September 1, 1989.

(b) If the claimant presents a written claim for damages to the surveyor during the 10-year limitations period, the period is extended for two years from the date the claim is presented.

(c) This section is a statute of repose and is independent of any other limitations period.

Added by Acts 1989, 71st Leg., ch. 1233, § 1, eff. Sept. 1, 1989. Amended by Acts 2001, 77th Leg., ch. 1173, § 1, eff. Sept. 1, 2001.

§ 16.012. Products Liability: Manufacturing Equipment

(a) In this section:

(1) "Claimant," "seller," and "manufacturer" have the meanings assigned by Section 82.001.

(2) "Products liability action" means any action against a manufacturer or seller for recovery of damages or other relief for harm allegedly caused by a defective product, whether the action is based in strict tort liability, strict products liability, negligence, misrepresentation, breach of express or implied warranty, or any other theory or combination of theories, and whether the relief sought is recovery of damages or any other legal or equitable relief, including a suit for:

(A) injury or damage to or loss of real or personal property;

(B) personal injury;

(C) wrongful death;

(D) economic loss; or

(E) declaratory, injunctive, or other equitable relief.

(b) Except as provided by Subsections (c), (d), and (d-1), a claimant must commence a products liability action against a manufacturer or seller of a product before the end of 15 years after the date of the sale of the product by the defendant.

(c) If a manufacturer or seller expressly warrants in writing that the product has a useful safe life of longer than 15 years, a claimant must commence a products liability action against that manufacturer or seller of the product before the end of the number of years warranted after the date of the sale of the product by that seller.

(d) This section does not apply to a products liability action seeking damages for personal injury or wrongful death in which the claimant alleges:

(1) the claimant was exposed to the product that is the subject of the action before the end of 15 years after the date the product was first sold;

(2) the claimant's exposure to the product caused the claimant's disease that is the basis of the action; and

(3) the symptoms of the claimant's disease did not, before the end of 15 years after the date of the first sale of the product by the defendant, manifest themselves to a degree and for a duration that would put a reasonable person on notice that the person suffered some injury.

(d-1) This section does not reduce a limitations period for a cause of action described by Subsection (d) that accrues before the end of the limitations period under this section.

(e) This section does not extend the limitations period within which a products liability action involving the product may be commenced under any other law.

(f) This section applies only to the sale and not to the lease of a product.

(g) This section does not apply to any claim to which the General Aviation Revitalization Act of 1994 (Pub. L. No. 103-298, 108 Stat. 1552 (1994), reprinted in note, 49 U.S.C. Section 40101) or its exceptions are applicable.

Added by Acts 1993, 73rd Leg., ch. 5, § 2 eff. Sept. 1, 1993. Amended by Acts 2003, 78th Leg., ch. 204, § 5.01, eff. Sept. 1, 2003.

Subchapter B. Limitations of Real Property Actions

§ 16.021. Definitions

In this subchapter:

(1) "Adverse possession" means an actual and visible appropriation of real property, commenced and continued under a claim of right that is inconsistent with and is hostile to the claim of another person.

(2) "Color of title" means a consecutive chain of transfers to the person in possession that:

(A) is not regular because of a muniment that is not properly recorded or is only in writing or because of a similar defect that does not want of intrinsic fairness or honesty; or

(B) is based on a certificate of headright, land warrant, or land scrip.

(3) "Peaceable possession" means possession of real property that is continuous and is not interrupted by an adverse suit to recover the property.

(4) "Title" means a regular chain of transfers of real property from or under the sovereignty of the soil.

Acts 1985, 69th Leg., ch. 959, § 1, eff. Sept. 1, 1985.

§ 16.022. Effect of Disability

(a) For the purposes of this subchapter, a person is under a legal disability if the person is:

(1) younger than 18 years of age, regardless of whether the person is married:

(2) of unsound mind; or

(3) serving in the United States Armed Forces during time of war.

(b) If a person entitled to sue for the recovery of real property or entitled to make a defense based on the title to real property is under a legal disability at the time title to the property vests or adverse possession commences, the time of the disability is not included in a limitations period.

(c) Except as provided by Sections 16.027 and 16.028, after the termination of the legal disability, a person has the same time to present a claim that is allowed to others under this chapter.

Amended by Acts 1987, 70th Leg., ch. 1049, § 57, eff. Sept. 1, 1987.

§ 16.023. Tacking of Successive Interests

To satisfy a limitations period, peaceable and adverse possession does not need to continue in the same person, but there must be privity of estate between each holder and his successor.

Acts 1985, 69th Leg., ch. 959, § 1, eff. Sept. 1, 1985.

§ 16.024. Adverse Possession: Three-Year Limitations Period

A person must bring suit to recover real property held by another in peaceable and adverse possession under title or color of title not later than three years after the day the cause of action accrues.

Acts 1985, 69th Leg., ch. 959, § 1, eff. Sept. 1, 1985.

§ 16.025. Adverse Possession: Five-Year Limitations Period

(a) A person must bring suit not later than five years after the day the cause of action accrues to recover real property held in peaceable and adverse possession by another who:

(1) cultivates, uses, or enjoys the property;

(2) pays applicable taxes on the property; and

(3) claims the property under a duly registered deed.

(b) This section does not apply to a claim based on a forged deed or a deed executed under a forged power of attorney.

Acts 1985, 69th Leg., ch. 959, § 1, eff. Sept. 1, 1985.

§ 16.026. Adverse Possession: 10-Year Limitations Period

(a) A person must bring suit not later than 10 years after the day the cause of action accrues to recover real property held in peaceable and adverse possession by another who cultivates, uses, or enjoys the property.

(b) Without a title instrument, peaceable and adverse possession is limited in this section to 160 acres, including improvements, unless the number of acres actually enclosed exceeds 160. If the number of enclosed acres exceeds 160 acres, peaceable and adverse possession extends to the real property actually enclosed.

(c) Peaceable possession of real property held under a duly registered deed or other memorandum of title that fixes the boundaries of the possessor's claim extends to the boundaries specified in the instrument.

Acts 1985, 69th Leg., ch. 959, § 1, eff. Sept. 1, 1985. Amended by Acts 1989, 71st Leg., ch. 764, § 1, eff. Sept. 1, 1989.

§ 16.027. Adverse Possession: 25-Year Limitations Period Notwithstanding Disability

A person, regardless of whether the person is or has been under a legal disability, must bring suit not later than 25 years after the day the cause of action accrues to recover real property held in peaceable and adverse possession by another who cultivates, uses, or enjoys the property.

Acts 1985, 69th Leg., ch. 959, § 1, eff. Sept. 1, 1985.

§ 16.028. Adverse Possession With Recorded Instrument: 25-Year Limitations Period

(a) A person, regardless of whether the person is or has been under a legal disability, may not maintain an action for the recovery of real property held for 25 years before the commencement of the action in peaceable and adverse possession by another who holds the property in good faith and under a deed or other instrument purporting to convey the property that is recorded in the deed records of the county where any part of the real property is located.

(b) Adverse possession of any part of the real property held under a recorded deed or other recorded instrument that purports to convey the property extends to and includes all of the property described in the instrument, even though the instrument is void on its face or in fact.

(c) A person who holds real property and claims title under this section has a good and marketable title to the property regardless of a disability arising at any time in the adverse claimant or a person claiming under the adverse claimant.

Acts 1985, 69th Leg., ch. 959, § 1, eff. Sept. 1, 1985.

§ 16.029. Evidence of Title to Land by Limitations

(a) In a suit involving title to real property that is not claimed by this state, it is prima facie evidence that the title to the property has passed from the person holding apparent record title to an opposing party if it is shown that:

(1) for one or more years during the 25 years preceding the filing of the suit the person holding apparent record title to the property did not exercise dominion over or pay taxes on the property; and

(2) during that period the opposing parties and those whose estate they own have openly exercised dominion over and have asserted a claim to the land and have paid taxes on it annually before becoming delinquent for as long as 25 years.

(b) This section does not affect a statute of limitations, a right to prove title by circumstantial evidence under the case law of this state, or a suit between a trustee and a beneficiary of the trust.

Acts 1985, 69th Leg., ch. 959, § 1, eff. Sept. 1, 1985.

§ 16.030. Title Through Adverse Possession

(a) If an action for the recovery of real property is barred under this chapter, the person who holds the property in peaceable and adverse possession has full title, precluding all claims.

(b) A person may not acquire through adverse possession any right or title to real property dedicated to public use.

Acts 1985, 69th Leg., ch. 959, § 1, eff. Sept. 1, 1985.

§ 16.031. Enclosed Land

(a) A tract of land that is owned by one person and that is entirely surrounded by land owned, claimed, or fenced by another is not considered enclosed by a fence that encloses any part of the surrounding land.

(b) Possession of the interior tract by the owner or claimant of the surrounding land is not peaceable and adverse possession as described by Section 16.026 unless:

(1) the interior tract is separated from the surrounding land by a fence; or

(2) at least one-tenth of the interior tract is cultivated and used for agricultural purposes or is used for manufacturing purposes.

Acts 1985, 69th Leg., ch. 959, § 1, eff. Sept. 1, 1985.

§ 16.032. Adjacent Land

Possession of land that belongs to another by a person owning or claiming 5,000 or more fenced acres that adjoin the land is not peaceable and adverse as described by Section 16.026 unless:

(1) the land is separated from the adjacent enclosed tract by a substantial fence;

(2) at least one-tenth of the land is cultivated and used for agricultural purposes or used for manufacturing purposes; or

(3) there is actual possession of the land.

Acts 1985, 69th Leg., ch. 959, § 1, eff. Sept. 1, 1985.

§ 16.033. Technical Defects in Instrument

(a) A person with a right of action for the recovery of real property conveyed by an instrument with one of the following defects must bring suit not later than four years after the day the instrument was recorded with the county clerk of the county where the real property is located:

(1) lack of the signature of a proper corporate officer, partner, or company officer, manager, or member;

(2) lack of a corporate seal;

(3) failure of the record to show the corporate seal used;

(4) failure of the record to show authority of the board of directors or stockholders of a corporation, partners of a partnership, or officers, managers, or members of a company;

(5) execution and delivery of the instrument by a corporation, partnership, or other company that had been dissolved, whose charter had expired, or whose franchise had been canceled, withdrawn, or forfeited;

(6) acknowledgment of the instrument in an individual, rather than a representative or official, capacity;

(7) execution of the instrument by a trustee without record of the authority of the trustee or proof of the facts recited in the instrument;

(8) failure of the record or instrument to show an acknowledgment or jurat that complies with applicable law; or

(9) wording of the stated consideration that may or might create an implied lien in favor of the grantor.

(b) This section does not apply to a forged instrument.

Acts 1985, 69th Leg., ch. 959, § 1, eff. Sept. 1, 1985. Amended by Acts 1993, 73rd Leg., ch. 291, § 1, eff. Sept. 1, 1993.

§ 16.034. Attorney's Fees

(a) In a suit for the possession of real property between a person claiming under record title to the property and one claiming by adverse possession, if the prevailing party recovers possession of the property from a person unlawfully in actual possession, the court may award costs and reasonable attorney's fees to the prevailing party.

(b) To recover attorney's fees, the person seeking possession must give the person unlawfully in possession a written demand for that person to vacate the premises. The demand must be given by registered or certified mail at least 10 days before filing the claim for recovery of possession.

(c) The demand must state that if the person unlawfully in possession does not vacate the premises within 10 days and a claim is filed by the person seeking possession, the court may enter a judgment against the person unlawfully in possession for costs and attorney's fees in an amount determined by the court to be reasonable.

Acts 1985, 69th Leg., ch. 959, § 1, eff. Sept. 1, 1985.

§ 16.035. Lien on Real Property

(a) A person must bring suit for the recovery of real property under a real property lien or the foreclosure of a real property lien not later than four years after the day the cause of action accrues.

(b) A sale of real property under a power of sale in a mortgage or deed of trust that creates a real property lien must be made not later than four years after the day the cause of action accrues.

(c) The running of the statute of limitations is not suspended against a bona fide purchaser for value, a lienholder, or a lessee who has no notice or knowledge of the suspension of the limitations period and who acquires an interest in the property when a cause of action on an outstanding real property lien has accrued for more than four years, except as provided by:

(1) Section 16.062, providing for suspension in the event of death; or

(2) Section 16.036, providing for recorded extensions of real property liens.

(d) On the expiration of the four-year limitations period, the real property lien and a power of sale to enforce the real property lien become void.

(e) If a series of notes or obligations or a note or obligation payable in installments is secured by a real property lien, the four-year limitations period does not begin to run until the maturity date of the last note, obligation, or installment.

(f) The limitations period under this section is not affected by Section 3.118, Business & Commerce Code.

(g) In this section, "real property lien" means:

(1) a superior title retained by a vendor in a deed of conveyance or a purchase money note; or

(2) a vendor's lien, a mortgage, a deed of trust, a voluntary mechanic's lien, or a voluntary materialman's lien on real estate, securing a note or other written obligation.

Acts 1985, 69th Leg., ch. 959, § 1, eff. Sept. 1, 1985. Amended by Acts 1997, 75th Leg., ch. 219, § 1, eff. May 23, 1997.

§ 16.036. Extension of Real Property Lien

(a) The party or parties primarily liable for a debt or obligation secured by a real property lien, as that term is defined in Section 16.035, may suspend the running of the four-year limitations period for real property liens through a written extension agreement as provided by this section.

(b) The limitations period is suspended and the lien remains in effect for four years after the extended maturity date of the debt or obligation if the extension agreement is:

(1) signed and acknowledged as provided by law for a deed conveying real property; and

(2) filed for record in the county clerk's office of the county where the real property is located.

(c) The parties may continue to extend the lien by entering, acknowledging, and recording additional extension agreements.

(d) The maturity date stated in the original instrument or in the date of the recorded renewal and extension is conclusive evidence of the maturity date of the debt or obligation.

(e) The limitations period under this section is not affected by Section 3.118, Business & Commerce Code.

Acts 1985, 69th Leg., ch. 959, § 1, eff. Sept. 1, 1985. Amended by Acts 1997, 75th Leg., ch. 219, § 2, eff. May 23, 1997.

§ 16.037. Effect of Extension of Real Property Lien on Third Parties

An extension agreement is void as to a bona fide purchaser for value, a lienholder, or a lessee who deals with real property affected by a real property lien without actual notice of the agreement and before the agreement is acknowledged, filed, and recorded.

Acts 1985, 69th Leg., ch. 959, § 1, eff. Sept. 1, 1985. Amended by Acts 1997, 75th Leg., ch. 219, § 3, eff. May 23, 1997.

Subchapter C. Residual Limitations Period

§ 16.051. Residual Limitations Period

Every action for which there is no express limitations period, except an action for the recovery of real property, must be brought not later than four years after the day the cause of action accrues.

Acts 1985, 69th Leg., ch. 959, § 1, eff. Sept. 1, 1985.

Subchapter D. Miscellaneous Provisions

§ 16.061. Rights Not Barred

(a) A right of action of this state or a political subdivision of the state, including a county, an incorporated city or town, a navigation district, a municipal utility district, a port authority, an entity acting under Chapter 54, Transportation Code, a school district, or an entity created under Section 52, Article III, or Section 59, Article XVI, Texas Constitution, is not barred by any of the following sections: 16.001-16.004, 16.006, 16.007, 16.021-16.028, 16.030-16.032, 16.035-16.037, 16.051, 16.062, 16.063, 16.065-16.067, 16.070, 16.071, 31.006, or 71.021.

(b) In this section:

(1) "Navigation district" means a navigation district organized under Section 52, Article III, or Section 59, Article XVI, Texas Constitution.

(2) "Port authority" has the meaning assigned by Section 60.402, Water Code.

(3) "Municipal utility district" means a municipal utility district created under Section 52, Article III, or Section 59, Article XVI, Texas Constitution.

Acts 1985, 69th Leg., ch. 959, § 1, eff. Sept. 1, 1985. Amended by Acts 1989, 71st Leg., ch. 2, § 4.02, eff. Aug. 28, 1989; Acts 1993, 73rd Leg., ch. 782, § 1, eff. Aug. 30, 1993; Amended by Acts 1997, 75th Leg., ch. 1070, § 47, eff. Sept. 1, 1997; Amended by Acts 2001, 77th Leg., ch. 1420, § 8.204, eff. Sept. 1, 2001.

§ 16.062. Effect of Death

(a) The death of a person against whom or in whose favor there may be a cause of action suspends the running of an applicable statute of limitations for 12 months after the death.

(b) If an executor or administrator of a decedent's estate qualifies before the expiration of the period provided by this section, the statute of limitations begins to run at the time of the qualification.

Acts 1985, 69th Leg., ch. 959, § 1, eff. Sept. 1, 1985.

§ 16.063. Temporary Absence From State

The absence from this state of a person against whom a cause of action may be maintained suspends the running of the applicable statute of limitations for the period of the person's absence.

Acts 1985, 69th Leg., ch. 959, § 1, eff. Sept. 1, 1985.

§ 16.064. Effect of Lack of Jurisdiction

(a) The period between the date of filing an action in a trial court and the date of a second filing of the same action in a different court suspends the running of the applicable statute of limitations for the period if:

(1) because of lack of jurisdiction in the trial court where the action was first filed, the action is dismissed or the judgment is set aside or annulled in a direct proceeding; and

(2) not later than the 60th day after the date the dismissal or other disposition becomes final, the action is commenced in a court of proper jurisdiction.

(b) This section does not apply if the adverse party has shown in abatement that the first filing was made with intentional disregard of proper jurisdiction.

Acts 1985, 69th Leg., ch. 959, § 1, eff. Sept. 1, 1985.

§ 16.065. Acknowledgment of Claim

An acknowledgment of the justness of a claim that appears to be barred by limitations is not admissible in evidence to defeat the law of limitations if made after the time that the claim is due unless the acknowledgment is in writing and is signed by the party to be charged.

Acts 1985, 69th Leg., ch. 959, § 1, eff. Sept. 1, 1985.

§ 16.066. Action on Foreign Judgment

(a) An action on a foreign judgment is barred in this state if the action is barred under the laws of the jurisdiction where rendered.

(b) An action against a person who has resided in this state for 10 years prior to the action may not be brought on a foreign judgment rendered more than 10 years before the commencement of the action in this state.

(c) In this section "foreign judgment" means a judgment or decree rendered in another state or a foreign country.

Acts 1985, 69th Leg., ch. 959, § 1, eff. Sept. 1, 1985.

§ 16.067. Claim Incurred Prior to Arrival in This State

(a) A person may not bring an action to recover a claim against a person who has moved to this state if the claim is barred by the law of limitations of the state or country from which the person came.

(b) A person may not bring an action to recover money from a person who has moved to this state and who was released from its payment by the bankruptcy or insolvency laws of the state or country from which the person came.

(c) A demand that is against a person who has moved to this state and was incurred prior to his arrival in this state is not barred by the law of limitations until the person has lived in this state for 12 months. This subsection does not affect the application of Subsections (a) and (b).

Acts 1985, 69th Leg., ch. 959, § 1, eff. Sept. 1, 1985.

§ 16.068. Amended and Supplemental Pleadings

If a filed pleading relates to a cause of action, cross action, counterclaim, or defense that is not subject to a plea of limitation when the pleading is filed, a subsequent amendment or supplement to the pleading that changes the facts or grounds of liability or defense is not subject to a plea of limitation unless the amendment or supplement is wholly based on a new, distinct, or different transaction or occurrence.

Acts 1985, 69th Leg., ch. 959, § 1, eff. Sept. 1, 1985.

§ 16.069. Counterclaim or Cross Claim

(a) If a counterclaim or cross claim arises out of the same transaction or occurrence that is the basis of an action, a party to the action may file the counterclaim or cross claim even though as a separate action it would be barred by limitation on the date the party's answer is required.

(b) The counterclaim or cross claim must be filed not later than the 30th day after the date on which the party's answer is required.

Acts 1985, 69th Leg., ch. 959, § 1, eff. Sept. 1, 1985.

§ 16.070. Contractual Limitations Period

(a) Except as provided by Subsection (b), a person may not enter a stipulation, contract, or agreement that purports to limit the time in which to bring suit on the stipulation, contract, or agreement to a period shorter than two years. A stipulation, contract, or agreement that establishes a limitations period that is shorter than two years is void in this state.

(b) This section does not apply to a stipulation, contract, or agreement relating to the sale or purchase of a business entity if a party to the stipulation, contract, or agreement pays or receives or is obligated to pay or entitled to receive consideration under the stipulation, contract, or agreement having an aggregate value of not less than $500,000.

Acts 1985, 69th Leg., ch. 959, § 1, eff. Sept. 1, 1985. Amended by Acts 1991, 72nd Leg., ch. 840, § 2, eff. Aug. 26, 1991.

§ 16.071. Notice Requirements

(a) A contract stipulation that requires a claimant to give notice of a claim for damages as a condition precedent to the right to sue on the contract is not valid unless the stipulation is reasonable. A stipulation that requires notification within less than 90 days is void.

(b) If notice is required, the claimant may notify any convenient agent of the company that requires the notice.

(c) A contract stipulation between the operator of a railroad, street railway, or interurban railroad and an employee or servant of the operator is void if it requires as a condition precedent to liability:

(1) the employee or servant to notify the system of a claim for damages for personal injury caused by negligence; or

(2) the spouse, parent, or child of a deceased employee or servant to notify the system of a claim of death caused by negligence.

(d) This section applies to a contract between a federal prime contractor and a subcontractor, except that the notice period stipulated in the subcontract may be for a period not less than the period stipulated in the prime contract, minus seven days.

(e) In a suit covered by this section or Section 16.070, it is presumed that any required notice has been given unless lack of notice is specifically pleaded under oath.

(f) This section does not apply to a contract relating to the sale or purchase of a business entity if a party to the contract pays or receives or is obligated to pay or receive consideration under the contract having an aggregate value of not less than $500,000.

Acts 1985, 69th Leg., ch. 959, § 1, eff. Sept. 1, 1985. Amended by Acts 1991, 72nd Leg., ch. 840, § 3, eff. Aug. 26, 1991.

§ 16.072. Saturday, Sunday, or Holiday

If the last day of a limitations period under any statute of limitations falls on a Saturday, Sunday, or holiday, the period for filing suit is extended to include the next day that the county offices are open for business.

Acts 1985, 69th Leg., ch. 959, § 1, eff. Sept. 1, 1985.

Subtitle C. Judgments

Chapter 37. Declaratory Judgments

Statutes in Context

Civil Practice and Remedies Code §§ 37.001–37.011 is the Texas version of the Uniform Declaratory Judgments Act. Of particular importance to trusts and estates is § 37.005 which gives the court broad authority to resolve any question which arises in the administration of a trust or estate, including the power to construe wills.

§ 37.001. Definition

In this chapter, "person" means an individual, partnership, joint-stock company, unincorporated association or society, or municipal or other corporation of any character.

Acts 1985, 69th Leg., ch. 959, § 1, eff. Sept. 1, 1985.

§ 37.002. Short Title, Construction, Interpretation

(a) This chapter may be cited as the Uniform Declaratory Judgments Act.

(b) This chapter is remedial; its purpose is to settle and to afford relief from uncertainty and insecurity with respect to rights, status, and other legal relations; and it is to be liberally construed and administered.

(c) This chapter shall be so interpreted and construed as to effectuate its general purpose to make uniform the law of those states that enact it and to harmonize, as far as possible, with federal laws and regulations on the subject of declaratory judgments and decrees.

Acts 1985, 69th Leg., ch. 959, § 1, eff. Sept. 1, 1985.

§ 37.003. Power of Courts to Render Judgment; Form and Effect

(a) A court of record within its jurisdiction has power to declare rights, status, and other legal relations whether or not further relief is or could be claimed. An action or proceeding is not open to objection on the ground that a declaratory judgment or decree is prayed for.

(b) The declaration may be either affirmative or negative in form and effect, and the declaration has the force and effect of a final judgment or decree.

(c) The enumerations in Sections 37.004 and 37.005 do not limit or restrict the exercise of the general powers conferred in this section in any proceeding in which declaratory relief is sought and a judgment or decree will terminate the controversy or remove an uncertainty.

Acts 1985, 69th Leg., ch. 959, § 1, eff. Sept. 1, 1985.

§ 37.004. Subject Matter of Relief

(a) A person interested under a deed, will, written contract, or other writings constituting a contract or whose rights, status, or other legal relations are affected by a statute, municipal ordinance, contract, or franchise may have determined any question of construction or validity arising under the instrument, statute, ordinance, contract, or franchise and obtain a declaration of rights, status, or other legal relations thereunder.

(b) A contract may be construed either before or after there has been a breach.

Acts 1985, 69th Leg., ch. 959, § 1, eff. Sept. 1, 1985.

§ 37.005. Declarations Relating to Trust or Estate

A person interested as or through an executor or administrator, including an independent executor or administrator, a trustee, guardian, other fiduciary, creditor, devisee, legatee, heir, next of kin, or cestui que trust in the administration of a trust or of the estate of a decedent, an infant, mentally incapacitated person, or insolvent may have a declaration of rights or legal relations in respect to the trust or estate:

(1) to ascertain any class of creditors, devisees, legatees, heirs, next of kin, or others;

(2) to direct the executors, administrators, or trustees to do or abstain from doing any particular act in their fiduciary capacity;

(3) to determine any question arising in the administration of the trust or estate, including questions of construction of wills and other writings; or

(4) to determine rights or legal relations of an independent executor or independent administrator regarding fiduciary fees and the settling of accounts.

Acts 1985, 69th Leg., ch. 959, § 1, eff. Sept. 1, 1985. Amended by Acts 1987, 70th Leg., ch. 167, § 3.08(a), eff. Sept. 1, 1987. Amended by Acts 1999, 76th Leg., ch. 855, § 10, eff. Sept. 1, 1999.

§ 37.006. Parties

(a) When declaratory relief is sought, all persons who have or claim any interest that would be affected by the declaration must be made parties. A declaration does not prejudice the rights of a person not a party to the proceeding.

(b) In any proceeding that involves the validity of a municipal ordinance or franchise, the municipality must be made a party and is entitled to be heard, and if the statute, ordinance, or franchise is alleged to be unconstitutional, the attorney general of the state must also be served with a copy of the proceeding and is entitled to be heard.

Acts 1985, 69th Leg., ch. 959, § 1, eff. Sept. 1, 1985.

§ 37.007. Jury Trial

If a proceeding under this chapter involves the determination of an issue of fact, the issue may be tried and determined in the same manner as issues of fact are tried and determined in other civil actions in the court in which the proceeding is pending.

Acts 1985, 69th Leg., ch. 959, § 1, eff. Sept. 1, 1985.

§ 37.008. Court Refusal to Render

The court may refuse to render or enter a declaratory judgment or decree if the judgment or decree would not terminate the uncertainty or controversy giving rise to the proceeding.

Acts 1985, 69th Leg., ch. 959, § 1, eff. Sept. 1, 1985.

§ 37.009. Costs

In any proceeding under this chapter, the court may award costs and reasonable and necessary attorney's fees as are equitable and just.

Acts 1985, 69th Leg., ch. 959, § 1, eff. Sept. 1, 1985.

§ 37.010. Review

All orders, judgments, and decrees under this chapter may be reviewed as other orders, judgments, and decrees.

Acts 1985, 69th Leg., ch. 959, § 1, eff. Sept. 1, 1985.

§ 37.011. Supplemental Relief

Further relief based on a declaratory judgment or decree may be granted whenever necessary or proper. The application must be by petition to a court having jurisdiction to grant the relief. If the application is deemed sufficient, the court shall, on reasonable notice, require any adverse party whose rights have been adjudicated by the declaratory judgment or decree to show cause why further relief should not be granted forthwith.

Acts 1985, 69th Leg., ch. 959, § 1, eff. Sept. 1, 1985.

Title 4. Liability in Tort

Chapter 71. Wrongful Death; Survival; Injuries Occurring Out of State

Statutes in Context

Civil Practice and Remedies Code §§ 71.001–71.052 deal with survival and wrongful death actions. The distinction between these two actions is important. A survival action is normally brought by the personal representative of the decedent for damages to which the decedent would have been entitled if the decedent had not died. The decedent may or may not have already filed suit for these damages prior to death. Any recovery is distributed as part of the decedent's estate. On the other hand, a wrongful death action is usually brought by the person(s) specified in § 71.004 (surviving spouse, children, or parents) and any recovery belongs to that person regardless of how the decedent's property would pass under intestacy or by will.

Subchapter A. Wrongful Death

§ 71.001. Definitions

In this subchapter:

(1) "Corporation" means a municipal, private, public, or quasi-public corporation other than a county or a common or independent school district.

(2) "Person" means an individual, association of individuals, joint-stock company, or corporation or a trustee or receiver of an individual, association of individuals, joint-stock company, or corporation.

(3) "Death" includes, for an individual who is an unborn child, the failure to be born alive.

(4) "Individual" includes an unborn child at every stage of gestation from fertilization until birth.

Acts 1985, 69th Leg., ch. 959, § 1, eff. Sept. 1, 1985. Amended by Acts 2003, 78th Leg., ch. 822, § 1.01, eff. Sept. 1, 2003.

§ 71.002. Cause of Action

(a) An action for actual damages arising from an injury that causes an individual's death may be brought if liability exists under this section.

(b) A person is liable for damages arising from an injury that causes an individual's death if the injury was caused by the person's or his agent's or servant's wrongful act, neglect, carelessness, unskillfulness, or default.

(c) A person is liable for damages arising from an injury that causes an individual's death if:

(1) the person is a proprietor, owner, charterer, or hirer of an industrial or public utility plant or of a railroad, street railway, steamboat, stagecoach, or other vehicle for the transportation of goods or passengers; and

(2) the injury was caused by the person's or his agent's or servant's wrongful act, neglect, carelessness, unskillfulness, or default.

(d) A person is liable for damages arising from an injury that causes an individual's death if:

(1) the person is a receiver, trustee, or other person in charge of or in control of a railroad, street railway, steamboat, stagecoach, or other vehicle for the transportation of goods or passengers, of an industrial or public utility plant, or of other machinery; and

(2) the injury was caused by:

(A) the person's wrongful act, neglect, carelessness, unskillfulness, or default;

(B) the person's servant's or agent's wrongful act, neglect, carelessness, unfitness, unskillfulness, or default; or

(C) a bad or unsafe condition of the railroad, street railway, or other machinery under the person's control or operation.

(e) A person is liable for damages arising from an injury that causes an individual's death if:

(1) the person is a receiver, trustee, or other person in charge of or in control of a railroad, street railway, steamboat, stagecoach, or other vehicle for the transportation of goods or passengers, of an industrial or public utility plant, or of other machinery; and

(2) the action could have been brought against the owner of the railroad, street railway, or other machinery if he had been acting as operator.

Acts 1985, 69th Leg., ch. 959, § 1, eff. Sept. 1, 1985.

§ 71.003. Application; Certain Conduct Excepted

(a) This subchapter applies only if the individual injured would have been entitled to bring an action for the injury if the individual had lived or had been born alive.

(b) This subchapter applies whether the injury occurs inside or outside this state.

(c) This subchapter does not apply to a claim for the death of an individual who is an unborn child that is brought against:

(1) the mother of the unborn child;

(2) a physician or other licensed health care provider, if the death is the intended result of a lawful medical procedure performed by the physician or health care provider with the requisite consent;

(3) a person who dispenses or administers a drug in accordance with law, if the death is the result of the dispensation or administration of the drug; or

(4) a physician or other health care provider licensed in this state, if the death directly or indirectly is caused by, associated with, arises out of, or relates to a lawful medical or health care practice or procedure of the physician or the health care provider.

Acts 1985, 69th Leg., ch. 959, § 1, eff. Sept. 1, 1985. Amended by Acts 2003, 78th Leg., ch. 822, § 1.02, eff. Sept. 1, 2003.

§ 71.004. Benefiting From and Bringing Action

(a) An action to recover damages as provided by this subchapter is for the exclusive benefit of the surviving spouse, children, and parents of the deceased.

(b) The surviving spouse, children, and parents of the deceased may bring the action or one or more of those individuals may bring the action for the benefit of all.

(c) If none of the individuals entitled to bring an action have begun the action within three calendar months after the death of the injured individual, his executor or administrator shall bring and prosecute the action unless requested not to by all those individuals.

Acts 1985, 69th Leg., ch. 959, § 1, eff. Sept. 1, 1985.

§ 71.005. Evidence Relating to Marital Status

In an action under this subchapter, evidence of the actual ceremonial remarriage of the surviving spouse is admissible, if it is true, but the defense is prohibited from directly or indirectly mentioning or alluding to a common-law marriage, an extramarital relationship, or the marital prospects of the surviving spouse.

Acts 1985, 69th Leg., ch. 959, § 1, eff. Sept. 1, 1985.

§ 71.0055. Evidence of Pregnancy

In an action under this subchapter for the death of an individual who is an unborn child, the plaintiff shall provide medical or other evidence that the mother of the individual was pregnant at the time of the individual's death.

Added by Acts 2003, 78th Leg., ch. 822, § 1.03, eff. Sept. 1, 2003.

§ 71.006. Effect of Felonious Act

An action under this subchapter is not precluded because the death is caused by a felonious act or because there may be a criminal proceeding in relation to the felony.

Acts 1985, 69th Leg., ch. 959, § 1, eff. Sept. 1, 1985.

§ 71.007. Ineffective Agreement

An agreement between the owner of a railroad, street railway, steamboat, stagecoach, or other vehicle for the transportation of goods or passengers,

of an industrial or public utility plant, or of other machinery and an individual, corporation, trustee, receiver, lessee, joint-stock association, or other entity in control of or operating the vehicle, plant, or other machinery does not release the owner or the entity controlling or operating the vehicle, plant, or other machinery from liability provided by this subchapter.
Acts 1985, 69th Leg., ch. 959, § 1, eff. Sept. 1, 1985.

§ 71.008. Death of Defendant

(a) If a defendant dies while an action under this subchapter is pending or if the individual against whom the action may have been instituted dies before the action is begun, the executor or administrator of the estate may be made a defendant, and the action may be prosecuted as though the defendant or individual were alive.

(b) A judgment in favor of the plaintiff shall be paid in due course of administration.
Acts 1985, 69th Leg., ch. 959, § 1, eff. Sept. 1, 1985.

§ 71.009. Exemplary Damages

When the death is caused by the wilful act or omission or gross negligence of the defendant, exemplary as well as actual damages may be recovered.
Acts 1985, 69th Leg., ch. 959, § 1, eff. Sept. 1, 1985.

§ 71.010. Award and Apportionment of Damages

(a) The jury may award damages in an amount proportionate to the injury resulting from the death.

(b) The damages awarded shall be divided, in shares as found by the jury in its verdict, among the individuals who are entitled to recover and who are alive at that time.
Acts 1985, 69th Leg., ch. 959, § 1, eff. Sept. 1, 1985.

§ 71.011. Damages Not Subject to Debts

Damages recovered in an action under this subchapter are not subject to the debts of the deceased.
Acts 1985, 69th Leg., ch. 959, § 1, eff. Sept. 1, 1985.

§ 71.012. Qualification of Foreign Personal Representative

If the executor or administrator of the estate of a nonresident individual is the plaintiff in an action under this subchapter, the foreign personal representative of the estate who has complied with the requirements of Section 95, Texas Probate Code, for the probate of a foreign will is not required to apply for ancillary letters testamentary under Section 105, Texas Probate Code, to bring and prosecute the action.
Added by Acts 1999, 76th Leg., ch. 382, § 1, eff. May 29, 1999.

Subchapter B. Survival

§ 71.021. Survival of Cause of Action

(a) A cause of action for personal injury to the health, reputation, or person of an injured person does not abate because of the death of the injured person or because of the death of a person liable for the injury.

(b) A personal injury action survives to and in favor of the heirs, legal representatives, and estate of the injured person. The action survives against the liable person and the person's legal representatives.

(c) The suit may be instituted and prosecuted as if the liable person were alive.
Acts 1985, 69th Leg., ch. 959, § 1, eff. Sept. 1, 1985.

§ 71.022. Qualification of Foreign Personal Representative

If the executor or administrator of the estate of a nonresident individual is the plaintiff in an action under this subchapter, the foreign personal representative of the estate who has complied with the requirements of Section 95, Texas Probate Code, for the probate of a foreign will is not required to apply for ancillary letters testamentary under Section 105, Texas Probate Code, to bring and prosecute the action.
Added by Acts 1999, 76th Leg., ch. 382, § 2, eff. May 29, 1999.

Subchapter C. Death or Injury Caused by Act or Omission Out of State

§ 71.031. Act or Omission Out of State

(a) An action for damages for the death or personal injury of a citizen of this state, of the United States, or of a foreign country may be enforced in the courts of this state, although the wrongful act, neglect, or default causing the death or injury takes place in a foreign state or country, if:

(1) a law of the foreign state or country or of this state gives a right to maintain an action for damages for the death or injury;

(2) the action is begun in this state within the time provided by the laws of this state for beginning the action;

(3) for a resident of a foreign state or country, the action is begun in this state within the time provided by the laws of the foreign state or country in which the wrongful act, neglect, or default took place; and

(4) in the case of a citizen of a foreign country, the country has equal treaty rights with the United States on behalf of its citizens.

(b) Except as provided by Subsection (a), all matters pertaining to procedure in the prosecution or maintenance of the action in the courts of this state are governed by the law of this state.

(c) The court shall apply the rules of substantive law that are appropriate under the facts of the case.
Acts 1985, 69th Leg., ch. 959, § 1, eff. Sept. 1, 1985. Amended by Acts 1997, 75th Leg., ch. 424, § 3, eff. May 29, 1997.

Chapter 84. Charitable Immunity and Liability

Statutes in Context

A charitable trust originally could not be liable for tort damages because of the doctrine of charitable immunity. In *Howle v. Camp Amon Carter*, 470 S.W.2d 629 (Tex. 1971), the Texas Supreme Court abolished charitable immunity for torts occurring after March 9, 1966. The Charitable Immunity and Liability Act of 1987, contained in Civil Practice and Remedies Code §§ 84.001–84.008, reinstates, in specified circumstances, charitable immunity for volunteers and limits the liability of employees of charities. Note that liability is restricted only for acts of ordinary negligence.

§ 84.001. Name of Act

This Act may be cited as the Charitable Immunity and Liability Act of 1987.

Added by Acts 1987, 70th Leg., ch. 370, § 1, eff. Sept. 1, 1987.

§ 84.002. Findings and Purposes

The Legislature of the State of Texas finds that:

(1) robust, active, bona fide, and well-supported charitable organizations are needed within Texas to perform essential and needed services;

(2) the willingness of volunteers to offer their services to these organizations is deterred by the perception of personal liability arising out of the services rendered to these organizations;

(3) because of these concerns over personal liability, volunteers are withdrawing from services in all capacities;

(4) these same organizations have a further problem in obtaining and affording liability insurance for the organization and its employees and volunteers;

(5) these problems combine to diminish the services being provided to Texas and local communities because of higher costs and fewer programs;

(6) the citizens of this state have an overriding interest in the continued and increased delivery of these services that must be balanced with other policy considerations; and

(7) because of the above conditions and policy considerations, it is the purpose of this Act to reduce the liability exposure and insurance costs of these organizations and their employees and volunteers in order to encourage volunteer services and maximize the resources devoted to delivering these services.

Added by Acts 1987, 70th Leg., ch. 370, § 1, eff. Sept. 1, 1987.

§ 84.003. Definitions

In this chapter:

(1) "Charitable organization" means:

(A) any organization exempt from federal income tax under Section 501(a) of the Internal Revenue Code of 1986[1] by being listed as an exempt organization in Section 501(c)(3) or 501(c)(4) of the code,[2] if it is a nonprofit corporation, foundation, community chest, or fund organized and operated exclusively for charitable, religious, prevention of cruelty to children or animals, youth sports and youth recreational, neighborhood crime prevention or patrol, fire protection or prevention, emergency medical or hazardous material response services, or educational purposes, including private primary or secondary schools, if accredited by a member association of the Texas Private School Accreditation Commission but excluding fraternities, sororities, and secret societies,or is organized and operated exclusively for the promotion of social welfare by being primarily engaged in promoting the common good and general welfare of the people in a community;

(B) any bona fide charitable, religious, prevention of cruelty to children or animals, youth sports and youth recreational, neighborhood crime prevention or patrol, or educational organization, excluding fraternities, sororities, and secret societies, or other organization organized and operated exclusively for the promotion of social welfare by being primarily engaged in promoting the common good and general welfare of the people in a community, and that:

(i) is organized and operated exclusively for one or more of the above purposes;

(ii) does not engage in activities which in themselves are not in furtherance of the purpose or purposes;

(iii) does not directly or indirectly participate or intervene in any political campaign on behalf of or in opposition to any candidate for public office;

(iv) dedicates its assets to achieving the stated purpose or purposes of the organization;

(v) does not allow any part of its net assets on dissolution of the organization to inure to the benefit of any group, shareholder, or individual; and

(vi) normally receives more than one-third of its support in any year from private or public gifts, grants, contributions, or membership fees;

(C) a homeowners association as defined by Section 528(c) of the Internal Revenue Code of 1986[3] or which is exempt from federal income tax under Section 501(a) of the Internal Revenue

---

[1] 26 U.S.C.A. § 501(a).

[2] 26 U.S.C.A. § 501(c)(3), 501(e)(4).

[3] 26 U.S.C.A. 528(c).

Code of 1986 by being listed as an exempt organization in Section 501(c)(4) of the code;

(D) a volunteer center, as that term is defined by Section 411.126, Government Code; or

(E) a local chamber of commerce that:

(i) is exempt from federal income tax under Section 501(a) of the Internal Revenue Code of 1986 by being listed as an exempt organization in Section 501(c)(6) of the code;

(ii) does not directly or indirectly participate or intervene in any political campaign on behalf of or in opposition to any candidate for public office; and

(iii) does not directly or indirectly contribute to a political action committee that makes expenditures to any candidates for public office.

(2) "Volunteer" means a person rendering services for or on behalf of a charitable organization who does not receive compensation in excess of reimbursement for expenses incurred. The term includes a person serving as a director, officer, trustee, or direct service volunteer, including a volunteer health care provider.

(3) "Employee" means any person, including an officer or director, who is in the paid service of a charitable organization, but does not include an independent contractor.

(4) (Repealed)

(5) "Volunteer health care provider" means an individual who voluntarily provides health care services without compensation or expectation of compensation and who is:

(A) an individual who is licensed to practice medicine under Subtitle B, Title 3, Occupations Code;

(B) a retired physician who is eligible to provide health care services, including a retired physician who is licensed but exempt from paying the required annual registration fee under Section 156.002, Occupations Code;

(C) a physician assistant licensed under Chapter 204, Occupations Code, or a retired physician assistant who is eligible to provide health care services under the law of this state;

(D) a registered nurse, including an advanced nurse practitioner or vocational nurse, licensed under Chapter 301, Occupations Code, or a retired vocational nurse or registered nurse, including a retired advanced nurse practitioner, who is eligible to provide health care services under the law of this state;

(E) a pharmacist licensed under Subtitle J, Title 3, Occupations Code, or a retired pharmacist who is eligible to provide health care services under the law of this state;

(F) a podiatrist licensed under Chapter 202, Occupations Code, or a retired podiatrist who is eligible to provide health care services under the law of this state;

(G) a dentist licensed under Subtitle D, Title 3, Occupations Code, or a retired dentist who is eligible to provide health care services under the law of this state;

(H) a dental hygienist licensed under Subtitle D, Title 3, Occupations Code, or a retired dental hygienist who is eligible to provide health care services under the law of this state; or

(I) an optometrist or therapeutic optometrist licensed under Chapter 351, Occupations Code, or a retired optometrist or therapeutic optometrist who is eligible to provide health care services under the law of this state.

(6) "Hospital system" means a system of hospitals and other health care providers located in this state that are under the common governance or control of a corporate parent.

(7) "Person responsible for the patient" means:

(A) the patient's parent, managing conservator, or guardian;

(B) the patient's grandparent;

(C) the patient's adult brother or sister;

(D) another adult who has actual care, control, and possession of the patient and has written authorization to consent for the patient from the parent, managing conservator, or guardian of the patient;

(E) an educational institution in which the patient is enrolled that has written authorization to consent for the patient from the parent, managing conservator, or guardian of the patient; or

(F) any other person with legal responsibility for the care of the patient.

Added by Acts 1987, 70th Leg., ch. 370, § 1, eff. Sept. 1, 1987. Amended by Acts 1989, 71st Leg., ch. 634, § 1, eff. Sept. 1, 1989. Amended by Acts 1997, 75th Leg., ch. 403, § 1, eff. Sept. 1, 1997; Acts 1999, 76th Leg., ch. 400, § 1, eff. Sept. 1, 1999; Acts 2001, 77th Leg., ch. 77, § 1, eff. May 14, 2001; Acts 2001, 77th Leg., ch. 538, § 1, eff. Sept. 1, 2001; Acts 2001, 77th Leg., ch. 1420, § 14.732, eff. Sept. 1, 2001; Acts 2003, 78th Leg., ch. 93, § 1, eff. Sept. 1, 2003; Acts 2003, 78th Leg., ch. 204, §§ 10.03, 10.04, & 18.03, eff. Sept. 1, 2003; Acts 2003, 78th Leg., ch. 553, § 2.001, eff. Sept. 1, 2003; Acts 2003, 78th Leg., ch. 895, § 1, eff. Sept. 1, 2003.

§ 84.004. Volunteer Liability

(a) Except as provided by Subsection (d) and Section 84.007, a volunteer of a charitable organization is immune from civil liability for any act or omission resulting in death, damage, or injury if the volunteer was acting in the course and scope of the volunteer's duties or functions including as an officer, director, or trustee within the organization.

(b) (Repealed)

(c) Except as provided by Subsection (d) and Section

84.007, a volunteer health care provider who is serving as a direct service volunteer of a charitable organization is immune from civil liability for any act or omission resulting in death, damage, or injury to a patient if:

(1) the volunteer commits the act or omission in the course of providing health care services to the patient;

(2) the services provided are within the scope of the license of the volunteer; and

(3) before the volunteer provides health care services, the patient or, if the patient is a minor or is otherwise legally incompetent, the person responsible for the patient signs a written statement that acknowledges:

(A) that the volunteer is providing care that is not administered for or in expectation of compensation; and

(B) the limitations on the recovery of damages from the volunteer in exchange for receiving the health care services.

(d) A volunteer of a charitable organization is liable to a person for death, damage, or injury to the person or his property proximately caused by any act or omission arising from the operation or use of any motor-driven equipment, including an airplane, to the extent insurance coverage is required by Chapter 601, Transportation Code, and to the extent of any existing insurance coverage applicable to the act or omission.

(e) The provisions of this section apply only to the liability of volunteers and do not apply to the liability of the organization for acts or omissions of volunteers.

(f) Subsection (c) applies even if:

(1) the patient is incapacitated due to illness or injury and cannot sign the acknowledgment statement required by that subsection; or

(2) the patient is a minor or is otherwise legally incompetent and the person responsible for the patient is not reasonably available to sign the acknowledgment statement required by that subsection.

Added by Acts 1987, 70th Leg., ch. 370, § 1, eff. Sept. 1, 1987. Amended by Acts 1997, 75th Leg., ch. 165, § 30.179, eff. Sept. 1, 1997; Acts 1999, 76th Leg., ch. 400, § 2, eff. Sept. 1, 1999; Acts 2003, 78th Leg., ch. 204, §§ 10.05, 18.01, 18.03, eff. Sept. 1, 2003.

§ 84.005. Employee Liability

Except as provided in Section 84.007 of this Act, in any civil action brought against an employee of a nonhospital charitable organization for damages based on an act or omission by the person in the course and scope of the person's employment, the liability of the employee is limited to money damages in a maximum amount of $500,000 for each person and $1,000,000 for each single occurrence of bodily injury or death and $100,000 for each single occurrence for injury to or destruction of property.

Added by Acts 1987, 70th Leg., ch. 370, § 1, eff. Sept. 1, 1987.

§ 84.006. Organization Liability

Except as provided in Section 84.007 of this Act, in any civil action brought against a nonhospital charitable organization for damages based on an act or omission by the organization or its employees or volunteers, the liability of the organization is limited to money damages in a maximum amount of $500,000 for each person and $1,000,000 for each single occurrence of bodily injury or death and $100,000 for each single occurrence for injury to or destruction of property.

Added by Acts 1987, 70th Leg., ch. 370, § 1, eff. Sept. 1, 1987.

§ 84.0061. Organizational Liability for Transportation Services Provided to Certain Welfare Recipients

(a) In this section, "religious charitable organization" means a charitable organization that is also a "religious organization" as the term is defined by Section 464.051, Health and Safety Code.

(b) Subject to Subsection (e), a religious charitable organization that owns or leases a motor vehicle is not liable for damages arising from the negligent use of the vehicle by a person to whom the organization has entrusted the vehicle to provide transportation services during the provision of those services described by Subsection (c) to a person who:

(1) is a recipient of:

(A) financial assistance under Chapter 31, Human Resources Code; or

(B) nutritional assistance under Chapter 33, Human Resources Code; and

(2) is participating in or applying to participate in:

(A) a work or employment activity under Chapter 31, Human Resources Code; or

(B) the food stamp employment and training program.

(c) Transportation services include transportation to and from the location of the:

(1) work, employment, or any training activity or program; or

(2) provider of any child-care services necessary for a person described by Subsection (b)(1) to participate in the work, employment, or training activity or program.

(d) Except as expressly provided in Subsection (b), this section does not limit, or in any way affect or diminish, other legal duties or causes of action arising from the use of a motor vehicle, including the condition of the vehicle itself and causes of action arising under Chapter 41.

(e) This section does not apply to any claim arising from injury, death, or property damage in which the operator of the vehicle was intoxicated, as the term is defined in Section 49.01, Penal Code.

Added by Acts 2001, 77th Leg., ch. 991, § 1, eff. June 15, 2001.

§ 84.0065. Organization Liability of Hospitals

(a) Except as provided by Section 84.007, in any civil action brought against a hospital or hospital system, or its employees, officers, directors, or volunteers, for damages based on an act or omission by the hospital or hospital system, or its employees, officers, directors, or volunteers, the liability of the hospital or hospital system is limited to money damages in a maximum amount of $500,000 for any act or omission resulting in death, damage, or injury to a patient if the patient or, if the patient is a minor or is otherwise legally incompetent, the person responsible for the patient signs a written statement that acknowledges:

(1) that the hospital is providing care that is not administered for or in expectation of compensation; and

(2) the limitations on the recovery of damages from the hospital in exchange for receiving the health care services.

(b) Subsection (a) applies even if:

(1) the patient is incapacitated due to illness or injury and cannot sign the acknowledgment statement required by that subsection; or

(2) the patient is a minor or is otherwise legally incompetent and the person responsible for the patient is not reasonably available to sign the acknowledgment statement required by that subsection.

Added by Acts 2003, 78th Leg., ch. 204, § 10.06, eff. Sept. 1, 2003.

§ 84.007. Applicability

(a) This chapter does not apply to an act or omission that is intentional, wilfully negligent, or done with conscious indifference or reckless disregard for the safety of others.

(b) This chapter does not limit or modify the duties or liabilities of a member of the board of directors or an officer to the organization or its members and shareholders.

(c) This chapter does not limit the liability of an organization or its employees or volunteers if the organization was formed substantially to limit its liability under this chapter.

(d) This chapter does not apply to organizations formed to dispose, remove, or store hazardous waste, industrial solid waste, radioactive waste, municipal solid waste, garbage, or sludge as those terms are defined under applicable state and federal law. This subsection shall be liberally construed to effectuate its purpose.

(e) Sections 84.005 and 84.006 of this chapter do not apply to a health care provider as defined in the Medical Liability and Insurance Improvement Act of Texas (Article 4590i, Vernon's Texas Civil Statutes), unless the provider is a federally funded migrant or community health center under the Public Health Service Act (42 U.S.C.A. Sections 254(b) and (c)) or is a nonprofit health maintenance organization created and operated by a community center under Section 534.101, Health and Safety Code, or unless the provider usually provides discounted services at or below costs based on the ability of the beneficiary to pay. Acceptance of Medicare or Medicaid payments will not disqualify a health care provider under this section. In no event shall Sections 84.005 and 84.006 of this chapter apply to a general hospital or special hospital as defined in Chapter 241, Health and Safety Code, or a facility or institution licensed under Subtitle C, Title 7, Health and Safety Code,[1] or Chapter 242, Health and Safety Code, or to any health maintenance organization created and operating under Chapter 843, Insurance Code, except for a nonprofit health maintenance organization created under Section 534.101, Health and Safety Code.

(f) This chapter does not apply to a governmental unit or employee of a governmental unit as defined in the Texas Tort Claims Act (Subchapter A, Chapter 101, Civil Practice and Remedies Code).

(g) Sections 84.005 and 84.006 of this Act do not apply to any charitable organization that does not have liability insurance coverage in effect on any act or omission to which this chapter applies. The coverage shall apply to the acts or omissions of the organization and its employees and volunteers and be in the amount of at least $500,000 for each person and $1,000,000 for each single occurrence for death or bodily injury and $100,000 for each single occurrence for injury to or destruction of property. The coverage may be provided under a contract of insurance or other plan of insurance authorized by statute and may be satisfied by the purchase of a $1,000,000 bodily injury and property damage combined single limit policy. Nothing in this chapter shall limit liability of any insurer or insurance plan in an action under Chapter 21, Insurance Code, or in an action for bad faith conduct, breach of fiduciary duty, or negligent failure to settle a claim.

(h) This chapter does not apply to:

(1) a statewide trade association that represents local chambers of commerce; or

(2) a cosponsor of an event or activity with a local chamber of commerce unless the cosponsor is a charitable organization under this chapter.

Added by Acts 1987, 70th Leg., ch. 370, § 1, eff. Sept. 1, 1987. Amended by Acts 1991, 72nd Leg., ch. 14, § 284(14), (20), eff. Sept. 1, 1991; Acts 1991, 72nd Leg., ch. 76, § 6, eff. Sept. 1, 1991. Amended by Acts 1997, 75th Leg., ch. 835, § 3, eff. Sept. 1, 1997; Acts 1997, 75th Leg., ch. 1297, § 1, eff. Sept. 1, 1997; Acts 2003, 78th Leg., ch. 93, § 2, eff. Sept. 1, 2003; Acts 2003, 78th Leg., ch. 204, § 18.02, eff. Sept. 1, 2003; Acts 2003, 78th Leg., ch. 1276, § 10A.507, eff. Sept. 1, 2003.

---

[1] V.T.C.A., Health and Safety Code § 571.001 et seq.

§ 84.008. Severability

If any clause or provision of this chapter or its application to any person or organization is held unconstitutional, such invalidity does not affect other clauses, provisions, or applications of this chapter that can be given effect without the invalid clause or provision and shall not affect or nullify the remainder of the Act or any other clause or provision, but the effect shall be confined to the clause or provision held to be invalid or unconstitutional and to this end the Act is declared to be severable.

Added by Acts 1987, 70th Leg., ch. 370, § 1, eff. Sept. 1, 1987.

Title 6. Miscellaneous Provisions

Chapter 133. Presumption of Death

Statutes in Context

A person missing for seven consecutive years is presumed dead under Civil Practice & Remedies Code § 133.001. See also Probate Code § 72 (allowing circumstantial evidence to prove death). Section 113.003 provides that if the person presumed dead is actually alive, that person is entitled to the return of the person's property along with rents, profits, and interest.

§ 133.001. Seven-Year Absence

Any person absenting himself for seven successive years shall be presumed dead unless it is proved that the person was alive within the seven-year period.

Added by Acts 1987, 70th Leg., ch. 167, § 3.15(a), eff. Sept. 1, 1987. Renumbered from V.T.C.A., Civil Practice & Remedies Code § 131.001 by Acts 1989, 71st Leg., ch. 2, § 16.01(4), eff. Aug. 28, 1989.

§ 133.002. Armed Services Certificate of Death

If a branch of the armed services issues a certificate declaring a person dead, the date of death is presumed to have occurred for all purposes as stated in the certificate. The certificate may be admitted in any court of competent jurisdiction as prima facie evidence of the date and place of the person's death.

Added by Acts 1987, 70th Leg., ch. 167, § 3.15(a), eff. Sept. 1, 1987. Renumbered from V.T.C.A., Civil Practice & Remedies Code § 131.002 by Acts 1989, 71st Leg., ch. 2, § 16.01(4), eff. Aug. 28, 1989.

§ 133.003. Restoration of Estate

(a) If an estate is recovered on a presumption of death under this chapter and if in a subsequent action or suit it is proved that the person presumed dead is living, the estate shall be restored to that person. The estate shall be restored with the rents and profits of the estate with legal interest for the time the person was deprived of the estate.

(b) A person delivering an estate or any part of an estate under this section to another under proper order of a court of competent jurisdiction is not liable for the estate or part of the estate.

(c) If the person recovering an estate on a presumption of death sells real property from the estate to a purchaser for value, the right of restoration under this section extends to the recovery of the purchase money received by the person, but does not extend to the recovery of the real property.

Added by Acts 1987, 70th Leg., ch. 167, § 3.15(a), eff. Sept. 1, 1987. Renumbered from V.T.C.A., Civil Practice & Remedies Code § 131.003 by Acts 1989, 71st Leg., ch. 2, § 16.01(4), eff. Aug. 28, 1989.

Chapter 137. Declaration for Mental Health Treatment

Statutes in Context

Chapter 137 authorizes a person to execute a Declaration for Mental Health Treatment which indicates the person's desires regarding the use of psychoactive medications, convulsive treatment, restraint, seclusion, and other mental health matters should a court determine that the person lacks the ability to make mental health treatment decisions. Section 137.011 provides a fill-in-the-blank form for the declarant to use. Two disinterested individuals must witness the declaration. The declaration does not need to be notarized.

§ 137.001. Definitions

In this chapter:

(1) "Adult" means a person 18 years of age or older or a person under 18 years of age who has had the disabilities of minority removed.

(2) "Attending physician" means the physician, selected by or assigned to a patient, who has primary responsibility for the treatment and care of the patient.

(3) "Declaration for mental health treatment" means a document making a declaration of preferences or instructions regarding mental health treatment.

(4) "Emergency" means a situation in which it is immediately necessary to treat a patient to prevent:

(A) probable imminent death or serious bodily injury to the patient because the patient:

(i) overtly or continually is threatening or attempting to commit suicide or serious bodily injury to the patient; or

(ii) is behaving in a manner that indicates that the patient is unable to satisfy the patient's need for nourishment, essential medical care, or self-protection; or

(B) imminent physical or emotional harm to another because of threats, attempts, or other acts of the patient.

(5) "Health care provider" means an individual or facility licensed, certified, or otherwise authorized to administer health care or treatment, for profit or otherwise, in the ordinary course of business or professional practice and includes a physician or other health care provider, a residential care provider, or an inpatient mental health facility as defined by Section 571.003, Health and Safety Code.

(6) "Incapacitated" means that, in the opinion of the court in a guardianship proceeding under Chapter XIII, Texas Probate Code, or in a medication hearing under Section 574.106, Health and Safety Code, a person lacks the ability to understand the nature and consequences of a proposed treatment, including the benefits, risks, and alternatives to the proposed treatment, and lacks the ability to make mental health treatment decisions because of impairment.

(7) "Mental health treatment" means electroconvulsive or other convulsive treatment, treatment of mental illness with psychoactive medication as defined by Section 574.101, Health and Safety Code, or emergency mental health treatment.

(8) "Principal" means a person who has executed a declaration for mental health treatment.

Added by Acts 1997, 75th Leg., ch. 1318, § 1, eff. Sept. 1, 1997. Amended by Acts 1999, 76th Leg., ch. 464, § 1, eff. June 18, 1999.

§ 137.002. Persons Who May Execute Declaration for Mental Health Treatment; Period of Validity

(a) An adult who is not incapacitated may execute a declaration for mental health treatment. The preferences or instructions may include consent to or refusal of mental health treatment.

(b) A declaration for mental health treatment is effective on execution as provided by this chapter. Except as provided by Subsection (c), a declaration for mental health treatment expires on the third anniversary of the date of its execution or when revoked by the principal, whichever is earlier.

(c) If the declaration for mental health treatment is in effect and the principal is incapacitated on the third anniversary of the date of its execution, the declaration remains in effect until the principal is no longer incapacitated.

Added by Acts 1997, 75th Leg., ch. 1318, § 1, eff. Sept. 1, 1997.

§ 137.003. Execution and Witnesses

(a) A declaration for mental health treatment must be signed by the principal in the presence of two or more subscribing witnesses.

(b) A witness may not, at the time of execution, be:

(1) the principal's health or residential care provider or an employee of that provider;

(2) the operator of a community health care facility providing care to the principal or an employee of an operator of the facility;

(3) a person related to the principal by blood, marriage, or adoption;

(4) a person entitled to any part of the estate of the principal on the death of the principal under a will, trust, or deed in existence or who would be entitled to any part of the estate by operation of law if the principal died intestate; or

(5) a person who has a claim against the estate of the principal.

(c) For a witness's signature to be effective, the witness must sign a statement affirming that, at the time the declaration for mental health treatment was signed, the principal:

(1) appeared to be of sound mind to make a mental health treatment decision;

(2) has stated in the witness's presence that the principal was aware of the nature of the declaration for mental health treatment and that the principal was signing the document voluntarily and free from any duress; and

(3) requested that the witness serve as a witness to the principal's execution of the document.

Added by Acts 1997, 75th Leg., ch. 1318, § 1, eff. Sept. 1, 1997.

§ 137.004. Health Care Provider to Act in Accordance With Declaration for Mental Health Treatment

A physician or other health care provider shall act in accordance with the declaration for mental health treatment when the principal has been found to be incapacitated. A physician or other provider shall continue to seek and act in accordance with the principal's informed consent to all mental health treatment decisions if the principal is capable of providing informed consent.

Added by Acts 1997, 75th Leg., ch. 1318, § 1, eff. Sept. 1, 1997.

§ 137.005. Limitation on Liability

(a) An attending physician, health or residential care provider, or person acting for or under an attending physician's or health or residential care provider's control is not subject to criminal or civil liability and has not engaged in professional misconduct for an act or omission if the act or omission is done in good faith under the terms of a declaration for mental health treatment.

(b) An attending physician, health or residential care provider, or person acting for or under an attending physician's or health or residential care provider's control does not engage in professional misconduct for:

(1) failure to act in accordance with a declara-

tion for mental health treatment if the physician, provider, or other person:

(A) was not provided with a copy of the declaration; and

(B) had no knowledge of the declaration after a good faith attempt to learn of the existence of a declaration; or

(2) acting in accordance with a directive for mental health treatment after the directive has expired or has been revoked if the physician, provider, or other person does not have knowledge of the expiration or revocation.

Added by Acts 1997. 75th Leg., ch. 1318, § 1, eff. Sept. 1, 1997.

§ 137.006. Discrimination Relating to Execution of Declaration for Mental Health Treatment

A health or residential care provider, health care service plan, insurer issuing disability insurance, self-insured employee benefit plan, or nonprofit hospital service plan may not:

(1) charge a person a different rate solely because the person has executed a declaration for mental health treatment;

(2) require a person to execute a declaration for mental health treatment before:

(A) admitting the person to a hospital, nursing home, or residential care home;

(B) insuring the person; or

(C) allowing the person to receive health or residential care;

(3) refuse health or residential care to a person solely because the person has executed a declaration for mental health treatment; or

(4) discharge the person solely because the person has or has not executed a declaration for mental health treatment.

Added by Acts 1997, 75th Leg., ch. 1318, § 1, eff. Sept. 1, 1997.

§ 137.007. Use and Effect of Declaration for Mental Health Treatment

(a) On being presented with a declaration for mental health treatment, a physician or other health care provider shall make the declaration a part of the principal's medical record. When acting in accordance with "a declaration for mental health treatment, a physician or other health care provider shall comply with the declaration to the fullest extent possible.

(b) If a physician or other provider is unwilling at any time to comply with a declaration for mental health treatment, the physician or provider may withdraw from providing treatment consistent with the exercise of independent medical judgment and must promptly:

(1) make a reasonable effort to transfer care for the principal to a physician or provider who is willing to comply with the declaration;

(2) notify the principal, or principal's guardian, if appropriate, of the decision to withdraw; and

(3) record in the principal's medical record the notification and, if applicable, the name of the physician or provider to whom the principal is transferred.

Added by Acts 1997, 75th Leg., ch. 1318, § 1, eff. Sept. 1, 1997. Amended by Acts 1999, 76th Leg., ch. 464, § 2, eff. June 18, 1999.

§ 137.008. Disregard of Declaration for Mental Health Treatment

(a) A physician or other health care provider may subject the principal to mental health treatment in a manner contrary to the principal's wishes as expressed in a declaration for mental health treatment only:

(1) if the principal is under an order for temporary or extended mental health services under Section 574.034 or 574.035, Health and Safety Code, and treatment is authorized in compliance with Section 574.106, Health and Safety Code; or

(2) in case of an emergency when the principal's instructions have not been effective in reducing the severity of the behavior that has caused the emergency.

(b) A declaration for mental health treatment does not limit any authority provided by Chapter 573 or 574, Health and Safety Code:

(1) to take a person into custody; or

(2) to admit or retain a person in a mental health treatment facility.

(c) This section does not apply to the use of electroconvulsive treatment or other convulsive treatment.

Added by Acts 1997, 75th Leg., ch. 1318, § 1, eff. Sept. 1, 1997. Amended by Acts 1999, 76th Leg., ch. 464, § 3, eff. June 18, 1999.

§ 137.009. Conflicting or Contrary Provisions

(a) Mental health treatment instructions contained in a declaration executed in accordance with this chapter supersede any contrary or conflicting instructions given by:

(1) a durable power of attorney under Chapter 135; or

(2) a guardian appointed under Chapter XIII, Texas Probate Code, after the execution of the declaration.

(b) Mental health treatment instructions contained in a declaration executed in accordance with this chapter shall be conclusive evidence of a declarant's preference in a medication hearing under Section 574.106, Health and Safety Code.

Added by Acts 1997, 75th Leg., ch. 1318, § 1, eff. Sept. 1, 1997.

§ 137.010. Revocation

(a) A declaration for mental health treatment is revoked when a principal who is not incapacitated:

(1) notifies a licensed or certified health or residential care provider of the revocation;

(2) acts in a manner that demonstrates a specific intent to revoke the declaration; or

(3) executes a later declaration for mental health treatment.

(b) A principal's health or residential care provider who is informed of or provided with a revocation of a declaration for mental health treatment immediately shall:

(1) record the revocation in the principal's medical record; and

(2) give notice of the revocation to any other health or residential care provider the provider knows to be responsible for the principal's care.

Added by Acts 1997, 75th Leg., ch. 1318, § 1, eff. Sept. 1, 1997. Amended by Acts 1999, 76th Leg., ch. 464, § 4, eff. June 18, 1999.

§ 137.011. Form of Declaration for Mental Health Treatment

The declaration for mental health treatment must be in substantially the following form:

DECLARATION FOR MENTAL HEALTH TREATMENT

I, ______________, being an adult of sound mind, wilfully and voluntarily make this declaration for mental health treatment to be followed if it is determined by a court that my ability to understand the nature and consequences of a proposed treatment, including the benefits, risks, and alternatives to the proposed treatment, is impaired to such an extent that I lack the capacity to make mental health treatment decisions. "Mental health treatment" means electroconvulsive or other convulsive treatment, treatment of mental illness with psychoactive medication, and preferences regarding emergency mental health treatment.

(OPTIONAL PARAGRAPH) I understand that I may become incapable of giving or withholding informed consent for mental health treatment due to the symptoms of a diagnosed mental disorder. These symptoms may include:

____

____

PSYCHOACTIVE MEDICATIONS

If I become incapable of giving or withholding informed consent for mental health treatment, my wishes regarding psychoactive medications are as follows:

_____ I consent to the administration of the following medications:

____

_____ I do not consent to the administration of the following medications:

____

_____ I consent to the administration of a federal Food and Drug Administration approved medication that was only approved and in existence after my declaration and that is considered in the same class of psychoactive medications as stated below:

____

____

Conditions or limitations: ______________________________________

____

____

CONVULSIVE TREATMENT

If I become incapable of giving or withholding informed consent for mental health treatment, my wishes regarding convulsive treatment are as follows:

_____ I consent to the administration of convulsive treatment.

_____ I do not consent to the administration of convulsive treatment.

Conditions or limitations: ______________________________________

____

PREFERENCES FOR EMERGENCY TREATMENT

In an emergency, I prefer the following treatment FIRST (circle one) Restraint/Seclusion/Medication.

In an emergency. I prefer the following treatment SECOND (circle one) Restraint/Seclusion/Medication.

In an emergency, I prefer the following "treatment THIRD (circle one) Restraint/Seclusion/Medication.

_____ I prefer a male/female to administer restraint, seclusion, and/or medications.

Options for treatment prior to use of restraint, seclusion, and/or medications:
____
____

Conditions or limitations: ____
____

ADDITIONAL PREFERENCES OR INSTRUCTIONS
____
____
____

Conditions or limitations: ____
____
____

Signature of Principal/Date: ____

STATEMENT OF WITNESSES

I declare under penalty of perjury that the principal's name has been represented to me by the principal, that the principal signed or acknowledged this declaration in my presence, that I believe the principal to be of sound mind, that the principal has affirmed that the principal is aware of the nature of the document and is signing it voluntarily and free from duress, that the principal requested that I serve as witness to the principal's execution of this document, and that I am not a provider of health or residential care to the principal, an employee of a provider of health or residential care to the principal, an operator of a community health care facility providing care to the principal, or an employee of an operator of a community health care facility providing care to the principal.

I declare that I am not related to the principal by blood, marriage, or adoption and that to the best of my knowledge I am not entitled to and do not have a claim against any part of the estate of the principal on the death of the principal under a will or by operation of law.

Witness Signature: ____
Print Name: ____
Date: ____
Address: ____
Witness Signature: ____
Print Name: ____
Date: ____
Address: ____

NOTICE TO PERSON MAKING A DECLARATION
FOR MENTAL HEALTH TREATMENT

This is an important legal document. It creates a declaration for mental health treatment. Before signing this document, you should know these important facts:

This document allows you to make decisions in advance about mental health treatment and specifically three types of mental health treatment: psychoactive medication, convulsive therapy, and emergency mental health treatment. The instructions that you include in this declaration will be followed only if a court believes that you are incapacitated to make treatment decisions. Otherwise, you will be considered able to give or withhold consent for the treatments.

This document will continue in effect for a period of three years unless you become incapacitated to participate in mental health treatment decisions. If this occurs, the directive will continue in effect until you are no longer incapacitated.

You have the right to revoke this document in whole or in part at any time you have not been determined to be incapacitated. YOU MAY NOT REVOKE THIS DECLARATION WHEN YOU ARE CONSIDERED BY A COURT TO BE INCAPACITATED. A revocation is effective when it is communicated to your attending physician or other health care provider.

If there is anything in this document that you do not understand, you should ask a lawyer to explain it to you. This declaration is not valid unless it is signed by two qualified witnesses who are personally known to you and who are present when you sign or acknowledge your signature.

Added by Acts 1997, 75th Leg., ch. 1318, § 1, eff. Sept. 1, 1997.

III.
CONSTITUTION OF THE STATE OF TEXAS

Article I. Bill of Rights

Statutes in Context

At common law, a person could not inherit land if the person was convicted or imprisoned for certain offenses, especially treason and other capital offenses. The English parliament abolished corruption of the blood by the mid-1800s and the practice is prohibited under Article I, § 21 of the Texas Constitution. Accordingly, an imprisoned person, even one on death row, may inherit property.

At common law, a person who was convicted of a felony forfeited all of the person's property to the government so there was no property for the person's heirs to inherit. Although most states have abolished forfeiture for most felonies, it is occasionally retained as a remedy for specific crimes. For example, under federal law, a person convicted of certain drug offenses forfeits a portion of the person's property to the government. 21 U.S.C. § 853. Forfeiture is prohibited by Article I, § 21 of the Texas Constitution.

The property of a person who committed suicide was subject to special rules at common law. If the intestate committed suicide to avoid punishment after committing a felony, the intestate's heirs took nothing. Instead, the real property escheated and personal property was forfeited. However, if the intestate committed suicide because of pain or exhaustion from living, only personal property was forfeited and real property still descended to the heirs. Article I, § 21 of the Texas Constitution abolishes these common-law rules and thus the property of a person who commits suicide passes just as if the death were caused by some other means.

See also Probate Code § 41.

Article I, § 21. Corruption of blood; forfeiture of estate; descent in case of suicide

No conviction shall work corruption of blood, or forfeiture of estate, and the estates of those who destroy their own lives shall descend or vest as in case of natural death.

Statutes in Context

Article I, § 26 adopts the common-law version of the Rule Against Perpetuities, that is, "a future interest not destructible by the owner of a prior interest cannot be valid unless it becomes vested at a date not more remote than twenty-one years after lives in being at the creation of such interest, plus the period of gestation. Any future interest so limited that it retains its indestructible and contingent character until a more remote time is invalid." Interpretive Commentary to Article I, § 21. The court must, however, reform transfers that violate the Rule under Property Code § 5.043. See also Property Code § 112.036 (indicating that the Rule does not apply to charitable trusts).

Article I, § 26. Perpetuities and monopolies; primogeniture or entailments

Perpetuities and monopolies are contrary to the genius of a free government, and shall never be allowed, nor shall the law of primogeniture or entailments ever be in force in this State.

Article XVI. General Provisions

Statutes in Context

Texas is a community property marital property jurisdiction and Article XVI, § 15 is the key constitutional provision which imposes this system. This Article also deals with a variety of other matters such as the partition of community property into separate property, the conversion of separate property into community property, and the creation of community property survivorship agreements. The legislature has more specifically described community and separate property rules in the Family, Probate, and Property Codes.

Article XVI, § 15. Separate and community property of husband and wife

All property, both real and personal, of a spouse owned or claimed before marriage, and that acquired afterward by gift, devise or descent, shall be the separate property of that spouse; and laws shall be passed more clearly defining the rights of the spouses, in relation to separate and community property; provided that persons about to marry and spouses, without the intention to defraud pre-existing creditors, may by written instrument from time to time partition between themselves all or part of their property, then existing or to be acquired, or exchange between themselves the community interest of one spouse or future

spouse in any property for the community interest of the other spouse or future spouse in other community property then existing or to be acquired, whereupon the portion or interest set aside to each spouse shall be and constitute a part of the separate property and estate of such spouse or future spouse; spouses also may from time to time, by written instrument, agree between themselves that the income or property from all or part of the separate property then owned or which thereafter might be acquired by only one of them, shall be the separate property of that spouse; if one spouse makes a gift of property to the other that gift is presumed to include all the income or property which might arise from that gift of property; spouses may agree in writing that all or part of their community property becomes the property of the surviving spouse on the death of a spouse; and spouses may agree in writing that all or part of the separate property owned by either or both of them shall be the spouses' community property.
Amended Nov. 2, 1999.

Statutes in Context

Following the authorization of Article XVI, § 49, the Texas Legislature has provided for certain personal property to be exempt from forced sale. See Property Code Chapter 42.

Article XVI, § 49. Protection of personal property from forced sale

The Legislature shall have power, and it shall be its duty, to protect by law from forced sale a certain portion of the personal property of all heads of families, and also of unmarried adults, male and female.

Statutes in Context

The source of the tremendous protection granted to Texas homesteads is Article XVI, § 50 of the Texas Constitution. This section establishes the protection without dollar value limitation and then lists exceptions, that is, situations in which the homestead is not protected. These exceptions are summarized as follows:

1. Purchase Money Liens—A purchase money lien is a lien on the homestead securing the purchase price in favor of the seller or lending bank. Purchase money liens are not subject to the homestead exemption, thus permitting the homestead to be foreclosed upon default. Article XVI, § 50(a)(1); Property Code § 41.001(b)(1).

2. Ad Valorem Taxes—A tax lien attaches automatically on the first of every year to all property on which property taxes are owed. Tax Code. § 32.01. The homestead is not exempt from forced sale to pay delinquent taxes. Article XVI, § 50(a)(2); Property Code § 41.001(b)(2).

3. Owelty of Partition Lien—Owelty of partition liens arise when there is an unequal division of co-tenancy property. For example, an unequal division of the homestead may arise in a divorce where the land on which the family home is situated is larger than the remaining portion of the land. Naturally, the house cannot be cut in half, so in such a scenario, the land may be partitioned unequally to keep the house in tact. Without the unequal partition in such a case, the entire land would need to be sold and the proceeds divided up equally. Upon an unequal division, the co-tenant with the lesser valued portion of property is entitled to a lien against the other co-tenant for the difference in value received. Homesteads are not exempt from owelty of partition liens. Article XVI, § 50(a)(3); Property Code § 41.001(b)(4).

4. Refinancing—The homestead may be encumbered by the refinancing of a valid lien against the homestead, including federal tax liens incurred from tax debt of either spouse. Article XVI, § 50(a)(4); Property Code § 41.001(b)(5). For example, if the bank has a purchase money lien against the homestead with an interest rate of 6 percent annum, the bank may offer homeowners to refinance the lien for an extra five years at 5 percent annum without risking the loss of its lien on the homestead.

5. Mechanic's and Materialman's Liens—Mechanic's and materialman's liens, that is, liens incurred in connection with improvements made upon the homestead, are valid against the homestead if: (1) a written contract was executed prior to the commencement of improvements or delivery of supplies, (2) the contract is signed by both spouses, and (3) the contract is properly recorded. Article XVI, § 50(a)(5); Property Code § 41.001(b)(3).

6. Home Equity Loan—A home equity loan arises when the homeowner uses an existing homestead as collateral for a loan based on the value of the property. Prior to 1998, a homeowner did not have the ability to use the homestead as collateral for a home equity loan. The recent amendment, permitting home equity loans, places no restrictions on the borrower's use of the money—it is not required that the loan proceeds be used on the homestead. Whatever the use of the proceeds, the homestead is not protected against a valid home equity loan. Article XVI, § 50(a)(6); Property Code § 41.001(b)(6). However, in an effort to protect the homeowner, the Constitution sets forth an extensive list of requirements which a creditor must satisfy before obtaining a valid lien against the homestead. On September 13, 2003, the voters of Texas approved an amendment to § 50 which permits a home equity loan to be granted as a line of credit as well as in the traditional lump sum.

7. Reverse Mortgage—A reverse mortgage is a home equity conversion strategy which uses the homestead as collateral for a loan in which the property owner receives a lump sum payment or regular periodic payments and in exchange the property owner gives up all or some of the home's equity. The mortgage is payable upon the death of the borrower or upon the abandonment of the homestead. Article

XVI, § 50(k)-(p). Prior to 1997, the use of the homestead as collateral for a reverse mortgage was prohibited. Now, a homestead used as collateral for a valid reverse mortgage is not protected against forced sale while in the hands of the borrower or any survivors claiming a survivor's homestead. Article XVI, § 50(a)(7); Property Code § 41.001(b)(7). However, the Constitution provides an extensive list of requirements that must be satisfied prior to entering into a valid reverse mortgage. On September 13, 2003, the voters of Texas approved an amendment to § 50 to permit the refinancing of a home equity loan with a reverse mortgage.

8. Manufactured Home Conversion and Refinance—The homestead is not protected from a lien which arose from the conversion and refinance of a personal property lien secured by a manufactured home to a lien on real property. Article XVI, § 50(a)(8).

9. Preexisting Lien—Although not expressly stated in Article XVI, § 50, a lien which existed against the property prior to it becoming a homestead normally has priority. *Stevenson v. Wilson*, 163 S.W.2d 1063 (Tex. Civ. App.—Waco 1942, no writ).

Article XVI, § 50. Homestead; protection from forced sale; mortgages, trust deeds and liens

(a) The homestead of a family, or of a single adult person, shall be, and is hereby protected from forced sale, for the payment of all debts except for:

(1) the purchase money thereof, or a part of such purchase money;

(2) the taxes due thereon;

(3) an owelty of partition imposed against the entirety of the property by a court order or by a written agreement of the parties to the partition, including a debt of one spouse in favor of the other spouse resulting from a division or an award of a family homestead in a divorce proceeding;

(4) the refinance of a lien against a homestead, including a federal tax lien resulting from the tax debt of both spouses, if the homestead is a family homestead, or from the tax debt of the owner;

(5) work and material used in constructing new improvements thereon, if contracted for in writing, or work and material used to repair or renovate existing improvements thereon if:

(A) the work and material are contracted for in writing, with the consent of both spouses, in the case of a family homestead, given in the same manner as is required in making a sale and conveyance of the homestead;

(B) the contract for the work and material is not executed by the owner or the owner's spouse before the fifth day after the owner makes written application for any extension of credit for the work and material, unless the work and material are necessary to complete immediate repairs to conditions on the homestead property that materially affect the health or safety of the owner or person residing in the homestead and the owner of the homestead acknowledges such in writing;

(C) the contract for the work and material expressly provides that the owner may rescind the contract without penalty or charge within three days after the execution of the contract by all parties, unless the work and material are necessary to complete immediate repairs to conditions on the homestead property that materially affect the health or safety of the owner or person residing in the homestead and the owner of the homestead acknowledges such in writing; and

(D) the contract for the work and material is executed by the owner and the owner's spouse only at the office of a third-party lender making an extension of credit for the work and material, an attorney at law, or a title company;

(6) an extension of credit that:

(A) is secured by a voluntary lien on the homestead created under a written agreement with the consent of each owner and each owner's spouse;

(B) is of a principal amount that when added to the aggregate total of the outstanding principal balances of all other indebtedness secured by valid encumbrances of record against the homestead does not exceed 80 percent of the fair market value of the homestead on the date the extension of credit is made;

(C) is without recourse for personal liability against each owner and the spouse of each owner, unless the owner or spouse obtained the extension of credit by actual fraud;

(D) is secured by a lien that may be foreclosed upon only by a court order;

(E) does not require the owner or the owner's spouse to pay, in addition to any interest, fees to any person that are necessary to originate, evaluate, maintain, record, insure, or service the extension of credit that exceed, in the aggregate, three percent of the original principal amount of the extension of credit;

(F) is not a form of open-end account that may be debited from time to time or under which credit may be extended from time to time unless the open-end account is a home equity line of credit;

(G) is payable in advance without penalty or other charge;

(H) is not secured by any additional real or personal property other than the homestead;

(I) is not secured by homestead property designated for agricultural use as provided by statutes governing property tax, unless such homestead property is used primarily for the production of milk;

(J) may not be accelerated because of a decrease in the market value of the homestead or because of the owner's default under other indebtedness not secured by a prior valid encumbrance against the homestead;

(K) is the only debt secured by the homestead at the time the extension of credit is made unless the other debt was made for a purpose described by Subsections (a)(1)-(a)(5) or Subsection (a)(8) of this section;

(L) is scheduled to be repaid:

(i) in substantially equal successive periodic monthly installments, not more often than every 14 days and not less often than monthly, beginning no later than two months from the date the extension of credit is made, each of which equals or exceeds the amount of accrued interest as of the date of the scheduled installment; or

(ii) if the extension of credit is a home equity line of credit, in periodic payments described under Subsection (t)(8) of this section;

(M) is closed not before:

(i) the 12th day after the later of the date that the owner of the homestead submits an application to the lender for the extension of credit or the date that the lender provides the owner a copy of the notice prescribed by Subsection (g) of this section; and

(ii) one business day after the date that the owner of the homestead receives a final itemized disclosure of the actual fees, points, interest, costs, and charges that will be charged at closing. If a bona fide emergency or another good cause exists and the lender obtains the written consent of the owner, the lender may provide the documentation to the owner or the lender may modify previously provided documentation on the date of closing; and

(iii) the first anniversary of the closing date of any other extension of credit described by Subsection (a)(6) of this section secured by the same homestead property, except a refinance described by Paragraph (Q)(x)(f) of this subdivision;

(N) is closed only at the office of the lender, an attorney at law, or a title company;

(O) permits a lender to contract for and receive any fixed or variable rate of interest authorized under statute;

(P) is made by one of the following that has not been found by a federal regulatory agency to have engaged in the practice of refusing to make loans because the applicants for the loans reside or the property proposed to secure the loans is located in a certain area:

(i) a bank, savings and loan association, savings bank, or credit union doing business under the laws of this state or the United States;

(ii) a federally chartered lending instrumentality or a person approved as a mortgagee by the United States government to make federally insured loans;

(iii) a person licensed to make regulated loans, as provided by statute of this state;

(iv) a person who sold the homestead property to the current owner and who provided all or part of the financing for the purchase; or

(v) a person who is related to the homestead property owner within the second degree of affinity or consanguinity; or

(vi) a person regulated by this state as a mortgage broker; and

(Q) is made on the condition that:

(i) the owner of the homestead is not required to apply the proceeds of the extension of credit to repay another debt except debt secured by the homestead or debt to another lender;

(ii) the owner of the homestead not assign wages as security for the extension of credit;

(iii) the owner of the homestead not sign any instrument in which blanks are left to be filled in;

(iv) the owner of the homestead not sign a confession of judgment or power of attorney to the lender or to a third person to confess judgment or to appear for the owner in a judicial proceeding;

(v) the lender, at the time the extension of credit is made, provide the owner of the homestead a copy of all documents signed by the owner related to the extension of credit;

(vi) the security instruments securing the extension of credit contain a disclosure that the extension of credit is the type of credit defined by Section 50(a)(6), Article XVI, Texas Constitution;

(vii) within a reasonable time after termination and full payment of the extension of credit, the lender cancel and return the promissory note to the owner of the homestead and give the owner, in recordable form, a release of the lien securing the extension of credit or a copy of an endorsement and assignment of the lien to a lender that is refinancing the extension of credit;

(viii) the owner of the homestead and any spouse of the owner may, within three days after the extension of credit is made, rescind the extension of credit without penalty or charge;

(ix) the owner of the homestead and the lender sign a written acknowledgment as to the fair market value of the homestead property on the date the extension of credit is made; and

(x) except as provided by Subparagraph (xi) of this paragraph, the lender or any holder of the note for the extension of credit shall forfeit all principal and interest of the extension of credit if the lender or holder fails to comply with the lender's or holder's obligations under the extension of credit and fails to correct the failure to comply not later than the 60th day after the date within a reasonable time after the lender or holder is notified by the borrower of the lender's failure to comply by:

(a) paying to the owner an amount equal to any overcharge paid by the owner under or related to the extension of credit if the owner has paid an amount that exceeds an amount stated in the applicable Paragraph (E), (G), or (O) of this subdivision;

(b) sending the owner a written acknowledgement that the lien is valid only in the amount that the extension of credit does not exceed the percentage described by Paragraph (B) of this subdivision, if applicable, or is not secured by property described under Paragraph (H) or (I) of this subdivision, if applicable;

(c) sending the owner a written notice modifying any other amount, percentage, term, or other provision prohibited by this section to a permitted amount, percentage, term, or other provision and adjusting the account of the borrower to ensure that the borrower is not required to pay more than an amount permitted by this section and is not subject to any other term or provision prohibited by this section;

(d) delivering the required documents to the borrower if the lender fails to comply with Subparagraph (v) of this paragraph or obtaining the appropriate signatures if the lender fails to comply with Subparagraph (ix) of this paragraph;

(e) sending the owner a written acknowledgement, if the failure to comply is prohibited by Paragraph (K) of this subdivision, that the accrual of interest and all of the owner's obligations under the extension of credit are abated while any prior lien prohibited under Paragraph (K) remains secured by the homestead; or

(f) if the failure to comply cannot be cured under Subparagraphs (x)(a)-(e) of this paragraph, curing the failure to comply by a refund or credit to the owner of $1,000 and offering the owner the right to refinance the extension of credit with the lender or holder for the remaining term of the loan at no cost to the owner on the same terms, including interest, as the original extension of credit with any modifications necessary to comply with this section or on terms on which the owner and the lender or holder otherwise agree that comply with this section; and

(xi) the lender or any holder of the note for the extension of credit shall forfeit all principal and interest of the extension of credit if the extension of credit is made by a person other than a person described under Paragraph (P) of this subdivision or if the lien was not created under a written agreement with the consent of each owner and each owner's spouse, unless each owner and each owner's spouse who did not initially consent subsequently consents;

(7) a reverse mortgage; or

(8) the conversion and refinance of a personal property lien secured by a manufactured home to a lien on real property, including the refinance of the purchase price of the manufactured home, the cost of installing the manufactured home on the real property, and the refinance of the purchase price of the real property.

(b) An owner or claimant of the property claimed as homestead may not sell or abandon the homestead without the consent of each owner and the spouse of each owner, given in such manner as may be prescribed by law.

(c) No mortgage, trust deed, or other lien on the homestead shall ever be valid unless it secures a debt described by this section, whether such mortgage, trust deed, or other lien, shall have been created by the owner alone, or together with his or her spouse, in case the owner is married. All pretended sales of the homestead involving any condition of defeasance shall be void.

(d) A purchaser or lender for value without actual knowledge may conclusively rely on an affidavit that designates other property as the homestead of the affiant and that states that the property to be conveyed or encumbered is not the homestead of the affiant.

(e) A refinance of debt secured by a homestead and described by any subsection under Subsections (a)(1) - (a)(5) that includes the advance of additional funds may not be secured by a valid lien against the homestead unless:

(1) the refinance of the debt is an extension of credit described by Subsection (a)(6) of this section; or

(2) the advance of all the additional funds is for reasonable costs necessary to refinance such debt or for a purpose described by Subsection (a)(2), (a)(3), or (a)(5) of this section.

(f) A refinance of debt secured by the homestead, any portion of which is an extension of credit described by Subsection (a)(6) of this section, may not be secured by a valid lien against the homestead unless the refinance of the debt is an extension of credit described by Subsection (a)(6) or (a)(7) of this section.

(g) An extension of credit described by Subsection (a)(6) of this section may be secured by a valid lien against homestead property if the extension of credit is not closed before the 12th day after the lender provides the owner with the following written notice on a separate instrument:

"NOTICE CONCERNING EXTENSIONS OF CREDIT DEFINED BY SECTION 50(a)(6), ARTICLE XVI, TEXAS CONSTITUTION:

"SECTION 50(a)(6), ARTICLE XVI, OF THE TEXAS CONSTITUTION ALLOWS CERTAIN LOANS TO BE SECURED AGAINST THE EQUITY IN YOUR HOME. SUCH LOANS ARE COMMONLY KNOWN AS EQUITY LOANS. IF YOU DO NOT REPAY THE LOAN OR IF YOU FAIL TO MEET THE TERMS OF THE LOAN, THE LENDER MAY FORECLOSE AND SELL YOUR HOME. THE CONSTITUTION PROVIDES THAT:

"(A) THE LOAN MUST BE VOLUNTARILY CREATED WITH THE CONSENT OF EACH OWNER OF YOUR HOME AND EACH OWNER'S SPOUSE;

"(B) THE PRINCIPAL LOAN AMOUNT AT THE TIME THE LOAN IS MADE MUST NOT EXCEED AN AMOUNT THAT, WHEN ADDED TO THE PRINCIPAL BALANCES OF ALL OTHER LIENS AGAINST YOUR HOME, IS MORE THAN 80 PERCENT OF THE FAIR MARKET VALUE OF YOUR HOME;

"(C) THE LOAN MUST BE WITHOUT RECOURSE FOR PERSONAL LIABILITY AGAINST YOU AND YOUR SPOUSE UNLESS YOU OR YOUR SPOUSE OBTAINED THIS EXTENSION OF CREDIT BY ACTUAL FRAUD;

(D) THE LIEN SECURING THE LOAN MAY BE FORECLOSED UPON ONLY WITH A COURT ORDER;

"(E) FEES AND CHARGES TO MAKE THE LOAN MAY NOT EXCEED 3 PERCENT OF THE LOAN AMOUNT;

"(F) THE LOAN MAY NOT BE AN OPEN-END ACCOUNT THAT MAY BE DEBITED FROM TIME TO TIME OR UNDER WHICH CREDIT MAY BE EXTENDED FROM TIME TO TIME UNLESS IT IS A HOME EQUITY LINE OF CREDIT;

"(C) YOU MAY PREPAY TILE LOAN WITHOUT PENALTY OR CHARGE

"(H) NO ADDITIONAL COLLATERAL MAY BE SECURITY FOR THE LOAN;

"(I) THE LOAN MAY NOT BE SECURED BY AGRICULTURAL HOMESTEAD PROPERTY, UNLESS THE AGRICULTURAL HOMESTEAD PROPERTY IS USED PRIMARILY FOR THE PRODUCTION OF MILK;

"(J) YOU ARE NOT REQUIRED TO REPAY THE LOAN EARLIER THAN AGREED SOLELY BECAUSE THE FAIR MARKET VALUE OF YOUR HOME DECREASES OR BECAUSE YOU DEFAULT ON ANOTHER LOAN THAT IS NOT SECURED BY YOUR HOME;

"(K) ONLY ONE LOAN DESCRIBED BY SECTION 50(a)(6), ARTICLE XVI, OF THE TEXAS CONSTITUTION MAY BE SECURED WITH YOUR HOME AT ANY GIVEN TIME;

"(L) THE LOAN MUST BE SCHEDULED TO BE REPAID IN PAYMENTS THAT EQUAL OR EXCEED THE AMOUNT OF ACCRUED INTEREST FOR EACH PAYMENT PERIOD;

"(M) THE LOAN MAY NOT CLOSE BEFORE 12 DAYS AFTER YOU SUBMIT A WRITTEN APPLICATION TO THE LENDER OR BEFORE 12 DAYS AFTER YOU RECEIVE THIS NOTICE, WHICHEVER DATE IS LATER; AND IF YOUR HOME WAS SECURITY FOR THE SAME TYPE OF LOAN WITHIN THE PAST YEAR, A NEW LOAN SECURED BY THE SAME PROPERTY MAY NOT CLOSE BEFORE ONE YEAR HAS PASSED FROM THE CLOSING DATE OF THE OTHER LOAN;

"(N) THE LOAN MAY CLOSE ONLY AT THE OFFICE OF THE LENDER, TITLE COMPANY, OR AN ATTORNEY AT LAW

"(O) THE LENDER MAY CHARGE ANY FIXED OR VARIABLE RATE OF INTEREST AUTHORIZED BY STATUTE;

"(P) ONLY A LAWFULLY AUTHORIZED LENDER MAY MAKE LOANS DESCRIBED BY SECTION 50(a)(6), ARTICLE XVI, OF THE TEXAS CONSTITUTION; AND

"(Q) LOANS DESCRIBED BY SECTION 50(a)(6), ARTICLE XVI, OF THE TEXAS CONSTITUTION MUST:

"(1) NOT REQUIRE YOU TO APPLY THE PROCEEDS TO ANOTHER DEBT EXCEPT A DEBT THAT IS SECURED BY YOUR HOME OR OWED TO ANOTHER LENDER;

"(2) NOT REQUIRE THAT YOU ASSIGN WAGES AS SECURITY;

"(3) NOT REQUIRE THAT YOU EXECUTE INSTRUMENTS WHICH HAVE BLANKS LEFT TO BE FILLED IN;

"(4) NOT REQUIRE THAT YOU SIGN A CONFESSION OF JUDGMENT OR POWER OF ATTORNEY TO ANOTHER PERSON TO CONFESS JUDGMENT OR APPEAR IN A LEGAL PROCEEDING ON YOUR BEHALF;

"(5) PROVIDE THAT YOU RECEIVE A COPY OF ALL DOCUMENTS YOU SIGN AT CLOSING;

"(6) PROVIDE THAT THE SECURITY INSTRUMENTS CONTAIN A DISCLOSURE THAT THIS LOAN IS A LOAN DEFINED BY SECTION 50(a)(6), ARTICLE XVI, OF THE TEXAS CONSTITUTION;

"(7) PROVIDE THAT WHEN THE LOAN IS PAID IN FULL, THE LENDER WILL SIGN AND GIVE YOU A RELEASE OF LIEN OR AN ASSIGNMENT OF THE LIEN, WHICHEVER IS APPROPRIATE;

"(8) PROVIDE THAT YOU MAY, WITHIN 3 DAYS AFTER CLOSING, RESCIND THE LOAN WITHOUT PENALTY OR CHARGE;

"(9) PROVIDE THAT YOU AND THE LENDER ACKNOWLEDGE THE FAIR MARKET VALUE OF YOUR HOME ON THE DATE THE LOAN CLOSES; AND

"(10) PROVIDE THAT THE LENDER WILL FORFEIT ALL PRINCIPAL AND INTEREST IF THE LENDER FAILS TO COMPLY WITH THE LENDER'S OBLIGATIONS UNLESS THE LENDER CURES THE FAILURE TO COMPLY AS PROVIDED BY SECTION 50(a)(6)(Q)(x), ARTICLE XVI, OF THE TEXAS CONSTITUTION; AND

"(R) IF THE LOAN IS A HOME EQUITY LINE OF CREDIT:

"(1) YOU MAY REQUEST ADVANCES, REPAY MONEY, AND REBORROW MONEY UNDER THE LINE OF CREDIT;
"(2) EACH ADVANCE UNDER THE LINE OF CREDIT MUST BE IN AN AMOUNT OF AT LEAST $4,000;
"(3) YOU MAY NOT USE A CREDIT CARD, DEBIT CARD, SOLICITATION CHECK, OR SIMILAR DEVICE TO OBTAIN ADVANCES UNDER THE LINE OF CREDIT;
"(4) ANY FEES THE LENDER CHARGES MAY BE CHARGED AND COLLECTED ONLY AT THE TIME THE LINE OF CREDIT IS ESTABLISHED AND THE LENDER MAY NOT CHARGE A FEE IN CONNECTION WITH ANY ADVANCE;
"(5) THE MAXIMUM PRINCIPAL AMOUNT THAT MAY BE EXTENDED, WHEN ADDED TO ALL OTHER DEBTS SECURED BY YOUR HOME, MAY NOT EXCEED 80 PERCENT OF THE FAIR MARKET VALUE OF YOUR HOME ON THE DATE THE LINE OF CREDIT IS ESTABLISHED;
"(6) IF THE PRINCIPAL BALANCE UNDER THE LINE OF CREDIT AT ANY TIME EXCEEDS 50 PERCENT OF THE FAIR MARKET VALUE OF YOUR HOME, AS DETERMINED ON THE DATE THE LINE OF CREDIT IS ESTABLISHED, YOU MAY NOT CONTINUE TO REQUEST ADVANCES UNDER THE LINE OF CREDIT UNTIL THE BALANCE IS LESS THAN 50 PERCENT OF THE FAIR MARKET VALUE; AND
"(7) THE LENDER MAY NOT UNILATERALLY AMEND THE TERMS OF THE LINE OF CREDIT.
"THIS NOTICE IS ONLY A SUMMARY OF YOUR RIGHTS UNDER THE TEXAS CONSTITUTION. YOUR RIGHTS ARE GOVERNED BY SECTION 50, ARTICLE XVI, OF THE TEXAS CONSTITUTION, AND NOT BY THIS NOTICE."

If the discussions with the borrower are conducted primarily in a language other than English, the lender shall, before closing, provide an additional copy of the notice translated into the written language in which the discussions were conducted.

(h) A lender or assignee for value may conclusively rely on the written acknowledgment as to the fair market value of the homestead property made in accordance with Subsection (a)(6)(Q)(ix) of this section if:

(1) the value acknowledged to is the value estimate in an appraisal or evaluation prepared in accordance with a state or federal requirement applicable to an extension of credit under Subsection (a)(6); and

(2) the lender or assignee does not have actual knowledge at the time of the payment of value or advance of funds by the lender or assignee that the fair market value stated in the written acknowledgment was incorrect.

(i) This subsection shall not affect or impair any right of the borrower to recover damages from the lender or assignee under applicable law for wrongful foreclosure. A purchaser for value without actual knowledge may conclusively presume that a lien securing an extension of credit described by Subsection (a)(6) of this section was a valid lien securing the extension of credit with homestead property if:

(1) the security instruments securing the extension of credit contain a disclosure that the extension of credit secured by the lien was the type of credit defined by Section 50(a)(6), Article XVI, Texas Constitution;

(2) the purchaser acquires the title to the property pursuant to or after the foreclosure of the voluntary lien; and

(3) the purchaser is not the lender or assignee under the extension of credit.

(j) Subsection (a)(6) and Subsections (e) - (i) of this section are not severable, and none of those provisions would have been enacted without the others. If any of those provisions are held to be preempted by the laws of the United States, all of those provisions are invalid. This subsection shall not apply to any lien or extension of credit made after January 1, 1998, and before the date any provision under Subsection (a)(6) or Subsections (e) - (i) is held to be preempted.

(k) "Reverse mortgage" means an extension of credit:

(1) that is secured by a voluntary lien on homestead property created by a written agreement with the consent of each owner and each owners spouse;

(2) that is made to a person who is or whose spouse is 62 years or older;

(3) that is made without recourse for personal liability against each owner and the spouse of each owner;

(4) under which advances are provided to a borrower based on the equity in a borrower s homestead;

(5) that does not permit tire lender to reduce the amoant or number of advances because of an adjustment in the interestate if periodic advances are to be made;

(6) that requires no payment of principal or interest until:

(A) all have died;

(B) the homestead property securing the loan is sold or otherwise transferred;

(C) all borrowers cease occupying the homestead property for a period of longer than 12 consecutive months without prior written approval from the lender: or

(D) the borrower:

(i) defaults on an obligation specified in the loan documents to repair and maintain, pay taxes and assessments on, or insure the homestead property;

(ii) commits actual fraud in connection with the loan; or

(iii) fails to maintain the priority of the lender's lien on the homestead property, after the lender gives notice to the borrower, by promptly discharging any lien that has priority or may obtain priority over the lender's lien within 10 days after the date the borrower receives the notice, unless the borrower:

(a) agrees in writing to the payment of the obligation secured by the lien in a manner acceptable to the lender;

(b) contests in good faith the lien by, or defends against enforcement of the lien in, legal proceedings so as to prevent the enforcement of the lien or forfeiture of any part of the homestead property; or

(c) secures from the holder of the lien an agreement satisfactory to the lender subordinating the lien to all amounts secured by the lender's lien on the homestead property;

(7) that provides that if the lender fails to make loan advances as required in the loan documents and if the lender fails to cure the default as required in the loan documents after notice from the borrower, the lender forfeits all principal and interest of the reverse mortgage, provided, however, that this subdivision does not apply when a governmental agency or instrumentality takes an assignment of the loan in order to cure the default;

(8) that is not made unless the owner of the homestead attests in writing that the owner received counseling regarding the advisability and availability of reverse mortgages and other financial alternatives;

(9) that requires the lender, at the time the loan is made, to disclose to the borrower by written notice the specific provisions contained in Subdivision (6) of this subsection under which the borrower is required to repay the loan;

(10) that does not permit the lender to commence foreclosure until the lender gives notice to the borrower, in the manner provided for a notice by mail related to the foreclosure of liens under Subsection (a)(6) of this section, that a ground for foreclosure exists and gives the borrower at least 30 days, or at least 20 days in the event of a default under Subdivision (6)(D)(iii) of this subsection, to:

(A) remedy the condition creating the ground for foreclosure;

(B) pay the debt secured by the homestead property from proceeds of the sale of the homestead property by the borrower or from any other sources: or

(C) convey the homestead property to the lender by a deed in lieu of foreclosure; and

(11) that is secured by a lien that may be foreclosed upon only by a court order, if the foreclosure is for a ground other than a ground stated by Subdivision (6)(A) or (B) of this subsection.

(l) Advances made under a reverse mortgage and interest on those advances have priority over a lien filed for record in the real property records in the county where the homestead property is located after the reverse mortgage is filed for record in the real property records of that county.

(m) A reverse mortgage may provide for an interest rate that is fixed or adjustable and may also provide for interest that is contingent on appreciation in the fair market value of the homestead property. Although payment of principal or interest shall not be required under a reverse mortgage until the entire loan becomes due and payable, interest may accrue and be compounded during the term of the loan as provided by the reverse mortgage loan agreement.

(n) A reverse mortgage that is secured by a valid lien against homestead property may be made or acquired without regard to the following provisions of any other law of this state:

(1) a limitation on the purpose and use of future advances or other mortgage proceeds;

(2) a limitation on future advances to a term of years or a limitation on the term of open-end account advances;

(3) a limitation on the term during which future advances take priority over intervening advances;

(4) a requirement that a maximum loan amount be stated in the reverse mortgage loan documents;

(5) a prohibition on balloon payments;

(6) a prohibition on compound interest and interest on interest;

(7) a prohibition on contracting for, charging, or receiving any rate of interest authorized by any law of this state authorizing a lender to contract for a rate of interest; and

(8) a requirement that a percentage of the reverse mortgage proceeds be advanced before the assignment of the reverse mortgage.

(o) For the purposes of determining eligibility under any statute relating to payments, allowances, benefits, or services provided on a means-tested basis by this state, including supplemental security income, low-income energy assistance, property tax relief, medical assistance, and general assistance:

(1) reverse mortgage loan advances made to a borrower are considered proceeds from a loan and not income; and

(2) undisbursed funds under a reverse mortgage loan are considered equity in a borrower's home and not proceeds from a loan.

(p) The advances made on a reverse mortgage loan under which more than one advance is made must be made according to the terms established by the loan documents by one or more of the following methods:

(1) at regular intervals;

(2) at regular intervals in which the amounts advanced may be reduced, for one or more advances, at the request of the borrower; or

(3) at any time by the lender, on behalf of the borrower, if the borrower fails to timely pay any of the following that the borrower is obligated to pay under the loan documents to the extent necessary

to protect the lender's interest in or the value of the homestead property:

(A) taxes;

(B) insurance;

(C) costs of repairs or maintenance performed by a person or company that is not an employee of the lender or a person or company that directly or indirectly controls, is controlled by, or is under common control with the lender;

(D) assessments levied against the homestead property; and

(E) any lien that has, or may obtain, priority over the lender's lien as it is established in the loan documents.

(q) To the extent that any statutes of this state, including without limitation, Section 41.001 of the Texas Property Code, purport to limit encumbrances that may properly be fixed on homestead property in a manner that does not permit encumbrances for extensions of credit described in Subsection (a)(6) or (a)(7) of this section, the same shall be superseded to the extent that such encumbrances shall be permitted to be fixed upon homestead property in the manner provided for by this amendment.

(r) The supreme court shall promulgate rules of civil procedure for expedited foreclosure proceedings related to the foreclosure of liens under Subsection (a)(6) of this section and to foreclosure of a reverse mortgage lien that requires a court order.

(s) The Finance Commission of Texas shall appoint a director to conduct research on the availability, quality, and prices of financial services and research the practices of business entities in the state that provide financial services under this section. The director shall collect information and produce reports on lending activity of those making loans under this section. The director shall report his or her findings to the legislature not later than December 1 of each year.

(t) A home equity line of credit is a form of an open-end account that may be debited from time to time, under which credit may be extended from time to time and under which:

(1) the owner requests advances, repays money, and reborrows money;

(2) any single debit or advance is not less than $4,000;

(3) the owner does not use a credit card, debit card, preprinted solicitation check, or similar device to obtain an advance;

(4) any fees described by Subsection (a)(6)(E) of this section are charged and collected only at the time the extension of credit is established and no fee is charged or collected in connection with any debit or advance;

(5) the maximum principal amount that may be extended under the account, when added to the aggregate total of the outstanding principal balances of all indebtedness secured by the homestead on the date the extension of credit is established, does not exceed an amount described under Subsection (a)(6)(B) of this section;

(6) no additional debits or advances are made if the total principal amount outstanding exceeds an amount equal to 50 percent of the fair market value of the homestead as determined on the date the account is established;

(7) the lender or holder may not unilaterally amend the extension of credit; and

(8) repayment is to be made in regular periodic installments, not more often than every 14 days and not less often than monthly, beginning not later than two months from the date the extension of credit is established, and:

(A) during the period during which the owner may request advances, each installment equals or exceeds the amount of accrued interest; and

(B) after the period during which the owner may request advances, installments are substantially equal.

(u) The legislature may by statute delegate one or more state agencies the power to interpret Subsections (a)(5)-(a)(7), (e)-(p), and (t), of this section. An act or omission does not violate a provision included in those subsections if the act or omission conforms to an interpretation of the provision that is:

(1) in effect at the time of the act or omission; and

(2) made by a state agency to which the power of interpretation is delegated as provided by this subsection or by an appellate court of this state or the United States.

Amended Nov. 7, 1995; Nov. 4, 1997, eff. Jan. 1, 1998; Nov. 2, 1999; Nov. 6, 2001; Sept. 13, 2003.

Statutes in Context

Homesteads are classified by property type as either a rural homestead or an urban homestead, and the size of the exemption varies depending on this classification. Whether a homestead is rural or urban is a question of fact. *Kimmey v. Goodrum*, 346 S.W.2d 901 (Tex. Civ. App.—Waco 1961, writ ref'd n.r.e).

1. Urban—Property Code § 41.002 defines "urban" homestead as property which, at the time of its designation, is located within a municipality and is served by police and fire protection as well as three of the following municipality services: electric, gas, sewer, storm sewer, and water. Beginning in 1999, the urban homestead is limited to ten acres. More than one lot may be designated as a person's urban homestead provided that the lots are contiguous and all lots making up the urban homestead do not exceed the ten acre limitation.

Historically, the urban homestead exemption was limited by value, rather than acreage. For example, in 1860, the urban homestead could not exceed $2,000 in value at the time of its designation. However, a

constitutional amendment in 1983 eliminated the dollar value limitation and restricted the urban homestead on the basis of acreage. From 1983 through 1999, the urban homestead was limited to one acre. Towards the end of 1999, the Texas Constitution was further amended, increasing the size of the urban homestead to ten acres.

2. Rural—Under the Constitution, rural homesteads are limited to 200 acres. Property Code § 41.002(b), however, provides that although a family may have a rural homestead of up to 200 acres, a single adult is limited to 100 acres. It is unclear whether the Property Code may cut back the number of acres for the single adult homestead.

The current version of the Property Code provides no definition of "rural" homestead. However, rural homestead is interpreted to mean homesteads that do not fall within the parameters of the urban homestead definition. *In re Rodriquez*, 282 B.R. 194, 199-200 (Bankr. N.D. Tex. 2002). This interpretation is consistent with previous versions of the Property Code, which provided "[a] homestead is considered to be rural if, at the time the designation is made, the property is not served by municipal utilities and fire and police protection." *See* Act of Aug. 28, 1989, 71st Leg., 2d C.S., ch. 391, § 2 (amended 1999) (current version at Property Code § 41.002(c) (replacing the definition of rural hometead with that of urban homestead)).

Note: The Constitution formerly provided for a third type of homestead, the business homestead. In 1999, a constitutional amendment eliminated the purely urban business homestead.

Article XVI, § 51. Amount of homestead; uses

The homestead, not in a town or city, shall consist of not more than two hundred acres of land, which may be in one or more parcels, with the improvements thereon; the homestead in a city, town or village, shall consist of lot or contiguous lots amounting to not more than 10 acres of land, together with any improvements on the land; provided, that the homestead in a city, town or village shall be used for the purposes of a home, or as both an urban home and a place to exercise a calling or business, of the homestead claimant, whether a single adult person, or the head of a family; provided also, that any temporary renting of the homestead shall not change the character of the same, when no other homestead has been acquired; provided further that a release or refinance of an existing lien against a homestead as to a part of the homestead does not create an additional burden on the part of the homestead property that is unreleased or subject to the refinance, and a new lien is not invalid only for that reason.

Amended Nov. 2, 1999.

Statutes in Context

1. Surviving Spouse—Upon the death of either the husband or wife (or both), the homestead property shall "descend and vest in like manner as other real property of the deceased." Probate Code § 283. However, the surviving spouse is entitled to retain a survivor's homestead right under Article XVI, § 52, for life or for so long as the survivor elects to use the homestead. This right protects the homestead against forced sale and partition so long as the surviving spouse chooses to use and occupy the homestead.

The survivor's homestead right may not be defeated by either spouse through the devise of the homestead in either party's will. Rather, the laws of testamentary disposition are subject to the survivor's homestead right. *White v. Sparks*, 118 S.W.2d 649 (Tex. Civ. App.—Dallas 1938, writ dism'd).

2. Minor Children—Upon the death of both parents, the homestead property will pass according to descent and distribution or under the deceased parent's will. However, much like the surviving spouse, the surviving minor children are entitled to a survivor's homestead under Article XVI, § 52. In asserting the surviving minor children's homestead entitlement, there is no requirement that the minor children resided with the deceased parent(s) prior to the parent's death. *National Union Fire Ins. Co. v. Olson*, 920 S.W.2d 458, 462 (Tex. App.—Austin 1996, no writ). The homestead right of surviving minor children is protected against forced sale as well as partition among heirs and will beneficiaries.

Parents are prevented from defeating the homestead rights of their minor children through a testamentary devise of the homestead property. However, the parents are not restricted from conveying or encumbering the homestead property while they are alive. *Hall v. Fields*, 17 S.W. 82 (Tex. 1891).

3. Unmarried Adult Children Remaining With the Family—Upon the death of both parents, unmarried adult children living at home may claim a statutory survivor's homestead that protects the homestead against forced sale under Probate Code § 271. However, an unmarried adult child has no special occupancy right and the homestead may be partitioned among the heirs. To claim a survivor's homestead, the parents must both be deceased and the adult child must be unmarried and living at home with the parents at the time of the last parent's death. *See Hunter v. NCNB Texas Nat'l Bank*, 857 S.W.2d 722 (Tex. App.—Houston [14th Dist.] 1993, writ denied).

Article XVI, § 52. Descent and distribution of homestead; restrictions on partition

On the death of the husband or wife, or both, the homestead shall descend and vest in like manner as other real property of the deceased, and shall be governed by the same laws of descent and distribution, but it shall not be partitioned among the heirs of the deceased during the lifetime of the surviving husband or wife, or so long as the survivor may elect to use or occupy the same as a homestead, or so long as the guardian of the minor children of the deceased may be permitted, under the order of the proper court having the jurisdiction, to use and occupy the same.

IV. CODE OF CRIMINAL PROCEDURE

Title 1. CODE OF CRIMINAL PROCEDURE OF 1965

LIMITATION AND VENUE

Chapter Twelve. LIMITATION

Statutes in Context

Article 12.01 contains the statute of limitations for various evil acts which may arise in the estate planning context such as when an executor or trustee steals or misapplies estate property or a person uses deception to obtain a signature on a will, trust, power of attorney, or other estate planning document.

Art. 12.01. [177-180] [225-228] [215-218] Felonies.

Except as provided in Article 12.03, felony indictments may be presented within these limits, and not afterward:

(1) no limitation:

(A) murder and manslaughter;

(B) sexual assault, if during the investigation of the offense biological matter is collected and subjected to forensic DNA testing and the testing results show that the matter does not match the victim or any other person whose identity is readily ascertained; or

(C) an offense involving leaving the scene of an accident under Section 550.021, Transportation Code, if the accident resulted in the death of a person;

(2) ten years from the date of the commission of the offense:

(A) theft of any estate, real, personal or mixed, by an executor, administrator, guardian or trustee, with intent to defraud any creditor, heir, legatee, ward, distributee, beneficiary or settlor of a trust interested in such estate;

(B) theft by a public servant of government property over which he exercises control in his official capacity;

(C) forgery or the uttering, using or passing of forged instruments;

(D) injury to a child, elderly individual, or disabled individual punishable as a felony of the first degree under Section 22.04, Penal Code; or

(E) sexual assault, except as provided by Subdivision (1) or (5); or

(F) arson;

(3) seven years from the date of the commission of the offense:

(A) misapplication of fiduciary property or property of a financial institution;

(B) securing execution of document by deception; or

(C) a violation under Sections 153.403(22)-(39), Tax Code;

(4) five years from the date of the commission of the offense:

(A) theft, burglary, robbery;

(B) kidnapping;

(C) injury to a child, elderly individual, or disabled individual that is not punishable as a felony of the first degree under Section 22.04, Penal Code; or

(D) abandoning or endangering a child;

(5) ten years from the 18th birthday of the victim of the offense:

(A) indecency with a child under Section 21.11(a)(1) or (2), Penal Code; or

(B) except as provided by Subdivision (1), sexual assault under Section 22.011(a)(2), Penal Code, or aggravated sexual assault under Section 22.021(a)(1)(B), Penal Code; or

(6) three years from the date of the commission of the offense: all other felonies.

Acts 1965, 59th Leg., vol. 2, p. 317, ch. 722. Amended by Acts 1973, 63rd Leg., p. 975, ch. 399, § 2(B), eff. Jan. 1, 1974; Acts 1975, 64th Leg., p. 478, ch. 203, § 5, eff. Sept. 1, 1975. Amended by Acts 1983, 68th Leg., p. 413, ch. 85, § 1, eff. Sept. 1, 1983; Acts 1983, 68th Leg., p. 5317, ch. 977, § 7, eff. Sept. 1, 1983; Acts 1985, 69th Leg., ch. 330, § 1, eff. Aug. 26, 1985; Acts 1987, 70th Leg., ch. 716, § 1, eff. Sept. 1, 1987; Acts 1991, 72nd Leg., ch. 565, § 6, eff. Sept. 1, 1991; Acts 1995, 74th Leg., ch. 476, § 1, eff. Sept. 1, 1995; Acts 1997, 75th Leg., ch. 740, § 1, eff. Sept. 1, 1997. Acts 1999, 76th Leg., ch. 39, § 1, eff. Sept. 1, 1999; Acts 1999, 76th Leg., ch. 1285, § 33, eff. Sept. 1, 2000; Acts 2001, 77th Leg., ch. 12., § 1, eff. Sept. 1, 2001; Acts 2001, 77th Leg., ch. 1479, § 1, eff. Sept. 1, 2001; Acts 2001, 77th Leg., ch. 1482, § 1, eff. Sept. 1, 2001; Acts 2003, 78th Leg., ch. 371, § 6, eff. Sept. 1, 2003; Acts 2003, 78th Leg., ch. 1276, § 5.001, eff. Sept. 1, 2003.

V.
RULES OF EVIDENCE

Article VI. WITNESSES

Statutes in Context

Courts normally seek whatever evidence is helpful when they interpret and construe wills. However, this ability may be restricted by state evidentiary rules, especially dead person's statutes (formerly referred to as "dead man's statutes"). These statutes limit the admissibility of evidence of what the testator did or said if the testimony is being offered by a party to the action. The policy supporting this limitation is that the testator is deceased and thus cannot rebut the statements made by a party who is obviously biased. Under older formulations of the rule, a party could not testify about any transaction or communication with the decedent. The modern version of Rule 601(b), however, only prohibits a party to the action from testifying with regard to uncorroborated oral statements of the decedent.

Rule 601. Competency and Incompetency of Witnesses

(a) General Rule. Every person is competent to be a witness except as otherwise provided in these rules. The following witnesses shall be incompetent to testify in any proceeding subject to these rules:

(1) *Insane Persons*. Insane persons who, in the opinion of the court, are in an insane condition of mind at the time when they are offered as a witness, or who, in the opinion of the court, were in that condition when the events happened of which they are called to testify.

(2) *Children*. Children or other persons who, after being examined by the court, appear not to possess sufficient intellect to relate transactions with respect to which they are interrogated.

(b) "Dead Man's Rule" in Civil Actions. In civil actions by or against executors, administrators, or guardians, in which judgment may be rendered for or against them as such, neither party shall be allowed to testify against the others as to any oral statement by the testator, intestate or ward, unless that testimony to the oral statement is corroborated or unless the witness is called at the trial to testify thereto by the opposite party; and, the provisions of this article shall extend to and include all actions by or against the heirs or legal representatives of a decedent based in whole or in part on such oral statement. Except for the foregoing, a witness is not precluded from giving evidence of or concerning any transaction with, any conversations with, any admissions of, or statement by, a deceased or insane party or person merely because the witness is a party to the action or a person interested in the event thereof. The trial court shall, in a proper case, where this rule prohibits an interested party or witness from testifying, instruct the jury that such person is not permitted by the law to give evidence relating to any oral statement by the deceased or ward unless the oral statement is corroborated or unless the party or witness is called at the trial by the opposite party.

(Effective March 1, 1998.)

Article VII. OPINIONS AND EXPERT TESTIMONY

Statutes in Context

Rule 704 permits a witness to testify regarding the witness's opinion of whether the testator had testamentary capacity when the testator executed the will even though such an opinion embraces an ultimate issue to be decided by the trier of fact.

Rule 704. Opinion on Ultimate Issue

Testimony in the form of an opinion or inference otherwise admissible is not objectionable because it embraces an ultimate issue to be decided by the trier of fact.

(Effective March 1, 1998.)

VI.
FAMILY CODE

Title 1. The Marriage Relationship

Subtitle A. Marriage

Chapter 2. The Marriage Relationship

Statutes in Context

Chapter 2 of the Family Code deals with the validity of marriages, both formal marriages and informal or "common law" marriages. These provisions are especially important in determining the identity of a decedent's surviving spouse for intestate succession purposes.

Subchapter D. Validity of Marriage

§ 2.301. Fraud, Mistake, or Illegality in Obtaining License

Except as otherwise provided by this chapter, the validity of a marriage is not affected by any fraud, mistake, or illegality that occurred in obtaining the marriage license.

Added by Acts 1997, 75th Leg., ch. 7, § 1, eff. April 17, 1997.

§ 2.302. Ceremony Conducted by Unauthorized Person

The validity of a marriage is not affected by the lack of authority of the person conducting the marriage ceremony if:

(1) there was a reasonable appearance of authority by that person; and

(2) at least one party to the marriage participated in the ceremony in good faith and that party treats the marriage as valid.

Added by Acts 1997, 75th Leg., ch. 7, § 1, eff. April 17, 1997.

Subchapter E. Marriage Without Formalities

Statutes in Context

Subchapter E explains when an informal or "common law" marriage is valid in Texas.

§ 2.401. Proof of Informal Marriage

(a) In a judicial, administrative, or other proceeding, the marriage of a man and woman may be proved by evidence that:

(1) a declaration of their marriage has been signed as provided by this subchapter; or

(2) the man and woman agreed to be married and after the agreement they lived together in this state as husband and wife and there represented to others that they were married.

(b) If a proceeding in which a marriage is to be proved as provided by Subsection (a)(2) is not commenced before the second anniversary of the date on which the parties separated and ceased living together, it is rebuttably presumed that the parties did not enter into an agreement to be married.

(c) A person under 18 years of age may not:

(1) be a party to an informal marriage; or

(2) execute a declaration of informal marriage under Section 2.402

Added by Acts 1997, 75th Leg., ch. 7, § 1, eff. April 17, 1997. Amended by Acts 1997, 75th Leg., ch. 1362, § 1, eff. Sept. 1, 1997.

§ 2.402. Declaration and Registration of Informal Marriage

(a) A declaration of informal marriage must be signed on a form prescribed by the bureau of vital statistics and provided by the county clerk. Each party to the declaration shall provide the information required in the form.

(b) The declaration form must contain:

(1) a heading entitled "Declaration and Registration of Informal Marriage, __________ County, Texas";

(2) spaces for each party's full name, including the woman's maiden surname, address, date of birth, place of birth, including city, county, and state, and social security number, if any;

(3) a space for indicating the type of document tendered by each party as proof of age and identity;

(4) printed boxes for each party to check "true" or "false" in response to the following statement: "The other party is not related to me as:

(A) an ancestor or descendant, by blood or adoption;

(B) a brother or sister, of the whole or half blood or by adoption;

(C) a parent's brother or sister, of the whole or half blood or by adoption; or

(D) a son or daughter of a brother or sister, of the whole or half blood or by adoption.";

(5) a printed declaration and oath reading: "I SOLEMNLY SWEAR (OR AFFIRM) THAT WE, THE UNDERSIGNED, ARE MARRIED TO EACH OTHER BY VIRTUE OF THE FOLLOWING FACTS: ON OR ABOUT (DATE) WE AGREED TO BE MARRIED, AND AFTER THAT DATE WE LIVED TOGETHER AS HUSBAND AND WIFE AND IN THIS STATE WE REPRESENTED TO OTHERS THAT WE WERE MARRIED. SINCE THE DATE OF MARRIAGE TO THE OTHER PARTY I HAVE NOT BEEN MARRIED TO ANY OTHER PERSON. THIS DECLARATION IS TRUE AND THE INFORMATION IN IT WHICH I HAVE GIVEN IS CORRECT.";

(6) spaces immediately below the printed declaration and oath for the parties' signatures; and

(7) a certificate of the county clerk that the parties made the declaration and oath and the place and date it was made.

(c) Repealed by Acts 1997, 75th Leg., ch. 1362, § 4, eff. Sept. 1, 1997.

Added by Acts 1997, 75th Leg., ch. 7, § 1, eff. April 17, 1997. Amended by Acts 1997, 75th Leg., ch. 1362, § 4, eff. Sept. 1, 1997.

§ 2.403. Proof of Identity and Age

The county clerk shall require proof of the identity and age of each party to the declaration of informal marriage to be established by a certified copy of the party's birth certificate or by some certificate, license, or document issued by this state or another state, the United States, or a foreign government.

Added by Acts 1997, 75th Leg., ch. 7, § 1, eff. April 17, 1997.

§ 2.404. Recording of Declaration of Informal Marriage

(a) The county clerk shall:

(1) determine that all necessary information is recorded on the declaration of informal marriage form and that all necessary documents are submitted to the clerk;

(2) administer the oath to each party to the declaration;

(3) have each party sign the declaration in the clerk's presence; and

(4) execute the clerk's certificate to the declaration.

(b) The county clerk may not certify or record the declaration if:

(1) either party fails to supply any information or provide any document required by this subchapter;

(2) either party is under 18 years of age; or

(3) either party checks "false" in response to the statement of relationship to the other party.

(c) On execution of the declaration, the county clerk shall record the declaration and all documents submitted with the declaration or note a summary of them on the declaration form, deliver the original of the declaration to the parties, and send a copy to the bureau of vital statistics.

(d) A declaration recorded as provided in this section is prima facie evidence of the marriage of the parties.

(e) At the time the parties sign the declaration, the clerk shall distribute to each party printed materials about acquired immune deficiency syndrome (AIDS) and human immunodeficiency virus (HIV). The clerk shall note on the declaration that the distribution was made. The materials shall be prepared and provided to the clerk by the Texas Department of Health and shall be designed to inform the parties about:

(1) the incidence and mode of transmission of AIDS and HIV;

(2) the local availability of medical procedures, including voluntary testing, designed to show or help show whether a person has AIDS or HIV infection, antibodies to HIV, or infection with any other probable causative agent of AIDS; and

(3) available and appropriate counseling services regarding AIDS and HIV infection.

Added by Acts 1997, 75th Leg., ch. 7, § 1, eff. April 17, 1997. Amended by Acts 1997, 75th Leg., ch. 1362, § 2, eff. Sept. 1, 1997.

§ 2.405. Violation by County Clerk; Penalty

A county clerk or deputy county clerk who violates this subchapter commits an offense. An offense under this section is a misdemeanor punishable by a fine of not less than $200 and not more than $500.

Subchapter F. Rights and Duties of Spouses

Statutes in Context

Section 2.501 codifies the fundamental duty of each spouse to support the other spouse.

§ 2.501. Duty to Support

(a) Each spouse has the duty to support the other spouse.

(b) A spouse who fails to discharge the duty of support is liable to any person who provides necessaries to the spouse to whom support is owed.

Added by Acts 1997, 75th Leg., ch. 7, § 1, eff. April 17, 1997.

Subtitle B. Property Rights and Liabilities

Chapter 3. Marital Property Rights and Liabilities

Subchapter A. General Rules for Separate and Community Property

Statutes in Context

Sections 3.001 - 3.006 contain the general rules for determining whether the property of a married individual is the separate property of one spouse or the community property of both spouses. See also Texas Constitution Article XVI, § 15.

§ 3.001. Separate Property

A spouse's separate property consists of:

(1) the property owned or claimed by the spouse before marriage;

(2) the property acquired by the spouse during marriage by gift, devise, or descent; and

(3) the recovery for personal injuries sustained by the spouse during marriage, except any recovery for loss of earning capacity during marriage.

Added by Acts 1997, 75th Leg., ch. 7, § 1, eff. April 17, 1997.

§ 3.002. Community Property

Community property consists of the property, other than separate property, acquired by either spouse during marriage.

Added by Acts 1997, 75th Leg., ch. 7, § 1, eff. April 17, 1997.

§ 3.003. Presumption of Community Property

(a) Property possessed by either spouse during or on dissolution of marriage is presumed to be community property.

(b) The degree of proof necessary to establish that property is separate property is clear and convincing evidence.

Added by Acts 1997, 75th Leg., ch. 7, § 1, eff. April 17, 1997.

§ 3.004. Recordation of Separate Property

(a) A subscribed and acknowledged schedule of a spouse's separate property may be recorded in the deed records of the county in which the parties, or one of them, reside and in the county or counties in which the real property is located.

(b) A schedule of a spouse's separate real property is not constructive notice to a good faith purchaser for value or a creditor without actual notice unless the instrument is acknowledged and recorded in the deed records of the county in which the real property is located.

Added by Acts 1997, 75th Leg., ch. 7, § 1, eff. April 17, 1997.

§ 3.005. Gifts Between Spouses

If one spouse makes a gift of property to the other spouse, the gift is presumed to include all the income and property that may arise from that property.

Added by Acts 1997, 75th Leg., ch. 7, § 1, eff. April 17, 1997.

§ 3.006. Proportional Ownership of Property by Marital Estates

If the community estate of the spouses and the separate estate of a spouse have an ownership interest in property, the respective ownership interests of the marital estates are determined by the rule of inception of title.

Added by Acts 1999, 76th Leg., ch. 692, § 1, eff. Sept. 1, 1999. Amended by Acts 2001, 77th Leg., ch. 838, § 3, eff. Sept. 1, 2001.

Subchapter B. Management, Control, and Disposition of Marital Property

Statutes in Context

Sections 3.101 – 3.104 address issues regarding the management, control, and disposition of separate and community property.

§ 3.101. Managing Separate Property

Each spouse has the sole management, control, and disposition of that spouse's separate property.

Added by Acts 1997, 75th Leg., ch. 7, § 1, eff. April 17, 1997.

§ 3.102. Managing Community Property

(a) During marriage, each spouse has the sole management, control, and disposition of the community property that the spouse would have owned if single, including:

(1) personal earnings;

(2) revenue from separate property;

(3) recoveries for personal injuries; and

(4) the increase and mutations of, and the revenue from, all property subject to the spouse's sole management, control, and disposition.

(b) If community property subject to the sole management, control, and disposition of one spouse is mixed or combined with community property subject to the sole management, control, and disposition of the other spouse, then the mixed or combined community property is subject to the joint management, control, and disposition of the spouses, unless the spouses provide otherwise by power of attorney in writing or other agreement.

(c) Except as provided by Subsection (a), community property is subject to the joint management, control, and disposition of the spouses unless the spouses provide otherwise by power of attorney in writing or other agreement.

Added by Acts 1997, 75th Leg., ch. 7, § 1, eff. April 17, 1997.

§ 3.103. Managing Earnings of Minor

Except as provided by Section 264.0111, during the marriage of the parents of an unemancipated minor for whom a managing conservator has not been appointed, the earnings of the minor are subject to the joint management, control, and disposition of the parents of the minor, unless otherwise provided by agreement of the parents or by judicial order.

Added by Acts 1997, 75th Leg., ch. 7, § 1, eff. April 17, 1997. Amended by Acts 2001, 77th Leg., ch. 964, § 1, eff. Sept. 1, 2001.

§ 3.104. Protection of Third Persons

(a) During marriage, property is presumed to be subject to the sole management, control, and disposition of a spouse if it is held in that spouse's name, as shown by muniment, contract, deposit of funds, or other evidence of ownership, or if it is in that spouse's possession and is not subject to such evidence of ownership.

(b) A third person dealing with a spouse is entitled to rely, as against the other spouse or anyone claiming from that spouse, on that spouse's authority to deal with the property if:

(1) the property is presumed to be subject to the sole management, control, and disposition of the spouse; and

(2) the person dealing with the spouse:

(A) is not a party to a fraud on the other spouse or another person; and

(B) does not have actual or constructive notice of the spouse's lack of authority.

Added by Acts 1997, 75th Leg., ch. 7, § 1, eff. April 17, 1997.

Subchapter C. Marital Property Liabilities

Statutes in Context

Sections 3.201 - 3.203 focus on the personal liability of each spouse and the liability of separate and community property for the debts of the spouses.

§ 3.201. Spousal Liability

(a) A person is personally liable for the acts of the person's spouse only if:

(1) the spouse acts as an agent for the person; or

(2) the spouse incurs a debt for necessaries as provided by Subchapter F, Chapter 2.

(b) Except as provided by this subchapter, community property is not subject to a liability that arises from an act of a spouse.

(c) A spouse does not act as an agent for the other spouse solely because of the marriage relationship.

Added by Acts 1997, 75th Leg., ch. 7, § 1, eff. April 17, 1997.

§ 3.202. Rules of Marital Property Liability

(a) A spouse's separate property is not subject to liabilities of the other spouse unless both spouses are liable by other rules of law.

(b) Unless both spouses are personally liable as provided by this subchapter, the community property subject to a spouse's sole management, control, and disposition is not subject to:

(1) any liabilities that the other spouse incurred before marriage; or

(2) any nontortious liabilities that the other spouse incurs during marriage.

(c) The community property subject to a spouse's sole or joint management, control, and disposition is subject to the liabilities incurred by the spouse before or during marriage.

(d) All community property is subject to tortious liability of either spouse incurred during marriage.

Added by Acts 1997, 75th Leg., ch. 7, § 1, eff. April 17, 1997.

§ 3.203. Order in Which Property is Subject to Execution

(a) A judge may determine, as deemed just and equitable, the order in which particular separate or community property is subject to execution and sale to satisfy a judgment, if the property subject to liability for a judgment includes any combination of:

(1) a spouse's separate property;

(2) community property subject to a spouse's sole management, control, and disposition;

(3) community property subject to the other spouse's sole management, control, and disposition; and

(4) community property subject to the spouses' joint management, control, and disposition.

(b) In determining the order in which particular property is subject to execution and sale, the judge shall consider the facts surrounding the transaction or occurrence on which the suit is based.

Added by Acts 1997, 75th Leg., ch. 7, § 1, eff. April 17, 1997.

Subchapter D. Management, Control, and Disposition of Marital Property Under Unusual Circumstances

Statutes in Context

Sections 3.301 - 3.309 explain how to handle the management, control, and disposition of marital property under unusual circumstances such as when a spouse is missing, permanently abandoned, or permanently separated.

§ 3.301. Missing, Abandoned, or Separated Spouse

(a) A spouse may file a sworn petition stating the facts that make it desirable for the petitioning spouse to manage, control, and dispose of community property described or defined in the petition that would otherwise be subject to the sole or joint management, control, and disposition of the other spouse if:

(1) the other spouse has disappeared and that spouse's location remains unknown to the petitioning spouse, unless the spouse is reported to be a prisoner of war or missing on public service;

(2) the other spouse has permanently abandoned the petitioning spouse; or

(3) the spouses are permanently separated.

(b) The petition may be filed in a court in the county in which the petitioner resided at the time the separation began, or the abandonment or disappearance occurred, not earlier than the 60th day after the date of the occurrence of the event. If both spouses are nonresidents of this state at the time the petition is filed, the petition may be filed in a court in a county in which any part of the described or defined community property is located.

Added by Acts 1997, 75th Leg., ch. 7, § 1, eff. April 17, 1997. Amended by Acts 2001, 77th Leg., ch. 217, § 23, eff. Sept. 1, 2001.

§ 3.302. Spouse Missing on Public Service

(a) If a spouse is reported by an executive department of the United States to be a prisoner of war or missing on the public service of the United States, the spouse of the prisoner of war or missing person may file a sworn petition stating the facts that make it desirable for the petitioner to manage, control, and dispose of the community property described or defined in the petition that would otherwise be subject to the sole or joint management, control, and disposition of the imprisoned or missing spouse.

(b) The petition may be filed in a court in the county in which the petitioner resided at the time the report was made not earlier than six months after the date of the notice that a spouse is reported to be a prisoner of war or missing on public service. If both spouses were nonresidents of this state at the time the report was made, the petition shall be filed in a court in a county in which any part of the described or defined property is located.

Added by Acts 1997, 75th Leg., ch. 7, § 1, eff. April 17, 1997.

§ 3.303. Appointment of Attorney

(a) Except as provided by Subsection (b), the court may appoint an attorney in a suit filed under this subchapter for the respondent.

(b) The court shall appoint an attorney in a suit filed under this subchapter for a respondent reported to be a prisoner of war or missing on public service.

(c) The court shall allow a reasonable fee for an appointed attorney's services as a part of the costs of the suit.

Added by Acts 1997, 75th Leg., ch. 7, § 1, eff. April 17, 1997.

§ 3.304. Notice of Hearing; Citation

(a) Notice of the hearing, accompanied by a copy of the petition, shall be issued and served on the attorney representing the respondent, if an attorney has been appointed.

(b) If an attorney has not been appointed for the respondent, citation shall be issued and served on the respondent as in other civil cases.

Added by Acts 1997, 75th Leg., ch. 7, § 1, eff. April 17, 1997.

§ 3.305. Citation by Publication

(a) If the residence of the respondent, other than a respondent reported to be a prisoner of war or missing on public service, is unknown, citation shall be published in a newspaper of general circulation published in the county in which the petition was filed. If that county has no newspaper of general circulation, citation shall be published in a newspaper of general circulation in an adjacent county or in the nearest county in which a newspaper of general circulation is published.

(b) The notice shall be published once a week for two consecutive weeks before the hearing, but the first notice may not be published after the 20th day before the date set for the hearing.

Added by Acts 1997, 75th Leg., ch. 7, § 1, eff. April 17, 1997.

§ 3.306. Court Order for Management, Control, and Disposition of Community Property

(a) After hearing the evidence in a suit under this subchapter, the court, on terms the court considers just and equitable, shall render an order describing or defining the community property at issue that will be subject to the management, control, and disposition of each spouse during marriage.

(b) The court may:

(1) impose any condition and restriction the court deems necessary to protect the rights of the respondent;

(2) require a bond conditioned on the faithful administration of the property; and

(3) require payment to the registry of the court of all or a portion of the proceeds of the sale of the property, to be disbursed in accordance with the court's further directions.

Added by Acts 1997, 75th Leg., ch. 7, § 1, eff. April 17, 1997.

§ 3.307. Continuing Jurisdiction of Court; Vacating Original Order

(a) The court has continuing jurisdiction over the court's order rendered under this subchapter.

(b) On the motion of either spouse, the court shall amend or vacate the original order after notice and hearing if:

(1) the spouse who disappeared reappears;

(2) the abandonment or permanent separation ends; or

(3) the spouse who was reported to be a prisoner of war or missing on public service returns.

Added by Acts 1997, 75th Leg., ch. 7, § 1, eff. April 17, 1997. Amended by Acts 2001, 77th Leg., ch. 217, § 24, eff. Sept. 1, 2001.

§ 3.308. Recording Order to Affect Real Property

An order authorized by this subchapter affecting real property is not constructive notice to a good faith purchaser for value or to a creditor without actual notice unless the order is recorded in the deed records of the county in which the real property is located.

Added by Acts 1997, 75th Leg., ch. 7, § 1, eff. April 17, 1997.

§ 3.309. Remedies Cumulative

The remedies provided in this subchapter are cumulative of other rights, powers, and remedies afforded spouses by law.

Added by Acts 1997, 75th Leg., ch. 7, § 1, eff. April 17, 1997.

Subchapter E. Equitable Interest of Community Estate in Enhanced Value of Separate Property

---

Statutes in Context

Sections 3.401 - 3.410 provide that a marital estate that makes an economic contribution to property owned by another marital estate has a claim for economic contribution with respect to the benefited estate. This claim does not create an ownership interest in the property nor does it affect the right to manage, control, or dispose of marital property. The claim matures when the first spouse dies and upon divorce.

---

§ 3.401. Definitions

In this subchapter:

(1) "Claim for economic contribution" means a claim made under this subchapter.

(2) "Economic contribution" means the contribution to a marital estate described by Section 3.402.

(3) "Equity" means, with respect to specific property owned by one or more marital estates, the amount computed by subtracting from the fair market value of the property as of a specific date the amount of a lawful lien specific to the property on that same date.

(4) "Marital estate" means one of three estates:

(A) the community property owned by the spouses together and referred to as the community marital estate;

(B) the separate property owned individually by the husband and referred to as a separate marital estate; or

(C) the separate property owned individually by the wife, also referred to as a separate marital estate.

(5) "Spouse" means a husband, who is a man, or a wife, who is a woman. A member of a civil union or similar relationship entered into in another state between persons of the same sex is not a spouse.

Added by Acts 1999, 76th Leg., ch. 692, § 2, eff. Sept. 1, 1999. Amended by Acts 2001, 77th Leg., ch. 838, § 2, eff. Sept. 1, 2001.

§ 3.402. Economic Contribution

(a) For purposes of this subchapter, "economic contribution" is the dollar amount of:

(1) the reduction of the principal amount of a debt secured by a lien on property owned before marriage, to the extent the debt existed at the time of marriage;

(2) the reduction of the principal amount of a debt secured by a lien on property received by a spouse by gift, devise, or descent during a marriage, to the extent the debt existed at the time the property was received;

(3) the reduction of the principal amount of that part of a debt, including a home equity loan:

(A) incurred during a marriage;

(B) secured by a lien on property; and

(C) incurred for the acquisition of, or for capital improvements to, property;

(4) the reduction of the principal amount of that part of a debt:

(A) incurred during a marriage;

(B) secured by a lien on property owned by a spouse;

(C) for which the creditor agreed to look for repayment solely to the separate marital estate of the spouse on whose property the lien attached; and

(D) incurred for the acquisition of, or for capital improvements to, property;

(5) the refinancing of the principal amount described by Subdivisions (1)-(4), to the extent the refinancing reduces that principal amount in a manner described by the appropriate subdivision; and

(6) capital improvements to property other than by incurring debt.

(b) "Economic contribution" does not include the dollar amount of:

(1) expenditures for ordinary maintenance and repair or for taxes, interest, or insurance; or

(2) the contribution by a spouse of time, toil, talent, or effort during the marriage.

Added by Acts 1999, 76th Leg., ch. 692, § 2, eff. Sept. 1, 1999. Amended by Acts 2001, 77th Leg., ch. 838, § 2, eff. Sept. 1, 2001.

§ 3.403. Claim Based on Economic Contribution

(a) A marital estate that makes an economic contribution to property owned by another marital estate has a claim for economic contribution with respect to the benefited estate.

(b) The amount of the claim under this section is equal to the product of:

(1) the equity in the benefited property on the date of dissolution of the marriage, the death of a spouse, or disposition of the property; multiplied by

(2) a fraction of which:

(A) the numerator is the economic contribution to the property owned by the benefited marital estate by the contributing marital estate; and

(B) the denominator is an amount equal to the sum of:

(i) the economic contribution to the property owned by the benefited marital estate by the contributing marital estate; and

(ii) the contribution by the benefited estate to the equity in the property owned by the benefited estate.

(b-1) The amount of the contribution by the benefited marital estate under Subsection (b)(2)(B)(ii) is measured by determining:

(1) if the benefited estate is the community property estate:

(A) the net equity of the community property estate in the property owned by the community property estate as of the date of the first economic contribution to that property by the contributing separate property estate; and

(B) any additional economic contribution to the equity in the property owned by the community property estate made by the benefited community property estate after the date described by Subdivision (A); or

(2) if the benefited estate is the separate property estate of a spouse:

(A) the net equity of the separate property estate in the property owned by the separate property estate as of the date of the first economic contribution to that property by the contributing community property estate or the separate property estate of the other spouse; and

(B) any additional contribution to the equity in the property owned by the separate property estate made by the benefited separate property estate after the date described by Subdivision (A).

(c) The amount of a claim under this section may be less than the total of the economic contributions made by the contributing estate, but may not cause the contributing estate to owe funds to the benefited estate.

(d) The amount of a claim under this section may not exceed the equity in the property on the date of dissolution of the marriage, the death of a spouse, or disposition of the property.

(e) The use and enjoyment of property during a marriage for which a claim for economic contribution to the property exists does not create a claim of an offsetting benefit against the claim.

Added by Acts 1999, 76th Leg., ch. 692, § 2, eff. Sept. 1, 1999. Amended by Acts 2001, 77th Leg., ch. 838, § 2, eff. Sept. 1, 2001; Acts 2003, 78th Leg., ch. 230, § 1, eff. Sept. 1, 2003.

§ 3.404. Application of Inception of Title Rule; Ownership Interest Not Created

(a) This subchapter does not affect the rule of inception of title under which the character of property is determined at the time the right to own or claim the property arises.

(b) The claim for economic contribution created under this subchapter does not create an ownership interest in property, but does create a claim against the property of the benefited estate by the contributing estate. The claim matures on dissolution of the marriage or the death of either spouse.

Added by Acts 1999, 76th Leg., ch. 692, § 2, eff. Sept. 1, 1999. Amended by Acts 2001, 77th Leg., ch. 838, § 2, eff. Sept. 1, 2001.

§ 3.405. Management Rights

This subchapter does not affect the right to manage, control, or dispose of marital property as provided by this chapter.

Added by Acts 1999, 76th Leg., ch. 692, § 2, eff. Sept. 1, 1999. Amended by Acts 2001, 77th Leg., ch. 838, § 2, eff. Sept. 1, 2001.

§ 3.406. Equitable Lien

(a) On dissolution of a marriage, the court shall impose an equitable lien on property of a marital estate to secure a claim for economic contribution in that property by another marital estate.

(b) On the death of a spouse, a court shall, on application for a claim of economic contribution brought by the surviving spouse, the personal representative of the estate of the deceased spouse, or any other person interested in the estate, as defined by Section 3, Texas Probate Code, impose an equitable lien on the property of a benefited marital estate to secure a claim for economic contribution by a contributing marital estate.

(c) Subject to homestead restrictions, an equitable lien under this section may be imposed on the entirety of a spouse's property in the marital estate and is not limited to the item of property that benefited from an economic contribution.

Added by Acts 1999, 76th Leg., ch. 692, § 2, eff. Sept. 1, 1999. Amended by Acts 2001, 77th Leg., ch. 838, § 2, eff. Sept. 1, 2001.

§ 3.407. Offsetting Claims

The court shall offset a claim for one marital estate's economic contribution in a specific asset of a second marital estate against the second marital estate's claim

for economic contribution in a specific asset of the first marital estate.
Added by Acts 2001, 77th Leg., ch. 838, § 2, eff. Sept. 1, 2001.

§ 3.408. Claim for Reimbursement

(a) A claim for economic contribution does not abrogate another claim for reimbursement in a factual circumstance not covered by this subchapter. In the case of a conflict between a claim for economic contribution under this subchapter and a claim for reimbursement, the claim for economic contribution, if proven, prevails.

(b) A claim for reimbursement includes:

(1) payment by one marital estate of the unsecured liabilities of another marital estate; and

(2) inadequate compensation for the time, toil, talent, and effort of a spouse by a business entity under the control and direction of that spouse.

(c) The court shall resolve a claim for reimbursement by using equitable principles, including the principle that claims for reimbursement may be offset against each other if the court determines it to be appropriate.

(d) Benefits for the use and enjoyment of property may be offset against a claim for reimbursement for expenditures to benefit a marital estate on property that does not involve a claim for economic contribution to the property.
Added by Acts 2001, 77th Leg., ch. 838, § 2, eff. Sept. 1, 2001.

§ 3.409. Nonreimbursable Claims

The court may not recognize a marital estate's claim for reimbursement for:

(1) the payment of child support, alimony, or spousal maintenance;

(2) the living expenses of a spouse or child of a spouse;

(3) contributions of property of a nominal value;

(4) the payment of a liability of a nominal amount; or

(5) a student loan owed by a spouse.
Added by Acts 2001, 77th Leg., ch. 838, § 2, eff. Sept. 1, 2001.

§ 3.410. Effect of Marital Property Agreements

A premarital or marital property agreement, whether executed before, on, or after September 1, 1999, that satisfies the requirements of Chapter 4 is effective to waive, release, assign, or partition a claim for economic contribution under this subchapter to the same extent the agreement would have been effective to waive, release, assign, or partition a claim for reimbursement under the law as it existed immediately before September 1, 1999, unless the agreement provides otherwise.
Added by Acts 2001, 77th Leg., ch. 838, § 2, eff. Sept. 1, 2001.

Chapter 4. Premarital and Marital Property Agreements

Subchapter A. Uniform Premarital Agreement Act

Statutes in Context

The Texas version of the Uniform Premarital Agreement Act are contained in §§ 4.001 - 4.010.

---

§ 4.001. Definitions

In this subchapter:

(1) "Premarital agreement" means an agreement between prospective spouses made in contemplation of marriage and to be effective on marriage.

(2) "Property" means an interest, present or future, legal or equitable, vested or contingent, in real or personal property, including income and earnings.
Added by Acts 1997, 75th Leg., ch. 7, § 1, eff. April 17, 1997.

§ 4.002. Formalities

A premarital agreement must be in writing and signed by both parties. The agreement is enforceable without consideration.
Added by Acts 1997, 75th Leg., ch. 7, § 1, eff. April 17, 1997.

§ 4.003. Content

(a) The parties to a premarital agreement may contract with respect to:

(1) the rights and obligations of each of the parties in any of the property of either or both of them whenever and wherever acquired or located;

(2) the right to buy, sell, use, transfer, exchange, abandon, lease, consume, expend, assign, create a security interest in, mortgage, encumber, dispose of, or otherwise manage and control property;

(3) the disposition of property on separation, marital dissolution, death, or the occurrence or nonoccurrence of any other event;

(4) the modification or elimination of spousal support;

(5) the making of a will, trust, or other arrangement to carry out the provisions of the agreement;

(6) the ownership rights in and disposition of the death benefit from a life insurance policy;

(7) the choice of law governing the construction of the agreement; and

(8) any other matter, including their personal rights and obligations, not in violation of public policy or a statute imposing a criminal penalty.

(b) The right of a child to support may not be adversely affected by a premarital agreement.
Added by Acts 1997, 75th Leg., ch. 7, § 1, eff. April 17, 1997.

§ 4.004. Effect of Marriage

A premarital agreement becomes effective on marriage.
Added by Acts 1997, 75th Leg., ch. 7, § 1, eff. April 17, 1997.

§ 4.005. Amendment or Revocation

After marriage, a premarital agreement may be amended or revoked only by a written agreement signed by the parties. The amended agreement or the revocation is enforceable without consideration.
Added by Acts 1997, 75th Leg., ch. 7, § 1, eff. April 17, 1997.

§ 4.006. Enforcement

(a) A premarital agreement is not enforceable if the party against whom enforcement is requested proves that:

(1) the party did not sign the agreement voluntarily; or

(2) the agreement was unconscionable when it was signed and, before signing the agreement, that party:

(A) was not provided a fair and reasonable disclosure of the property or financial obligations of the other party;

(B) did not voluntarily and expressly waive, in writing, any right to disclosure of the property or financial obligations of the other party beyond the disclosure provided; and

(C) did not have, or reasonably could not have had, adequate knowledge of the property or financial obligations of the other party.

(b) An issue of unconscionability of a premarital agreement shall be decided by the court as a matter of law.

(c) The remedies and defenses in this section are the exclusive remedies or defenses, including common law remedies or defenses.
Added by Acts 1997, 75th Leg., ch. 7, § 1, eff. April 17, 1997.

§ 4.007. Enforcement: Void Marriage

If a marriage is determined to be void, an agreement that would otherwise have been a premarital agreement is enforceable only to the extent necessary to avoid an inequitable result.
Added by Acts 1997, 75th Leg., ch. 7, § 1, eff. April 17, 1997.

§ 4.008. Limitation of Actions

A statute of limitations applicable to an action asserting a claim for relief under a premarital agreement is tolled during the marriage of the parties to the agreement. However, equitable defenses limiting the time for enforcement, including laches and estoppel, are available to either party.
Added by Acts 1997, 75th Leg., ch. 7, § 1, eff. April 17, 1997.

§ 4.009. Application and Construction

This subchapter shall be applied and construed to effect its general purpose to make uniform the law with respect to the subject of this subchapter among states enacting these provisions.
Added by Acts 1997, 75th Leg., ch. 7, § 1, eff. April 17, 1997.

§ 4.010. Short Title

This subchapter may be cited as the Uniform Premarital Agreement Act.
Added by Acts 1997, 75th Leg., ch. 7, § 1, eff. April 17, 1997.

Subchapter B. Marital Property Agreement

Statutes in Context

Sections 4.101 - 4.106 detail the procedure spouses should follow if they wish to partition separate property into community property. Compare §§ 4.201 - 4.206 which deal with the conversion of separate property into community property.

§ 4.101. Definition

In this subchapter, "property" has the meaning assigned by Section 4.001.
Added by Acts 1997, 75th Leg., ch. 7, § 1, eff. April 17, 1997.

§ 4.102. Partition or Exchange of Community Property

At any time, the spouses may partition or exchange between themselves all or part of their community property, then existing or to be acquired, as the spouses may desire. Property or a property interest transferred to a spouse by a partition or exchange agreement becomes that spouse's separate property. The partition or exchange of property includes future earnings and income arising from the property as the separate property of the owning spouse unless the spouses agree in a record that the future earnings and income will be community property after the partition or exchange.
Added by Acts 1997, 75th Leg., ch. 7, § 1, eff. April 17, 1997. Amended by Acts 2003, 78th Leg., ch. 230, § 2, eff. Sept. 1, 2003.

§ 4.103. Agreement Between Spouses Concerning Income or Property From Separate Property

At any time, the spouses may agree that the income or property arising from the separate property that is then owned by one of them, or that may thereafter be acquired, shall be the separate property of the owner.
Added by Acts 1997, 75th Leg., ch. 7, § 1, eff. April 17, 1997.

§ 4.104. Formalities

A partition or exchange agreement must be in writing and signed by both parties.
Added by Acts 1997, 75th Leg., ch. 7, § 1, eff. April 17, 1997.

§ 4.105. Enforcement

(a) A partition or exchange agreement is not enforceable if the party against whom enforcement is requested proves that:

(1) the party did not sign the agreement voluntarily; or

(2) the agreement was unconscionable when it was signed and, before execution of the agreement, that party:

(A) was not provided a fair and reasonable disclosure of the property or financial obligations of the other party;

(B) did not voluntarily and expressly waive, in writing, any right to disclosure of the property or financial obligations of the other party beyond the disclosure provided; and

(C) did not have, or reasonably could not have had, adequate knowledge of the property or financial obligations of the other party.

(b) An issue of unconscionability of a partition or exchange agreement shall be decided by the court as a matter of law.

(c) The remedies and defenses in this section are the exclusive remedies or defenses, including common law remedies or defenses.

Added by Acts 1997, 75th Leg., ch. 7, § 1, eff. April 17, 1997.

§ 4.106. Rights of Creditors and Recordation Under Partition or Exchange Agreement

(a) A provision of a partition or exchange agreement made under this subchapter is void with respect to the rights of a preexisting creditor whose rights are intended to be defrauded by it.

(b) A partition or exchange agreement made under this subchapter may be recorded in the deed records of the county in which a party resides and in the county in which the real property affected is located. An agreement made under this subchapter is constructive notice to a good faith purchaser for value or a creditor without actual notice only if the instrument is acknowledged and recorded in the county in which the real property is located.

Added by Acts 1997, 75th Leg., ch. 7, § 1, eff. April 17, 1997.

Subchapter C. Agreement to Convert Separate Property to Community Property

---

Statutes in Context

Sections 4.201 - 4.206 address the mechanism for spouses to convert separate property into community property. Texas law did not grant spouses the right to convert separate into community property until January 1, 2000 when an amendment to Texas Constitution Art. XVI, § 15 took effect. Compare §§ 4.101 - 4.106 which detail the procedure spouses should follow if they wish to partition separate property into community property.

---

§ 4.201. Definition

In this subchapter, "property" has the meaning assigned by Section 4.001.

Added by Acts 1999, 76th Leg., ch. 692, § 3, eff. Jan. 1, 2000.

§ 4.202. Agreement to Convert to Community Property

At any time, spouses may agree that all or part of the separate property owned by either or both spouses is converted to community property.

Added by Acts 1999, 76th Leg., ch. 692, § 3, eff. Jan. 1, 2000.

§ 4.203. Formalities of Agreement

(a) An agreement to convert separate property to community property:

(1) must be in writing and:

(A) be signed by the spouses;

(B) identify the property being converted; and

(C) specify that the property is being converted to the spouses' community property; and

(2) is enforceable without consideration.

(b) The mere transfer of a spouse's separate property to the name of the other spouse or to the name of both spouses is not sufficient to convert the property to community property under this subchapter.

Added by Acts 1999, 76th Leg., ch. 692, § 3, eff. Jan. 1, 2000.

§ 4.204. Management of Converted Property

Except as specified in the agreement to convert the property and as provided by Subchapter B, Chapter 3, and other law, property converted to community property under this subchapter is subject to:

(1) the sole management, control, and disposition of the spouse in whose name the property is held;

(2) the sole management, control, and disposition of the spouse who transferred the property if the property is not subject to evidence of ownership;

(3) the joint management, control, and disposition of the spouses if the property is held in the name of both spouses; or

(4) the joint management, control, and disposition of the spouses if the property is not subject to evidence of ownership and was owned by both spouses before the property was converted to community property.

Added by Acts 1999, 76th Leg., ch. 692, § 3, eff. Jan. 1, 2000.

§ 4.205. Enforcement

(a) An agreement to convert property to community property under this subchapter is not enforceable if the spouse against whom enforcement is sought proves that the spouse did not:

(1) execute the agreement voluntarily; or

(2) receive a fair and reasonable disclosure of the legal effect of converting the property to community property.

(b) An agreement that contains the following statement, or substantially similar words, prominently displayed in bold-faced type, capital letters, or underlined, is rebuttably presumed to provide a fair and reasonable disclosure of the legal effect of converting property to community property:

> "THIS INSTRUMENT CHANGES SEPARATE PROPERTY TO COMMUNITY PROPERTY. THIS MAY HAVE ADVERSE CONSEQUENCES DURING MARRIAGE AND ON TERMINATION OF THE MARRIAGE BY DEATH OR DIVORCE. FOR EXAMPLE:
> "EXPOSURE TO CREDITORS. IF YOU SIGN THIS AGREEMENT, ALL OR PART OF THE SEPARATE PROPERTY BEING CONVERTED TO COMMUNITY PROPERTY MAY BECOME SUBJECT TO THE LIABILITIES OF YOUR SPOUSE. IF YOU DO NOT SIGN THIS AGREEMENT, YOUR SEPARATE PROPERTY IS GENERALLY NOT SUBJECT TO THE LIABILITIES OF YOUR SPOUSE UNLESS YOU ARE PERSONALLY LIABLE UNDER ANOTHER RULE OF LAW.
> "LOSS OF MANAGEMENT RIGHTS. IF YOU SIGN THIS AGREEMENT, ALL OR PART OF THE SEPARATE PROPERTY BEING CONVERTED TO COMMUNITY PROPERTY MAY BECOME SUBJECT TO EITHER THE JOINT MANAGEMENT, CONTROL, AND DISPOSITION OF YOU AND YOUR SPOUSE OR THE SOLE MANAGEMENT, CONTROL, AND DISPOSITION OF YOUR SPOUSE ALONE. IN THAT EVENT, YOU WILL LOSE YOUR MANAGEMENT RIGHTS OVER THE PROPERTY. IF YOU DO NOT SIGN THIS AGREEMENT, YOU WILL GENERALLY RETAIN THOSE RIGHTS."
> "LOSS OF PROPERTY OWNERSHIP. IF YOU SIGN THIS AGREEMENT AND YOUR MARRIAGE IS SUBSEQUENTLY TERMINATED BY THE DEATH OF EITHER SPOUSE OR BY DIVORCE, ALL OR PART OF THE SEPARATE PROPERTY BEING CONVERTED TO COMMUNITY PROPERTY MAY BECOME THE SOLE PROPERTY OF YOUR SPOUSE OR YOUR SPOUSE'S HEIRS. IF YOU DO NOT SIGN THIS AGREEMENT, YOU GENERALLY CANNOT BE DEPRIVED OF OWNERSHIP OF YOUR SEPARATE PROPERTY ON TERMINATION OF YOUR MARRIAGE, WHETHER BY DEATH OR DIVORCE."

(c) If a proceeding regarding enforcement of an agreement under this subchapter occurs after the death of the spouse against whom enforcement is sought, the proof required by Subsection (a) may be made by an heir of the spouse or the personal representative of the estate of that spouse.
Added by Acts 1999, 76th Leg., ch. 692, § 3, eff. Jan. 1, 2000. Amended by Acts 2003, 78th Leg., ch. 230, § 3, eff. Sept. 1, 2003.

§ 4.206. Rights of Creditors; Recording

(a) A conversion of separate property to community property does not affect the rights of a preexisting creditor of the spouse whose separate property is being converted.

(b) A conversion of separate property to community property may be recorded in the deed records of the county in which a spouse resides and of the county in which any real property is located.

(c) A conversion of real property from separate property to community. property is constructive notice to a good faith purchaser for value or a creditor without actual notice only if the agreement to convert the property is acknowledged and recorded in the deed records of the county in which the real property is located.
Added by Acts 1999, 76th Leg., ch. 692, § 3, eff. Jan. 1, 2000.

Chapter 5. Homestead Rights

Statutes in Context

Sections 5.001 - 5.108 detail rules applicable to the sale of the homestead, both generally and in unusual circumstances such as when the location of a spouse is unknown.

Subchapter A. Sale of Homestead; General Rule

§ 5.001. Sale, Conveyance, or Encumbrance of Homestead

Whether the homestead is the separate property of either spouse or community property, neither spouse may sell, convey, or encumber the homestead without the joinder of the other spouse except as provided in this chapter or by other rules of law.
Added by Acts 1997, 75th Leg., ch. 7, § 1, eff. April 17, 1997.

§ 5.002. Sale of Separate Homestead After Spouse Judicially Declared Incapacitated

If the homestead is the separate property of a spouse and the other spouse has been judicially declared incapacitated by a court exercising original jurisdiction over guardianship and other matters under Chapter XIII, Texas Probate Code, the owner may sell, convey, or encumber the homestead without the joinder of the other spouse.
Amended by Acts 2001, 77th Leg., ch. 217, § 25, eff. Sept. 1, 2001.

§ 5.003. Sale of Community Homestead After Spouse Judicially Declared Incapacitated

If the homestead is the community property of the spouses and one spouse has been judicially declared incapacitated by a court exercising original jurisdiction over guardianship and other matters under Chapter XIII, Texas Probate Code, the competent spouse may sell, convey, or encumber the homestead without the joinder of the other spouse.
Added by Acts 1997, 75th Leg., ch. 7, § 1, eff. April 17, 1997. Renumbered from V.T.C.A., Family Code 5.107 and amended by Acts 2001, 77th Leg., ch. 217, § 29, eff. Sept. 1, 2001.

Subchapter B. Sale of Homestead Under Unusual Circumstances

§ 5.101. Sale of Separate Homestead Under Unusual Circumstances

If the homestead is the separate property of a spouse, that spouse may file a sworn petition that gives a description of the property, states the facts that make it desirable for the spouse to sell, convey, or encumber the homestead without the joinder of the other spouse, and alleges that the other spouse:

(1) has disappeared and that the location of the spouse remains unknown to the petitioning spouse;

(2) has permanently abandoned the homestead and the petitioning spouse;

(3) has permanently abandoned the homestead and the spouses are permanently separated; or

(4) has been reported by an executive department of the United States to be a prisoner of war or missing on public service of the United States.

Added by Acts 1997, 75th Leg., ch. 7, § 1, eff. April 17, 1997. Amended by Acts 2001, 77th Leg., ch. 217, § 26, eff. Sept. 1, 2001.

§ 5.102. Sale of Community Homestead Under Unusual Circumstances

If the homestead is the community property of the spouses, one spouse may file a sworn petition that gives a description of the property, states the facts that make it desirable for the petitioning spouse to sell, convey, or encumber the homestead without the joinder of the other spouse, and alleges that the other spouse:

(1) has disappeared and that the location of the spouse remains unknown to the petitioning spouse;

(2) has permanently abandoned the homestead and the petitioning spouse;

(3) has permanently abandoned the homestead and the spouses are permanently separated; or

(4) has been reported by an executive department of the United States to be a prisoner of war or missing on public service of the United States.

Added by Acts 1997, 75th Leg., ch. 7, § 1, eff. April 17, 1997. Amended by Acts 2001, 77th Leg., ch. 217, § 27, eff Sept. 1, 2001.

§ 5.103. Time for Filing Petition

The petitioning spouse may file the petition in a court of the county in which any portion of the property is located not earlier than the 60th day after the date of the occurrence of an event described by Sections 5.101(1)(3) and 5.102(1)(3) or not less than six months after the date the other spouse has been reported to be a prisoner of war or missing on public service.

Added by Acts 1997, 75th Leg., ch. 7, § 1, eff. April 17, 1997. Amended by Acts 2001, 77th Leg., ch. 217, § 28, eff. Sept. 1, 2001.

§ 5.104. Appointment of Attorney

(a) Except as provided by Subsection (b), the court may appoint an attorney in a suit filed under this subchapter for the respondent.

(b) The court shall appoint an attorney in a suit filed under this subchapter for a respondent reported to be a prisoner of war or missing on public service.

(c) The court shall allow a reasonable fee for the appointed attorney's services as a part of the costs of the suit.

Added by Acts 1997, 75th Leg., ch. 7, § 1, eff. April 17, 1997.

§ 5.105. Citation; Notice of Hearing

Citation and notice of hearing for a suit filed as provided by this subchapter shall be issued and served in the manner provided in Subchapter D, Chapter 3.

Added by Acts 1997, 75th Leg., ch. 7, § 1, eff. April 17, 1997.

§ 5.106. Court Order

(a) After notice and hearing, the court shall render an order the court deems just and equitable with respect to the sale, conveyance, or encumbrance of a separate property homestead.

(b) After hearing the evidence, the court, on terms the court deems just and equitable, shall render an order describing or defining the community property at issue that will be subject to the management, control, and disposition of each spouse during marriage.

(c) The court may:

(1) impose any conditions and restrictions the court deems necessary to protect the rights of the respondent;

(2) require a bond conditioned on the faithful administration of the property; and

(3) require payment to the registry of the court of all or a portion of the proceeds of the sale of the property to be disbursed in accordance with the court's further directions.

Added by Acts 1997, 75th Leg., ch. 7, § 1, eff. April 17, 1997.

§ 5.107. Renumbered as V.T.C.A., Family Code § 5.003 by Acts 2001, 77th Leg., ch. 217, § 29, eff. Sept. 1, 2001.

§ 5.108. Remedies and Powers Cumulative

The remedies and the powers of a spouse provided by this subchapter are cumulative of the other rights, powers, and remedies afforded the spouses by law.

Added by Acts 1997, 75th Leg., ch. 7, § 1, eff. April 17, 1997.

Subtitle C. Dissolution of Marriage

Chapter 7. Award of Marital Property

Statutes in Context

Chapter 7 explains how marital property is divided upon divorce. Generally, the court awards separate property to the spouse who owns the property while community property is divided in a manner that the court deems just and right after examining the rights of each spouse and any children of the marriage. Special rules are provided for the disposition of insurance, retirement, pension, and similar arrangements.

§ 7.001. General Rule of Property Division

In a decree of divorce or annulment, the court shall order a division of the estate of the parties in a manner that the court deems just and right, having due regard for the rights of each party and any children of the marriage.

Added by Acts 1997, 75th Leg., ch. 7, § 1, eff. April 17, 1997.

§ 7.002. Division of Property Under Special Circumstances

(a) In addition to the division of the estate of the parties required by Section 7.001, in a decree of divorce or annulment the court shall order a division of the following real and personal property, wherever situated, in a manner that the court deems just and right, having due regard for the rights of each party and any children of the marriage:

(1) property that was acquired by either spouse while domiciled in another state and that would have been community property if the spouse who acquired the property had been domiciled in this state at the time of the acquisition; or

(2) property that was acquired by either spouse in exchange for real or personal property and that would have been community property if the spouse who acquired the property so exchanged had been domiciled in this state at the time of its acquisition.

(b) In a decree of divorce or annulment, the court shall award to a spouse the following real and personal property, wherever situated, as the separate property of the spouse:

(1) property that was acquired by the spouse while domiciled in another state and that would have been the spouse's separate property if the spouse had been domiciled in this state at the time of acquisition; or

(2) property that was acquired by the spouse in exchange for real or personal property and that would have been the spouse's separate property if the spouse had been domiciled in this state at the time of acquisition.

(c) In a decree of divorce or annulment, the court shall confirm the following as the separate property of a spouse if partitioned or exchanged by written agreement of the spouses:

(1) income and earnings from the spouses' property, wages, salaries, and other forms of compensation received on or after January 1 of the year in which the suit for dissolution of marriage was filed; or

(2) income and earnings from the spouses' property, wages, salaries, and other forms of compensation received in another year during which the spouses were married for any part of the year.

Added by Acts 1997, 75th Leg., ch. 7, § 1, eff. April 17, 1997. Amended by Acts 1999, 76th Leg., ch. 692, § 4, eff. Sept. 1, 1999; Acts 2001, 77th Leg., ch. 838, § 4, eff. Sept. 1, 2001. Amended by Acts 2003, 78th Leg., ch. 230, § 4, eff. Sept. 1, 2003.

§ 7.003. Disposition of Retirement and Employment Benefits and Other Plans

In a decree of divorce or annulment, the court shall determine the rights of both spouses in a pension, retirement plan, annuity, individual retirement account, employee stock option plan, stock option, or other form of savings, bonus, profit-sharing, or other employer plan or financial plan of an employee or a participant, regardless of whether the person is self-employed, in the nature of compensation or savings.

Added by Acts 1997, 75th Leg., ch. 7, § 1, eff. April 17, 1997.

§ 7.004. Disposition of Rights in Insurance

In a decree of divorce or annulment, the court shall specifically divide or award the rights of each spouse in an insurance policy.

Added by Acts 1997, 75th Leg., ch. 7, § 1, eff. April 17, 1997.

§ 7.005. Insurance Coverage Not Specifically Awarded

(a) If in a decree of divorce or annulment the court does not specifically award all of the rights of the spouses in an insurance policy other than life insurance in effect at the time the decree is rendered, the policy remains in effect until the policy expires according to the policy's own terms.

(b) The proceeds of a valid claim under the policy are payable as follows:

(1) if the interest in the property insured was awarded solely to one former spouse by the decree, to that former spouse;

(2) if an interest in the property insured was awarded to each former spouse, to those former spouses in proportion to the interests awarded; or

(3) if the insurance coverage is directly related to the person of one of the former spouses, to that former spouse.

(c) The failure of either former spouse to change the endorsement on the policy to reflect the distribution of proceeds established by this section does not relieve the insurer of liability to pay the proceeds or any other obligation on the policy.

(d) This section does not affect the right of a former spouse to assert an ownership interest in an undivided life insurance policy, as provided by Subchapter D, Chapter 9.

Added by Acts 1997, 75th Leg., ch. 7, § 1, eff. April 17, 1997.

§ 7.006. Agreement Incident to Divorce or Annulment

(a) To promote amicable settlement of disputes in a suit for divorce or annulment, the spouses may enter into a written agreement concerning the division of the property and the liabilities of the spouses and maintenance of either spouse. The agreement may be revised or repudiated before rendition of the divorce or annulment unless the agreement is binding under another rule of law.

(b) If the court finds that the terms of the written agreement in a divorce or annulment are just and right, those terms are binding on the court. If the court approves the agreement, the court may set forth the agreement in full or incorporate the agreement by reference in the final decree.

(c) If the court finds that the terms of the written agreement in a divorce or annulment are not just and right, the court may request the spouses to submit a revised agreement or may set the case for a contested hearing.

Added by Acts 1997, 75th Leg., ch. 7, § 1, eff. April 17, 1997.

§ 7.007. Disposition of Claim for Economic Contribution or Claim for Reimbursement

(a) In a decree of divorce or annulment, the court shall determine the rights of both spouses in a claim for economic contribution as provided by Subchapter E, Chapter 3, and in a manner that the court considers just and right, having due regard for the rights of each party and any children of the marriage, shall:

(1) order a division of a claim for economic contribution of the community marital estate to the separate marital estate of one of the spouses;

(2) order that a claim for an economic contribution by one separate marital estate of a spouse to the community marital estate of the spouses be awarded to the owner of the contributing separate marital estate; and

(3) order that a claim for economic contribution of one separate marital estate in the separate marital estate of the other spouse be awarded to the owner of the contributing marital estate.

(b) In a decree of divorce or annulment, the court shall determine the rights of both spouses in a claim for reimbursement as provided by Subchapter E, Chapter 3, and shall apply equitable principles to:

(1) determine whether to recognize the claim after taking into account all the relative circumstances of the spouses; and

(2) order a division of the claim for reimbursement, if appropriate, in a manner that the court considers just and right, having due regard for the rights of each party and any children of the marriage.

Added by Acts 2001, 77th Leg., ch. 838, § 5, eff. Sept. 1, 2001.

Chapter 9. Post-Decree Proceedings

Subchapter D. Disposition of Undivided Beneficial Interest

Statutes in Context

Upon divorce, §§ 9.301 and 9.302 provide for the automatic revocation of an ex-spouse as the beneficiary of a life insurance policy or retirement plan unless one of the limited exceptions applies such as the ex-spouse redesignating the other former spouse after the divorce is final. However, it is highly likely these provisions will not apply to a policy or plan governed by the Employee Retirement Income Security Act (ERISA). The United States Supreme Court in *Egelhoff v. Egelhoff*, 532 U.S. 141 (2001), held that Washington provision altering the specified beneficiary upon divorce was preempted by ERISA. See *Heggy v. American Trading Employee Retirement Account Plan*, 56 S.W.3d 280 (Tex. App.—Houston [14th Dist.] 2001, no pet.) (holding that Family Code § 9.302 did not apply to a retirement account governed by ERISA and thus permitting the ex-spouse to receive the proceeds). But see *Keen v. Weaver*, __ S.W.3d ___, 46 Tex. Sup. Ct. J. 804 (Tex. 2003) (holding that a waiver of benefits in a divorce settlement prevented the ex-spouse from claiming the proceeds even though the beneficiary designation had not been changed to remove her as the beneficiary; the court rejected the lower court's application of the redesignation statute but reached the same result by enforcing the waiver under federal common law).

---

§ 9.301. Pre-Decree Designation of Ex-Spouse as Beneficiary of Life Insurance

(a) If a decree of divorce or annulment is rendered after an insured has designated the insured's spouse as a beneficiary under a life insurance policy in force at the time of rendition, a provision in the policy in favor of the insured's former spouse is not effective unless:

(1) the decree designates the insured's former spouse as the beneficiary;

(2) the insured redesignates the former spouse as the beneficiary after rendition of the decree; or

(3) the former spouse is designated to receive the proceeds in trust for, on behalf of, or for the benefit

of a child or a dependent of either former spouse.

(b) If a designation is not effective under Subsection (a), the proceeds of the policy are payable to the named alternative beneficiary or, if there is not a named alternative beneficiary, to the estate of the insured.

(c) An insurer who pays the proceeds of a life insurance policy issued by the insurer to the beneficiary under a designation that is not effective under Subsection (a) is liable for payment of the proceeds to the person or estate provided by Subsection (b) only if:

(1) before payment of the proceeds to the designated beneficiary, the insurer receives written notice at the home office of the insurer from an interested person that the designation is not effective under Subsection (a); and

(2) the insurer has not interpleaded the proceeds into the registry of a court of competent jurisdiction in accordance with the Texas Rules of Civil Procedure.

Added by Acts 1997, 75th Leg., ch. 7, § 1, eff. April 17, 1997.

§ 9.302. Pre-Decree Designation of Ex-Spouse as Beneficiary in Retirement Benefits and Other Financial Plans

(a) If a decree of divorce or annulment is rendered after a spouse, acting in the capacity of a participant, annuitant, or account holder, has designated the other spouse as a beneficiary under an individual retirement account, employee stock option plan, stock option, or other form of savings, bonus, profit-sharing, or other employer plan or financial plan of an employee or a participant in force at the time of rendition, the designating provision in the plan in favor of the other former spouse is not effective unless:

(1) the decree designates the other former spouse as the beneficiary;

(2) the designating former spouse redesignates the other former spouse as the beneficiary after rendition of the decree; or

(3) the other former spouse is designated to receive the proceeds or benefits in trust for, on behalf of, or for the benefit of a child or dependent of either former spouse.

(b) If a designation is not effective under Subsection (a), the benefits or proceeds are payable to the named alternative beneficiary or, if there is not a named alternative beneficiary, to the designating former spouse.

(c) A business entity, employer, pension trust, insurer, financial institution, or other person obligated to pay retirement benefits or proceeds of a financial plan covered by this section who pays the benefits or proceeds to the beneficiary under a designation of the other former spouse that is not effective under Subsection (a) is liable for payment of the benefits or proceeds to the person provided by Subsection (b) only if:

(1) before payment of the benefits or proceeds to the designated beneficiary, the payor receives written notice at the home office or principal office of the payor from an interested person that the designation of the beneficiary or fiduciary is not effective under Subsection (a); and

(2) the payor has not interpleaded the benefits or proceeds into the registry of a court of competent jurisdiction in accordance with the Texas Rules of Civil Procedure.

(d) This section does not affect the right of a former spouse to assert an ownership interest in an undivided pension, retirement, annuity, or other financial plan described by this section as provided by this subchapter.

(e) This section does not apply to the disposition of a beneficial interest in a retirement benefit or other financial plan of a public retirement system as defined by Section 802.001, Government Code.

Added by Acts 1997, 75th Leg., ch. 7, § 1, eff. April 17, 1997.

Title 2. Child in Relation to the Family

Subtitle A. Limitations of Minority

Chapter 31. Removal of Disabilities of Minority

Statutes in Context

Sections 31.001 - 31.007 explain how a minor may petition the court to have the disabilities of minority removed. If the minor is successful in removing the disabilities of minority, that minor is treated as an adult and thus, among other things, would have the capacity to contract. However, having the disabilities of minority removed does not cause the minor to be treated as reaching a particular age. For example, an individual must be 18 years old to execute a will under Probate Code § 57 (unless married, divorced, or in the armed forces). Under Family Code § 31.006, having the disabilities of minority removed does not cause the minor to be treated as reaching a statutorily specified prerequisite age. Consequently, the minor would continue to lack the legal capacity to execute a will.

§ 31.001. Requirements

(a) A minor may petition to have the disabilities of minority removed for limited or general purposes if the minor is:

(1) a resident of this state;

(2) 17 years of age, or at least 16 years of age and living separate and apart from the minor's parents, managing conservator, or guardian; and

(3) self-supporting and managing the minor's own financial affairs.

(b) A minor may file suit under this chapter in the minor's own name. The minor need not be represented by next friend.

Amended by Acts 1995, 74th Leg., ch. 20, § 1, eff. April 20, 1995.

§ 31.002. Requisites of Petition; Verification

(a) The petition for removal of disabilities of minority must state:

(1) the name, age, and place of residence of the petitioner;

(2) the name and place of residence of each living parent;

(3) the name and place of residence of the guardian of the person and the guardian of the estate, if any;

(4) the name and place of residence of the managing conservator, if any;

(5) the reasons why removal would be in the best interest of the minor; and

(6) the purposes for which removal is requested.

(b) A parent of the petitioner must verify the petition, except that if a managing conservator or guardian of the person has been appointed, the petition must be verified by that person. If the person who is to verify the petition is unavailable or that person's whereabouts are unknown, the guardian ad litem shall verify the petition.

Amended by Acts 1995, 74th Leg., ch. 20, § 1, eff. April 20, 1995.

§ 31.003. Venue

The petitioner shall file the petition in the county in which the petitioner resides.

Amended by Acts 1995, 74th Leg., ch. 20, § 1, eff. April 20, 1995.

§ 31.004. Guardian Ad Litem

The court shall appoint a guardian ad litem to represent the interest of the petitioner at the hearing.

Amended by Acts 1995, 74th Leg., ch. 20, § 1, eff. April 20, 1995.

§ 31.005. Order

The court by order, or the Texas Supreme Court by rule or order, may remove the disabilities of minority of a minor, including any restriction imposed by Chapter 32, if the court or the Texas Supreme Court finds the removal to be in the best interest of the petitioner. The order or rule must state the limited or general purposes for which disabilities are removed.

Amended by Acts 1995, 74th Leg., ch. 20, § 1, eff. April 20, 1995. Amended by Acts 1999, 76th Leg., ch. 1303, § 1, eff. Sept. 1, 1999.

§ 31.006. Effect of General Removal

Except for specific constitutional and statutory age requirements, a minor whose disabilities are removed for general purposes has the capacity of an adult, including the capacity to contract. Except as provided by federal law, all educational rights accorded to the parent of a student, including the right to make education decisions under Section 151.003(a)(10), transfer to the minor whose disabilities are removed for general purposes.

Amended by Acts 1995, 74th Leg., ch. 20, § 1, eff. April 20, 1995; Acts 2001, 77th Leg., ch. 767, § 9, eff. June 13, 2001.

§ 31.007. Registration of Order of Another State or Nation

(a) A nonresident minor who has had the disabilities of minority removed in the state of the minor's residence may file a certified copy of the order removing disabilities in the deed records of any county in this state.

(b) When a certified copy of the order of a court of another state or nation is filed, the minor has the capacity of an adult, except as provided by Section 31.006 and by the terms of the order.

Amended by Acts 1995, 74th Leg., ch. 20, § 1, eff. April 20, 1995.

Chapter 32. Consent to Treatment of Child by Non-Parent or Child

Statutes in Context

Chapter 32 explains when a non-parent may make medical, dental, psychological, and surgical treatment decisions for a child. Special provisions apply to immunization decisions.

Subchapter A. Consent to Medical, Dental, Psychological, and Surgical Treatment

§ 32.001. Consent by Non-Parent

(a) The following persons may consent to medical, dental, psychological, and surgical treatment of a child when the person having the right to consent as otherwise provided by law cannot be contacted and that person has not given actual notice to the contrary:

(1) a grandparent of the child;

(2) an adult brother or sister of the child;

(3) an adult aunt or uncle of the child;

(4) an educational institution in which the child is enrolled that has received written authorization to consent from a person having the right to consent;

(5) an adult who has actual care, control, and possession of the child and has written authorization to consent from a person having the right to consent;

(6) a court having jurisdiction over a suit affecting the parent-child relationship of which the child is the subject;

(7) an adult responsible for the actual care, control, and possession of a child under the jurisdiction of a juvenile court or committed by a juvenile court to the care of an agency of the state or county; or

(8) a peace officer who has lawfully taken custody of a minor, if the peace officer has reasonable grounds to believe the minor is in need of immediate medical treatment.

(b) The Texas Youth Commission may consent to the medical, dental, psychological, and surgical treatment of a child committed to it under Title 3 when the person having the right to consent has been contacted and that person has not given actual notice to the contrary.

(c) This section does not apply to consent for the immunization of a child.

(d) A person who consents to the medical treatment of a minor under Subsection (a)(7) or (8) is immune from liability for damages resulting from the examination or treatment of the minor, except to the extent of the person's own acts of negligence. A physician or dentist licensed to practice in this state, or a hospital or medical facility at which a minor is treated is immune from liability for damages resulting from the examination or treatment of a minor under this section, except to the extent of the person's own acts of negligence.

Amended by Acts 1995, 74th Leg., ch. 20, § 1, eff. April 20, 1995; Acts 1995, 74th Leg., ch. 751, § 5, eff. Sept. 1, 1995.

§ 32.002. Consent Form

(a) Consent to medical treatment under this subchapter must be in writing, signed by the person giving consent, and given to the doctor, hospital, or other medical facility that administers the treatment.

(b) The consent must include:

(1) the name of the child;

(2) the name of one or both parents, if known, and the name of any managing conservator or guardian of the child;

(3) the name of the person giving consent and the person's relationship to the child;

(4) a statement of the nature of the medical treatment to be given; and

(5) the date the treatment is to begin.

Amended by Acts 1995, 74th Leg., ch. 20, § 1, eff. April 20, 1995.

§ 32.003. Consent to Treatment by Child

(a) A child may consent to medical, dental, psychological, and surgical treatment for the child by a licensed physician or dentist if the child:

(1) is on active duty with the armed services of the United States of America;

(2) is:

(A) 16 years of age or older and resides separate and apart from the child's parents, managing conservator, or guardian, with or without the consent of the parents, managing conservator, or guardian and regardless of the duration of the residence; and

(B) managing the child's own financial affairs, regardless of the source of the income;

(3) consents to the diagnosis and treatment of an infectious, contagious, or communicable disease that is required by law or a rule to be reported by the licensed physician or dentist to a local health officer or the Texas Department of Health, including all diseases within the scope of Section 81.041, Health and Safety Code;

(4) is unmarried and pregnant and consents to hospital, medical, or surgical treatment, other than abortion, related to the pregnancy;

(5) consents to examination and treatment for drug or chemical addiction, drug or chemical dependency, or any other condition directly related to drug or chemical use; or

(6) is unmarried, is the parent of a child, and has actual custody of his or her child and consents to medical, dental, psychological, or surgical treatment for the child.

(b) Consent by a child to medical, dental, psychological, and surgical treatment under this section is not subject to disaffirmance because of minority.

(c) Consent of the parents, managing conservator, or guardian of a child is not necessary in order to authorize hospital, medical, surgical, or dental care under this section.

(d) A licensed physician, dentist, or psychologist may, with or without the consent of a child who is a patient, advise the parents, managing conservator, or guardian of the child of the treatment given to or needed by the child.

(e) A physician, dentist, psychologist, hospital, or medical facility is not liable for the examination and treatment of a child under this section except for the provider's or the facility's own acts of negligence.

(f) A physician, dentist, psychologist, hospital, or medical facility may rely on the written statement of the child containing the grounds on which the child has capacity to consent to the child's medical treatment.

Amended by Acts 1995, 74th Leg., ch. 20, § 1, eff. April 20, 1995; Acts 1995, 74th Leg., ch. 751, § 6, eff. Sept. 1, 1995; Acts 2001, 77th Leg., ch. 821, § 2.01, eff. June 14, 2001.

§ 32.004. Consent to Counseling

(a) A child may consent to counseling for:

(1) suicide prevention;

(2) chemical addiction or dependency; or

(3) sexual, physical, or emotional abuse.

(b) A licensed or certified physician, psychologist, counselor, or social worker having reasonable grounds to believe that a child has been sexually, physically, or emotionally abused, is contemplating suicide, or is suffering from a chemical or drug addiction or dependency may:

(1) counsel the child without the consent of the child's parents or, if applicable, managing conservator or guardian;

(2) with or without the consent of the child who is a client, advise the child's parents or, if applicable, managing conservator or guardian of the treatment given to or needed by the child; and

(3) rely on the written statement of the child containing the grounds on which the child has capacity to consent to the child's own treatment under this section.

(c) Unless consent is obtained as otherwise allowed by law, a physician, psychologist, counselor, or social worker may not counsel a child if consent is prohibited by a court order.

(d) A physician, psychologist, counselor, or social worker counseling a child under this section is not liable for damages except for damages resulting from the person's negligence or wilful misconduct.

(e) A parent, or, if applicable, managing conservator or guardian, who has not consented to counseling treatment of the child is not obligated to compensate a physician, psychologist, counselor, or social worker for counseling services rendered under this section.

Amended by Acts 1995, 74th Leg., ch. 20, § 1, eff. April 20, 1995.

§ 32.005. Examination Without Consent or Abuse or Neglect of Child

(a) Except as provided by Subsection (c), a physician, dentist, or psychologist having reasonable grounds to believe that a child's physical or mental condition has been adversely affected by abuse or neglect may examine the child without the consent of the child, the child's parents, or other person authorized to consent to treatment under this subchapter.

(b) An examination under this section may include X-rays, blood tests, photographs, and penetration of tissue necessary to accomplish those tests.

(c) Unless consent is obtained as otherwise allowed by law, a physician, dentist, or psychologist may not examine a child:

(1) 16 years of age or older who refuses to consent; or

(2) for whom consent is prohibited by a court order.

(d) A physician, dentist, or psychologist examining a child under this section is not liable for damages except for damages resulting from the physician's or dentist's negligence.

Amended by Acts 1995, 74th Leg., ch. 20, § 1, eff. April 20, 1995; Amended by Acts 1997, 75th Leg., ch. 575, § 1, eff. Sept. 1, 1997.

Subchapter B. Immunization

§ 32.101. Who May Consent to Immunization of Child

(a) In addition to persons authorized to consent to immunization under Chapter 151 and Chapter 153, the following persons may consent to the immunization of a child:

(1) a guardian of the child; and

(2) a person authorized under the law of another state or a court order to consent for the child.

(b) If the persons listed in Subsection (a) are not available and the authority to consent is not denied under Subsection (c), consent to the immunization of a child may be given by:

(1) a grandparent of the child;

(2) an adult brother or sister of the child;

(3) an adult aunt or uncle of the child;

(4) a stepparent of the child;

(5) an educational institution in which the child is enrolled that has written authorization to consent for the child from a parent, managing conservator, guardian, or other person who under the law of another state or a court order may consent for the child;

(6) another adult who has actual care, control, and possession of the child and has written authorization to consent for the child from a parent, managing conservator, guardian, or other person who, under the law of another state or a court order, may consent for the child;

(7) a court having jurisdiction of a suit affecting the parent-child relationship of which the minor is the subject;

(8) an adult having actual care, control, and possession of the child under an order of a juvenile court or by commitment by a juvenile court to the care of an agency of the state or county; or

(9) an adult having actual care, control, and possession of the child as the child's primary caregiver.

(c) A person otherwise authorized to consent under Subsection (a) may not consent for the child if the person has actual knowledge that a parent, managing conservator, guardian of the child, or other person who under the law of another state or a court order may consent for the child:

(1) has expressly refused to give consent to the immunization;

(2) has been told not to consent for the child; or

(3) has withdrawn a prior written authorization for the person to consent.

(d) The Texas Youth Commission may consent to the immunization of a child committed to it if a parent, managing conservator, or guardian of the minor or other person who, under the law of another state or court order, may consent for the minor has been contacted and:

(1) refuses to consent; and

(2) does not expressly deny to the Texas Youth Commission the authority to consent for the child.

(e) A person who consents under this section shall provide the health care provider with sufficient and accurate health history and other information about the minor for whom the consent is given and, if necessary, sufficient and accurate health history and information about the minor's family to enable the person who may consent to the minor's immunization and the health care provider to determine adequately the risks and benefits inherent in the proposed immunization and to determine whether immunization is advisable.

(f) Consent to immunization must meet the requirements of Section 32.002(a).

Amended by Acts 1995, 74th Leg., ch. 20, § 1, eff. April 20, 1995; Amended by Acts 1997, 75th Leg., ch. 165, § 7.09(a), eff. Sept. 1, 1997. Acts 1999, 76th Leg., ch. 62, § 6.02, eff. Sept. 1, 1999.

§ 32.102. Informed Consent to Immunization

(a) A person authorized to consent to the immunization of a child has the responsibility to ensure that the consent, if given, is an informed consent. The person authorized to consent is not required to be present when the immunization of the child is requested if a consent form that meets the requirements of Section 32.002 has been given to the health care provider.

(b) The responsibility of a health care provider to provide information to a person consenting to immunization is the same as the provider's responsibility to a parent.

(c) As part of the information given in the counseling for informed consent, the health care provider shall provide information to inform the person authorized to consent to immunization of the procedures available under the National Childhood Vaccine Injury Act of 1986 (42 U.S.C. § 300aa-1 et seq.) to seek possible recovery for unreimbursed expenses for certain injuries arising out of the administration of certain vaccines.

Amended by Acts 1995, 74th Leg., ch. 20, § 1, eff. April 20, 1995. Renumbered from § 32.103 and amended by Acts 1997, 75th Leg., ch. 165, § 7.09(b), (d), eff. Sept. 1, 1997.

§ 32.103. Limited Liability for Immunization

(a) In the absence of wilful misconduct or gross negligence, a health care provider who accepts the health history and other information given by a person who is delegated the authority to consent to the immunization of a child during the informed consent counseling is not liable for an adverse reaction to an immunization or for other injuries to the child resulting from factual errors in the health history or information given by the person to the health care provider.

(b) A person consenting to immunization of a child, a physician, nurse, or other health care provider, or a public health clinic, hospital, or other medical facility is not liable for damages arising from an immunization administered to a child authorized under this subchapter except for injuries resulting from the person's or facility's own acts of negligence.

Amended by Acts 1995, 74th Leg., ch 20, § 1, eff. April 20, 1995. Renumbered from § 32.104 by Acts 1997, 75th Leg., ch. 165, § 7.09(e), eff. Sept. 1, 1997.

§ 32.104. Renumbered.

Renumbered.

Renumbered as V.T.C.A., Family Code § 32.103 by Acts 1997, 75th Leg., ch. 165, § 7.09(e), eff. Sept. 1, 1997.

§ 32.105. Repealed.

Repealed.

Repealed by Acts 1997, 75th Leg., ch. 165, § 7.09(c), eff. Sept. 1, 1997.

Title 5. The Parent-Child Relationship and the Suit Affecting the Parent-Child Relationship

Subtitle B. Suits Affecting the Parent-Child Relationship

Chapter 154. Child Support

Subchapter A. Court-Ordered Child Support

Statutes in Context

Section 154.005 codifies an important exception to the effectiveness of spendthrift trust provisions which are generally enforceable under Property Code § 112.035. Assuming the court first imposes a child-support obligation on the parent who is the beneficiary of a spendthrift trust, the court may order the trustee to make payments for the support of the child notwithstanding the spendthrift provision. If a trust payment is mandatory, then the full amount of that payment may be reached. However, if the trust is discretionary, the court is limited to ordering child support payments from trust income.

§ 154.005. Payments of Support Obligation by Trust

(a) The court may order the trustees of a spendthrift or other trust to make disbursements for the support of a child to the extent the trustees are required to make payments to a beneficiary who is required to make child support payments as provided by this chapter.

(b) If disbursement of the assets of the trust is discretionary, the court may order child support payments from the income of the trust but not from the principal.

Added by Acts 1995, 74th Leg., ch. 20, § 1, eff. April 20, 1995.

Chapter 160. Uniform Parentage Act

Statutes in Context

Chapter 160 contains the Texas version of the Uniform Parentage Act.

Subchapter A. Application and Construction

§ 160.001. Application and Construction

This chapter shall be applied and construed to promote the uniformity of the law among the states that enact the Uniform Parentage Act.
Amended by Acts 2001, 77th Leg., ch. 821, § 1.01, eff. June 14, 2001.

§ 160.002. Conflicts Between Provisions

If a provision of this chapter conflicts with another provision of this title or another state statute or rule and the conflict cannot be reconciled, this chapter prevails.
Amended by Acts 2001, 77th Leg., ch. 821, § 1.01, eff. June 14, 2001.

Subchapter B. General Provisions

§ 160.101. Short Title

This chapter may be cited as the Uniform Parentage Act.
Amended by Acts 2001, 77th Leg., ch. 821, § 1.01, eff. June 14, 2001.

§ 160.102. Definitions

In this chapter:

(1) "Adjudicated father" means a man who has been adjudicated by a court to be the father of a child.

(2) "Assisted reproduction" means a method of causing pregnancy other than sexual intercourse. The term includes:

(A) intrauterine insemination;

(B) donation of eggs;

(C) donation of embryos;

(D) in vitro fertilization and transfer of embryos; and

(E) intracytoplasmic sperm injection.

(3) "Child" means an individual of any age whose parentage may be determined under this chapter.

(4) "Commence" means to file the initial pleading seeking an adjudication of parentage in a court of this state.

(5) "Determination of parentage" means the establishment of the parent-child relationship by the signing of a valid acknowledgment of paternity under Subchapter D or by an adjudication by a court.

(6) "Donor" means an individual who produces eggs or sperm used for assisted reproduction, regardless of whether the production is for consideration. The term does not include:

(A) a husband who provides sperm or a wife who provides eggs to be used for assisted reproduction by the wife; or

(B) a woman who gives birth to a child by means of assisted reproduction.

(7) "Ethnic or racial group" means, for purposes of genetic testing, a recognized group that an individual identifies as all or part of the individual's ancestry or that is identified by other information.

(8) "Genetic testing" means an analysis of an individual's genetic markers to exclude or identify a man as the father of a child or a woman as the mother of a child. The term includes an analysis of one or more of the following:

(A) deoxyribonucleic acid; and

(B) blood-group antigens, red-cell antigens, human-leukocyte antigens, serum enzymes, serum proteins, or red-cell enzymes.

(9) "Intended parents" means individuals who enter into an agreement providing that the individuals will be the parents of a child born to a gestational mother by means of assisted reproduction, regardless of whether either individual has a genetic relationship with the child.

(10) "Man" means a male individual of any age.

(11) "Parent" means an individual who has established a parent-child relationship under Section 160.201.

(12) "Paternity index" means the likelihood of paternity determined by calculating the ratio between:

(A) the likelihood that the tested man is the father of the child, based on the genetic markers of the tested man, the mother of the child, and the child, conditioned on the hypothesis that the tested man is the father of the child; and

(B) the likelihood that the tested man is not the father of the child, based on the genetic markers of the tested man, the mother of the child, and the child, conditioned on the hypothesis that the tested man is not the father of the child and that the father of the child is of the same ethnic or racial group as the tested man.

(13) "Presumed father" means a man who, by operation of law under Section 160.204, is recognized as the father of a child until that status is rebutted or confirmed in a judicial proceeding.

(14) "Probability of paternity" means the probability, with respect to the ethnic or racial group to which the alleged father belongs, that the alleged father is the father of the child, compared to a random, unrelated man of the same ethnic or racial group, expressed as a percentage incorporating the paternity index and a prior probability.

(15) "Record" means information that is inscribed on a tangible medium or that is stored in an electronic or other medium and is retrievable in a perceivable form.

(16) "Signatory" means an individual who authenticates a record and is bound by its terms.

(17) "Support enforcement agency" means a public official or public agency authorized to seek:

(A) the enforcement of child support orders or laws relating to the duty of support;

(B) the establishment or modification of child support;

(C) the determination of parentage;

(D) the location of child-support obligors and their income and assets; or

(E) the conservatorship of a child or the termination of parental rights.

Amended by Acts 2001, 77th Leg., ch. 821, § 1.01, eff. June 14, 2001.

§ 160.103. Scope of Chapter; Choice of Law

(a) This chapter governs every determination of parentage in this state.

(b) The court shall apply the law of this state to adjudicate the parent-child relationship. The applicable law does not depend on:

(1) the place of birth of the child; or

(2) the past or present residence of the child.

(c) This chapter does not create, enlarge, or diminish parental rights or duties under another law of this state.

Amended by Acts 2001, 77th Leg., ch. 821, § 1.01, eff. June 14, 2001; Acts 2003, 78th Leg., ch. 457, § 3, eff. Sept. 1, 2003.

§ 160.104. Authorized Courts

The following courts are authorized to adjudicate parentage under this chapter:

(1) a court with jurisdiction to hear a suit affecting the parent-child relationship under this title; or

(2) a court with jurisdiction to adjudicate parentage under another law of this state.

Amended by Acts 2001, 77th Leg., ch. 821, § 1.01, eff. June 14, 2001.

§ 160.105 Protection of Participants

A proceeding under this chapter is subject to the other laws of this state governing the health, safety, privacy, and liberty of a child or any other individual who may be jeopardized by the disclosure of identifying information, including the person's address, telephone number, place of employment, and social security number and the name of the child's day-care facility and school.

Amended by Acts 2001, 77th Leg., ch. 821, § 1.01, eff. June 14, 2001.

§ 160.106. Determination of Maternity

The provisions of this chapter relating to the determination of paternity apply to a determination of maternity.

Amended by Acts 2001, 77th Leg., ch. 821, § 1.01, eff. June 14, 2001.

Subchapter C. Parent-Child Relationship

Statutes in Context

Section 160.201 sets forth how the mother-child and father-child relationship is established. This determination is especially important when ascertaining the inheritance rights of children under Probate Code § 42.

§ 160.201. Establishment of Parent-Child Relationship

(a) The mother-child relationship is established between a woman and a child by:

(1) the woman giving birth to the child;

(2) an adjudication of the woman's maternity; or

(3) the adoption of the child by the woman.

(b) The father-child relationship is established between a man and a child by:

(1) an unrebutted presumption of the man's paternity of the child under Section 160.204;

(2) an effective acknowledgment of paternity by the man under Subchapter D,[1] unless the acknowledgment has been rescinded or successfully challenged;

(3) an adjudication of the man's paternity;

(4) the adoption of the child by the man; or

(5) the man's consenting to assisted reproduction by his wife under Subchapter H,[2] which resulted in the birth of the child.

Amended by Acts 2001, 77th Leg., ch. 821, § 1.01, eff. June 14, 2001.

§ 160.202. No Discrimination Based on Marital Status

A child born to parents who are not married to each other has the same rights under the law as a child born to parents who are married to each other.

Amended by Acts 2001, 77th Leg., ch. 821, § 1.01, eff. June 14, 2001.

§ 160.203. Consequences of Establishment of Parentage

Unless parental rights are terminated, a parent-child relationship established under this chapter applies for all purposes, except as otherwise provided by another law of this state.

Amended by Acts 2001, 77th Leg., ch. 821, § 1.01, eff. June 14, 2001.

---

[1] V.T.C.A., Family Code § 160.301 et seq.

[2] V.T.C.A., Family Code &sec; 160.701 et seq.

§ 160.204. Presumption of Paternity

(a) A man is presumed to be the father of a child if:

(1) he is married to the mother of the child and the child is born during the marriage;

(2) he is married to the mother of the child and the child is born before the 301st day after the date the marriage is terminated by death, annulment, declaration of invalidity, or divorce;

(3) he married the mother of the child before the birth of the child in apparent compliance with law, even if the attempted marriage is or could be declared invalid, and the child is born during the invalid marriage or before the 301st day after the date the marriage is terminated by death, annulment, declaration of invalidity, or divorce; or

(4) he married the mother of the child after the birth of the child in apparent compliance with law, regardless of whether the marriage is or could be declared invalid, he voluntarily asserted his paternity of the child, and:

(A) the assertion is in a record filed with the bureau of vital statistics;

(B) he is voluntarily named as the child's father on the child's birth certificate; or

(C) he promised in a record to support the child as his own; or

(5) during the first two years of the child's life, he continuously resided in the household in which the child resided and he represented to others that the child was his own.

(b) (1) A presumption of paternity established under this section may be rebutted only by an adjudication under Subchapter G[1]; or

(2) the filing of a valid denial of paternity by a presumed father in conjunction with the filing by another person of a valid acknowledgment of paternity as provided by Section 160.305.

Amended by Acts 2001, 77th Leg., ch. 821, § 1.01, eff. June 14, 2001; Acts 2003, 78th Leg., ch. 610, § 10, eff. Sept. 1, 2003; Acts 2003, 78th Leg., ch. 1248, § 1, eff. Sept. 1, 2003.

Subchapter D. Voluntary Acknowledgment of Paternity

Statutes in Context

Sections 160.301 - 160.316 provide a mechanism for a man to acknowledge his paternity of a child and thereafter to be treated as the child's father.

§ 160.301. Acknowledgment of Paternity

The mother of a child and a man claiming to be the biological father of the child may sign an acknowledgment of paternity with the intent to establish the man's paternity.

Added by Acts 2001, 77th Leg., ch. 821, § 1.01, eff. June 14, 2001. Amended by Acts 2003, 78th Leg., ch. 1248, § 2, eff. Sept. 1, 2003.

§ 160.302. Execution of Acknowledgment of Paternity

(a) An acknowledgment of paternity must:

(1) be in a record;

(2) be signed, or otherwise authenticated, under penalty of perjury by the mother and the man seeking to establish paternity;

(3) state that the child whose paternity is being acknowledged:

(A) does not have a presumed father or has a presumed father whose full name is stated; and

(B) does not have another acknowledged or adjudicated father;

(4) state whether there has been genetic testing and, if so, that the acknowledging man's claim of paternity is consistent with the results of the testing; and

(5) state that the signatories understand that the acknowledgment is the equivalent of a judicial adjudication of the paternity of the child and that a challenge to the acknowledgment is permitted only under limited circumstances and is barred after four years.

(b) An acknowledgment of paternity is void if it:

(1) states that another man is a presumed father of the child, unless a denial of paternity signed or otherwise authenticated by the presumed father is filed with the bureau of vital statistics;

(2) states that another man is an acknowledged or adjudicated father of the child; or

(3) falsely denies the existence of a presumed, acknowledged, or adjudicated father of the child.

(c) A presumed father may sign or otherwise authenticate an acknowledgment of paternity.

Added by Acts 2001, 77th Leg., ch. 821, § 1.01, eff. June 14, 2001.

§ 160.303. Denial of Paternity

A presumed father of a child may sign a denial of his paternity. The denial is valid only if:

(1) an acknowledgment of paternity signed or otherwise authenticated by another man is filed under Section 160.305;

(2) the denial is in a record and is signed or otherwise authenticated under penalty of perjury; and

(3) the presumed father has not previously:

(A) acknowledged paternity of the child, unless the previous acknowledgment has been rescinded under Section 160.307 or successfully challenged under Section 160.308; or

(B) been adjudicated to be the father of the child.

Added by Acts 2001, 77th Leg., ch. 821, § 1.01, eff. June 14, 2001.

[1] V.T.C.A., Family Code § 160.601 et seq.

§ 160.304. Rules for Acknowledgment and Denial of Paternity

(a) An acknowledgment of paternity and a denial of paternity may be contained in a single document or in different documents and may be filed separately or simultaneously. If the acknowledgment and denial are both necessary, neither document is valid until both documents are filed.

(b) An acknowledgment of paternity or a denial of paternity may be signed before the birth of the child.

(c) Subject to Subsection (a), an acknowledgment of paternity or denial of paternity takes effect on the date of the birth of the child or the filing of the document with the bureau of vital statistics, whichever occurs later.

(d) An acknowledgment of paternity or denial of paternity signed by a minor is valid if it otherwise complies with this chapter.

Added by Acts 2001, 77th Leg., ch. 821, § 1.01, eff. June 14, 2001.

§ 160.305. Effect of Acknowledgment or Denial of Paternity

(a) Except as provided by Sections 160.307 and 160.308, a valid acknowledgment of paternity filed with the bureau of vital statistics is the equivalent of an adjudication of the paternity of a child and confers on the acknowledged father all rights and duties of a parent.

(b) Except as provided by Sections 160.307 and 160.308, a valid denial of paternity filed with the bureau of vital statistics in conjunction with a valid acknowledgment of paternity is the equivalent of an adjudication of the nonpaternity of the presumed father and discharges the presumed father from all rights and duties of a parent.

Added by Acts 2001, 77th Leg., ch. 821, § 1.01, eff. June 14, 2001.

§ 160.306. Filing Fee Not Required

The bureau of vital statistics may not charge a fee for filing an acknowledgment of paternity or denial of paternity.

Added by Acts 2001, 77th Leg., ch. 821, § 1.01, eff. June 14, 2001.

§ 160.307. Proceeding for Rescission

A signatory may rescind an acknowledgment of paternity or denial of paternity by commencing a proceeding to rescind before the earlier of:

(1) the 60th day after the effective date of the acknowledgment or denial, as provided by Section 160.304; or

(2) the date of the first hearing in a proceeding to which the signatory is a party before a court to adjudicate an issue relating to the child, including a proceeding that establishes child support.

Added by Acts 2001, 77th Leg., ch. 821, § 1.01, eff. June 14, 2001.

§ 160.308. Challenge After Expiration of Period for Rescission

(a) After the period for rescission under Section 160.307 has expired, a signatory of an acknowledgment of paternity or denial of paternity may commence a proceeding to challenge the acknowledgment or denial only on the basis of fraud, duress, or material mistake of fact. The proceeding must be commenced before the fourth anniversary of the date the acknow-ledgment or denial is filed with the bureau of vital statistics.

(b) A party challenging an acknowledgment of paternity or denial of paternity has the burden of proof.

(c) Notwithstanding any other provision of this chapter, a collateral attack on an acknowledgment of paternity signed under this chapter may not be maintained after the fourth anniversary of the date the acknowledgment of paternity is filed with the bureau of vital statistics.

(d) For purposes of Subsection (a), evidence that, based on genetic testing, the man who is the signatory of an acknowledgement of paternity is not rebuttably identified as the father of a child in accordance with Section 160.505 constitutes a material mistake of fact.

Added by Acts 2001, 77th Leg., ch. 821, § 1.01, eff. June 14, 2001.

§ 160.309. Procedure for Rescission or Challenge

(a) Each signatory to an acknowledgment of paternity and any related denial of paternity must be made a party to a proceeding to rescind or challenge the acknowledgment or denial of paternity.

(b) For purposes of the rescission of or a challenge to an acknowledgment of paternity or denial of paternity, a signatory submits to the personal jurisdiction of this state by signing the acknowledgment or denial. The jurisdiction is effective on the filing of the document with the bureau of vital statistics.

(c) Except for good cause shown, while a proceeding is pending to rescind or challenge an acknowledgment of paternity or a denial of paternity, the court may not suspend the legal responsibilities of a signatory arising from the acknowledgment, including the duty to pay child support.

(d) A proceeding to rescind or to challenge an acknowledgment of paternity or a denial of paternity shall be conducted in the same manner as a proceeding to adjudicate parentage under Subchapter G.[1]

(e) At the conclusion of a proceeding to rescind or challenge an acknowledgment of paternity or a denial of paternity, the court shall order the bureau of vital statistics to amend the birth record of the child, if appropriate.

Added by Acts 2001, 77th Leg., ch. 821, § 1.01, eff. June 14, 2001.

---

[1] V.T.C.A., Family Code § 160.601 et seq.

§ 160.310. Ratification Barred

A court or administrative agency conducting a judicial or administrative proceeding may not ratify an unchallenged acknowledgment of paternity.

Added by Acts 2001, 77th Leg., ch. 821, § 1.01, eff. June 14, 2001.

§ 160.311. Full Faith and Credit

A court of this state shall give full faith and credit to an acknowledgment of paternity or a denial of paternity that is effective in another state if the acknowledgment or denial has been signed and is otherwise in compliance with the law of the other state.

Added by Acts 2001, 77th Leg., ch. 821, § 1.01, eff. June 14, 2001.

§ 160.312. Forms for Acknowledgment and Denial of Paternity

(a) To facilitate compliance with this subchapter, the bureau of vital statistics shall prescribe forms for the acknowledgment of paternity and the denial of paternity.

(b) A valid acknowledgment of paternity or denial of paternity is not affected by a later modification of the prescribed form.

Added by Acts 2001, 77th Leg., ch. 821, § 1.01, eff. June 14, 2001.

§ 160.313. Release of Information

The bureau of vital statistics may release information relating to the acknowledgment of paternity or denial of paternity to a signatory of the acknowledgment or denial and to the courts and Title IV-D agency of this or another state.

Added by Acts 2001, 77th Leg., ch. 821, § 1.01, eff. June 14, 2001.

§ 160.314. Adoption of Rules

The Title IV-D agency and the bureau of vital statistics may adopt rules to implement this subchapter.

Added by Acts 2001, 77th Leg., ch. 821, § 1.01, eff. June 14, 2001.

§ 160.315. Memorandum of Understanding

(a) The Title IV-D agency and the bureau of vital statistics shall adopt a memorandum of understanding governing the collection and transfer of information for the voluntary acknowledgment of paternity.

(b) The Title IV-D agency and the bureau of vital statistics shall review the memorandum semiannually and renew or modify the memorandum as necessary.

Added by Acts 2001, 77th Leg., ch. 821, § 1.01, eff. June 14, 2001.

§ 160.316. Suit to Contest Voluntary Statement of Paternity

(a) A man who executed a voluntary statement of paternity before September 1, 1999, and who, on the basis of that statement, is the subject of a final order declaring him to be a parent of the child who is the subject of the statement may file a suit affecting the parent-child relationship to contest the statement on the basis of fraud, duress, or material mistake of fact in the same manner that a person may contest an acknowledgment of paternity under Sections 160.308 and 160.309. For purposes of this subsection, evidence that, based on genetic testing, the man is not rebuttably identified as the father of a child in accordance with Section 160.505 constitutes a material mistake of fact.

(b) A suit filed under this section to contest a voluntary statement of paternity is not affected by an order with respect to the child that was rendered on the basis of that statement.

(c) The court, on a preliminary finding in a suit under this section that there is credible evidence of fraud, duress, or material mistake of fact regarding the execution of the voluntary statement of paternity, shall order genetic testing as provided by Subchapter F.[1] The person contesting the voluntary statement of paternity shall pay the cost of the testing.

(d) Except as provided by Subsection (e), if the results of the genetic testing do not rebuttably identify the man as the father of the child in accordance with Section 160.505, the court shall set aside:

(1) the final order declaring the man to be a parent of the child; and

(2) any other order with respect to the child that was rendered on the basis of the voluntary statement of paternity.

(e) The court may not set aside under Subsection (d) a final order declaring a man to be a parent of a child if the man who executed the voluntary statement of paternity:

(1) executed the statement knowing that he was not the father of the child; or

(2) subsequently adopted the child.

(f) If the court sets aside a final order as provided by Subsection (d), the court shall order the bureau of vital statistics to amend the birth record of the child. The court may not as a result of the order being set aside:

(1) require an obligee to repay child support paid by the man who executed the voluntary statement of paternity; or

(2) award damages to the man who executed the voluntary statement of paternity.

(g) A suit under this section must be filed before September 1, 2003.

(h) This section expires September 1, 2004.

Added by Acts 2001, 77th Leg., ch. 821, § 1.01, eff. June 14, 2001.

[1] V.T.C.A., Family Code § 160.501 et seq.

Subchapter E. Registry of Paternity

Statutes in Context

Sections 160.401 - 160.423 explain the operation of the registry of paternity which is established in the bureau of vital statistics.

§ 160.401. Establishment of Registry

A registry of paternity is established in the bureau of vital statistics.

Added by Acts 2001, 77th Leg., ch. 821, § 1.01, eff. June 14, 2001.

§ 160.402. Registration for Notification

(a) Except as otherwise provided by Subsection (b), a man who desires to be notified of a proceeding for the adoption of or the termination of parental rights regarding a child that he may have fathered may register with the registry of paternity:

(1) before the birth of the child; or

(2) not later than the 31st day after the date of the birth of the child.

(b) A man is entitled to notice of a proceeding described by Subsection (a) regardless of whether he registers with the registry of paternity if:

(1) a father-child relationship between the man and the child has been established under this chapter or another law; or

(2) the man commences a proceeding to adjudicate his paternity before the court has terminated his parental rights.

(c) A registrant shall promptly notify the registry in a record of any change in the information provided by the registrant. The bureau of vital statistics shall incorporate all new information received into its records but is not required to affirmatively seek to obtain current information for incorporation in the registry.

Added by Acts 2001, 77th Leg., ch. 821, § 1.01, eff. June 14, 2001.

§ 160.403. Notice of Proceeding

Notice of a proceeding to adopt or to terminate parental rights regarding a child must be given to a registrant who has timely registered with regard to that child. Notice must be given in a manner prescribed for service of process in a civil action.

Added by Acts 2001, 77th Leg., ch. 821, § 1.01, eff. June 14, 2001.

§ 160.404. Termination of Parental Rights: Failure to Register

The parental rights of a man alleged to be the father of a child may be terminated without notice as provided by Section 161.002 if the man:

(1) did not timely register with the bureau of vital statistics; and

(2) is not entitled to notice under Section 160.402 or 161.002.

Added by Acts 2001, 77th Leg., ch. 821, § 1.01, eff. June 14, 2001.

§ 160.411. Required Form

The bureau of vital statistics shall adopt a form for registering with the registry. The form must require the signature of the registrant. The form must state that:

(1) the form is signed under penalty of perjury;

(2) a timely registration entitles the registrant to notice of a proceeding for adoption of the child or for termination of the registrant's parental rights;

(3) a timely registration does not commence a proceeding to establish paternity;

(4) the information disclosed on the form may be used against the registrant to establish paternity;

(5) services to assist in establishing paternity are available to the registrant through the support enforcement agency;

(6) the registrant should also register in another state if the conception or birth of the child occurred in the other state;

(7) information on registries in other states is available from the bureau of vital statistics; and

(8) procedures exist to rescind the registration of a claim of paternity.

Added by Acts 2001, 77th Leg., ch. 821, § 1.01, eff. June 14, 2001.

§ 160.412. Furnishing of Information; Confidentiality

(a) The bureau of vital statistics is not required to attempt to locate the mother of a child who is the subject of a registration. The bureau of vital statistics shall send a copy of the notice of the registration to a mother who has provided an address.

(b) Information contained in the registry is confidential and may be released on request only to:

(1) a court or a person designated by the court;

(2) the mother of the child who is the subject of the registration;

(3) an agency authorized by another law to receive the information;

(4) a licensed child-placing agency;

(5) a support enforcement agency;

(6) a party, or the party's attorney of record, to a proceeding under this chapter or a proceeding to adopt or to terminate parental rights regarding a child who is the subject of the registration; and

(7) the registry of paternity in another state.

Added by Acts 2001, 77th Leg., ch. 821, § 1.01, eff. June 14, 2001.

§ 160.413. Offense: Unauthorized Release of Information

(a) A person commits an offense if the person intentionally releases information from the registry of paternity to another person, including an agency, that is not authorized to receive the information under Section 160.412.

(b) An offense under this section is a Class A misdemeanor.

Added by Acts 2001, 77th Leg., ch. 821, § 1.01, eff. June 14, 2001.

§ 160.414. Rescission of Registration

A registrant may rescind his registration at any time by sending to the registry a rescission in a record or another manner authenticated by him and witnessed or notarized.

Added by Acts 2001, 77th Leg., ch. 821, § 1.01, eff. June 14, 2001.

§ 160.415. Untimely Registration

If a man registers later than the 30th day after the date of the birth of the child, the bureau of vital statistics shall notify the registrant that the registration was not timely filed.

Added by Acts 2001, 77th Leg., ch. 821, § 1.01, eff. June 14, 2001.

§ 160.416. Fees for Registry

(a) A fee may not be charged for filing a registration or to rescind a registration.

(b) Except as otherwise provided by Subsection (c), the bureau of vital statistics may charge a reasonable fee for making a search of the registry and for furnishing a certificate.

(c) A support enforcement agency is not required to pay a fee authorized by Subsection (b).

Added by Acts 2001, 77th Leg., ch. 821, § 1.01, eff. June 14, 2001.

§ 160.421. Search of Appropriate Registry

(a) If a father-child relationship has not been established under this chapter, a petitioner for the adoption of or the termination of parental rights regarding the child must obtain a certificate of the results of a search of the registry.

(b) If the petitioner for the adoption of or the termination of parental rights regarding a child has reason to believe that the conception or birth of the child may have occurred in another state, the petitioner must obtain a certificate of the results of a search of the paternity registry, if any, in the other state.

Added by Acts 2001, 77th Leg., ch. 821, § 1.01, eff. June 14, 2001.

§ 160.422. Certificate of Search of Registry

(a) The bureau of vital statistics shall furnish a certificate of the results of a search of the registry on request by an individual, a court, or an agency listed in Section 160.412(b).

(b) The certificate of the results of a search must be signed on behalf of the bureau and state that:

(1) a search has been made of the registry; and

(2) a registration containing the information required to identify the registrant:

(A) has been found and is attached to the certificate; or

(B) has not been found.

(c) A petitioner must file the certificate of the results of a search of the registry with the court before a proceeding for the adoption of or termination of parental rights regarding a child may be concluded.

(d) A search of the registry is not required if the only man alleged to be the father of the child has signed a waiver of interest in, or relinguishment of parental rights with regard to, the child.

Added by Acts 2001, 77th Leg., ch. 821, § 1.01, eff. June 14, 2001.

§ 160.423. Admissibility of Certificate

A certificate of the results of a search of the registry in this state or of a paternity registry in another state is admissible in a proceeding for the adoption of or the termination of parental rights regarding a child and, if relevant, in other legal proceedings.

Added by Acts 2001, 77th Leg., ch. 821, § 1.01, eff. June 14, 2001.

Subchapter F. Genetic Testing

Statutes in Context

Sections 160.501 - 160. 511 govern genetic testing when used to determine parentage.

§ 160.501. Application of Subchapter

This subchapter governs genetic testing of an individual to determine parentage, regardless of whether the individual:

(1) voluntarily submits to testing; or

(2) is tested under an order of a court or a support enforcement agency.

Added by Acts 2001, 77th Leg., ch. 821, § 1.01, eff. June 14, 2001.

§ 160.502. Order for Testing

(a) Except as otherwise provided by this subchapter and by Subchapter G, a court shall order a child and other designated individuals to submit to genetic testing if the request is made by a party to a proceeding to determine parentage.

(b) If a request for genetic testing of a child is made before the birth of the child, the court or support enforcement agency may not order in utero testing.

(c) If two or more men are subject to court-ordered genetic testing, the testing may be ordered concurrently or sequentially.

Added by Acts 2001, 77th Leg., ch. 821, § 1.01, eff. June 14, 2001.

§ 160.503. Requirements for Genetic Testing

(a) Genetic testing must be of a type reasonably relied on by experts in the field of genetic testing. The testing must be performed in a testing laboratory accredited by:

(1) the American Association of Blood Banks, or a successor to its functions;

(2) the American Society for Histocompatibility and Immunogenetics, or a successor to its functions; or

(3) an accrediting body designated by the federal secretary of health and human services.

(b) A specimen used in genetic testing may consist of one or more samples, or a combination of samples, of blood, buccal cells, bone, hair, or other body tissue or fluid. The specimen used in the testing is not required to be of the same kind for each individual undergoing genetic testing.

(c) Based on the ethnic or racial group of an individual, the testing laboratory shall determine the databases from which to select frequencies for use in the calculation of the probability of paternity of the individual. If there is disagreement as to the testing laboratory's choice:

(1) the objecting individual may require the testing laboratory, not later than the 30th day after the date of receipt of the report of the test, to recalculate the probability of paternity using an ethnic or racial group different from that used by the laboratory;

(2) the individual objecting to the testing laboratory's initial choice shall:

(A) if the frequencies are not available to the testing laboratory for the ethnic or racial group requested, provide the requested frequencies compiled in a manner recognized by accrediting bodies; or

(B) engage another testing laboratory to perform the calculations; and

(3) the testing laboratory may use its own statistical estimate if there is a question regarding which ethnic or racial group is appropriate and, if available, shall calculate the frequencies using statistics for any other ethnic or racial group requested.

(d) If, after recalculation using a different ethnic or racial group, genetic testing does not rebuttably identify a man as the father of a child under Section 160.505, an individual who has been tested may be required to submit to additional genetic testing.

Added by Acts 2001, 77th Leg., ch. 821, § 1.01, eff. June 14, 2001.

§ 160.504. Report of Genetic Testing

(a) A report of the results of genetic testing must be in a record and signed under penalty of perjury by a designee of the testing laboratory. A report made under the requirements of this subchapter is self-authenticating.

(b) Documentation from the testing laboratory is sufficient to establish a reliable chain of custody that allows the results of genetic testing to be admissible without testimony if the documentation includes:

(1) the name and photograph of each individual whose specimens have been taken;

(2) the name of each individual who collected the specimens;

(3) the places in which the specimens were collected and the date of each collection;

(4) the name of each individual who received the specimens in the testing laboratory; and

(5) the dates the specimens were received.

Added by Acts 2001, 77th Leg., ch. 821, § 1.01, eff. June 14, 2001.

§ 160.505. Genetic Testing Results; Rebuttal

(a) A man is rebuttably identified as the father of a child under this chapter if the genetic testing complies with this subchapter and the results disclose:

(1) that the man has at least a 99 percent probability of paternity, using a prior probability of 0.5, as calculated by using the combined paternity index obtained in the testing; and

(2) a combined paternity index of at least 100 to 1.

(b) A man identified as the father of a child under Subsection (a) may rebut the genetic testing results only by producing other genetic testing satisfying the requirements of this subchapter that:

(1) excludes the man as a genetic father of the child; or

(2) identifies another man as the possible father of the child.

(c) Except as otherwise provided by Section 160.510, if more than one man is identified by genetic testing as the possible father of the child, the court shall order each man to submit to further genetic testing to identify the genetic father.

Added by Acts 2001, 77th Leg., ch. 821, § 1.01, eff. June 14, 2001.

§ 160.506. Costs of Genetic Testing

(a) Subject to the assessment of costs under Subchapter G,[1] the cost of initial genetic testing must be advanced:

(1) by a support enforcement agency, if the agency is providing services in the proceeding;

(2) by the individual who made the request;

(3) as agreed by the parties; or

(4) as ordered by the court.

(b) In cases in which the cost of genetic testing is advanced by the support enforcement agency, the

[1] V.T.C.A., Family Code § 160.601 et seq.

agency may seek reimbursement from a man who is rebuttably identified as the father.
Added by Acts 2001, 77th Leg., ch. 821, § 1.01, eff. June 14, 2001.

§ 160.507. Additional Genetic Testing

The court or the support enforcement agency shall order additional genetic testing on the request of a party who contests the result of the original testing. If the previous genetic testing identified a man as the father of the child under Section 160.505, the court or agency may not order additional testing unless the party provides advance payment for the testing.
Added by Acts 2001, 77th Leg., ch. 821, § 1.01, eff. June 14, 2001.

§ 160.508. Genetic Testing When All Individuals Not Available

(a) Subject to Subsection (b), if a genetic testing specimen for good cause and under circumstances the court considers to be just is not available from a man who may be the father of a child, a court may order the following individuals to submit specimens for genetic testing:

(1) the parents of the man;

(2) any brothers or sisters of the man;

(3) any other children of the man and their mothers; and

(4) other relatives of the man necessary to complete genetic testing.

(b) A court may not render an order under this section unless the court finds that the need for genetic testing outweighs the legitimate interests of the individual sought to be tested.
Added by Acts 2001, 77th Leg., ch. 821, § 1.01, eff. June 14, 2001.

§ 160.509. Deceased Individual

For good cause shown, the court may order genetic testing of a deceased individual.
Added by Acts 2001, 77th Leg., ch. 821, § 1.01, eff. June 14, 2001.

§ 160.510. Identical Brothers

(a) The court may order genetic testing of a brother of a man identified as the father of a child if the man is commonly believed to have an identical brother and evidence suggests that the brother may be the genetic father of the child.

(b) If each brother satisfies the requirements of Section 160.505 for being the identified father of the child and there is not another identical brother being identified as the father of the child, the court may rely on nongenetic evidence to adjudicate which brother is the father of the child.
Added by Acts 2001, 77th Leg., ch. 821, § 1.01, eff. June 14, 2001.

§ 160.511. Offense: Unauthorized Release of Specimen

(a) A person commits an offense if the person intentionally releases an identifiable specimen of another person for any purpose not relevant to the parentage proceeding and without a court order or the written permission of the person who furnished the specimen.

(b) An offense under this section is a Class A misdemeanor.
Added by Acts 2001, 77th Leg., ch. 821, § 1.01, eff. June 14, 2001.

Subchapter G. Proceeding to Adjudicate Parentage

Statutes in Context

Proceedings for a court adjudication of the parentage of a child are governed by §§ 160.601 - 160.637.

§ 160.601. Proceeding Authorized; Rules of Procedure

(a) A civil proceeding may be maintained to adjudicate the parentage of a child.

(b) The proceeding is governed by the Texas Rules of Civil Procedure.
Added by Acts 2001, 77th Leg., ch. 821, § 1.01, eff. June 14, 2001.

§ 160.602. Standing to Maintain Proceeding

(a) Subject to Subchapter D[1] and Sections 160.607 and 160.609 and except as provided by Subsection (b), a proceeding to adjudicate parentage may be maintained by:

(1) the child;

(2) the mother of the child;

(3) a man whose paternity of the child is to be adjudicated;

(4) the support enforcement agency or another government agency authorized by other law;

(5) an authorized adoption agency or licensed child-placing agency;

(6) a representative authorized by law to act for an individual who would otherwise be entitled to maintain a proceeding but who is deceased, is incapacitated, or is a minor; or

(7) a person related within the second degree by consanguinity to the mother of the child, if the mother is deceased, or

(8) a person who is an intended parent.

(b) After the date a child having no presumed, acknowledged, or adjudicated father becomes an

[1] V.T.C.A., Family Code § 160.301 et seq.

adult, a proceeding to adjudicate the parentage of the adult child may only be maintained by the adult child.
Added by Acts 2001, 77th Leg., ch. 821, § 1.01, eff. June 14, 2001. Amended by Acts 2003, 78th Leg., ch. 457, § 1, eff. Sept. 1, 2003; Acts 2003, 78th Leg., ch. 1248, § 3, eff. Sept. 1, 2003.

§ 160.603. Necessary Parties to Proceeding

The following individuals must be joined as parties in a proceeding to adjudicate parentage:

(1) the mother of the child; and

(2) a man whose paternity of the child is to be adjudicated.

Added by Acts 2001, 77th Leg., ch. 821, § 1.01, eff. June 14, 2001.

§ 160.604. Personal Jurisdiction

(a) An individual may not be adjudicated to be a parent unless the court has personal jurisdiction over the individual.

(b) A court of this state having jurisdiction to adjudicate parentage may exercise personal jurisdiction over a nonresident individual or the guardian or conservator of the individual if the conditions in Section 159.201 are satisfied.

(c) Lack of jurisdiction over one individual does not preclude the court from making an adjudication of parentage binding on another individual over whom the court has personal jurisdiction.
Added by Acts 2001, 77th Leg., ch. 821, § 1.01, eff. June 14, 2001.

§ 160.605. Venue

Venue for a proceeding to adjudicate parentage is in the county of this state in which:

(1) the child resides or is found;

(2) the respondent resides or is found if the child does not reside in this state; or

(3) a proceeding for probate or administration of the presumed or alleged father's estate has been commenced.

Added by Acts 2001, 77th Leg., ch. 821, § 1.01, eff. June 14, 2001.

§ 160.606. No Time Limitation: Child Having No Presumed, Acknowledged, or Adjudicated Father

A proceeding to adjudicate the parentage of a child having no presumed, acknowledged, or adjudicated father may be commenced at any time, including after the date:

(1) the child becomes an adult; or

(2) an earlier proceeding to adjudicate paternity has been dismissed based on the application of a statute of limitation then in effect.

Added by Acts 2001, 77th Leg., ch. 821, § 1.01, eff. June 14, 2001.

§ 160.607. Time Limitation: Child Having Presumed Father

(a) Except as otherwise provided by Subsection (b), a proceeding brought by a presumed father, the mother, or another individual to adjudicate the parentage of a child having a presumed father shall be commenced not later than the fourth anniversary of the date of the birth of the child.

(b) A proceeding seeking to disprove the father-child relationship between a child and the child's presumed father may be maintained at any time if the court determines that:

(1) the presumed father and the mother of the child did not live together or engage in sexual intercourse with each other during the probable time of conception; and

(2) the presumed father never represented to others that the child was his own.

Added by Acts 2001, 77th Leg., ch. 821, § 1.01, eff. June 14, 2001. Amended by Acts 2003, 78th Leg., ch. 1248, § 4, eff. Sept. 1, 2003.

§ 160.608. Authority to Deny Motion for Genetic Testing

(a) In a proceeding to adjudicate parentage, a court may deny a motion for an order for the genetic testing of the mother, the child, and the presumed father if the court determines that:

(1) the conduct of the mother or the presumed father estops that party from denying parentage; and

(2) it would be inequitable to disprove the father-child relationship between the child and the presumed father.

(b) In determining whether to deny a motion for an order for genetic testing under this section, the court shall consider the best interest of the child, including the following factors:

(1) the length of time between the date of the proceeding to adjudicate parentage and the date the presumed father was placed on notice that he might not be the genetic father;

(2) the length of time during which the presumed father has assumed the role of father of the child;

(3) the facts surrounding the presumed father's discovery of his possible nonpaternity;

(4) the nature of the relationship between the child and the presumed father;

(5) the age of the child;

(6) any harm that may result to the child if presumed paternity is successfully disproved;

(7) the nature of the relationship between the child and the alleged father;

(8) the extent to which the passage of time reduces the chances of establishing the paternity of another man and a child support obligation in favor of the child; and

(9) other factors that may affect the equities

arising from the disruption of the father-child relationship between the child and the presumed father or the chance of other harm to the child.

(c) In a proceeding involving the application of this section, a child who is a minor or is incapacitated must be represented by a guardian ad litem.

(d) A denial of a motion for an order for genetic testing must be based on clear and convincing evidence.

(e) If the court denies a motion for an order for genetic testing, the court shall issue an order adjudicating the presumed father to be the father of the child.

(f) This section applies to a proceeding to rescind or challenge an acknowledgment of paternity or a denial of paternity as provided by Section 160.309(d).

Added by Acts 2001, 77th Leg., ch. 821, § 1.01, eff. June 14, 2001. Amended by Acts 2003, 78th Leg., ch. 1248, § 5, eff. Sept. 1, 2003.

§ 160.609. Time Limitation: Child Having Acknowledged or Adjudicated Father

(a) If a child has an acknowledged father, a signatory to the acknowledgment or denial of paternity may commence a proceeding seeking to rescind the acknowledgment or denial or to challenge the paternity of the child only within the time allowed under Section 160.307 or 160.308.

(b) If a child has an acknowledged father or an adjudicated father, an individual, other than the child, who is not a signatory to the acknowledgment or a party to the adjudication and who seeks an adjudication of paternity of the child must commence a proceeding not later than the fourth anniversary of the effective date of the acknowledgment or adjudication.

Added by Acts 2001, 77th Leg., ch. 821, § 1.01, eff. June 14, 2001.

§ 160.610. Joinder of Proceedings

(a) Except as provided by Subsection (b), a proceeding to adjudicate parentage may be joined with a proceeding for adoption, termination of parental rights, possession of or access to a child, child support, divorce, annulment, or probate or administration of an estate or another appropriate proceeding.

(b) A respondent may not join a proceeding described by Subsection (a) with a proceeding to adjudicate parentage brought under Chapter 159.

Added by Acts 2001, 77th Leg., ch. 821, § 1.01, eff. June 14, 2001.

§ 160.611. Proceedings Before Birth

(a) A proceeding to determine parentage commenced before the birth of the child may not be concluded until after the birth of the child.

(b) In a proceeding described by Subsection (a), the following actions may be taken before the birth of the child:

(1) service of process;

(2) discovery; and

(3) except as prohibited by Section 160.502, collection of specimens for genetic testing.

Added by Acts 2001, 77th Leg., ch. 821, § 1.01, eff. June 14, 2001.

§ 160.612. Child as Party; Representation

(a) A minor child is a permissible party, but is not a necessary party to a proceeding under this subchapter.

(b) The court shall appoint an attorney ad litem to represent a child who is a minor or is incapacitated if the child is a party or the court finds that the interests of the child are not adequately represented.

Added by Acts 2001, 77th Leg., ch. 821, § 1.01, eff. June 14, 2001.

§ 160.621. Admissibility of Results of Genetic Testing; Expenses

(a) Except as otherwise provided by Subsection (c), a report of a genetic testing expert is admissible as evidence of the truth of the facts asserted in the report. The admissibility of the report is not affected by whether the testing was performed:

(1) voluntarily or under an order of the court or a support enforcement agency; or

(2) before or after the date of commencement of the proceeding.

(b) A party objecting to the results of genetic testing may call one or more genetic testing experts to testify in person or by telephone, videoconference, deposition, or another method approved by the court. Unless otherwise ordered by the court, the party offering the testimony bears the expense for the expert testifying.

(c) If a child has a presumed, acknowledged, or adjudicated father, the results of genetic testing are inadmissible to adjudicate parentage unless performed:

(1) with the consent of both the mother and the presumed, acknowledged, or adjudicated father; or

(2) under an order of the court under Section 160.502.

(d) Copies of bills for genetic testing and for prenatal and postnatal health care for the mother and child that are furnished to the adverse party on or before the 10th day before the date of a hearing are admissible to establish:

(1) the amount of the charges billed; and

(2) that the charges were reasonable, necessary, and customary.

Added by Acts 2001, 77th Leg., ch. 821, § 1.01, eff. June 14, 2001.

§ 160.622. Consequences of Declining Genetic Testing

(a) An order for genetic testing is enforceable by contempt.

(b) A court may adjudicate parentage contrary to the position of an individual whose paternity is being determined on the grounds that the individual declines to submit to genetic testing as ordered by the court.

(c) Genetic testing of the mother of a child is not a prerequisite to testing the child and a man whose paternity is being determined. If the mother is unavailable or declines to submit to genetic testing, the court may order the testing of the child and each man whose paternity is being adjudicated.

Added by Acts 2001, 77th Leg., ch. 821, § 1.01, eff. June 14, 2001.

§ 160.623. Admission of Paternity Authorized

(a) A respondent in a proceeding to adjudicate parentage may admit to the paternity of a child by filing a pleading to that effect or by admitting paternity under penalty of perjury when making an appearance or during a hearing.

(b) If the court finds that the admission of paternity satisfies the requirements of this section and that there is no reason to question the admission, the court shall render an order adjudicating the child to be the child of the man admitting paternity.

Added by Acts 2001, 77th Leg., ch. 821, § 1.01, eff. June 14, 2001.

§ 160.624. Temporary Order

(a) In a proceeding under this subchapter, the court shall render a temporary order for child support for a child if the order is appropriate and the individual ordered to pay child support:

(1) is a presumed father of the child;

(2) is petitioning to have his paternity adjudicated;

(3) is identified as the father through genetic testing under Section 160.505;

(4) is an alleged father who has declined to submit to genetic testing;

(5) is shown by clear and convincing evidence to be the father of the child; or

(6) is the mother of the child.

(b) A temporary order may include provisions for the possession of or access to the child as provided by other laws of this state.

Added by Acts 2001, 77th Leg., ch. 821, § 1.01, eff. June 14, 2001.

§ 160.631. Rules for Adjudication of Paternity

(a) The court shall apply the rules stated in this section to adjudicate the paternity of a child.

(b) The paternity of a child having a presumed, acknowledged, or adjudicated father may be disproved only by admissible results of genetic testing excluding that man as the father of the child or identifying another man as the father of the child.

(c) Unless the results of genetic testing are admitted to rebut other results of genetic testing, the man identified as the father of a child under Section 160.505 shall be adjudicated as being the father of the child.

(d) Unless the results of genetic testing are admitted to rebut other results of genetic testing, a man excluded as the father of a child by genetic testing shall be adjudicated as not being the father of the child.

(e) If the court finds that genetic testing under Section 160.505 does not identify or exclude a man as the father of a child, the court may not dismiss the proceeding. In that event, the results of genetic testing and other evidence are admissible to adjudicate the issue of paternity.

Added by Acts 2001, 77th Leg., ch. 821, § 1.01, eff. June 14, 2001.

§ 160.632. Jury Prohibited

The court shall adjudicate paternity of a child without a jury.

Added by Acts 2001, 77th Leg., ch. 821, § 1.01, eff. June 14, 2001.

§ 160.633. Hearings; Inspection of Records

(a) On the request of a party and for good cause shown, the court may order a proceeding under this subchapter closed to the public.

(b) A final order in a proceeding under this subchapter is available for public inspection. Other papers and records are available only with the consent of the parties or on order of the court for good cause.

Added by Acts 2001, 77th Leg., ch. 821, § 1.01, eff. June 14, 2001.

§ 160.634. Order on Default

The court shall issue an order adjudicating the paternity of a man who:

(1) after service of process, is in default; and

(2) is found by the court to be the father of a child.

Added by Acts 2001, 77th Leg., ch. 821, § 1.01, eff. June 14, 2001.

§ 160.635. Dismissal for Want of Prosecution

The court may issue an order dismissing a proceeding commenced under this chapter for want of prosecution only without prejudice. An order of dismissal for want of prosecution purportedly with prejudice is void and has only the effect of a dismissal without prejudice.

Added by Acts 2001, 77th Leg., ch. 821, § 1.01, eff. June 14, 2001.

§ 160.636. Order Adjudicating Parentage; Costs

(a) The court shall render an order adjudicating whether a man alleged or claiming to be the father is the parent of the child.

(b) An order adjudicating parentage must identify the child by name and date of birth.

(c) Except as otherwise provided by Subsection (d), the court may assess filing fees, reasonable attorney's fees, fees for genetic testing, other costs, and necessary travel and other reasonable expenses incurred in a proceeding under this subchapter. Attorney's fees awarded by the court may be paid directly to the attorney. An attorney who is awarded attorney's fees may enforce the order in the attorney's own name.

(d) The court may not assess fees, costs, or expenses against the support enforcement agency of this state or another state, except as provided by other law.

(e) On request of a party and for good cause shown, the court may order that the name of the child be changed.

(f) If the order of the court is at variance with the child's birth certificate, the court shall order the bureau of vital statistics to issue an amended birth record.

(g) On a finding of parentage, the court may order retroactive child support as provided by Chapter 154 and, on a proper showing, order a party to pay an equitable portion of all of the prenatal and postnatal health care expenses of the mother and the child.

(h) In rendering an order for retroactive child support under this section, the court shall use the child support guidelines provided by Chapter 154, together with any relevant factors.

Added by Acts 2001, 77th Leg., ch. 821, § 1.01, eff. June 14, 2001.

§ 160.637. Binding Effect of Determination of Parentage

(a) Except as otherwise provided by Subsection (b) or Section 160.316, a determination of parentage is binding on:

(1) all signatories to an acknowledgment or denial of paternity as provided by Subchapter D[1]; and

(2) all parties to an adjudication by a court acting under circumstances that satisfy the jurisdictional requirements of Section 159.201.

(b) A child is not bound by a determination of parentage under this chapter unless:

(1) the determination was based on an unrescinded acknowledgment of paternity and the acknowledgment is consistent with the results of genetic testing;

(2) the adjudication of parentage was based on a finding consistent with the results of genetic testing and the consistency is declared in the determination or is otherwise shown; or

(3) the child was a party or was represented in the proceeding determining parentage by an attorney ad litem.

(c) In a proceeding to dissolve a marriage, the court is considered to have made an adjudication of the parentage of a child if the court acts under circumstances that satisfy the jurisdictional requirements of Section 159.201, and the final order:

(1) expressly identifies the child as "a child of the marriage" or "issue of the marriage" or uses similar words indicating that the husband is the father of the child; or

(2) provides for the payment of child support for the child by the husband unless paternity is specifically disclaimed in the order.

(d) Except as otherwise provided by Subsection (b), a determination of parentage may be a defense in a subsequent proceeding seeking to adjudicate parentage by an individual who was not a party to the earlier proceeding.

(e) A party to an adjudication of paternity may challenge the adjudication only under the laws of this state relating to appeal, the vacating of judgments, or other judicial review.

Added by Acts 2001, 77th Leg., ch. 821, § 1.01, eff. June 14, 2001.

Subchapter H. Child of Assisted Reproduction

Statutes in Context

Modern medical technology permits children to be born via reproduction techniques that involve more than the traditional two people or years after the death of one of the parents. Examples of these methodologies include (1) *artificial insemination* (donated semen artificially introduced into the mother's vagina or uterus), (2) *in vitro fertilization* (donated egg and donated semen combined in a laboratory with the resulting embryo transferred to a donee), (3) *gamete intrafallopian transfer* (donated egg and donated sperm combined in a donee's fallopian tube), and (4) *embryo lavage and transfer* (fertilized egg removed from the donor and transferred to the donee's uterus).

Several options exist regarding the parentage of children born as a result of these techniques. The father could be (1) the supplier of the genetic material (sperm), (2) the husband of the supplier of the female genetic material (egg), or (3) the husband of the woman who gestates the child. Likewise, the mother could be (1) the supplier of the female genetic material, (2) the wife of the man who supplies the male genetic material, or (3) the woman who gestates the child even though this woman did not supply any genetic material (a surrogate mother).

Sections 160.701 - 160.763 resolve some, but not all, of the issues which arise regarding the individuals whom the law will treat as the parents of children conceived by means of assisted conception.

§ 160.701. Scope of Subchapter

This subchapter applies only to a child conceived by means of assisted reproduction.

Added by Acts 2001, 77th Leg., ch. 821, § 1.01, eff. June 14, 2001.

[1] V.T.C.A., Family Code § 160.301 et seq.

§ 160.702. Parental Status of Donor

A donor is not a parent of a child conceived by means of assisted reproduction.

Added by Acts 2001, 77th Leg., ch. 821, § 1.01, eff. June 14, 2001.

§ 160.703. Husband's Paternity of Child of Assisted Reproduction

If a husband provides sperm for or consents to assisted reproduction by his wife as provided by Section 160.704, he is the father of a resulting child.

Added by Acts 2001, 77th Leg., ch. 821, § 1.01, eff. June 14, 2001.

§ 160.704. Consent to Assisted Reproduction

(a) Consent by a married woman to assisted reproduction must be in a record signed by the woman and her husband. This requirement does not apply to the donation of eggs by a married woman for assisted reproduction by another woman.

(b) Failure by the husband to sign a consent required by Subsection (a) before or after the birth of the child does not preclude a finding that the husband is the father of a child born to his wife if the wife and husband openly treated the child as their own.

Added by Acts 2001, 77th Leg., ch. 821, § 1.01, eff. June 14, 2001.

§ 160.705. Limitation on Husband's Dispute of Paternity

(a) Except as otherwise provided by Subsection (b), the husband of a wife who gives birth to a child by means of assisted reproduction may not challenge his paternity of the child unless:

(1) before the fourth anniversary of the date of learning of the birth of the child he commences a proceeding to adjudicate his paternity; and

(2) the court finds that he did not consent to the assisted reproduction before or after the birth of the child.

(b) A proceeding to adjudicate paternity may be maintained at any time if the court determines that:

(1) the husband did not provide sperm for or, before or after the birth of the child, consent to assisted reproduction by his wife;

(2) the husband and the mother of the child have not cohabited since the probable time of assisted reproduction; and

(3) the husband never openly treated the child as his own.

(c) The limitations provided by this section apply to a marriage declared invalid after assisted reproduction.

Added by Acts 2001, 77th Leg., ch. 821, § 1.01, eff. June 14, 2001.

§ 160.706. Effect of Dissolution of Marriage

(a) If a marriage is dissolved before the placement of eggs, sperm, or embryos, the former spouse is not a parent of the resulting child unless the former spouse consented in a record that if assisted reproduction were to occur after a divorce the former spouse would be a parent of the child.

(b) The consent of a former spouse to assisted reproduction may be withdrawn by that individual in a record at any time before the placement of eggs, sperm, or embryos.

Added by Acts 2001, 77th Leg., ch. 821, § 1.01, eff. June 14, 2001.

§ 160.707. Parental Status of Deceased Spouse

If a spouse dies before the placement of eggs, sperm, or embryos, the deceased spouse is not a parent of the resulting child unless the deceased spouse consented in a record that if assisted reproduction were to occur after death the deceased spouse would be a parent of the child.

Added by Acts 2001, 77th Leg., ch. 821, § 1.01, eff. June 14, 2001.

Subchapter I. GESTATIONAL AGREEMENTS

Statutes in Context

The 2003 Texas Legislature authorized gestational agreements between a surrogate mother and the intended parents in Family Code §§ 160.751–160.762. If the agreement is properly validated, the woman who gave birth to the child will not be treated as the child's mother. Accordingly, this child would not inherit from or through the birth mother. Instead, the mother and father of the child will be the intended parents and inheritance rights will accrue accordingly.

§ 160.751. Definition

In thissubchapter, "gestational mother" means a woman who gives birth to a child conceived under a gestational agreement.

Added by Acts 2003, 78th Leg., ch. 457, § 2, eff. Sept. 1, 2003.

§ 160.752. Scope of Subchapter; Choice of Law

(a)Notwithstanding any other provision of this chapter or another law, this subchapter authorizes an agreement between a woman and the intended parents of a child in which the woman relinquishes all rights as a parent of a child conceived by means of assisted reproduction and that provides that the intended parents become the parents of the child.

(b) This subchapter controls over any other law with respect to a child conceived under a gestational agreement under this subchapter.

Added by Acts 2003, 78th Leg., ch. 457, § 2, eff. Sept. 1, 2003.

§ 160.753. Establishment of Parent-Child Relationship

(a) Notwithstanding any other provision of this chapter or another law, the mother-child relationship exists between a woman and a child by an adjudication confirming the woman as a parent of the child born to a gestational mother under a gestational agreement if the gestational agreement is validated under this subchapter or enforceable under other law, regardless of the fact that the gestational mother gave birth to the child.

(b) The father-child relationship exists between a child and a man by an adjudication confirming the man as a parent of the child born to a gestational mother under a gestational agreement if the gestational agreement is validated under this subchapter or enforceable under other law.

Added by Acts 2003, 78th Leg., ch. 457, § 2, eff. Sept. 1, 2003.

§ 160.754. Gestational Agreement Authorized

(a) A prospective gestational mother, her husband if she is married, each donor, and each intended parent may enter into a written agreement providing that:

(1) the prospective gestational mother agrees to pregnancy by means of assisted reproduction;

(2) the prospective gestational mother, her husband if she is married, and each donor other than the intended parents, if applicable, relinquish all parental rights and duties with respect to a child conceived through assisted reproduction;

(3) the intended parents will be the parents of the child; and

(4) the gestational mother and each intended parent agree to exchange throughout the period covered by the agreement all relevant information regarding the health of the gestational mother and each intended parent.

(b) The intended parents must be married to each other. Each intended parent must be a party to the gestational agreement.

(c) The gestational agreement must require that the eggs used in the assisted reproduction procedure be retrieved from an intended parent or a donor. The gestational mother's eggs may not be used in the assisted reproduction procedure.

(d) The gestational agreement must state that the physician who will perform the assisted reproduction procedure as provided by the agreement has informed the parties to the agreement of:

(1) the rate of successful conceptions and births attributable to the procedure, including the most recent published outcome statistics of the procedure at the facility at which it will be performed;

(2) the potential for and risks associated with the implantation of multiple embryos and consequent multiple births resulting from the procedure;

(3) the nature of and expenses related to the procedure;

(4) the health risks associated with, as applicable, fertility drugs used in the procedure, egg retrieval procedures, and egg or embryo transfer procedures; and

(5) reasonably foreseeable psychological effects resulting from the procedure.

(e) The parties to a gestational agreement must enter into the agreement before the 14th day preceding the date the transfer of eggs, sperm, or embryos to the gestational mother occurs for the purpose of conception or implantation.

(f) A gestational agreement does not apply to the birth of a child conceived by means of sexual intercourse.

(g) A gestational agreement may not limit the right of the gestational mother to make decisions to safeguard her health or the health of an embryo.

Added by Acts 2003, 78th Leg., ch. 457, § 2, eff. Sept. 1, 2003.

§ 160.755. Petition to Validate Gestational Agreement

(a) The intended parents and the prospective gestational mother under a gestational agreement may commence a proceeding to validate the agreement.

(b) A person may maintain a proceeding to validate a gestational agreement only if:

(1) the prospective gestational mother or the intended parents have resided in this state for the 90 days preceding the date the proceeding is commenced;

(2) the prospective gestational mother's husband, if she is married, is joined as a party to the proceeding; and

(3) a copy of the gestational agreement is attached to the petition.

Added by Acts 2003, 78th Leg., ch. 457, § 2, eff. Sept. 1, 2003.

§ 160.756. Hearing to Validate Gestational Agreement

(a) A gestational agreement must be validated as provided by this section.

(b) The court may validate a gestational agreement as provided by Subsection (c) only if the court finds that:

(1) the parties have submitted to the jurisdiction of the court under the jurisdictional standards of this chapter;

(2) the medical evidence provided shows that the intended mother is unable to carry a pregnancy to term and give birth to the child or is unable to carry the pregnancy to term and give birth to the child without unreasonable risk to her physical or mental health or to the health of the unborn child;

(3) unless waived by the court, an agency or other person has conducted a home study of the intended parents and has determined that the intended parents meet the standards of fitness applicable to adoptive parents;

(4) each party to the agreement has voluntarily

entered into and understands the terms of the agreement;

(5) the prospective gestational mother has had at least one previous pregnancy and delivery and carrying another pregnancy to term and giving birth to another child would not pose an unreasonable risk to the child's health or the physical or mental health of the prospective gestational mother; and

(6) the parties have adequately provided for which party is responsible for all reasonable health care expenses associated with the pregnancy, including providing for who is responsible for those expenses if the agreement is terminated.

(c) If the court finds that the requirements of Subsection (b) are satisfied, the court may render an order validating the gestational agreement and declaring that the intended parents will be the parents of a child born under the agreement.

(d) The court may validate the gestational agreement at the court's discretion. The court's determination of whether to validate the agreement is subject to review only for abuse of discretion.

Added by Acts 2003, 78th Leg., ch. 457, § 2, eff. Sept. 1, 2003.

§ 160.757. Inspection of Records

The proceedings, records, and identities of the parties to a gestational agreement under this subchapter are subject to inspection under the same standards of confidentiality that apply to an adoption under the laws of this state.

Added by Acts 2003, 78th Leg., ch. 457, § 2, eff. Sept. 1, 2003.

§ 160.758. Continuing, Exclusive Jurisdiction

Subject to Section 152.201, a court that conducts a proceeding under this subchapter has continuing, exclusive jurisdiction of all matters arising out of the gestational agreement until the date a child born to the gestational mother during the period covered by the agreement reaches 180 days of age.

Added by Acts 2003, 78th Leg., ch. 457, § 2, eff. Sept. 1, 2003.

§ 160.759. Termination of Gestational Agreement

(a) Before a prospective gestational mother becomes pregnant by means of assisted reproduction, the prospective gestational mother, her husband if she is married, or either intended parent may terminate a gestational agreement validated under Section 160.756 by giving written notice of the termination to each other party to the agreement.

(b) A person who terminates a gestational agreement under Subsection (a) shall file notice of the termination with the court. A person having the duty to notify the court who does not notify the court of the termination of the agreement is subject to appropriate sanctions.

(c) On receipt of the notice of termination, the court shall vacate the order rendered under Section 160.756 validating the gestational agreement.

(d) A prospective gestational mother and her husband, if she is married, may not be liable to an intended parent for terminating a gestational agreement if the termination is in accordance with this section.

Added by Acts 2003, 78th Leg., ch. 457, § 2, eff. Sept. 1, 2003.

§ 160.760. Parentage Under Validated Gestational Agreement

(a) On the birth of a child to a gestational mother under a validated gestational agreement, the intended parents shall file a notice of the birth with the court not later than the 300th day after the date assisted reproduction occurred.

(b) After receiving notice of the birth, the court shall render an order that:

(1) confirms that the intended parents are the child's parents;

(2) requires the gestational mother to surrender the child to the intended parents, if necessary; and

(3) requires the bureau of vital statistics to issue a birth certificate naming the intended parents as the child's parents.

(c) If a person alleges that a child born to a gestational mother did not result from assisted reproduction, the court shall order that scientifically accepted parentage testing be conducted to determine the child's parentage.

Added by Acts 2003, 78th Leg., ch. 457, § 2, eff. Sept. 1, 2003.

§ 160.761. Effect of Gestational Mother's Marriage After Validation of Agreement

If a gestational mother is married after the court renders an order validating a gestational agreement under this subchapter:

(1) the validity of the gestational agreement is not affected;

(2) the gestational mother's husband is not required to consent to the agreement; and

(3) the gestational mother's husband is not a presumed father of the child born under the terms of the agreement.

Added by Acts 2003, 78th Leg., ch. 457, § 2, eff. Sept. 1, 2003.

§ 160.762. Effect of Gestational Agreement that Is Not Validated

(a) A gestational agreement that is not validated as provided by this subchapter is unenforceable, regardless of whether the agreement is in a record.

(b) The parent-child relationship of a child born under a gestational agreement that is not validated as provided by this subchapter is determined as otherwise provided by this chapter.

(c) A party to a gestational agreement that is not validated as provided by this subchapter who is an intended parent under the agreement may be held liable for the support of a child born under the agreement, even if the agreement is otherwise unenforceable.

(d) The court may assess filing fees, reasonable attorney's fees, fees for genetic testing, other costs, and necessary travel and other reasonable expenses incurred in a proceeding under this section. Attorney's fees awarded by the court may be paid directly to the attorney. An attorney who is awarded attorney's fees may enforce the order in the attorney's own name.

Added by Acts 2003, 78th Leg., ch. 457, § 2, eff. Sept. 1, 2003.

§ 160.763. Health Care Facility Reporting Requirement

(a) The Texas Department of Health by rule shall develop and implement a confidential reporting system that requires each health care facility in this state at which assisted reproduction procedures are performed under gestational agreements to report statistics related to those procedures.

(b) In developing the reporting system, the department shall require each health care facility described by Subsection (a) to annually report:

(1) the number of assisted reproduction procedures under a gestational agreement performed at the facility during the preceding year; and

(2) the number and current status of embryos created through assisted reproduction procedures described by Subdivision (1) that were not transferred for implantation.

Added by Acts 2003, 78th Leg., ch. 457, § 2, eff. Sept. 1, 2003.

Chapter 161. Termination of the Parent-Child Relationship

Subchapter C. Hearing and Order

Statutes in Context

An order terminating parental rights under § 161.206 will not divest the child of the right to inherit from and through the parent unless the court order expressly removes inheritance rights.

---

§ 161.206. Order Terminating Parental Rights

(a) If the court finds by clear and convincing evidence grounds for termination of the parent-child relationship, it shall render an order terminating the parent-child relationship.

(b) Except as provided by Section 161.2061, an order terminating the parent-child relationship divests the parent and the child of all legal rights and duties with respect to each other, except that the child retains the right to inherit from and through the parent unless the court otherwise provides.

(c) Nothing in this chapter precludes or affects the rights of a biological or adoptive maternal or paternal grandparent to reasonable access under Chapter 153.

Added by Acts 1995, 74th Leg., ch. 20, § 1, eff. April 20, 1995. Amended by Acts 1995, 74th Leg., ch. 709, § 2, eff. Sept. 1, 1995; Acts 1995, 74th Leg., ch. 751, § 72, eff. Sept. 1, 1995; Acts 2003, 78th Leg., ch. 561, § 1, eff. Sept. 1, 2003.

§ 161.2061. Terms Regarding Limited Post-Termination Contact

(a) If the court finds it to be in the best interest of the child, the court may provide in an order terminating the parent-child relationship that the biological parent who filed an affidavit of voluntary relinquishment of parental rights under Section 161.103 shall have limited post-termination contact with the child as provided by Subsection (b) on the agreement of the biological parent and the Department of Protective and Regulatory Services.

(b) The order of termination may include terms that allow the biological parent to:

(1) receive specified information regarding the child;

(2) provide written communications to the child; and

(3) have limited access to the child.

(c) The terms of an order of termination regarding limited post-termination contact may be enforced only if the party seeking enforcement pleads and proves that, before filing the motion for enforcement, the party attempted in good faith to resolve the disputed matters through mediation.

(d) The terms of an order of termination under this section are not enforceable by contempt.

(e) The terms of an order of termination regarding limited post-termination contact may not be modified.

(f) An order under this section does not:

(1) affect the finality of a termination order; or

(2) grant standing to a parent whose parental rights have been terminated to file any action under this title other than a motion to enforce the terms regarding limited post-termination contact until the court renders a subsequent adoption order with respect to the child.

Added by Acts 2003, 78th Leg., ch. 561, § 2, eff. Sept. 1, 2003.

§ 161.2062. Provision for Limited Contact Between Biological Parent and Child

(a) An order terminating the parent-child relationship may not require that a subsequent adoption order include terms regarding limited post- termination contact between the child and a biological parent.

(b) The inclusion of a requirement for post-termination contact described by Subsection (a) in a termination order does not:

(1) affect the finality of a termination or subsequent adoption order; or

(2) grant standing to a parent whose parental rights have been terminated to file any action under this title after the court renders a subsequent adoption order with respect to the child.

Added by Acts 2003, 78th Leg., ch. 561, § 2, eff. Sept. 1, 2003.

Chapter 162. Adoption

Subchapter A. Adoption of a Child

Statutes in Context

Sections 162.001 - 162.025 govern the adoption of a child.

§ 162.001. Who May Adopt and be Adopted

(a) Subject to the requirements for standing to sue in Chapter 102, an adult may petition to adopt a child who may be adopted.

(b) A child residing in this state may be adopted if:

(1) the parent-child relationship as to each living parent of the child has been terminated or a suit for termination is joined with the suit for adoption;

(2) the parent whose rights have not been terminated is presently the spouse of the petitioner and the proceeding is for a stepparent adoption;

(3) the child is at least two years old, the parent-child relationship has been terminated with respect to one parent, the person seeking the adoption has been a managing conservator or has had actual care, possession, and control of the child for a period of six months preceding the adoption or is the child's former stepparent, and the nonterminated parent consents to the adoption; or

(4) the child is at least two years old, the parent-child relationship has been terminated with respect to one parent, and the person seeking the adoption is the child's former stepparent and has been a managing conservator or has had actual care, possession, and control of the child for a period of one year preceding the adoption.

(c) If an affidavit of relinquishment of parental rights contains a consent for the Department of Protective and Regulatory Services or a licensed child-placing agency to place the child for adoption and appoints the department or agency managing conservator of the child, further consent by the parent is not required and the adoption order shall terminate all rights of the parent without further termination proceedings.

Added by Acts 1995, 74th Leg., ch. 20, § 1, eff. April 20, 1995; Amended by Acts 1997, 75th Leg., ch. 561, § 14, eff. Sept. 1, 1997Acts 2003, 78th Leg., ch. 493, § 1, eff. Sept. 1, 2003.

§ 162.002. Prerequisites to Petition

(a) If a petitioner is married, both spouses must join in the petition for adoption.

(b) A petition in a suit for adoption or a suit for appointment of a nonparent managing conservator with authority to consent to adoption of a child must include:

(1) a verified allegation that there has been compliance with Subchapter B[1]; or

(2) if there has not been compliance with Subchapter B, a verified statement of the particular reasons for noncompliance.

Added by Acts 1995, 74th Leg., ch. 20, § 1, eff. April 20, 1995.

§ 162.0025. Repealed.

Repealed by Acts 2001, 77th Leg., ch. 133, § 7, eff. Sept. 1, 2001.

§ 162.003. Pre-adoptive Home Screening and Post-placement Report

In a suit for adoption, a pre-adoptive home screening and post-placement report must be conducted as provided in Chapter 107.

Added by Acts 1995, 74th Leg., ch. 20, § 1, eff. April 20, 1995. Amended by Acts 1995, 74th Leg., ch. 751, § 73, eff. Sept. 1, 1995; Acts 1995, 74th Leg., ch. 800, § 1, eff. Sept. 1, 1995; Acts 2001, 77th Leg., ch. 133, § 3, eff. Sept. 1, 2001.

§ 162.004. Repealed.

Repealed.

Repealed by Acts 2001, 77th Leg., ch. 133, § 7, eff. Sept. 1, 2001.

§ 162.0045. Preferential Setting

The court shall grant a motion for a preferential setting for a final hearing on an adoption and shall give precedence to that hearing over all other civil cases not given preference by other law if the social study has been filed and the criminal history for the person seeking to adopt the child has been obtained.

Added by Acts 1997, 75th Leg., ch. 561, § 15, eff. Sept. 1, 1997.

§ 162.005. Preparation of Health, Social, Educational, and Genetic History Report

(a) This section does not apply to an adoption by the child's:

(1) grandparent;

(2) aunt or uncle by birth, marriage, or prior adoption; or

(3) stepparent.

(b) Before placing a child for adoption, the Department of Protective and Regulatory Services, a licensed child-placing agency, or the child's parent or guardian shall compile a report on the available health, social, educational, and genetic history of the child to be adopted.

(c) The report shall include a history of physical, sexual, or emotional abuse suffered by the child, if any.

(d) If the child has been placed for adoption by a person or entity other than the department, a licensed

[1] V.T.C.A., Family Code § 162.101 et seq.

child-placing agency, or the child's parent or guardian, it is the duty of the person or entity who places the child for adoption to prepare the report.

(e) The person or entity who places the child for adoption shall provide the prospective adoptive parents a copy of the report as early as practicable before the first meeting of the adoptive parents with the child. The copy of the report shall be edited to protect the identity of birth parents and their families.

(f) The department, licensed child-placing agency, parent, guardian, person, or entity who prepares and files the original report is required to furnish supplemental medical, psychological, and psychiatric information to the adoptive parents if that information becomes available and to file the supplemental information where the original report is filed. The supplemental information shall be retained for as long as the original report is required to be retained.

Added by Acts 1995, 74th Leg., ch. 20, § 1, eff. April 20, 1995.

§ 162.006. Right to Examine Records

(a) The department, licensed child-placing agency, person, or entity placing a child for adoption shall inform the prospective adoptive parents of their right to examine the records and other information relating to the history of the child. The person or entity placing the child for adoption shall edit the records and information to protect the identity of the biological parents and any other person whose identity is confidential.

(b) The department, licensed child-placing agency, or court retaining a copy of the report shall provide a copy of the report that has been edited to protect the identity of the birth parents and any other person whose identity is confidential to the following persons on request:

(1) an adoptive parent of the adopted child;

(2) the managing conservator, guardian of the person, or legal custodian of the adopted child;

(3) the adopted child, after the child is an adult;

(4) the surviving spouse of the adopted child if the adopted child is dead and the spouse is the parent or guardian of a child of the deceased adopted child; or

(5) a progeny of the adopted child if the adopted child is dead and the progeny is an adult.

(c) A copy of the report may not be furnished to a person who cannot furnish satisfactory proof of identity and legal entitlement to receive a copy.

(d) A person requesting a copy of the report shall pay the actual and reasonable costs of providing a copy and verifying entitlement to the copy.

(e) The report shall be retained for 99 years from the date of the adoption by the department or licensed child-placing agency placing the child for adoption. If the agency ceases to function as a child-placing agency, the agency shall transfer all the reports to the department or, after giving notice to the department, to a transferee agency that is assuming responsibility for the preservation of the agency's adoption records. If the child has not been placed for adoption by the department or a licensed child-placing agency and if the child is being adopted by a person other than the child's stepparent, grandparent, aunt, or uncle by birth, marriage, or prior adoption, the person or entity who places the child for adoption shall file the report with the department, which shall retain the copies for 99 years from the date of the adoption.

Added by Acts 1995, 74th Leg., ch. 20, § 1, eff. April 20, 1995.

§ 162.0065. Editing Adoption Records in Department Placement

Notwithstanding any other provision of this chapter, in an adoption in which a child is placed for adoption by the Department of Protective and Regulatory Services, the department is not required to edit records to protect the identity of birth parents and other persons whose identity is confidential if the department determines that information is already known to the adoptive parents or is readily available through other sources, including the court records of a suit to terminate the parent-child relationship under Chapter 161.

Added by Acts 2003, 78th Leg., ch. 68, § 1, eff. Sept. 1, 2003.

§ 162.007. Contents of Health, Social, Educational, and Genetic History Report

(a) The health history of the child must include information about:

(1) the child's health status at the time of placement;

(2) the child's birth, neonatal, and other medical, psychological, psychiatric, and dental history information;

(3) a record of immunizations for the child; and

(4) the available results of medical, psychological, psychiatric, and dental examinations of the child.

(b) The social history of the child must include information, to the extent known, about past and existing relationships between the child and the child's siblings, parents by birth, extended family, and other persons who have had physical possession of or legal access to the child.

(c) The educational history of the child must include, to the extent known, information about:

(1) the enrollment and performance of the child in educational institutions;

(2) results of educational testing and standardized tests for the child; and

(3) special educational needs, if any, of the child.

(d) The genetic history of the child must include a description of the child's parents by birth and their parents, any other child born to either of the child's parents, and extended family members and must include, to the extent the information is available, information about:

(1) their health and medical history, including any genetic diseases and disorders;

(2) their health status at the time of placement;

(3) the cause of and their age at death;

(4) their height, weight, and eye and hair color;

(5) their nationality and ethnic background;

(6) their general levels of educational and professional achievements, if any;

(7) their religious backgrounds, if any;

(8) any psychological, psychiatric, or social evaluations, including the date of the evaluation, any diagnosis, and a summary of any findings;

(9) any criminal conviction records relating to a misdemeanor or felony classified as an offense against the person or family or public indecency or a felony violation of a statute intended to control the possession or distribution of a substance included in Chapter 481, Health and Safety Code; and

(10) any information necessary to determine whether the child is entitled to or otherwise eligible for state or federal financial, medical, or other assistance.

Added by Acts 1995, 74th Leg., ch. 20, § 1, eff. April 20, 1995.

§ 162.008. Filing of Health, Social, Educational, and Genetic History Report

(a) This section does not apply to an adoption by the child's:

(1) grandparent;

(2) aunt or uncle by birth, marriage, or prior adoption; or

(3) stepparent.

(b) A petition for adoption may not be granted until the following documents have been filed:

(1) a copy of the health, social, educational, and genetic history report signed by the child's adoptive parents; and

(2) if the report is required to be submitted to the bureau of vital statistics under Section 162.006(e), a certificate from the bureau acknowledging receipt of the report.

(c) A court having jurisdiction of a suit affecting the parent-child relationship may by order waive the making and filing of a report under this section if the child's biological parents cannot be located and their absence results in insufficient information being available to compile the report.

Added by Acts 1995, 74th Leg., ch. 20, § 1, eff. April 20, 1995. Amended by Acts 1999, 76th Leg., ch. 1390, § 20, eff. Sept. 1, 1999.

§ 162.0085. Criminal History Report Required

(a) In a suit affecting the parent-child relationship in which an adoption is sought, the court shall order each person seeking to adopt the child to obtain that person's own criminal history record information. The court shall accept under this section a person's criminal history record information that is provided by the Department of Protective and Regulatory Services or by a licensed child-placing agency that received the information from the department if the information was obtained not more than one year before the date the court ordered the history to be obtained.

(b) A person required to obtain information under Subsection (a) shall obtain the information in the manner provided by Section 411.128, Local Government Code.

Added by Acts 1995, 74th Leg., ch. 751, § 75, eff. Sept. 1, 1995; Acts 1995, 74th Leg., ch. 908, § 2, eff. Sept. 1, 1995; Amended by Acts 1997, 75th Leg., ch. 561, § 16, eff. Sept. 1, 1997.

§ 162.009. Residence With Petitioner

(a) The court may not grant an adoption until the child has resided with the petitioner for not less than six months.

(b) On request of the petitioner, the court may waive the residence requirement if the waiver is in the best interest of the child.

Added by Acts 1995, 74th Leg., ch. 20, § 1, eff. April 20, 1995.

§ 162.010. Consent Required

(a) Unless the managing conservator is the petitioner, the written consent of a managing conservator to the adoption must be filed. The court may waive the requirement of consent by the managing conservator if the court finds that the consent is being refused or has been revoked without good cause. A hearing on the issue of consent shall be conducted by the court without a jury.

(b) If a parent of the child is presently the spouse of the petitioner, that parent must join in the petition for adoption and further consent of that parent is not required.

(c) A child 12 years of age or older must consent to the adoption in writing or in court. The court may waive this requirement if it would serve the child's best interest.

Added by Acts 1995, 74th Leg., ch. 20, § 1, eff. April 20, 1995. Amended by Acts 1995, 74th Leg., ch. 751, § 76, eff. Sept. 1, 1995.

§ 162.011. Revocation of Consent

At any time before an order granting the adoption of the child is rendered, a consent required by Section 162.010 may be revoked by filing a signed revocation.

Added by Acts 1995, 74th Leg., ch. 20, § 1, eff. April 20, 1995.

§ 162.012. Direct or Collateral Attack

(a) Notwithstanding Rule 329, Texas Rules of Civil Procedure, the validity of an adoption order is not subject to attack after six months after the date the order was signed.

(b) The validity of a final adoption order is not subject to attack because a health, social, educational, and genetic history was not filed.

Added by Acts 1995, 74th Leg., ch. 20, § 1, eff. April 20, 1995; Amended by Acts 1997, 75th Leg., ch. 601, § 1, eff.

Sept. 1, 1997; Acts 1997, 75th Leg., ch. 600, § 2, eff. Jan. 1, 1998.

§ 162.013. Abatement or Dismissal

(a) If the sole petitioner dies or the joint petitioners die, the court shall dismiss the suit for adoption.

(b) If one of the joint petitioners dies, the proceeding shall continue uninterrupted.

(c) If the joint petitioners divorce, the court shall abate the suit for adoption. The court shall dismiss the petition unless the petition is amended to request adoption by one of the original petitioners.

Added by Acts 1995, 74th Leg., ch. 20, § 1, eff. April 20, 1995.

§ 162.014. Attendance at Hearing Required

(a) If the joint petitioners are husband and wife and it would be unduly difficult for one of the petitioners to appear at the hearing, the court may waive the attendance of that petitioner if the other spouse is present.

(b) A child to be adopted who is 12 years of age or older shall attend the hearing. The court may waive this requirement in the best interest of the child.

Added by Acts 1995, 74th Leg., ch. 20, § 1, eff. April 20, 1995.

§ 162.015. Race or Ethnicity

(a) In determining the best interest of the child, the court may not deny or delay the adoption or otherwise discriminate on the basis of race or ethnicity of the child or the prospective adoptive parents.

(b) This section does not apply to a person, entity, tribe, organization, or child custody proceeding subject to the Indian Child Welfare Act of 1978 (25 U.S.C. § 1901 et seq.). In this subsection "child custody proceeding" has the meaning provided by 25 U.S.C. § 1903.

Added by Acts 1995, 74th Leg., ch. 20, § 1, eff. April 20, 1995. Amended by Acts 1995, 74th Leg., ch. 751, § 77, eff. Sept. 1, 1995.

§ 162.016. Adoption Order

(a) If a petition requesting termination has been joined with a petition requesting adoption, the court shall also terminate the parent-child relationship at the same time the adoption order is rendered. The court must make separate findings that the termination is in the best interest of the child and that the adoption is in the best interest of the child.

(b) If the court finds that the requirements for adoption have been met and the adoption is in the best interest of the child, the court shall grant the adoption.

(c) The name of the child may be changed in the order if requested.

Added by Acts 1995, 74th Leg., ch. 20, § 1, eff. April 20, 1995.

Statutes in Context

An adopted child is, under § 162.017, entitled to inherit from and through the child's adoptive parents as though the child were the biological child of the parents. This is consistent with Probate Code § 40.

§ 162.017. Effect of Adoption

(a) An order of adoption creates the parent-child relationship between the adoptive parent and the child for all purposes.

(b) An adopted child is entitled to inherit from and through the child's adoptive parents as though the child were the biological child of the parents.

(c) The terms "child," "descendant," "issue," and other terms indicating the relationship of parent and child include an adopted child unless the context or express language clearly indicates otherwise.

(d) Nothing in this chapter precludes or affects the rights of a biological or adoptive maternal or paternal grandparent to reasonable access, as provided in Chapter 153.

Added by Acts 1995, 74th Leg., ch. 20, § 1, eff. April 20, 1995.

§ 162.018. Access to Information

(a) The adoptive parents are entitled to receive copies of the records and other information relating to the history of the child maintained by the department, licensed child-placing agency, person, or entity placing the child for adoption.

(b) The adoptive parents and the adopted child, after the child is an adult, are entitled to receive copies of the records that have been edited to protect the identity of the biological parents and any other person whose identity is confidential and other information relating to the history of the child maintained by the department, licensed child-placing agency, person, or entity placing the child for adoption.

(c) It is the duty of the person or entity placing the child for adoption to edit the records and information to protect the identity of the biological parents and any other person whose identity is confidential.

(d) At the time an adoption order is rendered, the court shall provide to the parents of an adopted child information provided by the bureau of vital statistics that describes the functions of the voluntary adoption registry under Subchapter E.[1] The licensed child-placing agency shall provide to each of the child's biological parents known to the agency, the information when the parent signs an affidavit of relinquishment of parental rights, affidavit of status of child, or affidavit of waiver of interest in a child. The information shall include the right of the child or biological parent to refuse

[1] V.T.C.A., Family Code § 162.401 et seq.

to participate in the registry. If the adopted child is 14 years old or older the court shall provide the information to the child.
Added by Acts 1995, 74th Leg., ch. 20, § 1, eff. April 20, 1995; Amended by Acts 1997, 75th Leg., ch. 561, § 17, eff. Sept. 1, 1997.

§ 162.019. Copy of Order
A copy of the adoption order is not required to be mailed to the parties as provided in Rules 119a and 239a, Texas Rules of Civil Procedure.
Added by Acts 1995, 74th Leg., ch. 20, § 1, eff. April 20, 1995.

§ 162.020. Withdrawal or Denial of Petition
If a petition requesting adoption is withdrawn or denied, the court may order the removal of the child from the proposed adoptive home if removal is in the child's best interest and may enter any order necessary for the welfare of the child.
Added by Acts 1995, 74th Leg., ch. 20, § 1, eff. April 20, 1995.

§ 162.021. Sealing File
(a) The court, on the motion of a party or on the court's own motion, may order the sealing of the file and the minutes of the court, or both, in a suit requesting an adoption.
(b) Rendition of the order does not relieve the clerk from the duty to send information regarding adoption to the bureau of vital statistics as required by this subchapter and Chapter 108.
Added by Acts 1995, 74th Leg., ch. 20, § 1, eff. April 20, 1995. Amended by Acts 1995, 74th Leg., ch. 751, § 78, eff. Sept. 1, 1995.

§ 162.022. Confidentiality Maintained by Clerk
The records concerning a child maintained by the district clerk after entry of an order of adoption are confidential. No person is entitled to access to the records or may obtain information from the records except for good cause under an order of the court that issued the order.
Added by Acts 1995, 74th Leg., ch. 20, § 1, eff. April 20, 1995.

§ 162.023. Adoption Order From Foreign Country
(a) Except as otherwise provided by law, an adoption order rendered to a resident of this state that is made by a foreign country shall be accorded full faith and credit by the courts of this state and enforced as if the order were rendered by a court in this state unless the adoption law or process of the foreign country violates the fundamental principles of human rights or the laws or public policy of this state.
(b) A person who adopts a child in a foreign country may register the order in this state. A petition for registration of a foreign adoption order may be combined with a petition for a name change. If the court finds that the foreign adoption order meets the requirements of Subsection (a), the court shall order the state registrar to:
(1) register the order under Chapter 192, Health and Safety Code; and
(2) file a certificate of birth for the child under Section 192.006, Health and Safety Code.
Added by Acts 2003, 78th Leg., ch. 19, § 1, eff. Sept. 1, 2003.

§ 162.025. Placement by Unauthorized Person; Offense
(a) A person who is not the natural or adoptive parent of the child, the legal guardian of the child, or a child-placing agency licensed under Chapter 42, Human Resources Code, commits an offense if the person:
(1) serves as an intermediary between a prospective adoptive parent and an expectant parent or parent of a minor child to identify the parties to each other; or
(2) places a child for adoption.
(b) It is not an offense under this section if a professional provides legal or medical services to:
(1) a parent who identifies the prospective adoptive parent and places the child for adoption without the assistance of the professional; or
(2) a prospective adoptive parent who identifies a parent and receives placement of a child for adoption without the assistance of the professional.
(c) An offense under this section is a Class B misdemeanor.
Added by Acts 1995, 74th Leg., ch. 411, § 1, eff. Sept. 1, 1995; Amended by Acts 1997, 75th Leg., ch. 561, § 18, eff. Sept. 1, 1997.

Subchapter F. Adoption of an Adult

Statutes in Context

Adoption of adults is governed by §§ 162.501 - 162.507.

§ 162.501. Adoption of Adult
The court may grant the petition of an adult residing in this state to adopt another adult according to this subchapter.
Added by Acts 1995, 74th Leg., ch. 20, § 1, eff. April 20, 1995.

§ 162.502. Jurisdiction
The petitioner shall file a suit to adopt an adult in the district court or a statutory county court granted jurisdiction in family law cases and proceedings by Chapter 25, Government Code, in the county of the petitioner's residence.

Added by Acts 1995, 74th Leg., ch. 20, § 1, eff. April 20, 1995.

§ 162.503. Requirements of Petition

(a) A petition to adopt an adult shall be entitled "In the Interest of ________, An Adult."

(b) If the petitioner is married, both spouses must join in the petition for adoption.

Added by Acts 1995, 74th Leg., ch. 20, § 1, eff. April 20, 1995.

§ 162.504. Consent

A court may not grant an adoption unless the adult consents in writing to be adopted by the petitioner.

Added by Acts 1995, 74th Leg., ch. 20, § 1, eff. April 20, 1995.

§ 162.505. Attendance Required

The petitioner and the adult to be adopted must attend the hearing. For good cause shown, the court may waive this requirement, by written order, if the petitioner or adult to be adopted is unable to attend.

Added by Acts 1995, 74th Leg., ch. 20, § 1, eff. April 20, 1995.

§ 162.506. Adoption Order

(a) The court shall grant the adoption if the court finds that the requirements for adoption of an adult are met.

(b) Notwithstanding that both spouses have joined in a petition for the adoption of an adult as required by Section 162.503(b), the court may grant the adoption of the adult to both spouses or, on request of the spouses, to only one spouse.

Added by Acts 1995, 74th Leg., ch. 20, § 1, eff. April 20, 1995. Amended by Acts 2003, 78th Leg., ch. 555, § 1, eff. Sept. 1, 2003.

Statutes in Context

An adopted adult is, under § 162.507, entitled to inherit from and through the child's adoptive parents as though the child were the biological child of the parents. The adopted adult may still inherit from the adult's biological parents. However, a biological parent may not inherit from or through the adopted adult. This is consistent with Probate Code § 40.

---

§ 162.507. Effect of Adoption

(a) The adopted adult is the son or daughter of the adoptive parents for all purposes.

(b) The adopted adult is entitled to inherit from and through the adopted adult's adoptive parents as though the adopted adult were the biological child of the adoptive parents.

(c) The adopted adult retains the right to inherit from the adult's biological parents. However, a biological parent may not inherit from or through an adopted adult.

Added by Acts 1995, 74th Leg., ch. 20, § 1, eff. April 20, 1995.

VII. FINANCE CODE

Title 3. Financial Institutions and Businesses

Subtitle F. Trust Companies

Chapter 182. Powers, Organization, and Financial Requirements

Subchapter A. Organization and Powers in General

Statutes in Context

Finance Code § 182.001 sets forth the general powers of a properly organized trust company in Texas. See Property Code § 112.008 which explains when a person has the capacity to be a trustee.

§ 182.001. Organization and General Powers of State Trust Company

(a) Subject to Subsection (g) and the other provisions of this chapter, one or more persons may organize and charter a state trust company as a state trust association or a limited trust association.

(b) A state trust company may engage in the trust business by:

(1) acting as trustee under a written agreement;

(2) receiving money and other property in its capacity as trustee for investment in real or personal property;

(3) acting as trustee and performing the fiduciary duties committed or transferred to it by order of a court;

(4) acting as executor, administrator, or trustee of the estate of a deceased person;

(5) acting as a custodian, guardian, conservator, or trustee for a minor or incapacitated person;

(6) acting as a successor fiduciary to a trust institution or other fiduciary;

(7) receiving for safekeeping personal property;

(8) acting as custodian, assignee, transfer agent, escrow agent, registrar, or receiver;

(9) acting as investment advisor, agent, or attorney in fact according to an applicable agreement;

(10) with the prior written approval of the banking commissioner and to the extent consistent with applicable fiduciary principles, engaging in a financial activity or an activity incidental or complementary to a financial activity, directly or through a subsidiary;

(11) exercising additional powers expressly conferred by rule of the finance commission; and

(12) exercising any incidental power that is reasonably necessary to enable it to fully exercise the powers expressly conferred according to commonly accepted fiduciary customs and usages.

(c) For purposes of other state law, a trust association is considered a corporation and a limited trust association is considered a limited liability company. To the extent consistent with this subtitle, a trust association may exercise the powers of a Texas business corporation and a limited trust association may exercise the powers of a Texas limited liability company as reasonably necessary to enable exercise of specific powers under this subtitle.

(d) A state trust company may contribute to a community fund or to a charitable, philanthropic, or benevolent instrumentality conducive to public welfare an amount that the state trust company's board considers appropriate and in the interests of the state trust company.

(e) Subject to Section 184.301, a state trust company may deposit trust funds with itself.

(f) A state trust company insured by the Federal Deposit Insurance Corporation may receive and pay deposits, with or without interest, made by the United States, the state, a county, or a municipality.

(g) In the exercise of discretion consistent with the purposes of this subtitle, the banking commissioner may require a state trust company to conduct an otherwise authorized activity through a subsidiary.

Added by Acts 1999, 76th Leg., ch. 62, § 7.16(a), eff. Sept. 1, 1999. Amended by Acts 2001, 77th Leg., ch. 528, § 20, eff. Sept. 1, 2001; Acts 2001, 77th Leg., ch. 1420, § 6.008(a), eff. Sept. 1, 2001.

Subtitle Z. Miscellaneous Provisions Relating to Financial Institutions and Businesses

Chapter 274. Substitute or Successor Fiduciary

Statutes in Context

Finance Code §§ 274.001 - 274.203 are often referred to as the "Substitute Fiduciary Act." This Act permits, under certain circumstances, one corporate fiduciary, such as a trustee or executor, to be substituted for another without obtaining court permission. The courts have held this Act to be constitutional. See *In re Estate of Touring*, 775 S.W.2d 39 (Tex. App.—Houston [14th Dist.] 1989, no writ).

The attorney who prepares a will or trust which names a corporate fiduciary should explain the potential operation of this Act to the client. If the client objects, the attorney should include a provision prohibiting a substitution as permitted by § 274.201.

Generally, the appointment of successor fiduciaries is governed by Property Code § 113.083 (trustees), Probate Code § 154A (independent executors), and Probate Code § 223 (dependent personal representatives).

Subchapter A. General Provisions

§ 274.001. Definitions

In this chapter:

(1) "Bank" has the meaning assigned by Section 2(c), Bank Holding Company Act of 1956 (12 U.S.C. § 1841 (c)) as amended, excluding a bank that does not have its main office or a branch located in this state.

(2) "Bank holding company" has the meaning assigned by Section 2(a), Bank Holding Company Act of 1956 (12 U.S.C. § 1841 (a)), as amended.

(3) "Commissioner" means the banking commissioner of Texas.

(4) "Fiduciary" means an entity responsible for managing a fiduciary account.

(5) "Fiduciary account" means an account with a situs of administration in this state involving the exercise of a corporate purpose specified by Section 182.001(b).

Acts 1997, 75th Leg., ch. 1008, § 1, eff. Sept. 1, 1997. Amended by Acts 1999, 76th Leg., ch. 62, § 7.51, eff. Sept. 1, 1999; Acts 1999, 76th Leg., ch. 344, § 2.030, eff. Sept. 1, 1999.

§ 274.002. Affiliated Bank

A bank is affiliated with a subsidiary trust company if more than 50 percent of the bank's voting stock is directly or indirectly owned by a bank holding company that owns more than 50 percent of the voting stock of the subsidiary trust company.

Acts 1997, 75th Leg., ch. 1008, § 1, eff. Sept. 1, 1997. Amended by Acts 1999, 76th Leg., ch. 344, § 2.030, eff. Sept. 1, 1999.

§ 274.003. Subsidiary Trust Company

An entity is a subsidiary trust company of a bank holding company if:

(1) the entity is a:

(A) corporation incorporated under Subchapter A, Chapter 182; or

(B) bank that is organized to conduct a trust business and any incidental business or to exercise trust powers; and

(2) more than 50 percent of the voting stock of the entity is directly or indirectly owned by the bank holding company.

Acts 1997, 75th Leg., ch. 1008, § 1, eff. Sept. 1, 1997. Amended by Acts 1999, 76th Leg., ch. 62, § 7.52, eff. Sept. 1, 1999; Acts 1999, 76th Leg., ch. 344, § 2.030, eff. Sept. 1, 1999.

Subchapter B. Subsidiary Trust Companies as Substitute or Successor Fiduciaries

§ 274.101. Agreement to Substitute Fiduciaries

(a) A subsidiary trust company may enter into an agreement with an affiliated bank of the company to substitute the company as fiduciary for the bank in each fiduciary account listed in the agreement, provided the situs of account administration is not moved outside of this state without the express written consent of all persons entitled to notice under Sections 274.103(a) and (c).

(b) The agreement must include:

(1) a list of each fiduciary account for which substitution is requested;

(2) a statement of whether the substitution will cause a change in the situs of administration of each fiduciary account; and

(3) the effective date of the substitution, which may not be before the 91st day after the date of the agreement.

(c) The agreement must be filed with the commissioner before the date the substitution takes effect.

(d) A fiduciary account may be removed from the operation of the agreement by the filing of an amendment to the agreement with the commissioner before the effective date stated in the agreement.

Acts 1997, 75th Leg., ch. 1008, § 1, eff. Sept. 1, 1997. Amended by Acts 1999, 76th Leg., ch. 344, § 2.031, eff. Sept. 1, 1999.

§ 274.102. Situs of Account Administration

The situs of administration of a fiduciary account is the county in this state in which the fiduciary maintains the office that is primarily responsible for dealing with the parties involved in the account.

Acts 1997, 75th Leg., ch. 1008, § 1, eff. Sept. 1, 1997. Amended by Acts 1999, 76th Leg., ch. 344, § 2.032, eff. Sept. 1, 1999.

§ 274.103. Notice of Substitution

(a) Not later than the 91st day before the effective date of a substitution under Section 274.101, the parties to the substitution agreement shall send notice of the substitution to:

(1) any other fiduciary;

(2) each surviving settler of a trust relating to the fiduciary account;

(3) each issuer of a security for which the affiliated bank administers the fiduciary account;

(4) the plan sponsor of each employee benefit plan relating to the fiduciary account;

(5) the principal of each agency account; and

(6) the guardian of the person of each ward that has the fiduciary account resulting from a guardianship.

(b) If the substitution does not cause a change in the situs of administration of a fiduciary account, the parties to the substitution agreement shall also send notice of the substitution to each person who is readily ascertainable as a beneficiary of the account because the person has received account statements or because a parent, conservator, or guardian of a minor beneficiary has received account statements on the minor's behalf.

(c) If the substitution causes a change in the situs of administration of a fiduciary account, the parties to the substitution agreement shall also send notice of the substitution to:

(1) each adult beneficiary of a trust relating to the account;

(2) each parent, conservator, or guardian of a minor beneficiary receiving or entitled to receive current distributions of income or principal from the account; and

(3) each person who individually or jointly has the power to remove the fiduciary being substituted.

(d) The notice must be sent by United States mail to the person's current address as shown on the fiduciary's records. The fiduciary shall make a reasonable attempt to ascertain the address of a person who does not have an address shown on the fiduciary's records.

Acts 1997, 75th Leg., ch. 1008, § 1, eff. Sept. 1, 1997.

§ 274.104. Form of Notice of Substitution

The notice required under Section 274.103 must be in writing and disclose:

(1) the effect the substitution of fiduciary will have on the situs of administration of the fiduciary account;

(2) the person's rights with respect to objecting to the substitution; and

(3) the liability of the existing fiduciary and the substitute fiduciary for their actions.

Acts 1997, 75th Leg., ch. 1008, § 1, eff. Sept. 1, 1997.

§ 274.105. Failure to Send Notice of Substitution; Defective Notice

(a) If the parties to a substitution agreement under Section 274.101 intentionally fail to send the required notice under Section 274.103, the substitution of the fiduciary is ineffective.

(b) If the parties unintentionally fail to send the required notice, the substitution of the fiduciary is not impaired.

(c) If a substitution of a fiduciary is ineffective because of a defect in the required notice, any action taken by a subsidiary trust company before the substitution is determined to be ineffective is valid if the action would have been valid if performed by the affiliated bank.

Acts 1997, 75th Leg., ch. 1008, § 1, eff. Sept. 1, 1997.

§ 274.106. Effective Date of Substitution of Fiduciaries

(a) The substitution takes effect on the effective date stated in the substitution agreement unless, not later than the 16th day before the effective date:

(1) each party entitled to receive notice of the substitution under Sections 274.103 (a) and (c) provides the affiliated bank with a written objection to the substitution; or

(2) a party entitled to receive notice of the substitution under Section 274.103 files a written petition in a court seeking to have the substitution denied under Section 274.107 and provides the affiliated bank with a copy of the petition.

(b) A substitution that is objected to under Subsection (a)(1) takes effect when:

(1) one of the parties objecting to the substitution removes the party's objection in writing; or

(2) the bank obtains a final court order approving the substitution.

(c) A substitution that is objected to under Subsection (a)(2) takes effect when:

(1) the petition is withdrawn or dismissed; or

(2) the court enters a final order denying the relief sought.

Acts 1997, 75th Leg., ch. 1008, § 1, eff. Sept. 1, 1997.

§ 274.107. Hearing on Agreement to Substitute Fiduciaries

(a) A court may deny the substitution if the court, after notice and hearing, determines:

(1) if the substitution will not cause a change in the situs of administration of a fiduciary account, that the substitution is materially detrimental to the account or to its beneficiaries; or

(2) if the substitution will cause a change in the situs of administration of a fiduciary account, that the substitution is not in the best interests of the account or its beneficiaries.

(b) The court shall allow a substitution that will cause the situs of administration of a fiduciary account to change if the court, after notice and hearing, determines that the substitution is in the best interests of the account and its beneficiaries.

(c) In a proceeding under this section, the court may award costs and reasonable and necessary attorney's fees as the court considers equitable and just.

Acts 1997, 75th Leg., ch. 1008, § 1, eff. Sept. 1, 1997.

§ 274.108. Subsidiary Trust Company as Substitute Fiduciary

On the effective date of the substitution as prescribed by Section 274.106, the subsidiary trust company:

(1) without the necessity of an instrument of transfer or conveyance, succeeds to all interest in property the affiliated bank holds for the fiduciary account being substituted; and

(2) without the necessity of judicial action or action by the creator of the fiduciary account, becomes fiduciary of the account and shall perform the duties and exercise the powers of a fiduciary in the same manner as if the company had originally been designated fiduciary.

Acts 1997, 75th Leg., ch. 1008, § 1, eff. Sept. 1, 1997.

§ 274.109. Notice of Change in Situs of Administration of Fiduciary Account Following Substitution

(a) If the fiduciary of a fiduciary account has changed as a result of a substitution agreement under Section 274.101, the substitute fiduciary shall send notice of a change in the situs of administration of the account after the substitution to each person entitled to notice under Sections 274.103 (a) and (c) not later than the 91st day before the effective date of the change.

(b) The notice must be sent by United States mail to the person's current address as shown on the fiduciary's records. The fiduciary shall make a reasonable attempt to ascertain the address of a person who does not have an address shown on the fiduciary's records.

(c) The notice must disclose:

(1) the effect that the change will have on the situs of administration of the account;

(2) the effective date of the change; and

(3) the person's rights with respect to objecting to the change.

Acts 1997, 75th Leg., ch. 1008, § 1, eff. Sept. 1, 1997.

§ 274.110. Failure to Send Notice of Change in Situs of Administration

(a) If the substitute fiduciary of a fiduciary account intentionally fails to send the required notice under Section 274.109, the change in the situs of administration is ineffective.

(b) If the substitute fiduciary unintentionally fails to send the required notice, the change in the situs of administration is not impaired.

Acts 1997, 75th Leg., ch. 1008, § 1, eff. Sept. 1, 1997.

§ 274.111. Effective Date of Change in Situs of Administration of Fiduciary Account

(a) A change in the situs of administration takes effect on the effective date stated in the notice under Section 274.109 unless, not later than the 16th day before the effective date:

(1) each party entitled to receive notice for the fiduciary account provides the subsidiary trust company with a written objection to the change; or

(2) a party entitled to receive notice files a written petition in a court seeking to have the change denied under Section 274.112 and provides the subsidiary trust company with a copy of the petition.

(b) A change that is objected to under Subsection (a)(1) takes effect when:

(1) one of the parties objecting to the change removes the party's objection in writing; or

(2) the subsidiary trust company obtains a final court order approving the change.

(c) A change that is objected to under Subsection (a)(2) takes effect when:

(1) the petition is withdrawn or dismissed; or

(2) the court enters a final order denying the relief sought.

Acts 1997, 75th Leg., ch. 1008, § 1, eff. Sept. 1, 1997.

§ 274.112. Hearing on Change in Situs of Administration of Fiduciary Account

(a) A court may allow the change in the situs of administration if the court, after notice and hearing, determines that the change is in the best interests of the fiduciary account and its beneficiaries. The court may deny the change if the court, after notice and hearing, determines that the change is not in the best interests of the account or its beneficiaries.

(b) In a proceeding under this section, the court may award costs and reasonable and necessary attorney's fees as the court considers equitable and just.

Acts 1997, 75th Leg., ch. 1008, § 1, eff. Sept. 1, 1997.

§ 274.113. Venue

(a) An action under this subchapter for a fiduciary account resulting from a decedent's estate or guardianship must be brought in the county provided for by the Texas Probate Code with respect to the probate of a will, issuance of letters testamentary or of administration, administration of a decedent's estate, appointment of a guardian, and administration of a guardianship.

(b) Except as provided by Subsection (c), an action under this subchapter regarding any other fiduciary account must be brought in the county of the situs of administration of the account, notwithstanding a statute that would set venue in the location of the fiduciary's principal office.

(c) A beneficiary of a fiduciary account described by Subsection (b) may elect to bring the action in the county in which the principal office of the first affiliated bank that transferred the account under this subchapter is located.
Acts 1997, 75th Leg., ch. 1008, § 1, eff. Sept. 1, 1997.

§ 274.114. Subsidiary Trust Company as Successor Fiduciary

For purposes of qualifying as successor fiduciary under a document creating a fiduciary account or a statute of this state relating to fiduciary accounts, a subsidiary trust company:

(1) is considered to have capital and surplus in an amount equal to the total of its capital and surplus and the capital and surplus of the bank holding company that owns the company; and

(2) is treated as a national bank unless it:

(A) is not a national bank under federal law; and

(B) has not entered into a substitution agreement with an affiliated bank of the company that is a national bank under federal law.

Acts 1997, 75th Leg., ch. 1008, § 1, eff. Sept. 1, 1997.

§ 274.115. Bond of Successor Fiduciary

If an affiliated bank of a subsidiary trust company has given bond to secure performance of its duties and the company qualifies as successor fiduciary, the company shall give bond to secure performance of its duties in the same manner as the bank.
Acts 1997, 75th Leg., ch. 1008, § 1, eff. Sept. 1, 1997.

§ 274.116. Responsibility for Subsidiary Trust Company

The bank holding company that owns a subsidiary trust company shall file with the commissioner an irrevocable undertaking to be fully responsible for the fiduciary acts and omissions of the subsidiary trust company.
Acts 1997, 75th Leg., ch. 1008, § 1, eff. Sept. 1, 1997.

Subchapter C. Banks Affiliated With Subsidiary Trust Companies

§ 274.201. Designation of Affiliated Bank as Fiduciary in Will

The prospective designation in a will or other instrument of an affiliated bank of a subsidiary trust company as fiduciary is also considered a designation of the company as fiduciary and confers on the company any discretionary power granted in the instrument unless:

(1) the bank and company agree in writing to have the designation of the bank as fiduciary be binding; or

(2) the creator of the fiduciary account, by appropriate language in the document creating the account, provides that the account is not eligible for substitution under this chapter.

Acts 1997, 75th Leg., ch. 1008, § 1, eff. Sept. 1, 1997.

§ 274.202. Liability of Affiliated Bank Acting as Fiduciary

After a substitution of a subsidiary trust company as fiduciary for an affiliated bank of the company, the bank remains liable for any action taken by the bank as a fiduciary.
Acts 1997, 75th Leg., ch. 1008, § 1, eff. Sept. 1, 1997.

§ 274.203. Deposit of Money With Affiliated Bank

(a) A subsidiary trust company may deposit with an affiliated bank of the company fiduciary money that is being held pending an investment, distribution, or payment of a debt if:

(1) the company maintains under its control as security for the deposit a separate fund of securities legal for trust investments pledged by the bank;

(2) the total market value of the securities is at all times at least equal to the amount of the deposit; and

(3) the fund of securities is designated as a separate fund.

(b) The bank may make periodic withdrawals from or additions to the fund of securities required by this section only if the required value is maintained.

(c) Income from securities in the fund belongs to the bank.

(d) Security for a deposit under this section is not required to the extent the deposit is insured or otherwise secured under law.
Acts 1997, 75th Leg., ch. 1008, § 1, eff. Sept. 1, 1997.

Title 4. Regulation of Interest, Loans, and Financed Transactions

Subtitle A. Interest

Chapter 302. Interest Rates

Subchapter A. General Provisions

Statutes in Context

A legacy (cash bequest) in a will earns interest at the legal rate as provided in Finance Code § 302.002. There is currently a conflict regarding the date from which the interest begins to accrue. Probate Code § 378B(f) provides that interest begins running one year after the date the court grants letters testamentary or letters of administration. The

2003 Texas Legislature simultaneously reenacted (with a mere technical amendment) this section while in another bill, repealed the section. The repealing bill enacted the Uniform Principal and Income Act which provides that interest is payable beginning on the first anniversary of the date of the decedent's death. See Property Code § 116.051(3)(A).

---

§ 302.002. Accrual of Interest When no Rate Specified

If a creditor has not agreed with an obligor to charge the obligor any interest, the creditor may charge and receive from the obligor legal interest at the rate of six percent a year on the principal amount of the credit extended beginning on the 30th day after the date on which the amount is due. If an obligor has agreed to pay to a creditor any compensation that constitutes interest, the obligor is considered to have agreed on the rate produced by the amount of that interest, regardless of whether that rate is stated in the agreement.

Acts 1997, 75th Leg., ch. 1008, § 1, eff. Sept. 1, 1997. Amended by Acts 1999, 76th Leg., ch. 62, § 7.18(a), eff. Sept. 1, 1999.

VIII.
Government Code

Title 2. Judicial Branch

Subtitle G. Attorneys

Appendix A. State Bar Rules

Article X. Discipline and Suspension of Members

Section 9. Texas Disciplinary Rules of Professional Conduct

I. Client-Lawyer Relationship

Statutes in Context

Rule 1.02(g) is of particular importance in the estate planning context because it provides guidance on what the attorney should do if the attorney reasonably believes that a client lacks legal competence to make decisions.

Rule 1.02. Scope and Objectives of Representation

(a) Subject to paragraphs (b), (c), (d), and (e), (f), and (g), a lawyer shall abide by a client's decisions:

(1) concerning the objectives and general methods of representation;

(2) whether to accept an offer of settlement of a matter, except as otherwise authorized by law;

(3) In a criminal case, after consultation with the lawyer, as to a plea to be entered, whether to waive jury trial, and whether the client will testify.

(b) A lawyer may limit the scope, objectives and general methods of the representation if the client consents after consultation.

(c) A lawyer shall not assist or counsel a client to engage in conduct that the lawyer knows is criminal or fraudulent. A lawyer may discuss the legal consequences of any proposed course of conduct with a client and may counsel and represent a client in connection with the making of a good faith effort to determine the validity, scope, meaning or application of the law.

(d) When a lawyer has confidential information clearly establishing that a client is likely to commit a criminal or fraudulent act that is likely to result in substantial injury to the financial interests or property of another, the lawyer shall promptly make reasonable efforts under the circumstances to dissuade the client from committing the crime or fraud.

(e) When a lawyer has confidential information clearly establishing that the lawyer's client has committed a criminal or fraudulent act in the commission of which the lawyer's services have been used, the lawyer shall make reasonable efforts under the circumstances to persuade the client to take corrective action.

(f) When a lawyer knows that a client expects representation not permitted by the rules of professional conduct or other law, the lawyer shall consult with the client regarding the relevant limitations on the lawyer's conduct.

(g) A lawyer shall take reasonable action to secure the appointment of a guardian or other legal representative for, or seek other protective orders with respect to, a client whenever the lawyer reasonably believes that the client lacks legal competence and that such action should be taken to protect the client.

Adopted by order of Oct. 17, 1989, eff. Jan. 1, 1990.

Statutes in Context

Rule 1.03 imposes a duty on the attorney to keep the client reasonably informed so the client may make informed decisions.

Rule 1.03. Communication

(a) A lawyer shall keep a client reasonably informed about the status of a matter and promptly comply with reasonable requests for information.

(b) A lawyer shall explain a matter to the extent reasonably necessary to permit the client to make informed decisions regarding the representation.

Adopted by order of Oct. 17, 1989, eff. Jan. 1, 1990.

Statutes in Context

Rule 1.05 focuses on the attorney's duty to keep client information confidential. Problems may arise if the attorney prepares the estate plans for more than one person from the same family such as husband and wife or parent and child.

Rule 1.05. Confidentiality of Information

(a) "Confidential information" includes both "privileged information" and "unprivileged client information." "Privileged information" refers to the information of a client protected by the lawyer-client privilege of Rule 503 of the Texas Rules of Evidence or of Rule 503 of the Texas Rules of Criminal Evidence or by the principles of attorney-client privilege governed by Rule 501 of the Federal Rules of Evidence for United States Courts and Magistrates. "Unprivileged client information" means all information relating to a client or furnished by the client, other than privileged information, acquired by the lawyer during the course of or by reason of the representation of the client.

(b) Except as permitted by paragraphs (c) and (d), or as required by paragraphs (e) and (f), a lawyer shall not knowingly:

(1) Reveal confidential information of a client or a former client to:

(i) a person that the client has instructed is not to receive the information; or

(ii) anyone else, other than the client, the client's representatives, or the members, associates, or employees of the lawyer's law firm.

(2) Use confidential information of a client to the disadvantage of the client unless the client consents after consultation.

(3) Use confidential information of a former client to the disadvantage of the former client after the representation is concluded unless the former client consents after consultation or the confidential information has become generally known.

(4) Use privileged information of a client for the advantage of the lawyer or of a third person, unless the client consents after consultation.

(c) A lawyer may reveal confidential information:

(1) When the lawyer has been expressly authorized to do so in order to carry out the representation.

(2) When the client consents after consultation.

(3) To the client, the client's representatives, or the members, associates, and employees of the lawyer's firm, except when otherwise instructed by the client.

(4) When the lawyer has reason to believe it is necessary to do so in order to comply with a court order, a Texas Disciplinary Rules of Professional Conduct, or other law.

(5) To the extent reasonably necessary to enforce a claim or establish a defense on behalf of the lawyer in a controversy between the lawyer and the client.

(6) To establish a defense to a criminal charge, civil claim or disciplinary complaint against the lawyer or the lawyer's associates based upon conduct involving the client or the representation of the client.

(7) When the lawyer has reason to believe it is necessary to do so in order to prevent the client from committing a criminal or fraudulent act.

(8) To the extent revelation reasonably appears necessary to rectify the consequences of a client's criminal or fraudulent act in the commission of which the lawyer's services had been used.

(d) A lawyer also may reveal unprivileged client information:

(1) When impliedly authorized to do so in order to carry out the representation.

(2) When the lawyer has reason to believe it is necessary to do so in order to:

(i) carry out the representation effectively;

(ii) defend the lawyer or the lawyer's employees or associates against a claim of wrongful conduct;

(iii) respond to allegations in any proceeding concerning the lawyer's representation of the client; or

(iv) prove the services rendered to a client, or the reasonable value thereof, or both, in an action against another person or organization responsible for the payment of the fee for services rendered to the client.

(e) When a lawyer has confidential information clearly establishing that a client is likely to commit a criminal or fraudulent act that is likely to result in death or substantial bodily harm to a person, the lawyer shall reveal confidential information to the extent revelation reasonably appears necessary to prevent the client from committing the criminal or fraudulent act.

(f) A lawyer shall reveal confidential information when required to do so by Rule 3.03(a)(2), 3.03(b), or by Rule 4.01(b).

Adopted by order of Oct. 17, 1989, eff. Jan. 1, 1990. Amended by order of Oct. 23, 1991.

Statutes in Context

Rule 1.08(b) prohibits an attorney from preparing a will not only if the attorney is a beneficiary, but also if the beneficiary is the attorney's parent, child, sibling, or spouse. There are two exceptions to the general admonition. The first exception is when the client is related to the donee. Although permitted, the prudent attorney should avoid drafting for relatives unless the disposition in the will is substantially similar to that which would occur under intestacy. The second exception is if the gift is not substantial. An attorney should not rely on this exception because although the attorney might not be risking loss of the attorney's law license for drafting the instrument, the attorney may still not receive the gift because of Probate Code § 58b. In addition, the determination of whether a gift is "substantial" is problematic. For example, a gift worth $50 might be substantial for a client whose net worth is $1,000 while a gift of $1 million might not be substantial for a client with a net worth of many billions of dollars.

Rule 1.08. Conflict of Interest: Prohibited Transactions

(a) A lawyer shall not enter into a business transaction with a client unless:

(1) the transaction and terms on which the lawyer acquires the interest are fair and reasonable to the client and are fully disclosed in a manner which can be reasonably understood by the client;

(2) the client is given a reasonable opportunity to seek the advice of independent counsel in the transaction; and

(3) the client consents in writing thereto.

(b) A lawyer shall not prepare an instrument giving the lawyer or a person related to the lawyer as a parent, child, sibling, or spouse any substantial gift from a client, including a testamentary gift, except where the client is related to the donee.

(c) Prior to the conclusion of all aspects of the matter giving rise to the lawyer's employment, a lawyer shall not make or negotiate an agreement with a client, prospective client, or former client giving the lawyer literary or media rights to a portrayal or account based in substantial part on information relating to the representation.

(d) A lawyer shall not provide financial assistance to a client in connection with pending or contemplated litigation or administrative proceedings, except that:

(1) a lawyer may advance or guarantee court costs, expenses of litigation or administrative proceedings, and reasonably necessary medical and living expenses, the repayment of which may be contingent on the outcome of the matter; and

(2) a lawyer representing an indigent client may pay court costs and expenses of litigation on behalf of the client.

(e) A lawyer shall not accept compensation for representing a client from one other than the client unless:

(1) the client consents;

(2) there is no interference with the lawyer's independence of professional judgment or with the client-lawyer relationship; and

(3) information relating to representation of a client is protected as required by Rule 1.05.

(f) A lawyer who represents two or more clients shall not participate in making an aggregate settlement of the claims of or against the clients, or in a criminal case an aggregated agreement to guilty or nolo contendere pleas, unless each client has consented after consultation, including disclosure of the existence and nature of all the claims or pleas involved and of the nature and extent of the participation of each person in the settlement.

(g) A lawyer shall not make an agreement prospectively limiting the lawyer's liability to a client for malpractice unless permitted by law and the client is independently represented in making the agreement, or settle a claim for such liability with an unrepresented client or former client with out first advising that person in writing that independent representation is appropriate in connection therewith.

(h) A lawyer shall not acquire a proprietary interest in the cause of action or subject matter of litigation the lawyer is conducting for a client, except that the lawyer may:

(1) acquire a lien granted by law to secure the lawyer's fee or expenses; and

(2) contract in a civil case with a client for a contingent fee that is permissible under Rule 1.04.

(i) If a lawyer would be prohibited by this Rule from engaging in particular conduct, no other lawyer while a member of or associated with that lawyer's firm may engage in that conduct.

(j) As used in this Rule, "business transactions" does not include standard commercial transactions between the lawyer and the client for products or services that the client generally markets to others.

Adopted by order of Oct. 17, 1989, eff. Jan. 1, 1990. Amended by order of Oct. 23, 1991.

Title 3. Legislative Branch

Subtitle B. Legislation

Chapter 311. Code Construction Act

Statutes in Context

The Code Construction Act applies to every Texas code enacted by the 60th or subsequent legislature as well as to any amendment, repeal, revision, or reenactment of any code provision passed by the 60th or later legislature. (A similar set of statutes applies to all other Texas statutes (Government Code §§ 312.001 -312.016)). The Act contains important definitions and construction rules which must be kept in mind when reading provisions of the Texas codes. Of particular importance in the estate planning context is § 311.005(6) which provides a definition of "signed."

Subchapter A. General Provisions

§ 311.001. Short Title

This chapter may be cited as the Code Construction Act.

Acts 1985, 69th Leg., ch. 479, § 1, eff. Sept. 1, 1985.

§ 311.002. Application

This chapter applies to:

(1) each code enacted by the 60th or a subsequent legislature as part of the state's continuing statutory revision program;

(2) each amendment, repeal, revision, and reenactment of a code or code provision by the 60th or a subsequent legislature;

(3) each repeal of a statute by a code; and

(4) each rule adopted under a code.

Acts 1985, 69th Leg., ch. 479, § 1, eff. Sept. 1, 1985.

§ 311.003. Rules Not Exclusive

The rules provided in this chapter are not exclusive but are meant to describe and clarify common situations in order to guide the preparation and construction of codes.

Acts 1985, 69th Leg., ch. 479, § 1, eff. Sept. 1, 1985.

§ 311.004. Citation of Codes

A code may be cited by its name preceded by the specific part concerned. Examples of citations are:

(1) Title 1, Business & Commerce Code;

(2) Chapter 5, Business & Commerce Code;

(3) Section 9.304, Business & Commerce Code;

(4) Section 15.06(a), Business & Commerce Code; and

(5) Section 17.18(b)(1)(B)(ii), Business & Commerce Code.

Acts 1985, 69th Leg., ch. 479, § 1, eff. Sept. 1, 1985. Amended by Acts 1985, 69th Leg., ch. 117, § 13(b), eff. Sept. 1, 1985.

§ 311.005. General Definitions

The following definitions apply unless the statute or context in which the word or phrase is used requires a different definition:

(1) "Oath" includes affirmation.

(2) "Person" includes corporation, organization, government or governmental subdivision or agency, business trust, estate, trust, partnership, association, and any other legal entity.

(3) "Population" means the population shown by the most recent federal decennial census.

(4) "Property" means real and personal property.

(5) "Rule" includes regulation.

(6) "Signed" includes any symbol executed or adopted by a person with present intention to authenticate a writing.

(7) "State," when referring to a part of the United States, includes any state, district, commonwealth, territory, and insular possession of the United States and any area subject to the legislative authority of the United States of America.

(8) "Swear" includes affirm.

(9) "United States" includes a department, bureau, or other agency of the United States of America.

(10) "Week" means seven consecutive days.

(11) "Written" includes any representation of words, letters, symbols, or figures.

(12) "Year" means 12 consecutive months.

(13) "Includes" and "including" are terms of enlargement and not of limitation or exclusive enumeration, and use of the terms does not create a presumption that components not expressed are excluded.

Acts 1985, 69th Leg., ch. 479, § 1, eff. Sept. 1, 1985. Amended by Acts 1989, 71st Leg., ch. 340, § 1, eff. Aug. 28, 1989.

§ 311.006. Internal References

In a code:

(1) a reference to a title, chapter, or section without further identification is a reference to a title, chapter, or section of the code; and

(2) a reference to a subtitle, subchapter, subsection, subdivision, paragraph, or other numbered or lettered unit without further identification is a reference to a unit of the next larger unit of the code in which the reference appears.

Added by Acts 1993, 73rd Leg., ch. 131, § 1, eff. May 11, 1993.

Subchapter B. Construction of Words and Phrases

§ 311.011. Common and Technical Usage of Words

(a) Words and phrases shall be read in context and construed according to the rules of grammar and common usage.

(b) Words and phrases that have acquired a technical or particular meaning, whether by legislative definition or otherwise, shall be construed accordingly.

Acts 1985, 69th Leg., ch. 479, § 1, eff. Sept. 1, 1985.

§ 311.012. Tense, Number, and Gender

(a) Words in the present tense include the future tense.

(b) The singular includes the plural and the plural includes the singular.

(c) Words of one gender include the other genders.

Acts 1985, 69th Leg., ch. 479, § 1, eff. Sept. 1, 1985.

§ 311.013. Authority and Quorum of Public Body

(a) A grant of authority to three or more persons as a public body confers the authority on a majority of the number of members fixed by statute.

(b) A quorum of a public body is a majority of the number of members fixed by statute.

Acts 1985, 69th Leg., ch. 479, § 1, eff. Sept. 1, 1985.

§ 311.014. Computation of Time

(a) In computing a period of days, the first day is excluded and the last day is included.

(b) If the last day of any period is a Saturday, Sunday, or legal holiday, the period is extended to include the next day that is not a Saturday, Sunday, or legal holiday.

(c) If a number of months is to be computed by counting the months from a particular day, the period ends on the same numerical day in the concluding month as the day of the month from which the computation is begun, unless there are not that many days

in the concluding month, in which case the period ends on the last day of that month.
Acts 1985, 69th Leg., ch. 479, § 1, eff. Sept. 1, 1985.

§ 311.015. Reference to a Series

If a statute refers to a series of numbers or letters, the first and last numbers or letters are included.
Acts 1985, 69th Leg., ch. 479, § 1, eff. Sept. 1, 1985.

§ 311.016. "May," "Shall," "Must," etc.

The following constructions apply unless the context in which the word or phrase appears necessarily requires a different construction or unless a different construction is expressly provided by statute:

(1) "May" creates discretionary authority or grants permission or a power.

(2) "Shall" imposes a duty.

(3) "Must" creates or recognizes a condition precedent.

(4) "Is entitled to" creates or recognizes a right.

(5) "May not" imposes a prohibition and is synonymous with "shall not."

(6) "Is not entitled to" negates a right.

(7) "Is not required to" negates a duty or condition precedent.

Added by Acts 1997, 75th Leg., ch. 220, § 1, eff. May 23, 1997.

Subchapter C. Construction of Statutes

§ 311.021. Intention in Enactment of Statutes

In enacting a statute, it is presumed that:

(1) compliance with the constitutions of this state and the United States is intended;

(2) the entire statute is intended to be effective;

(3) a just and reasonable result is intended;

(4) a result feasible of execution is intended; and

(5) public interest is favored over any private interest.

Acts 1985, 69th Leg., ch. 479, § 1, eff. Sept. 1, 1985.

§ 311.022. Prospective Operation of Statutes

A statute is presumed to be prospective in its operation unless expressly made retrospective.
Acts 1985, 69th Leg., ch. 479, § 1, eff. Sept. 1, 1985.

§ 311.023. Statute Construction Aids

In construing a statute, whether or not the statute is considered ambiguous on its face, a court may consider among other matters the:

(1) object sought to be attained;

(2) circumstances under which the statute was enacted;

(3) legislative history;

(4) common law or former statutory provisions, including laws on the same or similar subjects;

(5) consequences of a particular construction;

(6) administrative construction of the statute; and

(7) title (caption), preamble, and emergency provision.

Acts 1985, 69th Leg., ch. 479, § 1, eff. Sept. 1, 1985.

§ 311.024. Headings

The heading of a title, subtitle, chapter, subchapter, or section does not limit or expand the meaning of a statute.
Acts 1985, 69th Leg., ch. 479, § 1, eff. Sept. 1, 1985.

§ 311.025. Irreconcilable Statutes and Amendments

(a) Except as provided by Section 311.031(d), if statutes enacted at the same or different sessions of the legislature are irreconcilable, the statute latest in date of enactment prevails.

(b) Except as provided by Section 311.031(d), if amendments to the same statute are enacted at the same session of the legislature, one amendment without reference to another, the amendments shall be harmonized, if possible, so that effect may be given to each. If the amendments are irreconcilable, the latest in date of enactment prevails.

(c) In determining whether amendments are irreconcilable, text that is reenacted because of the requirement of Article III, Section 36, of the Texas Constitution is not considered to be irreconcilable with additions or omissions in the same text made by another amendment. Unless clearly indicated to the contrary, an amendment that reenacts text in compliance with that constitutional requirement does not indicate legislative intent that the reenacted text prevail over changes in the same text made by another amendment, regardless of the relative dates of enactment.

(d) In this section, the date of enactment is the date on which the last legislative vote is taken on the bill enacting the statute.

(e) If the journals or other legislative records fail to disclose which of two or more bills in conflict is latest in date of enactment, the date of enactment of the respective bills is considered to be, in order of priority:

(1) the date on which the last presiding officer signed the bill;

(2) the date on which the governor signed the bill; or

(3) the date on which the bill became law by operation of law.

Acts 1985, 69th Leg., ch. 479, § 1, eff. Sept. 1, 1985. Amended by Acts 1989, 71st Leg., ch. 340, § 2, eff. Aug. 28, 1989; Acts 1997, 75th Leg., ch. 220, § 2, eff. May 23, 1997.

§ 311.026. Special or Local Provision Prevails Over General

(a) If a general provision conflicts with a special or local provision, the provisions shall be construed, if possible, so that effect is given to both.

(b) If the conflict between the general provision and the special or local provision is irreconcilable, the special or local provision prevails as an exception to the

general provision, unless the general provision is the later enactment and the manifest intent is that the general provision prevail.
Acts 1985, 69th Leg., ch. 479, § 1, eff. Sept. 1, 1985.

§ 311.027. Statutory References

Unless expressly provided otherwise, a reference to any portion of a statute or rule applies to all reenactments, revisions, or amendments of the statute or rule.
Acts 1985, 69th Leg., ch. 479, § 1, eff. Sept. 1, 1985. Amended by Acts 1993, 73rd Leg., ch. 131, § 2, eff. May 11, 1993.

§ 311.028. Uniform Construction of Uniform Acts

A uniform act included in a code shall be construed to effect its general purpose to make uniform the law of those states that enact it.
Acts 1985, 69th Leg., ch. 479, § 1, eff. Sept. 1, 1985.

§ 311.029. Enrolled Bill Controls

If the language of the enrolled bill version of a statute conflicts with the language of any subsequent printing or reprinting of the statute, the language of the enrolled bill version controls.
Acts 1985, 69th Leg., ch. 479, § 1, eff. Sept. 1, 1985.

§ 311.030. Repeal of Repealing Statute

The repeal of a repealing statute does not revive the statute originally repealed nor impair the effect of any saving provision in it.
Acts 1985, 69th Leg., ch. 479, § 1, eff. Sept. 1, 1985.

§ 311.031. Saving Provisions

(a) Except as provided by Subsection (b), the reenactment, revision, amendment, or repeal of a statute does not affect:

(1) the prior operation of the statute or any prior action taken under it;

(2) any validation, cure, right, privilege, obligation, or liability previously acquired, accrued, accorded, or incurred under it;

(3) any violation of the statute or any penalty, forfeiture, or punishment incurred under the statute before its amendment or repeal; or

(4) any investigation, proceeding, or remedy concerning any privilege, obligation, liability, penalty, forfeiture, or punishment; and the investigation, proceeding, or remedy may be instituted, continued, or enforced, and the penalty, forfeiture, or punishment imposed, as if the statute had not been repealed or amended.

(b) If the penalty, forfeiture, or punishment for any offense is reduced by a reenactment, revision, or amendment of a statute, the penalty, forfeiture, or punishment, if not already imposed, shall be imposed according to the statute as amended.

(c) The repeal of a statute by a code does not affect an amendment, revision, or reenactment of the statute by the same legislature that enacted the code. The amendment, revision, or reenactment is preserved and given effect as part of the code provision that revised the statute so amended, revised, or reenacted.

(d) If any provision of a code conflicts with a statute enacted by the same legislature that enacted the code, the statute controls.
Acts 1985, 69th Leg., ch. 479, § 1, eff. Sept. 1, 1985.

§ 311.032. Severability of Statutes

(a) If any statute contains a provision for severability, that provision prevails in interpreting that statute.

(b) If any statute contains a provision for nonseverability, that provision prevails in interpreting that statute.

(c) In a statute that does not contain a provision for severability or nonseverability, if any provision of the statute or its application to any person or circumstance is held invalid, the invalidity does not affect other provisions or applications of the statute that can be given effect without the invalid provision or application, and to this end the provisions of the statute are severable.
Acts 1985, 69th Leg., ch. 479, § 1, eff. Sept. 1, 1985.

§ 311.034. Waiver of Sovereign Immunity

In order to preserve the legislature's interest in managing state fiscal matters through the appropriations process, a statute shall not be construed as a waiver of sovereign immunity unless the waiver is effected by clear and unambiguous language. In a statute, the use of "person," as defined by Section 311.005 to include governmental entities, does not indicate legislative intent, to waive sovereign immunity unless the context of the statute indicates no other reasonable construction.
Added by Acts 2001, 77th Leg., ch. 1158, § 8, eff. June 15, 2001.

Chapter 312. Construction of Laws

Statutes in Context

Sections §§ 312.001 -312.016 contain definitions and construction rules applicable to all Texas civil statutes which are very similar to those contained in the Code Construction Act (Government Code §§ 311.001 - 311.034).

Subchapter A. Construction Rules for Civil Statutes

§ 312.001. Application

This subchapter applies to the construction of all civil statutes.
Acts 1985, 69th Leg., ch. 479, § 1, eff. Sept. 1, 1985.

§ 312.002. Meaning of Words

(a) Except as provided by Subsection (b), words shall be given their ordinary meaning.

(b) If a word is connected with and used with reference to a particular trade or subject matter or is used as a word of art, the word shall have the meaning given by experts in the particular trade, subject matter, or art.
Acts 1985, 69th Leg., ch. 479, § 1, eff. Sept. 1, 1985.

§ 312.003. Tense, Number, and Gender

(a) Words in the present or past tense include the future tense.

(b) The singular includes the plural and the plural includes the singular unless expressly provided otherwise.

(c) The masculine gender includes the feminine and neuter genders.
Acts 1985, 69th Leg., ch. 479, § 1, eff. Sept. 1, 1985.

§ 312.004. Grants of Authority

A joint authority given to any number of officers or other persons may be executed by a majority of them unless expressly provided otherwise.
Acts 1985, 69th Leg., ch. 479, § 1, eff. Sept. 1, 1985.

§ 312.005. Legislative Intent

In interpreting a statute, a court shall diligently attempt to ascertain legislative intent and shall consider at all times the old law, the evil, and the remedy.
Acts 1985, 69th Leg., ch. 479, § 1, eff. Sept. 1, 1985.

§ 312.006. Liberal Construction

(a) The Revised Statutes are the law of this state and shall be liberally construed to achieve their purpose and to promote justice.

(b) The common law rule requiring strict construction of statutes in derogation of the common law does not apply to the Revised Statutes.
Acts 1985, 69th Leg., ch. 479, § 1, eff. Sept. 1, 1985.

§ 312.007. Repeal of Repealing Statute

The repeal of a repealing statute does not revive the statute originally repealed.
Acts 1985, 69th Leg., ch. 479, § 1, eff. Sept. 1, 1985.

§ 312.008. Statutory References

Unless expressly provided otherwise, a reference to any portion of a statute, rule, or regulation applies to all reenactments, revisions, or amendments of the statute, rule, or regulation.
Added by Acts 1993, 73rd Leg., ch. 131, § 3, eff. May 11, 1993.

Subchapter B. Miscellaneous Provisions

§ 312.011. Definitions

The following definitions apply unless a different meaning is apparent from the context of the statute in which the word appears:

(1) "Affidavit" means a statement in writing of a fact or facts signed by the party making it, sworn to before an officer authorized to administer oaths, and officially certified to by the officer under his seal of office.

(2) "Comptroller" means the state comptroller of public accounts.

(3) "Effects" includes all personal property and all interest in that property.

(4) "Governing body," if used with reference to a municipality, means the legislative body of a city, town, or village, without regard to the name or title given to any particular body.

(5) "Justice," when applied to a magistrate, means justice of the peace.

(6) "Land commissioner" means the Commissioner of the General Land Office.

(7) "Month" means a calendar month.

(8) "Oath" includes affirmation.

(9) "Official oath" means the oath required by Article XVI, Section 1, of the Texas Constitution.

(10) "Person" includes a corporation.

(11) "Preceding," when referring to a title, chapter, or article, means that which came immediately before.

(12) "Preceding federal census" or "most recent federal census" means the United States decennial census immediately preceding the action in question.

(13) "Property" includes real property, personal property, life insurance policies, and the effects of life insurance policies.

(14) "Signature" includes the mark of a person unable to write, and "subscribe" includes the making of such a mark.

(15) "Succeeding" means immediately following.

(16) "Swear" or "sworn" includes affirm or affirmed.

(17) "Written" or "in writing" includes any representation of words, letters, or figures, whether by writing, printing, or other means.

(18) "Year" means a calendar year.

(19) "Includes" and "including" are terms of enlargement and not of limitation or exclusive enumeration, and use of the terms does not create a presumption that components not expressed are excluded.

(20) "Population" means the population shown by the most recent federal decennial census.
Acts 1985, 69th Leg., ch. 479, § 1, eff. Sept. 1, 1985. Amended by Acts 1989, 71st Leg., ch. 340, § 3, eff. Aug. 28, 1989; Acts 1993, 73rd Leg., ch. 131, § 4, eff. May 11, 1993.

§ 312.012. Grammar and Punctuation

(a) A grammatical error does not vitiate a law. If the sentence or clause is meaningless because of the grammatical error, words and clauses may be transposed to give the law meaning.

(b) Punctuation of a law does not control or affect legislative intent in enacting the law.
Acts 1985, 69th Leg., ch. 479, § 1, eff. Sept. 1, 1985.

§ 312.013. Severability of Statutes

(a) Unless expressly provided otherwise, if any provision of a statute or its application to any person or circumstance is held invalid, the invalidity does not affect other provisions or applications of the statute that can be given effect without the invalid provision or application, and to this end the provisions of the statute are severable.

(b) This section does not affect the power or duty of a court to ascertain and give effect to legislative intent concerning severability of a statute.

Acts 1985, 69th Leg., ch. 479, § 1, eff. Sept. 1, 1985.

§ 312.014. Irreconcilable Amendments

(a) If statutes enacted at the same or different sessions of the legislature are irreconcilable, the statute latest in date of enactment prevails.

(b) If amendments to the same statute are enacted at the same session of the legislature, one amendment without reference to another, the amendments shall be harmonized, if possible, so that effect may be given to each. If the amendments are irreconcilable, the latest in date of enactment prevails.

(c) In determining whether amendments to the same statute enacted at the same session of the legislature are irreconcilable, text that is reenacted because of the requirement of Article III, Section 36, of the Texas Constitution is not considered to be irreconcilable with additions or omissions in the same text made by another amendment. Unless clearly indicated to the contrary, an amendment that reenacts text in compliance with that constitutional requirement does not indicate legislative intent that the reenacted text prevail over changes in the same text made by another amendment, regardless of the relative dates of enactment.

(d) In this section, the date of enactment is the date on which the last legislative vote is taken on the bill enacting the statute.

(e) If the journals or other legislative records fail to disclose which of two or more bills in conflict is latest in date of enactment, the date of enactment of the respective bills is considered to be, in order of priority:

(1) the date on which the last presiding officer signed the bill;

(2) the date on which the governor signed the bill; or

(3) the date on which the bill became law by operation of law.

Added by Acts 1989, 71st Leg., ch. 340, § 4, eff. Aug. 28, 1989. Amended by Acts 1997, 75th Leg., ch. 220, § 3, eff. May 23, 1997.

§ 312.015. Quorum

A majority of a board or commission established under law is a quorum unless otherwise specifically provided.

Added by Acts 1993, 73rd Leg., ch. 268, § 11, eff. Sept. 1, 1993.

§ 312.016. Standard Time

(a) The standard time in this state is the time at the 90th meridian longitude west from Greenwich, commonly known as "central standard time."

(b) The standard time in a region of this state that used mountain standard time before June 12, 1947, is the time at the 105th meridian longitude west from Greenwich, commonly known as "mountain standard time."

(c) Unless otherwise expressly provided, a reference in a statute, order, or rule to the time in which an act shall be performed means the appropriate standard time as provided by this section.

Added by Acts 1993, 73rd Leg., ch. 268, § 12, eff. Sept. 1, 1993.

Title 4. Executive Branch

Subtitle A. Executive Officers

Chapter 406. Notary Public; Commissioner of Deeds

Subchapter A. Notary Public

Statutes in Context

Government Code § 406.0165 provides a method for an individual who is physically unable to sign or make a mark to execute a document. This method is in addition to the proxy signatures methods already in existence such as Probate Code § 59(a) which permits a person to sign a will for the testator "by his direction and in his presence."

§ 406.0165. Signing Document for Individual With Disability

(a) A notary may sign the name of an individual who is physically unable to sign or make a mark on a document presented for notarization if directed to do so by that individual, in the presence of a witness who has no legal or equitable interest in any real or personal property that is the subject of, or is affected by, the document being signed. The notary shall require identification of the witness in the same manner as from an acknowledging person under Section 121.005, Civil Practice and Remedies Code.

(b) A notary who signs a document under this section shall write, beneath the signature, the following or a substantially similar sentence:

"Signature affixed by notary in the presence of (name of witness), a disinterested witness, under Section 406.0165, Government Code."

(c) A signature made under this section is effective as the signature of the individual on whose behalf the signature was made for any purpose. A subsequent bona fide purchaser for value may rely on the signature of the notary as evidence of the individual's consent to execution of the document.

(d) In this section, "disability" means a physical impairment that impedes the ability to sign or make a mark on a document.

Added by Acts 1997, 75th Leg., ch. 1218, § 1, eff. Sept. 1, 1997.

Subtitle G. Corrections

Chapter 501. Inmate Welfare

Subchapter A. General Welfare Provisions

Statutes in Context

Government Code § 501.017 provides details of the claim which the Texas Department of Criminal Justice has against the estate of an inmate who dies while incarcerated. The claim falls in Class 6 under Probate Code § 322.

§ 501.017. Cost of Confinement as Claim

(a) The department may establish a claim and lien against the estate of an inmate who dies while confined in a facility operated by or under contract with the department for the cost to the department of the inmate's confinement.

(b) The department may not enforce a claim or lien established under this section if the inmate has a surviving spouse or a surviving dependent or disabled child.

(c) The department shall adopt policies regarding recovery of the cost of confinement through enforcement of claims or liens established under this section.

Added by Acts 1989, 71st Leg., ch. 212, § 2.01, eff. Sept. 1, 1989. Renumbered from § 500.017 and amended by Acts 1991, 72nd Leg., ch. 16, § 10.01(a), eff. Aug. 26, 1991. Amended by Acts 1995, 74th Leg., ch. 321, § 1.084, eff. Sept. 1, 1995.

Title 5. Open Government; Ethics

Subtitle B. Ethics

Chapter 573. Degrees of Relationship; Nepotism Prohibitions

Subchapter B. Relationships by Consanguinity or by Affinity

Statutes in Context

Although Government Code §§ 573.021 - 573.025 are directly applicable only to the nepotism prohibitions on the conduct of various governmental officials and candidates, they are, by analogy, useful to see how a relationship may be determined in a probate context.

§ 573.021. Method of Computing Degree of Relationship

The degree of a relationship is computed by the civil law method.

Added by Acts 1993, 73rd Leg., ch. 268, § 1, eff. Sept. 1, 1993.

§ 573.022. Determination of Consanguinity

(a) Two individuals are related to each other by consanguinity if:

(1) one is a descendant of the other; or

(2) they share a common ancestor.

(b) An adopted child is considered to be a child of the adoptive parent for this purpose.

Added by Acts 1993, 73rd Leg., ch. 268, § 1, eff. Sept. 1, 1993.

§ 573.023. Computation of Degree of Consanguinity

(a) The degree of relationship by consanguinity between an individual and the individual's descendant is determined by the number of generations that separate them. A parent and child are related in the first degree, a grandparent and grandchild in the second degree, a great-grandparent and great-grandchild in the third degree and so on.

(b) If an individual and the individual's relative are related by consanguinity, but neither is descended from the other, the degree of relationship is determined by adding:

(1) the number of generations between the individual and the nearest common ancestor of the individual and the individual's relative; and

(2) the number of generations between the relative and the nearest common ancestor.

(c) An individual's relatives within the third degree by consanguinity are the individual's:

(1) parent or child (relatives in the first degree);

(2) brother, sister, grandparent, or grandchild (relatives in the second degree); and

(3) great-grandparent, great-grandchild, aunt who is a sister of a parent of the individual, uncle who is a brother of a parent of the individual, nephew who is a child of a brother or sister of the individual, or niece who is a child of a brother or sister of the individual (relatives in the third degree).

Added by Acts 1993, 73rd Leg., ch. 268, § 1, eff. Sept. 1, 1993.

§ 573.024. Determination of Affinity

(a) Two individuals are related to each other by affinity if:

(1) they are married to each other; or

(2) the spouse of one of the individuals is related by consanguinity to the other individual.

(b) The ending of a marriage by divorce or the death of a spouse ends relationships by affinity created by that marriage unless a child of that marriage is living, in which case the marriage is considered to continue as long as a child of that marriage lives.

(c) Subsection (b) applies to a member of the board of trustees of or an officer of a school district only until the youngest child of the marriage reaches the age of 21 years.

Added by Acts 1993, 73rd Leg., ch. 268, § 1, eff. Sept. 1, 1993. Amended by Acts 1995, 74th Leg., ch. 260, § 32, eff. May 30, 1995.

§ 573.025. Computation of Degree of Affinity

(a) A husband and wife are related to each other in the first degree by affinity. For other relationships by affinity, the degree of relationship is the same as the degree of the underlying relationship by consanguinity. For example: if two individuals are related to each other in the second degree by consanguinity, the spouse of one of the individuals is related to the other individual in the second degree by affinity.

(b) An individual's relatives within the third degree by affinity are:

(1) anyone related by consanguinity to the individual's spouse in one of the ways named in Section 573.023(c); and

(2) the spouse of anyone related to the individual by consanguinity in one of the ways named in Section 573.023(c).

Added by Acts 1993, 73rd Leg., ch. 268, § 1, eff. Sept. 1, 1993.

IX.
HEALTH AND SAFETY CODE

Title 2. Health

Subtitle H. Public Health Provisions

Chapter 166. Advance Directives

Statutes in Context

The Advance Directives Act authorizes three types of instruments to assist a person to plan for disability and death: (1) the directive to physicians, (2) the out-of-hospital do-not resuscitate order, and (3) the medical power of attorney. This Act was passed in 1999 and served to recodify and coordinate the separate statutes which had previously governed these instruments.

Sections 166.001 - 166.009 govern all three types of instruments. Subsequent sections address each of the three instruments in detail.

Subchapter A. GENERAL PROVISIONS

§ 166.001. Short Title

This chapter may be cited as the Advance Directives Act.

Added by Acts 1999, 76th Leg., ch. 450, § 1.02, eff. Sept. 1, 1999.

Statutes in Context

Section 166.002 provides important definitions which are applicable to all of Chapter 166. Be certain to compare and contrast the definitions of "irreversible condition" and "terminal condition."

§ 166.002. Definitions

In this chapter:

(1) "Advance directive" means:

(A) a directive, as that term is defined by Section 166.031;

(B) an out-of-hospital DNR order, as that term is defined by Section 166.081; or

(C) a medical power of attorney under Subchapter D.

(2) "Artificial nutrition and hydration" means the provision of nutrients or fluids by a tube inserted in a vein, under the skin in the subcutaneous tissues, or in the stomach (gastrointestinal tract).

(3) "Attending physician" means a physician selected by or assigned to a patient who has primary responsibility for a patient's treatment and care.

(4) "Competent" means possessing the ability, based on reasonable medical judgment, to understand and appreciate the nature and consequences of a treatment decision, including the significant benefits and harms of and reasonable alternatives to a proposed treatment decision.

(5) "Declarant" means a person who has executed or issued a directive under this chapter.

(6) "Ethics or medical committee" means a committee established under Sections 161.031-161.033.

(7) "Health care or treatment decision" means consent, refusal to consent, or withdrawal of consent to health care, treatment, service, or a procedure to maintain, diagnose, or treat an individual's physical or mental condition, including such a decision on behalf of a minor.

(8) "Incompetent" means lacking the ability, based on reasonable medical judgment, to understand and appreciate the nature and consequences of a treatment decision, including the significant benefits and harms of and reasonable alternatives to a proposed treatment decision.

(9) "Irreversible condition" means a condition, injury, or illness:

(A) that may be treated but is never cured or eliminated;

(B) that leaves a person unable to care for or make decisions for the person's own self; and

(C) that, without life-sustaining treatment provided in accordance with the prevailing standard of medical care, is fatal.

(10) "Life-sustaining treatment" means treatment that, based on reasonable medical judgment, sustains the life of a patient and without which the patient will die. The term includes both life-sustaining medications and artificial life support, such as mechanical breathing machines, kidney dialysis treatment, and artificial nutrition and hydration. The term does not include the administration of pain management medication or the performance of a medical procedure considered to be necessary to provide comfort care, or

any other medical care provided to alleviate a patient's pain.

(11) "Medical power of attorney" means a document delegating to an agent authority to make health care decisions executed or issued under Subchapter D.

(12) "Physician" means:

(A) a physician licensed by the Texas State Board of Medical Examiners; or

(B) a properly credentialed physician who holds a commission in the uniformed services of the United States and who is serving on active duty in this state.

(13) "Terminal condition" means an incurable condition caused by injury, disease, or illness that according to reasonable medical judgment will produce death within six months, even with available life-sustaining treatment provided in accordance with the prevailing standard of medical care. A patient who has been admitted to a program under which the person receives hospice services provided by a home and community support services agency licensed under Chapter 142 is presumed to have a terminal condition for purposes of this chapter.

(14) "Witness" means a person who may serve as a witness under Section 166.003.

(15) "Cardiopulmonary resuscitation" means any medical intervention used to restore circulatory or respiratory function that has ceased.

Added by Acts 1999, 76th Leg., ch. 450, § 1.02, eff. Sept. 1, 1999. Amended by Acts 2003, 78th Leg., ch. 1228, § 1, eff. June 6, 2003.

Statutes in Context

The proper method of witnessing advance directives is explained in § 166.003. Note that at least one of the witnesses must be a disinterested party to the declarant and the declarant's medical treatment.

---

§ 166.003. Witnesses

In any circumstance in which this chapter requires the execution of an advance directive or the issuance of a nonwritten advance directive to be witnessed:

(1) each witness must be a competent adult; and

(2) at least one of the witnesses must be a person who is not:

(A) a person designated by the declarant to make a treatment decision;

(B) a person related to the declarant by blood or marriage;

(C) a person entitled to any part of the declarant's estate after the declarant's death under a will or codicil executed by the declarant or by operation of law;

(D) the attending physician;

(E) an employee of the attending physician;

(F) an employee of a health care facility in which the declarant is a patient if the employee is providing direct patient care to the declarant or is an officer, director, partner, or business office employee of the health care facility or of any parent organization of the health care facility; or

(G) a person who, at the time the written advance directive is executed or, if the directive is a nonwritten directive issued under this chapter, at the time the nonwritten directive is issued, has a claim against any part of the declarant's estate after the declarant's death.

Added by Acts 1999, 76th Leg., ch. 450, § 1.02, eff. Sept. 1, 1999.

§ 166.004. Statement Relating to Advance Directive

(a) In this section, "health care provider" means:

(1) a hospital;

(2) an institution licensed under Chapter 242, including a skilled nursing facility;

(3) a home and community support services agency;

(4) a personal care facility; and

(5) a special care facility.

(b) A health care provider shall maintain written policies regarding the implementation of advance directives. The policies must include a clear and precise statement of any procedure the health care provider is unwilling or unable to provide or withhold in accordance with an advance directive.

(c) Except as provided by Subsection (g), the health care provider shall provide written notice to an individual of the written policies described by Subsection (b). The notice must be provided at the earlier of:

(1) the time the individual is admitted to receive services from the health care provider; or

(2) the time the health care provider begins providing care to the individual.

(d) If, at the time notice is to be provided under Subsection (c), the individual is incompetent or otherwise incapacitated and unable to receive the notice required by this section, the provider shall provide the required written notice, in the following order of preference, to:

(1) the individual's legal guardian;

(2) a person responsible for the health care decisions of the individual;

(3) the individual's spouse;

(4) the individual's adult child;

(5) the individual's parent; or

(6) the person admitting the individual.

(e) If Subsection (d) applies and except as provided by Subsection (f), if a health care provider is unable, after diligent search, to locate an individual listed by Subsection (d), the health care provider is not required to provide the notice.

(f) If an individual who was incompetent or otherwise incapacitated and unable to receive the notice required by this section at the time notice was to be provided under Subsection (c) later becomes able to receive the notice, the health care provider shall provide the written notice at the time the individual becomes able to receive the notice.

(g) This section does not apply to outpatient hospital services, including emergency services.

Added by Acts 1999, 76th Leg., ch. 450; § 1.02, eff. Sept. 1, 1999.

Statutes in Context

Section 166.005 provides that advance directives effective under the law of other jurisdictions will be given effect within the limitations of Texas law even if the directive does not meet the formalities of Texas law.

---

§ 166.005. Enforceability of Advance Directives Executed in Another Jurisdiction

An advance directive or similar instrument validly executed in another state or jurisdiction shall be given the same effect as an advance directive validly executed under the law of this state. This section does not authorize the administration, withholding, or withdrawal of health care otherwise prohibited by the laws of this state.

Added by Acts 1999, 76th Leg., ch. 450, § 1.02, eff. Sept. 1, 1999.

Statutes in Context

Insurance companies may not take into account the fact that an insured has or has not executed a directive in determining insurability or premiums. For example, a life insurance company may not offer lower premiums to an insured who does not sign a directive to physicians. Likewise, a health insurance company cannot require an insured to execute a directive as a condition of being covered by the policy. See §§ 116.006 and 116.007.

---

§ 166.006. Effect of Advance Directive on Insurance Policy and Premiums

(a) The fact that a person has executed or issued an advance directive does not:

(1) restrict, inhibit, or impair in any manner the sale, procurement, or issuance of a life insurance policy to that person; or

(2) modify the terms of an existing life insurance policy.

(b) Notwithstanding the terms of any life insurance policy, the fact that life-sustaining treatment is withheld or withdrawn from an insured qualified patient under this chapter does not legally impair or invalidate that person's life insurance policy and may not be a factor for the purpose of determining, under the life insurance policy, whether benefits are payable or the cause of death.

(c) The fact that a person has executed or issued or failed to execute or issue an advance directive may not be considered in any way in establishing insurance premiums.

Added by Acts 1999, 76th Leg., ch. 450, § 1.02, eff. Sept. 1, 1999.

§ 166.007. Execution of Advance Directive May Not be Required

A physician, health facility, health care provider, insurer, or health care service plan may not require a person to execute or issue an advance directive as a condition for obtaining insurance for health care services or receiving health care services.

Added by Acts 1999, 76th Leg., ch. 450, § 1.02, eff. Sept. 1, 1999.

Statutes in Context

Under § 166.008, if a declarant has executed more than one advance directive, the directive executed later in time controls.

---

§ 166.008. Conflict Between Advance Directives

To the extent that a treatment decision or an advance directive validly executed or issued under this chapter conflicts with another treatment decision or an advance directive executed or issued under this chapter, the treatment decision made or instrument executed later in time controls.

Added by Acts 1999, 76th Leg., ch. 450, § 1.02, eff. Sept. 1, 1999.

§ 166.009. Certain Life-Sustaining Treatment Not Required

This chapter may not be construed to require the provision of life-sustaining treatment that cannot be provided to a patient without denying the same treatment to another patient.

Added by Acts 1999, 76th Leg., ch. 450, § 1.02, eff. Sept. 1, 1999.

§ 166.010. Applicability of Federal Law Relating to Child Abuse and Neglect

This chapter is subject to applicable federal law and regulations relating to child abuse and neglect to the extent applicable to the state based on its receipt of federal funds.

Added by Acts 2003, 78th Leg., ch. 1228, § 2, eff. June 6, 2003.

Subchapter B. Directive to Physicians

Statutes in Context

A competent individual has the right to refuse medical treatment for any reason even if that refusal will lead to an otherwise preventable death. What happens, though, if the person is in a coma, brain damaged, or for some other reason cannot communicate the person's wishes? The person may have signed a directive to physicians or "living will" which expresses the person's desire not to be kept alive through the use of medical technology when the person is in a terminal condition and unable to communicate the person's wishes to decline further treatment.

California was the first state to statutorily authorize a person to make an advance statement regarding the use of life-sustaining procedures when its legislature enacted living will legislation in 1976. In 1977, Texas became the fifth state to enact similar legislation when it passed the Natural Death Act. This Act provided methods for a person to indicate the desire that his or her life not be prolonged with the use of artificial life-sustaining procedures when the person's death is inevitable. The 1999 Legislature recodified the Natural Death Act in a comprehensive Advance Directives Act which includes living wills, out-of-hospital do-not-resuscitate orders, and medical powers of attorney.

Many of your clients will be extremely interested in obtaining a living will. They are often discussed in the media and gain national attention when they are used to hasten the death of famous people like former President Richard Nixon and former first-lady Jacqueline Kennedy Onassis. In addition, the federal Patient Self-Determination Act, 42 U.S.C. § 1395cc(f), requires all hospitals, nursing homes, and other health care providers that participate in Medicare or Medicaid to give all patients at the time of their admission written information regarding their rights to refuse medical treatment under state law.

Sections 166.031 - 166.051 govern the creation and effect of directives to physicians.

§ 166.031. Definitions

In this subchapter:

(1) "Directive" means an instruction made under Section 166.032, 166.034, or 166.035 to administer, withhold, or withdraw life-sustaining treatment in the event of a terminal or irreversible condition.

(2) "Qualified patient" means a patient with a terminal or irreversible condition that has been diagnosed and certified in writing by the attending physician.

Amended by Acts 1993, 73rd Leg., ch. 107, § 5.04, eff. Aug. 30, 1993. Renumbered from § 672.002 and amended by Acts 1999, 76th Leg., ch. 450, § 1.03, eff. Sept. 1, 1999.

Statutes in Context

The formal requirements of a directive to physicians are detailed in § 166.032.

§ 166.032. Written Directive by Competent Adult; Notice to Physician

(a) A competent adult may at any time execute a written directive.

(b) The declarant must sign the directive in the presence of two witnesses who qualify under Section 166.003, at least one of whom must be a witness who qualifies under Section 166.003(2). The witnesses must sign the directive.

(c) A declarant may include in a directive directions other than those provided by Section 166.033 and may designate in a directive a person to make a treatment decision for the declarant in the event the declarant becomes incompetent or otherwise mentally or physically incapable of communication.

(d) A declarant shall notify the attending physician of the existence of a written directive. If the declarant is incompetent or otherwise mentally or physically incapable of communication, another person may notify the attending physician of the existence of the written directive. The attending physician shall make the directive a part of the declarant's medical record.

Amended by Acts 1997, 75th Leg., ch. 291, § 1, eff. Jan. 1, 1998. Renumbered from § 672.003 and amended by Acts 1999, 76th Leg., ch. 450, § 1.03, eff. Sept. 1, 1999.

Statutes in Context

Section 166.033 provides a fill-in-the-blank form which a person may use to create a directive to physicians. The use of this form is not required but it is in common use. Note that a declarant may provide individualized instructions in the area labeled "additional requests."

§ 166.033. Form of Written Directive

A written directive may be in the following form:

DIRECTIVE TO PHYSICIANS AND FAMILY OR SURROGATES

Instructions for completing this document:

This is an important legal document known as an Advance Directive. It is designed to help you communicate your wishes about medical treatment at some time in the future when you are unable to make your wishes known because of illness or injury. These wishes are usually based on personal values. In particular, you may want to consider what burdens or hardships of treatment you would be willing to accept for a particular amount of benefit obtained if you were seriously ill.

You are encouraged to discuss your values and wishes with your family or chosen spokesperson, as well as your physician. Your physician, other health care provider, or medical institution may provide you with various resources to assist you in completing your advance directive. Brief definitions are listed below and may aid you in your discussions and advance planning. Initial the treatment choices that best reflect your personal preferences. Provide a copy of your directive to your physician, usual hospital, and family or spokesperson. Consider a periodic review of this document. By periodic review, you can best assure that the directive reflects your preferences.

In addition to this advance directive, Texas law provides for two other types of directives that can be important during a serious illness. These are the Medical Power of Attorney and the Out-of-Hospital Do-Not-Resuscitate Order. You may wish to discuss these with your physician, family, hospital representative, or other advisers. You may also wish to complete a directive related to the donation of organs and tissues.

DIRECTIVE

I, _________, recognize that the best health care is based upon a partnership of trust and communication with my physician. My physician and I will make health care decisions together as long as I am of sound mind and able to make my wishes known. If there comes a time that I am unable to make medical decisions about myself because of illness or injury, I direct that the following treatment preferences be honored:

If, in the judgment of my physician, I am suffering with a terminal condition from which I am expected to die within six months, even with available life-sustaining treatment provided in accordance with prevailing standards of medical care:

_________ I request that all treatments other than those needed to keep me comfortable be discontinued or withheld and my physician allow me to die as gently as possible; OR

_________ I request that I be kept alive in this terminal condition using available life-sustaining treatment. (THIS SELECTION DOES NOT APPLY TO HOSPICE CARE.)

If, in the judgment of my physician, I am suffering with an irreversible condition so that I cannot care for myself or make decisions for myself and am expected to die without life-sustaining treatment provided in accordance with prevailing standards of care:

_________ I request that all treatments other than those needed to keep me comfortable be discontinued or withheld and my physician allow me to die as gently as possible; OR.

_________ I request that I be kept alive in this irreversible condition using available life-sustaining treatment. (THIS SELECTION DOES NOT APPLY TO HOSPICE CARE.)

Additional requests: (After discussion with your physician, you may wish to consider listing particular treatments in this space that you do or do not want in specific circumstances, such as artificial nutrition and fluids, intravenous antibiotics, etc. Be sure to state whether you do or do not want the particular treatment.)

____

____

____

After signing this directive, if my representative or I elect hospice care, I understand and agree that only those treatments needed to keep me comfortable would be provided and I would not be given available life-sustaining treatments.

If I do not have a Medical Power of Attorney, and I am unable to make my wishes known, I designate the following person(s) to make treatment decisions with my physician compatible with my personal values:

1._________

2._________

(If a Medical Power of Attorney has been executed, then an agent already has been named and you should not list additional names in this document.)

If the above persons are not available, or if I have not designated a spokesperson, I understand that a spokesperson will be chosen for me following standards specified in the laws of Texas. If, in the judgment of my physician, my death is imminent within minutes to hours, even with the use of all available medical treatment provided within the prevailing standard of care, I acknowledge that all treatments may be withheld or removed except those needed to maintain my comfort. I understand that under Texas law this directive has no effect if I have been diagnosed as pregnant. This directive will remain in effect until I revoke it. No other person may do so.

Signed _________

Date _________

City, County, State of Residence _________

Two competent adult witnesses must sign below, acknowledging the signature of the declarant. The witness designated as Witness 1 may not be a person designated to make a treatment decision for the patient and may not be related to the patient by blood or marriage. This witness may not be entitled to any part of the estate and may not have a claim against the estate of the patient. This witness may not be the attending physician or an employee of the attending physician. If this witness is an employee of a health care facility in which the patient is being cared for, this witness may not be involved in providing direct patient care to the patient. This witness may not be an officer, director, partner, or business office employee of a health care facility in which the patient is being cared for or of any parent organization of the health care facility.

Witness 1 _________

Witness 2 _________

Definitions:

"Artificial nutrition and hydration" means the provision of nutrients or fluids by a tube inserted in a vein, under the skin in the subcutaneous tissues, or in the stomach (gastrointestinal tract).

"Irreversible condition" means a condition, injury, or illness:

(1) that may be treated, but is never cured or eliminated;

(2) that leaves a person unable to care for or make decisions for the person's own self; and

(3) that, without life-sustaining treatment provided in accordance with the prevailing standard of medical care, is fatal.

Explanation: Many serious illnesses such as cancer, failure of major organs (kidney, heart, liver, or lung), and serious brain disease such as Alzheimer's dementia may be considered irreversible early on. There is no cure, but the patient may be kept alive for prolonged periods of time if the patient receives life-sustaining treatments. Late in the course of the same illness, the disease may be considered terminal when, even with treatment, the patient is expected to die. You may wish to consider which burdens of treatment you would be willing to accept in an effort to achieve a particular outcome. This is a very personal decision that you may wish to discuss with your physician, family, or other important persons in your life.

"Life-sustaining treatment" means treatment that, based on reasonable medical judgment, sustains the life of a patient and without which the patient will die. The term includes both life-sustaining medications and artificial life support such as mechanical breathing machines, kidney dialysis treatment, and artificial hydration and nutrition. The term does not include the administration of pain management medication, the performance of a medical procedure necessary to provide comfort care, or any other medical care provided to alleviate a patient's pain.

"Terminal condition" means an incurable condition caused by injury, disease, or illness that according to reasonable medical judgment will produce death within six months, even with available life-sustaining treatment provided in accordance with the prevailing standard of medical care.

Explanation: Many serious illnesses may be considered irreversible early in the course of the illness, but they may not be considered terminal until the disease is fairly advanced. In thinking about terminal illness and its treatment, you again may wish to consider the relative benefits and burdens of treatment and discuss your wishes with your physician, family, or other important

Amended by Acts 1997, 75th Leg., ch. 291, § 2, eff. Jan. 1, 1998. Renumbered from § 672.004 and amended by Acts 1999, 76th Leg., ch. 450, § 1.03, eff. Sept. 1, 1999.

Statutes in Context

Nonwritten directives such as by oral statements or gestures are permitted under § 166.034.

§ 166.034. Issuance of Nonwritten Directive by Competent Adult Qualified Patient

(a) A competent qualified patient who is an adult may issue a directive by a nonwritten means of communication.

(b) A declarant must issue the nonwritten directive in the presence of the attending physician and two witnesses who qualify under Section 166.003, at least one of whom must be a witness who qualifies under Section 166.003(2).

(c) The physician shall make the fact of the existence of the directive a part of the declarant's medical record, and the names of the witnesses shall be entered in the medical record.

Renumbered from § 672.005 and amended by Acts 1999, 76th Leg., ch. 450, § 1.03, eff. Sept. 1, 1999.

Statutes in Context

Section 166.035 explains when a directive may be executed on behalf of a minor.

§ 166.035. Execution of Directive on Behalf of Patient Younger Than 18 Years of Age

The following persons may execute a directive on behalf of a qualified patient who is younger than 18 years of age:

(1) the patient's spouse, if the spouse is an adult;

(2) the patient's parents; or

(3) the patient's legal guardian.

Renumbered from § 672.006 by Acts 1999, 76th Leg., ch. 450, § 1.03, eff. Sept. 1, 1999.

Statutes in Context

Directives do not have to be notarized and health care providers cannot require notarization or the use of a specific form under § 166.036.

§ 166.036. Notarized Document Not Required; Requirement of Specific Form Prohibited

(a) A written directive executed under Section 166.033 or 166.035 is effective without regard to whether the document has been notarized.

(b) A physician, health care facility, or health care professional may not require that:

(1) a directive be notarized; or

(2) a person use a form provided by the physician, health care facility, or health care professional.

Added by Acts 1999, 76th Leg., ch. 450, § 1.03, eff. Sept. 1, 1999.

Statutes in Context

Regardless of what a directive provides, a declarant may demand that life-sustaining procedures be given, even if the declarant is now incompetent or a minor according to § 166.037.

§ 166.037. Patient Desire Supersedes Directive

The desire of a qualified patient, including a qualified patient younger than 18 years of age, supersedes the effect of a directive.

Renumbered from § 672.007 and amended by Acts 1999, 76th Leg., ch. 450, § 1.03, eff. Sept. 1, 1999.

§ 166.038. Procedure When Declarant is Incompetent or Incapable of Communication

(a) This section applies when an adult qualified patient has executed or issued a directive and is incompetent or otherwise mentally or physically incapable of communication.

(b) If the adult qualified patient has designated a person to make a treatment decision as authorized by Section 166.032(c), the attending physician and the designated person may make a treatment decision in accordance with the declarant's directions.

(c) If the adult qualified patient has not designated a person to make a treatment decision, the attending physician shall comply with the directive unless the physician believes that the directive does not reflect the patient's present desire.

Renumbered from 672.008 and amended by Acts 1999, 76th Leg., ch. 450, § 1.03, eff. Sept. 1, 1999.

Statutes in Context

Section 166.039 explains when a decision to withhold or withdraw life-sustaining treatment may be made even if the patient has not executed a directive.

§ 166.039. Procedure When Person Has Not Executed or Issued a Directive and is Incompetent or Incapable of Communication

(a) If an adult qualified patient has not executed or issued a directive and is incompetent or otherwise mentally or physically incapable of communication, the attending physician and the patient's legal guardian or an agent under a medical power of attorney may make a treatment decision that may include a decision to withhold or withdraw life-sustaining treatment from the patient.

(b) If the patient does not have a legal guardian or an agent under a medical power of attorney, the attending physician and one person, if available, from one of the following categories, in the following priority, may make a treatment decision that may include a decision to withhold or withdraw life-sustaining treatment:

(1) the patient's spouse;

(2) the patient's reasonably available adult children;

(3) the patient's parents; or

(4) the patient's nearest living relative.

(c) A treatment decision made under Subsection (a) or (b) must be based on knowledge of what the patient would desire, if known.

(d) A treatment decision made under Subsection (b) must be documented in the patient's medical record and signed by the attending physician.

(e) If the patient does not have a legal guardian and a person listed in Subsection (b) is not available, a treatment decision made under Subsection (b) must be concurred in by another physician who is not involved in the treatment of the patient or who is a representative of an ethics or medical committee of the health care facility in which the person is a patient.

(f) The fact that an adult qualified patient has not executed or issued a directive does not create a presumption that the patient does not want a treatment decision to be made to withhold or withdraw life-sustaining treatment.

(g) A person listed in Subsection (b) who wishes to challenge a treatment decision made under this section must apply for temporary guardianship under Section 875, Texas Probate Code. The court may waive applicable fees in that proceeding.

Amended by Acts 1997, 75th Leg., ch. 291, § 3, eff. Jan. 1, 1998. Renumbered from § 672.009 and amended by Acts 1999, 76th Leg., ch. 450, § 1.03, eff. Sept. 1, 1999.

§ 166.040. Patient Certification and Prerequisites for Complying With Directive

(a) An attending physician who has been notified of the existence of a directive shall provide for the declarant's certification as a qualified patient on diagnosis of a terminal or irreversible condition.

(b) Before withholding or withdrawing life-sustaining treatment from a qualified patient under this subchapter, the attending physician must determine that the steps proposed to be taken are in accord with this subchapter and the patient's existing desires.

Renumbered from § 672.010 and amended by Acts 1999, 76th Leg., ch. 450, § 1.03, eff. Sept. 1, 1999.

Statutes in Context

A directive remains effective until it is revoked under § 166.041. In other words, a directive does not expire after a set period of time or when the declarant's medical condition changes.

§ 166.041. Duration of Directive

A directive is effective until it is revoked as prescribed by Section 166.042.

Renumbered from § 672.011 and amended by Acts 1999, 76th Leg., ch. 450, § 1.03, eff. Sept. 1, 1999.

Statutes in Context

The methods a declarant may use to revoke a directive are described in § 166.042. Note that the declarant does not have to be competent to revoke the directive in writing, orally, or by physical act.

§ 166.042. Revocation of Directive

(a) A declarant may revoke a directive at any time without regard to the declarant's mental state or competency. A directive may be revoked by:

(1) the declarant or someone in the declarant's presence and at the declarant's direction canceling, defacing, obliterating, burning, tearing, or otherwise destroying the directive;

(2) the declarant signing and dating a written revocation that expresses the declarant's intent to revoke the directive; or

(3) the declarant orally stating the declarant's intent to revoke the directive.

(b) A written revocation executed as prescribed by Subsection (a)(2) takes effect only when the declarant or a person acting on behalf of the declarant notifies the attending physician of its existence or mails the revocation to the attending physician. The attending physician or the physician's designee shall record in the patient's medical record the time and date when the physician received notice of the written revocation and shall enter the word "VOID" on each page of the copy of the directive in the patient's medical record.

(c) An oral revocation issued as prescribed by Subsection (a)(3) takes effect only when the declarant or a person acting on behalf of the declarant notifies the attending physician of the revocation. The attending physician or the physician's designee shall record in the patient's medical record the time, date, and place of the revocation, and, if different, the time, date, and place that the physician received notice of the revocation. The attending physician or the physician's designees shall also enter the word "VOID" on each page of the copy of the directive in the patient's medical record.

(d) Except as otherwise provided by this subchapter, a person is not civilly or criminally liable for failure

to act on a revocation made under this section unless the person has actual knowledge of the revocation.
Renumbered from § 672.012 and amended by Acts 1999, 76th Leg., ch. 450, § 1.03, eff. Sept. 1, 1999.

§ 166.043. Reexecution of Directive

A declarant may at any time reexecute a directive in accordance with the procedures prescribed by Section 166.032, including reexecution after the declarant is diagnosed as having a terminal or irreversible condition.
Renumbered from § 672.013 and amended by Acts 1999, 76th Leg., ch. 450, § 1.03, eff. Sept. 1, 1999.

Statutes in Context

Health care providers are protected from liability for withholding or withdrawing life-sustaining treatment under the conditions described in § 166.044.

---

§ 166.044. Limitation of Liability for Withholding or Withdrawing Life-Sustaining Procedures

(a) A physician or health care facility that causes life-sustaining treatment to be withheld or withdrawn from a qualified patient in accordance with this subchapter is not civilly liable for that action unless the physician or health care facility fails to exercise reasonable care when applying the patient's advance directive.

(b) A health professional, acting under the direction of a physician, who participates in withholding or withdrawing life-sustaining treatment from a qualified patient in accordance with this subchapter is not civilly liable for that action unless the health professional fails to exercise reasonable care when applying the patient's advance directive.

(c) A physician, or a health professional acting under the direction of a physician, who participates in withholding or withdrawing life-sustaining treatment from a qualified patient in accordance with this subchapter is not criminally liable or guilty of unprofessional conduct as a result of that action unless the physician or health professional fails to exercise reasonable care when applying the patient's advance directive.

(d) The standard of care that a physician, health care facility, or health care professional shall exercise under this section is that degree of care that a physician, health care facility, or health care professional, as applicable, of ordinary prudence and skill would have exercised under the same or similar circumstances in the same or a similar community.
Renumbered from § 672.015 and amended by Acts 1999, 76th Leg., ch. 450, § 1.03, eff. Sept. 1, 1999.

Statutes in Context

Health care providers may be liable for failing to effectuate a directive under the conditions described in § 166.045.

---

§ 166.045. Liability for Failure to Effectuate Directive

(a) A physician, health care facility, or health care professional who has no knowledge of a directive is not civilly or criminally liable for failing to act in accordance with the directive.

(b) A physician, or a health professional acting under the direction of a physician, is subject to review and disciplinary action by the appropriate licensing board for failing to effectuate a qualified patient's directive in violation of this subchapter or other laws of this state. This subsection does not limit remedies available under other laws of this state.

(c) If an attending physician refuses to comply with a directive or treatment decision and does not wish to follow the procedure established under Section 166.046, life-sustaining treatment shall be provided to the patient, but only until a reasonable opportunity has been afforded for the transfer of the patient to another physician or health care facility willing to comply with the directive or treatment decision.

(d) A physician, health professional acting under the direction of a physician, or health care facility is not civilly or criminally liable or subject to review or disciplinary action by the person's appropriate licensing board if the person has complied with the procedures outlined in Section 166.046.
Renumbered from § 672.016 and amended by Acts 1999, 76th Leg., ch. 450, § 1.03, eff. Sept. 1, 1999.

Statutes in Context

The procedures a physician must follow if the physician refuses to honor an advance directive are set forth in § 166.046.

---

§ 166.046. Procedure if Not Effectuating a Directive or Treatment Decision

(a) If an attending physician refuses to honor a patient's advance directive or health care or a treatment decision made by or on behalf of a patient, the physician's refusal shall be reviewed by an ethics or medical committee. The attending physician may not be a member of that committee. The patient shall be given life-sustaining treatment during the review.

(b) The patient or the person responsible for the health care decisions of the individual who has made the decision regarding the directive or treatment decision:

(1) may be given a written description of the ethics or medical committee review process and any other policies and procedures related to this section adopted by the health care facility;

(2) shall be informed of the committee review process not less than 48 hours before the meeting called to discuss the patient's directive, unless the time period is waived by mutual agreement;

(3) at the time of being so informed, shall be provided:

(A) a copy of the appropriate statement set forth in Section 166.052; and

(B) a copy of the registry list of health care providers and referral groups that have volunteered their readiness to consider accepting transfer or to assist in locating a provider willing to accept transfer that is posted on the website maintained by the Texas Health Care Information Council under Section 166.053; and

(4) is entitled to:

(A) attend the meeting; and

(B) receive a written explanation of the decision reached during the review process.

(c) The written explanation required by Subsection (b)(2)(B) must be included in the patient's medical record.

(d) If the attending physician, the patient, or the person responsible for the health care decisions of the individual does not agree with the decision reached during the review process under Subsection (b), the physician shall make a reasonable effort to transfer the patient to a physician who is willing to comply with the directive. If the patient is a patient in a health care facility, the facility's personnel shall assist the physician in arranging the patient's transfer to:

(1) another physician;

(2) an alternative care setting within that facility; or

(3) another facility.

(e) If the patient or the person responsible for the health care decisions of the patient is requesting life-sustaining treatment that the attending physician has decided and the review process has affirmed is inappropriate treatment, the patient shall be given available life-sustaining treatment pending transfer under Subsection (d). The patient is responsible for any costs incurred in transferring the patient to another facility. The physician and the health care facility are not obligated to provide life-sustaining treatment after the 10th day after the written decision required under Subsection (b) is provided to the patient or the person responsible for the health care decisions of the patient unless ordered to do so under Subsection (g).

(e-1) If during a previous admission to a facility a patient's attending physician and the review process under Subsection (b) have determined that life-sustaining treatment is inappropriate, and the patient is readmitted to the same facility within six months from the date of the decision reached during the review process conducted upon the previous admission, Subsections (b) through (e) need not be followed if the patient's attending physician and a consulting physician who is a member of the ethics or medical committee of the facility document on the patient's readmission that the patient's condition either has not improved or has deteriorated since the review process was conducted.

(f) Life-sustaining treatment under this section may not be entered in the patient's medical record as medically unnecessary treatment until the time period provided under Subsection (e) has expired.

(g) At the request of the patient or the person responsible for the health care decisions of the patient, the appropriate district or county court shall extend the time period provided under Subsection (e) only if the court finds, by a preponderance of the evidence, that there is a reasonable expectation that a physician or health care facility that will honor the patient's directive will be found if the time extension is granted.

(h) This section may not be construed to impose an obligation on a facility or a home and community support services agency licensed under Chapter 142 or similar organization that is beyond the scope of the services or resources of the facility or agency. This section does not apply to hospice services provided by a home and community support services agency licensed under Chapter 142.

Added by Acts 1999, 76th Leg., ch. 450, § 1.03, eff. Sept. 1, 1999. Amended by Acts 2003, 78th Leg., ch. 1228, §§ 2 & 3, eff. June 6, 2003.

Statutes in Context

A person who complies with a directive is not guilty of the crime of aiding suicide under Penal Code § 22.08.

§ 166.047. Honoring Directive Does Not Constitute Offense of Aiding Suicide

A person does not commit an offense under Section 22.08, Penal Code, by withholding or withdrawing life-sustaining treatment from a qualified patient in accordance with this subchapter.

Renumbered from § 672.017 and amended by Acts 1999, 76th Leg., ch. 450, § 1.03, eff. Sept. 1, 1999.

Statutes in Context

Section 166.048 describes the criminal offenses which are committed if a person conceals a declarant's advance directive, forges or falsifies a directive, or withholds information about the declarant's revocation of a directive.

§ 166.048. Criminal Penalty; Prosecution

(a) A person commits an offense if the person intentionally conceals, cancels, defaces, obliterates, or damages another person's directive without that person's consent. An offense under this subsection is a Class A misdemeanor.

(b) A person is subject to prosecution for criminal homicide under Chapter 19, Penal Code, if the person, with the intent to cause life-sustaining treatment to be withheld or withdrawn from another person contrary to the other person's desires, falsifies or forges a directive or intentionally conceals or withholds personal

knowledge of a revocation and thereby directly causes life-sustaining treatment to be withheld or withdrawn from the other person with the result that the other person's death is hastened.
Renumbered from § 672.018 and amended by Acts 1999, 76th Leg., ch. 450, § 1.03, eff. Sept. 1, 1999.

Statutes in Context

Health care providers may not withdraw or withhold life-sustaining treatment if the declarant is pregnant.

§ 166.049. Pregnant Patients

A person may not withdraw or withhold life-sustaining treatment under this subchapter from a pregnant patient.
Renumbered from § 672.019 and amended by Acts 1999, 76th Leg., ch. 450, § 1.03, eff. Sept. 1, 1999.

Statutes in Context

Voluntary euthanasia in which the euthanatizer actually kills the person at that person's request is not allowed under § 166.050.

§ 166.050. Mercy Killing Not Condoned

This subchapter does not condone, authorize, or approve mercy killing or permit an affirmative or deliberate act or omission to end life except to permit the natural process of dying as provided by this subchapter.
Renumbered from § 672.020 and amended by Acts 1999, 76th Leg., ch. 450, § 1.03, eff. Sept. 1, 1999.

§ 166.051. Legal Right or Responsibility Not Affected

This subchapter does not impair or supersede any legal right or responsibility a person may have to effect the withholding or withdrawal of life-sustaining treatment in a lawful manner, provided that if an attending physician or health care facility is unwilling to honor a patient's advance directive or a treatment decision to provide life-sustaining treatment, life-sustaining treatment is required to be provided the patient, but only until a reasonable opportunity has been afforded for transfer of the patient to another physician or health care facility willing to comply with the advance directive or treatment decision.
Renumbered from § 672.021 and amended by Acts 1999, 76th Leg., ch. 450, § 1.03, eff. Sept. 1, 1999.

Statutes in Context

In 2003, Texas enacted extensive procedures which must be followed when either (1) the attending physician wishes to cease life-sustaining treatment but the patient's advance directive or medical agent indicates that treatment should be continued; or (2) the attending physician wishes to continue life-sustaining treatment but the patient's advance directive or medical agent indicates that treatment should be withheld. §§ 166.052 – 166.053. These procedures will assist the patient in being transferred to a facility willing to comply with the advance directive or the agent's instructions.

§ 166.052. Statements Explaining Patient's Right to Transfer

(a) In cases in which the attending physician refuses to honor an advance directive or treatment decision requesting the provision of life-sustaining treatment, the statement required by Section 166.046(b)(2)(A) shall be in subtantially the following form:

When There Is A Disagreement About Medical Treatment: The Physician Recommends Against Life-Sustaining Treatment That You Wish To Continue

You have been given this information because you have requested life-sustaining treatment,* which the attending physician believes is not appropriate. This information is being provided to help you understand state law, your rights, and the resources available to you in such circumstances. It outlines the process for resolving disagreements about treatment among patients, families, and physicians. It is based upon Section 166.046 of the Texas Advance Directives Act, codified in Chapter 166 of the Texas Health and Safety Code.

When an attending physician refuses to comply with an advance directive or other request for life-sustaining treatment because of the physician's judgment that the treatment would be inappropriate, the case will be reviewed by an ethics or medical committee. Life-sustaining treatment will be provided through the review.

You will receive notification of this review at least 48 hours before a meeting of the committee related to your case. You are entitled to attend the meeting. With your agreement, the meeting may be held sooner than 48 hours, if possible.

You are entitled to receive a written explanation of the decision reached during the review process.

If after this review process both the attending physician and the ethics or medical committee conclude that life-sustaining treatment is inappropriate and yet you continue to request such treatment, then the following procedure will occur:

1. The physician, with the help of the health care facility, will assist you in trying to find a physician and facility willing to provide the requested treatment.
2. You are being given a list of health care providers and referral groups that have volunteered their readiness to consider accepting transfer, or to assist in locating a provider willing to accept transfer, maintained by the Texas Health Care Information Council. You may wish to contact providers or referral groups on the list or others of your choice to get help in arranging a transfer.
3. The patient will continue to be given life-sustaining treatment until he or she can be transferred to a willing provider for up to 10 days from the time you were given the committee's written decision that life-sustaining treatment is not appropriate.
4. If a transfer can be arranged, the patient will be responsible for the costs of the transfer.
5. If a provider cannot be found willing to give the requested treatment within 10 days, life-sustaining treatment may be withdrawn unless a court of law has granted an extension.

6. You may ask the appropriate district or county court to extend the 10-day period if the court finds that there is a reasonable expectation that a physician or health care facility willing to provide life-sustaining treatment will be found if the extension is granted.

* "Life-sustaining treatment" means treatment that, based on reasonable medical judgment, sustains the life of a patient and without which the patient will die. The term includes both life-sustaining medications and artificial life support, such as mechanical breathing machines, kidney dialysis treatment, and artificial nutrition and hydration. The term does not include the administration of pain management medication or the performance of a medical procedure considered to be necessary to provide comfort care, or any other medical care provided to alleviate a patient's pain.

(b) In cases in which the attending physician refuses to comply with an advance directive or treatment decision requesting the withholding or withdrawal of life-sustaining treatment, the statement required by Section 166.046(b)(3)(A) shall be in substantially the following form:

When There Is A Disagreement About Medical Treatment: The Physician Recommends Life-Sustaining Treatment That You Wish To Stop

You have been given this information because you have requested the withdrawal or withholding of life-sustaining treatment* and the attending physician refuses to comply with that request. The information is being provided to help you understand state law, your rights, and the resources available to you in such circumstances. It outlines the process for resolving disagreements about treatment among patients, families, and physicians. It is based upon Section 166.046 of the Texas Advance Directives Act, codified in Chapter 166 of the Texas Health and Safety Code.

When an attending physician refuses to comply with an advance directive or other request for withdrawal or withholding of life-sustaining treatment for any reason, the case will be reviewed by an ethics or medical committee. Life-sustaining treatment will be provided through the review.

You will receive notification of this review at least 48 hours before a meeting of the committee related to your case. You are entitled to attend the meeting. With your agreement, the meeting may be held sooner than 48 hours, if possible.

You are entitled to receive a written explanation of the decision reached during the review process.

If you or the attending physician do not agree with the decision reached during the review process, and the attending physician still refuses to comply with your request to withhold or withdraw life-sustaining treatment, then the following procedure will occur:

1. The physician, with the help of the health care facility, will assist you in trying to find a physician and facility willing to withdraw or withhold the life-sustaining treatment.

2. You are being given a list of health care providers and referral groups that have volunteered their readiness to consider accepting transfer, or to assist in locating a provider willing to accept transfer, maintained by the Texas Health Care Information Council. You may wish to contact providers or referral groups on the list or others of your choice to get help in arranging a transfer.

* "Life-sustaining treatment" means treatment that, based on reasonable medical judgment, sustains the life of a patient and without which the patient will die. The term includes both life-sustaining medications and artificial life support, such as mechanical breathing machines, kidney dialysis treatment, and artificial nutrition and hydration. The term does not include the administration of pain management medication or the performance of a medical procedure considered to be necessary to provide comfort care, or any other medical care provided to alleviate a patient's pain.

(c) An attending physician or health care facility may, if it chooses, include any additional information concerning the physician's or facility's policy, perspective, experience, or review procedure.

Added by Acts 2003, 78th Leg., ch. 1228, § 5, eff. June 6, 2003.

§ 166.053. Registry to Assist Transfers

(a) The Texas Health Care Information Council shall maintain a registry listing the identity of and contact information for health care providers and referral groups, situated inside and outside this state, that have voluntarily notified the council they may consider accepting or may assist in locating a provider willing to accept transfer of a patient under Section 166.045 or 166.046.

(b) The listing of a provider or referral group in the registry described in this section does not obligate the provider or group to accept transfer of or provide services to any particular patient.

(c) The Texas Health Care Information Council shall post the current registry list on its website in a form appropriate for easy comprehension by patients and persons responsible for the health care decisions of patients and shall provide a clearly identifiable link from its home page to the registry page. The list shall separately indicate those providers and groups that have indicated their interest in assisting the transfer of:

(1) those patients on whose behalf life-sustaining treatment is being sought;

(2) those patients on whose behalf the withholding or withdrawal of life-sustaining treatment is being sought; and

(3) patients described in both Subdivisions (1) and (2).

(d) The registry list described in this section shall include the following disclaimer:

"This registry lists providers and groups that have indicated to the Texas Health Care Information Council their interest in assisting the transfer of patients in the circumstances described, and is provided for information purposes only. Neither the Texas Health Care Information Council nor the State of Texas endorses or assumes any responsibility for any representation, claim, or act of the listed providers or groups."

Added by Acts 2003, 78th Leg., ch. 1228, § 5, eff. June 6, 2003.

Subchapter C. Out-of-Hospital Do-Not-Resuscitate Orders

Statutes in Context

The 1995 Texas Legislature authorized a physician, in accordance with his or her patient's wishes (or the wishes of the patient's legally authorized representative), to issue an order directing health care professionals acting in out-of-hospital settings, to refrain from initiating or continuing certain life-sustaining procedures. These provisions were recodified in 1999 as part of the Advance Directives Act. This order is designated as an Out-of-Hospital Do-Not-Resuscitate Order (OOH-DNR). OOH-DNR orders are effective when a patient, in a terminal condition, is in a setting such as a long-term care facility, hospice, or even a private home and health care professionals are called for assistance. The order also applies to situations where the person is in transport in an ambulance or other vehicle.

The policy underlying these provisions is to allow the natural process of dying by preventing the use of artificial life-sustaining measures, heroic or otherwise. However, the OOH-DNR order is effective only with respect to certain specified life-sustaining procedures including: (1) cardiopulmonary resuscitation, (2) advanced airway management, (3) artificial ventilation, (4) defibrillation, (5) transcutaneous cardiac pacing, and (6) other life-sustaining treatment specified by the Texas Board of Health. An OOH-DNR order may not authorize the withholding of any treatment designed to provide comfort, care, or pain relief nor the withholding of water and/or nutrition.

OOH-DNR orders are useful for terminally ill individuals who have reason to believe that their medical condition will result in a situation where a health care provider or emergency medical technician would take steps to initiate unwanted life-sustaining procedures. By executing OOH-DNR orders, these individuals may ensure that their wishes will be followed. The orders should relieve family members from the frustration of insisting that the person has a living will and does not want to endure certain procedures, even as the paramedics are going against those wishes and reviving the person. Additionally, the orders reduce the potential of a party honoring the person's wishes from being held criminally or civilly liable.

For an OOH-DNR order to be most effective, a person must wear an OOH-DNR identification device, as adopted by the Texas Board of Health, around his or her neck or wrist. This device allows medical personnel to immediately and conclusively determine that the person has executed a valid OOH–DNR order and that they are to act in accordance with the person's desires as evidenced by that order.

Sections 166.081 - 166.101 govern the execution and effect of OOH-DNR orders.

§ 166.081. Definitions

In this subchapter:

(1) Repealed.

(2) "DNR identification device" means an identification device specified by the board under Section 166.101 that is worn for the purpose of identifying a person who has executed or issued an out-of-hospital DNR order or on whose behalf an out-of-hospital DNR order has been executed or issued under this subchapter.

(3) "Emergency medical services" has the meaning assigned by Section 773.003.

(4) "Emergency medical services personnel" has the meaning assigned by Section 773.003.

(5) "Health care professionals" means physicians, physician assistants, nurses, and emergency medical services personnel and, unless the context requires otherwise, includes hospital emergency personnel.

(6) "Out-of-hospital DNR order":

(A) means a legally binding out-of-hospital do-not-resuscitate order, in the form specified by the board under Section 166.083, prepared and signed by the attending physician of a person, that documents the instructions of a person or the person's legally authorized representative and directs health care professionals acting in an out-of-hospital setting not to initiate or continue the following life-sustaining treatment:

(i) cardiopulmonary resuscitation;

(ii) advanced airway management;

(iii) artificial ventilation;

(iv) defibrillation;

(v) transcutaneous cardiac pacing; and

(vi) other life-sustaining treatment specified by the board under Section 166.101(a); and

(B) does not include authorization to withhold medical interventions or therapies considered necessary to provide comfort care or to alleviate pain or to provide water or nutrition.

(7) "Out-of-hospital setting" means a location in which health care professionals are called for assistance, including long-term care facilities, in-patient hospice facilities, private homes, hospital outpatient or emergency departments, physician's offices, and vehicles during transport.

(8) "Proxy" means a person designated and authorized by a directive executed or issued in accordance with Subchapter B to make a treatment decision for another person in the event the other

person becomes incompetent or otherwise mentally or physically incapable of communication.

(9) "Qualified relatives" means those persons authorized to execute or issue an out-of-hospital DNR order on behalf of a person who is incompetent or otherwise mentally or physically incapable of communication under Section 166.088.

(10) "Statewide out-of-hospital DNR protocol" means a set of statewide standardized procedures adopted by the board under Section 166.101(a) for withholding cardiopulmonary resuscitation and certain other life-sustaining treatment by health care professionals acting in out-of-hospital settings.

Added by Acts 1995, 74th Leg., ch. 965, § 10, eff. June 16, 1995. Renumbered from § 674.001 and amended by Acts 1999, 76th Leg., ch. 450, § 1.04, eff. Sept. 1, 1999. Amended by Acts 2003, 78th Leg., ch. 1228, § 8, eff. June 6, 2003.

Statutes in Context

Section 166.082 provides the requirements for a OOH-DNR order.

§ 166.082. Out-Of-Hospital DNR Order; Directive to Physicians

(a) A competent person may at any time execute a written out-of-hospital DNR order directing health care professionals acting in an out-of-hospital setting to withhold cardiopulmonary resuscitation and certain other life-sustaining treatment designated by the board.

(b) The declarant must sign the out-of-hospital DNR order in the presence of two witnesses who qualify under Section 166.003, at least one of whom must be a witness who qualifies under Section 166.003(2). The witnesses must sign the order. The attending physician of the declarant must sign the order and shall make the fact of the existence of the order and the reasons for execution of the order a part of the declarant's medical record.

(c) If the person is incompetent but previously executed or issued a directive to physicians in accordance with Subchapter B, the physician may rely on the directive as the person's instructions to issue an out-of-hospital DNR order and shall place a copy of the directive in the person's medical record. The physician shall sign the order in lieu of the person signing under Subsection (b).

(d) If the person is incompetent but previously executed or issued a directive to physicians in accordance with Subchapter B designating a proxy, the proxy may make any decisions required of the designating person as to an out-of-hospital DNR order and shall sign the order in lieu of the person signing under Subsection (b).

(e) If the person is now incompetent but previously executed or issued a medical power of attorney designating an agent, the agent may make any decisions required of the designating person as to an out-of-hospital DNR order and shall sign the order in lieu of the person signing under Subsection (b).

(f) The board, on the recommendation of the department, shall by rule adopt procedures for the disposition and maintenance of records of an original out-of-hospital DNR order and any copies of the order.

(g) An out-of-hospital DNR order is effective on its execution.

Added by Acts 1995, 74th Leg., ch. 965, § 10, eff. June 16, 1995. Renumbered from § 674.002 and amended by Acts 1999, 76th Leg., ch. 450, § 1.04, eff. Sept. 1, 1999.

Statutes in Context

The standard OOH-DNR form may be found at http://www.tdh.state.tx.us/hcqs/ems/dnr.pdf.

§ 166.083. Form of Out-Of-Hospital DNR Order

(a) A written out-of-hospital DNR order shall be in the standard form specified by board rule as recommended by the department.

(b) The standard form of an out-of-hospital DNR order specified by the board must, at a minimum, contain the following:

(1) a distinctive single-page format that readily identifies the document as an out-of-hospital DNR order;

(2) a title that readily identifies the document as an out-of-hospital DNR order;

(3) the printed or typed name of the person;

(4) a statement that the physician signing the document is the attending physician of the person and that the physician is directing health care professionals acting in out-of-hospital settings, including a hospital emergency department, not to initiate or continue certain life-sustaining treatment on behalf of the person, and a listing of those procedures not to be initiated or continued;

(5) a statement that the person understands that the person may revoke the out-of-hospital DNR order at any time by destroying the order and removing the DNR identification device, if any, or by communicating to health care professionals at the scene the person's desire to revoke the out-of-hospital DNR order;

(6) places for the printed names and signatures of the witnesses and attending physician of the person and the medical license number of the attending physician;

(7) a separate section for execution of the document by the legal guardian of the person, the person's proxy, an agent of the person having a medical power of attorney, or the attending physician attesting to the issuance of an out-of-hospital DNR order by nonwritten means of communication or acting in accordance with a previously executed or previously issued directive to physicians under Section 166.082(c) that includes the following:

(A) a statement that the legal guardian, the proxy, the agent, the person by nonwritten means of communication, or the physician directs that each listed life-sustaining treatment should not be initiated or continued in behalf of the person; and

(B) places for the printed names and signatures of the witnesses and, as applicable, the legal guardian, proxy, agent, or physician;

(8) a separate section for execution of the document by at least one qualified relative of the person when the person does not have a legal guardian, proxy, or agent having a medical power of attorney and is incompetent or otherwise mentally or physically incapable of communication, including:

(A) a statement that the relative of the person is qualified to make a treatment decision to withhold cardiopulmonary resuscitation and certain other designated life-sustaining treatment under Section 166.088 and, based on the known desires of the person or a determination of the best interest of the person, directs that each listed life-sustaining treatment should not be initiated or continued in behalf of the person; and

(B) places for the printed names and signatures of the witnesses and qualified relative of the person;

(9) a place for entry of the date of execution of the document;

(10) a statement that the document is in effect on the date of its execution and remains in effect until the death of the person or until the document is revoked;

(11) a statement that the document must accompany the person during transport;

(12) a statement regarding the proper disposition of the document or copies of the document, as the board determines appropriate; and

(13) a statement at the bottom of the document, with places for the signature of each person executing the document, that the document has been properly completed.

(c) The board may, by rule and as recommended by the department, modify the standard form of the out-of-hospital DNR order described by Subsection (b) in order to accomplish the purposes of this subchapter.

(d) A photocopy or other complete facsimile of the original written out-of-hospital DNR order executed under this subchapter may be used for any purpose for which the original written order may be used under this subchapter.

Added by Acts 1995, 74th Leg., ch. 965, § 10, eff. June 16, 1995. Renumbered from § 674.003 and amended by Acts 1999, 76th Leg., ch. 450, § 1.04, eff. Sept. 1, 1999.

Statutes in Context

Section 166.084 explains how a patient may issue an OOH-DNR order orally or by gesture.

---

§ 166.084. Issuance of Out-Of-Hospital DNR Order by Nonwritten Communication

(a) A competent person who is an adult may issue an out-of-hospital DNR order by nonwritten communication.

(b) A declarant must issue the nonwritten out-of-hospital DNR order in the presence of the attending physician and two witnesses who qualify under Section 166.003, at least one of whom must be a witness who qualifies under Section 166.003(2).

(c) The attending physician and witnesses shall sign the out-of-hospital DNR order in the place of the document provided by Section 166.083(b)(7) and the attending physician shall sign the document in the place required by Section 166.083(b)(13). The physician shall make the fact of the existence of the out-of-hospital DNR order a part of the declarant's medical record and the names of the witnesses shall be entered in the medical record.

(d) An out-of-hospital DNR order issued in the manner provided by this section is valid and shall be honored by responding health care professionals as if executed in the manner provided by Section 166.082.

Added by Acts 1995, 74th Leg., ch. 965, § 10, eff. June 16, 1995. Renumbered from § 674.004 and amended by Acts 1999, 76th Leg., ch. 450, § 1.04, eff. Sept. 1, 1999.

Statutes in Context

Under § 166.085, certain persons may execute an OOH-DNR order on behalf of a minor who is in a terminal or irreversible condition.

---

§ 166.085. Execution of Out-Of-Hospital DNR Order on Behalf of a Minor

(a) The following persons may execute an out-of-hospital DNR order on behalf of a minor:

(1) the minor's parents;

(2) the minor's legal guardian; or

(3) the minor's managing conservator.

(b) A person listed under Subsection (a) may not execute an out-of-hospital DNR order unless the minor has been diagnosed by a physician as suffering from a terminal or irreversible condition.

Added by Acts 1995, 74th Leg., ch. 965, § 10, eff. June 16, 1995. Renumbered from § 674.005 by Acts 1999, 76th Leg., ch. 450, § 1.04, eff. Sept. 1, 1999. Amended by Acts 2003, 78th Leg., ch. 1228, § 6, eff. June 6, 2003.

Statutes in Context

A competent person's request for treatment supersedes the instructions to withhold that treatment contained in an OOH-DNR order according to § 166.086.

---

§ 166.086. Desire of Person Supersedes Out-Of-Hospital DNR Order

The desire of a competent person, including a competent minor, supersedes the effect of an out-of-hospital DNR order executed or issued by or on behalf of the person when the desire is communicated to responding health care professionals as provided by this subchapter.

Added by Acts 1995, 74th Leg., ch. 965, § 10, eff. June 16, 1995. Renumbered from § 674.006 and amended by Acts 1999, 76th Leg., ch. 450, § 1.04, eff. Sept. 1, 1999.

§ 166.087. Procedure When Declarant is Incompetent or Incapable of Communication

(a) This section applies when a person 18 years of age or older has executed or issued an out-of-hospital DNR order and subsequently becomes incompetent or otherwise mentally or physically incapable of communication.

(b) If the adult person has designated a person to make a treatment decision as authorized by Section 166.032(c), the attending physician and the designated person shall comply with the out-of-hospital DNR order.

(c) If the adult person has not designated a person to make a treatment decision as authorized by Section 166.032(c), the attending physician shall comply with the out-of-hospital DNR order unless the physician believes that the order does not reflect the person's present desire.

Added by Acts 1995, 74th Leg., ch. 965, § 10, eff. June 16, 1995. Renumbered from § 674.007 and amended by Acts 1999, 76th Leg., ch. 450, § 1.04, eff. Sept. 1, 1999.

Statutes in Context

The circumstances under which a person may create an OOH-DNR order for a person who has not done so are explained in § 166.088.

§ 166.088. Procedure When Person Has Not Executed or Issued Out-Of-Hospital DNR Order and is Incompetent or Incapable of Communication

(a) If an adult person has not executed or issued an out-of-hospital DNR order and is incompetent or otherwise mentally or physically incapable of communication, the attending physician and the person's legal guardian, proxy, or agent having a medical power of attorney may execute an out-of-hospital DNR order on behalf of the person.

(b) If the person does not have a legal guardian, proxy, or agent under a medical power of attorney, the attending physician and at least one qualified relative from a category listed by Section 166.039(b), subject to the priority established under that subsection, may execute an out-of-hospital DNR order in the same manner as a treatment decision made under Section 166.039(b).

(c) A decision to execute an out-of-hospital DNR order made under Subsection (a) or (b) must be based on knowledge of what the person would desire, if known.

(d) An out-of-hospital DNR order executed under Subsection (b) must be made in the presence of at least two witnesses who qualify under Section 166.003, at least one of whom must be a witness who qualifies under Section 166.003(2).

(e) The fact that an adult person has not executed or issued an out-of-hospital DNR order does not create a presumption that the person does not want a treatment decision made to withhold cardiopulmonary resuscitation and certain other designated life-sustaining treatment designated by the board.

(f) If there is not a qualified relative available to act for the person under Subsection (b), an out-of-hospital DNR order must be concurred in by another physician who is not involved in the treatment of the patient or who is a representative of the ethics or medical committee of the health care facility in which the person is a patient.

(g) A person listed in Section 166.039(b) who wishes to challenge a decision made under this section must apply for temporary guardianship under Section 875, Texas Probate Code. The court may waive applicable fees in that proceeding.

Added by Acts 1995, 74th Leg., ch. 965, § 10, eff. June 16, 1995. Renumbered from § 674.008 and amended by Acts 1999, 76th Leg., ch. 450, § 1.04, eff. Sept. 1, 1999.

Statutes in Context

Section 166.089 explains how health care professionals should comply with an OOH-DNR order.

§ 166.089. Compliance With Out-Of-Hospital DNR Order

(a) When responding to a call for assistance, health care professionals shall honor an out-of-hospital DNR order in accordance with the statewide out-of-hospital DNR protocol and, where applicable, locally adopted out-of-hospital DNR protocols not in conflict with the statewide protocol if:

(1) the responding health care professionals discover an executed or issued out-of-hospital DNR order form on their arrival at the scene; and

(2) the responding health care professionals comply with this section.

(b) If the person is wearing a DNR identification device, the responding health care professionals must comply with Section 166.090.

(c) The responding health care professionals must establish the identity of the person as the person who executed or issued the out-of-hospital DNR order or for whom the out-of-hospital DNR order was executed or issued.

(d) The responding health care professionals must determine that the out-of-hospital DNR order form appears to be valid in that it includes:

(1) written responses in the places designated on the form for the names, signatures, and other

information required of persons executing or issuing, or witnessing the execution or issuance of, the order;

(2) a date in the place designated on the form for the date the order was executed or issued; and

(3) the signature of the declarant or persons executing or issuing the order and the attending physician in the appropriate places designated on the form for indicating that the order form has been properly completed.

(e) If the conditions prescribed by Subsections (a) through (d) are not determined to apply by the responding health care professionals at the scene, the out-of-hospital DNR order may not be honored and life-sustaining procedures otherwise required by law or local emergency medical services protocols shall be initiated or continued. Health care professionals acting in out-of-hospital settings are not required to accept or interpret an out-of-hospital DNR order that does not meet the requirements of this subchapter.

(f) The out-of-hospital DNR order form or a copy of the form, when available, must accompany the person during transport.

(g) A record shall be made and maintained of the circumstances of each emergency medical services response in which an out-of-hospital DNR order or DNR identification device is encountered, in accordance with the statewide out-of-hospital DNR protocol and any applicable local out-of-hospital DNR protocol not in conflict with the statewide protocol.

(h) An out-of-hospital DNR order executed or issued and documented or evidenced in the manner prescribed by this subchapter is valid and shall be honored by responding health care professionals unless the person or persons found at the scene:

(1) identify themselves as the declarant or as the attending physician, legal guardian, qualified relative, or agent of the person having a medical power of attorney who executed or issued the out-of-hospital DNR order on behalf of the person; and

(2) request that cardiopulmonary resuscitation or certain other life-sustaining treatment designated by the board be initiated or continued.

(i) If the policies of a health care facility preclude compliance with the out-of-hospital DNR order of a person or an out-of-hospital DNR order issued by an attending physician on behalf of a person who is admitted to or a resident of the facility, or if the facility is unwilling to accept DNR identification devices as evidence of the existence of an out-of-hospital DNR order, that facility shall take all reasonable steps to notify the person or, if the person is incompetent, the person's guardian or the person or persons having authority to make health care treatment decisions on behalf of the person, of the facility's policy and shall take all reasonable steps to effect the transfer of the person to the person's home or to a facility where the provisions of this subchapter can be carried out.

Added by Acts 1995, 74th Leg., ch. 965, § 10, eff. June 16, 1995. Renumbered from § 674.009 and amended by Acts 1999, 76th Leg., ch. 450, § 1.04, eff. Sept. 1, 1999.

Statutes in Context

A DNR identification device as authorized under § 166.090 acts as conclusive evidence that the person has a valid OOH-DNR order.

§ 166.090. DNR Identification Device

(a) A person who has a valid out-of-hospital DNR order under this subchapter may wear a DNR identification device around the neck or on the wrist as prescribed by board rule adopted under Section 166.101.

(b) The presence of a DNR identification device on the body of a person is conclusive evidence that the person has executed or issued a valid out-of-hospital DNR order or has a valid out-of-hospital DNR order executed or issued on the person's behalf. Responding health care professionals shall honor the DNR identification device as if a valid out-of-hospital DNR order form executed or issued by the person were found in the possession of the person.

Added by Acts 1995, 74th Leg., ch. 965, § 10, eff. June 16, 1995. Renumbered from § 674.010 and amended by Acts 1999, 76th Leg., ch. 450, § 1.04, eff. Sept. 1, 1999.

Statutes in Context

OOH-DNR orders are effective until revoked under § 166.091. They do not expire after a certain period of time or upon a change in the declarant's medical condition.

§ 166.091. Duration of Out-Of-Hospital DNR Order

An out-of-hospital DNR order is effective until it is revoked as prescribed by Section 166.092.

Added by Acts 1995, 74th Leg., ch. 965, § 10, eff. June 16, 1995. Renumbered from § 674.011 and amended by Acts 1999, 76th Leg., ch. 450, § 1.04, eff. Sept. 1, 1999.

Statutes in Context

Section 166.092 provides the methods for a declarant to revoke an OOH-DNR order.

§ 166.092. Revocation of Out-Of-Hospital DNR Order

(a) A declarant may revoke an out-of-hospital DNR order at any time without regard to the declarant's mental state or competency. An order may be revoked by:

(1) the declarant or someone in the declarant's presence and at the declarant's direction destroying

the order form and removing the DNR identification device, if any;

(2) a person who identifies himself or herself as the legal guardian, as a qualified relative, or as the agent of the declarant having a medical power of attorney who executed the out-of-hospital DNR order or another person in the person's presence and at the person's direction destroying the order form and removing the DNR identification device, if any;

(3) the declarant communicating the declarant's intent to revoke the order; or

(4) a person who identifies himself or herself as the legal guardian, a qualified relative, or the agent of the declarant having a medical power of attorney who executed the out-of-hospital DNR order orally stating the person's intent to revoke the order.

(b) An oral revocation under Subsection (a)(3) or (a)(4) takes effect only when the declarant or a person who identifies himself or herself as the legal guardian, a qualified relative, or the agent of the declarant having a medical power of attorney who executed the out-of-hospital DNR order communicates the intent to revoke the order to the responding health care professionals or the attending physician at the scene. The responding health care professionals shall record the time, date, and place of the revocation in accordance with the statewide out-of-hospital DNR protocol and rules adopted by the board and any applicable local out-of-hospital DNR protocol. The attending physician or the physician's designee shall record in the person's medical record the time, date, and place of the revocation and, if different, the time, date, and place that the physician received notice of the revocation. The attending physician or the physician's designee shall also enter the word "VOID" on each page of the copy of the order in the person's medical record.

(c) Except as otherwise provided by this subchapter, a person is not civilly or criminally liable for failure to act on a revocation made under this section unless the person has actual knowledge of the revocation.

Added by Acts 1995, 74th Leg., ch. 965, § 10, eff. June 16 1995. Renumbered from § 674.012 and amended by Acts 1999, 76th Leg., ch. 450, § 1.04, eff. Sept. 1, 1999.

§ 166.093. Reexecution of Out-Of-Hospital DNR Order

A declarant may at any time reexecute or reissue an out-of-hospital DNR order in accordance with the procedures prescribed by Section 166.082, including reexecution or reissuance after the declarant is diagnosed as having a terminal or irreversible condition.

Added by Acts 1995, 74th Leg., ch. 965, § 10, eff. June 16, 1995. Renumbered from § 674.013 and amended by Acts 1999, 76th Leg., ch. 450, § 1.04, eff. Sept. 1, 1999.

Statutes in Context

Health care professionals are protected from liability for following, or not following, an OOH-DNR order if they meet the requirements of §§ 166.094 or 166.095.

---

§ 166.094. Limitation on Liability for Withholding Cardiopulmonary Resuscitation and Certain Other Life-Sustaining Procedures

(a) A health care professional or health care facility or entity that in good faith causes cardiopulmonary resuscitation or certain other life-sustaining treatment designated by the board to be withheld from a person in accordance with this subchapter is not civilly liable for that action.

(b) A health care professional or health care facility or entity that in good faith participates in withholding cardiopulmonary resuscitation or certain other life-sustaining treatment designated by the board from a person in accordance with this subchapter is not civilly liable for that action.

(c) A health care professional or health care facility or entity that in good faith participates in withholding cardiopulmonary resuscitation or certain other life-sustaining treatment designated by the board from a person in accordance with this subchapter is not criminally liable or guilty of unprofessional conduct as a result of that action.

(d) A health care professional or health care facility or entity that in good faith causes or participates in withholding cardiopulmonary resuscitation or certain other life-sustaining treatment designated by the board from a person in accordance with this subchapter and rules adopted under this subchapter is not in violation of any other licensing or regulatory laws or rules of this state and is not subject to any disciplinary action or sanction by any licensing or regulatory agency of this state as a result of that action.

Added by Acts 1995, 74th Leg., ch. 965, § 10, eff. June 16, 1995. Renumbered from § 674.016 and amended by Acts 1999, 76th Leg., ch. 450, § 1.04, eff. Sept. 1, 1999.

§ 166.095. Limitation on Liability for Failure to Effectuate Out-Of-Hospital DNR Order

(a) A health care professional or health care facility or entity that has no actual knowledge of an out-of-hospital DNR order is not civilly or criminally liable for failing to act in accordance with the order.

(b) A health care professional or health care facility or entity is subject to review and disciplinary action by the appropriate licensing board for failing to effectuate an out-of-hospital DNR order. This subsection does not limit remedies available under other laws of this state.

(c) If an attending physician refuses to execute or comply with an out-of-hospital DNR order, the physician shall inform the person, the legal guardian or qualified relatives of the person, or the agent of the person having a medical power of attorney and, if the person or another authorized to act on behalf of the person so directs, shall make a reasonable effort to transfer the person to another physician who is willing to execute or comply with an out-of-hospital DNR order.

Added by Acts 1995, 74th Leg., ch. 965, § 10, eff. June 16, 1995. Renumbered from § 674.017 and amended by Acts 1999, 76th Leg., ch. 450, § 1.04, eff. Sept. 1, 1999.

Statutes in Context

A person who complies with an OOH-DNR order is not guilty of the crime of aiding suicide under Penal Code § 22.08

§ 166.096. Honoring Out-Of-Hospital DNR Order Does Not Constitute Offense of Aiding Suicide

A person does not commit an offense under Section 22.08, Penal Code, by withholding cardiopulmonary resuscitation or certain other life-sustaining treatment designated by the board from a person in accordance with this subchapter.

Added by Acts 1995, 74th Leg., ch. 965, § 10, eff. June 16, 1995. Renumbered from § 674.018 and amended by Acts 1999, 76th Leg., ch. 450, § 1.04, eff. Sept. 1, 1999.

Statutes in Context

Section 166.097 describes the criminal offenses which are committed if a person conceals a declarant's OOH-DNR order, forges or falsifies an order, or withholds information about the declarant's revocation of an order.

§ 166.097. Criminal Penalty; Prosecution

(a) A person commits an offense if the person intentionally conceals, cancels, defaces, obliterates, or damages another person's out-of-hospital DNR order or DNR identification device without that person's consent or the consent of the person or persons authorized to execute or issue an out-of-hospital DNR order on behalf of the person under this subchapter. An offense under this subsection is a Class A misdemeanor.

(b) A person is subject to prosecution for criminal homicide under Chapter 19, Penal Code, if the person, with the intent to cause cardiopulmonary resuscitation or certain other life-sustaining treatment designated by the board to be withheld from another person contrary to the other person's desires, falsifies or forges an out-of-hospital DNR order or intentionally conceals or withholds personal knowledge of a revocation and thereby directly causes cardiopulmonary resuscitation and certain other life-sustaining treatment designated by the board to be withheld from the other person with the result that the other person's death is hastened.

Added by Acts 1995, 74th Leg., ch. 965, § 10, eff. June 16, 1995. Renumbered from § 674.019 and amended by Acts 1999, 76th Leg., ch. 450, § 1.04, eff. Sept. 1, 1999.

Statutes in Context

Health care providers may not carry out an OOH-DNR order if the declarant is pregnant.

§ 166.098. Pregnant Persons

A person may not withhold cardiopulmonary resuscitation or certain other life-sustaining treatment designated by the board under this subchapter from a person known by the responding health care professionals to be pregnant.

Added by Acts 1995, 74th Leg., ch. 965, § 10, eff. June 16, 1995. Renumbered from § 674.020 and amended by Acts 1999, 76th Leg., ch. 450, § 1.04, eff. Sept. 1, 1999.

Statutes in Context

Voluntary euthanasia in which the euthanatizer actually kills the person at that person's request is not allowed under § 166.099.

§ 166.099. Mercy Killing Not Condoned

This subchapter does not condone, authorize, or approve mercy killing or permit an affirmative or deliberate act or omission to end life except to permit the natural process of dying as provided by this subchapter.

Added by Acts 1995, 74th Leg., ch. 965, § 10, eff. June 16, 1995. Renumbered from § 674.021 and amended by Acts 1999, 76th Leg., ch. 450, § 1.04, eff. Sept. 1, 1999.

§ 166.100. Legal Right or Responsibility Not Affected

This subchapter does not impair or supersede any legal right or responsibility a person may have under a constitution, other statute, regulation, or court decision to effect the withholding of cardiopulmonary resuscitation or certain other life-sustaining treatment designated by the board.

Added by Acts 1995, 74th Leg., ch. 965, § 10, eff. June 16, 1995. Renumbered from § 674.022 and amended by Acts 1999, 76th Leg., ch. 450, § 1.04, eff. Sept. 1, 1999.

§ 166.101. Duties of Department and Board

(a) The board shall, on the recommendation of the department, adopt all reasonable and necessary rules to carry out the purposes of this subchapter, including rules:

(1) adopting a statewide out-of-hospital DNR order protocol that sets out standard procedures for the withholding of cardiopulmonary resuscitation and certain other life-sustaining treatment by health care professionals acting in out-of-hospital settings;

(2) designating life-sustaining treatment that may be included in an out-of-hospital DNR order, including all procedures listed in Sections 166.081(6)(A)(i) through (v); and

(3) governing recordkeeping in circumstances in which an out-of-hospital DNR order or DNR identification device is encountered by responding health care professionals.

(b) The rules adopted by the board under Subsection (a) are not effective until approved by the Texas State Board of Medical Examiners.

(c) Local emergency medical services authorities may adopt local out-of-hospital DNR order protocols if the local protocols do not conflict with the statewide out-of-hospital DNR order protocol adopted by the board.

(d) The board by rule shall specify a distinctive standard design for a necklace and a bracelet DNR identification device that signifies, when worn by a person, that the possessor has executed or issued a valid out-of-hospital DNR order under this subchapter or is a person for whom a valid out-of-hospital DNR order has been executed or issued.

(e) The department shall report to the board from time to time regarding issues identified in emergency medical services responses in which an out-of-hospital DNR order or DNR identification device is encountered. The report may contain recommendations to the board for necessary modifications to the form of the standard out-of-hospital DNR order or the designated life-sustaining procedures listed in the standard out-of-hospital DNR order, the statewide out-of-hospital DNR order protocol, or the DNR identification devices.

Added by Acts 1995, 74th Leg., ch. 965, § 10, eff. June 16, 1995. Renumbered from § 674.023 and amended by Acts 1999, 76th Leg., ch. 450, § 1.04, eff. Sept. 1, 1999.

Statutes in Context

The 2003 Texas Legislature expanded the types of individuals who may honor a *physician's* do-not-resuscitate order in an out-of-hospital setting to include (1) licensed nurses and (2) anyone providing health care services in an out-of-hospital setting. § 116.102. Emergency medical services personnel responding to a call for assistance, however, may honor only a properly executed or issued out-of-hospital DNR order or a prescribed DNR identification device.

---

§ 166.102. Physician's DNR Order May be Honored by Health Care Personnel Other Than Emergency Medical Services Personnel

(a) Except as provided by Subsection (b), a licensed nurse or person providing health care services in an out-of-hospital setting may honor a physician's do-not-resuscitate order.

(b) When responding to a call for assistance, emergency medical services personnel shall honor only a properly executed or issued out-of-hospital DNR order or prescribed DNR identification device in accordance with this subchapter.

Added by Acts 2003, 78th Leg., ch. 1228, § 7, eff. June 6, 2003.

Subchapter D. Medical Power of Attorney

Statutes in Context

Traditionally, a person could not use a power of attorney to delegate the authority to make health care decisions. These decisions were considered too intimate to delegate. In addition, the existence of the patient's informed consent to any medical treatment was problematic because the agent, not the patient, would be making the decision. However, there are persuasive arguments in favor of this type of delegation. Medical decisions may then be made by a person specified by the patient. This person is likely to have a better understanding of how the patient would like to be treated than a guardian, doctor, or family member.

In 1982, the National Conference of Commissioners on Uniform State Laws approved the Model Health-Care Consent Act which included a provision permitting a person to transfer health care decision authority to a *health care representative*. The next year, California became the first state to address this issue when it enacted legislation approving a durable power of attorney for health care.

In 1989, Texas enacted extensive legislation authorizing a durable power of attorney for health care. The 1999 Legislature renamed this instrument as the medical power of attorney and recodified the enabling legislation in a comprehensive Advance Directives Act which also includes living wills and out-of-hospital do-not-resuscitate orders.

Sections 155.151 - 155.166 govern medical powers of attorney.

---

§ 166.151. Definitions

In this subchapter:

(1) "Adult" means a person 18 years of age or older or a person under 18 years of age who has had the disabilities of minority removed.

(2) "Agent" means an adult to whom authority to make health care decisions is delegated under a medical power of attorney.

(3) "Health care provider" means an individual or facility licensed, certified, or otherwise authorized to administer health care, for profit or otherwise, in the ordinary course of business or professional practice and includes a physician.

(4) "Principal" means an adult who has executed a medical power of attorney.

(5) "Residential care provider" means an individual or facility licensed, certified, or otherwise authorized to operate, for profit or otherwise, a residential care home.

Renumbered from V.T.C.A., Civil Practice & Remedies Code § 135.001 and amended by Acts 1999, 76th Leg., ch. 450, § 1.05, eff. Sept. 1, 1999.

Statutes in Context

Section 166.152 explains the scope of the agent's authority to make health care decisions for the principal. Note that the agent may not make certain decisions such as consenting to an abortion or to psychosurgery.

---

§ 166.152. Scope and Duration of Authority

(a) Subject to this subchapter or any express limitation on the authority of the agent contained in the medical power of attorney, the agent may make any health care decision on the principal's behalf that the principal could make if the principal were competent.

(b) An agent may exercise authority only if the principal's attending physician certifies in writing and files the certification in the principal's medical record that, based on the attending physician's reasonable medical judgment, the principal is incompetent.

(c) Notwithstanding any other provisions of this subchapter, treatment may not be given to or withheld from the principal if the principal objects regardless of whether, at the time of the objection:

(1) a medical power of attorney is in effect; or

(2) the principal is competent.

(d) The principal's attending physician shall make reasonable efforts to inform the principal of any proposed treatment or of any proposal to withdraw or withhold treatment before implementing an agent's advance directive.

(e) After consultation with the attending physician and other health care providers, the agent shall make a health care decision:

(1) according to the agent's knowledge of the principal's wishes, including the principal's religious and moral beliefs; or

(2) if the agent does not know the principal's wishes, according to the agent's assessment of the principal's best interests.

(f) Notwithstanding any other provision of this subchapter, an agent may not consent to:

(1) voluntary inpatient mental health services;

(2) convulsive treatment;

(3) psychosurgery;

(4) abortion; or

(5) neglect of the principal through the omission of care primarily intended to provide for the comfort of the principal.

(g) The power of attorney is effective indefinitely on execution as provided by this subchapter and delivery of the document to the agent, unless it is revoked as provided by this subchapter or the principal becomes competent. If the medical power of attorney includes an expiration date and on that date the principal is incompetent, the power of attorney continues to be effective until the principal becomes competent unless it is revoked as provided by this subchapter.

Renumbered from V.T.C.A., Civil Practice & Remedies Code § 135.002 and amended by Acts 1999, 76th Leg., ch. 450, § 1.05, eff. Sept. 1, 1999.

Statutes in Context

Certain individuals as enumerated in § 166.153 may not serve as an agent.

---

§ 166.153. Persons Who May Not Exercise Authority of Agent

A person may not exercise the authority of an agent while the person serves as:

(1) the principal's health care provider;

(2) an employee of the principal's health care provider unless the person is a relative of the principal;

(3) the principal's residential care provider; or

(4) an employee of the principal's residential care provider unless the person is a relative of the principal.

Renumbered from V.T.C.A., Civil Practice & Remedies Code § 135.003 by Acts 1999, 76th Leg., ch. 450, § 1.05, eff. Sept. 1, 1999.

Statutes in Context

Section 166.154 explains the formalities required for a valid medical power of attorney.

---

§ 166.154. Execution and Witnesses

(a) The medical power of attorney must be signed by the principal in the presence of two witnesses who qualify under Section 166.003, at least one of whom must be a witness who qualifies under Section 166.003(2). The witnesses must sign the document.

(b) If the principal is physically unable to sign, another person may sign the medical power of attorney with the principal's name in the principal's presence and at the principal's express direction.

Renumbered from V.T.C.A., Civil Practice & Remedies Code § 135.004 and amended by Acts 1999, 76th Leg., ch. 450, § 1.05, eff. Sept. 1, 1999.

Statutes in Context

The principal may revoke a medical power of attorney by following the procedures set forth in § 166.155.

---

§ 166.155. Revocation

(a) A medical power of attorney is revoked by:

(1) oral or written notification at any time by the principal to the agent or a licensed or certified

health or residential care provider or by any other act evidencing a specific intent to revoke the power, without regard to whether the principal is competent or the principal's mental state;

(2) execution by the principal of a subsequent medical power of attorney; or

(3) the divorce of the principal and spouse, if the spouse is the principal's agent, unless the medical power of attorney provides otherwise.

(b) A principal's licensed or certified health or residential care provider who is informed of or provided with a revocation of a medical power of attorney shall immediately record the revocation in the principal's medical record and give notice of the revocation to the agent and any known health and residential care providers currently responsible for the principal's care.

Renumbered from V.T.C.A., Civil Practice & Remedies Code § 135.005 and amended by Acts 1999, 76th Leg., ch. 450, § 1.05, eff. Sept. 1, 1999.

Statutes in Context

The division of authority between the principal's agent and a court-appointed guardian is detailed in § 166.156.

§ 166.156. Appointment of Guardian

(a) On motion filed in connection with a petition for appointment of a guardian or, if a guardian has been appointed, on petition of the guardian, a probate court shall determine whether to suspend or revoke the authority of the agent.

(b) The court shall consider the preferences of the principal as expressed in the medical power of attorney.

(c) During the pendency of the court's determination under Subsection (a), the guardian has the sole authority to make any health care decisions unless the court orders otherwise. If a guardian has not been appointed, the agent has the authority to make any health care decisions unless the court orders otherwise.

(d) A person, including any attending physician or health or residential care provider, who does not have actual knowledge of the appointment of a guardian or an order of the court granting authority to someone other than the agent to make health care decisions is not subject to criminal or civil liability and has not engaged in unprofessional conduct for implementing an agent's health care decision.

Renumbered from V.T.C.A., Civil Practice & Remedies Code § 135.006 and amended by Acts 1999, 76th Leg., ch. 450, § 1.05, eff. Sept. 1, 1999.

Statutes in Context

Section 166.157 gives the agent broad access to the patient's medical information so the agent may make informed health care decisions for the principal.

§ 166.157. Disclosure of Medical Information

Subject to any limitations in the medical power of attorney, an agent may, for the purpose of making a health care decision:

(1) request, review, and receive any information, oral or written, regarding the principal's physical or mental health, including medical and hospital records;

(2) execute a release or other document required to obtain the information; and

(3) consent to the disclosure of the information.

Renumbered from V.T.C.A., Civil Practice & Remedies Code § 135.007 and amended by Acts 1999, 76th Leg., ch. 450, § 1.05, eff. Sept. 1, 1999.

Statutes in Context

The health care provider's duty to follow the agent's directions is explained in § 166.158.

§ 166.158. Duty of Health or Residential Care Provider

(a) A principal's health or residential care provider and an employee of the provider who knows of the existence of the principal's medical power of attorney shall follow a directive of the principal's agent to the extent it is consistent with the desires of the principal, this subchapter, and the medical power of attorney.

(b) The attending physician does not have a duty to verify that the agent's directive is consistent with the principal's wishes or religious or moral beliefs.

(c) A principal's health or residential care provider who finds it impossible to follow a directive by the agent because of a conflict with this subchapter or the medical power of attorney shall inform the agent as soon as is reasonably possible. The agent may select another attending physician. The procedures established under Sections 166.045 and 166.046 apply if the agent's directive concerns providing, withholding, or withdrawing life-sustaining treatment.

(d) This subchapter may not be construed to require a health or residential care provider who is not a physician to act in a manner contrary to a physician's order.

Renumbered from V.T.C.A., Civil Practice & Remedies Code § 135.008 and amended by Acts 1999, 76th Leg., ch. 450, § 1.05, eff. Sept. 1, 1999.

Statutes in Context

Insurance companies may not require a person to sign a medical power of attorney as a condition of obtaining insurance and may not base insurance rates on whether the insured has signed a medical power of attorney under § 166.159.

§ 166.159. Discrimination Relating to Execution of Medical Power of Attorney

A health or residential care provider, health care service plan, insurer issuing disability insurance, self-insured employee benefit plan, or nonprofit hospital service plan may not:

(1) charge a person a different rate solely because the person has executed a medical power of attorney;

(2) require a person to execute a medical power of attorney before:

(A) admitting the person to a hospital, nursing home, or residential care home;

(B) insuring the person; or

(C) allowing the person to receive health or residential care; or

(3) refuse health or residential care to a person solely because the person has executed a medical power of attorney.

Renumbered from V.T.C.A., Civil Practice & Remedies Code § 135.009 and amended by Acts 1999, 76th Leg., ch. 450, § 1.05, eff. Sept. 1, 1999.

Statutes in Context

An agent is protected from civil and criminal liability if the agent complies with § 166.160.

---

§ 166.160. Limitation on Liability

(a) An agent is not subject to criminal or civil liability for a health care decision if the decision is made in good faith under the terms of the medical power of attorney and the provisions of this subchapter.

(b) An attending physician, health or residential care provider, or a person acting as an agent for or under the physician's or provider's control is not subject to criminal or civil liability and has not engaged in unprofessional conduct for an act or omission if the act or omission:

(1) is done in good faith under the terms of the medical power of attorney, the directives of the agent, and the provisions of this subchapter; and

(2) does not constitute a failure to exercise reasonable care in the provision of health care services.

(c) The standard of care that the attending physician, health or residential care provider, or person acting as an agent for or under the physician's or provider's control shall exercise under Subsection (b) is that degree of care that an attending physician, health or residential care provider, or person acting as an agent for or under the physician's or provider's control, as applicable, of ordinary prudence and skill would have exercised under the same or similar circumstances in the same or similar community.

(d) An attending physician, health or residential care provider, or person acting as an agent for or under the physician's or provider's control has not engaged in unprofessional conduct for:

(1) failure to act as required by the directive of an agent or a medical power of attorney if the physician, provider, or person was not provided with a copy of the medical power of attorney or had no knowledge of a directive; or

(2) acting as required by an agent's directive if the medical power of attorney has expired or been revoked but the physician, provider, or person does not have knowledge of the expiration or revocation.

Renumbered from V.T.C.A., Civil Practice & Remedies Code § 135.010 and amended by Acts 1999, 76th Leg., ch. 450, § 1.05, eff. Sept. 1, 1999.

Statutes in Context

The fact that an agent consents to medical treatment has no effect on the identity of the persons financially liable for the costs associated with that care under § 166.161.

---

§ 166.161. Liability for Health Care Costs

Liability for the cost of health care provided as a result of the agent's decision is the same as if the health care were provided as a result of the principal's decision.

Renumbered from V.T.C.A., Civil Practice & Remedies Code § 135.011 by Acts 1999, 76th Leg., ch. 450, § 1.05, eff. Sept. 1, 1999.

Statutes in Context

The principal must sign a statement indicating that the principal has received a disclosure statement and has understood its contents. The principal must sign this statement *before* signing the medical power of attorney. See § 166.162.

---

§ 166.162. Disclosure Statement

A medical power of attorney is not effective unless the principal, before executing the medical power of attorney, signs a statement that the principal has received a disclosure statement and has read and understood its contents.

Renumbered from V.T.C.A., Civil Practice & Remedies Code § 135.014 and amended by Acts 1999, 76th Leg., ch. 450, § 1.05, eff. Sept. 1, 1999.

Statutes in Context

Section 166.163 provides the form of the disclosure statement which the principal must receive before signing the medical power of attorney. Although not provided on the form, it is common practice to add a signature line at the end along with a statement that the principal has read and understood its contents. The principal should then sign this statement before signing the medical power of attorney.

---

§ 166.163. Form of Disclosure Statement

The disclosure statement must be in substantially the following form:

INFORMATION CONCERNING THE MEDICAL POWER OF ATTORNEY
THIS IS AN IMPORTANT LEGAL DOCUMENT. BEFORE SIGNING THIS DOCUMENT, YOU SHOULD KNOW THESE IMPORTANT FACTS:
Except to the extent you state otherwise, this document gives the person you name as your agent the authority to make any and all health care decisions for you in accordance with your wishes, including your religious and moral beliefs, when you are no longer capable of making them yourself. Because "health care" means any treatment, service, or procedure to maintain, diagnose, or treat your physical or mental condition, your agent has the power to make a broad range of health care decisions for you. Your agent may consent, refuse to consent, or withdraw consent to medical treatment and may make decisions about withdrawing or withholding life-sustaining treatment. Your agent may not consent to voluntary inpatient mental health services, convulsive treatment, psychosurgery, or abortion. A physician must comply with your agent's instructions or allow you to be transferred to another physician.

Your agent's authority begins when your doctor certifies that you lack the competence to make health care decisions.

Your agent is obligated to follow your instructions when making decisions on your behalf. Unless you state otherwise, your agent has the same authority to make decisions about your health care as you would have had.

It is important that you discuss this document with your physician or other health care provider before you sign it to make sure that you understand the nature and range of decisions that may be made on your behalf. If you do not have a physician, you should talk with someone else who is knowledgeable about these issues and can answer your questions. You do not need a lawyer's assistance to complete this document, but if there is anything in this document that you do not understand, you should ask a lawyer to explain it to you.

The person you appoint as agent should be someone you know and trust. The person must be 18 years of age or older or a person under 18 years of age who has had the disabilities of minority removed. If you appoint your health or residential care provider (e.g., your physician or an employee of a home health agency, hospital, nursing home, or residential care home, other than a relative), that person has to choose between acting as your agent or as your health or residential care provider; the law does not permit a person to do both at the same time.

You should inform the person you appoint that you want the person to be your health care agent. You should discuss this document with your agent and your physician and give each a signed copy. You should indicate on the document itself the people and institutions who have signed copies. Your agent is not liable for health care decisions made in good faith on your behalf.

Even after you have signed this document, you have the right to make health care decisions for yourself as long as you are able to do so and treatment cannot be given to you or stopped over your objection. You have the right to revoke the authority granted to your agent by informing your agent or your health or residential care provider orally or in writing or by your execution of a subsequent medical power of attorney. Unless you state otherwise, your appointment of a spouse dissolves on divorce.

This document may not be changed or modified. If you want to make changes in the document, you must make an entirely new one.

You may wish to designate an alternate agent in the event that your agent is unwilling, unable, or ineligible to act as your agent. Any alternate agent you designate has the same authority to make health care decisions for you.
THIS POWER OF ATTORNEY IS NOT VALID UNLESS IT IS SIGNED IN THE PRESENCE OF TWO COMPETENT ADULT WITNESSES. THE FOLLOWING PERSONS MAY NOT ACT AS ONE OF THE WITNESSES:

(1) the person you have designated as your agent;

(2) a person related to you by blood or marriage;

(3) a person entitled to any part of your estate after your death under a will or codicil executed by you or by operation of law;

(4) your attending physician;

(5) an employee of your attending physician;

(6) an employee of a health care facility in which you are a patient if the employee is providing direct patient care to you or is an officer, director, partner, or business office employee of the health care facility or of any parent organization of the health care facility; or

(7) a person who, at the time this power of attorney is executed, has a claim against any part of your estate after your death.

Renumbered from V.T.C.A., Civil Practice & Remedies Code § 135.015 and amended by Acts 1999, 76th Leg., ch. 450, § 1.05, eff. Sept. 1, 1999.

Statutes in Context

Section 166.164 contains the form which the principal completes and signs to appoint an agent to make health care decisions. Note that the principal may provide individualized instructions in the section labeled "limitations of the decision-making authority of my agent." Two witnesses are needed but the document does not need to be notarized.

§ 166.164. Form of Medical Power of Attorney

The medical power of attorney must be in substantially the following form:

MEDICAL POWER OF ATTORNEY DESIGNATION OF HEALTH CARE AGENT.
I,__________ (insert your name) appoint:
Name: ______________________________
Address: ____________________________
Phone: ______________________________

as my agent to make any and all health care decisions for me, except to the extent I state otherwise in this document. This medical power of attorney takes effect if I become unable to make my own health care decisions and this fact is certified in writing by my physician.

LIMITATIONS ON THE DECISION-MAKING AUTHORITY OF MY AGENT ARE AS FOLLOWS:

____

____

DESIGNATION OF ALTERNATE AGENT.

(You are not required to designate an alternate agent but you may do so. An alternate agent may make the same health care decisions as the designated agent if the designated agent is unable or unwilling to act as your agent. If the agent designated is your spouse, the designation is automatically revoked by law if your marriage is dissolved.)

If the person designated as my agent is unable or unwilling to make health care decisions for me, I designate the following persons to serve as my agent to make health care decisions for me as authorized by this document, who serve in the following order:

A. First Alternate Agent

Name: ______________________________

Address: ______________________________

Phone: ______________________________

B. Second Alternate Agent

Name: ______________________________

Address: ______________________________

Phone: ______________________________

The original of this document is kept at:

____

____

____

The following individuals or institutions have signed copies:

Name: ______________________________

Address: ______________________________

____

Name: ______________________________

Address: ______________________________

____

DURATION.

I understand that this power of attorney exists indefinitely from the date I execute this document unless I establish a shorter time or revoke the power of attorney. If I am unable to make health care decisions for myself when this power of attorney expires, the authority I have granted my agent continues to exist until the time I become able to make health care decisions for myself.

(IF APPLICABLE)

This power of attorney ends on the following date:

____

PRIOR DESIGNATIONS REVOKED.

I revoke any prior medical power of attorney.

ACKNOWLEDGMENT OF DISCLOSURE STATEMENT.

I have been provided with a disclosure statement explaining the effect of this document. I have read and understand that information contained in the disclosure statement.

(YOU MUST DATE AND SIGN THIS POWER OF ATTORNEY.)

I sign my name to this medical power of attorney on _____ day of _________ (month, year) at

____

(City and State)

____

(Signature)

____

(Print Name)

STATEMENT OF FIRST WITNESS.

I am not the person appointed as agent by this document. I am not related to the principal by blood or marriage. I would not be entitled to any portion of the principal's estate on the principal's death. I am not the attending physician of the principal or an employee of the attending physician. I have no claim against any portion of the principal's estate on the principal's death. Furthermore, if I am an employee of a health care facility in which the principal is a patient, I am not involved in providing direct patient care to the principal and am not an officer, director, partner, or business office employee of the health care facility or of any parent organization of the health care facility.

Signature: ______________________________

Print Name: ______________________________

Date: __________

Address: ______________________________

SIGNATURE OF SECOND WITNESS.

Signature: ______________________________

Print Name: ______________________________

Date: __________

Address: ______________________________

Renumbered from V.T.C.A., Civil Practice & Remedies Code § 135.016 and amended by Acts 1999, 76th Leg., ch. 450, § 1.05, eff. Sept. 1, 1999.

§ 166.165. Civil Action

(a) A person who is a near relative of the principal or a responsible adult who is directly interested in the principal, including a guardian, social worker, physician, or clergyman, may bring an action in district court to request that the medical power of attorney be revoked because the principal, at the time the medical power of attorney was signed:

(1) was not competent; or

(2) was under duress, fraud, or undue influence.

(b) The action may be brought in the county of the principal's residence or the residence of the person bringing the action.

(c) During the pendency of the action, the authority of the agent to make health care decisions continues in effect unless the district court orders otherwise.

Renumbered from V.T.C.A., Civil Practice & Remedies Code § 135.017 and amended by Acts 1999, 76th Leg., ch. 450, § 1.05, eff. Sept. 1, 1999.

§ 166.166. Other Rights or Responsibilities Not Affected

This subchapter does not limit or impair any legal right or responsibility that any person, including a physician or health or residential care provider, may have to make or implement health care decisions on behalf of a person, provided that if an attending physician or health care facility is unwilling to honor a patient's advance directive or a treatment decision to provide life-sustaining treatment, life-sustaining treatment is required to be provided the patient, but only until a reasonable opportunity has been afforded for transfer of the patient to another physician or health care facility willing to comply with the advance directive or treatment decision.

Renumbered from V.T.C.A., Civil Practice & Remedies Code § 135.018 and amended by Acts 1999, 76th Leg., ch. 450, § 1.05, eff. Sept. 1, 1999.

Title 4. Health Facilities

Subtitle F. Powers and Duties of Hospitals

Chapter 313. Consent to Medical Act

Statutes in Context

The Texas Legislature enacted the Consent to Medical Treatment Act in 1993. This Act empowers a surrogate to make certain decisions regarding an adult's medical treatment if that person is (1) in a hospital or residing in a nursing home; (2) is comatose, incapacitated, or otherwise mentally or physically incapable of communication; and (3) has not made other arrangements for medical treatment decisions.

The Act is designed to fill the gap in the previous health care scheme which left many patients without someone with the authority to make medical treatment decisions. Thus, the Act does not apply to the following situations: (1) a decision to withhold or withdraw life-sustaining treatment from a qualified terminal patient who had executed a directive to physicians, (2) an agent's decision under a medical power of attorney, (3) a consent to medical treatment of minors under the Family Code, (4) a consent for emergency care, (5) a hospital patient transfer, and (6) a guardian's decision if the guardian has authority to make medical treatment decisions.

§ 313.001. Short Title

This chapter may be cited as the Consent to Medical Treatment Act.

Added by Acts 1993, 73rd Leg., ch. 407, § 1, eff. Sept. 1, 1993.

§ 313.002. Definitions

In this chapter:

(1) "Adult" means a person 18 years of age or older or a person under 18 years of age who has had the disabilities of minority removed.

(2) "Attending physician" means the physician with primary responsibility for a patient's treatment and care.

(3) "Decision-making capacity" means the ability to understand and appreciate the nature and consequences of a decision regarding medical treatment and the ability to reach an informed decision in the matter.

(4) "Hospital" means a facility licensed under Chapter 241.

(5) "Incapacitated" means lacking the ability, based on reasonable medical judgment, to understand and appreciate the nature and consequences of a treatment decision, including the significant benefits and harms of and reasonable alternatives to any proposed treatment decision.

(6) "Medical treatment" means a health care treatment, service, or procedure designed to maintain or treat a patient's physical or mental condition, as well as preventative care.

(7) "Nursing home" means a facility licensed under Chapter 242.

(8) "Patient" means a person who is admitted to a hospital or residing in a nursing home.

(9) "Physician" means:

(A) a physician licensed by the Texas State Board of Medical Examiners; or

(B) a physician with proper credentials who holds a commission in a branch of the armed services of the United States and who is serving on active duty in this state.

(10) "Surrogate decision-maker" means an individual with decision-making capacity who is identified as the person who has authority to consent to medical treatment on behalf of an incapacitated patient in need of medical treatment.

Added by Acts 1993, 73rd Leg., ch. 407, § 1, eff. Sept. 1, 1993.

Statutes in Context

A surrogate may not make a health care decision if one of the situations enumerated in § 313.003 is true such as the existence of a health care agent.

§ 313.003. Exceptions and Application

(a) This chapter does not apply to:

(1) a decision to withhold or withdraw life-sustaining treatment from qualified terminal or irreversible patients under Subchapter B, Chapter 166;

(2) a health care decision made under a medical power of attorney under Subchapter D, Chapter 166, or under Chapter XII, Texas Probate Code;

(3) consent to medical treatment of minors under Chapter 32, Family Code;

(4) consent for emergency care under Chapter 773;

(5) hospital patient transfers under Chapter 241; or

(6) a patient's legal guardian who has the authority to make a decision regarding the patient's medical treatment.

(b) This chapter does not authorize a decision to withhold or withdraw life-sustaining treatment.

Added by Acts 1993, 73rd Leg., ch. 407, § 1, eff. Sept. 1, 1993. Amended by Acts 1999, 76th Leg., ch. 450, § 2.01, eff. Sept. 1, 1999.

Statutes in Context

Section 313.004 provides a priority order of individuals who are authorized to become a surrogate to make health care decisions.

§ 313.004. Consent for Medical Treatment

(a) If an adult patient in a hospital or nursing home is comatose, incapacitated, or otherwise mentally or physically incapable of communication, an adult surrogate from the following list, in order of priority, who has decision-making capacity, is available after a reasonably diligent inquiry, and is willing to consent to medical treatment on behalf of the patient may consent to medical treatment on behalf of the patient:

(1) the patient's spouse;

(2) an adult child of the patient who has the waiver and consent of all other qualified adult children of the patient to act as the sole decision-maker;

(3) a majority of the patient's reasonably available adult children;

(4) the patient's parents; or

(5) the individual clearly identified to act for the patient by the patient before the patient became incapacitated, the patient's nearest living relative, or a member of the clergy.

(b) Any dispute as to the right of a party to act as a surrogate decision-maker may be resolved only by a court of record having jurisdiction under Chapter V, Texas Probate Code.[1]

(c) Any medical treatment consented to under Subsection (a) must be based on knowledge of what the patient would desire, if known.

(d) Notwithstanding any other provision of this chapter, a surrogate decision-maker may not consent to:

(1) voluntary inpatient mental health services;

(2) electro-convulsive treatment; or

(3) the appointment of another surrogate decision-maker.

Added by Acts 1993, 73rd Leg., ch. 407, § 1, eff. Sept. 1, 1993.

Statutes in Context

A surrogate may make a health care decision only under the circumstances listed in § 313.005.

§ 313.005. Prerequisites for Consent

(a) If an adult patient in a hospital or nursing home is comatose, incapacitated, or otherwise mentally or physically incapable of communication and, according to reasonable medical judgment, is in need of medical treatment, the attending physician shall describe the:

(1) patient's comatose state, incapacity, or other mental or physical inability to communicate in the patient's medical record; and

(2) proposed medical treatment in the patient's medical record.

(b) The attending physician shall make a reasonably diligent effort to contact or cause to be contacted the persons eligible to serve as surrogate decision-makers. Efforts to contact those persons shall be recorded in detail in the patient's medical record.

(c) If a surrogate decision-maker consents to medical treatment on behalf of the patient, the attending physician shall record the date and time of the consent and sign the patient's medical record. The surrogate decision-maker shall countersign the patient's medical record or execute an informed consent form.

(d) A surrogate decision-maker's consent to medical treatment that is not made in person shall be reduced to writing in the patient's medical record, signed by the hospital or nursing home staff member receiving the consent, and countersigned in the patient's medical record or on an informed consent form by the surrogate decision-maker as soon as possible.

Added by Acts 1993, 73rd Leg., ch. 407, § 1, eff. Sept. 1, 1993.

Statutes in Context

The fact that a surrogate consents to medical treatment has no effect on the identity of the persons financially liable for the costs associated with that care under § 313.006.

§ 313.006. Liability for Medical Treatment Costs

Liability for the cost of medical treatment provided as a result of consent to medical treatment by a surrogate decision-maker is the same as the liability for that cost if the medical treatment were provided as a result of the patient's own consent to the treatment.

Added by Acts 1993, 73rd Leg., ch. 407, § 1, eff. Sept. 1, 1993.

Statutes in Context

A surrogate is protected from liability if the surrogate complies with § 313.007.

§ 313.007. Limitation on Liability

(a) A surrogate decision-maker is not subject to criminal or civil liability for consenting to medical care under this chapter if the consent is made in good faith.

(b) An attending physician, hospital, or nursing home or a person acting as an agent for or under the control of the physician, hospital, or nursing home is not subject to criminal or civil liability and has not engaged in unprofessional conduct if the medical treatment consented to under this chapter:

(1) is done in good faith under the consent to medical treatment; and

[1] V.A.T.S. Probate Code, § 72 et seq.

(2) does not constitute a failure to exercise due care in the provision of the medical treatment.
Added by Acts 1993, 73rd Leg., ch. 407, § 1, eff. Sept. 1, 1993.

Title 8. Death and Disposition of the Body

Subtitle A. Death

Chapter 671. Determination of Death and Autopsy Reports

Subchapter A. Determination of Death

Statutes in Context

Section 671.001 provides for the determination of death by traditional means (irreversible cessation of breathing and heart beating) as well as by irreversible cessation of all spontaneous brain function (brain death).

§ 671.001. Standard Used in Determining Death

(a) A person is dead when, according to ordinary standards of medical practice, there is irreversible cessation of the person's spontaneous respiratory and circulatory functions.

(b) If artificial means of support preclude a determination that a person's spontaneous respiratory and circulatory functions have ceased, the person is dead when, in the announced opinion of a physician, according to ordinary standards of medical practice, there is irreversible cessation of all spontaneous brain function. Death occurs when the relevant functions cease.

(c) Death must be pronounced before artificial means of supporting a person's respiratory and circulatory functions are terminated.

(d) A registered nurse or physician assistant may determine and pronounce a person dead in situations other than those described by Subsection (b) if permitted by written policies of a licensed health care facility, institution, or entity providing services to that person. Those policies must include physician assistants who are credentialed or otherwise permitted to practice at the facility, institution, or entity. If the facility, institution, or entity has an organized nursing staff and an organized medical staff or medical consultant, the nursing staff and medical staff or consultant shall jointly develop and approve those policies. The board shall adopt rules to govern policies for facilities, institutions, or entities that do not have organized nursing staffs and organized medical staffs or medical consultants.
Acts 1989, 71st Leg., ch. 678, § 1, eff. Sept. 1, 1989. Amended by Acts 1991, 72nd Leg., ch. 201, § 1, eff. Sept. 1, 1991. Amended by Acts 1995, 74th Leg., ch. 965, § 8, eff. June 16, 1995.

§ 671.002. Limitation of Liability

(a) A physician who determines death in accordance with Section 671.001(b) or a registered nurse or physician assistant who determines death in accordance with Section 671.001(d) is not liable for civil damages or subject to criminal prosecution for the physician's, registered nurse's, or physician assistant's actions or the actions of others based on the determination of death.

(b) A person who acts in good faith in reliance on a physician's, registered nurse's, or physician assistant's determination of death is not liable for civil damages or subject to criminal prosecution for the person's actions.
Acts 1989, 71st Leg., ch. 678, § 1, eff. Sept. 1, 1989. Amended by Acts 1991, 72nd Leg., ch. 201, § 2, eff. Sept. 1, 1991. Amended by Acts 1995, 74th Leg., ch. 965, § 9, eff. June 16, 1995.

Title 8. Death and Disposition of the Body

Subtitle B. Disposition of the Body

Chapter 691. Anatomical Board of the State of Texas

Subchapter B. Donation and Distribution of Bodies

Statutes in Context

Sections 691.024 - 691.030 regulate various matters relating to the distribution of dead bodies such as the persons who may claim the body for burial.

§ 691.024. Persons Who May Claim Body for Burial

(a) An officer, employee, or representative of the state, of a political subdivision, or of an institution is not required to give notice or deliver a body as required by Section 691.023 if the body is claimed for burial.

(b) A relative, bona fide friend, or representative of an organization to which the deceased belonged may claim the body for burial. The person in charge of the body shall release the body to the claimant without requiring payment when the person is satisfied that the claimed relationship exists.

(c) A claimant alleging to be a bona fide friend or a representative of an organization to which the deceased belonged must present a written statement of the relationship under which the claimant qualifies as a bona fide friend or organization representative.

(d) For purposes of this section, a bona fide friend means a person who is like one of the family, and does not include:

(1) an ordinary acquaintance;

(2) an officer, employee, or representative of the state, of a political subdivision, or of an institution

having charge of a body not claimed for burial or a body required to be buried at public expense;

(3) an employee of an entity listed in Subdivision (2) with which the deceased was associated; or

(4) a patient, inmate, or ward of an institution with which the deceased was associated.

(e) A person covered by Subsection (d) may qualify as a bona fide friend if the friendship existed before the deceased entered the institution.

Acts 1989, 71st Leg., ch. 678, § 1, eff. Sept. 1, 1989.

§ 691.025. Procedure After Death

(a) If a body is not claimed for burial immediately after death, the body shall be embalmed within 24 hours.

(b) For 72 hours after death, the person in charge of the institution having charge or control of the body shall make due effort to find a relative of the deceased and notify the relative of the death. If the person is not able to find a relative, the person shall file with the county clerk an affidavit stating that the person has made a diligent inquiry to find a relative and stating the inquiry the person made.

(c) A body that is not claimed for burial within 48 hours after a relative receives notification shall be delivered as soon as possible to the board or the board's representative.

(d) A relative of the deceased may claim the body within 60 days after the body has been delivered to an institution or other entity authorized to receive the body. The body shall be released without charge.

Acts 1989, 71st Leg., ch. 678, § 1, eff. Sept. 1, 1989.

§ 691.026. Body of Traveler

If an unclaimed body is the body of a traveler who died suddenly, the board shall direct the institution receiving the body to retain the body for six months for purposes of identification.

Acts 1989, 71st Leg., ch. 678, § 1, eff. Sept. 1, 1989.

§ 691.027. Autopsy

Only the board may grant permission to perform an autopsy on an unclaimed body. The board may grant permission after receiving a specific request for an autopsy that shows sufficient evidence of medical urgency.

Acts 1989, 71st Leg., ch. 678, § 1, eff. Sept. 1, 1989.

§ 691.028. Donation of Body by Written Instrument

(a) An adult living in this state who is of sound mind may donate his body by will or other written instrument to the board of a medical or dental school, or another donee authorized by the board, to be used for the advancement of medical science.

(b) To be effective, the donor must sign the will or other written instrument and it must be witnessed by two adults. The donor is not required to use a particular form or particular words in making the donation, but the will or other instrument must clearly convey the donor's intent.

(c) Appointment of an administrator or executor or acquisition of a court order is not necessary before the body may be delivered under this chapter.

(d) A donor may revoke a donation made under this section by executing a written instrument in a manner similar to the original donation.

Acts 1989, 71st Leg., ch. 678, § 1, eff. Sept. 1, 1989. Amended by Acts 2003, 78th Leg., ch. 948, § 6, eff. Sept. 1, 2003. Amended by Acts 2003, 78th Leg., ch. 948, § 6, eff. Sept. 1, 2003.

§ 691.029. Authority to Accept Bodies From Outside the State

The board may receive a body transported to the board from outside this state.

Acts 1989, 71st Leg., ch. 678, § 1, eff. Sept. 1, 1989.

§ 691.030. Board's Authority to Distribute Bodies and Anatomical Specimens

(a) The board or the board's representative shall distribute bodies donated to it and may redistribute bodies donated to medical or dental schools or other donees authorized by the board to schools and colleges of chiropractic, osteopathy, medicine, or dentistry incorporated in this state, to physicians, and to other persons as provided by this section.

(b) In making the distribution, the board shall give priority to the schools and colleges that need bodies for lectures and demonstrations.

(c) If the board has remaining bodies, the board or the board's representative shall distribute or redistribute those bodies to the schools and colleges proportionately and equitably according to the number of students in each school or college receiving instruction or demonstration in normal or morbid anatomy and operative surgery. The dean of each school or college shall certify that number to the board when required by the board.

(d) The board may transport a body or anatomical specimen to an authorized recipient in another state if the board determines that the supply of bodies or anatomical specimens in this state exceeds the need for bodies or anatomical specimens in this state and if:

(1) the deceased donated his body in compliance with Section 691.028 and at the time of the donation authorized the board to transport the body outside this state; or

(2) the body was donated in compliance with Chapter 692 (Texas Anatomical Gift Act) and the person authorized to make the donation under Section 692.004 authorized the board to transport the body outside this state.

Acts 1989, 71st Leg., ch. 678, § 1, eff. Sept. 1, 1989. Amended by Acts 2003, 78th Leg., ch. 948, § 7, eff. Sept. 1, 2003.

Chapter 692. Texas Anatomical Gift Act

Statutes in Context

Regardless of financial situation, each person has extremely valuable assets which can be transferred at death, namely the person's own body and its parts. Doctors perform over 20,000 organ transplants in the United States every year. Despite the media attention given to organ donation, organs are in short supply. As of 2001, over 75,000 people were waiting for organ transplants. Many people will find organ donation an exciting prospect because a high degree of self-satisfaction can come from the knowledge that donated organs will enhance or save lives. The American Bar Association urges all attorneys to discuss the topic of organ and tissue donations with their clients.

On the other hand, some people consider the use of their dead bodies for transplantation or research to be distasteful or contrary to their religious beliefs. In a way, organ donation is nothing more than cannibalism by technology. The argument is made that there is little difference between ingesting human flesh and having that flesh surgically inserted into the body; in both situations, part of a deceased person ends up inside a living person. A more widespread reason people refuse to donate organs is the fear that medical personnel may not work as hard to save the lives of organ donors as nondonors. The media are brimming with reports of people who were presumed dead but who were actually alive.

Organ donation has a relatively long history. Bones were first transplanted in 1878 and cornea transplants began in the 1940s. It was not until the kidney transplants of the 1950s, however, that the need for comprehensive organ donation law arose. The failure of then existing law to govern anatomical gifts uniformly and comprehensively led the National Conference of Commissioners on Uniform State Laws to approve the Uniform Anatomical Gift Act in 1968. Within five years, all fifty states and the District of Columbia substantially adopted the Act. Many states, but not Texas, have now enacted a revised version of the Act which was promulgated in 1987 to simplify the method of making anatomical gifts and to make it more likely that the donor's intentions will be carried out.

Chapter 692 contains the Texas enactment of the 1968 version of the Uniform Anatomical Gift Act.

§ 692.001. Short Title

This chapter may be cited as the Texas Anatomical Gift Act.

Acts 1989, 71st Leg., ch. 678, § 1, eff. Sept. 1, 1989.

§ 692.002. Definitions

In this chapter:

(1) "Bank or storage facility" means a facility licensed, accredited, or approved under the laws of any state to store human bodies or body parts.

(2) "Decedent" means a deceased person and includes a stillborn infant or fetus.

(3) "Donor" means a person who makes a gift of all or part of the person's body.

(4) "Donor card" means a card designed to be carried by a donor to evidence the donor's intentions with respect to organ, tissue, or eye donations.

(5) "Eye bank" means a nonprofit corporation chartered under the laws of this state to obtain, store, and distribute donor eyes to be used by ophthalmologists for corneal transplants, research, or other medical purposes.

(6) "Hospital" means a hospital:

(A) licensed, accredited, or approved under the laws of any state; or

(B) operated by the federal government, a state government, or a political subdivision of a state government.

(7) "Part" includes an organ, tissue, eye, bone, artery, blood, other fluid, and other parts of a human body.

(8) "Physician" means a physician licensed or authorized to practice under the laws of any state.

(9) "Qualified organ or tissue procurement organization" means an organization that procures and distributes organs or tissues for transplantation, research, or other medical purposes and that:

(A) is affiliated with a university or hospital or registered to operate as a nonprofit organization in this state for the primary purpose of organ or tissue procurement; and

(B) if the organization is an organ procurement organization, is certified to act as an organ procurement organization by the appropriate federal agency.

(10) "Transplant center" means a hospital that:

(A) maintains a waiting list;

(B) receives vascularized organs for the purpose of transplantation; and

(C) transplants organs into patients at the hospital.

(11) "Waiting list" means a patient waiting list of persons who are waiting for a vascular organ transplant.

Amended by Acts 1997, 75th Leg., ch. 225, § 2, eff. Sept. 1, 1997; Acts 1999, 76th Leg., ch. 615, § 1, eff. June 18, 1999.

Statutes in Context

A person who has testamentary capacity under Probate Code § 57 has the capacity to make an anatomical gift under § 692.003. In addition, a minor may make an anatomical gift if the minor obtains parental consent.

The donor may make an antomical gift in the donor's will. This method is not recommended because time is very critical. Many organs need to be

removed immediately to be useful and a client's will may not be located or read until it is too late. Accordingly, it is better for the donor to sign a card indicating the donor's wishes. The card should be small enough for the donor to carry in his or her wallet so it will be spotted in a timely fashion after the donor's death.

An anatomical gift card requires two witnesses and the donor's signature. Texas has not enacted the 1987 revision of the Uniform Anatomical Gift Act which dispenses with the witnessing requirement.

The donee need not secure the consent of any member of the donor's family for the gift to be effective. Nonetheless, many donees are reluctant to enforce their rights over the objection of close family members for fear of a lawsuit or bad publicity.

§ 692.003. Manner of Executing Gift of Own Body

(a) A person who has testamentary capacity under the Texas Probate Code may give all or part of the person's body for a purpose specified by Section 692.005. In addition, a person younger than 18 years of age who does not have testamentary capacity may make a gift on the person's driver's license or personal identification card, but that gift is not effective without the approval or consent of the person's parents or legal guardian if the person is younger than 18 years of age at the time of death.

(b) A person may make a gift under this section by will or by use of a document other than a will.

(c) A gift made by will is effective on the death of the testator without the necessity of probate. If the will is not probated or if the will is declared invalid for testamentary purposes, the gift is valid to the extent to which it has been acted on in good faith.

(d) A gift made by a document other than a will is effective on the death of the donor. The document may be a card designed to be carried by the donor. To be effective, the document must be signed by the donor in the presence of two witnesses. If the donor cannot sign the document, a person may sign the document for the donor at the donor's direction and in the presence of the donor and two witnesses. The witnesses to the signing of a document under this subsection must sign the document in the presence of the donor. Delivery of the document during the donor's lifetime is not necessary to make the gift valid.

(e) A gift made under this section by a person 18 years of age or older, including a gift made under Section 521.401, Transportation Code, shall be honored without obtaining the approval or consent of any other person.

Amended by Acts 1997, 75th Leg., ch. 165, § 30.211, eff. Sept. 1, 1997; Acts 1997, 75th Leg., ch. 225, § 3, eff. Sept. 1, 1997.

Statutes in Context

Close family members have the right to donate a person's organs even without the person's consent provided they have no actual notice of the person's contrary intent. Section 692.004 enumerates a priority order of these relatives with the person's spouse, adult children, parents, and adult siblings heading the list.

§ 692.004. Persons Who May Execute Gift

(a) The following persons, in the following priority, may give all or any part of a decedent's body for a purpose specified by Section 692.005:

(1) the decedent's spouse;

(2) the decedent's adult child;

(3) either of the decedent's parents;

(4) the decedent's adult brother or sister;

(5) the guardian of the person of the decedent at the time of death; or

(6) any other person authorized or under an obligation to dispose of the body.

(b) A person listed in Subsection (a) may make the gift only if:

(1) a person in a higher priority class is not available at the time of death;

(2) there is no actual notice of contrary indications by the decedent; and

(3) there is no actual notice of opposition by a member of the same or a higher priority class.

(c) A person listed in Subsection (a) may make the gift after death or immediately before death. The person must make the gift by a document signed by the person or by a telegraphic, recorded telephonic, or other recorded message.

Acts 1989, 71st Leg., ch. 678, § 1, eff. Sept. 1, 1989.

Statutes in Context

A donor may precisely designate the recipient of the anatomical gift and the purpose for which the gift may be used. For example, if the donor's sibling needs a kidney, the donor may specify that the only recipient of the donor's kidneys is this sibling. If the donor does not have a specific donee in mind, as is usually the case, the donor will not name a donee. Instead, any hospital may accept the gift. This is the normal scenario because the donor does not know when or where death will occur and which organs may be needed or useable. The donor may restrict the use of the gift even if no donee is named. Many people permit any organs to be taken for transplantation but do not want to relinquish their entire body, i.e., they do not want to be used as a cadaver for medical research or training. See §§ 692.005 and 692.006.

§ 692.005. Persons Who May Become Donees

(a) The following persons may be donees of gifts of bodies or parts of bodies:

(1) a qualified organ procurement organization, for distribution to another person who may be a donee under this section, to be used for transplantation;

(2) a hospital or physician, to be used only for therapy or transplantation;

(3) a bank or storage facility, to be used only therapy or transplantation;

(4) a person specified by a physician, to be used only for therapy or transplantation needed by the person;

(5) an eye bank the medical activities of which are directed by a physician; or

(6) the Anatomical Board of the State of Texas.

(b) The Anatomical Board of the State of Texas shall be the donee of gifts of bodies or parts of bodies made for education or research, which are subject to distribution by that board under Chapter 691.

Acts 1989, 71st Leg., ch. 678, § 1, eff. Sept. 1, 1989. Amended by Acts 1999, 76th Leg., ch. 615, § 2, eff. June 18, 1999; Acts 2003, 78th Leg., ch. 948, § 12, eff. Sept. 1, 2003.

§ 692.006. Designation of Donee or Physician

(a) A person may make a gift to a specified donee. If the person dies in this state and does not specify the donee and the gift is a vascular organ that is suitable for transplantation, a qualified organ procurement organization in this state is considered the specified donee. For any other gift that is not made to a specified donee, the attending physician may accept the gift as donee at the time of death or after death.

(b) If the gift is made to a specified donee who is not available at the time and place of death, the attending physician may accept the gift as donee at the time of death or after death unless the donor expressed an indication that the donor desired a different procedure.

(c) A physician who becomes a donee under Subsection (a) or (b) may not participate in the procedures for removing or transplanting a part.

(d) Notwithstanding Section 692.009, a donor may designate in the donor's will or document of gift the physician to perform the appropriate procedures. If the donor does not designate the physician, or if the physician is not available, the donee or other person authorized to accept the gift may employ or authorize any physician to perform the appropriate procedures.

Acts 1989, 71st Leg., ch. 678, § 1, eff. Sept. 1, 1989. Amended by Acts 1999, 76th Leg., ch. 615, § 3, eff. June 18, 1999.

§ 692.007. Delivery of Document

(a) If a donor makes a gift to a specified donee, the donor may deliver the will or document, or an executed copy, to the donee to expedite the appropriate procedures immediately after death. Delivery is not necessary to make the gift valid.

(b) The donor may deposit the will or other document, or an executed copy, in a hospital, registry office, or bank or storage facility that accepts the document for safekeeping or to facilitate the procedures after death.

(c) On or after the donor's death and on the request of an interested party, the person in possession of the document shall produce the document for examination.

Acts 1989, 71st Leg., ch. 678, § 1, eff. Sept. 1, 1989.

Statutes in Context

Section 692.008 explains how a donor may amend or revoke an anatomical gift document.

---

§ 692.008. Amendment or Revocation of Gift

(a) If the donor has delivered the will or other document, or executed copy, to a specified donee, the donor may amend or revoke the gift by:

(1) executing and delivering to the donee a signed statement;

(2) making an oral statement in the presence of two persons that is communicated to the donee;

(3) making a statement to an attending physician that is communicated to the donee; or

(4) executing a signed document that is found on the donor or found in the donor's effects.

(b) If the donor has not delivered the document of gift to the donee, the donor may revoke the gift in a manner prescribed by Subsection (a) or by destroying, canceling, or mutilating the document and each executed copy of the document.

(c) If the donor made the gift by will, the donor may revoke or amend the gift in a manner prescribed by Subsection (a) or in a manner prescribed for the amendment or revocation of a will.

Acts 1989, 71st Leg., ch. 678, § 1, eff. Sept. 1, 1989.

§ 692.009. Determination of Time of Death

The attending physician or, if none, the physician who certifies the death shall determine the time of death. That physician may not participate in the procedures for removing or transplanting a part.

Acts 1989, 71st Leg., ch. 678, § 1, eff. Sept. 1, 1989.

Statutes in Context

As with all gifts, the donee has the choice of accepting or rejecting an anatomical gift according to § 692.010.

---

§ 692.010. Acceptance or Rejection of Gift

(a) A donee may accept or reject a gift.

(b) If the donee or the donee's physician has actual notice of contrary indications by the decedent or has actual notice that a gift made under Section 692.004 is opposed by a member of the same or a higher priority class, the donee may not accept the gift.

(c) If a donee accepts a gift of an entire body, the decedent's surviving spouse or any other person authorized to give all or part of the body may authorize the body's embalming and have the use of the body for funeral services, subject to the terms of the gift.

(d) If a donee accepts a gift of a part, the donee shall cause the part to be removed from the body without unnecessary mutilation after death occurs and before the body is embalmed. After the part is removed, the surviving spouse, next of kin, or other person under

obligation to dispose of the body has custody of the body.
Acts 1989, 71st Leg., ch. 678, § 1, eff. Sept. 1, 1989.

§ 692.011. Examination for Medical Acceptability Authorized

A gift of all or part of a body authorizes any examination necessary to assure medical acceptability of the gift for the intended purposes.
Acts 1989, 71st Leg., ch. 678, § 1, eff. Sept. 1, 1989.

§ 692.012. Donee's Rights Superior

Except as prescribed by Section 692.015(a), a donee's rights that are created by a gift are superior to the rights of other persons.
Acts 1989, 71st Leg., ch. 678, § 1, eff. Sept. 1, 1989.

Statutes in Context

Sections 692.013 and 692.014 explain how hospitals are obligated to create protocols to identify potential organ donors and to discuss with their families the possibility of obtaining consent.

---

§ 692.013. Hospital Protocol

(a) Each hospital shall develop a protocol for identifying potential organ and tissue donors from among those persons who die in the hospital. The hospital shall make its protocol available to the public during the hospital's normal business hours.

(b) The protocol must:

(1) provide that the hospital use appropriately trained persons from an organ or tissue procurement organization to make inquiries relating to donations;

(2) encourage sensitivity to families' beliefs and circumstances in all discussions relating to the donations;

(3) establish guidelines based on accepted medical standards for determining if a person is medically suitable to donate organs or tissues; and

(4) provide for documentation of the inquiry and of its disposition in the decedent's medical records.

(c) The protocol must provide that an organ or tissue procurement organization is not required to make an inquiry under Section 692.014 if:

(1) the decedent is not medically suitable for donation based on the suitability guidelines established by the protocol; or

(2) the hospital or organ or tissue procurement organization has actual notice of an objection to the donation made by:

(A) the decedent;

(B) the person authorized to make the donation under Section 692.004, according to the priority established by that section; or

(C) an unavailable member of a higher priority class.

(d) An organ or tissue procurement organization that makes inquiries relating to donations shall develop a protocol for making those inquiries.
Acts 1989, 71st Leg., ch. 678, § 1, eff. Sept. 1, 1989. Amended by Acts 1991, 72nd Leg., ch. 291, § 3, eff. Sept. 1, 1991.

§ 692.014. Procedures

(a) At or near the time of notification of death, if it is unclear whether the decedent is or is not a donor, the organ or tissue procurement organization or its designee shall ask the person authorized to make an anatomical gift on behalf of the decedent under Section 692.004, according to the priority established by that section, whether the decedent is or is not a donor. The inquiry shall be made in accordance with the protocol established under Section 692.013 and with the procedures established under Subchapter Q, Chapter 521, Transportation Code.

(b) If the decedent is a donor 18 years of age or older, the decedent's anatomical gift made under Section 692.003, including a gift made under Section 521.401, Transportation Code, shall be honored without obtaining the approval or consent of any other person.

(c) A copy of the decedent's donor card or a decedent's driver's license or personal identification certificate with an affirmative statement of gift issued prior to September 1, 1997, is conclusive evidence of the decedent's status as a donor and serves as consent for the organ, tissue, or eye removal.

(d) If the decedent is not a declared donor, the organ or tissue procurement organization or its designee shall inform the person of the option to donate the decedent's organs, tissues, and eyes according to the procedures established under this chapter and under Subchapter Q, Chapter 521, Transportation Code.
Amended by Acts 1993, 73rd Leg., ch. 928, § 2, eff. Aug. 30, 1993; Acts 1997, 75th Leg., ch. 165, § 30.212, eff. Sept. 1, 1997; Acts 1997, 75th Leg., ch. 225, § 30.212, eff. Sept. 1, 1997.

§ 692.0145. Distribution of Vascular Organs for Transplantation

(a) A qualified organ procurement organization that receives the gift of a vascular organ that is suitable for transplantation shall distribute the organ for transplantation to an individual on a waiting list to be transplanted at a transplant center in this state.

(b) The qualified organ procurement organization may transfer a vascular organ to an out-of-state organ procurement organization or a suitable out-of-state recipient for transplantation if:

(1) a suitable recipient in this state cannot be found in a reasonable amount of time; or

(2) the transfer is made in accordance with a reciprocal agreement with an out-of-state organ procurement organization.
Added by Acts 1999, 76th Leg., ch. 615, § 4, eff. June 18, 1999.

§ 692.0147. Expired [December 31, 2000].

§ 692.015. Effect of Other Laws

(a) This chapter is subject to the laws of this state prescribing the powers and duties relating to autopsies.

(b) Sections 692.013 and 692.014 do not affect the laws relating to notification of the medical examiner or justice of the peace of each case of reportable death.

Acts 1989, 71st Leg., ch. 678, § 1, eff. Sept. 1, 1989.

Statutes in Context

Persons who in good faith act in accordance with the Anatomical Gift Act are protected from civil and criminal liability if they meet the requirements of § 692.016.

§ 692.016. Limitation of Liability

(a) A person who acts in good faith in accordance with this chapter is not liable for civil damages or subject to criminal prosecution for the person's action if the prerequisites for an anatomical gift are met under the laws applicable at the time and place the gift is made.

(b) A person who acts in good faith in accordance with Sections 692.013 and 692.014 is not liable as a result of the action except in the case of an act or omission of the person that is intentional, wilfully or wantonly negligent, or done with conscious indifference or reckless disregard. For purposes of this subsection, "good faith" in determining the appropriate person authorized to make a donation under Section 692.004 means making a reasonable effort to locate and contact the member or members of the highest priority class who are available at or near the time of death.

Acts 1989, 71st Leg., ch. 678, § 1, eff. Sept. 1, 1989. Amended by Acts 2001, 77th Leg., ch. 1388, § 1, eff. June 16. 2001.

Chapter 693. Removal of Body Parts, Body Tissue, and Corneal Tissue

Statutes in Context

Chapter 693 permits certain government officials to allow the removal of certain organs without the consent of the donor or the donor's family.

Subchapter A. Removal of Body Parts or Tissue

§ 693.001. Definition

In this subchapter, "visceral organ" means the heart, kidney, liver, or other organ or tissue that requires a patient support system to maintain the viability of the organ or tissue.

Acts 1989, 71st Leg., ch. 678, § 1, eff. Sept. 1, 1989.

Statutes in Context

Upon a request from a qualified organ procurement organization, the medical examiner may, if certain conditions are satisfied, permit the removal of organs from a decedent who died under circumstances requiring an inquest by the medical examiner even without the consent of a family member. See §§ 693.002 - 693.004.

§ 693.002. Removal of Body Part or Tissue from Decedent Who Died Under Circumstances Requiring an Inquest

(a)(1) On a request from a qualified organ procurement organization, as defined in Section 692.002, the medical examiner, justice of the peace, county judge, or physician designated by the justice of the peace or county judge may permit the removal of organs from a decedent who died under circumstances requiring an inquest by the medical examiner, justice of the peace, or county judge if consent is obtained pursuant to Section 693.003.

(2) If no autopsy is required, the organs to be transplanted shall be released in a timely manner to the qualified organ procurement organization, as defined in Section 692.002, for removal and transplantation.

(3) If an autopsy is required and the medical examiner, justice of the peace, county judge, or designated physician determines that the removal of the organs will not interfere with the subsequent course of an investigation or autopsy, the organs shall be released in a timely manner for removal and transplantation. The autopsy will be performed in a timely manner following the removal of the organs.

(4) If the medical examiner is considering withholding one or more organs of a potential donor for any reason, the medical examiner shall be present during the removal of the organs. In such case, the medical examiner may request a biopsy of those organs or deny removal of the anatomical gift. If the medical examiner denies removal of the anatomical gift, the medical examiner shall explain in writing the reasons for the denial. The medical examiner shall provide the explanation to:

(A) the qualified organ procurement organization; and

(B) any person listed in Section 693.004 who consented to the removal.

(5) If the autopsy is not being performed by a medical examiner and one or more organs may be withheld, the justice of the peace, county judge, or designated physician shall be present during the removal of the organs and may request the biopsy or deny removal of the anatomical gift. If removal of the anatomical gift is denied, the justice of the peace, county judge, or physician shall provide the written explanation required by Subdivisions (4)(A) and (B).

(6) If, in performing the duties required by this subsection, the medical examiner or, in those cases in which an autopsy is not performed by a medical examiner, the justice of the peace, county judge, or designated physician is required to be present at the hospital to examine the decedent prior to removal of the organs or during the procedure to remove the organs, the qualified organ procurement organization shall on request reimburse the county or the entity designated by the county for the actual costs incurred in performing such duties, not to exceed $1,000. Such reimbursements shall be deposited in the general fund of the county. The payment shall be applied to the additional costs incurred by the office of the medical examiner, justice of the peace, or county judge in performing such duties, including the cost of providing coverage beyond regular business hours. The payment shall be used to facilitate the timely procurement of organs in a manner consistent with the preservation of the organs for the purposes of transplantation.

(7) At the request of the medical examiner or, in those cases in which an autopsy is not performed by a medical examiner, the justice of the peace, county judge, or designated physician, the health care professional removing organs from a decedent who died under circumstances requiring an inquest shall file with the medical examiner, justice of the peace, or county judge a report detailing the condition of the organs removed and their relationship, if any, to the cause of death.

(b) On a request from a qualified tissue procurement organization, as defined in Section 692.002, the medical examiner may permit the removal of tissue believed to be clinically usable for transplants or other therapy or treatment from a decedent who died under circumstances requiring an inquest if consent is obtained pursuant to Section 693.003 or, if consent is not required by that section, no objection by a person listed in Section 693.004 is known by the medical examiner. If the medical examiner denies removal of the tissue, the medical examiner shall explain in writing the reasons for the denial. The medical examiner shall provide the explanation to:

(1) the qualified tissue procurement organization; and

(2) the person listed in Section 693.004 who consented to the removal.

(c) If the autopsy is not being performed by a medical examiner, the justice of the peace, county judge, or designated physician may permit the removal of tissue in the same manner as a medical examiner under Subsection (b). If removal of the anatomical gift is denied, the justice of the peace, county judge, or physician shall provide the written explanation required by Subsections (b)(1) and (2).

Acts 1989, 71st Leg., ch. 678, § 1, eff. Sept. 1, 1989. Amended by Acts 1995, 74th Leg., ch. 523, § 1, eff. June 13, 1995; Acts 2003, 78th Leg., ch. 1220, § 1, eff. July 1, 2003.

§ 693.003. Consent Required in Certain Circumstances

(a) A medical examiner or a person acting on the authority of a medical examiner may not remove a visceral organ unless the medical examiner or person obtains the consent of a person listed in Section 693.004.

(b) If a person listed in Section 693.004 is known and available within four hours after death is pronounced, a medical examiner or a person acting on the authority of a medical examiner may not remove a nonvisceral organ or tissue unless the medical examiner or person obtains that person's consent.

(c) If a person listed in Section 693.004 cannot be identified and contacted within four hours after death is pronounced and the medical examiner determines that no reasonable likelihood exists that a person can be identified and contacted during the four-hour period, the medical examiner may permit the removal of a nonvisceral organ or tissue.

Acts 1989, 71st Leg., ch. 678, § 1, eff. Sept. 1, 1989.

§ 693.004. Persons Who May Consent or Object to Removal

The following persons may consent or object to the removal of tissue or a body part:

(1) the decedent's spouse;

(2) the decedent's adult children, if there is no spouse;

(3) the decedent's parents, if there is no spouse or adult child; or

(4) the decedent's brothers or sisters, if there is no spouse, adult child, or parent.

Acts 1989, 71st Leg., ch. 678, § 1, eff. Sept. 1, 1989.

§ 693.005. Immunity from Damages in Civil Action

In a civil action brought by a person listed in Section 693.004 who did not object before the removal of tissue or a body part specified by Section 693.002, a medical examiner, justice of the peace, county judge, medical facility, physician acting on permission of a medical examiner, justice of the peace, or county judge, or person assisting a physician is not liable for damages on a theory of civil recovery based on a contention that the plaintiff's consent was required before the body part or tissue could be removed.

Acts 1989, 71st Leg., ch. 678, § 1, eff. Sept. 1, 1989. Amended by Acts 2003, 78th Leg., ch. 1220, § 1, eff. July 1, 2003.

Subchapter B. Removal of Corneal Tissue

Statutes in Context

Sections 693.011 - 693.024 authorize the justice of the peace or the medical examiner to permit the taking of corneal tissue if all of the following requirements are satisfied: the decedent/donor died under

circumstances requiring an inquest, no objection by the decedent's spouse is known (or if no spouse, decedent's adult children, or if no spouse and no adult children, the decedent's parents, or if no parents, adult children, or spouse, the decedent's brothers or sisters), and the removal of corneal tissue will not interfere with the subsequent course of an investigation or autopsy, or alter the decedent's postmortem facial appearance.

---

§ 693.011. Definition

In this subchapter, "eye bank" means a nonprofit corporation chartered under the laws of this state to obtain, store, and distribute donor eyes to be used by persons licensed to practice medicine for corneal transplants, research, or other medical purposes and the medical activities of which are directed by a person licensed to practice medicine in this state.
Acts 1989, 71st Leg., ch. 678, § 1, eff. Sept. 1, 1989.

§ 693.012. Removal of Corneal Tissue Permitted Under Certain Circumstances

On a request from an authorized official of an eye bank for corneal tissue, a justice of the peace or medical examiner may permit the removal of corneal tissue if:

(1) the decedent from whom the tissue is to be removed died under circumstances requiring an inquest by the justice of the peace or medical examiner;

(2) no objection by a person listed in Section 693.013 is known by the justice of the peace or medical examiner; and

(3) the removal of the corneal tissue will not interfere with the subsequent course of an investigation or autopsy or alter the decedent's postmortem facial appearance.

Acts 1989, 71st Leg., ch. 678, § 1, eff. Sept. 1, 1989.

§ 693.013. Persons Who May Object to Removal

The following persons may object to the removal of corneal tissue:

(1) the decedent's spouse;

(2) the decedent's adult children, if there is no spouse;

(3) the decedent's parents, if there is no spouse or adult child; or

(4) the decedent's brothers or sisters, if there is no spouse, adult child, or parent.

Acts 1989, 71st Leg., ch. 678, § 1, eff. Sept. 1, 1989.

§ 693.014. Immunity From Damages in Civil Action

(a) In a civil action brought by a person listed in Section 693.013 who did not object before the removal of corneal tissue, a medical examiner, justice of the peace, or eye bank official is not liable for damages on a theory of civil recovery based on a contention that the person's consent was required before the corneal tissue could be removed.

(b) Chapter 104, Civil Practice and Remedies Code, applies to a justice of the peace, medical examiner, and their personnel who remove, permit removal, or deny removal of corneal tissue under this subchapter as if the justice of the peace, medical examiner, and their personnel were state officers or employees.
Acts 1989, 71st Leg., ch. 678, § 1, eff. Sept. 1, 1989.

Subchapter C. Eye Enucleation

§ 693.021. Definition

In this chapter, "ophthalmologist" means a person licensed to practice medicine who specializes in treating eye diseases.
Acts 1989, 71st Leg., ch. 678, § 1, eff. Sept. 1, 1989.

§ 693.022. Persons Who May Enucleate Eye as Anatomical Gift

Only the following persons may Enucleate an eye that is an anatomical gift:

(1) a licensed physician;

(2) a licensed doctor of dental surgery or medical dentistry;

(3) a licensed embalmer; or

(4) a technician supervised by a physician.

Acts 1989, 71st Leg., ch. 678, § 1, eff. Sept. 1, 1989.

§ 693.023. Eye Enucleation Course

Each person, other than a licensed physician, who performs an eye enucleation must complete a course in eye enucleation taught by an ophthalmologist and must possess a certificate showing that the course has been completed.
Acts 1989, 71st Leg., ch. 678, § 1, eff. Sept. 1, 1989.

§ 693.024. Requisites of Eye Enucleation Course

The course in eye enucleation prescribed by Section 693.023 must include instruction in:

(1) the anatomy and physiology of the eye;

(2) maintaining a sterile field during the procedure;

(3) use of the appropriate instruments; and

(4) procedures for the sterile removal of the corneal button and the preservation of it in a preservative fluid.

Acts 1989, 71st Leg., ch. 678, § 1, eff. Sept. 1, 1989.

Subtitle C. Cemeteries

Chapter 711. General Provisions Relating to Cemeteries

Subchapter A. General Provisions

Statutes in Context

A significant number of individuals are deeply concerned about how their bodies will be disposed of upon

death. Many people have strong preferences regarding the disposition method, that is, burial or cremation. Other individuals wish to spell out the particulars of their funeral in great detail such as the location of the burial, whether the viewing is open or closed casket, the type of religious service, the inscription on the headstone, the kind of flowers and music, and the contents of the obituary. The legal systems of the ancient Greeks and Romans gave great weight to the deceased's instructions concerning bodily disposition. However, the common-law courts recognized no property rights in a dead body. This view gained widespread acceptance in the United States and thus a person's desires regarding disposition of the body were considered to be only precatory. A growing number of states have rejected this rule and recognize a person's right to determine the final disposition of the body.

The 1993 Texas Legislature took significant action to make it easier for a person to exercise the right to control the disposition of the person's remains when it made significant changes to § 711.002. Top priority for the disposition of remains is given to the expressed directions of the decedent. The directions must be in writing and may be contained in the following documents: (1) a will, (2) a prepaid funeral contract, or (3) a signed and acknowledged written instrument.

Second priority is granted to a special agent the decedent appointed for the purpose of controlling the disposition of the decedent's remains. This is a tremendous departure from normal agency law which provides that an agent's power, even one granted in a durable power, ends upon the principal's death. The statute supplies a model fill-in-the-blank form to make it simple and inexpensive for a person to appoint an agent, successor agents, and to state any special instructions. The agency appointment document must meet the following requirements: (1) substantially comply with the statutory form, (2) be properly completed, (3) be signed by the decedent, (4) be signed by the agent and each successor agent, and (5) contain an acknowledgment of the decedent's signature.

If the decedent left no binding instructions and did not properly appoint an agent, the following people in the priority listed have the right and duty to dispose of the decedent's remains: (1) the decedent's surviving spouse, (2) any one of the decedent's adult children, (3) either one of the decedent's parents, (4) any one of the decedent's adult siblings, and (5) any adult in the next degree of kinship determined as if the person died intestate.

The statute provides no penalty for failure to comply with the decedent's wishes.

---

§ 711.002. Disposition of Remains; Duty to Inter

(a) Unless a decedent has left directions in writing for the disposition of the decedent's remains as provided in Subsection (g), the following persons, in the priority listed, have the right to control the disposition, including cremation, of the decedent's remains, shall inter the remains, and are liable for the reasonable cost of interment:

(1) the person designated in a written instrument signed by the decedent;

(2) the decedent's surviving spouse;

(3) any one of the decedent's surviving adult children;

(4) either one of the decedent's surviving parents;

(5) any one of the decedent's surviving adult siblings; or

(6) any adult person in the next degree of kinship in the order named by law to inherit the estate of the decedent.

(b) The written instrument referred to in Subsection (a)(1) shall be in substantially the following form:

APPOINTMENT OF AGENT TO CONTROL
DISPOSITION OF REMAINS

I,
______________________________,
(your name and address)
being of sound mind, willfully and voluntarily make known my desire that, upon my death, the disposition of my remains shall be controlled by
______________________ (name of agent) in accordance with Section 711.002 of the Health and Safety Code and, with respect to that subject only, I hereby appoint such person as my agent (attorney-in-fact).

All decisions made by my agent with respect to the disposition of my remains, including cremation, shall be binding.

SPECIAL DIRECTIONS:
Set forth below are any special directions limiting the power granted to my agent:
____
____
____
____
____

AGENT:
Name:
____
Address:
____
Telephone Number:
____
Acceptance of Appointment:
____
(signature of agent)
Date of Signature: __________

SUCCESSORS:
If my agent dies, becomes legally disabled, resigns, or refuses to act, I hereby appoint the following persons (each to act alone and successively, in the order named) to serve as my agent (attorney-in-fact) to control the disposition of my remains as authorized by this document:
1. First Successor
Name:
____

Address:

Telephone Number:

Acceptance of Appointment:

(signature of first successor)
Date of Signature: ________

2. Second Successor
Name:

Address:

Telephone Number:

Acceptance of Appointment:

(signature of second successor)
Date of Signature:

DURATION:
This appointment becomes effective upon my death.

PRIOR APPOINTMENTS REVOKED:
I hereby revoke any prior appointment of any person to control the disposition of my remains.

RELIANCE:
I hereby agree that any cemetery organization, business operating a crematory or columbarium or both, funeral director or embalmer, or funeral establishment who receives a copy of this document may act under it. Any modification or revocation of this document is not effective as to any such party until that party receives actual notice of the modification or revocation. No such party shall be liable because of reliance on a copy of this document.

ASSUMPTION:
THE AGENT, AND EACH SUCCESSOR AGENT, BY ACCEPTING THIS APPOINTMENT, ASSUMES THE OBLIGATIONS PROVIDED IN, AND IS BOUND BY THE PROVISIONS OF, SECTION 711.002 OF THE HEALTH AND SAFETY CODE.
Signed this ________ day of _________, 19__.
______________ (your signature)
State of __________ County of _________
This document was acknowledged before me on _________ (date) by _________________ (name of principal).
__________________________ (signature of notarial officer)
(Seal, if any, of notary)
__________________________ (printed name)
My commission expires: _________

(c) A written instrument is legally sufficient under Subsection (a)(1) if the wording of the instrument complies substantially with Subsection (b), the instrument is properly completed, the instrument is signed by the decedent, the agent, and each successor agent, and the signature of the decedent is acknowledged. Such written instrument may be modified or revoked only by a subsequent written instrument that complies with this subsection.

(d) A person listed in Subsection (a) has the right, duty, and liability provided by that subsection only if there is no person in a priority listed before the person.

(e) If there is no person with the duty to inter under Subsection (a) and:

(1) an inquest is held, the person conducting the inquest shall inter the remains; and

(2) an inquest is not held, the county in which the death occurred shall inter the remains.

(f) A person who represents that the person knows the identity of a decedent and, in order to procure the disposition, including cremation, of the decedent's remains, signs an order or statement, other than a death certificate, warrants the identity of the decedent and is liable for all damages that result, directly or indirectly, from that warrant.

(g) A person may provide written directions for the disposition, including cremation, of the person's remains in a will, a prepaid funeral contract, or a written instrument signed and acknowledged by such person. The directions may govern the inscription to be placed on a grave marker attached to any plot in which the decedent had the right of sepulture at the time of death and in which plot the decedent is subsequently interred. The directions may be modified or revoked only by a subsequent writing signed and acknowledged by such person. The person otherwise entitled to control the disposition of a decedent's remains under this section shall faithfully carry out the directions of the decedent to the extent that the decedent's estate or the person controlling the disposition are financially able to do so.

(h) If the directions are in a will, they shall be carried out immediately without the necessity of probate. If the will is not probated or is declared invalid for testamentary purposes, the directions are valid to the extent to which they have been acted on in good faith.

(i) A cemetery organization, a business operating a crematory or columbarium or both, a funeral director or an embalmer, or a funeral establishment shall not be liable for carrying out the written directions of a decedent or the directions of any person who represents that the person is entitled to control the disposition of the decedent's remains.

(j) In the absence of evidence of a contrary intent, it is presumed that a married woman directs that her name, as it appears on the grave marker for the plot in which she is interred, include the same last name she used at the time of her death.

(k) Any dispute among any of the persons listed in Subsection (a) concerning their right to control the disposition, including cremation, of a decedent's remains shall be resolved by a court of competent jurisdiction. A cemetery organization or funeral establishment shall not be liable for refusing to accept the decedent's remains, or to inter or otherwise dispose of the decedent's remains, until it receives a court order or other suitable confirmation that the dispute has been resolved or settled.

Acts 1989, 71st Leg., ch. 678, § 1, eff. Sept. 1, 1989. Amended by Acts 1991, 72nd Leg., ch. 14, § 213, eff. Sept.

1, 1991. Amended by Acts 1993, 73rd Leg., ch. 634, § 2, eff. Sept. 1, 1993; Acts 1997, 75th Leg., ch. 967, § 1, eff. Sept. 1, 1997; Acts 1999, 76th Leg., ch. 1385, § 1, eff. Aug. 30, 1999.

Subchapter C. Cemetery Organizations

Statutes in Context

A burial plot is presumed to be the separate property of the person named as the grantee in the certificate of ownership or the deed to the plot under § 711.039. The spouse of the grantee has a vested right of interment for the spouse's remains in the plot while (1) the spouse is married to the plot owner, or (2) if the spouse is married to the plot owner at the time of the plot owner's death. Unless the spouse either (1) joins in a conveyance, or (2) consents in writing and attaches the consent to the conveyance, any attempted conveyance will not divest the spouse of the vested right of interment.

A plot owner who is interred in the plot and who wishes to transfer all rights in the plot must either (1) make a *specific* disposition of the plot by express reference to the plot in the plot owner's will (a gift of "all my property" would not transfer the burial plot), or (2) file and record a written declaration in the office of the cemetery organization. If the plot owner does not do so, then (1) a grave, niche, or crypt in the plot is reserved for the plot owner's surviving spouse, and (2) the plot owner's children, in order of need, have the right to be interred in any remaining locations in the plot without the consent of a person claiming an interest in the plot.

§ 711.039. Rights of Interment in Plot

(a) A plot in which the exclusive right of sepulture is conveyed is presumed to be the separate property of the person named as grantee in the certificate of ownership or other instrument of conveyance.

(b) The spouse of a person to whom the exclusive right of sepulture in a plot is conveyed has a vested right of interment of the spouse's remains in the plot while the spouse is married to the plot owner or if the spouse is married to the plot owner at the time of the owner's death.

(c) An attempted conveyance or other action without the joinder or written, attached consent of the spouse of the plot owner does not divest the spouse of the vested right of interment.

(d) The vested right of interment is terminated:

(1) on the final decree of divorce between the plot owner and the owner's former spouse unless the decree provides otherwise; or

(2) when the remains of the person having the vested right are interred elsewhere.

(e) Unless a plot owner who has the exclusive right of sepulture in a plot and who is interred in that plot has made a specific disposition of the plot by express reference to the plot in the owners will or by written declaration filed and recorded in the office of the cemetery organization:

(1) a grave, niche, or crypt in the plot shall be reserved for the surviving spouse of the plot owner; and

(2) the owner's children, in order of need, may be interred in any remaining graves, niches, or crypts of the plot without the consent of a person claiming an interest in the plot.

(f) The surviving spouse or a child of an interred plot owner may each waive his right of interment in the plot in favor of a relative of the owner or relative of the owner's spouse. The person in whose favor the waiver is made may be interred in the plot.

(g) The exclusive right of sepulture in an unused grave, niche, or crypt of a plot in which the plot owner has been interred may be conveyed only by:

(1) specific disposition of the unused grave, niche, or crypt by express reference to it in a will or by written declaration of the plot owner filed and recorded in the office of the cemetery organization; or

(2) the surviving spouse if any, and the heirs-at-law of the owner.

(h) Unless a deceased plot owner who has the exclusive right of sepulture in a plot and who is not interred in the plot has otherwise made specific disposition of the plot, the exclusive right of sepulture in the plot, except the one grave, niche, or crypt reserved for the surviving spouse, if any, vests on the death of the owner in the owner's heirs-at-law and may be conveyed by them.

Amended by Acts 1993, 73rd Leg., ch. 634, § 20, eff. Sept. 1, 1993; Acts 2001, 77th Leg., ch. 502, § 1, eff. Sept. 1, 2001.

Chapter 712. Perpetual Care Cemeteries

Subchapter B. Perpetual Care Trust Fund

Statutes in Context

Sections 712.021 and 712.030 address issues concerning perpetual care cemeteries.

§ 712.021. Establishment and Purposes of Fund

(a) A corporation that operates a perpetual care cemetery in this state shall have a fund established with a trust company or a bank with trust powers that is located in this state. The trust company or bank may not have more than one director who is also a director of the corporation.

(b) The principal of the fund may not be reduced voluntarily, and it must remain inviolable. The trustee shall maintain the principal of the fund separate from all operating funds of the corporation.

(c) In establishing a fund, the corporation may adopt plans for the general care, maintenance, and embellishment of its perpetual care cemetery.

(d) The fund and the trustee are governed by the Texas Trust Code (Section 111.001 et seq., Property Code).

(e) A corporation that establishes a fund may receive and hold for the fund and as a part of the fund or as an incident to the fund any property contributed to the fund.

(f) The fund and contributions to the fund are for charitable purposes. The perpetual care financed by the fund is:

(1) the discharge of a duty due from the corporation to persons interred and to be interred in its perpetual care cemetery; and

(2) for the benefit and protection of the public by preserving and keeping the perpetual care cemetery from becoming a place of disorder, reproach, and desolation in the community in which the perpetual care cemetery is located.

(g) The trustors of two or more perpetual care trust funds may establish a common trust fund in which deposits required by this chapter are made, provided that separate records of principal and income are maintained for each perpetual care cemetery for the benefit of which the common trust fund is established, and further provided that the income attributable to each perpetual care cemetery is used only for the perpetual care of that cemetery.

Acts 1989, 71st Leg., ch. 678, § 1, eff. Sept. 1, 1989. Amended by Acts 1993, 73rd Leg., ch. 634, § 31, eff. Sept. 1, 1993.

§ 712.030. Use of Gift for Special Care of Plot in Perpetual Care Cemetery

A trustee may take and hold property transferred to the trustee in trust in order to apply the principal, proceeds, or income of the property for any purpose consistent with the purpose of a corporation's perpetual care cemetery, including:

(1) the improvement or embellishment of any part of the perpetual care cemetery;

(2) the erection, renewal, repair, or preservation of a monument, fence, building, or other structure in the perpetual care cemetery;

(3) planting or cultivating plants in or around the perpetual care cemetery; or

(4) taking special care of or embellishing a plot, section, or building in the perpetual care cemetery.

Acts 1989, 71st Leg., ch. 678, § 1, eff. Sept. 1, 1989. Amended by Acts 1993, 73rd Leg., ch. 634, § 40, eff. Sept. 1, 1993.

X.
INSURANCE CODE

Title7. Life Insurance and Annuities

Subtitle A. Life Insurance in General

Chapter 1103. Life Insurance Policy Beneficiaries

Subchapter D. Forfeiture of BENEFICIARY'S Rights

Statutes in Context

Section 1103.151 provides that a beneficiary of a life insurance policy who wilfully kills the insured may not collect the proceeds and § 1103.152 explains how the contingent beneficiary in the policy is then normally entitled to the proceeds.

§ 1103.151. Forfeiture

A beneficiary of a life insurance policy or contract forfeits the beneficiary's interest in the policy or contract if the beneficiary is a principal or an accomplice in wilfully bringing about the death of the insured.
Added by Acts 2001, 77th Leg., ch. 1419, § 2, eff. June 1, 2003.

§ 1103.152. Payment of Proceeds to Contingent Beneficiary or to Relative

(a) Except as provided by Subsection (b), if a beneficiary of a life insurance policy or contract forfeits an interest in the policy or contract under Section 1103.151, a contingent beneficiary named by the insured in the policy or contract is entitled to receive the proceeds of the policy or contract.

(b) A contingent beneficiary is not entitled to receive the proceeds of a life insurance policy or contract if the contingent beneficiary forfeits an interest in the policy or contract under Section 1103.151.

(c) If there is not a contingent beneficiary entitled to receive the proceeds of a life insurance policy or contract under Subsection (a), the nearest relative of the insured is entitled to receive those proceeds.
Added by Acts 2001, 77th Leg., ch. 1419, § 2, eff. June 1, 2003.

Chapter 1104. Life Insurance and Annuity Contracts Issued to Certain Persons

Subchapter B. Trustee Named as Beneficiary of Life Insurance Policy

Statutes in Context

A trustee of an inter vivos trust or testamentary may be named as the beneficiary of a life insurance policy under §§ 1104.021 - 1104.025. This is consistent with Property Code § 111.004(12).

§ 1104.021. Trustee Named as Beneficiary in Policy

(a) An individual may make a trust agreement providing that the proceeds of a life insurance policy insuring the individual be made payable to a trustee named as beneficiary in the policy. The validity of a trust agreement or declaration of trust that designates a beneficiary of a life insurance policy is not affected by whether any corpus of the trust exists in addition to the right of the trustee to receive insurance proceeds.

(b) Life insurance policy proceeds described by Subsection (a) shall be paid to the trustee. The trustee shall hold and dispose of the proceeds as provided by the trust agreement.
Added by Acts 2001, 77th Leg., ch. 1419, § 2, eff. June 1, 2003.

§ 1104.022. Trustee Named as Beneficiary in Will

(a) A life insurance policy may provide that the beneficiary of the policy be a trustee designated by will in accordance with the policy provisions and the requirements of the insurance company.

(b) Except as provided by Subsection (c), on probate of a will described by Subsection (a), the life insurance policy proceeds shall be paid to the trustee. The trustee shall hold and dispose of the proceeds as provided under the terms of the will as the will existed on the date of the testator's death and in the same manner as other testamentary trusts are administered.

(c) Except as otherwise provided by agreement with the insurance company during the life of the insured, the insurance company shall pay the life insurance policy proceeds to the executors, administrators, or assigns of the insured if, during the 18-month period beginning on the first day after the date of the insured's death:

(1) a qualified trustee does not make to the insurance company a claim to the proceeds; or

(2) the insurance company is provided satisfactory evidence showing that there is or will be no trustee to receive the proceeds.

Added by Acts 2001, 77th Leg., ch. 1419, § 2, eff. June 1, 2003.

§ 1104.023. Debts; Inheritance Tax

Life insurance policy proceeds received by a trustee under this subchapter are not subject to debts of the insured or to inheritance tax to any greater extent than if the proceeds were payable to a beneficiary other than the executor or administrator of the insured's estate.

Added by Acts 2001, 77th Leg., ch. 1419, § 2, eff. June 1, 2003.

§ 1104.024. Commingling

Life insurance policy proceeds received by a trustee under this subchapter may be commingled with any other assets properly coming into the trust.

Added by Acts 2001, 77th Leg., ch. 1419, § 2, eff. June 1, 2003.

§ 1104.025. Certain Prior Beneficiary Designations Not Affected

This subchapter does not affect the validity of a life insurance policy beneficiary designation made before July 1, 1967, that names as beneficiary a trustee of a trust established by will.

Added by Acts 2001, 77th Leg., ch. 1419, § 2, eff. June 1, 2003.

Chapter 1108. Benefits Exempt From Seizure

Statutes in Context

Sections 1108.001 - 1108.102 protect payments from many life insurance policies and annuity plans from creditors of both the insured and the beneficiary.

Subchapter A. General Provisions

§ 1108.001. Construction With Other Law

The exemptions under this chapter are in addition to the exemptions from garnishment, attachment, execution, or other seizure under Chapter 42, Property Code.

Added by Acts 2001, 77th Leg., ch. 1419, § 2, eff. June 1, 2003.

§ 1108.002. Annuity Contracts

For purposes of regulation under this code, an annuity contract is considered an insurance policy or contract if the annuity contract is issued:

(1) by a life, health, or accident insurance company, including a mutual company or fraternal benefit society; or

(2) under an annuity or benefit plan used by an employer or individual.

Added by Acts 2001, 77th Leg., ch. 1419, § 2, eff. June 1, 2003.

Subchapter B. Exemptions From Seizure

§ 1108.051. Exemptions for Certain Insurance and Annuity Benefits

(a) Except as provided by Section 1108.053, this section applies to any benefits, including the cash value and proceeds of an insurance policy, to be provided to an insured or beneficiary under:

(1) an insurance policy or annuity contract issued by a life, health, or accident insurance company, including a mutual company or fraternal benefit society; or

(2) an annuity or benefit plan used by an employer or individual.

(b) Notwithstanding any other provision of this code, insurance or annuity benefits described by Subsection (a):

(1) inure exclusively to the benefit of the person for whose use and benefit the insurance or annuity is designated in the policy or contract; and

(2) are fully exempt from:

(A) garnishment, attachment, execution, or other seizure;

(B) seizure, appropriation, or application by any legal or equitable process or by operation of law to pay a debt or other liability of an insured or of a beneficiary, either before or after the benefits are provided; and

(C) a demand in a bankruptcy proceeding of the insured or beneficiary.

Added by Acts 2001, 77th Leg., ch. 1419, § 2, eff. June 1, 2003.

§ 1108.052. Exemptions Unaffected by Beneficiary Designation

The exemptions provided by Section 1108.051 apply regardless of whether:

(1) the power to change the beneficiary is reserved to the insured; or

(2) the insured or the insured's estate is a contingent beneficiary.

Added by Acts 2001, 77th Leg., ch. 1419, § 2, eff. June 1, 2003.

§ 1108.053. Exceptions to Exemptions

The exemptions provided by Section 1108.051 do not apply to:

(1) a premium payment made in fraud of a creditor, subject to the applicable statute of limitations for recovering the payment;

(2) a debt of the insured or beneficiary secured by a pledge of the insurance policy or the proceeds of the policy; or

(3) a child support lien or levy under Chapter 157, Family Code.

Added by Acts 2001, 77th Leg., ch. 1419, § 2, eff. June 1, 2003. Amended by Acts 2003, 78th Leg., ch. 1276, § 10A.301(a), eff. Sept. 1, 2003.

Subchapter C. Assignment of Benefits

§ 1108.101. Assignment Generally

This chapter does not prevent an insured, owner, or annuitant from assigning, in accordance with the terms of the policy or contract:

(1) any benefits to be provided under an insurance policy or annuity contract to which this chapter applies; or

(2) any other rights under the policy or contract.

Added by Acts 2001, 77th Leg., ch. 1419, § 2, eff. June 1, 2003.

§ 1108.102. Certain Assignments Void

If an insurance policy, annuity contract, or annuity or benefit plan described by Section 1108.051 prohibits a beneficiary from assigning or commuting benefits to be provided or other rights under the policy, contract, or plan, an assignment or commutation or attempted assignment or commutation of the benefits or rights by the beneficiary is void.

Added by Acts 2001, 77th Leg., ch. 1419, § 2, eff. June 1, 2003.

Chapter 1111. Life and Viatical Settlements and Accelerated Term Life Insurance Benefits

Statutes in Context

Two innovative uses of life insurance can provide valuable benefits to an insured while the insured is still alive but facing a rapidly approaching death. One technique involves a life insurance policy that requires the insurer to prepay all or a portion of the death benefit to the insured when the insured has a disabling or life-threatening condition which doctors predict will cause death within a relatively short period of time. These provisions are referred to by terms such as *accelerated death benefit*, *living needs benefit*, *acceleration-of-life-insurance benefit*, and *living payout option*. The insured may then use the proceeds to offset health care expenses. Depending on the debilitating extent of the illness, the extra money also may allow the insured to enjoy the remainder of the insured's life to its fullest such as by taking a vacation before the insured becomes too ill to do so. Some policies also will provide benefits to pay for a life-saving organ transplant. State governments have been quick to authorize insurance companies to offer policies that contain accelerated benefits. By the end of 1991, the insurance commissions of all states had authorized accelerated benefits.

The other technique provides basically the same result but through a different means. In a *viatical settlement*, a third party purchases the life insurance policy of an insured (the *viator*) who has a life-threatening disease or illness. The insured receives a one-time payment which usually ranges from 50 to 80 percent of the policy's face value or the insured may elect to receive periodic payments. Most purchasers require the insured to have two years or less to live. The shorter the insured's life expectancy, the greater the purchase price will be. The purchaser becomes the owner of the policy and typically names itself as the beneficiary. The purchaser continues to pay any required premiums and receives the policy's entire face value when the insured dies.

Chapter 1111 regulates viatical settlements in §§ 1111.001 -1111.006 and accelerated term life insurance benefits in §§ 1111.051 - 1111.053.

Subchapter A. Life and Viatical Settlements

§ 1111.001. Definitions

In this subchapter:

(1) "Life settlement" means an agreement that is solicited, negotiated, offered, entered into, delivered, or issued for delivery in this state under which a person pays anything of value that is:

(A) less than the expected death benefit of a policy insuring the life of an individual who does not have a catastrophic or life-threatening illness or condition; and

(B) paid in return for the policy owner's or certificate holder's assignment, transfer, bequest, devise, or sale of the death benefit under or ownership of the policy.

(2) "Person" means an individual, corporation, trust, partnership, association, or any other legal entity.

(3) "Viatical settlement" means an agreement that is solicited, negotiated, offered, entered into, delivered, or issued for delivery in this state under which a person pays anything of value that is:

(A) less than the expected death benefit of a policy insuring the life of an individual who has a catastrophic or life-threatening illness or condition; and

(B) paid in return for the policy owner's or certificate holder's assignment, transfer, bequest, devise, or sale of the death benefit under or ownership of the policy.

Added by Acts 2001, 77th Leg., ch. 1419, § 2, eff. June 1, 2003.

§ 1111.002. Purpose

The purpose of this subchapter is to:

(1) provide for registration of persons engaged in the business of life or viatical settlements; and

(2) provide consumer protection for a person who may sell or otherwise transfer the person's life insurance policy.

Added by Acts 2001, 77th Leg., ch. 1419, § 2, eff. June 1, 2003.

§ 1111.003. Rules; Registration and Regulation

(a) To implement this subchapter, the commissioner shall adopt reasonable rules relating to life settlements and relating to viatical settlements.

(b) The rules adopted by the commissioner under this section must include rules governing:

(1) registration of a person engaged in the business of life settlements;

(2) registration of a person engaged in the business of viatical settlements;

(3) approval of contract forms;

(4) disclosure requirements;

(5) prohibited practices relating to:

(A) unfair discrimination in the provision of life or viatical settlements; and

(B) referral fees paid by persons engaged in the business of life or viatical settlements;

(6) assignment or resale of life insurance policies;

(7) maintenance of appropriate confidentiality of personal and medical information; and

(8) the responsibility of a registrant to ensure compliance with this subchapter and rules relating to life or viatical settlements after the registration is revoked, suspended, or otherwise lapses.

(c) The commissioner may not adopt a rule establishing a price or fee for the sale or purchase of a life settlement. This subsection does not prohibit the commissioner from adopting a rule relating to an unjust price or fee for the sale or purchase of a life settlement.

(d) The commissioner may not adopt a rule that regulates the actions of an investor providing money to a life or viatical settlement company.

Added by Acts 2001, 77th Leg., ch. 1419, § 2, eff. June 1, 2003.

§ 1111.004. Annual Fee for Registration

The commissioner may adopt rules requiring payment of an annual fee in connection with registration. The fee may not exceed $250.

Added by Acts 2001, 77th Leg., ch. 1419, § 2, eff. June 1, 2003.

§ 1111.005. Denial, Suspension, or Revocation of Registration; Enforcement

(a) The commissioner may suspend or revoke a registration or deny an application for registration if the commissioner determines that the registrant or applicant, individually or through any officer, director, or shareholder of the registrant or applicant:

(1) wilfully violated:

(A) this subchapter;

(B) an applicable provision of this code or another insurance law of this state; or

(C) a rule adopted under a law described by Paragraph (A) or (B);

(2) intentionally made a material misstatement in the application for registration;

(3) obtained or attempted to obtain registration by fraud or misrepresentation;

(4) misappropriated, converted to the registrant's or applicant's own use, or illegally withheld money belonging to a party to a life or viatical settlement;

(5) was guilty of fraudulent or dishonest practices;

(6) materially misrepresented the terms of business conducted under this subchapter or any other provision of this code or another insurance law of this state;

(7) made or issued, or caused to be made or issued, a statement materially misrepresenting or making incomplete comparisons regarding the material terms of any business conducted under this subchapter; or

(8) was convicted of a felony or was convicted of a misdemeanor involving moral turpitude or fraud.

(b) An applicant or registrant whose registration has been denied, suspended, or revoked under this section may not file another application for registration before the first anniversary of the effective date of the denial, suspension, or revocation or, if judicial review of the denial, suspension, or revocation is sought, the first anniversary of the date of the final court order or decree affirming the action. The commissioner may deny an application filed after that period unless the applicant shows good cause why the denial, suspension, or revocation of the previous registration should not bar the issuance of a new registration.

(c) In addition to an action taken against a person under Subsection (a) or (b), the commissioner may take against the person any action that the commissioner may take against a person engaged in the business of insurance who violates a statute or rule.

Added by Acts 2001, 771h Leg., ch. 1419, § 2, eff. June 1, 2003.

§ 1111.006. Applicability of Other Insurance Laws

The following laws apply to a person engaged in the business of life or viatical settlements:

(1) Articles 1.10, 1.10D, 1.19, and 21.21;

(2) Chapters 82, 83, and 84;

(3) Sections 31.002, 32.001, 32.002, 32.003, 32.021, 32.023, 32.041, 38.001, 81.004, 801.056, and 862.052; and

(4) Subchapter C, Chapter 36.

Added by Acts 2001, 77th Leg., ch. 1419, § 2, eff. June 1, 2003.

Subchapter B. Accelerated Term Life Insurance Benefits

§ 1111.051. Definitions

In this subchapter:

(1) "Accelerated benefit" means a benefit paid to an insured instead of a portion of a death benefit.

(2) "Death benefit" means a benefit payable to a beneficiary on the death of an insured.

(3) "Long-term care illness" means an illness or physical condition that results in the inability to perform the activities of daily life or the substantial and material duties of any occupation.

(4) "Terminal illness" means an illness or physical condition, including a physical injury, that can reasonably be expected to result in death within not more than two years.

Added by Acts 2001, 77th Leg., ch. 1419, § 2, eff. June 1, 2003.

§ 1111.052. Authority to Pay Accelerated Term Life Benefits

An insurer may pay an accelerated benefit under an individual or group term life insurance policy or certificate if:

(1) the insurer has received a written medical opinion, satisfactory to the insurer, that the insured has:

(A) a terminal illness;

(B) a long-term care illness; or

(C) an illness or physical condition that is likely to cause permanent disability or premature death, including:

(i) acquired immune deficiency syndrome (AIDS);

(ii) a malignant tumor;

(iii) a condition that requires an organ transplant; or

(iv) a coronary artery disease that results in acute infarction or requires surgery; and

(2) the amount of the accelerated benefit is deducted from:

(A) the amount of the death benefit payable under the policy or certificate; and

(B) any amount the insured would otherwise be entitled to convert to an individual contract.

Added by Acts 2001, 77th Leg., ch. 1419, § 2, eff. June 1, 2003. Amended by Acts 2003, 78th Leg., ch. 1276, § 10A.302, eff. Sept. 1, 2003.

§ 1111.053. Rules

The commissioner may adopt rules to implement this subchapter.

Added by Acts 2001, 77th Leg., ch. 1419, § 2, eff. June 1, 2003.

XI.
PENAL CODE

Title 5. Offenses Against the Person

Chapter 22. Assaultive Offenses

Statutes in Context

Assisted suicide arises when the person committing suicide needs help in procuring the means to commit the act such as a weapon, drugs, or Dr. Jack Kevorkian's "suicide machine." The person, however, self-administers the lethal agent by pulling the trigger, swallowing the pills, turning on the gas, or the like. If a doctor assists the person in procuring the fatal drugs, the term *physician-assisted suicide* is often used. Assisted suicide in general is sometimes called *passive euthanasia* because the euthanatizer merely supplies the means of death rather than directly causing the death. Assisted suicide can be contrasted with *voluntary euthanasia* in which the euthanatizer actually kills the person at that person's request. The term *involuntary euthanasia* is reserved for cases where the euthanatizer kills a person out of reasons of mercy but where the person did not specifically request to be killed.

Most state legislatures have enacted statutes such as § 22.08 of the Texas Penal Code which make it a crime to assist someone to commit suicide. These statutes withstood constitutional muster in the United States Supreme Court case of *Vacco v. Quill*, 117 S. Ct. 2293 (1997). The Court held that the United States Constitution does not guarantee a person the right to die and that states can prohibit assisted suicide. However, the Court indicated that a state may decide to authorize and regulate assisted suicide. As of August 2003, Oregon is the only state to permit its citizens to seek assistance in procuring the means to commit suicide.

Note that withholding or withdrawing life-sustaining procedures under a valid directive to physicians or out-of-hospital do-not-resuscitate order is not considered aiding suicide. *See* Health and Safety Code §§ 166.047 and 166.096.

§ 22.08. Aiding Suicide

(a) A person commits an offense if, with intent to promote or assist the commission of suicide by another, he aids or attempts to aid the other to commit or attempt to commit suicide.

(b) An offense under this section is a Class C misdemeanor unless the actor's conduct causes suicide or attempted suicide that results in serious bodily injury, in which event the offense is a state jail felony.

Acts 1973, 63rd Leg., p. 883, ch. 399, § 1, eff. Jan. 1, 1974. Amended by Acts 1993, 73rd Leg., ch. 900, § 1.01, eff. Sept. 1, 1994.

Title7. Offenses Against Property

Chapter 32. Fraud

Subchapter D. Other Deceptive Practices

Statutes in Context

Section 32.45 provides criminal penalties when a fiduciary such as an executor, administrator, trustee, or guardian misapplies property, that is, deals with the property contrary to the terms of the instrument (trust, will, etc.) or any law prescribing the custody or disposition of the property (Probate Code, Property Code, etc.). Note that the fiduciary's conduct must be intentional, knowing, or reckless. Mere negligent conduct will not give rise to a criminal offense although it may subject the fiduciary to civil liability. No actual loss to the property or gain to the fiduciary is necessary. All that must occur is that the property be handled in a manner that involves substantial risk of loss.

§ 32.45. Misapplication of Fiduciary Property or Property of Financial Institution

(a) For purposes of this section:

(1) "Fiduciary" includes:

(A) trustee, guardian, administrator, executor, conservator, and receiver;

(B) an attorney in fact or agent appointed under a durable power of attorney as provided by Chapter XII, Texas Probate Code.

(C) any other person acting in a fiduciary capacity, but not a commercial bailee unless the commercial bailee is a party in a motor fuel sales agreement with a distributor or supplier, as those terms are defined by Section 153.001, Tax Code; and

(D) an officer, manager, employee, or agent carrying on fiduciary functions on behalf of a fiduciary.

(2) "Misapply" means deal with property contrary to:

(A) an agreement under which the fiduciary holds the property; or

(B) a law prescribing the custody or disposition of the property.

(b) A person commits an offense if he intentionally, knowingly, or recklessly misapplies property he holds as a fiduciary or property of a financial institution in a manner that involves substantial risk of loss to the owner of the property or to a person for whose benefit the property is held.

(c) An offense under this section is:

(1) a Class C misdemeanor if the value of the property misapplied is less than $20;

(2) a Class B misdemeanor if the value of the property misapplied is $20 or more but less than $500;

(3) a Class A misdemeanor if the value of the property misapplied is $500 or more but less than $1,500;

(4) a state jail felony if the value of the property misapplied is $1,500 or more but less than $20,000;

(5) a felony of the third degree if the value of the property misapplied is $20,000 or more but less than $100,000;

(6) a felony of the second degree if the value of the property misapplied is $100,000 or more but less than $200,000; or

(7) a felony of the first degree if the value of the property misapplied is $200,000 or more.

[Subsection (d) as added by Acts 2003, 78th Leg., ch. 198, § 2.137, eff. Sept. 1, 2003.]

(d) With the consent of the appropriate local county or district attorney, the attorney general has concurrent jurisdiction with that consenting local prosecutor to prosecute an offense under this section that involves the state Medicaid program.

[Subsection (d) as added by Acts 2003, 78th Leg., ch. 257, § 14, eff. Sept. 1, 2003.]

(d) With the consent of the appropriate local county or district attorney, the attorney general has concurrent jurisdiction with that consenting local prosecutor to prosecute an offense under this section that involves the state Medicaid program.

[Subsection (d) as added by Acts 2003, 78th Leg., ch. 432, § 3, eff. Sept. 1, 2003.]

(d) An offense described for purposes of punishment by Subsections (c)(1)-(6) is increased to the next higher category of offense if it is shown on the trial of the offense that the offense was committed against an elderly individual as defined by Section 22.04.

Acts 1973, 63rd Leg., p. 883, ch. 399, § 1, eff. Jan. 1, 1974. Amended by Acts 1991, 72nd Leg., ch. 565, § 2, eff. Sept. 1, 1991; Acts 1993, 73rd Leg., ch. 900, § 1.01, eff. Sept. 1, 1994; Amended by Acts 1997, 75th Leg., ch. 1036, § 14, eff. Sept. 1, 1997; Acts 2001, 77th Leg., ch 1047, § 1, eff. Sept. 1, 2001; Acts 2003, 78th Leg., ch. 198, § 2.137, eff. Sept. 1, 2003; Acts 2003, 78th Leg., ch. 257, § 14, eff. Sept. 1, 2003; Acts 2003, 78th Leg., ch. 432, § 3, eff. Sept. 1, 2003.

Statutes in Context

A person who fraudulently destroys, alters, or conceals a will, trust, power of attorney, or other writing may be subject to criminal liability under § 32.47.

§ 32.47. Fraudulent Destruction, Removal, or Concealment of Writing

(a) A person commits an offense if, with intent to defraud or harm another, he destroys, removes, conceals, alters, substitutes, or otherwise impairs the verity, legibility, or availability of a writing, other than a governmental record.

(b) For purposes of this section, "writing" includes:

(1) printing or any other method of recording information;

(2) money, coins, tokens, stamps, seals, credit cards, badges, trademarks;

(3) symbols of value, right, privilege, or identification; and

(4) universal product codes, labels, price tags, or markings on goods.

(c) Except as provided in Subsection (d), an offense under this section is a Class A misdemeanor.

(d) An offense under this section is a state jail felony if the writing:

(1) is a will or codicil of another, whether or not the maker is alive or dead and whether or not it has been admitted to probate; or

(2) is a deed, mortgage, deed of trust, security instrument, security agreement, or other writing for which the law provides public recording or filing, whether or not the writing has been acknowledged.

Acts 1973, 63rd Leg., p. 883, ch. 399, § 1, eff. Jan. 1, 1974. Amended by Acts 1993, 73rd Leg., ch. 900, § 1.01, eff. Sept. 1, 1994; Acts 2001, 77th Leg., ch. 21, § 1, eff. Sept. 1, 2001.

XII.
Probate Code

Chapter I. General Provisions

§ 1. Short Title

This Act shall be known, and may be cited, as the "Texas Probate Code."

Acts 1955, 54th Leg., p. 88, ch. 55, eff. Jan. 1, 1956.

§ 2. Effective Date and Application

(a) Effective Date. This Code shall take effect and be in force on and after January 1, 1956. The procedure herein prescribed shall govern all probate proceedings in county and probate courts brought after the effective date of this Act, and also all further procedure in proceedings in probate then pending, except to the extent that in the opinion of the court, with respect to proceedings in probate then pending, its application in particular proceedings or parts thereof would not be feasible or would work injustice, in which event the former procedure shall apply.

(b) Rights Not Affected. No act done in any proceeding commenced before this Code takes effect, and no accrued right, shall be impaired by the provisions of this Code. When a right is acquired, extinguished, or barred upon the expiration of a prescribed period of time which has commenced to run by the provision of any statute in force before this Code takes effect, such provision shall remain in force and be deemed a part of this Code with respect to such right. All things properly done under any previously existing statute prior to the taking effect of this Code shall be treated as valid. Where citation or other process or notice is issued and served in compliance with existing statutes prior to the taking effect of this Code, the party upon whom such citation or other process has been served shall have the time provided for under such previously existing statutes in which to comply therewith.

(c) Subdivisions Have No Legal Effect. The division of this Code into Chapters, Parts, Sections, Subsections, and Paragraphs is solely for convenience and shall have no legal effect.

(d) Severability. If any provision of this Code, or the application thereof to any person or circumstance, is held invalid, such invalidity shall not affect other provisions or applications of the Code which can be given effect without the invalid provision or application, and to this end the provisions of this Code are declared to be severable, and the Legislature hereby states that it would have enacted such portions of the Code which can lawfully be given effect regardless of the possible invalidity of other provisions of the Code.

(e) Nature of Proceeding. The administration of the estate of a decedent, from the filing of the application for probate and administration, or for administration, until the decree of final distribution and the discharge of the last personal representative, shall be considered as one proceeding for purposes of jurisdiction. The entire proceeding is a proceeding in rem.

Acts 1955, 54th Leg., p. 88, ch. 55, eff. Jan. 1, 1956. Amended by Acts 1993, 73rd Leg., ch. 957, § 2, eff. Sept. 1, 1993.

Statutes in Context

The definitions in § 3 apply to the entire Probate Code except as otherwise provided by Chapter XIII which governs guardianships.

Some terms are defined contrary to their traditional meanings. For example, the term "devise," which usually refers to a gift of real property in a will, is defined to encompass gifts of both real and personal property in subsection (h). Likewise, "legacy," which normally refers to a gift of money (personal property) in a will, is deemed to include gifts of real property as well by subsection (s).

"Heirs" include anyone who is entitled to property under intestate succession under subsection (o). The surviving spouse is considered an heir even though at common law, the surviving spouse was not an heir (not a blood relative). A person who takes under a will is not properly called an heir.

The term "will" is defined in subsection (ff) to include a variety of testamentary instruments including codicils and instruments which do not actually make at-death distributions of property such as documents which merely appoint an executor or guardian, revoke another will, or direct how property may not be distributed.

Courts will sometimes ignore the plain language of the definitions. For example, in *Heien v. Crabtree*, 369 S.W.2d 28 (Tex. 1963), the Texas Supreme Court refused to treat a child who was adopted by estoppel as a "child" under subsection (b) despite the language of the definition stating that the term includes a child adopted "by acts of estoppel."

The definitions apply to these terms *as used in the Probate Code*. The definitions do not necessarily

apply when they are used in a will or other estate planning document.

§ 3. Definitions and Use of Terms

Except as otherwise provided by Chapter XIII of this Code, when used in this Code, unless otherwise apparent from the context:

(a) "Authorized corporate surety" means a domestic or foreign corporation authorized to do business in the State of Texas for the purpose of issuing surety, guaranty or indemnity bonds guaranteeing the fidelity of executors and administrators.

(b) "Child" includes an adopted child, whether adopted by any existing or former statutory procedure or by acts of estoppel, but, unless expressly so stated herein, does not include a child who has no presumed father.

(c) "Claims" include liabilities of a decedent which survive, including taxes, whether arising in contract or in tort or otherwise, funeral expenses, the expense of a tombstone, expenses of administration, estate and inheritance taxes, and debts due such estates.

(d) "Corporate fiduciary" means a financial institution as defined by Section 201.101, Finance Code, having trust powers, existing or doing business under the laws of this state, another state, or the United States, which is authorized by law to act under the order or appointment of any court of record, without giving bond, as receiver, trustee, executor, administrator, or, although without general depository powers, depository for any moneys paid into court, or to become sole guarantor or surety in or upon any bond required to be given under the laws of this state.

(e) "County Court" and "Probate Court" are synonymous terms and denote county courts in the exercise of their probate jurisdiction, courts created by statute and authorized to exercise original probate jurisdiction, and district courts exercising probate jurisdiction in contested matters.

(f) "County Judge," "Probate Judge," and "Judge" denote the presiding judge of any court having original jurisdiction over probate proceedings, whether it be a county court in the exercise of its probate jurisdiction, a court created by statute and authorized to exercise probate jurisdiction, or a district court exercising probate jurisdiction in contested matters.

(g) "Court" denotes and includes both a county court in the exercise of its probate jurisdiction, a court created by statute and authorized to exercise original probate jurisdiction, or a district court exercising original probate jurisdiction in contested matters.

(h) "Devise," when used as a noun, includes a testamentary disposition of real or personal property, or of both. When used as a verb, "devise" means to dispose of real or personal property, or of both, by will.

(i) "Devisee" includes legatee.

(j) "Distributee" denotes a person entitled to the estate of a decedent under a lawful will, or under the statutes of descent and distribution.

(k) "Docket" means the probate docket.

(l) "Estate" denotes the real and personal property of a decedent, both as such property originally existed and as from time to time changed in form by sale, reinvestment, or otherwise, and as augmented by any accretions and additions thereto (including any property to be distributed to the representative of the decedent by the trustee of a trust which terminates upon the decedent's death) and substitutions therefor, and as diminished by any decreases therein and distributions therefrom.

(m) "Exempt property" refers to that property of a decedent's estate which is exempt from execution or forced sale by the Constitution or laws of this State, and to the allowance in lieu thereof.

(n) Repealed by Acts 1995, 74th Leg., ch. 1039, § 73(1), eff. Sept. 1, 1995.

(o) "Heirs" denote those persons, including the surviving spouse, who are entitled under the statutes of descent and distribution to the estate of a decedent who dies intestate.

(p) "Incapacitated" or "Incapacitated person" means:

(1) a minor;

(2) an adult individual who, because of a physical or mental condition, is substantially unable to provide food, clothing, or shelter for himself or herself, to care for the individual's own physical health, or to manage the individual's own financial affairs; or

(3) a person who must have a guardian appointed to receive funds due the person from any governmental source.

(q) "Independent executor" means the personal representative of an estate under independent administration as provided in Section 145 of this Code. The term "independent executor" includes the term "independent administrator."

(r) "Interested persons" or "persons interested" means heirs, devisees, spouses, creditors, or any others having a property right in, or claim against, the estate being administered; and anyone interested in the welfare of a minor or incompetent ward.

(s) "Legacy" includes any gift or devise by will, whether of personalty or realty. "Legatee" includes any person entitled to a legacy under a will.

(t) "Minors" are all persons under eighteen years of age who have never been married or who have not had disabilities of minority removed for general purposes.

(u) "Minutes" means the probate minutes.

(v) "Mortgage" or "Lien" includes deed of trust, vendor's lien, chattel mortgage, mechanic's, materialman's or laborer's lien, judgment, attachment or garnishment lien, pledge by hypothecation, and Federal or State tax liens.

(w) "Net estate" means the real and personal property of a decedent, exclusive of homestead rights, exempt property, the family allowance and enforceable claims against the estate.

(x) "Person" includes natural persons and corporations.

(y) Repealed by Acts 1995, 74th Leg., ch. 1039, § 73(1), eff. Sept. 1, 1995.

(z) "Personal property" includes interests in goods, money, choses in action, evidence of debts, and chattels real.

(aa) "Personal representative" or "Representative" includes executor, independent executor, administrator, independent administrator, temporary administrator, together with their successors. The inclusion of independent executors herein shall not be held to subject such representatives to control of the courts in probate matters with respect to settlement of estates except as expressly provided by law.

(bb) "Probate matter," "Probate proceedings," "Proceeding in probate," and "Proceedings for probate" are synonymous and include a matter or proceeding relating to the estate of a decedent.

(cc) "Property" includes both real and personal property.

(dd) "Real property" includes estates and interests in lands, corporeal or incorporeal, legal or equitable, other than chattels real.

(ee) "Surety" includes both personal and corporate sureties.

(ff) "Will" includes codicil; it also includes a testamentary instrument which merely:

(1) appoints an executor or guardian;

(2) directs how property may not be disposed of; or

(3) revokes another will.

(gg) The singular number includes the plural; the plural number includes the singular.

(hh) The masculine gender includes the feminine and neuter.

(ii) "Statutory probate court" means a statutory court designated as a statutory probate court under Chapter 25, Government Code. A county court at law exercising probate jurisdiction is not a statutory probate court under this Code unless the court is designated a statutory probate court under Chapter 25, Government Code.

(jj) "Next of kin" includes an adopted child or his or her descendents and the adoptive parent of the adopted child.

(kk) "Charitable organization" means:

(1) a nonprofit corporation, trust, community chest, fund, foundation, or other entity that is exempt from federal income tax under Section 501(c)(3) of the Internal Revenue Code of 1986[1] because the entity is organized and operated exclusively for religious, charitable, scientific, educational, or literary purposes, testing for public safety, prevention of cruelty to children or animals, or promotion of amateur sports competition; or

(2) any other entity or organization that is organized and operated exclusively for the purposes listed in Section 501(c)(3) of the Internal Revenue Code of 1986.

[1] 26 U.S.C.A. § 501(c)(3).

(ll) "Governmental agency of the state" means:

(1) an incorporated city or town, a county, a public school district, a special-purpose district or authority, or a district, county, or justice of the peace court;

(2) a board, commission, department, office, or other agency in the executive branch of state government, including an institution of higher education as defined by Section 61.003, Education Code;

(3) the legislature or a legislative agency; and

(4) the supreme court, the court of criminal appeals, a court of appeals, or the State Bar of Texas or another judicial agency having statewide jurisdiction.

(mm) "Ward" is a person for whom a guardian has been appointed.

Subsec. (n) amended by Acts 1985, 69th Leg., ch. 591, § 1, eff. Sept. 1, 1985; Subsec. (p) amended by Acts 1985, 69th Leg., ch. 159, § 1, eff. Sept. 1, 1985; Subsec. (y) amended by Acts 1985, 69th Leg., ch. 159, § 2, eff. Sept. 1, 1985; Subsec. (b) amended by Acts 1989, 71st Leg., ch. 375, § 33, eff. Sept. 1, 1989; Subsecs. (kk), (ll) added by Acts 1989, 71st Leg., ch. 1035, § 1, eff. Sept. 1, 1989; subsec. (n) amended by Acts 1991, 72nd Leg., ch. 14, § 284(96), eff. Sept. 1, 1991; Subsec. (ff) amended by Acts 1991, 72nd Leg., ch. 895, § 1, eff. Sept. 1, 1991. Amended by Acts 1993, 73rd Leg., ch. 957, § 3, eff. Sept. 1, 1993; Subsec. (n) repealed by Acts 1995, 74th Leg., ch. 1039, § 73(1), eff. Sept. 1, 1995; Subsec. (p) amended by Acts 1995, 74th Leg., ch. 1039, § 4, eff. Sept. 1, 1995; Subsec. (y) repealed by Acts 1995, 74th Leg., ch. 1039, § 73(1), eff. Sept. 1, 1995; Subsec. (mm) added by Acts 1995, 74th Leg., ch. 1039, § 4, eff. Sept. 1, 1995; Subsec. (ii) amended by Acts 1997, 75th Leg., ch. 52, § 1, eff. Sept. 1, 1997; Subsec. (d) amended by Acts 1999, 76th Leg., ch. 344, § 6.001, eff. Sept. 1, 1999; Subsec. (p) amended by Acts 1999, 76th Leg., ch. 379, § 1, eff. Sept. 1, 1999.

§ 4. Jurisdiction of County Court With Respect to Probate Proceedings

The county court shall have the general jurisdiction of a probate court. It shall probate wills, grant letters testamentary and of administration, settle accounts of personal representatives, and transact all business appertaining to estates subject to administration, including the settlement, partition, and distribution of such estates.

Acts 1955, 54th Leg., p. 88, ch. 55, eff. Jan. 1, 1956. Amended by Acts 1993, 73rd Leg., ch. 957, § 4, eff. Sept. 1, 1993.

Statutes in Context

Ascertaining which court has jurisdiction to hear matters relating to intestate succession, wills, and estate administration depends on the type of courts that exist in the county. There are three possibilities. First, if the county has only a constitutional county court (that is, no statutory probate court and no statutory court exercising probate jurisdiction) estate matters are filed in the constitutional county court. This situation is

common in rural (low population) counties. Second, if the county has a statutory court exercising probate jurisdiction, but no statutory probate court, then the parties may file in either the constitutional county court or the statutory court with probate jurisdiction. Third, if the county has a statutory probate court, all probate proceedings are filed with the statutory probate court. Counties with statutory probate courts include Bexar, Dallas, Denton, El Paso, Galveston, Harris, Hidalgo, Tarrant, and Travis. A statutory probate court also has concurrent jurisdiction with the district court in the situations listed in subsection (e) which includes all actions involving inter vivos trusts.

If the action is brought in a constitutional county court in a county with no statutory probate court or statutory court exercising probate jurisdiction and a dispute arises, the parties may demand that the action be transferred to the district court. After resolving the specific dispute, the district court will remand the case back to the constitutional county court. If the estate is probated in a constitutional county court in a county with a statutory court exercising probate jurisdiction (not a statutory probate court), then the parties may demand a transfer to the statutory court. Once the case is transferred, it remains in the statutory court. Transfer from the constitutional county court also may occur upon the court's own motion. Finally, if the estate is probated in a statutory probate court, all estate matters remain with that court; transfer is not available.

Regardless of the court mandated or chosen for the proceeding, the court has jurisdiction to hear all matters incident to the estate as defined in § 5B.

A final order (but not an interlocutory order) of any court exercising probate jurisdiction is appealable to the courts of appeals. In *Crowson v. Wakeham*, 897 S.W.2d 779 (Tex. 1995), the Supreme Court of Texas held that an order in a probate case is final for appellate purposes when (1) a statute declares that a specified phase of the probate proceedings are final and appealable, (2) the order disposes of all issues in the phase of the proceeding for which it was brought, or (3) a particular order is made final by a severance order meeting the usual severance criteria.

§ 5. Jurisdiction With Respect to Probate Proceedings

(a) (Repealed)

(b) In those counties in which there is no statutory probate court, county court at law, or other statutory court exercising the jurisdiction of a probate court, all applications, petitions, and motions regarding probate and administrations shall be filed and heard in the county court. In contested probate matters, the judge of the county court may on the judge's own motion or shall on the motion of any party to the proceeding, according to the motion:

(1) request the assignment of a statutory probate court judge to hear the contested portion of the proceeding, as provided by Section 25.0022, Government Code; or

(2) transfer the contested portion of the proceeding to the district court, which may then hear the contested matter as if originally filed in district court.

(b-1) If the judge of the county court has not transferred a contested probate matter to the district court at the time a party files a motion for assignment of a statutory probate court judge, the county judge shall grant the motion and may not transfer the matter to district court unless the party withdraws the motion.

(b-2) A statutory probate court judge assigned to a contested probate matter as provided by Subsection (b) of this section has the jurisdiction and authority granted to a statutory probate court by Sections 5A and 5B of this code. On resolution of a contested matter, including an appeal of a matter, to which a statutory probate court judge has been assigned, the statutory probate court judge shall transfer the resolved portion of the case to the county court for further proceedings not inconsistent with the orders of the statutory probate court judge.

(b-3) In contested matters transferred to the district court, the district court has the general jurisdiction of a probate court. On resolution of a contested matter, including an appeal of a matter, the district court shall transfer the resolved portion of the case to the county court for further proceedings not inconsistent with the orders of the district court.

(b-4) The county court shall continue to exercise jurisdiction over the management of the estate with the exception of the contested matter until final disposition of the contested matter is made by the assigned statutory probate court judge or the district court.

(b-5) If a contested portion of the proceeding is transferred to a district court under Subsection (b-3) of this section, the clerk of the district court may perform in relation to the transferred portion of the proceeding any function a county clerk may perform in that type of contested proceeding.

(c) In those counties in which there is no statutory probate court, but in which there is a county court at law or other statutory court exercising the jurisdiction of a probate court, all applications, petitions, and motions regarding probate and administrations shall be filed and heard in those courts and the constitutional county court, rather than in the district courts, unless otherwise provided by law. The judge of a county court may hear any of those matters regarding probate or administrations sitting for the judge of any other county court. In contested probate matters, the judge of the constitutional county court may on the judge's own motion, and shall on the motion of a party to the proceeding, transfer the proceeding to the county court at law or a statutory court exercising the jurisdiction of a probate court other than a statutory probate court. The court to which the proceeding is transferred may hear the proceeding as if originally filed in the court.

(d) In those counties in which there is a statutory probate court, all applications, petitions, and motions regarding probate or administrations shall be filed and heard in the statutory probate court.

(e) A statutory probate court has concurrent jurisdiction with the district court in all personal injury, survival, or wrongful death actions by or against a person in the person's capacity as a personal representative, in all actions involving an inter vivos trust, in all actions involving a charitable trust, and in all actions involving a personal representative of an estate in which each other party aligned with the personal representative is not an interested person in that estate.

(f) All courts exercising original probate jurisdiction shall have the power to hear all matters incident to an estate. When a surety is called on to perform in place of an administrator, all courts exercising original probate jurisdiction may award judgment against the personal representative in favor of his surety in the same suit.

(g) All final orders of any court exercising original probate jurisdiction shall be appealable to the courts of appeals.

(h) A statutory probate court has jurisdiction over any matter appertaining to an estate or incident to an estate and has jurisdiction over any cause of action in which a personal representative of an estate pending in the statutory probate court is a party.

(i) A statutory probate court may exercise the pendent and ancillary jurisdiction necessary to promote judicial efficiency and economy.

Subsec. (b) amended by Acts 1983, 68th Leg., p. 5434, ch. 1015, § 1, eff. Aug. 29, 1983; Subsecs. (b), (c) amended by Acts 1983, 68th Leg., p. 4122, ch. 647, § 2, eff. Sept. 1, 1983; Subsec. (b) amended by Acts 1985, 69th Leg., ch. 159, § 3, eff. Sept. 1, 1985; amended by Acts 1987, 70th Leg., ch. 459, § 4, eff. Sept. 1, 1987. Amended by Acts 1989, 71st Leg., ch. 1035, § 2, eff. Sept. 1, 1989; Subsecs. (a), (b), (c), (e) amended by Acts 1993, 73rd Leg., ch. 957, § 5, eff. Sept. 1, 1993; Subsec. (g) added by Acts 1997, 75th Leg., ch. 1435, § 3, eff. Sept. 1, 1997; Subsec. (b) amended by Acts 1999, 76th Leg., ch. 1389, § 1, eff. Aug. 30, 1999. Amended by Acts 2001, 77th Leg., ch. 63, § 1, eff. Sept. 1, 2001. Amended by Acts 2003, 78th Leg., ch.1060, §§ 1, 2, & 16, eff. Sept. 1, 2003.

Statutes in Context

Section 5A defines the phrases "appertaining to estates" and "incident to estates" and provides additional guidance regarding the jurisdiction of statutory probate courts. The precise extent of the jurisdiction of the various courts is a matter of frequent litigation and the legislature has amended § 5B on a regular basis to clarify the issue.

Generally, there are two ways an action may be appertaining to or incident to an estate to give a statutory probate court jurisdiction. First, the cause of action may be expressly listed in § 5A(b) and second, the controlling issue in the suit may be the settlement, partition, or distribution of an estate. *In re Swepi*, 85 S.W.3d 800 (Tex. 2002).

---

§ 5A. Matters Appertaining and Incident to an Estate

(a) In proceedings in the constitutional county courts and statutory county courts at law, the phrases "appertaining to estates" and "incident to an estate" in this Code include the probate of wills, the issuance of letters testamentary and of administration, the determination of heirship, and also include, but are not limited to, all claims by or against an estate, all actions for trial of title to land incident to an estate and for the enforcement of liens thereon incident to an estate, all actions for trial of the right of property incident to an estate, and actions to construe wills, and generally all matters relating to the settlement, partition, and distribution of estates of deceased persons.

(b) In proceedings in the statutory probate courts, the phrases "appertaining to estates" and "incident to an estate" in this Code include the probate of wills, the issuance of letters testamentary and of administration, and the determination of heirship, and also include, but are not limited to, all claims by or against an estate, all actions for trial of title to land and for the enforcement of liens thereon, all actions for trial of the right of property, all actions to construe wills, the interpretation and administration of testamentary trusts and the applying of constructive trusts, and generally all matters relating to the collection, settlement, partition, and distribution of estates of deceased persons. All statutory probate courts may, in the exercise of their jurisdiction, notwithstanding any other provisions of this Code, hear all suits, actions, and applications filed against or on behalf of any heirship proceeding or decedent's estate, including estates administered by an independent executor; all such suits, actions, and applications are appertaining to and incident to an estate. This subsection shall be construed in conjunction with and in harmony with Section 145 and all other sections of this Code dealing with independent executors, but shall not be construed so as to increase permissible judicial control over independent executors. Except for situations in which the jurisdiction of a statutory probate court is concurrent with that of a district court as provided by Section 5(e) of this Code or any other court, any cause of action appertaining to estates or incident to an estate shall be brought in a statutory probate court.

(c) (Repealed)

(d) (Repealed)

(e) (Repealed)

(f) Notwithstanding any other provision of this chapter, the proper venue for an action by or against a personal representative for personal injury, death, or property damages is determined under Section 15.007, Civil Practice and Remedies Code.

Added by Acts 1979, 66th Leg., p. 1741, ch. 713, § 3, eff. Aug. 27, 1979. Subsec. (b) amended by Acts 1985, 69th Leg., ch. 875, § 1, eff. Aug. 26, 1985; Acts 1987, 70th Leg., ch. 459, § 1, eff. Sept. 1, 1987. Amended by Acts 1989, 71st Leg., ch. 1035, § 3, eff. Sept. 1, 1989; Subsecs. (a), (b) amended by Acts 1993, 73rd Leg., ch. 957, § 6, eff. Sept. 1,

1993; Subsec. (b) amended by Acts 1997, 75th Leg., ch. 1302, § 1, eff. Sept. 1, 1997; Subsec. (b) amended by Acts 1999, 76th Leg., ch. 64, § 1, eff. Sept. 1, 1999; Subsec. (e) amended by Acts 1999, 76th Leg., ch. 64, § 1, eff. Sept. 1, 1999. Amended by Acts 2003, 78th Leg., ch.204, § 3.05, eff. Sept. 1, 2003; Acts 2003, 78th Leg., ch. 1060, §§ 3, 4 & 16, eff. Sept. 1, 2003.

Statutes in Context

A statutory probate court judge may transfer a case pending in a district, county, or statutory court to the statutory probate court if it is appertaining to or incident to an estate already pending in the statutory probate court. The judge is not, however, obligated to make the transfer; it is discretionary. *In re Azle Manor, Inc.*, 83 S.W.3d 410 (Tex. App. — Fort Worth 2002, no pet.).

§ 5B. Transfer of Proceeding

(a) A judge of a statutory probate court, on the motion of a party to the action or on the motion of a person interested in an estate, may transfer to his court from a district, county, or statutory court a cause of action appertaining to or incident to an estate pending in the statutory probate court or a cause of action in which a personal representative of an estate pending in the statutory probate court is a party and may consolidate the transferred cause of action with the other proceedings in the statutory probate court relating to that estate.

(b) Notwithstanding any other provision of this chapter, the proper venue for an action by or against a personal representative for personal injury, death, or property damages is determined under Section 15.007, Civil Practice and Remedies Code.

Added by Acts 1983, 68th Leg., p. 5228, ch. 958, § 1, eff. Sept. 1, 1983. Amended by Acts 1999, 76th Leg., ch. 1431, § 1, eff. Sept. 1, 1999. Amended by Acts 2003, 78th Leg., ch. 204, § 3.06, eff. Sept. 1, 2003.

§ 5C. Actions to Collect Delinquent Property Taxes

(a) This section applies only to a decedent's estate that:

(1) is being administered in a pending probate proceeding;

(2) owns or claims an interest in property against which a taxing unit has imposed ad valorem taxes that are delinquent; and

(3) is not being administered as an independent administration under Section 145 of this code.

(b) Notwithstanding any provision of this code to the contrary, if the probate proceedings are pending in a foreign jurisdiction or in a county other than the county in which the taxes were imposed, a suit to foreclose the lien securing payment of the taxes or to enforce personal liability for the taxes must be brought under Section 33.41, Tax Code, in a court of competent jurisdiction in the county in which the taxes were imposed.

(c) If the probate proceedings have been pending for four years or less in the county in which the taxes were imposed, the taxing unit may present a claim for the delinquent taxes against the estate to the personal representative of the estate in the probate proceedings.

(d) If the taxing unit presents a claim against the estate under Subsection (c) of this section:

(1) the claim of the taxing unit is subject to each applicable provision in Parts 4 and 5, Chapter VIII,[1] of this code that relates to a claim or the enforcement of a claim in a probate proceeding; and

(2) the taxing unit may not bring a suit in any other court to foreclose the lien securing payment of the taxes or to enforce personal liability for the delinquent taxes before the first day after the fourth anniversary of the date the application for the probate proceeding was filed.

(e) To foreclose the lien securing payment of the delinquent taxes, the taxing unit must bring a suit under Section 33.41, Tax Code, in a court of competent jurisdiction for the county in which the taxes were imposed if:

(1) the probate proceedings have been pending in that county for more than four years; and

(2) the taxing unit did not present a delinquent tax claim under Subsection (c) of this section against the estate in the probate proceeding.

(f) In a suit brought under Subsection (e) of this section, the taxing unit:

(1) shall make the personal representative of the decedent's estate a party to the suit; and

(2) may not seek to enforce personal liability for the taxes against the estate of the decedent.

Added by Acts 1999, 76th Leg., ch. 1481, § 36, eff. Sept. 1, 1999.

Statutes in Context

The venue rules provided in § 6, as applied to the administration of estates and related matters, trump the normal venue rules found in the Rules of Civil Procedure. Proper venue is based on the decedent's domicile at death.

If the decedent was domiciled or had a fixed place of residence in Texas, the appropriate venue is the county of the decedent's domicile or residence at the time of death. It is not relevant where the decedent died, where the decedent's heirs or beneficiaries live, or where the decedent's real or personal property is located.

If the decedent dies in Texas but has no place of residence in Texas, then the appropriate venue is either in the county (1) where the decedent's principal property is located, or (2) where the decedent died. The county in which the application for probate is filed first has priority under Probate Code § 8.

If the decedent did not die in Texas and did not reside in Texas, the appropriate venue is in the county where the nearest next of kin reside. If the decedent

[1] V.A.T.S. Probate Code, § 294 et seq. or § 331 et seq.

has no next of kin in Texas, then the appropriate venue is the county in which the decedent's principal estate is located. The typical reason for probate proceedings in Texas for a person who did not reside or die in Texas is because the decedent owned real property located in Texas.

---

§ 6. Venue for Probate of Wills and Administration of Estates of Decedents

Wills shall be admitted to probate, and letters testamentary or of administration shall be granted:

(a) In the county where the deceased resided, if he had a domicile or fixed place of residence in this State.

(b) If the deceased had no domicile or fixed place of residence in this State but died in this State, then either in the county where his principal property was at the time of his death, or in the county where he died.

(c) If he had no domicile or fixed place of residence in this State, and died outside the limits of this State, then in any county in this State where his nearest of kin reside.

(d) But if he had no kindred in this State, then in the county where his principal estate was situated at the time of his death.

(e) In the county where the applicant resides, when administration is for the purpose only of receiving funds or money due to a deceased person or his estate from any governmental source or agency; provided, that unless the mother or father or spouse or adult child of the deceased is applicant, citation shall be served personally on the living parents and spouses and adult children, if any, of the deceased person, or upon those who are alive and whose addresses are known to the applicant.

Acts 1955, 54th Leg., p. 88, ch. 55, eff. Jan. 1, 1956.

§ 8. Concurrent Venue and Transfer of Proceedings

(a) Concurrent Venue. When two or more courts have concurrent venue of an estate, the court in which application for probate proceedings thereon is first filed shall have and retain jurisdiction of the estate to the exclusion of the other court or courts. The proceedings shall be deemed commenced by the filing of an application averring facts sufficient to confer venue; and the proceeding first legally commenced shall extend to all of the property of the estate. Provided, however, that a bona fide purchaser of real property in reliance on any such subsequent proceeding, without knowledge of its invalidity, shall be protected in such purchase unless the decree admitting the will to probate or granting administration in the prior proceeding shall be recorded in the office of the county clerk of the county in which such property is located.

(b) Proceedings in More Than One County. If proceedings for probate are commenced in more than one county, they shall be stayed except in the county where first commenced until final determination of venue in the county where first commenced. If the proper venue is finally determined to be in another county, the clerk, after making and retaining a true copy of the entire file in the case, shall transmit the original file to the proper county, and proceedings shall thereupon be had in the proper county in the same manner as if the proceedings had originally been instituted therein.

(c) Transfer of Proceeding

(1) Transfer for Want of Venue. If it appears to the court at any time before the final decree that the proceeding was commenced in a court which did not have priority of venue over such proceeding, the court shall, on the application of any interested person, transfer the proceeding to the proper county by transmitting to the proper court in such county the original file in such case, together with certified copies of all entries in the minutes theretofore made, and administration of the estate in such county shall be completed in the same manner as if the proceeding had originally been instituted therein; but, if the question as to priority of venue is not raised before final decree in the proceedings is announced, the finality of such decree shall not be affected by any error in venue.

(2) Transfer for Convenience of the Estate. If it appears to the court at any time before the estate is closed that it would be in the best interest of the estate, the court, in its discretion, may order the proceeding transferred to the proper court in any other county in this State. The clerk of the court from which the proceeding is transferred shall transmit to the court to which the proceeding is transferred the original file in the proceeding and a certified copy of the entries in the index.

(d) Validation of Prior Proceedings. When a proceeding is transferred to another county under any provision of this Section of this Code, all orders entered in connection with the proceeding shall be valid and shall be recognized in the second court, provided such orders were made and entered in conformance with the procedure prescribed by this Code.

(e) Jurisdiction to Determine Venue. Any court in which there has been filed an application for proceedings in probate shall have full jurisdiction to determine the venue of such proceeding, and of any proceeding relating thereto, and its determination shall not be subject to collateral attack.

Acts 1955, 54th Leg., p. 88, ch. 55, eff. Jan. 1, 1956. Subsec. (c)(2) amended by Acts 1983, 68th Leg., p. 4754, ch. 833, § 1, eff. Sept. 1, 1983; Acts 1987, 70th Leg., ch. 786, § 1, eff. Aug. 31, 1987. Amended by Acts 2003, 78th Leg., ch. 1060, § 5, eff. Sept. 1, 2003.

§ 9. Defects in Pleading

No defect of form or substance in any pleading in probate shall be held by any court to invalidate such pleading, or any order based upon such pleading, unless the defect has been timely objected to and called to the attention of the court in which such proceedings were or are pending.

Acts 1955, 54th Leg., p. 88, ch. 55, eff. Jan. 1, 1956.

Statutes in Context

An individual may have a strong motivation to have a testator's will deemed invalid and ineffective to dispose of the testator's property. First, this person could be an heir who would receive more under intestacy than the will. Or, second, this person could be a beneficiary of a prior will who would receive a smaller gift under the more recent will.

A person must have a pecuniary interest in the estate to contest the proceedings. *Logan v. Thomason*, 202 S.W.2d 212, 215 (Tex. 1947) ("An interest resting on sentiment or sympathy, or any other basis other than gain or loss of money or its equivalent, is insufficient."). See also Probate Code § 3(r) defining "person interested."

The timing of a will contest is of particular importance. First, the timing determines which party has the burden of proof. If the contest action is brought before the probate of the will, then the party admitting the will to probate has the burden to prove that the will is valid. On the other hand, if the contest action is brought after the will has been admitted to probate, the party contesting the will has the burden to prove that there is a deficiency in the will. Second, will contests are subject to the statute of limitations set forth in Probate Code § 93.

§ 10. Persons Entitled to Contest Proceedings

Any person interested in an estate may, at any time before any issue in any proceeding is decided upon by the court, file opposition thereto in writing and shall be entitled to process for witnesses and evidence, and to be heard upon such opposition, as in other suits.

Acts 1955, 54th Leg., p. 88, ch. 55, eff. Jan. 1, 1956.

Statutes in Context

Unlike many states, Texas law does not expressly require that the beneficiaries of a will be given notice or made a party to a will contest action except for certain schools and charities as provided in § 10A. *See Wojcik v. Wesolick*, 97 S.W.3d 335 (Tex. App. — Houston [14th Dist.] 2003, no pet. h.), *but see*, *Kotz v. Kotz*, 613 S.W.2d 760, 761 (Tex. Civ. App. — Beaumont 1981, no writ), and *Jennings v. Srp*, 521 S.W.2d 326, 328-329 (Tex. Civ. App. — Corpus Christi 1975, no writ).

§ 10A. Necessary Party

(a) An institution of higher education as defined by Section 61.003, Education Code, a private institution of higher education, or a charitable organization is a necessary party to a will contest or will construction suit involving a will in which the institution or organization is a distributee.

(b) If an institution or organization is a necessary party under Subsection (a) of this section, the court shall serve the institution or organization in the manner provided for service on other parties by this code.

Added by Acts 1989, 71st Leg., ch. 1035, § 4, eff. Sept. 1, 1989. Amended by Acts 1991, 72nd Leg., ch. 675, § 1, eff. Sept. 1, 1991.

Statutes in Context

The ability of litigants to obtain evidence of a decedent's testamentary capacity was greatly enhanced by the legislature's enactment of Probate Code § 10B in 1997. This section provides that a party to a will contest, or a proceeding in which a party relies on the mental or testamentary capacity of a decedent as part of the party's claim or defense, is entitled to production of all communications or records that are relevant to the decedent's condition.

§ 10B. Communications or Records Relating to Decedent's Condition Before Death

Notwithstanding the Medical Practice Act (Article 4495b, Vernon's Texas Civil Statutes), a person who is a party to a will contest or a proceeding in which a party relies on the mental or testamentary capacity of a decedent before the decedent's death as part of the party's claim or defense is entitled to production of all communications or records relevant to the decedent's condition before the decedent's death. On receipt of a subpoena of communications or records under this section and proof of filing of the will contest or proceeding, by file-stamped copy, the appropriate physician, hospital, medical facility, custodian of records, or other person in possession of the communications or records shall release the communications or records to the party requesting the records without further authorization.

Added by Acts 1997, 75th Leg., ch. 1302, § 2, eff. Sept. 1, 1997. Amended by Acts 1999, 76th Leg., ch. 855, § 1, eff. Sept. 1, 1999.

Statutes in Context

The lower courts of Texas have recognized the tort of tortious interference with inheritance rights. See *King v. Acker*, 725 S.W.2d 750 (Tex. App. — Houston [1st Dist.] 1987, no writ). However, the courts have not delineated exactly what actions would constitute tortious interference. Taking an opposite approach, the 2003 Legislature enacted § 10C which declares that certain specified actions may *not* be considered tortious interference, that is, the filing or contesting in probate court of any pleading relating to a decedent's estate will not constitute tortious interference.

§ 10C. Effect of Filing or Contesting Pleading

(a) The filing or contesting in probate court of any pleading relating to a decedent's estate does not constitute tortious interference with inheritance of the estate.

(b) This section does not abrogate any rights of a person under Rule 13, Texas Rules of Civil Procedure, or Chapter 10, Civil Practice and Remedies Code.

Added by Acts 2003, 78th Leg., ch.1060, § 6, eff. Sept. 1, 2003.

§ 11. Applications and Other Papers to be Filed With Clerk

All applications for probate proceedings, complaints, petitions and all other papers permitted or required by law to be filed in the court in probate matters, shall be filed with the county clerk of the proper county who shall file the same and endorse on each paper the date filed and the docket number, and his official signature.
Acts 1955, 54th Leg., p. 88, ch. 55, eff. Jan. 1, 1956.

§ 12. Costs and Security Therefor

(a) Applicability of Laws Regulating Costs. The provisions of law regulating costs in ordinary civil cases shall apply to all matters in probate when not expressly provided for in this Code.

(b) Security for Costs Required, When. When any person other than the personal representative of an estate files an application, complaint, or opposition in relation to the estate, he may be required by the clerk to give security for the probable cost of such proceeding before filing the same; or any one interested in the estate, or any officer of the court, may, at any time before the trial of such application, complaint, or opposition, obtain from the court, upon written motion, an order requiring such party to give security for the probable costs of such proceeding. The rules governing civil suits in the county court respecting this subject shall control in such cases.

(c) Suit for Fiduciary. No security for costs shall be required of an executor or administrator appointed by a court of this state in any suit brought by him in his fiduciary character.
Acts 1955, 54th Leg., p. 88, ch. 55, eff. Jan. 1, 1956. Subsec. (c) added by Acts 1985, 69th Leg., ch. 959, § 4, eff. Sept. 1, 1985; amended by Acts 1993, 73rd Leg., ch. 957, § 7, eff. Sept. 1, 1993.

§ 13. Judge's Probate Docket

The county clerk shall keep a record book to be styled "Judge's Probate Docket," and shall enter therein:

(a) The name of each person upon whose person or estate proceedings are had or sought to be had.

(b) The name of the executor or administrator or of the applicant for letters.

(c) The date of the filing of the original application for probate proceedings.

(d) A minute of each order, judgment, decree, and proceeding had in each estate, with the date thereof.

(e) A number for each estate upon the docket in the order in which proceedings are commenced, and each paper filed in an estate shall be given the corresponding docket number of the estate.
Acts 1955, 54th Leg., p. 88, ch. 55, eff. Jan. 1, 1956. Amended by Acts 1993, 73rd Leg., ch. 957, § 8, eff. Sept. 1, 1993.

§ 14. Claim Docket

The county clerk shall also keep a record book to be styled "Claim Docket," and shall enter therein all claims presented against an estate for approval by the court. This docket shall be ruled in sixteen columns at proper intervals from top to bottom, with a short note of the contents at the top of each column. One or more pages shall be assigned to each estate. The following information shall be entered in the respective columns beginning with the first or marginal column: The names of claimants in the order in which their claims are filed; the amount of the claim; its date; the date of filing; when due; the date from which it bears interest; the rate of interest; when allowed by the executor or administrator; the amount allowed; the date of rejection; when approved; the amount approved; when disapproved; the class to which the claim belongs; when established by judgment of a court; the amount of such judgment.
Acts 1955, 54th Leg., p. 88, ch. 55, eff. Jan. 1, 1956. Amended by Acts 1993, 73rd Leg., ch. 957, § 9, eff. Sept. 1, 1993.

§ 15. Case Files

The county clerk shall maintain a case file for each decedent's estate in which a probate proceeding has been filed. The case file must contain all orders, judgments, and proceedings of the court and any other probate filing with the court, including all:

(1) applications for the probate of wills and for the granting of administration;

(2) citations and notices, whether published or posted, with the returns thereon;

(3) wills and the testimony upon which the same are admitted to probate, provided that the substance only of depositions shall be recorded;

(4) bonds and official oaths;

(5) inventories, appraisements, and lists of claims;

(6) exhibits and accounts;

(7) reports of hiring, renting, or sale;

(8) applications for sale or partition of real estate and reports of sale and of commissioners of partition;

(9) applications for authority to execute leases for mineral development, or for pooling or unitization of lands, royalty, or other interest in minerals, or to lend or invest money; and

(10) reports of lending or investing money.

Acts 1955, 54th Leg., p. 88, ch. 55, eff. Jan. 1, 1956. Amended by Acts 1993, 73rd Leg., ch. 957, § 10, eff. Sept. 1, 1993; Acts 1999, 76th Leg., ch. 67, § 1, eff. Sept. 1, 1999.

§ 16. Probate Fee Book

The county clerk shall keep a record book styled "Probate Fee Book," and shall enter therein each item of costs which accrues to the officers of the court, together with witness fees, if any, showing the party to whom the costs or fees are due, the date of the accrual of the same, the estate or party liable therefor, and the

date on which any such costs or fees are paid.
Acts 1955, 54th Leg., p. 88, ch. 55, eff. Jan. 1, 1956.

§ 17. Maintaining Records in Lieu of Record Books

In lieu of keeping the record books described by Sections 13, 14, and 16 of this code, the county clerk may maintain the information relating to a person's or estate's probate proceedings maintained in those record books on a computer file, on microfilm, in the form of a digitized optical image, or in another similar form of data compilation.
Added by Acts 1999, 76th Leg., ch. 67, § 1, eff. Sept. 1, 1999.

§ 17A. Index

The county clerk shall properly index each record book, and shall keep it open for public inspection, but shall not let it out of his custody.
Acts 1955, 54th Leg., p. 88, ch. 55, eff. Jan. 1, 1956. Renumbered from V.A.T.S. Probate Code, § 17 and amended by Acts 1999, 76th Leg., ch. 67, § 1, eff. Sept. 1, 1999.

§ 18. Use of Records as Evidence

The record books or individual case files, including records on a computer file, on microfilm, in the form of a digitized optical image, or in another similar form of data compilation described in preceding sections of this code, or certified copies or reproductions of the records, shall be evidence in any court of this state.
Acts 1955, 54th Leg., p. 88, ch. 55, eff. Jan. 1, 1956. Amended by Acts 1999, 76th Leg., ch. 67, § 1, eff. Sept. 1, 1999.

§ 19. Call of the Dockets

The judge of the court in which probate proceedings are pending, at such times as he shall determine, shall call the estates of decedents in their regular order upon both the probate and claim dockets and make such orders as shall be necessary.
Acts 1955, 54th Leg., p. 88, ch. 55, eff. Jan. 1, 1956. Amended by Acts 1993, 73rd Leg., ch. 957, § 11, eff. Sept. 1, 1993.

§ 20. Clerk May Set Hearings

Whenever, on account of the county judge's absence from the county seat, or his being on vacation, disqualified, ill, or deceased, such judge is unable to designate the time and place for hearing a probate matter pending in his court, authority is hereby vested in the county clerk of the county in which such matter is pending to designate such time and place, entering such setting on the judge's docket and certifying thereupon why such judge is not acting by himself. If, after service of such notices and citations as required by law with reference to such time and place of hearing has been perfected, no qualified judge is present for the hearing, the same shall automatically be continued from day to day until a qualified judge is present to hear and determine the matter.
Acts 1955, 54th Leg., p. 88, ch. 55, eff. Jan. 1, 1956.

Statutes in Context

Any party has the right to a jury trial in a contested probate action under § 21.

---

§ 21. Trial by Jury

In all contested probate and mental illness proceedings in the district court or in the county court or statutory probate court, county court at law or other statutory court exercising probate jurisdiction, the parties shall be entitled to trial by jury as in other civil actions.
Acts 1955, 54th Leg., p. 88, ch. 55, eff. Jan. 1, 1956. Amended by Acts 1973, 63rd Leg., p. 1685, ch. 610, § 2.

§ 22. Evidence

In proceedings arising under the provisions of this Code, the rules relating to witnesses and evidence that govern in the District Court shall apply so far as practicable except that where a will is to be probated, and in other probate matters where there is no opposing party or attorney of record upon whom notice and copies of interrogatories may be served, service may be had by posting notice of intention to take depositions for a period of ten days as provided in this Code governing posting of notices. When such notice is filed with the clerk, a copy of the interrogatories shall also be filed, and at the expiration of ten days, commission may issue for taking the depositions, and the judge may file cross-interrogatories where no one appears, if he so desires.
Acts 1955, 54th Leg., p. 88, ch. 55, eff. Jan. 1, 1956.

§ 23. Decrees and Signing of Minutes

All decisions, orders, decrees, and judgments of the county court in probate matters shall be rendered in open court except in cases where it is otherwise specially provided. The probate minutes shall be approved and signed by the judge on the first day of each month, except, however, that if the first day of the month falls on a Sunday, such approval shall be entered on the preceding or succeeding day.
Acts 1955, 54th Leg., p. 88, ch. 55, eff. Jan. 1, 1956.

§ 24. Enforcement of Orders

The county or probate judge may enforce obedience to all his lawful orders against executors and administrators by attachment and imprisonment, but no such imprisonment shall exceed three days for any one offense, unless otherwise expressly so provided in this Code.
Acts 1955, 54th Leg., p. 88, ch. 55, eff. Jan. 1, 1956. Amended by Acts 1993, 73rd Leg., ch. 957, § 12, eff. Sept. 1, 1993.

§ 25. Executions

Executions in probate matters shall be directed "to any sheriff or any constable within the State of Texas," made returnable in sixty days, and shall be attested and signed by the clerk officially under the seal of the court.

All proceedings under such executions shall be governed by the laws regulating proceedings under executions issued from the District Court so far as applicable. Provided, however, that no execution directed to the sheriff or any constable of a specific county within this State shall be held defective if such execution was properly executed within such county by such officer.
Acts 1955, 54th Leg., p. 88, ch. 55, eff. Jan. 1, 1956.

§ 26. Attachments for Property

Whenever complaint in writing, under oath, shall be made to the county or probate judge by any person interested in the estate of a decedent that the executor or administrator is about to remove said estate, or any part thereof, beyond the limits of the State, such judge may order a writ to issue, directed "to any sheriff or any constable within the State of Texas," commanding him to seize such estate, or any part thereof, and hold the same subject to such further orders as such judge shall make on such complaint. No such writ shall issue unless the complainant shall give bond, in such sum as the judge shall require, payable to the executor or administrator of such estate, conditioned for the payment of all damages and costs that shall be recovered for the wrongful suing out of such writ. Provided, however, that no writ of attachment directed to the sheriff or any constable of a specific county within this State shall be held defective if such writ was properly executed within such county by such officer.
Acts 1955, 54th Leg., p. 88, ch. 55, eff. Jan. 1, 1956. Amended by Acts 1993, 73rd Leg., ch. 957, § 13, eff. Sept. 1, 1993.

§ 27. Enforcement of Specific Performance

When any person shall sell property and enter into bond or other written agreement to make title thereto, and shall depart this life without having made such title, the owner of such bond or written agreement or his legal representatives, may file a complaint in writing in the court of the county where the letters testamentary or of administration on the estate of the deceased obligor were granted, and cause the personal representative of such estate to be cited to appear at a date stated in the citation and show cause why specific performance of such bond or written agreement should not be decreed. Such bond or other written agreement shall be filed with such complaint, or good cause shown under oath why the same cannot be filed; and if it cannot be so filed, the same or the substance thereof shall be set forth in the complaint. After the service of the citation, the court shall hear such complaint and the evidence thereon, and, if satisfied from the proof that such bond or written agreement was legally executed by the testator or intestate, and that the complainant has a right to demand specific performance thereof, a decree shall be made ordering the personal representative to make title to the property, according to the tenor of the obligation, fully describing the property in such decree. When a conveyance is made under the provisions of this Section, it shall refer to and identify the decree of the court authorizing it, and, when delivered, shall vest in the person to whom made all the right and title which the testator or intestate had to the property conveyed; and such conveyance shall be prima facie evidence that all requirements of the law have been complied with in obtaining the same.
Acts 1955, 54th Leg., p. 88, ch. 55, eff. Jan. 1, 1956.

§ 28. Personal Representative to Serve Pending Appeal of Appointment

Pending appeals from orders or judgments appointing administrators or temporary administrators, the appointees shall continue to act as such and shall continue the prosecution of any suits then pending in favor of the estate.
Acts 1955, 54th Leg., p. 88, ch. 55, eff. Jan. 1, 1956. Amended by Acts 1975, 64th Leg., p. 2196, ch. 701, § 3, eff. June 21, 1975. Amended by Acts 1993, 73rd Leg., ch. 957, § 14, eff. Sept. 1, 1993.

Statutes in Context

While appeal bonds are normally required, no bond is required when an appeal is made by the personal representative unless the appeal personally concerns the personal representative.

---

§ 29. Appeal Bonds of Personal Representatives

When an appeal is taken by an executor or administrator, no bond shall be required, unless such appeal personally concerns him, in which case he must give the bond.
Acts 1955, 54th Leg., p. 88, ch. 55, eff. Jan. 1, 1956. Amended by Acts 1993, 73rd Leg., ch. 957, § 15, eff. Sept. 1, 1993.

Statutes in Context

A bill of review is filed for the purpose of getting a decision revised or corrected upon a showing of error. It may be filed by an interested party and is filed in the court where the estate was administered. A bill of review may be filed within two years of the date of the decision. Thus, a bill of review may be filed even though it is too late to appeal.

---

§ 31. Bill of Review

Any person interested may, by a bill of review filed in the court in which the probate proceedings were had, have any decision, order, or judgment rendered by the court, or by the judge thereof, revised and corrected on showing error therein; but no process or action under such decision, order or judgment shall be stayed except by writ of injunction, and no bill of review shall be filed after two years have elapsed from the date of such decision, order, or judgment.
Acts 1955, 54th Leg., p. 88, ch. 55, eff. Jan. 1, 1956. Amended by Acts 1993, 73rd Leg., ch. 957, § 16, eff. Sept. 1, 1993.

§ 32. Common Law Applicable

The rights, powers and duties of executors and administrators shall be governed by the principles of the common law, when the same do not conflict with the provisions of the statutes of this State.

Acts 1955, 54th Leg., p. 88, ch. 55, eff. Jan. 1, 1956. Amended by Acts 1993, 73rd Leg., ch. 957, § 17, eff. Sept. 1, 1993.

Statutes in Context

Section 33 provides extensive instructions on how notice and citations are to be given using a variety of delivery methods including personal service, posting, publication, and mailing.

---

§ 33. Issuance, Contents, Service, and Return of Citation, Notices, and Writs in Probate Matters

(a) When Citation or Notice Necessary. No person need be cited or otherwise given notice except in situations in which this Code expressly provides for citation or the giving of notice; provided, however, that even though this Code does not expressly provide for citation, or the issuance or return of notice in any probate matter, the court may, in its discretion, require that notice be given, and prescribe the form and manner of service and return thereof.

(b) Issuance by the Clerk or by Personal Representative. The county clerk shall issue necessary citations, writs, and process in probate matters, and all notices not required to be issued by personal representatives, without any order from the court, unless such order is required by a provision of this Code.

(c) Contents of Citation, Writ, and Notice. Citation and notices issued by the clerk shall be signed and sealed by him, and shall be styled "The State of Texas." Notices required to be given by a personal representative shall be in writing and shall be signed by the representative in his official capacity. All citations and notices shall be directed to the person or persons to be cited or notified, shall be dated, and shall state the style and number of the proceeding, the court in which it is pending, and shall describe generally the nature of the proceeding or matter to which the citation or notice relates. No precept directed to an officer is necessary. A citation or notice shall direct the person or persons cited or notified to appear by filing a written contest or answer, or to perform other acts required of him or them and shall state when and where such appearance or performance is required. No citation or notice shall be held to be defective because it contains a precept directed to an officer authorized to serve it. All writs and other process except citations and notices shall be directed "To any sheriff or constable within the State of Texas," but shall not be held defective because directed to the sheriff or any constable of a specific county if properly served within the named county by such officer.

(d) Where No Specific Form of Notice, Service, or Return is Prescribed, or When Provisions Are Insufficient or Inadequate. In all situations in which this Code requires that notice be given, or that a person be cited, and in which a specific method of giving such notice or of citing such person, or a specific method of service and return of such citation or notice is not given, or an insufficient or inadequate provision appears with respect to any of such matters, or when any interested person so requests, such notice or citation shall be issued, served, and returned in such manner as the court, by written order, shall direct in accordance with this Code and the Texas Rules of Civil Procedure, and shall have the same force and effect as if the manner of service and return had been specified in this Code.

(e) Service of Citation or Notice Upon Personal Representatives. Except in instances in which this Code expressly provides another method of service, any notice or citation required to be served upon any personal representative or receiver shall be served by the clerk issuing such citation or notice. The clerk shall serve the same by sending the original thereof by registered or certified mail to the attorney of record for the personal representative or receiver, but if there is no attorney of record, to the personal representative or receiver.

(f) Methods of Serving Citations and Notices.

(1) Personal Service. Where it is provided that personal service shall be had with respect to a citation or notice, any such citation or notice must be served upon the attorney of record for the person to be cited. Notwithstanding the requirement of personal service, service may be made upon such attorney by any of the methods hereinafter specified for service upon an attorney. If there is no attorney of record in the proceeding for such person, or if an attempt to make service upon the attorney was unsuccessful, a citation or notice directed to a person within this State must be served by the sheriff or constable upon the person to be cited or notified, in person, by delivering to him a true copy of such citation or notice at least ten (10) days before the return day thereof, exclusive of the date of service. Where the person to be cited or notified is absent from the State, or is a nonresident, such citation or notice may be served by any disinterested person competent to make oath of the fact. Said citation or notice shall be returnable at least ten (10) days after the date of service, exclusive of the date of service. The return of the person serving the citation or notice shall be endorsed on or attached to same; it shall show the time and place of service, certify that a true copy of the citation or notice was delivered to the person directed to be served, be subscribed and sworn to before some officer authorized by the laws of this State to take affidavits, under the hand and official seal of such officer, and returned to the county clerk who issued same. If in either case such citation or notice is returned with the notation that the person sought to be served, whether within or without this State, cannot be found, the clerk shall issue a new citation or notice directed to

the person or persons sought to be served and service shall be by publication.

(2) Posting. When citation or notice is required to be posted, it shall be posted by the sheriff or constable at the courthouse door of the county in which the proceedings are pending, or at the place in or near the courthouse where public notices customarily are posted, for not less than ten (10) days before the return day thereof, exclusive of the date of posting. The clerk shall deliver the original and a copy of such citation or notice to the sheriff or any constable of the proper county, who shall post said copy as herein prescribed and return the original to the clerk, stating in a written return thereon the time when and the place where he posted such copy. The date of posting shall be the date of service. When posting of notice by a personal representative is authorized or required, the method herein prescribed shall be followed, such notices to be issued in the name of the representative, addressed and delivered to, posted and returned by, the proper officer, and filed with the clerk.

(3) Publication. When a person is to be cited or notified by publication, the citation or notice shall be published once in a newspaper of general circulation in the county in which the proceedings are pending, and said publication shall be not less than ten (10) days before the return day thereof, exclusive of the date of publication. The date of publication which said newspaper bears shall be the date of service. If no newspaper is published, printed, or of general circulation, in the county where citation or notice is to be had, service of such citation or notice shall be by posting.

(4) Mailing.

(A) When any citation or notice is required or permitted to be served by registered or certified mail, other than notices required to be given by personal representatives, the clerk shall issue such citation or notice and shall serve the same by sending the original thereof by registered or certified mail. Any notice required to be given by a personal representative by registered or certified mail shall be issued by him, and he shall serve the same by sending the original thereof by registered or certified mail. In either case the citation or notice shall be mailed with instructions to deliver to the addressee only, and with return receipt requested. The envelope containing such citation or notice shall be addressed to the attorney of record in the proceeding for the person to be cited or notified, but if there is none, or if returned undelivered, then to the person to be cited or notified. A copy of such citation or notice, together with the certificate of the clerk, or of the personal representative, as the case may be, showing the fact and date of mailing, shall be filed and recorded. If a receipt is returned, it shall be attached to the certificate.

(B) When any citation or notice is required or permitted to be served by ordinary mail, the clerk, or the personal representative when required by statute or by order of the court, shall serve the same by mailing the original to the person to be cited or notified. A copy of such citation or notice, together with a certificate of the person serving the same showing the fact and time of mailing, shall be filed and recorded.

(C) When service is made by mail, the date of mailing shall be the date of service. Service by mail shall be made not less than twenty (20) days before the return day thereof, exclusive of the date of service.

(D) If a citation or notice served by mailing is returned undelivered, a new citation or notice shall be issued, and such citation or notice shall be served by posting.

(g) Return of Citation or Notice. All citations and notices issued by the clerk and served by personal service, by mail, by posting, or by publication, shall be returnable to the court from which issued on the first Monday after the service is perfected.

(h) Sufficiency of Return in Cases of Posting. In any probate matter where citation or notice is required to be served by posting, and such citation or notice is issued in conformity with the applicable provision of this Code, the citation or notice and the service and return thereof shall be sufficient and valid if any sheriff or constable posts a copy or copies of such citation or notice at the place or places prescribed by this Code on a day which is sufficiently prior to the return day named in such citation or notice for the period of time for which such citation or notice is required to be posted to elapse before the return day of such citation or notice, and the fact that such sheriff or constable makes his return on such citation or notice and returns same into court before the period of time elapses for which such citation or notice is required to be posted, shall not affect the sufficiency or validity of such citation or notice or the service or return thereof, even though such return is made, and such citation or notice is returned into court, on the same day it is issued.

(i) Proof of Service. Proof of service in all cases requiring notice or citation, whether by publication, posting, mailing, or otherwise, shall be filed before the hearing. Proof of service made by a sheriff or constable shall be made by the return of service. Service made by a private person shall be proved by the affidavit of the person. Proof of service by publication shall be made by the affidavit of the publisher or that of an employee of the publisher, which affidavit shall show the date the issue of the newspaper bore, and have attached to or embodied in it a copy of the published notice or citation. In the case of service by mail, proof shall be made by the certificate of the clerk, or the affidavit of the personal representative or other person making such service, stating the fact and time of mailing. In the case of service by registered or certified mail, the return receipt shall be attached to the certificate, if a receipt has been returned.

(j) Request for Notice. At any time after an application is filed for the purpose of commencing any proceeding in probate, including, but not limited to, a proceeding for the probate of a will, grant of letters testamentary or of administration and determination of heirship, any person interested in the estate may file with the clerk a request in writing that he be notified of any and all, or of any specifically designated, motions, applications, or pleadings filed by any person, or by any particular persons specifically designated in the request. The fees and costs for such notices shall be borne by the person requesting them, and the clerk may require a deposit to cover the estimated costs of furnishing such person with the notice or notices requested. The clerk shall thereafter send to such person by ordinary mail copies of any of the documents specified in the request. Failure of the clerk to comply with the request shall not invalidate any proceeding.

Acts 1955, 54th Leg., p. 88, ch. 55, eff. Jan. 1, 1956. Amended by Acts 1957, 55th Leg., p. 53, ch. 31, § 1, eff. Aug. 22, 1957; Acts 1971, 62nd Leg., p. 967, ch. 173, § 1, eff. Jan. 1, 1972. Subsec. (j) amended by Acts 1993, 73rd Leg., ch. 957, § 18, eff. Sept. 1, 1993.

Statutes in Context

If a party has an attorney of record in a case, all notices are to be served on the attorney rather than the party under § 34.

§ 34. Service on Attorney

If any attorney shall have entered his appearance of record for any party in any proceeding in probate, all citations and notices required to be served on the party in such proceeding shall be served on the attorney, and such service shall be in lieu of service upon the party for whom the attorney appears. All notices served on attorneys in accordance with this section may be served by registered or certified mail or by delivery to the attorney in person. They may be served by a party to the proceeding or his attorney of record, or by the proper sheriff or constable, or by any other person competent to testify. A written statement by an attorney of record, or the return of the officer, or the affidavit of any other person showing service shall be prima facie evidence of the fact of service.

Acts 1955, 54th Leg., p. 88, ch. 55, eff. Jan. 1, 1956. Amended by Acts 1971, 62nd Leg., p. 970, ch. 173, § 2, eff. Jan. 1, 1972.

Statutes in Context

Normally, a judge has the discretion whether to appoint an attorney ad litem to represent an unborn, unascertained, unknown, nonresident, or incompetent party. However, in a determination of heirship proceeding, the judge is *required* to appoint an attorney ad litem under Probate Code § 53(c).

§ 34A. Attorneys Ad Litem

Except as provided by Section 53(c) of this code, the judge of a probate court may appoint an attorney ad litem to represent the interests of a person having a legal disability, a nonresident, an unborn or unascertained person, or an unknown heir in any probate proceeding. Each attorney ad litem appointed under this section is entitled to reasonable compensation for services in the amount set by the court and to be taxed as costs in the proceeding.

Added by Acts 1983, 68th Leg., p. 747, ch. 178, § 1, eff. Aug. 29, 1983. Amended by Acts 1987, 70th Leg., ch. 467, § 1, eff. Sept. 1, 1987; Acts 1993, 73rd Leg., ch. 957, § 19, eff. Sept. 1, 1993; Acts 2001, 77th Leg., ch. 664, § 1, eff. Sept. 1, 2001.

§ 35. Waiver of Notice

Any person legally competent who is interested in any hearing in a proceeding in probate may, in person or by attorney, waive in writing notice of such hearing. A trustee may make such a waiver on behalf of the beneficiary of his trust. A consul or other representative of a foreign government, whose appearance has been entered as provided by law on behalf of any person residing in a foreign country, may make such waiver of notice on behalf of such person. Any person who submits to the jurisdiction of the court in any hearing shall be deemed to have waived notice thereof.

Acts 1955, 54th Leg., p. 88, ch. 55, eff. Jan. 1, 1956. Amended by Acts 1993, 73rd Leg., ch. 957, § 20, eff. Sept. 1, 1993.

Statutes in Context

The judge has the duty to use reasonable diligence to make certain that personal representatives in dependent administrations are performing their duties properly. The judge, however, does not have this responsibility with respect to independent personal representatives who are not supervised by the court.

§ 36. Duty and Responsibility of Judge

(a) It shall be the duty of each county and probate court to use reasonable diligence to see that personal representatives of estates being administered under orders of the court and other officers of the court perform the duty enjoined upon them by law pertaining to such estates. The judge shall annually, if in his opinion the same be necessary, examine the condition of each of said estates and the solvency of the bonds of personal representatives of estates. He shall, at any time he finds that the personal representative's bond is not sufficient to protect such estate, require such personal representatives to execute a new bond in accordance with law. In each case, he shall notify the personal representative, and the sureties on the bond, as provided by law; and should damage or loss result to estates through the gross neglect of the judge to use reasonable diligence in the performance of his duty, he shall be liable on his bond to those damaged by such neglect.

(b) The court may request an applicant or court-appointed fiduciary to produce other information identifying an applicant, decedent, or personal representative, including social security numbers, in addition to identifying information the applicant or fiduciary is required to produce under this code. The court shall maintain the information required under this subsection, and the information may not be filed with the clerk.

Acts 1955, 54th Leg., p. 88, ch. 55, eff. Jan. 1, 1956. Amended by Acts 1975, 64th Leg., p. 979, ch. 375, § 1, eff. June 19, 1975. Amended by Acts 1993, 73rd Leg., ch. 957, § 21, eff. Sept. 1, 1993; Acts 1997, 75th Leg., ch. 1302, § 3, eff. Sept. 1, 1997.

Statutes in Context

A testator often protects the will and other important documents by placing them in a safe deposit box. Sections 36B-36F provide guidelines for certain parties, such as a spouse, parent, adult descendent, or executor, to gain access to the safe deposit box for the purpose of obtaining the decedent's will as well as a burial plot deed and life insurance policies. These provisions provide procedures for both court and non-court ordered access.

§ 36B. Examination of Documents or Safe Deposit Box With Court Order

(a) A judge of a court having probate jurisdiction of a decedent's estate may order a person to permit a court representative named in the order to examine a decedent's documents or safe deposit box if it is shown to the judge that:

(1) the person may possess or control the documents or that the person leased the safe deposit box to the decedent; and

(2) the documents or safe deposit box may contain a will of the decedent, a deed to a burial plot in which the decedent is to be buried, or an insurance policy issued in the decedent's name and payable to a beneficiary named in the policy.

(b) The court representative shall examine the decedent's documents or safe deposit box in the presence of:

(1) the judge ordering the examination or an agent of the judge; and

(2) the person who has possession or control of the documents or who leased the safe deposit box or, if the person is a corporation, an officer of the corporation or an agent of an officer.

Added by Acts 1981, 67th Leg., 1st C.S., p. 193, ch. 17, art. 3, § 1, eff. Sept. 1, 1981.

§ 36C. Delivery of Document With Court Order

(a) A judge who orders an examination by a court representative of a decedent's documents or safe deposit box under Section 36B of this code may order the person who possesses or controls the documents or who leases the safe deposit box to permit the court representative to take possession of the following documents:

(1) a will of the decedent;

(2) a deed to a burial plot in which the decedent is to be buried; or

(3) an insurance policy issued in the decedent's name and payable to a beneficiary named in the policy.

(b) The court representative shall deliver:

(1) the will to the clerk of a court that has probate jurisdiction and that is located in the same county as the court of the judge who ordered the examination;

(2) the burial plot deed to the person designated by the judge in the order for the examination; or

(3) the insurance policy to a beneficiary named in the policy.

(c) A court clerk to whom a will is delivered under Subsection (b) of this section shall issue a receipt for the will to the court representative who delivers it.

Added by Acts 1981, 67th Leg., 1st C.S., p. 193, ch. 17, art. 3, § 1, eff. Sept. 1, 1981.

§ 36D. Examination of Document or Safe Deposit Box Without Court Order

(a) A person who possesses or controls a document delivered by a decedent for safekeeping or who leases a safe deposit box to a decedent may permit any of the following persons to examine the document or the contents of the safe deposit box:

(1) the spouse of the decedent;

(2) a parent of the decedent;

(3) a descendant of the decedent who is at least 18 years old; or

(4) a person named as executor of the decedent's estate in a copy of a document that the person has and that appears to be a will of the decedent.

(b) The examination shall be conducted in the presence of the person who possesses or controls the document or who leases the safe deposit box or, if the person is a corporation, an officer of the corporation.

Added by Acts 1981, 67th Leg., 1st C.S., p. 193, ch. 17, art. 3, § 1, eff. Sept. 1, 1981.

§ 36E. Delivery of Document Without Court Order

(a) A person who permits an examination of a decedent's document or safe deposit box under Section 36D of this code may deliver:

(1) a document appearing to be the decedent's will to the clerk of a court that has probate jurisdiction and that is located in the county in which the decedent resided or to the person named in the document as an executor of the decedent's estate;

(2) a document appearing to be a deed to a burial plot in which the decedent is to be buried or appearing to give burial instructions to the person making the examination; or

(3) a document appearing to be an insurance policy on the decedent's life to a beneficiary named in the policy.

(b) A person who has leased a safe deposit box to the decedent shall keep a copy of a document appearing to be a will that the person delivers under Subsection (a) of this section. The person shall keep the copy for four years after the day of delivery.

(c) A person may not deliver a document under Subsection (a) of this section unless requested to do so by the person examining the document and unless the person examining the document issues a receipt for the document to the person who is to deliver it.

Added by Acts 1981, 67th Leg., 1st C.S., p. 193, ch. 17, art. 3, § 1, eff. Sept. 1, 1981.

§ 36F. Restriction on Removal of Contents of Safe Deposit Box

A person may not remove the contents of a decedent's safe deposit box except as provided by Section 36C or 36E of this code or except as provided by another law.

Added by Acts 1981, 67th Leg., 1st C.S., p. 193, ch. 17, art. 3, § 1, eff. Sept. 1, 1981.

Chapter II. Descent and Distribution

Statutes in Context

The new owner of a person's property upon death depends on two main factors — first, the type of asset and, second, whether the decedent made a valid will. Certain property, commonly referred to as *non-probate assets*, is controlled by the terms of the property arrangement itself. Examples of these arrangements include land held in joint tenancy with survivorship rights and contractual arrangements which specify the at-death owner such as life insurance and pay on death accounts at banks, savings and loan associations, and other financial institutions. The passage of the remaining property, the *probate estate*, depends on whether the decedent died after executing a valid will which disposed of all of the decedent's probate property.

Chapter II of the Probate Code governs what happens when a person dies without a valid will or dies with a valid will which does not encompass all of the person's probate estate. When this happens, the person's probate property which is not covered by a valid will is distributed through a process called *intestate succession*. A person may die totally intestate, that is, *intestate as to the person*, if the person did not leave any type of valid will. A person may also die partially intestate, that is, *intestate as to property*, if the person's valid will fails to dispose of all of the person's probate estate.

Statutes in Context

Title to the decedent's property passes to the heirs or beneficiaries immediately upon the decedent's death regardless of the length of time occupied by the administration process. *See Welder v. Hitchcock*, 617 S.W.2d 294 (Tex. Civ. App. — Corpus Christi 1981, writ ref'd n.r.e.) (declaring that "there is no shorter interval of time than between the death of a decedent and the vesting of his estate in his heirs"). This title is, however, subject to the claims of the decedent's creditors.

However, if a personal representative is appointed, that person has a superior right to possess all of the decedent's probate assets owned at the time of death. It may be difficult for the personal representative to collect this property because family members often take the decedent's property, especially personal property in the decedent's home, shortly after death despite having no authority to do so.

§ 37. Passage of Title Upon Intestacy and Under a Will

When a person dies, leaving a lawful will, all of his estate devised or bequeathed by such will, and all powers of appointment granted in such will, shall vest immediately in the devisees or legatees of such estate and the donees of such powers; and all the estate of such person, not devised or bequeathed, shall vest immediately in his heirs at law; subject, however, to the payment of the debts of the testator or intestate, except such as is exempted by law, and subject to the payment of court-ordered child support payments that are delinquent on the date of the person's death; and whenever a person dies intestate, all of his estate shall vest immediately in his heirs at law, but with the exception aforesaid shall still be liable and subject in their hands to the payment of the debts of the intestate and the delinquent child support payments; but upon the issuance of letters testamentary or of administration upon any such estate, the executor or administrator shall have the right to possession of the estate as it existed at the death of the testator or intestate, with the exception aforesaid; and he shall recover possession of and hold such estate in trust to be disposed of in accordance with the law.

Acts 1955, 54th Leg., p. 88, ch. 55, eff. Jan. 1, 1956. Amended by Acts 1969, 61st Leg., p. 1703, ch. 556, § 2, eff. June 10, 1969. Amended by Acts 1981, 67th Leg., p. 2537, ch. 674, § 3, eff. Sept. 1, 1981.

Statutes in Context

Under modern law, an heir, will beneficiary, life insurance beneficiary, or beneficiary of a survivorship agreement may disclaim or renounce the person's interest. In the normal course of events, heirs and beneficiaries do not disclaim. Most people like the idea of getting something for free. However, there are many good reasons why a person may desire to forego the offered bounty. Four of the most common reasons are as follows: (1) the property may be undesirable or accompanied by an onerous burden (e.g., littered with leaky barrels of toxic chemical waste or subject to back taxes exceeding the value of the land); (2) the heir or beneficiary may believe that it is wrong to benefit from the death of another and refuse the property on moral or religious grounds; (3) an heir or beneficiary who is in debt may disclaim the property to prevent the property from being taken by the person's creditors; and (4) the heir or beneficiary may disclaim to reduce the person's transfer tax burden (a "qualified disclaimer" under I.R.C. § 2518).

Section 37A provides the formal requirements for effectuating a disclaimer. The heir must disclaim in a written and acknowledged (notarized) document. The writing must be filed in the court handling the estate of the decedent not later than 9 months after the deceased's death. The heir must give notice of disclaimer to the executor or administrator of the estate by personal service or by registered or certified mail.

The heir or beneficiary may "pick and choose" which assets to disclaim but if the person accepts the property, the right to disclaim is waived. Even a relatively small exercise of dominion or control over the property may prevent disclaimer. *See Badouh v. Hale*, 22 S.W.3d 392 (Tex. 2000) (holding that a beneficiary who used property she expected to receive under a will as collateral for a loan prior to the testator's death could not disclaim because such a use was the exercise of dominion and control).

Once a valid disclaimer is made, the disclaimant is treated as predeceasing the person from whom the disclaimant is taking. The disclaimed property then passes under intestacy, the will, or the contract as if the disclaimant had died first. The disclaimant cannot specify the new owner of the disclaimed property. *See Welder v. Hitchcock*, 617 S.W.2d 294 (Tex. Civ. App. — Corpus Christi 1981, writ ref'd n.r.e.) (holding that the disclaimed property passes as if the disclaiming person is dead *vis-à-vis* the disclaimed property, not the entire estate).

Once made, a disclaimer is irrevocable.

Disclaimers are an effective method for a debtor to prevent property to be inherited, received under a will, or taken under a survivorship agreement from falling into the hands of a creditor. The disclaimer is not a fraudulent conveyance and thus it may not be set aside by the disclaimant's creditors. However, the United States Supreme Court has held that a disclaimer will not defeat a federal tax lien. *Drye v. United States*, 528 U.S. 49 (1999).

---

§ 37A. Means of Evidencing Disclaimer or Renunciation of Property or Interest Receivable From a Decedent

Any person, or the guardian of an incapacitated person, the personal representative of a deceased person, or the guardian ad litem of an unborn or unascertained person, with prior court approval of the court having, or which would have, jurisdiction over such guardian, personal representative, or guardian ad litem, or any independent executor of a deceased person, without prior court approval, who may be entitled to receive any property as a beneficiary and who intends to effect disclaimer irrevocably on or after September 1, 1977, of the whole or any part of such property shall evidence same as herein provided. A disclaimer evidenced as provided herein shall be effective as of the death of decedent and shall relate back for all purposes to the death of the decedent and is not subject to the claims of any creditor of the disclaimant. Unless the decedent's will provides otherwise, the property subject to the disclaimer shall pass as if the person disclaiming or on whose behalf a disclaimer is made had predeceased the decedent and a future interest that would otherwise take effect in possession or enjoyment after the termination of the estate or interest that is disclaimed takes effect as if the disclaiming beneficiary had predeceased the decedent. Failure to comply with the provisions hereof shall render such disclaimer ineffective except as an assignment of such property to those who would have received same had the person attempting the disclaimer died prior to the decedent. The term "property" as used in this section shall include all legal and equitable interests, powers, and property, whether present or future, whether vested or contingent, and whether beneficial or burdensome, in whole or in part. The term "disclaimer" as used in this section shall include "renunciation." In this section "beneficiary" includes a person who would have been entitled, if the person had not made a disclaimer, to receive property as a result of the death of another person by inheritance, under a will, by an agreement between spouses for community property with a right of survivorship, by a joint tenancy with a right of survivorship, or by any other survivorship agreement, account, or interest in which the interest of the decedent passes to a surviving beneficiary, by an insurance, annuity, endowment, employment, deferred compensation, or other contract or arrangement, or under a pension, profit sharing, thrift, stock bonus, life insurance, survivor income, incentive, or other plan or program providing retirement, welfare, or fringe benefits with respect to an employee or a self-employed individual. Nothing in this section shall be construed to preclude a subsequent disclaimer by any person who shall be entitled to property as a result of a disclaimer. The following shall apply to such disclaimers:

(a) Written Memorandum of Disclaimer and Filing Thereof. In the case of property receivable by a beneficiary, the disclaimer shall be evidenced by a written memorandum, acknowledged before a notary public or other person authorized to take acknowledgements of conveyances of real estate. Unless the beneficiary is a charitable organization or governmental agency of the state, a written memorandum of disclaimer disclaiming a present interest shall be filed not later than nine months after the death of the decedent and a written memorandum of disclaimer disclaiming a future interest may be filed not later than nine months after the event determining that the taker of the property or interest is finally ascertained and his interest is indefeasibly vested. If the beneficiary is a charitable organization or a governmental agency of the state, a written memorandum of disclaimer disclaiming a present or future interest shall be filed not later than nine months after the beneficiary receives the notice required by Section 128A of this code. The written memorandum of disclaimer shall be filed in the probate court in which the decedent's will has been probated or in which proceedings have been commenced for the administration of the decedent's estate or which has before it an application for either of the same; provided, however, if the administration of the decedent's estate is closed, or after the expiration of one year following the date of the issuance of letters testamentary in an independent administration, or if there has been no will of the decedent probated or filed for probate, or if no administration of the decedent's estate has been commenced, or if no application for administration of the decedent's estate has been filed, the written memorandum of disclaimer shall be filed with the county clerk of the county of the decedent's residence, or, if the decedent is not a resident of this state but real property or an interest therein located in this state is disclaimed, a written memorandum of disclaimer shall be filed with the county clerk of the county in which such real property or interest therein is located, and recorded by such county clerk in the deed records of that county.

(b) Notice of Disclaimer. Unless the beneficiary is a charitable organization or governmental agency of the state, copies of any written memorandum of disclaimer shall be delivered in person to, or shall be mailed by registered or certified mail to and received by, the legal representative of the transferor of the interest or the holder of legal title to the property to which the disclaimer relates not later than nine months after the death of the decedent or, if the interest is a future interest, not later than nine months after the date the person who will receive the property or interest is finally ascertained and the person's interest is indefeasibly vested. If the beneficiary is a charitable organization or government agency of the state, the notices required by this section shall be filed not later than nine months after the beneficiary receives the notice required by Section 128A of this code.

(c) Power to Provide for Disclaimer. Nothing herein shall prevent a person from providing in a will, insurance policy, employee benefit agreement, or other instrument for the making of disclaimers by a beneficiary of an interest receivable under that instrument and for the disposition of disclaimed property in a manner different from the provisions hereof.

(d) Irrevocability of Disclaimer. Any disclaimer filed and served under this section shall be irrevocable.

(e) Partial Disclaimer. Any person who may be entitled to receive any property as a beneficiary may disclaim such property in whole or in part, including but not limited to specific powers of invasion, powers of appointment, and fee estate in favor of life estates; and a partial disclaimer or renunciation, in accordance with the provisions of this section, shall be effective whether the property so renounced or disclaimed constitutes a portion of a single, aggregate gift or constitutes part or all of a separate, independent gift; provided, however, that a partial disclaimer shall be effective only with respect to property expressly described or referred to by category in such disclaimer; and provided further, that a partial disclaimer of property which is subject to a burdensome interest created by the decedent's will shall not be effective unless such property constitutes a gift which is separate and distinct from undisclaimed gifts.

(f) Partial Disclaimer by Spouse. Without limiting Subsection (e) of this section, a disclaimer by the decedent's surviving spouse of a transfer by the decedent is not a disclaimer by the surviving spouse of all or any part of any other transfer from the decedent to or for the benefit of the surviving spouse, regardless of whether the property or interest that would have passed under the disclaimed transfer passes because of the disclaimer to or for the benefit of the surviving spouse by the other transfer.

(g) Disclaimer After Acceptance. No disclaimer shall be effective after the acceptance of the property by the beneficiary. For the purpose of this section, acceptance shall occur only if the person making such disclaimer has previously taken possession or exercised dominion and control of such property in the capacity of beneficiary.

(h) Interest in Trust Property. A beneficiary who accepts an interest in a trust is not considered to have a direct or indirect interest in trust property that relates to a licensed or permitted business and over which the beneficiary exercises no control. Direct or indirect beneficial ownership of not more than five percent of any class of equity securities that is registered under the Securities Exchange Act of 1934 shall not be deemed to be an ownership interest in the business of the issuer of such securities within the meaning of any statute, pursuant thereto.

Added by Acts 1971, 62nd Leg., p. 2954, ch. 979, § 1, eff. Aug. 30, 1971. Amended by Acts 1977, 65th Leg., p. 1918, ch. 769, § 1, eff. Aug. 29, 1977; Acts 1979, 66th Leg., p. 1741, ch. 713, § 4, eff. Aug. 27, 1979. Amended by Acts 1987, 70th Leg., ch. 467, § 2, eff. Sept. 1, 1987; Acts 1991, 72nd Leg., ch. 895, § 2, eff. Sept. 1, 1991; Acts 1993, 73rd Leg., ch. 846, § 1, eff. Sept. 1, 1993; Acts 1995, 74th Leg., ch. 1039, § 5, eff. Sept. 1, 1995.

Statutes in Context

Once an heir or beneficiary receives the property through intestate succession, by will, or as the beneficiary of a life insurance policy, the person may assign his/her interest in the property to a third person. Unlike with a disclaimer under § 37A, the heir or beneficiary will be liable for transfer taxes and the property will become subject to the creditors of the heir or beneficiary.

§ 37B. Assignment of Property Received from a Decedent

(a) A person entitled to receive property or an interest in property from a decedent under a will, by inheritance, or as a beneficiary under a life insurance contract, and who does not disclaim the property under Section 37A of this code, may assign the property or interest in property to any person.

(b) The assignment may, at the request of the assignor, be filed as provided for the filing of a disclaimer under Section 37A(a) of this code. The filing requires the service of notice under Section 37A(b) of this code.

(c) Failure to comply with the provisions of Section 37A of this code does not affect an assignment under this section.

(d) An assignment under this section is a gift to the assignee and is not a disclaimer or renunciation under Section 37A of this code.

(e) An assignment that would defeat a spendthrift provision imposed in a trust may not be made under this section.

Added by Acts 1985, 69th Leg., ch. 880, § 1, eff. Sept. 1, 1985.

Statutes in Context

The 2003 Texas Legislature enacted § 37C to explain when an inter vivos gift will be treated as being in satisfaction of a testamentary gift. The provision is analogous to the existing provision dealing with advancements in an intestacy context under Probate Code § 44.

An inter vivos gift will be considered in partial or total satisfaction of a testamentary gift only if one of the following three conditions is satisfied:

(1) The testator's will expressly indicates that the inter vivos gift is to be deducted from the testamentary gift.

(2) The testator declares in a contemporaneous writing that the inter vivos gift is either (a) to be deducted from the testamentary gift or (b) is in satisfaction of the testamentary gift.

(3) The beneficiary acknowledges in writing that the inter vivos gift is in satisfaction of the testamentary gift.

The value of property the testator gives in partial satisfaction of a testamentary gift is determined at the earlier of the date when (a) the beneficiary acquires possession of or enjoys the property or (b) when the testator dies.

Note the "interesting" placement of this new provision. The Legislature included the section in the intestacy chapter (Chapter II – Descent and Distribution) rather than in the chapter dealing with wills (Chapter IV – Execution and Revocation of Wills).

---

§ 37C. Satisfaction of Devise

(a) Property given to a person by a testator during the testator's lifetime is considered a satisfaction, either wholly or partly, of a devise to the person if:

(1) the testator's will provides for deduction of the lifetime gift;

(2) the testator declares in a contemporaneous writing that the lifetime gift is to be deducted from or is in satisfaction of the devise; or

(3) the devisee acknowledges in writing that the lifetime gift is in satisfaction of the devise.

(b) Property given in partial satisfaction of a devise shall be valued as of the earlier of the date on which the devisee acquires possession of or enjoys the property or the date on which the testator dies.

Added by Acts 2003, 78th Leg., ch. 1060, § 7, eff. Sept. 1, 2003.

Statutes in Context

Early in the evolution of civilization, societies developed customs and laws to control the transmission of a person's property after death. Our modern intestacy laws are traced originally to the Anglo-Saxons. The Norman Conquest of 1066 A.D. played a significant role in the development of these rules. William the Conqueror was irritated that English landowners refused to recognize his right to the English Crown after his victory. Accordingly, William took ownership of all land by force and instituted the Norman form of feudalism. Under this system, the Crown was the true owner of all real property with others holding the property in a hierarchical scheme under which lower-ranked holders owed various financial and service-oriented duties to higher-ranked holders.

As a result, real property became the most essential element in the political, economic, and social structure of the Middle Ages. The Crown and its tough royal courts controlled the *descent* of real property. The basic features of descent included the following rules. (1) Male heirs inherited real property to the exclusion of female heirs unless no male heir existed. The reason underlying this discriminatory preference for male over female heirs was based on the feudal incidents of ownership. One of the primary duties of lower-ranked holders of property was to provide military service to higher-ranked holders. Under the then existing social climate, women were deemed unable to perform these services and thus were not able to inherit realty if a male heir existed. (2) If two or more males were equally related to the decedent, the oldest male would inherit all of the land to the total exclusion of the younger males. This is the rule of *primogeniture*. Primogeniture was applied because the Crown thought it was too impractical to divide the duty to provide military services as well as to subdivide the property. (3) If there were no male heirs and several female heirs, each female heir shared equally.

Before the industrial revolution, personal property was of lesser importance. There were no machines or corporate securities about which to worry. Instead, most chattels were of relatively little value such as clothing, furniture, jewelry, and livestock. Thus, the Crown permitted the church and its courts to govern the *distribution* of personal property. The ecclesiastical courts based distribution on canon law which had its foundation in Roman law. In general, personal property was distributed equally among equally related heirs. There was no preference for male heirs and the ages of the heirs were irrelevant.

After centuries of movement toward a unified system, the English Parliament passed the *Administration of Estates Act* in 1925 which abolished primogeniture and the preference for male heirs as well as providing uniform rules for all types of property. Most intestacy statutes in the United States make no distinction based on the age and sex of the heirs nor between the descent of real property and the distribution of personal property. However, Texas and a few other states retain this latter common law principle and provide different intestacy schemes for real and personal property under certain circumstances.

The intestate distribution scheme in Texas is derived mainly from three sections of the Probate Code: § 38 (distribution of property of a single decedent and the separate property of a married decedent), § 45 (distribution of the community property of a married decedent), and § 43 (determination of the type of distribution). Below is a summary of these sections assuming that the decedent died on or after September 1, 1993.

A. IDENTIFY MARITAL STATUS OF DECEDENT AND PROPERTY WHICH NEEDS TO BE DISTRIBUTED

1. If Married — Community Property & Separate Property

2. If Unmarried — Individual Property

B. DISTRIBUTION OF COMMUNITY PROPERTY OF MARRIED PERSON — § 45

1. If No Surviving Descendants

All community to surviving spouse. Surviving spouse retains the one-half of the community that the surviving spouse owned once the marriage was dissolved by death and inherits the deceased spouse's one-half of the community.

2. If Surviving Children or Their Descendants

a. No Non-Spousal Descendants

Surviving spouse takes all if all of the deceased spouse's surviving descendants are also descendants of the surviving spouse.

Note that for spouses dying before September 1, 1993, the deceased spouse's one-half of the community property was not inherited by the surviving spouse. Instead, the deceased spouse' share passed to the deceased spouse's descendants.

b. Non-Spousal Descendants

If any of the deceased spouse's surviving descendants are not also descendants of the surviving spouse, then the community is divided.

(1) Surviving Spouse

Retains ½ interest that surviving souse already owned by virtue of it being community property.

(2) Children and Descendants of Deceased Spouse

Receive deceased spouse's ½.

All deceased spouse's descendants are treated as a group regardless of whether the other parent is or is not the surviving spouse.

C. DISTRIBUTION OF SEPARATE PROPERTY OF MARRIED PERSON — § 38(b)

Unlike most states, Texas has retained a vestige of the common law distinction between the descent of real property and the distribution of personal property.

If the intestate was in the midst of a real estate transaction at the time of death, it becomes significant to determine whether the intestate's interest is real or personal property. Texas courts hold that *equitable conversion* occurs. Thus, after a contract for the purchase and sale of real property is signed but before closing, the seller is treated as owning personal property (the right to the sales proceeds) and the buyer as owing real property (the right to specifically enforce the contract). *Parson v. Wolfe*, 676 S.W.2d 689 (Tex. App.—Amarillo 1984, no writ).

1. Surviving Descendants

a. Personal Property

1/3 to surviving spouse.

2/3 to children or descendants.

b. Real Property

Life estate in 1/3 to surviving spouse.

Outright 2/3 and the remainder of surviving spouse's life estate to children or descendants

2. No Surviving Descendants

a. Personal Property

All to surviving spouse.

b. Real Property

(1) Surviving Parents or Siblings or Their Descendants

½ to surviving spouse.

½ to parents and siblings as if the intestate died without a surviving spouse.

(2) No Surviving Parents, Siblings, or Their Descendants

All to surviving spouse.

D. INDIVIDUAL PROPERTY DISTRIBUTION (UNMARRIED INTESTATE) — § 38(a)

1. Descendants Survive

All to descendants.

2. No Descendants Survive But Surviving Parents

a. Both Parents Survive

Each parent gets ½.

b. One Parent Survives as well as Siblings or Sibling's Descendants

½ to surviving parent; ½ to siblings and their descendants.

c. One Parent Survives but No Siblings nor Sibling's Descendants

All to surviving parent.

3. No Descendants and No Parents Survive

All to siblings and their descendants.

4. No Descendants, Surviving Parent, Siblings or Their Descendants

Estate divided into two halves (moieties) with one half going to paternal grandparents, uncles, cousins, etc. and the other half to the maternal side. Texas does not have a *laughing heir* statute preventing these remote relatives from inheriting.

If one side of the family has completely died out, the entire estate will pass to the surviving side. *State v. Estate of Loomis*, 553 S.W.2d 166 (Tex. Civ. App.—Tyler 1977, writ ref'd).

5. No Surviving Heirs

The property will **escheat** to the state of Texas under Property Code § 71.001.

E. TYPE OF DISTRIBUTION — § 43

Whenever individuals such as children, grandchildren, siblings and their descendants, cousins, etc. are heirs, you must determine how to divide their shares among them.

1. Per Capita

If the takers are all of the *same degree* of relationship to the intestate, then they take per capita, i.e., each heir takes the same amount.

For example, if all takers are children, each takes an equal share. If all children are deceased, then each grandchild takes an equal share.

2. Per Capita by Representation

If the takers are of *different degrees* of relationship to decedent, e.g., children and grandchildren, the younger generation takers share what the older generation taker would have received had that person survived.

For example, assume that Grandfather had three children; two predeceased. 1/3 passes to the surviving child, with 1/3 passing to the children of each deceased child (grandchildren). If each deceased child had a different number of grandchildren, the shares of the grandchildren will be different. (e.g., if one deceased child had two children, each gets 1/6; if the other deceased child had three children, each gets 1/9).

EXAMPLES

Example 1. Wilma, a widow, dies intestate survived by her only son, Sammy, and her father, Frank. How is Wilma's property distributed?

Answer: Wilma's entire estate passes to Sammy.

Example 2. Harry, a widower, dies intestate survived by his mother, Mary, and his two brothers, Bruce and Bob. How is Harry's property distributed?

Answer: One-half of Harry's estate passes to Mary. Bruce and Bob each receive one-quarter.

Example 3. Husband (H) and Wife (W) have three children, Amy (A), Brad (B), and Charles (C). All three children are married and have children of their own. A has one child, Mike (M). B has three children, Nancy (N), Opie (O), and Pat (P). C's children are Robert (R) and Susan (S). H died intestate with both community and separate property. In addition, H owned real and personal property of each type.

a. How would H's property be distributed?

Answer: All of H's community property is now owned by W; W keeps the one-half she owned by virtue of it being community property and W inherits H's one-half.

W receives one-third of H's separate personal property. Each of A, B, and C receive two-ninths of H's separate personal property.

W receives a life estate in one-third of H's separate real property. Each of A, B, and C receive two-ninths outright in H's separate real property as well as one-third of the remainder in W's life estate.

b. Assume that both B and C predeceased H. How would H's property be distributed?

Answer: All of H's community property is now owned by W; W keeps the one-half she owned by virtue of it being community property and W inherits H's one-half.

W receives one-third of H's separate personal property. A receives two-ninths of H's separate personal property, each of N, O, and P receive two-twenty-sevenths and each of R and S receive one-ninth.

W receives a life estate in one-third of H's separate real property. A receives two-ninths outright in H's separate real property plus one-third of the remainder in W's life estate. Each of N, O, and P receive two-twenty-sevenths outright in H's separate real property plus one-ninth of the remainder in W's life estate. Each of R and S receive one-ninth outright in H's separate real property plus one-sixth of the remainder in W's life estate.

c. Assume that A, B, and C predeceased H. How would H's property be distributed?

Answer: All of H's community property is now owned by W; W keeps the one-half she owned by virtue of it being community property and W inherits H's one-half.

W receives one-third of H's separate personal property. Each of the six grandchildren (M, N, O, P, R, and S) receive one-ninth of H's separate personal property.

W receives a life estate in one-third of H's separate real property. Each of the six grandchildren receive one-ninth outright in H's separate real property plus one-sixth of the remainder in W's life estate.

d. Answer questions (a), (b), and (c) assuming that A's mother is X instead of W.

Answer: Only the distribution of community property in each case is different. In each situation, W would only retain her one-half of the community. H's share of the community property passes to his descendants because not all of his descendants are descendants of W. In (a), each of A, B, and C would get one-sixth of the total community (one-third of H's one-half). In (b), A would receive one-sixth, each of N, O, and P, one-eighteenth, and each of R and S, one-twelfth. In (c), each grandchild would receive one-twelfth of the total community.

Example 4. Mother and Father, now deceased, had three children, Arthur, Bill, and Chris. Arthur died survived by his wife, Peggy, and their two children, Linda and Ken. Bill is unmarried and childless. Chris is married to Wendy and they have no children. Chris died intestate with both community and separate property. In addition, Chris owned real and personal property of each type. How would Chris's property be distributed?

Answer: Wendy receives all the community property, all separate personal property, and one-half of the separate real property. Bill receives one-quarter of the separate real property and Linda and Ken each receive one-eighth of the separate real property.

§ 38. Persons Who Take Upon Intestacy

(a) Intestate Leaving No Husband or Wife. Where any person, having title to any estate, real, personal or mixed, shall die intestate, leaving no husband or wife, it shall descend and pass in parcenary to his kindred, male and female, in the following course:

1. To his children and their descendants.

2. If there be no children nor their descendants, then to his father and mother, in equal portions. But if only the father or mother survive the intestate, then his estate shall be divided into two equal portions, one of which shall pass to such survivor, and the other half shall pass to the brothers and sisters of the deceased, and to their descendants; but if there be none such, then the whole estate shall be inherited by the surviving father or mother.

3. If there be neither father nor mother, then the whole of such estate shall pass to the brothers and sisters of the intestate, and to their descendants.

4. If there be none of the kindred aforesaid, then the inheritance shall be divided into two moieties, one of which shall go to the paternal and the other to the maternal kindred, in the following course: To the grandfather and grandmother in equal portions, but if only one of these be living, then the estate shall be divided into two equal parts, one of which shall go to such survivor, and the other shall go to the descendant or descendants of such deceased grandfather or grandmother. If there be no such descendants, then the whole estate shall be inherited by the surviving grandfather or grandmother. If there be no surviving grandfather or grandmother, then the whole of such estate shall go to their descendants, and so on without end, passing in like manner to the nearest lineal ancestors and their descendants.

(b) Intestate Leaving Husband or Wife. Where any person having title to any estate, real, personal or mixed, other than a community estate, shall die intestate as to such estate, and shall leave a surviving husband or wife, such estate of such intestate shall descend and pass as follows:

1. If the deceased have a child or children, or their descendants, the surviving husband or wife shall take one-third of the personal estate, and the balance of such personal estate shall go to the child or children of the deceased and their descendants. The surviving husband or wife shall also be entitled to an estate for life, in one-third of the land of the intestate, with remainder to the child or children of the intestate and their descendants.

2. If the deceased have no child or children, or their descendants, then the surviving husband or wife shall be entitled to all the personal estate, and to one-half of the lands of the intestate, without remainder to any person, and the other half shall pass and be inherited according to the rules of descent and distribution; provided, however, that if the deceased has neither surviving father nor mother nor surviving brothers or sisters, or their descendants, then the surviving husband or wife shall be entitled to the whole of the estate of such intestate.

Acts 1955, 54th Leg., p. 88, ch. 55, eff. Jan. 1, 1956.

Statutes in Context

The common law policy of keeping real property in the blood line of the original owner led to the development of the principle of *ancestral property*. This doctrine applied if an individual inherited real property and then died intestate without surviving descendants or first-line collateral relatives. Under this doctrine, real property inherited from the intestate's paternal side of the family would pass to the paternal collateral relatives and property inherited from the maternal side would pass to the maternal collateral relatives.

Section 39 provides that the doctrine of ancestral property does not apply in Texas by stating that the intestate is treated as the original purchaser of all property.

---

§ 39. No Distinction Because of Property's Source

There shall be no distinction in regulating the descent and distribution of the estate of a person dying intestate between property which may have been derived by gift, devise or descent from the father, and that which may have been derived by gift, devise or descent from the mother; and all the estate to which such intestate may have had title at the time of death shall descend and vest in the heirs of such person in the same manner as if he had been the original purchaser thereof.

Acts 1955, 54th Leg., p. 88, ch. 55, eff. Jan. 1, 1956.

Statutes in Context

The ability of a person to adopt a non-biological person and cause that person to be treated as a biological child was recognized thousands of years ago by societies such as the ancient Greeks, Romans, and Egyptians. However, the concept of adoption was beyond the grasp of common law attorneys and courts. The idea that a person could have "parents" other than the biological mother and father was unthinkable. In fact, English law did not recognize adoption until 1926. Accordingly, modern law relating to adoption developed in the United States with Vermont and Texas taking the lead when their legislatures enacted adoption statutes in 1850.

Section 40 details the effect of adoption on intestate distribution. The rights of three parties are at issue: (1) the adopted child; (2) the adoptive parents; and (3) the biological parents. Adopted children will inherit from and through the adoptive parents and, unlike in many states, also from and through the biological parents. Adoptive parents are entitled to inherit from and through the adopted child. The inheritance rights of the biological parents, on the other hand, are cut off – biological parents do not inherit from or

through their child who was given up for adoption. *See also* Family Code §§ 162.017 (adoption of minors) and 162.507 (adoption of adults).

A decree terminating the parent-child relationship may specifically remove the child's right to inherit from and through a biological parent. *See* Family Code § 161.206.

Adoption by estoppel, also called *equitable adoption*, occurs when a "parent" acts as though the "parent" has adopted the "child" even though a formal court-approved adoption never occurred. Typically, the "child" must prove that there was an agreement to adopt and the courts will look at circumstantial evidence to establish the agreement. Thus, when the "parent" dies, the adopted by estoppel child is entitled to share in the estate just as if an adoption had actually occurred.

The result is different, however, if the adopted by estoppel child dies. The adoptive by estoppel parents and their kin are prohibited from inheriting from or through the adopted by estoppel child. The courts explain that it is the parents' fault that a formal adoption did not take place and thus the equities are not in their favor. As a result, the child's biological kin are the child's heirs. See *Heien v. Crabtree*, 369 S.W.2d 28 (Tex. 1963).

§ 40. Inheritance By and From an Adopted Child

For purposes of inheritance under the laws of descent and distribution, an adopted child shall be regarded as the child of the parent or parents by adoption, such adopted child and its descendants inheriting from and through the parent or parents by adoption and their kin the same as if such child were the natural child of such parent or parents by adoption, and such parent or parents by adoption and their kin inheriting from and through such adopted child the same as if such child were the natural child of such parent or parents by adoption. The natural parent or parents of such child and their kin shall not inherit from or through said child, but said child shall inherit from and through its natural parent or parents. Nothing herein shall prevent any parent by adoption from disposing of his property by will according to law. The presence of this Section specifically relating to the rights of adopted children shall in no way diminish the rights of such children, under the laws of descent and distribution or otherwise, which they acquire by virtue of their inclusion in the definition of "child" which is contained in this Code.

Acts 1955, 54th Leg., p. 88, ch. 55, eff. Jan. 1, 1956. Amended by Acts 1989, 71st Leg., ch. 375, § 34, eff. Sept. 1, 1989.

§ 41. Matters Affecting and Not Affecting the Right to Inherit

Statutes in Context

Posthumous heirs are heirs conceived but not yet born when the intestate dies. Section 41(a) provides that posthumous lineal heirs (e.g., children and grandchildren) will inherit from the intestate, but posthumous non-lineal heirs (e.g., nieces and nephews) will not inherit.

(a) Persons Not in Being. No right of inheritance shall accrue to any persons other than to children or lineal descendants of the intestate, unless they are in being and capable in law to take as heirs at the time of the death of the intestate.

Statutes in Context

The term "half-blood" refers to collateral relatives who share only one common ancestor. For example, a brother and sister who have the same mother but different fathers would be half-siblings. On the other hand, if the brother and sister have the same parents, they would be related by the "whole-blood" because they share the same common ancestors.

At common law, half-blooded heirs could not inherit real property from a half-blooded intestate although they were entitled to inherit personal property. This strict rule with its emphasis on blood relationships has been modified by the states. States adopt one of three modern approaches: (1) The majority of states have totally eliminated the distinction between half- and whole-blooded relatives in determining inheritance rights. Thus, half-blooded collaterals inherit just as if they were of the whole-blood. (2) Some states like Texas adopt the Scottish rule which provides that half-blooded collaterals receive half shares. (3) A few states permit half-blooded collateral heirs to inherit only if there is no whole-blooded heir of the same degree. Remember that the distinction between whole and half-blooded heirs is relevant only if distribution is being made to collateral heirs of the intestate.

A simple way to determine the proper distribution to half- and whole-blooded heirs under § 41(b) is to calculate the total number of shares by creating two shares for each whole-blooded heir and one share for each half-blooded heir. Each whole-blooded heir receives two of these shares and each half-blooded heir receives one. For example, if there are three sibling heirs, Whole Blood Arthur, Half Blood Brenda, and Half Blood Charlie, four shares would be created (two for Arthur and one each for Brenda and Charlie). The estate would be distributed with Arthur receiving two shares (1/2 of the estate) and Brenda and Charlie receiving one share each (1/4 of the estate).

(b) Heirs of Whole and Half Blood. In situations where the inheritance passes to the collateral kindred of the intestate, if part of such collateral be of the whole blood, and the other part be of the half blood only, of the intestate, each of those of half blood shall inherit only half so much as each of those of the whole blood; but if all be of the half blood, they shall have whole portions.

Statutes in Context

At common law, a noncitizen could not acquire or transmit real property through intestacy. This rule made sense because the landowner owed duties to the Crown which would be difficult to enforce if the landowner was not a citizen. On the other hand, noncitizens from friendly countries could both acquire and transmit personal property through intestacy.

Under § 41(c), noncitizens are treated no differently than citizens when it comes to inheritance rights. Note, however, that during the World Wars, the U.S. government restricted the inheritance rights of citizens of enemy nations.

(c) Alienage. No person is disqualified to take as an heir because he or a person through whom he claims is or has been an alien.

Statutes in Context

Corruption of blood refers to a common law principle that prevented a person from inheriting land if the person was convicted or imprisoned for certain offenses, especially treason and other capital crimes. Article I, § 21 of the Texas Constitution prohibits corruption of blood and § 41(d) restates this prohibition. Accordingly, an imprisoned person, even one on death row, may inherit property.

Forfeiture refers to a common law principle that caused all the property of a person who was convicted of a felony to be forfeited to the government so there was no property for the person's heirs to inherit. Article I, § 21 of the Texas Constitution prohibits forfeiture and § 41(d) restates this prohibition. Note, however, that under federal law, a person convicted of certain drug offenses forfeits a portion of the person's property to the government. 21 U.S.C. § 853.

To prevent murderers from benefiting from their evil acts, most state legislatures have enacted statutes prohibiting murderers from inheriting. These provisions are often referred to as *slayers' statutes.* Section 41(d), however, only applies if a beneficiary of a life insurance policy is convicted and sentenced as a principal or accomplice in wilfully bringing about the death of the insured. Texas courts resort to the constructive trust principle to prevent the murdering heir from inheriting. Legal title does pass to the murderer but equity treats the murderer as a constructive trustee of the title because of the unconscionable mode of its acquisition and then compels the murderer to convey it to the heirs of the deceased, exclusive of the murder. See *Pritchett v. Henry*, 287 S.W.2d 546 (Tex. Civ. App. — Beaumont 1955, writ dism'd).

The property of a person who committed suicide was subject to special rules at common law. If the intestate committed suicide to avoid punishment after committing a felony, the intestate's heirs took nothing. Instead, the real property escheated and personal property was forfeited. However, if the intestate committed suicide because of pain or exhaustion from living, only personal property was forfeited and real property still descended to the heirs. Article I, § 21 of the Texas Constitution abolishes these common-law rules and thus the property of a person who commits suicide passes just as if the death were caused by some other means. Section 41(d) restates the Constitutional provision.

(d) Convicted Persons and Suicides. No conviction shall work corruption of blood or forfeiture of estate, except in the case of a beneficiary in a life insurance policy or contract who is convicted and sentenced as a principal or accomplice in wilfully bringing about the death of the insured, in which case the proceeds of such insurance policy or contract shall be paid as provided in the Insurance Code of this State, as same now exists or is hereafter amended; nor shall there be any forfeiture by reason of death by casualty; and the estates of those who destroy their own lives shall descend or vest as in the case of natural death.

Acts 1955, 54th Leg., p. 88, ch. 55, eff. Jan. 1, 1956. Amended by Acts 1969, 61st Leg., p. 1922, ch. 641, § 2, eff. June 12, 1969.

Statutes in Context

At common law, a child born outside of a valid marriage was considered as having no parents (*filius nullius*). Thus, a nonmarital child did not inherit from or through the child's biological mother or father. Likewise, the biological parents could not inherit from or through the child. However, the nonmarital child did retain the right to inherit from the child's spouse and descendants. If the child died intestate with neither a surviving spouse nor descendants, the child's property escheated to the government.

This harsh treatment of nonmarital children, formerly referred to by pejorative terms such as "illegitimate children" or "bastards," has been greatly alleviated under modern law. In the 1977 United States Supreme Court case of *Trimble v. Gordon*, 430 U.S. 726 (1977), the Court held that marital and nonmarital children must be treated the same when determining heirs under intestacy statutes. The Court held that discriminating against non-marital children was a violation of the equal protection clause of the 14th Amendment.

One year later, the Supreme Court retreated from its broad holding in *Trimble*. In the five-four decision of *Lalli v. Lalli*, 439 U.S. 259 (1978), the Court held that a state may have legitimate reasons to apply a more demanding standard for nonmarital children to inherit from their fathers than from their mothers. The Court cited several justifications for this unequal treatment including the more efficient and orderly administration of estates, the avoidance of spurious claims, the maintenance of the finality of judgments, and the inability of the purported father to contest the child's paternity allegations.

Section 42(a) permits the nonmarital child to inherit from and through the biological mother (and vice versa) without any difference in the amount of maternity proof from that which a marital child is required to produce. On the other hand, Texas imposes higher standards on a nonmarital child to inherit from the father. Section 42(b), in conjunction with the referenced provisions of the Family Code, enumerates how a person may be considered the child of a man and thus entitled to inherit.

Texas also permits the nonmarital child to prove paternity after the purported father has died. In an attempt to limit the number of false claims, Texas imposes a higher standard of proof of paternity in post-death actions, that is, there must be clear and convincing evidence of paternity. DNA evidence is especially helpful in making this determination.

---

§ 42. Inheritance Rights of Children

(a) Maternal Inheritance. For the purpose of inheritance, a child is the child of his biological or adopted mother, so that he and his issue shall inherit from his mother and from his maternal kindred, both descendants, ascendants, and collaterals in all degrees, and they may inherit from him and his issue.

(b) Paternal Inheritance. (1) For the purpose of inheritance, a child is the child of his biological father if the child is born under circumstances described by Section 160.201, Family Code, is adjudicated to be the child of the father by court decree as provided by Chapter 160, Family Code, was adopted by his father, or if the father executed an acknowledgment of paternity as provided by Subchapter D, Chapter 160, Family Code, or a like statement properly executed in another jurisdiction, so that he and his issue shall inherit from his father and from his paternal kindred, both descendants, ascendants, and collaterals in all degrees, and they may inherit from him and his issue. A person claiming to be a biological child of the decedent, who is not otherwise presumed to be a child of the decedent, or claiming inheritance through a biological child of the decedent, who is not otherwise presumed to be a child of the decedent, may petition the probate court for a determination of right of inheritance. If the court finds by clear and convincing evidence that the purported father was the biological father of the child, the child is treated as any other child of the decedent for the purpose of inheritance and he and his issue may inherit from his paternal kindred, both descendants, ascendants, and collaterals in all degrees, and they may inherit from him and his issue. This section does not permit inheritance by a purported father of a child, whether recognized or not, if the purported father's parental rights have been terminated.

(2) A person who purchases for valuable consideration any interest in real or personal property of the heirs of a decedent, who in good faith relies on the declarations in an affidavit of heirship that does not include a child who at the time of the sale or contract of sale of the property is not a presumed child of the decedent and has not under a final court decree or judgment been found to be entitled to treatment under this subsection as a child of the decedent, and who is without knowledge of the claim of that child, acquires good title to the interest that the person would have received, as purchaser, in the absence of any claim of the child not included in the affidavit. This subdivision does not affect the liability, if any, of the heirs for the proceeds of any sale described by this subdivision to the child who was not included in the affidavit of heirship.

(c) Homestead Rights, Exempt Property, and Family Allowances. A child as provided by Subsections (a) and (b) of this section is a child of his mother, and a child of his father, for the purpose of determining homestead rights, distribution of exempt property, and the making of family allowances.

(d) Marriages Void and Voidable. The issue of marriages declared void or voided by annulment shall be treated in the same manner as issue of a valid marriage.

Subsec. (b) amended by Acts 1987, 70th Leg., ch. 464, § 1, eff. Sept. 1, 1987. Amended by Acts 1989, 71st Leg., ch. 375, § 35, eff. Sept. 1, 1989. Subsec. (b)(1) amended by Acts 1997, 75th Leg., ch. 165, § 7.54, eff. Sept. 1, 1997; amended by Acts 1997, 75th Leg., ch. 1302, § 4, eff. Sept. 1, 1997; amended by Acts 2001, 77th Leg., ch. 821, § 2.18, eff. June 14, 2001.

Statutes in Context

Whenever individuals such as children, grandchildren, siblings and their descendants, cousins, etc., are heirs, one must determine how to divide their shares among them. If the takers are all of the *same degree* of relationship to the intestate, then they take *per capita*, i.e., each heir takes the same amount. For example, if all takers are children, each takes an equal share. If all children are deceased, then each grandchild takes an equal share.

If the takers are of *different degrees* of relationship to the decedent, e.g., children and grandchildren, the younger-generation takers share what the older-generation taker would have received had that person survived, that is, *per capita with representation*. (Note that the term "per stirpes" as used in the caption to § 43 is a misnomer. *Per stirpes* refers to a distribution where shares are determined by the number of individuals in the first generation, even if they have all predeceased the intestate.) For example, assume that Grandfather had three children; two predeceased. one-third passes to the surviving child, with one-third passing to the children of each deceased child (grandchildren). If each deceased child had a different number of grandchildren, the shares of the grandchildren will be different (e.g., if one deceased child had two children, each gets one-sixth; if the other deceased child had three children, each gets one-ninth).

See the examples in the *Statutes in Context* for § 38.

---

§ 43. Determination of Per Capita and Per Stirpes Distribution

When the intestate's children, descendants, brothers, sisters, uncles, aunts, or any other relatives of the deceased standing in the first or same degree alone come into the distribution upon intestacy, they shall take per capita, namely: by persons; and, when a part of them being dead and a part living, the descendants of those dead shall have right to distribution upon intestacy, such descendants shall inherit only such portion of said property as the parent through whom they inherit would be entitled to if alive.

Acts 1955, 54th Leg., p. 88, ch. 55, eff. Jan. 1, 1956. Amended by Acts 1991, 72nd Leg., ch. 895, § 3, eff. Sept. 1, 1991.

Statutes in Context

An *advancement* is a special type of inter vivos gift. The advancer (donor) anticipates dying intestate and the advancee (donee) is an individual who is likely to be one of the advancer's heirs. Although the gift is irrevocable and unconditional, the advancer intends the advancement to be an early distribution from the advancer's estate. Thus, the advancee's share of the advancer's estate is reduced to compensate for the advancement.

When the advancer dies intestate, the advanced property is treated as if it were still in the advancer's probate estate when computing the size of the intestate shares. Thus, the advancee receives a smaller share in the estate because the advancee already has part of the advancer's estate, that is, the advancement. This equalization process is referred to as *going into hotchpot*.

Section 44 provides that property given during an intestate's life to an heir is an advancement only if (1) the decedent acknowledges the advancement in a contemporaneous writing at the time of or prior to the transfer, or (2) the heir acknowledges in writing, at any time, that the transfer of property is to be treated as an advancement.

Example 1 Intestate had three children, Arthur, Brenda, and Charles. Intestate made a $100,000 advancement to Arthur. Intestate died with a distributable probate estate of $500,000. What is the proper distribution of Intestate's estate?

Arthur receives $100,000, Brenda receives $200,000, and Charles receives $200,000. Because the $100,000 gift to Arthur was an advancement, that amount is treated as if it were still in Intestate's estate. Thus, Intestate's estate is distributed as if it contained $600,000. Intestate had three children and thus each child is entitled to a per capita share of $200,000. Because Arthur has already received $100,000 by way of the advancement, he is entitled only to an additional $100,000 from Intestate's estate. Brenda and Charles each receive their share from Intestate's estate. The hotchpot process ensures that each child receives an equal share from Intestate accounting for both inter vivos and at-death transfers.

Example 2 Intestate had three children, Arthur, Brenda, and Charles. Intestate made a $100,000 advancement to Arthur. Intestate died with a distributable probate estate of $50,000. What is the proper distribution of Intestate's estate?

Arthur receives none of Intestate's estate, Brenda receives $25,000 and Charles receives $25,000. Like other inter vivos gifts, advancements are irrevocable. Thus, Arthur is under no obligation to actually return the advanced amount to Intestate's estate. Arthur is not indebted for the advanced amount. Instead, Arthur simply does not share in Intestate's estate because he has already received property in excess of the share to which he would be entitled under a hotpotch computation. Thus, Intestate's entire estate is distributed to Brenda and Charles.

Example 3 Intestate had three children, Arthur, Brenda, and Charles. Intestate advanced two assets to Arthur, a house worth $100,000 at the time of the advancement and a car worth $30,000 at the time of the advancement. Intestate died with a distributable probate estate of $500,000. At the time of Intestate's death, the house had appreciated to $300,000 and the car had depreciated to $1,000. What is the proper distribution of Intestate's estate?

Arthur receives $80,000, Brenda receives $210,000, and Charles receives $210,000. Advancements are valued as of the date of the advancement under § 44(b). Thus, subsequent appreciation and depreciation of advanced property is ignored when going into hotchpot. The house valued at $100,000 and the car valued at $30,000 come into hotchpot. The value of the hotchpot, that is, advancements plus Intestate's estate, is $630,000. Each of the three children is entitled to $210,000. Because Arthur already received advancements valued at $130,000, he receives only $80,000 from the estate. Brenda and Charles each receive a full $210,000 share because neither of them had received an advancement.

Example 4 Intestate had three children, Arthur, Brenda, and Charles. Intestate made a $100,000 advancement to Arthur. Arthur died survived by his two children, Sam and Susan. Subsequently, Intestate died with a distributable probate estate of $500,000. What is the proper distribution of Intestate's estate?

Under § 44(c), the advancement is not considered because Arthur did not survive Intestate and thus hotchpot does not occur unless Intestate specified in writing that the advancement is to be brought into hotchpot even if Intestate predeceases Arthur. Accordingly, Brenda and Charles would each receive one-third of Intestate's probate estate (approximately $166,666) while Sam and Susan would each receive one-sixth (approximately $83,333). The policy behind this approach is that the advancee's heirs may not have received the advanced property or its value from the advancee's estate.

The analogous concept to advancements in a will context is called *satisfaction* and is governed by § 37C.

---

§ 44. Advancements

(a) If a decedent dies intestate as to all or a portion of the decedent's estate, property the decedent gave during the decedent's lifetime to a person who, on the date of the decedent's death, is the decedent's heir, or property received by a decedent's heir under a nontestamentary transfer under Chapter XI[1] of this code is an advancement against the heir's intestate share only if:

(1) the decedent declared in a contemporaneous writing or the heir acknowledged in writing that the gift or nontestamentary transfer is an advancement; or

(2) the decedent's contemporaneous writing or the heir's written acknowledged otherwise indicates that the gift or nontestamentary transfer is to be taken into account in computing the division and distribution of the decedent's intestate estate.

(b) For purposes of Subsection (a) of this section, property that is advanced is valued at the time the heir came into possession or enjoyment of the property or at the time of the decedent's death, whichever occurs first.

(c) If the recipient of the property fails to survive the decedent, the property is not taken into account in computing the division and distribution of the decedent's intestate estate, unless the decedent's contemporaneous writing provides otherwise.

Acts 1955, 54th Leg., p. 88, ch. 55, eff. Jan. 1, 1956. Amended by Acts 1993, 73rd Leg., ch. 846, § 4, eff. Sept. 1, 1993.

Statutes in Context

Section 45 provides the intestate distribution scheme for community property. See the *Statutes in Context* to § 38 for a discussion of this provision.

Note that the distribution of community property was considerably different prior to September 1, 1993; the deceased spouse's half of the community passed to the deceased spouse's children even if all of the deceased spouse's children were also children of the surviving spouse.

Issues may arise regarding the identity and/or existence of a surviving spouse, especially if an informal or common law marriage is involved. *See* Family Code § 2.401.

---

§ 45. Community Estate

(a) On the intestate death of one of the spouses to a marriage, the community property estate of the deceased spouse passes to the surviving spouse if:

(1) no child or other descendant of the deceased spouse survives the deceased spouse; or

(2) all surviving children and descendants of the deceased spouse are also children or descendants of the surviving spouse.

(b) On the intestate death of one of the spouses to a marriage, if a child or other descendant of the deceased spouse survives the deceased spouse and the child or descendant is not a child or descendant of the surviving spouse, one-half of the community estate is retained by the surviving spouse and the other one-half passes to the children or descendants of the deceased spouse. The descendants shall inherit only such portion of said property to which they would be entitled under Section 43 of this code. In every case, the community estate passes charged with the debts against it.

Acts 1955, 54th Leg., p. 88, ch. 55, eff. Jan. 1, 1956. Amended by Acts 1991, 72nd Leg., ch. 895, § 4, eff. Sept. 1, 1991; Acts 1993, 73rd Leg., ch. 846, § 33, eff. Sept. 1, 1993.

Statutes in Context

A *joint tenancy* is a type of concurrent property ownership. A joint tenant's rights end at death in favor of the surviving joint tenants. Thus, when a joint tenant dies, the deceased tenant's share is divided equally among the surviving joint tenants. The rights of these surviving joint tenants are superior to the deceased tenant's heirs or beneficiaries.

At common law, the survivorship feature attached automatically to a joint tenancy. The presumption of survivorship often led to unanticipated property distributions as co-owners held as joint tenants when they intended to hold as tenants in common. Nonlegally trained individuals did not appreciate the significant difference between these two types of concurrent ownership. Consequently, § 46(a) provides that the survivorship feature does not attach to a joint tenancy unless it is expressly stated in the instrument.

Survivorship agreements for community property are covered separately in §§ 451-462.

---

§ 46. Joint Tenancies

(a) If two or more persons hold an interest in property jointly, and one joint owner dies before severance, the interest of the decedent in the joint estate shall not survive to the remaining joint owner or owners but shall pass by will or intestacy from the decedent as if the decedent's interest had been severed. The joint owners may agree in writing, however, that the interest of any joint owner who dies shall survive to the surviving joint owner or owners, but no such agreement shall be inferred from the mere fact that the property is held in joint ownership.

(b) Subsection (a) does not apply to agreements between spouses regarding their community property. Agreements between spouses regarding rights of survivorship in community property are governed by Part 3 of Chapter XI of this code.[1]

Acts 1955, 54th Leg., p. 88, ch. 55, eff. Jan. 1, 1956. Amended by Acts 1961, 57th Leg., p. 233, ch. 120, § 1, eff.

---

[1] Section 436 et seq.

[1] V.A.T.S. Probate Code § 451 et seq.

May 15, 1961; Acts 1969, 61st Leg., p. 1922, ch. 641, § 3, eff. June 12, 1969. Amended by Acts 1981, 67th Leg., p. 895, ch. 319, § 1, eff. Sept. 1, 1981; Acts 1987, 70th Leg., ch. 678, § 2; Acts 1989, 71st Leg., ch. 655, § 1, eff. Aug. 28, 1989.

Statutes in Context

To be an heir, will beneficiary, recipient of property held in a joint tenancy with survivorship rights, or beneficiary of a life insurance policy, an individual must outlive the decedent. At common law, survival for only a mere instant was needed. This rule led to many proof problems as family members tried to establish that one person outlived the other or vice versa. Some of these cases read like horror novels as the courts evaluate evidence of which person twitched, gurgled, or gasped longer. See *Glover v. Davis*, 366 S.W.2d 227 (Tex. 1963).

To remedy this problem, § 47 imposes a survival period of 120 hours (5 days). If a person survives the decedent but dies prior to the expiration of the survival period, the property passes as if the person had actually predeceased the decedent.

---

§ 47. Requirement of Survival by 120 Hours

(a) Survival of Heirs. A person who fails to survive the decedent by 120 hours is deemed to have predeceased the decedent for purposes of homestead allowance, exempt property, and intestate succession, and the decedent's heirs are determined accordingly, except as otherwise provided in this section. If the time of death of the decedent or of the person who would otherwise be an heir, or the times of death of both, cannot be determined, and it cannot be established that the person who would otherwise be an heir has survived the decedent by 120 hours, it is deemed that the person failed to survive for the required period. This subsection does not apply where its application would result in the escheat of an intestate estate.

(b) Disposal of Community Property. When a husband and wife have died, leaving community property, and neither the husband nor wife survived the other by 120 hours, one-half of all community property shall be distributed as if the husband had survived, and the other one-half thereof shall be distributed as if the wife had survived. The provisions of this subsection apply to proceeds of life or accident insurance which are community property and become payable to the estate of either the husband or the wife, as well as to other kinds of community property.

(c) Survival of Devisees or Beneficiaries. A devisee who does not survive the testator by 120 hours is treated as if he predeceased the testator, unless the will of the decedent contains some language dealing explicitly with simultaneous death or deaths in a common disaster, or requiring that the devisee survive the testator or survive the testator for a stated period in order to take under the will. If property is so disposed of that the right of a beneficiary to succeed to any interest therein is conditional upon his surviving another person, the beneficiary shall be deemed not to have survived unless he or she survives the person by 120 hours. However, if any interest in property is given alternatively to one of two or more beneficiaries, with the right of each to take being dependent upon his surviving the other or others, and all shall die within a period of less than 120 hours, the property shall be divided into as many equal portions as there are beneficiaries, and those portions shall be distributed respectively to those who would have taken in the event that each beneficiary had survived.

(d) Joint Owners. If any real or personal property, including community property with a right of survivorship, shall be so owned that one of two joint owners is entitled to the whole on the death of the other, and neither survives the other by 120 hours, these assets shall be distributed one-half as if one joint owner had survived and the other one-half as if the other joint owner had survived. If there are more than two joint owners and all have died within a period of less than 120 hours, these assets shall be divided into as many equal portions as there are joint owners and these portions shall be distributed respectively to those who would have taken in the event that each joint owner survived.

(e) Insured and Beneficiary. When the insured and a beneficiary in a policy of life or accident insurance have died within a period of less than 120 hours, the insured shall be deemed to have survived the beneficiary for the purpose of determining the rights under the policy of the beneficiary or beneficiaries as such. The provisions of this subsection shall not prevent the application of subsection (b) above to the proceeds of life or accident insurance which are community property.

(f) Instruments Providing Different Disposition. When provision has been made in the case of wills, living trusts, deeds, or contracts of insurance, or any other situation, for disposition of property different from the provisions of this Section, this Section shall not apply.

Acts 1955, 54th Leg., p. 88, ch. 55, eff. Jan. 1, 1956. Amended by Acts 1965, 59th Leg., p. 279, ch. 119, § 1, eff. Aug. 30, 1965; Acts 1979, 66th Leg., p. 1743, ch. 713, § 6, eff. Aug. 27, 1979. Subsec. (d) amended by Acts 1993, 73rd Leg., ch. 846, § 5, eff. Sept. 1, 1993.

Chapter III. Determination Of Heirship

Statutes in Context

If the decedent died intestate, the court will make a determination of the identity of the heirs. If there is no need for an estate administration, this *determination of heirship* may be all that is required to prove that title to property passed from the intestate to the heirs. The court will open an administration only if one is necessary to pay debts or to partition property among the

heirs. Sections 48-56 relate to steps which must be taken for a formal determination of heirship.

The analogous proceeding for a testate decedent is to probate the will as a muniment of title as discussed in §§ 89A-89C.

§ 48. Proceedings to Declare Heirship. When and Where Instituted

(a) When a person dies intestate owning or entitled to real or personal property in Texas, and there shall have been no administration in this State upon his estate; or when there has been a will probated in this State or elsewhere, or an administration in this State upon the estate of such decedent, and any real or personal property in this State has been omitted from such will or from such administration, or no final disposition thereof has been made in such administration, the court of the county in which such proceedings were last pending, or in the event no will of such decedent has been admitted to probate in this State, and no administration has been granted in this State upon the estate of such decedent, then the court of the county in which any of the real property belonging to such estate is situated, or if there is no such real estate, then of the county in which any personal property belonging to such estate is found, may determine and declare in the manner hereinafter provided who are the heirs and only heirs of such decedent, and their respective shares and interests, under the laws of this State, in the estate of such decedent, and proceedings therefor shall be known as proceedings to declare heirship.

(b) If an application for determination of heirship is filed within four (4) years from the date of the death of the decedent, the applicant may request that the court determine whether a necessity for administration exists. The court shall hear evidence upon the issue and make a determination thereof in its judgment.

(c) Notwithstanding any other provision of this section, a probate court in which the proceedings for the guardianship of the estate of a ward who dies intestate were pending at the time of the death of the ward may, if there is no administration pending in the estate, determine and declare who are the heirs and only heirs of the ward, and their respective shares and interests, under the laws of this State, in the estate of the ward.

Acts 1955, 54th Leg., p. 88, ch. 55, eff. Jan. 1, 1956. Amended by Acts 1971, 62nd Leg., p. 971, ch. 173, § 4, eff. Jan. 1, 1972; Acts 1977, 65th Leg., p. 1521, ch. 616, § 1, eff. Aug. 29, 1977.

§ 49. Who May Institute Proceedings to Declare Heirship

(a) Such proceedings may be instituted and maintained in any of the instances enumerated above by any person or persons claiming to be the owner of the whole or a part of the estate of such decedent, or by the guardian of the estate of a ward, if the proceedings are instituted and maintained in the probate court in which the proceedings for the guardianship of the estate were pending at the time of the death of the ward. In such a case an application shall be filed in a proper court stating the following information:

(1) the name of the decedent and the time and place of death;

(2) the names and residences of the decedent's heirs, the relationship of each heir to the decedent, and the true interest of the applicant and each of the heirs in the estate of the decedent;

(3) all the material facts and circumstances within the knowledge and information of the applicant that might reasonably tend to show the time or place of death or the names or residences of all heirs, if the time or place of death or the names or residences of all the heirs are not definitely known to the applicant;

(4) a statement that all children born to or adopted by the decedent have been listed;

(5) a statement that each marriage of the decedent has been listed with the date of the marriage, the name of the spouse, and if the marriage was terminated, the date and place of termination, and other facts to show whether a spouse has had an interest in the property of the decedent;

(6) whether the decedent died testate and if so, what disposition has been made of the will;

(7) a general description of all the real and personal property belonging to the estate of the decedent; and

(8) an explanation for the omission of any of the foregoing information that is omitted from the application.

(b) Such application shall be supported by the affidavit of each applicant to the effect that, insofar as is known to such applicant, all the allegations of such application are true in substance and in fact and that no such material fact or circumstance has, within the affiant's knowledge, been omitted from such application. The unknown heirs of such decedent, all persons who are named in the application as heirs of such decedent, and all persons who are, at the date of the filing of the application, shown by the deed records of the county in which any of the real property described in such application is situated to own any share or interest in any such real property, shall be made parties in such proceeding.

Acts 1955, 54th Leg., p. 88, ch. 55, eff. Jan. 1, 1956. Amended by Acts 1971, 62nd Leg., p. 971, ch. 173, § 4, eff. Jan. 1, 1972; Acts 1977, 65th Leg., p. 1522, ch. 616, § 2, eff. Aug. 29, 1977; Acts 1979, 66th Leg., p. 1744, ch. 713, § 7, eff. Aug. 27, 1979. Subsec. (a) amended by Acts 1983, 68th Leg., p. 629, ch. 139, § 1, eff. Sept. 1, 1983; Acts 1985, 69th Leg., ch. 693, § 1, eff. Sept. 1, 1985.

§ 50. Notice

(a) Citation shall be served by registered or certified mail upon all distributees 12 years of age or older whose names and addresses are known, or whose names and addresses can be learned through the exercise of reasonable diligence, provided that the court may in its discretion require that service of citation shall be made by personal service upon some or all of those named as distributees in the application. Citation shall be served as provided by this subsection on the parent, managing conservator, or guardian of a distributee who is younger than 12 years of age, if the name and address of the parent, managing conservator, or guardian is known or can be reasonably ascertained.

(b) If the address of a person or entity on whom citation is required to be served cannot be ascertained, citation shall be served on the person or entity by publication in the county in which the proceedings are commenced, and if the decedent resided in another county, then a citation shall also be published in the county of the decedent's last residence. To determine whether there are any other heirs, citation shall also be served on unknown heirs by publication in the manner provided by this subsection.

(c) Except in proceedings in which there is service of citation by publication as provided by Subsection (b) of this section, citation shall also be posted in the county in which the proceedings are commenced and in the county of the decedent's last residence.

(d) A party to the proceedings who has executed the application need not be served by any method.

(e) A parent, managing conservator, guardian, attorney ad litem, or guardian ad litem of a distributee who is at least 12 years of age but younger than 19 years of age may not waive citation required to be served on the distributee under this section.

Acts 1955, 54th Leg., p. 88, ch. 55, eff. Jan. 1, 1956. Amended by Acts 1971, 62nd Leg., p. 971, ch. 173, § 4, eff. Jan. 1, 1972; Acts 1979, 66th Leg., p. 1745, ch. 713, § 8, eff. Aug. 27, 1979. Subsecs. (a), (b) amended by Acts 1997, 75th Leg., ch. 1130, § 1, eff. Sept. 1, 1997. Subsecs. (b) amended by and (e) added by Acts 2001, 77th Leg., ch. 664, § 2, eff. Sept. 1, 2001.

§ 51. Transfer of Proceeding When Will Probated or Administration Granted

If an administration upon the estate of any such decedent shall be granted in the State, or if the will of such decedent shall be admitted to probate in this State, after the institution of a proceeding to declare heirship, the court in which such proceeding is pending shall, by an order entered of record therein, transfer the cause to the court of the county in which such administration shall have been granted, or such will shall have been probated, and thereupon the clerk of the court in which such proceeding was originally filed shall send to the clerk of the court named in such order, a certified transcript of all pleadings, docket entries, and orders of the court in such cause. The clerk of the court to which such cause shall be transferred shall file the transcript and record the same in the minutes of the court and shall docket such cause, and the same shall thereafter proceed as though originally filed in that court. The court, in its discretion, may consolidate the cause so transferred with the pending proceeding.

Acts 1955, 54th Leg., p. 88, ch. 55, eff. Jan. 1, 1956. Amended by Acts 1971, 62nd Leg., p. 971, ch. 173, § 4, eff. Jan. 1, 1972.

Statutes in Context

Some title companies, oil landpersons, and financial institutions may rely on a affidavit of heirship, standing alone without a formal determination of heirship, to clear defects in title to real property.

§ 52. Recorded Instruments as Prima Facie Evidence

(a) A statement of facts concerning the family history, genealogy, marital status, or the identity of the heirs of a decedent shall be received in a proceeding to declare heirship, or in a suit involving title to real or personal property, as prima facie evidence of the facts therein stated, if the statement is contained in either an affidavit or any other instrument legally executed and acknowledged or sworn to before, and certified by, an officer authorized to take acknowledgments or oaths as applicable, or any judgment of a court of record, and if the affidavit or instrument has been of record for five years or more in the deed records of any county in this state in which such real or personal property is located at the time the suit is instituted, or in the deed records of any county of this state in which the decedent had his domicile or fixed place of residence at the time of his death. If there is any error in the statement of facts in such recorded affidavit or instrument, the true facts may be proved by anyone interested in the proceeding in which said affidavit or instrument is offered in evidence.

(b) An affidavit of facts concerning the identity of heirs of a decedent as to an interest in real property that is filed in a proceeding or suit described by Subsection (a) of this section may be in the form described by Section 52A of this code.

(c) An affidavit of facts concerning the identity of heirs of a decedent does not affect the rights of an omitted heir or a creditor of the decedent as otherwise provided by law. This statute shall be cumulative of all other statutes on the same subject, and shall not be construed as abrogating any right to present evidence or to rely on an affidavit of facts conferred by any other statute or rule of law.

Acts 1955, 54th Leg., p. 88, ch. 55, eff. Jan. 1, 1956. Amended by Acts 1969, 61st Leg., p. 1922, ch. 641, § 4, eff. June 12, 1969. Amended by Acts 1991, 72nd Leg., ch. 895, § 5, eff. Sept. 1, 1991; Acts 1999, 76th Leg., ch. 1538, § 1, eff. Sept. 1, 1999.

§ 52A. Form of Affidavit of Facts Concerning Identity of Heirs

An affidavit of facts concerning the identity of heirs of a decedent may be in substantially the following form:

AFFIDAVIT OF FACTS CONCERNING THE IDENTITY OF HEIRS

Before me, the undersigned authority, on this day personally appeared __________ ("Affiant") (insert name of affiant) who, being first duly sworn, upon his/her oath states:

1. My name is __________ (insert name of affiant), and I live at __________ (insert address of affiant's residence). I am personally familiar with the family and marital history of __________ ("Decedent") (insert name of decedent), and I have personal knowledge of the facts stated in this affidavit.
2. I knew decedent from __________ (insert date) until __________ (insert date). Decedent died on __________ (insert date of death). Decedent's place of death was __________ (insert place of death). At the time of decedent's death, decedent's residence was __________ (insert address of decedent's residence).
3. Decedent's marital history was as follows: __________ (insert marital history and, if decedent's spouse is deceased, insert date and place of spouse's death).
4. Decedent had the following children: __________ (insert name, birth date, name of other parent, and current address of child or date of death of child and descendants of deceased child, as applicable, for each child).
5. Decedent did not have or adopt any other children and did not take any other children into decedent's home or raise any other children, except: __________ (insert name of child or names of children, or state "none").
6. (Include if decedent was not survived by descendants.) Decedent's mother was: __________ (insert name, birth date, and current address or date of death of mother, as applicable).
7. (Include if decedent was not survived by descendants.) Decedent's father was: __________ (insert name, birth date, and current address or date of death of father, as applicable).
8. (Include if decedent was not survived by descendants or by both mother and father.) Decedent had the following siblings: __________ (insert name, birth date, and current address or date of death of each sibling and parents of each sibling and descendants of each deceased sibling, as applicable, or state "none").
9. (Optional.) The following persons have knowledge regarding the decedent, the identity of decedent's children, if any, parents, or siblings, if any: __________ (insert names of persons with knowledge, or state "none").
10. Decedent died without leaving a written will. (Modify statement if decedent left a written will.)
11. There has been no administration of decedent's estate. (Modify statement if there has been administration of decedent's estate.)
12. Decedent left no debts that are unpaid, except: __________ (insert list of debts, or state "none").
13. There are no unpaid estate or inheritance taxes, except: __________ (insert list of unpaid taxes, or state "none").
14. To the best of my knowledge, decedent owned an interest in the following real property: __________ (insert list of real property in which decedent owned an interest, or state "none").
15. (Optional.) The following were the heirs of decedent: __________ (insert names of heirs).
16. (Insert additional information as appropriate, such as size of the decedent's estate.)

Signed this _____ day of __________, _____.

____
(signature of affiant)
State of __________
County of __________
Sworn to and subscribed to before me on __________ (date) by __________ (insert name of affiant).

____
(signature of notarial officer)
(Seal, if any, of notary) ________________
(printed name)
My commission expires: __________

Added by Acts 1999, 76th Leg., ch. 1538, § 2, eff. Sept. 1, 1999.

§ 53. Evidence; Unknown Parties and Incapacitated Persons

(a) The court in its discretion may require all or any part of the evidence admitted in a proceeding to declare heirship to be reduced to writing, and subscribed and sworn to by the witnesses, respectively, and filed in the cause, and recorded in the minutes of the court.

(b) If it appears to the court that there are or may be living heirs whose names or whereabouts are unknown, or that any defendant is an incapacitated person, the court may, in its discretion, appoint an attorney ad litem or guardian ad litem to represent the interests of any such persons. The court may not appoint an attorney ad litem or guardian ad litem unless the court finds that the appointment is necessary to protect the interests of the living heir or incapacitated person.

(c) The court shall appoint an attorney ad litem to represent the interests of unknown heirs.

Acts 1955, 54th Leg., p. 88, ch. 55, eff. Jan. 1, 1956. Amended by Acts 1971, 62nd Leg., p. 971, ch. 173, § 4, eff. Jan. 1, 1972. Subsec. (b) amended by Acts 1995, 74th Leg., ch. 1039, § 6, eff. Sept. 1, 1995; Sec. heading amended by Acts 2001, 77th Leg., ch. 664, § 3, eff. Sept. 1, 2001; Subsec. (c) added by Acts 2001, 77th Leg., ch. 664, § 4, eff. Sept. 1, 2001.

§ 54. Judgment

The judgment of the court in a proceeding to declare heirship shall declare the names and places of residence of the heirs of the decedent, and their respective shares and interests in the real and personal property of such decedent. If the proof is in any respect deficient, the judgment shall so state.

Acts 1955, 54th Leg., p. 88, ch. 55, eff. Jan. 1, 1956. Amended by Acts 1971, 62nd Leg., p. 971, ch. 173, § 4, eff. Jan. 1, 1972.

§ 55. Effect of Judgment

(a) Such judgment shall be a final judgment, and may be appealed or reviewed within the same time limits and in the same manner as may other judgments in probate matters at the instance of any interested person. If any person who is an heir of the decedent is not served with citation by registered or certified mail, or by personal service, he may at any time within four years from the date of such judgment have the same corrected by bill of review, or upon proof of actual fraud, after the passage of any length of time, and may recover from the heirs named in the judgment, and those claiming under them who are not bona fide purchasers for value, his just share of the property or its value.

(b) Although such judgment may later be modified, set aside, or nullified, it shall nevertheless be conclusive in any suit between any heir omitted from the judgment and a bona fide purchaser for value who has purchased real or personal property after entry of the judgment without actual notice of the claim of the omitted heir. Similarly, any person who has delivered funds or property of the decedent to the persons declared to be heirs in the judgment, or has engaged in any other transaction with them, in good faith, after entry of such judgment, shall not be liable therefor to any person.

(c) If the court states in its judgment that there is no necessity for administration on the estate, such recital shall constitute authorization to all persons owing any money to the estate of the decedent, or having custody of any property of such estate, or acting as registrar or transfer agent of any evidence of interest, indebtedness, property, or right belonging to the estate, and to persons purchasing from or otherwise dealing with the heirs as determined in the judgment, to pay, deliver, or transfer such property or evidence of property rights to such heirs, or to purchase property from such heirs, without liability to any creditor of the estate or other person. Such heirs shall be entitled to enforce their right to payment, delivery, or transfer by suit. Nothing in this chapter shall affect the rights or remedies of the creditors of the decedent except as provided in this subsection.

Acts 1955, 54th Leg., p. 88, ch. 55, eff. Jan. 1, 1956. Amended by Acts 1971, 62nd Leg., p. 971, ch. 173, § 4, eff. Jan. 1, 1972; Acts 1979, 66th Leg., p. 1746, ch. 713, § 9, eff. Aug. 27, 1979.

§ 56. Filing of Certified Copy of Judgment

A certified copy of such judgment may be filed for record in the office of the county clerk of the county in which any of the real property described in such judgment is situated, and recorded in the deed records of such county, and indexed in the name of such decedent as grantor and of the heirs named in such judgment as grantees; and, from and after such filing, such judgment shall constitute constructive notice of the facts set forth therein.

Acts 1955, 54th Leg., p. 88, ch. 55, eff. Jan. 1, 1956.

Chapter IV. Execution and Revocation of Wills

Statutes in Context

The only way for a person to avoid having the probate estate pass to heirs under the law of intestate succession is to execute a valid will. A person has, however, no right to make a will. The United States Supreme Court confirmed that "[r]ights of succession to the property of a deceased . . . are of statutory creation, and the dead hand rules succession only by sufferance. Nothing in the Federal Constitution forbids the legislature of a state to limit, condition, or even abolish the power of testamentary disposition over property within its jurisdiction." *Irving Trust Co. v. Day*, 314 U.S. 556, 562 (1942).

Although not required to do so, the Texas Legislature has granted individuals the privilege of designating the recipients of their property upon death. Because the ability to execute a will is a privilege, a will typically has no effect unless the testator has precisely followed all the requirements. Texas, like most states, demands strict compliance with the statutorily mandated requirements. A few states, however, have adopted a *substantial compliance* rule which grants the court a *dispensing power* to excuse a harmless error if there is clear and convincing evidence that the testator intended the document to be a will.

Many states have a *savings statute* which permits a will that does not meet the requirements of a valid will under local law to nonetheless be effective under certain circumstances. Texas does not have a savings statute.

There are four main requirements of a valid will: (1) legal capacity (§ 57), (2) testamentary capacity (§ 57 and case law thereunder), (3) testamentary intent (case law), and (4) formalities (attested wills under § 59, holographic wills under § 60, and nuncupative wills under §§ 64-65). Whenever you are asked to determine if a document purporting to be a will is valid, you must begin your analysis by ascertaining whether the testator satisfied each of these four requirements.

Statutes in Context

Section 57 requires that the testator have both legal and testamentary capacity to execute a will.

The testator has legal capacity if the testator is either (1) age 18 or older, (2) currently or previously married, or (3) a current member of the armed forces of the United States.

A testator has testamentary capacity ("sound mind") if the testator has (1) sufficient mental ability to understand the act in which the testator was engaged, (2) sufficient mental ability to understand the effect of making a will (that is, to dispose of property upon death), (3) sufficient mental ability to understand the general nature and extent of the testator's property, (4) sufficient mental ability to know the testator's next of kin and the natural objects of the testator's bounty and their claims upon the testator, and (5) memory sufficient to collect in the testator's mind the elements of the business to be transacted and to hold them long enough to perceive at least their obvious relation to each other and to form a reasonable judgment as to them. *Stephen v. Coleman*, 533 S.W.2d 444 (Tex. Civ. App. — Fort Worth 1976, writ ref'd n.r.e.).

§ 57. Who May Execute a Will

Every person who has attained the age of eighteen years, or who is or has been lawfully married, or who is a member of the armed forces of the United States or of the auxiliaries thereof or of the maritime service at the time the will is made, being of sound mind, shall have the right and power to make a last will and testament, under the rules and limitations prescribed by law.

Acts 1955, 54th Leg., p. 88, ch. 55, eff. Jan. 1, 1956. Amended by Acts 1967, 60th Leg., p. 801, ch. 334, § 1, eff. Aug. 28, 1967.

Statutes in Context

Section 58(b) authorizes a *negative will*, that is, a will which does not provide for the disposition of property but rather merely states that a named heir may not take by intestacy. Negative provisions were not enforced under the common law.

Section 58(c) provides that the contents of any specifically gifted item are not included in the gift unless the gift expressly includes the contents. Intangible property such as stock and titled personal property such as motor vehicles, are not considered contents. For example, if the will devises "my home to Son," the contents of the real property will not pass to Son. However, if the will devises "my house and its contents to Son" and upon testator's death the home contains furniture, stock certificates, and a car, Son would receive the furniture, but not the stock or car.

§ 58. Interests Which May Pass Under a Will

(a) Every person competent to make a last will and testament may thereby devise and bequeath all the estate, right, title, and interest in property the person has at the time of the person's death, subject to the limitations prescribed by law.

(b) A person who makes a last will and testament may:

(1) disinherit an heir; and

(2) direct the disposition of property or an interest passing under the will or by intestacy.

(c) A legacy of personal property does not include any contents of the property unless the will directs that the contents are included in the legacy. A devise of real property does not include any personal property located on or associated with the real property or any contents of personal property located on the real property unless the will directs that the personal property or contents are included in the devise.

(d) In this section:

(1) "Contents" means tangible personal property, other than titled personal property, found inside of or on a specifically bequeathed or devised item. The term includes clothing, pictures, furniture, coin collections, and other items of tangible personal property that do not require a formal transfer of title and that are located in another item of tangible personal property such as a cedar chest or other furniture.

(2) "Titled personal property" includes all tangible personal property represented by a certificate of title, certificate of ownership, written label, marking, or designation that signifies ownership by a person. The term includes a motor vehicle, motor home, motorboat, or other similar property that requires a formal transfer of title.

Acts 1955, 54th Leg., p. 88, ch. 55, eff. Jan. 1, 1956. Amended by Acts 1991, 72nd Leg., ch. 895, § 6, eff. Sept. 1, 1991; Acts 1993, 73rd Leg., ch. 846, § 6, eff. Sept. 1, 1993; Subsecs. (c), (d) amended by Acts 1995, 74th Leg., ch. 642, § 1, eff. Sept. 1, 1995.

Statutes in Context

Section 58a authorizes the use of a *pour-over* provision in a will, that is, a testamentary gift to an inter vivos trust. Pour-over provisions are very common because a testator may wish to obtain the benefits of a trust but not want to create the trust in the testator's will. Reasons a testator may prefer the pour-over technique include (1) an inter vivos trust is easier to amend than a will; (2) an inter vivos trust can serve as a receptacle for a variety of other assets, such as life insurance proceeds and annuity payments, to provide a unified disposition of the testator's property; and (3) the testator may pour over into a trust created by someone else, such as a spouse.

Section 58a is based on the 1991 version of the Uniform Testamentary Additions to Trusts Act. Innovations in this act include (1) the testator's ability to pour over to an inter vivos trust which, although placed in writing, has not actually been created because no property has yet been transferred to the trust (in other words, the testamentary gift may provide the initial funding of the trust) and (2) the pour-over property is governed by the current terms of the trust, not those in effect when the testator died. Thus, if a testator leaves property to a trust created by someone else who is still alive, the potential exists

for that person to make amendments to the trust after the testator's death which may change the identity of the beneficiaries and how the trust property is spent or managed.

***See* Insurance Code §§ 1104.021 through 1104.025 for additional provisions applicable to life insurance which is payable to the trustee named in the policy.**

§ 58a. Devises or Bequests to Trustees

(a) A testator may validly devise or bequeath property in a will to the trustee of a trust established or to be established:

(1) during the testator's lifetime by the testator, by the testator and another person, or by another person, including a funded or unfunded life insurance trust, in which the settlor has reserved any or all rights of ownership of the insurance contracts; or

(2) at the testator's death by the testator's devise or bequest to the trustee, if the trust is identified in the testator's will and its terms are in a written instrument, other than a will, that is executed before, with, or after the execution of the testator's will or in another person's will if that other person has predeceased the testator, regardless of the existence, size, or character of the corpus of the trust.

(b) A devise or bequest is not invalid because the trust is amendable or revocable or because the trust was amended after the execution of the will or the testator's death.

(c) Unless the testator's will provides otherwise, property devised or bequeathed to a trust described by Subsection (a) of this section is not held under a testamentary trust of the testator. The property becomes a part of the trust to which it is devised or bequeathed and must be administered and disposed of in accordance with the provisions of the instrument establishing the trust, including any amendments to the instrument made before or after the testator's death.

(d) Unless the testator's will provides otherwise, a revocation or termination of the trust before the testator's death causes the devise or bequest to lapse.

Added by Acts 1961, 57th Leg., p. 43, ch. 29, § 1. Amended by Acts 1993, 73rd Leg., ch. 846, § 7, eff. Sept. 1, 1993.

Statutes in Context

Section 58b voids a testamentary gift made to an attorney or someone closely connected to the attorney (i.e., heir or employee) when the attorney is also the attorney who drafted the will. This section, however, does not apply to wills prepared by an attorney if the attorney is the testator's spouse, ascendant or descendant, or related within the third degree of consanguinity or affinity. *See* Government Code §§ 573.021 - 573.025 (definitions of "consanguinity" and "affinity" by analogy).

***See also* Disciplinary Rule of Professional Conduct 1.08(b) (in the Government Code).**

§ 58b. Devises and Bequests That Are Void

(a) A devise or bequest of property in a will to an attorney who prepares or supervises the preparation of the will or a devise or bequest of property in a will to an heir or employee of the attorney who prepares or supervises the preparation of the will is void.

(b) This section does not apply to:

(1) a devise or bequest made to a person who:

(A) is the testator's spouse;

(B) is an ascendant or descendant of the testator; or

(C) is related within the third degree by consanguinity or affinity to the testator; or

(2) a bona fide purchaser for value from a devisee in a will.

Added by Acts 1997, 75th Leg., ch. 1054, § 1, eff. Sept. 1, 1997. Subsec. (b) amended by Acts 2001, 77th Leg., ch. 527, § 1, eff. June 11, 2001.

Statutes in Context

The 2003 Texas Legislature clarified whether a residuary clause will be deemed to exercise a power of appointment held by the testator by enacting Probate Code § 58c. A residuary clause or a clause purporting to dispose of all of the testator's property will exercise a power of appointment in favor of the will beneficiary only if one of the following two conditions is satisfied:

(1) The testator makes a specific reference to the power of appointment in the will.

(2) There is some other indication in a writing (but not necessarily the will itself) that the testator intended to include the property subject to the power of appointment in the will.

§ 58c. Exercise of Power of Appointment

A testator may not exercise a power of appointment through a residuary clause in the testator's will or through a will providing for general disposition of all the testator's property unless:

(1) the testator makes a specific reference to the power in the will; or

(2) there is some other indication in writing that the testator intended to include the property subject to the power in the will.

Added by Acts 2003, 78th Leg., ch. 1060, § 8, eff. Sept. 1, 2003.

Statutes in Context

Section 59 sets forth the formalities necessary for an attested will.

1. In Writing The statute does not indicate what the will is to be written on or written with. See Government Code § 311.005(11) for a definition of "written."

2. Signed by Testator The Probate Code does not explain what constitutes a signature but the Code Construction Act (Government Code § 311.005(6)) provides

that a signature is any symbol executed or adopted by a person with present intent to authenticate a writing. Accordingly, initials, marks, and nicknames are sufficient.

A proxy may sign the testator's name provided the signature is placed on the will (1) by the testator's direction and (2) in the testator's presence. *See also* Government Code § 406.0165 for when a notary may sign as a proxy in the presence of a witness if the testator is physically unable to sign.

Section 59(a) does not specify a location for the testator's signature. *See Lawson v. Dawson's Estate*, 53 S.W. 64 (Tex. Civ. App. — 1899, writ ref'd) (holding with regard to a holographic will that the location of the testator's signature is "of secondary consequence").

3. Attested by at Least Two Witnesses The witnesses must be credible, that is, competent to testify in court under the applicable evidence rules. *See Moos v. First State Bank*, 60 S.W.2d 888 (Tex. Civ. App. 1933, writ dism'd w.o.j.). The witnesses only need to be above the age of 14. *See* Probate Code §§ 61-62 for what happens if the witness is also a beneficiary of the will.

The witnesses do not need to know they are witnessing a will. In other words, *publication* is not required in Texas. *See Davis v. Davis*, 45 S.W.2d 240 (Tex. Civ. App. — Beaumont 1931, no writ). The witnesses only need to have the intent to give validity to the document as an act of the testator.

The witnesses must attest using "their names" in "their own handwriting." Thus, attestation by mark or by proxy is not allowed.

Although § 59(a) states that the witnesses must "subscribe" (that is, attest at the end of the will), the courts have not read this requirement strictly. *See Fowler v. Stagner*, 55 Tex. 393 (1881).

The witnesses must attest "in the presence of the testator." The courts have interpreted this to mean a *conscious presence*, that is, "the attestation must occur where testator, unless blind, is able to see it from his actual position at the time, or at most, from such position as slightly altered, where he has the power readily to make the alteration without assistance." *Nichols v. Rowan*, 442 S.W.2d 21 (Tex. Civ. App. — San Antonio 1967, writ ref'd n.r.e.). Note that Texas law, unlike many states, does *not* require (1) the witnesses to attest in each other's presence or (2) the testator to sign the will in the presence of the witnesses.

Although the testator should sign the will before the witnesses attest, Texas courts have not been strict in this regard. Instead, they have followed the continuous transaction view so that as long as "the execution and attestation of a will occurs at the same time and place and forms part of one transaction, it is immaterial that the witnesses subscribe before the testator signs." *James v. Haupt*, 573 S.W.2d 285, 289 (Tex. Civ. App. — Tyler 1978, writ ref'd n.r.e.).

Section 59(b) provides the testator with the option of adding a *self-proving affidavit* to the will. Virtually all wills contain this affidavit because it substitutes for the in-court testimony of the witnesses when the will is probated thereby saving considerable time and expense. In the past, problems arose if the testator and/or the witnesses signed the affidavit but not the will. The courts consistently held that the will and the affidavit were separate documents and thus a signature on the self-proving affidavit could not substitute for a missing signature on the will. *See Boren v. Boren*, 402 S.W.2d 728 (Tex. 1966). The 1991 Texas Legislature amended § 59(b) to alleviate this harsh result. Now, a signature on the affidavit may be used to prove the will but the will is then no longer considered self-proved and the testimony of the witnesses will be needed to probate the will.

§ 59. Requisites of a Will

(a) Every last will and testament, except where otherwise provided by law, shall be in writing and signed by the testator in person or by another person for him by his direction and in his presence, and shall, if not wholly in the handwriting of the testator, be attested by two or more credible witnesses above the age of fourteen years who shall subscribe their names thereto in their own handwriting in the presence of the testator. Such a will or testament may, at the time of its execution or at any subsequent date during the lifetime of the testator and the witnesses, be made self-proved, and the testimony of the witnesses in the probate thereof may be made unnecessary, by the affidavits of the testator and the attesting witnesses, made before an officer authorized to administer oaths under the laws of this State. Provided that nothing shall require an affidavit or certificate of any testator or testatrix as a prerequisite to self-proof of a will or testament other than the certificate set out below. The affidavits shall be evidenced by a certificate, with official seal affixed, of such officer attached or annexed to such will or testament in form and contents substantially as follows:

THE STATE OF TEXAS COUNTY OF ____________

Before me, the undersigned authority, on this day personally appeared ____________, ____________, and ____________, known to me to be the testator and the witnesses, respectively, whose names are subscribed to the annexed or foregoing instrument in their respective capacities, and, all of said persons being by me duly sworn, the said ____________, testator, declared to me and to the said witnesses in my presence that said instrument is his last will and testament, and that he had willingly made and executed it as his free act and deed; and the said witnesses, each on his oath stated to me, in the presence and hearing of the said testator, that the said testator had declared to them that said instrument is his last will and testament, and that he executed same as such and wanted each of them to sign it as a witness; and upon their oaths each witness stated further that they did sign the same as witnesses in the presence of the said testator and at his request; that he was at that time eighteen years of age or over (or being under such age, was or had been lawfully married, or was then a member of the armed forces of the United States or of an auxiliary thereof or of the Maritime Service) and was of sound mind; and that each of said witnesses was then at least fourteen years of age.

____
Testator

____
Witness

____
Witness

Subscribed and sworn to before me by the said ________, testator, and by the said ______________ and ______________, witnesses, this ____________ day of ____________ A.D. ____________.

(SEAL)

(Signed) ____________________________________

(Official Capacity of Officer)

(b) An affidavit in form and content substantially as provided by Subsection (a) of this section is a "self-proving affidavit." A will with a self-proving affidavit subscribed and sworn to by the testator and witnesses attached or annexed to the will is a "self-proved will." Substantial compliance with the form of such affidavit shall suffice to cause the will to be self-proved. For this purpose, an affidavit that is subscribed and acknowledged by the testator and subscribed and sworn to by the witnesses would suffice as being in substantial compliance. A signature on a self-proving affidavit is considered a signature to the will if necessary to prove that the will was signed by the testator or witnesses, or both, but in that case, the will may not be considered a self-proved will.

(c) A self-proved will may be admitted to probate without the testimony of any subscribing witness, but otherwise it shall be treated no differently than a will not self-proved. In particular and without limiting the generality of the foregoing, a self-proved will may be contested, or revoked or amended by a codicil in exactly the same fashion as a will not self-proved.

Acts 1955, 54th Leg., p. 88, ch. 55, eff. Jan. 1, 1956. Amended by Acts 1961, 57th Leg., p. 936, ch. 412, § 1, eff. June 17, 1961; Acts 1969, 61st Leg., p. 1922, ch. 641, § 5, eff. June 12, 1969; Acts 1971, 62nd Leg., p. 974, ch. 173, § 5, eff. Jan. 1, 1972. Amended by Acts 1991, 72nd Leg., ch. 895, § 7, eff. Sept. 1, 1991.

Statutes in Context

A *contractual will* refers to a will that is either (a) executed in whole or in part as the consideration for a contract, or (b) not revoked as the consideration for a contract. The contract must meet all the requirements for a valid contract under applicable Texas law.

To ensure that only the wills of testators who actually intend to be bound are deemed contractual, § 59A requires that (1) the will state that a contract exists along with the material terms of the contract or (2) the contract be proved by a binding and enforceable written agreement such as a premarital agreement, divorce property settlement, or buy-sell agreement. The statute further provides that joint wills (a single testamentary instrument that contains the wills of two or more persons, such as a husband and wife) and reciprocal wills (separate wills which contain parallel dispositive provisions) are not presumably contractual. Nonetheless, to avoid the unintended creation of a contractual will, it may be prudent to include an anticontract provision.

If the testator executed the will prior to September 1, 1979, the contractual nature of the will may be established by extrinsic evidence.

§ 59A. Contracts Concerning Succession

(a) A contract to make a will or devise, or not to revoke a will or devise, if executed or entered into on or after September 1, 1979, can be established only by:

(1) provisions of a written agreement that is binding and enforceable; or

(2) provisions of a will stating that a contract does exist and stating the material provisions of the contract.

(b) The execution of a joint will or reciprocal wills does not by itself suffice as evidence of the existence of a contract.

Added by Acts 1979, 66th Leg., p. 1746, ch. 713, § 10, eff. Aug. 27, 1979. Amended by Acts 2003, 78th Leg., ch. 1060, § 9, eff. Sept. 1, 2003.

Statutes in Context

A *holographic* will is prepared in the testator's own handwriting. Section 60 exempts holographic wills from the attestation requirement. This special treatment is justified by the aura of validity that surrounds a handwritten document because of the reduced chance of forgery and enhanced assurance of authenticity resulting from the large sample of the testator's writing.

The will must be "wholly" in the testator's own handwriting. Texas courts have adopted the surplusage approach which means that nonholographic material will not injure the holographic character of the will as long as the nonholographic material is not necessary to complete the instrument and does not affect its meaning. *See Maul v. Williams*, 39 S.W.2d 1107 (Tex. Comm'n App. 1934, holding approved).

A holographic will may be made self-proved. Because the self-proving affidavit is a separate instrument, it does not need to be holographic.

§ 60. Exception Pertaining to Holographic Wills

Where the will is written wholly in the handwriting of the testator, the attestation of the subscribing witnesses may be dispensed with. Such a will may be made self-proved at any time during the testator's lifetime by the attachment or annexation thereto of an affidavit by the testator to the effect that the instrument is his last will; that he was at least eighteen years of age when he executed it (or, if under such age, was or had been lawfully married, or was then a member of the armed forces of the United States or of an auxiliary thereof or of the Maritime Service); that he was of sound mind; and that he has not revoked such instrument.

Acts 1955, 54th Leg., p. 88, ch. 55, eff. Jan. 1, 1956. Amended by Acts 1969, 61st Leg., p. 1922, ch. 641, § 6, eff. June 12, 1969.

Statutes in Context

A testamentary gift to a beneficiary who is also a witness to the will is presumed void under the Texas *purging* statute, § 61. The testimony of an interested witness about the attestation is suspect because the witness has a motive to lie. There are three exceptions to this rule. The first exception applies if the witness would be an heir if the testator had actually died intestate in which case the witness may receive the gift provided it does not exceed the share of the testator's estate the witness could take under intestate succession. With regard to the smaller of the gift under the will or the intestate share, the witness has no motive to lie because the witness will receive that amount regardless of the validity of the will. The second exception is if the will can "be otherwise established" such as by the testimony of another witness. The third exception is detailed in § 62.

§ 61. Bequest to Witness

Should any person be a subscribing witness to a will, and also be a legatee or devisee therein, if the will cannot be otherwise established, such bequest shall be void, and such witness shall be allowed and compelled to appear and give his testimony in like manner as if no such bequest had been made. But, if in such case the witness would have been entitled to a share of the estate of the testator had there been no will, he shall be entitled to as much of such share as shall not exceed the value of the bequest to him in the will.

Acts 1955, 54th Leg., p. 88, ch. 55, eff. Jan. 1, 1956.

Statutes in Context

Section 62 provides the third exception to the interested witness rule set forth in § 61. If the testimony of the witness-beneficiary is corroborated by a disinterested and credible person, the witness-beneficiary may retain the testamentary gift. Note that this person does not have to be an attesting witness to the will. For example, this person could be the attorney who supervised the will execution ceremony.

§ 62. Corroboration of Testimony of Interested Witness

In the situation covered by the preceding Section, the bequest to the subscribing witness shall not be void if his testimony proving the will is corroborated by one or more disinterested and credible persons who testify that the testimony of the subscribing witness is true and correct, and such subscribing witness shall not be regarded as an incompetent or non-credible witness under Section 59 of this Code.

Acts 1955, 54th Leg., p. 88, ch. 55, eff. Jan. 1, 1956.

Statutes in Context

Section 63 provides two methods for revoking a will.

1. Subsequent Writing The testator may revoke a will in a new will, codicil, or other written declaration. The revocation may be express ("I hereby revoke all prior wills and codicils.") or it may be by implication (the testator's old will left Blackacre to Able and the new will leaves Blackacre to Brenda). The formalities for the revocation instrument are the same as for a will.

2. Physical Act The testator may revoke a will by "destroying or canceling" the will such as by tearing up the will, drawing a dark line through the testator's signature, or burning the will. Revocation by physical act is an "all or nothing" arrangement, that is, Texas law does not permit partial revocation by physical act. Thus, if the testator merely draws lines through certain provisions or makes interlineations on a nonholographic will, these self-help changes will not be given effect; the will is probated as originally written. *See Leatherwood v. Stephens*, 24 S.W.2d 819 (Tex. Comm'n App. 1930, judgment adopted).

The physical act may be performed by a proxy provided it is done in the testator's presence.

§ 63. Revocation of Wills

No will in writing, and no clause thereof or devise therein, shall be revoked, except by a subsequent will, codicil, or declaration in writing, executed with like formalities, or by the testator destroying or canceling the same, or causing it to be done in his presence.

Acts 1955, 54th Leg., p. 88, ch. 55, eff. Jan. 1, 1956.

Statutes in Context

A *nuncupative* will is an oral or spoken will. The common law had a long history of recognizing nuncupative wills for personal property. Beginning with the Statute of Frauds of 1677, however, legislatures have increased the number of restrictions and conditions on their use. The Wills Act of 1837 eliminated oral wills except for soldiers and sailors.

Courts and legislatures in the United States do not favor nuncupative wills because of the difficulty of proof and potential for fraud. Nonetheless, Texas still permits nuncupative wills under the limited circumstances set forth in §§ 64-65.

Section 64 provides that nuncupative wills may be used only for the disposition of personal property; real property may not be devised orally.

§ 64. Capacity to Make a Nuncupative Will

Any person who is competent to make a last will and testament may dispose of his personal property by a nuncupative will made under the conditions and limitations prescribed in this Code.

Acts 1955, 54th Leg., p. 88, ch. 55, eff. Jan. 1, 1956.

Statutes in Context

Section 65 imposes limitations on nuncupative wills in addition to the restriction to personal property set forth in § 64.

1. Last Sickness The testator must be about ready to die when the testator speaks the testamentary words. The courts have strictly interpreted this element requiring the testator to be "in extremis," that is, overtaken by sudden and violent sickness so the testator has no time or opportunity to make a written will. *See McClain v. Adams*, 146 S.W.2d 373 (Tex. Comm'n App. 1941).

2. Location The testator must speak the testamentary words either (1) at home, (2) at a place where the testator resided for 10 days or more before speaking the words, or (3) at any location if the testator is taken sick away from home and then dies before returning home.

3. Value of Bequeathed Property A nuncupative will may dispose of no more than $30 worth of personal property unless there are at least three witnesses who heard the testator speak the testamentary words.

See § 86 for the special provisions relating to the proving of a nuncupative will.

§ 65. Requisites of a Nuncupative Will

No nuncupative will shall be established unless it be made in the time of the last sickness of the deceased, at his home or where he has resided for ten days or more next preceding the date of such will, except when the deceased is taken sick away from home and dies before he returns to such home; nor when the value exceeds Thirty Dollars, unless it be proved by three credible witnesses that the testator called on a person to take notice or bear testimony that such is his will, or words of like import.

Acts 1955, 54th Leg., p. 88, ch. 55, eff. Jan. 1, 1956.

Statutes in Context

Parents have no obligation to provide testamentary gifts for their children, even if they are minors. Thus, a parent may intentionally disinherit one or more of the parent's children. However, to protect a child from an accidental or inadvertent disinheritance, state legislatures have enacted statutes which may provide a forced share of the parent's estate for a *pretermitted* (omitted) child under certain circumstances. Section 67 contains the rules for determining whether a pretermitted child is entitled to a forced share of the testator's estate.

To qualify as a pretermitted child, the child must be born or adopted *after* the testator executes the will. A child is not pretermitted merely because the child is not a beneficiary of the will.

A pretermitted child will not be entitled to a forced share if (1) the testator provided for the pretermitted child in the will such as by a class gift to "children," (2) the testator provided for the pretermitted child with a non-probate asset such as a life insurance policy or a P.O.D. account, or (3) the testator mentioned the pretermitted child in the will (for example, "I intentionally make no provision for any child who may be hereafter born or adopted.").

If the will makes no gift to the testator's children (i.e., (1) the testator had a child when the testator executed the will but left nothing to this child, or (2) the testator had no living child when the testator executed the will), then the share of each pretermitted child is determined as follows. First, ascertain the amount of the estate not passing to the pretermitted child's other parent (remember that the testator's spouse may not be the child's other parent). Second, give the pretermitted child a share of this amount as if the testator had died intestate with no surviving spouse. The other beneficiaries will receive proportionately less to make up the pretermitted child's share.

If the will provides for at least one of the testator's then living children, then the pretermitted child's share is determined as follows. First, ascertain the amount of the estate given to the testator's children. Second, ascertain the number of children named as beneficiaries in the testator's will and the number of pretermitted children. Add these two figures together. Third, divide the amount of the estate given to the testator's children (step 1) by the figure in step 2 (children beneficiaries + pretermitted children). Each pretermitted child will receive this amount and the gifts to the other children beneficiaries will be reduced proportionately.

Example 1 Husband and Wife have three children, Art, Brenda, and Charles. After Wife executed her will, she had a fourth child, Paul. Husband is Paul's father and Wife's will does not mention or provide for Paul. To how much is Paul entitled under the following circumstances:

(a) Wife's will gives her entire estate to Husband. Paul is entitled to nothing because Wife's entire estate was left to Paul's other parent (Husband).

(b) Wife's will gives $25,000 to Husband and the residuary to the American Red Cross. Paul is entitled to one-quarter of the residuary estate. Husband will still receive $25,000 and the American Red Cross will receive three-quarters of the residuary estate.

(c) Wife's will gives her entire estate to the American Red Cross. Paul is entitled to one-quarter of the residuary estate with the balance passing to the American Red Cross.

(d) Wife's will gives $50,000 to Art, $30,000 to Brenda, and $20,000 to Charles. Paul is entitled to $25,000 (Wife left a total of $100,000 to her children, the total number of will beneficiary and pretermitted children is four; $100,000/4 = $25,000). The beneficiary children receive proportionately less, that is, Art will receive $37,500, Brenda will receive $22,500, and Charles will receive $15,000.

(e) Wife's will leaves $100,000 to Art. Paul is entitled to $50,000 and Art's gift is reduced to $50,000. Brenda and Charles still receive nothing.

(f) Wife named Paul as a beneficiary of her life insurance policy. Paul is entitled to nothing from Wife's estate.

Example 2 After executing her will, Wife has her first and only child, Paul. Wife's will does not mention or provide for Paul. To how much is Paul entitled under the following circumstances assuming that Husband is Paul's father?

(a) Wife's will gives her entire estate to Husband. Paul is entitled to nothing because Wife left her entire estate to Paul's other parent (Husband).

(b) Wife's will gives $25,000 to Husband and the residuary to the American Red Cross. Paul is entitled to the entire residuary. Husband still receives $25,000 and the American Red Cross receives nothing.

(c) Wife's will gives her entire estate to the American Red Cross. Paul is entitled to Wife's entire estate.

Example 3 After Husband married Wife (both childless prior to the marriage), Husband executed a will leaving his entire estate to Wife. This will did not mention or provide for any subsequent children. As a result of an affair Husband had with Sarah, Paul was born and paternity has been properly established. To how much is Paul entitled upon Husband's death? Paul will receive Husband's entire estate because Wife is not Paul's other parent.

---

§ 67. Pretermitted Child

(a) Whenever a pretermitted child is not mentioned in the testator's will, provided for in the testator's will, or otherwise provided for by the testator, the pretermitted child shall succeed to a portion of the testator's estate as provided by Subsection (a)(1) or (a)(2) of this section.

(1) If the testator has one or more children living when he executes his last will, and:

(A) No provision is made therein for any such child, a pretermitted child succeeds to the portion of the testator's separate and community estate to which the pretermitted child would have been entitled pursuant to Section 38(a) of this code had the testator died intestate without a surviving spouse owning only that portion of his estate not devised or bequeathed to the parent of the pretermitted child.

(B) Provision, whether vested or contingent, is made therein for one or more of such children, a pretermitted child is entitled to share in the testator's estate as follows:

(i) The portion of the testator's estate to which the pretermitted child is entitled is limited to the disposition made to children under the will.

(ii) The pretermitted child shall receive such share of the testator's estate, as limited in Subparagraph (i), as he would have received had the testator included all pretermitted children with the children upon whom benefits were conferred under the will, and given an equal share of such benefits to each such child.

(iii) To the extent that it is feasible, the interest of the pretermitted child in the testator's estate shall be of the same character, whether an equitable or legal life estate or in fee, as the interest that the testator conferred upon his children under the will.

(2) If the testator has no child living when he executes his last will, the pretermitted child succeeds to the portion of the testator's separate and community estate to which the pretermitted child would have been entitled pursuant to Section 38(a) of this code had the testator died intestate without a surviving spouse owning only that portion of his estate not devised or bequeathed to the parent of the pretermitted child.

(b) The pretermitted child may recover the share of the testator's estate to which he is entitled either from the other children under Subsection (a)(1)(B) or the testamentary beneficiaries under Subsections (a)(1)(A) and (a)(2) other than the parent of the pretermitted child, ratably, out of the portions of such estate passing to such persons under the will. In abating the interests of such beneficiaries, the character of the testamentary plan adopted by the testator shall be preserved to the maximum extent possible.

(c) A "pretermitted child," as used in this section, means a child of a testator who, during the lifetime of the testator, or after his death, is born or adopted after the execution of the will of the testator.

(d) For the purposes of this section, a child is provided for or a provision is made for a child if a disposition of property to or for the benefit of the pretermitted child, whether vested or contingent, is made:

(1) in the testator's will, including a devise or bequest to a trustee as authorized by Section 58(a) of this code; or

(2) outside the testator's will and is intended to take effect at the testator's death.

Acts 1955, 54th Leg., p. 88, ch. 55, eff. Jan. 1, 1956. Amended by Acts 1989, 71st Leg., ch. 1035, § 5, eff. Sept. 1, 1989; Acts 1991, 72nd Leg., ch. 895, § 8, eff. Sept. 1, 1991; Acts 1993, 73rd Leg., ch. 846, § 8, eff. Sept. 1, 1993; Acts 2003, 78th Leg., ch. 1060, § 10, eff. Sept. 1, 2003.

Statutes in Context

Deceased individuals cannot take and hold title to property. Accordingly, a testamentary gift intended for a beneficiary who died before the testator will not take effect, that is, the gift *lapses*. Lapse also may occur if a beneficiary biologically outlives the testator but is legally treated as predeceasing the testator. For example, the beneficiary may disclaim the gift (§ 37A) or fail to satisfy the survival period imposed by the will or § 47.

To determine the proper distribution of a lapsed gift, the courts begin by ascertaining the testator's intent as reflected by the express terms of the will. If the will provides a substitute taker in the event of lapse, that alternate beneficiary will receive the gift. If the will requires survivorship (e.g., "to my surviving children" or "to such of my children as shall survive me"), only the surviving beneficiaries are entitled to share in the gift. If the will is silent, however, § 68, the *anti-lapse* statute, may provide a substitute beneficiary.

Section 68(a) provides a substitute beneficiary if four conditions are satisfied. (1) The deceased beneficiary must be either a descendant of the testator or a descendant of the testator's parents (i.e., siblings, nieces, and nephews). (2) The beneficiary must die during the testator's lifetime or be treated as dying during the testator's lifetime. (3) The predeceased beneficiary must have left at least one surviving descendant. (4) A surviving descendant of the deceased beneficiary must survive the testator.

If all four requirements are met, then the gift to the predeceased beneficiary does not lapse and instead passes to the descendants of the predeceased beneficiary on a per capita with representation basis.

Section 68(a) applies to class gifts, as well as to gifts to individuals, as long as the class member was alive at the date the testator executed the will.

Section 68(c) addresses the issue of a partial lapse in the residuary clause when the clause lacks survivorship language. For example, assume that a valid will leaves the residuary estate to two of testator's friends, Bill and George. If Bill dies before the testator, George will receive the entire residuary estate. Section 68(c) implies survivorship language even though the will is silent. Remember that survivorship language is implied only in residuary gifts (that is, not in specific or general gifts).

§ 68. Prior Death of Legatee

(a) If a devisee who is a descendant of the testator or a descendant of a testator's parent is deceased at the time of the execution of the will, fails to survive the testator, or is treated as if the devisee predeceased the testator by Section 47 of this code or otherwise, the descendants of the devisee who survived the testator by 120 hours take the devised property in place of the devisee. The property shall be divided into as many shares as there are surviving descendants in the nearest degree of kinship to the devisee and deceased persons in the same degree whose descendants survived the testator. Each surviving descendant in the nearest degree receives one share, and the share of each deceased person in the same degree is divided among his descendants by representation. For purposes of this section, a person who would have been a devisee under a class gift if the person had survived the testator is treated as a devisee unless the person died before the date the will was executed.

(b) Except as provided by Subsection (a) of this section, if a devise or bequest, other than a residuary devise or bequest, fails for any reason, the devise or bequest becomes a part of the residuary estate.

(c) Except as provided by Subsection (a) of this section, if the residuary estate is devised to two or more persons and the share of one of the residuary devisees fails for any reason, the residuary devisee's share passes to the other residuary devisees, in proportion to the residuary devisee's interest in the residuary estate.

(d) Except as provided by Subsection (a) of this section, if all residuary devisees are dead at the time of the execution of the will, fail to survive the testator, or are treated as if they predeceased the testator, the residuary estate passes as if the testator had died intestate.

(e) This section applies unless the testator's last will and testament provides otherwise. For example, a devise or bequest in the testator's will such as "to my surviving children" or "to such of my children as shall survive me" prevents the application of Subsection (a) of this section.

Acts 1955, 54th Leg., p. 88, ch. 55, eff. Jan. 1, 1956. Amended by Acts 1991, 72nd Leg., ch. 895, § 9, eff. Sept. 1, 1991. Subsecs. (a), (e) amended by Acts 1993, 73rd Leg., ch. 846, § 9, eff. Sept. 1, 1993.

Statutes in Context

Divorce was not a common occurrence in the early history of England or the United States. Thus, there is little common law addressing the ramifications of a divorce on a will executed during marriage which made a gift to a person who is now an ex-spouse. Early decisions usually held that the divorce had no effect on the will. The courts realized that a testator probably did not intend for the property to pass to an ex-spouse but felt that they had no legal basis for voiding the gift.

Section 69 provides that upon divorce, all provisions of a will executed during marriage in favor of an ex-spouse are void. The balance of the will remains effective as written. Thus, the ex-spouse would not be able to take as a beneficiary or serve in a fiduciary capacity such as the executor of the will, the guardian of any minor children, or the trustee of a testamentary trust. If the spouses remarry each other and remain married until the first spouse dies, the will remains effective as originally written. The testator also may include a provision validating a gift in favor of a spouse regardless of whether the spouses are married or divorced at the time of the testator's death.

The property left to the ex-spouse beneficiary passes under the will as if the ex-spouse had predeceased the testator.

See Family Code §§ 9.301 & 9.302 for similar provisions applicable to life insurance polices and retirement plans. The Trust Code does not have an analogous provision when an ex-spouse is named as a beneficiary of a trust.

§ 69. Voidness Arising From Divorce

(a) If, after making a will, the testator is divorced or the testator's marriage is annulled, all provisions in the will in favor of the testator's former spouse, or appointing such spouse to any fiduciary capacity under the will or with respect to the estate or person of the testator's children, must be read as if the former spouse failed to survive the testator, and shall be null and void and of no effect unless the will expressly provides otherwise.

(b) A person who is divorced from the decedent or whose marriage to the decedent has been annulled is not a surviving spouse unless, by virtue of a subsequent marriage, the person is married to the decedent at the time of death.

Acts 1955, 54th Leg., p. 88, ch. 55, eff. Jan. 1, 1956. Amended by Acts 1979, 66th Leg., p. 1746, ch. 713, § 12, eff. Aug. 27, 1979. Subsec. (a) amended by Acts 1995, 74th Leg., ch. 642, § 2, eff. Sept. 1, 1995; Acts 1997, 75th Leg., ch. 1302, § 5, eff. Sept. 1, 1997.

Statutes in Context

A judge in a divorce action would sometimes issue an order preventing a party from changing his or her will during the pendancy of the divorce. The Texas Legislature added § 69A in 1993 to prohibit this practice.

---

§ 69A. Changing Wills

(a) A court may not prohibit a person from executing a new will or a codicil to an existing will.

(b) Notwithstanding Section 3(g) of this code, in this section, "court" means a constitutional county court, district court, or statutory county court, including a statutory probate court.

Added by Acts 1993, 73rd Leg., ch. 120, § 1, eff. Sept. 1, 1993.

§ 70. Provision in Will for Management of Separate Property

The husband or wife may, by last will and testament, give to the survivor of the marriage the power to keep testator's separate property together until each of the several distributees shall become of lawful age, and to manage and control the same under the provisions of law relating to community property, and subject to such other restrictions as are imposed by such will; provided, that any child or distributee entitled to any part of said property shall, at any time upon becoming of age, be entitled to receive his distributive portion of said estate.

Acts 1955, 54th Leg., p. 88, ch. 55, eff. Jan. 1, 1956.

Statutes in Context

Section 70A provides rules for determining who is entitled to increases in securities which occur between the time the testator executed the will and the testator's death. Generally, cash dividends are not included in a gift of securities but stock splits and stock dividends are included.

---

§ 70A. Increase in Securities; Accessions

(a) Unless the will clearly provides otherwise, a devise of securities that are owned by the testator on the date of execution of the will includes the following additional securities subsequently acquired by the testator as a result of the testator's ownership of the devised securities:

(1) securities of the same organization acquired because of action initiated by the organization or any successor, related, or acquiring organization, including stock splits, stock dividends, and new issues of stock acquired in a reorganization, redemption, or exchange, other than securities acquired through the exercise of purchase options or through a plan of reinvestment; and

(2) securities of another organization acquired as a result of a merger, consolidation, reorganization, or other distribution by the organization or any successor, related, or acquiring organization, including stock splits, stock dividends, and new issues of stock acquired in a reorganization, redemption, or exchange, other than securities acquired through the exercise of purchase options or through a plan of reinvestment.

(b) Unless the will clearly provides otherwise, a devise of securities does not include a cash distribution relating to the securities and accruing before death, whether or not the distribution is paid before death.

(c) In this section:

(1) "Securities" has the meaning assigned by Section 4, The Securities Act (Article 581-4, Vernon's Texas Civil Statutes), and its subsequent amendments.

(2) "Stock" means securities.

Added by Acts 1993, 73rd Leg., ch. 846, § 10, eff. Sept. 1, 1993.

Statutes in Context

Section 71 provides a procedure for a testator to deposit the will with the clerk of the court for safekeeping. Thus, when a person dies, it is prudent for those interested in the estate to check with the county court clerk in every county in which the decedent has resided. The deposit has no legal effect and does not enhance the likelihood of the will being deemed valid.

---

§ 71. Deposit of Will With Court During Testator's Lifetime

(a) Deposit of Will. A will may be deposited by the person making it, or by another person for him, with the county clerk of the county of the testator's residence. Before accepting any will for deposit, the clerk may require such proof as shall be satisfactory to him concerning the testator's identity and residence. The clerk, on being paid a fee of Three Dollars therefor, shall receive and keep the will, and shall give a certificate of deposit for it. All wills so filed shall be numbered by the clerk in consecutive order, and all certificates of deposit shall bear like numbers respectively.

(b) How Will Shall Be Enclosed. Every will intended to be deposited with a county clerk shall be enclosed in a sealed wrapper, which shall have indorsed thereon "Will of," followed by the name, address and signature of the testator. The wrapper must also be indorsed with the name and current address of each person who shall be notified of the deposit of the will after the death of the testator.

(c) Index To Be Kept of All Wills Deposited. Each county clerk shall keep an index of all wills so deposited with him.

(d) To Whom Will Shall Be Delivered. During the lifetime of the testator, a will so deposited shall be delivered only to the testator, or to another person authorized by him by a sworn written order. Upon delivery of the will to the testator or to a person so authorized by him, the certificate of deposit issued for the will shall be surrendered by the person to whom delivery of the will is made; provided, however, that in lieu of the surrender of such certificate, the clerk may, in his discretion, accept and file an affidavit by the testator to the effect that the certificate of deposit has been lost, stolen, or destroyed.

(e) Proceedings Upon Death of Testator. If there shall be submitted to the clerk an affidavit to the effect that the testator of any will deposited with the clerk has died, or if the clerk shall receive any other notice or proof of the death of such testator which shall suffice to convince him that the testator is deceased, the clerk shall notify by registered mail with return receipt requested the person or persons named on the indorsement of the wrapper of the will that the will is on deposit in his office, and, upon request, he shall deliver the will to such person or persons, taking a receipt therefor. If the notice by registered mail is returned undelivered, or if a clerk has accepted a will which does not specify on the wrapper the person or persons to whom it shall be delivered, the clerk shall open the wrapper and inspect the will. If an executor is named in the will, he shall be notified by registered mail, with return receipt requested, that the will is on deposit, and, upon request, the clerk shall deliver the will to the person so named as executor. If no executor is named in the will, or if the person so named is deceased, or fails to take the will within thirty days after the clerk's notice to him is mailed, or if notice to the person so named is returned undelivered, the clerk shall give notice by registered mail, with return receipt requested, to the devisees and legatees named in the will that the will is on deposit, and, upon request, the clerk shall deliver the will to any or all of such devisees and legatees.

(f) Depositing Has No Legal Significance. These provisions for the depositing of a will during the lifetime of a testator are solely for the purpose of providing a safe and convenient repository for such a will, and no will which has been so deposited shall be treated for purposes of probate any differently than any will which has not been so deposited. In particular, and without limiting the generality of the foregoing, a will which is not deposited shall be admitted to probate upon proof that it is the last will and testament of the testator, notwithstanding the fact that the same testator has on deposit with the court a prior will which has been deposited in accordance with the provisions of this Code.

(g) Depositing Does Not Constitute Notice. The fact that a will has been deposited as provided herein shall not constitute notice of any character, constructive or otherwise, to any person as to the existence of such will or as to the contents thereof.

Acts 1955, 54th Leg., p. 88, ch. 55, eff. Jan. 1, 1956.

Chapter V. Probate and Grant of Administration

Part 1. Estates of Decedents

Statutes in Context

The validity of a will may not be determined while the testator is still alive. Section 72 does not authorize *ante-mortem* probate.

Section 72 also provides a procedure for dealing with the estate of a person whose death is proved only by circumstantial evidence.

---

§ 72. Proceedings Before Death; Administration in Absence of Direct Evidence of Death; Distribution; Limitation of Liability; Restoration of Estate; Validation of Proceedings

(a) The probate of a will or administration of an estate of a living person shall be void; provided, however, that the court shall have jurisdiction to determine the fact, time and place of death, and where application is made for the grant of letters testamentary or of administration upon the estate of a person believed to be dead and there is no direct evidence that such person is dead but the death of such person shall be proved by circumstantial evidence to the satisfaction of the court, such letters shall be granted. Distribution of the estate to the persons entitled thereto shall not be made by the personal representative until after the expiration of three (3) years from the date such letters are granted. If in a subsequent action such person shall be proved by direct evidence to have been living at any time subsequent to the date of grant of such letters, neither the personal representative nor anyone who shall deliver said estate or any part thereof to another under orders of the court shall be liable therefor; and provided further, that such person shall be entitled to restoration of said estate or the residue thereof with the rents and profits therefrom, except real or personal property sold by the personal representative or any distributee, his successors or assigns, to bona fide purchasers for value, in which case the right of such person to the restoration shall be limited to the proceeds of such sale or the residue thereof with the increase thereof. In no event shall the bonds of such personal representative be void provided, however, that the surety shall have no liability for any acts of the personal representative which were done in compliance with or approved by an order of the court. Probate proceedings upon estates of persons believed to be dead brought prior to the effective date of this Act and all such probate proceedings then pending, except such probate proceedings contested in any litigation pending on the effective date of this Act, are hereby validated insofar as the court's finding of death of such person is concerned.

(b) In any case in which the fact of death must be proved by circumstantial evidence, the court, at the request of any interested person, may direct that citation be issued to the person supposed to be dead, and served upon him by publication and by posting, and by such additional means as the court may by its order direct. After letters testamentary or of administration have been issued, the court may also direct the personal representative to make a search for the person supposed to be dead by notifying law enforcement agencies and public welfare agencies in appropriate locations that such person has disappeared, and may further direct that the applicant engage the services of an investigative agency to make a search for such person. The expenses of search and notices shall be taxed as costs and shall be paid out of the property of the estate.

Acts 1955, 54th Leg., p. 88, ch. 55, eff. Jan. 1, 1956. Amended by Acts 1959, 56th Leg., p. 950, ch. 442, § 1, eff. May 30, 1959; Acts 1971, 62nd Leg., p. 975, ch. 173, § 7, eff. Jan. 1, 1972.

Statutes in Context

A will must usually be probated within 4 years of the testator's death. However, § 73(a) permits a court to permit a "late" probate if the proponent of the will was "not in default." The courts have been quite lenient and have accepted a variety of reasons for the proponent's tardiness. *See Kamoos v. Woodward*, 570 S.W.2d 6 (Tex. Civ. App. — San Antonio 1978, writ ref'd n.r.e.).

§ 73. Period for Probate

(a) No will shall be admitted to probate after the lapse of four years from the death of the testator unless it be shown by proof that the party applying for such probate was not in default in failing to present the same for probate within the four years aforesaid; and in no case shall letters testamentary be issued where a will is admitted to probate after the lapse of four years from the death of the testator.

(b) If any person shall purchase real or personal property from the heirs of a decedent more than four years from the date of the death of the decedent, for value, in good faith, and without knowledge of the existence of a will, such purchaser shall be held to have good title to the interest which such heir or heirs would have had in the absence of a will, as against the claims of any devisees or legatees under any will which may thereafter be offered for probate.

Acts 1955, 54th Leg., p. 88, ch. 55, eff. Jan. 1, 1956. Amended by Acts 1971, 62nd Leg., p. 976, ch. 173, § 8, eff. Jan. 1, 1972.

Statutes in Context

Section 74 provides that the application for the administration of an estate must usually be filed within 4 years of the decedent's death. A "late" administration is allowed if it is necessary to recover property due to the estate of the decedent.

§ 74. Time to File Application for Letters Testamentary or Administration

All applications for the grant of letters testamentary or of administration upon an estate must be filed within four years after the death of the testator or intestate; provided, that this section shall not apply in any case where administration is necessary in order to receive or recover funds or other property due to the estate of the decedent.

Acts 1955, 54th Leg., p. 88, ch. 55, eff. Jan. 1, 1956. Amended by Acts 1971, 62nd Leg., p. 976, ch. 173, § 8, eff. Jan. 1, 1972.

Statutes in Context

After a testator dies, the custodian of the will does not have a duty to probate the will. Instead, § 75 merely requires that the custodian deliver the will to the clerk of the court. The statute provides procedures, including imprisonment of the custodian, which may be used if the custodian is unwilling to deliver the will.

§ 75. Duty and Liability of Custodian of Will

Upon receiving notice of the death of a testator, the person having custody of the testator's will shall deliver it to the clerk of the court which has jurisdiction of the estate. On sworn written complaint that any person has the last will of any testator, or any papers belonging to the estate of a testator or intestate, the county judge shall cause said person to be cited by personal service to appear before him and show cause why he should not deliver such will to the court for probate, or why he should not deliver such papers to the executor or administrator. Upon the return of such citation served, unless delivery is made or good cause shown, if satisfied that such person had such will or papers at the time of filing the complaint, such judge may cause him to be arrested and imprisoned until he shall so deliver them. Any person refusing to deliver such will or papers shall also be liable to any person aggrieved for all damages sustained as a result of such refusal, which damages may be recovered in any court of competent jurisdiction.

Acts 1955, 54th Leg., p. 88, ch. 55, eff. Jan. 1, 1956.

§ 76. Persons Who May Make Application

An executor named in a will or any interested person may make application to the court of a proper county:

(a) For an order admitting a will to probate, whether the same is written or unwritten, in his possession or not, is lost, is destroyed, or is out of the State.

(b) For the appointment of the executor named in the will.

(c) For the appointment of an administrator, if no executor is designated in the will, or if the person so named is disqualified, or refuses to serve, or is dead, or resigns, or if there is no will. An application for probate may be combined with an application for the appointment of an executor or administrator; and a person interested in either the probate of the will or the appointment of a personal representative may apply for both.

Acts 1955, 54th Leg., p. 88, ch. 55, eff. Jan. 1, 1956.

Statutes in Context

To serve as a personal representative of a decedent's estate, the person must be qualified under § 77 and not disqualified under § 78. Section 77 provides a list in priority order of the persons who are qualified to serve. Note that the court may appoint co-personal representatives.

---

§ 77. Order of Persons Qualified to Serve

Letters testamentary or of administration shall be granted to persons who are qualified to act, in the following order:

(a) To the person named as executor in the will of the deceased.

(b) To the surviving husband or wife.

(c) To the principal devisee or legatee of the testator.

(d) To any devisee or legatee of the testator.

(e) To the next of kin of the deceased, the nearest in order of descent first, and so on, and next of kin includes a person and his descendants who legally adopted the deceased or who have been legally adopted by the deceased.

(f) To a creditor of the deceased.

(g) To any person of good character residing in the county who applies therefor.

(h) To any other person not disqualified under the following Section.

When applicants are equally entitled, letters shall be granted to the applicant who, in the judgment of the court, is most likely to administer the estate advantageously, or they may be granted to any two or more of such applicants.

Acts 1955, 54th Leg., p. 88, ch. 55, eff. Jan. 1, 1956. Amended by Acts 1979, 66th Leg., p. 1763, ch. 713, § 34, eff. Aug. 27, 1979.

Statutes in Context

Section 78 enumerates the persons who are disqualified from serving as a personal representative.

---

§ 78. Persons Disqualified to Serve as Executor or Administrator

No person is qualified to serve as an executor or administrator who is:

(a) An incapacitated person;

(b) A convicted felon, under the laws either of the United States or of any state or territory of the United States, or of the District of Columbia, unless such person has been duly pardoned, or his civil rights restored, in accordance with law;

(c) A non-resident (natural person or corporation) of this State who has not appointed a resident agent to accept service of process in all actions or proceedings with respect to the estate, and caused such appointment to be filed with the court;

(d) A corporation not authorized to act as a fiduciary in this State; or

(e) A person whom the court finds unsuitable.

Acts 1955, 54th Leg., p. 88, ch. 55, eff. Jan. 1, 1956. Amended by Acts 1957, 55th Leg., p. 53, ch. 31, § 2a, eff. Aug. 22, 1957; Acts 1969, 61st Leg., p. 1922, ch. 641, § 7, eff. June 12, 1969. Amended by Acts 1995, 74th Leg., ch. 1039, § 7, eff. Sept. 1, 1995.

§ 79. Waiver of Right to Serve

The surviving husband or wife, or, if there be none, the heirs or any one of the heirs of the deceased to the exclusion of any person not equally entitled, may, in open court, or by power of attorney duly authenticated and filed with the county clerk of the county where the application is filed, renounce his right to letters testamentary or of administration in favor of another qualified person, and thereupon the court may grant letters to such person.

Acts 1955, 54th Leg., p. 88, ch. 55, eff. Jan. 1, 1956.

Statutes in Context

If a creditor seeks an administration, § 80 provides a means for an interested person to defeat the application.

---

§ 80. Prevention of Administration

(a) Method of Prevention. When application is made for letters of administration upon an estate by a creditor, and other interested persons do not desire an administration thereupon, they can defeat such application:

(1) By the payment of the claim of such creditor; or

(2) By proof to the satisfaction of the court that such claim is fictitious, fraudulent, illegal, or barred by limitation; or

(3) By executing a bond payable to, and to be approved by, the judge in double the amount of such creditor's debt, conditioned that the obligors will pay the debt of such applicant upon the establishment thereof by suit in any court in the county having jurisdiction of the amount.

(b) Filing of Bond. The bond provided for, when given and approved, shall be filed with the county clerk, and any creditor for whose protection it was executed may sue thereon in his own name for the recovery of his debt.

(c) Bond Secured by Lien. A lien shall exist on all of the estate in the hands of the distributees of such estate, and those claiming under them with notice of such lien, to secure the ultimate payment of the bond provided for herein.

Acts 1955, 54th Leg., p. 88, ch. 55, eff. Jan. 1, 1956.

Statutes in Context

Section 81 enumerates the contents of an application for letters testamentary depending on the type of will involved and whether it can be produced in court.

---

§ 81. Contents of Application for Letters Testamentary

(a) For Probate of a Written Will. A written will shall, if within the control of the applicant, be filed with the application for its probate, and shall remain in the custody of the county clerk unless removed therefrom by order of a proper court. An application for probate of a written will shall state:

(1) The name and domicile of each applicant.

(2) The name, age if known, and domicile of the decedent, and the fact, time, and place of death.

(3) Facts showing that the court has venue.

(4) That the decedent owned real or personal property, or both, describing the same generally, and stating its probable value.

(5) The date of the will, the name and residence of the executor named therein, if any, and if none be named, then the name and residence of the person to whom it is desired that letters be issued, and also the names and residences of the subscribing witnesses, if any.

(6) Whether a child or children born or adopted after the making of such will survived the decedent, and the name of each such survivor, if any.

(7) That such executor or applicant, or other person to whom it is desired that letters be issued, is not disqualified by law from accepting letters.

(8) Whether the decedent was ever divorced, and if so, when and from whom.

(9) Whether the state, a governmental agency of the state, or a charitable organization is named by the will as a devisee.

The foregoing matters shall be stated and averred in the application to the extent that they are known to the applicant, or can with reasonable diligence be ascertained by him, and if any of such matters is not stated or averred in the application, the application shall set forth the reason why such matter is not so stated and averred.

(b) For Probate of Written Will Not Produced. When a written will cannot be produced in court, in addition to the requirements of Subsection (a) hereof, the application shall state:

(1) The reason why such will cannot be produced.

(2) The contents of such will, as far as known.

(3) The date of such will and the executor appointed therein, if any, as far as known.

(4) The name, age, marital status, and address, if known, and the relationship to the decedent, if any, of each devisee, and of each person who would inherit as an heir in the absence of a valid will, and, in cases of partial intestacy, of each heir.

(c) Nuncupative Wills. An application for probate of a nuncupative will shall contain all applicable statements required with respect to written wills in the foregoing subsections and also:

(1) The substance of testamentary words spoken.

(2) The names and residences of the witnesses thereto.

Acts 1955, 54th Leg., p. 88, ch. 55, eff. Jan. 1, 1956. Amended by Acts 1971, 62nd Leg., p. 976, ch. 173, § 9, eff. Jan. 1, 1972. Subsec. (a) amended by Acts 1987, 70th Leg., ch. 463, § 1, eff. Sept. 1, 1987. Amended by Acts 1989, 71st Leg., ch. 1035, § 6, eff. Sept. 1, 1989; Subsec. (a) amended by Acts 1997, 75th Leg., ch. 1302, § 6, eff. Sept. 1, 1997.

Statutes in Context

Section 82 enumerates the requirements of an application for letters of administration for an intestate decedent.

---

§ 82. Contents of Application for Letters of Administration

An application for letters of administration when no will, written or oral, is alleged to exist shall state:

(a) The name and domicile of the applicant, relationship to the decedent, if any, and that the applicant is not disqualified by law to act as administrator;

(b) The name and intestacy of the decedent, and the fact, time and place of death;

(c) Facts necessary to show venue in the court to which the application is made;

(d) Whether the decedent owned real or personal property, with a statement of its probable value;

(e) The name, age, marital status and address, if known, and the relationship, if any, of each heir to the decedent;

(f) If known by the applicant at the time of the filing of the application, whether children were born to or adopted by the decedent, with the name and the date and place of birth of each;

(g) If known by the applicant at the time of the filing of the application, whether the decedent was ever divorced, and if so, when and from whom; and

(h) That a necessity exists for administration of the estate, alleging the facts which show such necessity.

Acts 1955, 54th Leg., p. 88, ch. 55, eff. Jan. 1, 1956.

Amended by Acts 1979, 66th Leg., p. 1746, ch. 713, § 13, eff. Aug. 27, 1979. Amended by Acts 1987, 70th Leg., ch. 463, § 2, eff. Sept. 1, 1987; Acts 1997, 75th Leg., ch. 1302, § 7, eff. Sept. 1, 1997.

§ 83. Procedure Pertaining to a Second Application

(a) Where Original Application Has Not Been Heard. If, after an application for the probate of a will or for the appointment of a general personal representative has been filed, and before such application has been heard, an application for the probate of a will of the decedent, not theretofore presented for probate, is filed, the court shall hear both applications together and determine what instrument, if any, should be admitted to probate, or whether the decedent died intestate.

(b) Where First Will Has Been Admitted to Probate. If, after a will has been admitted to probate, an application for the probate of a will of the decedent, not theretofore presented for probate, is filed, the court shall determine whether the former probate should be set aside, and whether such other will should be admitted to probate, or whether the decedent died intestate.

(c) Where Letters of Administration Have Been Granted. Whenever letters of administration shall have been granted upon an estate, and it shall afterwards be discovered that the deceased left a lawful will, such will may be proved in the manner provided for the proof of wills; and, if an executor is named in such will, and he is not disqualified, he shall be allowed to qualify and accept as such executor, and the letters previously granted shall be revoked; but, if no such executor be named in the will, or if the executor named be disqualified, be dead, or shall renounce the executorship, or shall neglect or otherwise fail or be unable to accept and qualify within twenty days after the date of the probate of the will, or shall neglect for a period of thirty days after the discovery of such will to present it for probate, then administration with the will annexed of the estate of such testator shall be granted as in other cases. All acts done by the first administrator, prior to the qualification of the executor or of the administrator with the will annexed, shall be as valid as if no such will had been discovered.
Acts 1955, 54th Leg., p. 88, ch. 55, eff. Jan. 1, 1956.

Statutes in Context

Section 84 explains how to prove a written will which is physically produced in court. If the will is self-proved, no additional proof is needed. *See* §§ 59 (attested wills) and 60 (holographic wills).

---

§ 84. Proof of Written Will Produced in Court

(a) Self-Proved Will. If a will is self-proved as provided in this Code, no further proof of its execution with the formalities and solemnities and under the circumstances required to make it a valid will shall be necessary.

(b) Attested Written Will. If not self-proved as provided in this Code, an attested written will produced in court may be proved:

(1) By the sworn testimony or affidavit of one or more of the subscribing witnesses thereto, taken in open court.

(2) If all the witnesses are non-residents of the county, or those who are residents are unable to attend court, by the sworn testimony of any one or more of them by deposition, either written or oral, taken in the same manner and under the same rules as depositions taken in other civil actions; or, if no opposition in writing to such will is filed on or before the date set for hearing thereon, then by the sworn testimony or affidavit of two witnesses taken in open court, or by deposition in the manner provided herein, to the signature or the handwriting evidenced thereby of one or more of the attesting witnesses, or of the testator, if he signed the will; or, if it be shown under oath to the satisfaction of the court that, diligent search having been made, only one witness can be found who can make the required proof, then by the sworn testimony or affidavit of such one taken in open court, or by deposition in the manner provided herein, to such signatures or handwriting.

(3) If none of the witnesses is living, or if all of such witnesses are members of the armed forces of the United States of America or of any auxiliary thereof, or of the armed forces reserve of the United States of America or of any auxiliary thereof, or of the Maritime Service, and are beyond the jurisdiction of the court, by two witnesses to the handwriting of one or both of the subscribing witnesses thereto, or of the testator, if signed by him, and such proof may be either by sworn testimony or affidavit taken in open court, or by deposition, either written or oral, taken in the same manner and under the same rules as depositions taken in other civil actions; or, if it be shown under oath to the satisfaction of the court that, diligent search having been made, only one witness can be found who can make the required proof, then by the sworn testimony or affidavit of such one taken in open court, or by deposition in the manner provided herein, to such signatures or handwriting.

(c) Holographic Will. If not self-proved as provided in this Code, a will wholly in the handwriting of the testator may be proved by two witnesses to his handwriting, which evidence may be by sworn testimony or affidavit taken in open court, or, if such witnesses are non-residents of the county or are residents who are unable to attend court, by deposition, either written or oral, taken in the same manner and under the same rules as depositions taken in other civil actions.

(d) Depositions if No Contest Filed. If no contest has been filed, depositions for the purpose of establishing a will may be taken in the same manner as provided in this Code for the taking of depositions

where there is no opposing party or attorney of record upon whom notice and copies of interrogatories may be served; and, in such event, this Subsection, rather than the preceding portions of this Section which provide for the taking of depositions under the same rules as depositions in other civil actions, shall be applicable.
Acts 1955, 54th Leg., p. 88, ch. 55, eff. Jan. 1, 1956. Amended by Acts 2003, 78th Leg., ch. 1060, §11, eff. Sept. 1, 2003.

Statutes in Context

Section 85 explains the additional proof which is necessary if the original will is not physically produced in court (e.g., the original is lost, hidden, withheld by disgruntled heir, accidentally destroyed, etc.). Note that a copy of the will is insufficient to prove its contents; the contents must be proved "by the testimony of a credible witness who has read [the original] or heard it read."

§ 85. Proof of Written Will Not Produced in Court

A written will which cannot be produced in court shall be proved in the same manner as provided in the preceding Section for an attested written will or an holographic will, as the case may be, and the same amount and character of testimony shall be required to prove such will as is required to prove a written will produced in court; but, in addition thereto, the cause of its non-production must be proved, and such cause must be sufficient to satisfy the court that it cannot by any reasonable diligence be produced, and the contents of such will must be substantially proved by the testimony of a credible witness who has read it or heard it read.
Acts 1955, 54th Leg., p. 88, ch. 55, eff. Jan. 1, 1956. Amended by Acts 2003, 78th Leg., ch. 1060, § 11, eff. Sept. 1, 2003.

Statutes in Context

Section 86 explains the additional proof which is necessary if the will is oral. *See* §§ 64 and 65.

§ 86. Proof of Nuncupative Will

(a) Notice and Proof of Nuncupative Will. No nuncupative will shall be proved within fourteen days after the death of the testator, or until those who would have been entitled by inheritance, had there been no will, have been summoned to contest the same, if they desire to do so.

(b) Testimony Pertaining to Nuncupative Wills. After six months have elapsed from the time of speaking the alleged testamentary words, no testimony shall be received to prove a nuncupative will, unless the testimony or the substance thereof shall have been committed to writing within six days after making the will.

(c) When Value of Estate Exceeds Thirty Dollars. When the value of the estate exceeds Thirty Dollars, a nuncupative will must be proved by three credible witnesses that the testator called on a person to take notice or bear testimony that such is his will, or words of like import.
Acts 1955, 54th Leg., p. 88, ch. 55, eff. Jan. 1, 1956.

§ 87. Testimony to Be Committed to Writing

All testimony taken in open court upon the hearing of an application to probate a will shall be committed to writing at the time it is taken, and subscribed, and sworn to in open court by the witness or witnesses, and filed by the clerk; provided, however, that in any contested case, the court may, upon agreement of the parties, and in the event of no agreement on its own motion, dismiss this requirement.
Acts 1955, 54th Leg., p. 88, ch. 55, eff. Jan. 1, 1956. Amended by Acts 1971, 62nd Leg., p. 976, ch. 173, § 9, eff. Jan. 1, 1972.

Statutes in Context

Section 88 enumerates the items which the applicant must prove to receive letters testamentary or letters of administration.

§ 88. Proof Required for Probate and Issuance of Letters Testamentary or of Administration

(a) General Proof. Whenever an applicant seeks to probate a will or to obtain issuance of letters testamentary or of administration, he must first prove to the satisfaction of the court:

(1) That the person is dead, and that four years have not elapsed since his decease and prior to the application; and

(2) That the court has jurisdiction and venue over the estate; and

(3) That citation has been served and returned in the manner and for the length of time required by this Code; and

(4) That the person for whom letters testamentary or of administration are sought is entitled thereto by law and is not disqualified.

(b) Additional Proof for Probate of Will. To obtain probate of a will, the applicant must also prove to the satisfaction of the court:

(1) If the will is not self-proved as provided by this Code, that the testator, at the time of executing the will, was at least eighteen years of age, or was or had been lawfully married, or was a member of the armed forces of the United States or of the auxiliaries thereof, or of the Maritime Service of the United States, and was of sound mind; and

(2) If the will is not self-proved as provided by this Code, that the testator executed the will with the formalities and solemnities and under the circumstances required by law to make it a valid will; and

(3) That such will was not revoked by the testator.

(c) Additional Proof for Issuance of Letters Testamentary. If letters testamentary are to be granted, it must appear to the court that proof required for the probate of the will has been made, and, in addition, that the person to whom the letters are to be granted is named as executor in the will.

(d) Additional Proof for Issuance of Letters of Administration. If letters of administration are to be granted, the applicant must also prove to the satisfaction of the court that there exists a necessity for and administration upon such estate.

(e) Proof Required Where Prior Letters Have Been Granted. If letters testamentary or of administration have previously been granted upon the estate, the applicant need show only that the person for whom letters are sought is entitled thereto by law and is not disqualified.

Acts 1955, 54th Leg., p. 88, ch. 55, eff. Jan. 1, 1956. Amended by Acts 1969, 61st Leg., p. 1922, ch. 641, § 8, eff. June 12, 1969.

§ 89. Action of Court on Probated Will

Upon the completion of hearing of an application for the probate of a will, if the Court be satisfied that such will should be admitted to probate, an order to that effect shall be entered. Certified copies of such will and the order, or of the record thereof, and the record of testimony, may be recorded in other counties, and may be used in evidence, as the original might be, on the trial of the same matter in any other court, when taken there by appeal or otherwise.

Acts 1955, 54th Leg., p. 88, ch. 55, eff. Jan. 1, 1956. Amended by Acts 1961, 57th Leg., p. 1072, ch. 480, § 1, eff. Aug. 28, 1961. Amended by Acts 1983, 68th Leg., p. 1155, ch. 260, § 1, eff. Sept. 1, 1983; Acts 1993, 73rd Leg., ch. 846, § 11, eff. Sept. 1, 1993.

Statutes in Context

Sections 89A-89C detail how to probate a will as a muniment of title. This procedure is extremely efficient and cost-effective because there is no administration of the estate (no executor is appointed; no letters testamentary are issued). Instead, the testator's will is proved to be valid and the court order admitting the will to probate documents title transfer to the beneficiaries and gives authority to all those who hold the testator's property to deliver it to the beneficiaries. To use the procedure, however, the testator's estate must have no unpaid debts (except those secured by real property) or the court must determine for another reason that there is no necessity for administration. Sometimes the beneficiaries will pay the testator's debts out of their own pockets so that this procedure may be used.

The muniment of title procedure is also used for "late" probates which are permitted under § 73. *See also* § 128B (heirs must receive notice of late probate).

---

§ 89A. Contents of Application for Probate of Will as Muniment of Title

(a) A written will shall, if within the control of the applicant, be filed with the application for probate as a muniment of title, and shall remain in the custody of the county clerk unless removed from the custody of the clerk by order of a proper court. An application for probate of a will as a muniment of title shall state:

(1) The name and domicile of each applicant.

(2) The name, age if known, and domicile of the decedent, and the fact, time, and place of death.

(3) Facts showing that the court has venue.

(4) That the decedent owned real or personal property, or both, describing the property generally, and stating its probable value.

(5) The date of the will, the name and residence of the executor named in the will, if any, and the names and residences of the subscribing witnesses, if any.

(6) Whether a child or children born or adopted after the making of such will survived the decedent, and the name of each such survivor, if any.

(7) That there are no unpaid debts owing by the estate of the testator, excluding debts secured by liens on real estate.

(8) Whether the decedent was ever divorced, and if so, when and from whom.

(9) Whether the state, a governmental agency of the state, or a charitable organization is named by the will as a devisee.

The foregoing matters shall be stated and averred in the application to the extent that they are known to the applicant, or can with reasonable diligence be ascertained by the applicant, and if any of such matters is not stated or averred in the application, the application shall set forth the reason why such matter is not so stated and averred.

(b) When a written will cannot be produced in court, in addition to the requirements of Subsection (a) of this section, the application shall state:

(1) The reason why such will cannot be produced.

(2) The contents of such will, to the extent known.

(3) The date of such will and the executor appointed in the will, if any, to the extent known.

(4) The name, age, marital status, and address, if known, and the relationship to the decedent, if any, of each devisee, and of each person who would inherit as an heir in the absence of a valid will, and, in cases of partial intestacy, of each heir.

(c) An application for probate of a nuncupative will as muniment of title shall contain all applicable statements required with respect to written wills in the foregoing subsections and also:

(1) The substance of testamentary words spoken.

(2) The names and residences of the witnesses thereto.

Added by Acts 1997, 75th Leg., ch. 540, § 1, eff. Sept. 1, 1997. Subsec. (a) amended by Acts 2001, 77th Leg., ch. 10, § 1, eff. Sept. 1, 2001.

§ 89B. Proof Required for Probate of a Will as a Muniment of Title

(a) General Proof. Whenever an applicant seeks to probate a will as a muniment of title, the applicant must first prove to the satisfaction of the court:

(1) That the person is dead, and that four years have not elapsed since the person's death and prior to the application; and

(2) That the court has jurisdiction and venue over the estate; and

(3) That citation has been served and returned in the manner and for the length of time required by this Code; and

(4) That there are no unpaid debts owing by the estate of the testator, excluding debts secured by liens on real estate.

(b) To obtain probate of a will as a muniment of title, the applicant must also prove to the satisfaction of the court:

(1) If the will is not self-proved as provided by this Code, that the testator, at the time of executing the will, was at least 18 years of age, or was or had been lawfully married, or was a member of the armed forces of the United States or of the auxiliaries of the armed forces of the United States, or of the Maritime Service of the United States, and was of sound mind; and

(2) If the will is not self-proved as provided by this Code, that the testator executed the will with the formalities and solemnities and under the circumstances required by law to make it a valid will; and

(3) That such will was not revoked by the testator.

Added by Acts 1997, 75th Leg., ch. 540, § 1 eff. Sept. 1, 1997.

§ 89C. Probate of Wills as Muniments of Title

(a) In each instance where the court is satisfied that a will should be admitted to probate, and where the court is further satisfied that there are no unpaid debts owing by the estate of the testator, excluding debts secured by liens on real estate, or for other reason finds that there is no necessity for administration upon such estate, the court may admit such will to probate as a muniment of title.

(b) If a person who is entitled to property under the provisions of the will cannot be ascertained solely by reference to the will or if a question of construction of the will exists, on proper application and notice as provided by Chapter 37, Civil Practice and Remedies Code, the court may hear evidence and include in the order probating the will as a muniment of title a declaratory judgment construing the will or determining those persons who are entitled to receive property under the will and the persons' shares or interests in the estate. The judgment is conclusive in any suit between any person omitted from the judgment and a bona fide purchaser for value who has purchased real or personal property after entry of the judgment without actual notice of the claim of the omitted person to an interest in the estate. Any person who has delivered property of the decedent to a person declared to be entitled to the property under the judgment or has engaged in any other transaction with the person in good faith after entry of the judgment is not liable to any person for actions taken in reliance on the judgment.

(c) The order admitting a will to probate as a muniment of title shall constitute sufficient legal authority to all persons owing any money to the estate of the decedent, having custody of any property, or acting as registrar or transfer agent of any evidence of interest, indebtedness, property, or right belonging to the estate, and to persons purchasing from or otherwise dealing with the estate, for payment or transfer, without liability, to the persons described in such will as entitled to receive the particular asset without administration. The person or persons entitled to property under the provisions of such wills shall be entitled to deal with and treat the properties to which they are so entitled in the same manner as if the record of title thereof were vested in their names.

(d) Unless waived by the court, before the 181st day, or such later day as may be extended by the court, after the date a will is admitted to probate as a muniment of title, the applicant for probate of the will shall file with the clerk of the court a sworn affidavit stating specifically the terms of the will that have been fulfilled and the terms of the will that have been unfulfilled. Failure of the applicant for probate of the will to file such affidavit shall not otherwise affect title to property passing under the terms of the will.

Added by Acts 1993, 73rd Leg., ch. 846, § 12, eff. Sept. 1, 1993. Renumbered from V.A.T.S. Probate Code, § 89A by Acts 1997, 75th Leg., ch. 540, § 1, eff. Sept. 1, 1997.

§ 90. Custody of Probated Wills

All original wills, together with the probate thereof, shall be deposited in the office of the county clerk of the county wherein the same shall have been probated, and shall there remain, except during such time as they may be removed for inspection to another place upon order by the court where probated. If the court shall order an original will to be removed to another place for inspection, the person removing such original will shall give a receipt therefor, and the clerk of the court shall make and retain a copy of such original will.

Acts 1955, 54th Leg., p. 88, ch. 55, eff. Jan. 1, 1956.

§ 91. When Will Not in Custody of Court, or Oral

If for any reason a written will is not in the custody of the court, or if the will is oral, the court shall find the contents thereof by written order, and certified copies of same as so established by the court may be recorded in other counties, and may be used in evidence, as in the case of certified copies of written wills in the custody of the court.

Acts 1955, 54th Leg., p. 88, ch. 55, eff. Jan. 1, 1956.

§ 92. Period for Probate Does Not Affect Settlement

Where letters testamentary or of administration shall have once been granted, any person interested in the administration of the estate may proceed, after any lapse of time, to compel settlement of the estate when it does not appear from the record that the administration thereof has been closed.

Acts 1955, 54th Leg., p. 88, ch. 55, eff. Jan. 1, 1956.

Statutes in Context

Section 93 provides the statute of limitations for contesting a will. If the con4test ground is not based on fraud, the period is 2 years from the date the court admitted the will to probate. However, if the contest ground is based on forgery or other fraud, the 2-year period runs from the discovery of the forgery or fraud. Incapacitated persons as defined in § 3(p) have 2 years from the removal of their disabilities to begin the contest.

---

§ 93. Period for Contesting Probate

After a will has been admitted to probate, any interested person may institute suit in the proper court to contest the validity thereof, within two years after such will shall have been admitted to probate, and not afterward, except that any interested person may institute suit in the proper court to cancel a will for forgery or other fraud within two years after the discovery of such forgery or fraud, and not afterward. Provided, however, that incapacitated persons shall have two years after the removal of their disabilities within which to institute such contest.

Acts 1955, 54th Leg., p. 88, ch. 55, eff. Jan. 1, 1956. Amended by Acts 2001, 77th Leg., ch. 292, § 3, eff. May 23, 2001.

Statutes in Context

A will has no legal effect until it is probated. Under § 94, a beneficiary has no claim to the devised or bequeathed property until the will is admitted to probate.

---

§ 94. No Will Effectual Until Probated

Except as hereinafter provided with respect to foreign wills, no will shall be effectual for the purpose of proving title to, or the right to the possession of, any real or personal property disposed of by the will, until such will has been admitted to probate.

Acts 1955, 54th Leg., p. 88, ch. 55, eff. Jan. 1, 1956.

Part 2. Procedure Pertaining to Foreign Wills

Statutes in Context

Sections 95-107A address the procedures for handling "foreign" (that is, non-Texas) wills.

1. Non-Texas Domiciliary With Non-Texas Will

a. Will Probated in Decedent's Domiciliary Jurisdiction If the will is probated in the decedent's domiciliary state or country, the will need not meet the requirements of Texas law to be effective to dispose of Texas property. The only grounds a contestant may use to attack the will in Texas are (1) the foreign proceedings are not properly authenticated, (2) the will was previously rejected by a Texas court, and (3) the will has been set aside by a court in the domiciliary jurisdiction. *See* §§ 95(b)(1), 95(d)(1), 95(e), and 100(a).

b. Will Admitted in Non-Domiciliary Jurisdiction If the will has already been probated in a state or county which was not the decedent's domicile at death, the will may be contested in Texas on any ground that would prevent a Texas will from gaining admission to probate. See §§ 95(b)(2), 95(d)(2), and 100(b).

c. Will Not Admitted Anywhere If the will has not been admitted in any other state or county, the proponent may bring an original probate in Texas. The will may be contested on any ground that would prevent a Texas will from gaining admission to probate. See §§ 103 and 104.

d. Rejected in Domiciliary Jurisdiction A rejection of a foreign will by the decedent's domiciliary jurisdiction is conclusive in Texas unless the ground for rejection in the domiciliary jurisdiction would not have been a valid ground for rejecting the will under Texas law. For example, assume that the testator died with an unwitnessed holographic will in a state which requires witnesses on all wills. Because Texas recognizes holographic wills without witnesses (§ 60), this will could be probated in Texas even though it was rejected by the domiciliary state. *See* § 102.

2. Texas Domiciliary with Non-Texas Will The will must meet all Texas requirements. Texas does not have a *savings statute*, that is, a statute which provides that a will is effective in Texas if it would have been valid in the state or country in which it was originally executed.

---

§ 95. Probate of Foreign Will Accomplished by Filing and Recording

(a) Foreign Will May Be Probated. The written will of a testator who was not domiciled in Texas at the time of his death which would affect any real or personal property in this State, may be admitted to probate upon proof that it stands probated or established in any of the United States, its territories, the District of Columbia, or any foreign nation.

(b) Application and Citation.

(1) Will probated in domiciliary jurisdiction. If a foreign will has been admitted to probate or established in the jurisdiction in which the testator was domiciled at the time of his death, the application need state only that probate is requested on the basis of the authenticated copy of the foreign proceedings in which the will was probated or established. No citation or notice is required.

(2) Will probated in non-domiciliary jurisdiction. If a foreign will has been admitted to probate or established in any jurisdiction other than the domicile of the testator at the time of his death, the application for its probate shall contain all of the information required in an application for the probate of a domestic will, and shall also set out the name and address of each devisee and each person who will be entitled to a portion of the estate as an heir in the absence of a will. Citations shall be issued and served on each such devisee and heir by registered or certified mail.

(c) Copy of Will and Proceedings To Be Filed. A copy of the will and of the judgment, order, or decree by which it was admitted to probate or otherwise established, attested by and with the original signature of the clerk of the court or of such other official as has custody of such will or is in charge of probate records, with the seal of the court affixed, if there is a seal, together with a certificate containing the original signature of the judge or presiding magistrate of such court that the said attestation is in due form, shall be filed with the application. Original signatures shall not be required for recordation in the deed records pursuant to Sections 96 through 99 or Section 107 of this code.

(d) Probate Accomplished by Recording.

(1) Will admitted in domiciliary jurisdiction. If the will has been probated or established in the jurisdiction in which the testator was domiciled at the time of his death, it shall be the ministerial duty of the clerk to record such will and the evidence of its probate or establishment in the minutes of the court. No order of the court is necessary. When so filed and recorded, the will shall be deemed to be admitted to probate, and shall have the same force and effect for all purposes as if the original will had been probated by order of the court, subject to contest in the manner and to the extent hereinafter provided.

(2) Will admitted in non-domiciliary jurisdiction. If the will has been probated or established in another jurisdiction not the domicile of the testator, its probate in this State may be contested in the same manner as if the testator had been domiciled in this State at the time of his death. If no contest is filed, the clerk shall record such will and the evidence of its probate or establishment in the minutes of the court, and no order of the court shall be necessary. When so filed and recorded, it shall be deemed to be admitted to probate, and shall have the same force and effect for all purposes as if the original will had been probated by order of the court, subject to contest in the manner and to the extent hereafter provided.

(e) Effect of Foreign Will on Local Property. If a foreign will has been admitted to probate or established in the jurisdiction in which the testator was domiciled at the time of his death, such will, when probated as herein provided, shall be effectual to dispose of both real and personal property in this State irrespective of whether such will was executed with the formalities required by this Code.

(f) Protection of Purchasers. When a foreign will has been probated in this State in accordance with the procedure prescribed in this section for a will that has been admitted to probate in the domicile of the testator, and it is later proved in a proceeding brought for that purpose that the foreign jurisdiction in which the will was admitted to probate was not in fact the domicile of the testator, the probate in this State shall be set aside. If any person has purchased property from the personal representative or any legatee or devisee, in good faith and for value, or otherwise dealt with any of them in good faith, prior to the commencement of the proceeding, his title or rights shall not be affected by the fact that the probate in this State is subsequently set aside.

Acts 1955, 54th Leg., p. 88, ch. 55, eff. Jan. 1, 1956. Amended by Acts 1971, 62nd Leg., p. 976, ch. 173, § 9, eff. Jan. 1, 1972. Subsec. (c) amended by Acts 1999, 76th Leg., ch. 755, § 1, eff. Sept. 1, 1999.

§ 96. Filing and Recording Foreign Will in Deed Records

When any will or testamentary instrument conveying or in any manner disposing of land in this State has been duly probated according to the laws of any of the United States, or territories thereof, or the District of Columbia, or of any country out of the limits of the United States, a copy thereof and of its probate which bears the attestation, seal and certificate required by the preceding Section, may be filed and recorded in the deed records in any county of this State in which said real estate is situated, in the same manner as deeds and conveyances are required to be recorded under the laws of this State, and without further proof or authentication; provided that the validity of such a will or testamentary instrument filed under this Section may be contested in the manner and to the extent hereinafter provided.

Acts 1955, 54th Leg., p. 88, ch. 55, eff. Jan. 1, 1956.

§ 97. Proof Required for Recording in Deed Records

A copy of such foreign will or testamentary instrument, and of its probate attested as provided above, together with the certificate that said attestation is in due form, shall be prima facie evidence that said will or testamentary instrument has been duly admitted to probate, according to the laws of the state, territory, district, or country wherein it has allegedly been admitted to probate, and shall be sufficient to authorize the same to be recorded in the deed records in the proper county or counties in this State.

Acts 1955, 54th Leg., p. 88, ch. 55, eff. Jan. 1, 1956. Amended by Acts 1969, 61st Leg., p. 1925, ch. 641, § 9, eff. June 12, 1969.

§ 98. Effect of Recording Copy of Will in Deed Records

Every such foreign will, or testamentary instrument, and the record of its probate, which shall be attested

and proved, as hereinabove provided, and delivered to the county clerk of the proper county in this State to be recorded in the deed records, shall take effect and be valid and effectual as a deed of conveyance of all property in this State covered by said foreign will or testamentary instrument; and the record thereof shall have the same force and effect as the record of deeds or other conveyances of land from the time when such instrument is delivered to the clerk to be recorded, and from that time only.
Acts 1955, 54th Leg., p. 88, ch. 55, eff. Jan. 1, 1956. Amended by Acts 1969, 61st Leg., p. 1925, ch. 641, § 9, eff. June 12, 1969.

§ 99. Recording in Deed Records Serves as Notice of Title

The record of any such foreign will, or testamentary instrument, and of its probate, duly attested and proved and filed for recording in the deed records of the proper county, shall be notice to all persons of the existence of such will or testamentary instrument, and of the title or titles conferred thereby.
Acts 1955, 54th Leg., p. 88, ch. 55, eff. Jan. 1, 1956. Amended by Acts 1969, 61st Leg., p. 1925, ch. 641, § 9, eff. June 12, 1969.

§ 100. Contest of Foreign Wills

(a) Will Admitted in Domiciliary Jurisdiction. A foreign will that has been admitted to probate or established in the jurisdiction in which the testator was domiciled at the time of his death, and either admitted to probate in this State or filed in the deed records of any county of this State, may be contested by any interested person but only upon the following grounds:

(1) That the foreign proceedings were not authenticated in the manner required for ancillary probate or recording in the deed records.

(2) That the will has been finally rejected for probate in this State in another proceeding.

(3) That the probate of the will has been set aside in the jurisdiction in which the testator died domiciled.

(b) Will Probated in Non-Domiciliary Jurisdiction. A foreign will that has been admitted to probate or established in any jurisdiction other than that of the testator's domicile at the time of his death may be contested on any grounds that are the basis for the contest of a domestic will. If a will has been probated in this State in accordance with the procedure applicable for the probate of a will that has been admitted in the state of domicile, without the service of citation required for a will admitted in another jurisdiction that is not the domicile of the testator, and it is proved that the foreign jurisdiction in which the will was probated was not in fact the domicile of the testator, the probate in this State shall be set aside. If otherwise entitled, the will may be reprobated in accordance with the procedure prescribed for the probate of a will admitted in a non-domiciliary jurisdiction, or it may be admitted to original probate in this State in the same or a subsequent proceeding.

(c) Time and Method. A foreign will that has been admitted to ancillary probate in this State or filed in the deed records in this State may be contested by the same procedures, and within the same time limits, as wills admitted to probate in this State in original proceedings.
Acts 1955, 54th Leg., p. 88, ch. 55, eff. Jan. 1, 1956. Amended by Acts 1971, 62nd Leg., p. 976, ch. 173, § 9, eff. Jan. 1, 1972.

§ 101. Notice of Contest of Foreign Will

Within the time permitted for the contest of a foreign will in this State, verified notice may be filed and recorded in the minutes of the court in this State in which the will was probated, or the deed records of any county in this State in which such will was recorded, that proceedings have been instituted to contest the will in the foreign jurisdiction where it was probated or established. Upon such filing and recording, the force and effect of the probate or recording of the will shall cease until verified proof is filed and recorded that the foreign proceedings have been terminated in favor of the will, or that such proceedings were never actually instituted.
Acts 1955, 54th Leg., p. 88, ch. 55, eff. Jan. 1, 1956. Amended by Acts 1969, 61st Leg., p. 1925, ch. 641, § 9, eff. June 12, 1969.

§ 102. Effect of Rejection of Will in Domiciliary Proceedings

Final rejection of a will or other testamentary instrument from probate or establishment in the jurisdiction in which the testator was domiciled shall be conclusive in this State, except where the will or other testamentary instrument has been rejected solely for a cause which is not ground for rejection of a will of a testator who died domiciled in this State, in which case the will or testamentary instrument may nevertheless be admitted to probate or continue to be effective in this State.
Acts 1955, 54th Leg., p. 88, ch. 55, eff. Jan. 1, 1956. Amended by Acts 1971, 62nd Leg., p. 976, ch. 173, § 9, eff. Jan. 1, 1972.

§ 103. Original Probate of Foreign Will in This State

Original probate of the will of a testator who died domiciled outside this State which, upon probate, may operate upon any property in this State, and which is valid under the laws of this State, may be granted in the same manner as the probate of other wills is granted under this Code, if the will does not stand rejected from probate or establishment in the jurisdiction where the testator died domiciled, or if it stands rejected from probate or establishment in the jurisdiction where the testator died domiciled solely for a cause which is not ground for rejection of a will of a testator who died domiciled in this State. The court may delay passing

on the application for probate of a foreign will pending the result of probate or establishment, or of a contest thereof, at the domicile of the testator.
Acts 1955, 54th Leg., p. 88, ch. 55, eff. Jan. 1, 1956.

§ 104. Proof of Foreign Will in Original Probate Proceeding

If a testator dies domiciled outside this State, a copy of his will, authenticated in the manner required by this Code, shall be sufficient proof of the contents of the will to admit it to probate in an original proceeding in this State if no objection is made thereto. This Section does not authorize the probate of any will which would not otherwise be admissible to probate, or, in case objection is made to the will, relieve the proponent from offering proof of the contents and legal sufficiency of the will as otherwise required, except that the original will need not be produced unless the court so orders.
Acts 1955, 54th Leg., p. 88, ch. 55, eff. Jan. 1, 1956. Amended by Acts 1969, 61st Leg., p. 1925, ch. 641, § 9, eff. June 12, 1969.

§ 105. Executor of Will Probated in Another Jurisdiction

When a foreign will is admitted to ancillary probate in accordance with Section 95 of this Code, the executor named in such will shall be entitled to receive, upon application, letters testamentary upon proof that he has qualified as such in the jurisdiction in which the will was admitted to probate, and that he is not disqualified to serve as executor in this State. After such proof is made, the court shall enter an order directing that ancillary letters testamentary be issued to him. If letters of administration have previously been granted by such court in this State to any other person, such letters shall be revoked upon the application of the executor after personal service of citation upon the person to whom such letters were granted.
Acts 1955, 54th Leg., p. 88, ch. 55, eff. Jan. 1, 1956. Amended by Acts 1969, 61st Leg., p. 1925, ch. 641, § 9, eff. June 12, 1969.

Statutes in Context

Section 105A explains when a non-Texas bank or trust company may serve as an executor or trustee in Texas. Basically, the statute adopts a reciprocity approach, that is, the foreign entity may serve in Texas if a Texas bank or trust company may serve as a fiduciary in the foreign jurisdiction.

§ 105A. Appointment and Service of Foreign Banks and Trust Companies in Fiduciary Capacity

(a) A corporate fiduciary that does not have its main office or a branch office in this state, hereinafter called "foreign corporate fiduciaries", having the corporate power to so act, may be appointed and may serve in the State of Texas as trustee (whether of a personal or corporate trust), executor, administrator, guardian of the estate, or in any other fiduciary capacity, whether the appointment be by will, deed, agreement, declaration, indenture, court order or decree, or otherwise, when and to the extent that the home state of the corporate fiduciary grants authority to serve in like fiduciary capacity to a corporate fiduciary whose home state is this state.

(b) Before qualifying or serving in the State of Texas in any fiduciary capacity, as aforesaid, such a foreign corporate fiduciary shall file in the office of the Secretary of the State of the State of Texas (1) a copy of its charter, articles of incorporation or of association, and all amendments thereto, certified by its secretary under its corporate seal; (2) a duly executed instrument in writing, by its terms of indefinite duration and irrevocable, appointing the Secretary of State and his successors its agent for service of process upon whom all notices and processes issued by any court of this state may be served in any action or proceeding relating to any trust, estate, fund or other matter within this state with respect to which such foreign corporate fiduciary is acting in any fiduciary capacity, including the acts or defaults of such foreign corporate fiduciary with respect to any such trust, estate or fund; and (3) a written certificate of designation, which may be changed from time to time thereafter by the filing of a new certificate of designation, specifying the name and address of the officer, agent or other person to whom such notice or process shall be forwarded by the Secretary of State. Upon receipt of such notice or process, it shall be the duty of the Secretary of State forthwith to forward same by registered or certified mail to the officer, agent or other person so designated. Service of notice or process upon the Secretary of State as agent for such a foreign corporate fiduciary shall in all ways and for all purposes have the same effect as if personal service had been had within this state upon such foreign corporate fiduciary.

(c) Any foreign corporate fiduciary acting in a fiduciary capacity in this state in strict accordance with the provisions of this Section shall not be deemed to be doing business in the State of Texas within the meaning of Article 8.01 of the Texas Business Corporation Act; and shall be deemed qualified to serve in such capacity under the provisions of Section 105 of this Code.

(d) The provisions hereof are in addition to, and not a limitation on, the provisions of Subtitle F or G, Title 3, Finance Code.

(e) Any foreign corporate fiduciary which shall violate any provision of this Section 105a shall be guilty of a misdemeanor and, upon conviction thereof, shall be subject to a fine of not exceeding Five Thousand Dollars ($5,000.00), and may, in the discretion of the court, be prohibited from thereafter serving in this state in any fiduciary capacity.
Subsecs. (c), (d) amended by Acts 1995, 74th Leg., ch. 914, § 10, eff. Sept. 1, 1995; Subsec. (c) amended by Acts 1997, 75th Leg., ch. 769, § 5, eff. Sept. 1, 1997. Amended by Acts 1999, 76th Leg., ch. 344, § 6.002, eff. Sept. 1, 1999; Subsec.

(d) amended by Acts 2001, 77th Leg., ch. 1420, § 6.029, eff. Sept. 1, 2001.

§ 106. When Foreign Executor to Give Bond

A foreign executor shall not be required to give bond if the will appointing him so provides. If the will does not exempt him from giving bond, the provisions of this Code with respect to the bonds of domestic representatives shall be applicable.

Acts 1955, 54th Leg., p. 88, ch. 55, eff. Jan. 1, 1956. Amended by Acts 1971, 62nd Leg., p. 976, ch. 173, § 9, eff. Jan. 1, 1972.

§ 107. Power of Sale of Foreign Executor or Trustee

When by any foreign will recorded in the deed records of any county in this state in the manner provided herein, power is given an executor or trustee to sell any real or personal property situated in this state, no order of a court of this state shall be necessary to authorize such executor or trustee to make such sale and execute proper conveyance, and whenever any particular directions are given by a testator in any such will respecting the sale of any such property situated in this state, belonging to his estate, the same shall be followed unless such directions have been annulled or suspended by order of a court of competent jurisdiction.

Acts 1955, 54th Leg., p. 88, ch. 55, eff. Jan. 1, 1956. Amended by Acts 1969, 61st Leg., p. 1925, ch. 641, § 9, eff. June 12, 1969.

§ 107A. Suit for the Recovery of Debts by a Foreign Executor or Administrator

(a) On giving notice by registered or certified mail to all creditors of the decedent in this state who have filed a claim against the estate of the decedent for a debt due to the creditor, a foreign executor or administrator of a person who was a nonresident at the time of death may prosecute a suit in this state for the recovery of debts due to the decedent.

(b) The plaintiff's letters testamentary or letters of administration granted by a competent tribunal, properly authenticated, shall be filed with the suit.

(c) By filing suit in this state for the recovery of a debt due to the decedent, a foreign executor or administrator submits personally to the jurisdiction of the courts of this state in a proceeding relating to the recovery of a debt due by his decedent to a resident of this state. Jurisdiction under this subsection is limited to the money or value of personal property recovered in this state by the foreign executor or administrator.

(d) Suit may not be maintained in this state by a foreign executor or administrator if there is an executor or administrator of the decedent qualified by a court of this state or if there is pending in this state an application for appointment as an executor or administrator.

Added by Acts 1977, 65th Leg., p. 1190, ch. 457, § 1, eff. Aug. 29, 1977.

Part 3. Emergency Intervention Proceedings; Funeral and Burial Expenses

Statutes in Context

Sections 108-114 provide a method for a person qualified to serve as an administrator under § 77 to obtain court permission in an accelerated time frame to (1) obtain access to the decedent's funds to pay for the decedent's funeral and burial expenses and (2) to obtain access to the decedent's rented residence (e.g., an apartment) to remove and protect the decedent's personal property. The application cannot be filed earlier than the third day after the decedent's death or later than the nintieth day after the decedent's death.

§ 108. Time to File Emergency Application

An applicant may file an application requesting emergency intervention by a court exercising probate jurisdiction to provide for the payment of funeral and burial expenses or the protection and storage of personal property owned by the decedent that was located in rented accommodations on the date of the decedent's death with the clerk of the court in the county of domicile of the decedent or the county in which the rental accommodations that contain the decedent's personal property are located. The application must be filed not earlier than the third day after the date of the decedent's death and not later than the 90th day after the date of the decedent's death.

Added by Acts 1993, 73rd Leg., ch. 712, § 7, eff. Sept. 1, 1993. Amended by Acts 1995, 74th Leg., ch. 642, § 6, eff. Sept. 1, 1995. Renumbered from V.A.T.S. Probate Code, § 520 and amended by Acts 1997, 75th Leg., ch. 199, § 1, eff. Sept. 1, 1997.

§ 109. Eligible Applicants for Emergency Intervention

A person qualified to serve as an administrator under Section 77 of this code may file an emergency intervention application.

Added by Acts 1993, 73rd Leg., ch. 712, § 7, eff. Sept. 1, 1993. Renumbered from V.A.T.S. Probate Code, § 521 and amended by Acts 1997, 75th Leg., ch. 199, § 1, eff. Sept. 1, 1997.

§ 110. Requirements for Emergency Intervention

An applicant may file an emergency application with the court under Section 108 of this code only if an application has not been filed and is not pending under Section 81, 82, 137, or 145 of this code and the applicant:

(1) needs to obtain funds for the funeral and burial of the decedent; or

(2) needs to gain access to rental accommodations in which the decedent's personal property is located and the applicant has been denied access to those accommodations.

Added by Acts 1995, 74th Leg., ch. 642, § 7, eff. Sept. 1, 1995. Renumbered from V.A.T.S. Probate Code, § 521A and amended by Acts 1997, 75th Leg., ch. 199, § 1, eff. Sept. 1, 1997.

§ 111. Contents of Emergency Intervention Application for Funeral and Burial Expenses

(a) An application for emergency intervention to obtain funds needed for a decedent's funeral and burial expenses must be sworn and must contain:

(1) the name, address, social security number, and interest of the applicant;

(2) the facts showing an immediate necessity for the issuance of an emergency intervention order under this section by the court;

(3) the date of the decedent's death, place of death, decedent's residential address, and the name and address of the funeral home holding the decedent's remains;

(4) any known or ascertainable heirs and devisees of the decedent and the reason:

(A) the heirs and devisees cannot be contacted; or

(B) the heirs and devisees have refused to assist in the decedent's burial;

(5) a description of funeral and burial procedures necessary and a statement from the funeral home that contains a detailed and itemized description of the cost of the funeral and burial procedures; and

(6) the name and address of an individual, entity, or financial institution, including an employer, that is in possession of any funds of or due to the decedent, and related account numbers and balances, if known by the applicant.

(b) The application shall also state whether there are any written instructions from the decedent relating to the type and manner of funeral or burial the decedent would like to have. The applicant shall attach the instructions, if available, to the application and shall fully comply with the instructions. If written instructions do not exist, the applicant may not permit the decedent's remains to be cremated unless the applicant obtains the court's permission to cremate the decedent's remains.

Added by Acts 1993, 73rd Leg., ch. 712, § 7, eff. Sept. 1, 1993. Amended by Acts 1995, 74th Leg., ch. 642, § 8, eff. Sept. 1, 1995. Renumbered from V.A.T.S. Probate Code, § 522 and amended by Acts 1997, 75th Leg., ch. 199, § 1, eff. Sept. 1, 1997.

§ 112. Contents for Emergency Intervention Application for Access to Personal Property

An application for emergency intervention to gain access to rental accommodations of a decedent at the time of the decedent's death that contain the decedent's personal property must be sworn and must contain:

(1) the name, address, social security number, and interest of the applicant;

(2) the facts showing an immediate necessity for the issuance of an emergency intervention order by the court;

(3) the date and place of the decedent's death, the decedent's residential address, and the name and address of the funeral home holding the decedent's remains;

(4) any known or ascertainable heirs and devisees of the decedent and the reason:

(A) the heirs and devisees cannot be contacted; or

(B) the heirs and devisees have refused to assist in the protection of the decedent's personal property;

(5) the type and location of the decedent's personal property and the name of the person in possession of the property; and

(6) the name and address of the owner or manager of the decedent's rental accommodations and whether access to the accommodations is necessary.

Added by Acts 1995, 74th Leg., ch. 642, § 9, eff. Sept. 1, 1995. Renumbered from V.A.T.S. Probate Code, § 522A and amended by Acts 1997, 75th Leg., ch. 199, § 1, eff. Sept. 1, 1997.

§ 113. Orders of Emergency Intervention

(a) If the court determines on review of an application filed under Section 108 of this code that emergency intervention is necessary to obtain funds needed for a decedent's funeral and burial expenses, the court may order funds of the decedent held by an employer, individual, or financial institution to be paid directly to a funeral home only for reasonable and necessary attorney's fees for the attorney who obtained the order granted under this section, for court costs for obtaining the order, and for funeral and burial expenses not to exceed $5,000 as ordered by the court to provide the decedent with a reasonable, dignified, and appropriate funeral and burial.

(b) If the court determines on review of an application filed under Section 108 of this code that emergency intervention is necessary to gain access to accommodations rented by the decedent at the time of the decedent's death that contain the decedent's personal property, the court may order one or more of the following:

(1) the owner or agent of the rental accommodations shall grant the applicant access to the accommodations at a reasonable time and in the presence of the owner or agent;

(2) the applicant and owner or agent of the rental accommodations shall jointly prepare and file with the court a list that generally describes the decedent's property found at the premises;

(3) the applicant or the owner or agent of the rental accommodations may remove and store the decedent's property at another location until claimed by the decedent's heirs;

(4) the applicant has only the powers that are specifically stated in the order and that are necessary to protect the decedent's property that is the subject of the application; or

(5) funds of the decedent held by an employer, individual, or financial institution to be paid to the applicant for reasonable and necessary attorney's fees and court costs for obtaining the order.

(c) The court clerk may issue certified copies of an emergency intervention order on request of the applicant only until the 90th day after the date the order was signed or the date a personal representative is qualified, whichever occurs first.

(d) A person who is furnished with a certified copy of an emergency intervention order within the period described by Subsection (c) of this section is not personally liable for the person's actions that are taken in accordance with and in reliance on the order.

Added by Acts 1993, 73rd Leg., ch. 712, § 7, eff. Sept. 1, 1993. Amended by Acts 1995, 74th Leg., ch. 642, § 10, eff. Sept. 1, 1995. Renumbered from V.A.T.S. Probate Code, § 523 and amended by Acts 1997, 75th Leg., ch. 199, § 1, eff. Sept. 1, 1997.

§ 114. Termination

(a) All power and authority of an applicant under an emergency intervention order cease to be effective or enforceable on the 90th day after the date the order was issued or on the date a personal representative is qualified, whichever occurs first.

(b) If a personal representative has not been appointed when an emergency intervention order issued under Section 113(b) of this code ceases to be effective, a person who is in possession of the decedent's personal property that is the subject of the order, without incurring civil liability, may:

(1) release the property to the decedent's heirs; or

(2) dispose of the property under Subchapter C, Chapter 54, Property Code[1] or Section 7.209 or 7.210, Business & Commerce Code.

Added by Acts 1993, 73rd Leg., ch. 712, § 7, eff. Sept. 1, 1993. Amended by Acts 1995, 74th Leg., ch. 642, § 11, eff. Sept. 1, 1995. Renumbered from V.A.T.S. Probate Code, § 524 and amended by Acts 1997, 75th Leg., ch. 199, § 1, eff. Sept. 1, 1997.

Statutes in Context

Section 115 permits the person serving as the executor of a deceased spouse's will or the deceased spouse's next of kin to file an application to limit the right of the surviving spouse to control the deceased spouse's burial or cremation. The purpose of this procedure is to prevent a spouse who is suspected of being involved in the deceased spouse's death from burying or cremating the deceased spouse's body and thereby concealing or destroying potentially inculpatory evidence. *See also* Health & Safety Code § 711.002.

---

[1] V.T.C.A., Property Code § 54.041 et seq.

§ 115. Limitation on Right of Surviving Spouse to Control Deceased's Burial or Cremation

(a) An application under this section may be filed by:

(1) the executor of the deceased's will; or

(2) the next of kin of the deceased, the nearest in order of descent first, and so on, and next of kin includes the deceased's descendants who legally adopted the deceased or who have been legally adopted by the deceased.

(b) An application under this section must be under oath and must establish:

(1) whether the deceased died intestate or testate;

(2) the surviving spouse is alleged to be a principal or accomplice in a wilful act which resulted in the death of the deceased; and

(3) good cause exists to limit the right of the surviving spouse to control the burial and interment or cremation of the deceased spouse.

(c) After notice and hearing, without regard to whether the deceased died intestate or testate, a court may limit the right of a surviving spouse, whether or not the spouse has been designated by the deceased's will as the executor of a deceased spouse's estate, to control the burial and interment or cremation of the deceased spouse if the court finds that there is good cause to believe that the surviving spouse is the principal or an accomplice in a wilful act which resulted in the death of the deceased spouse.

(d) If the court limits the surviving spouse's right of control, as provided by Subsection (c), the court shall designate and authorize a person to make burial or cremation arrangements.

Added by Acts 1995, 74th Leg., ch. 642, § 12, eff. Sept. 1, 1995. Renumbered from V.A.T.S. Probate Code, § 525 and amended by Acts 1997, 75th Leg., ch. 199, § 1, eff. Sept. 1, 1997.

Part 4. Citations and Notices

Statutes in Context

Notice of an application for the probate of a written will produced in court and for letters of administration is served by posting under § 128. The notice of the action is merely placed on the courthouse door or a nearby location under § 33(f)(2). Unlike in many states, will beneficiaries and heirs do not receive personal service or service by mail. The posting procedure has been deemed to satisfy the due process requirements of the U.S. Constitution. *See Estate of Ross*, 672 S.W.2d 315 (Tex. App. — Eastland 1984, writ ref'd n.r.e.), *cert. denied*, *Holmes v. Ross*, 470 U.S. 1084 (1985). Methods of service more likely to give actual (as contrasted to constructive) notice are required if the proponent is attempting to probate a written will not produced in court, a nuncupative will, or a will more than 4 years after the testator's death (*see* § 128B).

---

§ 128. Citations With Respect to Applications for Probate or for Issuance of Letters

(a) Where Application Is for Probate of a Written Will Produced in Court or for Letters of Administration. When an application for the probate of a written will produced in court, or for letters of administration, is filed with the clerk, he shall issue a citation to all parties interested in such estate, which citation shall be served by posting and shall state:

(1) That such application has been filed, and the nature of it.

(2) The name of the deceased and of the applicant.

(3) The time when such application will be acted upon.

(4) That all persons interested in the estate should appear at the time named therein and contest said application, should they desire to do so.

(b) Where Application Is for Probate of a Written Will Not Produced or of a Nuncupative Will. When the application is for the probate of a nuncupative will, or of a written will which cannot be produced in court, the clerk shall issue a citation to all parties interested in such estate, which citation shall contain substantially the statements made in the application for probate, and the time when, place where, and the court before which such application will be acted upon. If the heirs of the testator be residents of this state, and their residence be known, the citation shall be served upon them by personal service. Service of such citation may be made by publication in the following cases:

(1) When the heirs are non-residents of this state; or

(2) When their names or their residences are unknown; or

(3) When they are transient persons.

(c) No Action Until Service Is Had. No application for the probate of a will or for the issuance of letters shall be acted upon until service of citation has been made in the manner provided herein.

Acts 1955, 54th Leg., p. 88, ch. 55, eff. Jan. 1, 1956.

Statutes in Context

Generally, the beneficiaries of a will are not entitled to notice that a will has been admitted to probate. However, if the beneficiary is a government agency or charity, § 128A requires notice.

§ 128A. Notice to Certain Entities After Probate

(a) If the address of the entity can be ascertained with reasonable diligence, an applicant under Section 81 of this code shall give the state, a governmental agency of the state, or a charitable organization notice that the entity is named as a devisee in a written will, a written will not produced, or a nuncupative will that has been admitted to probate.

(b) The notice required by Subsection (a) of this section must be given not later than the 30th day after the date of the probate of the will.

(c) The notice must be in writing and state the county in which the will was admitted to probate. A copy of the application and the order admitting the will to probate and, if the application is for probate of a written will, a copy of the will must be attached to the notice.

(d) An entity entitled to notice under Subsection (a) of this section must be notified by registered or certified mail, return receipt requested.

(e) The applicant must file a copy of the notice with the court in which the will was admitted to probate.

Added by Acts 1989, 71st Leg., ch. 1035, § 7, eff. Sept. 1, 1989.

Statutes in Context

See Statutes in Context to § 128.

§ 128B. Notice When Will Probated After Four Years

(a) Except as provided by Subsection (b) of this section, an applicant for the probate of a will under Section 73(a) of this code must give notice by service of process to each of the testator's heirs whose address can be ascertained by the applicant with reasonable diligence. The notice must be given before the probate of the testator's will.

(b) Notice under Subsection (a) of this section is not required to be provided to an heir who has delivered to the court an affidavit signed by the heir stating that the heir does not object to the offer of the testator's will for probate.

(c) The notice required by this section and an affidavit described by Subsection (b) of this section must also contain a statement that:

(1) the testator's property will pass to the testator's heirs if the will is not admitted to probate; and

(2) the person offering the testator's will for probate may not be in default for failing to present the will for probate during the four-year period immediately following the testator's death.

(d) If the address of any of the testator's heirs cannot be ascertained by the applicant with reasonable diligence, the court shall appoint an attorney ad litem to protect the interests of the unknown heirs after an application for the probate of a will is made under Section 73(a) of this code.

(e) In the case of an application for the probate of a will of a testator who has had another will admitted to probate, this section applies to a beneficiary of the testator's probated will instead of the testator's heirs.

Added by Acts 1999, 76th Leg., ch. 855, § 2, eff. Sept. 1, 1999.

§ 129. Validation of Prior Modes of Service of Citation

(a) In all cases where written wills produced in court have been probated prior to June 14, 1927, after publication of citation as provided by the then Article 28 of the Revised Civil Statutes of Texas (1925), without service of citation, the action of the courts in admitting said wills to probate is hereby validated in so far as service of citation is concerned.

(b) In all cases where written wills produced in court have been probated or letters of administration have been granted prior to May 18, 1939, after citation, as provided by the then Article 3334, Title 54, of the Revised Civil Statutes of Texas (1925), without service of citation as provided for in the then Article 3336, Title 54, of the Revised Civil Statutes of Texas (1925) as amended by Acts 1935, 44th Legislature, page 659, Chapter 273, Section 1, such service of citation and the action of the court in admitting said wills to probate and granting administration upon estates, are hereby validated in so far as service of citation is concerned.

(c) In all cases where written wills have been probated or letters of administration granted, prior to June 12, 1941, upon citation or notice duly issued by the clerk in conformance with the requirements of the then Article 3333 of Title 54 of the Revised Civil Statutes of Texas (1925), as amended, but not directed to the sheriff or any constable of the county wherein the proceeding was pending, and such citation or notice having been duly posted by the sheriff or any constable of said county and returned for or in the time, manner, and form required by law, such citation or notice and return thereof and the action of the court in admitting said wills to probate or granting letters of administration upon estates, are hereby validated in so far as said citation or notice, and the issuance, service and return thereof are concerned.

Acts 1955, 54th Leg., p. 88, ch. 55, eff. Jan. 1, 1956.

§ 129A. Service by Publication or Other Substituted Service

Notwithstanding any other provisions of this part of this chapter, if an attempt to make service under this part of this chapter is unsuccessful, service may be made in the manner provided by Rule 109 or 109a, Texas Rules of Civil Procedure, for the service of a citation on a party by publication or other substituted service.

Added by Acts 1993, 73rd Leg., ch. 712, § 2, eff. Sept. 1, 1993.

Chapter VI. Special Types of Administration

Part 1. Temporary Administration in the Interest of Estates of Dependents

Statutes in Context

Section 131A permits the court to appoint a temporary administrator to protect a decedent's estate. Any person, even one who does not qualify as an interested person under § 3(r), may request a temporary administration.

§ 131A. Appointment of Temporary Administrators

(a) If a county judge determines that the interest of a decedent's estate requires the immediate appointment of a personal representative, he shall, by written order, appoint a temporary administrator with limited powers as the circumstances of the case require. The duration of the appointment must be specified in the court's order and may not exceed 180 days unless the appointment is made permanent as provided by Subsection (j) of this section.

(b) Any person may file with the clerk of the court a written application for the appointment of a temporary administrator of a decedent's estate under this section. The application must be verified and must include the information required by Section 81 of this code if the decedent died testate or Section 82 of this code if the decedent died intestate and an affidavit that sets out:

(1) the name, address, and interest of the applicant;

(2) the facts showing an immediate necessity for the appointment of a temporary administrator;

(3) the requested powers and duties of the temporary administrator;

(4) a statement that the applicant is entitled to letters of temporary administration and is not disqualified by law from serving as a temporary administrator; and

(5) a description of the real and personal property that the applicant believes to be in the decedent's estate.

(c) An order of appointment must:

(1) designate the appointee as "temporary administrator" of the decedent's estate for the specified period;

(2) define the powers conferred on the appointee; and

(3) set the amount of bond to be given by the appointee.

(d) On the date of the order, the appointee shall file with the county clerk a bond in the amount ordered by the court.

(e) Not later than the third day after the date on which an appointee qualifies, the county clerk shall issue to the appointee letters of appointment that set forth the powers to be exercised by the appointee as ordered by the court.

(f) On the date that the county clerk issues letters of appointment, the county clerk shall post a notice of the appointment to all interested persons on the courthouse door.

(g) On the date the county clerk issues letters of appointment, the appointee shall notify the known heirs of the decedent of his appointment by certified mail, return receipt requested.

(h) A notice required by Subsection (f) or (g) of this section must state that:

(1) an interested person or an heir may request a hearing to contest the appointment not later than the 15th day after the date that the letters of appointment are issued;

(2) if no contest is made within the period specified by the notice, the appointment will continue for the time specified in the order of appointment; and

(3) the court may make the appointment permanent.

(i) If an interested person or an heir requests a hearing to contest the appointment of a temporary administrator, a hearing shall be held and a determination made not later than the 10th day after the date the request was made. If a request is not made on or before the 15th day after the date that the letters of appointment are issued, the appointment of a temporary administrator continues for the period specified in the order, unless made permanent under Subsection (j) of this section. During the pendency of a contest of the appointment of a temporary administrator, the temporary appointee shall continue to act as administrator of the estate to the extent of the powers conferred by his appointment. If the court sets aside the appointment, the court may require the temporary administrator to prepare and file, under oath, a complete exhibit of the condition of the estate and detail the disposition the temporary administrator has made of the property of the estate.

(j) At the conclusion of the term of appointment of a temporary administrator, the court may, by written order, make the appointment permanent if the permanent appointment is in the interest of the estate.

Added by Acts 1987, 70th Leg., ch. 460, § 2, eff. Sept. 1, 1987. Subsec. (e) amended by Acts 1989, 71st Leg., ch. 1035, § 8, eff. Sept. 1, 1989; Subsec. (b) amended by Acts 1997, 75th Leg., ch. 540, § 2, eff. Sept. 1, 1997.

Statutes in Context

Section 132 provides for the creation of a temporary administration pending the contest of a will if no executor has yet to be appointed.

---

§ 132. Temporary Administration Pending Contest of a Will or Administration

(a) Appointment of Temporary Administrator. Pending a contest relative to the probate of a will or the granting of letters of administration, the court may appoint a temporary administrator, with such limited powers as the circumstances of the case require; and such appointment may continue in force until the termination of the contest and the appointment of an executor or administrator with full powers. The power of appointment in this Subsection is in addition to the court's power of appointment under Section 131A of this Code.

(b) Additional Powers Relative to Claims. When temporary administration has been granted pending a will contest, or pending a contest on an application for letters of administration, the court may, at any time during the pendency of the contest, confer upon the temporary administrator all the power and authority of a permanent administrator with respect to claims against the estate, and in such case the court and the temporary administrator shall act in the same manner as in permanent administration in connection with such matters as the approval or disapproval of claims, the payment of claims, and the making of sales of real or personal property for the payment of claims; provided, however, that in the event such power and authority is conferred upon a temporary administrator, he shall be required to give bond in the full amount required of a permanent administrator. The provisions of this Subsection are cumulative and shall not be construed to exclude the right of the court to order a temporary administrator to do any and all of the things covered by this Subsection in other cases where the doing of such things shall be necessary or expedient to preserve the estate pending final determination of the contest.

Acts 1955, 54th Leg., p. 88, ch. 55, eff. Jan. 1, 1956. Subsec. (a) amended by Acts 1987, 70th Leg., ch. 460, § 3, eff. Sept. 1, 1987.

§ 133. Powers of Temporary Administrators

Temporary administrators shall have and exercise only such rights and powers as are specifically expressed in the order of the court appointing them, and as may be expressed in subsequent orders of the court. Where a court, by a subsequent order, extends the rights and powers of a temporary administrator, it may require additional bond commensurate with such extension. Any acts performed by temporary administrators that are not so expressly authorized shall be void.

Acts 1955, 54th Leg., p. 88, ch. 55, eff. Jan. 1, 1956. Amended by Acts 1993, 73rd Leg., ch. 957, § 25, eff. Sept. 1, 1993.

§ 134. Accounting

At the expiration of a temporary appointment, the appointee shall file with the clerk of the court a sworn list of all property of the estate which has come into his hands, a return of all sales made by him, and a full exhibit and account of all his acts as such appointee.

Acts 1955, 54th Leg., p. 88, ch. 55, eff. Jan. 1, 1956.

§ 135. Closing Temporary Administration

The list, return, exhibit, and account so filed shall be acted upon by the court and, whenever temporary letters shall expire or cease to be of effect for any cause, the court shall immediately enter an order requiring such temporary appointee forthwith to deliver the estate remaining in his possession to the person or persons legally entitled to its possession. Upon proof of such delivery, the appointee shall be discharged and the sureties on his bond released as to any future liability.

Acts 1955, 54th Leg., p. 88, ch. 55, eff. Jan. 1, 1956. Amended by Acts 1993, 73rd Leg., ch. 957, § 26, eff. Sept. 1, 1993.

Part 3. Small Estates

Statutes in Context

Sections 137-138 provide a short-form method for handling an intestate estate when the total value of the intestate's property, not including homestead and exempt property, does not exceed $50,000. This procedure is inexpensive and quick and thus is often preferred to a normal administration. Note, however, that the only real property which may be transferred in this manner is the homestead. The estate of a wealthy person might qualify for this procedure because the decedent's wealth may be in non-probate assets and the decedent's homestead.

§ 137. Collection of Small Estates Upon Affidavit

(a) The distributees of the estate of a decedent who dies intestate shall be entitled thereto, to the extent that the assets, exclusive of homestead and exempt property, exceed the known liabilities of said estate, exclusive of liabilities secured by homestead and exempt property, without awaiting the appointment of a personal representative when:

(1) No petition for the appointment of a personal representative is pending or has been granted; and

(2) Thirty days have elapsed since the death of the decedent; and

(3) The value of the entire assets of the estate, not including homestead and exempt property, does not exceed $50,000; and

(4) There is filed with the clerk of the court having jurisdiction and venue an affidavit sworn to by two disinterested witnesses, by all such distributees that have legal capacity, and, if the facts warrant, by the natural guardian or next of kin of any minor or the guardian of any other incapacitated person who is also a distributee, which affidavit shall be examined by the judge of the court having jurisdiction and venue; and

(5) The affidavit shows the existence of the foregoing conditions and includes a list of all of the known assets and liabilities of the estate, the names and addresses of the distributees, and the relevant family history facts concerning heirship that show the distributees' rights to receive the money or property of the estate or to have such evidences of money, property, or other rights of the estate as are found to exist transferred to them as heirs or assignees; and

(6) The judge, in the judge's discretion, finds that the affidavit conforms to the terms of this section and approves the affidavit; and

(7) A copy of the affidavit, certified to by said clerk, is furnished by the distributees of the estate to the person or persons owing money to the estate, having custody or possession of property of the estate, or acting as registrar, fiduciary or transfer agent of or for evidences of interest, indebtedness, property, or other right belonging to the estate.

(b) This section does not affect the disposition of property under the terms of a will or other testamentary document nor, except as provided by Subsection (c) of this section, does it transfer title to real property.

(c) Title to a decedent's homestead that is the only real property in a decedent's estate may be transferred on an affidavit that meets the requirements of this section. An affidavit that is used to transfer title to a homestead under this section must be recorded in the deed records of a county in which the homestead is located. A bona fide purchaser for value may rely on a recorded affidavit under this section. A bona fide purchaser for value without actual or constructive notice of an heir who is not disclosed in a recorded affidavit under this section acquires title to a homestead free of the interests of the undisclosed heir, but the bona fide purchaser remains subject to any claim a creditor of the decedent has by law. A purchaser has constructive notice of an heir who is not disclosed in a recorded affidavit under this section if an affidavit, judgment of heirship, or title transaction in the chain of title in the deed records identifies the heir of the decedent who is not disclosed in the affidavit as an heir of the decedent. An heir who is not disclosed in a recorded affidavit under this section may recover from an heir who receives consideration from a purchaser in a transfer for value of title to a homestead passing under the affidavit.

(d) If the judge approves the affidavit under this section, the affidavit is to be recorded as an official public record under Chapter 194, Local Government Code. If the county has not adopted a microfilm or microphotographic process under Chapter 194, Local Government Code, the county clerk shall provide and keep in his office an appropriate book labeled "Small Estates," with an accurate index showing the name of the decedent and reference to land, if any, involved, in which he shall record every such affidavit so filed, upon being paid his legal recording fee.

Acts 1955, 54th Leg., p. 88, ch. 55, eff. Jan. 1, 1956. Amended by Acts 1957, 55th Leg., p. 53, ch. 31, § 4, eff. Aug. 22, 1957; Acts 1969, 61st Leg., p. 1978, ch. 670, § 1, eff. Sept. 1, 1969; Acts 1975, 64th Leg., p. 1402, ch. 543, § 1, eff. Sept. 1, 1975; Acts 1977, 65th Leg., p. 361, ch. 177, § 1, eff. May 29, 1977; Acts 1979, 66th Leg., p. 1747, ch. 713, § 14, eff. Aug. 27, 1979. Amended by Acts 1983, 68th Leg., p. 4560, ch. 757, § 1, eff. Sept. 1, 1983; Acts 1993, 73rd Leg., ch. 594, § 1, eff. Sept. 1, 1993; Acts 1995, 74th Leg., ch. 642, § 3, eff. Sept. 1, 1995; Subsec. (a) amended by Acts 1995, 74th Leg., ch. 1039, § 8, eff. Sept. 1, 1995; amended by Acts 1997, 75th Leg., ch. 540, § 3, eff. Sept. 1, 1997.

§ 138. Effect of Affidavit

The person making payment, delivery, transfer or issuance pursuant to the affidavit described in the preceding Section shall be released to the same extent as if made to a personal representative of the decedent, and shall not be required to see to the application thereof or to inquire into the truth of any statement in the affidavit, but the distributees to whom payment, delivery, transfer, or issuance is made shall be answerable therefor to any person having a prior right and be accountable to any personal representative thereafter appointed. In addition, the person or persons who execute the affidavit shall be liable for any damage or loss to any person which arises from any payment, delivery, transfer, or issuance made in reliance on such affidavit. If the person to whom such affidavit is delivered refuses to pay, deliver, transfer, or issue the property as above provided, such property may be recovered in an action brought for such purpose by or on behalf of the distributees entitled thereto, upon proof of the facts required to be stated in the affidavit.

Acts 1955, 54th Leg., p. 88, ch. 55, eff. Jan. 1, 1956. Amended by Acts 1995, 74th Leg., ch. 642, § 4, eff. Sept. 1, 1995.

Statutes in Context

Sections 139-142 provide a procedure for a court to dispense with administration if (1) the decedent is survived by a spouse or minor children and (2) the value of the estate, not including homestead and exempt property, does not exceed the family allowance. Administration is not necessary because there would be no property for the decedent's creditors or will beneficiaries to reach.

§ 139. Application for Order of No Administration

If the value of the entire assets of an estate, not including homestead and exempt property, does not exceed the amount to which the surviving spouse and minor children of the decedent are entitled as a family allowance, there may be filed by or on behalf of the surviving spouse or minor children an application in any court of proper venue for administration, or, if an application for the appointment of a personal representative has been filed but not yet granted, then in the court where such application has been filed, requesting the court to make a family allowance and to enter an order that no administration shall be necessary. The application shall state the names of the heirs or devisees, a list of creditors of the estate together with the amounts of the claims so far as the same are known, and a description of all real and personal property belonging to the estate, together with the estimated value thereof according to the best knowledge and information of the applicant, and the liens and encumbrances thereon, with a prayer that the court make a family allowance and that, if the entire assets of the estate, not including homestead and exempt property, are thereby exhausted, the same be set aside to the surviving spouse and minor children, as in the case of other family allowances provided for by this Code.

Acts 1955, 54th Leg., p. 88, ch. 55, eff. Jan. 1, 1956.

§ 140. Hearing and Order Upon the Application

Upon the filing of an application for no administration such as that provided for in the preceding Section, the court may hear the same forthwith without notice, or at such time and upon such notice as the court requires. Upon the hearing of the application, if the court finds that the facts contained therein are true and that the expenses of last illness, funeral charges, and expenses of the proceeding have been paid or secured, the court shall make a family allowance and, if the entire assets of the estate, not including homestead and exempt property, are thereby exhausted, shall order that no administration be had of the estate and shall assign to the surviving spouse and minor children the whole of the estate, in the same manner and with the same effect as provided in this Code for the making of family allowances to the surviving spouse and minor children.

Acts 1955, 54th Leg., p. 88, ch. 55, eff. Jan. 1, 1956.

§ 141. Effect of Order

The order that no administration be had on the estate shall constitute sufficient legal authority to all persons owing any money, having custody of any property, or acting as registrar or transfer agent of any evidence of interest, indebtedness, property, or right, belonging to the estate, and to persons purchasing from or otherwise dealing with the estate, for payment or transfer to the persons described in the order as entitled to receive the estate without administration, and the persons so described in the order shall be entitled to enforce their right to such payment or transfer by suit.

Acts 1955, 54th Leg., p. 88, ch. 55, eff. Jan. 1, 1956.

§ 142. Proceeding to Revoke Order

At any time within one year after the entry of an order of no administration, and not thereafter, any interested person may file an application to revoke the same, alleging that other property has been discovered, or that property belonging to the estate was not included in the application for no administration, or that the property described in the application was incorrectly valued, and that if said property were added, included, or correctly valued, as the case may be, the total value of the property would exceed that necessary to justify the court in ordering no administration. Upon proof of any of such grounds, the court shall revoke the order of no administration. In case of any contest as to the value of any property, the court may appoint two appraisers to appraise the same in accordance with the procedure hereinafter provided for inventories and appraisements, and the appraisement of such appraisers shall be received in evidence but shall not be conclusive.

Acts 1955, 54th Leg., p. 88, ch. 55, eff. Jan. 1, 1956.

Statutes in Context

Section 143 provides for summary proceedings for certain insolvent estates even after a personal representative has been appointed. The statute refers to "claims of Classes One to Four" from § 322. Note that § 322 has been amended many times since § 143 was enacted in 1955 and thus the referenced claims are not the same as when § 143 originally took effect.

§ 143. Summary Proceedings for Small Estates After Personal Representative Appointed

Whenever, after the inventory, appraisement, and list of claims has been filed by a personal representative, it is established that the estate of a decedent, exclusive of the homestead and exempt property and family allowance to the surviving spouse and minor children, does not exceed the amount sufficient to pay the claims of Classes One to Four, inclusive, as claims are hereinafter classified, the personal representative shall, upon order of the court, pay the claims in the order provided and to the extent permitted by the assets of the estate subject to the payment of such claims, and thereafter present his account with an application for the settlement and allowance thereof. Thereupon the court, with or without notice, may adjust, correct, settle, allow or disallow such account, and, if the account is settled and allowed, may decree final distribution, discharge the personal representative, and close the administration.
Acts 1955, 54th Leg., p. 88, ch. 55, eff. Jan. 1, 1956.

Part 4. Independent Administration

Statutes in Context

Texas was a pioneer in the area of non-court-supervised administrations since the first independent administration statutes were enacted in 1843. Independent administrations are extremely common because they are faster, economical, and more convenient than court-supervised (dependent) administrations. Once the personal representative files the inventory, appraisement, and list of claims, the personal representative administers the estate without court involvement.

Section 145 explains when an independent administration is possible. (1) The testator's will may expressly authorize independent administration. Although no special language is needed, most attorneys track the statutory language as follows: "I appoint [name] as independent executor. I direct that there shall be no action in the probate court in the settlement of my estate other than the probating and recording of this will, and the return of an inventory, appraisement, and list of claims of my estate." *See* § 145(b). (2) If the testator did not specify the executor to be independent, all of the beneficiaries may agree under § 145(c). However, if the will expressly prohibits independent administration, the court will not authorize independent administration. *See* § 145(o). (3) If the decedent died intestate, the heirs may agree to an independent administration under § 145(c).

§ 145. Independent Administration

(a) Independent administration of an estate may be created as provided in Subsections (b) through (e) of this section.

(b) Any person capable of making a will may provide in his will that no other action shall be had in the county court in relation to the settlement of his estate than the probating and recording of his will, and the return of an inventory, appraisement, and list of claims of his estate.

(c) In situations where an executor is named in a decedent's will, but the will does not provide for independent administration of the decedent's estate as provided in Subsection (b) of this section, all of the distributees of the decedent may agree on the advisability of having an independent administration and collectively designate in the application for probate of the decedent's will the executor named in the will to serve as independent executor and request in the application that no other action shall be had in the county court in relation to the settlement of the decedent's estate other than the probating and recording of the decedent's will, and the return of an inventory, appraisement, and list of claims of the decedent's estate. In such case the county court shall enter an order granting independent administration and appointing the person, firm, or corporation designated in the application as independent executor, unless the county court finds that it would not be in the best interest of the estate to do so.

(d) In situations where no executor is named in the decedent's will, or in situations where each executor named in the will is deceased or is disqualified to serve as executor or indicates by affidavit filed with the application for administration of the decedent's estate his inability or unwillingness to serve as executor, all of the distributees of the decedent may agree on the advisability of having an independent administration and collectively designate in the application for probate of the decedent's will a qualified person, firm, or corporation to serve as independent administrator and request in the application that no other action shall be had in the county court in relation to the settlement of the decedent's estate other than the probating and recording of the decedent's will, and the return of an inventory, appraisement, and list of claims of the decedent's estate. In such case the county court shall enter an order granting independent administration and appointing the person, firm, or corporation designated in the application as independent administrator, unless the county court finds that it would not be in the best interest of the estate to do so.

(e) All of the distributees of a decedent dying intestate may agree on the advisability of having an independent administration and collectively designate in the application for administration of the decedent's estate a qualified person, firm, or corporation to serve as independent administrator and request in the application that no other action shall be had in the county court in relation to the settlement of the decedent's estate other than the return of an inventory, appraisement, and list of claims of the decedent's estate. In such case the county court shall enter an order granting independent administration and appointing the person, firm, or corporation designated in the application as independent administrator, unless the county court finds that it would not be in the best interest of the estate to do so.

(f) In those cases where an independent administration is sought under the provisions of Subsections (c) through (e) above, all distributees shall be served with citation and notice of the application for independent administration unless the distributee waives the issuance or service of citation or enters an appearance in court.

(g) In no case shall any independent administrator be appointed by any court to serve in any intestate administration until those parties seeking the appointment of said independent administrator offer clear and convincing evidence to the court that they constitute all of the said decedent's heirs.

(h) When an independent administration has been created, and the order appointing an independent executor has been entered by the county court, and the inventory, appraisement, and list aforesaid has been filed by the executor and approved by the county court, as long as the estate is represented by an independent executor, further action of any nature shall not be had in the county court except where this Code specifically and explicitly provides for some action in the county court.

(i) If a distributee described in Subsections (c) through (e) of this section is an incapacitated person, the guardian of the person of the distributee may sign the application on behalf of the distributee. If the county court finds that either the granting of independent administration or the appointment of the person, firm, or corporation designated in the application as independent executor would not be in the best interests of the incapacitated person, then, notwithstanding anything to the contrary in Subsections (c) through (e) of this section, the county court shall not enter an order granting independent administration of the estate. If such distributee who is an incapacitated person has no guardian of the person, the county court may appoint a guardian ad litem to make application on behalf of the incapacitated person if the county court considers such an appointment necessary to protect the interest of the distributees.

(j) If a trust is created in the decedent's will, the person or class of persons first eligible to receive the income from the trust, when determined as if the trust were to be in existence on the date of the decedent's death, shall, for the purposes of Subsections (c) and (d) of this section, be deemed to be the distributee or distributees on behalf of such trust, and any other trust or trusts coming into existence upon the termination of such trust, and are authorized to apply for independent administration on behalf of the trusts without the consent or agreement of the trustee or any other beneficiary of the trust, or the trustee or any beneficiary of any other trust which may come into existence upon the termination of such trust.

(k) If a life estate is created either in the decedent's will or by law, the life tenant or life tenants, when determined as if the life estate were to commence on the date of the decedent's death, shall, for the purposes of Subsections (c) through (e) of this section, be deemed to be the distributee or distributees on behalf of the entire estate created, and are authorized to apply for independent administration on behalf of the estate without the consent or approval of any remainderman.

(l) If a decedent's will contains a provision that a distributee must survive the decedent by a prescribed period of time in order to take under the decedent's will, then, for the purposes of determining who shall be the distributee under Subsections (c), (d), (h), and (i) of this section, it shall be presumed that the distributees living at the time of the filing of the application for probate of the decedent's will survived the decedent by the prescribed period.

(m) In the case of all decedents, whether dying testate or intestate, for the purposes of determining who shall be the distributees under Subsections (c), (d), (e), (h), and (i) of this section, it shall be presumed that no distributee living at the time the application for independent administration is filed shall subsequently disclaim any portion of such distributee's interest in the decedent's estate.

(n) If a distributee of a decedent's estate should die and if by virtue of such distributee's death such distributee's share of the decedent's estate shall become payable to such distributee's estate, then the deceased distributee's personal representative may sign the application for independent administration of the decedent's estate under Subsections (c), (d), (e), (h), and (i) of this section.

(o) Notwithstanding anything to the contrary in this section, a person capable of making a will may provide in his will that no independent administration of his estate may be allowed. In such case, his estate, if administered, shall be administered and settled under the direction of the county court as other estates are required to be settled.

(p) If an independent administration of a decedent's estate is created pursuant to Subsections (c), (d), or (e) of this section, then, unless the county court shall waive bond on application for waiver, the independent executor shall be required to enter into bond payable to and to be approved by the judge and his or her successors in a sum that is found by the judge to be adequate under all circumstances, or a bond with one surety in a sum that is found by the judge to be adequate under all circumstances, if the surety is an authorized corporate surety. This subsection does not repeal any other section of this Code.

(q) Absent proof of fraud or collusion on the part of a judge, no judge may be held civilly liable for the commission of misdeeds or the omission of any required act of any person, firm, or corporation designated as an independent executor or independent administrator under Subsections (c), (d), and (e) of the section. Section 36 of this code does not apply to the appointment of an independent executor or administrator under Subsection (c), (d), or (e) of this section.

(r) A person who declines to serve or resigns as independent executor or administrator of a decedent's estate may be appointed an executor or administrator of the estate if the estate will be administered and settled under the direction of the court.

Acts 1955, 54th Leg., p. 88, ch. 55, eff. Jan. 1, 1956. Amended by Acts 1957, 55th Leg., p. 53, ch. 31, § 2(b); Acts 1977, 65th Leg., p. 1061, ch. 390, § 3, eff. Sept. 1, 1977; Acts 1979, 66th Leg., p. 1750, ch. 713, § 16, eff. Aug. 27, 1979. Subsec. (r) added by Acts 1991, 72nd Leg., ch. 895, § 10, eff. Sept. 1, 1991; Subsec. (q) amended by Acts 1993, 73rd Leg., ch. 846, § 15, eff. Sept. 1, 1993; Subsec. (i) amended by Acts 1995, 74th Leg., ch. 1039, § 9, eff. Sept. 1, 1995.

Statutes in Context

The independent executor deals with creditors and sets aside exempt property and allowances just like a dependent executor but without court involvement under § 146. Note, however, that the courts have held that §§ 309, 310, and 313 do not apply to independent administrations. *See Bunting v. Pearson*, 430 S.W.2d 470 (Tex. 1968).

---

§ 146. Payment of Claims and Delivery of Exemptions and Allowances

(a) Duty of the Independent Executor. An independent executor, in the administration of an estate, independently of and without application to, or any action in or by the court:

(1) shall give the notices required under Sections 294 and 295;

(2) may give the notice permitted under Section 294(d) and bar a claim under that subsection;

(3) shall approve, classify, and pay, or reject, claims against the estate in the same order of priority, classification, and proration prescribed in this Code; and

(4) shall set aside and deliver to those entitled thereto exempt property and allowances for support, and allowances in lieu of exempt property, as prescribed in this Code, to the same extent and result as if the independent executor's actions had been accomplished in, and under orders of, the court.

(b) Secured Claims for Money. Within six months after the date letters are granted or within four months after the date notice is received under Section 295, whichever is later, a creditor with a claim for money secured by real or personal property of the estate must give notice to the independent executor of the creditor's election to have the creditor's claim approved as a matured secured claim to be paid in due course of administration. If the election is not made, the claim is a preferred debt and lien against the specific property securing the indebtedness and shall be paid according to the terms of the contract that secured the lien, and the claim may not be asserted against other assets of the estate. The independent executor may pay the claim before the claim matures if paying the claim before maturity is in the best interest of the estate.

(c) Liability of Independent Executor. An independent executor, in the administration of an estate, may pay at any time and without personal liability a claim for money against the estate to the extent approved and classified by the personal representative if:

(1) the claim is not barred by limitations; and

(2) at the time of payment, the independent executor reasonably believes the estate will have sufficient assets to pay all claims against the estate.

(d) Notice Required of Unsecured Creditor. An unsecured creditor who has a claim for money against an estate and receives a notice under Section 294(d) shall give notice to the independent executor of the nature and amount of the claim not later than the 120th day after the date on which the notice is received or the claim is barred.

(e) Placement of Notice. Notice required by Subsections (b) and (d) must be contained in:

(1) a written instrument that is hand-delivered with proof of receipt or mailed by certified mail, return receipt requested, to the independent executor or the executor's attorney;

(2) a pleading filed in a lawsuit with respect to the claim; or

(3) a written instrument or pleading filed in the court in which the administration of the estate is pending.

Acts 1955, 54th Leg., p. 88, ch. 55, eff. Jan. 1, 1956. Amended by Acts 1957, 55th Leg., p. 53, ch. 31, § 2(c), eff. Aug. 21, 1957. Amended by Acts 1995, 74th Leg., ch. 1054, § 1, eff. Jan. 1, 1996. Subsec. (b) amended by and Subsecs. (d), (e) added by Acts 1997, 75th Leg., ch. 1302, § 8, eff. Sept. 1, 1997.

§ 147. Enforcement of Claims by Suit

Any person having a debt or claim against the estate may enforce the payment of the same by suit against the independent executor; and, when judgment is recovered against the independent executor, the execution shall run against the estate of the decedent in the hands of the independent executor which is subject to such debt. The independent executor shall not be required to plead to any suit brought against him for money until after six months from the date that an independent administration was created and the order appointing an independent executor was entered by the county court.

Acts 1955, 54th Leg., p. 88, ch. 55, eff. Jan. 1, 1956. Amended by Acts 1975, 64th Leg., p. 980, ch. 376, § 1, eff. June 19, 1975; Acts 1977, 65th Leg., p. 1064, ch. 390, § 4, eff. Sept. 1, 1977.

§ 148. Requiring Heirs to Give Bond

When an independent administration is created and the order appointing an independent executor is entered by the county court, any person having a debt against such estate may, by written complaint filed in the county court where such order was entered, cause all distributees of the estate, heirs at law, and other persons entitled to any portion of such estate under the will, if any, to be cited by personal service to appear before such county court and execute a bond for an amount equal to the amount of the creditor's claim or the full value of such estate, as shown by the inventory and list of claims, whichever is the smaller, such bond to be payable to the judge, and his successors, and to be approved by said judge, and conditioned that all obligors shall pay all debts that shall be established against such estate in the manner provided by law. Upon the return of the citation served, unless such person so entitled to any portion of the estate, or some of them, or some other person for them, shall execute such bond to the satisfaction of the county court, such estate shall thereafter be administered and settled under the direction of the county court as other estates are required to be settled. If the bond is executed and approved, the independent administration shall proceed. Creditors of the estate may sue on such bond, and shall be entitled to judgment thereon for the amount of their debt, or they may have their action against those in possession of the estate.

Acts 1955, 54th Leg., p. 88, ch. 55, eff. Jan. 1, 1956. Amended by Acts 1977, 65th Leg., p. 1064, ch. 390, § 5, eff. Sept. 1, 1977; Acts 1979, 66th Leg., p. 1750, ch. 713, § 17, eff. Aug. 27, 1979.

§ 149. Requiring Independent Executor to Give Bond

When it has been provided by will, regularly probated, that an independent executor appointed by such will shall not be required to give bond for the management of the estate devised by such will, the direction shall be observed, unless it be made to appear at any time that such independent executor is mismanaging the property, or has betrayed or is about to betray his trust, or has in some other way become disqualified, in which case, upon proper proceedings had for that purpose, as in the case of executors or administrators acting under orders of the court, such executor may be required to give bond.

Acts 1955, 54th Leg., p. 88, ch. 55, eff. Jan. 1, 1956.

Statutes in Context

The independent executor does not need to render annual accountings. Instead, accountings are required only under the circumstances described in the Code, that is, (1) if an interested person demands an accounting 15 months or more after the date the independent executor was appointed (§ 149A) or (2) an interested person petitions the court for an accounting and distribution after 2 years from the date of the creation of the independent administration (§ 149B).

---

§ 149A. Accounting

(a) Interested Person May Demand Accounting. At any time after the expiration of fifteen months from the date that an independent administration was created and the order appointing an independent executor was entered by the county court, any person interested in the estate may demand an accounting from the independent executor. The independent executor shall thereupon furnish to the person or persons making the demand an exhibit in writing, sworn and subscribed by the independent executor, setting forth in detail:

1. The property belonging to the estate which has come into his hands as executor.
2. The disposition that has been made of such property.
3. The debts that have been paid.
4. The debts and expenses, if any, still owing by the estate.
5. The property of the estate, if any, still remaining in his hands.
6. Such other facts as may be necessary to a full and definite understanding of the exact condition of the estate.
7. Such facts, if any, that show why the administration should not be closed and the estate distributed.

Any other interested person shall, upon demand, be entitled to a copy of any exhibit or accounting that has been made by an independent executor in compliance with this section.

(b) Enforcement of Demand. Should the independent executor not comply with a demand for an accounting authorized by this section within sixty days after receipt of the demand, the person making the demand may compel compliance by an action in the county court, as that term is defined by Section 3 of this code. After a hearing, the court shall enter an order requiring the accounting to be made at such time as it deems proper under the circumstances.

(c) Subsequent Demands. After an initial accounting has been given by an independent executor, any person interested in an estate may demand subsequent periodic accountings at intervals of not less than twelve months, and such subsequent demands may be enforced in the same manner as an initial demand.

(d) Remedies Cumulative. The right to an accounting accorded by this section is cumulative of any other remedies which persons interested in an estate may have against the independent executor thereof.

Added by Acts 1971, 62nd Leg., p. 980, ch. 173, § 10, eff. Jan. 1, 1972. Amended by Acts 1973, 63rd Leg., p. 412, ch. 184, § 1, eff. May 25, 1973; Acts 1977, 65th Leg., p. 1065, ch. 390, § 6, eff. Sept. 1, 1977; Subsec. (b) amended by Acts 1999, 76th Leg., ch. 855, § 3, eff. Sept. 1, 1999.

§ 149B. Accounting and Distribution

(a) In addition to or in lieu of the right to an accounting provided by Section 149A of this code, at any time after the expiration of two years from the date that an independent administration was created and the order appointing an independent executor was entered, a person interested in the estate may petition the county court, as that term is defined by Section 3 of this code, for an accounting and distribution. The court may order an accounting to be made with the court by the independent executor at such time as the court deems proper. The accounting shall include the information that the court deems necessary to determine whether any part of the estate should be distributed.

(b) On receipt of the accounting and, after notice to the independent executor and a hearing, unless the court finds a continued necessity for administration of the estate, the court shall order its distribution by the independent executor to the persons entitled to the property. If the court finds there is a continued necessity for administration of the estate, the court shall order the distribution of any portion of the estate that the court finds should not be subject to further administration by the independent executor. If any portion of the estate that is ordered to be distributed is incapable of distribution without prior partition or sale, the court shall order partition and distribution, or sale, in the manner provided for the partition and distribution of property incapable of division in estates administered under the direction of the county court.

(c) If all the property in the estate is ordered distributed by the executor and the estate is fully administered, the court also may order the independent executor to file a final account with the court and may enter an order closing the administration and terminating the power of the independent executor to act as executor.

Added by Acts 1979, 66th Leg., p. 1751, ch. 713, § 18, eff. Aug. 27, 1979. Subsecs. (a) and (b) amended by Acts 1985, 69th Leg., ch. 882, § 1, eff. Aug. 26, 1985; Subsec. (a) amended by Acts 1987, 70th Leg., ch. 760, § 1, eff. Aug. 31, 1987; Subsec. (b) amended by Acts 1987, 70th Leg., ch. 565, § 1, eff. June 18, 1987; Subsec. (a) amended by Acts 1999, 76th Leg., ch. 855, § 4, eff. Sept. 1, 1999.

Statutes in Context

Section 149C provides the procedures for removing an independent executor. The court may order the costs, expenses, and reasonable attorney's fees of the party seeking removal to be paid out of the estate. The removed independent executor is entitled to reimbursement for expenses assuming the defense is in good faith even if the person is removed from office.

---

§ 149C. Removal of Independent Executor

(a) The county court, as that term is defined by Section 3 of this code, on its own motion or on motion of any interested person, after the independent executor has been cited by personal service to answer at a time and place fixed in the notice, may remove an independent executor when:

(1) the independent executor fails to return within ninety days after qualification, unless such time is extended by order of the court, an inventory of the property of the estate and list of claims that have come to his knowledge;

(2) sufficient grounds appear to support belief that he has misapplied or embezzled, or that he is about to misapply or embezzle, all or any part of the property committed to his care;

(3) he fails to make an accounting which is required by law to be made;

(4) he fails to timely file the notice required by Section 128A of this code;

(5) he is proved to have been guilty of gross misconduct or gross mismanagement in the performance of his duties; or

(6) he becomes an incapacitated person, or is sentenced to the penitentiary, or from any other cause becomes legally incapacitated from properly performing his fiduciary duties.

(b) The order of removal shall state the cause of removal and shall direct by order the disposition of the assets remaining in the name or under the control of the removed executor. The order of removal shall require that letters issued to the removed executor shall be surrendered and that all letters shall be canceled of record. If an independent executor is removed by the court under this section, the court may, on application, appoint a successor independent executor as provided by Section 154A of this code.

(c) An independent executor who defends an action for his removal in good faith, whether successful or not, shall be allowed out of the estate his necessary expenses and disbursements, including reasonable attorney's fees, in the removal proceedings.

(d) Costs and expenses incurred by the party seeking removal incident to removal of an independent executor appointed without bond, including reasonable attorney's fees and expenses, may be paid out of the estate.

Added by Acts 1979, 66th Leg., p. 1751, ch. 713, § 19, eff. Aug. 27, 1979. Subsec. (d) added by Acts 1987, 70th Leg., ch. 719, § 1, eff. Aug. 31, 1987. Subsec. (a) amended by Acts 1989, 71st Leg., ch. 1035, § 10, eff. Sept. 1, 1989; amended by Acts 1995, 74th Leg., ch. 1039, § 10, eff. Sept. 1, 1995; amended by Acts 1999, 76th Leg., ch. 855, § 5, eff. Sept. 1, 1999.

§ 149D. Distribution of Remaining Estate Pending Judicial Discharge

(a) On or before filing an action under Section 149E of this code, the independent executor must distribute to the beneficiaries of the estate any of the remaining assets or property of the estate that remains in the hands of the independent executor after all of the estate's debts have been paid, except for a reasonable reserve of assets that the independent executor may retain in a fiduciary capacity pending court approval of the final account.

(b) The court may review the amount of assets on reserve and may order the independent executor to make further distributions under this section.

Added by Acts 1999, 76th Leg., ch. 855, § 6, eff. Sept. 1, 1999.

Statutes in Context

Section 149E permits the court to discharge an independent executor so that the executor will have a court order indicating that he or she is not liable for any matters relating to the past administration of the estate which have been fully and fairly disclosed.

§ 149E. Judicial Discharge of Independent Executor

(a) After an estate has been administered and if there is no further need for an independent administration of the estate, the independent executor of the estate may file an action for declaratory judgment under Chapter 37, Civil Practice and Remedies Code, seeking to discharge the independent executor from any liability involving matters relating to the past administration of the estate that have been fully and fairly disclosed.

(b) On the filing of an action under this section, each beneficiary of the estate shall be personally served with citation, except for a beneficiary who has waived the issuance and service of citation.

(c) In a proceeding under this section, the court may require the independent executor to file a final account that includes any information the court considers necessary to adjudicate the independent executor's request for a discharge of liability. The court may audit, settle, or approve a final account filed under this subsection.

Added by Acts 1999, 76th Leg., ch. 855, § 6, eff. Sept. 1, 1999.

§ 149F. Court Costs and Other Charges Related to Final Account in Judicial Discharge

(a) Except as ordered by the court, the independent executor is entitled to pay from the estate legal fees, expenses, or other costs of a proceeding incurred in relation to a final account required under Section 149E of this code.

(b) The independent executor shall be personally liable to refund any amount not approved by the court as a proper charge against the estate.

Added by Acts 1999, 76th Leg., ch. 855, § 6, eff. Sept. 1, 1999.

§ 149G. Rights and Remedies Cumulative

The rights and remedies conferred by Sections 149D, 149E, and 149F of this code are cumulative of other rights and remedies to which a person interested in the estate may be entitled under law.

Added by Acts 1999, 76th Leg., ch. 855, § 6, eff. Sept. 1, 1999.

§ 150. Partition and Distribution or Sale of Property Incapable of Division

If the will does not distribute the entire estate of the testator, or provide a means for partition of said estate, or if no will was probated, the independent executor may file his final account in the county court in which the will was probated, or if no will was probated, in the county court in which the order appointing the independent executor was entered, and ask for either partition and distribution of the estate or an order of sale of any portion of the estate alleged by the independent executor and found by the court to be incapable of a fair and equal partition and distribution, or both; and the same either shall be partitioned and distributed or shall be sold, or both, in the manner provided for the partition and distribution of property and the sale of property incapable of division in estates administered under the direction of the county court.

Acts 1955, 54th Leg., p. 88, ch. 55, eff. Jan. 1, 1956. Amended by Acts 1977, 65th Leg., p. 1065, ch. 390, § 7, eff. Sept. 1, 1977; Acts 1979, 66th Leg., p. 1752, ch. 713, § 20, eff. Aug. 27, 1979.

Statutes in Context

There is no requirement that an independent administration be closed. The Code, however, provides two methods for closing the administration. (1) Section 151 permits the independent executor to file a *closing report*, verified by affidavit, after all debts are paid to the extent possible and the residue, if any, is distributed to the heirs or beneficiaries. The court takes no action on the affidavit. (2) Section 152 permits an heir or beneficiary to petition the court for an order closing the estate.

Section 151(d) prohibits an independent executor from requiring that a beneficiary or heir sign a release or waiver of rights against the executor as a condition of delivery of the property.

§ 151. Closing Independent Administration by Affidavit

(a) Filing of Affidavit. When all of the debts known to exist against the estate have been paid, or when they have been paid so far as the assets in the hands of the independent executor will permit, when there is no pending litigation, and when the independent executor has distributed to the persons entitled thereto all assets of the estate, if any, remaining after payment of debts, the independent executor may file with the court:

(1) a closing report verified by affidavit that shows:

(i) The property of the estate which came into the hands of the independent executor;

(ii) The debts that have been paid;

(iii) The debts, if any, still owing by the estate;

(iv) The property of the estate, if any, remaining on hand after payment of debts; and

(v) The names and residences of the persons to whom the property of the estate, if any, remaining on hand after payment of debts has been distributed; and

(2) signed receipts or other proof of delivery of property to the distributees named in the closing report if the closing report reflects that there was property remaining on hand after payment of debts.

(b) Effect of Filing the Affidavit. (1) The filing of such an affidavit and proof of delivery, if required, shall terminate the independent administration and the power and authority of the independent executor, but shall not relieve the independent executor from liability for any mismanagement of the estate or from liability for any false statements contained in the affidavit. When such an affidavit has been filed, persons dealing with properties of the estate, or with claims against the estate, shall deal directly with the distributees of the estate; and the acts of such distributees with respect to such properties or claims shall in all ways be valid and binding as regards the persons with whom they deal, notwithstanding any false statements made by the independent executor in such affidavit.

(2) If the independent executor is required to give bond, the independent executor's filing of the affidavit and proof of delivery, if required, automatically releases the sureties on the bond from all liability for the future acts of the principal.

(c) Authority to Transfer Property of a Decedent After Filing the Affidavit. An independent executor's affidavit closing the independent administration shall constitute sufficient legal authority to all persons owing any money, having custody of any property, or acting as registrar or transfer agent or trustee of any evidence of interest, indebtedness, property, or right that belongs to the estate, for payment or transfer without additional administration to the persons described in the will as entitled to receive the particular asset or who as heirs at law are entitled to receive the asset. The persons described in the will as entitled to receive the particular asset or the heirs at law entitled to receive the asset may enforce their right to the payment or transfer by suit.

(d) Delivery Subject to Receipt or Proof of Delivery. An independent executor may not be required to deliver tangible or intangible personal property to a distributee unless the independent executor shall receive, at or before the time of delivery of the property, a signed receipt or other proof of delivery of the property to the distributee. An independent executor shall not require a waiver or release from the distributee as a condition of delivery of property to a distributee.

(e) Community Administration. A community administrator may use the procedures in this section to terminate community administration under Section 175 of this code. The independent executor's filing of the affidavit releases the sureties on the community administrator's bond from all liability for the future acts of the principal.

Acts 1955, 54th Leg., p. 88, ch. 55, eff. Jan. 1, 1956. Amended by Acts 1979, 66th Leg., p. 1752, ch. 713, § 21, eff. Aug. 27, 1979. Amended by Acts 1991, 72nd Leg., ch. 895, § 11, eff. Sept. 1, 1991; Subsec. (a) amended by Acts 1995, 74th Leg., ch. 642, § 5, eff. Sept. 1, 1995.

Statutes in Context

See the Statutes in Context to § 151.

---

§ 152. Closing Independent Administration Upon Application by Distributee

(a) At any time after an estate has been fully administered and there is no further need for an independent administration of such estate, any distributee may file an application to close the administration; and, after citation upon the independent executor, and upon hearing, the court may enter an order:

(1) requiring the independent executor to file a verified report meeting the requirements of Section 151(a) of this code;

(2) closing the administration;

(3) terminating the power of the independent executor to act as such; and

(4) releasing the sureties on any bond the independent executor was required to give from all liability for the future acts of the principal.

(b) The order of the court closing the independent administration shall constitute sufficient legal authority to all persons owing any money, having custody of any property, or acting as registrar or transfer agent or trustee of any evidence of interest, indebtedness, property, or right that belongs to the estate, for payment or transfer without additional administration to the persons described in the will as entitled to receive the particular asset or who as heirs at law are entitled to receive the asset. The persons described in the will as entitled to receive the particular asset or the heirs at law entitled to receive the asset may enforce their right to the payment or transfer by suit.

Acts 1955, 54th Leg., p. 88, ch. 55, eff. Jan. 1, 1956. Amended by Acts 1979, 66th Leg., p. 1752, ch. 713, § 22, eff. Aug. 27, 1979. Subsec. (a) amended by Acts 1991, 72nd Leg., ch. 895, § 12, eff. Sept. 1, 1991.

§ 153. Issuance of Letters

At any time before the authority of an independent executor has been terminated in the manner set forth in the preceding Sections, the clerk shall issue such number of letters testamentary as the independent executor shall request.

Acts 1955, 54th Leg., p. 88, ch. 55, eff. Jan. 1, 1956.

§ 154. Powers of an Administrator Who Succeeds an Independent Executor

(a) Grant of Powers by Court. Whenever a person has died, or shall die, testate, owning property in Texas, and such person's will has been or shall be admitted to probate by the proper court, and such probated will names an independent executor or executors, or trustees acting in the capacity of independent executors, to execute the terms and provisions of said will, and such will grants to such independent executor, or executors, or trustees acting in the capacity of independent executors, the power to raise or borrow money and to mortgage, and such independent executor, or executors, or trustees, have died or shall die, resign, fail to qualify, or be removed from office, leaving unexecuted parts or portions of the will of the testator, and an administrator with the will annexed is appointed by the court having jurisdiction of the estate, and an administrator's bond is filed and approved by the court, then in all such cases, the court may, in addition to the powers conferred upon such administrator under other provisions of the laws of Texas, authorize, direct, and empower such administrator to do and perform the acts and deeds, clothed with the rights, powers, authorities, and privileges, and subject to the limitations, set forth in the subsequent portions of this Section.

(b) Power to Borrow Money and Mortgage or Pledge Property. The court, upon application, citation, and hearing, may, by its order, authorize, direct, and empower such administrator to raise or borrow such sums of money and incur such obligations and debts as the court shall, in its said order, direct, and to renew and extend same from time to time, as the court, upon application and order, shall provide; and, if authorized by the court's order, to secure such loans, obligations, and debts, by pledge or mortgage upon property or assets of the estate, real, personal, or mixed, upon such terms and conditions, and for such duration of time, as the court shall deem to be to the best interest of the estate, and by its order shall prescribe; and all such loans, obligations, debts, pledges, and mortgages shall be valid and enforceable against the estate and against such administrator in his official capacity.

(c) Powers Limited to Those Granted by the Will. The court may order and authorize such administrator to have and exercise the powers and privileges set forth in the preceding Subsections hereof only to the extent that same are granted to or possessed by the independent executor, or executors, or trustees acting in the capacity of independent executors, under the terms of the probated will of such deceased person, and then only in such cases as it appears, at the hearing of the application, that at the time of the appointment of such administrator, there are outstanding and unpaid obligations and debts of the estate, or of the independent executor, or executors, or trustees, chargeable against the estate, or unpaid expenses of administration, or when the court appointing such administrator orders the business of such estate to be carried on and it becomes necessary, from time to time, under orders of the court, for such administrator to borrow money and incur obligations and indebtedness in order to protect and preserve the estate.

(d) Powers Other Than Those Relating to Borrowing Money and Mortgaging or Pledging Property. The court, in addition, may, upon application, citation, and hearing, order, authorize and empower such administrator to assume, exercise, and discharge, under the orders and directions of said court, made from time to time, all or such part of the rights, powers, and authorities vested in and delegated to, or possessed by, the independent executor, or executors, or trustees acting in the capacity of independent executors, under the terms of the will of such deceased person, as the court finds to be to the best interest of the estate and shall, from time to time, order and direct.

(e) Application for Grant of Powers. The granting to such administrator by the court of some, or all, of the powers and authorities set forth in this Section shall be upon application filed by such administrator with the county clerk, setting forth such facts as, in the judgment of the administrator, require the granting of the power or authority requested.

(f) Citation. Upon the filing of such application, the clerk shall issue citation to all persons interested in the estate, stating the nature of the application, and requiring such persons to appear on the return day named in such citation and show cause why such application should not be granted, should they choose to do so. Such citation shall be served by posting.

(g) Hearing and Order. The court shall hear such application and evidence thereon, upon the return day named in the citation, or thereafter, and, if satisfied a necessity exists and that it would be to the best interest of the estate to grant said application in whole or in part, the court shall so order; otherwise, the court shall refuse said application.

Acts 1955, 54th Leg., p. 88, ch. 55, eff. Jan. 1, 1956.

§ 154A. Court-Appointed Successor Independent Executor

(a) If the will of a person who dies testate names an independent executor who, having qualified, fails for any reason to continue to serve, or is removed for cause by the court, and the will does not name a successor independent executor or if each successor executor named in the will fails for any reason to qualify as executor or indicates by affidavit filed with the application for an order continuing independent administration his inability or unwillingness to serve as successor independent executor, all of the distributees of the decedent as of the filing of the application for an order continuing independent administration may apply to the county court for the appointment of a qualified person, firm, or corporation to serve as successor independent executor. If the county court finds that continued administration of the estate is necessary, the county court shall enter an order continuing independent administration and appointing the person, firm, or corporation designated in the application as successor independent executor, unless the county court finds that it would not be in the best interest of the estate to do so. Such successor shall serve with all of the powers and privileges granted to his predecessor independent executor.

(b) If a distributee described in this section is an incapacitated person, the guardian of the person of the distributee may sign the application on behalf of the distributee. If the county court finds that either the continuing of independent administration or the appointment of the person, firm, or corporation designated in the application as successor independent executor would not be in the best interest of the incapacitated person, then, notwithstanding anything to the contrary in Subsection (a) of this section, the county court shall not enter an order continuing independent administration of the estate. If the distributee is an incapacitated person and has no guardian of the person, the court may appoint a guardian ad litem to make application on behalf of the incapacitated person if the county court considers such an appointment necessary to protect the interest of such distributee.

(c) If a trust is created in the decedent's will, the person or class of persons first eligible to receive the income from the trust, determined as if the trust were to be in existence on the date of the filing of the application for an order continuing independent administration, shall, for the purposes of this section, be deemed to be the distributee or distributees on behalf of such trust, and any other trust or trusts coming into existence upon the termination of such trust, and are authorized to apply for an order continuing independent administration on behalf of the trust without the consent or agreement of the trustee or any other beneficiary of the trust, or the trustee or any beneficiary of any other trust which may come into existence upon the termination of such trust.

(d) If a life estate is created either in the decedent's will or by law, and if a life tenant is living at the time of the filing of the application for an order continuing independent administration, then the life tenant or life tenants, determined as if the life estate were to commence on the date of the filing of the application for an order continuing independent administration, shall, for the purposes of this section, be deemed to the distributee or distributees on behalf of the entire estate created, and are authorized to apply for an order continuing independent administration on behalf of the estate without the consent or approval of any remainderman.

(e) If a decedent's will contains a provision that a distributee must survive the decedent by a prescribed period of time in order to take under the decedent's will, for the purposes of determining who shall be the distributee under this section, it shall be presumed that the distributees living at the time of the filing of the application for an order continuing independent administration of the decedent's estate survived the decedent for the prescribed period.

(f) In the case of all decedents, whether dying testate or intestate, for the purposes of determining who shall be the distributees under this section, it shall be presumed that no distributee living at the time the application for an order continuing independent administration of the decedent's estate is filed shall subsequently disclaim any portion of such distributee's interest in the decedent's estate.

(g) If a distributee of a decedent's estate should die, and if by virtue of such distributee's death such distributee's share of the decedent's estate shall become payable to such distributee's estate, then the deceased distributee's personal representative may sign the application for an order continuing independent administration of the decedent's estate under this section.

(h) If a successor independent executor is appointed pursuant to this section, then, unless the county court shall waive bond on application for waiver, the successor independent executor shall be required to enter into bond payable to and to be approved by the judge and his or her successors in a sum that is found by the judge to be adequate under all circumstances, or a bond with one surety in a sum that is found by the judge to be adequate under all circumstances, if the surety is an authorized corporate surety.

(i) Absent proof of fraud or collusion on the part of a judge, the judge may not be held civilly liable for the commission of misdeeds or the omission of any required act of any person, firm, or corporation designated as a successor independent executor under this section. Section 36 of this code does not apply to an appointment of a successor independent executor under this section.

Added by Acts 1977, 65th Leg., p. 1066, ch. 390, § 8, eff. Sept. 1, 1977. Amended by Acts 1979, 66th Leg., p. 1753, ch. 713, § 23, eff. Aug. 27, 1979. Subsec. (i) added by Acts 1993, 73rd Leg., ch. 846, § 16, eff. Sept. 1, 1993; Subsec. (b) amended by Acts 1995, 74th Leg., ch. 1039, § 11, eff. Sept. 1, 1995.

Part 5. Administration of Community Property

Statutes in Context

Sections 155-156 provide that no administration is necessary for community property if the spouse died intestate and all community property passes to the surviving spouse (that is, either the deceased spouse had no surviving descendants or all of the deceased spouse's descendants were also descendants of the surviving spouse).

§ 155. Administration of Community Property

When a husband or wife dies intestate and the community property passes to the survivor, no administration thereon, community or otherwise, shall be necessary.

Acts 1955, 54th Leg., p. 88, ch. 55, eff. Jan. 1, 1956. Amended by Acts 1971, 62nd Leg., p. 980, ch. 173, § 11, eff. Jan. 1, 1972.

§ 156. Liability of Community Property for Debts

The community property subject to the sole or joint management, control, and disposition of a spouse dur-

ing marriage continues to be subject to the liabilities of that spouse upon death. In addition, the interest that the deceased spouse owned in any other nonexempt community property passes to his or her heirs or devisees charged with the debts which were enforceable against such deceased spouse prior to his or her death. In the administration of community estates, the survivor or personal representative shall keep a separate, distinct account of all community debts allowed or paid in the administration and settlement of such estate.
Acts 1955, 54th Leg., p. 88, ch. 55, eff. Jan. 1, 1956. Amended by Acts 1971, 62nd Leg., p. 980, ch. 173, § 11, eff. Jan. 1, 1972.

Statutes in Context

Section 160 permits the surviving spouse to administer the community property in both testate and intestate situations provided no personal representative has yet been appointed. This procedure is often called an *unqualified community administration*.

§ 160. Powers of Surviving Spouse When No Administration Is Pending

(a) When no one has qualified as executor or administrator of the estate of a deceased spouse, the surviving spouse, whether the husband or wife, as the surviving partner of the marital partnership, without qualifying as community administrator as hereinafter provided, has power to sue and be sued for the recovery of community property; to sell, mortgage, lease, and otherwise dispose of community property for the purpose of paying community debts; to collect claims due to the community estate; and has such other powers as shall be necessary to preserve the community property, discharge community obligations, and wind up community affairs.

(b) If an affidavit stating that the affiant is the surviving spouse and that no one has qualified as executor or administrator of the estate of the deceased spouse is furnished to a person owing money to the community estate for current wages at the time of the death of the deceased spouse, the person making payment or delivering to the affiant the deceased spouse's final paycheck for wages, including unpaid sick pay or vacation pay, if any, is released from liability to the same extent as if the payment or delivery was made to a personal representative of the deceased spouse. The person is not required to inquire into the truth of the affidavit. The affiant to whom the payment or delivery is made is answerable to any person having a prior right and is accountable to any personal representative who is appointed. The affiant is liable for any damage or loss to any person that arises from a payment or delivery made in reliance on the affidavit.

(c) This section does not affect the disposition of the property of the deceased spouse.
Acts 1955, 54th Leg., p. 88, ch. 55, eff. Jan. 1, 1956. Amended by Acts 1993, 73rd Leg., ch. 846, § 17, eff. Sept. 1, 1993.

Statutes in Context

Sections 161-177 explain the procedure called *qualified community administration*. The surviving spouse must formally qualify to obtain powers similar to those of an independent executor but only with respect to the community property. This procedure is available only if (1) the deceased spouse's will names no executor, (2) the executor named in the deceased spouse's will fails to serve, or (3) the deceased spouse died intestate. The surviving spouse serving as the community administrator has no control over the deceased spouse's separate property.

§ 161. Community Administration

Whenever an interest in community property passes to someone other than the surviving spouse, the surviving spouse may qualify as community administrator in the manner hereinafter provided if

(a) The deceased spouse failed to name an executor in his will, or

(b) If the executor named in the will of the deceased spouse is for any reason unable or unwilling to qualify as such, or

(c) If the deceased spouse died intestate.
Acts 1955, 54th Leg., p. 88, ch. 55, eff. Jan. 1, 1956. Amended by Acts 1971, 62nd Leg., p. 980, ch. 173, § 11, eff. Jan. 1, 1972.

§ 162. Application for Community Administration

A surviving spouse who desires to qualify as a community administrator shall, within four years after the death of the other spouse, file a written application in the court having venue over the estate of the deceased spouse, stating:

(a) That the other spouse is dead, setting forth the time and place of such death; and

(b) The name and residence of each person to whom an interest in community property has passed by the will of the decedent or by intestacy; and

(c) That there is a community estate between the deceased spouse and the applicant, and the facts that authorize the applicant to be appointed as community administrator; and

(d) That, by virtue of facts set forth in the application, the court has venue over the estate of the deceased spouse; and

(e) If the applicant desires that appraisers be appointed, that not less than one nor more than three appraisers should be appointed to appraise such estate.
Acts 1955, 54th Leg., p. 88, ch. 55, eff. Jan. 1, 1956. Amended by Acts 1971, 62nd Leg., p. 980, ch. 173, § 11, eff. Jan. 1, 1972.

§ 163. Appointment of Appraisers

If the appointment of appraisers is requested by the applicant, or by any interested person, the judge shall, without notice or citation, enter an order appointing

appraisers to appraise such estate as in other administrations.
Acts 1955, 54th Leg., p. 88, ch. 55, eff. Jan. 1, 1956. Amended by Acts 1971, 62nd Leg., p. 980, ch. 173, § 11, eff. Jan. 1, 1972.

§ 164. Inventory, Appraisement, and List of Claims

The surviving spouse, with the assistance of the appraisers, if any be appointed, shall make out a full, fair, and complete inventory, appraisement, and list of claims of the community estate as in other administrations, shall attach thereto a list of all indebtedness owing by said community estate to other parties, giving the amount of each debt and the name of the party or parties to whom it is owing, and his or their post-office address, and shall return same to the court within ninety (90) days after the date of the order appointing apprisers, if any be appointed, unless a longer time shall be granted by the court. If no appraisers be appointed, such return shall be made within ninety (90) days after the date of the application for community administration, unless a longer time shall be granted by the court. In either event, the court may, for good cause shown, require the filing of the inventory and appraisement within a shorter period of time. Such inventory, list of claims, and list of indebtedness of such community estate shall be sworn to by said surviving spouse, and said inventory, appraisement, and list of claims owing said community estate shall be sworn to by said appraisers, if any appraisers have been appointed.
Acts 1955, 54th Leg., p. 88, ch. 55, eff. Jan. 1, 1956. Amended by Acts 1971, 62nd Leg., p. 980, ch. 173, § 11, eff. Jan. 1, 1972.

§ 165. Bond of Community Administrator

The community administrator shall at the time the inventory, appraisement, and list of claims are returned, present to the court a bond with two or more good and sufficient sureties, payable to and to be approved by the judge and his successors in a sum as is found by the judge to be adequate under all the circumstances, or a bond with one surety in a sum as is found by the judge to be adequate under all the circumstances, if the surety is an authorized corporate surety. The condition of the bond shall be that such surviving spouse will faithfully administer such community estate and will, after the payment of debts with which such property is properly chargeable, deliver to such person or persons as shall be entitled to receive the same the portion of the community estate devised or bequeathed to them under the terms of the will of the deceased spouse, or which passes to them under the laws of descent and distribution. Either spouse may by will apportion community indebtedness as between the devisees and legatees of such testator and the surviving spouse, but this shall not include the power to charge the community share of the surviving spouse with more than the portion of the community debts for which it would otherwise be liable.
Acts 1955, 54th Leg., p. 88, ch. 55, eff. Jan. 1, 1956. Amended by Acts 1965, 59th Leg., p. 717, ch. 339, § 1, eff. June 9, 1965; Acts 1971, 62nd Leg., p. 982, ch. 173, § 12, eff. Jan. 1, 1972.

§ 166. Order of the Court

When such inventory, appraisement, list of claims, and bond are returned to the judge, he shall examine the same and approve or disapprove them by an order to that effect and, when approved, the order approving them shall also authorize the survivor as community administrator to control, manage, and dispose of the community property in accordance with the provisions of this Code.
Acts 1955, 54th Leg., p. 88, ch. 55, eff. Jan. 1, 1956.

§ 167. Powers of Community Administrator

When the order mentioned in the preceding section has been entered, the survivor, without any further action in the court, shall have the power to control, manage, and dispose of the community property, as provided in this Code, as fully and completely as if he or she were the sole owner thereof, and to sue and be sued with regard to the same; and a certified copy of the order of the court shall be evidence of the qualification and right of such survivor. After paying community debts outstanding at the death of the deceased spouse, the qualified community administrator may carry on as statutory trustee for the owners of the community estate, investing and reinvesting the funds of the estate and continuing the operation of community enterprises until the termination of the trust as provided in this Code. The qualified community administrator is not entitled to mortgage community property to secure debts incurred for his individual benefit, or otherwise to appropriate the community estate to his individual benefit; but he may transfer or encumber his individual interest in the community estate.
Acts 1955, 54th Leg., p. 88, ch. 55, eff. Jan. 1, 1956. Amended by Acts 1971, 62nd Leg., p. 982, ch. 173, § 13, eff. Jan. 1, 1972.

§ 168. Accounting by Survivor

The survivor, whether qualified as community administrator or not, shall keep a fair and full account and statement of all community debts and expenses paid by him, and of the disposition made of the community property; and, upon final partition of such estate, shall deliver to the heirs, devisees or legatees of the deceased spouse their interest in such estate, and the increase and profits of the same, after deducting therefrom the proportion of the community debts chargeable thereto, unavoidable losses, necessary and reasonable expenses, and a reasonable commission for the management of the same. Neither the survivor nor his bondsmen shall be liable for losses sustained by the estate, except when the survivor has been guilty of gross negligence or bad faith.
Acts 1955, 54th Leg., p. 88, ch. 55, eff. Jan. 1, 1956. Amended by Acts 1971, 62nd Leg., p. 982, ch. 173, § 13, eff. Jan. 1, 1972.

§ 169. Payment of Debts

The community administrator shall pay all just and legal community debts within the time, and according to the classification, and in the order prescribed for the payment of debts in other administrations. Where there is a deficiency of assets to pay all claims of the same class, such claims shall be paid pro rata.
Acts 1955, 54th Leg., p. 88, ch. 55, eff. Jan. 1, 1956.

§ 170. New Appraisement or New Bond

Any person interested in a community estate may cause a new appraisement to be made of the same, or may cause a new bond to be required of the survivor, for the same causes and in like manner as provided in other administrations.
Acts 1955, 54th Leg., p. 88, ch. 55, eff. Jan. 1, 1956.

§ 171. Creditor May Require Exhibit

Any creditor of the community estate whose claim has not been paid in full, after the lapse of one year from the filing of the inventory, appraisement, list of claims, and bond by the survivor, may by written application to the court cause such survivor to be cited by personal service to appear and make an exhibit to the court in writing and under oath, showing fully and specifically:

(a) The debts that have been presented to him against such community estate and their class; and

(b) The debts that have been paid by him and those that remain unpaid, and the class of each; and

(c) The property that has been disposed of by him, and the amount received therefor; and

(d) The property remaining on hand; and

(e) An account of losses, expenses, and commissions.
Acts 1955, 54th Leg., p. 88, ch. 55, eff. Jan. 1, 1956.

§ 172. Action of Court Upon Exhibit

When such exhibit has been returned to the court and filed, the court shall examine the same and hear exceptions and objections thereto, and evidence in support of or against same. Should it appear to the court from such exhibit or from other evidence that such community estate has been improperly administered, or that there are still assets of said estate that are liable for the payment of the applicant's debt, or any part thereof, the court shall enter an order requiring the survivor to pay such debt, or a part thereof, as the evidence may show to be proper; and, should he neglect the same for thirty days after the date of such order, the following proceedings shall be had:

(a) If said debt be for the amount of One Thousand Dollars or less, exclusive of interest, the court shall order citation to issue for the sureties upon the bond of such survivor, citing them by personal service to appear before such court at a regular term thereof, and show cause why judgment should not be rendered against them for such debt and costs, which citation shall be returnable as in other civil suits; and the proceedings in such case shall be the same as in other civil suits in said court.

(b) If the amount due and payable to such creditor exceeds One Thousand Dollars, exclusive of interest, the creditor may have his action against such survivor and the sureties upon his bond in the District Court of the county where the survivor's bond is filed.
Acts 1955, 54th Leg., p. 88, ch. 55, eff. Jan. 1, 1956.

§ 173. Approval of Exhibit

If, after examining the exhibit and after receiving evidence in support of or against the same, the court is satisfied that the estate has been fairly administered in conformity to law, and that there remains no further property of such estate for the payment of debts, the court shall enter an order approving such exhibit and directing the same to be recorded, and shall also in such order declare the community administration closed.
Acts 1955, 54th Leg., p. 88, ch. 55, eff. Jan. 1, 1956.

§ 174. Failure to File Exhibit

Should the survivor, after being duly cited, fail to file an exhibit as required, the court shall proceed as if the creditor's right to the payment of his claim had been fully established.
Acts 1955, 54th Leg., p. 88, ch. 55, eff. Jan. 1, 1956.

§ 175. Termination of Community Administration

After the lapse of twelve months from the filing of the bond of the survivor, the community administration may be terminated whenever termination is desired by either the survivor or the persons entitled to the share of the deceased spouse, or to any portion thereof. Partition and distribution of the community estate may be had and the administration closed either by proceedings as in other independent administration or by proceedings in the appropriate District Court. When the community administration is closed, the community administrator shall be discharged and his bondsmen released from further liability.
Acts 1955, 54th Leg., p. 88, ch. 55, eff. Jan. 1, 1956.

§ 176. Remarriage of Surviving Spouse

The remarriage of a surviving spouse shall not terminate the surviving spouse's powers or liabilities as a qualified community administrator or administratrix; nor shall it terminate his or her powers as a surviving partner.
Acts 1955, 54th Leg., p. 88, ch. 55, eff. Jan. 1, 1956. Amended by Acts 1979, 66th Leg., p. 39, ch. 24, § 23, eff. Aug. 27, 1979.

§ 177. Distribution of Powers Among Personal Representatives and Surviving Spouse

(a) When Community Administrator Has Qualified. The qualified community administrator is entitled to administer the entire community estate, including the part which was by law under the management of the deceased spouse during the continuance of the marriage.

(b) When No Community Administrator Has Qualified. When a personal representative of the estate of a deceased spouse has duly qualified, the personal representative is authorized to administer, not only the separate property of the deceased spouse, but also the community property which was by law under the management of the deceased spouse during the continuance of the marriage and all of the community property that was by law under the joint control of the spouses during the continuance of the marriage. The surviving spouse, as surviving partner of the marital partnership, is entitled to retain possession and control of all community property which was legally under the sole management of the surviving spouse during the continuance of the marriage and to exercise over that property all the powers elsewhere in this part of this code authorized to be exercised by the surviving spouse when there is no administration pending on the estate of the deceased spouse. The surviving spouse may by written instrument filed with the clerk waive any right to exercise powers as community survivor, and in such event the personal representative of the deceased spouse shall be authorized to administer upon the entire community estate.
Acts 1955, 54th Leg., p. 88, ch. 55, eff. Jan. 1, 1956. Amended by Acts 1971, 62nd Leg., p. 982, ch. 173, § 13, eff. Jan. 1, 1972. Subsec. (b) amended by Acts 2001, 77th Leg., ch. 10, § 2, eff. Sept. 1, 2001.

Chapter VII. Executors and Administrators

Part 1. Appointment and Issuance of Letters

Statutes in Context

Letters are typically one-page documents issued under the seal of the court which indicate that the personal representative has been appointed by the court and has qualified. *See* § 183. The personal representative may then show this certificate as evidence of the representative's authority when dealing with estate matters or collecting estate property. Third parties who deal with a person who has letters are usually protected from liability to the heirs or beneficiaries if the executor mismanages the property. See § 188. Consequently, third parties often want to retain an original letter for their files. Because the cost of letters is nominal, often under $10.00 per copy, the personal representative should estimate the number of letters needed before qualifying and obtain all the necessary letters at the same time to prevent multiple trips to the courthouse and the associated time and monetary cost.

Section 178 enumerates the circumstances under which the court will grant either letters testamentary or letters of administration. Note that if letters of administration are issued with respect to a testate decedent, the administration is said to be *with the will annexed* (also called an *administration c.t.a. (cum testamento annexo)*).

§ 178. When Letters Testamentary or of Administration Shall Be Granted

(a) Letters Testamentary. When a will has been probated, the court shall, within twenty days thereafter, grant letters testamentary, if permitted by law, to the executor or executors appointed by such will, if any there be, or to such of them as are not disqualified, and are willing to accept the trust and qualify according to law.

(b) Letters of Administration. When a person shall die intestate, or where no executor is named in a will, or where the executor is dead or shall fail or neglect to accept and qualify within twenty days after the probate of the will, or shall neglect for a period of thirty days after the death of the testator to present the will for probate, then administration of the estate of such intestate, or administration with the will annexed of the estate of such testator, shall be granted, should administration appear to be necessary. No administration of any estate shall be granted unless there exists a necessity therefor, such necessity to be determined by the court hearing the application. Such necessity shall be deemed to exist if two or more debts exist against the estate, or if or when it is desired to have the county court partition the estate among the distributees, but mention of these two instances of necessity for administration shall not prevent the court from finding other instances of necessity upon proof before it.

(c) Failure to Issue Letters Within Prescribed Time. Failure of a court to issue letters testamentary within the twenty day period prescribed by this Section shall not affect the validity of any letters testamentary which are issued subsequent to such period, in accordance with law.
Acts 1955, 54th Leg., p. 88, ch. 55, eff. Jan. 1, 1956.

§ 179. Opposition to Grant of Letters of Administration

When application is made for letters of administration, any person may at any time before the application is granted, file his opposition thereto in writing, and may apply for the grant of letters to himself or to any other person; and, upon the trial, the court shall grant letters to the person that may seem best entitled to them, having regard to applicable provisions of this Code, without further notice than that of the original application.
Acts 1955, 54th Leg., p. 88, ch. 55, eff. Jan. 1, 1956.

§ 180. Effect of Finding That No Necessity for Administration Exists

When application is filed for letters of administration and the court finds that there exists no necessity for administration of the estate, the court shall recite in its order refusing the application that no necessity

for administration exists. An order of the court containing such recital shall constitute sufficient legal authority to all persons owing any money, having custody of any property, or acting as registrar or transfer agent of any evidence of interest, indebtedness, property, or right belonging to the estate, and to persons purchasing or otherwise dealing with the estate, for payment or transfer to the distributees of the decedent, and such distributees shall be entitled to enforce their right to such payment or transfer by suit.
Acts 1955, 54th Leg., p. 88, ch. 55, eff. Jan. 1, 1956.

§ 181. Orders Granting Letters Testamentary or of Administration

When letters testamentary or of administration are granted, the court shall make an order to that effect, which shall specify:

(a) The name of the testator or intestate; and

(b) The name of the person to whom the grant of letters is made; and

(c) If bond is required, the amount thereof; and

(d) If any interested person shall apply to the court for the appointment of an appraiser or appraisers, or if the court deems an appraisal necessary, the name of not less than one nor more than three disinterested persons appointed to appraise the estate and return such appraisement to the court; and

(e) That the clerk shall issue letters in accordance with said order when the person to whom said letters are granted shall have qualified according to law.
Acts 1955, 54th Leg., p. 88, ch. 55, eff. Jan. 1, 1956. Amended by Acts 1967, 60th Leg., p. 1815, ch. 697, § 1, eff. Aug. 28, 1967; Acts 1969, 61st Leg., p. 1922, ch. 641, § 10, eff. June 12, 1969.

Statutes in Context

The clerk will not issue letters until the personal representative qualifies, that is, posts any required bond and takes the oath of office. *See* § 189.

§ 182. When Clerk Shall Issue Letters

Whenever an executor or administrator has been qualified in the manner required by law, the clerk of the court granting the letters testamentary or of administration shall forthwith issue and deliver the letters to such executor or administrator. When two or more persons qualify as executors or administrators, letters shall be issued to each of them so qualifying.
Acts 1955, 54th Leg., p. 88, ch. 55, eff. Jan. 1, 1956.

§ 183. What Constitutes Letters

Letters testamentary or of administration shall be a certificate of the clerk of the court granting the same, attested by the seal of such court, and stating that the executor or administrator, as the case may be, has duly qualified as such as the law requires, the date of such qualification, and the name of the deceased.
Acts 1955, 54th Leg., p. 88, ch. 55, eff. Jan. 1, 1956.

§ 186. Letters or Certificate Made Evidence

Letters testamentary or of administration or a certificate of the clerk of the court which granted the same, under the seal of such court, that said letters have been issued, shall be sufficient evidence of the appointment and qualification of the personal representative of an estate and of the date of qualification.
Acts 1955, 54th Leg., p. 88, ch. 55, eff. Jan. 1, 1956. Amended by Acts 1993, 73rd Leg., ch. 957, § 28, eff. Sept. 1, 1993.

§ 187. Issuance of Other Letters

When letters have been destroyed or lost, the clerk shall issue other letters in their stead, which shall have the same force and effect as the original letters. The clerk shall also issue any number of letters as and when requested by the person or persons who hold such letters.
Acts 1955, 54th Leg., p. 88, ch. 55, eff. Jan. 1, 1956.

§ 188. Rights of Third Persons Dealing With Executors or Administrators

When an executor or administrator, legally qualified as such, has performed any acts as such executor or administrator in conformity with his authority and the law, such acts shall continue to be valid to all intents and purposes, so far as regards the rights of innocent purchasers of any of the property of the estate from such executor or administrator, for a valuable consideration, in good faith, and without notice of any illegality in the title to the same, notwithstanding such acts or the authority under which they were performed may afterward be set aside, annulled, and declared invalid.
Acts 1955, 54th Leg., p. 88, ch. 55, eff. Jan. 1, 1956.

Part 2. Oaths and Bonds of Personal Representatives

Statutes in Context

Section 189 explains that a personal representative is "qualified" after posting any required bond and taking the oath of office.

§ 189. How Executors, Administrators, and Guardians Shall Qualify

A personal representative shall be deemed to have duly qualified when he shall have taken and filed his oath and made the required bond, had the same approved by the judge, and filed it with the clerk. In case of an executor who is not required to make bond, he shall be deemed to have duly qualified when he shall have taken and filed his oath required by law.
Acts 1955, 54th Leg., p. 88, ch. 55, eff. Jan. 1, 1956. Amended by Acts 1993, 73rd Leg., ch. 957, § 29, eff. Sept. 1, 1993.

Statutes in Context

Section 190 sets forth the oaths which personal representatives must take and file before receiving letters.

§ 190. Oaths of Executors and Administrators

(a) Executor, or Administrator With Will Annexed. Before the issuance of letters testamentary or of administration with the will annexed, the person named as executor, or appointed administrator with the will annexed, shall take and subscribe an oath in form substantially as follows: "I do solemnly swear that the writing which has been offered for probate is the last will of __________, so far as I know or believe, and that I will well and truly perform all the duties of executor of said will (or of administrator with the will annexed, as the case may be) of the estate of said ________."

(b) Administrator. Before the issuance of letters of administration, the person appointed administrator shall take and subscribe an oath in form substantially as follows: "I do solemnly swear that __________, deceased, died without leaving any lawful will (or that the named executor in any such will is dead or has failed or neglected to offer the same for probate, or to accept and qualify as executor, within the time required, as the case may be), so far as I know or believe, and that I will well and truly perform all the duties of administrator of the estate of said deceased."

(c) Temporary Administrator. Before the issuance of temporary letters of administration, the person appointed temporary administrator shall take and subscribe an oath in form substantially as follows: "I do solemnly swear that I will well and truly perform the duties of temporary administrator of the estate of __________, deceased, in accordance with the law, and with the order of the court appointing me such administrator."

(d) Filing and Recording of Oaths. All such oaths may be taken before any officer authorized to administer oaths, and shall be filed with the clerk of the court granting the letters, and shall be recorded in the minutes of such court.

Acts 1955, 54th Leg., p. 88, ch. 55, eff. Jan. 1, 1956.

Statutes in Context

The personal representative should take the oath and post any required bond within 20 days of the order granting letters under § 192.

§ 192. Time for Taking Oath and Giving Bond

The oath of a personal representative may be taken and subscribed, or his bond may be given and approved, at any time before the expiration of twenty days after the date of the order granting letters testamentary or of administration, as the case may be, or before such letters shall have been revoked for a failure to qualify within the time allowed. All such oaths may be taken before any person authorized to administer oaths under the laws of this State.

Acts 1955, 54th Leg., p. 88, ch. 55, eff. Jan. 1, 1956. Amended by Acts 1993, 73rd Leg., ch. 957, § 30, eff. Sept. 1, 1993.

Statutes in Context

Personal representatives in Texas must post bond unless one of the exceptions in § 195 applies. The bond is to protect the estate creditors, beneficiaries, and heirs from the personal representative wasting, mismanaging, or misapplying the estate. Section 194 explains how the court establishes the amount of the bond and the methods for posting the bond.

§ 194. Bonds of Personal Representatives of Estates

Except when bond is not required under the provisions of this Code, before the issuance of letters testamentary or of administration, the recipient of letters shall enter into bond conditioned as required by law, payable to the county judge or probate judge of the county in which the probate proceedings are pending and to his successors in office. Such bonds shall bear the written approval of either of such judges in his official capacity, and shall be executed and approved in accordance with the following rules:

1. Court to Fix Penalty. The penalty of the bond shall be fixed by the judge, in an amount deemed sufficient to protect the estate and its creditors, as hereinafter provided.

2. Bond to Protect Creditors Only, When. If the person to whom letters testamentary or of administration is granted is also entitled to all of the decedent's estate, after payment of debts, the bond shall be in an amount sufficient to protect creditors only, notwithstanding the rules applicable generally to bonds of personal representatives of estates.

3. Before Fixing Penalty, Court to Hear Evidence. In any case where a bond is, or shall be, required of a personal representative of an estate, the court shall, before fixing the penalty of the bond, hear evidence and determine:

(a) The amount of cash on hand and where deposited, and the amount of cash estimated to be needed for administrative purposes, including operation of a business, factory, farm or ranch owned by the estate, and expenses of administration for one (1) year; and

(b) The revenue anticipated to be received in the succeeding twelve (12) months from dividends, interest, rentals, or use of real or personal property belonging to the estate and the aggregate amount of any installments or periodical payments to be collected; and

(c) The estimated value of certificates of stock, bonds, notes, or securities of the estate or ward, the name of the depository, if any, in which said assets are held for safekeeping, the face value of life insurance or other policies payable to the person on whose estate administration is sought, or to such estate, and such other personal property as is owned by the estate, or by one under disability; and

(d) The estimated amount of debts due and owing by the estate or ward.

4. Penalty of Bond. The penalty of the bond shall be fixed by the judge in an amount equal to the estimated value of all personal property belonging to the estate, or to the person under disability, together with an additional amount to cover revenue anticipated to be derived during the succeeding twelve (12) months from interest, dividends, collectible claims, the aggregate amount of any installments or periodical payments exclusive of income derived or to be derived from federal social security payments, and rentals for use of real and personal property; provided, that the penalty of the original bond shall be reduced in proportion to the amount of cash or value of securities or other assets authorized or required to be deposited or placed in safekeeping by order of court, or voluntarily made by the representative or by his sureties as hereinafter provided in Subdivisions 6 and 7 hereof.

5. Agreement as to Deposit of Assets. It shall be lawful, and the court may require such action when deemed in the best interest of an estate, for a personal representative to agree with the surety or sureties, either corporate or personal, for the deposit of any or all cash, and safekeeping of other assets of the estate in a financial institution as defined by Section 201.101, Finance Code, with its main office or a branch office in this state and qualified to act as a depository in this State under the laws of this State or of the United States, if such deposit is otherwise proper, in such manner as to prevent the withdrawal of such moneys or other assets without the written consent of the surety, or an order of the court made on such notice to the surety as the court shall direct. No such agreement shall in any manner release from or change the liability of the principal or sureties as established by the terms of the bond.

6. Deposits Authorized or Required, When. Cash or securities or other personal assets of an estate or which an estate is entitled to receive may, and if deemed by the court in the best interest of such estate shall, be deposited or placed in safekeeping as the case may be, in one or more of the depositories hereinabove described upon such terms as shall be prescribed by the court. The court in which the proceedings are pending, upon its own motion, or upon written application of the representative or of any other person interested in the estate may authorize or require additional assets of the estate then on hand or as they accrue during the pendency of the probate proceedings to be deposited or held in safekeeping as provided above. The amount of the bond of the personal representative shall be reduced in proportion to the cash so deposited, or the value of the securities or other assets placed in safekeeping. Such cash so deposited, or securities or other assets held in safekeeping, or portions thereof, may be withdrawn from a depository only upon order of the court, and the bond of the personal representative shall be increased in proportion to the amount of cash or the value of securities or other assets so authorized to be withdrawn.

7. Representative May Deposit Cash or Securities of His Own in Lieu of Bond. It shall be lawful for the personal representative of an estate, in lieu of giving surety or sureties on any bond which shall be required of him, or for the purpose of reducing the amount of such bond, to deposit out of his own assets cash or securities acceptable to the court, with a depository such as named above or with any other corporate depository approved by the court, if such deposit is otherwise proper, said deposit to be equal in amount or value to the amount of the bond required, or the bond reduced by the value of assets so deposited.

8. Rules Applicable to Making and Handling Deposits in Lieu of Bond or to Reduce Penal Sum of Bond. (a) A receipt for a deposit in lieu of surety or sureties shall be issued by the depository, showing the amount of cash or, if securities, the amount and description thereof, and agreeing not to disburse or deliver the same except upon receipt of a certified copy of an order of the court in which the proceedings are pending, and such receipt shall be attached to the representative's bond and be delivered to and filed by the county clerk after approval by the judge.

(b) The amount of cash or securities on deposit may be increased or decreased, by order of the court from time to time, as the interest of the estate shall require.

(c) Deposits in lieu of sureties on bonds, whether of cash or securities, may be withdrawn or released only on order of a court having jurisdiction.

(d) Creditors shall have the same rights against the representative and such deposits as are provided for recovery against sureties on a bond.

(e) The court may on its own motion, or upon written application by the representative or by any other person interested in the estate, require that adequate bond be given by the representative in lieu of such deposit, or authorize withdrawal of the deposit and substitution of a bond with sureties therefor. In either case, the representative shall file a sworn statement showing the condition of the estate, and unless the same be filed within twenty (20) days after being personally served with notice of the filing of an application by another, or entry of the court's motion, he shall be subject to removal as in other cases. The deposit may not be released or withdrawn until the court has been satisfied as to the condition of the estate, has determined the amount of bond, and has received and approved the bond.

9. Withdrawal of Deposits When Estate Closed. Upon the closing of an estate, any such deposit or portion thereof remaining on hand, whether of the assets of the representative, or of the assets of the estate, or of the surety, shall be released by order of court and paid over to the person or persons entitled thereto. No writ of attachment or garnishment shall lie against the deposit, except as to claims of creditors of the estate being administered, or persons interested therein, including distributees and wards, and then only in the event distribution has been ordered by the court, and to the extent only of such distribution as shall have been ordered.

10. Who May Act as Sureties. The surety or sureties on said bonds may be authorized corporate sureties, or personal sureties.

11. Procedure When Bond Exceeds Fifty Thousand Dollars ($50,000). When any such bond shall exceed Fifty Thousand Dollars ($50,000) in penal sum, the court may require that such bond be signed by two (2) or more authorized corporate sureties, or by one such surety and two (2) or more good and sufficient personal sureties. The estate shall pay the cost of a bond with corporate sureties.

12. Qualifications of Personal Sureties. If the sureties be natural persons, there shall not be less than two (2), each of whom shall make affidavit in the manner prescribed in this Code, and the judge shall be satisfied that he owns property within this State, over and above that exempt by law, sufficient to qualify as a surety as required by law. Except as provided by law, only one surety is required if the surety is an authorized corporate surety; provided, a personal surety, instead of making affidavit, or creating a lien on specific real estate when such is required, may, in the same manner as a personal representative, deposit his own cash or securities, in lieu of pledging real property as security, subject, so far as applicable, to the provisions covering such deposits when made by personal representatives.

13. Bonds of Temporary Appointees. In case of a temporary administrator, the bond shall be in such sum as the judge shall direct.

14. Increased or Additional Bonds When Property Sold, Rented, Leased for Mineral Development, or Money Borrowed or Invested. The provisions in this Section with respect to deposit of cash and safekeeping of securities shall cover, so far as they may be applicable, the orders to be entered by the court when real or personal property of an estate has been authorized to be sold or rented, or money borrowed thereon, or when real property, or an interest therein, has been authorized to be leased for mineral development or subjected to unitization, the general bond having been found insufficient.

Acts 1955, 54th Leg., p. 88, ch. 55, eff. Jan. 1, 1956. Amended by Acts 1957, 55th Leg., p. 53, ch. 31, § 6(b), eff. Aug. 22, 1957; Acts 1971, 62nd Leg., p. 983, ch. 173, § 14, eff. Jan. 1, 1972; Acts 1979, 66th Leg., p. 1754, ch. 713, § 25, eff. Aug. 27, 1979. Amended by Acts 1993, 73rd Leg., ch. 957, § 31, eff. Sept. 1, 1993; Subsec. 5 amended by Acts 1999, 76th Leg., ch. 344, § 6.003, eff. Sept. 1, 1999.

Statutes in Context

A personal representative is excused from the requirement of posting bond in the following situations: (1) the testator waived bond in the testator's will (§ 195(a)), (2) a corporate fiduciary is serving as the personal representative (§ 195(b)), or (3) the court waives bond for an independent executor (§ 145(p)). It is very common for a testator to waive bond in the will to save the estate, and hence the beneficiaries, the cost of the bond.

---

§ 195. When No Bond Required

(a) By Will. Whenever any will probated in a Texas court directs that no bond or security be required of the person or persons named as executors, the court finding that such person or persons are qualified, letters testamentary shall be issued to the persons so named, without requirement of bond.

(b) Corporate Fiduciary Exempted From Bond. If a personal representative is a corporate fiduciary, as said term is defined in this Code, no bond shall be required.

Acts 1955, 54th Leg., p. 88, ch. 55, eff. Jan. 1, 1956. Subsec. (a) amended by Acts 1995, 74th Leg., ch. 1039, § 12, eff. Sept. 1, 1995.

§ 196. Form of Bond

The following form, or the same in substance, may be used for the bonds of personal representatives:

> "The State of Texas
> "County of _____
> "Know all men by these presents that we, A.B., as principal, and E.F., as sureties, are held and firmly bound unto the county (or probate) judge of the County of _____, and his successors in office, in the sum of _____ Dollars; conditioned that the above bound A.B., who has been appointed executor of the last will and testament of J.C., deceased (or has been appointed by the said judge of _____ County, administrator with the will annexed of the estate of J.C., deceased, or has been appointed by the said judge of _____ County, administrator of the estate of J.C., deceased, or has been appointed by the said judge of _____ County, temporary administrator of the estate of J.C., deceased, as the case may be), shall well and truly perform all of the duties required of him by law under said appointment."

Acts 1955, 54th Leg., p. 88, ch. 55, eff. Jan. 1, 1956. Amended by Acts 1993, 73rd Leg., ch. 957, § 32, eff. Sept. 1, 1993.

§ 197. Bonds to Be Filed

All bonds required by preceding provisions of this Code shall be subscribed by both principals and sureties, and, when approved by the court, be filed with the clerk.

Acts 1955, 54th Leg., p. 88, ch. 55, eff. Jan. 1, 1956.

§ 198. Bonds of Joint Representatives

When two or more persons are appointed representatives of the same estate or person and are required by the provisions of this Code or by the court to give a bond, the court may require either a separate bond from each or one joint bond from all of them.

Acts 1955, 54th Leg., p. 88, ch. 55, eff. Jan. 1, 1956.

§ 199. Bonds of Married Persons

When a married person is appointed personal representative, the person may, jointly with, or without, his or her spouse, execute such bond as the law requires; and such bond shall bind the person's separate estate, but shall bind his or her spouse only if signed by the spouse.

Acts 1955, 54th Leg., p. 88, ch. 55, eff. Jan. 1, 1956. Amended by Acts 1979, 66th Leg., p. 39, ch. 24, § 24, eff. Aug. 27, 1979.

§ 200. Bond of Married Person Under Eighteen Years of Age

When a person under eighteen years of age who is or has been married shall accept and qualify as executor or administrator, any bond required to be executed by him shall be as valid and binding for all purposes as if he were of lawful age.

Acts 1955, 54th Leg., p. 88, ch. 55, eff. Jan. 1, 1956. Amended by Acts 1975, 64th Leg., p. 105, ch. 45, § 3, eff. Sept. 1, 1975. Amended by Acts 1993, 73rd Leg., ch. 957, § 33, eff. Sept. 1, 1993.

§ 201. (a) Affidavit of Personal Surety; (b) Lien on Specific Property, When Required; (c) Subordination of Lien Authorized

(a) Affidavit of Personal Surety. Before the judge may consider a bond with personal sureties, each person offered as surety shall execute an affidavit stating the amount of his assets, reachable by creditors, of a value over and above his liabilities, the total of the worth of such sureties to be equal to at least double the amount of the bond, and such affidavit shall be presented to the judge for his consideration and, if approved, shall be attached to and form part of the bond.

(b) Lien on Specific Property, When Required. If the judge finds that the estimated value of personal property of the estate which cannot be deposited or held in safekeeping as hereinabove provided is such that personal sureties cannot be accepted without the creation of a specific lien on real property of such sureties, he shall enter an order requiring that each surety designate real property owned by him within this State subject to execution, of a value over and above all liens and unpaid taxes, equal at least to the amount of the bond, giving an adequate legal description of such property, all of which shall be incorporated in an affidavit by the surety, approved by the judge, and be attached to and form part of the bond. If compliance with such order is not had, the judge may in his discretion require that the bond be signed by an authorized corporate surety, or by such corporate surety and two (2) or more personal sureties.

(c) Subordination of Lien Authorized. If a personal surety who has been required to create a lien on specific real estate desires to lease such property for mineral development, he may file his written application in the court in which the proceedings are pending, requesting subordination of such lien to the proposed lease, and the judge of such court may, in his discretion, enter an order granting such application. A certified copy of such order, filed and recorded in the deed records of the proper county, shall be sufficient to subordinate such lien to the rights of a lessee, in the proposed lease.

Acts 1955, 54th Leg., p. 88, ch. 55, eff. Jan. 1, 1956. Amended by Acts 1957, 55th Leg., p. 53, ch. 31, § 6(c).

§ 202. Bond as Lien on Real Property of Surety

When a personal surety has been required by the court to create a lien on specific real property as a condition of his acceptance as surety on a bond, a lien on the real property of the surety in this State which is described in the affidavit of the surety, and only upon such property, shall arise as security for the performance of the obligation of the bond. The clerk of the court shall, before letters are issued to the representative, cause to be mailed to the office of the county clerk of each county in which is located any real property as set forth in the affidavit of the surety, a statement signed by the clerk, giving a sufficient description of such real property, the name of the principal and sureties, the amount of the bond, and the name of the estate and the court in which the bond is given. The county clerk to whom such statement is sent shall record the same in the deed records of the county. All such recorded statements shall be duly indexed in such manner that the existence and character of the liens may conveniently be determined, and such recording and indexing of such statement shall constitute and be constructive notice to all persons of the existence of such lien on such real property situated in such county, effective as of date of such indexing.

Acts 1955, 54th Leg., p. 88, ch. 55, eff. Jan. 1, 1956. Amended by Acts 1957, 55th Leg., p. 53, ch. 31, § 6(d).

§ 203. When New Bond May Be Required

A personal representative may be required to give a new bond in the following cases:

(a) When the sureties upon the bond, or any one of them, shall die, remove beyond the limits of the state, or become insolvent; or

(b) When, in the opinion of the court, the sureties upon any such bond are insufficient; or

(c) When, in the opinion of the court, any such bond is defective; or

(d) When the amount of any such bond is insufficient; or

(e) When the sureties, or any one of them, petitions the court to be discharged from future liability upon such bond; or

(f) When the bond and the record thereof have been lost or destroyed.

Acts 1955, 54th Leg., p. 88, ch. 55, eff. Jan. 1, 1956.

§ 204. Demand for New Bond by Interested Person

Any person interested in an estate may, upon application in writing filed with the county clerk of the county where the probate proceedings are pending, alleging that the bond of the personal representative is insufficient or defective, or has been, together with the record thereof, lost or destroyed, cause such representative to be cited to appear and show cause why he should not give a new bond.

Acts 1955, 54th Leg., p. 88, ch. 55, eff. Jan. 1, 1956.

§ 205. Judge to Require New Bond

When it shall be known to him that any such bond is in any respect insufficient or that it has, together with the record thereof, been lost or destroyed, the judge

shall without delay cause the representative to be cited to show cause why he should not give a new bond.
Acts 1955, 54th Leg., p. 88, ch. 55, eff. Jan. 1, 1956.

§ 206. Order Requiring New Bond

Upon the return of a citation ordering a personal representative to show cause why he should not give a new bond, the judge shall, on the day named therein for the hearing of the matter, proceed to inquire into the sufficiency of the reasons for requiring a new bond; and, if satisfied that a new bond should be required, he shall enter an order to that effect, stating in such order the amount of such new bond, and the time within which it shall be given, which shall not be later than twenty days from the date of such order.
Acts 1955, 54th Leg., p. 88, ch. 55, eff. Jan. 1, 1956.

§ 207. Order Suspends Powers of Personal Representative

When a personal representative is required to give a new bond, the order requiring such bond shall have the effect to suspend his powers, and he shall not thereafter pay out any money of said estate or do any other official act, except to preserve the property of the estate, until such new bond has been given and approved.
Acts 1955, 54th Leg., p. 88, ch. 55, eff. Jan. 1, 1956.

§ 208. Decrease in Amount of Bond

A personal representative required to give bond may at any time file with the clerk a written application to the court to have his bond reduced. Forthwith the clerk shall issue and cause to be posted notice to all persons interested and to the surety or sureties on the bond, apprising them of the fact and nature of the application and of the time when the judge will hear the application. The judge, in his discretion, upon the submission of proof that a smaller bond than the one in effect will be adequate to meet the requirements of the law and protect the estate, and upon the approval of an accounting filed at the time of the application, may permit the filing of a new bond in a reduced amount.
Acts 1955, 54th Leg., p. 88, ch. 55, eff. Jan. 1, 1956.

§ 209. Discharge of Sureties Upon Execution of New Bond

When a new bond has been given and approved, an order shall be entered discharging the sureties upon the former bond from all liability for the future acts of the principal.
Acts 1955, 54th Leg., p. 88, ch. 55, eff. Jan. 1, 1956.

§ 210. Release of Sureties Before Estate Fully Administered

The sureties upon the bond of a personal representative, or any one of them, may at any time file with the clerk a petition to the court in which the proceedings are pending, praying that such representative be required to give a new bond and that petitioners be discharged from all liability for the future acts of such representative; whereupon, such representative shall be cited to appear and give a new bond.
Acts 1955, 54th Leg., p. 88, ch. 55, eff. Jan. 1, 1956.

§ 211. Release of Lien Before Estate Fully Administered

If a personal surety who has given a lien on specific real property as security applies to the court to have the lien released, the court shall order the release requested, if the court is satisfied that the bond is sufficient without the lien on such property, or if sufficient other real or personal property of the surety is substituted on the same terms and conditions required for the lien which is to be released. If such personal surety who requests the release of the lien does not offer a lien on other real or personal property, and if the court is not satisfied of the sufficiency of the bond without the substitution of other property, the court shall order the personal representative to appear and give a new bond.
Acts 1955, 54th Leg., p. 88, ch. 55, eff. Jan. 1, 1956.

§ 212. Release of Recorded Lien on Surety's Property

A certified copy of the court's order describing the property, and releasing the lien, filed with the county clerk of the county where the property is located, and recorded in the deed records, shall have the effect of cancelling the lien on such property.
Acts 1955, 54th Leg., p. 88, ch. 55, eff. Jan. 1, 1956.

§ 213. Revocation of Letters for Failure to Give Bond

If at any time a personal representative fails to give bond as required by the court, within the time fixed by this Code, another person may be appointed in his stead.
Acts 1955, 54th Leg., p. 88, ch. 55, eff. Jan. 1, 1956.

Statutes in Context

The court may require a personal representative to give bond even if bond was not originally needed, e.g., the testator's will waived bond. *See* §§ 214-217.

---

§ 214. Executor or Guardian Without Bond Required to Give Bond

Where no bond is required of an executor appointed by will, any person having a debt, claim, or demand against the estate, to the justice of which oath has been made by himself, his agent, or attorney, or any other person interested in such estate, whether in person or as the representative of another, may file a complaint in writing in the court where such will is probated, and the court shall thereupon cite such executor to appear and show cause why he should not be required to give bond.
Acts 1955, 54th Leg., p. 88, ch. 55, eff. Jan. 1, 1956. Amended by Acts 1993, 73rd Leg., ch. 957, § 34, eff. Sept. 1, 1993.

§ 215. Order Requiring Bond

Upon hearing such complaint, if it appears to the court that such executor is wasting, mismanaging, or misapplying such estate, and that thereby a creditor may probably lose his debt, or that thereby some person's interest in the estate may be diminished or lost, the court shall enter an order requiring such executor to give bond within ten days from the date of such order.

Acts 1955, 54th Leg., p. 88, ch. 55, eff. Jan. 1, 1956. Amended by Acts 1993, 73rd Leg., ch. 957, § 34, eff. Sept. 1, 1993.

§ 216. Bond in Such Case

Such bond shall be for an amount sufficient to protect the estate and its creditors, to be approved by, and payable to, the judge, conditioned that said executor will well and truly administer such estate, and that he will not waste, mismanage, or misapply the same.

Acts 1955, 54th Leg., p. 88, ch. 55, eff. Jan. 1, 1956. Amended by Acts 1993, 73rd Leg., ch. 957, § 34, eff. Sept. 1, 1993.

§ 217. Failure to Give Bond

Should the executor fail to give such bond within ten days after the order requiring him to do so, then if the judge does not extend the time, he shall, without citation, remove such executor and appoint some competent person in his stead who shall administer the estate according to the provisions of such will or the law, and who, before he enters upon the administration of said estate, shall take the oath required of an administrator with the will annexed, and shall give bond in the same manner and in the same amount provided in this Code for the issuance of original letters of administration.

Acts 1955, 54th Leg., p. 88, ch. 55, eff. Jan. 1, 1956. Amended by Acts 1993, 73rd Leg., ch. 957, § 34, eff. Sept. 1, 1993.

§ 218. Bonds Not Void Upon First Recovery

The bonds of personal representatives shall not become void upon the first recovery, but may be put in suit and prosecuted from time to time until the whole amount thereof shall have been recovered.

Acts 1955, 54th Leg., p. 88, ch. 55, eff. Jan. 1, 1956.

Part 3. Revocation of Letters, Death, Resignation, and Removal

Statutes in Context

Section 220 explains how the court will appoint a replacement personal representative if the currently serving representative dies, resigns, or is removed. This section also handles a variety of other situations where a replacement may be appropriate.

§ 220. Appointment of Successor Representative

(a) Because of Death, Resignation or Removal. When a person duly appointed a personal representative fails to qualify, or, after qualifying, dies, resigns, or is removed, the court may, upon application appoint a successor if there be necessity therefor, and such appointment may be made prior to the filing of, or action upon, a final accounting. In case of death, the legal representatives of the deceased person shall account for, pay, and deliver to the person or persons legally entitled to receive the same, all the property of every kind belonging to the estate entrusted to his care, at such time and in such manner as the court shall order. Upon the finding that a necessity for the immediate appointment of a successor representative exists, the court may appoint such successor without citation or notice.

(b) Because of Existence of Prior Right. Where letters have been granted to one, and another whose right thereto is prior and who has not waived such right and is qualified, applies for letters, the letters previously granted shall be revoked and other letters shall be granted to the applicant.

(c) When Named Executor Becomes an Adult. If one named in a will as executor is not an adult when the will is probated and letters in any capacity have been granted to another, such nominated executor, upon proof that he has become an adult and is not otherwise disqualified, shall be entitled to have such former letters revoked and appropriate letters granted to him. And if the will names two or more persons as executor, any one or more of whom are minors when such will is probated, and letters have been issued to such only as are adults, said minor or minors, upon becoming adults, if not otherwise disqualified, shall be permitted to qualify and receive letters.

(d) Upon Return of Sick or Absent Executor. If one named in a will as executor was sick or absent from the State when the testator died, or when the will was proved, and therefore could not present the will for probate within thirty days after the testator's death, or accept and qualify as executor within twenty days after the probate of the will, he may accept and qualify as executor within sixty days after his return or recovery from sickness, upon proof to the court that he was absent or ill; and, if the letters have been issued to others, they shall be revoked.

(e) When Will Is Discovered After Administration Granted. If it is discovered after letters of administration have been issued that the deceased left a lawful will, the letters shall be revoked and proper letters issued to the person or persons entitled thereto.

(f) When Application and Service Necessary. Except when otherwise expressly provided in this Code, letters shall not be revoked and other letters granted except upon application, and after personal service of citation on the person, if living, whose letters are sought to be revoked, that he appear and show cause why such application should not be granted.

(g) Payment or Tender of Money Due During Vacancy. Money or other thing of value falling due to an estate while the office of the personal representative is vacant may be paid, delivered, or tendered to the clerk of the court for credit of the estate, and the

debtor, obligor, or payor shall thereby be discharged of the obligation for all purposes to the extent and purpose of such payment or tender. If the clerk accepts such payment or tender, he shall issue a proper receipt therefor.
Acts 1955, 54th Leg., p. 88, ch. 55, eff. Jan. 1, 1956. Amended by Acts 1969, 61st Leg., p. 1922, ch. 641, § 11, eff. June 12, 1969. Subsecs. (c), (d), (g) amended by Acts 1993, 73rd Leg., ch. 957, § 35, eff. Sept. 1, 1993.

Statutes in Context

Section 221 addresses issues regarding the resignation of a personal representative.

§ 221. Resignation

(a) Application to Resign. A personal representative who wishes to resign his trust shall file with the clerk his written application to the court to that effect, accompanied by a full and complete exhibit and final account, duly verified, showing the true condition of the estate entrusted to his care.

(b) Successor Representatives. If the necessity exists, the court may immediately accept a resignation and appoint a successor, but shall not discharge the person resigning, or release him or the sureties on his bond until final order or judgment shall have been rendered on his final account.

(c) Citation. Upon the filing of an application to resign, supported by exhibit and final account, the clerk shall call the application to the attention of the judge, who shall set a date for a hearing upon the matter. The clerk shall then issue a citation to all interested persons, showing that proper application has been filed, and the time and place set for hearing, at which time said persons may appear and contest the exhibit and account. The citation shall be posted, unless the court directs that it be published.

(d) Hearing. At the time set for hearing, unless it has been continued by the court, if the court finds that citation has been duly issued and served, he shall proceed to examine such exhibit and account, and hear all evidence for and against the same, and shall, if necessary, restate, and audit and settle the same. If the court is satisfied that the matters entrusted to the applicant have been handled and accounted for in accordance with law, he shall enter an order of approval, and require that the estate remaining in the possession of the applicant, if any, be delivered to the person or persons entitled by law to receive it.

(e) Requisites of Discharge. No resigning personal representative shall be discharged until the application has been heard, the exhibit and account examined, settled, and approved, and until he has satisfied the court that he has delivered the estate, if there be any remaining in his possession, or has complied with all lawful orders of the court with relation to his trust.

(f) Final Discharge. When the resigning applicant has complied in all respects with the orders of the court, an order shall be made accepting the resignation, discharging the applicant, and, if he is under bond, his sureties.
Acts 1955, 54th Leg., p. 88, ch. 55, eff. Jan. 1, 1956. Subsec. (d) amended by Acts 1993, 73rd Leg., ch. 957, § 36, eff. Sept. 1, 1993.

Statutes in Context

A nonresident of Texas may serve as a personal representative only if the nonresident appoints a resident agent to accept service of process in all actions or proceedings with respect to the estate. *See* § 78(c). Section 221A provides guidance for how the personal representative may change the resident agent.

§ 221A. Change of Resident Agent

(a) A personal representative may change its resident agent to accept service of process in a probate proceeding or other action relating to the estate by filing a statement of the change titled "Designation of Successor Resident Agent" with the court in which the probate proceeding is pending. The statement must contain the names and addresses of the:

(1) personal representative;
(2) resident agent; and
(3) successor resident agent.

(b) The designation of a successor resident agent made in a statement filed under this section takes effect on the date on which the statement is filed with the court.
Added by Acts 1999, 76th Leg., ch. 855, § 7, eff. Sept. 1, 1999.

Statutes in Context

A nonresident of Texas may serve as a personal representative only if the nonresident appoints a resident agent to accept service of process in all actions or proceedings with respect to the estate. *See* § 78(c). Section 221B provides guidance for how the resident agent may resign.

§ 221B. Resignation of Resident Agent

(a) A resident agent of a personal representative may resign as the resident agent by giving notice to the personal representative and filing with the court in which the probate proceeding is pending a statement titled "Resignation of Resident Agent" that:

(1) contains the name of the personal representative;

(2) contains the address of the personal representative most recently known by the resident agent;

(3) states that notice of the resignation has been given to the personal representative and that the personal representative has not designated a successor resident agent; and

(4) contains the date on which the notice of the resignation was given to the personal representative.

(b) The resident agent shall send, by certified mail, return receipt requested, a copy of a resignation statement filed under Subsection (a) of this section to:

(1) the personal representative at the address most recently known by the agent; and

(2) each party in the case or the party's attorney or other designated representative of record.

(c) The resignation of a resident agent takes effect on the date on which the court enters an order accepting the agent's resignation. A court may not enter an order accepting the agent's resignation unless the agent complies with the requirements of this section.

Added by Acts 1999, 76th Leg., ch. 855, § 7, eff. Sept. 1, 1999.

Statutes in Context

Section 222 explains how a court may remove a personal representative from office. Subsection (a) enumerates when the removal may occur without notice to the personal representative while subsection (b) lists the circumstances where notice to the personal representative is needed before the court may issue an order of removal. *See also* § 149C (removal of independent executor). Reinstatement is thereafter possible under § 222A.

---

§ 222. Removal

(a) Without Notice. (1) The court, on its own motion or on motion of any interested person, and without notice, may remove any personal representative, appointed under provisions of this Code, who:

(A) Neglects to qualify in the manner and time required by law;

(B) Fails to return within ninety days after qualification, unless such time is extended by order of the court, an inventory of the property of the estate and list of claims that have come to his knowledge;

(C) Having been required to give a new bond, fails to do so within the time prescribed;

(D) Absents himself from the State for a period of three months at one time without permission of the court, or removes from the State;

(E) Cannot be served with notices or other processes because of the fact that the:

(i) personal representative's whereabouts are unknown;

(ii) personal representative is eluding service; or

(iii) personal representative is a nonresident of this state who does not have a resident agent to accept service of process in any probate proceeding or other action relating to the estate; or

(F) Has misapplied, embezzled, or removed from the State, or is about to misapply, embezzle, or remove from the State, all or any part of the property committed to the personal representative's care.

(2) The court may remove a personal representative under Paragraph (F), Subdivision (1), of this subsection only on the presentation of clear and convincing evidence given under oath.

(b) With Notice. The court may remove a personal representative on its own motion, or on the complaint of any interested person, after the personal representative has been cited by personal service to answer at a time and place fixed in the notice, when:

(1) Sufficient grounds appear to support belief that he has misapplied, embezzled, or removed from the state, or that he is about to misapply, embezzle, or remove from the state, all or any part of the property committed to his care;

(2) He fails to return any account which is required by law to be made;

(3) He fails to obey any proper order of the court having jurisdiction with respect to the performance of his duties;

(4) He is proved to have been guilty of gross misconduct, or mismanagement in the performance of his duties;

(5) He becomes an incapacitated person, or is sentenced to the penitentiary, or from any other cause becomes incapable of properly performing the duties of his trust;

(6) As executor or administrator, he fails to make a final settlement within three years after the grant of letters, unless the time be extended by the court upon a showing of sufficient cause supported by oath; or

(7) As executor or administrator, he fails to timely file the notice required by Section 128A of this code.

(c) Order of Removal. The order of removal shall state the cause thereof. It shall require that any letters issued to the one removed shall, if he has been personally served with citation, be surrendered, and that all such letters be cancelled of record, whether delivered or not. It shall further require, as to all the estate remaining in the hands of a removed person, delivery thereof to the person or persons entitled thereto, or to one who has been appointed and has qualified as successor representative.

Acts 1955, 54th Leg., p. 88, ch. 55, eff. Jan. 1, 1956. Amended by Acts 1969, 61st Leg., p. 1922, ch. 641, § 11, eff. June 12, 1969. Subsec. (b) amended by Acts 1989, 71st Leg., ch. 1035, § 11, eff. Sept. 1, 1989; Subsecs. (a), (b) amended by Acts 1993, 73rd Leg., ch. 905, § 11, eff. Sept. 1, 1993; Subsecs. (b), (c) amended by Acts 1993, 73rd Leg., ch. 957, § 37, eff. Sept. 1, 1993; Subsecs. (a), (b) amended by Acts 1995, 74th Leg., ch. 1039, § 13, eff. Sept. 1, 1995; Subsec. (a) amended by Acts 1999, 76th Leg., ch. 855, § 8, eff. Sept. 1, 1999.

§ 222A. Reinstatement After Removal

(a) Not later than the 10th day after the date the court signs the order of removal, a personal representative who is removed under Subsection (a)(1)(F) or (G), Section 222, of this code may file an application with the court for a hearing to determine whether the personal representative should be reinstated.

(b) On the filing of an application for a hearing under this section, the court clerk shall issue a notice stating that the application for reinstatement was filed, the name of the decedent, and the name of the applicant. The clerk shall issue the notice to the applicant and to the successor representative of the decedent's estate. The notice must cite all persons interested in the estate to appear at the time and place stated in the notice if they wish to contest the application.

(c) If, at the conclusion of a hearing under this section, the court is satisfied by a preponderance of the evidence that the applicant did not engage in the conduct that directly led to the applicant's removal, the court shall set aside an order appointing a successor representative, if any, and shall enter an order reinstating the applicant as personal representative of the ward or estate.

(d) If the court sets aside the appointment of a successor representative under this section, the court may require the successor representative to prepare and file, under oath, an accounting of the estate and to detail the disposition the successor has made of the property of the estate.

Added by Acts 1993, 73rd Leg., ch. 905, § 12, eff. Sept. 1, 1993. Amended by Acts 2003, 78th Leg., ch. 1060, § 12, eff. Sept. 1, 2003.

Part 4. Subsequent Personal Representatives

Statutes in Context

Sections 223-227 outline the rights and obligations of subsequent personal representatives.

§ 223. Further Administration With or Without Will Annexed

Whenever any estate is unrepresented by reason of the death, removal, or resignation of the personal representative of such estate, the court shall grant further administration of the estate when necessary, and with the will annexed where there is a will, upon application therefor by a qualified person interested in the estate. Such appointments shall be made on notice and after hearing, as in case of original appointments, except that when the court finds that there is a necessity for the immediate appointment of a successor representative, such successor may be appointed upon application but without citation or notice.

Acts 1955, 54th Leg., p. 88, ch. 55, eff. Jan. 1, 1956. Amended by Acts 1969, 61st Leg., p. 1922, ch. 641, § 11, eff. June 12, 1969.

§ 224. Successors Succeed to Prior Rights, Powers, and Duties

When a representative of the estate not administered succeeds another, he shall be clothed with all rights, powers, and duties of his predecessor, except such rights and powers conferred on the predecessor by will which are different from those conferred by this Code on personal representatives generally. Subject to this exception, the successor shall proceed to administer such estate in like manner as if his administration were a continuation of the former one. He shall be required to account for all the estate which came into the hands of his predecessor and shall be entitled to any order or remedy which the court has power to give in order to enforce the delivery of the estate and the liability of the sureties of his predecessor for so much as is not delivered. He shall be excused from accounting for such of the estate as he has failed to recover after due diligence.

Acts 1955, 54th Leg., p. 88, ch. 55, eff. Jan. 1, 1956.

§ 225. Additional Powers of Successor Appointee

In addition, such appointee may make himself, and may be made, a party to suits prosecuted by or against his predecessors. He may settle with the predecessor, and receive and receipt for all such portion of the estate as remains in his hands. He may bring suit on the bond or bonds of the predecessor in his own name and capacity, for all the estate that came into the hands of the predecessor and has not been accounted for by him.

Acts 1955, 54th Leg., p. 88, ch. 55, eff. Jan. 1, 1956.

§ 226. Subsequent Executors Also Succeed to Prior Rights and Duties

Whenever an executor shall accept and qualify after letters of administration shall have been granted upon the estate, such executor shall, in like manner, succeed to the previous administrator, and he shall administer the estate in like manner as if his administration were a continuation of the former one, subject, however, to any legal directions of the testator contained in the will in relation to the estate.

Acts 1955, 54th Leg., p. 88, ch. 55, eff. Jan. 1, 1956. Amended by Acts 1993, 73rd Leg., ch. 957, § 38, eff. Sept. 1, 1993.

§ 227. Successors Return of Inventory, Appraisement, and List of Claims

An appointee who has been qualified to succeed to a prior personal representative shall make and return to the court an inventory, appraisement, and list of claims of the estate, within ninety days after being qualified, in like manner as is required of original appointees; and he shall also in like manner return additional inventories, appraisements, and lists of claims. In all orders appointing successor representatives of estates, the court shall appoint appraisers as in original appointments upon the application of any person interested in the estate.

Acts 1955, 54th Leg., p. 88, ch. 55, eff. Jan. 1, 1956. Amended by Acts 1969, 61st Leg., p. 1922, ch. 641, § 11, eff. June 12, 1969.

Part 5. General Powers of Personal Representatives

Statutes in Context

The standard of care which a personal representative must use when dealing with estate property is that of

a prudent person. *See McLendon v. McLendon*, 862 S.W.2d 662 (Tex. App. – Dallas 1993, *writ denied*).

§ 230. Care of Property of Estates

The executor or administrator shall take care of the property of the estate of his testator or intestate as a prudent man would take of his own property, and if there be any buildings belonging to the estate, he shall keep the same in good repair, extraordinary casualties excepted, unless directed not to do so by an order of the court.

Acts 1955, 54th Leg., p. 88, ch. 55, eff. Jan. 1, 1956. Amended by Acts 1975, 64th Leg., p. 268, ch. 114, § 1, eff. April 30, 1975. Amended by Acts 1993, 73rd Leg., ch. 957, § 39, eff. Sept. 1, 1993.

Statutes in Context

The personal representative has a duty to collect all of the decedent's property under § 233. This right is superior to that of the heirs or beneficiaries. *See* § 37.

§ 232. Representative of Estate Shall Take Possession of Personal Property and Records

The personal representative of an estate, immediately after receiving letters, shall collect and take into possession the personal property, record books, title papers, and other business papers of the estate, and all such in his possession shall be delivered to the person or persons legally entitled thereto when the administration has been closed or a successor has received letters.

Acts 1955, 54th Leg., p. 88, ch. 55, eff. Jan. 1, 1956.

Statutes in Context

Section 233 provides the personal representative with guidance in collecting the decedent's property. The section also explains when and how the personal representative may hire an attorney on a contingency fee basis to assist in the recovery and collection process.

§ 233. Collection of Claims and Recovery of Property

(a) Every personal representative of an estate shall use ordinary diligence to collect all claims and debts due the estate and to recover possession of all property of the estate to which its owners have claim or title, provided there is a reasonable prospect of collecting such claims or of recovering such property. If he wilfully neglects to use such diligence, he and the sureties on his bond shall be liable, at the suit of any person interested in the estate, for the use of the estate, for the amount of such claims or the value of such property as has been lost by such neglect.

(b) Except as provided by Subsection (c) of this section, a personal representative may enter into a contract to convey, or may convey, a contingent interest in any property sought to be recovered, not exceeding one-third thereof, for services of attorneys, subject only to approval of the court in which the estate is being administered.

(c) A personal representative, including an independent executor or independent administrator, may convey or contract to convey for services of an attorney a contingent interest that exceeds one-third of the property sought to be recovered under this section only on the approval of the court in which the estate is being administered. The court must approve a contract entered into or conveyance made under this section before an attorney performs any legal services. A contract entered into or conveyance made in violation of this section is void, unless the court ratifies or reforms the contract or documents relating to the conveyance to the extent necessary to cause the contract or conveyance to meet the requirements of this section.

(d) In approving a contract or conveyance under Subsection (b) or (c) of this section for services of an attorney, the court shall consider:

(1) the time and labor that will be required, the novelty and difficulty of the questions to be involved, and the skill that will be required to perform the legal services properly;

(2) the fee customarily charged in the locality for similar legal services;

(3) the value of property recovered or sought to be recovered by the personal representative under this section;

(4) the benefits to the estate that the attorney will be responsible for securing; and

(5) the experience and ability of the attorney who will be performing the services.

(e) On satisfactory proof to the court, a personal representative of an estate is entitled to all necessary and reasonable expenses incurred by the personal representative in collecting or attempting to collect a claim or debt owed to the estate or in recovering or attempting to recover property to which the estate has a title or claim.

Acts 1955, 54th Leg., p. 88, ch. 55, eff. Jan. 1, 1956. Amended by Acts 1993, 73rd Leg., ch. 848, § 1, eff. Sept. 1, 1993.

§ 233A. Suits by Executors or Administrators

Suits for the recovery of personal property, debts, or damages and suits for title or possession of lands or for any right attached to or growing out of the same or for injury or damage done thereto may be instituted by executors or administrators appointed in this state; and judgment in such cases shall be conclusive, but may be set aside by any person interested for fraud or collusion on the part of such executor or administrator.

Added by Acts 1985, 69th Leg., ch. 959, § 3, eff. Sept. 1, 1985. Amended by Acts 1993, 73rd Leg., ch. 957, § 40, eff. Sept. 1, 1993.

Statutes in Context

Unlike an independent executor, a dependent executor must seek court approval before taking almost all actions with respect to the estate. Section 234(a)

enumerates when court approval is needed while § 234(b) lists a few situations where the personal representative may act without court order.

---

§ 234. Exercise of Powers With and Without Court Order

(a) Powers To Be Exercised Under Order of the Court. The personal representative of the estate of any person may, upon application and order authorizing same, renew or extend any obligation owing by or to such estate. When a personal representative deems it for the interest of the estate, he may, upon written application to the court, and by order granting authority:

(1) Purchase or exchange property;

(2) Take claims or property for the use and benefit of the estate in payment of any debt due or owing to the estate;

(3) Compound bad or doubtful debts due or owing to the estate;

(4) Make compromises or settlements in relation to property or claims in dispute or litigation;

(5) Compromise or pay in full any secured claim which has been allowed and approved as required by law against the estate by conveying to the holder of such claim the real estate or personalty securing the same, in full payment, liquidation, and satisfaction thereof, and in consideration of cancellation of notes, deeds of trust, mortgages, chattel mortgages, or other evidences of liens securing the payment of such claim;

(6) Abandon the administration of property of the estate that is burdensome or worthless. Abandoned real or personal property may be foreclosed by a secured party, trustee, or mortgagee without further order of the court.

(b) Powers To Be Exercised Without Court Order. The personal representative of the estate of any person may, without application to or order of the court, exercise the powers listed below, provided, however, that a personal representative under court control may apply and obtain an order if doubtful of the propriety of the exercise of any such powers:

(1) Release liens upon payment at maturity of the debt secured thereby;

(2) Vote stocks by limited or general proxy;

(3) Pay calls and assessments;

(4) Insure the estate against liability in appropriate cases;

(5) Insure property of the estate against fire, theft, and other hazards;

(6) Pay taxes, court costs, bond premiums.

Acts 1955, 54th Leg., p. 88, ch. 55, eff. Jan. 1, 1956. Amended by Acts 1971, 62nd Leg., p. 984, ch. 173, § 15, eff. Jan. 1, 1972. Subsec. (a) amended by Acts 1997, 75th Leg., ch. 1302, § 9, eff. Sept. 1, 1997.

§ 235. Possession of Property Held in Common Ownership

If the estate holds or owns any property in common, or as part owner with another, the representative of the estate shall be entitled to possession thereof in common with the other part owner or owners in the same manner as other owners in common or joint owners would be entitled.

Acts 1955, 54th Leg., p. 88, ch. 55, eff. Jan. 1, 1956.

§ 238. Operation of Farm, Ranch, Factory, or Other Business

If the estate owns a farm, ranch, factory, or other business, the disposition of which has not been specifically directed by will, and if the same be not required to be sold at once for the payment of debts or other lawful purposes, the representative, upon order of the court, shall carry on the operation of such farm, ranch, factory, or other business, or cause the same to be done, or rent the same, as shall appear to be for the best interest of the estate. In deciding, the court shall consider the condition of the estate, and the necessity that may exist for future sale of such property or business for the payment of debts, claims, or other lawful expenditures, and shall not extend the time of renting any of the property beyond what appears consistent with the speedy settlement of the estate of a deceased person or the settlement of his estate.

Acts 1955, 54th Leg., p. 88, ch. 55, eff. Jan. 1, 1956. Amended by Acts 1993, 73rd Leg., ch. 957, § 41, eff. Sept. 1, 1993.

§ 238A. Administration of Partnership Interest by Personal Representative

If the decedent was a partner in a general partnership and the articles of partnership provide that, on the death of a partner, his or her executor or other personal representative shall be entitled to the place of the deceased partner in the firm, the executor or other personal representative so contracting to come into the partnership shall, to the extent allowed by law, be liable to third persons only to the extent of the deceased partner's capital in the partnership and the estate's assets held by the executor or other personal representative. This section does not exonerate an executor or other personal representative from liability for his or her negligence.

Added by Acts 1979, 66th Leg., p. 71, ch. 46, § 1, eff. April 11, 1979.

§ 239. Payment or Credit of Income

In all cases where the estate of a deceased person is being administered under the direction, control, and orders of a court in the exercise of its probate jurisdiction, upon the application of the executor or administrator of said estate, or of any interested party, after notice thereof has been given by posting, if it appears from evidence introduced at the hearing upon said application, and the court finds, that the reasonable market value of the assets of the estate then on hand, exclusive of the annual income therefrom, is at least twice the aggregate amount of all unpaid debts, administration expenses, and legacies, and that no creditor or legatee of the estate has then appeared and objected, the court may order and direct the executor or administrator to pay to, or credit to the account of, those persons who the court finds will own the assets of the estate when the administration thereon is completed, and in the same proportions, such part of the annual net income received by or accruing to said estate, as the court believes and finds can conveniently be paid to such owners without prejudice to the rights of creditors, legatees, or other interested parties. Nothing herein contained shall authorize the court to order paid over to such owners of the estate any part of the corpus or principal of the estate, except as otherwise provided by sections of this Code; provided, however, in this connection, bonuses, rentals, and royalties received for, or from, an oil, gas, or other mineral lease shall be treated and regarded as income, and not as corpus or principal.

Acts 1955, 54th Leg., p. 88, ch. 55, eff. Jan. 1, 1956. Amended by Acts 1973, 63rd Leg., p. 407, ch. 182, § 1, eff. May 25, 1973.

Statutes in Context

Section 240 provides that the acts of one of several co-personal representatives are valid except that all personal representatives must join in a conveyance of real property. Accordingly, a testator must take great care in the appointment of multiple personal representatives because the act of one (as contrasted with all or a majority) is binding under most circumstances.

§ 240. Joint Executors or Administrators

Should there be more than one executor or administrator of the same estate at the same time, the acts of one of them as such executor or administrator shall be as valid as if all had acted jointly; and, in case of the death, resignation or removal of an executor or administrator, if there be a co-executor or co-administrator of such estate, he shall proceed with the administration as if no such death, resignation or removal had occurred. Provided, however, that this Section shall not be construed to authorize one of several executors or administrators to convey real estate, but in such case all the executors or administrators who have qualified as such and are acting as such shall join in the conveyance, unless the court, after due hearing, authorizes less than all to act.

Acts 1955, 54th Leg., p. 88, ch. 55, eff. Jan. 1, 1956.

Part 6. Compensation, Expenses, and Court Costs

Statutes in Context

The testator may establish the amount of compensation for a personal representative by including a provision in the will (e.g., a fixed amount, a "reasonable" amount, or no compensation). *See Stanley v. Henderson*, 162 S.W.2d 95 (Tex. 1942). If the will is silent, the personal representative is entitled to compensation as set forth in § 241 provided the court finds that the personal representative managed the estate prudently.

The amount of the compensation is basically a commission on what the personal representative expends and collects, unless it is "too easy" to justify the compensation. The personal representative is entitled to 5 percent of the sums received in cash (e.g., selling estate assets) plus 5 percent of the sums paid out in cash (e.g., paying debts). However, this commission is not available for collecting cash on hand, bank accounts, or life insurance policies nor for making payments to the beneficiaries or heirs.

The personal representative can attempt to get a larger amount of compensation by showing that the personal representative is managing a business or farm or that the 5 percent commission is unreasonably low.

§ 241. Compensation of Personal Representatives

(a) Executors, administrators, and temporary administrators shall be entitled to receive a commission of five per cent (5%) on all sums they may actually receive in cash, and the same per cent on all sums they may actually pay out in cash, in the administration of the estate on a finding by the court that the executor or administrator has taken care of and managed the estate in compliance with the standards of this code; provided, no commission shall be allowed for receiving funds belonging to the testator or intestate which were on hand or were held for the testator or intestate at the time of his death in a financial institution or a brokerage firm, including cash or a cash equivalent held in a checking account, savings account, certificate of deposit, or money market account; nor for collecting the proceeds of any life insurance policy; nor for paying out cash to the heirs or legatees as such; provided, further, however, that in no event shall the executor or administrator be entitled in the aggregate to more than five per cent (5%) of the gross fair market value of the estate subject to administration. If the executor or administrator manages a farm, ranch, factory, or other business of the estate, or if the compensation as calculated above is unreasonably low, the court may allow him reasonable compensation for his services, including unusual effort to collect funds or life insurance. For this purpose, the county court shall have jurisdiction to receive, consider, and act on applications from independent executors. The court may, on application of an interested person or on its own motion, deny a commission allowed by this subsection in whole or in part if:

(1) the court finds that the executor or administrator has not taken care of and managed estate property prudently; or

(2) the executor or administrator has been removed under Section 149C or 222 of this code.

(b) Definition. In this section, "financial institution" means an organization authorized to do business

under state or federal laws relating to financial institutions, including banks and trust companies, savings banks, building and loan associations, savings and loan companies or associations, and credit unions.
Acts 1955, 54th Leg., p. 88, ch. 55, eff. Jan. 1, 1956. Amended by Acts 1957, 55th Leg., p. 53, ch. 31, § 8. Amended by Acts 1987, 70th Leg., ch. 919, § 1, eff. Sept. 1, 1987; Sec. (a) amended by Acts 1991, 72nd Leg., ch. 468, § 1, eff. Sept. 1, 1991; Sec. (c) added by Acts 1991, 72nd Leg., ch. 468, § 2, eff. Sept. 1, 1991. Amended by Acts 1993, 73rd Leg., ch. 957, § 42, eff. Sept. 1, 1993.

Statutes in Context

Section 242 allows the personal representative to be reimbursed for all necessary and reasonable expenses, including attorneys' fees, incurred in administering the estate.

§ 242. Expenses Allowed

Personal representatives of estates shall also be entitled to all necessary and reasonable expenses incurred by them in the preservation, safe-keeping, and management of the estate, and in collecting or attempting to collect claims or debts, and in recovering or attempting to recover property to which the estate has a title or claim, and all reasonable attorney's fees, necessarily incurred in connection with the proceedings and management of such estate, on satisfactory proof to the court.
Acts 1955, 54th Leg., p. 88, ch. 55, eff. Jan. 1, 1956.

Statutes in Context

Section 243 explains when a person may be reimbursed from the estate for expenses incurred in (1) attempting to probate a will or (2) defending a will already admitted to probate, provided the actions are both in good faith and with just cause.

§ 243. Allowance for Defending Will

When any person designated as executor in a will or an alleged will, or as administrator with the will or alleged will annexed, defends it or prosecutes any proceeding in good faith, and with just cause, for the purpose of having the will or alleged will admitted to probate, whether successful or not, he shall be allowed out of the estate his necessary expenses and disbursements, including reasonable attorney's fees, in such proceedings. When any person designated as a devisee, legatee, or beneficiary in a will or an alleged will, or as administrator with the will or alleged will annexed, defends it or prosecutes any proceeding in good faith, and with just cause, for the purpose of having the will or alleged will admitted to probate, whether successful or not, he may be allowed out of the estate his necessary expenses and disbursements, including reasonable attorney's fees, in such proceedings.
Acts 1955, 54th Leg., p. 88, ch. 55, eff. Jan. 1, 1956. Amended by Acts 1983, 68th Leg., p. 5227, ch. 957, § 1, eff. Sept. 1, 1983; Acts 1987, 70th Leg., ch. 462, § 1, eff. Sept. 1, 1987.

§ 244. Expense Accounts

All expense charges shall be made in writing, showing specifically each item of expense and the date thereof, and shall be verified by affidavit of the representative, filed with the clerk and entered on the claim docket, and shall be acted on by the court in like manner as other claims against the estate.
Acts 1955, 54th Leg., p. 88, ch. 55, eff. Jan. 1, 1956.

§ 245. When Costs Are Adjudged Against Representative

When a personal representative neglects to perform a required duty or if a personal representative is removed for cause, the personal representative and the sureties on the personal representative's bond are liable for:

(1) costs of removal and other additional costs incurred that are not authorized expenditures, as defined by this code; and

(2) reasonable attorney's fees incurred in removing the personal representative or in obtaining compliance regarding any statutory duty the personal representative has neglected.

Acts 1955, 54th Leg., p. 88, ch. 55, eff. Jan. 1, 1956. Amended by Acts 1977, 65th Leg., p. 1171, ch. 448, § 3, eff. Aug. 29, 1977. Amended by Acts 1983, 68th Leg., p. 631, ch. 140, § 1, eff. Aug. 29, 1983. Amended by Acts 2003, 78th Leg., ch. 1060, § 13, eff. Sept. 1, 2003.

Chapter VIII. Proceedings During Administration

Part 1. Inventory, Appraisement, and List of Claims

Statutes in Context

If an interested person applies or if the court deems it necessary, the court will appoint appraisers to value the property in the decedent's estate. These values will be included on the inventory required by § 250. The appraiser's fee is provided for in § 253.

§ 248. Appointment of Appraisers

At any time after the grant of letters testamentary or of administration, upon the application of any interested person or if the court shall deem necessary, the court shall appoint not less than one nor more than three disinterested persons, citizens of the county in which letters were granted, to appraise the property of the estate. In such event and when part of the estate is situated in a county other than the county in which letters were granted, if the court shall deem necessary it may appoint not less than one nor more than three disinterested persons, citizens of the county where such part of the estate is situated, to appraise the property of the estate situated therein.

Acts 1955, 54th Leg., p. 88, ch. 55, eff. Jan. 1, 1956. Amended by Acts 1967, 60th Leg., p. 1815, ch. 697, § 2, eff. Aug. 28, 1967; Amended by Acts 1993, 73rd Leg., ch. 957, § 44, eff. Sept. 1, 1993.

§ 249. Failure of Appraisers to Serve

If any appraiser so appointed shall fail or refuse to act, the court shall by a like order or orders remove such appraiser and appoint another appraiser or appraisers, as the case shall require.
Acts 1955, 54th Leg., p. 88, ch. 55, eff. Jan. 1, 1956. Amended by Acts 1967, 60th Leg., p. 1816, ch. 697, § 3, eff. Aug. 28, 1967.

Statutes in Context

The personal representative in both dependent and independent administrations must file an inventory, appraisement, and list of claims within 90 days after qualification. This document helps the creditors to determine which assets are available to pay their claims and thus provides them with valuable insight into how they should proceed to have the best chance of getting paid. Additionally, the inventory helps the heirs and beneficiaries to determine the property to which they may be entitled.

The inventory must include all real property located in Texas and all personal property wherever located. (Out of state real property is not listed because Texas courts have no jurisdiction over this property.) Non-probate assets, that is, property which passes outside of the probate process such as survivorship interests and life insurance proceeds, are not included in the inventory.

If the decedent was married at the time of death, the inventory must designate whether the property is separate or community.

---

§ 250. Inventory and Appraisement

Within ninety days after his qualification, unless a longer time shall be granted by the court, the representative shall file with the clerk of court a verified, full and detailed inventory, in one written instrument, of all the property of such estate which has come to his possession or knowledge, which inventory shall include:

(a) all real property of the estate situated in the State of Texas;

(b) all personal property of the estate wherever situated. The representative shall set out in the inventory his appraisement of the fair market value of each item thereof as of the date of death in the case of grant of letters testamentary or of administration, as the case may be; provided that if the court shall appoint an appraiser or appraisers of the estate, the representative shall determine the fair market value of each item of the inventory with the assistance of such appraiser or appraisers and shall set out in the inventory such appraisement. The inventory shall specify what portion of the property, if any, is separate property and what portion, if any, is community property. If any property is owned in common with others, the interest owned by the estate shall be shown, together with the names and relationship, if known, of co-owners. Such inventory, when approved by the court and duly filed with the clerk of court, shall constitute for all purposes the inventory and appraisement of the estate referred to in this Code. The court for good cause shown may require the filing of the inventory and appraisement at a time prior to ninety days after the qualification of the representative.
Acts 1955, 54th Leg., p. 88, ch. 55, eff. Jan. 1, 1956. Amended by Acts 1967, 60th Leg., p. 1816, ch. 697, § 4, eff. Aug. 28, 1967;Amended by Acts 1993, 73rd Leg., ch. 957, § 45, eff. Sept. 1, 1993.

Statutes in Context

The list of claims is part of the inventory and appraisement. The list is of claims due or owing to the decedent's estate, that is, claims on which the decedent was a creditor. It is not a list of claims against the decedent's estate.

---

§ 251. List of Claims

There shall also be made out and attached to said inventory a full and complete list of all claims due or owing to the estate, which shall state:

(a) The name of each person indebted to the estate and his address when known.

(b) The nature of such debt, whether by note, bill, bond, or other written obligation, or by account or verbal contract.

(c) The date of such indebtedness, and the date when the same was or will be due.

(d) The amount of each claim, the rate of interest thereon, and time for which the same bears interest.

(e) In the case of decedent's estate, which of such claims are separate property and which are of the community.

(f) What portion of the claims, if any, is held in common with others, giving the names and the relationships, if any, of other part owners, and the interest of the estate therein.
Acts 1955, 54th Leg., p. 88, ch. 55, eff. Jan. 1, 1956.

Statutes in Context

The inventory, appraisement, and list of claims must be supported by the personal representative's sworn affidavit.

---

§ 252. Affidavit to be Attached

The representative of the estate shall also attach to such inventory and list of claims his affidavit subscribed and sworn to before an officer in the county authorized by law to administer oaths, that the said inventory and list of claims are a true and complete statement of the property and claims of the estate that have come to his knowledge.
Acts 1955, 54th Leg., p. 88, ch. 55, eff. Jan. 1, 1956.

§ 253. Fees of Appraisers

Each appraiser appointed by the court, as herein authorized, shall be entitled to receive a minimum compensation of Five Dollars ($5) per day, payable out of the estate, for each day that he actually serves in performance of his duties as such.

Acts 1955, 54th Leg., p. 88, ch. 55, eff. Jan. 1, 1956. Amended by Acts 1957, 55th Leg., p. 53, ch. 31, § 9.

Statutes in Context

The court will either approve or disapprove the inventory, appraisement, and list of claims under § 255.

---

§ 255. Action by the Court

Upon return of the inventory, appraisement, and list of claims, the judge shall examine and approve, or disapprove, them, as follows:

(a) Order of Approval. Should the judge approve the inventory, appraisement, and list of claims, he shall issue an order to that effect.

(b) Order of Disapproval. Should the judge not approve the inventory, appraisement, or list of claims, or any of them, an order to that effect shall be entered, and it shall further require the return of another inventory, appraisement, and list of claims, or whichever of them is disapproved, within a time specified in such order, not to exceed twenty days from the date of the order; and the judge may also, if deemed necessary, appoint new appraisers.

Acts 1955, 54th Leg., p. 88, ch. 55, eff. Jan. 1, 1956.

§ 256. Discovery of Additional Property

If, after the filing of the inventory and appraisement, property or claims not included in the inventory shall come to the possession or knowledge of the representative, he shall forthwith file with the clerk of court a verified, full and detailed supplemental inventory and appraisement.

Acts 1955, 54th Leg., p. 88, ch. 55, eff. Jan. 1, 1956. Amended by Acts 1967, 60th Leg., p. 1816, ch. 697, § 5, eff. Aug. 28, 1967.

§ 257. Additional Inventory or List of Claims Required by Court

Any representative of an estate, on the written complaint of any interested person that property or claims of the estate have not been included in the inventory and list of claims filed, shall be cited to appear before the court in which the cause is pending and show cause why he should not be required to make and return an additional inventory or list of claims, or both. After hearing such complaint, and being satisfied of the truth thereof, the court shall enter its order requiring such additional inventory or list of claims, or both, to be made and returned in like manner as original inventories, and within such time, not to exceed twenty days, from the date of said order, as may be fixed by the court, but to include only property or claims theretofore not inventoried or listed.

Acts 1955, 54th Leg., p. 88, ch. 55, eff. Jan. 1, 1956.

§ 258. Correction Required When Inventory, Appraisement, or List of Claims Erroneous or Unjust

Any person interested in an estate who deems an inventory, appraisement, or list of claims returned therein erroneous or unjust in any particular may file a complaint in writing setting forth and pointing out the alleged erroneous or unjust items, and cause the representative to be cited to appear before the court and show cause why such errors should not be corrected. If, upon the hearing of such complaint, the court be satisfied from the evidence that the inventory, appraisement, or list of claims is erroneous or unjust in any particular as alleged in the complaint, an order shall be entered specifying the erroneous or unjust items and the corrections to be made, and appointing appraisers to make a new appraisement correcting such erroneous or unjust items and requiring the return of said new appraisement within twenty days from the date of the order. The court may also, on its own motion or that of the personal representative of the estate, have a new appraisal made for the purposes above set out.

Acts 1955, 54th Leg., p. 88, ch. 55, eff. Jan. 1, 1956.

§ 259. Effect of Reappraisement

When any reappraisement is made, returned, and approved by the court, it shall stand in place of the original appraisement. Not more than one reappraisement shall be made, but any person interested in the estate may object to the reappraisement either before or after it is approved, and if the court finds that the reappraisement is erroneous or unjust, the court shall appraise the property upon the basis of the evidence before it.

Acts 1955, 54th Leg., p. 88, ch. 55, eff. Jan. 1, 1956.

§ 260. Failure of Joint Personal Representatives to Return an Inventory, Appraisement, and List of Claims

If there be more than one representative qualified as such, any one or more of them, on the neglect of the others, may make and return an inventory and appraisement and list of claims; and the representative so neglecting shall not thereafter interfere with the estate or have any power over same; but the representative so returning shall have the whole administration, unless, within sixty days after the return, the delinquent or delinquents shall assign to the court in writing and under oath a reasonable excuse which the court may deem satisfactory; and if no excuse is filed or if the excuse filed is not deemed sufficient, the court shall enter an order removing any and all such delinquents and revoking their letters.

Acts 1955, 54th Leg., p. 88, ch. 55, eff. Jan. 1, 1956.

§ 261. Use of Inventories, Appraisements, and Lists of Claims as Evidence

All inventories, appraisements, and lists of claims which have been taken, returned, and approved in ac-

cordance with law, or the record thereof, or copies of either the originals or the record thereof, duly certified under the seal of the county court affixed by the clerk, may be given in evidence in any of the courts of this State in any suit by or against the representative of the estate, but shall not be conclusive for or against him, if it be shown that any property or claims of the estate are not shown therein, or that the value of the property or claims of the estate actually was in excess of that shown in the appraisement and list of claims.
Acts 1955, 54th Leg., p. 88, ch. 55, eff. Jan. 1, 1956.

Part 2. Withdrawing Estates of Deceased Persons from Administration

Statutes in Context

After the filing of the inventory, appraisement, and list of claims, a person entitled to the estate may ask the court to withdraw the estate from administration by posting a bond at least double the gross appraised value of the estate. See §§ 262-269.

§ 262. Executor or Administrator Required to Report on Condition of Estate

At any time after the return of inventory, appraisement, and list of claims of a deceased person, any one entitled to a portion of the estate may, by a written complaint filed in the court in which such case is pending, cause the executor or administrator of the estate to be cited to appear and render under oath an exhibit of the condition of the estate.
Acts 1955, 54th Leg., p. 88, ch. 55, eff. Jan. 1, 1956.

§ 263. Bond Required to Withdraw Estate From Administration

When the executor or administrator has rendered the required exhibit, the persons entitled to such estate, or any of them, or any persons for them, may execute and deliver to the court a bond payable to the judge, and his successors in office, to be approved by the court, for an amount equal to at least double the gross appraised value of the estate as shown by the appraisement and list of claims returned, conditioned that the persons who execute such bond shall pay all the debts against the estate not paid that have been or shall be allowed by the executor or administrator and approved by the court, or that have been or shall be established by suit against said estate, and will pay to the executor or administrator any balance that shall be found to be due him by the judgment of the court on his exhibit.
Acts 1955, 54th Leg., p. 88, ch. 55, eff. Jan. 1, 1956.

§ 264. Court's Order

When such bond has been given and approved, the court shall thereupon enter an order directing and requiring the executor or administrator to deliver forthwith to all persons entitled to any portion of the estate the portion or portions of such estate to which they are entitled.
Acts 1955, 54th Leg., p. 88, ch. 55, eff. Jan. 1, 1956.

§ 265. Order of Discharge

When an estate has been so withdrawn from further administration, an order shall be entered discharging the executor or administrator and declaring the administration closed.
Acts 1955, 54th Leg., p. 88, ch. 55, eff. Jan. 1, 1956.

§ 266. Lien on Property of Estate Withdrawn From Administration

A lien shall exist on all of the estate withdrawn from administration in the hands of the distributees, and those claiming under them with notice of such lien, to secure the ultimate payment of the aforesaid bond and of the debts and claims secured thereby.
Acts 1955, 54th Leg., p. 88, ch. 55, eff. Jan. 1, 1956.

§ 267. Partition of Estate Withdrawn From Administration

Any person entitled to any portion of the estate withdrawn from further administration may, on written application to the court, cause a partition and distribution to be made among the persons entitled thereto, in accordance with the provisions of this Code pertaining to the partition and distribution of estates.
Acts 1955, 54th Leg., p. 88, ch. 55, eff. Jan. 1, 1956.

§ 268. Creditors May Sue on Bond

Any creditor of an estate withdrawn from administration whose debt or claim is unpaid and is not barred by limitation shall have the right to sue on the bond in his own name, and shall be entitled to judgment thereon for such debt or claim as he shall establish against the estate.
Acts 1955, 54th Leg., p. 88, ch. 55, eff. Jan. 1, 1956.

§ 269. Creditors May Sue Distributees

Any creditor of an estate withdrawn from administration whose debt or claim is unpaid and is not barred by limitation may sue any distributee who has received any of the estate, or he may sue all the distributees together, but no one of such distributees shall be liable beyond his just proportion according to the amount of the estate he shall have received in the distribution.
Acts 1955, 54th Leg., p. 88, ch. 55, eff. Jan. 1, 1956.

Part 3. Setting Apart Homestead and Other Exempt Property, and Fixing the Family Allowance

Statutes in Context

A homestead is "the dwelling house constituting the family residence, together with the land on which it is situated and the appurtenances connected therewith." *Farrington v. First Nat'l Bank of Bellville,* 753 S.W.2d

248 (Tex. App. — Houston [1st Dist.] 1988, *writ denied*). Homesteads are classified by property type as either a rural homestead or an urban homestead, and the size of the exemption varies depending on this classification. *See Statutes in Context* to Texas Constitution Article XVI, § 51.

The source of the tremendous protection granted to Texas homesteads is Article XVI, § 50 of the Texas Constitution. This section establishes the protection without dollar value limitation and then lists exceptions, that is, situations in which the homestead is not protected. *See Statutes in Context* to Texas Constitution Article XVI, § 50.

§ 270. Liability of Homestead for Debts

The homestead shall not be liable for the payment of any of the debts of the estate, except for:

(1) the purchase money thereof;

(2) the taxes due thereon;

(3) work and material used in constructing improvements thereon if the requirements of Section 50(a)(5), Article XVI, Texas Constitution, are met;

(4) an owelty of partition imposed against the entirety of the property by court order or by a written agreement of the parties to the partition, including a debt of one spouse in favor of the other spouse resulting from a division or an award of a family homestead in a divorce proceeding;

(5) the refinance of a lien against a homestead, including a federal tax lien resulting from the tax debt of both spouses, if the homestead is a family homestead, or from the tax debt of the decedent;

(6) an extension of credit on the homestead if the requirements of Section 50(a)(6), Article XVI, Texas Constitution, are met; or

(7) a reverse mortgage.

Acts 1955, 54th Leg., p. 88, ch. 55, eff. Jan. 1, 1956. Amended by Acts 1979, 66th Leg., p. 35, ch. 24, § 1, eff. Aug. 27, 1979. Amended by Acts 1999, 76th Leg., ch. 487, § 1, eff. Sept. 1, 1999; Acts 1999, 76th Leg., ch. 855, § 9, eff. Sept. 1, 1999.

Statutes in Context

The exempt property which the court sets aside includes the homestead as discussed in § 270 as well as exempt personal property under Property Code §§ 42.001 - 42.005.

§ 271. Exempt Property to Be Set Apart

(a) Unless an affidavit is filed under Subsection (b) of this section, immediately after the inventory, appraisement, and list of claims have been approved, the court shall, by order, set apart for the use and benefit of the surviving spouse and minor children and unmarried children remaining with the family of the deceased, all such property of the estate as is exempt from execution or forced sale by the constitution and laws of the state.

(b) Before the approval of the inventory, appraisement, and list of claims, a surviving spouse, any person who is authorized to act on behalf of minor children of the deceased, or any unmarried children remaining with the family of the deceased may apply to the court to have exempt property set aside by filing an application and a verified affidavit listing all of the property that the applicant claims is exempt. The applicant bears the burden of proof by a preponderance of the evidence at any hearing on the application. The court shall set aside property of the decedent's estate that the court finds is exempt.

Acts 1955, 54th Leg., p. 88, ch. 55, eff. Jan. 1, 1956. Amended by Acts 1979, 66th Leg., p. 35, ch. 24, § 2, eff. Aug. 27, 1979; Amended by Acts 1993, 73rd Leg., ch. 846, § 18, eff. Sept. 1, 1993.

Statutes in Context

For a discussion of the rights of the surviving spouse, minor children, and unmarried children living at home to occupy the homestead, *see Statutes in Context* to Texas Constitution Article XVI, § 52.

§ 272. To Whom Delivered

The exempt property set apart to the surviving spouse and children shall be delivered by the executor or administrator without delay as follows: (a) If there be a surviving spouse and no children, or if the children be the children of the surviving spouse, the whole of such property shall be delivered to the surviving spouse. (b) If there be children and no surviving spouse, such property, except the homestead, shall be delivered to such children if they be of lawful age, or to their guardian if they be minors. (c) If there be children of the deceased of whom the surviving spouse is not the parent, the share of such children in such exempted property, except the homestead, shall be delivered to such children if they be of lawful age, or to their guardian, if they be minors. (d) In all cases, the homestead shall be delivered to the surviving spouse, if there be one, and if there be no surviving spouse, to the guardian of the minor children and unmarried children, if any, living with the family.

Acts 1955, 54th Leg., p. 88, ch. 55, eff. Jan. 1, 1956. Amended by Acts 1979, 66th Leg., p. 35, ch. 24, § 3, eff. Aug. 27, 1979.

Statutes in Context

If the decedent did not have a homestead (e.g., the decedent lived in rental accommodations), then other property up to a value of $15,000 may be set aside instead. Likewise, if the decedent did not have exempt personal property, an allowance of up to $5,000 of other property may be set aside. Note that these "in lieu of" values are significantly less than the amounts available if the actual exempt property is in the estate (unlimited value of homestead; larger dollar values for exempt personal property).

§ 273. Allowance in Lieu of Exempt Property

In case there should not be among the effects of the deceased all or any of the specific articles exempted from execution or forced sale by the Constitution and laws of this state, the court shall make a reasonable allowance in lieu thereof, to be paid to such surviving spouse and children, or such of them as there are, as hereinafter provided. The allowance in lieu of a homestead shall in no case exceed $15,000 and the allowance for other exempted property shall in no case exceed $5,000, exclusive of the allowance for the support of the surviving spouse and minor children which is hereinafter provided for.

Acts 1955, 54th Leg., p. 88, ch. 55, eff. Jan. 1, 1956. Amended by Acts 1977, 65th Leg., p. 351, ch. 172, § 1, eff. Aug. 29, 1977; Acts 1979, 66th Leg., p. 35, ch. 24, § 4, eff. Aug. 27, 1979; Amended by Acts 1993, 73rd Leg., ch. 846, § 19, eff. Sept. 1, 1993.

§ 274. How Allowance Paid

The allowance made in lieu of any of the exempted property shall be paid either in money out of the funds of the estate that come to the hands of the executor or administrator, or in any property of the deceased that such surviving spouse or children, if they be of lawful age, or their guardian if they be minors, shall choose to take at the appraisement, or a part thereof, or both, as they shall select; provided, however, that property specifically bequeathed or devised to another may be so taken, or may be sold to raise funds for the allowance as hereinafter provided, only if the other available property shall be insufficient to provide the allowance.

Acts 1955, 54th Leg., p. 88, ch. 55, eff. Jan. 1, 1956. Amended by Acts 1979, 66th Leg., p. 36, ch. 24, § 5, eff. Aug. 27, 1979.

§ 275. To Whom Allowance Paid

The allowance in lieu of exempt property shall be paid by the executor or administrator, as follows: (a) If there be a surviving spouse and no children, or if all the children be the children of the surviving spouse, the whole shall be paid to such surviving spouse.

(b) If there be children and no surviving spouse, the whole shall be paid to and equally divided among them if they be of lawful age, but if any of such children are minors, their shares shall be paid to their guardian or guardians.

(c) If there be a surviving spouse, and children of the deceased, some of whom are not children of the surviving spouse, the surviving spouse shall receive one-half of the whole, plus the shares of the children of whom the survivor is the parent, and the remaining shares shall be paid to the children of whom the survivor is not the parent, or, if they are minors, to their guardian.

Acts 1955, 54th Leg., p. 88, ch. 55, eff. Jan. 1, 1956. Amended by Acts 1979, 66th Leg., p. 36, ch. 24, § 6, eff. Aug. 27, 1979.

§ 276. Sale to Raise Allowance

If there be no property of the deceased that such surviving spouse or children are willing to take for such allowance, or not a sufficiency, and there be no funds, or not sufficient funds, of the estate in the hands of such executor or administrator to pay such allowance, or any part thereof, the court, on the application in writing of such surviving spouse and children, shall order a sale of so much of the estate for cash as will be sufficient to raise the amount of such allowance, or a part thereof, as the case requires.

Acts 1955, 54th Leg., p. 88, ch. 55, eff. Jan. 1, 1956. Amended by Acts 1979, 66th Leg., p. 36, ch. 24, § 7, eff. Aug. 27, 1979.

§ 277. Preference of Liens

If property upon which there is a valid subsisting lien or encumbrance shall be set apart to the surviving spouse or children as exempt property, or appropriated to make up allowances made in lieu of exempt property or for the support of the surviving spouse or children, the debts secured by such lien shall, if necessity requires, be either paid or continued as against such property. This provision applies to all estates, whether solvent or insolvent.

Acts 1955, 54th Leg., p. 88, ch. 55, eff. Jan. 1, 1956. Amended by Acts 1979, 66th Leg., p. 36, ch. 24, § 8, eff. Aug. 27, 1979.

Statutes in Context

If the estate is solvent, the exempt personal property passes to the heirs or beneficiaries under § 278. Although this may seem to harm the surviving spouse and minor children, it actually does not because if the estate is solvent, there will be property to award a family allowance under § 286.

§ 278. When Estate Is Solvent

If, upon a final settlement of the estate, it shall appear that the same is solvent, the exempted property, except the homestead or any allowance in lieu thereof, shall be subject to partition and distribution among the heirs and distributees of such estate in like manner as the other property of the estate.

Acts 1955, 54th Leg., p. 88, ch. 55, eff. Jan. 1, 1956.

Statutes in Context

If the estate is insolvent, the surviving spouse and children retain the exempt property free and clear of the claims of creditors as well as of the decedent's beneficiaries or heirs under § 279. This rule does not, however, actually deprive the beneficiaries or heirs of their property because if the property were not given to the surviving spouse and children, the estate creditors would have been able to reach it and the beneficiaries and heirs would not have received it anyway.

§ 279. When Estate is Insolvent

Should the estate, upon final settlement, prove to be insolvent, the title of the surviving spouse and children to all the property and allowances set apart or paid

to them under the provisions of this Code shall be absolute, and shall not be taken for any of the debts of the estate except as hereinafter provided.
Acts 1955, 54th Leg., p. 88, ch. 55, eff. Jan. 1, 1956. Amended by Acts 1979, 66th Leg., p. 37, ch. 24, § 9, eff. Aug. 27, 1979.

§ 280. Exempt Property Not Considered in Determining Solvency

In ascertaining whether an estate is solvent or insolvent, the exempt property set apart to the surviving spouse or children, or the allowance in lieu thereof, and the family allowance hereinafter provided for, shall not be estimated or considered as assets of the estate.
Acts 1955, 54th Leg., p. 88, ch. 55, eff. Jan. 1, 1956. Amended by Acts 1979, 66th Leg., p. 37, ch. 24, § 10, eff. Aug. 27, 1979.

Statutes in Context

Exempt personal property is liable for the payment of the decedent's funeral and last sickness expenses up to a total of $15,000. *See* § 322 (defining "Class 1" claims).

---

§ 281. Exempt Property Liable for Certain Debts

The exempt property, other than the homestead or any allowance made in lieu thereof, shall be liable for the payment of Class 1 claims, but such property shall not be liable for any other debts of the estate.
Acts 1955, 54th Leg., p. 88, ch. 55, eff. Jan. 1, 1956; Amended by Acts 1997, 75th Leg., ch. 1302, § 10, eff. Sept. 1, 1997.

§ 282. Nature of Homestead Property Immaterial

The homestead rights of the surviving spouse and children of the deceased are the same whether the homestead be the separate property of the deceased or community property between the surviving spouse and the deceased, and the respective interests of such surviving spouse and children shall be the same in one case as in the other.
Acts 1955, 54th Leg., p. 88, ch. 55, eff. Jan. 1, 1956. Amended by Acts 1979, 66th Leg., p. 37, ch. 24, § 11, eff. Aug. 27, 1979.

Statutes in Context

For a discussion of the rights of the surviving spouse, minor children, and unmarried children living at home to occupy the homestead, *see Statutes in Context* to Texas Constitution Article XVI, § 52.

---

§ 283. Homestead Rights of Surviving Spouse

On the death of the husband or wife, leaving a spouse surviving, the homestead shall descend and vest in like manner as other real property of the deceased and shall be governed by the same laws of descent and distribution.
Acts 1955, 54th Leg., p. 88, ch. 55, eff. Jan. 1, 1956. Amended by Acts 1979, 66th Leg., p. 37, ch. 24, § 12, eff. Aug. 27, 1979.

§ 284. When Homestead Not Partitioned

The homestead shall not be partitioned among the heirs of the deceased during the lifetime of the surviving spouse, or so long as the survivor elects to use or occupy the same as a homestead, or so long as the guardian of the minor children of the deceased is permitted, under the order of the proper court having jurisdiction, to use and occupy the same.
Acts 1955, 54th Leg., p. 88, ch. 55, eff. Jan. 1, 1956. Amended by Acts 1979, 66th Leg., p. 37, ch. 24, § 13, eff. Aug. 27, 1979.

§ 285. When Homestead Can Be Partitioned

When the surviving spouse dies or sells his or her interest in the homestead, or elects no longer to use or occupy the same as a homestead, or when the proper court no longer permits the guardian of the minor children to use and occupy the same as a homestead, it may be partitioned among the respective owners thereof in like manner as other property held in common.
Acts 1955, 54th Leg., p. 88, ch. 55, eff. Jan. 1, 1956. Amended by Acts 1979, 66th Leg., p. 37, ch. 24, § 14, eff. Aug. 27, 1979.

Statutes in Context

Sections 286-293 provide an allowance for the surviving spouse and minor children based on need. There is no allowance if the spouse or minor child has adequate property. *See* § 288. (There is also no allowance for an unmarried child remaining with the family.)

Unlike many states, there is no statutorily set maximum amount. The amount is based on what is necessary to support the surviving spouse or minor children for one year from the time of death. *See* § 287. This amount is treated as a debt of the estate. In other words, it does not reduce the value of property the surviving spouse and minor children receive under the will or by intestacy (that is, the family allowance is not an advancement or satisfaction).

---

§ 286. Family Allowance to Surviving Spouses and Minors

(a) Unless an affidavit is filed under Subsection (b) of this section, immediately after the inventory, appraisement, and list of claims have been approved, the court shall fix a family allowance for the support of the surviving spouse and minor children of the deceased.

(b) Before the approval of the inventory, appraisement, and list of claims, a surviving spouse or any person who is authorized to act on behalf of minor children of the deceased may apply to the court to have the court fix the family allowance by filing an applica-

tion and a verified affidavit describing the amount necessary for the maintenance of the surviving spouse and minor children for one year after the date of the death of the decedent and describing the spouse's separate property and any property that minor children have in their own right. The applicant bears the burden of proof by a preponderance of the evidence at any hearing on the application. The court shall fix a family allowance for the support of the surviving spouse and minor children of the deceased.
Acts 1955, 54th Leg., p. 88, ch. 55, eff. Jan. 1, 1956. Amended by Acts 1979, 66th Leg., p. 38, ch. 24, § 15, eff. Aug. 27, 1979; Amended by Acts 1993, 73rd Leg., ch. 846, § 20, eff. Sept. 1, 1993.

§ 287. Amount of Family Allowance

Such allowance shall be of an amount sufficient for the maintenance of such surviving spouse and minor children for one year from the time of the death of the testator or intestate. The allowance shall be fixed with regard to the facts or circumstances then existing and those anticipated to exist during the first year after such death. The allowance may be paid either in a lump sum or in installments, as the court shall order.
Acts 1955, 54th Leg., p. 88, ch. 55, eff. Jan. 1, 1956. Amended by Acts 1979, 66th Leg., p. 38, ch. 24, § 16, eff. Aug. 27, 1979.

§ 288. When Family Allowance Not Made

No such allowance shall be made for the surviving spouse when the survivor has separate property adequate to the survivor's maintenance; nor shall such allowance be made for the minor children when they have property in their own right adequate to their maintenance.
Acts 1955, 54th Leg., p. 88, ch. 55, eff. Jan. 1, 1956. Amended by Acts 1979, 66th Leg., p. 38, ch. 24, § 17, eff. Aug. 27, 1979.

§ 289. Order Fixing Family Allowance

When an allowance has been fixed, an order shall be entered stating the amount thereof, providing how the same shall be payable, and directing the executor or administrator to pay the same in accordance with law.
Acts 1955, 54th Leg., p. 88, ch. 55, eff. Jan. 1, 1956.

Statutes in Context

The family allowance has priority over the claims of other creditors except for the first $15,000 of funeral and last illness expenses. See § 322 (defining "Class 1" claims).

---

§ 290. Family Allowance Preferred

The family allowance made for the support of the surviving spouse and minor children of the deceased shall be paid in preference to all other debts or charges against the estate, except Class 1 claims.
Acts 1955, 54th Leg., p. 88, ch. 55, eff. Jan. 1, 1956. Amended by Acts 1979, 66th Leg., p. 38, ch. 24, § 18, eff. Aug. 27, 1979; Amended by Acts 1997, 75th Leg., ch. 1302, § 11, eff. Sept. 1, 1997.

§ 291. To Whom Family Allowance Paid

The executor or administrator shall apportion and pay the family allowance:

(a) To the surviving spouse, if there be one, for the use of the survivor and the minor children, if such children be the survivor's.

(b) If the surviving spouse is not the parent of such minor children, or of some of them, the portion of such allowance necessary for the support of such minor child or children of which the survivor is not the parent shall be paid to the guardian or guardians of such child or children.

(c) If there be no surviving spouse, the allowance to the minor child or children shall be paid to the guardian or guardians of such minor child or children.

(d) If there be a surviving spouse and no minor child or children, the entire allowance shall be paid to the surviving spouse.
Acts 1955, 54th Leg., p. 88, ch. 55, eff. Jan. 1, 1956. Amended by Acts 1979, 66th Leg., p. 38, ch. 24, § 19, eff. Aug. 27, 1979.

§ 292. May Take Property for Family Allowance

The surviving spouse, or the guardian of the minor children, as the case may be, shall have the right to take in payment of such allowance, or any part thereof, any of the personal property of the estate at its appraised value as shown by the appraisement; provided, however, that property specifically devised or bequeathed to another may be so taken, or may be sold to raise funds for the allowance as hereinafter provided, only if the other available property shall be insufficient to provide the allowance.
Acts 1955, 54th Leg., p. 88, ch. 55, eff. Jan. 1, 1956. Amended by Acts 1979, 66th Leg., p. 39, ch. 24, § 20, eff. Aug. 27, 1979.

§ 293. Sale to Raise Funds for Family Allowance

If there be no personal property of the deceased that the surviving spouse or guardian is willing to take for such allowance, or not a sufficiency of them, and if there be no funds or not sufficient funds in the hands of such executor or administrator to pay such allowance, or any part thereof, then the court, as soon as the inventory, appraisement, and list of claims are returned and approved, shall order a sale of so much of the estate for cash as will be sufficient to raise the amount of such allowance, or a part thereof, as the case requires.
Acts 1955, 54th Leg., p. 88, ch. 55, eff. Jan. 1, 1956. Amended by Acts 1979, 66th Leg., p. 39, ch. 24, § 21, eff. Aug. 27, 1979.

Part 4. Presentment and Payment of Claims

Statutes in Context

The personal representative must alert the decedent's creditors that the decedent has died and that the court has appointed a personal representative. This information permits the creditors to take the proper steps to present their claims so they can get paid. There are four types of notice.

1. Notice to Comptroller of Public Accounts. The personal representative must give notice to the comptroller of public accounts within one month of receiving letters if the decedent remitted or should have remitted taxes administered by the comptroller. Service is by certified or registered mail. *See* § 294(a). Because the personal representative may not yet know whether the decedent remitted or should have remitted these taxes, it may be good practice to give the notice in all cases.

2. General Notice to Creditors. Within one month of receiving letters, the personal representative must publish notice in a newspaper in the county where letters were issued. *See* § 294(a). In large population counties, this notice is often published in specialized legal newspapers rather than the local paper.

3. Notice to Unsecured Creditors. The personal representative has the option to give notice by certified or registered mail to the unsecured creditors of the estate (e.g., credit card issuers and utility providers). If the creditor does not present a claim within 4 months of receipt of the notice, the creditor is barred from pursuing the claim even if the statute of limitations on the claim has not otherwise run. This provision is often called the *non-claim statute. See* § 294(d).

4. Notice to Secured Creditors. *See Statutes in Context* to § 295.

§ 294. Notice by Representative of Appointment

(a) Giving of Notice Required. Within one month after receiving letters, personal representatives of estates shall send to the comptroller of public accounts by certified or registered mail if the decedent remitted or should have remitted taxes administered by the comptroller of public accounts and publish in some newspaper, printed in the county where the letters were issued, if there be one, a notice requiring all persons having claims against the estate being administered to present the same within the time prescribed by law. The notice shall include the date of issuance of letters held by the representative, the address to which claims may be presented, and an instruction of the representative's choice that claims be addressed in care of the representative, in care of the representative's attorney, or in care of "Representative, Estate of ________" (naming the estate).

(b) Proof of Publication. A copy of such printed notice, together with the affidavit of the publisher, duly sworn to and subscribed before a proper officer, to the effect that the notice was published as provided in this Code for the service of citation or notice by publication, shall be filed in the court where the cause is pending.

(c) When No Newspaper Printed in the County. When no newspaper is printed in the county, the notice shall be posted and the return made and filed as required by this Code.

(d) Permissive Notice to Unsecured Creditors. At any time before an estate administration is closed, the personal representative may give notice by certified or registered mail, with return receipt requested, to an unsecured creditor having a claim for money against the estate expressly stating that the creditor must present a claim within four months after the date of the receipt of the notice or the claim is barred, if the claim is not barred by the general statutes of limitation. The notice must include:

(1) the dates of issuance of letters held by the representative;

(2) the address to which claims may be presented; and

(3) an instruction of the representative's choice that the claim be addressed in care of:

(A) the representative;

(B) the representative's attorney; or

(C) "Representative, Estate of" (naming the estate).

Acts 1955, 54th Leg., p. 88, ch. 55, eff. Jan. 1, 1956; Subsec. (a) amended by Acts 1981, 67th Leg., p. 243, ch. 102, § 9, eff. Aug. 31, 1981; Subsec. (a) amended by Acts 1991, 72nd Leg., ch. 464, § 1, eff. Aug. 26, 1991; Subsec. (a) amended by and (d) added by Acts 1995, 74th Leg., ch. 1054, § 2, eff. Jan. 1, 1996.

Statutes in Context

Within 2 months of receiving letters, the personal representative must give notice to the holders of claims which are secured by mortgages, deeds of trust, Article 9 security interests, etc. Service is by registered or certified mail. *See* § 295.

§ 295. Notice to Holders of Secured Claims

(a) When notice required for secured claimants. Within two months after receiving letters, the personal representative of an estate shall give notice of the issuance of such letters to each and every person known to the personal representative to have a claim for money against the estate of a decedent that is secured by real or personal property of the estate. Within a reasonable time after the personal representative obtains actual knowledge of the existence of a person having a secured claim for money and to whom notice was not previously given, the personal representative shall give notice to the person of the issuance of letters.

(b) How notice shall be given. The notice stating the original grant of letters shall be given by mailing same by certified or registered mail, with return receipt requested, addressed to the record holder of such indebtedness or claim at the record holder's last known post office address.

(c) Proof of service of notice. A copy of each notice required by Subsection (a) of this section and a copy of the return receipt and an affidavit of the representative, stating that said notice was mailed as required by law, giving the name of the person to whom the notice was mailed, if not shown on the notice or receipt, shall be filed with the clerk of the court from which letters were issued.

Acts 1955, 54th Leg., p. 88, ch. 55, eff. Jan. 1, 1956; Subsec. (b) amended by Acts 1987, 70th Leg., ch. 461, § 1, eff. Sept. 1, 1987. Amended by Acts 1991, 72nd Leg., ch. 895, § 13, eff. Sept. 1, 1991; Subsecs. (a), (b) amended by Acts 1993, 73rd Leg., ch. 957, § 46, eff. Sept. 1, 1993. Amended by Acts 1995, 74th Leg., ch. 1054, § 3, eff. Jan. 1, 1996.

§ 296. One Notice Sufficient

If the notices required by the two preceding Sections have been given by a former representative, or by one where several are acting, that shall be sufficient, and need not be repeated by any successor or co-representative.

Acts 1955, 54th Leg., p. 88, ch. 55, eff. Jan. 1, 1956.

§ 297. Penalty for Failure to Give Notice

If the representative fails to give the notices required in preceding Sections, or to cause such notices to be given, the representative and the sureties on the representative's bond shall be liable for any damage which any person suffers by reason of such neglect, unless it appears that such person had notice otherwise.

Acts 1955, 54th Leg., p. 88, ch. 55, eff. Jan. 1, 1956; Amended by Acts 1995, 74th Leg., ch. 1054, § 4, eff. Jan. 1, 1996.

Statutes in Context

Normally, a creditor may present a claim anytime before the estate is closed. There are two main exceptions to this rule: (1) if the statute of limitations on the claim has run or (2) an unsecured creditor did not present the claim within 4 months after receiving notice. *See* § 298. (*See also* Civil Practice & Remedies Code § 16.062 which extends the running of a limitations period for 12 months after the decedent's death, unless a personal representative is appointed sooner, in which case limitations resumes running at the time the personal representative qualifies.)

§ 298. Claims Against Estates of Decedents

(a) Time for Presentation of Claims. A claim may be presented to the personal representative at any time before the estate is closed if suit on the claim has not been barred by the general statutes of limitation. If a claim of an unsecured creditor for money is not presented within four months after the date of receipt of the notice permitted by Section 294(d), the claim is barred.

(b) Claims Barred by Limitation Not to Be Allowed or Approved. No claims for money against a decedent, or against the estate of the decedent, on which a suit is barred under Subsection (a) of this section, Section 313, or Section 317(a) or by a general statute of limitation applicable thereto shall be allowed by a personal representative. If allowed by the representative and the court is satisfied that the claim is barred or that limitation has run, the claim shall be disapproved.

Acts 1955, 54th Leg., p. 88, ch. 55, eff. Jan. 1, 1956. Amended by Acts 1971, 62nd Leg., p. 2992, ch. 988, § 1, eff. June 15, 1971; Amended by Acts 1993, 73rd Leg., ch. 957, § 47, eff. Sept. 1, 1993; Acts 1995, 74th Leg., ch. 1054, § 5, eff. Jan. 1, 1996.

Statutes in Context

Section 299 provides that the statute of limitations is tolled when a creditor files or deposits a claim for money.

§ 299. Tolling of General Statutes of Limitation

The general statutes of limitation are tolled on the date:

(1) a claim for money is filed or deposited with the clerk; or

(2) suit is brought against the personal representative of an estate with respect to a claim of the estate that is not required to be presented to the personal representative.

Acts 1955, 54th Leg., p. 88, ch. 55, eff. Jan. 1, 1956; Amended by Acts 1997, 75th Leg., ch. 1302, § 12, eff. Sept. 1, 1997.

Statutes in Context

The creditor must submit a sworn affidavit supporting the claim under § 301.

§ 301. Claims for Money Must be Authenticated

No personal representative of a decedent's estate shall allow, and the court shall not approve, a claim for money against such estate, unless such claim be supported by an affidavit that the claim is just and that all legal offsets, payments, and credits known to the affiant have been allowed. If the claim is not founded on a written instrument or account, the affidavit shall also state the facts upon which the claim is founded. A photostatic copy of any exhibit or voucher necessary to prove a claim may be offered with and attached to the claim in lieu of the original.

Acts 1955, 54th Leg., p. 88, ch. 55, eff. Jan. 1, 1956; Amended by Acts 1993, 73rd Leg., ch. 957, § 48, eff. Sept. 1, 1993; Acts 1995, 74th Leg., ch. 1054, § 6, eff. Jan. 1, 1996.

§ 302. When Defects of Form Are Waived

Any defect of form, or claim of insufficiency of exhibits or vouchers presented, shall be deemed waived

by the personal representative unless written objection thereto has been made within thirty days after presentment of the claim, and filed with the county clerk.
Acts 1955, 54th Leg., p. 88, ch. 55, eff. Jan. 1, 1956.

§ 303. Evidence Concerning Lost or Destroyed Claims

If evidence of a claim is lost or destroyed, the claimant or an authorized representative or agent of the claimant, may make affidavit to the fact of such loss or destruction, stating the amount, date, and nature of the claim and when due, and that the same is just, and that all legal offsets, payments and credits known to the affiant have been allowed, and that the claimant is still the owner of the claim; and the claim must be proved by disinterested testimony taken in open court, or by oral or written deposition, before the claim is approved. If such claim is allowed or approved without such affidavit, or if it is approved without satisfactory proof, such allowance or approval shall be void.
Acts 1955, 54th Leg., p. 88, ch. 55, eff. Jan. 1, 1956; Amended by Acts 1995, 74th Leg., ch. 1054, § 7, eff. Jan. 1, 1996.

§ 304. Authentication of Claim by Others Than Individual Owners

An authorized officer or representative of a corporation or other entity shall make the affidavit required to authenticate a claim of such corporation or entity. When an affidavit is made by an officer of a corporation, or by an executor, administrator, trustee, assignee, agent, representative, or attorney, it shall be sufficient to state in such affidavit that the person making it has made diligent inquiry and examination, and that he believes that the claim is just and that all legal offsets, payments, and credits made known to the affiant have been allowed.
Acts 1955, 54th Leg., p. 88, ch. 55, eff. Jan. 1, 1956; Amended by Acts 1993, 73rd Leg., ch. 957, § 49, eff. Sept. 1, 1993; Acts 1995, 74th Leg., ch. 1054, § 8, eff. Jan. 1, 1996.

Statutes in Context

A secured creditor must determine how the creditor wants the claim handled. The creditor must make this election by the later of (a) 4 months after the receipt of notice or (b) 6 months after letters are issued. *See* § 306(b)

1. Preferred Debt and Lien. If the creditor elects preferred debt and lien status, the creditor receives top priority over the collateral. However, if the value of the collateral is less than the debt, the creditor will not have a right to recover the deficiency from the estate. *See* § 306(d). Preferred debt and lien status is presumed unless the creditor affirmatively elects otherwise. *See* § 306(b).

2. Matured Secured Claim. If the creditor elects matured secured claim status, the creditor retains the right to seek a deficiency if the value of the collateral is less than the amount owed. However, the creditor must subordinate the claim to (a) the first $15,000 of funeral and last illness expenses, (b) the family allowance, and (c) administration and other expenses. *See* § 306(c).

---

§ 306. Method of Handling Secured Claims for Money

(a) Specifications of Claim. When a secured claim for money against an estate is presented, the claimant shall specify therein, in addition to all other matters required to be specified in claims:

(1) Whether it is desired to have the claim allowed and approved as a matured secured claim to be paid in due course of administration, in which event it shall be so paid if allowed and approved; or

(2) Whether it is desired to have the claim allowed, approved, and fixed as a preferred debt and lien against the specific property securing the indebtedness and paid according to the terms of the contract which secured the lien, in which event it shall be so allowed and approved if it is a valid lien; provided, however, that the personal representative may pay said claim prior to maturity if it is for the best interest of the estate to do so.

(b) Time for Specification of Secured Claim. Within six months after the date letters are granted, or within four months after the date notice is received under Section 295 of this code, whichever is later, the secured creditor may present the creditor's claim and shall specify whether the claim is to be allowed and approved under Paragraph (1) or (2) of Subsection (a) of this section. If a secured claim is not presented within the time prescribed by this subsection or if the claim is presented without specifying how the claim is to be paid, it shall be treated as a claim to be paid in accordance with Paragraph (2) of Subsection (a) hereof.

(c) Matured Secured Claims. If a claim has been allowed and approved as a matured secured claim under Paragraph (1) of Subsection (a) of this section, the claim shall be paid in due course of administration and the secured creditor is not entitled to exercise any other remedies in a manner that prevents the preferential payment of claims and allowances described by Paragraphs (1) through (3) of Section 320(a) of this code.

(d) Approved Claim as Preferred Lien Against Property. When an indebtedness has been allowed and approved under Paragraph (2) of Subsection (a) hereof, no further claim shall be made against other assets of the estate by reason thereof, but the same thereafter shall remain a preferred lien against the property securing same, and the property shall remain security for the debt in any distribution or sale thereof prior to final maturity and payment of the debt.

(e) Payment of Maturities on Preferred Debt and Lien Claims. If property securing a claim allowed, approved, and fixed under Paragraph (2) of Subsection (a) hereof is not sold or distributed within six months from the date letters are granted, the representative of the estate shall promptly pay all maturities which have accrued on the debt according to the terms thereof, and shall perform all the terms of any contract securing same. If the representative defaults in such payment or performance, on application of the claimholder, the court shall:

(1) require the sale of said property subject to the unmatured part of such debt and apply the proceeds of the sale to the liquidation of the maturities;

(2) require the sale of the property free of the lien and apply the proceeds to the payment of the whole debt; or

(3) authorize foreclosure by the claimholder as provided by Subsections (f) through (k) of this section.

(f) Foreclosure of Preferred Liens. An application by a claimholder under Subsection (e) of this section to foreclose the claimholder's lien or security interest on property securing a claim that has been allowed, approved, and fixed under Paragraph (2) of Subsection (a) of this section shall be supported by affidavit of the claimholder that:

(1) describes the property or part of the property to be sold by foreclosure;

(2) describes the amounts of the claimholder's outstanding debt;

(3) describes the maturities that have accrued on the debt according to the terms of the debt;

(4) describes any other debts secured by a mortgage, lien, or security interest against the property that are known by the claimholder;

(5) contains a statement that the claimholder has no knowledge of the existence of any debts secured by the property other than those described by the application; and

(6) requests permission for the claimholder to foreclose the claimholder's mortgage, lien, or security interest.

(g) Citation. On the filing of an application, the clerk shall issue citation by personal service to the personal representative and to any person described by the application as having other debts secured by a mortgage, lien, or security interest against the property and by posting to any other person interested in the estate. The citation must require the person to appear and show cause why foreclosure should or should not be permitted.

(h) Setting of Hearing on Application. When an application is filed, the clerk shall immediately notify the judge. The judge shall schedule in writing a date for a hearing on the application. The judge may, by entry on the docket or otherwise, continue the hearing for a reasonable time to allow an interested person to obtain an appraisal or other evidence concerning the fair market value of the property that is the subject of the application. If the interested person requests an unreasonable time for a continuance, the person must show good cause for the continuance.

(i) Hearing. (1) At the hearing, if the court finds that there is a default in payment or performance under the contract that secures the payment of the claim, the court shall:

(A) require the sale of the property subject to the unmatured part of the debt and apply the proceeds of the sale to the liquidation of the maturities;

(B) require the sale of the property free of the lien and apply the proceeds to the payment of the whole debt; or

(C) authorize foreclosure by the claimholder as provided by Subsection (f) of this section.

(2) When the court grants a claimholder the right of foreclosure, the court shall authorize the claimholder to foreclose the claimholder's mortgage, lien, or security interest in accordance with the provisions of the document creating the mortgage, lien, or security interest or in any other manner allowed by law. In the discretion of the court and based on the evidence presented at the hearing, the court may fix a minimum price for the property to be sold by foreclosure that does not exceed the fair market value of the property. If the court fixes a minimum price, the property may not be sold at the foreclosure sale for a lower price.

(j) Appeal. Any person interested in the estate may appeal an order issued under Subsection (i)(1)(C) of this section.

(k) Unsuccessful Foreclosure. If a foreclosure sale authorized under this section is conducted and the property is not sold because no bid at the sale met the minimum price set by the court, the claimholder may file another application under Subsection (f) of this section. The court may, in the court's discretion, eliminate or modify the minimum price requirement and grant permission for another foreclosure sale.

Acts 1955, 54th Leg., p. 88, ch. 55, eff. Jan. 1, 1956; Subsec. (d) amended by Acts 1993, 73rd Leg., ch. 957, § 50, eff. Sept. 1, 1993. Amended by Acts 1995, 74th Leg., ch. 1054, § 9, eff. Jan. 1, 1996. Subsecs. (e), (f), (i), (j) amended by Acts 1997, 75th Leg., ch. 1302, § 13, eff. Sept. 1, 1997.

§ 307. Claims Providing for Attorney's Fees

If the instrument evidencing or supporting a claim provides for attorney's fees, then the claimant may include as a part of the claim the portion of such fee that he has paid or contracted to pay to an attorney to prepare, present, and collect such claim.

Acts 1955, 54th Leg., p. 88, ch. 55, eff. Jan. 1, 1956.

§ 308. Depositing Claims With Clerk

Claims may also be presented by depositing same, with vouchers and necessary exhibits and affidavit attached, with the clerk, who, upon receiving same, shall advise the representative of the estate, or the representative's attorney, by letter mailed to the representative's last known address, of the deposit of same. Should the representative fail to act on said claim within thirty days after it is deposited, then it shall be presumed to be rejected. Failure of the clerk to give notice as required herein shall not affect the validity of

the presentment or the presumption of rejection because not acted upon within said thirty day period. The clerk shall enter a deposited claim on the claim docket.
Acts 1955, 54th Leg., p. 88, ch. 55, eff. Jan. 1, 1956; Amended by Acts 1995, 74th Leg., ch. 1054, § 10, eff. Jan. 1, 1996.

Statutes in Context

A personal representative in a dependent administration has three options once a creditor presents a claim.

1. Accept. The personal representative may accept the claim which means that the personal representative agrees that the creditor's claim is valid. It does not mean that the claim will actually get paid; the claim merely goes in the stack of valid claims to be paid according to the priority rules set forth in the Code.

2. Reject. The personal representative may reject the claim, that is, indicate that the personal representative will not pay the claim. The creditor in a dependent (but not independent) administration must then bring suit within 90 days of the rejection or else the claim is barred. *See* § 313. *See also Statutes in Context* to § 146.

3. Do Nothing. If the personal representative takes no action with respect to the claim within 30 days, the claim is deemed rejected. *See* § 310. This then triggers the running of the creditor's obligation in a dependent administration to bring suit within 90 days under § 313.

Section 309 does not apply to independent administrations. *See Bunting v. Pearson*, 430 S.W.2d 470 (Tex. 1968).

---

§ 309. Memorandum of Allowance or Rejection of Claim

When a duly authenticated claim against an estate is presented to the representative, or deposited with the clerk as heretofore provided, the representative shall, within thirty days after the claim is presented or deposited, endorse thereon, annex thereto, or file with the clerk a memorandum signed by the representative, stating the date of presentation or depositing of the claim, and that the representative allows or rejects it, or what portion thereof the representative allows or rejects.
Acts 1955, 54th Leg., p. 88, ch. 55, eff. Jan. 1, 1956; Amended by Acts 1995, 74th Leg., ch. 1054, § 11, eff. Jan. 1, 1996.

Statutes in Context

Section 310 does not apply to independent administrations. See *Bunting v. Pearson*, 430 S.W.2d 470 (Tex. 1968).

---

§ 310. Failure to Endorse or Annex Memorandum

The failure of a representative of an estate to timely allow or reject a claim under Section 309 of this code shall constitute a rejection of the claim. If the claim is thereafter established by suit, the costs shall be taxed against the representative, individually, or the representative may be removed on the written complaint of any person interested in the claim, after personal service of citation, hearing, and proof, as in other cases of removal.
Acts 1955, 54th Leg., p. 88, ch. 55, eff. Jan. 1, 1956; Amended by Acts 1995, 74th Leg., ch. 1054, § 12, eff. Jan. 1, 1996.

§ 311. When Claims Entered in Docket

After a claim against an estate has been presented to and allowed or rejected by the personal representative, in whole or in part, the claim must be filed with the county clerk of the proper county. The clerk shall enter the claim on the claim docket.
Acts 1955, 54th Leg., p. 88, ch. 55, eff. Jan. 1, 1956. Amended by Acts 1971, 62nd Leg., p. 2992, ch. 988, § 2, eff. June 15, 1971; Amended by Acts 1993, 73rd Leg., ch. 957, § 51, eff. Sept. 1, 1993; Acts 1995, 74th Leg., ch. 1054, § 13, eff. Jan. 1, 1996.

§ 312. Contest of Claims, Action by Court, and Appeals

(a) Contest of Claims. Any person interested in an estate may, at any time before the court has acted upon a claim, appear and object in writing to the approval of the same, or any part thereof, and in such case the parties shall be entitled to process for witnesses, and the court shall hear proof and render judgment as in ordinary suits.

(b) Court's Action Upon Claims. All claims which have been allowed and entered upon the claim docket for a period of ten days shall be acted upon by the court and be either approved in whole or in part or rejected, and they shall also at the same time be classified by the court.

(c) Hearing on Claims. Although a claim may be properly authenticated and allowed, if the court is not satisfied that it is just, the court shall examine the claimant and the personal representative under oath, and hear other evidence necessary to determine the issue. If not then convinced that the claim is just, the court shall disapprove it.

(d) Order of the Court. When the court has acted upon a claim, the court shall also endorse thereon, or annex thereto, a written memorandum dated and signed officially, stating the exact action taken upon such claim, whether approved or disapproved, or approved in part or rejected in part, and stating the classification of the claim. Such orders shall have the force and effect of final judgments.

(e) Appeal. When a claimant or any person interested in an estate shall be dissatisfied with the action of the court upon a claim, the claimant or person may appeal therefrom to the courts of appeals, as from other judgments of the county court in probate matters.
Acts 1955, 54th Leg., p. 88, ch. 55, eff. Jan. 1, 1956. Amended by Acts 1975, 64th Leg., p. 2196, ch. 701, § 4,

eff. June 21, 1975; Subsecs. (a), (e) amended by Acts 1993, 73rd Leg., ch. 957, § 52, eff. Sept. 1, 1993; Subsecs. (c) to (e) amended by Acts 1995, 74th Leg., ch. 1054, § 14, eff. Jan. 1, 1996.

Statutes in Context

Section 313 does not apply to independent administrations. See *Bunting v. Pearson*, 430 S.W.2d 470 (Tex. 1968).

§ 313. Suit on Rejected Claim

When a claim or a part thereof has been rejected by the representative, the claimant shall institute suit thereon in the court of original probate jurisdiction in which the estate is pending within ninety days after such rejection, or the claim shall be barred. When a rejected claim is sued on, the endorsement made on or annexed thereto, or any memorandum of rejection filed with respect to the claim, shall be taken to be true without further proof, unless denied under oath. When a rejected claim or part thereof has been established by suit, no execution shall issue, but the judgment shall be filed in the court in which the cause is pending, entered upon the claim docket, classified by the court, and handled as if originally allowed and approved in due course of administration.

Amended by Acts 1995, 74th Leg., ch. 1054, § 15, eff. Jan. 1, 1996; Acts 2001, 77th Leg., ch. 10, § 3, eff. Sept. 1, 2001.

Statutes in Context

A claim for money must first be presented and rejected before the creditor may sue on the claim. However, this requirement does not apply to a claim which is not "for money" such as an unliquidated tort claim or a claim based on quantum meruit for services rendered.

§ 314. Presentment of Claims a Prerequisite for Judgment

No judgment shall be rendered in favor of a claimant upon any claim for money which has not been legally presented to the representative of an estate, and rejected by the representative or by the court, in whole or in part.

Acts 1955, 54th Leg., p. 88, ch. 55, eff. Jan. 1, 1956; Amended by Acts 1993, 73rd Leg., ch. 957, § 53, eff. Sept. 1, 1993; Acts 1995, 74th Leg., ch. 1054, § 16, eff. Jan. 1, 1996.

§ 315. Costs of Suit With Respect to Claims

All costs incurred in the probate court with respect to claims shall be taxed as follows:

(a) If allowed and approved, the estate shall pay the costs.

(b) If allowed, but disapproved, the claimant shall pay the costs.

(c) If rejected, but established by suit, the estate shall pay the costs.

(d) If rejected, but not established by suit, the claimant shall pay the costs, except as provided by Section 310 of this code.

(e) In suits to establish a claim after rejection in part, if the claimant fails to recover judgment for a greater amount than was allowed or approved, the claimant shall pay all costs.

Acts 1955, 54th Leg., p. 88, ch. 55, eff. Jan. 1, 1956; Amended by Acts 1995, 74th Leg., ch. 1054, § 17, eff. Jan. 1, 1996.

§ 316. Claims Against Personal Representatives

The naming of an executor in a will shall not operate to extinguish any just claim which the deceased had against the person named as executor; and, in all cases where a personal representative is indebted to the testator or intestate, the representative shall account for the debt in the same manner as if it were cash in the representative's hands; provided, however, that if said debt was not due at the time of receiving letters, the representative shall be required to account for it only from the date when it becomes due.

Acts 1955, 54th Leg., p. 88, ch. 55, eff. Jan. 1, 1956; Amended by Acts 1995, 74th Leg., ch. 1054, § 18, eff. Jan. 1, 1996.

Statutes in Context

Section 317 provides special rules for claims which a personal representative has against the estate the personal representative is administering.

§ 317. Claims by Personal Representatives

(a) By Executors or Administrators. The foregoing provisions of this Code relative to the presentation of claims against an estate shall not be construed to apply to any claim of a personal representative against the testator or intestate; but a personal representative holding such claim shall file the same in the court granting the letters, verified by affidavit as required in other cases, within six months after the representative has qualified, or such claim shall be barred.

(b) Action on Such Claims. When a claim by a personal representative has been filed with the court within the required time, such claim shall be entered upon the claim docket and acted upon by the court in the same manner as in other cases, and, when the claim has been acted upon by the court, an appeal from the judgment of the court may be taken as in other cases.

(c) Provisions Not Applicable to Certain Claims. The foregoing provisions relative to the presentment of claims shall not be so construed as to apply to a claim:

(1) of any heir, devisee, or legatee who claims in such capacity;

(2) that accrues against the estate after the granting of letters for which the representative of the estate has contracted; or

(3) for delinquent ad valorem taxes against a decedent's estate that is being administered in probate in:

(A) a county other than the county in which the taxes were imposed; or

(B) the same county in which the taxes were imposed, if the probate proceedings have been pending for more than four years.

Acts 1955, 54th Leg., p. 88, ch. 55, eff. Jan. 1, 1956; Amended by Acts 1993, 73rd Leg., ch. 957, § 54, eff. Sept. 1, 1993; Acts 1995, 74th Leg., ch. 1054, § 19, eff. Jan. 1, 1996; Subsec. (c) amended by Acts 1999, 76th Leg., ch. 1481, § 37, eff. Sept., 1, 1999.

§ 318. Claims Not Allowed After Order for Partition and Distribution

No claim for money against the estate of a decedent shall be allowed by a personal representative and no suit shall be instituted against the representative on any such claim, after an order for final partition and distribution has been made; but, after such an order has been made, the owner of any claim not barred by the laws of limitation shall have an action thereon against the heirs, devisees, legatees, or creditors of the estate, limited to the value of the property received by them in distributions from the estate.

Acts 1955, 54th Leg., p. 88, ch. 55, eff. Jan. 1, 1956; Amended by Acts 1995, 74th Leg., ch. 1054, § 20, eff. Jan. 1, 1996.

§ 319. Claims Not to be Paid Unless Approved

No claim for money against the estate of a decedent, or any part thereof, shall be paid until it has been approved by the court or established by the judgment of a court of competent jurisdiction.

Acts 1955, 54th Leg., p. 88, ch. 55, eff. Jan. 1, 1956; Amended by Acts 1993, 73rd Leg., ch. 957, § 55, eff. Sept. 1, 1993.

Statutes in Context

Sections 320 and 322 provide the priority order for the payment of claims. However, other factors may come into play in determining the payment order. Below is a priority order which attempts to combine the priority rules in a unified list.

1. Federal government claims, e.g., the federal tax lien. 31 U.S.C. § 3713(a). However, federal claims do not have priority over funeral expenses or the family allowance because the decedent did not owe those while alive. (Federal claims do have priority over expenses of last illness because those expenses were obligations of the decedent.)
2. Secured creditor who has preferred debt and lien status vis-à-vis the collateral only. *See* § 306(a)(2).
3. Homestead (or the allowance in lieu thereof). *See* § 281.
4. Funeral expenses and expenses of last sickness up to a combined total of $15,000. *See* §§ 320(a)(1) and 322 (Class 1).
5. Exempt personal property. *See* § 281.
6. Family allowance. *See* §§ 290 and 320(a)(2).
7. Administration and related expenses. *See* §§ 320(a)(3) and 322 (Class 2).
8. Secured creditor who elected matured secured claim status vis-à-vis the collateral only. *See* § 322 (Class 3).
9. Delinquent child support. *See* § 322 (Class 4).
10. Certain Texas tax claims. *See* § 322 (Class 5).
11. Confinement claims. *See* § 322 (Class 6) and Government Code § 501.017.
12. State medical assistance payments. *See* § 322 (Class 7).
13. Unsecured claims approved by the personal representative (may include deficiency amounts of secured claimants who elected matured secured claim status. *See* § 322 (Class 8).
14. Beneficiaries and heirs. *See* § 322B for the abatement order of testamentary gifts.

§ 320. Order of Payment of Claims and Allowances

(a) Priority of Payments. Personal representatives, when they have funds in their hands belonging to the estate, shall pay in the following order:

(1) Funeral expenses and expenses of last sickness, in an amount not to exceed Fifteen Thousand Dollars.

(2) Allowances made to the surviving spouse and children, or to either.

(3) Expenses of administration and the expenses incurred in the preservation, safekeeping, and management of the estate.

(4) Other claims against the estate in the order of their classification.

(b) Sale of Mortgaged Property. If a personal representative has the proceeds of a sale that has been made for the satisfaction of a mortgage, lien, or security interest, and the proceeds, or any part of the proceeds, are not required for the payment of any debts against the estate that have a preference over the mortgage, lien, or security interest, the personal representative shall pay the proceeds to any holder of a mortgage, lien, or security interest. If there is more than one mortgage, lien, or security interest against the property, the personal representative shall pay the holders in the order of the holders' priority. If the personal representative fails to pay proceeds under this subsection, a holder, on proof of the failure to pay, may obtain an order from the court directing the payment to be made.

(c) Claimant's Petition. A claimant whose claim has not been paid may petition the court for determination of his claim at any time before it is barred by the applicable statute of limitations and upon due proof procure an order for its allowance and payment from the estate.

(d) Permissive Order of Payment. After the sixth month after the date letters are granted and on application by the personal representative stating that the personal representative has no actual knowledge of any outstanding enforceable claims against the estate other than the claims already approved and classified by the court, the court may order the personal representative to pay any claim that is allowed and approved.

Acts 1955, 54th Leg., p. 88, ch. 55, eff. Jan. 1, 1956. Amended by Acts 1975, 64th Leg., p. 1818, ch. 554, § 1, eff. Sept. 1, 1975; Acts 1977, 65th Leg., p. 352, ch. 173, § 1, eff. Aug. 29, 1977; Acts 1979, 66th Leg., p. 1876, ch. 758, § 1, eff. Aug. 27, 1979; Subsec. (a) amended by Acts 1987, 70th Leg., ch. 461, § 2, eff. Sept. 1, 1987. Amended by Acts 1993, 73rd Leg., ch. 957, § 56, eff. Sept. 1, 1993; Acts 1995, 74th Leg., ch. 1054, § 21, eff. Jan. 1, 1996; Acts 1997, 75th Leg., ch. 540, § 4, eff. Sept. 1, 1997; Subsec. (a) amended by Acts 1997, 75th Leg., ch. 1361, § 1, eff. Sept. 1, 1997.

§ 320A. Funeral Expenses

When personal representatives pay claims for funeral expenses and for items incident thereto, such as tombstones, grave markers, crypts or burial plots, they shall charge the whole of such claims to the decedent's estate and shall charge no part thereof to the community share of a surviving spouse.

Added by Acts 1967, 60th Leg., p. 768, ch. 321, § 1, eff. May 27, 1967; Amended by Acts 1995, 74th Leg., ch. 1054, § 22, eff. Jan. 1, 1996.

§ 321. Deficiency of Assets

When there is a deficiency of assets to pay all claims of the same class, other than secured claims for money, the claims in such class shall be paid pro rata, as directed by the court, and in the order directed. No personal representative shall be allowed to pay the claims, whether the estate is solvent or insolvent, except with the pro rata amount of the funds of the estate that have come to hand.

Acts 1955, 54th Leg., p. 88, ch. 55, eff. Jan. 1, 1956; Amended by Acts 1993, 73rd Leg., ch. 957, § 57, eff. Sept. 1, 1993; Acts 1995, 74th Leg., ch. 1054, § 23, eff. Jan. 1, 1996.

Statutes in Context

See *Statutes in Context* to § 320.

§ 322. Classification of Claims Against Estates of Decedent

Claims against an estate of a decedent shall be classified and have priority of payment, as follows:

Class 1. Funeral expenses and expenses of last sickness for a reasonable amount to be approved by the court, not to exceed a total of Fifteen Thousand Dollars, with any excess to be classified and paid as other unsecured claims.

Class 2. Expenses of administration and expenses incurred in the preservation, safekeeping, and management of the estate including fees and expenses awarded under Section 243 of this code.

Class 3. Secured claims for money under Section 306(a)(1), including tax liens, so far as the same can be paid out of the proceeds of the property subject to such mortgage or other lien, and when more than one mortgage, lien, or security interest shall exist upon the same property, they shall be paid in order of their priority.

Class 4. Claims for the principal amount of and accrued interest on delinquent child support and child support arrearages that have been confirmed and reduced to money judgment, as determined under Subchapter F, Chapter 157, Family Code.[1]

Class 5. Claims for taxes, penalties, and interest due under Title 2, Tax Code;[2] Chapter 8, Title 132, Revised Statutes;[3] Section 81.111, Natural Resources Code; the Municipal Sales and Use Tax Act (Chapter 321, Tax Code); Section 451.404, Transportation Code; or Subchapter I, Chapter 452, Transportation Code.[4]

Class 6. Claims for the cost of confinement established by the institutional division of the Texas Department of Criminal Justice under Section 501.017 LOC., Local Government Code.

Class 7. Claims for repayment of medical assistance payments made by the state under Chapter 32, Human Resources Code, to or for the benefit of the decedent.

Class 8. All other claims.

Acts 1955, 54th Leg., p. 88, ch. 55, eff. Jan. 1, 1956. Amended by Acts 1971, 62nd Leg., p. 2992, ch. 988, § 3, eff. June 15, 1971; Acts 1979, 66th Leg., p. 869, ch. 394, § 1, eff. Aug. 27, 1979; Amended by Acts 1981, 67th Leg., p. 242, ch. 102, § 8, eff. Aug. 31, 1981; Acts 1981, 67th Leg., p. 1785, ch. 389, § 38A, 39(l), eff. Jan. 1, 1982; Acts 1987, 70th Leg., ch. 1049, § 51, eff. Sept. 1, 1987; Acts 1987, 70th Leg., ch. 1052, § 2.07, eff. Sept. 1, 1987; Acts 1989, 71st Leg., ch. 2, § 14.27(a)(6), eff. Aug. 28, 1989; Acts 1989, 71st Leg., ch. 1035, § 13, eff. Sept. 1, 1989; Acts 1995, 74th Leg., ch. 1054, § 24, eff. Jan. 1, 1996; Acts 1997, 75th Leg., ch. 165, § 30.243, eff. Sept. 1, 1997; Acts 1997, 75th Leg., ch. 1361, § 2, eff. Sept. 1, 1997; Acts 1999, 76th Leg., ch. 69, § 1, eff. Sept. 1, 1999; Acts 2003, 78th Leg., ch. 1060, § 14, eff. Sept. 1, 2003.

Statutes in Context

The testator's estate may be subject to a tax on the privilege of making gratuitous transfers upon the testator's death, that is, the federal or Texas estate tax. What testamentary gifts bear the burden of these tax obligations? Some states do not have any special rules for tax liabilities. In other words, gifts abate to pay tax liabilities just like they do to pay other claims against the estate. On the other hand, an increasing number of states, including Texas in § 322A, have tax apportionment statutes so that the amount of each gift is reduced by the amount of estate tax attributable to the transfer. In effect, each transfer is reduced by its fair share of the tax rather than being subsidized

[1] V.T.C.A., Family Code § 157.261 et seq.
[2] V.T.C.A., Tax Code § 101.001 et seq.
[3] Vernon's Ann.Civ.St. art. 8801 et seq.
[4] V.T.C.A., Transportation Code § 452.401 et seq.

by lower ranking gifts. Tax apportionment prevents the residual gift, which is often the most important gift in the will, from bearing the entire estate tax burden in addition to all of the other claims against the estate.

State and federal governments include many non-probate transfers in a testator's taxable estate. Section 322A covers these non-probate assets as well as testamentary transfers. Federal law mandates that life insurance beneficiaries and recipients under powers of appointment shoulder their fair share of transfer taxes. *See* I.R.C. §§ 2206 and 2207. Texas extends apportionment to other transfers, such as multiple-party bank accounts, survivorship rights, and trusts over which the testator held the power of revocation.

Section 322A is designed to carry out the testator's presumed intent. The legislature believed that most testators would want each transfer, be it probate or non-probate, to be responsible for its own tax. If the testator does not agree, the testator may provide otherwise in the will and those instructions will prevail over the apportionment statute. Note that the apportionment statute may be inadvertently trumped if the testator includes a generic clause in the will such as, "The executor shall pay all taxes payable because of my death from my residuary estate." *See Peterson v. Mayse*, 993 S.W.2d 217 (Tex. App. — Tyler 1999, *writ denied*).

---

§ 322A. Apportionment of Taxes

(a) In this section:

(1) "Estate" means the gross estate of a decedent as determined for the purpose of estate taxes.

(2) "Estate tax" means any estate, inheritance, or death tax levied or assessed on the property of a decedent's estate, because of the death of a person, imposed by federal, state, local, or foreign law, including the federal estate tax and the additional inheritance tax imposed by Chapter 211, Tax Code, and including interest and penalties imposed in addition to those taxes. Estate tax does not include a tax imposed under Section 2701(d)(1)(A), Internal Revenue Code of 1986 (26 U.S.C. § 2701 (d)).

(3) "Person" includes a trust, natural person, partnership, association, joint stock company, corporation, government, political subdivision, or governmental agency.

(4) "Person interested in the estate" means a person, or a fiduciary on behalf of that person, who is entitled to receive, or who has received, from a decedent or because of the death of the decedent, property included in the decedent's estate for purposes of the estate tax, but does not include a creditor of the decedent or of the decedent's estate.

(5) "Representative" means the representative, executor, or administrator of an estate, or any other person who is required to pay estate taxes assessed against the estate.

(b)(1) The representative shall charge each person interested in the estate a portion of the total estate tax assessed against the estate. The portion of each estate tax that is charged to each person interested in the estate must represent the same ratio as the taxable value of that person's interest in the estate included in determining the amount of the tax bears to the total taxable value of all the interests of all persons interested in the estate included in determining the amount of the tax. In apportioning an estate tax under this subdivision, the representative shall disregard a portion of the tax that is apportioned under the law imposing the tax, otherwise apportioned by federal law, or apportioned as otherwise provided by this section.

(2) Subdivision (1) of this subsection does not apply to the extent the decedent in a written inter vivos or testamentary instrument disposing of or creating an interest in property specifically directs the manner of apportionment of estate tax or grants a discretionary power of apportionment to another person. A direction for the apportionment or nonapportionment of estate tax is limited to the estate tax on the property passing under the instrument unless the instrument is a will that provides otherwise.

(3) If under Subdivision (2) of this subsection directions for the apportionment of an estate tax in two or more instruments executed by the same person conflict, the instrument disposing of or creating an interest in the property to be taxed controls. If directions for the apportionment of estate tax in two or more instruments executed by different persons conflict, the direction of the person in whose estate the property is included controls.

(4) Subdivisions (2) and (3) of this subsection do not grant or enlarge the power of a person to apportion estate tax to property passing under an instrument created by another person in excess of the estate tax attributable to the property. Subdivisions (2) and (3) of this subsection do not apply to the extent federal law directs a different manner of apportionment.

(c) Any deduction, exemption, or credit allowed by law in connection with the estate tax inures to a person interested in the estate as provided by Subsections (d)-(f) of this section.

(d) If the deduction, exemption, or credit is allowed because of the relationship of the person interested in the estate to the decedent, or because of the purpose of the gift, the deduction, exemption, or credit inures to the person having the relationship or receiving the gift, unless that person's interest in the estate is subject to a prior present interest that is not allowable as a deduction. The estate tax apportionable to the person having the present interest shall be paid from the corpus of the gift or the interest of the person having the relationship.

(e) A deduction for property of the estate that was previously taxed and a credit for gift taxes or death taxes of a foreign country that were paid by the decedent or his estate inures proportionally to all persons interested in the estate who are liable for a share of the estate tax.

(f) A credit for inheritance, succession, or estate taxes, or taxes of a similar nature applicable to property or interests includable in the estate, inures to the persons interested in the estate who are chargeable with payment of a portion of those taxes to the extent that the credit reduces proportionately those taxes.

(g) To the extent that property passing to or in trust for a surviving spouse or a charitable, public, or similar gift or devise is not an allowable deduction for purposes of the estate tax solely because of an inheritance tax or other death tax imposed on and deductible from the property, the property is not included in the computation provided for by Subsection (b) of this section, and to that extent no apportionment is made against the property. The exclusion provided by this subsection does not apply if the result would be to deprive the estate of a deduction otherwise allowable under Section 2053(d), Internal Revenue Code of 1986,[1] relating to deductions for state death taxes on transfers for public, charitable, or religious uses.

(h) Except as provided by Subsection (i)(3) of this section, an interest in income, an estate for years or for life, or another temporary interest in any property or fund is not subject to apportionment. The estate tax apportionable to the temporary interest and the remainder, if any, is chargeable against the corpus of the property or the funds that are subject to the temporary interest and remainder.

(i)(1) In this subsection, "qualified real property" has the meaning assigned by Section 2032A, Internal Revenue Code of 1986 (26 U.S.C. § 2032A).

(2) If an election is made under Section 2032A, Internal Revenue Code of 1986 (26 U.S.C. § 2032A), the representative shall apportion estate taxes according to the amount of federal estate tax that would be payable if the election were not made. The amount of the reduction of the estate tax resulting from the election shall be applied to reduce the amount of the estate tax allocated based on the value of the qualified real property that is the subject of the election. If the amount applied to reduce the taxes allocated based on the value of the qualified real property is greater than the amount of those taxes, the excess shall be applied to the portion of the taxes allocated for all other property. This amount is to be apportioned under Subsection (b)(1) of this section.

(3) If additional federal estate tax is imposed under Section 2032A(c), Internal Revenue Code of 1986 (26 U.S.C. § 2032A) because of an early disposition or cessation of a qualified use, the additional tax shall be equitably apportioned among the persons who have an interest in the portion of the qualified real property to which the additional tax is attributable in proportion to their interests. The additional tax is a charge against such qualified real property. If the qualified real property is split between one or more life or term interests and remainder interests, the additional tax shall be apportioned to each person whose action or cessation of use caused the imposition of additional tax, unless all persons with an interest in the qualified real property agree in writing to dispose of the property, in which case the additional tax shall be apportioned among the remainder interests.

(j) (Repealed)

(k) If the date for the payment of any portion of an estate tax is extended, the amount of the extended tax shall be apportioned to the persons who receive the specific property that gives rise to the extension. Those persons are entitled to the benefits and shall bear the burdens of the extension.

(l) If federal law directs the apportionment of the federal estate tax, a similar state tax shall be apportioned in the same manner.

(m) Interest on an extension of estate tax and interest and penalties on a deficiency shall be apportioned equitably to reflect the benefits and burdens of the extension or deficiency and of any tax deduction associated with the interest and penalties, but if the assessment or penalty and interest is due to delay caused by the negligence of the representative, the representative shall be charged with the amount of assessed penalty and interest.

(n) If property includable in an estate does not come into possession of the representative obligated to pay the estate tax, the representative shall recover from each person interested in the estate the amount of the estate tax apportioned to the person under this section or assign to persons affected by the tax obligation the representative's right of recovery. The obligation to recover a tax under this subsection does not apply if:

(1) the duty is waived by the parties affected by the tax obligation or by the instrument under which the representative derives powers; or

(2) in the reasonable judgment of the representative, proceeding to recover the tax is not cost-effective.

(o) If a representative cannot collect from a person interested in the estate an unpaid amount of estate tax apportioned to the person, the amount not collected shall be apportioned among the other persons interested in the estate who are subject to apportionment in the same manner as provided by Subsection (b)(1) of this section. A person who is charged with or who pays an apportioned amount under this subsection because another person failed to pay an amount of estate tax apportioned to the person has a right of reimbursement for that amount from the person who failed to pay the tax. The representative may enforce the right of reimbursement, or the person who is charged with or who pays an apportioned amount under this subsection may enforce the right of reimbursement directly by an assignment from the representative. A person assigned the right under this subsection is subrogated to the rights of the representative. A representative who has a right of reimbursement may petition a court to determine the right of reimbursement.

[1] 26 U.S.C.A. § 2053(d).

(p) This section shall be applied after giving effect to any disclaimers made in accordance with Section 37A of this code.

(q) Interest and penalties assessed against the estate by a taxing authority shall be apportioned among and charged to the persons interested in the estate in the manner provided by Subsection (b) of this section, unless, on application by any person interested in the estate, the court determines that the proposed apportionment is not equitable or that the assessment of interest or penalties was caused by a breach of fiduciary duty of a representative. If the apportionment is not equitable, the court may apportion interest and penalties in an equitable manner. If the assessment of interest or penalties was caused by a breach of fiduciary duty of a representative, the court may charge the representative with the amount of the interest and penalties assessed attributable to his conduct.

(r) Expenses reasonably incurred by a representative in determination of the amount, apportionment, or collection of the estate tax shall be apportioned among and charged to persons interested in the estate in the manner provided by Subsection (b) of this section unless, on application by any person interested in the estate, the court determines that the proposed apportionment is not equitable. If the court determines that the assessment is not equitable, the court may apportion the expenses in an equitable manner.

(s) For the purposes of this section, "court" means a court in which proceedings for administration of the estate are pending or have been completed or, if no proceedings are pending or have been completed, a court in which venue lies for the administration of the estate of the decedent.

(t) A representative who has possession of any property of an estate that is distributable to a person interested in the estate may withhold from that property an amount equal to the person's apportioned share of the estate tax.

(u) A representative shall recover from any person interested in the estate the unpaid amount of the estate tax apportioned and charged to the person under this section, unless the representative determines in good faith that an attempt to recover this amount would be economically impractical.

(v) A representative required to recover unpaid amounts of estate tax apportioned to persons interested in the estate under this section may not be required to initiate the necessary actions until the expiration of 90 days after the date of the final determination of the amount of the estate tax by the Internal Revenue Service. A representative who initiates an action under this section within a reasonable time after the 90-day period is not subject to any liability or surcharge because any portion of the estate tax apportioned to any person interested in the estate was collectible at a time following the death of the decedent but thereafter became uncollectible.

(w) A representative acting in another state may initiate an action in a court of this state to recover a proportionate amount of the federal estate tax, of an estate tax payable to another state, or of a death duty due by a decedent's estate to another state, from a person interested in the estate who is domiciled in this state or owns property in this state subject to attachment or execution. In the action, a determination of apportionment by the court having jurisdiction of the administration of the decedent's estate in the other state is prima facie correct. This section applies only if the state in which the determination of apportionment was made affords a substantially similar remedy.

(x) A reference in this section to a section of the Internal Revenue Code of 1986 refers to the section as it exists at the time in question. The reference also includes a corresponding section of a subsequent Internal Revenue Code and the referenced section as renumbered if it is renumbered.

(y) The prevailing party in an action initiated by a person for the collection of estate taxes from a person interested in the estate to whom estate taxes were apportioned and charged under Subsection (b) of this section shall be awarded necessary expenses, including reasonable attorney's fees.

Added by Acts 1987, 70th Leg., ch. 742, § 1, eff. Sept. 1, 1987. Amended by Acts 1991, 72nd Leg., ch. 410, § 1, eff. Sept. 1, 1991; Acts 2003, 78th Leg., ch. 1060, § 16, eff. Sept. 1, 2003.

Statutes in Context

A testator may attempt to give away more property in the testator's will than the testator is actually able to give. This could occur because the testator misjudged the value of the testator's estate. Just because a testator leaves a $500,000 legacy in the testator's will does not mean the testator actually has that money to give. The testator may also not have accounted for all of the testator's debts, including funeral and burial costs and expenses of last illness. In most situations, the claims of creditors have priority over assertions to property by beneficiaries.

Abatement is the reduction or elimination of a testamentary gift to pay an obligation of the estate or a testamentary gift of a higher priority. The abatement order is set forth in § 322B.

---

§ 322B. Abatement of Bequests

(a) Except as provided by Subsections (b)-(d) of this section, a decedent's property is liable for debts and expenses of administration other than estate taxes, and bequests abate in the following order:

(1) property not disposed of by will, but passing by intestacy;

(2) personal property of the residuary estate;

(3) real property of the residuary estate;

(4) general bequests of personal property;

(5) general devises of real property;

(6) specific bequests of personal property; and

(7) specific devises of real property.

(b) This section does not affect the requirements for payment of a claim of a secured creditor who elects to have the claim continued as a preferred debt and lien against specific property under Section 306 of this code.

(c) This section does not apply to the payment of estate taxes under Section 322A of this code.

(d) A decedent's intent, as expressed in a will, controls over the abatement of bequests provided by this section.

Added by Acts 1987, 70th Leg., ch. 742, § 2, eff. Sept. 1, 1987.

§ 323. Joint Obligation

When two or more persons are jointly bound for the payment of a debt, or for any other purpose, upon the death of any of the persons so bound, the decedent's estate shall be charged by virtue of such obligation in the same manner as if the obligors had been bound severally as well as jointly.

Acts 1955, 54th Leg., p. 88, ch. 55, eff. Jan. 1, 1956; Amended by Acts 1995, 74th Leg., ch. 1054, § 25, eff. Jan. 1, 1996.

§ 324. Representatives Not to Purchase Claims

It shall be unlawful, and cause for removal, for a personal representative whether acting under appointment by will or under orders of the court, to purchase for the personal representative's own use or for any purposes whatsoever, any claim against the estate the personal representative represents. Upon written complaint by any person interested in the estate, and satisfactory proof of violation of this provision, after citation and hearing, the court shall enter its order cancelling the claim, and no part thereof shall be paid out of the estate; and the court may, in the court's discretion, remove such representative.

Acts 1955, 54th Leg., p. 88, ch. 55, eff. Jan. 1, 1956; Amended by Acts 1993, 73rd Leg., ch. 957, § 58, eff. Sept. 1, 1993; Acts 1995, 74th Leg., ch. 1054, § 26, eff. Jan. 1, 1996.

§ 326. Owner May Obtain Order for Payment

Any creditor of an estate of a decedent whose claim, or part thereof, has been approved by the court or established by suit, may, at any time after twelve months from the granting of letters testamentary, upon written application and proof showing that the estate has on hand sufficient available funds, obtain an order directing that payment be made; or, if there are no available funds, and if to await the receipt of funds from other sources would unreasonably delay payment, the court shall then order sale of property of the estate sufficient to pay the claim; provided, the representative of the estate shall have first been cited on such written complaint to appear and show cause why such order should not be made.

Acts 1955, 54th Leg., p. 88, ch. 55, eff. Jan. 1, 1956.

§ 328. Liability for Nonpayment of Claims

(a) Procedure to Force Payment. If any representative of an estate shall fail to pay on demand any money ordered by the court to be paid to any person, except to the State Treasury, when there are funds of the estate available, the person or claimant entitled to such payment, upon affidavit of the demand and failure to pay, shall be authorized to have execution issued against the property of the estate for the amount due, with interest and costs; or

(b) Penalty Against Representative. Upon return of the execution not satisfied, or merely upon the affidavit of demand and failure to pay, the court may cite the representative and the sureties on the representative's bond to show cause why they should not be held liable for such debt, interest, costs, and damages. Upon return of citation duly served, if good cause to the contrary be not shown, the court shall render judgment against the representative and sureties so cited, in favor of the holder of such claim, for the amount theretofore ordered to be paid or established by suit, and remaining unpaid, together with interest and costs, and also for damages upon the amount neglected to be paid, at the rate of five per cent per month for each month, or fraction thereof, that the payment was neglected to be paid after demand made therefor, which damages may be collected in any court of competent jurisdiction.

Acts 1955, 54th Leg., p. 88, ch. 55, eff. Jan. 1, 1956; Subsec. (b) amended by Acts 1995, 74th Leg., ch. 1054, § 27, eff. Jan. 1, 1996.

Statutes in Context

Section 329 explains when and how a personal representative may borrow money for estate administration purposes.

---

§ 329. Borrowing Money

(a) Circumstances Under Which Money May Be Borrowed. Any real or personal property of an estate may be mortgaged or pledged by deed of trust or otherwise as security for an indebtedness, under order of the court, when necessary for any of the following purposes:

(1) For the payment of any ad valorem, income, gift, estate, inheritance, or transfer taxes upon the transfer of an estate or due from a decedent or the estate, regardless of whether such taxes are assessed by a state, or any of its political subdivisions, or by the federal government or by a foreign country; or

(2) For payment of expenses of administration, including sums necessary for operation of a business, farm, or ranch owned by the estate; or

(3) For payment of claims allowed and approved, or established by suit, against the estate; or

(4) To renew and extend a valid, existing lien.

(b) Procedure for Borrowing Money. When it is necessary to borrow money for any of the aforementioned purposes, or to create or extend a lien upon property of the estate as security, a sworn application for such authority shall be filed with the court, stating fully and in detail the circumstances which the representative of the estate believes make necessary the granting of such authority. Thereupon, the clerk shall issue and cause to be posted a citation to all interested persons, stating the nature of the application and requiring such persons, if they choose so to do, to appear and show cause, if any, why such application should not be granted.

(c) Order Authorizing Such Borrowing, or Extension of Lien. The court, if satisfied by the evidence adduced at the hearing upon said application that it is to the interest of the estate to borrow money, or to extend and renew an existing lien, shall issue its order to that effect, setting out the terms and conditions of the authority granted; provided, however, the loan or renewal shall not be for a term longer than three years from the granting of original letters to the representative of such estate, but the court may authorize an extension of such lien for not more than one additional year without further citation or notice. If a new lien is created on property of an estate, the court may require that the representative's general bond be increased, or an additional bond given, for the protection of the estate and the creditors, as for the sale of real property belonging to the estate.

Acts 1955, 54th Leg., p. 88, ch. 55, eff. Jan. 1, 1956. Amended by Acts 1973, 63rd Leg., p. 408, ch. 182, § 3, eff. May 25, 1973; Subsec. (a) amended by Acts 1987, 70th Leg., ch. 766, § 1, eff. Aug. 31, 1987; Subsecs. (a), (c) amended by Acts 1993, 73rd Leg., ch. 957, § 59, eff. Sept. 1, 1993; Acts 1995, 74th Leg., ch. 1054, § 28, eff. Jan. 1, 1996.

Part 5. Sales

Statutes in Context

Part 5 provides extensive (endless) guidance on how a personal representative sells estate property. The personal representative must ask the court for permission to sell, the court sets a hearing, citation is given to the interested parties, a hearing is conducted, the court authorizes the sale, the personal representative sells the property, the personal representative reports the sale to the court, and then the court approves the sale.

However, if the testator authorized the executor to sell estate property in the will, no court action is necessary. *See* § 332. Accordingly, it is extremely common for a will to grant the executor the power to sell.

§ 331. Court Must Order Sales

Except as hereinafter provided, no sale of any property of an estate shall be made without an order of court authorizing the same. The court may order property sold for cash or on credit, at public auction or privately, as it may consider most to the advantage of the estate, except when otherwise specially provided herein.

Acts 1955, 54th Leg., p. 88, ch. 55, eff. Jan. 1, 1956.

§ 332. Sales Authorized by Will

Whenever by the terms of a will an executor is authorized to sell any property of the testator, no order of court shall be necessary to authorize the executor to make such sale, and the sale may be made at public auction or privately as the executor deems to be in the best interest of the estate and may be made for cash or upon such credit terms as the executor shall determine; provided, that when particular directions are given by a testator in his will respecting the sale of any property belonging to his estate, the same shall be followed, unless such directions have been annulled or suspended by order of the court.

Acts 1955, 54th Leg., p. 88, ch. 55, eff. Jan. 1, 1956.

§ 333. Certain Personal Property to be Sold

(a) The representative of an estate, after approval of inventory and appraisement, shall promptly apply for an order of the court to sell at public auction or privately, for cash or on credit not exceeding six months, all of the estate that is liable to perish, waste, or deteriorate in value, or that will be an expense or disadvantage to the estate if kept. Property exempt from forced sale, specific legacies, and personal property necessary to carry on a farm, ranch, factory, or any other business which it is thought best to operate, shall not be included in such sales.

(b) In determining whether to order the sale of an asset under Subsection (a) of this section, the court shall consider:

(1) the representative's duty to take care of and manage the estate as a person of ordinary prudence, discretion, and intelligence would exercise in the management of the person's own affairs; and

(2) whether the asset constitutes an asset that a trustee is authorized to invest under Chapter 117 or Subchapter F, Chapter 113, Property Code.[1]

Acts 1955, 54th Leg., p. 88, ch. 55, eff. Jan. 1, 1956; Amended by Acts 1993, 73rd Leg., ch. 846, § 21, eff. Sept. 1, 1993; Acts 2003, 78th Leg., ch. 1103, § 14, eff. Jan. 1, 2004.

§ 334. Sales of Other Personal Property

Upon application by the personal representative of the estate or by any interested person, the court may order the sale of any personal property of the estate not required to be sold by the preceding Section, including growing or harvested crops or livestock, but not including exempt property or specific legacies, if the court finds that so to do would be in the best interest of the estate in order to pay expenses of administration, funeral expenses, expenses of last illness, allowances, or claims against the estate, from the proceeds of the sale of such property. In so far as possible, applications and orders for the sale of personal property shall conform to the requirements hereinafter set forth for applications and orders for the sale of real estate.

Acts 1955, 54th Leg., p. 88, ch. 55, eff. Jan. 1, 1956.

[1] V.T.C.A. Property Code, § 113.171 et seq.

§ 335. Special Provisions Pertaining to Livestock

When the personal representative of an estate has in his possession any livestock which he deems necessary or to the advantage of the estate to sell, he may, in addition to any other method provided by law for the sale of personal property, obtain authority from the court in which the estate is pending to sell such livestock through a bonded livestock commission merchant, or a bonded livestock auction commission merchant. Such authority may be granted by the court upon written and sworn application by the personal representative, or by any person interested in the estate, describing the livestock sought to be sold, and setting out the reasons why it is deemed necessary or to the advantage of the estate that the application be granted. The court shall forthwith consider any such application, and may, in its discretion, hear evidence for or against the same, with or without notice, as the facts warrant. If the application be granted, the court shall enter its order to that effect, and shall authorize delivery of the livestock to any bonded livestock commission merchant or bonded livestock auction commission merchant for sale in the regular course of business. The commission merchant shall be paid his usual and customary charges, not to exceed five per cent of the sale price, for the sale of such livestock. A report of such sale, supported by a verified copy of the merchant's account of sale, shall be made promptly by the personal representative to the court, but no order of confirmation by the court is required to pass title to the purchaser of such livestock.

Acts 1955, 54th Leg., p. 88, ch. 55, eff. Jan. 1, 1956. Amended by Acts 2001, 77th Leg., ch. 443, § 1, eff. Sept. 1, 2001.

§ 336. Sales of Personal Property at Public Auction

All sales of personal property at public auction shall be made after notice has been issued by the representative of the estate and posted as in case of posting for original proceedings in probate, unless the court shall otherwise direct.

Acts 1955, 54th Leg., p. 88, ch. 55, eff. Jan. 1, 1956.

§ 337. Sales of Personal Property on Credit

No more than six months credit may be allowed when personal property is sold at public auction, based upon the date of such sale. The purchaser shall be required to give his note for the amount due, with good and solvent personal security, before delivery of such property can be made to him, but security may be waived if delivery is not to be made until the note, with interest, has been paid.

Acts 1955, 54th Leg., p. 88, ch. 55, eff. Jan. 1, 1956.

§ 338. Sale of Mortgaged Property

Any creditor holding a claim secured by a valid mortgage or other lien, which has been allowed and approved or established by suit, may obtain from the court in which the estate is pending an order that said property, or so much thereof as necessary to satisfy his claim, shall be sold, by filing his written application therefor. Upon the filing of such application, the clerk shall issue citation requiring the representative of the estate to appear and show cause why such application should not be granted. If it appears to the court that it would be advisable to discharge the lien out of the general assets of the estate or that it be refinanced, he may so order; otherwise, he shall grant the application and order that the property be sold at public or private sale, as deemed best, as in ordinary cases of sales of real estate.

Acts 1955, 54th Leg., p. 88, ch. 55, eff. Jan. 1, 1956.

§ 339. Sales of Personal Property to be Reported; Decree Vests Title

All sales of personal property shall be reported to the court, and the laws regulating sales of real estate as to confirmation or disapproval of sales shall apply, but no conveyance shall be necessary. The decree confirming the sale of personal property shall vest the right and title of the estate of the intestate in the purchaser who has complied with the terms of the sale, and shall be prima facie evidence that all requirements of the law in making the sale have been met. The representative of an estate may, upon request, issue a bill of sale without warranty to the purchaser as evidence of title, the expense thereof to be borne by the purchaser.

Acts 1955, 54th Leg., p. 88, ch. 55, eff. Jan. 1, 1956; Amended by Acts 1993, 73rd Leg., ch. 957, § 60, eff. Sept. 1, 1993.

§ 340. Selection of Real Property to be Sold for Payment of Debts

Real property of the estate which is selected to be sold for the payment of expenses or claims shall be that which the court deems most advantageous to the estate to be sold.

Acts 1955, 54th Leg., p. 88, ch. 55, eff. Jan. 1, 1956.

§ 341. Application for Sale of Real Estate

Application may be made to the court for an order to sell property of the estate when it appears necessary or advisable in order to:

(1) Pay expenses of administration, funeral expenses and expenses of last sickness of decedents, and allowances and claims against the estates of decedents.

(2) Dispose of any interest in real property of the estate of a decedent, when it is deemed to the best interest of the estate to sell such interest.

Acts 1955, 54th Leg., p. 88, ch. 55, eff. Jan. 1, 1956. Amended by Acts 1969, 61st Leg., p. 2030, ch. 695, § 1, eff. June 12, 1969; Acts 1973, 63rd Leg., p. 408, ch. 182, § 4, eff. May 25, 1973; Acts 1975, 64th Leg., p. 975, ch. 372, § 1, eff. June 19, 1975; Acts 1975, 64th Leg., p. 976, ch. 373, § 1, eff. June 19, 1975; Acts 1979, 66th Leg., p. 1755, ch. 713, § 27, eff. Aug. 27, 1979; Amended by Acts 1993, 73rd Leg., ch. 957, § 61, eff. Sept. 1, 1993.

§ 342. Contents of Application for Sale of Real Estate

An application for the sale of real estate shall be in writing, shall describe the real estate or interest in or part thereof sought to be sold, and shall be accompanied by an exhibit, verified by affidavit, showing fully and in detail the condition of the estate, the charges and claims that have been approved or established by suit, or that have been rejected and may yet be established, the amount of each such claim, the property of the estate remaining on hand liable for the payment of such claims, and any other facts tending to show the necessity or advisability of such sale.

Acts 1955, 54th Leg., p. 88, ch. 55, eff. Jan. 1, 1956.

§ 343. Setting of Hearing on Application

Whenever an application for the sale of real estate is filed, it shall immediately be called to the attention of the judge by the clerk, and the judge shall designate in writing a day for hearing said application, any opposition thereto, and any application for the sale of other land, together with the evidence pertaining thereto. The judge may, by entries on the docket, continue such hearing from time to time until he is satisfied concerning the application.

Acts 1955, 54th Leg., p. 88, ch. 55, eff. Jan. 1, 1956. Amended by Acts 1979, 66th Leg., p. 1755, ch. 713, § 28, eff. Aug. 27, 1979.

§ 344. Citation and Return on Application

Upon the filing of such application and exhibit, the clerk shall issue a citation to all persons interested in the estate, describing the land or interest or part thereof sought to be sold, requiring them to appear at the time set by the court as shown in the citation and show cause why the sale should not be made, if they so elect. Service of such citation shall be by posting.

Acts 1955, 54th Leg., p. 88, ch. 55, eff. Jan. 1, 1956.

§ 345. Opposition to Application

When an application for an order of sale is made, any person interested in the estate may, before an order is made thereon, file his opposition to the sale, in writing, or may make application for the sale of other property of the estate.

Acts 1955, 54th Leg., p. 88, ch. 55, eff. Jan. 1, 1956.

§ 346. Order of Sale

If satisfied upon hearing that the sale of the property of the estate described in the application is necessary or advisable, the court shall order the sale to be made; otherwise, the court may deny the application and may, if it deems best, order the sale of other property the sale of which would be more advantageous to the estate. An order for the sale of real estate shall specify:

(a) The property to be sold, giving such description as will identify it; and

(b) Whether the property is to be sold at public auction or at private sale, and, if at public auction, the time and place of such sale; and

(c) The necessity or advisability of the sale and its purpose; and

(d) Except in cases in which no general bond is required, that, having examined the general bond of the representative of the estate, the court finds it to be sufficient as required by law, or finds the same to be insufficient and specifies the necessary or increased bond, as the case may be; and

(e) That the sale shall be made and the report returned in accordance with law; and

(f) The terms of the sale.

Acts 1955, 54th Leg., p. 88, ch. 55, eff. Jan. 1, 1956.

§ 347. Procedure When Representative Neglects to Apply for Sale

When the representative of an estate neglects to apply for an order to sell sufficient property to pay the charges and claims against the estate that have been allowed and approved, or established by suit, any interested person may, upon written application, cause such representative to be cited to appear and make a full exhibit of the condition of such estate, and show cause why a sale of the property should not be ordered. Upon hearing such application, if the court is satisfied that a sale of the property is necessary or advisable in order to satisfy such claims, it shall enter an order of sale as provided in the preceding Section.

Acts 1955, 54th Leg., p. 88, ch. 55, eff. Jan. 1, 1956.

§ 348. Permissible Terms of Sale of Real Estate

(a) For Cash or Credit. The real estate may be sold for cash, or for part cash and part credit, or the equity in land securing an indebtedness may be sold subject to such indebtedness, or with an assumption of such indebtedness, at public or private sale, as appears to the court to be for the best interest of the estate. When real estate is sold partly on credit, the cash payment shall not be less than one-fifth of the purchase price, and the purchaser shall execute a note for the deferred payments payable in monthly, quarterly, semi-annual or annual installments, of such amounts as appears to the court to be for the best interest of the estate, to bear interest from date at a rate of not less than four percent (4%) per annum, payable as provided in such note. Default in the payment of principal or interest, or any part thereof when due, shall, at the election of the holder of such note, mature the whole debt. Such note shall be secured by vendor's lien retained in the deed and in the note upon the property sold, and be further secured by deed of trust upon the property sold, with the usual provisions for foreclosure and sale upon failure to make the payments provided in the deed and notes.

(b) Reconveyance Upon Redemption. When an estate owning real estate by virtue of foreclosure of vendor's lien or mortgage belonging to the estate, ei-

ther by judicial sale or by a foreclosure suit or through sale under deed of trust or by acceptance of a deed in cancellation of a lien or mortgage owned by the estate, and it appears to the court that an application to redeem the property foreclosed upon has been made by the former owner of the real estate to any corporation or agency now created or hereafter to be created by any Act or Acts of the Congress of the United States or of the State of Texas in connection with legislation for the relief of owners of mortgaged or encumbered homes, farms, ranches, or other real estate, and it further appears to the court that it would be to the best interest of the estate to own bonds of one of the above named federal or state corporations or agencies instead of the real estate, then upon proper application and proof, the court may dispense with the provisions of credit sales as provided above, and may order reconveyance of the property to the former mortgage debtor, or former owner, reserving vendor's lien notes for the total amount of the indebtedness due or for the total amount of bonds which the corporation or agency above named is under its rules and regulations allowed to advance, and, upon obtaining such an order, it shall be proper for the representative to indorse and assign the notes so obtained over to any one of the corporations or agencies above named in exchange for bonds of that corporation or agency.
Acts 1955, 54th Leg., p. 88, ch. 55, eff. Jan. 1, 1956. Amended by Acts 1959, 56th Leg., p. 636, ch. 290, § 1, eff. May 30, 1959.

§ 349. Public Sales of Real Estate

(a) Notice of Sale. Except as hereinafter provided, all public sales of real estate shall be advertised by the representative of the estate by a notice published in the county in which the estate is pending, as provided in this Code for publication of notices or citations. Reference shall be made to the order of sale, the time, place, and the required terms of sale, and a brief description of the property to be sold shall be given. It need not contain field notes, but if rural property, the name of the original survey, the number of acres, its locality in the county, and the name by which the land is generally known, if any, shall be given.

(b) Method of Sale. All public sales of real estate shall be made at public auction to the highest bidder.

(c) Time and Place of Sale. All such sales shall be made in the county in which the proceedings are pending, at the courthouse door of said county, or other place in such county where sales of real estate are specifically authorized to be made, on the first Tuesday of the month after publication of notice shall have been completed, between the hours of ten o'clock A.M. and four o'clock P.M., provided, that if deemed advisable by the court, he may order such sale to be made in the county in which the land is situated, in which event notice shall be published both in such county and in the county where the proceedings are pending.

(d) Continuance of Sales. If sales are not completed on the day advertised, they may be continued from day to day by making public announcement verbally of such continuance at the conclusion of the sale each day, such continued sales to be within the same hours as hereinbefore prescribed. If sales are so continued, the fact shall be shown in the report of sale made to the court.

(e) Failure of Bidder to Comply. When any person shall bid off property of an estate offered for sale at public auction, and shall fail to comply with the terms of sale, such property shall be readvertised and sold without any further order; and the person so defaulting shall be liable to pay to the representative of the estate, for its benefit, ten per cent of the amount of his bid, and also any deficiency in price on the second sale, such amounts to be recovered by such representative by suit in any court having jurisdiction of the amount claimed, in the county in which the sale was made.
Acts 1955, 54th Leg., p. 88, ch. 55, eff. Jan. 1, 1956.

§ 350. Private Sales of Real Estate

All private sales of real estate shall be made in such manner as the court directs in its order of sale, and no further advertising, notice, or citation concerning such sale shall be required, unless the court shall direct otherwise.
Acts 1955, 54th Leg., p. 88, ch. 55, eff. Jan. 1, 1956. Amended by Acts 1979, 66th Leg., p. 1755, ch. 713, § 29, eff. Aug. 27, 1979.

§ 351. Sales of Easements and Right of Ways

It shall be lawful to sell and convey easements and rights of ways on, under, and over the lands of an estate being administered under orders of a court, regardless of whether the proceeds of such a sale are required for payment of charges or claims against the estate, or for other lawful purposes. The procedure for such sales shall be the same as now or hereafter provided by law for sales of real property of estates of decedents at private sale.
Acts 1955, 54th Leg., p. 88, ch. 55, eff. Jan. 1, 1956; Amended by Acts 1993, 73rd Leg., ch. 957, § 62, eff. Sept. 1, 1993.

Statutes in Context

Self-dealing is generally not allowed, that is, the personal representative may not purchase estate property. However, § 352 permits the personal representative to purchase if (1) the testator granted express permission in the will or (2) the court finds that it is in the best interest of the estate to permit the personal representative to purchase estate property after giving notice the distributees and creditors.

---

§ 352. Representative Purchasing Property of the Estate

(a) Except as provided by Subsection (b), (c), or (d) of this section, the personal representative of an estate shall not become the purchaser, directly or indirectly, of any property of the estate sold by him, or by any co-representative if one be acting.

(b) A personal representative of an estate may purchase property from the estate if the will, duly admitted to probate, appointing the personal representative expressly authorizes the sale.

(c) A personal representative of a decedent may purchase property from the estate of the decedent in compliance with the terms of a written executory contract signed by the decedent, including a contract for deed, earnest money contract, buy/sell agreement, or stock purchase or redemption agreement.

(d) After issuing the notice required by this subsection, a personal representative of an estate, including an independent administrator, may purchase property from the estate on the court's determination that the sale is in the best interest of the estate. The personal representative shall give notice by certified mail, return receipt requested, unless the court requires another form of notice, to each distributee of a deceased person's estate and to each creditor whose claim remains unsettled after presenting a claim within six months of the original grant of letters. The court may require additional notice or it may allow for the waiver of the notice required for a sale made under this subsection.

(e) If a purchase is made in violation of this section, any person interested in the estate may file a written complaint with the court in which the proceedings are pending, and upon service of citation upon the representative, after hearing and proof, such sale shall be by the court declared void, and shall be set aside by the court and the property ordered to be reconveyed to the estate. All costs of the sale, protest, and suit, if found necessary, shall be adjudged against the representative.

Acts 1955, 54th Leg., p. 88, ch. 55, eff. Jan. 1, 1956; Amended by Acts 1985, 69th Leg., ch. 709, § 1, eff. Aug. 26, 1985; Subsecs. (a) and (c) amended by Acts 1989, 71st Leg., ch. 651, § 1, eff. June 14, 1989; Subsecs. (a), (d) and (e) amended by Acts 1991, 72nd Leg., ch. 895, § 14, eff. Sept. 1, 1991; Subsecs. (c) and (d) amended by Acts 1993, 73rd Leg., ch. 957, § 63, eff. Sept. 1, 1993.

§ 353. Reports of Sale

All sales of real property of an estate shall be reported to the court ordering the same within thirty days after the sales are made. Reports shall be in writing, sworn to, and filed with the clerk, and noted on the probate docket. They shall show:

(a) The date of the order of sale.

(b) The property sold, describing it.

(c) The time and place of sale.

(d) The name of the purchaser.

(e) The amount for which each parcel of property or interest therein was sold.

(f) The terms of the sale, and whether made at public auction or privately.

(g) Whether the purchaser is ready to comply with the order of sale.

Acts 1955, 54th Leg., p. 88, ch. 55, eff. Jan. 1, 1956.

§ 354. Bond on Sale of Real Estate

If the personal representative of the estate is not required by this Code to furnish a general bond, the sale may be confirmed by the court if found to be satisfactory and in accordance with law. Otherwise, before any sale of real estate is confirmed, the court shall determine whether the general bond of said representative is sufficient to protect the estate after the proceeds of the sale are received. If the court so finds, the sale may be confirmed. If the general bond be found insufficient, the sale shall not be confirmed until and unless the general bond be increased to the amount required by the court, or an additional bond given, and approved by the court. The increase, or the additional bond, shall be equal to the amount for which such real estate is sold, plus, in either instance, such additional sum as the court shall find necessary and fix for the protection of the estate; provided, that where the real estate sold is encumbered by a lien to secure a claim against the estate and is sold to the owner or holder of such secured claim and is in full payment, liquidation, and satisfaction thereof, no increased general bond or additional bond shall be required except for the amount of cash, if any, actually paid to the representative of the estate in excess of the amount necessary to pay, liquidate, and satisfy such claim in full.

Acts 1955, 54th Leg., p. 88, ch. 55, eff. Jan. 1, 1956.

§ 355. Action of Court on Report of Sale

After the expiration of five days from the filing of a report of sale, the court shall inquire into the manner in which the sale was made, hear evidence in support of or against such report, and determine the sufficiency or insufficiency of the representative's general bond, if any has been required and given; and, if he is satisfied that the sale was for a fair price, was properly made and in conformity with law, and has approved any increased or additional bond which may have been found necessary to protect the estate, the court shall enter a decree confirming such sale, showing conformity with the foregoing provisions of the Code, and authorizing the conveyance of the property to be made by the representative of the estate upon compliance by the purchaser with the terms of the sale, detailing such terms. If the court is not satisfied that the sale was for a fair price, was properly made, and in conformity with law, an order shall be made setting the same aside and ordering a new sale to be made, if necessary. The action of the court in confirming or disapproving a report of sale shall have the force and effect of a final judgment; and any person interested in the estate or in the sale shall have the right to have such decrees reviewed as in other final judgments in probate proceedings.

Acts 1955, 54th Leg., p. 88, ch. 55, eff. Jan. 1, 1956. Amended by Acts 1975, 64th Leg., p. 2197, ch. 701, § 6, eff. June 21, 1975.

§ 356. Deed Conveys Title to Real Estate

When real estate is sold, the conveyance shall be by proper deed which shall refer to and identify the de-

cree of the court confirming the sale. Such deed shall vest in the purchaser all right, title, and interest of the estate to such property, and shall be prima facie evidence that said sale has met all applicable requirements of the law.
Acts 1955, 54th Leg., p. 88, ch. 55, eff. Jan. 1, 1956.

§ 357. Delivery of Deed, Vendor's and Deed of Trust Lien

After a sale is confirmed by the court and the terms of sale have been complied with by the purchaser, the representative of the estate shall forthwith execute and deliver to the purchaser a proper deed conveying the property. If the sale is made partly on credit, the vendor's lien securing the purchase money note or notes shall be expressly retained in said deed, and in no event waived, and before actual delivery of said deed to purchaser, he shall execute and deliver to the representative of the estate a vendor's lien note or notes, with or without personal sureties as the court shall have ordered, and also a deed of trust or mortgage on the property as further security for the payment of said note or notes. Upon completion of the transaction, the personal representative shall promptly file or cause to be filed and recorded in the appropriate records in the county where the land is situated said deed of trust or mortgage.
Acts 1955, 54th Leg., p. 88, ch. 55, eff. Jan. 1, 1956.

§ 358. Penalty for Neglect

Should the representative of an estate neglect to comply with the preceding Section, or to file the deed of trust securing such lien in the proper county, he and the sureties on his bond shall, after complaint and citation, be held liable for the use of the estate, for all damages resulting from such neglect, which damages may be recovered in any court of competent jurisdiction, and he may be removed by the court.
Acts 1955, 54th Leg., p. 88, ch. 55, eff. Jan. 1, 1956.

Part 6. Hiring and Renting

Statutes in Context

Part 6 provides guidance to the personal representative who wishes to rent estate property. Short-term leases are permitted without court order under § 359 while court permission is needed for leases more than one year in length. *See* § 361.

§ 359. Hiring or Renting Without Order of Court

The personal representative of an estate may, without order of court, rent any of its real property or hire out any of its personal property, either at public auction or privately, as may be deemed in the best interest of the estate, for a period not to exceed one year.
Acts 1955, 54th Leg., p. 88, ch. 55, eff. Jan. 1, 1956.

§ 360. Liability of Personal Representative

If property of the estate is hired or rented without an order of court, the personal representative shall be required to account to the estate for the reasonable value of the hire or rent of such property, to be ascertained by the court upon satisfactory evidence, upon sworn complaint of any person interested in the estate.
Acts 1955, 54th Leg., p. 88, ch. 55, eff. Jan. 1, 1956.

§ 361. Order to Hire or Rent

Representatives of estates, if they prefer, may, and, if the proposed rental period exceeds one year, shall, file a written application with the court setting forth the property sought to be hired or rented. If the court finds that it would be to the interest of the estate, he shall grant the application and issue an order which shall describe the property to be hired or rented, state whether such hiring or renting shall be at public auction or privately, whether for cash or on credit, and, if on credit, the extent of same and the period for which the property may be rented. If to be hired or rented at public auction, the court shall also prescribe whether notice thereof shall be published or posted.
Acts 1955, 54th Leg., p. 88, ch. 55, eff. Jan. 1, 1956.

§ 362. Procedure in Case of Neglect to Rent Property

Any person interested in an estate may file his written and sworn complaint in a court where such estate is pending, and cause the personal representative of such estate to be cited to appear and show cause why he did not hire or rent any property of the estate, and the court, upon hearing such complaint, shall make such order as seems for the best interest of the estate.
Acts 1955, 54th Leg., p. 88, ch. 55, eff. Jan. 1, 1956.

§ 363. When Property is Hired or Rented on Credit

When property is hired or rented on credit, possession thereof shall not be delivered until the hirer or renter has executed and delivered to the representative of the estate a note with good personal security for the amount of such hire or rent; and, if any such property so hired or rented is delivered without receiving such security, the representative and the sureties on his bond shall be liable for the full amount of such hire or rent; provided, that when the hire or rental is payable in installments, in advance of the period of time to which they relate, this Section shall not apply.
Acts 1955, 54th Leg., p. 88, ch. 55, eff. Jan. 1, 1956.

§ 364. Property Hired or Rented to be Returned in Good Condition

All property hired or rented, with or without an order of court, shall be returned to the possession of the estate in as good condition, reasonable wear and tear excepted, as when hired or rented, and it shall be the duty and responsibility of the representative of the estate to see that this is done, to report to the court any

loss, damage or destruction of property hired or rented, and to ask for authority to take such action as is necessary; failing so to do, he and the sureties on his bond shall be liable to the estate for any loss or damage suffered through such fault.
Acts 1955, 54th Leg., p. 88, ch. 55, eff. Jan. 1, 1956.

§ 365. Report of Hiring or Renting

(a) When any property of the estate with an appraised value of Three Thousand Dollars or more has been hired or rented, the representative shall, within thirty days thereafter, file with the court a sworn and written report, stating:

(1) The property involved and its appraised value.

(2) The date of hiring or renting, and whether at public auction or privately.

(3) The name of the person or persons hiring or renting such property.

(4) The amount of such hiring or rental.

(5) Whether the hiring or rental was for cash or on credit, and, if on credit, the length of time, the terms, and the security taken therefor.

(b) When the value of the property involved is less than Three Thousand Dollars, the hiring or renting thereof may be reported upon in the next annual or final account which shall be filed as required by law.
Acts 1955, 54th Leg., p. 88, ch. 55, eff. Jan. 1, 1956.

§ 366. Action of Court on Report

At any time after five days from the time such report of hiring or renting is filed, it shall be examined by the court and approved and confirmed by order of the court if found just and reasonable; but, if disapproved, the estate shall not be bound and the court may order another offering of the property for hire or rent, in the same manner and subject to the same rules heretofore provided. If the report has been approved and it later appears that, by reason of any fault of the representative of the estate, the property has not been hired or rented for its reasonable value, the court shall cause the representative of the estate and his sureties to appear and show cause why the reasonable value of hire or rent of such property shall not be adjudged against him.
Acts 1955, 54th Leg., p. 88, ch. 55, eff. Jan. 1, 1956.

Part 7. Mineral Leases, Pooling or Unitization Agreements, and Other Matters Relating to Mineral Properties

Statutes in Context

Part 7 provides the personal representative with guidance for dealing with mineral interests of the decedent's estate.

§ 367. Mineral Leases After Public Notice

(a) Certain Words and Terms Defined. As used throughout in this Part of this Chapter, the words "land" or "interest in land" include minerals or any interest in any of such minerals in place. The word "property" includes land, minerals in place, whether solid, liquid or gaseous, as well as an interest of any kind in such property, including royalty, owned by the estate. "Mineral development" includes exploration, by geophysical or by any other means, drilling, mining, developing, and operating, and producing and saving oil, other liquid hydrocarbons, gas (including all liquid hydrocarbons in the gaseous phase in the reservoir), gaseous elements, sulphur, metals, and all other minerals, solid or otherwise.

(b) Mineral Leases, With or Without Pooling or Unitization. Personal representatives of the estates of decedents, appointed and qualified under the laws of this State, and acting solely under orders of court, may be authorized by the court in which the probate proceedings on such estates are pending to make, execute, and deliver leases, with or without unitization clauses or pooling provisions, providing for the exploration for, and development and production of, oil, other liquid hydrocarbons, gas (including all liquid hydrocarbons in the gaseous phase), metals, and other solid minerals, and other minerals, or any of such minerals in place, belonging to such estates.

(c) Rules Concerning Applications, Orders, Notices, and Other Essential Matters. All such leases, with or without pooling provisions or unitization clauses, shall be made and entered into pursuant to and in conformity with the following rules:

1. Contents of Application. The representative of the estate shall file with the county clerk of the county where the probate proceeding is pending his written application, addressed to the court or the judge of such court, asking for authority to lease property of the estate for mineral exploration and development, with or without pooling provisions or unitization clauses. The application shall (a) describe the property fully enough by reference to the amount of acreage, the survey name or number, or abstract number, or other description adequately identifying the property and its location in the county in which situated; (b) specify the interest thought to be owned by the estate, if less than the whole, but asking for authority to include all interest owned by the estate, if that be the intention; and (c) set out the reasons why such particular property of the estate should be leased. Neither the name of any proposed lessee, nor the terms, provisions, or form of any desired lease, need be set out or suggested in any such application for authority to lease for mineral development.

2. Order Designating Time and Place for Hearing Application

(a) Duties of Clerk and Judge. When an application to lease, as above prescribed, is filed, the county clerk shall immediately call the filing of such application to the attention of the court, and the judge shall promptly make and enter a brief order designating the time and place for the hearing of such application.

(b) Continuance of Hearing. If the hearing is not had at the time originally designated by the court or by timely order or orders of continuance duly entered, then, in such event, the hearing shall be automatically continued, without further notice, to the same hour or time the following day (except Sundays and holidays on which the county courthouse is officially closed to business) and from day to day until the application is finally acted upon and disposed of by order of the court. No notice of such automatic continuance shall be required.

3. Notice of Application to Lease, Service of Notice, and Proof of Service

(a) Notice and Its Contents. The personal representative, and not the county clerk, shall give notice in writing of the time designated by the judge for the hearing on the application to lease. The notice shall be directed to all persons interested in the estate. It shall state the date on which the application was filed, describe briefly the property sought to be leased, specifying the fractional interest sought to be leased if less than the entire interest in the tract or tracts identified, state the time and place designated by the judge for the hearing, and be dated.

(b) Service of Notice. The personal representative shall give at least ten days notice, exclusive of the date of notice and of the date set for hearing, by publication in one issue of a newspaper of general circulation in the county in which the proceeding is pending, or, if there be no such newspaper, then by posting by the personal representative or at his instance. The date of notice when published shall be the date the newspaper bears.

4. Preceding Requirements Mandatory. In the absence of: (a) a written order originally designating a time and place for hearing; (b) a notice issued by the personal representative of the estate in compliance with such order; and (c) proof of publication or posting of such notice as required, any order of the judge or court authorizing any acts to be performed pursuant to said application shall be null and void.

5. Hearing on Application to Lease and Order Thereon. At the time and place designated for the hearing, or at any time to which it shall have been continued as hereinabove provided, the judge shall hear such application, requiring proof as to the necessity or advisability of leasing for mineral development the property described in the application and in the notice; and, if he is satisfied that the application is in due form, that notice has been duly given in the manner and for the time required by law, that the proof of necessity or advisability of leasing is sufficient, and that the application should be granted, then an order shall be entered so finding, and authorizing the making of one or more leases, with or without pooling provisions or unitization clauses (with or without cash consideration if deemed by the court to be in the best interest of the estate) affecting and covering the property, or portions thereof, described in the application. Said order authorizing leasing shall also set out the following mandatory contents:

(a) The name of the lessee.

(b) The actual cash consideration, if any, to be paid by the lessee.

(c) Finding that the personal representative is exempted by law from giving bond, if that be a fact and if not a fact, then a finding as to whether or not the representative's general bond on file is sufficient to protect the personal property on hand, inclusive of any cash bonus to be paid, if any. If the court finds the general bond insufficient to meet these requirements, the order shall show the amount of increased or additional bond required to cover the deficiency.

(d) A complete exhibit copy, either written or printed, of each lease thus authorized to be made, shall either be set out in the order or attached thereto and incorporated by reference in said order and made a part thereof. It shall show the name of the lessee, the date of the lease, an adequate description of the property being leased, the delay rental, if any, to be paid to defer commencement of operations, and all other terms and provisions authorized; provided, that if no date of the lease appears in such exhibit copy, or in the court's order, then the date of the court's order shall be considered for all purposes as the date of the authorized lease, and if the name and address of the depository bank, or either of them, for receiving rental is not shown in said exhibit copy, the same may be inserted or caused to be inserted in the lease by the estate's personal representative at the time of its execution, or at any other time agreeable to the lessee, his successors, or assigns.

6. Conditional Validity of Lease; Bond; Time of Execution; Confirmation Not Needed. If, upon the hearing of an application for authority to lease, the court shall grant the same as above provided, the personal representative of the estate shall then be fully authorized to make, within thirty days after date of the judge's order, but not afterwards unless an extension be granted by the court upon sworn application showing good cause, the lease or leases as evidenced by the aforesaid true exhibit copies, in accordance with said order; but, unless the personal representative is not required to give a general bond, no such lease, for which a cash consideration is required, though ordered, executed, and delivered, shall be valid unless the order authorizing same actually makes findings with respect to the general bond, and, in case such bond has been found insufficient, then unless and until the bond has been increased, or an additional bond given, as required by the court's order, with the sureties required by law, has been approved by the judge and filed with the clerk of the court in which the proceedings are pending. In the event two or more leases on different lands are authorized by the same order, the general bond shall be increased, or additional bonds given, to cover all. It shall not be necessary for the judge to make any order confirming such leases.

7. Term of Lease Binding. Every such lease, when executed and delivered in compliance with the rules hereinabove set out, shall be valid and binding upon the property or interest therein owned by the estate and covered by the lease for the full duration of the term as provided therein, subject only to its terms and conditions, even though the primary term shall extend beyond the date when the estate shall have been closed in accordance with law; provided the authorized primary term shall not exceed five (5) years, subject to terms and provisions of the lease extending it beyond the primary term by paying production, by bona fide drilling or reworking operations, whether in or on the same or additional well or wells, with no cessation of operations of more than sixty (60) consecutive days before production has been restored or obtained, or by the provisions of the lease relating to a shut-in gas well.

7(a). Validation of Certain Provisions of Leases Heretofore Executed by Personal Representatives. As to any valid mineral lease heretofore executed and delivered in compliance with the provisions of the Texas Probate Code and which lease is still in force, any provisions of any such lease continuing such lease in force after its five (5) year primary term by a shut-in gas well are hereby validated; provided, however, that this provision shall not be applicable to any such provision of any such lease which is involved in any lawsuit pending in this state on the effective date of this Act wherein the validity of such provision is an issue.

8. Amendment of Leases. Any oil, gas, and mineral lease heretofore or hereafter executed by a personal representative pursuant to the Texas Probate Code may be amended by an instrument which provides that a shut-in gas well on the land covered by the lease or on land pooled with all or some part thereof shall continue such lease in force after its five (5) year primary term. Such instrument shall be executed by the personal representative, with the approval of the court, and on such terms and conditions as may be prescribed therein.

Acts 1955, 54th Leg., p. 88, ch. 55, eff. Jan. 1, 1956. Amended by Acts 1957, 55th Leg., p. 53, ch. 31, § 10(a); Acts 1961, 57th Leg., p. 441, ch. 215, § 1 to 3, eff. May 25, 1961; Subsec. (b) amended by Acts 1993, 73rd Leg., ch. 957, § 64, eff. Sept. 1, 1993.

§ 368. Mineral Leases at Private Sale

(a) Authorization Allowed. Notwithstanding the preceding mandatory requirements for setting a time and place for hearing of an application to lease and the issuance, service, and return of notice, the court may authorize the making of oil, gas, and mineral leases at private sale (without public notice or advertising) if, in the opinion of the court, sufficient facts are set out in the application required above to show that it would be more advantageous to the estate that a lease be made privately and without compliance with said mandatory requirements mentioned above. Leases so authorized may include pooling provisions or unitization clauses as in other cases.

(b) Action of the Court When Public Advertising Not Required. At any time after the expiration of five (5) days and prior to the expiration of ten (10) days from the date of filing and without an order setting time and place of hearing, the court shall hear the application to lease at private sale and shall inquire into the manner in which the proposed lease has been or will be made, and shall hear evidence for or against the same; and, if satisfied that the lease has been or will be made for a fair and sufficient consideration and on fair terms, and has been or will be properly made in conformity with law, the court shall enter an order authorizing the execution of such lease without the necessity of advertising, notice, or citation, said order complying in all other respects with the requirements essential to the validity of mineral leases as hereinabove set out, as if advertising or notice were required. No order confirming a lease or leases made at private sale need be issued, but no such lease shall be valid until the increased or additional bond required by the court, if any, has been approved by the court and filed with the clerk of the court.

Acts 1955, 54th Leg., p. 88, ch. 55, eff. Jan. 1, 1956. Amended by Acts 1957, 55th Leg., p. 53, ch. 31, § 10(b).

§ 369. Pooling or Unitization of Royalty or Minerals

(a) Authorization for Pooling or Unitization. When an existing lease or leases on property owned by the estate does not adequately provide for pooling or unitization, the court may authorize the commitment of royalty or mineral interests in oil, liquid hydrocarbons, gas (including all liquid hydrocarbons in the gaseous phase in the reservoir), gaseous elements, and other minerals, or any one or more of them, owned by the estate being administered, to agreements that provide for the operation of areas as a pool or unit for the exploration, development, and production of all such minerals, where the court finds that the pool or unit to which the agreement relates will be operated in such a manner as to protect correlative rights, or to prevent the physical or economic waste of oil, liquid hydrocarbons, gas (including all liquid hydrocarbons in the gaseous phase in the reservoir), gaseous elements, or other mineral subject thereto, and that it is to the best interest of the estate to execute the agreement. Any agreement so authorized to be executed may, among others things, provide:

(1) That operations incident to the drilling of or production from a well upon any portion of a pool or unit shall be deemed for all purposes to be the conduct of operations upon or production from each separately owned tract in the pool or unit.

(2) That any lease covering any part of the area committed to a pool or unit shall continue in force in its entirety as long as oil, gas, or other mineral subject to the agreement is produced in paying quantities from any part of the pooled or unitized area, or as long as operations are conducted as provided in the lease on any part of the pooled or unitized area, or as long as there is a shut-in gas well on any part of the pooled or unitized area, if the presence of such shut-in gas well is a ground for continuation of the lease by the terms of said lease.

(3) That the production allocated by the agreement to each tract included in a pool or unit shall, when produced, be deemed for all purposes to have been produced from such tract by a well drilled thereon.

(4) That the royalties provided for on production from any tract or portion thereof within the pool or unit shall be paid only on that portion of the production allocated to the tract in accordance with the agreement.

(5) That the dry gas, before or after extraction of hydrocarbons, may be returned to a formation underlying any lands or leases committed to the agreement, and that no royalties are required to be paid on the gas so returned.

(6) That gas obtained from other sources or other lands may be injected into a formation underlying any lands or leases committed to the agreement, and that no royalties are required to be paid on the gas so injected when same is produced from the unit.

(b) Procedure for Authorizing Pooling or Unitization. Pooling or unitization, when not adequately provided for by an existing lease or leases on property owned by the estate, may be authorized by the court in which the proceedings are pending pursuant to and in conformity with the following rules:

(1) Contents of Application. The personal representative of the estate shall file with the county clerk of the county where the probate proceeding is pending his written application for authority (a) to enter into pooling or unitization agreements supplementing, amending, or otherwise relating to, any existing lease or leases covering property owned by the estate, or (b) to commit royalties or other interest in minerals, whether subject to lease or not, to a pooling or unitization agreement. The application shall also (c) describe the property sufficiently, as required in original application to lease, (d) describe briefly the lease or leases, if any, to which the interest of the estate is subject, and (e) set out the reasons why the proposed agreement concerning such property should be made. A true copy of the proposed agreement shall be attached to the application and by reference made a part thereof, but the agreement shall not be recorded in the minutes. The clerk shall immediately, after such application is filed, call it to the attention of the judge.

(2) Notice Not Necessary. No notice of the filing of such application by advertising, citation, or otherwise, is required.

(3) Hearing of Application. A hearing on such application may be held by the judge at any time agreeable to the parties to the proposed agreement, and the judge shall hear proof and satisfy himself as to whether or not it is to the best interest of the estate that the proposed agreement be authorized. The hearing may be continued from day to day and from time to time as the court finds to be necessary.

(4) Action of Court and Contents of Order. If the court finds that the pool or unit to which the agreement relates will be operated in such a manner as to protect correlative rights or to prevent the physical or economic waste of oil, liquid hydrocarbons, gas (including all liquid hydrocarbons in the gaseous phase in the reservoir), gaseous elements, or other mineral subject thereto; that it is to the best interest of the estate that the agreement be executed; and that the agreement conforms substantially with the permissible provisions of Subsection (a) hereof, he shall enter an order setting out the findings made by him, authorizing execution of the agreement (with or without payment of cash consideration according to the agreement). If cash consideration is to be paid for the agreement, findings as to the necessity of increased or additional bond, as in making of leases upon payment of the cash bonus therefor, shall also be made, and no such agreement shall be valid until the increased or additional bond required by the court, if any, has been approved by the judge and filed with the clerk. The date of the court's order shall be the effective date of the agreement, if not stipulated in such agreement.

Acts 1955, 54th Leg., p. 88, ch. 55, eff. Jan. 1, 1956. Amended by Acts 1961, 57th Leg., p. 441, ch. 215, § 4, eff. May 25, 1961.

§ 370. Special Ancillary Instruments Which May Be Executed Without Court Order

As to any valid mineral lease or pooling or unitization agreement, executed on behalf of the estate prior to the effective date of this Code, or pursuant to its provisions, or by a former owner of land, minerals, or royalty affected thereby, the personal representative of the estate which is being administered may, without further order of the court, and without consideration, execute division orders, transfer orders, instruments of correction, instruments designating depository banks for the reception of delay rentals or shut-in gas well royalty to accrue or become payable under the terms of any such lease or leases, and similar instruments pertaining to any such lease or agreement and the property covered thereby.

Acts 1955, 54th Leg., p. 88, ch. 55, eff. Jan. 1, 1956. Amended by Acts 1957, 55th Leg., p. 53, ch. 31, § 10(c).

§ 371. Procedure When Representative of Estate Neglects to Apply for Authority

When the personal representative of an estate shall neglect to apply for authority to subject property of the estate to a lease for mineral development, pooling or unitization, or to commit royalty or other interest in minerals to pooling or unitization, any person interested in the estate may, upon written application filed with the county clerk, cause such representative to be cited to show cause why it is not for the best interest of the estate for such a lease to be made, or such an agreement entered into. The clerk shall immediately call the filing of such application to the attention of the judge of the court in which the probate proceedings are pending, and the judge shall set a time and place for a hearing on the application, and the representative of the estate shall be cited to appear and show cause why the execution of such lease or agreement should not be ordered. Upon hearing, if satisfied from the proof that it would be in the best interest of the estate, the court shall enter an order requiring the personal representative forthwith to file his application to subject such property of the estate to a lease for mineral development, with or without pooling or unitization provisions, or to commit royalty or other minerals to unitization, as the case may be. The procedure prescribed with respect to original application to lease, or with respect to original application for authority to commit royalty or minerals to pooling or unitization, whichever is appropriate, shall then be followed.

Acts 1955, 54th Leg., p. 88, ch. 55, eff. Jan. 1, 1956.

§ 372. Validation of Certain Leases and Pooling or Unitization Agreements Based on Previous Statutes

All presently existing leases on the oil, gas, or other minerals, or one or more of them, belonging to the estates of decedents, and all agreements with respect to pooling, or unitization thereof, or one or more of them, or any interest therein, with like properties of others having been authorized by the court having venue, and executed and delivered by the executors, administrators, or other fiduciaries of their estates in substantial conformity to the rules set forth in statutes heretofore existing, providing for only seven days notice in some instances, and also for a brief order designating a time and place for hearing, are hereby validated in so far as said period of notice is concerned, and in so far as the absence of any order setting a time and place for hearing is concerned; provided, this shall not apply to any lease or pooling or unitization agreement involved in any suit pending on the effective date of this Code wherein either the length of time of said notice or the absence of such order is in issue.

Acts 1955, 54th Leg., p. 88, ch. 55, eff. Jan. 1, 1956; Amended by Acts 1993, 73rd Leg., ch. 957, § 65, eff. Sept. 1, 1993.

Part 8. Partition and Distribution of Estates of Decedents

Statutes in Context

Distribution of the estate is typically done when the administration is finished. However, an heir or beneficiary may request partial distribution at any time or total distribution after 12 months have passed from the date the court issued letters.

§ 373. Application for Partition and Distribution of Estates of Decedents

(a) Who May Apply. At any time after the expiration of twelve months after the original grant of letters testamentary or of administration, the executor or administrator, or the heirs, devisees, or legatees of the estate, or any of them, may, by written application filed in the court in which the estate is pending, request the partition and distribution of the estate.

(b) Contents of Application. The application shall state:

(1) The name of the person whose estate is sought to be partitioned and distributed; and

(2) The names and residences of all persons entitled to shares of such estate, and whether adults or minors; and, if these facts be unknown to the applicant, it shall be so stated in the application; and

(3) The reasons why partition and distribution should be had.

(c) Partial Distribution. At any time after the original grant of letters testamentary or of administration, and the filing and approval of the inventory, the executor or administrator, or the heirs, devisees, or legatees of the estate, or any of them, may, by written application filed in the court in which the estate is pending, request a distribution of any portion of the estate. All interested parties shall be personally cited, as in other distributions, including known creditors. The court may upon proper citation and hearing distribute any portion of the estate it deems advisable. In the event a distribution is to be made to one or more heirs or devisees, and not to all the heirs or devisees, the court shall require a refunding bond in an amount to be determined by the court to be filed with the court and, upon its approval, the court shall order the distribution of that portion of the estate, unless such requirement is waived in writing and the waiver is filed with the court by all interested parties. This section shall apply to corpus as well as income, notwithstanding any other provisions of this Code.

Acts 1955, 54th Leg., p. 88, ch. 55, eff. Jan. 1, 1956. Amended by Acts 1973, 63rd Leg., p. 408, ch. 182, § 2, eff. May 25, 1973.

§ 374. Citation of Interested Persons

Upon the filing of such application, the clerk shall issue a citation which shall state the name of the person whose estate is sought to be partitioned and dis-

tributed, and the date upon which the court will hear the application, and the citation shall require all persons interested in the estate to appear and show cause why such partition and distribution should not be made. Such citation shall be personally served upon each person residing in the state entitled to a share of the estate whose address is known; and, if there be any such persons whose identities or addresses are not known, or who are not residents of this state, or are residents of but absent from this state, such citation shall be served by publication.
Acts 1955, 54th Leg., p. 88, ch. 55, eff. Jan. 1, 1956.

§ 375. Citation of Executor or Administrator

When application for partition and distribution is made by any person other than the executor or administrator, such representative shall also be cited to appear and answer the application and to file in court a verified exhibit and account of the condition of the estate, as in the case of final settlements.
Acts 1955, 54th Leg., p. 88, ch. 55, eff. Jan. 1, 1956.

§ 377. Facts to be Ascertained Upon Hearing

At the hearing upon the application for partition and distribution, the court shall ascertain:

(a) The residue of the estate subject to partition and distribution, which shall be ascertained by deducting from the entire assets of such estate remaining on hand the amount of all debts and expenses of every kind which have been approved or established by judgment, but not paid, or which may yet be established by judgment, and also the probable future expenses of administration.

(b) The persons who are by law entitled to partition and distribution, and their respective shares.

(c) Whether advancements have been made to any of the persons so entitled and their nature and value. If advancements have been made, the court shall require the same to be placed in hotchpotch as required by the law governing intestate succession.
Acts 1955, 54th Leg., p. 88, ch. 55, eff. Jan. 1, 1956.

§ 378. Decree of the Court

If the court is of the opinion that the estate should be partitioned and distributed, it shall enter a decree which shall state:

(a) The name and address, if known, of each person entitled to a share of the estate, specifying those who are known to be minors, and the names of their guardians, or the guardians ad litem, and the name of the attorney appointed to represent those who are unknown or who are not residents of the state.

(b) The proportional part of the estate to which each is entitled.

(c) A full description of all the estate to be distributed.

(d) That the executor or administrator retain in his hands for the payment of all debts, taxes, and expenses of administration a sufficient amount of money or property for that purpose, specifying the amount of money or the property to be so retained.
Acts 1955, 54th Leg., p. 88, ch. 55, eff. Jan. 1, 1956.

Statutes in Context

Section 378A helps assure that marital deduction pecuniary gifts which authorize in-kind distribution of assets meet the "fairly representative" test and thus qualify for the deduction.

---

§ 378A. Satisfaction of Pecuniary Bequests

(a) Unless the governing instrument provides otherwise, if an executor, administrator, or trustee is authorized under the will or trust of a decedent to satisfy a pecuniary bequest, devise, or transfer in trust in kind with assets at their value for federal estate tax purposes, in satisfaction of a gift intended to qualify, or that otherwise would qualify, for a United States estate tax marital deduction, the executor, administrator, or trustee, in order to implement the bequest, devise, or transfer, shall distribute assets, including cash, fairly representative of appreciation or depreciation in the value of all property available for distribution in satisfaction of the pecuniary bequest, devise, or transfer.

(b) Unless the governing instrument provides otherwise, if a will or trust contains a pecuniary bequest, devise, or transfer that may be satisfied by distributing assets in kind and if the executor, administrator, or trustee determines to fund the bequest, devise, or transfer by distributing assets in kind, the property shall, for the purpose of funding the bequest, devise, or transfer, be valued at its value on the date or dates of distribution.
Added by Acts 1987, 70th Leg., ch. 1110, § 1, eff. Sept. 1, 1987. Amended by Acts 1991, 72nd Leg., ch. 895, § 15, eff. Sept. 1, 1991.

Statutes in Context

Income from a gifted item that accrues after death but before distribution is given to the beneficiary, less the cost of taxes, repairs, insurance, management fees, etc.

A legacy (cash bequest) in a will earns interest at the legal rate as provided in Finance Code § 302.002. There is currently a conflict regarding the date from which the interest begins to accrue. Probate Code § 378B(f) provides that interest begins running one year after the date the court grants letters testamentary or letters of administration. The 2003 Texas Legislature simultaneously reenacted (with a mere technical amendment) this section while in another bill, repealed the section. The repealing bill enacted the Uniform Principal and Income Act which provides that interest is payable beginning on the first anniversary of the date of the decedent's death. *See* Property Code § 116.051(3)(A).

---

§ 378B. Allocation of Income and Expenses During Administration of Decedent's Estate

(a) Except as provided by Subsection (b) of this section and unless the will provides otherwise, all expenses incurred in connection with the settlement of a decedent's estate, including debts, funeral expenses, estate taxes, penalties relating to estate taxes, and family allowances, shall be charged against the principal of the estate. Fees and expenses of an attorney, accountant, or other professional advisor, commissions and expenses of a personal representative, court costs, and all other similar fees or expenses relating to the administration of the estate and interest relating to estate taxes shall be allocated between the income and principal of the estate as the executor determines in its discretion to be just and equitable.

(b) Unless the will provides otherwise, income from the assets of a decedent's estate that accrues after the death of the testator and before distribution, including income from property used to discharge liabilities, shall be determined according to the rules applicable to a trustee under the Texas Trust Code (Subtitle B, Title 9, Property Code)[1] and distributed as provided by Chapter 116, Property Code, and Subsections (c), and (d) of this section.

(c) The income from the property bequeathed or devised to a specific devisee shall be distributed to the devisee after reduction for property taxes, ordinary repairs, insurance premiums, interest accrued after the death of the testator, other expenses of management and operation of the property, and other taxes, including the taxes imposed on the income that accrues during the period of administration and that is payable to the devisee.

(d) The balance of the net income shall be distributed to all other devisees after reduction for the balance of property taxes, ordinary repairs, insurance premiums, interest accrued, other expenses of management and operation of all property from which the estate is entitled to income, and taxes imposed on income that accrues during the period of administration and that is payable or allocable to the devisees, in proportion to the devisees' respective interests in the undistributed assets of the estate.

(e) (Repealed)

[subsection (f) repealed by Acts 2003, 78th Leg., ch. 659, § 4, eff. Jan. 1, 2004.]

[subsection (f) as amended by Acts 2003, 78th Leg., ch. 1060, § 15, eff. Sept. 1, 2003.]

(f) A devisee of a pecuniary bequest, whether or not in trust, shall be paid interest on the bequest at the legal rate of interest as provided by Section 302.002, Finance Code, and its subsequent amendments, beginning one year after the date the court grants letters testamentary or letters of administration.

(g) Income received by a trustee under this section shall be treated as income of the trust as provided by Section 116.101, Property Code.

(h) In this section, "undistributed assets" includes funds used to pay debts, administration expenses, and federal and state estate, inheritance, succession, and generation-skipping transfer taxes until the date of payment of the debts, expenses, and taxes. Except as required by Sections 2055 and 2056 of the Internal Revenue Code of 1986 (26 U.S.C. § 2055 and 2056), and its subsequent amendments, the frequency and method of determining the beneficiaries' respective interests in the undistributed assets of the estate shall be in the executor's sole and absolute discretion. The executor may consider all relevant factors, including administrative convenience and expense and the interests of the various beneficiaries of the estate in order to reach a fair and equitable result among beneficiaries.

(i) Chapter 116, Property Code, prevails to the extent of any conflict between this section and Chapter 116, Property Code.

Added by Acts 1993, 73rd Leg., ch. 846, § 24, eff. Sept. 1, 1993. Amended by Acts 2003, 78th Leg., ch. 659, §§ 3 & 4, eff. Jan. 1, 2004; Acts 2003, 78th Leg., ch. 1060, § 15, eff. Sept. 1, 2003.

§ 379. Partition When Estate Consists of Money or Debts Only

If the estate to be distributed shall consist only of money or debts due the estate, or both, the court shall fix the amount to which each distributee is entitled, and shall order the payment and delivery thereof by the executor or administrator.

Acts 1955, 54th Leg., p. 88, ch. 55, eff. Jan. 1, 1956.

§ 380. Partition and Distribution When Property is Capable of Division

(a) Appointment of Commissioners. If the estate does not consist entirely of money or debts due the estate, or both, the court shall appoint three or more discreet and disinterested persons as commissioners, to make a partition and distribution of the estate, unless the court has already determined that the estate is incapable of partition.

(b) Writ of Partition and Service Thereof. When commissioners are appointed, the clerk shall issue a writ of partition directed to the commissioners appointed, commanding them to proceed forthwith to make partition and distribution in accordance with the decree of the court, a copy of which decree shall accompany the writ, and also command them to make due return of said writ, with their proceedings under it, on a date named in the writ. Such writ shall be served by delivering the same and the accompanying copy of the decree of partition to any one of the commissioners appointed, and by notifying the other commissioners, verbally or otherwise, of their appointment, and such service may be made by any person.

(c) Partition by Commissioners. The commissioners shall make a fair, just, and impartial partition and distribution of the estate in the following order:

(1) Of the land or other property, by allotting to each distributee a share in each parcel or shares in one or more parcels, or one or more parcels separately, either with or without the addition of a share or shares of other parcels, as shall be most for the

[1] V.T.C.A. Property Code, § 111.001 et seq.

interest of the distributees; provided, the real estate is capable of being divided without manifest injury to all or any of the distributees.

(2) If the real estate is not capable of a fair, just and equal division in kind, but may be made so by allotting to one or more of the distributees a proportion of the money or other personal property to supply the deficiency or deficiencies, the commissioners shall have power to make, as nearly as may be, an equal division of the real estate and supply the deficiency of any share or shares from the money or other property.

(3) The commissioners shall proceed to make a like division in kind, as nearly as may be, of the money and other personal property, and shall determine by lot, among equal shares, to whom each particular share shall belong.

(d) Report of Commissioners. The commissioners, having divided the whole or any part of the estate, shall make to the court a written sworn report containing a statement of the property divided by them, and also a particular description of the property allotted to each distributee, and its value. If it be real estate that has been divided, the report shall contain a general plat of said land with the division lines plainly set down and with the number of acres in each share. The report of a majority of the commissioners shall be sufficient.

(e) Action of the Court. Upon the return of such report, the court shall examine the same carefully and hear all exceptions and objections thereto, and evidence in favor of or against the same, and if it be informal, shall cause said informality to be corrected. If such division shall appear to have been fairly made according to law, and no valid exceptions are taken to it, the court shall approve it, and shall enter a decree vesting title in the distributees of their respective shares or portions of the property as set apart to them by the commissioners; otherwise, the court may set aside said report and division and order a new partition to be made.

(f) Delivery of Property. When the report of commissioners to make partition has been approved and ordered to be recorded, the court shall order the executor or administrator to deliver to the distributees their respective shares of the estate on demand, including all the title deeds and papers belonging to the same.

(g) Fees of Commissioners. Commissioners thus appointed who actually serve in partitioning and distributing an estate shall be entitled to receive Five Dollars each for every day that they are necessarily engaged in the performance of their duties as such commissioners, to be taxed and paid as other costs in cases of partition.

Acts 1955, 54th Leg., p. 88, ch. 55, eff. Jan. 1, 1956.

§ 381. Partition and Distribution When Property of an Estate is Incapable of Division

(a) Finding by the Court. When, in the opinion of the court, the whole or any portion of an estate is not capable of a fair and equal partition and distribution, the court shall make a special finding in writing, specifying therein the property incapable of division.

(b) Order of Sale. When the court has found that the whole or any portion of the estate is not capable of fair and equal division, it shall order a sale of all property which it has found not to be capable of such division. Such sale shall be made by the executor or administrator in the same manner as when sales of real estate are made for the purpose of satisfying debts of the estate, and the proceeds of such sale, when collected, shall be distributed by the court among those entitled thereto.

(c) Purchase by Distributee. At such sale, if any distributee shall buy any of the property, he shall be required to pay or secure only such amount of his bid as exceeds the amount of his share of such property.

(d) Applicability of Provisions Relating to Sales of Real Estate. The provisions of this Code relative to reports of sales of real estate, the giving of an increased general or additional bond upon sales of real estate, and to the vesting of title to the property sold by decree or by deed, shall also apply to sales made under this Section.

Acts 1955, 54th Leg., p. 88, ch. 55, eff. Jan. 1, 1956.

§ 382. Property Located in Another County

(a) Court May Order Sale. When any portion of the estate to be partitioned lies in another county and cannot be fairly partitioned without prejudice to the interests of the distributees, the commissioners may report such facts to the court in writing; whereupon, if satisfied that the said property cannot be fairly divided, or that its sale would be more advantageous to the distributees, the court may order a sale thereof, which sale shall be conducted in the same manner as is provided in this Code for the sale of property which is not capable of fair and equal division.

(b) Court May Appoint Additional Commissioners. If the court is not satisfied that such property cannot be fairly and advantageously divided, or that its sale would be more advantageous to the distributees, three or more commissioners may be appointed in each county where any portion of the estate so reported is situated, and the same proceedings shall be had thereon as are provided in this Code for commissioners to make partition.

Acts 1955, 54th Leg., p. 88, ch. 55, eff. Jan. 1, 1956.

§ 384. Damages for Neglect to Deliver Property

If any executor or administrator shall neglect to deliver to the person entitled thereto, when demanded, any portion of an estate ordered to be delivered, such person may file with the clerk of the court his written complaint alleging the fact of such neglect, the date of his demand, and other relevant facts, whereupon the clerk shall issue a citation to be served personally on such representative, apprising him of the complaint and citing him to appear before the court and answer, if he so desires, at the time designated in the citation.

If at the hearing the court finds that the citation was duly served and returned and that the representative is guilty of such neglect, the court shall enter an order to that effect, and the representative shall be liable to such complainant in damages at the rate of ten per cent of the amount or appraised value of the share so withheld, per month, for each and every month or fraction thereof that the share is and/or has been so withheld after date of demand, which damages may be recovered in any court of competent jurisdiction.
Acts 1955, 54th Leg., p. 88, ch. 55, eff. Jan. 1, 1956.

§ 385. Partition of Community Property

(a) Application for Partition. When a husband or wife shall die leaving any community property, the survivor may, at any time after letters testamentary or of administration have been granted, and an inventory, appraisement, and list of the claims of the estate have been returned, make application in writing to the court which granted such letters for a partition of such community property.

(b) Bond and Action of the Court. The survivor shall execute and deliver to the judge of said court a bond with a corporate surety or two or more good and sufficient personal sureties, payable to and approved by said judge, for an amount equal to the value of the survivor's interest in such community property, conditioned for the payment of one-half of all debts existing against such community property, and the court shall proceed to make a partition of said community property into two equal moieties, one to be delivered to the survivor and the other to the executor or administrator of the deceased. The provisions of this Code respecting the partition and distribution of estates shall apply to such partition so far as the same are applicable.

(c) Lien Upon Property Delivered. Whenever such partition is made, a lien shall exist upon the property delivered to the survivor to secure the payment of the aforementioned bond; and any creditor of said community estate may sue in his own name on such bond, and shall have judgment thereon for one-half of such debt as he shall establish, and for the other one-half he shall be entitled to be paid by the executor or administrator of the deceased.
Acts 1955, 54th Leg., p. 88, ch. 55, eff. Jan. 1, 1956.

§ 386. Partition of Property Jointly Owned

Any person having a joint interest with the estate of a dececent in any property, real or personal, may make application to the court from which letters testamentary or of administration have been granted thereon to have a partition thereof, whereupon the court shall make a partition of said property between the applicant and the estate of the deceased; and all the provisions of this Code in relation to the partition and distribution of estates shall govern partition hereunder, so far as the same are applicable.
Acts 1955, 54th Leg., p. 88, ch. 55, eff. Jan. 1, 1956.

§ 387. Expense of Partition

Expense of partition of the estate of a decedent shall be paid by the distributees pro rata. The portion of the estate allotted each distributee shall be liable for his portion of such expense, and, if not paid, the court may order execution therefor in the names of the persons entitled thereto.
Acts 1955, 54th Leg., p. 88, ch. 55, eff. Jan. 1, 1956.

Part 10A. Stocks, Bonds, and Other Personal Property

Statutes in Context

Section 398A permits corporate securities and other personal property to be held in the name of a nominee (e.g., a stock broker).

---

§ 398A. Holding of Stocks, Bonds, and Other Personal Property by Personal Representatives in Name of Nominee

Unless otherwise provided by will, a personal representative may cause stocks, bonds, and other personal property of an estate to be registered and held in the name of a nominee without mention of the fiduciary relationship in any instrument or record constituting or evidencing title thereto. The personal representative is liable for the acts of the nominee with respect to any property so registered. The records of the personal representative shall at all times show the ownership of the property. Any property so registered shall be in the possession and control of the personal representative at all times and be kept separate from his individual property.
Added by Acts 1969, 61st Leg., p. 2106, ch. 719, § 1, eff. Sept. 1, 1969.

Part 11. Annual Accounts and Other Exhibits

Statutes in Context

Part 11 requires that the dependent personal representative prepare detailed accounts each year. The accounting must include all vouchers and receipts and it must be supported by a sworn affidavit.

---

§ 399. Annual Accounts Required

(a) Estates of Decedents Being Administered Under Order of Court. The personal representative of the estate of a decedent being administered under order of court shall, upon the expiration of twelve (12) months from the date of qualification and receipt of letters, return to the court an exhibit in writing under oath setting forth a list of all claims against the estate that were presented to him within the period covered by the account, specifying which have been allowed by him, which have been paid, which have been rejected and the date when rejected, which have been sued upon, and the condition of the suit, and show:

(1) All property that has come to his knowledge or into his possession not previously listed or inventoried as property of the estate.

(2) Any changes in the property of the estate which have not been previously reported.

(3) A complete account of receipts and disbursements for the period covered by the account, and the source and nature thereof, with receipts of principal and income to be shown separately.

(4) A complete, accurate and detailed description of the property being administered, the condition of the property and the use being made thereof, and, if rented, the terms upon and the price for which rented.

(5) The cash balance on hand and the name and location of the depository wherein such balance is kept; also, any other sums of cash in savings accounts or other form, deposited subject to court order, and the name and location of the depository thereof.

(6) A detailed description of personal property of the estate, which shall, with respect to bonds, notes, and other securities, include the names of obligor and obligee, or if payable to bearer, so state; the date of issue and maturity; the rate of interest; serial or other identifying numbers; in what manner the property is secured; and other data necessary to identify the same fully, and how and where held for safekeeping.

(7) A statement that, during the period covered by the account, all tax returns due have been filed and that all taxes due and owing have been paid and a complete account of the amount of the taxes, the date the taxes were paid, and the governmental entity to which the taxes were paid.

(8) If any tax return due to be filed or any taxes due to be paid are delinquent on the filing of the account, a description of the delinquency and the reasons for the delinquency.

(9) A statement that the personal representative has paid all the required bond premiums for the accounting period.

(b) Annual Reports Continue Until Estate Closed. Each personal representative of the estate of a decedent shall continue to file annual accounts conforming to the essential requirements of those in Subsection (a) hereof as to changes in the assets of the estate after rendition of the former account so that the true condition of the estate, with respect to money, securities, and other property, can be ascertained by the court or by any interested person, by adding to the balances forward the receipts, and then subtracting the disbursements. The description of property sufficiently described in an inventory or previous account may be by reference thereto.

(c) Supporting Vouchers, etc., Attached to Accounts. Annexed to all annual accounts of representatives of estates shall be:

(1) Proper vouchers for each item of credit claimed in the account, or, in the absence of such voucher, the item must be supported by evidence satisfactory to the court. Original vouchers may, upon application, be returned to the representative after approval of his account.

(2) An official letter from the bank or other depository in which the money on hand of the estate is deposited, showing the amounts in general or special deposits.

(3) Proof of the existence and possession of securities owned by the estate, or shown by the accounting, as well as other assets held by a depository subject to orders of the court, the proof to be by one of the following means:

a. By an official letter from the bank or other depository wherein said securities or other assets are held for safekeeping; provided, that if such depository is the representative, the official letter shall be signed by a representative of such depository other than the one verifying the account; or

b. By a certificate of an authorized representative of the corporation which is surety on the representative's bonds; or

c. By a certificate of the clerk or a deputy clerk of a court of record in this State; or

d. By an affidavit of any other reputable person designated by the court upon request of the representative or other interested party.

Such certificate or affidavit shall be to the effect that the affiant has examined the assets exhibited to him by the representative as assets of the estate in which the accounting is made, and shall describe the assets by reference to the account or otherwise sufficiently to identify those so exhibited, and shall state the time when and the place where exhibited. In lieu of using a certificate or an affidavit, the representative may exhibit the securities to the judge of the court who shall endorse on the account, or include in his order with respect thereto, a statement that the securities shown therein as on hand were in fact exhibited to him, and that those so exhibited were the same as those shown in the account, or note any variance. If the securities are exhibited at any place other than where deposited for safekeeping, it shall be at the expense and risk of the representative. The court may require additional evidence as to the existence and custody of such securities and other personal property as in his discretion he shall deem proper; and may require the representative to exhibit them to the court, or any person designated by him, at any time at the place where held for safekeeping.

(d) Verification of Account. The representative filing the account shall attach thereto his affidavit that it contains a correct and complete statement of the matters to which it relates.

Acts 1955, 54th Leg., p. 88, ch. 55, eff. Jan. 1, 1956. Amended by Acts 1957, 55th Leg., p. 53, ch. 31, § 11(a); Subsec. (a) amended by Acts 1993, 73rd Leg., ch. 712, § 4, eff. Sept. 1, 1993. Amended by Acts 1993, 73rd Leg., ch.

957, § 66, eff. Sept. 1, 1993; Subsec. (a) amended by Acts 1997, 75th Leg., ch. 1403, § 1, eff. Sept. 1, 1997.

§ 400. Penalty for Failure to File Annual Account

Should any personal representative of an estate fail to return any annual account required by preceding sections of this Code, any person interested in said estate may, upon written complaint, or the court upon its own motion may, cause the personal representative to be cited to return such account, and show cause for such failure. If he fails to return said account after being so cited, or fails to show good cause for his failure so to do, the court, upon hearing, may revoke the letters of such representative, and may fine him in a sum not to exceed Five Hundred Dollars ($500). He and his sureties shall be liable for any fine imposed, and for all damages and costs sustained by reason of such failure, which may be recovered in any court of competent jurisdiction.

Acts 1955, 54th Leg., p. 88, ch. 55, eff. Jan. 1, 1956. Amended by Acts 1957, 55th Leg., p. 53, ch. 31, § 11(b); Amended by Acts 1993, 73rd Leg., ch. 957, § 67, eff. Sept. 1, 1993.

§ 401. Action Upon Annual Accounts

These rules shall govern the handling of annual accounts:

(a) They shall be filed with the county clerk, and the filing thereof shall be noted forthwith upon the judge's docket.

(b) Before being considered by the judge, the account shall remain on file ten (10) days.

(c) At any time after the expiration of ten (10) days after the filing of an annual account, the judge shall consider same, and may continue the hearing thereon until fully advised as to all items of said account.

(d) No accounting shall be approved unless possession of cash, listed securities, or other assets held in safekeeping or on deposit under order of court has been proved as required by law.

(e) If the account be found incorrect, it shall be corrected. When corrected to the satisfaction of the court, it shall be approved by an order of court, and the court shall then act with respect to unpaid claims, as follows:

(1) Order for Payment of Claims in Full. If it shall appear from the exhibit, or from other evidence, that the estate is wholly solvent, and that the representative has in his hands sufficient funds for the payment of every character of claims against the estate, the court shall order immediate payment to be made of all claims allowed and approved or established by judgment.

(2) Order for Pro Rata Payment of Claims. If it shall appear from the account, or from other evidence, that the funds on hand are not sufficient for the payment of all the said claims, or if the estate is insolvent and the personal representative has any funds on hand, the court shall order such funds to be applied to the payment of all claims having a preference in the order of their priority if they, or any of them, be still unpaid, and then to the payment pro rata of the other claims allowed and approved or established by final judgment, taking into consideration also the claims that were presented within twelve (12) months after the granting of administration, and those which are in suit or on which suit may yet be instituted.

Acts 1955, 54th Leg., p. 88, ch. 55, eff. Jan. 1, 1956. Amended by Acts 1957, 55th Leg., p. 53, ch. 31, § 11(c).

§ 402. Additional Exhibits of Estates of Decedents

At any time after the expiration of fifteen months from the original grant of letters to an executor or administrator, any interested person may, by a complaint in writing filed in the court in which the estate is pending, cause the representative to be cited to appear and make an exhibit in writing under oath, setting forth fully, in connection with previous exhibits, the condition of the estate he represents; and, if it shall appear to the court by said exhibit, or by other evidence, that said representative has any funds of the estate in his hands subject to distribution among the creditors of the estate, the court shall order the same to be paid out to them according to the provisions of this Code; or any representative may voluntarily present such exhibit to the court; and, if he has any of the funds of the estate in his hands subject to distribution among the creditors of the estate, a like order shall be made.

Acts 1955, 54th Leg., p. 88, ch. 55, eff. Jan. 1, 1956.

§ 403. Penalty for Failure to File Exhibits or Reports

Should any personal representative fail to file any exhibit or report required by this Code, any person interested in the estate may, upon written complaint filed with the clerk of the court, cause him to be cited to appear and show cause why he should not file such exhibit or report; and, upon hearing, the court may order him to file such exhibit or report, and, unless good cause be shown for such failure, the court may revoke the letters of such personal representative and may fine him in an amount not to exceed One Thousand Dollars.

Acts 1955, 54th Leg., p. 88, ch. 55, eff. Jan. 1, 1956.

Part 12. Final Settlement, Accounting, and Discharge

Statutes in Context

Part 12 explains how a dependent administration is closed.

§ 404. Closing Administration of Estates of Decedents

Administration of the estates of decedents shall be settled and closed when all the debts known to exist

against the estate of a deceased person have been paid, or when they have been paid so far as the assets in the hands of an administrator or executor of such estate will permit, and when there is no further need for administration.
Acts 1955, 54th Leg., p. 88, ch. 55, eff. Jan. 1, 1956. Amended by Acts 1975, 64th Leg., p. 104, ch. 45, § 2, eff. Sept. 1, 1975; Amended by Acts 1985, 69th Leg., ch. 881, § 2, eff. Aug. 26, 1985; Subsec. (c) amended by Acts 1989, 71st Leg., ch. 1035, § 15, eff. Sept. 1, 1989; Subsec. (a) amended by Acts 1993, 73rd Leg., ch. 712, § 5, eff. Sept. 1, 1993; Acts 1999, 76th Leg., ch. 826, § 1, eff. June 18, 1999.

§ 405. Account for Final Settlement of Estates of Decedents

When administration of the estate of a decedent is to be settled and closed, the personal representative of such estate shall present to the court his verified account for final settlement. In such account it shall be sufficient to refer to the inventory without describing each item of property in detail, and to refer to and adopt any and all proceedings had in the administration concerning sales, renting or hiring, leasing for mineral development, or any other transactions on behalf of the estate including exhibits, accounts, and vouchers previously filed and approved, without restating the particular items thereof. Each final account, however, shall be accompanied by proper vouchers in support of each item thereof not already accounted for and shall show, either by reference to any proceedings authorized above or by statement of the facts:

1. The property belonging to the estate which has come into the hands of the executor or administrator.
2. The disposition that has been made of such property.
3. The debts that have been paid.
4. The debts and expenses, if any, still owing by the estate.
5. The property of the estate, if any, still remaining on hand.
6. The persons entitled to receive such estate, their relationship to the decedent, and their residence, if known, and whether adults or minors, and, if minors, the names of their guardians, if any.
7. All advancements or payments that have been made, if any, by the executor or administrator from such estate to any such person.
8. The tax returns due that have been filed and the taxes due and owing that have been paid and a complete account of the amount of taxes, the date the taxes were paid, and the governmental entity to which the taxes were paid.
9. If any tax return due to be filed or any taxes due to be paid are delinquent on the filing of the account, a description of the delinquency and the reasons for the delinquency.
10. The personal representative has paid all required bond premiums.

Acts 1955, 54th Leg., p. 88, ch. 55, eff. Jan. 1, 1956; Amended by Acts 1993, 73rd Leg., ch. 712, § 6, eff. Sept. 1, 1993; Acts 1993, 73rd Leg., ch. 957, § 69, eff. Sept. 1, 1993; Acts 1997, 75th Leg., ch. 1403, § 2, eff. Sept. 1, 1997.

§ 405A. Delivery of Property

The court may permit a resident executor or administrator who has any of the estate of a ward to deliver the estate to a duly qualified and acting guardian of the ward.
Added by Acts 1995, 74th Leg., ch. 1039, § 14, eff. Sept. 1, 1995.

§ 406. Procedure in Case of Neglect or Failure to File Final Account; Payments Due Meantime

(a) If a personal representative charged with the duty of filing a final account fails or neglects so to do at the proper time, the court shall, upon its own motion, or upon the written complaint of any one interested in the decedent's estate which has been administered, cause such representative to be cited to appear and present such account within the time specified in the citation.

(b) If the whereabouts of the personal representative and heirs of a decedent are unknown and a complaint has not been filed by anyone interested in the decedent's estate, the court may, on or after the fourth anniversary after the last date on which letters testamentary or of administration are issued by the court clerk, close the estate without a final accounting and without appointing a successor personal representative.
Amended by Acts 1993, 73rd Leg., ch. 898, § 1, eff. June 19, 1993; Acts 1993, 73rd Leg., ch. 957, § 70, eff. Sept. 1, 1993; Acts 1999, 76th Leg., ch. 827, § 1, eff. Sept. 1, 1999.

§ 407. Citation Upon Presentation of Account for Final Settlement

Upon the filing of an account for final settlement by temporary or permanent personal representatives of the estates of decedents, citation shall contain a statement that such final account has been filed, the time and place when it will be considered by the court, and a statement requiring the person or persons cited to appear and contest the same if they see proper. Such citation shall be issued by the county clerk to the persons and in the manner set out below.

1. In case of the estates of deceased persons, notice shall be given by the personal representative to each heir or beneficiary of the decedent by certified mail, return receipt requested, unless another type of notice is directed by the court by written order. The notice must include a copy of the account for final settlement.
2. If the court deems further additional notice necessary, it shall require the same by written order. In its discretion, the court may allow the waiver of notice of an account for final settlement in a proceeding concerning a decedent's estate.

Acts 1955, 54th Leg., p. 88, ch. 55, eff. Jan. 1, 1956. Amended by Acts 1959, 56th Leg., p. 641, ch. 294, § 1, eff. May 30, 1959; Acts 1979, 66th Leg., p. 1755, ch. 713, § 30, eff. Aug. 27, 1979; Amended by Acts 1983, 68th Leg., p. 4558, ch. 756, § 1, eff. Sept. 1, 1983; Acts 1993, 73rd Leg., ch. 957, § 71, eff. Sept. 1, 1993.

§ 408. Action of the Court

(a) Action Upon Account. Upon being satisfied that citation has been duly served upon all persons interested in the estate, the court shall examine the account for final settlement and the vouchers accompanying the same, and, after hearing all exceptions or objections thereto, and evidence in support of or against such account, shall audit and settle the same, and restate it if that be necessary.

(b) Distribution of Remaining Property. Upon final settlement of an estate, if there be any of such estate remaining in the hands of the personal representative, the court shall order that a partition and distribution be made among the persons entitled to receive such estate.

(c) Discharge of Representative When No Property Remains. If, upon such settlement, there be none of the estate remaining in the hands of the representative, he shall be discharged from his trust and the estate ordered closed.

(d) Discharge When Estate Fully Administered. Whenever the representative of an estate has fully administered the same in accordance with this Code and the orders of the court, and his final account has been approved, and he has delivered all of said estate remaining in his hands to the person or persons entitled to receive the same, it shall be the duty of the court to enter an order discharging such representative from his trust, and declaring the estate closed.

Acts 1955, 54th Leg., p. 88, ch. 55, eff. Jan. 1, 1956. Amended by Acts 1979, 66th Leg., p. 1877, ch. 758, § 4, eff. Aug. 27, 1979; Subsec. (b) amended by Acts 1993, 73rd Leg., ch. 957, § 72, eff. Sept. 1, 1993.

§ 409. Money Becoming Due Pending Final Discharge

Until the order of final discharge of the personal representative is entered in the minutes of the court, money or other thing of value falling due to the estate while the account for final settlement is pending may be paid, delivered, or tendered to the personal representative, who shall issue receipt therefor, and the obligor and/or payor shall be thereby discharged of the obligation for all purposes.

Acts 1955, 54th Leg., p. 88, ch. 55, eff. Jan. 1, 1956; Amended by Acts 1993, 73rd Leg., ch. 957, § 73, eff. Sept. 1, 1993.

§ 410. Inheritance Taxes Must be Paid

No final account of an executor or administrator shall be approved, and no estate of a decedent shall be closed, unless the final account shows, and the court finds, that all inheritance taxes due and owing to the State of Texas with respect to all interests and properties passing through the hands of the representative have been paid.

Acts 1955, 54th Leg., p. 88, ch. 55, eff. Jan. 1, 1956; Amended by Acts 1989, 71st Leg., ch. 1035, § 16, eff. Sept. 1, 1989.

§ 412. Offsets, Credits, and Bad Debts

In the settlement of any of the accounts of the personal representative of an estate, all debts due the estate which the court is satisfied could not have been collected by due diligence, and which have not been collected, shall be excluded from the computation.

Acts 1955, 54th Leg., p. 88, ch. 55, eff. Jan. 1, 1956.

§ 414. Procedure if Representative Fails to Deliver Estate

If any personal representative of an estate, upon final settlement, shall neglect to deliver to the person entitled thereto when demanded any portion of an estate or any funds or money in his hands ordered to be delivered, such person may file with the clerk of the court his written complaint alleging the fact of such neglect, the date of his demand, and other relevant facts, whereupon the clerk shall issue a citation to be served personally upon such representative, apprising him of the complaint and citing him to appear before the court and answer, if he so desires, at the time designated in the citation. If at the hearing the court finds that the citation was duly served and returned and that the representative is guilty of the neglect charged, the court shall enter an order to that effect, and the representative shall be liable to such person in damages at the rate of ten per cent of the amount or appraised value of the money or estate so withheld, per month, for each and every month or fraction thereof that said estate or money or funds is and/or has been so withheld after date of demand, which damages may be recovered in any court of competent jurisdiction.

Acts 1955, 54th Leg., p. 88, ch. 55, eff. Jan. 1, 1956; Amended by Acts 1993, 73rd Leg., ch. 957, § 74, eff. Sept. 1, 1993.

Chapter X. Payment of Estates into State Treasury

Statutes in Context

Under certain circumstances, the personal representative may be ordered to pay unclaimed estate funds to the comptroller under Chapter X. However, the relationship of these provisions to the unclaimed property provisions of Chapters 74 and 75 of the Property Code is unclear.

---

§ 427. When Estates to be Paid Into State Treasury

If any person entitled to a portion of an estate, except a resident minor without a guardian, shall not demand his portion from the executor or administrator within six months after an order of court approving the report of commissioners of partition, or within six months after the settlement of the final account of an executor or administrator, as the case may be, the court by written order shall require the executor or administrator to pay so much of said portion as is in money to the comptroller; and such portion as is in other property he shall order the executor or administrator to sell on such terms as the court thinks best, and, when the proceeds of such sale are collected, the court shall order the same to be paid to the comptroller, in all such cases allowing the executor or administrator reasonable compensation for his services. A suit to recover proceeds of the sale is governed by Section 433 of this Code.

Acts 1955, 54th Leg., p. 88, ch. 55, eff. Jan. 1, 1956; Amended by Acts 1991, 72nd Leg., ch. 153, § 27, eff. Sept. 1, 1991; Acts 1997, 75th Leg., ch. 1423, § 15.01, eff. Sept. 1, 1997.

§ 428. Indispensability of Comptroller as Party

The comptroller is an indispensable party to any judicial or administrative proceeding concerning the disposition and handling of any portion of an estate that is or may be payable to the comptroller under Section 427 of this Code. Whenever an order shall be made by the court for an executor or administrator to pay any funds to the comptroller under Section 427 of this Code, the clerk of the court in which such order is made shall serve on the comptroller by personal service of citation a certified copy of such order within five days after the same has been made.

Acts 1955, 54th Leg., p. 88, ch. 55, eff. Jan. 1, 1956; Amended by Acts 1991, 72nd Leg., ch. 153, § 27, eff. Sept. 1, 1991; Acts 1997, 75th Leg., ch. 1423, § 15.02, eff. Sept. 1, 1997.

§ 429. Penalty for Neglect to Notify Comptroller

Any clerk who shall neglect to have served on the comptroller by personal citation a certified copy of any such order within the time prescribed by Section 428 of this Code shall be liable in a penalty of One Hundred Dollars, to be recovered in an action in the name of the state, after personal service of citation, on the information of any citizen, one-half of which penalty shall be paid to the informer and the other one-half to the state.

Acts 1955, 54th Leg., p. 88, ch. 55, eff. Jan. 1, 1956; Amended by Acts 1991, 72nd Leg., ch. 153, § 27, eff. Sept. 1, 1991; Acts 1997, 75th Leg., ch. 1423, § 15.03, eff. Sept. 1, 1997.

§ 430. Receipt of Comptroller

Whenever an executor or administrator pays the comptroller any funds of the estate he represents, under the preceding provisions of this Code, he shall take from the comptroller a receipt for such payment, with official seal attached, and shall file the same with the clerk of the court ordering such payment; and such receipt shall be recorded in the minutes of the court.

Acts 1955, 54th Leg., p. 88, ch. 55, eff. Jan. 1, 1956; Amended by Acts 1997, 75th Leg., ch. 1423, § 15.04, eff. Sept. 1, 1997.

§ 431. Penalty for Failure to Make Payments to Comptroller

When an executor or administrator fails to pay to the comptroller any funds of an estate which he has been ordered by the court so to pay, within 30 days after such order has been made, such executor or administrator shall, after personal service of citation charging such failure and after proof thereof, be liable to pay out of his own estate to the comptroller damages thereon at the rate of five per cent per month for each month, or fraction thereof, that he fails to make such payment after 30 days from such order, which damages may be recovered in any court of competent jurisdiction.

Acts 1955, 54th Leg., p. 88, ch. 55, eff. Jan. 1, 1956; Amended by Acts 1991, 72nd Leg., ch. 153, § 28, eff. Sept. 1, 1991; Acts 1997, 75th Leg., ch. 1423, § 15.05, eff. Sept. 1, 1997.

§ 432. Comptroller May Enforce Payment and Collect Damages

The Comptroller shall have the right in the name of the state to apply to the court in which the order for payment was made to enforce the payment of funds which the executor or administrator has failed to pay to him pursuant to order of court, together with the payment of any damages that shall have accrued under the provisions of the preceding section of this code, and the court shall enforce such payment in like manner as other orders of payment are required to be enforced. The comptroller shall also have the right to institute suit in the name of the state against such executor or administrator, and the sureties on his bond, for the recovery of the funds so ordered to be paid and such damages as have accrued. The county attorney or criminal district attorney of the county, the district attorney of the district, or the attorney general, at the election of the comptroller and with the approval of the attorney general, shall represent the comptroller in all such proceedings, and shall also represent the interests of the state in all other matters arising under any provisions of this Code.

Acts 1955, 54th Leg., p. 88, ch. 55, eff. Jan. 1, 1956; Amended by Acts 1991, 72nd Leg., ch. 153, § 28, eff. Sept. 1, 1991; Acts 1997, 75th Leg., ch. 1423, § 15.06, eff. Sept. 1, 1997.

§ 433. Suit for the Recovery of Funds Paid to the Comptroller

(a) Mode of Recovery. When funds of an estate have been paid to the comptroller, any heir, devisee, or legatee of the estate, or their assigns, or any of them, may recover the portion of such funds to which he, she, or they are entitled. The person claiming such funds shall institute suit on or before the fourth anniversary of the date of the order requiring payment to the comptroller, by petition filed in the district court of Travis County, against the comptroller, setting forth the plaintiff's right to such funds, and the amount claimed by him.

(b) Citation. Upon the filing of such petition, the clerk shall issue a citation for the comptroller, to be served by personal service, to appear and represent the interest of the state in such suit. As the comptroller elects and with the approval of the attorney general, the attorney general, the county attorney or criminal district attorney for the county, or the district attorney for the district shall represent the comptroller.

(c) Procedure. The proceedings in such suit shall be governed by the rules for other civil suits; and, should the plaintiff establish his right to the funds claimed, he shall have a judgment therefor, which shall specify the amount to which he is entitled; and a certified copy of such judgment shall be sufficient authority for the comptroller to pay the same.

(d) Costs. The costs of any such suit shall in all cases be adjudged against the plaintiff, and he may be required to secure the costs.

Acts 1955, 54th Leg., p. 88, ch. 55, eff. Jan. 1, 1956; Subsecs. (a), (b) amended by Acts 1991, 72nd Leg., ch. 153, § 29, eff. Sept. 1, 1991; Acts 1997, 75th Leg., ch. 1423, § 15.07, eff. Sept. 1, 1997.

Chapter XI. Nontestamentary Transfers

Part 1. Multiple-Party Accounts

Statutes in Context

Multiple-party accounts, such as checking accounts, savings accounts, and certificates of deposit, are contractual arrangements for the deposit of money with financial institutions such as state or national banks, savings and loan associations, and credit unions. The disposition of the funds remaining in these accounts upon the death of one of the depositors depends on the type of account, the account contract, and the applicable state law.

Multiple-party accounts are important non-probate transfer mechanisms because these accounts are widely used, easy to understand, and inexpensive to obtain. Chapter XI, Part 1, address the four commonly recognized types of multiple-party accounts: (1) the *joint account*, which may transfer ownership rights to the account's balance to the surviving party; (2) the *agency* or *convenience account*, which does not transfer the balance upon the death of one of the parties; (3) the *payable on death account*, which causes the balance to belong to the surviving pay-on-death payees upon the death of the depositors; and (4) the *trust account*, under which the beneficiaries receive the account balance upon outliving all trustees.

§ 436. Definitions

In this part:

(1) "Account" means a contract of deposit of funds between a depositor and a financial institution, and includes a checking account, savings account, certificate of deposit, share account, and other like arrangement.

(2) "Beneficiary" means a person named in a trust account as one for whom a party to the account is named as trustee.

(3) "Financial institution" means an organization authorized to do business under state or federal laws relating to financial institutions, including, without limitation, banks and trust companies, savings banks, building and loan associations, savings and loan companies or associations, credit unions, and brokerage firms that deal in the sales and purchases of stocks, bonds, and other types of securities.

(4) "Joint account" means an account payable on request to one or more of two or more parties whether or not there is a right of survivorship.

(5) "Multiple-party account" means a joint account, a convenience account, a P.O.D. account, or a trust account. It does not include accounts established for deposit of funds of a partnership, joint venture, or other association for business purposes, or accounts controlled by one or more persons as the duly authorized agent or trustee for a corporation, unincorporated association, charitable or civic organization, or a regular fiduciary or trust account where the relationship is established other than by deposit agreement.

(6) "Net contribution" of a party to a joint account as of any given time is the sum of all deposits made to that account by or for him, less all withdrawals made by or for him which have not been paid to or applied to the use of any other party, plus a pro rata share of any interest or dividends included in the current balance. The term includes, in addition, any proceeds of deposit life insurance added to the account by reason of the death of the party whose net contribution is in question.

(7) "Party" means a person who, by the terms of the account, has a present right, subject to request, to payment from a multiple-party account. A P.O.D. payee or beneficiary of a trust account is a party only after the account becomes payable to him by reason of his surviving the original payee or trustee. Unless the context otherwise requires, it includes a guardian, personal representative, or assignee, including an attaching creditor, of a party. It also includes a person identified as a trustee of an account for another whether or not a beneficiary is named, but it does not include a named beneficiary unless the beneficiary has a present right of withdrawal.

(8) "Payment" of sums on deposit includes withdrawal, payment on check or other directive of a party, and any pledge of sums on deposit by a party

and any set-off, or reduction or other disposition of all or part of an account pursuant to a pledge.

(9) "Proof of death" includes a certified copy of a death certificate or the judgment or order of a court in a proceeding where the death of a person is proved by circumstantial evidence to the satisfaction of the court as provided by Section 72 of this code.

(10) "P.O.D. account" means an account payable on request to one person during lifetime and on his death to one or more P.O.D. payees, or to one or more persons during their lifetimes and on the death of all of them to one or more P.O.D. payees.

(11) "P.O.D. payee" means a person designated on a P.O.D. account as one to whom the account is payable on request after the death of one or more persons.

(12) "Request" means a proper request for withdrawal, or a check or order for payment, which complies with all conditions of the account, including special requirements concerning necessary signatures and regulations of the financial institution, but if the financial institution conditions withdrawal or payment on advance notice, for purposes of this part the request for withdrawal or payment is treated as immediately effective and a notice of intent to withdraw is treated as a request for withdrawal.

(13) "Sums on deposit" means the balance payable on a multiple-party account including interest, dividends, and in addition any deposit life insurance proceeds added to the account by reason of the death of a party.

(14) "Trust account" means an account in the name of one or more parties as trustee for one or more beneficiaries where the relationship is established by the form of the account and the deposit agreement with the financial institution and there is no subject of the trust other than the sums on deposit in the account. It is not essential that payment to the beneficiary be mentioned in the deposit agreement. A trust account does not include a regular trust account under a testamentary trust or a trust agreement which has significance apart from the account, or a fiduciary account arising from a fiduciary relation such as attorney-client.

(15) "Withdrawal" includes payment to a third person pursuant to check or other directive of a party.

Added by Acts 1979, 66th Leg., p. 1756, ch. 713, § 31, eff. Aug. 27, 1979; Subsecs. (3), (5) amended by Acts 1993, 73rd Leg., ch. 846, § 25, eff. Sept. 1, 1993.

Statutes in Context

The right to withdraw funds from a multiple-party account is a separate issue from the ownership of those funds. For example, a party to a joint account may have the right to withdraw funds but does not necessarily own those funds.

---

§ 437. Ownership as Between Parties and Others

The provisions of Sections 438 through 440 of this code that concern beneficial ownership as between parties, or as between parties and P.O.D. payees or beneficiaries of multiple-party accounts, are relevant only to controversies between these persons and their creditors and other successors, and have no bearing on the power of withdrawal of these persons as determined by the terms of account contracts.

Added by Acts 1979, 66th Leg., p. 1756, ch. 713, § 31, eff. Aug. 27, 1979; Amended by Acts 1981, 67th Leg., p. 895, ch. 319, § 2, eff. Sept. 1, 1981.

Statutes in Context

Section 438 explains who owns the funds in a multiple-party account while the original parties are all still alive.

1. Joint Account. The funds in a joint account belong to the parties in proportion to their net contributions, that is, what the party deposited, minus what the party withdrew, plus a proportionate share of the interest. *See* § 436(6).

2. P.O.D. Account. The funds in a P.O.D. account belong to the original payees. The P.O.D. payees have no ownership rights.

3. Trust Account. The funds in a trust account belong to the trustee and the beneficiary has no rights unless there is a contrary intent shown by the account terms or deposit agreement or there is clear and convincing evidence of an irrevocable trust.

---

§ 438. Ownership During Lifetime

(a) A joint account belongs, during the lifetime of all parties, to the parties in proportion to the net contributions by each to the sums on deposit, unless there is clear and convincing evidence of a different intent.

(b) A P.O.D. account belongs to the original payee during his lifetime and not to the P.O.D. payee or payees. If two or more parties are named as original payees, during their lifetimes rights as between them are governed by Subsection (a) of this section.

(c) Unless a contrary intent is manifested by the terms of the account or the deposit agreement or there is other clear and convincing evidence of an irrevocable trust, a trust account belongs beneficially to the trustee during his lifetime, and if two or more parties are named as trustee on the account, during their lifetimes beneficial rights as between them are governed by Subsection (a) of this section. If there is an irrevocable trust, the account belongs beneficially to the beneficiary.

Added by Acts 1979, 66th Leg., p. 1756, ch. 713, § 31, eff. Aug. 27, 1979.

Statutes in Context

Section 438A governs convenience accounts which are used as a primitive type of agency relationship to, for example, allow someone to assist the depositor in

writing checks when the depositor is unable to do so (e.g., disabled, stationed out of the country in the military, on vacation, etc.).

All funds in the account belong to the party, not the co-signer, although both the party and the co-signer have the right to withdraw the funds. When the party dies, the entire account passes into the party's estate. The co-signer has no survivorship rights.

§ 438A. Convenience Account

(a) If an account is established at a financial institution by one or more parties in the names of the parties and one or more convenience signers and the terms of the account provide that the sums on deposit are paid or delivered to the parties or to the convenience signers "for the convenience" of the parties, the account is a convenience account.

(b) The making of a deposit in a convenience account does not affect the title to the deposit.

(c) A party to a convenience account is not considered to have made a gift of the deposit or of any additions or accruals to the deposit to a convenience signer.

(d) On the death of the last surviving party, a convenience signer shall have no right of survivorship in the account and ownership of the account remains in the estate of the last surviving party.

(e) If an addition is made to the account by anyone other than a party, the addition and accruals to the addition are considered to have been made by a party.

(f) All deposits to a convenience account and additions and accruals to the deposits may be paid to a party or to a convenience signer. The financial institution is completely released from liability for a payment made from the account before the financial institution receives notice in writing signed by the party not to make the payment in accordance with the terms of the account. After receipt of the notice from a party, the financial institution may require a party to approve any further payments from the account.

(g) If the financial institution makes a payment of the sums on deposit in a convenience account to a convenience signer after the death of the last surviving party and before the financial institution has received written notice of the last surviving party's death, the financial institution is completely released from liability for the payment. If a financial institution makes payment to the personal representative of the deceased last surviving party's estate after the death of the last surviving party and before service on the financial institution of a court order prohibiting payment, the financial institution is released to the extent of the payment from liability to any person claiming a right to the funds. The receipt by the representative to whom payment is made is a complete release and discharge of the financial institution.

Added by Acts 1993, 73rd Leg., ch. 795, § 1, eff. Aug. 30, 1993; Acts 1993, 73rd Leg., ch. 846, § 27, eff. Sept. 1, 1993. Amended by Acts 2003, 78th Leg., ch. 658, § 1, eff. Sept. 1, 2003.

Statutes in Context

Section 439 governs ownership of the funds in a multiple-party account when one or more of the parties dies.

1. Joint Account. The net contributions of the deceased party pass into the deceased party's estate unless there is an express survivorship agreement. Unlike many states, the presumption in Texas is that a joint account does not have the survivorship feature. (Note that this is consistent with § 46(a).) The survivorship feature exists only if there is (a) a written agreement, (b) signed by the deceased party (if community property is involved, both spouses must sign under § 451), (c) which expressly makes the deceased party's interest survive to the surviving party. Extrinsic evidence is not admissible to establish the survivorship feature.

The statute contains "safe harbor" language to create the survivorship feature, that is, "On the death of one party to a joint account, all sums in the account on the date of the death vest in and belong to the surviving party as his or her separate property and estate." Note that a mere authorization of payment of funds to the survivor does not create the survivorship feature. The right to withdraw is not equated with ownership rights. *See Stauffer v. Henderson*, 801 S.W.2d 858 (Tex. 1990).

2. P.O.D. Account. The funds in a P.O.D. account belong to the surviving P.O.D. payees only after all original P.O.D. payees are dead.

3. Trust Account. The funds in a trust account belong to the surviving beneficiaries only after all trustees are dead.

§ 439. Right of Survivorship

(a) Sums remaining on deposit at the death of a party to a joint account belong to the surviving party or parties against the estate of the decedent if, by a written agreement signed by the party who dies, the interest of such deceased party is made to survive to the surviving party or parties. Notwithstanding any other law, an agreement is sufficient to confer an absolute right of survivorship on parties to a joint account under this subsection if the agreement states in substantially the following form: "On the death of one party to a joint account, all sums in the account on the date of the death vest in and belong to the surviving party as his or her separate property and estate." A survivorship agreement will not be inferred from the mere fact that the account is a joint account. If there are two or more surviving parties, their respective ownerships during lifetime shall be in proportion to their previous ownership interests under Section 438 of this code augmented by an equal share for each survivor of any interest the decedent may have owned in the account immediately before his death, and the right of survivorship continues between the surviving parties if a written agreement signed by a party who dies so provides.

(b) If the account is a P.O.D. account and there is a written agreement signed by the original payee or payees, on the death of the original payee or on the death of the survivor of two or more original payees, any sums remaining on deposit belong to the P.O.D. payee or payees if surviving, or to the survivor of them if one or more P.O.D. payees die before the original payee. If two or more P.O.D. payees survive, there is no right of survivorship in event of death of a P.O.D. payee thereafter unless the terms of the account or deposit agreement expressly provide for survivorship between them.

(c) If the account is a trust account and there is a written agreement signed by the trustee or trustees, on death of the trustee or the survivor of two or more trustees, any sums remaining on deposit belong to the person or persons named as beneficiaries, if surviving, or to the survivor of them if one or more beneficiaries die before the trustee dies. If two or more beneficiaries survive, there is no right of survivorship in event of death of any beneficiary thereafter unless the terms of the account or deposit agreement expressly provide for survivorship between them.

(d) In other cases, the death of any party to a multiple-party account has no effect on beneficial ownership of the account other than to transfer the rights of the decedent as part of his estate.

Added by Acts 1979, 66th Leg., p. 1756, ch. 713, § 31, eff. Aug. 27, 1979; Subsec. (a) amended by Acts 1987, 70th Leg., ch. 297, § 1, eff. Aug. 31, 1987; Subsecs. (b), (c) amended by Acts 1993, 73rd Leg., ch. 846, § 26, eff. Sept. 1, 1993.

Statutes in Context

A financial institution may use the form provided in § 439A to achieve predicable results and to give the customer understandable information regarding the workings of multiple-party accounts. However, few banks actually use the suggested form.

§ 439A. Uniform Single-Party or Multiple-Party Account Form

(a) A contract of deposit that contains provisions substantially the same as in the form provided by Subsection (b) of this section establishes the type of account selected by a party. The provisions of this part of Chapter XI of this code govern an account selected under the form, other than a single-party account without a P.O.D. designation. A contract of deposit that does not contain provisions substantially the same as in the form provided by Subsection (b) of this section is governed by the provisions of this chapter applicable to the account that most nearly conforms to the depositor's intent.

(b) A financial institution may use the following form to establish the type of account selected by a party:

UNIFORM SINGLE-PARTY OR MULTIPLE-PARTY ACCOUNT SELECTION FORM NOTICE: THE TYPE OF ACCOUNT YOU SELECT MAY DETERMINE HOW PROPERTY PASSES ON YOUR DEATH. YOUR WILL MAY NOT CONTROL THE DISPOSITION OF FUNDS HELD IN SOME OF THE FOLLOWING ACCOUNTS.

Select one of the following accounts by placing your initials next to the account selected:

____ (1) SINGLE-PARTY ACCOUNT WITHOUT "P.O.D." (PAYABLE ON DEATH) DESIGNATION. The party to the account owns the account. On the death of the party, ownership of the account passes as a part of the party's estate under the party's will or by intestacy.

Enter the name of the party:

____

____ (2) SINGLE-PARTY ACCOUNT WITH "P.O.D." (PAYABLE ON DEATH) DESIGNATION. The party to the account owns the account. On the death of the party, ownership of the account passes to the P.O.D. beneficiaries of the account. The account is not a part of the party's estate.

Enter the name of the party:

____

Enter the name or names of the P.O.D. beneficiaries:

____

____

____ (3) MULTIPLE-PARTY ACCOUNT WITHOUT RIGHT OF SURVIVORSHIP. The parties to the account own the account in proportion to the parties' net contributions to the account. The financial institution may pay any sum in the account to a party at any time. On the death of a party, the party's ownership of the account passes as a part of the party's estate under the party's will or by intestacy.

Enter the names of the parties:

____

____

____

____ (4) MULTIPLE-PARTY ACCOUNT WITH RIGHT OF SURVIVORSHIP. The parties to the account own the account in proportion to the parties' net contributions to the account. The financial institution may pay any sum in the account to a party at any time. On the death of a party, the party's ownership of the account passes to the surviving parties.

Enter the names of the parties:

____

____

____ (5) MULTIPLE-PARTY ACCOUNT WITH RIGHT OF SURVIVORSHIP AND P.O.D. (PAYABLE ON DEATH) DESIGNATION. The parties to the account own the account in proportion to the parties' net contributions to the account. The financial institution may pay any sum in the account to a party at any time. On the death of the last surviving party, the ownership of the account passes to the P.O.D. beneficiaries.

Enter the names of the parties:

____

Enter the name or names of the P.O.D. beneficiaries:

____

____ (6) CONVENIENCE ACCOUNT. The parties to the account own the account. One or more convenience signers to the account may make account transactions for a party. A convenience signer does not own the account. On the death of the last surviving party, ownership of the account passes as a part of the last surviving party's estate under the last surviving party's will or by intestacy. The financial institution may pay funds in the account to a convenience signer before the financial institution receives notice of the death of the last surviving party. The payment to a convenience signer does not affect the parties' [party's] ownership of the account.

Enter the names of the parties:

____

____

Enter the names of the convenience signers:

____

____

____ (7) TRUST ACCOUNT. The parties named as trustees to the account own the account in proportion to the parties' net contributions to the account. A trustee may withdraw funds from the account. A beneficiary may not withdraw funds from the account before all trustees are deceased. On the death of the last surviving trustee, the ownership of the account passes to the beneficiary. The trust account is not a part of a trustee's estate and does not pass under the trustee's will or by intestacy, unless the trustee survives all of the beneficiaries and all other trustees.

Enter the name or names of the trustees:

____

Enter the name or names of the beneficiaries:

____

(c) A financial institution shall be deemed to have adequately disclosed the information provided in this section if the financial institution uses the form set forth in Subsection (b) of this section. If a financial institution varies the format of the form set forth in Subsection (b) of this section, then such financial institution may make disclosures in the account agreement or in any other form which adequately discloses the information provided in this section.

(d) A financial institution may combine any of the provisions and vary the format of the selections form and notices described in Subsection (b) of this section provided that the customer receives adequate disclosure of the ownership rights and there is appropriate indication of the names of the parties. This may be accomplished in a universal account form with options listed for selection and additional disclosures provided in the account agreement, or in any other manner which adequately discloses the information provided in this section.

Added by Acts 1993, 73rd Leg., ch. 795, § 2, eff. Aug. 30, 1993. Amended by Acts 2003, 78th Leg., ch.658, § 2, eff. Sept. 1, 2003.

§ 440. Effect of Written Notice to Financial Institution

The provisions of Section 439 of this code as to rights of survivorship are determined by the form of the account at the death of a party. Notwithstanding any other provision of the law, this form may be altered by written order given by a party to the financial institution to change the form of the account or to stop or vary payment under the terms of the account. The order or request must be signed by a party, received by the financial institution during the party's lifetime, and not countermanded by other written order of the same party during his lifetime.

Added by Acts 1979, 66th Leg., p. 1756, ch. 713, § 31, eff. Aug. 27, 1979.

§ 441. Accounts and Transfers Nontestamentary

Transfers resulting from the application of Section 439 of this code are effective by reason of the account contracts involved and this statute and are not to be considered as testamentary or subject to the testamentary provisions of this code.

Added by Acts 1979, 66th Leg., p. 1756, ch. 713, § 31, eff. Aug. 27, 1979.

Statutes in Context

Section 442 provides that funds in a multiple-party account are available to pay the debts of a deceased depositor but only as a last resort after all other estate assets are exhausted. Thus, although multiple-party accounts are considered non-probate in nature, they may still be involved in the probate process if the funds are needed to pay debts or other claims against the estate.

§ 442. Rights of Creditors

No multiple-party account will be effective against an estate of a deceased party to transfer to a survivor sums needed to pay debts, taxes, and expenses of administration, including statutory allowances to the surviving spouse and minor children, if other assets of the estate are insufficient. No multiple-party account will be effective against the claim of a secured creditor who has a lien on the account. A party to a multiple-party account may pledge the account or otherwise create a security interest in the account without the joinder of, as appropriate, a P.O.D. payee, a beneficiary, a convenience signer, or any other party to a joint account, regardless of whether there is a right of survivorship. A convenience signer may not pledge or otherwise create a security interest in an account. Not later than the 30th day after the date on which a security interest on a multiple-party account is perfected, a secured creditor that is a financial institution the accounts of which are insured by the Federal Deposit Insurance Corporation shall provide written notice of the pledge of the account to any other party to the account who did not create the security interest. The notice must be sent by certified mail to any other party at the last address the party provided to the depository bank and is not required to be provided to a P.O.D. payee, a beneficiary, or a convenience signer. A party, P.O.D.

payee, or beneficiary who receives payment from a multiple-party account after the death of a deceased party shall be liable to account to the deceased party's personal representative for amounts the decedent owned beneficially immediately before his death to the extent necessary to discharge the claims and charges mentioned above remaining unpaid after application of the decedent's estate, but is not liable in an amount greater than the amount that the party, P.O.D. payee, or beneficiary received from the multiple-party account. No proceeding to assert this liability shall be commenced unless the personal representative has received a written demand by a surviving spouse, a creditor, or one acting for a minor child of the decedent, and no proceeding shall be commenced later than two years following the death of the decedent. Sums recovered by the personal representative shall be administered as part of the decedent's estate. This section shall not affect the right of a financial institution to make payment on multiple-party accounts according to the terms thereof, or make it liable to the estate of a deceased party unless before payment the institution received written notice from the personal representative stating the sums needed to pay debts, taxes, claims, and expenses of administration.

Added by Acts 1979, 66th Leg., p. 1756, ch. 713, § 31, eff. Aug. 27, 1979. Amended by Acts 2003, 78th Leg., ch. 564, § 1, eff. Sept. 1, 2003.

§ 443. Protection of Financial Institutions

Sections 444 through 449 of this code govern the liability of financial institutions that make payments as provided in this chapter and the set-off rights of the institutions.

Added by Acts 1979, 66th Leg., p. 1756, ch. 713, § 31, eff. Aug. 27, 1979.

§ 444. Payment on Signature of One Party

Financial institutions may enter into multiple-party accounts to the same extent that they may enter into single-party accounts. A multiple-party account may be paid, on request, to any one or more of the parties. A financial institution shall not be required to inquire as to the source of funds received for deposit to a multiple-party account, or to inquire as to the proposed application of any sum withdrawn from an account, for purposes of establishing net contributions.

Added by Acts 1979, 66th Leg., p. 1756, ch. 713, § 31, eff. Aug. 27, 1979.

§ 445. Payment of Joint Account After Death or Disability

Any sums in a joint account may be paid, on request, to any party without regard to whether any other party is incapacitated or deceased at the time the payment is demanded, but payment may not be made to the personal representative or heirs of a deceased party unless proofs of death are presented to the financial institution showing that the decedent was the last surviving party or unless there is no right of survivorship under Section 439 of this code. A financial institution that pays a sum from a joint account to a surviving party to that account pursuant to a written agreement under Section 439(a) of this code is not liable to an heir, devisee, or beneficiary of the decedent's estate.

Added by Acts 1979, 66th Leg., p. 1756, ch. 713, § 31, eff. Aug. 27, 1979; Amended by Acts 1987, 70th Leg., ch. 297, § 2, eff. Aug. 31, 1987.

§ 446. Payment of P.O.D. Account

A P.O.D. account may be paid, on request, to any original party to the account. Payment may be made, on request, to the P.O.D. payee or to the personal representative or heirs of a deceased P.O.D. payee upon presentation to the financial institution of proof of death showing that the P.O.D. payee survived all persons named as original payees. Payment may be made to the personal representative or heirs of a deceased original payee if proof of death is presented to the financial institution showing that his decedent was the survivor of all other persons named on the account either as an original payee or as P.O.D. payee.

Added by Acts 1979, 66th Leg., p. 1756, ch. 713, § 31, eff. Aug. 27, 1979.

§ 447. Payment of Trust Account

A trust account may be paid, on request, to any trustee. Unless the financial institution has received written notice that the beneficiary has a vested interest not dependent upon his surviving the trustee, payment may be made to the personal representative or heirs of a deceased trustee if proof of death is presented to the financial institution showing that his decedent was the survivor of all other persons named on the account either as trustee or beneficiary. Payment may be made, on request, to the beneficiary upon presentation to the financial institution of proof of death showing that the beneficiary or beneficiaries survived all persons named as trustees.

Added by Acts 1979, 66th Leg., p. 1756, ch. 713, § 31, eff. Aug. 27, 1979.

§ 448. Discharge from Claims

Payment made as provided by Section 444, 445, 446, or 447 of this code discharges the financial institution from all claims for amounts so paid whether or not the payment is consistent with the beneficial ownership of the account as between parties, P.O.D. payees, or beneficiaries, or their successors. The protection here given does not extend to payments made after a financial institution has received written notice from any party able to request present payment to the effect that withdrawals in accordance with the terms of the account should not be permitted. Unless the notice is withdrawn by the person giving it, the successor of any deceased party must concur in any demand for withdrawal if the financial institution is to be protected under this section. No other notice or any other information shown to have been available to a financial institution shall affect its right to the protection provided here. The protection

here provided shall have no bearing on the rights of parties in disputes between themselves or their successors concerning the beneficial ownership of funds in, or withdrawn from, multiple-party accounts.
Added by Acts 1979, 66th Leg., p. 1756, ch. 713, § 31, eff. Aug. 27, 1979.

§ 449. Set-Off to Financial Institution

Without qualifying any other statutory right to set-off or lien and subject to any contractual provision, if a party to a multiple-party account is indebted to a financial institution, the financial institution has a right to set-off against the account in which the party has or had immediately before his death a present right of withdrawal. The amount of the account subject to set-off is that proportion to which the debtor is, or was immediately before his death, beneficially entitled, and in the absence of proof of net contributions, to an equal share with all parties having present rights of withdrawal.
Added by Acts 1979, 66th Leg., p. 1756, ch. 713, § 31, eff. Aug. 27, 1979.

Part 2. Provisions Relating to Effect of Death

Statutes in Context

Section 450 authorizes a wide range of arrangements which provide for payment or transfer upon death. These designations are effective to transfer property outside of probate.

§ 450. Provisions for Payment or Transfer at Death

(a) Any of the following provisions in an insurance policy, contract of employment, bond, mortgage, promissory note, deposit agreement, employees' trust, retirement account, deferred compensation arrangement, custodial agreement, pension plan, trust agreement, conveyance of real or personal property, securities, accounts with financial institutions as defined in Part 1 of this chapter, mutual fund account, or any other written instrument effective as a contract, gift, conveyance, or trust is deemed to be nontestamentary, and this code does not invalidate the instrument or any provision:

(1) that money or other benefits theretofore due to, controlled, or owned by a decedent shall be paid after his death to a person designated by the decedent in either the instrument or a separate writing, including a will, executed at the same time as the instrument or subsequently;

(2) that any money due or to become due under the instrument shall cease to be payable in event of the death of the promisee or the promissor before payment or demand; or

(3) that any property which is the subject of the instrument shall pass to a person designated by the decedent in either the instrument or a separate writing, including a will, executed at the same time as the instrument or subsequently.

(b) Nothing in this section limits the rights of creditors under other laws of this state.

(c) In this section:

(1) "Employees' trust" means:

(A) a trust that forms a part of a stock-bonus, pension, or profit-sharing plan under Section 401, Internal Revenue Code of 1954 (26 U.S.C.A. Sec. 401 (1986));

(B) a pension trust under Chapter 111, Property Code; and

(C) an employer-sponsored benefit plan or program, or any other retirement savings arrangement, including a pension plan created under Section 3, Employee Retirement Income Security Act of 1974 (29 U.S.C.A. Sec. 1002 (1986)), regardless of whether the plan, program, or arrangement is funded through a trust.

(2) "Individual retirement account" means a trust, custodial arrangement, or annuity under Section 408(a) or (b), Internal Revenue Code of 1954 (26 U.S.C.A. Sec. 408 (1986)).

(3) "Retirement account" means a retirement-annuity contract, an individual retirement account, a simplified employee pension, or any other retirement savings arrangement.

(4) "Retirement-annuity contract" means an annuity contract under Section 403, Internal Revenue Code of 1954 (26 U.S.C.A. Sec. 403 (1986)).

(5) "Simplified employee pension" means a trust, custodial arrangement, or annuity under Section 408, Internal Revenue Code of 1954 (26 U.S.C.A. Sec. 408 (1986)).

Subsec. (a) amended by Acts 1987, 70th Leg., ch. 94, § 1, eff. Aug. 31, 1987; Subsec. (c) added by Acts 1987, 70th Leg., ch. 94, § 2, eff. Aug. 31, 1987; Subsec. (a) amended by Acts 1997, 75th Leg., ch. 1302, § 14, eff. Sept. 1, 1997; Acts 2001, 77th Leg., ch. 284, § 1, eff. May 22, 2001.

Part 3. Community Property with Right of Survivorship

Statutes in Context

Community property could not be held in survivorship form until 1987 when Article XVI, § 15 of the Texas Constitution was amended to authorize community property survivorship agreements. Sections 451-462 provide guidance with respect to these agreements.

§ 451. Right of Survivorship

At any time, spouses may agree between themselves that all or part of their community property, then existing or to be acquired, becomes the property of the surviving spouse on the death of a spouse.
Added by Acts 1989, 71st Leg., ch. 655, § 2, eff. Aug. 28, 1989.

Statutes in Context

A community property survivorship agreement must be (1) in writing, (2) signed by *both* spouses (not just the deceased spouse), and (3) contain express survivorship language.

§ 452. Formalities

An agreement between spouses creating a right of survivorship in community property must be in writing and signed by both spouses. If an agreement in writing is signed by both spouses, the agreement shall be sufficient to create a right of survivorship in the community property described in the agreement if it includes any of the following phrases:

(1) "with right of survivorship";

(2) "will become the property of the survivor";

(3) "will vest in and belong to the surviving spouse"; or

(4) "shall pass to the surviving spouse."

An agreement that otherwise meets the requirements of this part, however, shall be effective without including any of those phrases.

Added by Acts 1989, 71st Leg., ch. 655, § 2, eff. Aug. 28, 1989.

§ 453. Ownership and Management During Marriage

Property subject to an agreement between spouses creating a right of survivorship in community property remains community property during the marriage of the spouses. Such an agreement does not affect the rights of the spouses concerning management, control, and disposition of the property subject to the agreement unless the agreement provides otherwise.

Added by Acts 1989, 71st Leg., ch. 655, § 2, eff. Aug. 28, 1989.

§ 454. Transfers Nontestamentary

Transfers at death resulting from agreements made in accordance with this part of this code are effective by reason of the agreement involved and are not testamentary transfers. Such transfers are not subject to the provisions of this code applicable to testamentary transfers except as expressly provided otherwise in this code.

Added by Acts 1989, 71st Leg., ch. 655, § 2, eff. Aug. 28, 1989.

§ 455. Revocation

An agreement between spouses made in accordance with this part of this code may be revoked in accordance with the terms of the agreement. If the agreement does not provide a method for revocation, the agreement may be revoked by a written instrument signed by both spouses or by a written instrument signed by one spouse and delivered to the other spouse. The agreement may be revoked with respect to specific property subject to the agreement by the disposition of such property by one or both of the spouses if such disposition is not inconsistent with specific terms of the agreement and applicable law.

Added by Acts 1989, 71st Leg., ch. 655, § 2, eff. Aug. 28, 1989.

§ 456. Proof of Agreement

(a) Application for Adjudication. An agreement between spouses creating a right of survivorship in community property that satisfies the requirements of this part is effective without an adjudication. After the death of a spouse, however, the surviving spouse or the personal representative of the surviving spouse may apply to the court for an order stating that the agreement satisfies the requirements of this code and is effective to create a right of survivorship in community property. The original agreement shall be filed with the application for an adjudication. An application for an adjudication under this section must include:

(1) the name and domicile of the surviving spouse;

(2) the name and former domicile of the decedent and the fact, time, and place of death;

(3) facts establishing venue in the court; and

(4) the social security number of the decedent, if known.

(b) Proof Required. An applicant for an adjudication under this section must prove to the satisfaction of the court:

(1) that the spouse whose community property interest is at issue is dead;

(2) that the court has jurisdiction and venue;

(3) that the agreement was executed with the formalities required by law;

(4) that the agreement was not revoked; and

(5) that citation has been served and returned in the manner and for the length of time required by this code.

(c) Method of Proof. The deceased spouse's signature to the agreement may be proved by the sworn testimony of one witness taken in open court, by the affidavit of one witness, or by the deposition of one witness, either written or oral, taken in the same manner and under the same rules as depositions in other civil actions. If the surviving spouse is competent to make an oath, the surviving spouse's signature to the agreement may be proved by the sworn testimony of the surviving spouse taken in open court, by the affidavit of the surviving spouse, or by the deposition of the surviving spouse either written or oral, taken in the same manner and under the same rules as depositions in other civil actions. If the surviving spouse is not competent to make an oath, the surviving spouse's signature to the agreement may be proved in the manner provided above for the proof of the deceased spouse's signature.

(d) Venue. An application for an adjudication under this section must be filed in the county of proper venue for administration of the deceased spouse's estate.

Added by Acts 1989, 71st Leg., ch. 655, § 2, eff. Aug. 28, 1989.

§ 457. Action of Court on Agreement

On completion of a hearing on an application under Section 456 of this code, if the court is satisfied that the requisite proof has been made, an order adjudging the agreement valid shall be entered. Certified copies of the agreement and order may be recorded in other counties and may be used in evidence, as the original might be, on the trial of the same matter in any other court, on appeal or otherwise.
Added by Acts 1989, 71st Leg., ch. 655, § 2, eff. Aug. 28, 1989.

§ 458. Effect of Order

An agreement between spouses creating a right of survivorship in community property that satisfies the requirements of this code is effective and enforceable without an adjudication. If an order adjudging such an agreement valid is obtained, however, the order shall constitute sufficient authority to all persons owing money, having custody of any property, or acting as registrar or transfer agent of any evidence of interest, indebtedness, property, or right, that is subject to the provisions of the agreement, and to persons purchasing from or otherwise dealing with the surviving spouse for payment or transfer to the surviving spouse, and the surviving spouse may enforce his or her right to such payment or transfer.
Added by Acts 1989, 71st Leg., ch. 655, § 2, eff. Aug. 28, 1989.

§ 459. Custody of Adjudicated Agreements

An original agreement creating a right of survivorship in community property that has been adjudicated together with the order adjudging it valid shall be deposited in the office of the county clerk of the county in which it was adjudicated and shall remain there, except during such time when it may be removed for inspection to another place on order of the court where adjudicated. If the court orders an original agreement to be removed to another place for inspection, the person removing the original agreement shall give a receipt therefor, and the clerk of the court shall make and retain a copy of the original agreement.
Added by Acts 1989, 71st Leg., ch. 655, § 2, eff. Aug. 28, 1989.

§ 460. Protection of Persons or Entities Acting Without Knowledge or Notice

(a) Personal Representatives. If the personal representative of a decedent's estate has no actual knowledge of the existence of an agreement creating a right of survivorship in community property in the decedent's surviving spouse, the personal representative shall not be liable to the surviving spouse or to any person claiming from the surviving spouse for selling, exchanging, distributing, or otherwise disposing of the property or an interest therein.

(b) Purchaser without Notice of Survivorship Agreement.

(1) If any person or entity purchases real or personal property from a person claiming from a decedent more than six months after the date of the decedent's death, for value, and without notice of the existence of an agreement creating a right of survivorship in the property in the decedent's surviving spouse, the purchaser shall have good title to the interest which the person claiming from the decedent would have had in the absence of the agreement, as against the claims of the surviving spouse or any person claiming from the surviving spouse.

(2) If any person or entity purchases real or personal property from the personal representative of a decedent's estate, for value, and without notice of the existence of an agreement creating a right of survivorship in the property in the decedent's surviving spouse, the purchaser shall have good title to the interest which the personal representative would have had the power to convey in the absence of the agreement, as against the claims of the surviving spouse or any person claiming from the surviving spouse.

(c) Purchaser without Notice of Revocation of Survivorship Agreement. If any person or entity purchases real or personal property from a decedent's surviving spouse more than six months after the date of the decedent's death, for value, and:

(1) with respect to real or personal property, the purchaser has received an original or certified copy of an agreement purporting to create a right of survivorship in such property in the decedent's surviving spouse, purportedly signed by the decedent and the surviving spouse; or

(2) with respect to real property, an agreement purporting to create a right of survivorship in such property in the decedent's surviving spouse, purportedly signed by the decedent and the surviving spouse, is properly recorded in a county in which a part of the property is located; and the purchaser has no notice that the agreement was revoked, the purchaser shall have good title to the interest which the surviving spouse would have had in the absence of a revocation of the agreement, as against the claims of the personal representative of the decedent's estate and all persons claiming from the decedent or the personal representative of the decedent's estate.

(d) Debtors, Transfer Agents, and Other Persons Acting without Notice of Survivorship Agreement. If any person or entity owing money to a decedent or having custody of any property or acting as registrar or transfer agent of any evidence of interest, indebtedness, property, or right which was owned by a decedent prior to death has no actual knowledge of an agreement creating a right of survivorship in such property in the decedent's surviving spouse, that person or entity may pay or transfer such property to the personal representative of the decedent's estate or to the heirs, legatees, or devisees of the decedent's estate if no administration is pending on the estate, and the person or entity shall be discharged from all claims for amounts or property so paid or transferred.

(e) Debtors, Transfer Agents, and Persons Acting without Notice of Revocation of Survivorship Agreement. If any person or entity owing money to a decedent or having custody of any property or acting as registrar or transfer agent of any evidence of interest, indebtedness, property, or right which was owned by a decedent prior to death is presented with the original or a certified copy of an agreement creating a right of survivorship in such property in the decedent's surviving spouse, purportedly signed by the decedent and the decedent's surviving spouse and if such person or entity has no actual knowledge that the agreement was revoked, that person or entity may pay or transfer such property to the decedent's surviving spouse and shall be discharged from all claims for amounts or property so paid or transferred.

(f) Definitions. Under this section:

(1) a person or entity has "actual knowledge" of an agreement creating a right of survivorship in community property or of the revocation of such an agreement only if the person or entity has received written notice or has received the original or a certified copy of the agreement or revoking instrument;

(2) a person or entity has "notice" of an agreement creating a right of survivorship in community property or the revocation of such an agreement if the person or entity has actual knowledge of the agreement or revocation or, with respect to real property, if the agreement or revoking instrument is properly recorded in the county in which the real property is located; and

(3) a "certified copy" is a copy of an official record or of a document authorized by law to be recorded or filed and actually recorded or filed in a public office, certified as correct in accordance with the provisions of Rule 902 of the Texas Rules of Civil Evidence.

(g) Other Cases. Except as expressly provided in this section, the provisions of this section do not affect the rights of a surviving spouse or person claiming from the surviving spouse in disputes with persons claiming from a decedent or the successors of any of them concerning a beneficial interest in property or the proceeds therefrom, subject to a right of survivorship pursuant to an agreement that satisfies the requirements of this code.

Added by Acts 1989, 71st Leg., ch. 655, § 2, eff. Aug. 28, 1989.

§ 461. Rights of Creditors

The provisions of Part 1 of this chapter govern the rights of creditors in multiple-party accounts, as defined by Section 436 of Part 1. Except as expressly provided above in this section, the community property subject to the sole or joint management, control, and disposition of a spouse during marriage continues to be subject to the liabilities of that spouse upon death without regard to a right of survivorship in the decedent's surviving spouse under an agreement made in accordance with the provisions of this part. The surviving spouse shall be liable to account to the deceased spouse's personal representative for the property received by the surviving spouse pursuant to a right of survivorship to the extent necessary to discharge such liabilities. No proceeding to assert such a liability shall be commenced unless the personal representative has received a written demand by a creditor, and no proceeding shall be commenced later than two years following the death of the decedent. Property recovered by the personal representative shall be administered as part of the decedent's estate. This section does not affect the protection given to persons and entities under Section 460 of this code unless, before payment or transfer to the surviving spouse, the person or entity received a written notice from the decedent's personal representative stating the amount needed to satisfy the decedent's liabilities.

Added by Acts 1989, 71st Leg., ch. 655, § 2, eff. Aug. 28, 1989.

§ 462. Coordination with Part 1 of Chapter XI

The provisions of Part 1 of this chapter apply to multiple-party accounts held by spouses with a right of survivorship to the extent that such provisions are not inconsistent with the provisions of this part.

Added by Acts 1989, 71st Leg., ch. 655, § 2, eff. Aug. 28, 1989.

Chapter XII. Durable Power of Attorney Act

Statutes in Context

A power of attorney is a formal method of creating an agency relationship under which one person has the ability to act in the place of another. The person granting authority is called the *principal* and the person who obtains the authority is the *agent* or *attorney-in-fact*. Note that in this context, the term "attorney" is not synonymous with "lawyer" and thus any competent person may serve as an agent even if the person has no legal training.

Under traditional agency law, an agent's authority terminates when the principal becomes incompetent because the principal is no longer able to monitor the agent's conduct. This rule prevented powers of attorney from being used as a disability planning technique. In 1954, Virginia became the first state to authorize a *durable* power of attorney which provides that the agent retains the authority to act even if the principal is incompetent. All states now have legislation sanctioning durable powers of attorney. The Texas provisions are found in Chapter XII.

§ 481. Short Title

This chapter may be cited as the Durable Power of Attorney Act.

Added by Acts 1993, 73rd Leg., ch. 49, § 1, eff. Sept. 1, 1993.

Statutes in Context

The requirements for a valid durable power of attorney are as follows: (1) the instrument must be in writing (oral statements are insufficient), (2) the principal must be an adult, (3) the principal must sign the instrument, (4) the instrument must name an agent, (5) the instrument must expressly provide that the agent's authority either (a) continues even after the principal becomes disabled or (b) begins when the agent becomes disabled (the *springing* power of attorney), and (6) the power of attorney must be acknowledged. Note that no witnesses are needed and the durable power of attorney does not need to be filed with the court.

---

§ 482. Definition

A "durable power of attorney" means a written instrument that:

(1) designates another person as attorney in fact or agent;

(2) is signed by an adult principal;

(3) contains the words "This power of attorney is not affected by subsequent disability or incapacity of the principal," or "This power of attorney becomes effective on the disability or incapacity of the principal," or similar words showing the principal's intent that the authority conferred on the attorney in fact or agent shall be exercised notwithstanding the principal's subsequent disability or incapacity; and

(4) is acknowledged by the principal before an officer authorized to take acknowledgments to deeds of conveyance and to administer oaths under the laws of this state or any other state.

Added by Acts 1993, 73rd Leg., ch. 49, § 1, eff. Sept. 1, 1993.

Statutes in Context

The durable power of attorney does not lapse merely because it is not used for a prolonged period of time. *See* § 483.

---

§ 483. Duration

A durable power of attorney does not lapse because of the passage of time unless the instrument creating the power of attorney specifically states a time limitation.

Added by Acts 1993, 73rd Leg., ch. 49, § 1, eff. Sept. 1, 1993.

§ 484. Effect of Acts by Attorney in Fact or Agent During Incapacity of Principal

All acts done by an attorney in fact or agent pursuant to a durable power of attorney during any period of disability or incapacity of the principal have the same effect and inure to the benefit of and bind the principal and the principal's successors in interest as if the principal were not disabled or incapacitated.

Added by Acts 1993, 73rd Leg., ch. 49, § 1, eff. Sept. 1, 1993.

Statutes in Context

The appointment of a permanent guardian of the principal's estate will terminate the agent's authority under § 485(a).

---

§ 485. Relation of Attorney in Fact or Agent to Court-Appointed Guardian of Estate

(a) If, after execution of a durable power of attorney, a court of the principal's domicile appoints a permanent guardian of the estate of the principal, the powers of the attorney in fact or agent terminate on the qualification of the guardian of the estate, and the attorney in fact or agent shall deliver to the guardian of the estate all assets of the estate of the ward in the attorney's or agent's possession and shall account to the guardian of the estate as the attorney or agent would to the principal had the principal terminated his powers.

(b) If, after execution of a durable power of attorney, a court of the principal's domicile appoints a temporary guardian of the estate of the principal, the court may suspend the powers of the attorney in fact or agent on the qualification of the temporary guardian of the estate until the date on which the term of the temporary guardian expires.

(c) Subsection (b) of this section may not be construed to prohibit the application for or issuance of a temporary restraining order under applicable law.

Added by Acts 1993, 73rd Leg., ch. 49, § 1, eff. Sept. 1, 1993. Amended by Acts 2001, 77th Leg., ch. 217, § 1, eff. Sept. 1, 2001.

Statutes in Context

Generally, the designation of a spouse as an agent is automatically revoked upon the principal's divorce from the spouse under § 485A.

---

§ 485A. Effect of Principal's Divorce or Marriage Annulment if Former Spouse is Attorney in Fact or Agent

If, after execution of a durable power of attorney, the principal is divorced from a person who has been appointed the principal's attorney in fact or agent or the principal's marriage to a person who has been appointed the principal's attorney in fact or agent is annulled, the powers of the attorney in fact or agent granted to the principal's former spouse shall terminate on the date on which the divorce or annulment of marriage is granted by a court, unless otherwise expressly provided by the durable power of attorney.

Added by Acts 1997, 75th Leg., ch. 455, § 1, eff. Sept. 1, 1997.

§ 486. Knowledge of Death, Guardian of Estate, Revocation, Divorce, or Marriage Annulment; Good-Faith Acts

(a) The revocation by, the death of, or the qualification of a guardian of the estate of a principal who has executed a durable power of attorney does not revoke or terminate the agency as to the attorney in fact, agent, or other person who, without actual knowledge of the termination of the power by revocation, by the principal's death, or by the qualification of a guardian of the estate of the principal, acts in good faith under or in reliance on the power.

(b) The divorce of a principal from a person who has been appointed the principal's attorney in fact or agent before the date on which the divorce is granted or the annulment of the marriage of a principal and a person who has been appointed the principal's attorney in fact or agent before the date the annulment is granted does not revoke or terminate the agency as to a person other than the principal's former spouse if the person acts in good faith under or in reliance on the power.

(c) Any action taken under this section, unless otherwise invalid or unenforceable, binds successors in interest of the principal.

Added by Acts 1993, 73rd Leg., ch. 49, § 1, eff. Sept. 1, 1993. Amended by Acts 1997, 75th Leg., ch. 455, § 2, eff. Sept. 1, 1997.

§ 487. Affidavit of Lack of Knowledge or Termination of Power; Recording; Good-Faith Reliance

(a) As to acts undertaken in good-faith reliance on the durable power of attorney, an affidavit executed by the attorney in fact or agent under a durable power of attorney stating that the attorney in fact or agent did not have at the time of exercise of the power actual knowledge of the termination of the power by revocation, by the principal's death, by the principal's divorce or the annulment of the marriage of the principal if the attorney in fact or agent was the principal's spouse, or by the qualification of a guardian of the estate of the principal is conclusive proof as between the attorney in fact or agent and a person other than the principal or the principal's personal representative dealing with the attorney in fact or agent of the nonrevocation or nontermination of the power at that time.

(b) As to acts undertaken in good-faith reliance on the durable power of attorney, an affidavit executed by the attorney in fact or agent under a durable power of attorney stating that the principal is disabled or incapacitated, as defined by the power, is conclusive proof as between the attorney in fact or agent and a person other than the principal or the principal's personal representative dealing with the attorney in fact or agent of the disability or incapacity of the principal at that time.

(c) If the exercise of the power of attorney requires execution and delivery of any instrument that is to be recorded, an affidavit executed under Subsection (a) or (b) of this section, when authenticated for record, may also be recorded.

(d) This section does not affect any provision in a durable power of attorney for its termination by expiration of time or occurrence of an event other than express revocation.

(e) When a durable power of attorney is used, a third party who relies in good faith on the acts of an attorney in fact or agent within the scope of the power of attorney is not liable to the principal.

Added by Acts 1993, 73rd Leg., ch. 49, § 1, eff. Sept. 1, 1993. Amended by Acts 1997, 75th Leg., ch. 455, § 3, eff. Sept. 1, 1997.

§ 487A. Effect of Bankruptcy Proceeding

After execution of a durable power of attorney, the filing of a voluntary or involuntary petition in bankruptcy in connection with the principal's debts does not revoke or terminate the agency as to the principal's attorney in fact or agent. Any act the attorney in fact or agent may undertake with respect to the principal's property is subject to the limitations and requirements of the United States Bankruptcy Code until a final determination is made in the bankruptcy proceeding.

Added by Acts 2001, 77th Leg., ch. 73, § 1, eff. Sept. 1, 2001.

§ 488. Revocation of Durable Power of Attorney

Unless otherwise provided by the durable power of attorney, a revocation of a durable power of attorney is not effective as to a third party relying on the power of attorney until the third party receives actual notice of the revocation.

Added by Acts 1993, 73rd Leg., ch. 49, § 1, eff. Sept. 1, 1993.

Statutes in Context

The durable power of attorney will need to be recorded if the agent uses it with respect to a real property transaction. *See* § 489.

---

§ 489. Recording Durable Power of Attorney for Real Property Transactions

A durable power of attorney for a real property transaction requiring the execution and delivery of an instrument that is to be recorded, including a release, assignment, satisfaction, mortgage, security agreement, deed of trust, encumbrance, deed of conveyance, oil, gas, or other mineral lease, memorandum of a lease, lien, or other claim or right to real property, shall be recorded in the office of the county clerk of the county in which the property is located.

Added by Acts 1993, 73rd Leg., ch. 49, § 1, eff. Sept. 1, 1993.

Statutes in Context

The agent's duty to inform the principal with respect to actions taken and to account for them is set forth in § 489B.

---

§ 489B. Duty to Inform and Account

(a) The attorney in fact or agent is a fiduciary and has a duty to inform and to account for actions taken pursuant to the power of attorney.

(b) The attorney in fact or agent shall timely inform the principal of all actions taken pursuant to the power of attorney. Failure of the attorney in fact or agent to inform timely, as to third parties, shall not invalidate any action of the attorney in fact or agent.

(c) The attorney in fact or agent shall maintain records of each action taken or decision made by the attorney in fact or agent.

(d) The principal may demand an accounting by the attorney in fact or agent. Unless otherwise directed by the principal, the accounting shall include:

(1) the property belonging to the principal that has come to the attorney in fact's or agent's knowledge or into the attorney in fact's or agent's possession;

(2) all actions taken or decisions made by the attorney in fact or agent;

(3) a complete account of receipts, disbursements, and other actions of the attorney in fact or agent, including their source and nature, with receipts of principal and income shown separately;

(4) a listing of all property over which the attorney in fact or agent has exercised control, with an adequate description of each asset and its current value if known to the attorney in fact or agent;

(5) the cash balance on hand and the name and location of the depository where the balance is kept;

(6) all known liabilities; and

(7) such other information and facts known to the attorney in fact or agent as may be necessary to a full and definite understanding of the exact condition of the property belonging to the principal.

(e) Unless directed otherwise by the principal, the attorney in fact or agent shall also provide to the principal all documentation regarding the principal's property.

(f) The attorney in fact or agent shall maintain all records until delivered to the principal, released by the principal, or discharged by a court.

(g) If the attorney in fact or agent fails or refuses to inform the principal, provide documentation, or deliver the accounting within 60 days (or such longer or shorter time that the principal demands or a court may order), the principal may file suit to compel the attorney in fact or agent to deliver the accounting, to deliver the assets, or to terminate the power of attorney.

(h) This section shall not limit the right of the principal to terminate the power of attorney or to make additional requirements of or to give additional instructions to the attorney in fact or agent.

(i) Wherever in this chapter a principal is given an authority to act, that shall include not only the principal but also any person designated by the principal, a guardian of the estate of the principal, or other personal representative of the principal.

(j) The rights set out in this section and chapter are cumulative of any other rights or remedies the principal may have at common law or other applicable statutes and not in derogation of those rights.

Added by Acts 2001, 77th Leg., ch. 1056, § 1, eff. Sept. 1, 2001.

Statutes in Context

Section 490 contains a form which the principal may use to create a durable power of attorney. The form provides a list of powers which the agent is presumed to have unless the principal crosses out the power. Each of the listed powers is explained in great detail by a later statutory provision. It is important for the principal to read the statutory provisions so that the principal fully understands the scope of the powers which the principal is granting to the agent.

The principal has a choice of making the power effective immediately (the default choice) or effective only upon incapacity (the *springing* power). Debate exists regarding which effective date is better. The principal often feels there is no need to grant any authority until the agent's actions are actually needed. However, third parties may be reluctant to accept a springing agent's authority for fear that the principal is not actually incapacitated. A compromise option is for the agent to make the power effective immediately but have the agent's attorney (or some other trusted person) keep the document and deliver it to the agent at the appropriate time.

---

§ 490. Statutory Durable Power of Attorney

(a) The following form is known as a "statutory durable power of attorney." A person may use a statutory durable power of attorney to grant an attorney in fact or agent powers with respect to a person's property and financial matters. A power of attorney in substantially the following form has the meaning and effect prescribed by this chapter. The validity of a power of attorney as meeting the requirements of a statutory durable power of attorney is not affected by the fact that one or more of the categories of optional powers listed in the form are struck or the form includes specific limitations on or additions to the attorney in fact's or agent's powers.

The following form is not exclusive, and other forms of power of attorney may be used.

STATUTORY DURABLE POWER OF ATTORNEY

NOTICE: THE POWERS GRANTED BY THIS DOCUMENT ARE BROAD AND SWEEPING. THEY ARE EXPLAINED IN THE DURABLE POWER OF ATTORNEY ACT, CHAPTER XII, TEXAS PROBATE CODE. IF YOU HAVE ANY QUESTIONS ABOUT THESE POWERS, OBTAIN COMPETENT LEGAL ADVICE. THIS DOCUMENT DOES NOT AUTHORIZE ANYONE TO MAKE MEDICAL AND OTHER HEALTH-CARE DECISIONS FOR YOU. YOU MAY

REVOKE THIS POWER OF ATTORNEY IF YOU LATER WISH TO DO SO.

I, _________ (insert your name and address), appoint _________ (insert the name and address of the person appointed) as my agent (attorney-in-fact) to act for me in any lawful way with respect to all of the following powers except for a power that I have crossed out below.

TO WITHHOLD A POWER, YOU MUST CROSS OUT EACH POWER WITHHELD.

Real property transactions;

Tangible personal property transactions;

Stock and bond transactions;

Commodity and option transactions;

Banking and other financial institution transactions;

Business operating transactions;

Insurance and annuity transactions;

Estate, trust, and other beneficiary transactions;

Claims and litigation;

Personal and family maintenance;

Benefits from social security, Medicare, Medicaid, or other governmental programs or civil or military service;

Retirement plan transactions;

Tax matters.

IF NO POWER LISTED ABOVE IS CROSSED OUT, THIS DOCUMENT SHALL BE CONSTRUED AND INTERPRETED AS A GENERAL POWER OF ATTORNEY AND MY AGENT (ATTORNEY IN FACT) SHALL HAVE THE POWER AND AUTHORITY TO PERFORM OR UNDERTAKE ANY ACTION I COULD PERFORM OR UNDERTAKE IF I WERE PERSONALLY PRESENT.

SPECIAL INSTRUCTIONS:

Special instructions applicable to gifts (initial in front of the following sentence to have it apply):

I grant my agent (attorney in fact) the power to apply my property to make gifts, except that the amount of a gift to an individual may not exceed the amount of annual exclusions allowed from the federal gift tax for the calendar year of the gift.

ON THE FOLLOWING LINES YOU MAY GIVE SPECIAL INSTRUCTIONS LIMITING OR EXTENDING THE POWERS GRANTED TO YOUR AGENT.

____

____

____

____

____

____

____

____

____

____

UNLESS YOU DIRECT OTHERWISE ABOVE, THIS POWER OF ATTORNEY IS EFFECTIVE IMMEDIATELY AND WILL CONTINUE UNTIL IT IS REVOKED.

CHOOSE ONE OF THE FOLLOWING ALTERNATIVES BY CROSSING OUT THE ALTERNATIVE NOT CHOSEN:

(A) This power of attorney is not affected by my subsequent disability or incapacity.

(B) This power of attorney becomes effective upon my disability or incapacity.

YOU SHOULD CHOOSE ALTERNATIVE (A) IF THIS POWER OF ATTORNEY IS TO BECOME EFFECTIVE ON THE DATE IT IS EXECUTED.

IF NEITHER (A) NOR (B) IS CROSSED OUT, IT WILL BE ASSUMED THAT YOU CHOSE ALTERNATIVE (A).

If Alternative (B) is chosen and a definition of my disability or incapacity is not contained in this power of attorney, I shall be considered disabled or incapacitated for purposes of this power of attorney if a physician certifies in writing at a date later than the date this power of attorney is executed that, based on the physician's medical examination of me, I am mentally incapable of managing my financial affairs. I authorize the physician who examines me for this purpose to disclose my physical or mental condition to another person for purposes of this power of attorney. A third party who accepts this power of attorney is fully protected from any action taken under this power of attorney that is based on the determination made by a physician of my disability or incapacity.

I agree that any third party who receives a copy of this document may act under it. Revocation of the durable power of attorney is not effective as to a third party until the third party receives actual notice of the revocation. I agree to indemnify the third party for any claims that arise against the third party because of reliance on this power of attorney.

If any agent named by me dies, becomes legally disabled, resigns, or refuses to act, I name the following (each to act alone and successively, in the order named) as successor(s) to that agent: ____________.

Signed this _____ day of ____________, 19__

____

(your signature)

State of ______________________ County of

____

This document was acknowledged before me on ______________________ (date) by

____

(name of principal)

____

(signature of notarial officer)

(Seal, if any, of notary)

____

(printed name)

My commission expires: __________

THE ATTORNEY IN FACT OR AGENT, BY ACCEPTING OR ACTING UNDER THE APPOINTMENT, ASSUMES THE FIDUCIARY AND OTHER LEGAL RESPONSIBILITIES OF AN AGENT.

(b) A statutory durable power of attorney is legally sufficient under this chapter if the wording of the form complies substantially with Subsection (a) of this section, the form is properly completed, and the signature of the principal is acknowledged.

(c) Repealed by Acts 1997, 75th Leg., ch. 455, § 7, eff. Sept. 1, 1997.

Added by Acts 1993, 73rd Leg., ch. 49, § 1, eff. Sept. 1, 1993. Subsec. (a) amended by Acts 1997, 75th Leg., ch. 455, § 4, eff. Sept. 1, 1997; Subsec. (c) repealed by Acts 1997, 75th Leg., ch. 455, § 7, eff. Sept. 1, 1997.

Statutes in Context

Sections 491-505 provide detailed explanations of the powers granted in the statutory form.

---

§ 491. Construction of Powers Generally

The principal, by executing a statutory durable power of attorney that confers authority with respect to any class of transactions, empowers the attorney in fact or agent for that class of transactions to:

(1) demand, receive, and obtain by litigation, action, or otherwise any money or other thing of value to which the principal is, may become, or may claim to be entitled;

(2) conserve, invest, disburse, or use any money or other thing of value received on behalf of the principal for the purposes intended;

(3) contract in any manner with any person, on terms agreeable to the attorney in fact or agent, to accomplish a purpose of a transaction and perform, rescind, reform, release, or modify the contract or another contract made by or on behalf of the principal;

(4) execute, acknowledge, seal, and deliver a deed, revocation, mortgage, lease, notice, check, release, or other instrument the agent considers desirable to accomplish a purpose of a transaction;

(5) prosecute, defend, submit to arbitration, settle, and propose or accept a compromise with respect to a claim existing in favor of or against the principal or intervene in an action or litigation relating to the claim;

(6) seek on the principal's behalf the assistance of a court to carry out an act authorized by the power of attorney;

(7) engage, compensate, and discharge an attorney, accountant, expert witness, or other assistant;

(8) keep appropriate records of each transaction, including an accounting of receipts and disbursements;

(9) prepare, execute, and file a record, report, or other document the attorney in fact or agent considers necessary or desirable to safeguard or promote the principal's interest under a statute or governmental regulation;

(10) reimburse the attorney in fact or agent for expenditures made in exercising the powers granted by the durable power of attorney; and

(11) in general, do any other lawful act that the principal may do with respect to a transaction.

Added by Acts 1993, 73rd Leg., ch. 49, § 1, eff. Sept. 1, 1993.

§ 492. Construction of Power Relating to Real Property Transactions

In a statutory durable power of attorney, the language conferring authority with respect to real property transactions empowers the attorney in fact or agent without further reference to a specific description of the real property to:

(1) accept as a gift or as security for a loan or reject, demand, buy, lease, receive, or otherwise acquire an interest in real property or a right incident to real property;

(2) sell, exchange, convey with or without covenants, quitclaim, release, surrender, mortgage, encumber, partition, consent to partitioning, subdivide, apply for zoning, rezoning, or other governmental permits, plat or consent to platting, develop, grant options concerning, lease or sublet, or otherwise dispose of an estate or interest in real property or a right incident to real property;

(3) release, assign, satisfy, and enforce by litigation, action, or otherwise a mortgage, deed of trust, encumbrance, lien, or other claim to real property that exists or is claimed to exist;

(4) do any act of management or of conservation with respect to an interest in real property, or a right incident to real property, owned or claimed to be owned by the principal, including power to:

(A) insure against a casualty, liability, or loss;

(B) obtain or regain possession or protect the interest or right by litigation, action, or otherwise;

(C) pay, compromise, or contest taxes or assessments or apply for and receive refunds in connection with them;

(D) purchase supplies, hire assistance or labor, or make repairs or alterations in the real property; and

(E) manage and supervise an interest in real property, including the mineral estate, by, for example, entering into a lease for oil, gas, and mineral purposes, making contracts for development of the mineral estate, or making pooling and unitization agreements;

(5) use, develop, alter, replace, remove, erect, or install structures or other improvements on real property in which the principal has or claims to have an estate, interest, or right;

(6) participate in a reorganization with respect to real property or a legal entity that owns an interest in or right incident to real property, receive and hold shares of stock or obligations received in a plan or reorganization, and act with respect to the shares or obligations, including:

(A) selling or otherwise disposing of the shares or obligations;

(B) exercising or selling an option, conversion, or similar right with respect to the shares or obligations; and

(C) voting the shares or obligations in person or by proxy;

(7) change the form of title of an interest in or right incident to real property; and

(8) dedicate easements or other real property in which the principal has or claims to have an interest to public use, with or without consideration.

Added by Acts 1993, 73rd Leg., ch. 49, § 1, eff. Sept. 1, 1993. Amended by Acts 1997, 75th Leg., ch. 455, § 5, eff. Sept. 1, 1997.

§ 493. Construction of Power Relating to Tangible Personal Property Transactions

In a statutory durable power of attorney, the language conferring general authority with respect to tangible personal property transactions empowers the attorney in fact or agent to:

(1) accept as a gift or as security for a loan, reject, demand, buy, receive, or otherwise acquire ownership or possession of tangible personal property or an interest in tangible personal property;

(2) sell, exchange, convey with or without covenants, release, surrender, mortgage, encumber, pledge, hypothecate, create a security interest in, pawn, grant options concerning, lease or sublet to others, or otherwise dispose of tangible personal property or an interest in tangible personal property;

(3) release, assign, satisfy, or enforce by litigation, action, or otherwise a mortgage, security interest, encumbrance, lien, or other claim on behalf of the principal, with respect to tangible personal property or an interest in tangible personal property; and

(4) do an act of management or conservation with respect to tangible personal property or an interest in tangible personal property on behalf of the principal, including:

(A) insuring against casualty, liability, or loss;

(B) obtaining or regaining possession or protecting the property or interest by litigation, action, or otherwise;

(C) paying, compromising, or contesting taxes or assessments or applying for and receiving refunds in connection with taxes or assessments;

(D) moving from place to place;

(E) storing for hire or on a gratuitous bailment; and

(F) using, altering, and making repairs or alterations.

Added by Acts 1993, 73rd Leg., ch. 49, § 1, eff. Sept. 1, 1993.

§ 494. Construction of Power Relating to Stock and Bond Transactions

In a statutory durable power of attorney, the language conferring authority with respect to stock and bond transactions empowers the attorney in fact or agent to buy, sell, and exchange stocks, bonds, mutual funds, and all other types of securities and financial instruments other than commodity futures contracts and call and put options on stocks and stock indexes, receive certificates and other evidences of ownership with respect to securities, exercise voting rights with respect to securities in person or by proxy, enter into voting trusts, and consent to limitations on the right to vote.

Added by Acts 1993, 73rd Leg., ch. 49, § 1, eff. Sept. 1, 1993.

§ 495. Construction of Power Relating to Commodity and Option Transactions

In a statutory durable power of attorney, the language conferring authority with respect to commodity and option transactions empowers the attorney in fact or agent to buy, sell, exchange, assign, settle, and exercise commodity futures contracts and call and put options on stocks and stock indexes traded on a regulated options exchange and establish, continue, modify, or terminate option accounts with a broker.

Added by Acts 1993, 73rd Leg., ch. 49, § 1, eff. Sept. 1, 1993.

§ 496. Construction of Power Relating to Banking and Other Financial Institution Transactions

In a statutory durable power of attorney, the language conferring authority with respect to banking and other financial institution transactions empowers the attorney in fact or agent to:

(1) continue, modify, or terminate an account or other banking arrangement made by or on behalf of the principal;

(2) establish, modify, or terminate an account or other banking arrangement with a bank, trust company, savings and loan association, credit union, thrift company, brokerage firm, or other financial institution selected by the attorney in fact or agent;

(3) hire a safe deposit box or space in a vault;

(4) contract to procure other services available from a financial institution as the attorney in fact or agent considers desirable;

(5) withdraw by check, order, or otherwise money or property of the principal deposited with or left in the custody of a financial institution;

(6) receive bank statements, vouchers, notices, or similar documents from a financial institution and act with respect to them;

(7) enter a safe deposit box or vault and withdraw or add to the contents;

(8) borrow money at an interest rate agreeable to the attorney in fact or agent and pledge as security real or personal property of the principal necessary to borrow, pay, renew, or extend the time of payment of a debt of the principal;

(9) make, assign, draw, endorse, discount, guarantee, and negotiate promissory notes, bills of exchange, checks, drafts, or other negotiable or nonnegotiable paper of the principal, or payable to the principal or the principal's order, to receive the cash

or other proceeds of those transactions, to accept a draft drawn by a person on the principal, and to pay the principal when due;

(10) receive for the principal and act on a sight draft, warehouse receipt, or other negotiable or nonnegotiable instrument;

(11) apply for and receive letters of credit, credit cards, and traveler's checks from a financial institution and give an indemnity or other agreement in connection with letters of credit; and

(12) consent to an extension of the time of payment with respect to commercial paper or a financial transaction with a financial institution.

Added by Acts 1993, 73rd Leg., ch. 49, § 1, eff. Sept. 1, 1993.

§ 497. Construction of Power Relating to Business Operation Transactions

In a statutory durable power of attorney, the language conferring authority with respect to business operating transactions empowers the attorney in fact or agent to:

(1) operate, buy, sell, enlarge, reduce, or terminate a business interest;

(2) to the extent that an agent is permitted by law to act for a principal and subject to the terms of the partnership agreement:

(A) perform a duty or discharge a liability or exercise a right, power, privilege, or option that the principal has, may have, or claims to have under a partnership agreement, whether or not the principal is a general or limited partner;

(B) enforce the terms of a partnership agreement by litigation, action, or otherwise; and

(C) defend, submit to arbitration, settle, or compromise litigation or an action to which the principal is a party because of membership in the partnership;

(3) exercise in person or by proxy or enforce by litigation, action, or otherwise a right, power, privilege, or option the principal has or claims to have as the holder of a bond, share, or other instrument of similar character and defend, submit to arbitration, settle, or compromise a legal proceeding to which the principal is a party because of a bond, share, or similar instrument;

(4) with respect to a business owned solely by the principal:

(A) continue, modify, renegotiate, extend, and terminate a contract made with an individual or a legal entity, firm, association, or corporation by or on behalf of the principal with respect to the business before execution of the power of attorney;

(B) determine:

(i) the location of its operation;

(ii) the nature and extent of its business;

(iii) the methods of manufacturing, selling, merchandising, financing, accounting, and advertising employed in its operation;

(iv) the amount and types of insurance carried; and

(v) the mode of engaging, compensating, and dealing with its accountants, attorneys, and other agents and employees;

(C) change the name or form of organization under which the business is operated and enter into a partnership agreement with other persons or organize a corporation to take over all or part of the operation of the business; and

(D) demand and receive money due or claimed by the principal or on the principal's behalf in the operation of the business and control and disburse the money in the operation of the business;

(5) put additional capital into a business in which the principal has an interest;

(6) join in a plan of reorganization, consolidation, or merger of the business;

(7) sell or liquidate a business or part of it at the time and on the terms that the attorney in fact or agent considers desirable;

(8) establish the value of a business under a buyout agreement to which the principal is a party;

(9) prepare, sign, file, and deliver reports, compilations of information, returns, or other papers with respect to a business that are required by a governmental agency, department, or instrumentality or that the attorney in fact or agent considers desirable and make related payments; and

(10) pay, compromise, or contest taxes or assessments and do any other act that the attorney in fact or agent considers desirable to protect the principal from illegal or unnecessary taxation, fines, penalties, or assessments with respect to a business, including attempts to recover, in any manner permitted by law, money paid before or after the execution of the power of attorney.

Added by Acts 1993, 73rd Leg., ch. 49, § 1, eff. Sept. 1, 1993.

§ 498. Construction of Power Relating to Insurance Transactions

In a statutory durable power of attorney, the language conferring authority with respect to insurance and annuity transactions empowers the attorney in fact or agent to:

(1) continue, pay the premium or assessment on, modify, rescind, release, or terminate a contract procured by or on behalf of the principal that insures or provides an annuity to either the principal or another person, whether or not the principal is a beneficiary under the contract;

(2) procure new, different, or additional contracts of insurance and annuities for the principal or the principal's spouse, children, and other dependents and select the amount, type of insurance or annuity, and mode of payment;

(3) pay the premium or assessment on or modify, rescind, release, or terminate a contract of insurance or annuity procured by the attorney in fact or agent;

(4) designate the beneficiary of the contract, except that an attorney in fact or agent may be named a beneficiary of the contract or an extension, renewal, or substitute for the contract only to the extent the attorney in fact or agent was named as a beneficiary under a contract procured by the principal before executing the power of attorney;

(5) apply for and receive a loan on the security of the contract of insurance or annuity;

(6) surrender and receive the cash surrender value;

(7) exercise an election;

(8) change the manner of paying premiums;

(9) change or convert the type of insurance contract or annuity with respect to which the principal has or claims to have a power described in this section;

(10) change the beneficiary of a contract of insurance or annuity, except that the attorney in fact or agent may be designated a beneficiary only to the extent authorized by Subdivision (4) of this section;

(11) apply for and procure government aid to guarantee or pay premiums of a contract of insurance on the life of the principal;

(12) collect, sell, assign, hypothecate, borrow on, or pledge the interest of the principal in a contract of insurance or annuity; and

(13) pay from proceeds or otherwise, compromise or contest, or apply for refunds in connection with a tax or assessment levied by a taxing authority with respect to a contract of insurance or annuity or its proceeds or liability accruing because of the tax or assessment.

Added by Acts 1993, 73rd Leg., ch. 49, § 1, eff. Sept. 1, 1993.

§ 499. Construction of Power Relating to Estate, Trust, and Other Beneficiary Transactions

In a statutory durable power of attorney, the language conferring authority with respect to estate, trust, and other beneficiary transactions empowers the attorney in fact or agent to act for the principal in all matters that affect a trust, probate estate, guardianship, conservatorship, escrow, custodianship, or other fund from which the principal is, may become, or claims to be entitled, as a beneficiary, to a share or payment, including to:

(1) accept, reject, disclaim, receive, receipt for, sell, assign, release, pledge, exchange, or consent to a reduction in or modification of a share in or payment from the fund;

(2) demand or obtain by litigation, action, or otherwise money or any other thing of value to which the principal is, may become, or claims to be entitled because of the fund;

(3) initiate, participate in, or oppose a legal or judicial proceeding to ascertain the meaning, validity, or effect of a deed, will, declaration of trust, or other instrument or transaction affecting the interest of the principal;

(4) initiate, participate in, or oppose a legal or judicial proceeding to remove, substitute, or surcharge a fiduciary;

(5) conserve, invest, disburse, or use anything received for an authorized purpose; and

(6) transfer all or part of an interest of the principal in real property, stocks, bonds, accounts with financial institutions, insurance, and other property to the trustee of a revocable trust created by the principal as settlor.

Added by Acts 1993, 73rd Leg., ch. 49, § 1, eff. Sept. 1, 1993.

§ 500. Construction of Power Relating to Claims and Litigation

In a statutory durable power of attorney, the language conferring general authority with respect to claims and litigation empowers the attorney in fact or agent to:

(1) assert and prosecute before a court or administrative agency a claim, a claim for relief, a counterclaim, or an offset or defend against an individual, a legal entity, or a government, including suits to recover property or other thing of value, to recover damages sustained by the principal, to eliminate or modify tax liability, or to seek an injunction, specific performance, or other relief;

(2) bring an action to determine adverse claims, intervene in an action or litigation, and act as amicus curiae;

(3) in connection with an action or litigation, procure an attachment, garnishment, libel, order of arrest, or other preliminary, provisional, or intermediate relief and use an available procedure to effect or satisfy a judgment, order, or decree;

(4) in connection with an action or litigation, perform any lawful act the principal could perform, including acceptance of tender, offer of judgment, admission of facts, submission of a controversy on an agreed statement of facts, consent to examination before trial, and binding of the principal in litigation;

(5) submit to arbitration, settle, and propose or accept a compromise with respect to a claim or litigation;

(6) waive the issuance and service of process on the principal, accept service of process, appear for the principal, designate persons on whom process directed to the principal may be served, execute and file or deliver stipulations on the principal's behalf, verify pleadings, seek appellate review, procure and give surety and indemnity bonds, contract and pay for the preparation and printing of records and briefs, or receive and execute and file or deliver a consent, waiver, release, confession of judgment, satisfaction of judgment, notice, agreement, or other instrument in connection with the prosecution, settlement, or defense of a claim or litigation;

(7) act for the principal with respect to bankruptcy or insolvency proceedings, whether voluntary or involuntary, concerning the principal or

some other person, with respect to a reorganization proceeding or a receivership or application for the appointment of a receiver or trustee that affects an interest of the principal in real or personal property or other thing of value; and

(8) pay a judgment against the principal or a settlement made in connection with a claim or litigation and receive and conserve money or other thing of value paid in settlement of or as proceeds of a claim or litigation.

Added by Acts 1993, 73rd Leg., ch. 49, § 1, eff. Sept. 1, 1993.

§ 501. Construction of Power Relating to Personal and Family Maintenance

In a statutory durable power of attorney, the language conferring authority with respect to personal and family maintenance empowers the attorney in fact or agent to:

(1) perform the acts necessary to maintain the customary standard of living of the principal, the principal's spouse and children, and other individuals customarily or legally entitled to be supported by the principal, including providing living quarters by purchase, lease, or other contract, or paying the operating costs, including interest, amortization payments, repairs, and taxes on premises owned by the principal and occupied by those individuals;

(2) provide for the individuals described by Subdivision (1) of this section normal domestic help, usual vacations and travel expenses, and funds for shelter, clothing, food, appropriate education, and other current living costs;

(3) pay necessary medical, dental, and surgical care, hospitalization, and custodial care for the individuals described by Subdivision (1) of this section;

(4) continue any provision made by the principal, for the individuals described by Subdivision (1) of this section, for automobiles or other means of transportation, including registering, licensing, insuring, and replacing the automobiles or other means of transportation;

(5) maintain or open charge accounts for the convenience of the individuals described by Subdivision (1) of this section and open new accounts the attorney in fact or agent considers desirable to accomplish a lawful purpose; and

(6) continue payments incidental to the membership or affiliation of the principal in a church, club, society, order, or other organization or to continue contributions to those organizations.

Added by Acts 1993, 73rd Leg., ch. 49, § 1, eff. Sept. 1, 1993.

§ 502. Construction of Power Relating to Benefits From Certain Governmental Programs or Civil or Military Service

In a statutory durable power of attorney, the language conferring authority with respect to benefits from social security, Medicare, Medicaid, or other governmental programs or civil or military service empowers the attorney in fact or agent to:

(1) execute vouchers in the name of the principal for allowances and reimbursements payable by the United States, a foreign government, or a state or subdivision of a state to the principal, including allowances and reimbursements for transportation of the individuals described by Section 501(1) of this code, and for shipment of their household effects;

(2) take possession and order the removal and shipment of property of the principal from a post, warehouse, depot, dock, or other place of storage or safekeeping, either governmental or private, and execute and deliver a release, voucher, receipt, bill of lading, shipping ticket, certificate, or other instrument for that purpose;

(3) prepare, file, and prosecute a claim of the principal to a benefit or assistance, financial or otherwise, to which the principal claims to be entitled under a statute or governmental regulation;

(4) prosecute, defend, submit to arbitration, settle, and propose or accept a compromise with respect to any benefits the principal may be entitled to receive; and

(5) receive the financial proceeds of a claim of the type described in this section and conserve, invest, disburse, or use anything received for a lawful purpose.

Added by Acts 1993, 73rd Leg., ch. 49, § 1, eff. Sept. 1, 1993.

§ 503. Construction of Power Relating to Retirement Plan Transactions

(a) In a statutory durable power of attorney, the language conferring authority with respect to retirement plan transactions empowers the attorney in fact or agent to do any lawful act the principal may do with respect to a transaction relating to a retirement plan, including to:

(1) apply for service or disability retirement benefits;

(2) select payment options under any retirement plan in which the principal participates, including plans for self-employed individuals;

(3) designate or change the designation of a beneficiary or benefits payable by a retirement plan, except that an attorney in fact or agent may be named a beneficiary only to the extent the attorney in fact or agent was a named beneficiary under the retirement plan before the durable power of attorney was executed;

(4) make voluntary contributions to retirement plans if authorized by the plan;

(5) exercise the investment powers available under any self-directed retirement plan;

(6) make "rollovers" of plan benefits into other retirement plans;

(7) borrow from, sell assets to, and purchase assets from retirement plans if authorized by the plan;

(8) waive the right of the principal to be a beneficiary of a joint or survivor annuity if the principal is a spouse who is not employed;

(9) receive, endorse, and cash payments from a retirement plan;

(10) waive the right of the principal to receive all or a portion of benefits payable by a retirement plan; and

(11) request and receive information relating to the principal from retirement plan records.

(b) In this section, "retirement plan" means:

(1) an employee pension benefit plan as defined by Section 1002, Employee Retirement Income Security Act of 1974 (ERISA) (29 U.S.C. § 1002), without regard to the provisions of Section (2)(B) of that section;

(2) a plan that does not meet the definition of an employee benefit plan under ERISA because the plan does not cover common law employees;

(3) a plan that is similar to an employee benefit plan under ERISA, regardless of whether it is covered by Title I of ERISA, including a plan that provides death benefits to the beneficiary of employees; and

(4) an individual retirement account or annuity or a self-employed pension plan or similar plan or account.

Added by Acts 1993, 73rd Leg., ch. 49, § 1, eff. Sept. 1, 1993. Amended by Acts 1997, 75th Leg., ch. 455, § 6, eff. Sept. 1, 1997.

§ 504. Construction of Power Relating to Tax Matters

In a statutory durable power of attorney, the language conferring authority with respect to tax matters empowers the attorney in fact or agent to:

(1) prepare, sign, and file federal, state, local, and foreign income, gift, payroll, Federal Insurance Contributions Act, and other tax returns, claims for refunds, requests for extension of time, petitions regarding tax matters, and any other tax-related documents, including receipts, offers, waivers, consents, including consents and agreements under Section 2032A, Internal Revenue Code of 1986 (26 U.S.C. § 2032A), closing agreements, and any power of attorney form required by the Internal Revenue Service or other taxing authority with respect to a tax year on which the statute of limitations has not run and 25 tax years following that tax year;

(2) pay taxes due, collect refunds, post bonds, receive confidential information, and contest deficiencies determined by the Internal Revenue Service or other taxing authority;

(3) exercise any election available to the principal under federal, state, local, or foreign tax law; and

(4) act for the principal in all tax matters for all periods before the Internal Revenue Service and any other taxing authority.

Added by Acts 1993, 73rd Leg., ch. 49, § 1, eff. Sept. 1, 1993.

§ 505. Existing Interest; Foreign Interests

The powers described in Sections 492 through 504 of this code may be exercised equally with respect to an interest the principal has at the time the durable power of attorney is executed or acquires later, whether or not the property is located in this state and whether or not the powers are exercised or the durable power of attorney is executed in this state.

Added by Acts 1993, 73rd Leg., ch. 49, § 1, eff. Sept. 1, 1993.

§ 506. Uniformity of Application and Construction

This chapter shall be applied and construed to effect its general purpose to make uniform the law with respect to the subject of this chapter among states enacting it.

Added by Acts 1993, 73rd Leg., ch. 49, § 1, eff. Sept. 1, 1993.

Chapter XIII. Guardianship

Statutes in Context

Guardians may be needed for minors and adult incapacitated individuals. There are two main types of guardians: a guardian of the *person* who is in charge of the ward's physical needs (§ 767) and a guardian of the *estate* of who is in charge of the ward's property and financial affairs (§ 768).

The guardianship provisions of the Probate Code were originally integrated with the decedents' estates provisions. In 1993, they were split. In many respects, the guardianship provisions still closely mirror the decedents' estates provisions.

Part 1. General Provisions

Subpart A. Definitions; Purpose; Applicability; Proceedings in Rem

§ 601. Definitions

In this chapter:

(1) "Attorney ad litem" means an attorney who is appointed by a court to represent and advocate on behalf of a proposed ward, an incapacitated person, or an unborn person in a guardianship proceeding.

(2) "Authorized corporate surety" means a domestic or foreign corporation authorized to do business in this state to issue surety, guaranty, or indemnity bonds guaranteeing the fidelity of guardians.

(3) "Child" includes a biological or adopted child, whether adopted by a parent under a statutory procedure or by acts of estoppel.

(4) "Claims" includes a liability against the estate of a minor or an incapacitated person and debts due to the estate of a minor or an incapacitated person.

(5) "Community administrator" means a spouse who is authorized to manage, control, and dispose of the entire community estate on the judicial declaration of incapacity of the other spouse, including the part of the community estate that the other

spouse legally has the power to manage in the absence of the incapacity.

(6) "Corporate fiduciary" means a financial institution as defined by Section 201.101, Finance Code, having trust powers, existing or doing business under the laws of this state, another state, or the United States, that is authorized by law to act under the order or appointment of any court of record, without giving bond, as a guardian, receiver, trustee, executor, or administrator, or, although without general depository powers, as a depository for any money paid into court, or to become sole guarantor or surety in or on any bond required to be given under the laws of this state.

(7) "Court investigator" means a person appointed by a statutory probate court under Section 25.0025, Government Code.

(8) "Court" or "probate court" means a county court in the exercise of its probate jurisdiction, a court created by statute and authorized to exercise original probate jurisdiction, or a district court exercising original probate jurisdiction in contested matters.

(9) "Estate" or "guardianship estate" means the real and personal property of a ward or deceased ward, both as the property originally existed and as has from time to time changed in form by sale, reinvestment, or otherwise, and as augmented by any accretions and additions to (including any property to be distributed to the representative of the deceased ward by the trustee of a trust that terminates on the ward's death) or substitutions for the property, and as diminished by any decreases to or distributions from the property.

(10) "Exempt property" refers to that property of a deceased ward's estate that is exempt from execution or forced sale by the constitution or laws of this state, and to the allowance in lieu of the property.

(11) "Guardian" means a person who is appointed guardian under Section 693 of this code, or a temporary or successor guardian. Except as expressly provided otherwise, "guardian" includes the guardian of the estate and the guardian of the person of an incapacitated person.

(12) "Guardian ad litem" means a person who is appointed by a court to represent the best interests of an incapacitated person in a guardianship proceeding.

(13) "Guardianship program" means a local, county, or regional program that provides guardianship and related services to an incapacitated person or other person who needs assistance in making decisions concerning the person s own welfare or financial affairs.

(14) "Incapacitated person" means:

(A) a minor;

(B) an adult individual who, because of a physical or mental condition, is substantially unable to provide food, clothing, or shelter for himself or herself, to care for the individual's own physical health, or to manage the individual's own financial affairs; or

(C) a person who must have a guardian appointed to receive funds due the person from any governmental source.

(15) "Interested persons" or "persons interested" means an heir, devisee, spouse, creditor, or any other person having a property right in, or claim against, the estate being administered or a person interested in the welfare of an incapacitated person, including a minor.

(16) "Minor" means a person who is younger than 18 years of age and who has never been married or who has not had the person's disabilities of minority removed for general purposes.

(17) "Minutes" means the guardianship minutes.

(18) "Mortgage" or "lien" includes a deed of trust; vendor's lien; chattel mortgage; mechanic's, materialman's, or laborer's lien; judgment, attachment, or garnishment lien; pledge by hypothecation; and a federal or state tax lien.

(19) "Next of kin" includes an adopted child, the descendants of an adopted child, and the adoptive parent of an adopted child.

(20) "Parent" means the mother of a child, a man presumed to be the biological father of a child, a man who has been adjudicated to be the biological father of a child by a court of competent jurisdiction, or an adoptive mother or father of a child, but does not include a parent as to whom the parent-child relationship has been terminated.

(21) "Person" includes natural persons, corporations, and guardianship programs.

(22) "Personal property" includes an interest in goods, money, choses in action, evidence of debts, and chattels real.

(23) "Personal representative" or "representative" includes a guardian, and a successor guardian.

(24) "Private professional guardian" means a person, other than an attorney or a corporate fiduciary, who is engaged in the business of providing guardianship services.

(25) "Proceedings in guardianship," "guardianship matter," "guardianship matters," "guardianship proceeding," and "proceedings for guardianship" are synonymous and include a matter or proceeding relating to a guardianship or any other matter addressed by this chapter.

(26) "Property" includes both real and personal property.

(27) "Proposed ward" means a person alleged to be incapacitated in a guardianship proceeding.

(28) "Real property" includes estates and interests in lands, corporeal or incorporeal, legal or equitable, other than chattels real.

(29) "Statutory probate court" means a statutory court designated as a statutory probate court under Chapter 25, Government Code. A county court at law exercising probate jurisdiction is not a statutory

probate court under this chapter unless the court is designated a statutory probate court under Chapter 25, Government Code.

(30) "Surety" includes a personal and a corporate surety.

(31) "Ward" is a person for whom a guardian has been appointed.

(32) The singular number includes the plural; the plural number includes the singular.

(33) The masculine gender includes the feminine and neuter.

Added by Acts 1993, 73rd Leg., ch. 957, § 1, eff. Sept. 1, 1993. Amended by Acts 1995, 74th Leg., ch. 1039, § 15, eff. Sept. 1, 1995; Subsec. (17) amended by Acts 1997, 75th Leg., ch. 1376, § 1, eff. Sept. 1, 1997; Subsec. (29) amended by Acts 1997, 75th Leg., ch. 52, § 2, eff. Sept. 1, 1997; Subsec. (5) amended by Acts 1999, 76th Leg., ch. 344, § 6.005, eff. Sept. 1, 1999. Amended by Acts 1999, 76th Leg., ch. 379, § 2, eff. Sept. 1, 1999; Acts 2001, 77th Leg., ch. 217, § 2, eff. Sept. 1, 2001.

§ 602. Policy; Purpose of Guardianship

A court may appoint a guardian with full authority over an incapacitated person or may grant a guardian limited authority over an incapacitated person as indicated by the incapacitated person's actual mental or physical limitations and only as necessary to promote and protect the well-being of the person. If the person is not a minor, the court may not use age as the sole factor in determining whether to appoint a guardian for the person. In creating a guardianship that gives a guardian limited power or authority over an incapacitated person, the court shall design the guardianship to encourage the development or maintenance of maximum self-reliance and independence in the incapacitated person.

Added by Acts 1993, 73rd Leg., ch. 957, § 1, eff. Sept. 1, 1993.

§ 603. Laws Applicable to Guardianships

(a) To the extent applicable and not inconsistent with other provisions of this code, the laws and rules governing estates of decedents apply to and govern guardianships.

(b) A reference in other sections of this code or in other law to a person who is mentally, physically, or legally incompetent, a person who is judicially declared incompetent, an incompetent or an incompetent person, a person of unsound mind, or a habitual drunkard means an incapacitated person.

Added by Acts 1993, 73rd Leg., ch. 957, § 1, eff. Sept. 1, 1993.

§ 604. Proceeding In Rem

From the filing of the application for the appointment of a guardian of the estate or person, or both, until the guardianship is settled and closed under this chapter, the administration of the estate of a minor or other incapacitated person is one proceeding for purposes of jurisdiction and is a proceeding in rem.

Added by Acts 1993, 73rd Leg., ch. 957, § 1, eff. Sept. 1, 1993.

Part 2. Guardianship Proceedings and Matters

Subpart A. Jurisdiction

§ 605. County Court Jurisdiction

The county court has the general jurisdiction of a probate court. The county court shall appoint guardians of minors and other incapacitated persons, grant letters of guardianship, settle accounts of guardians, and transact all business appertaining to estates subject to guardianship, including the settlement, partition, and distribution of the estates. The county court may also enter other orders as may be authorized under this chapter.

Added by Acts 1993, 73rd Leg., ch. 957, § 1, eff. Sept. 1, 1993.

§ 606. Jurisdiction with Respect to Guardianship Proceedings

(a) (Repealed)

(b) In those counties in which there is no statutory probate court, county court at law, or other statutory court exercising the jurisdiction of a probate court, all applications, petitions, and motions regarding guardianships, mental health matters, and other matters covered by this chapter shall be filed and heard in the county court. In contested guardianship matters, the judge of the county court may on the judge's own motion, or shall on the motion of any party to the proceeding, according to the motion:

(1) request the assignment of a statutory probate court judge to hear the contested portion of the proceeding, as provided by Section 25.0022, Government Code; or

(2) transfer the contested portion of the proceeding to the district court, which may hear the transferred contested matter as if originally filed in the district court.

(b-1) If the judge of the county court has not transferred a contested guardianship matter to the district court at the time a party files a motion for assignment of a statutory probate court judge, the county judge shall grant the motion and may not transfer the matter to the district court unless the party withdraws the motion.

(b-2) A statutory probate court judge assigned to a contested guardianship matter as provided by Subsection (b) of this section has the jurisdiction and authority granted to a statutory probate court by Sections 607 and 608 of this code. On resolution of a contested matter, including an appeal of a matter, to which a statutory probate court judge has been assigned, the statutory probate court judge shall transfer the resolved portion of the case to the county court for further proceedings not inconsistent with the orders of the statutory probate court judge.

(b-3) In contested matters transferred to the district court the district court has the general jurisdiction of a probate court. On resolution of a contested matter, including an appeal of a matter, the district court shall transfer the resolved portion of the case to the county court for further proceedings not inconsistent with the orders of the district court.

(b-4) The county court shall continue to exercise jurisdiction over the management of the guardianship with the exception of the contested matter until final disposition of the contested matter is made by the assigned judge or the district court.

(b-5) If a contested portion of the proceeding is transferred to a district court under Subsection (b-3) of this section , the clerk of the district court may perform in relation to the transferred portion of the proceeding any function a county clerk may perform in that type of contested proceeding.

(c) In those counties in which there is no statutory probate court, but in which there is a county court at law or other statutory court exercising the jurisdiction of a probate court, all applications, petitions, and motions regarding guardianships, mental health matters, or other matters addressed by this chapter shall be filed and heard in those courts and the constitutional county court unless otherwise provided by law. The judge of a county court may hear any of those matters sitting for the judge of any other county court. Except as provided by Section 608 of this code, in contested guardianship matters, the judge of the constitutional county court may on the judge's own motion, and shall on the motion of a party to the proceeding, transfer the proceeding to the county court at law or a statutory court exercising the jurisdiction of a probate court other than a statutory probate court. The court to which the proceeding is transferred may hear the proceeding as if originally filed in the court.

(d) In those counties in which there is a statutory probate court, all applications, petitions, and motions regarding guardianships, mental health matters, or other matters addressed by this chapter shall be filed and heard in the statutory probate court.

(e) A court that exercises original probate jurisdiction has the power to hear all matters incident to an estate. After a guardianship of the estate of a ward is required to be settled as provided by Section 745 of this chapter, the court exercising original probate jurisdiction over the settling of the former ward's estate has the jurisdiction to hear:

(1) an action brought by or on behalf of the former ward against a former guardian of the ward for alleged misconduct arising from the performance of the person's duties as guardian;

(2) an action against a former guardian of the former ward that is brought by a surety that is called on to perform in place of the former guardian;

(3) a claim for the payment of compensation, expenses, and court costs and any other matter authorized under Subpart H, Part 2, of this chapter;

(4) a matter related to an authorization made or duty performed by a guardian under Subpart C, Part 4, of this chapter; and

(5) any other matter related or appertaining to a guardianship estate that a court exercising original probate jurisdiction is specifically authorized to hear under this chapter.

(f) When a surety is called on to perform in place of a guardian or former guardian, a court exercising original probate jurisdiction, including jurisdiction exercised under Subsection (e)(2) of this section, may award judgment against the guardian or former guardian in favor of the surety of the guardian or former guardian in the same suit.

(g) A final order of a court that exercises original probate jurisdiction is appealable to a court of appeals.

(h) A statutory probate court has concurrent jurisdiction with the district court in all personal injury, survival, or wrongful death actions by or against a person in the person's capacity as a guardian and in all actions involving a guardian in which each other party aligned with the guardian is not an interested person in the guardianship.

(i) A statutory probate court has jurisdiction over any matter appertaining to an estate or incident to an estate and has jurisdiction over any cause of action in which a guardian in a guardianship proceeding pending in the statutory probate court is a party.

(j) A statutory probate court may exercise the pendent and ancillary jurisdiction necessary to promote judicial efficiency and economy.

Added by Acts 1993, 73rd Leg., ch. 957, § 1, eff. Sept. 1, 1993. Subsec. (b) amended by Acts 1995, 74th Leg., ch. 1039, § 16, eff. Sept. 1, 1995; Subsec. (e) amended by Acts 1995, 74th Leg., ch. 1039, § 17, eff. Sept. 1, 1995; Subsec. (b) amended by Acts 1999, 76th Leg., ch. 1389, § 2, eff. Aug. 30, 1999. Amended by Acts 2001, 77th Leg., ch. 63, § 2, eff. Sept. 1, 2001; Subsec. (c) amended by Acts 2001, 77th Leg., ch. 1174, § 1, eff. Sept. 1, 2001; Subsecs. (e), (f) amended by and (g) added by Acts 2001, 77th Leg., ch. 484, § 1, eff. Sept. 1, 2001. Amended by Acts 2003, 78th Leg., ch.549, §§ 1, 2, 3, 4, 5 & 33, eff. Sept. 1, 2003.

§ 607. Matters Appertaining and Incident to an Estate

(a) In a proceeding in a constitutional county court or a statutory county court at law, the phrases "appertaining to estates" and "incident to an estate" in this chapter include the appointment of guardians, the issuance of letters of guardianship, a claim by or against a guardianship estate, all actions for trial of title to land incident to a guardianship estate and for the enforcement of liens incident to a guardianship estate, all actions for trial of the right of property incident to a guardianship estate, and generally all matters relating to the settlement, partition, and distribution of a guardianship estate.

(b) In a proceeding in a statutory probate court, the phrases "appertaining to estates" and "incident to an estate" in this chapter include the appointment of guardians, the issuance of letters of guardianship, all claims by or against a guardianship estate, all actions for trial of title to land and for the enforcement of liens on the land, all actions for trial of the right of property, and generally all matters relating to the collection, settlement, partition, and distribution of a guardianship estate. A statutory probate court, in the exercise of its jurisdiction and notwithstanding any other provision of this chapter, may hear all suits, actions, and applications filed against or on behalf of any guardianship; all such suits, actions, and applications are appertaining to and incident to an estate. Except for situations in which the jurisdiction of a statutory probate court is concurrent with that of a district court or any other court, any cause of action appertaining to or incident to a guardianship estate shall be brought in a statutory probate court.

(c) (Repealed)

(d) (Repealed)

(e) Notwithstanding any other provision of this chapter, the proper venue for an action by or against a personal representative for personal injury, death, or property damages is determined under Section 15.007, Civil Practice and Remedies Code.

Added by Acts 1993, 73rd Leg., ch. 957, § 1, eff. Sept. 1, 1993. Subsec. (b) amended by Acts 1999, 76th Leg., ch. 10, § 1, eff. Sept. 1, 1999; Subsec. (e) amended by Acts 1999, 76th Leg., ch. 10, § 2, eff. Sept. 1, 1999. Amended by Acts 2003, 78th Leg., ch. 204, § 3.07, eff. Sept. 1, 2003; Acts 2003, 78th Leg., ch.549, §§ 6 & 33, eff. Sept. 1, 2003.

§ 608. Transfer of Guardianship Proceeding

A judge of a statutory probate court, on the motion of a party to the action or of a person interested in a guardianship, may transfer to the judge's court from a district, county, or statutory court a cause of action appertaining to or incident to a guardianship estate that is pending in the statutory probate court or a cause of action relating to a guardianship in which a guardian, ward, or proposed ward in a guardianship pending in the statutory probate court is a party and may consolidate the transferred cause of action with the other proceedings in the statutory probate court relating to the guardianship estate.

Added by Acts 1993, 73rd Leg., ch. 957, § 1, eff. Sept. 1, 1993. Amended by Acts 1999, 76th Leg., ch. 1431, § 2, eff. Sept. 1, 1999; Acts 2003, 78th Leg., ch. 549, § 7, eff. Sept. 1, 2003.

§ 609. Contested Guardianship of the Person of a Minor

(a) If an interested person contests an application for the appointment of a guardian of the person of a minor or an interested person seeks the removal of a guardian of the person of a minor, the judge, on the judge's own motion, may transfer all matters relating to the guardianship of the person of the minor to a court of competent jurisdiction in which a suit affecting the parent-child relationship under the Family Code is pending.

(b) The probate court that transfers a proceeding under this section to a court with proper jurisdiction over suits affecting the parent-child relationship shall send to the court to which the transfer is made the complete files in all matters affecting the guardianship of the person of the minor and certified copies of all entries in the minutes. The transferring court shall keep a copy of the transferred files. If the transferring court retains jurisdiction of the guardianship of the estate of the minor or of another minor who was the subject of the suit, the court shall send a copy of the complete files to the court to which the transfer is made and shall keep the original files.

(c) The court to which a transfer is made under this section shall apply the procedural and substantive provisions of the Family Code, including Sections 155.005 and 155.205, in regard to enforcing an order rendered by the court from which the proceeding was transferred.

Added by Acts 1993, 73rd Leg., ch. 957, § 1, eff. Sept. 1, 1993. Subsec. (c) amended by Acts 1997, 75th Leg., ch. 77, § 1, eff. Sept. 1, 1997; amended by Acts 1997, 75th Leg., ch. 165, § 7.55, eff. Sept. 1, 1997.

Subpart B. Venue

§ 610. Venue for Appointment of Guardian

(a) Except as otherwise authorized by this section, a proceeding for the appointment of a guardian for the person or estate, or both, of an incapacitated person shall be brought in the county in which the proposed ward resides or is located on the date the application is filed or in the county in which the principal estate of the proposed ward is located.

(b) A proceeding for the appointment of a guardian for the person or estate, or both, of a minor may be brought:

(1) in the county in which both the minor's parents reside;

(2) if the parents do not reside in the same county, in the county in which the parent who is the sole managing conservator of the minor resides, or in the county in which the parent who is the joint managing conservator with the greater period of physical possession of and access to the minor resides;

(3) if only one parent is living and the parent has custody of the minor, in the county in which that parent resides;

(4) if both parents are dead but the minor was in the custody of a deceased parent, in the county in which the last surviving parent having custody resided; or

(5) if both parents of a minor child have died in a common disaster and there is no evidence that the parents died other than simultaneously, in the county in which both deceased parents resided at the time of their simultaneous deaths if they resided in the same county.

(c) A proceeding for the appointment of a guardian who was appointed by will may be brought in the county in which the will was admitted to probate or in the county of the appointee's residence if the appointee resides in this state.

(d) Repealed by Acts 1999, 76th Leg., ch. 379, § 10, eff. Sept. 1, 1999.

Added by Acts 1993, 73rd Leg., ch. 957, § 1, eff. Sept. 1, 1993. Subsec. (d) repealed by Acts 1999, 76th Leg., ch. 379, § 10, eff. Sept. 1, 1999.

§ 611. Concurrent Venue and Transfer for Want of Venue

(a) If two or more courts have concurrent venue of a guardianship matter, the court in which an application for a guardianship proceeding is initially filed has and retains jurisdiction of the guardianship matter. A proceeding is considered commenced by the filing of an application alleging facts sufficient to confer venue, and the proceeding initially legally commenced extends to all of the property of the guardianship estate.

(b) If a guardianship proceeding is commenced in more than one county, it shall be stayed except in the county in which it was initially commenced until final determination of proper venue is made by the court in the county in which it was initially commenced.

(c) If it appears to the court at any time before the guardianship is closed that the proceeding was commenced in a court that did not have venue over the proceeding, the court shall, on the application of any interested person, transfer the proceeding to the proper county.

(d) When a proceeding is transferred to another county under a provision of this chapter, all orders entered in connection with the proceeding shall be valid and shall be recognized in the court to which the guardianship was ordered transferred, if the orders were made and entered in conformance with the procedures prescribed by this code.

Added by Acts 1993, 73rd Leg., ch. 957, § 1, eff. Sept. 1, 1993.

§ 612. Application for Transfer of Guardianship to Another County

When a guardian or any other person desires to remove the transaction of the business of the guardianship from one county to another, the person shall file a written application in the court in which the guardianship is pending stating the reason for moving the transaction of business.

Added by Acts 1993, 73rd Leg., ch. 957, § 1, eff. Sept. 1, 1993.

§ 613. Notice

(a) On filing an application to remove a guardianship to another county, the sureties on the bond of the guardian shall be cited by personal service to appear and show cause why the application should not be granted.

(b) If an application is filed by a person other than the guardian, the guardian shall be cited by personal service to appear and show cause why the application should not be granted.

Added by Acts 1993, 73rd Leg., ch. 957, § 1, eff. Sept. 1, 1993.

§ 614. Court Action

On hearing an application under Section 612 of this code, if good cause is not shown to deny the application and it appears that removal of the guardianship is in the best interests of the ward, the court shall enter an order authorizing the removal on payment on behalf of the estate of all accrued costs.

Added by Acts 1993, 73rd Leg., ch. 957, § 1, eff. Sept. 1, 1993.

§ 615. Transcript of Record

When an order of removal is made under Section 614 of this code, the clerk shall record any unrecorded papers of the guardianship required to be recorded and make out a complete certified transcript of all the orders, decrees, judgments, and proceedings in the guardianship. On payment of the clerk's fees, the clerk shall transmit the transcript, with the original papers in the case, to the county clerk of the county to which the guardianship was ordered removed.

Added by Acts 1993, 73rd Leg., ch. 957, § 1, eff. Sept. 1, 1993.

§ 616. Removal Effective

The order removing a guardianship does not take effect until:

(1) the transcript required by Section 615 of this code is filed in the office of the county clerk of the county to which the guardianship was ordered removed; and

(2) a certificate under the clerk's official seal and reporting the filing of the transcript is filed in the court ordering the removal by the county clerk of the county to which the guardianship was ordered removed.

Added by Acts 1993, 73rd Leg., ch. 957, § 1, eff. Sept. 1, 1993.

§ 617. Continuation of Guardianship

When a guardianship is removed from one county to another in accordance with this subpart, the guardianship proceeds in the court to which it was removed as if it had been originally commenced in that court. It is not necessary to record in the receiving court any of the papers in the case that were recorded in the court from which the case was removed.

Added by Acts 1993, 73rd Leg., ch. 957, § 1, eff. Sept. 1, 1993.

§ 618. New Guardian Appointed on Removal

If it appears to the court that removal of the guardianship is in the best interests of the ward, but that because of the removal it will be unduly expensive or unduly inconvenient to the estate for the guardian of the estate to continue to serve in that capacity, the court may in its order of removal revoke the letters of guardianship and appoint a new guardian, and the former

guardian shall account for and deliver the estate as provided by this chapter in a case in which a guardian resigns.
Added by Acts 1993, 73rd Leg., ch. 957, § 1, eff. Sept. 1, 1993.

Subpart C. Duties and Records of Clerk

§ 621. Application and Other Papers to be Filed With Clerk

(a) An application for a guardianship proceeding, a complaint, petition, or other paper permitted or required by law to be filed in the court in guardianship matters shall be filed with the county clerk of the proper county.

(b) The county clerk shall file the paper received under this section and endorse on each paper the date filed, the docket number, and the clerk's official signature.
Added by Acts 1993, 73rd Leg., ch. 957, § 1, eff. Sept. 1, 1993.

§ 622. Costs and Security

(a) The laws regulating costs in ordinary civil cases apply to a guardianship matter unless otherwise expressly provided by this chapter.

(b) When a person other than the guardian, attorney ad litem, or guardian ad litem files an application, complaint, or opposition in relation to a guardianship matter, the clerk may require the person to give security for the probable costs of the guardianship proceeding before filing. A person interested in the guardianship or in the welfare of the ward, or an officer of the court, at any time before the trial of an application, complaint, or opposition in relation to a guardianship matter, may obtain from the court, on written motion, an order requiring the person who filed the application, complaint, or opposition to give security for the probable costs of the proceeding. The rules governing civil suits in the county court relating to this subject control in these cases.

(c) No security for costs shall be required of a guardian, attorney ad litem, or guardian ad litem appointed under this chapter by a court of this state in any suit brought by the guardian, attorney ad litem, or guardian ad litem in their respective fiduciary capacities.
Added by Acts 1993, 73rd Leg., ch. 957, § 1, eff. Sept. 1, 1993.

§ 623. Judge's Guardianship Docket

(a) The county clerk shall keep a record book to be styled "Judge's Guardianship Docket" and shall enter in the record book:

(1) the name of each person on whose person or estate a proceeding is had or is sought to be had;

(2) the name of the guardian of the estate or person or of the applicant for letters;

(3) the date the original application for a guardianship proceeding was filed;

(4) a minute, including the date, of each order, judgment, decree, and proceeding in each estate; and

(5) a number of each guardianship on the docket in the order in which a proceeding is commenced.

(b) Each paper filed in a guardianship proceeding shall be given the corresponding docket number of the estate.
Added by Acts 1993, 73rd Leg., ch. 957, § 1, eff. Sept. 1, 1993.

§ 624. Claim Docket

The county clerk shall keep a record book to be styled "Claim Docket" and shall enter in the claim docket all claims presented against a guardianship for court approval. The claim docket shall be ruled in 16 columns at proper intervals from top to bottom, with a short note of the contents at the top of each column. One or more pages shall be assigned to each guardianship. The following information shall be entered in the respective columns beginning with the first or marginal column: The names of claimants in the order in which their claims are filed; the amount of the claim; its date; the date of filing; when due; the date from which it bears interest; the rate of interest; when allowed by the guardian; the amount allowed; the date of rejection; when approved; the amount approved; when disapproved; the class to which the claim belongs; when established by judgment of a court; the amount of the judgment.
Added by Acts 1993, 73rd Leg., ch. 957, § 1, eff. Sept. 1, 1993.

§ 625. Case Files

The county clerk shall maintain a case file for each person's filed guardianship proceedings. The case file must contain all orders, judgments, and proceedings of the court and any other guardianship filing with the court, including all:

(1) applications for the granting of guardianship;

(2) citations and notices, whether published or posted, with the returns on the citations and notices;

(3) bonds and official oaths;

(4) inventories, appraisements, and lists of claims;

(5) exhibits and accounts;

(6) reports of hiring, renting, or sale;

(7) applications for sale or partition of real estate and reports of sale and of commissioners of partition;

(8) applications for authority to execute leases for mineral development, or for pooling or unitization of lands, royalty, or other interest in minerals, or to lend or invest money;

(9) reports of lending or investing money; and

(10) reports of guardians of the persons.

Added by Acts 1993, 73rd Leg., ch. 957, § 1, eff. Sept. 1, 1993. Amended by Acts 1999, 76th Leg., ch. 67, § 2, eff. Sept. 1, 1999.

§ 626. Guardianship Fee Book

The county clerk shall keep a record book styled "Guardianship Fee Book" and shall enter in the guardianship fee book each item of costs that accrue to the officers of the court, with witness fees, if any, showing the:

(1) party to whom the costs or fees are due;

(2) date of the accrual of the costs or fees;

(3) guardianship or party liable for the costs or fees; and

(4) date on which the costs or fees are paid.

Added by Acts 1993, 73rd Leg., ch. 957, § 1, eff. Sept. 1, 1993.

§ 627. Maintaining Records in Lieu of Record Books

In lieu of keeping the record books described by Sections 623, 624, and 626 of this code, the county clerk may maintain the information relating to a person's guardianship proceeding maintained in those record books on a computer file, on microfilm, in the form of a digitized optical image, or in another similar form of data compilation.

Added by Acts 1999, 76th Leg., ch. 67, § 2, eff. Sept. 1, 1999.

§ 627A. Index

The county clerk shall properly index the records and keep the index open for public inspection but may not release the index from the clerk's custody.

Added by Acts 1993, 73rd Leg., ch. 957, § 1, eff. Sept. 1, 1993. Renumbered from § 627 and amended by Acts 1999, 76th Leg., ch. 67, § 2, eff. Sept. 1, 1999.

§ 628. Use of Records as Evidence

The record books or individual case files, including records on a computer file, on microfilm, in the form of a digitized optical image, or in another similar form of data compilation described in other sections of this chapter, or certified copies or reproductions of the records, shall be evidence in any court of this state.

Added by Acts 1993, 73rd Leg., ch. 957, § 1, eff. Sept. 1, 1993. Amended by Acts 1999, 76th Leg., ch. 67, § 2, eff. Sept. 1, 1999.

§ 629. Call of the Dockets

The judge of the court in which a guardianship proceeding is pending, as the judge determines, shall call guardianship matters in their regular order on both the guardianship and claim dockets and shall make necessary orders.

Added by Acts 1993, 73rd Leg., ch. 957, § 1, eff. Sept. 1, 1993.

§ 630. Clerk May Set Hearings

If the county judge is absent from the county seat or is on vacation, disqualified, ill, or deceased and is unable to designate the time and place for hearing a guardianship matter pending in the judge's court, the county clerk of the county in which the matter is pending may designate the time and place for hearing, entering the setting on the judge's docket and certifying on the docket the reason that the judge is not acting to set the hearing. If a qualified judge is not present for the hearing, after service of the notices and citations required by law with reference to the time and place of hearing has been perfected, the hearing is automatically continued from day to day until a qualified judge is present to hear and determine the matter.

Added by Acts 1993, 73rd Leg., ch. 957, § 1, eff. Sept. 1, 1993.

§ 631. Clerk's Duties

(a) If the proper venue is finally determined to be in another county, the clerk, after making and retaining a true copy of the entire file in the case, shall transmit the original file to the proper county, and a proceeding shall be held in the proper county in the same manner as if the proceeding had originally been instituted in the proper county.

(b) By transmitting to the proper court in the proper county for venue purposes the original file in the case, with certified copies of all entries in the minutes made in the file, an administration of the guardianship in the proper county for venue purposes shall be completed in the same manner as if the proceeding had originally been instituted in that county.

(c) The clerk of the court from which the proceeding is transferred shall transmit to the court to which the proceeding is transferred the original file in the proceeding and a certified copy of the entries in the minutes that relate to the proceeding.

Added by Acts 1993, 73rd Leg., ch. 957, § 1, eff. Sept. 1, 1993.

Subpart D. Service and Notice

§ 632. Issuance, Contents, Service, and Return of Citation, Notices, and Writs in Guardianship Matters

(a) A person does not need to be cited or otherwise given notice in a guardianship matter except in situations in which this chapter expressly provides for citation or the giving of notice. If this chapter does not expressly provide for citation or the issuance or return of notice in a guardianship matter, the court may require that notice be given. If the court requires that notice be given, the court shall prescribe the form and manner of service and return of service.

(b) Unless a court order is required by a provision of this chapter, the county clerk shall issue without a court order necessary citations, writs, and process in guardianship matters and all notices not required to be issued by guardians.

(c) A citation and notice issued by the clerk shall be signed and sealed by the clerk and shall be styled "The State of Texas." A notice required to be given by a guardian shall be in writing and signed by the guardian in the guardian's official capacity. A citation or notice shall be dated and directed to the person that is being cited or notified and must state the style and number of the proceeding and the court in which the proceeding is pending and must describe generally the nature of the proceeding or matter to which the citation or notice relates. A precept directed to an officer is not necessary. A citation or notice must direct the person cited or notified to appear by filing a written contest or answer or perform other required acts. A citation or notice must state when and where an appearance or performance by a person cited or notified is required. A citation or notice is not defective because it contains a precept directed to an officer authorized to serve it. A writ or other process other than a citation or notice shall be directed "To any sheriff or constable within the State of Texas" and may not be held defective because it is directed to the sheriff or any constable of a specific county if the writ or other process is properly served within the named county by an officer authorized to serve it.

(d) In all situations in which this chapter requires that notice be given or that a person be cited, and in which a specific method of giving the notice or citing the person, or a specific method of service and return of the citation or notice is not given, or an insufficient or inadequate provision appears with respect to any matter relating to citation or notice, or on request of an interested person, notice or citation shall be issued, served, and returned in the manner the court, by written order, directs in accordance with this chapter and the Texas Rules of Civil Procedure and has the same force and effect as if the manner of service and return had been specified in this chapter.

(e) Except in instances in which this chapter expressly provides for another method of service, a notice or citation required to be served on a guardian or receiver shall be served by the clerk that issues the citation or notice. The clerk shall serve the citation or notice by sending the original citation or notice by registered or certified mail to the attorney of record for the guardian or receiver or to the guardian or receiver, if the guardian or receiver does not have an attorney of record.

(f)(1) In cases in which it is provided that personal service shall be had with respect to a citation or notice, the citation or notice must be served on the attorney of record for the person who is being cited or notified. Notwithstanding the requirement of personal service, service may be made on the attorney by any method specified under this chapter for service on an attorney. If there is no attorney of record in the proceeding for the person who is being cited or notified, or if an attempt to make service on the attorney was unsuccessful, a citation or notice directed to a person within this state must be served in person by the sheriff or constable on the person who is being cited or notified by delivering to the person a true copy of the citation or notice at least 10 days before the return day on the citation or notice, exclusive of the date of service. If the person who is being cited or notified is absent from the state or is a nonresident, the citation or notice may be served by a disinterested person competent to make oath of the fact. The citation or notice served by a disinterested person shall be returnable at least 10 days after the date of service, exclusive of the date of service. The return of the person serving the citation or notice shall be endorsed on or attached to the citation or notice. The return must show the time and place of service, certify that a true copy of the citation or notice was delivered to the person directed to be served, be subscribed and sworn to before an officer authorized by the laws of this state to take affidavits, under the hand and official seal of the officer, and returned to the county clerk who issued the citation or notice. If the citation or notice is returned with the notation that the person sought to be served, whether or not within this state, cannot be found, the clerk shall issue a new citation or notice directed to the person sought to be served and service shall be by publication.

(2) When citation or notice is required to be posted, the sheriff or constable shall post the citation or notice at the courthouse door of the county in which the proceeding is pending, or at the place in or near the courthouse where public notices customarily are posted, for at least 10 days before the return day of the citation or notice, exclusive of the date of posting. The clerk shall deliver the original and a copy of the citation or notice to the sheriff or a constable of the proper county, who shall post the copy as prescribed by this section and return the original to the clerk, stating in a written return of the copy the time when and the place where the sheriff or constable posted the copy. The date of posting is the date of service. When posting of notice by a guardian is authorized or required, the method prescribed by this section shall be followed. The notice is to be issued in the name of the guardian, addressed and delivered to, posted and returned by, the proper officer, and filed with the clerk.

(3) When a person is to be cited or notified by publication, the citation or notice shall be published once in a newspaper of general circulation in the county in which the proceeding is pending, and the publication shall be not less than 10 days before the return date of the citation or notice, exclusive of the date of publication. The date of publication of the newspaper in which the citation or notice is published appears is the date of service. If there is no newspaper of general circulation published or printed in the county in which citation or notice is to be had, service of the citation or notice shall be by posting.

(4)(A) When a citation or notice is required or permitted to be served by registered or certified mail, other than a notice required to be given by a guardian, the clerk shall issue the citation or notice and shall serve the citation or notice by sending the original citation or notice by registered or certified mail. A guardian shall issue notice required to be given by the guardian by registered or certified mail, and the guardian shall serve the notice by sending the original notice by registered or certified mail. The citation or notice shall be mailed return receipt requested with instructions to deliver to the addressee only. The envelope containing the citation or notice shall be addressed to the attorney of record in the proceeding for the person who is being cited or notified, but if there is no attorney of record, or if the citation or notice is returned undelivered, the envelope containing the citation or notice shall be addressed to the person who is being cited or notified. A copy of the citation or notice and the certificate of the clerk or guardian showing the fact and date of mailing shall be filed and recorded. If a receipt is returned, it shall be attached to the certificate.

(B) When a citation or notice is required or permitted to be served by ordinary mail, the clerk or the guardian when required by statute or court order, shall serve the citation or notice by mailing the original to the person being cited or notified. A copy of the citation or notice and a certificate of the person serving the citation or notice that shows the fact and time of mailing shall be filed and recorded.

(C) When service is made by mail, the date of mailing is the date of service. Service by mail must be made not less than 20 days before the return day of the citation or notice, exclusive of the date of service.

(D) If a citation or notice served by mail is returned undelivered, a new citation or notice shall be issued, and the new citation or notice shall be served by posting.

(g) A citation or notice issued by the clerk and served by personal service, by mail, by posting, or by publication shall be returned to the court from which the citation or notice was issued on the first Monday after the service is perfected.

(h) In a guardianship matter in which citation or notice is required to be served by posting and issued in conformity with the applicable provision of this code, the citation or notice and the service of and return of the citation or notice is sufficient and valid if a sheriff or constable posts a copy of the citation or notice at the place or places prescribed by this chapter on a day that is sufficiently before the return day contained in the citation or notice for the period of time for which the citation or notice is required to be posted to elapse before the return day of the citation or notice. The sufficiency or validity of the citation or notice or the service of or return of the service of the citation or notice is not affected by the fact that the sheriff or constable makes his return on the citation or notice and returns the citation or notice to the court before the period elapses for which the citation or notice is required to be posted, even though the return is made, and the citation or notice is returned to the court, on the same day it is issued.

(i) Proof of service by publication, posting, mailing, or otherwise in all cases requiring notice or citation shall be filed before a hearing. Proof of service made by a sheriff or constable shall be made by the return of service. Service made by a private person shall be proved by the person's affidavit. Proof of service by publication shall be made by an affidavit of the publisher or of an employee of the publisher that shows the issue date of the newspaper that carried the notice or citation and that has attached to or embodied in the affidavit a copy of the notice or citation. Proof of service by mail shall be made by the certificate of the clerk, or the affidavit of the guardian or other person that makes the service that states the fact and time of mailing. The return receipt must be attached to the certificate, if a receipt has been returned if service is made by registered or certified mail.

(j) At any time after an application is filed for the purpose of commencing a guardianship proceeding, a person interested in the estate or welfare of a ward or an incapacitated person may file with the clerk a written request that the person be notified of any or all specifically designated motions, applications, or pleadings filed by any person, or by a person specifically designated in the request. The person who makes the request is responsible for the fees and costs associated with the documents specified in the request. The clerk may require a deposit to cover the estimated costs of furnishing the person with the requested notice. The clerk by ordinary mail shall send to the requesting person a copy of any document specified in the request. A proceeding is not invalid if the clerk fails to comply with the request under this subsection.

Added by Acts 1993, 73rd Leg., ch. 957, § 1, eff. Sept. 1, 1993.

§ 633. Notice and Citation

(a) On the filing of an application for guardianship, notice shall be issued and served as provided by this section.

(b) The court clerk shall issue a citation stating that the application for guardianship was filed, the name of the proposed ward, the name of the applicant, and the name of the person to be appointed guardian as provided in the application, if that person is not the applicant. The citation must cite all persons interested in the welfare of the proposed ward to appear at the time and place stated in the notice if they wish to contest the application. The citation shall be posted.

(c) The sheriff or other officer shall personally serve citation to appear and answer the application for guardianship on:

(1) a proposed ward who is 12 years of age or older;

(2) the parents of a proposed ward if the whereabouts of the parents are known or can be reasonably ascertained;

(3) any court-appointed conservator or person having control of the care and welfare of the proposed ward;

(4) a proposed ward's spouse if the whereabouts of the spouse are known or can be reasonably ascertained; and

(5) the person named in the application to be appointed guardian, if that person is not the applicant.

(d) The applicant shall mail a copy of the application for guardianship and a notice containing the information required in the citation issued under Subsection (b) of this section by registered or certified mail, return receipt requested, or by any other form of mail that provides proof of delivery, to the following persons, if their whereabouts are known or can be reasonably ascertained:

(1) all adult children of a proposed ward;

(2) all adult siblings of a proposed ward;

(3) the administrator of a nursing home facility or similar facility in which the proposed ward resides;

(4) the operator of a residential facility in which the proposed ward resides;

(5) a person whom the applicant knows to hold a power of attorney signed by the proposed ward;

(6) a person designated to serve as guardian of the proposed ward by a written declaration under Section 679 of this code, if the applicant knows of the existence of the declaration;

(7) a person designated to serve as guardian of the proposed ward in the probated will of the last surviving parent of the ward; and

(8) a person designated to serve as guardian of the proposed ward by a written declaration of the proposed ward's last surviving parent, if the declarant is deceased and the applicant knows of the existence of the declaration.

(9) each person named as next of kin in the application for guardianship as required by Section 682(10) or (12) of this code.

(d-1) The applicant shall file with the court:

(1) a copy of any notice required by Subsection (d) of this section and the proofs of delivery of the notice; and

(2) an affidavit sworn to by the applicant or the applicant's attorney stating:

(A) that the notice was mailed as required by Subsection (d) of this section; and

(B) the name of each person to whom the notice was mailed, if the person's name is not shown on the proof of delivery.

(e) A person other than the proposed ward who is entitled to receive notice or personal service of citation under Subsections (c) and (d) of this section may choose, in person or by attorney ad litem, by writing filed with the clerk, to waive the receipt of notice or the issuance and personal service of citation.

(f) The court may not act on an application for the creation of a guardianship until the Monday following the expiration of the 10-day period beginning the date service of notice and citation has been made as provided by Subsections (b), (c), and (d)(1) of this section and the applicant has complied with Subsection (d-1) of this section. The validity of a guardianship created under this chapter is not affected by the failure of the applicant to comply with the requirements of Subsections (d)(2)-(9) of this section.

(g) It is not necessary for a person who files an application for the creation of a guardianship under this chapter to be served with citation or waive the issuance and personal service of citation under this section.

Added by Acts 1995, 74th Leg., ch. 1039, § 18, eff. Sept. 1, 1995. Subsecs. (d), (I) amended by Acts 1997, 75th Leg., ch. 77, § 2, eff. Sept. 1, 1997; Subsec. (b) amended by Acts 1999, 76th Leg., ch. 997, § 1, eff. Sept. 1, 1999; Subsec. (c) amended by Acts 1999, 76th Leg., ch. 379, § 3, eff. Sept. 1, 1999; Subsec. (c) amended by Acts 1999, 76th Leg., ch. 997, § 1, eff. Sept. 1, 1999; Subsec. (c) amended by Acts 2001, 77th Leg., ch. 940, § 1, eff. Sept. 1, 2001; Subsec. (c) amended by Acts 2001, 77th Leg., ch. 1174, § 2, eff. Sept. 1, 2001; Subsec. (d) amended by Acts 2001, 77th Leg., ch. 940, § 1, eff. Sept. 1, 2001; Subsec. (d) amended by Acts 2001, 77th Leg., ch. 1174, § 2, eff. Sept. 1, 2001; Subsec. (f) amended by Acts 2001, 77th Leg., ch. 940, § 1, eff. Sept. 1, 2001; Subsec. (f) amended by Acts 2001, 77th Leg., ch. 1174, § 2, eff. Sept. 1, 2001. Amended by Acts 2003, 78th Leg., ch. 549, § 8, eff. Sept. 1, 2003.

§ 634. Service on Attorney

(a) If an attorney has entered an appearance on record for a party in a guardianship proceeding, a citation or notice required to be served on the party shall be served on the attorney. Service on the attorney of record is in lieu of service on the party for whom the attorney appears. Except as provided by Section 633(e) of this code, an attorney ad litem may not waive personal service of citation.

(b) A notice served on an attorney under this section may be served by registered or certified mail, return receipt requested, by any other form of mail requiring proof of delivery, or by delivery to the attorney in person. A party to the proceeding or the party's attorney of record, an appropriate sheriff or constable, or another person who is competent to testify may serve notice or citation to an attorney under this section.

(c) A written statement by an attorney of record, the return of the officer, or the affidavit of a person that shows service is prima facie evidence of the fact of service.

Added by Acts 1993, 73rd Leg., ch. 957, § 1, eff. Sept. 1, 1993. Amended by Acts 2003, 78th Leg., ch. 549, § 9, eff. Sept. 1, 2003.

§ 635. Waiver of Notice

A competent person who is interested in a hearing in a guardianship proceeding, in person or by attorney, may waive in writing notice of the hearing. A consul or other representative of a foreign government, whose appearance has been entered as provided by law on behalf of a person residing in a foreign country, may waive notice on behalf of the person. A person who submits to the jurisdiction of the court in a hearing is deemed to have waived notice of the hearing.

Added by Acts 1993, 73rd Leg., ch. 957, § 1, eff. Sept. 1, 1993.

§ 636. Notices to Department of Veterans Affairs by Guardians

When an annual or other account of funds, or an application for the expenditure of or investment of funds is filed by a guardian whose ward is a beneficiary of the Department of Veterans Affairs, or when a claim against the estate of a ward who is a beneficiary of the Department of Veterans Affairs is filed, the court shall set a date for the hearing of the account, application, petition, or claim to be held not less than 20 days from the date of the filing of the account, application, petition, or claim. The person who files the account, application, petition, or claim shall give notice of the date of the filing to the office of the Department of Veterans Affairs in whose territory the court is located by mailing to the office a certified copy of the account, application, petition, or claim not later than five days after the date of the filing. An office of the Department of Veterans Affairs, through its attorney, may waive the service of notice and the time within which a hearing may be had in those cases.

Added by Acts 1993, 73rd Leg., ch. 957, § 1, eff. Sept. 1, 1993. Amended by Acts 1995, 74th Leg., ch. 1039, § 19, eff. Sept. 1, 1995.

Subpart E. Trial and Hearing Matters

§ 641. Defects in Pleading

A court may not invalidate a pleading in a guardianship matter or an order based on the pleading based on a defect of form or substance in the pleading, unless the defect has been timely objected to and called to the attention of the court in which the proceeding was or is pending.

Added by Acts 1993, 73rd Leg., ch. 957, § 1, eff. Sept. 1, 1993.

§ 642. Standing to Commence or Contest Proceeding

(a) Except as provided by Subsection (b) of this section, any person has the right to commence any guardianship proceeding, including a proceeding for complete restoration of a ward's capacity or modification of a ward's guardianship, or to appear and contest any guardianship proceeding or the appointment of a particular person as guardian.

(b) A person who has an interest that is adverse to a proposed ward or incapacitated person may not:

(1) file an application to create a guardianship for the proposed ward or incapacitated person;

(2) contest the creation of a guardianship for the proposed ward or incapacitated person;

(3) contest the appointment of a person as a guardian of the person or estate, or both, of the proposed ward or incapacitated person; or

(4) contest an application for complete restoration of a ward's capacity or modification of a ward's guardianship.

(c) The court shall determine by motion in limine the standing of a person who has an interest that is adverse to a proposed ward or incapacitated person.

Added by Acts 1993, 73rd Leg., ch. 957, § 1, eff. Sept. 1, 1993. Subsec. (c) added by Acts 1995, 74th Leg., ch. 1039, § 20, eff. Sept. 1, 1995; Subsecs. (a), (b) amended by Acts 1999, 76th Leg., ch. 829, § 2, eff. Sept. 1, 1999.

§ 643. Trial by Jury

A party in a contested guardianship proceeding is entitled, on request, to a jury trial.

Added by Acts 1993, 73rd Leg., ch. 957, § 1, eff. Sept. 1, 1993.

§ 644. Hearing by Submission

(a) A court may consider by submission a motion or application filed under this chapter unless the proceeding is:

(1) contested; or

(2) an application for the appointment of a guardian.

(b) The burden of proof at a hearing on a motion or application that is being considered by the court on submission is on the party who is seeking relief under the motion or application.

(c) The court may consider a person's failure to file a response to a motion or application that may be considered on submission as a representation that the person does not oppose the motion or application.

(d) A person's request for oral argument is not a response to a motion or application under this section.

(e) The court, on its own motion, may order oral argument on a motion or application that may be considered by submission.

Added by Acts 1993, 73rd Leg., ch. 957, § 1, eff. Sept. 1, 1993. Amended by Acts 1995, 74th Leg., ch. 1039, § 21, eff. Sept. 1, 1995.

§ 645. Guardians Ad Litem

(a) The judge may appoint a guardian ad litem to represent the interests of an incapacitated person in a guardianship proceeding.

(b) A guardian ad litem is entitled to reasonable compensation for services in the amount set by the court to be taxed as costs in the proceeding.

(c) A guardian ad litem is an officer of the court. The guardian ad litem shall protect the incapacitated person in a manner that will enable the court to determine what action will be in the best interests of the incapacitated person.

(d) If a guardian ad litem is appointed under Section 681(4) of this code, the fees and expenses of the guardian ad litem are costs of the litigation proceeding that made the appointment necessary.

(e) In the interest of judicial economy, the court may appoint as guardian ad litem under Section 681(4) of this code the person who has been appointed attorney ad litem under Section 646 of this code or the person who is serving as an ad litem for the benefit of the ward in any other proceeding.

Added by Acts 1993, 73rd Leg., ch. 957, § 1, eff. Sept. 1, 1993.

§ 645A. Immunity

(a) A guardian ad litem appointed under Section 645, 683, or 694A of this code to represent the interests of an incapacitated person in a guardianship proceeding involving the creation, modification, or termination of a guardianship is not liable for civil damages arising from a recommendation made or an opinion given in the capacity of guardian ad litem.

(b) Subsection (a) of this section does not apply to a recommendation or opinion that is:

(1) wilfully wrongful;

(2) given with conscious indifference or reckless disregard to the safety of another;

(3) given in bad faith or with malice; or

(4) grossly negligent.

Added by Acts 2003, 78th Leg., ch. 622, § 1, eff. Sept. 1, 2003.

§ 646. Appointment of Attorney ad Litem and Interpreter

(a) In a proceeding under this chapter for the appointment of a guardian, the court shall appoint an attorney ad litem to represent the interests of the proposed ward. The attorney shall be supplied with copies of all of the current records in the case and may have access to all of the proposed ward's relevant medical, psychological, and intellectual testing records.

(b) To be eligible for appointment as an attorney ad litem, a person must have the certification required by Section 647A of this code.

(c) A person whose certificate has expired must obtain a new certificate to be eligible for appointment as an attorney ad litem.

(d) At the time of the appointment of the attorney ad litem, the court shall also appoint a language interpreter or a sign interpreter if necessary to ensure effective communication between the proposed ward and the attorney.

Added by Acts 1993, 73rd Leg., ch. 957, § 1, eff. Sept. 1, 1993. Subsecs. (b) to (d) amended by Acts 1995, 74th Leg., ch. 1039, § 22, eff. Sept. 1, 1995; Subsec. (e) repealed by Acts 1995, 74th Leg., ch. 1039, § 74, eff. Sept. 1, 1995; Subsec. (a) amended by Acts 1999, 76th Leg., ch. 379, § 4, eff. Sept. 1, 1999. Amended by Acts 1999, 76th Leg., ch. 716, § 1, eff. Sept. 1, 1999.

§ 647. Duties of Attorney Ad Litem

(a) An attorney ad litem appointed under Section 646 of this code to represent a proposed ward shall, within a reasonable time before the hearing, interview the proposed ward. To the greatest extent possible, the attorney shall discuss with the proposed ward the law and facts of the case, the proposed ward's legal options regarding disposition of the case, and the grounds on which guardianship is sought.

(b) Before the hearing, the attorney shall review the application for guardianship, certificates of current physical, medical, and intellectual examinations, and all of the proposed ward's relevant medical, psychological, and intellectual testing records.

Added by Acts 1993, 73rd Leg., ch. 957, § 1, eff. Sept. 1, 1993.

§ 647A. Certification Requirement for Certain Court-Appointed Attorneys

(a) A court-appointed attorney in any guardianship proceeding must be certified by the State Bar of Texas or a person or other entity designated by the state bar as having successfully completed a course of study in guardianship law and procedure sponsored by the state bar or its designee.

(b) For certification under this section, the state bar shall require three hours of credit.

(c) Except as provided by Subsection (e) of this section, a certificate issued under this section expires on the second anniversary of the date the certificate is issued.

(d) To be eligible to be appointed by a court to represent a person at a guardianship proceeding, an attorney whose certificate has expired must obtain a new certificate.

(e) A new certificate obtained by a person who previously has been issued a certificate under this section expires on the fourth anniversary of the date the new certificate is issued if the person has been certified each of the four years immediately preceding the date the new certificate is issued.

Added by Acts 1999, 76th Leg., ch. 716, § 2, eff. Sept. 1, 1999.

§ 648. Court Visitor Program

(a) Each statutory probate court shall operate a court visitor program to assess the conditions of wards and proposed wards. Another court that has jurisdiction over a guardianship proceeding may operate a court visitor program in accordance with the population needs and financial abilities of the jurisdiction. A court that operates a court visitor program shall use persons willing to serve without compensation to the greatest extent possible.

(b) On request by any interested person, including a ward or proposed ward, or on its own motion, and at any time before the appointment of a guardian or during the pendency of a guardianship of the person or estate, a court may appoint a court visitor to evaluate the ward or proposed ward and provide a written report that substantially complies with Subsection (c) of this section.

(c) A court visitor's report must include:

(1) a description of the nature and degree of capacity and incapacity of the ward or proposed ward, including the medical history of the ward or proposed ward, if reasonably available and not waived by the court;

(2) a medical prognosis and a list of the treating physicians of the ward or proposed ward, when appropriate;

(3) a description of the living conditions and circumstances of the ward or proposed ward;

(4) a description of the social, intellectual, physical, and educational condition of the ward or proposed ward;

(5) a statement that the court visitor has personally visited or observed the ward or proposed ward;

(6) a statement of the date of the most recent visit by the guardian, if one has been appointed;

(7) a recommendation as to any modifications needed in the guardianship or proposed guardianship, including removal or denial of the guardianship; and

(8) any other information required by the court.

(d) The court visitor shall file the report not later than the 14th day after the date of the evaluation conducted by the court visitor, and the court visitor making the report must swear, under penalty of perjury, to its accuracy to the best of the court visitor's knowledge and belief.

(e) A court visitor who has not expressed a willingness to serve without compensation is entitled to reasonable compensation for services in an amount set by the court and to be taxed as costs in the proceeding.

(f) This section does not apply to a guardianship that is created only because it is necessary for a person to have a guardian appointed to receive funds from a governmental source.

Added by Acts 1993, 73rd Leg., ch. 957, § 1, eff. Sept. 1, 1993. Subsec. (f) added by Acts 1995, 74th Leg., ch. 1039, § 23, eff. Sept. 1, 1995.

§ 648A. Duties of Court Investigator

(a) On the filing of an application for guardianship under Section 682 of this code, a court investigator shall investigate the circumstances alleged in the application to determine whether a less restrictive alternative than guardianship is appropriate.

(b) A court investigator shall:

(1) supervise the court visitor program established under Section 648 of this code and in that capacity serve as the chief court visitor;

(2) investigate a complaint received from any person about a guardianship and report to the judge, if necessary; and

(3) perform other duties as assigned by the judge or required by this code.

(c) After making an investigation under Subsection (a) or (b) of this section, a court investigator shall file with the court a report of the court investigator's findings and conclusions. Disclosure to a jury of the contents of a court investigator's report is subject to the Texas Rules of Civil Evidence. In a contested case, the court investigator shall provide copies of the report to the attorneys for the parties before the earlier of:

(1) the seventh day after the day the report is completed; or

(2) the 10th day before the day the trial is scheduled to begin.

(d) Nothing in this section supersedes any duty or obligation of another to report or investigate abuse or neglect under any statute of this state.

Added by Acts 1995, 74th Leg., ch. 1039, § 24, eff. Sept. 1, 1995. Subsec. (b) amended by Acts 1999, 76th Leg., ch. 829, § 3, eff. Sept. 1, 1999.

§ 649. Evidence

In a guardianship proceeding, the rules relating to witnesses and evidence that govern in the district court apply as far as practicable. If there is no opposing party or attorney of record on whom to serve notice and copies of interrogatories, service may be had by posting notice of the intention to take depositions for a period of 10 days as provided by this chapter in the provisions governing a posting of notice. When notice by posting under this section is filed with the clerk, a copy of the interrogatories shall also be filed. At the expiration of the 10-day period, commission may issue for taking the depositions and the judge may file cross-interrogatories if no person appears.

Added by Acts 1993, 73rd Leg., ch. 957, § 1, eff. Sept. 1, 1993.

§ 650. Decrees and Signing of Minutes

A decision, order, decree, or judgment of the court in a guardianship matter must be rendered in open court, except in a case in which it is otherwise expressly provided. The judge shall approve and sign the guardianship minutes on the first day of each month. If the first day of the month falls on a Saturday, Sunday, or legal holiday, the judge's approval shall be entered on the preceding or succeeding day.

Added by Acts 1993, 73rd Leg., ch. 957, § 1, eff. Sept. 1, 1993.

§ 651. Enforcement of Orders

The judge may enforce obedience to an order entered against a guardian by attachment and imprisonment. An imprisonment of a guardian may not exceed three days for any one offense, unless expressly provided otherwise in this chapter.

Added by Acts 1993, 73rd Leg., ch. 957, § 1, eff. Sept. 1, 1993.

Subpart F. Post-Trial Matters

§ 653. Execution

An execution in a guardianship matter shall be directed "To any sheriff or any constable within the State of Texas," made returnable in 60 days, and attested and signed by the clerk officially under the seal of the court. A proceeding under an execution in a guardianship matter is governed so far as applicable by the laws regulating a proceeding under an execution issued from the district court. An execution directed to the sheriff or a constable of a specific county in this state may not be held defective if the execution was properly executed within the county by the officer to whom the direction for execution was given.

Added by Acts 1993, 73rd Leg., ch. 957, § 1, eff. Sept. 1, 1993.

§ 654. Attachment for Property

When a complaint in writing and under oath that the guardian is about to remove the estate or any part of the estate beyond the limits of the state is made to the judge by a person interested in the estate of a minor or other incapacitated person, the judge may order a writ to issue, directed "To any sheriff or any constable within the State of Texas," commanding the sheriff or constable to seize the estate or any part of the estate and to hold the estate subject to further court order. The judge may not issue a writ unless the complainant gives a bond, in the sum the judge requires, payable to the guardian of the estate and conditioned on payment of all damages and costs that shall be recovered for a wrongful suit out of the writ. A writ of attachment directed to the sheriff or a constable of a specific county in this state is not defective if the writ was properly executed within the county by the officer to whom the direction to seize the estate was given.
Added by Acts 1993, 73rd Leg., ch. 957, § 1, eff. Sept. 1, 1993.

§ 655. Guardian to Serve Pending Appeal of Appointment

Pending an appeal from an order or judgment appointing a guardian, an appointee shall continue to act as guardian and shall continue the prosecution of a pending suit in favor of the guardianship.
Added by Acts 1993, 73rd Leg., ch. 957, § 1, eff. Sept. 1, 1993.

§ 656. Appeal Bond of Guardian

When a guardian appeals, a bond is not required, unless the appeal personally concerns the guardian, in which case the guardian must give the bond.
Added by Acts 1993, 73rd Leg., ch. 957, § 1, eff. Sept. 1, 1993.

§ 657. Bill of Review

A person interested, including a ward, by bill of review filed in the court in which a guardianship proceeding took place, may have a decision, order, or judgment rendered by the court, revised and corrected if an error is shown on the decision, order, or judgment. A process or action under the decision, order, or judgment is not stayed except by writ of injunction. A bill of review may not be filed after two years have elapsed from the date of the decision, order, or judgment. A person with a disability has two years after the removal of the person's respective disability to apply for a bill of review.
Added by Acts 1993, 73rd Leg., ch. 957, § 1, eff. Sept. 1, 1993.

Subpart G. Letters of Guardianship

§ 659. Issuance of Letters of Guardianship

(a) When a person who is appointed guardian has qualified under Section 699 of this code, the clerk shall issue to the guardian a certificate under seal, stating the fact of the appointment, of the qualification, the date of the appointment and qualification, and the date the letters of guardianship expire. The certificate issued by the clerk constitutes letters of guardianship.

(b) All letters of guardianship expire one year and four months after the date of issuance unless renewed.

(c) The clerk may not renew letters of guardianship relating to the appointment of a guardian of the estate until the court receives and approves the guardian's annual accounting. The clerk may not renew letters of guardianship relating to the appointment of a guardian of the person until the court receives and approves the annual report. If the guardian's annual accounting or annual report is disapproved or not timely filed, the clerk may not issue further letters of guardianship to the delinquent guardian unless ordered by the court.

(d) Regardless of the date the court approves an annual accounting or annual report for purposes of this section, a renewal relates back to the date the original letters of guardianship are issued, unless the accounting period has been changed as provided by this chapter, in which case a renewal relates back to the first day of the accounting period.
Added by Acts 1993, 73rd Leg., ch. 957, § 1, eff. Sept. 1, 1993. Amended by Acts 1995, 74th Leg., ch. 1039, § 25, eff. Sept. 1, 1995.

§ 660. Letters or Order Made Evidence

(a) Letters of guardianship or a certificate under seal of the clerk of the court that granted the letters issued under Section 659 of this code is sufficient evidence of the appointment and qualification of the guardian and of the date of qualification.

(b) The court order that appoints the guardian is evidence of the authority granted to the guardian and of the scope of the powers and duties that the guardian may exercise only after the date letters of guardianship or a certificate has been issued under Section 659 of this code.
Added by Acts 1993, 73rd Leg., ch. 957, § 1, eff. Sept. 1, 1993. Amended by Acts 1995, 74th Leg., ch. 1039, § 26, eff. Sept. 1, 1995.

§ 661. Issuance of New Letters

When letters of guardianship have been destroyed or lost, the clerk shall issue new letters that have the same force and effect as the original letters. The clerk shall also issue any number of letters on request of the person who holds the letters.
Added by Acts 1993, 73rd Leg., ch. 957, § 1, eff. Sept. 1, 1993.

§ 662. Rights of Third Persons Dealing With Guardian

When a guardian who has qualified performs any act as guardian that is in conformity with the guardian's authority and the law, the guardian's act continues to be valid for all intents and purposes in regard to the rights of an innocent purchaser of the property of the guardianship estate who purchased the

property from the guardian for a valuable consideration, in good faith, and without notice of any illegality in the title to the property, even if the guardian's act or the authority under which the act was performed may later be set aside, annulled, or declared invalid.
Added by Acts 1993, 73rd Leg., ch. 957, § 1, eff. Sept. 1, 1993.

§ 663. Validation of Certain Letters of Guardianship

All presently existing letters of guardianship issued to a nonresident guardian, with or without the procedure provided in this subpart, in whole or in part, and with or without a notice or citation required of resident guardians, are validated as of each letter's date, insofar as the absence of the procedure, notice, or citations is concerned. An otherwise valid conveyance, mineral lease, or other act of a nonresident guardian qualified and acting in connection with the letters of guardianship under supporting orders of a county or probate court of this state are validated. This section does not apply to any letters, conveyance, lease, or other act of a nonresident guardian under this section if the absence of the procedure, notice, or citation involving the letters, conveyance, lease, or other act of the nonresident guardian is an issue in a lawsuit pending in this state on September 1, 1993.
Added by Acts 1993, 73rd Leg., ch. 957, § 1, eff. Sept. 1, 1993.

Subpart H. Compensation, Expenses, and Court Costs

§ 665. Compensation of Guardians and Temporary Guardians

(a) The court may authorize compensation for a guardian or a temporary guardian serving as a guardian of the person alone from available funds of the ward's estate or other funds available for that purpose. The court shall set the compensation in an amount not exceeding five percent of the ward's gross income. In determining whether to authorize compensation for a guardian under this section, the court shall consider the ward's monthly income from all sources and whether the ward receives medical assistance under the state Medicaid program.

(b) The guardian or temporary guardian of an estate is entitled to reasonable compensation on application to the court at the time the court approves any annual accounting or final accounting filed by the guardian or temporary guardian under this chapter. A fee of five percent of the gross income of the ward's estate and five percent of all money paid out of the estate is considered reasonable under this subsection if the court finds that the guardian or temporary guardian has taken care of and managed the estate in compliance with the standards of this chapter.

(c) On application of an interested person or on its own motion, the court may review and modify the amount of compensation authorized under Subsection (b) of this section if the court finds that the amount is unreasonably low when considering the services rendered as guardian or temporary guardian.

(d) A finding of unreasonably low compensation may not be established under Subsection (c) of this section solely because the amount of compensation is less than the usual and customary charges of the person or entity serving as guardian or temporary guardian.

(e) The court, on application of an interested person or on its own motion, may deny a fee authorized under this section in whole, or in part, if:

(1) the court finds that the guardian or temporary guardian has not adequately performed the duties required of a guardian or temporary guardian under this chapter; or

(2) the guardian or temporary guardian has been removed for cause.

(f) Except as provided by Subsection (c) of this section for a fee that is determined by the court to be unreasonably low, the aggregate fee of the guardian of the person and guardian of the estate may not exceed an amount equal to five percent of the gross income of the ward's estate plus five percent of all money paid out of the estate.

(g) If the estate of a ward is insufficient to pay for the services of a private professional guardian or a licensed attorney serving as guardian of the ward's person, the court may authorize compensation for that guardian if funds in the county treasury are budgeted for that purpose.

(h) In this section:

(1) "Gross income" does not include Department of Veterans Affairs or Social Security benefits received by a ward.

(2) "Money paid out" does not include any money loaned, invested, or paid over on the settlement of the guardianship or a tax-motivated gift made by the ward.

Added by Acts 1993, 73rd Leg., ch. 957, § 1, eff. Sept. 1, 1993. Amended by Acts 1995, 74th Leg., ch. 1039, § 27, eff. Sept. 1, 1995; Acts 1999, 76th Leg., ch. 905, § 1, eff. Sept. 1, 1999; Subsec. (a) amended by Acts 2001, 77th Leg., ch. 217, § 3, eff. Sept. 1, 2001. Amended by Acts 2001, 77th Leg., ch. 953, § 1, eff. Sept. 1, 2001.

§ 665A. Payment for Professional Services

The court shall order the payment of a fee set by the court as compensation to the attorneys, mental health professionals, and interpreters appointed under Section 646 or 687 of this code, as applicable, to be taxed as costs in the case. If after examining the proposed ward's assets the court determines the proposed ward is unable to pay for services provided by an attorney, a mental health professional, or an interpreter appointed under Section 646 or 687 of this code, as applicable, the county is responsible for the cost of those services.
Added by Acts 1995, 74th Leg., ch. 1039, § 28, eff. Sept. 1, 1995.

§ 665B. Compensation of Certain Attorneys

(a) A court that creates a guardianship for a ward under this chapter, on request of a person who filed an application to be appointed guardian of the proposed ward or for the appointment of another suitable person as guardian of the proposed ward, may authorize compensation of an attorney who represents the person who filed the application at the application hearing, regardless of whether the person is appointed the ward's guardian, from:

(1) available funds of the ward's estate; or

(2) the county treasury if:

(A) the ward's estate is insufficient to pay for the services provided by the attorney; and

(B) funds in the county treasury are budgeted for that purpose.

(b) The court may not authorize compensation under this section unless the court finds that the applicant acted in good faith and for just cause in the filing and prosecution of the application.

Added by Acts 1995, 74th Leg., ch. 1039, § 28, eff. Sept. 1, 1995. Subsec. (a) amended by Acts 1999, 76th Leg., ch. 905, § 2, eff. Sept. 1, 1999. Amended by Acts 2003, 78th Leg., ch. 549, § 10, eff. Sept. 1, 2003.

§ 665C. Compensation for Collection of Claims and Recovery of Property

(a) Except as provided by Subsection (b) of this section, a guardian of an estate may enter into a contract to convey, or may convey, a contingent interest in any property sought to be recovered, not exceeding one-third thereof for services of attorneys, subject only to the approval of the court in which the estate is being administered.

(b) A guardian of an estate may convey or contract to convey for services of attorneys a contingent interest that exceeds one-third of the property sought to be recovered under this section only on the approval of the court in which the estate is being administered. The court must approve a contract entered into or conveyance made under this section before an attorney performs any legal services. A contracted entered into or conveyance made in violation of this section is void, unless the court ratifies or reforms the contract or documents relating to the conveyance to the extent necessary to cause the contract or conveyance to meet the requirements of this section.

(c) In approving a contract or conveyance under Subsection (a) or (b) of this section for services of an attorney, the court shall consider:

(1) the time and labor that will be required, the novelty and difficulty of the questions to be involved, and the skill that will be required to perform the legal services properly;

(2) the fee customarily charged in the locality for similar legal services;

(3) the value of property recovered or sought to be recovered by the personal representative under this section;

(4) the benefits to the estate that the attorney will be responsible for securing; and

(5) the experience and ability of the attorney who will be performing the services.

(d) On satisfactory proof to the court, a guardian of an estate is entitled to all necessary and reasonable expenses incurred by the guardian in collecting or attempting to collect a claim or debt owed to the estate or in recovering or attempting to recover property to which the estate has a title or claim.

Added by Acts 1995, 74th Leg., ch. 1039, § 28, eff. Sept. 1, 1995.

§ 666. Expenses Allowed

A guardian is entitled to be reimbursed from the guardianship estate for all necessary and reasonable expenses incurred in performing any duty as a guardian, including reimbursement for the payment of reasonable attorney's fees necessarily incurred by the guardian in connection with the management of the estate or any other guardianship matter.

Added by Acts 1993, 73rd Leg., ch. 957, § 1, eff. Sept. 1, 1993. Amended by Acts 2001, 77th Leg., ch. 953, § 2, eff. Sept. 1, 2001.

§ 667. Expense Account

All expense charges shall be:

(1) in writing, showing specifically each item of expense and the date of the expense;

(2) verified by affidavit of the guardian;

(3) filed with the clerk; and

(4) paid only if the payment is authorized by court order.

Added by Acts 1993, 73rd Leg., ch. 957, § 1, eff. Sept. 1, 1993. Amended by Acts 2001, 77th Leg., ch. 953, § 3, eff. Sept. 1, 2001.

§ 668. Costs Adjudged Against Guardian

When costs are incurred because a guardian neglects to perform a required duty or if a guardian is removed for cause, the guardian and the sureties on the guardian's bond are liable for:

(1) costs of removal and other additional costs incurred that are not authorized expenditures under this chapter; and

(2) reasonable attorney's fees incurred in removing the guardian or in obtaining compliance regarding any statutory duty the guardian has neglected.

Added by Acts 1993, 73rd Leg., ch. 957, § 1, eff. Sept. 1, 1993.

§ 669. Costs Against Guardianship

(a) Except as provided by Subsection (b), in a guardianship matter, the cost of the proceeding, including the cost of the guardian ad litem or court visitor, shall be paid out of the guardianship estate, or, if the estate is insufficient to pay for the cost of the proceeding, the cost of the proceeding shall be paid out of the county treasury, and the judgment of the court shall be issued accordingly.

(b) If a court denies an application for the appointment of a guardian under this chapter based on the

recommendation of a court investigator, the applicant shall pay the cost of the proceeding.
Added by Acts 1993, 73rd Leg., ch. 957, § 1, eff. Sept. 1, 1993. Amended by Acts 1995, 74th Leg., ch. 1039, s 29, eff. Sept. 1, 1995.

Subpart I. Duty and Responsibility of Court

§ 671. Judge's Duty

(a) The court shall use reasonable diligence to determine whether a guardian is performing all of the duties required of the guardian that pertain to the guardian's ward.

(b) The judge, at least annually, shall examine the well-being of each ward of the court and the solvency of the bonds of the guardians of the estates.

(c) If after examining the solvency of a guardian's bond under this section a judge determines that the guardian's bond is not sufficient to protect the ward or the ward's estate, the judge shall require the guardian to execute a new bond.

(d) The judge shall notify the guardian and the sureties on the bond as provided by law. If damage or loss results to a guardianship or ward because of gross neglect of the judge to use reasonable diligence in the performance of the judge's duty under this section, the judge shall be liable on the judge's bond to those damaged by the judge's neglect.

(e) The court may request an applicant or court-appointed fiduciary to produce other information identifying an applicant, ward, or guardian, including social security numbers, in addition to identifying information the applicant or fiduciary is required to produce under this code. The court shall maintain the information required under this subsection, and the information may not be filed with the clerk.
Added by Acts 1993, 73rd Leg., ch. 957, § 1, eff. Sept. 1, 1993. Subsec. (e) added by Acts 1997, 75th Leg., ch. 77, § 3, eff. Sept. 1, 1997.

§ 672. Annual Determination Whether Guardianship Should be Continued, Modified, or Terminated

(a) A court in which a guardianship proceeding is pending shall review annually each guardianship in which the application to create the guardianship was filed after September 1, 1993, and may review annually any other guardianship to determine whether the guardianship should be continued, modified, or terminated.

(b) In reviewing a guardianship as provided by Subsection (a) of this section, a statutory probate court may:

(1) review any report prepared by a court investigator under Section 648A of this code;

(2) review any report prepared by a court visitor under Section 648 of this code;

(3) conduct a hearing; or

(4) review an annual account prepared under Section 741 of this code or a report prepared under Section 743 of this code.

(c) In reviewing a guardianship as provided by Subsection (a) of this section, a court that is not a statutory probate court may use any appropriate method determined by the court according to the court's caseload and the resources available to the court.

(d) A determination under this section must be in writing and filed with the clerk.

(e) This section does not apply to a guardianship that is created only because it is necessary for a person to have a guardian appointed to receive funds from a governmental source.
Added by Acts 1995, 74th Leg., ch. 1039, § 30, eff. Sept. 1, 1995.

Subpart J. Liability of Guardian for Conduct of Ward

§ 673. Liability

A person is not liable to a third person solely because the person has been appointed guardian of a ward under this chapter.
Added by Acts 1993, 73rd Leg., ch. 957, § 1, eff. Sept. 1, 1993.

Part 3. Appointment and Qualification of Guardians

Subpart A. Appointment

§ 675. Rights and Powers Retained by Ward

An incapacitated person for whom a guardian is appointed retains all legal and civil rights and powers except those designated by court order as legal disabilities by virtue of having been specifically granted to the guardian.
Added by Acts 1993, 73rd Leg., ch. 957, § 1, eff. Sept. 1, 1993.

Statutes in Context

Section 676 explains how a guardian of a minor is selected. Upon the surviving parent's death or incapacity, the court will give great deference to a designation of a guardian in the parent's will or other written document (see § 677A).

---

§ 676. Guardians of Minors

(a) Except as provided by Section 680 of this code, the selection of a guardian for a minor is governed by this section.

(b) If the parents live together, both parents are the natural guardians of the person of the minor children by the marriage, and one of the parents is entitled to be appointed guardian of the children's estates. If the parents disagree as to which parent should be appointed, the court shall make the appointment on the basis of which parent is better qualified to serve in that capacity. If one parent is dead, the survivor is the natural guardian of the person of the minor children and is entitled to be appointed guardian of their estates. The rights of parents who do not live together are equal, and the guardianship of their minor children shall be assigned to one or the other, considering only the best interests of the children.

(c) In appointing a guardian for a minor orphan:

(1) if the last surviving parent did not appoint a guardian, the nearest ascendant in the direct line of the minor is entitled to guardianship of both the person and the estate of the minor;

(2) if more than one ascendant exists in the same degree in the direct line, one ascendant shall be appointed, according to circumstances and considering the best interests of the minor;

(3) if the minor has no ascendant in the direct line, the nearest of kin shall be appointed, and if there are two or more persons in the same degree of kinship, one shall be appointed, according to circumstances and considering the best interests of the minor; and

(4) if no relative of the minor is eligible to be guardian, or if no eligible person applies to be guardian, the court shall appoint a qualified person as guardian.

(d) Notwithstanding Subsection (b) of this section and Section 690 of this code, the surviving parent of a minor may by will or written declaration appoint any eligible person to be guardian of the person of the parent's minor children after the death of the parent or in the event of the parent's incapacity.

(e) After the death of the surviving parent of a minor or if the court finds the surviving parent is an incapacitated person, as appropriate, the court shall appoint the person designated in the will or declaration to serve as guardian of the person of the parent's minor children in preference to those otherwise entitled to serve as guardian under this chapter unless the court finds that the designated guardian is disqualified, is dead, refuses to serve, or would not serve the best interests of the minor children.

(f) On compliance with this chapter, an eligible person is also entitled to be appointed guardian of the children's estates after the death of the parent or in the event of the parent's incapacity.

(g) The powers of a person appointed to serve as the designated guardian of the person or estate, or both, of a minor child solely because of the incapacity of the minor's surviving parent and in accordance with this section and Section 677A of this code terminate when a probate court enters an order finding that the surviving parent is no longer an incapacitated person.

Added by Acts 1993, 73rd Leg., ch. 957, § 1, eff. Sept. 1, 1993. Subsec. (d) amended by Acts 1995, 74th Leg., ch. 304, § 1, eff. Sept. 1, 1995; Subsec. (d) amended by and (e) to (g) added by Acts 2001, 77th Leg., ch. 217, § 4, eff. Sept. 1, 2001.

Statutes in Context

Section 677 explains how a guardian of a non-minor is selected. Upon the surviving parent's death or incapacity, the court will give great deference to a designation of a guardian in the parent's will or other written document (*see* § 677A).

---

§ 677. Guardians of Persons Other Than Minors

(a) The court shall appoint a guardian for a person other than a minor according to the circumstances and considering the best interests of the ward. If the court finds that two or more eligible persons are equally entitled to be appointed guardian:

(1) the ward's spouse is entitled to the guardianship in preference to any other person if the spouse is one of the eligible persons;

(2) the eligible person nearest of kin to the ward is entitled to the guardianship if the ward's spouse is not one of the eligible persons; or

(3) the court shall appoint the eligible person who is best qualified to serve as guardian if:

(A) the persons entitled to serve under Subdivisions (1) and (2) of this section refuse to serve;

(B) two or more persons entitled to serve under Subdivision (2) of this section are related in the same degree of kinship to the ward; or

(C) neither the ward's spouse or any person related to the ward is an eligible person.

(b) The surviving parent of an adult individual who is an incapacitated person may by will or written declaration appoint an eligible person to be guardian of the person of the adult individual after the parent's death or in the event of the parent's incapacity if the parent is the guardian of the person of the adult individual.

(c) After the death of the surviving parent of an adult individual who is an incapacitated person or if the court finds the surviving parent becomes an incapacitated person after being appointed the individual's guardian, as appropriate, the court shall appoint the person designated in the will or declaration to serve as guardian in preference to those otherwise entitled to serve as guardian under this chapter unless the court finds that the designated guardian is disqualified, is dead, refuses to serve, or would not serve the best interests of the adult individual.

(d) On compliance with this chapter, the eligible person appointed under Subsection (c) of this section is also entitled to be appointed guardian of the adult individual's estate after the death of the individual's parent or in the event of the parent's incapacity if the individual's parent is the guardian of the individual's estate.

(e) The powers of a person appointed to serve as the designated guardian of the person or estate, or both, of an adult individual solely because of the incapacity of the individual's surviving parent and in accordance with this section and Section 677A of this code terminate when a probate court enters an order finding that the surviving parent is no longer an incapacitated person and reappointing the surviving parent as the individual's guardian.

Added by Acts 1993, 73rd Leg., ch. 957, § 1, eff. Sept. 1, 1993. Amended by Acts 1995, 74th Leg., ch. 304, § 2, eff. Sept. 1, 1995; Subsec. (b) amended by and (c) to (e) added by Acts 2001, 77th Leg., ch. 217, § 5, eff. Sept. 1, 2001.

Statutes in Context

Section 677A sets forth the requirements for non-testamentary guardian declarations by a parent of a minor or adult who is in need of a guardian. Separate rules exist for holographic and attested declarations. A suggested form is also provided.

§ 677A. Written Declarations by Certain Parents to Appoint Guardians for Their Children

(a) A written declaration appointing an eligible person to be guardian of the person of the parent's child under Section 676(d) or 677(b) of this code must be signed by the declarant and be:

(1) written wholly in the handwriting of the declarant; or

(2) attested to in the presence of the declarant by at least two credible witnesses 14 years of age or older who are not named as guardian or alternate guardian in the declaration.

(b) A declaration that is not written wholly in the handwriting of the declarant may be signed by another person for the declarant under the direction of and in the presence of the declarant.

(c) A declaration described by Subsection (a)(2) of this section may have attached a self-proving affidavit signed by the declarant and the witnesses attesting to the competence of the declarant and the execution of the declaration.

(d) The declaration and any self-proving affidavit may be filed with the court at any time after the application for appointment of a guardian is filed and before a guardian is appointed.

(e) If the designated guardian does not qualify, is dead, refuses to serve, resigns, or dies after being appointed guardian, or is otherwise unavailable to serve as guardian, the court shall appoint the next eligible designated alternate guardian named in the declaration. If the guardian and all alternate guardians do not qualify, are dead, refuse to serve, or later die or resign, the court shall appoint another person to serve as otherwise provided by this code.

(f) The declarant may revoke a declaration in any manner provided for the revocation of a will under Section 63 of this code, including the subsequent reexecution of the declaration in the manner required for the original declaration.

(g) A declaration and affidavit may be in any form adequate to clearly indicate the declarant's intention to designate a guardian for the declarant's child. The following form may, but need not, be used:

DECLARATION OF APPOINTMENT OF GUARDIAN FOR MY CHILDREN <C>IN THE EVENT OF MY DEATH OR INCAPACITY

I, ________, make this Declaration to appoint as guardian for my child or children, listed as follows, in the event of my death or incapacity:

__________ __________

__________ __________

__________ __________

(add blanks as appropriate)

I designate ________ to serve as guardian of the person of my (child or children), ________ as first alternate guardian of the person of my (child or children), ________ as second alternate guardian of the person of my (child or children), and ________ as third alternate guardian of the person of my (child or children).

I direct that the guardian of the person of my (child or children) serve (with or without) bond.

(If applicable) I designate ________ to serve as guardian of the estate of my (child or children), ________ as first alternate guardian of the estate of my (child or children), ________ as second alternate guardian of the estate of my (child or children), and ________ as third alternate guardian of the estate of my (child or children).

If any guardian or alternate guardian dies, does not qualify, or resigns, the next named alternate guardian becomes guardian of my (child or children).

Signed this day of ________ 20__.

____

Declarant

__________ __________

Witness Witness

SELF-PROVING AFFIDAVIT

Before me, the undersigned authority, on this date personally appeared the declarant, and ________ and ________ as witnesses, and all being duly sworn, the declarant said that the above instrument was his or her Declaration of Appointment of Guardian for the Declarant's Children in the Event of Declarant's Death or Incapacity and that the declarant had made and executed it for the purposes expressed in the declaration. The witnesses declared to me that they are each 14 years of age or older, that they saw the declarant sign the declaration, that they signed the declaration as witnesses, and that the declarant appeared to them to be of sound mind.

____

Declarant

__________ __________

Affiant Affiant

Subscribed and sworn to before me by the above named declarant and affiants on this _____ day of ________ 20__.

____

Notary Public in and for the State of Texas

My Commission expires:

____

(h) In this section, "self-proving affidavit" means an affidavit the form and content of which substantially complies with the requirements of Subsection (g) of this section.

Added by Acts 1995, 74th Leg., ch. 304, § 3, eff. Sept. 1, 1995. Subsec. (a) amended by Acts 1997, 75th Leg., ch. 77, § 4, eff. Sept. 1, 1997; Subsec. (e) amended by Acts 1999, 76th Leg., ch. 1078, § 2, eff. Sept. 1, 1999. Amended by Acts 2001, 77th Leg., ch. 217, § 6, eff. Sept. 1, 2001.

§ 677B. Proof of Written Declaration of Certain Parents to Designate Children's Guardian

(a) In this section:

(1) "Declaration" means a written declaration of a person that:

(A) appoints a guardian for the person's child under Section 676(d) or 677(b) of this code; and

(B) satisfies the requirements of Section 677A of this code.

(2) "Self-proving affidavit" means an affidavit the form and content of which substantially complies with the requirements of Section 677A(g) of this code.

(3) "Self-proving declaration" includes a self-proving affidavit that is attached or annexed to a declaration.

(b) If a declaration is self-proved, the court may admit the declaration into evidence without the testimony of witnesses attesting to the competency of the declarant and the execution of the declaration. Additional proof of the execution of the declaration with the formalities and solemnities and under the circumstances required to make it a valid declaration is not necessary.

(c) At any time during the declarant's lifetime, a written declaration described by Section 677A(a)(1) of this code may be made self-proved in the same form and manner a will written wholly in the handwriting of a testator is made self-proved under Section 60 of this code.

(d) A properly executed and witnessed self-proving declaration and affidavit, including a declaration and affidavit described by Section 677A(c) of this code, are prima facie evidence that the declarant was competent at the time the declarant executed the declaration and that the guardian named in the declaration would serve the best interests of the ward.

(e) A written declaration described by Section 677A(a)(1) of this code that is not self-proved may be proved in the same manner a will written wholly in the handwriting of the testator is proved under Section 84 of this code.

(f) A written declaration described by Section 677A(a)(2) of this code that is not self-proved may be proved in the same manner an attested written will produced in court is proved under Section 84 of this code.

Added by Acts 2001, 77th Leg., ch. 217, § 7, eff. Sept. 1, 2001.

§ 678. Presumption Concerning Best Interest

It is presumed not to be in the best interests of a ward to appoint a person as guardian of the ward if the person has been finally convicted of any sexual offense, sexual assault, aggravated assault, aggravated sexual assault, injury to a child, to an elderly individual, or to a disabled individual, abandoning or endangering a child, or incest.

Added by Acts 1993, 73rd Leg., ch. 957, § 1, eff. Sept. 1, 1993. Amended by Acts 1995, 74th Leg., ch. 612, § 1, eff. Aug. 28, 1995.

Statutes in Context

Historically, most courts held that they were not required to give weight to an incompetent person's preference for a guardian. An incompetent's opinion was inherently suspect because a person lacking the capacity to handle property may lack the capacity to select a proper guardian and may be more susceptible to undue influence. The modern trend adopted by Texas in § 679 is to permit a competent individual to designate the individual the person would like the court to appoint as the person's guardian before the onset of incompetency. Thus, should the need for a guardian arise, the court may follow the person's intent which was expressed at a time when the person was competent to do so.

A self-designation of guardian may be holographic or attested. Section 679 sets forth the requirements along with a suggested form.

A declarant may also disqualify a person from serving as a guardian even though the person would otherwise have priority under § 677. This allows the declarant to, for example, designate the "good" child and disqualify the "bad" child.

Debate exists over whether the same individuals should be named in the self-designation of guardian as in the durable power of attorney (§ 490) and the medical power of attorney (Health & Safety Code § 166.164). One school of thought is that by naming the same persons, there will be consistency if an "evil" person attempts to take over from the agents by being named as a guardian. On the other hand, if different people are named, it is easier for the agents to be held accountable in case their conduct is less than honorable.

---

§ 679. Designation of Guardian Before Need Arises

(a) A person other than an incapacitated person may designate by a written declaration persons to serve as guardian of the person of the declarant or the estate of the declarant if the declarant becomes incapacitated. The declaration must be signed by the declarant and be:

(1) written wholly in the handwriting of the declarant; or

(2) attested to in the presence of the declarant by at least two credible witnesses 14 years of age or older who are not named as guardian or alternate guardian in the declaration.

(b) A declarant may, in the declaration, disqualify named persons from serving as guardian of the declarant's person or estate, and the persons named may not be appointed guardian under any circumstances.

(c) A declaration that is not written wholly in the handwriting of a declarant may be signed by another person for the declarant under the direction of and in the presence of the declarant.

(d) A declaration described by Subsection (a)(2) of this section may have attached a selfproving affidavit signed by the declarant and the witnesses attesting to the competence of the declarant and the execution of the declaration.

(e) The declaration and any self-proving affidavit may be filed with the court at any time after the application for appointment of a guardian is filed and before a guardian is appointed.

(f) Unless the court finds that the person designated in the declaration to serve as guardian is disqualified or would not serve the best interests of the ward, the court shall appoint the person as guardian in preference to those otherwise entitled to serve as guardian under this code. If the designated guardian does not qualify, is dead, refuses to serve, resigns, or dies after being appointed guardian, or is otherwise unavailable to serve as guardian, the court shall appoint the next eligible designated alternate guardian named in the declaration. If the guardian and all alternate guardians do not qualify, are dead, refuse to serve, or later die or resign, the court shall appoint another person to serve as otherwise provided by this code.

(g) The declarant may revoke a declaration in any manner provided for the revocation of a will under Section 63 of this code, including the subsequent reexecution of the declaration in the manner required for the original declaration.

(h) If a declarant designates the declarant's spouse to serve as guardian under this section, and the declarant is subsequently divorced from that spouse before a guardian is appointed, the provision of the declaration designating the spouse has no effect.

(i) A declaration and affidavit may be in any form adequate to clearly indicate the declarant's intention to designate a guardian. The following form may, but need not, be used:

I, __________, make this Declaration of Guardian, to operate if the need for a guardian for me later arises.

DECLARATION OF GUARDIAN IN THE EVENT OF LATER INCAPACITY OR NEED OF GUARDIAN

1. I designate __________ to serve as guardian of my person, __________ as first alternate guardian of my person, __________ as second alternate guardian of my person, and __________ as third alternate guardian of my person.
2. I __________ designate to serve as guardian of my estate, __________ as first alternate guardian of my estate, __________ as second alternate guardian of my estate, and __________ as third alternate guardian of my estate.
3. If any guardian or alternate guardian dies, does not qualify, or resigns, the next named alternate guardian becomes my guardian.
4. I expressly disqualify the following persons from serving as guardian of my person: __________, __________, and __________.
5. I expressly disqualify the following persons from serving as guardian of my estate: __________, __________, and __________.

Signed this ______ day of ______, 20__.

____
Declarant

______________________________ ______________________________
Witness Witness

SELF-PROVING AFFIDAVIT

Before me, the undersigned authority, on this date personally appeared the declarant, and __________ and __________ as witnesses, and all being duly sworn, the declarant said that the above instrument was his or her Declaration of Guardian and that the declarant had made and executed it for the purposes expressed in the declaration. The witnesses declared to me that they are each 14 years of age or older, that they saw the declarant sign the declaration, that they signed the declaration as witnesses, and that the declarant appeared to them to be of sound mind.

____
Declarant

______________________________ ______________________________
Witness Witness

Subscribed and sworn to before me by the above named declarant and affiants on this _____ day of _____, 20__.

____
Notary Public in and for the State of Texas
My Commission expires:
____

(j) In this section, "self-proving affidavit" means an affidavit the form and content of which substantially complies with the requirements of Subsection (i) of this section.
Added by Acts 1993, 73rd Leg., ch. 957, § 1, eff. Sept. 1, 1993. Amended by Acts 2001, 77th Leg., ch. 217, § 8, eff. Sept. 1, 2001.

§ 679A. Proof of Written Declaration to Designate Guardian Before Need Arises

(a) In this section:

(1) "Declaration" means a written declaration of a person that:

(A) designates another person to serve as a guardian of the person or estate of the declarant; and

(B) satisfies the requirements of Section 679 of this code.

(2) "Self-proving affidavit" means an affidavit the form and content of which substantially complies with the requirements of Section 679(i) of this code.

(3) "Self-proving declaration" includes a self-proving affidavit that is attached or annexed to a declaration.

(b) If a declaration is self-proved, the court may admit the declaration into evidence without the testimony of witnesses attesting to the competency of the declarant and the execution of the declaration. Additional proof of the execution of the declaration with the formalities and solemnities and under the circumstances required to make it a valid declaration is not necessary.

(c) At any time during the declarant's lifetime, a written declaration described by Section 679(a)(1) of this code may be made self-proved in the same form and manner a will written wholly in the handwriting of a testator is made self-proved under Section 60 of this code.

(d) A properly executed and witnessed self-proving declaration and affidavit, including a declaration and affidavit described by Section 679(d) of this code, are prima facie evidence that the declarant was competent at the time the declarant executed the declaration and that the guardian named in the declaration would serve the best interests of the ward.

(e) A written declaration described by Section 679(a)(1) of this code that is not self-proved may be proved in the same manner a will written wholly in the handwriting of the testator is proved under Section 84 of this code.

(f) A written declaration described by Section 679(a)(2) of this code that is not self-proved may be proved in the same manner an attested written will produced in court is proved under Section 84 of this code.
Added by Acts 2001, 77th Leg., ch. 217, § 9, eff. Sept. 1, 2001.

§ 680. Selection of Guardian by Minor

(a) When an application is filed for the guardianship of the person or estate, or both, of a minor at least 12 years of age, the minor, by writing filed with the clerk, may choose the guardian if the court approves the choice and finds that the choice is in the best interest of the minor.

(b) A minor at least 12 years of age may select another guardian of either the minor's person or estate, or both, if the minor has a guardian appointed by the court or the minor has a guardian appointed by will or written declaration of the parent of the minor and that guardian dies, resigns, or is removed from guardianship. If the court is satisfied that the person selected is suitable and competent and that the appointment of the person is in the best interest of the minor, it shall make the appointment and revoke the letters of guardianship of the former guardian. The minor shall make the selection by filing an application in open court in person or by attorney.
Added by Acts 1993, 73rd Leg., ch. 957, § 1, eff. Sept. 1, 1993. Amended by Acts 1995, 74th Leg., ch. 1039, § 31, eff. Sept. 1, 1995.

§ 681. Persons Disqualified to Serve as Guardians

A person may not be appointed guardian if the person is:

(1) a minor;

(2) a person whose conduct is notoriously bad;

(3) an incapacitated person;

(4) a person who is a party or whose parent is a party to a lawsuit concerning or affecting the welfare of the proposed ward, unless the court:

(A) determines that the lawsuit claim of the person who has applied to be appointed guardian is not in conflict with the lawsuit claim of the proposed ward; or

(B) appoints a guardian ad litem to represent the interests of the proposed ward throughout the litigation of the ward's lawsuit claim;

(5) a person indebted to the proposed ward unless the person pays the debt before appointment;

(6) a person asserting a claim adverse to the proposed ward or the proposed ward's property, real or personal;

(7) a person who, because of inexperience, lack of education, or other good reason, is incapable of properly and prudently managing and controlling the ward or the ward's estate;

(8) a person, institution, or corporation found unsuitable by the court;

(9) a person disqualified in a declaration made under Section 679 of this code; or

(10) a nonresident person who has not filed with the court the name of a resident agent to accept service of process in all actions or proceedings relating to the guardianship.
Added by Acts 1993, 73rd Leg., ch. 957, § 1, eff. Sept. 1, 1993. Amended by Acts 1995, 74th Leg., ch. 1039, § 32, eff. Sept. 1, 1995.

§ 682. Application; Contents

Any person may commence a proceeding for the appointment of a guardian by filing a written application in a court having jurisdiction and venue. The application must be sworn to by the applicant and state:

(1) the name, sex, date of birth, and address of the proposed ward;

(2) the name, relationship, and address of the person the applicant desires to have appointed as guardian;

(3) whether guardianship of the person or estate, or both, is sought;

(4) the nature and degree of the alleged incapacity, the specific areas of protection and assistance requested, and the limitation of rights requested to be included in the court's order of appointment;

(5) the facts requiring that a guardian be appointed and the interest of the applicant in the appointment;

(6) the nature and description of any guardianship of any kind existing for the proposed ward in any other state;

(7) the name and address of any person or institution having the care and custody of the proposed ward;

(8) the approximate value and description of the proposed ward's property, including any compensation, pension, insurance, or allowance to which the proposed ward may be entitled;

(9) the name and address of any person whom the applicant knows to hold a power of attorney signed by the proposed ward and a description of the type of power of attorney;

(10) if the proposed ward is a minor and if known by the applicant:

(A) the name of each parent of the proposed ward and state the parent's address or that the parent is deceased;

(B) the name and age of each sibling, if any, of the proposed ward and state the sibling's address or that the sibling is deceased; and

(C) if each of the proposed ward's parents and siblings are deceased, the names and addresses of the proposed ward's next of kin who are adults;

(11) if the proposed ward is a minor, whether the minor was the subject of a legal or conservatorship proceeding within the preceding two-year period and, if so, the court involved, the nature of the proceeding, and the final disposition, if any, of the proceeding;

(12) if the proposed ward is an adult and if known by the applicant:

(A) the name of the proposed ward's spouse, if any, and state the spouse's address or that the spouse is deceased;

(B) the name of each of the proposed ward's parents and state the parent's address or that the parent is deceased;

(C) the name and age of each of the proposed ward's siblings, if any, and state the sibling's address or that the sibling is deceased;

(D) the name and age of each of the proposed ward's children, if any, and state the child's address or that the child is deceased; and

(E) if the proposed ward's spouse and each of the proposed ward's parents, siblings, and children are deceased, or, if there is no spouse, parent, adult sibling, or adult child, the names and addresses of the proposed ward's next of kin who are adults;

(13) facts showing that the court has venue over the proceeding; and

(14) if applicable, that the person whom the applicant desires to have appointed as a guardian is a private professional guardian who has complied with the requirements of Section 697 of this code.

Added by Acts 1993, 73rd Leg., ch. 957, § 1, eff. Sept. 1, 1993. Amended by Acts 1997, 75th Leg., ch. 77, § 5, eff. Sept. 1, 1997; Acts 1997, 75th Leg., ch. 1376, § 2, eff. Sept. 1, 1997; Acts 1999, 76th Leg., ch. 829, § 4, eff. Sept. 1, 1999. Amended by Acts 2003, 78th Leg., ch. 549, § 11, eff. Sept. 1, 2003.

§ 682A. Application for Appointment of Guardian for Certain Persons

(a) If a minor is a person who, because of incapacity, will require a guardianship after the ward is no longer a minor, a person may file an application under Section 682 of this code for the appointment of a guardian of the person or the estate, or both, of the proposed ward not earlier than the 180th day before the proposed ward's 18th birthday. If the application is heard before the proposed ward's 18th birthday, a guardianship created under this section may not take effect and the person appointed guardian may not give a bond or take the oath as required under Section 700 or 702 of this code until the proposed ward's 18th birthday.

(b) Notwithstanding Section 694(b) of this code, the guardianship of the person of a minor who is the subject of an application for the appointment of a guardian of the person filed under Subsection (a) of this section is settled and closed when:

(1) the court, after a hearing on the application, determines that the appointment of a guardian of the person for the proposed ward is not necessary; or

(2) the guardian appointed by the court after a hearing on the application has qualified under Section 699 of this code.

Added by Acts 1999, 76th Leg., ch. 904, § 1, eff. Sept. 1, 1999. Subsec. (a) amended by Acts 2001, 77th Leg., ch. 217, § 10, eff. Sept. 1, 2001.

§ 683. Court's Initiation of Guardianship Proceedings

(a) If a court has probable cause to believe that a person domiciled or found in the county in which the court is located is an incapacitated person, and the person does not have a guardian in this state, the court shall appoint a guardian ad litem or court investigator to investigate and file an application for the appointment of a guardian of the person or estate, or both, of the person believed to be incapacitated.

(b) To establish probable cause under this section, the court may require:

(1) an information letter about the person believed to be incapacitated that is submitted by an interested person and satisfies the requirements of Section 683A of this code; or

(2) a written letter or certificate from a physician who has examined the person believed to be incapacitated that satisfies the requirements of Section 687(a) of this code, except that the letter must be dated not earlier than the 120th day before the date of the filing of an application under Subsection (a) of this section and be based on an examination the physician performed not earlier than the 120th day before that date.

(c) A court that creates a guardianship for a ward under this chapter may authorize compensation of a guardian ad litem who files an application under Subsection (a) of this section from available funds of the ward's estate. If after examining the ward's assets the court determines the ward is unable to pay for services provided by the guardian ad litem, the court may authorize compensation from the county treasury.

Added by Acts 1993, 73rd Leg., ch. 957, § 1, eff. Sept. 1, 1993. Amended by Acts 1999, 76th Leg., ch. 905, § 3, eff. Sept. 1, 1999.

§ 683A. Information Letter

An information letter under Section 683(b)(1) of this code about a person believed to be incapacitated may:

(1) include the name, address, telephone number, county of residence, and date of birth of the person;

(2) state whether the residence of the person is a private residence, health care facility, or other type of residence;

(3) describe the relationship between the interested person and the person;

(4) contain the names and telephone numbers of any known friends and relatives of the person;

(5) state whether a guardian of the person or estate of the person has been appointed in this state;

(6) state whether the person has executed a power of attorney and, if so, the designee's name, address, and telephone number;

(7) describe any property of the person, including the estimated value of that property;

(8) list any amount and source of monthly income of the person; and

(9) describe the nature and degree of the person's alleged incapacity and include a statement of whether the person is in imminent danger of serious impairment to the person's physical health, safety, or estate.

Added by Acts 1999, 76th Leg., ch. 905, § 4, eff. Sept. 1, 1999.

§ 684. Findings Required

(a) Before appointing a guardian, the court must find by clear and convincing evidence that:

(1) the proposed ward is an incapacitated person;

(2) it is in the best interest of the proposed ward to have the court appoint a person as guardian of the proposed ward; and

(3) the rights of the proposed ward or the proposed ward's property will be protected by the appointment of a guardian.

(b) Before appointing a guardian, the court must find by a preponderance of the evidence that:

(1) the court has venue of the case;

(2) the person to be appointed guardian is eligible to act as guardian and is entitled to appointment, or, if no eligible person entitled to appointment applies, the person appointed is a proper person to act as guardian;

(3) if a guardian is appointed for a minor, the guardianship is not created for the primary purpose of enabling the minor to establish residency for enrollment in a school or school district for which the minor is not otherwise eligible for enrollment; and

(4) the proposed ward is totally without capacity as provided by this code to care for himself or herself and to manage the individual's property, or the proposed ward lacks the capacity to do some, but not all, of the tasks necessary to care for himself or herself or to manage the individual's property.

(c) The court may not grant an application to create a guardianship unless the applicant proves each element required by this code. A determination of incapacity of an adult proposed ward, other than a person who must have a guardian appointed to receive funds due the person from any governmental source, must be evidenced by recurring acts or occurrences within the preceding six-month period and not by isolated instances of negligence or bad judgment.

(d) A court may not appoint a guardian of the estate of a minor when a payment of claims is made under Section 887 of this code.

(e) A certificate of the executive head or a representative of the bureau, department, or agency of the government, to the effect that the appointment of a guardian is a condition precedent to the payment of any funds due the proposed ward from that governmental entity, is prima facie evidence of the necessity for the appointment of a guardian.

Added by Acts 1993, 73rd Leg., ch. 957, § 1, eff. Sept. 1, 1993. Amended by Acts 1995, 74th Leg., ch. 1039, § 33, eff. Sept. 1, 1995; Subsec. (b) amended by Acts 1997, 75th Leg., ch. 1376, § 3, eff. Sept. 1, 1997; Subsec. (c) amended by Acts 1999, 76th Leg., ch. 379, § 5, eff. Sept. 1, 1999.

§ 685. Hearing for Appointment of Guardian; Right to Jury Trial

(a) A proposed ward must be present at a hearing to appoint a guardian unless the court, on the record or in the order, determines that a personal appearance is not necessary. The court may close the hearing if the proposed ward or the proposed ward's counsel requests a closed hearing.

(b) The proposed ward is entitled, on request, to a jury trial.

(c) At the hearing, the court shall:

(1) inquire into the ability of any allegedly incapacitated adult person to feed, clothe, and shelter himself or herself, to care for the individual's own physical health, and to manage the individual's property or financial affairs;

(2) ascertain the age of any proposed ward who is a minor;

(3) inquire into the governmental reports for any person who must have a guardian appointed to receive funds due the person from any governmental source; and

(4) inquire into the qualifications, abilities, and capabilities of the person seeking to be appointed guardian.

Added by Acts 1993, 73rd Leg., ch. 957, § 1, eff. Sept. 1, 1993. Subsec. (a) amended by Acts 1995, 74th Leg., ch. 1039, § 34, eff. Sept. 1, 1995; Subsecs. (a), (c) amended by Acts 1999, 76th Leg., ch. 379, § 6, eff. Sept. 1, 1999.

§ 686. Use of Records in Hearing to Appoint Guardian

(a) Before a hearing may be held for the appointment of a guardian, current and relevant medical, psychological, and intellectual testing records of the proposed ward must be provided to the attorney ad litem appointed to represent the proposed ward unless:

(1) the proposed ward is a minor or a person who must have a guardian appointed to receive funds due the person from any governmental source; or

(2) the court makes a finding on the record that no current or relevant records exist and examining the proposed ward for the purpose of creating the records is impractical.

(b) Current medical, psychological, and intellectual testing records are a sufficient basis for a determination of guardianship.

(c) The findings and recommendations contained in the medical, psychological, and intellectual testing records are not binding on the court.

Added by Acts 1993, 73rd Leg., ch. 957, § 1, eff. Sept. 1, 1993. Subsec. (a) amended by Acts 1999, 76th Leg., ch. 379, § 7, eff. Sept. 1, 1999.

§ 687. Examinations and Reports

(a) The court may not grant an application to create a guardianship for an incapacitated person, other than a minor, person whose alleged incapacity is mental retardation, or person for whom it is necessary to have a guardian appointed only to receive funds from a governmental source, unless the applicant presents to the court a written letter or certificate from a physician licensed in this state that is dated not earlier than the 120th day before the date of the filing of the application and based on an examination the physician performed not earlier than the 120th day before the date of the filing of the application. The letter or certificate must:

(1) describe the nature and degree of incapacity, including the medical history if reasonably available;

(2) provide a medical prognosis specifying the estimated severity of the incapacity;

(3) state how or in what manner the proposed ward's ability to make or communicate responsible decisions concerning himself or herself is affected by the person's physical or mental health;

(4) state whether any current medication affects the demeanor of the proposed ward or the proposed ward's ability to participate fully in a court proceeding;

(5) describe the precise physical and mental conditions underlying a diagnosis of senility, if applicable; and

(6) include any other information required by the court.

(b) Except as provided by Subsection (c) of this section, if the court determines it is necessary, the court may appoint the necessary physicians to examine the proposed ward. The court must make its determination with respect to the necessity for a physician's examination of the proposed ward at a hearing held for that purpose. Not later than the fourth day before the date of the hearing, the applicant shall give to the proposed ward and the proposed ward's attorney ad litem written notice specifying the purpose and the date and time of the hearing. A physician who examines the proposed ward, other than a physician or psychologist who examines the proposed ward under Subsection (c) of this section, shall make available to an attorney ad litem appointed to represent the proposed ward, for inspection, a written letter or certificate from the physician that complies with the requirements of Subsection (a) of this section.

(c) If the basis of the proposed ward's alleged incapacity is mental retardation, the proposed ward shall be examined by a physician or psychologist licensed in this state or certified by the Texas Department of Mental Health and Mental Retardation to perform the examination, unless there is written documentation filed with the court that shows that the proposed ward has been examined according to the rules adopted by the Texas Department of Mental Health and Mental Retardation not earlier than 24 months before the date of a hearing to appoint a guardian for the proposed ward. The physician or psychologist shall conduct the examination according to the rules adopted by the Texas Department of Mental Health and Mental Retardation and shall submit written findings and recommendations to the court.

Added by Acts 1995, 74th Leg., ch. 1039, § 35, eff. Sept. 1, 1995. Subsec. (a) amended by Acts 1999, 76th Leg., ch. 379, § 8, eff. Sept. 1, 1999; Subsec. (b) amended by Acts 2001, 77th Leg., ch. 1174, § 3, eff. Sept. 1, 2001. Amended by Acts 2003, 78th Leg., ch. 549, § 12, eff. Sept. 1, 2003.

§ 689. Preference of Ward

Before appointing a guardian, the court shall make a reasonable effort to consider the incapacitated person's

preference of the person to be appointed guardian and, to the extent not inconsistent with other provisions of this chapter, shall give due consideration to the preference indicated by the incapacitated person.
Added by Acts 1993, 73rd Leg., ch. 957, § 1, eff. Sept. 1, 1993.

§ 690. Persons Appointed Guardian

Only one person may be appointed as guardian of the person or estate, but one person may be appointed guardian of the person and another of the estate, if it is in the best interest of the ward. Nothing in this section prohibits the joint appointment of a husband and wife, of joint managing conservators, or of coguardians appointed under the laws of a jurisdiction other than this state.
Added by Acts 1993, 73rd Leg., ch. 957, § 1, eff. Sept. 1, 1993. Amended by Acts 1995, 74th Leg., ch. 1039, § 36, eff. Sept. 1, 1995.

§ 692. Dismissal of Application

If it is found that an adult person possesses the capacity to care for himself or herself and to manage the individual's property as would a reasonably prudent person, the court shall dismiss the application for guardianship.
Added by Acts 1993, 73rd Leg., ch. 957, § 1, eff. Sept. 1, 1993. Amended by Acts 1995, 74th Leg., ch. 1039, § 38, eff. Sept. 1, 1995.

§ 693. Order of Court

(a) If it is found that the proposed ward is totally without capacity as provided by this code to care for himself or herself and to manage the individual's property, the court may appoint a guardian of the individual's person or estate, or both, with full authority over the incapacitated person except as provided by law. An order appointing a guardian under this subsection must contain findings of fact and specify:

(1) the information required by Subsection (c) of this section;

(2) that the guardian has full authority over the incapacitated person; and

(3) if necessary, the amount of funds from the corpus of the person's estate the court will allow the guardian to expend for the education and maintenance of the person under Section 776 of this code.

(b) If it is found that the person lacks the capacity to do some, but not all, of the tasks necessary to care for himself or herself or to manage the individual's property, the court may appoint a guardian with limited powers and permit the individual to care for himself or herself or to manage the individual's property commensurate with the individual's ability.

An order appointing a guardian under this subsection must contain findings of fact and specify:

(1) the information required by Subsection (c) of this section;

(2) the specific powers, limitations, or duties of the guardian with respect to the care of the person or the management of the person's property by the guardian; and

(3) if necessary, the amount of funds from the corpus of the person's estate the court will allow the guardian to expend for the education and maintenance of the person under Section 776 of this code.

(c) The order of the court appointing a guardian must specify:

(1) the name of the person appointed;

(2) the name of the ward;

(3) whether the guardian is of the person or the estate, or of both, of the ward;

(4) the amount of any bond required;

(5) if it is a guardianship of the estate and the court deems an appraisal is necessary, one or more but not more than three disinterested persons to appraise the estate and to return the appraisement to the court; and

(6) that the clerk will issue letters of guardianship to the person appointed when the person has qualified according to law.

(d) An order appointing a guardian may not duplicate or conflict with the powers and duties of any other guardian.

(e) An order appointing a guardian or a successor guardian may specify a period of not more than one year during which a petition for adjudication that the incapacitated person no longer requires the guardianship may not be filed without special leave.
Added by Acts 1993, 73rd Leg., ch. 957, § 1, eff. Sept. 1, 1993. Amended by Acts 1995, 74th Leg., ch. 1039, § 39, eff. Sept. 1, 1995.

§ 694. Term of Appointment of Guardian

(a) Unless otherwise discharged as provided by law, a guardian remains in office until the estate is closed.

(b) The guardianship shall be settled and closed when the incapacitated person:

(1) dies and, if the person was married, the person's spouse qualifies as survivor in community;

(2) is found by the court to have full capacity to care for himself or herself and to manage the person's property;

(3) is no longer a minor; or

(4) no longer must have a guardian appointed to receive funds due the person from any governmental source.

(c) An order appointing a guardian or a successor guardian may specify a period of not more than one year during which a petition for adjudication that the incapacitated person no longer requires the guardianship may not be filed without special leave.

(d) A request for an order under this section may be made by informal letter to the court. A person who knowingly interferes with the transmission of the request to the court may be adjudged guilty of contempt of court.

(e) If a nonresident guardian of a nonresident ward qualifies as guardian under this chapter, the guardianship of any resident guardian may be terminated.

(f) Repealed by Acts 1999, 76th Leg., ch. 379, § 10, eff. Sept. 1, 1999.

Added by Acts 1993, 73rd Leg., ch. 957, § 1, eff. Sept. 1, 1993. Amended by Acts 1995, 74th Leg., ch. 1039, § 40, eff. Sept. 1, 1995; Subsec. (b) amended by Acts 1999, 76th Leg., ch. 379, § 9, eff. Sept. 1, 1999; Subsec. (f) repealed by Acts 1999, 76th Leg., ch. 379, § 10, eff. Sept. 1, 1999.

§ 694A. Complete Restoration of Ward's Capacity or Modification of Guardianship

(a) A ward or any person interested in the ward's welfare may file a written application with the court for an order:

(1) finding that the ward is no longer an incapacitated person and ordering the settlement and closing of the guardianship;

(2) finding that the ward lacks the capacity to do some or all of the tasks necessary to provide food, clothing, or shelter for himself or herself, to care for the ward's own physical health, or to manage the ward's own financial affairs and granting additional powers or duties to the guardian; or

(3) finding that the ward has the capacity to do some, but not all, of the tasks necessary to provide food, clothing, or shelter for himself or herself, to care for the ward's own physical health, or to manage the ward's own financial affairs and:

(A) limiting the powers or duties of the guardian; and

(B) permitting the ward to care for himself or herself or to manage the ward's own financial affairs commensurate with the ward's ability.

(b) A ward may make a request for an order under this section by informal letter to the court. A person who knowingly interferes with the transmission of the request to the court may be adjudged guilty of contempt of court.

(c) On receipt of an informal letter under Subsection (b) of this section, the court shall appoint the court investigator or a guardian ad litem to file an application under Subsection (a) of this section on the ward's behalf. A guardian ad litem appointed under this subsection may also be appointed by the court to serve as attorney ad litem under Section 694C of this code.

(d) When an application is filed under this section, citation shall be served on the ward's guardian and on the ward if the ward is not the applicant.

(e) Except as otherwise provided by the court, on good cause shown by the applicant, a person may not reapply for complete restoration of a ward's capacity or modification of a ward's guardianship before the first anniversary of the date of the hearing on the last preceding application.

Added by Acts 1995, 74th Leg., ch. 1039, § 41, eff. Sept. 1, 1995. Amended by Acts 1999, 76th Leg., ch. 829, § 5, eff. Sept. 1, 1999.

§ 694B. Contents of Application

An application filed under Section 694A of this code must be sworn to by the applicant and must:

(1) contain the name, sex, date of birth, and address of the ward;

(2) contain the name and address of any person serving as guardian of the person of the ward on the date the application is filed;

(3) contain the name and address of any person serving as guardian of the estate of the ward on the date the application is filed;

(4) state the nature and description of the ward's guardianship;

(5) state the specific areas of protection and assistance and any limitation of rights that exist;

(6) state whether the relief being sought is:

(A) a restoration of the ward's capacity because the ward is no longer an incapacitated person;

(B) the granting of additional powers or duties to the guardian; or

(C) the limitation of powers granted to or duties performed by the guardian;

(7) if the relief being sought under the application is described by Subdivision (6)(B) or (C) of this section, state:

(A) the nature and degree of the ward's incapacity;

(B) the specific areas of protection and assistance to be provided to the ward and requested to be included in the court's order; and

(C) any limitation of the ward's rights requested to be included in the court's order;

(8) state the approximate value and description of the ward's property, including any compensation, pension, insurance, or allowance to which the ward is or may be entitled; and

(9) if the ward is 60 years of age or older, contain the names and addresses, to the best of the applicant's knowledge, of the ward's spouse, siblings, and children or, if there is no known spouse, sibling, or child, the names and addresses of the ward's next of kin.

Added by Acts 1999, 76th Leg., ch. 829, § 6, eff. Sept. 1, 1999.

§ 694C. Appointment of Attorney ad Litem

(a) The court shall appoint an attorney ad litem to represent a ward in a proceeding for the complete restoration of the ward's capacity or for the modification of the ward's guardianship.

(b) Unless otherwise provided by the court, an attorney ad litem appointed under this section shall represent the ward only for purposes of the restoration or modification proceeding.

Added by Acts 1999, 76th Leg., ch. 829, § 6, eff. Sept. 1, 1999.

§ 694D. Hearing

(a) At a hearing on an application for complete restoration of a ward's capacity or modification of a ward's guardianship, the court shall consider only evidence regarding the ward's mental or physical capacity at the time of the hearing that is relevant to the restoration of capacity or modification of the guardianship, as appropriate.

(b) The party who filed the application has the burden of proof at the hearing.

Added by Acts 1999, 76th Leg., ch. 829, § 6, eff. Sept. 1, 1999.

§ 694E. Findings Required

(a) Before ordering the settlement and closing of the guardianship under an application filed under Section 694A of this code, the court must find by a preponderance of the evidence that the ward is no longer partially or fully incapacitated.

(b) Before granting additional powers to the guardian or requiring the guardian to perform additional duties under an application filed under Section 694A of this code, the court must find by a preponderance of the evidence that the current nature and degree of the ward's incapacity warrants a modification of the guardianship and that some or all of the ward's rights need to be further restricted.

(c) Before limiting the powers granted to or duties required to be performed by the guardian under an application filed under Section 694A of this code, the court must find by a preponderance of the evidence that the current nature and degree of the ward's incapacity warrants a modification of the guardianship and that some of the ward's rights need to be restored.

Added by Acts 1999, 76th Leg., ch. 829, § 6, eff. Sept. 1, 1999.

§ 694F. Examinations and Reports Relating to Complete Restoration of Ward's Capacity or Modification of Guardianship

(a) The court may not grant an order completely restoring a ward's capacity or modifying a ward's guardianship under an application filed under Section 694A of this code unless, in addition to other requirements prescribed by this code, the applicant presents to the court a written letter or certificate from a physician licensed in this state that is dated not earlier than the 120th day before the date of the filing of the application or dated after the date on which the application was filed but before the date of the hearing. The letter or certificate must:

(1) describe the nature and degree of incapacity, including the medical history if reasonably available, or state that, in the physician's opinion, the ward has the capacity to provide food, clothing, and shelter for himself or herself, to care for the ward's own physical health, and to manage the financial affairs of the ward;

(2) provide a medical prognosis specifying the estimated severity of any incapacity;

(3) state how or in what manner the ward's ability to make or communicate responsible decisions concerning himself or herself is affected by the person's physical or mental health;

(4) state whether any current medication affects the demeanor of the ward or the ward's ability to participate fully in a court proceeding;

(5) describe the precise physical and mental conditions underlying a diagnosis of senility, if applicable; and

(6) include any other information required by the court.

(b) If the court determines it is necessary, the court may appoint the necessary physicians to examine the ward in the same manner and to the same extent as a ward is examined by a physician under Section 687 of this code.

Added by Acts 1999, 76th Leg., ch. 829, § 6, eff. Sept. 1, 1999.

§ 694G. Order of Complete Restoration of Ward's Capacity

If the court finds that a ward is no longer an incapacitated person, the order completely restoring the ward's capacity must contain findings of fact and specify:

(1) the information required by Section 694J of this code;

(2) that the ward is no longer an incapacitated person;

(3) that there is no further need for a guardianship of the person or estate of the ward;

(4) that the guardian is required to:

(A) immediately settle the guardianship in accordance with this chapter; and

(B) deliver all of the remaining guardianship estate to the ward; and

(5) that the clerk shall revoke letters of guardianship when the guardianship is finally settled and closed.

Added by Acts 1999, 76th Leg., ch. 829, § 6, eff. Sept. 1, 1999. Amended by Acts 2001, 77th Leg., ch. 484, § 2, eff. Sept. 1, 2001; Acts 2001, 77th Leg., ch. 1174, § 4, eff. Sept. 1, 2001.

§ 694H. Modification of Guardianship

If the court finds that a guardian's powers or duties should be expanded or limited, the order modifying the guardianship must contain findings of fact and specify:

(1) the information required by Section 694J of this code;

(2) the specific powers, limitations, or duties of the guardian with respect to the care of the ward or the management of the property of the ward, as appropriate;

(3) the specific areas of protection and assistance to be provided to the ward;

(4) any limitation of the ward's rights; and

(5) that the clerk shall modify the letters of guardianship to the extent applicable to conform to the order.

Added by Acts 1999, 76th Leg., ch. 829. § 6, eff. Sept. 1, 1999.

§ 694I. Dismissal of Application

If the court finds that a modification of the ward's guardianship is not necessary, including that the ward's capacity has not been restored, the court shall dismiss the application and enter an order that contains findings of fact and specifies:

(1) the information required by Section 694J of this code; and

(2) that the powers, limitations, or duties of the guardian with respect to the care of the ward or the management of the ward's property will remain unchanged.

Added by Acts 1999, 76th Leg., ch. 829, § 6, eff. Sept. 1, 1999.

§ 694J. Contents of Order

(a) A court order entered with respect to a request made under Section 694A of this code to completely restore a ward's capacity or modify a ward's guardianship must:

(1) contain the name of the guardian;

(2) contain the name of the ward; and

(3) state whether the type of guardianship being addressed at the proceeding is a:

(A) guardianship of the person;

(B) guardianship of the estate; or

(C) guardianship of both the person and the estate.

(b) In an order described by this section, the court may not grant a power to a guardian or require the guardian to perform a duty that is a power granted to or a duty required to be performed by another guardian.

Added by Acts 1999, 76th Leg., ch. 829, § 6, eff. Sept. 1, 1999.

§ 694K. Attorney Retained on Ward's Behalf

(a) A ward may retain an attorney for a proceeding involving the complete restoration of the ward's capacity or modification of the ward's guardianship.

(b) The court may order that compensation for services provided by an attorney retained under this section be paid from funds in the ward's estate only if the court finds that the attorney had a good-faith belief that the ward had the capacity necessary to retain the attorney's services.

Added by Acts 1999, 76th Leg., ch. 829, § 6, eff. Sept. 1, 1999.

§ 695. Appointment of Successor Guardian

(a) If a guardian dies, resigns, or is removed, the court may, on application and on service of notice as directed by the court, appoint a successor guardian.

(b) A successor guardian has the powers and rights and is subject to all of the duties of the preceding guardian.

Added by Acts 1993, 73rd Leg., ch. 957, § 1, eff. Sept. 1, 1993.

§ 695A. Successor Guardians for Wards of Guardianship Programs or Governmental Entities

(a) If a guardianship program or governmental entity serving as a guardian for a ward under this chapter becomes aware of a family member or friend of the ward or any other interested person who is willing and able to serve as the ward's successor guardian, the program or entity shall notify the court in which the guardianship is pending of the individual's willingness and ability.

(b) When the court is notified of the existence of a proposed successor guardian under Subsection (a) of this section or the court otherwise becomes aware of a family member, friend, or any other interested person who is willing and able to serve as a successor guardian for a ward of a guardianship program or governmental entity, the court shall determine whether the proposed successor guardian is qualified to serve under this chapter as the ward's successor guardian.

(c) If the court finds under Subsection (b) of this section that the proposed successor guardian for a ward is not disqualified from being appointed as the ward's successor guardian under Section 681 of this code and that the appointment is in the ward's best interests, the guardianship program or governmental entity serving as the ward's guardian or the court, on the court's own motion, may file an application to appoint the individual as the ward's successor guardian. Service of notice on an application filed under this subsection shall be made as directed by the court.

Added by Acts 1999, 76th Leg., ch. 906, § 1, eff. Sept. 1, 1999.

§ 696. Appointment of Private Professional Guardians

A court may not appoint a private professional guardian to serve as a guardian or permit a private professional guardian to continue to serve as a guardian under this code if the private professional guardian has not complied with the requirements of Section 697 of this code.

Added by Acts 1993, 73rd Leg., ch. 957, § 1, eff. Sept. 1, 1993.

§ 697. Registration of Private Professional Guardians

(a) A private professional guardian must apply annually to the clerk of the county having venue over the proceeding for the appointment of a guardian for certification. The application must include a sworn statement containing the following information concerning a private professional guardian or each person who represents or plans to represent the interests of a ward as a guardian on behalf of the private professional guardian:

(1) educational background and professional experience;

(2) three or more professional references;

(3) the names of all of the wards the private professional guardian or person is or will be serving as a guardian;

(4) the aggregate fair market value of the property of all wards that is being or will be managed by the private professional guardian or person;

(5) place of residence, business address, and business telephone number; and

(6) whether the private professional guardian or person has ever been removed as a guardian by the court or resigned as a guardian in a particular case, and, if so, a description of the circumstances causing the removal or resignation, and the style of the suit, the docket number, and the court having jurisdiction over the proceeding.

(b) The application must be accompanied by a nonrefundable fee set by the clerk in an amount necessary to cover the cost of administering this section.

(c) The term of the certification begins on the date that the requirements are met and extends through December 31 of the initial year. After the initial year of certification, the term of the certification begins on January 1 and ends on December 31 of each year. A renewal application must be completed during December of the year preceding the year for which the renewal is requested.

(d) The clerk shall bring the information received under this section to the judge's attention for review. The judge shall use the information only in determining whether to appoint, remove, or continue the appointment of a private professional guardian.

(e) Not later than February 1 of each year, the clerk shall submit to the Health and Human Services Commission the names and business addresses of private professional guardians who have satisfied the certification requirements under this section during the preceding year.

Added by Acts 1993, 73rd Leg., ch. 957, § 1, eff. Sept. 1, 1993. Subsec. (a) amended by and Subsec. (e) added by Acts 1999, 76th Leg., ch. 1116, § 2, eff. Sept. 1, 1999.

§ 698. Access to Criminal History Records

(a) The clerk of the county having venue over the proceeding for the appointment of a guardian shall obtain criminal history record information that is maintained by the Department of Public Safety or the Federal Bureau of Investigation identification division relating to:

(1) a private professional guardian;

(2) each person who represents or plans to represent the interests of a ward as a guardian on behalf of the private professional guardian; or

(3) each person employed by a private professional guardian who will:

(A) have personal contact with a ward or proposed ward;

(B) exercise control over and manage a ward's estate; or

(C) perform any duties with respect to the management of a ward's estate.

(b) The criminal history record information obtained under this section is for the exclusive use of the court and is privileged and confidential. The criminal history record information may not be released or otherwise disclosed to any person or agency except on court order or consent of the person being investigated. The clerk may destroy the criminal history information records after the records are used for the purposes authorized by this section.

(c) The court shall use the information obtained under this section only in determining whether to appoint, remove, or continue the appointment of a private professional guardian.

(d) A person commits an offense if the person releases or discloses any information received under this section without the authorization prescribed by Subsection (b) of this section. An offense under this subsection is a Class A misdemeanor.

(e) The clerk may charge a reasonable fee sufficient to recover the costs of obtaining criminal history information records authorized by Subsection (a) of this section.

Added by Acts 1993, 73rd Leg., ch. 957, § 1, eff. Sept. 1, 1993. Subsec. (a) amended by Acts 1999, 76th Leg., ch. 1116, § 3, eff. Sept. 1, 1999.

Subpart B. Qualification

§ 699. How Guardians Qualify

A guardian is deemed to have duly qualified when the guardian has taken and filed the oath required under Section 700 of this code, has made the required bond, and has filed it with the clerk, and has the bond approved by the judge. A guardian who is not required to make bond, is deemed to have duly qualified when the guardian has taken and filed the required oath.

Added by Acts 1993, 73rd Leg., ch. 957, § 1, eff. Sept. 1, 1993.

§ 700. Oath of Guardian

(a) The guardian shall take an oath to discharge faithfully the duties of guardian for the person or estate, or both, of a ward.

(b) A representative of the Department of Protective and Regulatory Services shall take the oath required by Subsection (a) of this section if the department is appointed guardian.

Added by Acts 1993, 73rd Leg., ch. 957, § 1, eff. Sept. 1, 1993. Amended by Acts 1997, 75th Leg., ch. 1022, § 101, eff. Sept. 1, 1997.

§ 701. Time for Taking Oath and Giving Bond

Except as provided by Section 682A(a) of this code, the oath of a guardian may be taken and subscribed, or the bond of a guardian may be given and approved, at any time before the expiration of the 20th day after the date of the order granting letters of guardianship, or before the letters have been revoked for a failure to qualify within the time allowed. An oath may be taken before any person authorized to administer oaths under the laws of this state.

Added by Acts 1993, 73rd Leg., ch. 957, § 1, eff. Sept. 1, 1993. Amended by Acts 2001, 77th Leg., ch. 217, § 11, eff. Sept. 1, 2001.

§ 702. Bond Required of Guardian of the Person or Estate

(a) Except as provided by Subsections (b) and (c) of this section, a guardian of the person or of the estate of a ward is required to give bond.

(b) A bond is not required to be given by a guardian that is:

(1) a corporate fiduciary, as defined by Section 601 of this code; or

(2) a guardianship program operated by a county.

(c) When a will that is made by a surviving parent and is probated in a court in this state or a written declaration that is made by a surviving parent directs that the guardian appointed in the will or declaration serve without bond, the court finding that the person is qualified shall issue letters of guardianship of the person to the person named to be appointed guardian in the will or declaration without requirement of bond. The court may not waive the requirement of a bond for the guardian of the estate of a ward, regardless of whether a surviving parent's will or declaration directs the court to waive the bond.

Added by Acts 1993, 73rd Leg., ch. 957, § 1, eff. Sept. 1, 1993. Subsec. (b) amended by Acts 1995, 74th Leg., ch. 642, § 13, eff. Sept. 1, 1995. Amended by Acts 1995, 74th Leg., ch. 1039, § 42, eff. Sept. 1, 1995; Subsec. (b) amended by Acts 1997, 75th Leg., ch. 924, § 1, eff. Sept. 1, 1997; Subsec. (c) amended by Acts 1999, 76th Leg., ch. 1078, § 1, eff. Sept. 1, 1999; Subsec. (b) amended by Acts 2001, 77th Leg., ch. 217, § 12, eff. Sept. 1, 2001.

§ 702A. Types of Bonds Acceptable for Guardian of the Person

(a) This section applies only to a bond required to be posted by a guardian of the person of a ward when there is no guardian of the ward's estate.

(b) To ensure the performance of the guardian's duties, the court may accept only:

(1) a corporate surety bond;

(2) a personal surety bond;

(3) a deposit of money instead of a surety bond; or

(4) a personal bond.

(c) In determining the appropriate type and amount of bond to set for the guardian, the court shall consider:

(1) the familial relationship of the guardian to the ward;

(2) the guardian's ties to the community;

(3) the guardian's financial condition;

(4) the guardian's past history of compliance with the court; and

(5) the reason the guardian may have previously been denied a corporate surety bond.

Added by Acts 1997, 75th Leg., ch. 924, § 2, eff. Sept. 1, 1997.

§ 703. Bond of Guardian of the Estate

(a) Except when bond is not required under this chapter, before being issued letters of guardianship of estates, the recipient of letters shall give a bond that is conditioned as required by law and that is payable to the judge of the county in which the guardianship proceedings are pending or to the judge's successors in office. A bond of the guardian of the estate must have the written approval of either of the judges in the judge's official capacity and shall be executed and approved in accordance with Subsections (b)-(q) of this section.

(b) The judge shall set the penalty of the bond in an amount that is sufficient to protect the guardianship and its creditors, as provided by this chapter.

(c) If a bond is or will be required of a guardian of an estate, the court, before setting the penalty of the bond, shall hear evidence and determine:

(1) the amount of cash on hand and where deposited, and the amount of cash estimated to be needed for administrative purposes, including the operation of a business, factory, farm, or ranch owned by the guardianship estate, and administrative expenses for one year;

(2) the revenue anticipated to be received in the succeeding 12 months from dividends, interest, rentals, or use of real or personal property belonging to the guardianship estate and the aggregate amount of any installments or periodic payments to be collected;

(3) the estimated value of certificates of stock, bonds, notes, or securities of the ward, the name of the depository in which the stocks, bonds, notes, or securities of the ward are held for safekeeping, the face value of life insurance or other policies payable to the person on whose guardianship administration is sought or to the person's estate, and other personal property that is owned by the guardianship, or by a person with a disability; and

(4) the estimated amount of debts due and owing by the ward.

(d) The judge shall set the penalty of the bond in an amount equal to the estimated value of all personal property belonging to the ward, with an additional amount to cover revenue anticipated to be derived during the succeeding 12 months from interest, dividends, collectible claims, the aggregate amount of any installments or periodic payments exclusive of income derived or to be derived from federal social security payments, and rentals for use of real and personal property, provided that the penalty of the original bond shall be reduced in proportion to the amount of cash or value of securities or other assets authorized or required to be deposited or placed in safekeeping by court order, or voluntarily made by the guardian or by the sureties on the bond of the guardian as provided in Subsections (f) and (g) of this section.

(e) If the court considers it to be in the best interests of the ward, the court may require that the guardian and the corporate or personal sureties on the bond of the guardian of the ward agree to deposit any or all cash and safekeeping of other assets of the guardianship estate in a financial institution as defined by Section 201.101, Finance Code, with its main office or a branch office in this state and qualified to act as a depository in this state under the laws of this state or of the United States, and, if the depository is otherwise proper, the court may require the deposit to be made in a manner so as to prevent the withdrawal of the money or other assets in the guardianship estate without the written consent of the surety or on court order made on the notice to the surety. An agreement made by a guardian and the sureties on the bond of the guardian under this section does not release from liability or change the liability of the principal or sureties as established by the terms of the bond.

(f) Cash, securities, or other personal assets of a ward that a ward is entitled to receive may, and if it is deemed by the court in the best interests of the ward shall, be deposited or placed in safekeeping in one or more of the depositories described in this section on the terms prescribed by the court. The court in which the guardianship proceeding is pending, on its own motion or on written application of the guardian or of any other person interested in the ward, may authorize or require additional assets of the guardianship estate then on hand or as they accrue during the pendency of the guardianship proceeding to be deposited or held in safekeeping as provided by this section. The amount of the guardian's bond shall be reduced in proportion to the cash deposited or the value of the securities or other assets placed in safekeeping. Cash that is deposited, securities or other assets held in safekeeping, or portions of the cash, securities, or other assets held in safekeeping may be withdrawn from a depository only on court order. The bond of the guardian shall be increased in proportion to the amount of cash or the value of securities or other assets that are authorized to be withdrawn.

(g) In lieu of giving a surety or sureties on a bond that is required of the guardian, or for purposes of reducing the amount of the bond, the guardian of an estate may deposit out of the guardian's own assets cash or securities that are acceptable to the court with a financial institution as defined by Section 201.101, Finance Code, with its main office or a branch office in this state. If the deposit is otherwise proper, the deposit must be equal in amount or value to the amount of the bond required or the bond shall be reduced by the value of assets that are deposited.

(h) The depository shall issue a receipt for a deposit in lieu of a surety showing the amount of cash or, if securities, the amount and description of the securities and agreeing not to disburse or deliver the cash or securities except on receipt of a certified copy of an order of the court in which the proceeding is pending. The receipt must be attached to the guardian's bond and be delivered to and filed by the county clerk after the receipt is approved by the judge.

(i) The amount of cash or securities on deposit may be increased or decreased by court order from time to time as the interests of the guardianship shall require.

(j) A cash or security deposit in lieu of a surety on the bond may be withdrawn or released only on order of a court that has jurisdiction.

(k) A creditor has the same rights against the guardian and the deposits as are provided for recovery against sureties on a bond.

(l) The court on its own motion or on written application by the guardian or any other person interested in the guardianship may require that the guardian give adequate bond in lieu of the deposit or may authorize withdrawal of the deposit and substitution of a bond with sureties on the bond. In either case, the guardian shall file a sworn statement showing the condition of the guardianship. The guardian is subject to removal as in other cases if the guardian does not file the sworn statement before the 21st day after the guardian is personally served with notice of the filing of the application or before the 21st day after the date the court enters its motion. The deposit may not be released or withdrawn until the court is satisfied as to the condition of the guardianship estate, determines the amount of bond, and receives and approves the bond.

(m) On the closing of a guardianship, a deposit or a portion of a deposit that remains on hand, whether of the assets of the guardian, the guardianship, or surety, shall be released by court order and paid to the person entitled to the assets. A writ of attachment or garnishment does not lie against the deposit except as to claims of creditors of the guardianship being administered or of persons interested in the guardianship, including distributees and wards, and only if the court has ordered distribution, and only to the extent of the ordered distribution.

(n) The surety on the bond may be an authorized corporate or personal surety.

(o) When the bond is more than $50,000, the court may require that the bond be signed by two or more authorized corporate sureties or by one corporate surety and two or more good and sufficient personal sureties. The guardianship shall pay the cost of a bond with corporate sureties.

(p) If the sureties are natural persons, there may not be less than two sureties, each of whom shall make affidavit in the manner prescribed by this chapter. The judge must be satisfied that each surety owns property in this state, over and above that exempt by law, sufficient to qualify as a surety as required by law. Except as otherwise provided by law, only one surety is required if the surety is an authorized corporate surety. A personal surety, instead of making an affidavit or creating a lien on specific real estate when an affidavit or lien is required, may deposit the personal surety's own cash or securities in the same manner as a guardian in lieu of pledging real property as security, subject to the provisions covering the deposits when made by guardians.

(q) If the guardian is a temporary guardian, the judge shall set the amount of the bond.

(r) The provisions of this section relating to the deposit of cash and safekeeping of securities cover, as far as they may apply, the orders entered by the court when:

(1) real or personal property of a guardianship has been authorized to be sold or rented;

(2) money is borrowed from the guardianship;

(3) real property, or an interest in real property, has been authorized to be leased for mineral development or made subject to unitization;

(4) the general bond has been found insufficient; or

(5) money is borrowed or invested on behalf of a ward.

(s) In determining the amount of the bond, the court may not take into account the assets of the estate that are placed in a management trust under Subpart N, Part 4,[1] of this code.

Added by Acts 1993, 73rd Leg., ch. 957, § 1, eff. Sept. 1, 1993. Subsecs. (e), (g) amended by Acts 1999, 76th Leg., ch. 344, § 6.006, eff. Sept. 1, 1999.

§ 704. Form of Bond

The following form, or the same in substance, may be used for the bonds of guardians:

> "The State of Texas
>
> "County of ________
>
> "Know all men by these presents that we, A.B., as principal, and E.F., as sureties, are held and firmly bound to the county judge of the County of ____ and his successors in office, in the sum of $ ____; conditioned that the above bound A.B., who has been appointed by the judge of the county as guardian or temporary guardian of the person or of the estate, or both, ________, stating in each case whether or not the person is a minor or an incapacitated person other than a minor, shall well and truly perform all of the duties required of the guardian or temporary guardian of the estate by law under appointment."

Added by Acts 1993, 73rd Leg., ch. 957, § 1, eff. Sept. 1, 1993.

§ 705. Bond to be Filed

A bond required under this chapter shall be subscribed by the principals and sureties, and shall be filed with the clerk when approved by the court.

Added by Acts 1993, 73rd Leg., ch. 957, § 1, eff. Sept. 1, 1993.

§ 706. Bond of Joint Guardians

When two or more persons are appointed guardians and are required to give a bond by the court or under this chapter, the court may require either a separate bond from each person or one joint bond from all of the persons.

Added by Acts 1993, 73rd Leg., ch. 957, § 1, eff. Sept. 1, 1993.

§ 707. Bond of Married Persons

When a married person is appointed guardian, the person may jointly execute, with or without, the person's spouse, the bond required by law. The bond shall bind the person's separate estate and may bind the person's spouse only if the bond is signed by the spouse.

Added by Acts 1993, 73rd Leg., ch. 957, § 1, eff. Sept. 1, 1993.

[1] Section 867 et seq.

§ 708. Bond of Married Person Younger Than 18 Years of Age

When a person who is younger than 18 years of age and is or has been married accepts and qualifies as guardian, a bond required to be executed by the person shall be as valid and binding for all purposes as if the person were of lawful age.

Added by Acts 1993, 73rd Leg., ch. 957, § 1, eff. Sept. 1, 1993.

§ 708A. Bond of Guardianship Program

The judge may require a guardianship program that is appointed guardian under this chapter to file one bond that:

(1) meets all the conditions required under this chapter; and

(2) is in an amount that is sufficient to protect the guardianship and the creditors of the guardianship of all of the wards of the guardianship program.

Added by Acts 1993, 73rd Leg., ch. 957, § 1, eff. Sept. 1, 1993.

§ 709. Affidavit of Personal Surety; Lien on Specific Property When Required; Subordination of Lien Authorized

(a) Before a judge considers a bond with a personal surety, each personal surety shall execute an affidavit stating the amount of the surety's assets, reachable by creditors, of a value over and above the surety's liabilities. The total of the surety's worth must be equal to at least double the amount of the bond. The affidavit shall be presented to the judge for the judge's consideration and, if approved, shall be attached to and form part of the bond.

(b) If the judge finds that the estimated value of personal property of the guardianship that cannot be deposited or held in safekeeping as provided by this section is such that personal sureties cannot be accepted without the creation of a specific lien on the real property of the sureties, the judge shall enter an order requiring that each surety designate real property owned by the surety in this state subject to execution. The designated property must be of a value over and above all liens and unpaid taxes, equal at least to the amount of the bond, giving an adequate legal description of the property, all of which shall be incorporated in an affidavit by the surety, approved by the judge, and attached to and form part of the bond. If the surety does not comply with the order, the judge may require that the bond be signed by an authorized corporate surety or by an authorized corporate surety and two or more personal sureties.

(c) If a personal surety who has been required to create a lien on specific real estate desires to lease the real property for mineral development, the personal surety may file the surety's written application in the court in which the proceeding is pending to request subordination of the lien to the proposed lease. The judge of the court in which the proceeding is pending may enter an order granting the application. A certified copy

of an order entered under this subsection that is filed and recorded in the deed records of the proper county is sufficient to subordinate the lien to the rights of a lessee in the proposed lease.
Added by Acts 1993, 73rd Leg., ch. 957, § 1, eff. Sept. 1, 1993.

§ 710. Bond as Lien on Real Property of Surety

When a personal surety is required by the court to create a lien on specific real property as a condition of the personal surety's acceptance as surety on a bond, a lien on the surety's real property in this state that is described in the affidavit of the surety, and only on the property, shall arise as security for the performance of the obligation of the bond. Before letters are issued to the guardian, the clerk of the court shall mail to the office of the county clerk of each county in which any real property set forth in the surety's affidavit is located a statement signed by the clerk that gives a sufficient description of the real property, the name of the principal and sureties, the amount of the bond, the name of the guardianship, and the court in which the bond is given. The county clerk to whom such statement is sent shall record the statement in the deed records of the county. The recorded statement shall be duly indexed in such a manner that the existence and character of a lien may conveniently be determined, and the recording and indexing of the statement is constructive notice to a person of the existence of the lien on the real property located in the county, effective as of the date of the indexing.
Added by Acts 1993, 73rd Leg., ch. 957, § 1, eff. Sept. 1, 1993.

§ 711. When New Bond May be Required

A guardian may be required to give a new bond when:

(1) one of the sureties on the bond dies, removes beyond the limits of the state, or becomes insolvent;

(2) in the opinion of the court, the sureties on the bond are insufficient;

(3) in the opinion of the court, the bond is defective;

(4) the amount of the bond is insufficient;

(5) one of the sureties petitions the court to be discharged from future liability on the bond; or

(6) the bond and the record of the bond has been lost or destroyed.

Added by Acts 1993, 73rd Leg., ch. 957, § 1, eff. Sept. 1, 1993.

§ 712. Demand for New Bond by Interested Person

A person interested in a guardianship may allege, on application in writing that is filed with the county clerk of the county in which the guardianship proceeding is pending, that the guardian's bond is insufficient or defective or has been, with the record of the bond, lost or destroyed, and may cause the guardian to be cited to appear and show cause why the guardian should not give a new bond.
Added by Acts 1993, 73rd Leg., ch. 957, § 1, eff. Sept. 1, 1993.

§ 713. Judge to Require New Bond

When it is made known to a judge that a bond is insufficient or that the bond has, with the record of the bond, been lost or destroyed, the judge without delay shall cause the guardian to be cited to show cause why the guardian should not give a new bond.
Added by Acts 1993, 73rd Leg., ch. 957, § 1, eff. Sept. 1, 1993.

§ 714. Order Requiring New Bond

On the return of a citation ordering a guardian to show cause why the guardian should not give a new bond, the judge on the day contained in the return of citation as the day for the hearing of the matter, shall proceed to inquire into the sufficiency of the reasons for requiring a new bond. If the judge is satisfied that a new bond should be required, the judge shall enter an order to that effect that states the amount of the new bond and the time within which the new bond shall be given, which may not be later than 20 days from the date of the order issued by the judge under this section.
Added by Acts 1993, 73rd Leg., ch. 957, § 1, eff. Sept. 1, 1993.

§ 715. Order Suspends Powers of Guardians

When a guardian is required to give a new bond, the order requiring the bond has the effect of suspending the guardian's powers, and the guardian may not pay out any money of the guardianship or do any other official act, except to preserve the property of the guardianship, until a new bond has been given and approved.
Added by Acts 1993, 73rd Leg., ch. 957, § 1, eff. Sept. 1, 1993.

§ 716. Decrease in Amount of Bond

A guardian required to give bond at any time may file with the clerk a written application to the court to have the bond reduced. After an application has been filed by the guardian under this section, the clerk shall issue and cause to be posted notice to all persons interested in the estate and to a surety on the bond, apprising the persons and surety of the fact and nature of the application and of the time at which the judge will hear the application. The judge may permit the filing of a new bond in a reduced amount on the submission of proof that a smaller bond than the one in effect will be adequate to meet the requirements of the law and protect the guardianship and on the approval of an accounting filed at the time of the application.
Added by Acts 1993, 73rd Leg., ch. 957, § 1, eff. Sept. 1, 1993.

§ 717. Discharge of Sureties on Execution of New Bond

When a new bond has been given and approved, the judge shall enter an order discharging the sureties

on the former bond from all liability for the future acts of the principal.
Added by Acts 1993, 73rd Leg., ch. 957, § 1, eff. Sept. 1, 1993.

§ 718. Release of Sureties Before Guardianship Fully Administered

A surety on the guardian's bond at any time may file with the clerk a petition with the court in which the proceeding is pending, praying that the guardian be required to give a new bond and that the petitioner be discharged from all liability for the future acts of the guardian. If a petition is filed, the guardian shall be cited to appear and give a new bond.
Added by Acts 1993, 73rd Leg., ch. 957, § 1, eff. Sept. 1, 1993.

§ 719. Release of Lien Before Guardianship Fully Administered

If a personal surety who has given a lien on specific real property as security applies to the court to have the lien released, the court shall order the release requested if the court is satisfied that the bond is sufficient without the lien on the property or if sufficient other real or personal property of the surety is substituted on the same terms and conditions required for the lien that is to be released. If the personal surety who requests the release of the lien does not offer a lien on other real or personal property and if the court is not satisfied that the bond is sufficient without the substitution of other property, the court shall order the guardian to appear and give a new bond.
Added by Acts 1993, 73rd Leg., ch. 957, § 1, eff. Sept. 1, 1993.

§ 720. Release of Recorded Lien on Surety's Property

A certified copy of the court order that describes the property, releases the lien, and is filed with the county clerk and recorded in the deed records of the county in which the property is located has the effect of cancelling the lien on the property.
Added by Acts 1993, 73rd Leg., ch. 957, § 1, eff. Sept. 1, 1993.

§ 721. Revocation of Letters for Failure to Give Bond

If a guardian of a ward fails to give the bond required by the court within the time required under this chapter, another person may be appointed guardian of the ward.
Added by Acts 1993, 73rd Leg., ch. 957, § 1, eff. Sept. 1, 1993.

§ 722. Guardian Without Bond Required to Give Bond

If a bond is not required of an individual guardian of the estate, a person who has a debt, claim, or demand against the guardianship, to the justice of which oath has been made by the person, the person's agent or attorney, or any other person interested in the guardianship, in person or as the representative of another person, may file a complaint under oath in writing in the court in which the guardian was appointed, and the court, after a complaint is filed under this section, shall cite the guardian to appear and show cause why the guardian should not be required to give bond.
Added by Acts 1993, 73rd Leg., ch. 957, § 1, eff. Sept. 1, 1993.

§ 723. Order Requiring Bond

On hearing a complaint under Section 722 of this code, if it appears to the court that a guardian is wasting, mismanaging, or misapplying the guardianship estate and that a creditor may probably lose his debt, or that a person's interest in the guardianship may be diminished or lost, the court shall enter an order requiring the guardian to give a bond not later than the 10th day after the date of the order.
Added by Acts 1993, 73rd Leg., ch. 957, § 1, eff. Sept. 1, 1993.

§ 724. Amount of Bond

A bond that is required under Section 723 of this code shall be in an amount that is sufficient to protect the guardianship and its creditors. The bond shall be approved by and payable to the judge and shall be conditioned that the guardian will well and truly administer the guardianship and that the guardian will not waste, mismanage, or misapply the guardianship estate.
Added by Acts 1993, 73rd Leg., ch. 957, § 1, eff. Sept. 1, 1993.

§ 725. Failure to Give Bond

If the guardian fails to give the bond required under Section 723 of this code, and the judge does not extend the time, the judge, without citation, shall remove the guardian and appoint a competent person as guardian of the ward who:

(1) shall administer the guardianship according to the provisions of a will or law;

(2) shall take the oath required of a guardian as the case may be before the person enters on the administration of the guardianship; and

(3) shall give bond in the same manner and in the same amount provided in this chapter for the issuance of original letters of guardianship.

Added by Acts 1993, 73rd Leg., ch. 957, § 1, eff. Sept. 1, 1993.

§ 726. Bonds Not Void on First Recovery

The bond of a guardian is not void on the first recovery, but the bond may be sued on and prosecuted from time to time until the whole amount of the bond is recovered.
Added by Acts 1993, 73rd Leg., ch. 957, § 1, eff. Sept. 1, 1993.

Part 4. Administration of Guardianship

Subpart A. Inventory, Appraisement, and List of Claims

§ 727. Appointment of Appraisers

After letters of guardianship of the estate have been granted and on the application of any interested person, or if the court deems it necessary, the court shall appoint at least one but not more than three disinterested persons who are citizens of the county in which letters were granted to appraise the property of the ward. If the court appoints an appraiser under this section and part of the estate is located in a county other than the county in which letters were granted, the court may appoint at least one but not more than three disinterested persons who are citizens of the county in which the part of the estate is located to appraise the property of the estate located in the county if the court considers it necessary to appoint an appraiser.

Added by Acts 1993, 73rd Leg., ch. 957, § 1, eff. Sept. 1, 1993.

§ 728. Failure of Appraiser to Serve

If an appraiser appointed under Section 727 of this code fails or refuses to act, the court shall remove the appraiser and appoint one or more appraisers.

Added by Acts 1993, 73rd Leg., ch. 957, § 1, eff. Sept. 1, 1993.

§ 729. Inventory and Appraisement

(a) Not later than the 30th day after the date the guardian of the estate qualifies as guardian, unless a longer time is granted by the court, the guardian of the estate shall file with the clerk of the court a verified, full and detailed inventory, in one written instrument, of all the property of the ward that has come into the guardian's possession or knowledge. The inventory filed by the guardian under this section must include:

(1) all real property of the ward that is located in this state; and

(2) all personal property of the ward wherever located.

(b) The guardian shall set out in the inventory the guardian's appraisement of the fair market value of each item of the property on the date of the grant of letters of guardianship. If the court appoints an appraiser of the estate, the guardian shall determine the fair market value of each item of the inventory with the assistance of the appraiser and shall set out in the inventory the appraisement made by the appraiser.

(c) An inventory made under this section must specify what portion of the property is separate property and what portion is community property. If any property is owned in common with other persons, the interest owned by the ward shall be shown in the inventory, together with the names and relationship, if known, of co-owners.

(d) The inventory, when approved by the court and duly filed with the clerk of court, is for purposes of this chapter the inventory and appraisement of the estate referred to in this chapter.

(e) The court for good cause shown may require the filing of the inventory and appraisement at a time not later than the 90th day after the date of qualification of the guardian.

Added by Acts 1993, 73rd Leg., ch. 957, § 1, eff. Sept. 1, 1993. Amended by Acts 2003, 78th Leg., ch. 549, § 13, eff. Sept. 1, 2003.

§ 730. List of Claims

The guardian shall make and attach to an inventory under Section 729 of this code a full and complete list of all claims due or owing to the ward that must state:

(1) the name of each person indebted to the ward and the address of the person if known;

(2) the nature of the debt, whether it is a note, bill, bond, or other written obligation or whether it is an account or verbal contract;

(3) the date of the indebtedness and the date when the debt is or was due;

(4) the amount of each claim, the rate of interest on each claim, and time for which the claim bears interest; and

(5) what portion of the claim is held in common with others, including the names and the relationships of other part owners and the interest of the estate in the claim.

Added by Acts 1993, 73rd Leg., ch. 957, § 1, eff. Sept. 1, 1993.

§ 731. Affidavit Attached

The guardian of the estate shall attach to the inventory and list of claims the guardian's affidavit subscribed and sworn to before an officer in the county authorized by law to administer oaths that the inventory and list of claims are a true and complete statement of the property and claims of the estate that have come to the guardian's knowledge.

Added by Acts 1993, 73rd Leg., ch. 957, § 1, eff. Sept. 1, 1993.

§ 732. Appraiser Fees

An appraiser appointed by the court is entitled to receive a reasonable fee for the performance of the appraiser's duties as an appraiser that are to be paid out of the estate.

Added by Acts 1993, 73rd Leg., ch. 957, § 1, eff. Sept. 1, 1993.

§ 733. Court Action

(a) On return of the inventory, appraisement, and list of claims, the judge shall examine and approve or disapprove the inventory, appraisement, or list of claims as follows:

(1) if the judge approves the inventory, appraisement, and list of claims, the judge shall issue an order to that effect; and

(2) if the judge does not approve the inventory, appraisement, or list of claims, the judge shall enter an order to that effect.

(b) The court order shall require the return of another inventory, appraisement, and list of claims, or whichever of them is disapproved, within a time specified in the order but not later than 20 days after the date of the order. The judge may appoint new appraisers if the judge deems it necessary.
Added by Acts 1993, 73rd Leg., ch. 957, § 1, eff. Sept. 1, 1993.

§ 734. Discovery of Additional Property

The guardian of the estate shall promptly file with the clerk of court a verified, full, and detailed supplemental inventory and appraisement if property or claims that are not included in the inventory come to the guardian's possession or knowledge after the guardian files the inventory and appraisement required under Section 729 of this code.
Added by Acts 1993, 73rd Leg., ch. 957, § 1, eff. Sept. 1, 1993.

§ 735. Additional Inventory or List of Claims

(a) On the written complaint of an interested person that property or claims of the estate have not been included in the inventory and list of claims filed by the guardian, the guardian of an estate shall be cited to appear before the court in which the cause is pending and show cause why the guardian should not be required to make and return an additional inventory or list of claims, or both.

(b) After hearing a complaint filed under this section and being satisfied of the truth of the complaint, the court shall enter an order requiring the additional inventory or list of claims, or both, to be made and returned in like manner as the original inventory, not later than 20 days after the date of the order, as may be set by the court. The additional inventory or list of claims must include only property or claims that were not inventoried or listed by the guardian.
Added by Acts 1993, 73rd Leg., ch. 957, § 1, eff. Sept. 1, 1993.

§ 736. Correction When Inventory, Appraisement, or List of Claims Erroneous or Unjust

A person interested in an estate who deems an inventory, appraisement, or list of claims returned by the guardian erroneous or unjust in any particular form may file a written complaint that sets forth and points out the alleged erroneous or unjust items and cause the guardian to be cited to appear before the court and show cause why the errors should not be corrected. On the hearing of a complaint filed under this section, if the court is satisfied from the evidence that the inventory, appraisement, or list of claims is erroneous or unjust in any particular form as alleged in the complaint, the court shall enter an order that specifies the erroneous or unjust items and the corrections to be made and that appoints an appraiser to make a new appraisement correcting the erroneous or unjust items and requires the return of the new appraisement not later than the 20th day after the date of the order. The court may also, on its own motion or on motion of the guardian of the estate, have a new appraisal made for the purposes described by this section.
Added by Acts 1993, 73rd Leg., ch. 957, § 1, eff. Sept. 1, 1993.

§ 737. Effect of Reappraisement

When a reappraisement is made, returned, and approved by the court, the reappraisement stands in place of the original appraisement. Not more than one reappraisement shall be made, but any person interested in the estate may object to the reappraisement before or after the reappraisement is approved. If the court finds that the reappraisement is erroneous or unjust, the court shall appraise the property on the basis of the evidence before the court.
Added by Acts 1993, 73rd Leg., ch. 957, § 1, eff. Sept. 1, 1993.

§ 738. Failure of Joint Guardians to Return an Inventory, Appraisement, and List of Claims

If there is more than one qualified guardian of the estate, one or more of the guardians, on the neglect of the other guardians, may make and return an inventory and appraisement and list of claims. The guardian so neglecting may not thereafter interfere with the estate or have any power over the estate. The guardian that returns an inventory, appraisement, and list of claims has the whole administration, unless, not later than the 60th day after the date of return, each of the delinquent guardians assigns to the court in writing and under oath a reasonable excuse that the court may deem satisfactory. If no excuse is filed or if the excuse filed by a delinquent guardian is insufficient, the court shall enter an order removing the delinquent guardian and revoking the guardian's letters.
Added by Acts 1993, 73rd Leg., ch. 957, § 1, eff. Sept. 1, 1993.

§ 739. Use of Inventories, Appraisements, and Lists of Claims as Evidence

All inventories, appraisements, and lists of claims that have been taken, returned, and approved in accordance with the law, or the record of an inventory, appraisement, or list of claims, or copies of either the originals or the record, duly certified under the seal of the county court affixed by the clerk, may be given in evidence in any of the courts of this state in any suit by or against the guardian of the estate, but may not be conclusive for or against the guardian of the estate if it is shown that any property or claims of the estate are not shown in the inventory, appraisement, or list of claims or that the value of the property or claims of the estate actually was in excess of the value shown in the appraisement and list of claims.

Added by Acts 1993, 73rd Leg., ch. 957, § 1, eff. Sept. 1, 1993.

Subpart B. Annual Accounts, Reports, and Other Exhibits

§ 741. Annual Accounts Required

(a) Not later than the 60th day after the expiration of 12 months from the date of qualification, unless the court extends that time period, the guardian of the estate of a ward shall return to the court an exhibit in writing under oath setting forth a list of all claims against the estate that were presented to the guardian within the period covered by the account and specifying which claims have been allowed, paid, or rejected by the guardian and the date when any claim was rejected and which claims have been the subject of a lawsuit and the status of the lawsuit, and showing:

(1) all property that has come to the guardian's knowledge or into the guardian's possession that has not been previously listed or inventoried as property of the ward;

(2) any changes in the property of the ward that have not been previously reported;

(3) a complete account of receipts and disbursements for the period covered by the account, and the source and nature of the receipts and disbursements, with receipts of principal and income shown separately;

(4) a complete, accurate, and detailed description of the property being administered, the condition of the property, and the use being made of the property and, if rented, the terms of the rental and the price for which the property is being rented;

(5) the cash balance on hand and the name and location of the depository where the cash balance is kept and any other sums of cash in savings accounts or other form, deposited subject to court order, and the name and location of the depository of the cash; and

(6) a detailed description of personal property of the estate, that, with respect to bonds, notes, and other securities, includes the names of obligor and obligee, or if payable to bearer, so state; the date of issue and maturity; the rate of interest; serial or other identifying numbers; in what manner the property is secured; and other data necessary to identify the same fully, and how and where held for safekeeping.

(b) A guardian of the estate shall file annual accounts conforming to the essential requirements of those in Subsection (a) of this section as to changes in the assets of the estate after rendition of the former account so that the true condition of the estate, with respect to money or securities or other property, can be ascertained by the court or by any interested person, by adding to the balances forward the receipts, and then subtracting the disbursements. The description of property sufficiently described in an inventory or previous account may be by reference to the property.

(c) The following shall be annexed to all annual accounts of guardians of estates:

(1) proper vouchers for each item of credit claimed in the account, or, in the absence of a voucher, the item must be supported by evidence satisfactory to the court, and original vouchers may, on application, be returned to the guardian after approval of the guardian's account;

(2) an official letter from the bank or other depository in which the money on hand of the estate or ward is deposited that shows the amounts in general or special deposits; and

(3) proof of the existence and possession of securities owned by the estate, or shown by the accounting, and other assets held by a depository subject to court order, the proof by one of the following means:

(A) an official letter from the bank or other depository that holds the securities or other assets for safekeeping; provided, that if the depository is the representative, the official letter shall be signed by a representative of the depository other than the depository that verifies the account;

(B) a certificate of an authorized representative of the corporation that is the surety on the representative's bonds;

(C) a certificate of the clerk or a deputy clerk of a court of record in this state; or

(D) an affidavit of any other reputable person designated by the court on request of the guardian or other interested party.

(d) A certificate or affidavit under this section shall be to the effect that the affiant has examined the assets exhibited to the affiant by the guardian as assets of the estate in which the accounting is made, shall describe the assets by reference to the account or otherwise sufficiently to identify those assets exhibited, and shall state the time when and the place where the assets were exhibited. Instead of using a certificate or an affidavit, the representative may exhibit the securities to the judge of the court who shall endorse on the account, or include in the judge's order with respect to the account, a statement that the securities shown to the judge as on hand were in fact exhibited to the judge and that those securities exhibited to the judge were the same as those shown in the account, or note any variance. If the securities are exhibited at any place other than where deposited for safekeeping, it shall be at the expense and risk of the representative. The judge may require additional evidence as to the existence and custody of the securities and other personal property as in the judge's discretion the judge considers proper, and the judge may require the representative to exhibit the securities to the judge, or any person designated by the judge, at any time at the place where the securities are held for safekeeping.

(e) The guardian of the estate filing the account shall attach to the account the guardian's affidavit that:

(1) the account contains a correct and complete statement of the matters to which the account relates;

(2) the guardian has paid the bond premium for the next accounting period;

(3) the guardian has filed all tax returns of the ward due during the accounting period; and

(4) the guardian has paid all taxes the ward owed during the accounting period, showing:

(A) the amount of the taxes;

(B) the date the guardian paid the taxes; and

(C) the name of the governmental entity to which the guardian paid the taxes.

(f) If the guardian, on the ward's behalf, has not filed a tax return or paid taxes that are due on the filing of the account under this section, the guardian of the estate filing the account shall attach to the account a description of the taxes and the reasons for the guardian's failure to file the return or pay the taxes.

(g) If the estate produces negligible or fixed income, the court has the power to waive the filing of annual accounts, and the court may permit the guardian to receive all income and apply it to the support, maintenance, and education of the ward and account to the court for income and corpus of the estate when the estate must be closed.

Added by Acts 1993, 73rd Leg., ch. 957, § 1, eff. Sept. 1, 1993.

§ 742. Action on Annual Accounts

(a) The rules in this section govern the handling of annual accounts.

(b) Annual accounts shall be filed with the county clerk, and the filing of the accounts shall be noted on the judge's docket.

(c) Before being considered by the judge, the account must remain on file for 10 days.

(d) After the expiration of 10 days after the filing of an annual account, the judge shall consider the annual account, and may continue the hearing on the account until the judge is fully advised as to all items of the account.

(e) An accounting may not be approved unless possession of cash, listed securities, or other assets held in safekeeping or on deposit under court order has been proved as required by law.

(f) If an account is found to be incorrect, it shall be corrected. When corrected to the satisfaction of the court, the account shall be approved by a court order, and the court shall act with respect to unpaid claims, as follows:

(1) if it appears from the exhibit, or from other evidence, that the estate is wholly solvent, and that the guardian has sufficient funds for the payment of every claim against the estate, the court shall order immediate payment made of all claims allowed and approved or established by judgment; and

(2) if it appears from the account, or from other evidence, that the funds on hand are not sufficient for the payment of all the claims, or if the estate is insolvent and the guardian has any funds on hand, the court shall order the funds to be applied to the payment of all claims having a preference in the order of their priority if any claim is still unpaid, and then to the payment pro rata of the other claims allowed and approved or established by final judgment, taking into consideration also the claims that were presented not later than 12 months after the date of the granting of letters of guardianship and those claims that are in suit or on which suit may yet be instituted.

Added by Acts 1993, 73rd Leg., ch. 957, § 1, eff. Sept. 1, 1993. Subsec. (f) amended by Acts 1995, 74th Leg., ch. 1039, § 43, eff. Sept. 1, 1995.

§ 743. Reports of Guardians of the Person

(a) The guardian of the person of a ward shall return to the court a sworn, written report showing each item of receipts and disbursements for the support and maintenance of the ward, the education of the ward when necessary, and support and maintenance of the ward's dependents, when authorized by order of court.

(b) The guardian of the person, whether or not there is a separate guardian of the estate, shall submit to the court an annual report by sworn affidavit that contains the following information:

(1) the guardian's current name, address, and phone number;

(2) the ward's current:

(A) name, address, and phone number; and

(B) age and date of birth;

(3) the type of home in which the ward resides, described as the ward's own; a nursing, guardian's, foster, or boarding home; a relative's home, and the ward's relationship to the relative; a hospital or medical facility; or other type of residence;

(4) the length of time the ward has resided in the present home and, if there has been a change in the ward's residence in the past year, the reason for the change;

(5) the date the guardian most recently saw the ward, and how frequently the guardian has seen the ward in the past year;

(6) a statement indicating whether or not the guardian has possession or control of the ward's estate;

(7) the following statements concerning the ward's health during the past year:

(A) whether the ward's mental health has improved, deteriorated, or remained unchanged, and a description if there has been a change; and

(B) whether the ward's physical health has improved, deteriorated, or remained unchanged, and a description if there has been a change;

(8) a statement concerning whether or not the ward has regular medical care, and the ward's treatment or evaluation by any of the following persons during the last year, including the name of that person, and the treatment involved:

(A) a physician;

(B) a psychiatrist, psychologist, or other mental health care provider;

(C) a dentist;

(D) a social or other caseworker; or

(E) another individual who provided treatment;

(9) a description of the ward's activities during the past year, including recreational, educational, social, and occupational activities, or if no activities are available or if the ward is unable or has refused to participate in them, a statement to that effect;

(10) the guardian's evaluation of the ward's living arrangements as excellent, average, or below average, including an explanation if the conditions are below average;

(11) the guardian's evaluation of whether the ward is content or unhappy with the ward's living arrangements;

(12) the guardian's evaluation of unmet needs of the ward;

(13) a statement of whether or not the guardian's power should be increased, decreased, or unaltered, including an explanation if a change is recommended;

(14) a statement that the guardian has paid the bond premium for the next reporting period; and

(15) any additional information the guardian desires to share with the court regarding the ward, including whether the guardian has filed for emergency detention of the ward under Subchapter A, Chapter 573, Health and Safety Code, and if applicable, the number of times the guardian has filed and the dates of the applications.

(15) any additional information the guardian desires to share with the court regarding the ward, including whether the guardian has filed for emergency detention of the ward under Subchapter A, Chapter 573, Health and Safety Code, and if applicable, the number of times the guardian has filed and the dates of the applications.

(c) If the ward is deceased, the guardian shall provide the court with the date and place of death, if known, in lieu of the information about the ward otherwise required to be provided in the annual report.

(d) Unless the judge is satisfied that the facts stated are true, he shall issue orders as are necessary for the best interests of the ward.

(e) If the judge is satisfied that the facts stated in the report are true, the court shall approve the report.

(f) The court on the court's own motion may waive the costs and fees related to the filing of a report approved under Subsection (e) of this section.

(g) Once each year for the duration of the guardianship, a guardian of the person shall file the report that contains the information required by Subsections (a) and (b) of this section. Except as provided by Subsection (h) of this section, the report must cover a 12-month reporting period that begins on the date the guardian qualifies to serve.

(h) The court may change a reporting period for purposes of this section but may not extend a reporting period so that it covers more than 12 months.

(i) Each report is due not later than the 60th day after the date on which the reporting period ends.

(j) A guardian of the person may complete and file the report required under this section without the assistance of an attorney.

Added by Acts 1993, 73rd Leg., ch. 957, § 1, eff. Sept. 1, 1993. Subsec. (a) amended by Acts 1995, 74th Leg., ch. 1039, § 44, eff. Sept. 1, 1995; Subsecs. (e) to (i) added by Acts 1995, 74th Leg., ch. 1039, § 45, eff. Sept. 1, 1995; Subsec. (b) amended by Acts 1997, 75th Leg., ch. 1403, § 3, eff. Sept. 1, 1997; Subsec. (j) added by Acts 1999, 76th Leg., ch. 905, § 5, eff. Sept. 1, 1999. Amended by Acts 2003, 78th Leg., ch. 692, § 1, eff. Sept. 1, 2003.

§ 744. Penalty for Failure to File Accountings, Exhibits, or Reports

If a guardian fails to file any accounting, exhibit, report of the guardian of the person, or other report required by this chapter, any person interested in the estate may, on written complaint filed with the clerk of the court, or the court on its own motion, may cause the guardian to be cited to appear and show cause why the guardian should not file the account, exhibit, or report; and, on hearing, the court may order the guardian to file the account, exhibit, or report, and, unless good cause is shown for the failure to file the account, exhibit, or report, the court may fine the guardian an amount not to exceed $1,000, revoke the letters of the guardian, or fine the guardian an amount not to exceed $1,000 and revoke the letters of the guardian.

Added by Acts 1993, 73rd Leg., ch. 957, § 1, eff. Sept. 1, 1993. Amended by Acts 1995, 74th Leg., ch. 1039, § 46, eff. Sept. 1, 1995.

Subpart C. Final Settlement, Accounting, and Discharge

§ 745. Settling Guardianships of the Estate

(a) A guardianship of the estate of a ward shall be settled when:

(1) a minor ward dies or becomes an adult by becoming 18 years of age, or by removal of disabilities of minority according to the law of this state, or by marriage;

(2) an incapacitated ward dies, or is decreed as provided by law to have been restored to full legal capacity;

(3) the spouse of a married ward has qualified as survivor in community and the ward owns no separate property;

(4) the estate of a ward becomes exhausted;

(5) the foreseeable income accruing to a ward or to his estate is so negligible that maintaining the guardianship in force would be burdensome;

(6) all of the assets of the estate have been placed in a management trust under Subpart N, Part 4, of this code and the court determines that a guardianship for the ward is no longer necessary; or

(7) the court determines for any other reason that a guardianship for the ward is no longer necessary.

(b) In a case arising under Subsection (a)(5) of this section, the court may authorize the income to be paid to a parent, or other person who has acted as guardian of the ward, to assist in the maintenance of the ward and without liability to account to the court for the income.

(c) When the estate of a minor ward consists only of cash or cash equivalents in an amount of $100,000 or less, the guardianship of the estate may be terminated and the assets paid to the county clerk of the county in which the guardianship proceeding is pending, and the clerk shall manage the funds as provided by Section 887 of this code.

(d) In the settlement of a guardianship, the court may appoint an attorney ad litem to represent the interests of the ward, and may allow the attorney reasonable compensation for services provided by the attorney out of the ward's estate.

Added by Acts 1993, 73rd Leg., ch. 957, § 1, eff. Sept. 1, 1993. Subsec. (c) amended by Acts 1995, 74th Leg., ch. 1039, § 47, eff. Sept. 1, 1995; Sec. heading amended by Acts 2001, 77th Leg., ch. 484, § 3, eff. Sept. 1, 2001; Subsec. (a) amended by Acts 2001, 77th Leg., ch. 484, § 4, eff. Sept. 1, 2001; Subsec. (c) amended by Acts 2001, 77th Leg., ch. 127, § 1, eff. Sept. 1, 2001; Subsec. (c) amended by Acts 2001, 77th Leg., ch. 217, § 13, eff. Sept. 1, 2001; Subsec. (c) amended by Acts 2001, 77th Leg., ch. 1174, § 5, eff. Sept. 1, 2001; Subsec. (d) amended by Acts 2001, 77th Leg., ch. 484, § 4, eff. Sept. 1, 2001. Amended by Acts 2003, 78th Leg., ch. 549, § 14, eff. Sept. 1, 2003.

§ 746. Payment of Funeral Expenses and Other Debts on Death of Ward

Before the guardianship of a person or estate of a ward is closed on the death of a ward, the guardian, subject to the approval of the court, may make all funeral arrangements, pay for the funeral expenses out of the estate of the deceased ward, and pay all other debts out of the estate. If a personal represe§ntative of the estate of a deceased ward is appointed, the court shall on the written complaint of the personal representative cause the guardian to be cited to appear and present a final account as provided in Section 749 of this code.

Added by Acts 1993, 73rd Leg., ch. 957, § 1, eff. Sept. 1, 1993. Amended by Acts 2001, 77th Leg., ch. 484, § 5, eff. Sept. 1, 2001.

§ 747. Termination of Guardianship of the Person

(a) When the guardianship of an incapacitated person is required to be settled as provided by Section 745 of this code, the guardian of the person shall deliver all property of the ward in the possession or control of the guardian to the emancipated ward or other person entitled to the property. If the ward is deceased, the guardian shall deliver the property to the personal representative of the deceased ward's estate or other person entitled to the property.

(b) If there is no property of the ward in the possession or control of the guardian of the person, the guardian shall, not later than the 60th day after the date on which the guardianship is required to be settled, file with the court a sworn affidavit that states the reason the guardianship was terminated and to whom the property of the ward in the guardian's possession was delivered. The judge may issue orders as necessary for the best interests of the ward or of the estate of a deceased ward. This section does not discharge a guardian of the person from liability for breach of the guardian's fiduciary duties.

Added by Acts 1993, 73rd Leg., ch. 957, § 1, eff. Sept. 1, 1993. Subsec. (a) amended by Acts 2001, 77th Leg., ch. 484, § 6, eff. Sept. 1, 2001. Amended by Acts 2003, 78th Leg., ch. 586, § 1, eff. Sept. 1, 2003.

§ 748. Payment by Guardian of Taxes or Expenses

Notwithstanding any other provision of this chapter, a probate court in which proceedings to declare heirship are maintained may order the payment by the guardian of any and all taxes or expenses of administering the estate and may order the sale of properties in the ward's estate, when necessary, for the purpose of paying the taxes or expenses of administering the estate or for the purpose of distributing the estate among the heirs.

Added by Acts 1993, 73rd Leg., ch. 957, § 1, eff. Sept. 1, 1993.

§ 749. Account for Final Settlement of Estates of Wards

When a guardianship of the estate is required to be settled, the guardian shall present to the court the guardian's verified account for final settlement. In the account it shall be sufficient to refer to the inventory without describing each item of property in detail and to refer to and adopt any and all guardianship proceedings that concern sales, renting or hiring, leasing for mineral development, or any other transaction on behalf of the guardianship estate, including an exhibit, account, or voucher previously filed and approved, without restating the particular items. Each final account shall be accompanied by proper vouchers in support of each item not already accounted for and shall show, either by reference to any proceedings authorized above or by statement of the facts:

(1) the property, rents, revenues, and profits received by the guardian, and belonging to the ward, during the term of the guardianship;

(2) the disposition made of the property, rents, revenues, and profits;

(3) the expenses and debts against the estate that remain unpaid, if any;

(4) the property of the estate that remains in the hands of the guardian, if any;

(5) that the guardian has paid all required bond premiums;

(6) the tax returns the guardian has filed during the guardianship;

(7) the amount of taxes the ward owed during the guardianship that the guardian has paid;

(8) a complete account of the taxes the guardian has paid during the guardianship, including the amount of the taxes, the date the guardian paid the taxes, and the name of the governmental entity to which the guardian paid the taxes;

(9) a description of all current delinquencies in the filing of tax returns and the payment of taxes and a reason for each delinquency; and

(10) other facts as appear necessary to a full and definite understanding of the exact condition of the guardianship.

Added by Acts 1993, 73rd Leg., ch. 957, § 1, eff. Sept. 1, 1993. Amended by Acts 1997, 75th Leg., ch. 1403, § 4, eff. Sept. 1, 1997; Acts 2001, 77th Leg., ch. 484, § 7, eff. Sept. 1, 2001.

§ 750. Procedure in Case of Neglect or Failure to File Final Account or Report

(a) If a guardian charged with the duty of filing a final account or report fails or neglects so to do at the proper time, the court may, on the court's own motion, or on the written complaint of the emancipated ward or anyone interested in the ward or the ward's estate, shall cause the guardian to be cited to appear and present the account or report within the time specified in the citation.

(b) If a written complaint has not been filed by anyone interested in the guardianship of a person or estate of a minor or deceased ward, the court may, on or after the third anniversary after the date of the death of the ward or after the date the minor reaches the age of majority, remove the estate from the court's active docket without a final accounting and without appointing a successor personal representative.

(c) If a complaint has not been filed by anyone interested in the estate of a ward whose whereabouts are unknown to the court, the court may, on or after the fourth anniversary after the ward's whereabouts became unknown to the court, remove the estate from the court's active docket without a final accounting and without appointing a successor personal representative.

Added by Acts 1993, 73rd Leg., ch. 957, § 1, eff. Sept. 1, 1993.

§ 751. Citation on Presentation of Account for Final Settlement

(a) On the filing of an account for final settlement by a guardian of the estate of a ward, citation must contain a statement that the final account has been filed, the time and place when it will be considered by the court, and a statement requiring the person cited to appear and contest the final account if the person determines it is proper. The county clerk shall issue the citation to the following persons and in the manner provided by this section.

(b) If a ward is a living resident of this state who is 14 years of age or older, and the ward's residence is known, the ward shall be cited by personal service, unless the ward, in person or by attorney, by writing filed with the clerk, waives the issuance and personal service of citation.

(c) If one who has been a ward is deceased, the ward's executor or administrator, if one has been appointed, shall be personally served, but no service is required if the executor or administrator is the same person as the guardian.

(d) If a ward's residence is unknown, or if the ward is a nonresident of this state, or if the ward is deceased and no representative of the ward's estate has been appointed and qualified in this state, the citation to the ward or to the ward's estate shall be by publication, unless the court by written order directs citation by posting.

(e) If the court deems further additional notice necessary, it shall require the additional notice by written order. In its discretion, the court may allow the waiver of notice of an account for final settlement in a guardianship proceeding.

Added by Acts 1993, 73rd Leg., ch. 957, § 1, eff. Sept. 1, 1993.

§ 752. Court Action; Closing of Guardianship of Ward's Estate

(a) On being satisfied that citation has been duly served on all persons interested in the estate, the court shall examine the account for final settlement and the vouchers accompanying the account. After hearing all exceptions or objections to the account and evidence in support of or against the account, the court shall audit and settle the same, and restate it if that is necessary.

(b) On final settlement of an estate, if there is any part of the estate remaining in the hands of the guardian, the court shall order that it be delivered, in case of a ward, to the ward, or in the case of a deceased ward, to the personal representative of the deceased ward's estate if one has been appointed, or to any other person legally entitled to the estate.

(c) If on final settlement of an estate there is no part of the estate remaining in the hands of the guardian, the court shall discharge the guardian from the guardian's trust and order the estate closed.

(d) When the guardian of an estate has fully administered the estate in accordance with this chapter and the orders of the court and the guardian's final account has been approved, and the guardian has delivered all of the estate remaining in the guardian's hands to any person entitled to receive the estate, the court shall enter an order discharging the guardian from the guardian's trust, and declaring the estate closed.

Added by Acts 1993, 73rd Leg., ch. 957, § 1, eff. Sept. 1, 1993. Sec. heading amended by Acts 2001, 77th Leg., ch. 484, § 8, eff. Sept. 1, 2001.

§ 753. Money Becoming Due Pending Final Discharge

Money or any other thing of value falling due to the estate or ward while the account for final settlement is pending, other than money or any other thing of value

held under Section 703(c) of this code, until the order of final discharge of the guardian is entered in the minutes of the court, may be paid, delivered, or tendered to the emancipated ward, the guardian, or the personal representative of the deceased ward's estate, who shall issue a receipt for the money or other thing of value, and the obligor or payor shall be discharged of the obligation for all purposes.
Added by Acts 1993, 73rd Leg., ch. 957, § 1, eff. Sept. 1, 1993.

§ 754. Inheritance Taxes Must be Paid

If the guardian has been ordered to make payment of inheritance taxes under this code, an estate of a deceased ward may not be closed unless the final account shows and the court finds that all inheritance taxes due and owing to this state with respect to all interests and properties passing through the hands of the guardian have been paid.
Added by Acts 1993, 73rd Leg., ch. 957, § 1, eff. Sept. 1, 1993.

§ 755. Appointment of Attorney to Represent Ward

When the ward is dead and there is no executor or administrator of the ward's estate, or when the ward is a nonresident, or the ward's residence is unknown, the court may appoint an attorney ad litem to represent the interest of the ward in the final settlement with the guardian, and shall allow the attorney reasonable compensation out of the ward's estate for any services provided by the attorney.
Added by Acts 1993, 73rd Leg., ch. 957, § 1, eff. Sept. 1, 1993.

§ 756. Offsets, Credits, and Bad Debts

In the settlement of any of the accounts of the guardian of an estate, all debts due the estate that the court is satisfied could not have been collected by due diligence, and that have not been collected, shall be excluded from the computation.
Added by Acts 1993, 73rd Leg., ch. 957, § 1, eff. Sept. 1, 1993.

§ 757. Accounting for Labor or Services of a Ward

The guardian of a ward shall account for the reasonable value of the labor or services of the ward of the guardian, or the proceeds of the labor or services, if the labor or services have been rendered by the ward, but the guardian is entitled to reasonable credits for the board, clothing, and maintenance of the ward.
Added by Acts 1993, 73rd Leg., ch. 957, § 1, eff. Sept. 1, 1993.

§ 758. Procedure if Representative Fails to Deliver Estate

If a guardian, on final settlement or termination of the guardianship of the estate, neglects to deliver to the person entitled when legally demanded any portion of the estate or any funds or money in the hands of the guardian ordered to be delivered, a person entitled to the estate, funds, or money may file with the clerk of the court a written complaint alleging the fact of the guardian's neglect, the date of the person's demand, and other relevant facts. After the person files a complaint under this section, the clerk shall issue a citation to be served personally on the guardian, appraising the guardian of the complaint and citing the guardian to appear before the court and answer, if the guardian desires, at the time designated in the citation. If at the hearing the court finds that the citation was duly served and returned and that the guardian is guilty of the neglect charged, the court shall enter an order to that effect, and the guardian shall be liable to the person who filed the complaint in damages at the rate of 10 percent of the amount or appraised value of the money or estate withheld, per month, for each month or fraction of a month that the estate or money of a guardianship of the estate, or on termination of guardianship of the person, or funds is or has been withheld by the guardian after the date of demand, which damages may be recovered in any court of competent jurisdiction.
Added by Acts 1993, 73rd Leg., ch. 957, § 1, eff. Sept. 1, 1993.

Subpart D. Revocation of Letters, Death, Resignation, and Removal

§ 759. Appointment of Successor Guardian

(a) In case of the death of the guardian of the person or of the estate of a ward, a personal representative of the deceased guardian shall account for, pay, and deliver to a person legally entitled to receive the property, all the property belonging to the guardianship that is entrusted to the care of the representative, at the time and in the manner as the court orders. On a finding that a necessity for the immediate appointment of a successor guardian exists, the court may appoint a successor guardian without citation or notice.

(b) If letters have been granted to a person, and another person whose right to be appointed successor guardian is prior and who has not waived the right and is qualified, applies for letters, the letters previously granted shall be revoked and other letters shall be granted to the applicant.

(c) If a person named in a will as guardian is not an adult when the will is probated and letters in any capacity have been granted to another person, the nominated guardian, on proof that the nominated guardian has become an adult and is not otherwise disqualified from serving as a guardian, is entitled to have the former letters revoked and appropriate letters granted to the nominated guardian. If the will names two or more persons as guardian, any one or more of whom are minors when the will is probated and letters have been issued to the persons who are adults, a minor, on becoming an adult, if not otherwise disqualified, is permitted to qualify and receive letters.

(d) If a person named in a will as guardian was ill or absent from the state when the testator died, or when the will was proved, and for that reason could not present the will for probate not later than the 30th day after the testator's death, or accept and qualify as guardian not later than the 20th day after the date the will was probated, the person may accept and qualify as guardian not later than the 60th day after the person's return or recovery from illness, on proof to the court that the person was absent or ill. If the letters have been issued to another person, the letters shall be revoked.

(e) If it is discovered after letters of guardianship have been issued that the deceased person left a lawful will, the letters shall be revoked and proper letters of guardianship issued to a person entitled to receive the letters.

(f) Except when otherwise expressly provided in this chapter, letters may not be revoked and other letters granted except on application, and after personal service of citation on the person, if living, whose letters are sought to be revoked, that the person appear and show cause why the application should not be granted.

(g) Money or any other thing of value falling due to a ward while the office of the guardian is vacant may be paid, delivered, or tendered to the clerk of the court for credit of the ward, and the debtor, obligor, or payor shall be discharged of the obligation for all purposes to the extent and purpose of the payment or tender. If the clerk accepts the payment or tender, the clerk shall issue a proper receipt for the payment or tender.

(h) The court may appoint as successor guardian a spouse, parent, or child of a proposed ward who has been disqualified from serving as guardian because of a litigation conflict under Section 681(4) of this code on removal of the conflict that caused the initial disqualification if the spouse, parent, or child is otherwise qualified to serve as a guardian.

Added by Acts 1993, 73rd Leg., ch. 957, § 1, eff. Sept. 1, 1993. Subsec. (a) amended by Acts 1995, 74th Leg., ch. 1039, § 48, eff. Sept. 1, 1995.

§ 760. Resignation

(a) A guardian of the estate who wishes to resign the guardian's trust shall file with the clerk a written application to the court to that effect, accompanied by a full and complete exhibit and final account, duly verified, showing the true condition of the guardianship estate entrusted to the guardian's care. A guardian of the person who wishes to resign the guardian's trust shall file with the clerk a written application to the court to that effect, accompanied by a report setting forth the information required in the annual report required under this chapter, duly verified, showing the condition of the ward entrusted to the guardian's care.

(b) If the necessity exists, the court may immediately accept a resignation and appoint a successor but may not discharge the person resigning as guardian of the estate or release the person or the sureties on the person's bond until final order or judgment is rendered on the final account of the guardian.

(c) On the filing of an application to resign, supported by an exhibit and final account, the clerk shall call the application to the attention of the judge, who shall set a date for a hearing on the matter. The clerk shall then issue a citation to all interested persons, showing that proper application has been filed and the time and place set for hearing, at which time the interested persons may appear and contest the exhibit and account or report. The citation shall be posted, unless the court directs that it be published.

(d) At the time set for hearing, unless it has been continued by the court, if the court finds that citation has been duly issued and served, the court shall proceed to examine the exhibit and account or report and hear all evidence for and against the exhibit, account, or report and shall, if necessary, restate, and audit and settle the exhibit, account, or report. If the court is satisfied that the matters entrusted to the applicant have been handled and accounted for in accordance with the law, the court shall enter an order of approval and require that the estate remaining in the possession of the applicant, if any, be delivered to the person entitled by law to receive it. A guardian of the person is required to comply with all orders of the court concerning the ward of the guardian.

(e) A resigning guardian may not be discharged until the application has been heard, the exhibit and account or report examined, settled, and approved, and the guardian has satisfied the court that the guardian has delivered the estate, if there is any part of the estate remaining in the possession of the guardian, or has complied with all orders of the court with relation to the guardian's trust.

(f) When the resigning guardian has complied in all respects with the orders of the court, an order shall be made accepting the resignation, discharging the applicant, and, if the applicant is under bond, the sureties of the guardian.

(g) The court at any time may order a resigning guardian who has all or part of the estate of a ward to deliver all or part of the ward's estate to a person who has been appointed and has qualified as successor guardian.

Added by Acts 1993, 73rd Leg., ch. 957, § 1, eff. Sept. 1, 1993. Subsec. (g) added by Acts 1995, 74th Leg., ch. 1039, § 49, eff. Sept. 1, 1995.

§ 760A. Change of Resident Agent

(a) A guardian may change its resident agent to accept service of process in a guardianship proceeding or other matter relating to the guardianship by filing a statement of the change entitled "Designation of Successor Resident Agent" with the court in which the guardianship proceeding is pending. The statement must contain the names and addresses of the:

(1) guardian;

(2) resident agent; and

(3) successor resident agent.

(b) The designation of a successor resident agent made in a statement filed under this section takes effect on the date on which the statement is filed with the court.

Added by Acts 2001, 77th Leg., ch. 217, § 14, eff. Sept. 1, 2001.

§ 760B. Resignation of Resident Agent

(a) A resident agent of a guardian may resign as the resident agent by giving notice to the guardian and filing with the court in which the guardianship proceeding is pending a statement entitled "Resignation of Resident Agent" that:

(1) contains the name of the guardian;

(2) contains the address of the guardian most recently known by the resident agent;

(3) states that notice of the resignation has been given to the guardian and that the guardian does not have a resident agent; and

(4) contains the date on which the notice of the resignation was given to the guardian.

(b) The resident agent shall send, by certified mail, return receipt requested, a copy of a resignation statement filed under Subsection (a) of this section to:

(1) the guardian at the address most recently known by the agent; and

(2) each party in the case or the party's attorney or other designated representative of record.

(c) The resignation of a resident agent takes effect on the date on which the court enters an order accepting the agent's resignation. A court may not enter an order accepting the agent's resignation unless the agent complies with the requirements of this section.

Added by Acts 2001, 77th Leg., ch. 217, § 14, eff. Sept. 1, 2001.

§ 761. Removal

(a) The court, on its own motion or on motion of any interested person, including the ward, and without notice, may remove any guardian, appointed under this chapter, who:

(1) neglects to qualify in the manner and time required by law;

(2) fails to return within 90 days after qualification, unless the time is extended by order of the court, an inventory of the property of the guardianship estate and list of claims that have come to the guardian's knowledge;

(3) having been required to give a new bond, fails to do so within the time prescribed;

(4) absents himself from the state for a period of three months at one time without permission of the court, or removes from the state;

(5) cannot be served with notices or other processes because of the fact that:

(A) the guardian's whereabouts are unknown;

(B) the guardian is eluding service; or

(C) the guardian is a nonresident of this state who does not have a resident agent to accept service of process in any guardianship proceeding or other matter relating to the guardianship;

(6) has misapplied, embezzled, or removed from the state, or is about to misapply, embezzle, or remove from the state, all or any part of the property committed to the guardian's care; or

(7) has cruelly treated a ward, or has neglected to educate or maintain the ward as liberally as the means of the ward and the condition of the ward's estate permit.

(b) The court may remove a personal representative under Subsection (a)(6) or (7) of this section only on the presentation of clear and convincing evidence given under oath.

(c) The court may remove a guardian on its own motion, or on the complaint of an interested person, after the guardian has been cited by personal service to answer at a time and place set in the notice, when:

(1) sufficient grounds appear to support belief that the guardian has misapplied, embezzled, or removed from the state, or that the guardian is about to misapply, embezzle, or remove from the state, all or any part of the property committed to the care of the guardian;

(2) the guardian fails to return any account or report that is required by law to be made;

(3) the guardian fails to obey any proper order of the court having jurisdiction with respect to the performance of the guardian's duties;

(4) the guardian is proved to have been guilty of gross misconduct or mismanagement in the performance of the duties of the guardian;

(5) the guardian becomes incapacitated, or is sentenced to the penitentiary, or from any other cause becomes incapable of properly performing the duties of the guardian's trust;

(6) as guardian of the person, the guardian cruelly treats the ward, or neglects to educate or maintain the ward as liberally as the means of the ward's estate and the ward's ability or condition permit;

(7) the guardian interferes with the ward's progress or participation in programs in the community;

(8) the guardian fails to comply with the requirements of Section 697 of this code; or

(9) the court determines that, because of the dissolution of the joint guardians' marriage, the termination of the guardians' joint appointment and the continuation of only one of the joint guardians as the sole guardian is in the best interest of the ward,

(d) The order of removal shall state the cause of the removal. It must require that any letters issued to the person who is removed shall, if the removed person has been personally served with citation, be surrendered and that all those letters be cancelled of record, whether or not delivered. It must further require, as to all the estate remaining in the hands of a removed person, delivery of the estate to the person or persons entitled to the estate, or to one who has been appointed and has qualified as successor guardian, and as to the person of a ward, that control be relinquished as required in the order.

(e) If a joint guardian is removed under Subsection (c)(9) of this section, the other joint guardian is entitled to continue to serve as the sole guardian unless removed for a reason other than the dissolution of the joint guardians' marriage.

(f) If the necessity exists, the court may immediately appoint a successor but may not discharge the person removed as guardian of the estate or release the person or the sureties on the person's bond until final order or judgment is rendered on the final account of the guardian.

(g) The court at any time may order a person removed as guardian under this section who has all or part of the estate of a ward to deliver all or part of the ward's estate to a person who has been appointed and has qualified as successor guardian.

Added by Acts 1993, 73rd Leg., ch. 957, § 1, eff Sept. 1, 1993. Subsecs. (e), (f) added by Acts 1995, 74th Leg., ch. 1039, § 50, eff. Sept. 1, 1995. Amended by Acts 2001, 77th Leg., ch. 217, § 15, eff. Sept. 1, 2001.

§ 762. Reinstatement After Removal

(a) Not later than the 10th day after the date the court signs the order of removal, a personal representative who is removed under Subsection (a)(6) or (7), Section 761, of this code may file an application with the court for a hearing to determine whether the personal representative should be reinstated.

(b) On the filing of an application for a hearing under this section, the court clerk shall issue a notice stating that the application for reinstatement was filed, the name of the ward, and the name of the applicant. The clerk shall issue the notice to the applicant, the ward, a person interested in the welfare of the ward, or the ward's estate, and, if applicable, a person who has control of the care and custody of the ward. The notice must cite all persons interested in the estate or welfare of the ward to appear at the time and place stated in the notice if they wish to contest the application.

(c) If, at the conclusion of a hearing under this section, the court is satisfied by a preponderance of the evidence that the applicant did not engage in the conduct that directly led to the applicant's removal, the court shall set aside an order appointing a successor representative, if any, and shall enter an order reinstating the applicant as personal representative of the ward or estate.

(d) If the court sets aside the appointment of a successor representative under this section, the court may require the successor representative to prepare and file, under oath, an accounting of the estate and to detail the disposition the successor has made of the property of the estate.

Added by Acts 1993, 73rd Leg., ch. 957, § 1, eff. Sept. 1, 1993. Amended by Acts 2003, 78th Leg., ch. 549, § 15, eff. Sept. 1, 2003.

§ 763. Additional Powers of Successor Guardian

In addition, a successor guardian may make himself, and may be made, a party to a suit prosecuted by or against the predecessor of the successor guardian. The successor guardian may settle with the predecessor and receive and receipt for all the portion of the estate as remains in the hands of the successor guardian. The successor guardian may bring suit on the bond or bonds of the predecessor in the guardian's own name and capacity for all the estate that came into the hands of the predecessor and has not been accounted for by the predecessor.

Added by Acts 1993, 73rd Leg., ch. 957, § 1, eff. Sept. 1, 1993.

§ 764. Subsequent Guardians Succeed to Prior Rights and Duties

Whenever a guardian shall accept and qualify after letters of guardianship are granted on the estate, the guardian shall, in like manner, succeed to the previous guardian, and the guardian shall administer the estate in like manner as if the administration by the guardian were a continuation of the former one.

Added by Acts 1993, 73rd Leg., ch. 957, § 1, eff. Sept. 1, 1993.

§ 765. Successors' Return of Inventory, Appraisement, and List of Claims

A successor guardian who has qualified to succeed a prior guardian shall make and return to the court an inventory, appraisement, and list of claims of the estate, not later than the 30th day after the date the successor guardian qualifies as guardian, in the same manner as is required of an original appointee. The successor guardian shall in like manner as is required of an original appointee return additional inventories, appraisements, and lists of claims. In all orders appointing a successor guardian, the court shall appoint an appraiser as in original appointments on the application of any person interested in the estate.

Added by Acts 1993, 73rd Leg., ch. 957, § 1, eff. Sept. 1, 1993. Amended by Acts 2003, 78th Leg., ch. 549, § 16, eff. Sept. 1, 2003.

Subpart E. General Duties and Powers of Guardians

§ 767. Powers and Duties of Guardians of the Person

The guardian of the person is entitled to the charge and control of the person of the ward, and the duties of the guardian correspond with the rights of the guardian. A guardian of the person has:

(1) the right to have physical possession of the ward and to establish the ward's legal domicile;

(2) the duty of care, control, and protection of the ward;

(3) the duty to provide the ward with clothing, food, medical care, and shelter;

(4) the power to consent to medical, psychiatric, and surgical treatment other than the inpatient psychiatric commitment of the ward; and

(5) on application to and order of the court, the power to establish a trust in accordance with 42 U.S.C. Section 1396p(d)(4)(B), as amended, and direct that the income of the ward as defined by that section be paid directly to the trust, solely for the purpose of the ward's eligibility for medical assistance under Chapter 32, Human Resources Code.

(b) Notwithstanding Subsection (a)(4) of this section, a guardian of the person of a ward has the power to transport the ward to an inpatient mental health facility for a preliminary examination in accordance with Subchapters A and C, Chapter 573, Health and Safety Code.

Added by Acts 1993, 73rd Leg., ch. 957, § 1, eff. Sept. 1, 1993. Amended by Acts 2003, 78th Leg., ch. 549, § 17, eff. Sept. 1, 2003; Acts 2003, 78th Leg., ch. 692, § 2, eff. Sept. 1, 2003.

§ 768. General Powers and Duties of Guardian of the Estate

The guardian of the estate of a ward is entitled to the possession and management of all property belonging to the ward, to collect all debts, rentals, or claims that are due to the ward, to enforce all obligations in favor of the ward, and to bring and defend suits by or against the ward; but, in the management of the estate, the guardian is governed by the provisions of this chapter. It is the duty of the guardian of the estate to take care of and manage the estate as a prudent person would manage the person's own property except as otherwise provided by this chapter. The guardian of the estate shall account for all rents, profits, and revenues that the estate would have produced by such prudent management.

Added by Acts 1993, 73rd Leg., ch. 957, § 1, eff. Sept. 1, 1993. Amended by Acts 2003, 78th Leg., ch. 549, §18, eff. Sept. 1, 2003.

§ 769. Summary of Powers of Guardian of Person and Estate

The guardian of both the person of and estate of a ward has all the rights and powers and shall perform all the duties of the guardian of the person and of the guardian of the estate.

Added by Acts 1993, 73rd Leg., ch. 957, § 1, eff. Sept. 1, 1993. Amended by Acts 2003, 78th Leg., ch. 549, § 18, eff. Sept. 1, 2003.

§ 770. Care of Ward; Commitment

(a) The guardian of an adult may expend funds of the guardianship as provided by court order to care for and maintain the incapacitated person. The guardian may apply for residential care and services provided by a public or private facility on behalf of an incapacitated person who has decision-making ability if the person agrees to be placed in the facility. The guardian shall report the condition of the person to the court at regular intervals at least annually, unless the court orders more frequent reports. If the person is receiving residential care in a public or private residential care facility, the guardian shall include in any report to the court a statement as to the necessity for continued care in the facility.

(b) Except as provided by Subsection (c) or (d) of this section, a guardian may not voluntarily admit an incapacitated person to a public or private in-patient psychiatric facility or to a residential facility operated by the Texas Department of Mental Health and Mental Retardation for care and treatment. If care and treatment in a psychiatric or a residential facility are necessary, the person or the person's guardian may

(1) apply for services under Section 593.027 or 593.028, Health and Safety Code;

(2) apply to a court to commit the person under Subtitle D, Title 7, Health and Safety Code (Persons with Mental Retardation Act),[1] Subtitle C, Title 7, Health and Safety Code (Texas Mental Health Code),[2] or Chapter 462, Health and Safety Code; or

(3) transport the ward to an inpatient mental health facility for a preliminary examination in accordance with Subchapters A and C, Chapter 573, Health and Safety Code.

(c) A guardian of a person younger than 16 years of age may voluntarily admit an incapacitated person to a public or private inpatient psychiatric facility for care and treatment.

(d) A guardian of a person may voluntarily admit an incapacitated person to a residential care facility for emergency care or respite care under Section 593.027 or 593.028, Health and Safety Code; or

Added by cts 1993, 73rd Leg., ch. 957, § 1, eff. Sept. 1, 1993. Amended by Acts 2003, 78th Leg., ch. 692, § 3, eff. Sept. 1, 2003.

§ 770A. Administration of Medication

(a) In this section, "psychoactive medication" has the meaning assigned by Section 574.101, Health and Safety Code.

(b) If a person under a protective custody order as provided by Subchapter B, Chapter 574, Health and Safety Code, is a ward who is not a minor, the guardian of the person of the ward may consent to the administration of psychoactive medication as prescribed by the ward's treating physician regardless of the ward's expressed preferences regarding treatment with psychoactive medication.

Added by Acts 2003, 78th Leg., ch. 692, § 4, eff. Sept. 1, 2003.

Subpart F. Specific Duties and Powers of Guardians

§ 771. Guardian of Estate: Possession of Personal Property and Records

The guardian of an estate, immediately after receiving letters of guardianship, shall collect and take into

[1] V.T.C.A., Health & Safety Code § 591.001 et seq.
[2] V.T.C.A., Health & Safety Code § 571.001 et seq.

possession the personal property, record books, title papers, and other business papers of the ward and shall deliver the personal property, books, or papers, of the ward to a person who is legally entitled to that property when the guardianship has been closed or a successor guardian has received letters.
Added by Acts 1993, 73rd Leg., ch. 957, § 1, eff. Sept. 1, 1993.

§ 772. Collection of Claims and Recovery of Property

Every guardian of an estate shall use ordinary diligence to collect all claims and debts due the ward and to recover possession of all property of the ward to which the ward has claim or title, if there is a reasonable prospect of collecting the claims or of recovering the property. If the guardian wilfully neglects to use ordinary diligence, the guardian and the sureties on the guardian's bond shall be liable, at the suit of any person interested in the estate, for the use of the estate, for the amount of the claims or for the value of the property that has been lost due to the guardian's neglect.
Added by Acts 1993, 73rd Leg., ch. 957, § 1, eff. Sept. 1, 1993. Amended by Acts 1995, 74th Leg., ch. 1039, § 51, eff. Sept. 1, 1995.

§ 773. Suit by Guardian of Estate

A guardian of a ward's estate appointed in this state may institute suits for the recovery of personal property, debts, or damages and suits for title to or possession of land or for any right attached to or growing out of the same or for injury or damage done. Judgment in those cases shall be conclusive but may be set aside by any person interested for fraud or collusion on the part of the guardian.
Added by Acts 1993, 73rd Leg., ch. 957, § 1, eff. Sept. 1, 1993. Amended by Acts 1995, 74th Leg., ch. 1039, § 52, eff. Sept. 1, 1995.

§ 774. Exercise of Power With or Without Court Order

(a) On application, and if authorized by an order, the guardian of the estate may renew or extend any obligation owed by or to the ward. On written application to the court and when a guardian of the estate deems it is in the best interest of the estate, the guardian may, if authorized by an order of the court:

(1) purchase or exchange property;

(2) take a claim or property for the use and benefit of the estate in payment of a debt due or owing to the estate;

(3) compound a bad or doubtful debt due or owing to the estate;

(4) make a compromise or a settlement in relation to property or a claim in dispute or litigation;

(5) compromise or pay in full any secured claim that has been allowed and approved as required by law against the estate by conveying to the holder of the secured claim the real estate or personalty securing the claim, in full payment, liquidation, and satisfaction of the claim, and in consideration of cancellation of a note, deed of trust, mortgage, chattel mortgage, or other evidence of a lien that secures the payment of the claim;

(6) abandon worthless or burdensome property and the administration of that property. Abandoned real or personal property may be foreclosed on by a secured party, trustee, or mortgagee without further order of the court;

(7) purchase a prepaid funeral benefits contract; and

(8) establish a trust in accordance with 42 U.S.C. Section 1396p(d)(4)(B), as amended, and direct that the income of the ward as defined by that section be paid directly to the trust, solely for the purpose of the ward's eligibility for medical assistance under Chapter 32, Human Resources Code.

(b) The guardian of the estate of a person, without application to or order of the court, may exercise the following powers provided, however, that a guardian may apply and obtain an order if doubtful of the propriety of the exercise of any such power:

(1) release a lien on payment at maturity of the debt secured by the lien;

(2) vote stocks by limited or general proxy;

(3) pay calls and assessments;

(4) insure the estate against liability in appropriate cases;

(5) insure property of the estate against fire, theft, and other hazards; and

(6) pay taxes, court costs, and bond premiums.
Added by Acts 1993, 73rd Leg., ch. 957, § 1, eff. Sept. 1, 1993. Subsec. (a) amended by Acts 1997, 75th Leg., ch. 77, § 6, eff. Sept. 1, 1997: Subsec. (a) amended by Acts 2001, 77th Leg., ch. 305, § 1, eff. Sept. 1, 2001. Amended by Acts 2003, 78th Leg., ch. 549, § 19, eff. Sept. 1, 2003.

§ 775. Possession of Property Held in Common Ownership

If the ward holds or owns any property in common, or as part owner with another person, the guardian of the estate is entitled to possession of the property of the ward held or owned in common with a part owner in the same manner as another owner in common or joint owner would be entitled.
Added by Acts 1993, 73rd Leg., ch. 957, § 1, eff. Sept. 1, 1993.

§ 776. Sums Allowable for Education and Maintenance of Ward

(a) Subject to Section 777 of this code, if a monthly allowance for the ward was not ordered in the court's order appointing a guardian, the guardian of the estate shall file an application with the court requesting a monthly allowance to be expended from the income and corpus of the ward's estate for the education and maintenance of the ward and the maintenance of the ward's property.

(a-1) The guardian must file the application requesting the monthly allowance not later than the 30th day after the date on which the guardian qualifies as guardian or the date specified by the court, whichever is later. The application must clearly separate amounts requested for education and maintenance of the ward from amounts requested for maintenance of the ward's property.

(a-2) In determining the amount of the monthly allowance for the ward and the ward's property, the court shall consider the condition of the estate and the income and corpus of the estate necessary to pay the reasonably anticipated regular education and maintenance expenses of the ward and maintenance expenses of the ward's property. The court's order setting a monthly allowance must specify the types of expenditures the guardian may make on a monthly basis for the ward or the ward's property. An order setting a monthly allowance does not affect the guardian's duty to account for expenditures of the allowance in the annual account required by Section 741 of this code.

(a-3) When different persons have the guardianship of the person and estate of a ward, the guardian of the estate shall pay to the guardian of the person the monthly allowance set by the court, at a time specified by the court, for the education and maintenance of the ward. If the guardian of the estate fails to pay to the guardian of the person the monthly allowance set by the court, the guardian of the estate shall be compelled to make the payment by court order after the guardian is duly cited to appear.

(b) When a guardian has in good faith expended funds from the income and corpus of the estate of the ward for support and maintenance of the ward and the expenditures exceed the monthly allowance authorized by the court, the guardian shall file a motion with the court requesting approval of the expenditures. The court may approve the excess expenditures if:

(1) the expenditures were made when it was not convenient or possible for the guardian to first secure court approval;

(2) the proof is clear and convincing that the expenditures were reasonable and proper;

(3) the court would have granted authority in advance to make the expenditures; and

(4) the ward received the benefits of the expenditures.

Added by Acts 1993, 73rd Leg., ch. 957, § 1, eff. Sept. 1, 1993. Subsec. (b) amended by Acts 1995, 74th Leg., ch. 1039, § 53, eff. Sept. 1, 1995. Amended by Acts 2003, 78th Leg., ch. 549, § 20, eff. Sept. 1, 2003.

§ 776A. Sums Allowable for Education and Maintenance of Ward's Spouse or Dependent

(a) Subject to Section 777 of this code and on application to the court, the court may order the guardian of the estate of a ward to expend funds from the ward's estate for the education and maintenance of the ward's spouse or dependent.

(b) In determining whether to order the expenditure of funds from a ward's estate for the ward's spouse or dependent, as appropriate, in accordance with this section, the court shall consider:

(1) the circumstances of the ward, the ward's spouse, and the ward's dependents;

(2) the ability and duty of the ward's spouse to support himself or herself and the ward's dependent;

(3) the size of the ward's estate;

(4) a beneficial interest the ward or the ward's spouse or dependent has in a trust; and

(5) an existing estate plan, including a trust or will, that provides a benefit to the ward's spouse or dependent.

(c) A person who makes an application to the court under this section shall mail notice of the application by certified mail to all interested persons.

Added by Acts 1997, 75th Leg., ch. 77, § 7, eff. Sept. 1, 1997.

§ 777. Sums Allowed Parents for Education and Maintenance of Minor Ward

(a) Except as provided by Subsection (b) of this section, a parent who is the guardian of the person of a ward who is 17 years of age or younger may not use the income or the corpus from the ward's estate for the ward's support, education, or maintenance.

(b) A court with proper jurisdiction may authorize the guardian of the person to spend the income or the corpus from the ward's estate to support, educate, or maintain the ward if the guardian presents clear and convincing evidence to the court that the ward's parents are unable without unreasonable hardship to pay for all of the expenses related to the ward's support.

Added by Acts 1993, 73rd Leg., ch. 957, § 1, eff. Sept. 1, 1993.

§ 778. Title of Wards Not to be Disputed

A guardian or the heirs, executors, administrators, or assigns of a guardian may not dispute the right of the ward to any property that came into the possession of the guardian as guardian of the ward, except property that is recovered from the guardian or property on which there is a personal action pending.

Added by Acts 1993, 73rd Leg., ch. 957, § 1, eff. Sept. 1, 1993.

§ 779. Operation of Farm, Ranch, Factory, or Other Business

If the ward owns a farm, ranch, factory, or other business and if the farm, ranch, factory, or other business is not required to be sold at once for the payment of debts or other lawful purposes, the guardian of the estate on order of the court shall carry on the operation of the farm, ranch, factory, or other business, or cause the same to be done, or rent the same, as shall appear to be for the best interests of the estate. In deciding, the court shall consider the condition of the estate and the necessity that may exist for the future sale of the property or business for the payment of a debt, claim, or other lawful expenditure and may not extend the time of renting any of the property beyond

what appears consistent with the maintenance and education of a ward or the settlement of the estate of the ward.
Added by Acts 1993, 73rd Leg., ch. 957, § 1, eff. Sept. 1, 1993.

§ 780. Administration of Partnership Interest by Guardian

If the ward was a partner in a general partnership and the articles of partnership provide that, on the incapacity of a partner, the guardian of the estate of the partner is entitled to the place of the incapacitated partner in the firm, the guardian who contracts to come into the partnership shall, to the extent allowed by law, be liable to a third person only to the extent of the incapacitated partner's capital in the partnership and the assets of the estate of the partner that are held by the guardian. This section does not exonerate a guardian from liability for the negligence of the guardian.
Added by Acts 1993, 73rd Leg., ch. 957, § 1, eff. Sept. 1, 1993.

§ 781. Borrowing Money

(a) The guardian may mortgage or pledge any real or personal property of a guardianship estate by deed of trust or otherwise as security for an indebtedness, under court order, when necessary for any of the following purposes:

(1) for the payment of any ad valorem, income, gift, or transfer taxes due from a ward, regardless of whether the taxes are assessed by a state, a political subdivision of the state, the federal government, or a foreign country;

(2) for the payment of any expenses of administration, including sums necessary for the operation of a business, farm, or ranch owned by the estate;

(3) for the payment of any claims allowed and approved, or established by suit, against the ward or the estate of the ward;

(4) to renew and extend a valid, existing lien;

(5) to make improvements or repairs to the real estate of the ward if:

(A) the real estate of the ward is not revenue producing but could be made revenue producing by certain improvements and repairs; or

(B) the revenue from the real estate could be increased by making improvements or repairs to the real estate;

(6) court-authorized borrowing of money that the court finds to be in the best interests of the ward for the purchase of a residence for the ward or a dependent of the ward; and

(7) if the guardianship is kept open after the death of the ward, funeral expenses of the ward and expenses of the ward's last illness.

(b) When it is necessary to borrow money for any of the purposes authorized under Subsection (a) of this section, or to create or extend a lien on property of the estate as security, a sworn application for the authority to borrow money shall be filed with the court, stating fully and in detail the circumstances that the guardian of the estate believes make necessary the granting of the authority. On the filing of an application under this subsection, the clerk shall issue and cause to be posted a citation to all interested persons, stating the nature of the application and requiring the interested persons to appear and show cause why the application should not be granted.

(c) If the court is satisfied by the evidence adduced at the hearing on the application that it is in the interest of the ward or the ward's estate to borrow money under Subsection (b) of this section, or to extend and renew an existing lien, the court shall issue an order to that effect, setting out the terms and conditions of the authority granted. The term of the loan or renewal shall be for the length of time that the court determines to be for the best interests of the ward or the ward's estate. If a new lien is created on the property of a guardianship estate, the court may require that the guardian's general bond be increased, or that an additional bond be given, for the protection of the guardianship estate and its creditors, as for the sale of real property belonging to the estate.
Added by Acts 1993, 73rd Leg., ch. 957, § 1, eff. Sept. 1, 1993.

§ 782. Powers, Duties, and Obligations of Guardian of Person Entitled to Government Funds

(a) A guardian of the person for whom it is necessary to have a guardian appointed to receive funds from a governmental source has the power to administer only the funds received from the governmental source, all earnings, interest, or profits derived from the funds, and all property acquired with the funds. The guardian has the power to receive the funds and pay out the expenses of administering the guardianship and the expenses for the support, maintenance, or education of the ward or the ward's dependents. Expenditures for the support, maintenance, or education of the ward or the ward's dependents may not exceed $12,000 during any 12-month period without the court's approval.

(b) All acts performed before September 1, 1993, by guardians of the estate of a person for whom it is necessary to have a guardian appointed to receive and disburse funds that are due the person from a governmental source are validated if the acts are performed in conformance with orders of a court that has venue with respect to the support, maintenance, and education of the ward or the ward's dependents and the investment of surplus funds of the ward under this chapter and if the validity of the act is not an issue in a probate proceeding or civil lawsuit that is pending on September 1, 1993.
Added by Acts 1993, 73rd Leg., ch. 957, § 1, eff. Sept. 1, 1993. Amended by Acts 1995, 74th Leg., ch. 1039, § 54, eff. Sept. 1, 1995.

Subpart G. Claims Procedures

§ 783. Notice by Guardian of Appointment

(a) Within one month after receiving letters, personal representatives of estates shall send to the comptroller of public accounts by certified or registered mail if the ward remitted or should have remitted taxes administered by the comptroller of public accounts and publish in some newspaper, printed in the county where the letters were issued, if there be one, a notice requiring all persons having a claim against the estate being administered to present the claim within the time prescribed by law. The notice must include the time of issuance of letters held by the representative, the address to which a claim may be presented, and an instruction of the representative's choice that a claim be addressed in care of the representative, in care of the representative's attorney, or in care of "Representative, Estate of ________" (naming the estate).

(b) A copy of the printed notice, with the affidavit of the publisher, duly sworn to and subscribed before a proper officer, to the effect that the notice was published as provided in this chapter for the service of citation or notice by publication, shall be filed in the court in which the cause is pending.

(c) When no newspaper is printed in the county, the notice shall be posted and the return made and filed as required by this chapter.

Added by Acts 1993, 73rd Leg., ch. 957, § 1, eff. Sept. 1, 1993. Subsec. (a) amended by Acts 1997, 75th Leg., ch. 77, § 8, eff. Sept. 1, 1997.

§ 784. Notice to Holders of Recorded Claims

(a) Within four months after receiving letters, the guardian of an estate shall give notice of the issuance of the letters to each and every person having a claim for money against the estate of a ward if the claim is secured by a deed of trust, mortgage, or vendor's, mechanic's or other contractor's lien on real estate belonging to the estate.

(b) Within four months after receiving letters, the guardian of an estate shall give notice of the issuance of the letters to each person having an outstanding claim for money against the estate of a ward if the guardian has actual knowledge of the claim.

(c) The notice stating the original grant of letter shall be given by mailing the notice by certified mail or registered letter, with return receipt requested, addressed to the record holder of the indebtedness or claim at the last known post office address of the record holder.

(d) A copy of each notice required by Subsection (a) of this section, with the return receipt and an affidavit of the representative, stating that the notice was mailed as required by law, giving the name of the person to whom the notice was mailed, if not shown on the notice or receipt, shall be filed in the court from which letters were issued.

(e) In the notice required by Subsection (b) of this section, the guardian of the estate may expressly state in the notice that the unsecured creditor must present a claim not later than the 120th day after the date on which the unsecured creditor receives the notice or the claim is barred, if the claim is not barred by the general statutes of limitation. The notice under this subsection must include:

(1) the address to which claims may be presented; and

(2) an instruction that the claim be filed with the clerk of the court issuing the letters of guardianship.

Added by Acts 1993, 73rd Leg., ch. 957, § 1, eff. Sept. 1, 1993. Subsec. (c) added by Acts 2001, 77th Leg., ch. 1174, § 6, eff. Sept. 1, 2001.

§ 785. One Notice Sufficient; Penalty for Failure to Give Notice

(a) If the notice required by Section 784 of this code has been given by a former representative, or by one when several representatives are acting, the notice given by the former representative or co-representative is sufficient and need not be repeated by any successor or co-representative.

(b) If the guardian fails to give the notice required in other sections of this chapter or to cause the notices to be given, the guardian and the sureties on the bond of the guardian shall be liable for any damage that any person suffers because of the neglect, unless it appears that the person had notice otherwise.

Added by Acts 1993, 73rd Leg., ch. 957, § 1, eff. Sept. 1, 1993.

§ 786. Claims Against Wards

(a) A claim may be presented to the guardian of the estate at any time when the estate is not closed and when suit on the claim has not been barred by the general statutes of limitation. A claim of an unsecured creditor for money that is not presented within the time prescribed by the notice of presentment permitted by Section 784(e) of this code is barred.

(b) A claim against a ward on which a suit is barred by a general statute of limitation applicable to the claim may not be allowed by a guardian. If allowed by the guardian and the court is satisfied that limitation has run, the claim shall be disapproved.

Added by Acts 1993, 73rd Leg., ch. 957, § 1, eff. Sept. 1, 1993. Subsec. (a) amended by Acts 2001, 77th Leg., ch. 1174, § 7, eff. Sept. 1, 2001.

§ 787. Tolling of General Statutes of Limitation

The general statutes of limitation are tolled:

(1) by filing a claim that is legally allowed and approved; or

(2) by bringing a suit on a rejected and disapproved claim not later than the 90th day after the date of rejection or disapproval.

Added by Acts 1993, 73rd Leg., ch. 957, § 1, eff. Sept. 1, 1993.

§ 788. Claims Must be Authenticated

Except as provided by this section, with respect to the payment of an unauthenticated claim by a guardian, a guardian of the estate may not allow and the court may not approve a claim for money against the estate, unless the claim is supported by an affidavit that the claim is just and that all legal offsets, payments, and credits known to the affiant have been allowed. If the claim is not founded on a written instrument or account, the affidavit must also state the facts on which the claim is founded. A photostatic copy of an exhibit or voucher necessary to prove a claim under this section may be offered with and attached to the claim instead of the original.

Added by Acts 1993, 73rd Leg., ch. 957, § 1, eff. Sept. 1, 1993.

§ 789. When Defects of Form are Waived

Any defect of form or claim of insufficiency of exhibits or vouchers presented is deemed waived by the guardian unless written objection to the form, exhibit, or voucher is made not later than the 30th day after the date of presentment of the claim and is filed with the county clerk.

Added by Acts 1993, 73rd Leg., ch. 957, § 1, eff. Sept. 1, 1993.

§ 790. Evidence Concerning Lost or Destroyed Claims

If evidence of a claim is lost or destroyed, the claimant or a representative of the claimant may make affidavit to the fact of the loss or destruction, stating the amount, date, and nature of the claim and when due, that the claim is just, that all legal offsets, payments, and credits known to the affiant have been allowed, and that the claimant is still the owner of the claim. The claim must be proved by disinterested testimony taken in open court, or by oral or written deposition, before the claim is approved. If the claim is allowed or approved without the affidavit or if the claim is approved without satisfactory proof, the allowance or approval is void.

Added by Acts 1993, 73rd Leg., ch. 957, § 1, eff. Sept. 1, 1993.

§ 791. Authentication of Claim by Others Than Individual Owners

The cashier, treasurer, or managing official of a corporation shall make the affidavit required to authenticate a claim of the corporation. When an affidavit is made by an officer of a corporation, or by an executor, administrator, guardian, trustee, assignee, agent, or attorney, it is sufficient to state in the affidavit that the person making the affidavit has made diligent inquiry and examination and that the person believes that the claim is just and that all legal offsets, payments, and credits made known to the person making the affidavit have been allowed.

Added by Acts 1993, 73rd Leg., ch. 957, § 1, eff. Sept. 1, 1993.

§ 792. Guardian's Payment of Unauthenticated Claims

A guardian may pay an unauthenticated claim against the estate of the guardian's ward that the guardian believes to be just, but the guardian and the sureties on the bond of the guardian shall be liable for the amount of any payment of the claim if the court finds that the claim is not just.

Added by Acts 1993, 73rd Leg., ch. 957, § 1, eff. Sept. 1, 1993.

§ 793. Method of Handling Secured Claims

(a) When a secured claim against a ward is presented, the claimant shall specify in the claim, in addition to all other matters required to be specified in claims:

(1) whether the claim shall be allowed and approved as a matured secured claim to be paid in due course of administration, in which event it shall be so paid if allowed and approved; or

(2) whether the claim shall be allowed, approved, and fixed as a preferred debt and lien against the specific property securing the indebtedness and paid according to the terms of the contract that secured the lien, in which event it shall be so allowed and approved if it is a valid lien; provided, however, the guardian may pay the claim prior to maturity if it is in the best interests of the estate to do so.

(b) If a secured claim is not presented within the time provided by law, it shall be treated as a claim to be paid in accordance with Subsection (a)(2) of this section.

(c) When an indebtedness has been allowed and approved under Subsection (a)(2) of this section, no further claim shall be made against other assets of the estate because of the indebtedness, but the claim remains a preferred lien against the property securing the claim, and the property remains security for the debt in any distribution or sale of the property before final maturity and payment of the debt.

(d) If property that secures a claim allowed, approved, and fixed under Subsection (a)(2) of this section is not sold or distributed not later than the 12th month after the date letters of guardianship are granted, the guardian of the estate shall promptly pay all maturities that have accrued on the debt according to the terms of the maturities and shall perform all the terms of any contract securing the maturities. If the guardian defaults in the payment or performance, the court, on motion of the claim holder, shall require the sale of the property subject to the unmatured part of the debt and apply the proceeds of the sale to the liquidation of the maturities or, at the option of the claim holder, a motion may be made in a like manner to require the sale of the property free of the lien and to apply the proceeds to the payment of the whole debt.

Added by Acts 1993, 73rd Leg., ch. 957, § 1, eff. Sept. 1, 1993.

§ 794. Claims Providing for Attorney's Fees

If the instrument that evidences or supports a claim provides for attorney's fees, the claimant may include as a part of the claim the portion of the fee that the claimant has paid or contracted to pay to an attorney to prepare, present, and collect the claim.
Added by Acts 1993, 73rd Leg., ch. 957, § 1, eff. Sept. 1, 1993.

§ 795. Depositing Claims With Clerk

A claim may also be presented by depositing the claim, with vouchers and necessary exhibits and affidavit attached to the claim, with the clerk. The clerk, on receiving the claim, shall advise the guardian of the estate or the guardian's attorney by letter mailed to the last known address of the guardian of the deposit of the claim. If the guardian fails to act on the claim within 30 days after it is filed, the claim is presumed to be rejected. Failure of the clerk to give notice as required under this section does not affect the validity of the presentment or the presumption of rejection of the claim because not acted on within the 30-day period.
Added by Acts 1993, 73rd Leg., ch. 957, § 1, eff. Sept. 1, 1993.

§ 796. Memorandum of Allowance or Rejection of Claim

When a duly authenticated claim against a guardianship estate is presented to the guardian or filed with the clerk as provided by this subpart, the guardian shall, not later than the 30th day after the date the claim is presented or filed, endorse or annex to the claim a memorandum signed by the guardian stating the time of presentation or filing of the claim and that the guardian allows or rejects the claim, or what portion of the claim the guardian allows or rejects.
Added by Acts 1993, 73rd Leg., ch. 957, § 1, eff. Sept. 1, 1993.

§ 797. Failure to Endorse or Annex Memorandum

The failure of a guardian of an estate to endorse on or annex to a claim presented to the guardian, or the failure of a guardian to allow or reject the claim or portion of the claim within 30 days after the claim was presented constitutes a rejection of the claim. If the claim is later established by suit, the costs shall be taxed against the guardian, individually, or the guardian may be removed as in other cases of removal on the written complaint of any person interested in the claim, after personal service of citation, hearing, and proof.
Added by Acts 1993, 73rd Leg., ch. 957, § 1, eff. Sept. 1, 1993.

§ 798. Claims Entered in Docket

After a claim against a ward's estate has been presented to and allowed by the guardian, either in whole or in part, the claim shall be filed with the county clerk of the proper county who shall enter it on the claim docket.
Added by Acts 1993, 73rd Leg., ch. 957, § 1, eff. Sept. 1, 1993.

§ 799 Contest of Claims, Action by Court, and Appeals

(a) Any person interested in a ward, at any time before the court has acted on a claim, may appear and object in writing to the approval of the claim, or any part of the claim. The parties are entitled to process for witnesses, and the court shall hear proof and render judgment as in ordinary suits.

(b) The court shall either approve in whole or in part or reject a claim that has been allowed and entered on the claim docket for a period of 10 days and shall at the same time classify the claim.

(c) Although a claim may be properly authenticated and allowed, if the court is not satisfied that it is just, the court shall examine the claimant and the guardian under oath and hear other evidence necessary to determine the issue. If after the examination and hearing the court is not convinced that the claim is just, the court shall disapprove the claim.

(d) When the court has acted on a claim, the court shall endorse on or annex to the claim a written memorandum dated and signed officially that states the exact action taken by the court on the claim, whether the court approved or disapproved the claim or approved in part or rejected in part the claim, and that states the classification of the claim. An order under this subsection has the force and effect of a final judgment.

(e) When a claimant or any person interested in a ward is dissatisfied with the action of the court on a claim, the claimant or person interested may appeal the action to the courts of appeals, as from other judgments of the county court in probate matters.
Added by Acts 1993, 73rd Leg., ch. 957, § 1, eff. Sept. 1, 1993.

§ 800. Suit on Rejected Claim

When a claim or a part of a claim has been rejected by the guardian, the claimant shall institute suit on the claim in the court of original probate jurisdiction in which the guardianship is pending or in any other court of proper jurisdiction not later than the 90th day after the date of the rejection of the claim or the claim is barred. When a rejected claim is sued on, the endorsement made on or annexed to the claim is taken to be true without further proof, unless denied under oath. When a rejected claim or part of a claim has been established by suit, no execution shall issue but the judgment shall be certified not later than the 30th day after the date of rendition if the judgment is from a court other than the court of original probate jurisdiction, filed in the court in which the cause is pending entered on the claim docket, classified by the court, and handled as if originally allowed and approved in due course of administration.
Added by Acts 1993, 73rd Leg., ch. 957, § 1, eff. Sept. 1, 1993.

§ 801. Presentment of Claims a Prerequisite for Judgment

(a) A judgment may not be rendered in favor of a claimant on any claim for money that has not been legally presented to the guardian of the estate of the ward and rejected by the guardian or by the court, in whole or in part.

(b) Subsection (a) does not apply to a claim for delinquent ad valorem taxes against the estate of a ward that is being administered in probate in a county other than the county in which the taxes were imposed.

Added by Acts 1993, 73rd Leg., ch. 957, § 1, eff. Sept. 1, 1993. Amended by Acts 1999, 76th Leg., ch. 1481, § 38, eff. Sept. 1, 1999.

§ 802. Costs of Suit With Respect to Claims

All costs incurred in the probate court with respect to claims are taxed as follows:

(1) if allowed and approved, the guardianship estate shall pay the costs;

(2) if allowed, but disapproved, the claimant shall pay the costs;

(3) if rejected, but established by suit, the guardianship estate shall pay the costs;

(4) if rejected, but not established by suit, the claimant shall pay the costs; or

(5) in suits to establish a claim after rejection in part, if the claimant fails to recover judgment for a greater amount than was allowed or approved, the claimant shall pay all costs.

Added by Acts 1993, 73rd Leg., ch. 957, § 1, eff. Sept. 1, 1993.

§ 803. Claims by Guardians

(a) A claim that a guardian of the person or estate held against the ward at the time of the appointment of the guardian, or that has since accrued, shall be verified by affidavit as required in other cases and presented to the clerk of the court in which the guardianship is pending. The clerk shall enter the claim on the claim docket, after which it shall take the same course as other claims.

(b) When a claim by a guardian has been filed with the court within the required time, the claim shall be entered on the claim docket and acted on by the court in the same manner as in other cases. When the claim has been acted on by the court, an appeal from the judgment of the court may be taken as in other cases.

Added by Acts 1993, 73rd Leg., ch. 957, § 1, eff. Sept. 1, 1993.

§ 804. Claims Not to be Paid Unless Approved

Except as provided for payment at the risk of a guardian of an unauthenticated claim, a claim for money against the estate of a ward or any part of a claim may not be paid until it has been approved by the court or established by the judgment of a court of competent jurisdiction.

Added by Acts 1993, 73rd Leg., ch. 957, § 1, eff. Sept. 1, 1993.

§ 805. Order of Payment of Claims

(a) The guardian shall pay a claim against the estate of the guardian's ward that has been allowed and approved or established by suit, as soon as practicable, in the following order, except as provided by Subsection (b) of this section:

(1) expenses for the care, maintenance, and education of the ward or the ward's dependents;

(2) funeral expenses of the ward and expenses of the ward's last illness, if the guardianship is kept open after the death of the ward as provided under this chapter, except that any claim against the estate of a ward that has been allowed and approved or established by suit before the death of the ward shall be paid before the funeral expenses and expenses of the last illness;

(3) expenses of administration; and

(4) other claims against the ward or the ward's estate.

(b) If the estate is insolvent, the guardian shall give first priority to the payment of a claim relating to the administration of the guardianship. The guardian shall pay other claims against the ward's estate in the order prescribed by Subsection (a) of this section.

(c) A claimant whose claim has not been paid may petition the court for determination of the claim at any time before it is barred by the applicable statute of limitations and on due proof procure an order for its allowance and payment from the estate.

Added by Acts 1993, 73rd Leg., ch. 957, § 1, eff. Sept. 1, 1993. Amended by Acts 1997, 75th Leg., ch. 1403, § 5, eff. Sept. 1, 1997.

§ 806. Deficiency of Assets

When there is a deficiency of assets to pay all claims of the same class, the claims in the same class shall be paid pro rata, as directed by the court, and in the order directed. A guardian may not be allowed to pay any claims, whether the estate is solvent or insolvent, except with the pro rata amount of the funds of the guardianship estate that have come to hand.

Added by Acts 1993, 73rd Leg., ch. 957, § 1, eff. Sept. 1, 1993.

§ 807. Guardian Not to Purchase Claims

A guardian may not purchase for the guardian's own use or for any purposes whatsoever a claim against the guardianship the guardian represents. On written complaint by a person interested in the guardianship estate and satisfactory proof of violation of this provision, the court after citation and hearing shall enter its order cancelling the claim and no part of the claim shall be paid out of the guardianship. The judge may remove the guardian for a violation of this section.

Added by Acts 1993, 73rd Leg., ch. 957, § 1, eff. Sept. 1, 1993.

§ 808. Proceeds of Sale of Mortgaged Property

When a guardian has on hand the proceeds of a sale that has been made for the satisfaction of a mortgage

or other lien and the proceeds, or any part of the proceeds, are not required for the payment of any debts against the estate that have a preference over the mortgage or other lien, the guardian shall pay the proceeds to a holder of the mortgage or other lien. If the guardian fails to pay the proceeds as required by this section, the holder, on proof of the mortgage or other lien, may obtain an order from the court directing the payment to be made.
Added by Acts 1993, 73rd Leg., ch. 957, § 1, eff. Sept. 1, 1993.

§ 809. Liability for Nonpayment of Claims

(a) If a guardian of an estate fails to pay on demand any money ordered by the court to be paid to any person, except to the state treasury, when there are funds of the guardianship estate available, the person or claimant entitled to the payment, on affidavit of the demand and failure to pay, is authorized to have execution issued against the property of the guardianship for the amount due, with interest and costs.

(b) On return of the execution not satisfied, or merely on the affidavit of demand and failure to pay, the court may cite the guardian and the sureties on the bond of the guardian to show cause why the guardian or the sureties should not be held liable for the debt, interest, costs, or damages. On return of citation duly served, if good cause to the contrary is not shown, the court shall render judgment against the guardian and sureties that are cited under this subsection in favor of the holder of the claim for the unpaid amount ordered to be paid or established by suit, with interest and costs, and for damages on the amount neglected to be paid, at the rate of five percent per month for each month or fraction of a month that the payment was neglected to be paid after demand was made for payment. The damages may be collected in any court of competent jurisdiction.
Added by Acts 1993, 73rd Leg., ch. 957, § 1, eff. Sept. 1, 1993.

Subpart H. Sales

§ 811. Court Must Order Sales

Except as provided by this subpart, the sale of any property of the ward may not be made without an order of court authorizing the sale. The court may order property sold for cash or on credit, at public auction or privately, as it may consider most to the advantage of the estate, except when otherwise specifically provided in this chapter.
Added by Acts 1993, 73rd Leg., ch. 957, § 1, eff. Sept. 1, 1993.

§ 812. Certain Personal Property to be Sold

(a) The guardian of an estate, after approval of inventory and appraisement, shall promptly apply for an order of the court to sell at public auction or privately, for cash or on credit not exceeding six months, all of the estate that is liable to perish, waste, or deteriorate in value or that will be an expense or disadvantage to the estate if kept. Property exempt from forced sale, a specific legacy, or personal property necessary to carry on a farm, ranch, factory, or any other business that it is thought best to operate, may not be included in a sale under this section.

(b) In determining whether to order the sale of an asset under Subsection (a) of this section, the court shall consider:

(1) the guardian's duty to take care of and manage the estate as a person of ordinary prudence, discretion, and intelligence would exercise in the management of the person's own affairs; and

(2) whether the asset constitutes an asset that a trustee is authorized to invest under Chapter 117 or Subchapter F, Chapter 113, Property Code.[1]

Added by Acts 1993, 73rd Leg., ch. 957, § 1, eff. Sept. 1, 1993. Amended by Acts 2003, 78th Leg., ch. 1103, § 15, eff. Jan. 1, 2004.

§ 813. Sales of Other Personal Property

On application by the guardian of the estate or by any interested person, the court may order the sale of any personal property of the estate not required to be sold by Section 812 of this code, including growing or harvested crops or livestock but not including exempt property, if the court finds that the sale of the property would be in the best interests of the ward or the ward's estate in order to pay expenses of the care, maintenance, and education of the ward or the ward's dependents, expenses of administration, allowances, or claims against the ward or the ward's estate, and funeral expenses of the ward and expenses of the ward's last illness, if the guardianship is kept open after the death of the ward, from the proceeds of the sale of the property. Insofar as possible, applications and orders for the sale of personal property must conform to the requirements set forth under this chapter for applications and orders for the sale of real estate.
Added by Acts 1993, 73rd Leg., ch. 957, § 1, eff. Sept. 1, 1993.

§ 814. Special Provisions Pertaining to Livestock

(a) When the guardian of an estate has in the guardian's possession any livestock that the guardian deems necessary or to the advantage of the estate to sell, the guardian may, in addition to any other method provided by law for the sale of personal property, obtain authority from the court in which the estate is pending to sell the livestock through a bonded livestock commission merchant or a bonded livestock auction commission merchant.

(b) On written and sworn application by the guardian or by any person interested in the estate that describes the livestock sought to be sold and that sets out

[1] V.T.C.A., Property Code § 113.171 et seq.

the reasons why it is deemed necessary or to the advantage of the estate that the application be granted, the court may authorize the sale. The court shall consider the application and may hear evidence for or against the application, with or without notice, as the facts warrant.

(c) If the application is granted, the court shall enter its order to that effect and shall authorize delivery of the livestock to any bonded livestock commission merchant or bonded livestock auction commission merchant for sale in the regular course of business. The commission merchant shall be paid the merchant's usual and customary charges, not to exceed five percent of the sale price, for the sale of the livestock. A report of the sale, supported by a verified copy of the merchant's account of sale, shall be made promptly by the guardian to the court, but no order of confirmation by the court is required to pass title to the purchaser of the livestock.

Added by Acts 1993, 73rd Leg., ch. 957, § 1, eff. Sept. 1, 1993. Amended by Acts 2003, 78th Leg., ch. 549, § 21, eff. Sept. 1, 2003.

§ 815. Sales of Personal Property at Public Auction

All sales of personal property at public auction shall be made after notice has been issued by the guardian of the estate and posted as in case of posting for original proceedings in probate, unless the court shall otherwise direct.

Added by Acts 1993, 73rd Leg., ch. 957, § 1, eff. Sept. 1, 1993.

§ 816. Sales of Personal Property on Credit

No more than six months' credit may be allowed when personal property is sold at public auction, based on the date of the sale. The purchaser shall be required to give his note for the amount due, with good and solvent personal security, before delivery of the property can be made to the purchaser, but security may be waived if delivery is not to be made until the note, with interest, has been paid.

Added by Acts 1993, 73rd Leg., ch. 957, § 1, eff. Sept. 1, 1993.

§ 817. Sale of Mortgaged Property

On the filing of a written application, a creditor who holds a claim that is secured by a valid mortgage or other lien and that has been allowed and approved or established by suit may obtain from the court in which the guardianship is pending an order that the property, or so much of the property as necessary to satisfy the creditor's claim, shall be sold. On the filing of the application, the clerk shall issue citation requiring the guardian of the estate to appear and show cause why an application filed under this section should not be granted. If it appears to the court that it would be advisable to discharge the lien out of the general assets of the estate or that it be refinanced, the court may so order. Otherwise, the court shall grant the application and order that the property be sold at public or private sale, as the court considers best, as in ordinary cases of sales of real estate.

Added by Acts 1993, 73rd Leg., ch. 957, § 1, eff. Sept. 1, 1993.

§ 818. Sales of Personal Property Reported; Decree Vests Title

All sales of personal property shall be reported to the court. The laws regulating the confirmation or disapproval of sales of real estate apply to sales of personal property, but no conveyance shall be necessary. The decree confirming the sale of personal property shall vest the right and title of the estate of the ward in the purchaser who has complied with the terms of the sale and shall be prima facie evidence that all requirements of the law in making the sale have been met. The guardian of an estate may, on request, issue a bill of sale without warranty to the purchaser as evidence of title. The expense of the bill of sale if requested is to be borne by the purchaser.

Added by Acts 1993, 73rd Leg., ch. 957, § 1, eff. Sept. 1, 1993.

§ 819. Selection of Real Property Sold for Payment of Debts

Real property of the ward that is selected to be sold for the payment of expenses or claims shall be that property that the court deems most advantageous to the guardianship to be sold.

Added by Acts 1993, 73rd Leg., ch. 957, § 1, eff. Sept. 1, 1993.

§ 820. Application for Sale of Real Estate

An application may be made to the court for an order to sell real property of the estate when it appears necessary or advisable in order to:

(1) pay expenses of administration, allowances, and claims against the ward or the ward's estate, and to pay funeral expenses of the ward and expenses of the ward's last illness, if the guardianship is kept open after the death of the ward;

(2) make up the deficiency when the income of a ward's estate, the personal property of the ward's estate, and the proceeds of previous sales, are insufficient to pay for the education and maintenance of the ward or to pay debts against the estate;

(3) dispose of property of the ward's estate that consists in whole or in part of an undivided interest in real estate when it is deemed in the best interests of the estate to sell the interest;

(4) dispose of real estate of a ward, any part of which is nonproductive or does not produce sufficient revenue to make a fair return on the value of the real estate, when the improvement of the real estate with a view to making it productive is not deemed advantageous or advisable and it appears that the sale of the real estate and the investment of the money derived from the sale of the real estate would be in the best interests of the estate; or

(5) conserve the estate of a ward by selling mineral interest or royalties on minerals in place owned by a ward.

Added by Acts 1993, 73rd Leg., ch. 957, § 1, eff. Sept. 1, 1993.

§ 821. Contents of Application for Sale of Real Estate

An application for the sale of real estate shall be in writing, must describe the real estate or an interest in or part of the real estate sought to be sold, and shall be accompanied by an exhibit, verified by affidavit that shows fully and in detail:

(1) the condition of the estate;

(2) the charges and claims that have been approved or established by suit, or that have been rejected and may be established later;

(3) the amount of each claim that has been approved or established by suit, or that has been rejected but may be established later;

(4) the property of the estate remaining on hand liable for the payment of those claims; and

(5) any other facts that show the necessity or advisability of the sale.

Added by Acts 1993, 73rd Leg., ch. 957, § 1, eff. Sept. 1, 1993.

§ 822. Setting of Hearing on Application

When an application for the sale of real estate is filed, it shall immediately be called to the attention of the judge by the clerk. The judge shall designate in writing a day for hearing the application, any opposition to the application, and any application for the sale of other land, with the evidence pertaining to the application. The judge may, by entries on the docket, continue the hearing from time to time until the judge is satisfied concerning the application.

Added by Acts 1993, 73rd Leg., ch. 957, § 1, eff. Sept. 1, 1993.

§ 823. Citation and Return on Application

On the filing of an application for the sale of real estate under Section 820 of this code and exhibit, the clerk shall issue a citation to all persons interested in the guardianship that describes the land or interest or part of the land or interest sought to be sold and that requires the persons to appear at the time set by the court as shown in the citation and show cause why the sale should not be made, if they so elect. Service of citation shall be by posting.

Added by Acts 1993, 73rd Leg., ch. 957, § 1, eff. Sept. 1, 1993.

§ 824. Opposition to Application

When an application for an order of sale is made, a person interested in the guardianship, before an order of sale is made by the court, may file the person's opposition to the sale, in writing, or may make application for the sale of other property of the estate.

Added by Acts 1993, 73rd Leg., ch. 957, § 1, eff. Sept. 1, 1993.

§ 825. Order of Sale

If satisfied on hearing that the sale of the property of the guardianship described in the application made under Section 820 of this code is necessary or advisable, the court shall order the sale to be made. Otherwise, the court may deny the application and, if the court deems best, may order the sale of other property the sale of which would be more advantageous to the estate. An order for the sale of real estate must specify:

(1) the property to be sold, giving a description that will identify the property;

(2) whether the property is to be sold at public auction or at private sale, and, if at public auction, the time and place of the sale;

(3) the necessity or advisability of the sale and its purpose;

(4) except in cases in which no general bond is required, that, having examined the general bond of the representative of the estate, the court finds it to be sufficient as required by law, or finds the bond to be insufficient and specifies the necessary or increased bond;

(5) that the sale shall be made and the report returned in accordance with law; and

(6) the terms of the sale.

Added by Acts 1993, 73rd Leg., ch. 957, § 1, eff. Sept. 1, 1993.

§ 826. Procedure When Guardian Neglects to Apply For Sale

When the guardian of an estate neglects to apply for an order to sell sufficient property to pay the charges and claims against the estate that have been allowed and approved or established by suit, an interested person, on written application, may cause the guardian to be cited to appear and make a full exhibit of the condition of the estate, and show cause why a sale of the property should not be ordered. On hearing an application made under this section, if the court is satisfied that a sale of the property is necessary or advisable in order to satisfy the claims, it shall enter an order of sale as provided by Section 825 of this code.

Added by Acts 1993, 73rd Leg., ch. 957, § 1, eff. Sept. 1, 1993.

§ 827. Permissible Terms of Sale of Real Estate

(a) The real estate may be sold for cash, or for part cash and part credit, or the equity in land securing an indebtedness may be sold subject to the indebtedness, or with an assumption of the indebtedness, at public or private sale, as appears to the court to be in the best interests of the estate. When real estate is sold partly on credit, the cash payment may not be less than one-fifth of the purchase price, and the purchaser shall execute a note for the deferred payments payable in monthly, quarterly, semiannual or annual installments, of the amounts as appear to the court to be for the best interests of the guardianship, to bear interest from date at a rate of not less than four percent per annum, payable as provided in the note. Default in the payment of principal or interest, or any part of the payment when due, at the election of the holder of the note, matures the whole debt. The note shall be secured by vendor's lien retained in the deed and in the note on the property sold and shall be further secured by deed of trust on the property sold, with the usual provisions for foreclosure and sale on failure to make the payments provided in the deed and the note.

(b) When an estate owning real estate by virtue of foreclosure of a vendor's lien or mortgage belonging to the estate either by judicial sale or by a foreclosure suit, by sale under deed of trust, or by acceptance of a deed in cancellation of a lien or mortgage owned by the estate, and it appears to the court that an application to redeem the property foreclosed on has been made by the former owner of the real estate to any corporation or agency created by any act of the Congress of the United States or of this state in connection with legislation for the relief of owners of mortgaged or encumbered homes, farms, ranches, or other real estate and that it would be in the best interests of the estate to own bonds of one of the above named federal or state corporations or agencies instead of the real estate, then on proper application and proof, the court may dispense with the provisions of credit sales as provided by Subsection (a) of this section, and may order reconveyance of the property to the former mortgage debtor, or former owner, reserving vendor's lien notes for the total amount of the indebtedness due or for the total amount of bonds that the corporation or agency above named is under its rules and regulations allowed to advance. On obtaining the order, it shall be proper for the guardian to endorse and assign the notes so obtained over to any one of the corporations or agencies above named in exchange for bonds of that corporation or agency.

Added by Acts 1993, 73rd Leg., ch. 957, § 1, eff. Sept. 1, 1993.

§ 828. Public Sale of Real Estate

(a) Except as otherwise provided by this chapter, all public sales of real estate shall be advertised by the guardian of the estate by a notice published in the county in which the estate is pending, as provided by this chapter for publication of notices or citations. A reference in the notice shall be made to the order of sale, the time, place, and the required terms of sale, and a brief description of the property to be sold. A reference made under this section does not have to contain field notes, but if the real estate consists of rural property, the name of the original survey, the number of acres, its locality in the county, and the name by which the land is generally known must be contained in the reference.

(b) All public sales of real estate shall be made at public auction to the highest bidder.

(c) All public sales of real estate shall be made in the county in which the guardianship proceedings are pending, at the courthouse door of the county, or at another place in the county where sales of real estate are specifically authorized to be made, on the first Tuesday of the month after publication of notice has been completed, between the hours of 10 a.m. and 4 p.m. If deemed advisable by the court, the court may order the sale to be made in the county in which the land is located, in which event notice shall be published both in that county and in the county in which the proceedings are pending.

(d) If a sale is not completed on the day advertised, the sale may be continued from day to day by making an oral public announcement of the continuance at the conclusion of the sale each day. The continued sale is to be made within the same hours as prescribed by Subsection (c) of this section. If sales are so continued, the fact shall be shown in the report of sale made to the court.

(e) When a person who bids on property of a guardianship estate offered for sale at public auction fails to comply with the terms of sale, the property shall be readvertised and sold without any further order. The person who defaults shall be liable to pay to the guardian of the estate, for the benefit of the estate, 10 percent of the amount of the person's bid and any deficiency in price on the second sale. The guardian shall recover the amounts by suit in any court in the county in which the sale was made that has jurisdiction over the amount claimed.

Added by Acts 1993, 73rd Leg., ch. 957, § 1, eff. Sept. 1, 1993.

§ 829. Private Sale of Real Estate

All private sales of real estate shall be made in the manner the court directs in its order of sale, and no further advertising, notice, or citation concerning the sale shall be required unless the court shall direct otherwise.

Added by Acts 1993, 73rd Leg., ch. 957, § 1, eff. Sept. 1, 1993.

§ 830. Sales of Easements and Rights of Way

The guardian may sell and convey easements and rights of way on, under, and over the land of a guardianship estate that is being administered under orders of a court, regardless of whether the proceeds of the sale are required for payment of charges or claims against the estate, or for other lawful purposes. The procedure for the sale is the same as provided by law for a sale of real property of wards at private sale.

Added by Acts 1993, 73rd Leg., ch. 957, § 1, eff. Sept. 1, 1993.

§ 831. Guardian Purchasing Property of the Estate

(a) Except as provided by Subsection (b) or (c) of this section, the guardian of an estate may not purchase, directly or indirectly, any property of the estate sold by the guardian, or by any co-representative of a guardian.

(b) A guardian may purchase property from the estate in compliance with the terms of a written executory contract signed by the ward before the ward became incapacitated, including a contract for deed, earnest money contract, buy/sell agreement, or stock purchase or redemption agreement.

(c) After issuing the notice required by this subsection, a guardian of an estate may purchase property from the estate on the court's determination that the sale is in the best interest of the estate. The guardian shall give notice by certified mail, return receipt requested, unless the court requires another form of notice, to each distributee of a deceased person's estate and to each creditor whose claim remains unsettled after presenting a claim within six months of the original grant of letters. In the case of an application filed by the guardian of the estate of a ward, the court shall appoint an attorney ad litem to represent the ward with respect to the sale. The court may require additional notice or it may allow for the waiver of the notice required for a sale made under this subsection.

(d) If a purchase is made in violation of this section, a person interested in the estate may file a written complaint with the court in which the guardianship proceedings are pending. On service of citation on the guardian and after hearing and proof, the court shall declare the sale void, set aside the sale, and order that the property be reconveyed to the estate. All costs of the sale, protest, and suit, if found necessary, shall be adjudged against the guardian.

Added by Acts 1993, 73rd Leg., ch. 957, § 1, eff. Sept. 1, 1993.

§ 832. Report of Sale

A sale of real property of an estate shall be reported to the court that orders the sale not later than the 30th day after the date the sale is made. A report must be in writing, sworn to, filed with the clerk, and noted on the probate docket. A report made under this section must contain:

(1) the date of the order of sale;

(2) a description of the property sold;

(3) the time and place of sale;

(4) the name of the purchaser;

(5) the amount for which each parcel of property or interest in the parcel of property was sold;

(6) the terms of the sale, and whether the sale was private or made at a public auction; and

(7) whether the purchaser is ready to comply with the order of sale.

Added by Acts 1993, 73rd Leg., ch. 957, § 1, eff. Sept. 1, 1993.

§ 833. Bond on Sale of Real Estate

If the guardian of the estate is not required by this chapter to furnish a general bond, the court may confirm the sale if the court finds the sale is satisfactory and in accordance with law. Otherwise, before a sale of real estate is confirmed, the court shall determine whether the general bond of the guardian is sufficient to protect the estate after the proceeds of the sale are received. If the court finds the bond is sufficient, the court may confirm the sale. If the general bond is found by the court to be insufficient, the court may not confirm the sale until the general bond is increased to the amount required by the court, or an additional bond is given and approved by the court. The increase in the amount of the bond, or the additional bond, shall be equal to the amount for which the real estate is sold in addition to any additional sum the court finds necessary and sets for the protection of the estate. If the real estate sold is encumbered by a lien to secure a claim against the estate, is sold to the owner or holder of the secured claim, and is in full payment, liquidation, and satisfaction of the claim, an increased general bond or additional bond may not be required except for the amount of cash actually paid to the guardian of the estate in excess of the amount necessary to pay, liquidate, and satisfy the claim in full.

Added by Acts 1993, 73rd Leg., ch. 957, § 1, eff. Sept. 1, 1993.

§ 834. Action of Court on Report of Sale

After the expiration of five days from the date a report of sale is filed under Section 832 of this code, the court shall inquire into the manner in which the sale was made, hear evidence in support of or against the report, and determine the sufficiency or insufficiency of the guardian's general bond, if any has been required and given. If the court is satisfied that the sale was for a fair price, was properly made, and conforms with the law and the court has approved any increased or additional bond that may have been found necessary to protect the estate, the court shall enter a decree confirming the sale showing conformity with other provisions of this chapter relating to the sale and authorizing the conveyance of the property to be made by the guardian of the estate on compliance by the purchaser with the terms of the sale, detailing those terms. If the court is not satisfied that the sale was for a fair price, was properly made, and conforms with the law, the court shall issue an order that sets the sale aside and order a new sale to be made, if necessary. The action of the court in confirming or disapproving a report of sale has the force and effect of a final judgment. Any person interested in the guardianship estate or in the sale has the right to have the decrees reviewed as in other final judgments in probate proceedings.

Added by Acts 1993, 73rd Leg., ch. 957, § 1, eff. Sept. 1, 1993.

§ 835. Deed Conveys Title to Real Estate

When real estate is sold, the conveyance of real estate shall be by proper deed that refers to and identifies the decree of the court that confirmed the sale. The deed shall vest in the purchaser all right, title, and interest of the estate to the property and shall be prima facie evidence that the sale has met all applicable requirements of the law.

Added by Acts 1993, 73rd Leg., ch. 957, § 1, eff. Sept. 1, 1993.

§ 836. Delivery of Deed, Vendor's Lien, and Deed of Trust Lien

After a sale is confirmed by the court and one purchaser has complied with the terms of sale, the guardian of the estate shall execute and deliver to the purchaser a proper deed conveying the property. If the sale is made partly on credit, the vendor's lien securing a purchase money note shall be expressly retained in the deed and may not be waived. Before actual delivery of the deed to the purchaser, the purchaser shall execute and deliver to the guardian of the estate a vendor's lien note, with or without personal sureties as the court has ordered and a deed of trust or mortgage on the property as further security for the payment of the note. On completion of the transaction, the guardian shall promptly file and record in the appropriate records in the county where the land is located the deed of trust or mortgage.
Added by Acts 1993, 73rd Leg., ch. 957, § 1, eff. Sept. 1, 1993.

§ 837. Penalty for Neglect

If the guardian of an estate neglects to comply with Section 836 of this code or fails to file the deed of trust securing the lien in the proper county, the guardian, after complaint and citation, may be removed. The guardian and the sureties on the bond of the guardian shall be held liable for the use of the estate and for all damages resulting from the neglect of the guardian. Damages under this section may be recovered in a court of competent jurisdiction.
Added by Acts 1993, 73rd Leg., ch. 957, § 1, eff. Sept. 1, 1993.

Subpart I. Hiring and Renting

§ 839. Hiring or Renting Without Order of Court

The guardian of an estate, without court order, may rent any real property of the estate or hire out any personal property of the estate for one year or less, either at public auction or privately, as may be deemed in the best interests of the estate.
Added by Acts 1993, 73rd Leg., ch. 957, § 1, eff. Sept. 1, 1993.

§ 840. Liability of Guardian

If property of the guardianship estate is hired or rented without court order, on the sworn complaint of any person interested in the estate, the guardian of the estate shall be required to account to the estate for the reasonable value of the hire or rent of the property to be ascertained by the court on satisfactory evidence.
Added by Acts 1993, 73rd Leg., ch. 957, § 1, eff. Sept. 1, 1993.

§ 841. Order to Hire or Rent

A guardian of an estate may file a written application with the court setting forth the property sought to be hired or rented. If the proposed rental period is one year or more, the guardian of the estate shall file a written application with the court setting forth the property sought to be hired or rented. If the court finds that it would be in the interests of the estate, the court shall grant the application and issue an order that describes the property to be hired or rented and states whether the hiring or renting shall be at public auction or privately, whether for cash or on credit, and, if on credit, the extent of the credit and the period for which the property may be rented. If the property is to be hired or rented at public auction, the court shall prescribe whether notice shall be published or posted.
Added by Acts 1993, 73rd Leg., ch. 957, § 1, eff. Sept. 1, 1993.

§ 842. Procedure in Case of Neglect to Rent Property

A person interested in a guardianship may file a written and sworn complaint in a court in which the estate is pending and cause the guardian of the estate to be cited to appear and show cause why the guardian did not hire or rent any property of the estate. The court, on hearing the complaint, shall make an order that is in the best interests of the estate.
Added by Acts 1993, 73rd Leg., ch. 957, § 1, eff. Sept. 1, 1993.

§ 843. Property Hired or Rented on Credit

When property is hired or rented on credit, possession of the property may not be delivered until the hirer or renter has executed and delivered to the guardian of the estate a note with good personal security for the amount of the hire or rental. If the property that is hired or rented is delivered without the receipt of the security required under this section, the guardian and the sureties on the bond of the guardian shall be liable for the full amount of the hire or rental. This section does not apply to a hire or rental that is paid in installments in advance of the period of time to which they relate.
Added by Acts 1993, 73rd Leg., ch. 957, § 1, eff. Sept. 1, 1993.

§ 844. Property Hired or Rented Returned in Good Condition

All property that is hired or rented, with or without a court order, shall be returned to the possession of the guardianship in as good a condition, reasonable wear and tear excepted, as when the property was hired or rented. It shall be the duty and responsibility of the guardian of the estate to see that the property is returned as provided by this section, to report to the court any loss, damage, or destruction of property that is hired or rented under this chapter, and to ask for authority to take action as is necessary. If the guardian fails to act as required by this section, the guardian and the sureties on the bond of the guardian shall be liable to the guardianship for any loss or damage suffered through the fault of the guardian to act as required under this section.

Added by Acts 1993, 73rd Leg., ch. 957, § 1, eff. Sept. 1, 1993.

§ 845. Report of Hiring or Renting

(a) When any property of the guardianship estate with an appraised value of $3,000 or more has been hired or rented, the guardian of the estate, not later than the 30th day after the date of the hire or rental, shall file with the court a sworn and written report that states:

(1) the property involved and its appraised value;

(2) the date of hiring or renting, and whether at public auction or privately;

(3) the name of the person who hired or rented the property;

(4) the amount of the hiring or rental; and

(5) whether the hiring or rental was for cash or on credit, and, if on credit, the length of time, the terms, and the security taken for the hiring or rental.

(b) When the value of the property involved is less than $3,000, the hiring or renting of the property may be reported in the next annual or final account that is to be filed as required by law.

Added by Acts 1993, 73rd Leg., ch. 957, § 1, eff. Sept. 1, 1993.

§ 846. Court Action on Report

After five days from the time the report of the hiring or rental is filed, the court shall examine the report and shall approve and confirm the hiring or rental by court order if the court finds the hire or rental just and reasonable. If the court disapproves the hiring or rental, the guardianship may not be bound and the court may order another offering of the property for hire or rent in the same manner and subject to the same rules provided in this chapter for property for hire or rent. If the report has been approved by the court and it later appears that, due to the fault of the guardian of the estate, the property has not been hired or rented for its reasonable value, the court shall cause the guardian of the estate and the sureties on the bond of the guardian to appear and show cause why the reasonable value of the hire or rental of the property should not be adjudged against the guardian or sureties.

Added by Acts 1993, 73rd Leg., ch. 957, § 1, eff. Sept. 1, 1993.

Subpart J. Mineral Leases, Pooling or Unitization Agreements, and Other Matters Relating to Mineral Properties

§ 847. Mineral Leases After Public Notice

(a) In this subpart:

(1) "Land" or "interest in land" includes minerals or any interest in any of the minerals in place.

(2) "Mineral development" includes exploration, by geophysical or by any other means, drilling, mining, developing, and operating, and producing and saving oil, other liquid hydrocarbons, gas (including all liquid hydrocarbons in the gaseous phase in the reservoir), gaseous elements, sulphur, metals, and all other minerals, solid or otherwise.

(3) "Property" includes land, minerals in place, whether solid, liquid, or gaseous, as well as an interest of any kind in the property, including royalty, owned by the estate.

(b) A guardian acting solely under an order of a court, may be authorized by the court in which the guardianship proceeding is pending to make, execute, and deliver leases, with or without unitization clauses or pooling provisions, that provide for the exploration for, and development and production of, oil, other liquid hydrocarbons, gas (including all liquid hydrocarbons in the gaseous phase), metals, and other solid minerals, and other minerals, or any of those minerals in place, belonging to the estate.

(c) All leases authorized by Subsection (b) of this section, with or without pooling provisions or utilization clauses, shall be made and entered into pursuant to and in conformity with Subsections (d)-(m) of this section.

(d) The guardian of the estate shall file a written application with the court seeking authority to lease property of the estate for mineral exploration and development, with or without pooling provisions or unitization clauses. The name of any proposed lessee or the terms, provisions, or form of any desired lease do not need to be set out or suggested in the application. The application shall:

(1) describe the property fully enough by reference to the amount of acreage, the survey name or number, abstract number, or other description that adequately identifies the property and its location in the county in which the property is located;

(2) specify the interest thought to be owned by the estate if less than the whole, but asking for authority to include all interest owned by the estate if that is the intention; and

(3) set out the reasons why the particular property of the estate should be leased.

(e) When an application to lease is filed, under this section, the county clerk shall immediately call the filing of the application to the attention of the court. The judge shall promptly make and enter a brief order designating the time and place for the hearing of the application. If the hearing does not take place at the time originally designated by the court or by timely order of continuance duly entered, the hearing shall be automatically continued without further notice to the same hour or time the following day, except Sundays and holidays on which the county courthouse is officially closed to business, and from day to day until the application is finally acted on and disposed of by order of the court. No notice of the automatic continuance shall be required.

(f) The guardian shall give written notice directed to all persons interested in the estate of the time designated by the judge for the hearing on the application to lease. The notice must be dated, state the date on which the application was filed, describe briefly the property sought to be leased, specify the fractional interest sought to be leased if less than the entire interest in the tract identified, and state the time and place designated by the judge for the hearing. Exclusive of the date of notice and of the date set for hearing, the guardian shall give at least 10 days' notice by publishing in one issue of a newspaper of general circulation in the county in which the proceeding is pending or by posting if there is no newspaper in the county. Posting under this section may be done at the guardian's instance. The date of notice when published shall be the date the newspaper bears.

(g) A court order authorizing any acts to be performed pursuant to the application is null and void in the absence of:

(1) a written order originally designating a time and place for hearing;

(2) a notice issued by the guardian of the estate in compliance with the order; and

(3) proof of publication or posting of the notice as required.

(h) At the time and place designated for the hearing, or at any time to which the hearing has been continued as provided by this section, the judge shall hear the application and require proof as to the necessity or advisability of leasing for mineral development the property described in the application and in the notice. If the judge is satisfied that the application is in due form, that notice has been duly given in the manner and for the time required by law, that the proof of necessity or advisability of leasing is sufficient, and that the application should be granted, the judge shall enter an order so finding and authorizing the making of one or more leases, with or without pooling provisions or unitization clauses (with or without cash consideration if deemed by the court to be in the best interest of the estate) that affects and covers the property or portions of the property described in the application. The order that authorizes the leasing must also set out the following mandatory contents:

(1) the name of the lessee;

(2) the actual cash consideration, if any, to be paid by the lessee;

(3) a finding that the guardian is exempt by law from giving bond if that is a fact, and if the guardian is required to give a bond, then a finding as to whether or not the guardian's general bond on file is sufficient to protect the personal property on hand, inclusive of any cash bonus to be paid; but if the court finds the general bond is insufficient to meet these requirements, the order shall show the amount of increased or additional bond required to cover the deficiency;

(4) a complete exhibit copy, either written or printed, of each lease authorized to be made, either set out in, attached to, incorporated by reference in, or made a part of the order.

(i) An exhibit copy must show the name of the lessee, the date of the lease, an adequate description of the property being leased, the delay rental, if any, to be paid to defer commencement of operations, and all other terms and provisions authorized. If no date of the lease appears in the exhibit copy or in the court's order, then the date of the court's order is considered for all purposes as the date of the authorized lease. If the name and address of a depository bank for receiving rental is not shown in the exhibit copy, the name or address of the depository bank may be inserted or caused to be inserted in the lease by the estate's guardian at the time of its execution or at any other time agreeable to the lessee, his successors, or assigns.

(j) On the hearing of an application for authority to lease, if the court grants the authority to lease, the guardian of the estate is fully authorized to make, not later than the 30th day after the date of the judge's order, unless an extension is granted by the court on a sworn application showing good cause, the lease as evidenced by the true exhibit copies in accordance with the order. Unless the guardian is not required to give a general bond, a lease for which a cash consideration is required, though ordered, executed, and delivered, is not valid unless the order authorizing the lease actually makes a finding with respect to the general bond. If the general bond has been found insufficient, the lease is not valid until the bond has been increased or an additional bond given with the sureties required by law as required by the court order, has been approved by the judge, and has been filed with the clerk of the court in which the proceeding is pending. If two or more leases on different lands are authorized by the same order, the general bond shall be increased or additional bonds given to cover all. It is not necessary for the judge to make any order confirming the leases.

(k) Every lease when executed and delivered in compliance with the rules set out in this section shall be valid and binding on the property or interest owned by the estate and covered by the lease for the full duration of the term as provided in the lease and is subject only to its terms and conditions even though the primary term extends beyond the date when the estate is closed in accordance with law. In order for a lease to be valid and binding on the property or interest owned by the estate under this section, the authorized primary term in the lease may not exceed five years, subject to terms and provisions of the lease extending it beyond the primary term by paying production, by bona fide drilling or reworking operations, whether in or on the same or additional well or wells with no cessation of operations of more than 60 consecutive days before production has been restored or obtained, or by the provisions of the lease relating to a shut-in gas well.

(l) As to any existing valid mineral lease executed and delivered in compliance with this chapter before September 1, 1993, a provision of the lease continuing the lease in force after its five-year primary term by a shut-in gas well is validated, unless the validity of the provision is an issue in a lawsuit pending in this state on September 1, 1993.

(m) Any oil, gas, and mineral lease executed by a guardian under this chapter may be amended by an instrument that provides that a shut-in gas well on the land covered by the lease or on land pooled with all or some part of the land covered by the lease shall continue the lease in force after its five-year primary term. The instrument shall be executed by the guardian, with court approval, and on the terms and conditions as may be prescribed in the instrument.

Added by Acts 1993, 73rd Leg., ch. 957, § 1, eff. Sept. 1, 1993.

§ 848. Mineral Leases at Private Sale

(a) Notwithstanding the mandatory requirements for setting a time and place for hearing of an application to lease under Section 847 of this code and the issuance, service, and return of notice, the court may authorize the making of oil, gas, and mineral leases at private sale without public notice or advertising if, in the opinion of the court, sufficient facts are set out in the application to show that it would be more advantageous to the estate that a lease be made privately and without compliance with the mandatory requirements under Section 847 of this code. Leases authorized under this section may include pooling provisions or unitization clauses as in other cases.

(b) At any time after the expiration of five days and before the expiration of the 10th day after the date of filing and without an order setting the time and place of hearing, the court shall hear the application to lease at a private sale. The court shall inquire into the manner in which the proposed lease has been or will be made and shall hear evidence for or against the application. If the court is satisfied that the lease has been or will be made for a fair and sufficient consideration and on fair terms and has been or will be properly made in conformity with the law, the court shall enter an order authorizing the execution of the lease without the necessity of advertising, notice, or citation. An order entered under this subsection must comply in all other respects with the requirements essential to the validity of mineral leases set out in this chapter as if advertising or notice were required. An order that confirms a lease made at a private sale does not need to be issued. A lease made at a private sale is not valid until the increased or additional bond required by the court, if any, has been approved by the court and filed with the clerk of the court.

Added by Acts 1993, 73rd Leg., ch. 957, § 1, eff. Sept. 1, 1993.

§ 849. Pooling or Unitization of Royalty or Minerals

(a) When an existing lease on property owned by the estate does not adequately provide for pooling or unitization, the court may authorize the commitment of royalty or mineral interests in oil, liquid hydrocarbons, gas (including all liquid hydrocarbons in the gaseous phase in the reservoir), gaseous elements, and other minerals or any one or more of them owned by the estate being administered to agreements that provide for the operation of areas as a pool or unit for the exploration, development, and production of all those minerals, if the court finds that the pool or unit to which the agreement relates will be operated in such a manner as to protect correlative rights, or to prevent the physical or economic waste of oil, liquid hydrocarbons, gas (including all liquid hydrocarbons in the gaseous phase in the reservoir), gaseous elements, or other mineral subject thereto, and that it is in the best interests of the estate to execute the agreement. Any agreement so authorized to be executed may provide that:

(1) operations incident to the drilling of or production from a well on any portion of a pool or unit are deemed for all purposes to be the conduct of operations on or production from each separately owned tract in the pool or unit;

(2) any lease covering any part of the area committed to a pool or unit shall continue in force in its entirety as long as oil, gas, or other mineral subject to the agreement is produced in paying quantities from any part of the pooled or unitized area, as long as operations are conducted as provided in the lease on any part of the pooled or unitized area, or as long as there is a shut-in gas well on any part of the pooled or unitized area if the presence of the shut-in gas well is a ground for continuation of the lease on the terms of the lease;

(3) the production allocated by the agreement to each tract included in a pool or unit shall, when produced, be deemed for all purposes to have been produced from the tract by a well drilled on the tract;

(4) the royalties provided for on production from any tract or portion of a tract within the pool or unit shall be paid only on that portion of the production allocated to the tract in accordance with the agreement;

(5) the dry gas, before or after extraction of hydrocarbons, may be returned to a formation underlying any lands or leases committed to the agreement, and that no royalties are required to be paid on the gas so returned; and

(6) gas obtained from other sources or another tract of land may be injected into a formation underlying any land or lease committed to the agreement, and that no royalties are required to be paid on the gas so injected when same is produced from the unit.

(b) Pooling or unitization, when not adequately provided for by an existing lease on property owned by the estate, may be authorized by the court in which the proceeding is pending pursuant to and in conformity with Subsections (c)-(g) of this section.

(c) The guardian of the estate shall file with the county clerk of the county in which the guardianship proceeding is pending the guardian's written application for authority to enter into a pooling or unitization agreement supplementing, amending, or otherwise relating to, any existing lease covering property owned by the estate, or to commit royalties or other interest in minerals, whether subject to lease or not, to a pooling or unitization agreement. The application must also describe the property sufficiently as required in the original application to lease, describe briefly the lease to which the interest of the estate is subject, and set out the reasons the proposed agreement concerning the property should be made. A true copy of the proposed agreement shall be attached to the application and by reference made a part of the application, but the agreement may not be recorded in the minutes. The clerk shall immediately, after the application is filed, call it to the attention of the judge.

(d) Notice of the filing of the application by advertising, citation, or otherwise is not required.

(e) The judge may hold a hearing on the application at a time that is agreeable to the parties to the proposed agreement. The judge shall hear proof and be satisfied as to whether it is in the best interests of the estate that the proposed agreement be authorized. The hearing may be continued from day to day and from time to time as the court finds to be necessary.

(f) If the court finds that the pool or unit to which the agreement relates will be operated in such a manner as to protect correlative rights or to prevent the physical or economic waste of oil, liquid hydrocarbons, gas (including all liquid hydrocarbons in the gaseous phase in the reservoir), gaseous elements, or other mineral subject to the pool or unit, that it is in the best interests of the estate that the agreement be executed, and that the agreement conforms substantially with the permissible provisions of Subsection (a) of this section, the court shall enter an order setting out the findings made by the court and authorizing execution of the agreement, with or without payment of cash consideration according to the agreement. If cash consideration is to be paid for the agreement, the court shall make a finding as to the necessity of increased or additional bond as a finding is made in the making of leases on payment of the cash bonus for the lease. The agreement is not valid until the increased or additional bond required by the court, if any, has been approved by the judge and filed with the clerk. If the date is not stipulated in the agreement, the date of the court's order shall be the effective date of the agreement.

Added by Acts 1993, 73rd Leg., ch. 957, § 1, eff. Sept. 1, 1993.

§ 850. Special Ancillary Instruments Executed Without Court Order

As to any valid mineral lease or pooling or unitization agreement, executed on behalf of the estate before September 1, 1993, pursuant to provisions, or by a former owner of land, minerals, or royalty affected by the lease, pooling, or unitization agreement, the guardian of the estate that is being administered, without further order of the court and without consideration, may execute division orders, transfer orders, instruments of correction, instruments designating depository banks for the reception of delay rentals or shut-in gas well royalty to accrue or become payable under the terms of the lease, or similar instruments pertaining to the lease or agreement and the property covered by the lease or agreement.

Added by Acts 1993, 73rd Leg., ch. 957, § 1, eff. Sept. 1, 1933.

§ 851. Procedure When Guardian of Estate Neglects to Apply for Authority

When the guardian of an estate neglects to apply for authority to subject property of the estate to a lease for mineral development, pooling, or unitization, or authority to commit royalty or other interest in minerals to pooling or unitization, any person interested in the estate, on written application filed with the county clerk, may cause the guardian to be cited to show cause why it is not in the best interests of the estate for the lease to be made or an agreement to be entered into. The clerk shall immediately call the filing of the application under this section to the attention of the judge of the court in which the guardianship proceeding is pending. The judge shall set a time and place for a hearing on the application. The guardian of the estate shall be cited to appear and show cause why the execution of the lease or agreement should not be ordered. On hearing and if satisfied from the proof that it would be in the best interests of the estate, the court shall enter an order requiring the guardian to file the guardian's application to subject the property of the estate to a lease for mineral development, with or without pooling or unitization provisions, or to commit royalty or other minerals to unitization, as the case may be. The procedures prescribed with respect to original application to lease or with respect to original application for authority to commit royalty or minerals to pooling or unitization shall be followed.

Added by Acts 1993, 73rd Leg., ch. 957, § 1, eff. Sept. 1, 1993.

§ 852. Validation of Certain Leases and Pooling or Unitization Agreements Based on Previous Statutes

All leases on the oil, gas, or other minerals existing on September 1, 1993, belonging to the estates of minors or other incapacitated persons and all agreements with respect to the pooling or unitization of oil, gas, or other minerals or any interest in oil, gas, or other minerals with like properties of others that have been authorized by the court having venue, executed, and delivered by a guardian or other fiduciary of the estate of a minor or incapacitated person in substantial conformity to the rules set forth in statutes on execution or delivery providing for only seven days' notice in some instances and for a brief order designating a time and place for hearing, are validated insofar as the period of notice or absence of an order setting a time and place for hearing is concerned, unless the length of time of the notice or the absence of the order is an issue in a lease or pooling or unitization

agreement that is involved in a lawsuit pending on September 1, 1993.
Added by Acts 1993, 73rd Leg., ch. 957, § 1, eff. Sept. 1, 1993.

Subpart K. Partition of Ward's Estate in Realty

§ 853. Partition of Ward's Interest in Realty

(a) If a ward owns an interest in real estate in common with another part owner or one or more part owners, and if, in the opinion of the guardian of the estate, it is in the best interests of the ward's estate to partition the real estate, the guardian may agree on a partition with the other part owners subject to the approval of the court in which the guardianship proceeding is pending.

(b) When a guardian has reached an agreement with the other part owners on how to partition the real estate, the guardian shall file with the court an application to have the agreement approved. The application filed by the guardian under this subsection shall describe the land that is to be divided and shall state why it is in the best interests of the ward's estate to partition the real estate and shall show that the proposed partition agreement is fair and just to the ward's estate.

(c) When the application required by Subsection (b) of this section is filed, the county clerk shall immediately call the filing of the application to the attention of the judge of the court in which the guardianship proceeding is pending. The judge shall designate a day to hear the application. The application must remain on file at least 10 days before any orders are made, and the judge may continue the hearing from time to time until the judge is satisfied concerning the application.

(d) If the judge is satisfied that the proposed partition of the real estate is in the best interests of the ward's estate, the court shall enter an order approving the partition and directing the guardian to execute the necessary agreement for the purpose of carrying the order and partition into effect.

(e) When a guardian has executed an agreement or will execute an agreement to partition any land in which the ward has an interest without court approval as provided by this section, the guardian shall file with the court in which the guardianship proceedings are pending an application for the approval and ratification of the partition agreement. The application must refer to the agreement in such a manner that the court can fully understand the nature of the partition and the land being divided. The application must state that, in the opinion of the guardian, the agreement is fair and just to the ward's estate and is in the best interests of the estate. When the application is filed, a hearing shall be held on the application as provided by Subsection (c) of this section. If the court is of the opinion that the partition is fairly made and that the partition is in the best interests of the ward's estate, the court shall enter an order ratifying and approving the partition agreement. When the partition is ratified and approved, the partition shall be effective and binding as if originally executed after a court order.

(f) If the guardian of the estate of a ward is of the opinion that it is in the best interests of the ward's estate that any real estate that the ward owns in common with others should be partitioned, the guardian may bring a suit in the court in which the guardianship proceeding is pending against the other part owner or part owners for the partition of the real estate. The court, if after hearing the suit is satisfied that the necessity for the partition of the real estate exists, may enter an order partitioning the real estate to the owner of the real estate.
Added by Acts 1993, 73rd Leg., ch. 957, § 1, eff. Sept. 1, 1993.

Subpart L. Investments and Loans of Estates of Wards

§ 854. Guardian Required to Keep Estate Invested Under Certain Circumstances

(a) The guardian of the estate is not required to invest funds that are immediately necessary for the education, support, and maintenance of the ward or others the ward supports, if any, as provided by this chapter. The guardian of the estate shall invest any other funds and assets available for investment unless the court orders otherwise under this subpart.

(b) The court may, on its own motion or on written request of a person interested in the guardianship, cite the guardian to appear and show cause why the estate is not invested or not properly invested. At any time after giving notice to all parties, the court may conduct a hearing to protect the estate, except that the court may not hold a final hearing on whether the estate is properly invested until the 31st day after the date the guardian was originally cited to appear under this subsection. On the hearing of the court's motion or a request made under this section, the court shall render an order the court considers to be in the best interests of the ward.

(c) The court may appoint a guardian ad litem for the limited purpose of representing the ward's best interests with respect to the investment of the ward's property at a hearing under this section.
Added by Acts 2003, 78th Leg., ch. 549, § 22, eff. Sept. 1, 2003.

§ 855. Standard for Management and Investments

(a) In acquiring, investing, reinvesting, exchanging, retaining, selling, supervising, and managing a ward's estate, a guardian of the estate shall exercise the judgment and care under the circumstances then prevailing that persons of ordinary prudence, discretion, and intelligence exercise in the management of their own affairs, considering the probable income from as well as the probable increase in value and the safety of their capital. The guardian shall also consider all other relevant factors, including:

(1) the anticipated costs of supporting the ward;

(2) the ward's age, education, current income, ability to earn additional income, net worth, and liabilities;

(3) the nature of the ward's estate; and

(4) any other resources reasonably available to the ward.

(a-1) In determining whether a guardian has exercised the standard of investment required by this section with respect to an investment decision, the court shall, absent fraud or gross negligence, take into consideration the investment of all the assets of the estate over which the guardian has management or control, rather than taking into consideration the prudence of only a single investment made by the guardian.

(b) A guardian of the estate is considered to have exercised the standard required by this section with respect to investing the ward's estate if the guardian invests in the following:

(1) bonds or other obligations of the United States;

(2) tax-supported bonds of this state;

(3) except as limited by Subsections (c) and (d) of this section, tax-supported bonds of a county, district, political subdivision, or incorporated city or town in this state;

(4) shares or share accounts of a state savings and loan association or savings bank with its main office or a branch office in this state if the payment of the shares or share accounts is insured by the Federal Deposit Insurance Corporation;

(5) the shares or share accounts of a federal savings and loan association or savings bank with its main office or a branch office in this state if the payment of the shares or share accounts is insured by the Federal Deposit Insurance Corporation;

(6) collateral bonds of companies incorporated under the laws of this state, having a paid-in capital of $1,000,000 or more, when the bonds are a direct obligation of the company that issues the bonds and are specifically secured by first mortgage real estate notes or other securities pledged with a trustee; or

(7) interest-bearing time deposits that may be withdrawn on or before one year after demand in a bank that does business in this state where the payment of the time deposits is insured by the Federal Deposit Insurance Corporation.

(c) The bonds of a county, district, or subdivision may be purchased only if the net funded debt of the county, district, or subdivision that issues the bonds does not exceed 10 percent of the assessed value of taxable property in the county, district, or subdivision.

(d) The bonds of a city or town may be purchased only if the net funded debt of the city or town does not exceed 10 percent of the assessed value of taxable property in the city or town less that part of the debt incurred for acquisition or improvement of revenue-producing utilities, the revenues of which are not pledged to support other obligations of the city or town.

(e) The limitations in Subsections (c) and (d) of this section do not apply to bonds issued for road purposes in this state under Section 52, Article III, of the Texas Constitution that are supported by a tax unlimited as to rate or amount.

(f) In this section, "net funded debt" means the total funded debt less sinking funds on hand.

(g) The court may modify or eliminate the guardian's duty to keep the estate invested or the standard required by this section with regard to investments of estate assets on a showing by clear and convincing evidence that the modification or elimination is in the best interests of the ward and the ward's estate.

Added by Acts 1993, 73rd Leg., ch. 957, § 1, eff. Sept. 1, 1993. Subsec. (b) amended by Acts 1999, 76th Leg., ch. 344, § 6.007, eff. Sept. 1, 1999. Amended by Acts 2003, 78th Leg., ch. 549, §§ 23 & 24, eff. Sept. 1, 2003.

§ 855A. Retention of Assets

(a) A guardian of the estate may retain without court approval until the first anniversary of the date of receipt any property received into the guardianship estate at its inception or added to the estate by gift, devise, inheritance, mutation, or increase, without regard to diversification of investments and without liability for any depreciation or loss resulting from the retention. The guardian shall care for and manage the retained assets as a person of ordinary prudence, discretion, and intelligence would in caring for and managing the person's own affairs.

(b) On application and a hearing, the court may render an order authorizing the guardian to continue retaining the property after the period prescribed by Subsection (a) of this section if the retention is an element of the guardian's investment plan as provided by this subpart.

Added by Acts 2003, 78th Leg., ch. 549, § 25, eff. Sept. 1, 2003.

§ 855B. Procedure for Making Investments or Retaining Estate Assets

(a) Not later than the 180th day after the date on which the guardian of the estate qualified as guardian or another date specified by the court, the guardian shall file a written application with the court for an order:

(1) authorizing the guardian to:

(A) develop and implement an investment plan for estate assets;

(B) declare that one or more estate assets must be retained, despite being underproductive with respect to income or overall return; or

(C) loan estate funds, invest in real estate or make other investments, or purchase a life, term, or endowment insurance policy or an annuity contract; or

(2) modifying or eliminating the guardian's duty to invest the estate.

(b) On hearing the application under this section and on a finding by the preponderance of the evidence that the action requested in the application is in the best interests of the ward and the ward's estate, the court shall render an order granting the authority requested in the application or an order modifying or eliminating the guardian's duty to keep the estate invested. The order must state in reasonably specific terms:

(1) the nature of the investment, investment plan, or other action requested in the application and authorized by the court;

(2) when an investment must be reviewed and reconsidered by the guardian; and

(3) whether the guardian must report the guardian's review and recommendations to the court.

(c) The fact that an account or other asset is the subject of a specific or general gift under a ward's will, if any, or that a ward has funds, securities, or other property held with a right of survivorship does not prevent:

(1) a guardian of the estate from taking possession and control of the asset or closing the account; or

(2) the court from authorizing an action or modifying or eliminating a duty with respect to the possession, control, or investment of the account or other asset.

(d) The procedure prescribed by this section does not apply if a different procedure is prescribed for an investment or sale by a guardian. A guardian is not required to follow the procedure prescribed by this section with respect to an investment or sale that is specifically authorized by other law.

Added by Acts 2003, 78th Leg., ch. 549, § 25, eff. Sept. 1, 2003.

§ 856. Other Investments

[repealed by Acts 2003, 78th Leg., ch. 549, § 35, eff. Sept. 1, 2003.]

[text below as amended by Acts 2003, 78th Leg., ch. 1103, § 16, eff. Sept. 1, 2003.]

(a) If a guardian of an estate deems it is in the best interests of the ward the guardian is appointed to represent to invest on behalf of the ward in the Texas Tomorrow Constitutional Trust Fund established by Subchapter F, Chapter 54, Education Code,[1] or to invest in or sell any property or security in which a trustee is authorized to invest by either Chapter 117 or Subchapter F, Chapter 113, of the Texas Trust Code (Subtitle B, Title 9, Property Code),[2] and the investment or sale is not expressly permitted by other sections of this chapter, the guardian may file a written application in the court in which the guardianship is pending that asks for an order authorizing the guardian to make the desired investment or sale and states the reason why the guardian is of the opinion that the investment or sale would be beneficial to the ward. A citation or notice is not necessary under this subsection unless ordered by the court.

(b) On the hearing of the application filed under this section, the court shall enter an order authorizing the investment or sale if the court is satisfied that the investment or sale will be beneficial to the ward. The court order must specify the investment or sale to be made and contain other directions as the court finds advisable.

(c) The procedure specified in this section does not need to be followed in making an investment or sale specifically authorized by other statutes and does not apply if a different procedure is prescribed for an investment or sale by a guardian.

Added by Acts 1993, 73rd Leg., ch. 957, § 1, eff. Sept. 1, 1993. Subsec. (a) amended by Acts 1997, 75th Leg., ch. 434, § 1, eff. Sept. 1, 1997. Repealed by Acts 2003, 78th Leg., ch. 549, § 35, eff. Sept. 1, 2003; amended by Acts 2003, 78th Leg., ch. 1103, § 16, eff. Sept. 1, 2003.

§ 857. Investment in or Continued Investment in Life Insurance or Annuities

(a) In this section, "life insurance company" means a stock or mutual legal reserve life insurance company that maintains the full legal reserves required under the laws of this state and that is licensed by the State Board of Insurance to transact the business of life insurance in this state.

(b) The guardian of the estate may invest in life, term, or endowment insurance policies, or in annuity contracts, or both, issued by a life insurance company or administered by the Veterans Administration, subject to conditions and limitations in this section.

(c) The guardian shall first apply to the court for an order that authorizes the guardian to make the investment. The application filed under this subsection must include a report that shows:

(1) in detail the financial condition of the estate at the time the application is made;

(2) the name and address of the life insurance company from which the policy or annuity contract is to be purchased and that the company is licensed by the State Board of Insurance to transact that business in this state on the date the application is filed, or that the policy or contract is administered by the Veterans Administration;

(3) a statement of the face amount and plan of the policy of insurance sought to be purchased and of the amount, frequency, and duration of the annuity payments to be provided by the annuity contract sought to be purchased;

(4) a statement of the amount, frequency, and duration of the premiums required by the policy or annuity contract; and

(5) a statement of the cash value of the policy or annuity contract at its anniversary nearest the 21st birthday of the ward, assuming that all premiums to the anniversary are paid and that there is no indebtedness against the policy or contract incurred in accordance with its terms.

(d) An insurance policy must be issued on the life of the ward, or the father, mother, spouse, child,

[1] V.T.C.A., Education Code § 54.6001 et seq.

[2] V.T.C.A., Property Code § 111.001 et seq.

brother, sister, grandfather, or grandmother of the ward or a person in whose life the ward may have an insurable interest.

(e) Only the ward, the ward's estate, or the father, mother, spouse, child, brother, sister, grandfather, or grandmother of the ward may be a beneficiary of the insurance policy and of the death benefit of the annuity contract, and the ward must be the annuitant in the annuity contract.

(f) The control of the policy or the annuity contract and of the incidents of ownership in the policy or annuity contract is vested in the guardian during the life and disability of the ward.

(g) The policy or annuity contract may not be amended or changed during the life and disability of the ward except on application to and order of the court.

(h) If a life, term, or endowment insurance policy or a contract of annuity is owned by the ward when a proceeding for the appointment of a guardian is begun, and it is made to appear that the company issuing the policy or contract of annuity is a life insurance company as defined by this section or the policy or contract is administered by the Veterans Administration, the policy or contract may be continued in full force and effect. All future premiums may be paid out of surplus funds of the ward's estate. The guardian shall apply to the court for an order to continue the policy or contract, or both, according to the existing terms of the policy or contract or to modify the policy or contract to fit any new developments affecting the welfare of the ward. Before any application filed under this subsection is granted, the guardian shall file a report in the court that shows in detail the financial condition of the ward's estate at the time the application is filed.

(i) The court, if satisfied by the application and the evidence adduced at the hearing that it is in the interests of the ward to grant the application, shall enter an order granting the application.

(j) A right, benefit, or interest that accrues under an insurance or annuity contract that comes under the provisions of this section shall become the exclusive property of the ward when the ward's disability is terminated.

Added by Acts 1993, 73rd Leg., ch. 957, § 1, eff. Sept. 1, 1993. Amended by Acts 2003, 78th Leg., ch. 549, § 26, eff. Sept. 1, 2003.

§ 858. Loans and Security for Loans

(a) If, at any time, the guardian of the estate has on hand money belonging to the ward in an amount that provides a return that is more than is necessary for the education, support, and maintenance of the ward and others the ward supports, if applicable, the guardian may lend the money for a reasonable rate of interest. The guardian shall take the note of the borrower for the money that is loaned, secured by a mortgage with a power of sale on unencumbered real estate located in this state worth at least twice the amount of the note, or by collateral notes secured by vendor's lien notes, as collateral, or the guardian may purchase vendor's lien notes if at least one-half has been paid in cash or its equivalent on the land for which the notes were given.

(b) A guardian of the estate is considered to have obtained a reasonable rate of interest for a loan for purposes of Subsection (a) of this section if the rate of interest is at least equal to 120 percent of the applicable short-term, midterm, or long-term interest rate under Section 7520, Internal Revenue Code of 1986, as amended, for the month during which the loan was made.

(c) Except as provided by this subsection, a guardian of the estate who loans estate money with the court's approval on security approved by the court is not personally liable if the borrower is unable to repay the money and the security fails. If the guardian committed fraud or was negligent in making or managing the loan, including in collecting on the loan, the guardian and the guardian's surety are liable for the loss sustained by the guardianship estate as a result of the fraud or negligence.

(d) Except as provided by Subsection (e) of this section, a guardian of the estate who lends estate money may not pay or transfer any money to consummate the loan until the guardian:

(1) submits to an attorney for examination all bonds, notes, mortgages, abstracts, and other documents relating to the loan; and

(2) receives a written opinion from the attorney stating that the documents under Subdivision (1) of this subsection are regular and that the title to relevant bonds, notes, or real estate is clear.

(e) A guardian of the estate may obtain a mortgagee's title insurance policy on any real estate loan in lieu of an abstract and attorney's opinion under Subsection (d) of this section.

(f) The borrower shall pay attorney's fees for any legal services required by this section.

(g) Not later than the 30th day after the date the guardian of the estate loans money from the estate, the guardian shall file with the court a written report, accompanied by an affidavit, stating fully the facts related to the loan. This subsection does not apply to a loan made in accordance with a court order.

(h) This section does not apply to an investment in a debenture, bond, or other publicly traded debt security.

Added by Acts 1993, 73rd Leg., ch. 957, § 1, eff. Sept. 1, 1993. Amended by Acts 2003, 78th Leg., ch. 549, § 27, eff. Sept. 1, 2003.

§ 860. Guardian's Investments in Real Estate

(a) The guardian of the estate may invest estate assets in real estate if:

(1) the guardian believes that the investment is in the best interests of the ward;

(2) there are on hand sufficient additional assets to provide a return sufficient to provide for:

(A) the education, support, and maintenance of the ward and others the ward supports, if applicable; and

(B) the maintenance, insurance, and taxes on the real estate in which the guardian wishes to invest;

(3) the guardian files a written application with the court requesting a court order authorizing the guardian to make the desired investment and stating the reasons why the guardian is of the opinion that the investment would be for the benefit of the ward; and

(4) the court renders an order authorizing the investment as provided by this section.

(b) When an application is filed by the guardian under this section, the judge's attention shall be called to the application, and the judge shall make investigation as necessary to obtain all the facts concerning the investment. The judge may not render an opinion or make an order on the application until 10 days from the date of the filing of the application have expired. On the hearing of the application, if the court is satisfied that the investment benefits the ward, the court shall issue an order that authorizes the guardian to make the investment. The order shall specify the investment to be made and contain other directions the court thinks are advisable.

(c) When a contract is made for the investment of money in real estate under court order, the guardian shall report the contract in writing to the courts. The court shall inquire fully into the contract. If satisfied that the investment will benefit the estate of the ward and that the title of the real estate is valid and unencumbered, the court may approve the contract and authorize the guardian to pay over the money in performance of the contract. The guardian may not pay any money on the contract until the contract is approved by court order to that effect.

(d) When the money of the ward has been invested in real estate, the title to the real estate shall be made to the ward. The guardian shall inventory, appraise, manage, and account for the real estate as other real estate of the ward.

Added by Acts 1993, 73rd Leg., ch. 957, § 1, eff. Sept. 1, 1993. Amended by Acts 2003, 78th Leg., ch. 549, § 28, eff. Sept. 1, 2003.

§ 861. Opinion of Attorney With Respect to Loans

When the guardian of the estate of a ward lends the money of the ward, the guardian may not pay over or transfer any money in consummation of the loan until the guardian has submitted to a reputable attorney for examination all bonds, notes, mortgages, documents, abstracts, and other papers pertaining to the loan and the guardian has received a written opinion from the attorney that all papers pertaining to the loan are regular and that the title to the bonds, notes, or real estate is good. The attorney's fee shall be paid by the borrower. The guardian may obtain a mortgagee's title insurance policy on any real estate loan instead of an abstract and attorney's opinion.

Added by Acts 1993, 73rd Leg., ch. 957, § 1, eff. Sept. 1, 1993. Amended by Acts 1995, 74th Leg., ch. 1039, § 55, eff. Sept. 1, 1995.

§ 862. Report of Loans

Not later than the 30th day after the date money belonging to a ward's estate is lent, the guardian of the ward's estate shall report to the court in writing, verified by affidavit, stating fully the facts of the loan, unless the loan was made pursuant to a court order.

Added by Acts 1993, 73rd Leg., ch. 957, § 1, eff. Sept. 1, 1993. Amended by Acts 1995, 74th Leg., ch. 1039, § 56, eff. Sept. 1, 1995.

§ 863. Liability of Guardian and Guardian's Surety

(a) In addition to any other remedy authorized by law, if the guardian of the estate fails to invest or lend estate assets in the manner provided by this subpart, the guardian and the guardian's surety are liable for the principal and the greater of:

(1) the highest legal rate of interest on the principal during the period the guardian failed to invest or lend the assets; or

(2) the overall return that would have been made on the principal if the principal were invested in the manner provided by this subpart.

(b) In addition to the liability under Subsection (a) of this section, the guardian and the guardian's surety are liable for attorney's fees, litigation expenses, and costs related to a proceeding brought to enforce this.

Added by Acts 1993, 73rd Leg., ch. 957, § 1, eff. Sept. 1, 1993. Amended by Acts 2003, 78th Leg., ch. 549, § 29, eff. Sept. 1, 2003.

Subpart M. Tax Motivated and Charitable Gifts

§ 865. Power to Make Tax-Motivated Gifts

(a) On application of the guardian of the estate or any interested party and after the posting of notice, the court, after hearing, may enter an order that authorizes the guardian to apply the principal or income of the ward's estate that is not required for the support of the ward or the ward's family during the ward's lifetime toward the establishment of an estate plan for the purpose of minimizing income, estate, inheritance, or other taxes payable out of the ward's estate on a showing that the ward will probably remain incapacitated during the ward's lifetime. On the ward's behalf, the court may authorize the guardian to make gifts, outright or in trust, of the ward's personal property or real estate to or for the benefit of:

(1) an organization to which charitable contributions may be made under the Internal Revenue Code and in which it is shown the ward would reasonably have an interest;

(2) the ward's spouse, descendant, or other person related to the ward by blood or marriage who are identifiable at the time of the order;

(3) a devisee under the ward's last validly executed will, trust, or other beneficial instrument if the instrument exists; and

(4) a person serving as guardian of the ward if the person is eligible under either Subdivision (2) or (3) of this subsection.

(b) The person making an application to the court under this section shall outline the proposed estate plan and set forth all the benefits that are to be derived from the estate plan. The application must indicate that the planned disposition is consistent with the ward's intentions if the ward's intentions can be ascertained. If the ward's intentions cannot be ascertained, the ward will be presumed to favor reduction in the incidence of the various forms of taxation and the partial distribution of the ward's estate as provided by this section.

(c) The court may appoint a guardian ad litem for the ward or any interested party at any stage of the proceedings if it is deemed advisable for the protection of the ward or the interested party.

(d) A subsequent modification of an approved plan may be made by similar application to the court.

(e) A person who makes an application to the court under this section shall mail notice of the application by certified mail to:

(1) all devisees under a will, trust, or other beneficial instrument relating to the ward's estate;

(2) the ward's spouse;

(3) the ward's dependents; and

(4) any other person as directed by the court.

Added by Acts 1993, 73rd Leg., ch. 957, § 1, eff. Sept. 1, 1993. Subsec. (a) amended by and Subsec. (e) added by Acts 1997, 75th Leg., ch. 77, § 9, eff. Sept. 1, 1997.

§ 865A. Inspection of Certain Instrument for Estate Planning Purposes

(a) On the filing of an application under Section 865 of this code, the guardian of the ward's estate may apply to the court for an order to seek an in camera inspection of a true copy of a will, codicil, trust, or other estate planning instrument of the ward as a means of obtaining access to the instrument for purposes of establishing an estate plan under Section 865 of this code.

(b) An application filed under this section must:

(1) be sworn to by the guardian;

(2) list all of the instruments requested for inspection; and

(3) state one or more reasons supporting the necessity to inspect each requested instrument for the purpose described by Subsection (a) of this section.

(c) A person who files an application under this section shall send a copy of the application to:

(1) each person who has custody of an instrument listed in the application;

(2) the ward's spouse;

(3) the ward's dependents;

(4) all devisees under a will, trust, or other beneficial instrument relating to the ward's estate; and

(5) any other person as directed by the court.

(d) Notice required by Subsection (c) of this section must be delivered by certified mail to a person described by Subsection (c)(2), (3), (4), or (5) of this section and by registered or certified mail to a person described by Subsection (c)(1) of this section. After the 10th day after the date on which the applicant complies with the notice requirement, the applicant may request that a hearing be held on the application. Notice of the date, time, and place of the hearing must be given by the applicant to each person described by Subsection (c)(1) of this section when the court sets a date for a hearing on the application.

(e) After the conclusion of a hearing on the application and on a finding that there is good cause for an in camera inspection of a requested instrument, the court shall direct the person that has custody of the requested will, codicil, trust. or other estate planning instrument to deliver a true copy of the instrument to the court for in camera inspection only. After conducting an in camera review of the instrument, the court, if good cause exists, shall release all or part of the instrument to the applicant only for the purpose described by Subsection (a) of this section.

(f) The court may appoint a guardian ad litem for the ward or an interested party at any stage of the proceedings if it is considered advisable for the protection of the ward or the interested party.

(g) An attorney does not violate the attorney-client privilege solely by complying with a court order to release an instrument subject to this section. Notwithstanding Section 22.004, Government Code, the supreme court may not amend or adopt rules in conflict with this subsection.

Added by Acts 2001, 77th Leg., ch. 217, § 16, eff. Sept. 1, 2001.

§ 866. Contributions

(a) The guardian of the estate may at any time file the guardian's sworn application in writing with the county clerk requesting an order from the court in which the guardianship is pending authorizing the guardian to contribute from the income of the ward's estate a specific amount of money as stated in the application, to one or more:

(1) designated corporations, trusts, or community chests, funds, or foundations, organized and operated exclusively for religious, charitable, scientific, literary, or educational purposes; or

(2) designated nonprofit federal, state, county, or municipal projects operated exclusively for public health or welfare.

(b) When an application is filed under this section, the county clerk shall immediately call the filing of the application to the attention of the judge of the court. The judge, by written order filed with the clerk, shall designate a day to hear the application. The application shall remain on file at least 10 days before the hearing is held. The judge may postpone or continue the hearing from time to time until the judge is satisfied concerning the application.

(c) On the conclusion of a hearing under this section, the court may enter an order authorizing the guardian to make a contribution from the income of the ward's estate to a particular donee designated in the application and order if the court is satisfied and finds from the evidence that:

(1) the amount of the proposed contribution stated in the application will probably not exceed 20 percent of the net income of the ward's estate for the current calendar year;

(2) the net income of the ward's estate for the current calendar year exceeds, or probably will exceed, $25,000;

(3) the full amount of the contribution, if made, will probably be deductible from the ward's gross income in determining the net income of the ward under applicable federal income tax laws and rules;

(4) the condition of the ward's estate justifies a contribution in the proposed amount; and

(5) the proposed contribution is reasonable in amount and is for a worthy cause.

Added by Acts 1993, 73rd Leg., ch. 957, § 1, eff. Sept. 1, 1993.

Subpart N. Management Trusts

§ 867. Creation of Management Trust

(a) In this section, "financial institution" means a financial institution, as defined by Section 201.101, Finance Code, that has trust powers and exists and does business under the laws of this or another state or the United States.

(b) On application by the guardian of a ward or by a ward's attorney ad litem or an incapacitated person's guardian ad litem at any time after the date of the ad litem's appointment under Section 646 or another provision of this code, the court in which the guardianship proceeding is pending may enter an order that creates for the ward's or incapacitated person's benefit a trust for the management of guardianship funds or funds of the incapacitated person's estate if the court finds that the creation of the trust is in the ward's or incapacitated person's best interests. Except as provided by Subsections (c) and (d) of this section, the court shall appoint a financial institution to serve as trustee of the trust.

(c) If the value of the trust's principal is $50,000 or less, the court may appoint a person other than a financial institution to serve as trustee of the trust only if the court finds the appointment to be in the ward's best interests.

(d) If the value of the trust's principal is more than $50,000, the court may appoint a person other than a financial institution to serve as trustee of the trust only if the court finds that:

(1) no financial institution is willing to serve as trustee; and

(2) the appointment is in the ward's best interests.

(e) Before making a finding that there is no financial institution willing to serve as trustee under Subsection (d)(1) of this section, the court must check any list of corporate fiduciaries located in this state that is maintained at the office of the presiding judge of the statutory probate courts or at the principal office of the Texas Bankers Association.

(f) The order shall direct the guardian or another person to deliver all or part of the assets of the guardianship to a person or corporate fiduciary appointed by the court as trustee of the trust. The order shall include terms, conditions, and limitations placed on the trust. The court shall maintain the trust under the same cause number as the guardianship proceeding.

Added by Acts 1993, 73rd Leg., ch. 957, § 1, eff. Sept. 1, 1993. Amended by Acts 1995, 74th Leg., ch. 1039, § 57, eff. Sept. 1, 1995; Acts 1997, 75th Leg., ch. 1375, § 1, eff. Sept. 1, 1997; Acts 2001, 77th Leg., ch. 994, § 1, eff. Sept. 1, 2001.

§ 868. Terms of Management Trust

(a) Except as provided by Subsection (d) of this section, a trust created under Section 867 of this code must provide that:

(1) the ward is the sole beneficiary of the trust;

(2) the trustee may disburse an amount of the trust's principal or income as the trustee determines is necessary to expend for the health, education, support, or maintenance of the ward;

(3) the income of the trust that the trustee does not disburse under Subdivision (2) of this subsection must be added to the principal of the trust;

(4) if the trustee is a corporate fiduciary, the trustee serves without giving a bond; and

(5) the trustee, on annual application to the court and subject to the court's approval, is entitled to receive reasonable compensation for services that the trustee provided to the ward as the ward's trustee that is:

(A) to be paid from the trust's income, principal, or both; and

(B) determined in the same manner as compensation of a guardian of an estate under Section 665 of this code.

(b) The trust may provide that a trustee make a distribution, payment, use, or application of trust funds for the health, education, support, or maintenance of the ward or of another person whom the ward is legally obligated to support, as necessary and without the intervention of a guardian or other representative of the ward, to:

(1) the ward's guardian;

(2) a person who has physical custody of the ward or another person whom the ward is legally obligated to support; or

(3) a person providing a good or service to the ward or another person whom the ward is legally obligated to support.

(c) A provision in a trust created under Section 867 that relieves a trustee from a duty, responsibility, or liability imposed by this subpart or Subtitle B, Title 9, Property Code, is enforceable only if:

(1) the provision is limited to specific facts and circumstances unique to the property of that trust and is not applicable generally to the trust; and

(2) the court creating or modifying the trust makes a specific finding that there is clear and convincing evidence that the inclusion of the provision is in the best interests of the beneficiary of the trust.

(d) When creating or modifying a trust, the court may omit or modify terms required by Subsection (a)(1) or (2) of this section only if the court determines that the omission or modification:

(1) is necessary and appropriate for the ward to be eligible to receive public benefits or assistance under a state or federal program that is not otherwise available to the ward; and

(2) is in the ward's best interests.

(e) The court may include additional provisions in a trust created or modified under this section if the court determines an addition does not conflict with Subsection (a) and, if appropriate, Subsection (d) of this section.

(f) If the trustee determines that it is in the best interest of the ward, the trustee may invest funds of the trust in the Texas tomorrow fund established by Subchapter F, Chapter 54, Education Code.

Added by Acts 1993, 73rd Leg., ch. 957, § 1, eff. Sept. 1, 1993. Subsec. (b) amended by Acts 1995, 74th Leg., ch. 1039, § 58, eff. Sept. 1, 1995. Subsec. (c) added by Acts 1995, 74th Leg., ch. 1039, § 59, eff. Sept. 1, 1995; Subsecs. (a), (b) amended by Acts 1997, 75th Leg., ch. 1375, § 2, eff. Sept. 1, 1997; Subsec. (c) repealed by Acts 1997, 75th Leg., ch. 1375, § 6, eff. Sept. 1, 1997; Subsecs. (d), (e) added by Acts 1997, 75th Leg., ch. 1375, § 2, eff. Sept. 1, 1997; Subsec. (f) added by Acts 1999, 76th Leg., ch. 94, § 2, eff. May 17, 1999; Subsec. (a) amended by Acts 2001, 77th Leg., ch. 994. § 2, eff. Sept. 1, 2001. Amended by Acts 2003, 78th Leg., ch. 1154, § 4, eff. Sept. 1, 2003.

§ 868A. Discharge of Guardian of Estate and Continuation of Trust

On or at any time after the creation of a trust under this subpart, the court may discharge the guardian of the ward's estate only if a guardian of the ward's person remains and the court determines that the discharge is in the ward's best interests.

Added by Acts 1997, 75th Leg., ch. 1375, § 3, eff. Sept. 1, 1997. Amended by Acts 2003, 78th Leg., ch. 549, § 30, eff. Sept. 1, 2003.

§ 868B. Bond Requirement for Certain Trustees

The court shall require a person, other than a corporate fiduciary, serving as trustee to file with the county clerk a bond in an amount equal to the value of the trust's principal and projected annual income and with the conditions the court determines are necessary.

Added by Acts 2001, 77th Leg., ch. 994, § 3, eff. Sept. 1, 2001.

§ 869. Trust Amendment, Modification, or Revocation

(a) The court may amend, modify, or revoke the trust at any time before the date of the trust's termination.

(b) The ward or guardian of the ward's estate may not revoke the trust.

Added by Acts 1993, 73rd Leg., ch. 957, § 1, eff. Sept. 1, 1993.

§ 869A. Successor Trustee

The court may appoint a successor trustee if the trustee resigns, becomes ineligible, or is removed.

Added by Acts 1995, 74th Leg., ch. 1039, § 60, eff. Sept. 1, 1995. Amended by Acts 2001, 77th Leg., ch. 994, § 4, eff. Sept. 1, 2001.

§ 869B. Applicability of Texas Trust Code

(a) A trust created under Section 867 of this code is subject to Subtitle B, Title 9, Property Code.

(b) To the extent of a conflict between Subtitle B, Title 9, Property Code, and a provision of this subpart or of the trust, the provision of the subpart or trust controls.

Added by Acts 1997, 75th Leg., ch. 1375, § 3, eff. Sept. 1, 1997.

§ 869C. Jurisdiction Over Trust Matters

A court that creates a trust under Section 867 of this code has the same jurisdiction to hear matters relating to the trust as the court has with respect to the guardianship and other matters covered by this chapter.

Added by Acts 1997, 75th Leg., ch. 1375, § 3, eff. Sept. 1, 1997.

§ 870. Termination of Trust

(a) If the ward is a minor, the trust terminates:

(1) on the death of the ward or the ward's 18th birthday, whichever is earlier; or

(2) on the date provided by court order which may not be later than the ward's 25th birthday.

(b) If the ward is an incapacitated person other than a minor, the trust terminates on the date the court determines that continuing the trust is no longer in the ward's best interests or on the death of the ward.

Added by Acts 1993, 73rd Leg., ch. 957, § 1, eff. Sept. 1, 1993. Subsec. (b) amended by Acts 1995, 74th Leg., ch. 1039, § 61, eff. Sept. 1, 1995; amended by Acts 1997, 75th Leg., ch. 1375, § 4, eff. Sept. 1, 1997.

§ 871. Annual Accounting

(a) The trustee shall prepare and file with the court an annual accounting of transactions in the trust in the same manner and form that is required of a guardian under this chapter.

(b) The trustee shall provide a copy of the annual account to the guardian of the ward's estate or person.

(c) The annual account is subject to court review and approval in the same manner that is required of an annual account prepared by a guardian under this chapter.

Added by Acts 1993, 73rd Leg., ch. 957, § 1, eff. Sept. 1, 1993.

§ 872. Liability

The guardian of the person or of the estate of the ward or the surety on the bond of the guardian is not liable for an act or omission of the trustee.

Added by Acts 1993, 73rd Leg., ch. 957, § 1, eff. Sept. 1, 1993. Amended by Acts 1995, 74th Leg., ch. 1039, § 62, eff. Sept. 1, 1995.

§ 873. Distribution of Trust Property

Unless otherwise provided by the court, the trustee shall:

(1) prepare a final account in the same form and manner that is required of a guardian under Section 749 of this code; and

(2) on court approval, distribute the principal or any undistributed income of the trust:

(A) to the ward when the trust terminates on its own terms;

(B) to the successor trustee on appointment of a successor trustee; or

(C) to the representative of the deceased ward's estate on the ward's death.

Added by Acts 1993, 73rd Leg., ch. 957, § 1, eff. Sept. 1, 1993. Amended by Acts 1995, 74th Leg., ch. 1039, § 63, eff. Sept. 1, 1995.

Part 5. Special Proceedings and Orders

Subpart A. Temporary Guardianships

§ 875. Temporary Guardian—Procedure

(a) If a court is presented with substantial evidence that a person may be a minor or other incapacitated person, and the court has probable cause to believe that the person or person's estate, or both, requires the immediate appointment of a guardian, the court shall appoint a temporary guardian with limited powers as the circumstances of the case require.

(b) The person retains all rights and powers that are not specifically granted to the person's temporary guardian by court order.

(c) A sworn, written application for the appointment of a temporary guardian shall be filed before the court appoints a temporary guardian. The application must state:

(1) the name and address of the person who is the subject of the guardianship proceeding;

(2) the danger to the person or property alleged to be imminent;

(3) the type of appointment and the particular protection and assistance being requested;

(4) the facts and reasons supporting the allegations and requests;

(5) the name, address, and qualification of the proposed temporary guardian;

(6) the name, address, and interest of the applicant; and

(7) if applicable, that the proposed temporary guardian is a private professional guardian who has complied with the requirements of Section 697 of this code.

(d) On the filing of an application for temporary guardianship, the court shall appoint an attorney to represent the proposed ward in all guardianship proceedings in which independent counsel has not been retained by or on behalf of the proposed ward.

(e) On the filing of an application for temporary guardianship, the clerk shall issue notice that shall be served on the respondent, the respondent's appointed attorney, and the proposed temporary guardian named in the application, if that person is not the applicant. The notice must describe the rights of the parties and the date, time, place, purpose, and possible consequences of a hearing on the application. A copy of the application must be attached to the notice.

(f)(1) A hearing shall be held not later than the 10th day after the date of the filing of the application for temporary guardianship unless the hearing date is postponed as provided by Subdivision (2) of this subsection. At a hearing under this section, the respondent has the right to:

(A) receive prior notice;

(B) have representation by counsel;

(C) be present;

(D) present evidence and confront and cross-examine witnesses; and

(E) a closed hearing if requested by the respondent or the respondent's attorney.

(2) The respondent or the respondent's attorney may consent to postpone the hearing on the application for temporary guardianship for a period not to exceed 30 days after the date of the filing of the application.

(3) Every application for temporary guardianship takes precedence over all matters except older matters of the same character.

(4) Immediately after an application for temporary guardianship is filed, the court shall issue an order that sets a certain date for hearing on the application for temporary guardianship.

(5) On one day's notice to the party who filed the application for temporary guardianship, the respondent or the respondent's attorney may appear and move for the dismissal of the application for temporary guardianship. If a motion is made for dismissal of the application for temporary guardianship, the court shall hear and determine the motion as expeditiously as the ends of justice require.

(6) If the applicant is not the proposed temporary guardian, a temporary guardianship may not be granted before a hearing on the application required by Subdivision (1) of this subsection unless the proposed temporary guardian appears in court.

(g) If at the conclusion of the hearing required by Subsection (f)(1) of this section the court determines that the applicant has established that there is substantial evidence that the person is a minor or other incapacitated person, that there is imminent danger that the physical health or safety of the respondent will be seriously impaired, or that the respondent's estate will be seriously damaged or dissipated unless immediate action is taken, the court shall appoint a temporary guardian by written order. The court shall assign to the temporary guardian only those powers and duties that are necessary to protect the respondent against the imminent danger shown. The court shall set bond according to Subpart B, Part 3, of this chapter. The reasons for the temporary guardianship and the powers and duties of the temporary guardian must be described in the order of appointment.

(h) Except as provided by Subsection (k) of this section, a temporary guardianship may not remain in effect for more than 60 days.

(i) If the court appoints a temporary guardian after the hearing required by Subsection (F)(1) of this section, all court costs, including attorney's fees, may be assessed as provided in Section 665A, 665B, or 669 of this code.

(j) The court may not customarily or ordinarily appoint the Department of Protective and Regulatory Services as a temporary guardian under this section. The appointment of the department as a temporary guardian under this section should be made only as a last resort.

(k) If an application for a temporary guardianship, for the conversion of a temporary guardianship to a permanent guardianship, or for a permanent guardianship is challenged or contested, the court, on the court's own motion or on the motion of any interested party, may appoint a new temporary guardian or grant a temporary restraining order under Rule 680, Texas Rules of Civil Procedure, or both, without issuing additional citation if the court finds that the appointment or the issuance of the order is necessary to protect the proposed ward or the proposed ward's estate.

(l) A temporary guardian appointed under Subsection (k) of this section must qualify in the same form and manner required of a guardian under this code. The term of the temporary guardian expires at the conclusion of the hearing challenging or contesting the application or on the date a permanent guardian the court appoints for the proposed ward qualifies to serve as the ward's guardian.

Added by Acts 1993, 73rd Leg., ch. 957, § 1, eff. Sept. 1, 1993. Subsecs. (c), (i) amended by Acts 1995, 74th Leg., ch. 1039, § 64, eff. Sept. 1, 1995; Subsec. (j) amended by Acts 1995, 74th Leg., ch. 76, § 8.074, eff. Sept. 1, 1995; Subsecs. (j), (k) amended by Acts 1995, 74th Leg., ch. 1039, § 64, eff. Sept. 1, 1995; Subsecs. (e), (f) amended by Acts 1999, 76th Leg., ch. 997, § 2, eff. Sept. 1, 1999; Subsec. (c) amended by Acts 2001, 77th Leg., ch. 217, § 17, eff. Sept. 1, 2001. Amended by Acts 2003, 78th Leg., ch. 277, § 1, eff. Sept. 1, 2003.

§ 876. Authority of Temporary Guardian

When the temporary guardian files the oath and bond required under this chapter, the court order appointing the temporary guardian takes effect without the necessity for issuance of letters of guardianship. The clerk shall note compliance with oath and bond requirements by the appointed guardian on a certificate attached to the order. The order shall be evidence of the temporary guardian's authority to act within the scope of the powers and duties set forth in the order. The clerk may not issue certified copies of the order until the oath and bond requirements are satisfied.

Added by Acts 1993, 73rd Leg., ch. 957, § 1, eff. Sept. 1, 1993.

§ 877. Powers of Temporary Guardian

All the provisions of this chapter relating to the guardianship of persons and estates of incapacitated persons apply to a temporary guardianship of the persons and estates of incapacitated persons, insofar as the same may be made applicable.

Added by Acts 1993, 73rd Leg., ch. 957, § 1, eff. Sept. 1, 1993.

§ 878. Accounting

At the expiration of a temporary appointment, the appointee shall file with the clerk of the court a sworn list of all property of the estate that has come into the hands of the appointee, a return of all sales made by the appointee, and a full exhibit and account of all of the appointee's acts as temporary appointee.

Added by Acts 1993, 73rd Leg., ch. 957, § 1, eff. Sept. 1, 1993.

§ 879. Closing Temporary Guardianship

The court shall act on the list, return, exhibit, and account filed under Section 878 of this code. Whenever temporary letters expire or cease to be effective for any reason, the court shall immediately enter an order requiring the temporary appointee to deliver the estate remaining in the temporary appointee's possession to the person who is legally entitled to the possession of the estate. The temporary appointee shall be discharged and the sureties on the bond of the temporary appointee shall be released as to future liability on proof that the appointee delivered the property as required by this section.

Added by Acts 1993, 73rd Leg., ch. 957, § 1, eff. Sept. 1, 1993.

Subpart B. Guardianships for Nonresidents

§ 881. Nonresident Guardian

(a) A nonresident of this state may be appointed and qualified as guardian or coguardian of a nonresident ward's estate located in this state in the same manner provided by this code for the appointment and qualification of a resident as guardian of the estate of an incapacitated person if:

(1) a court of competent jurisdiction in the geographical jurisdiction in which the nonresident resides appointed the nonresident guardian;

(2) the nonresident is qualified as guardian or as a fiduciary legal representative by whatever name known in the foreign jurisdiction of the property or estate of the ward located in the jurisdiction of the foreign court; and

(3) with the written application for appointment in the county court of any county in this state in which all or part of the ward's estate is located, the nonresident files a complete transcript of the proceedings from the records of the court in which the nonresident applicant was appointed, showing the applicant's appointment and qualification as the guardian or fiduciary legal representative of the ward's property or estate.

(b) The transcript required by Subsection (a) of this section must be certified to and attested by the clerk of the foreign court or the officer of the court charged by law with custody of the court records, under the court seal, if any. The certificate of the judge, chief justice, or presiding magistrate, as applicable, of the foreign court must be attached to the transcript, certifying that the attestation of the transcript by the clerk or legal custodian of the court records is in correct form.

(c) If the nonresident applicant meets the requirements of this section, without the necessity of any notice or citation, the court shall enter an order appointing the nonresident. After the nonresident applicant qualifies in the manner required of resident guardians and files with the court a power of attorney appointing a resident agent to accept service of process in all actions or proceedings with respect to the estate, the clerk shall issue the letters of guardianship to the nonresident guardian.

(d) After qualification, the nonresident guardian shall file an inventory and appraisement of the estate of the ward in this state subject to the jurisdiction of the court, as in ordinary cases, and is subject to all applicable provisions of this code with respect to the handling and settlement of estates by resident guardians.

(e) A resident guardian who has any of the estate of a ward may be ordered by the court to deliver the estate to a duly qualified and acting guardian of the ward.

Added by Acts 1993, 73rd Leg., ch. 957, § 1, eff. Sept. 1, 1993; Subsec. (e) added by Acts 1995, 74th Leg., ch. 1039, § 65, eff. Sept. 1, 1995.

§ 881A. Nonresident Guardian's Removal of Ward's Property From State

A nonresident guardian, regardless of whether the nonresident guardian is qualified under this code, may remove personal property of the ward out of the state if:

(1) the removal does not conflict with the tenure of the property or the terms and limitations of the guardianship under which the property is held; and

(2) all debts known to exist against the estate in this state are paid or secured by bond payable to and approved by the judge of the court in which guardianship proceedings are pending in this state.

Added by Acts 1995, 74th Leg., ch. 1039, § 66, eff. Sept. 1, 1995.

§ 882. Nonresident as Ward

Guardianship of the estate of a nonresident incapacitated person who owns property in this state may be granted, if necessary, in the same manner as for the property of a resident of this state. A court in the county in which the principal estate of the ward is located has jurisdiction to appoint a guardian. The court shall take all actions and make all necessary orders with respect to the estate of the ward for the maintenance, support, care, or education of the ward, out of the proceeds of the ward's estate, in the same manner as if the ward were a resident of this state and was sent abroad by the court for education or treatment. If a qualified nonresident guardian of the estate later qualifies in this state under Section 881 of this code, the court shall close the resident guardianship.

Added by Acts 1993, 73rd Leg., ch. 957, § 1, eff. Sept. 1, 1993.

Subpart C. Incapacitated Spouse and Community Property

§ 883. Incapacitated Spouse

(a) Except as provided by Subsection (c) of this section, when a husband or wife is judicially declared to be incapacitated:

(1) the other spouse, in the capacity of surviving partner of the marital partnership, acquires full power to manage, control, and dispose of the entire community estate as community administrator. including the part of the community estate that the incapacitated spouse legally has the power to manage in the absence of the incapacity, without an administration; and

(2) if the incapacitated spouse owns separate property, the court shall appoint the other spouse or another person or entity, in the order of precedence established under Section 677 of this code, as guardian of the estate to administer only the separate property of the incapacitated spouse.

(b) The spouse who is not incapacitated is presumed to be suitable and qualified to serve as community administrator. The qualification of a guardian of the estate of the separate property of an incapacitated spouse as required under Subsection (a) of this section does not deprive the competent spouse of the right to manage, control, and dispose of the entire community estate as provided in this chapter.

(c) If a spouse who is not incapacitated is removed as community administrator or if the court finds that the spouse who is not incapacitated would be disqualified to serve as guardian under Section 681 of this code or is not suitable to serve as community administrator for any other reason, the court:

(1) shall appoint a guardian of the estate for the incapacitated spouse if the court:

(A) has not appointed a guardian of the estate under Subsection (a)(2) of this section; or

(B) has appointed the spouse who is not incapacitated as guardian of the estate under Subsection (a)(2) of this section;

(2) after taking into consideration the financial circumstances of the spouses and any other relevant factors, may order the spouse who is not incapacitated to deliver to the guardian of the estate of the incapacitated spouse a portion, not to exceed one-half, of the community property that is subject to the spouses' joint management, control, and disposition under Section 3.102, Family Code; and

(3) shall authorize the guardian of the estate of the incapacitated spouse to administer:

(A) any separate property of the incapacitated spouse;

(B) any community property that is subject to the incapacitated spouse's sole management, control, and disposition under Section 3.102, Family Code;

(C) any community property delivered to the guardian of the estate under Subdivision (2) of this subsection; and

(D) any income earned on property described in this subsection.

(d) On a person's removal as community administrator or on qualification of a guardian of the estate of the person's incapacitated spouse under Subsection (c) of this section, as appropriate, a spouse who is not incapacitated shall continue to administer:

(1) the person's own separate property;

(2) any community property that is subject to the person's sole management, control, and disposition under Section 3.102, Family Code;

(3) any community property subject to the spouses' joint management, control, and disposition under Section 3.102, Family Code, unless the person is required to deliver a portion of that community property to the guardian of the estate of the person's incapacitated spouse under Subsection (c)(2) of this section, in which event, the person shall continue to administer only the portion of the community property remaining after delivery; and

(4) any income earned on property described in this subsection the person is authorized to administer.

(e) The duties and obligations between spouses, including the duty to support the other spouse, and the rights of any creditor of either spouse are not affected by the manner in which community property is administered under this section.

(f) This section does not partition community property between an incapacitated spouse and a spouse who is not incapacitated.

(g) If the court renders an order directing the guardian of the estate of the incapacitated spouse to administer certain community property as provided by Subsection (c) of this section, the community property administered by the guardian is considered the incapacitated spouse's community property, subject to the incapacitated spouse's sole management, control, and disposition under Section 3.102, Family Code. If the court renders an order directing the spouse who is not incapacitated to administer certain community property as provided by Subsection (d) of this section, the community property administered by the spouse who is not incapacitated is considered that spouse's community property, subject to that spouse's sole management, control, and disposition under Section 3.102, Family Code.

(h) An order described by Subsection (g) of this section does not affect the enforceability of a creditor's claim existing on the date the court renders the order.

Added by Acts 1993, 73rd Leg., ch. 957, § 1, eff. Sept. 1, 1993. Amended by Acts 2001, 77th Leg., ch. 217, § 18, eff. Sept. 1, 2001. Amended by Acts 2003, 78th Leg., ch. 549, § 31, eff. Sept. 1, 2003.

§ 883A. Recovery of Capacity

The special powers of management, control, and disposition vested in the community administrator by this chapter shall terminate when the decree of a court of competent jurisdiction finds that the mental capacity of the incapacitated spouse has been recovered.

Added by Acts 1995, 74th Leg., ch. 1039, § 67, eff. Sept. 1, 1995. Amended by Acts 2001, 77th Leg., ch. 217, § 19, eff. Sept. 1, 2001.

§ 883B. Accounting, Inventory, and Appraisement by Community Administrator

(a) On its own motion or on the motion of an interested person for good cause shown, the court may order a community administrator to file a verified, full, and detailed inventory and appraisement of:

(1) any community property that is subject to the incapacitated spouse's sole management, control, and disposition under Section 3.102, Family Code;

(2) any community property subject to the spouses' joint management, control, and disposition under Section 3.102, Family Code; and

(3) any income earned on property described in this subsection.

(b) At any time after the expiration of 15 months after the date that a community administrator's spouse is judicially declared to be incapacitated, the court, on its own motion or on the motion of an interested person for good cause shown, may order the community administrator to prepare and file an accounting of:

(1) any community property that is subject to the incapacitated spouse's sole management, control, and disposition under Section 3.102, Family Code:

(2) any community property subject to the spouses' joint management, control, and disposition under Section 3.102, Family Code; and

(3) any income earned on property described in this subsection.

(c) An inventory and appraisement ordered under Subsection (a) of this section must:

(1) be prepared in the same form and manner that is required of a guardian under Section 729 of this code; and

(2) be filed not later than the 90th day after the date on which the order is issued.

(d) An accounting ordered under Subsection (b) of this section must:

(1) be prepared in the same form and manner that is required of a guardian under Section 741 of this code, except that the requirement that an accounting be filed annually with the county clerk does not apply; and

(2) be filed not later than the 60th day after the date on which the order is issued.

(e) After an initial accounting has been filed by a community administrator under this section, the court, on the motion of an interested person for good cause shown may order the community administrator to file subsequent periodic accountings at intervals of not less than 12 months.

Added by Acts 2001, 77th Leg., ch. 217, § 20, eff. Sept. 1, 2001.

§ 883C. Removal of Community Administrator

(a) A court, on its own motion or on the motion of an interested person and after the community administrator has been cited by personal service to answer at a time and place specified in the notice, may remove a community administrator if:

(1) the community administrator fails to comply with a court order for an inventory and appraisement, accounting, or subsequent accounting under Section 883B of this code;

(2) sufficient grounds appear to support belief that the community administrator has misapplied or embezzled, or that the community administrator is about to misapply or embezzle, all or any part of the property committed to the care of the community administrator;

(3) the community administrator is proved to have been guilty of gross misconduct or gross mismanagement in the performance of duties as community administrator; or

(4) the community administrator becomes an incapacitated person, is sentenced to the penitentiary, or for any other reason becomes legally incapacitated from properly performing the community administrator's fiduciary duties.

(b) The order of removal must state the cause of removal and shall direct by order the disposition of the assets remaining in the name or under the control of the removed community administrator.

(c) A community administrator who defends an action for the removal of the community administrator in good faith, regardless of whether successful, is entitled to recover from the incapacitated spouse's part of the community estate the community administrator's necessary expenses and disbursements in the removal proceedings, including reasonable attorney's fees.

Added by Acts 2001, 77th Leg., ch. 217, § 20, eff. Sept. 1, 2001.

§ 883D. Appointment of Attorney ad Litem for Incapacitated Spouse

(a) The court shall appoint an attorney ad litem to represent the interests of an incapacitated spouse in a proceeding to remove a community administrator or other proceeding brought under this subpart.

(b) The attorney ad litem may demand from the community administrator an accounting or inventory and appraisement of the incapacitated spouse's part of the community estate being managed by the community administrator.

(c) A community administrator shall comply with a demand made under this section not later than the 60th day after the date on which the community administrator receives the demand.

(d) An accounting or inventory and appraisement returned under this section must be prepared in the form and manner required by the attorney ad litem, and the attorney ad litem may require the community administrator to file the accounting and inventory and appraisement with the court.

Added by Acts 2001, 77th Leg., ch. 217, § 20, eff. Sept. 1, 2001.

§ 884. Delivery to Spouse

A guardian of the estate of an incapacitated married person who, as guardian, is administering community property as part of the estate of the ward, shall deliver on demand the community property to the spouse who is not incapacitated if the spouse becomes community administrator under Section 883 of this code.

Added by Acts 1993, 73rd Leg., ch. 957, § 1, eff. Sept. 1, 1993. Amended by Acts 2001, 77th Leg., ch. 217, § 21, eff. Sept. 1, 2001.

§ 884A. Lawsuit Information

A person whose spouse is judicially declared to be incapacitated and who acquires the power to manage, control, and dispose of the entire community estate under Section 883 of this code shall inform the court in writing of any suit filed by or on behalf of the person that:

(1) is a suit for dissolution of the marriage of the person and the person's incapacitated spouse; or

(2) names the incapacitated spouse as a defendant.

Added by Acts 2001, 77th Leg., ch. 217, § 22, eff. Sept. 1, 2001.

Subpart D. Receivership for Minors and Other Incapacitated Persons

§ 885. Receivership

(a) When the estate of a minor or other incapacitated person or any portion of the estate of the minor or other incapacitated person appears in danger of injury, loss, or waste and in need of a guardianship or other representative and there is no guardian of the estate who is qualified in this state and a guardian is not needed, the county judge of the county in which the minor or other incapacitated person resides or in which the endangered estate is located shall enter an order, with or without application, appointing a suitable person as receiver to take charge of the estate. The court order shall require a receiver appointed under this section to give bond as in ordinary receiverships in an amount the judge deems necessary to protect the estate. The court order shall specify the duties and powers of the receiver as the judge deems necessary for the protection, conservation, and preservation of the estate. The clerk shall enter an order made under this section on the minutes of the court. The person who is appointed as receiver shall make and submit a bond for the judge's approval and shall file the bond, when approved, with the clerk. The person who is appointed receiver shall proceed to take charge of the endangered estate pursuant to the powers and duties vested in the person by the order of appointment and subsequent orders made by the judge.

(b) During the pendency of the receivership, when the needs of the minor or other incapacitated person require the use of the income or corpus of the estate for the education, clothing, or subsistence of the minor or other incapacitated person, the judge, with or without application, shall enter an order on the minutes of the court that appropriates an amount of income or corpus that is sufficient for that purpose. The receiver shall use the amount appropriated by the court to pay a claim for the education, clothing, or subsistence of the minor or other incapacitated person that is presented to the judge for approval and ordered by the judge to be paid.

(c) During the pendency of the receivership, when the receiver has on hand an amount of money that belongs to the minor or other incapacitated person that is in excess of the amount needed for current necessities and expenses, the receiver, under direction of the judge, may invest, lend, or contribute the excess money or any portion of the money in the manner, for the security, and on the terms and conditions provided by this chapter for investments, loans, or contributions by guardians. The receiver shall report to the judge all transactions made under this subsection in the same manner that a report is required of a guardian under this chapter.

(d) All necessary expenses incurred by the receiver in administering the estate may be rendered monthly to the judge in the form of a sworn statement of account that includes a report of the receiver's acts, the condition of the estate, the status of the threatened danger to the estate, and the progress made toward abatement of the danger. If the judge is satisfied that the statement is correct and reasonable in all respects, the judge shall promptly enter an order approving the expenses and authorizing the receiver to be reimbursed from the funds of the estate in the receiver's hands. A receiver shall be compensated for services rendered in the receiver's official capacity in the same manner and amount as provided by this chapter for similar services rendered by guardians of estates.

(e) When the threatened danger has abated and the estate is no longer liable to injury, loss, or waste because there is no guardian or other representative of the estate, the receiver shall report to the judge, file with the clerk a full and final sworn account of all property of the estate the receiver received, had on hand when the receivership was pending, all sums paid out, all acts performed by the receiver with respect to the estate, and all property of the estate that remains in the receiver's hands on the date of the report. On the filing of the report, the clerk shall issue and cause to be posted a notice to all persons interested in the welfare of the minor or other incapacitated person and shall give personal notice to the person who has custody of the minor or other incapacitated person to appear before the judge at a time and place specified in the notice and contest the report and account if the person desires.

(f) If on hearing the receiver's report and account the judge is satisfied that the danger of injury, loss, or waste to the estate has abated and that the report and account are correct, the judge shall enter an order finding that the danger of injury, loss, or waste to the estate has abated and shall direct the receiver to deliver the estate to the person from whom the receiver took possession as receiver, to the person who has custody of the minor or other incapacitated person, or to another person as the judge may find is entitled to possession of the estate. A person who receives the estate under this subsection shall execute and file with the clerk an appropriate receipt for the estate that is delivered to the person. The judge's order shall discharge the receivership and the sureties on the bond of the receiver. If the judge is not satisfied that the danger has abated, or if the judge is not satisfied with the receiver's report and account, the judge shall enter an order that continues the receivership in effect until the judge is satisfied that the danger has abated or is satisfied with the report and account.

(g) An order or a bond, report, account, or notice in a receivership proceeding must be recorded in the minutes of the court.

Added by Acts 1993, 73rd Leg., ch. 957, § 1, eff. Sept. 1, 1993.

Subpart E. Payment of Claims without Guardianship

§ 887. Payment of Claims Without Guardianship and Administration of Terminated Guardianship Assets

(a) When a resident person who is a minor or other incapacitated person, or the former ward of a guardianship terminated under Subpart C, Part 4, of this code,[1] who are referred to in this section as "creditor," are without a legal guardian of the person's estate, and

[1] V.A.T.S. Probate Code, § 745 et seq.

the person is entitled to money in an amount that is $100,000 or less, the right to which is liquidated and is uncontested in any pending lawsuit, the debtor may pay the money to the county clerk of the county in which the creditor resides to the account of the creditor, giving the creditor's name, the creditor's social security identification number, the nature of the creditor's disability, and, if the creditor is a minor, the minor's age, and the creditor's postoffice address. The receipt for the money signed by the clerk is binding on the creditor as of the date of receipt and to the extent of the payment. The clerk, by letter mailed to the address given by the debtor, shall apprise the creditor of the fact that the deposit was made. On receipt of the payment by the clerk, the clerk shall call the receipt of the payment to the court's attention and shall invest the money as authorized under this chapter pursuant to court order in the name and for the account of the minor or other person entitled to the money. Any increase, dividend, or income from an investment made under this section shall be credited to the account of the minor or other person entitled to the investment. Any money that is deposited under the terms of this section that has not been paid out shall be subject to the provisions of this chapter not later than October 1, 1993.

(b) Not later than March 1 of each calendar year, the clerk of the court shall make a written report to the court of the status of an investment made by the clerk under this section. The report must contain:

(1) the amount of the original investment or the amount of the investment at the last annual report, whichever is later;

(2) any increase, dividend, or income from such investment since the last annual report;

(3) the total amount of the investment and all increases, dividends, or income at the date of the report; and

(4) the name of the depository or the type of investment.

(c) The father or mother, or unestranged spouse, of the creditor, with priority being given to the spouse who resides in this state or if there is no spouse and both father and mother are dead or are nonresidents of this state, then the person who resides in this state who has actual custody of the creditor, as custodian and on filing with the clerk written application and bond approved by the county judge of the county, may withdraw the money from the clerk for the use and benefit of the creditor, the bond to be in double the amount of the money and to be payable to the judge or the judge's successors in office and to be conditioned that the custodian will use the money for the creditor's benefit under directions of the court and that the custodian, when legally called on to do so, will faithfully account to the creditor and the creditor's heirs or legal representatives for the money and any increase to the money on the removal of the disability to which the creditor is subject, or on the creditor's death, or the appointment of a guardian for the creditor. A fee or commission may not be allowed to the custodian for taking care of, handling, or expending the money withdrawn by the custodian.

(d) When the custodian has expended the money in accordance with directions of the court or has otherwise complied with the terms of the custodian's bond by accounting for the money and any increase in the money, the custodian shall file with the county clerk of the county the custodian's sworn report of the custodian's accounting. The filing of the custodian's report, when approved by the court, operates as a discharge of the person as custodian and of the person's sureties from all further liability under the bond. The court shall satisfy itself that the report is true and correct and may require proof as in other cases.

(e) When a nonresident minor, a nonresident person who is adjudged by a court of competent jurisdiction to be incapacitated, or the former ward of a guardianship terminated under Subpart C, Part 4, of this code who has no legal guardian qualified in this state is entitled to money in an amount that is not more than $100,000 owing as a result of transactions within this state, the right to which is liquidated and is uncontested in any pending lawsuit in this state, the debtor in this state may pay the money to the guardian of the creditor who is duly qualified in the domiciliary jurisdiction or to the county clerk of any county in this state in which real property owned by the nonresident person is located. If the person is not known to own any real property in any county in this state the debtor has the right to pay the money to the county clerk of the county of this state in which the debtor resides. In either case, the debtor's payment to the clerk is for the use and benefit and for the account of the nonresident creditor. The receipt for the payment signed by the clerk that recites the name of the creditor and the post office address of the creditor, if known, is binding on the creditor as of the date and to the extent of the payment. The clerk shall handle the money paid to the clerk by the debtor in the same manner as provided for cases of payments to the accounts of residents of this state under Subsections (a)-(d) of this section. All applicable provisions of Subsections (a)-(d) of this section apply to the handling and disposition of money or any increase, dividend, or income paid to the clerk for the use, benefit, and account of the nonresident creditor.

(f) If a person who is authorized to withdraw the money does not withdraw the money from the clerk as provided for in this section, the creditor, after termination of the creditor's disability, or the subsequent personal representative of the creditor or the creditor's heirs may withdraw, at any time and without special bond for the purpose, the money on simply exhibiting to the clerk an order of the county or probate court of the county where the money is held by the clerk that directs the clerk to deliver the money to the creditor, to the creditor's personal representative, or to the creditor's heirs named in the order. Before the court issues an order under this subsection, the person's identity and the person's credentials must be proved to the court's satisfaction.

(g) When it is made to appear to the judge of a county court, district court, or other court of this state, by an affidavit executed by the superintendent, business manager, or field representative of any eleemosynary institution of this state, that a certain inmate in the institution is a person who has a mental disability, an incapacitated person, or a person whose mental illness or mental incapacity, or both, renders the person incapable of caring for himself and of managing the person's own property and financial affairs, there is no known legal guardian appointed for the estate of the inmate, and there is on deposit in the court registry a certain sum of money that belongs to the inmate that does not exceed $10,000, the court may order the disposition of the funds as provided by this subsection. The court, on satisfactory proof by affidavit or otherwise that the inmate is a person who has a mental disability, an incapacitated person, or a person whose mental illness or mental incapacity, or both, renders the inmate incapable of caring for the inmate's self and of managing the inmate's own property and financial affairs and is without a legally appointed guardian of the inmate's estate, may by order direct the clerk of the court to pay the money to the institution for the use and benefit of the inmate. The state institution to which the payment is made may not be required to give bond or security for receiving the fund from the court registry, and the receipt from the state institution for the payment, or the canceled check or warrant by which the payment was made, shall be sufficient evidence of the disposition of the payment. The clerk of the court is relieved of further responsibility for the disposition. On receipt of the money, the institution shall deposit all of the amount of money received to the trust account of the inmate. The money deposited by the institution in the trust account is to be used by or for the personal use of the owner of the trust account under the rules or custom of the institution in the expenditure of the funds by the inmate or for the use and benefit of the inmate by the responsible officer of the institution. This subsection is cumulative of all other laws affecting the rights of a person who has a mental disability, an incapacitated person, or a person who has a mental illness and affecting money that belongs to the person as an inmate of a state eleemosynary institution. If the inmate dies leaving a balance in the inmate's trust account, the balance may be applied to the burial expenses of the inmate or applied to the care, support, and treatment account of the inmate at the eleemosynary institution. After the expenditure of all funds in the trust account or after the death of the inmate, the responsible officer shall furnish a statement of expenditures of the funds to the nearest relative who is entitled to receive the statement, A copy of the statement shall be filed with the court that first granted the order to dispose of the funds in accordance with the provisions of this chapter.

Added by Acts 1993, 73rd Leg., ch. 957, § 1, eff. Sept. 1, 1993. Subsecs. (a), (e) amended by Acts 1997, 75th Leg., ch. 295, § 1, eff. Sept. 1, 1997; Subsec. (a) amended by Acts 2001, 77th Leg., ch. 127, § 2, eff. Sept. 1, 2001; Subsec. (a) amended by Acts 2001. 77th Leg., ch. 1174, § 8, eff. Sept. 1, 2001; Subsec. (e) amended by Acts 2001, 77th Leg., ch. 127, § 2, eff. Sept. 1, 2001; Subsec. (e) amended by Acts 2001, 77th Leg., ch. 1174, § 8, eff. Sept. 1, 2001.

Subpart F. Sale of Property of Minors and Certain Wards

§ 889. Sale of Property of a Minor by a Parent Without Guardianship

(a) When a minor has an interest in real or personal property and the net value of the interest does not exceed $100,000, a natural or adoptive parent, or the managing conservator, of a minor who is not a ward may apply to the court for an order to sell the minor's interest in the property without being appointed guardian. A minor may not disaffirm a sale of property pursuant to a court order under this section.

(b) The parent shall apply to the court under oath for the sale of the property. Venue for the application under this section is the same as venue for an application for the appointment of a guardian for a minor. The application must contain:

(1) a legal description of the real property and a description that identifies the personal property;

(2) the name of the minor and the minor's interest in the property;

(3) the name of the purchaser;

(4) a statement that the sale of the minor's interest in the property is for cash; and

(5) a statement that all funds received by the parent shall be used for the use and benefit of the minor.

(c) On receipt of the application, the court shall set the application for hearing at a date not earlier than five days from the date of the filing of the application. If the court deems it necessary, the court may cause citation to be issued.

(d) At the time of the hearing of the application filed under this section, the court shall order the sale of the property if the court is satisfied from the evidence that the sale is in the best interests of the minor. The court may require an independent appraisal of the property to be sold to establish the minimum sale price.

(e) When the court enters the order of sale, the purchaser of the property shall pay the proceeds of the sale belonging to the minor into the court registry.

(f) Nothing in this section prevents the proceeds deposited in the registry from being withdrawn from the court registry under Section 887 of this code.

Added by Acts 1993, 73rd Leg., ch. 957, § 1, eff. Sept. 1, 1993. Subsec. (a) amended by Acts 1995, 74th Leg., ch. 1039, § 68, eff. Sept. 1, 1995; Subsec. (f) amended by Acts 1995, 74th Leg., ch. 1039, § 69, eff. Sept. 1, 1995; Subsec. (a) amended by Acts 1997, 75th Leg., ch. 295, § 2, eff. Sept. 1, 1997; Subsec. (a) amended by Acts 2001, 77th Leg., ch. 127, § 3, eff. Sept. 1, 2001; Subsec. (a) amended by Acts 2001, 77th Leg., ch. 1174, § 9, eff. Sept. 1, 2001.

§ 890. Sale of Property of Ward Without Guardianship of the Estate

(a) This section applies only to a ward who has a guardian of the person but does not have a guardian of the estate.

(b) When a ward has an interest in real or personal property in an estate and the net value of the interest does not exceed $100,000, the guardian may apply under oath to the court for an order to sell the ward's interest in the property without being appointed guardian of the estate. A ward may not disaffirm a sale of property pursuant to a court order under this section.

(c) Venue for an application under this section is the same as venue for an application for the appointment of a guardian for the ward. The application must contain the same information required by Section 859(b) of this code.

(d) On receipt of the application, the court shall set the application for hearing at a date not earlier than five days from the date of the filing of the application. If the court considers it necessary, the court may cause citation to be issued.

(e) The procedures and evidentiary requirements for a hearing of an application filed under this section are the same as the procedures and evidentiary requirements for a hearing of an application filed under Section 889 of this code.

(f) When the court enters the order of sale, the purchaser of the property shall pay the proceeds of the sale belonging to the ward into the court registry.

(g) Nothing in this section prevents the proceeds deposited in the court registry from being withdrawn as prescribed by Section 887 of this code.

Added by Acts 1997, 75th Leg., ch. 295, § 4, eff. Sept. 1, 1997. Subsec. (b) amended by Acts 2001, 77th Leg., ch. 127, § 4, eff. Sept. 1, 2001; Subsec. (b) amended by Acts 2001, 77th Leg., ch. 1174, § 10, eff. Sept. 1, 2001.

Subpart G. Interstate Guardianships

§ 891. Transfer of Guardianship to Foreign Jurisdiction

(a) A guardian of the person or estate of a ward may apply with the court that has jurisdiction over the guardianship to transfer the guardianship to a court in a foreign jurisdiction if the ward has moved permanently to the foreign jurisdiction.

(b) Notice of the application to transfer a guardianship under this section shall be served personally on the ward and shall be given to the foreign court to which the guardianship is to be transferred.

(c) On the court's own motion or on the motion of the ward or any interested person, the court shall hold a hearing to consider the application to transfer the guardianship.

(d) The court shall transfer a guardianship to a foreign court if the court determines the transfer is in the best interests of the ward. The transfer of the guardianship must be made contingent on the acceptance of the guardianship in the foreign jurisdiction. To facilitate the orderly transfer of the guardianship, the court shall coordinate efforts with the appropriate foreign court.

Added by Acts 2001, 77th Leg., ch. 479, § 1, eff. Sept. 1, 2001.

§ 892. Receipt and Acceptance of Foreign Guardianship

(a) A guardian appointed by a foreign court to represent an incapacitated person who is residing in this state or intends to move to this state may file an application with a court in which the ward resides or intends to reside to have the guardianship transferred to the court.

(b) Notice of the application for receipt and acceptance of a foreign guardianship under this section shall be served personally on the ward and shall be given to the foreign court from which the guardianship is to be transferred.

(c) If an application for receipt and acceptance of a foreign guardianship is filed in two or more courts with jurisdiction, the proceeding shall be heard in the court with jurisdiction over the application filed on the earliest date if venue is otherwise proper in that court. A court that does not have venue to hear the application shall transfer the proceeding to the proper court.

(d) In reviewing an application for receipt and acceptance of a foreign guardianship, the court should determine:

(1) that the proposed guardianship is not a collateral attack on an existing or proposed guardianship in another jurisdiction in this or another state; and

(2) for a guardianship in which a court in one or more states may have jurisdiction, that the application has been filed in the court that is best suited to consider the matter.

(e) On the court's own motion or on the motion of the ward or any interested person, the court shall hold a hearing to consider the application for receipt and acceptance of a foreign guardianship.

(f) The court shall grant an application for receipt and acceptance of a foreign guardianship if the transfer of the guardianship from the foreign jurisdiction is in the best interests of the ward. In granting an application under this subsection, the court shall give full faith and credit to the provisions of the foreign guardianship order concerning the determination of the ward's incapacity and the rights, powers, and duties of the guardian.

(g) The court shall coordinate efforts with the appropriate foreign court to facilitate the orderly transfer of the guardianship.

(h) The denial of an application for receipt and acceptance of a guardianship under this section does not affect the right of a guardian appointed by a foreign court to file an application to be appointed guardian of the incapacitated person under Section 682 of this code.

Added by Acts 2001, 77th Leg., ch. 479, § 1, eff. Sept. 1, 2001.

§ 893. Review of Transferred Guardianship

Not later than the 90th day after the date a court grants an application for receipt and acceptance of a foreign guardianship under Section 892 of this code, the court shall hold a hearing to consider modifying the administrative procedures or requirements of the transferred guardianship in accordance with local and state law.

Added by Acts 2001, 77th Leg., ch. 479, § 1, eff. Sept. 1, 2001.

Subpart H. Contracts in Arts, Entertainment, Advertisement, and Sports

§ 901. Definitions

In this subpart:

(1) "Advertise" means to solicit or induce, through print or electronic media, including radio, television, computer, or direct mail, to purchase consumer goods or services.

(2) "Advertisement contract" means a contract under which a person is employed or agrees to advertise consumer goods or services.

(3) "Artist" means:

(A) an actor who performs in a motion picture, theatrical, radio, television, or other entertainment production;

(B) a musician or musical director;

(C) a director or producer of a motion picture, theatrical, radio, television, or other entertainment production;

(D) a writer;

(E) a cinematographer;

(F) a composer, lyricist, or arranger of musical compositions;

(G) a dancer or choreographer of musical productions;

(H) a model; or

(I) any other individual who renders analogous professional services in a motion picture, theatrical, radio, television, or other entertainment production.

(4) "Arts and entertainment contract" means a contract under which:

(A) an artist is employed or agrees to render services in a motion picture, theatrical, radio, television, or other entertainment production; or

(B) a person agrees to purchase, secure, sell, lease, license, or otherwise dispose of literary, musical, or dramatic tangible or intangible property or any rights in that property for use in the field of entertainment, including a motion picture, television, the production of phonograph records, or theater.

(5) "Consumer goods" means goods that are used or bought for use primarily for personal, family, or household purposes.

(6) "Sports contract" means a contract under which an athlete is employed or agrees to participate, compete, or engage in a sports or athletic activity at a professional or amateur sports event or athletic event.

Added by Acts 2001, 77th Leg., ch. 799, § 1, eff. Sept. 1, 2001.

§ 902. Construction

This subpart may not be construed to authorize the making of a contract that binds a minor beyond the seventh anniversary of the date of the contract.

Added by Acts 2001, 77th Leg., ch. 799, § 1, eff. Sept. 1, 2001.

§ 903. Approval of Certain Contracts of Minors; Not Voidable

(a) A court, on petition of the guardian of the estate of the minor, may enter an order approving for purposes of this subpart an arts and entertainment contract, advertisement contract, or sports contract that is entered into by a minor. The court may approve the contract only after the guardian of the minor's estate provides to the other party to the contract notice of the petition and an opportunity to request a hearing in the manner provided by the court.

(b) The approval of a contract under this section extends to the contract as a whole and any of the terms and provisions of the contract, including any optional or conditional provision in the contract relating to the extension or termination of its term.

(c) A court may withhold approval of a contract under which part of the minor's net earnings under the contract will be set aside as provided by Section 904 of this code until the guardian of the minor's estate executes and files with the court written consent to the making of the order.

(d) An otherwise valid contract approved under this section may not be voidable solely on the ground that it was entered into by a person during the age of minority.

(e) Each parent of the minor is a necessary party to a proceeding brought under this section.

Added by Acts 2001, 77th Leg., ch. 799, § 1, eff. Sept. 1, 2001.

§ 904. Net Earnings of Minor; Set Aside and Preservation

(a) In this section, "net earnings" means the total amount to be received for the services of the minor under the contract less:

(1) the sum required by law to be paid as taxes to any government or governmental agency;

(2) a reasonable sum to be expended for the support, care, maintenance, education, and training of the minor;

(3) fees and expenses paid in connection with procuring the contract or maintaining employment of the minor; and

(4) attorney's fees for services rendered in connection with the contract or any other business of the minor.

(b) Notwithstanding any other law, the court may require in an order approving a contract under Section 903 of this code that a portion of the net earnings of the minor under the contract be set aside and preserved for the benefit of the minor in a trust created under Section 867 of this code or a similar trust created under the laws of another state. The amount to be set aside under this subsection must be a reasonable amount as determined by the court.

Added by Acts 2001, 77th Leg., ch. 799, § 1, eff. Sept. 1, 2001.

§ 905. Guardian Ad Litem

The court may appoint a guardian ad litem for a minor who has entered into an arts and entertainment contract, advertisement contract, or sports contract if the court finds that appointment of the ad litem would be in the best interest of the minor.

Added by Acts 2001, 77th Leg., ch. 799, § 1, eff. Sept. 1, 2001.

XIII.
PROPERTY CODE

Title 2. Conveyances

Chapter 5. Conveyances

Subchapter A. General Provisions

Statutes in Context

At common law, a fee simple was granted only if the words of limitation "and his heirs" were used. Section 5.001 reverses the common law presumption so that a grant "to A" results in A receiving a fee simple.

§ 5.001. Fee Simple

(a) An estate in land that is conveyed or devised is a fee simple unless the estate is limited by express words or unless a lesser estate is conveyed or devised by construction or operation of law. Words previously necessary at common law to transfer a fee simple estate are not necessary.

(b) This section applies only to a conveyance occurring on or after February 5, 1840.

Acts 1983, 68th Leg., p. 3480, ch. 576, § 1, eff. Jan. 1, 1984.

§ 5.002. Failing as a Conveyance

An instrument intended as a conveyance of real property or an interest in real property that, because of this chapter, fails as a conveyance in whole or in part is enforceable to the extent permitted by law as a contract to convey the property or interest.

Acts 1983, 68th Leg., p. 3480, ch. 576, § 1, eff. Jan. 1, 1984.

§ 5.003. Partial Conveyance

(a) An alienation of real property that purports to transfer a greater right or estate in the property than the person making the alienation may lawfully transfer alienates only the right or estate that the person may convey.

(b) Neither the alienation by deed or will of an estate on which a remainder depends nor the union of the estate with an inheritance by purchase or descent affects the remainder.

Acts 1983, 68th Leg., p. 3480, ch. 576, § 1, eff. Jan. 1, 1984.

§ 5.004. Conveyance by Authorized Officer

(a) A conveyance of real property by an officer legally authorized to sell the property under a judgment of a court within the state passes absolute title to the property to the purchaser.

(b) This section does not affect the rights of a person who is not or who does not claim under a party to the conveyance or judgment.

Acts 1983, 68th Leg., p. 3480, ch. 576, § 1, eff. Jan. 1, 1984.

§ 5.005. Aliens

An alien has the same real and personal property rights as a United States citizen.

Acts 1983, 68th Leg., p. 3481, ch. 576, § 1, eff. Jan. 1, 1984.

§ 5.009. Duties of Life Tenant

(a) Subject to Subsection (b), if the life tenant of a legal life estate is given the power to sell and reinvest any life tenancy property, the life tenant is subject, with respect to the sale and investment of the property, to all of the fiduciary duties of a trustee imposed by the Texas Trust Code (Subtitle B, Title 9, Property Code)[1] or the common law of this state.

(b) A life tenant may retain, as life tenancy property, any real property originally conveyed to the life tenant without being subject to the fiduciary duties of a trustee; however, the life tenant is subject to the common law duties of a life tenant.

Acts 1993, 73rd Leg., ch. 846, § 34, eff. Sept. 1, 1993. Renumbered from § 5.008 by Acts 1995, 74th Leg., ch. 76, § 17.01(42), eff. Sept. 1, 1995.

Subchapter C. Future Estates

§ 5.041. Future Estates

A person may make an inter vivos conveyance of an estate of freehold or inheritance that commences in the future, in the same manner as by a will.

Acts 1983, 68th Leg., p. 3483, ch. 576, § 1, eff. Jan. 1, 1984.

Statutes in Context

Section 5.042 abolishes many of the arcane common law rules regarding conveyances such as the Rule in Shelley's case and the Doctrine of Worthier Title.

§ 5.042. Abolition of Common-Law Rules

(a) The common-law rules known as the rule in Shelley's case, the rule forbidding a remainder to the grantor's heirs, the doctrine of worthier title, and the

[1] V.T.C.A., Property Code § 111.001 et seq.

doctrine or rule prohibiting an existing lien upon part of a homestead from extending to another part of the homestead not charged with the debts secured by the existing lien upon part of the homestead do not apply in this state.

(b) A deed, will, or other conveyance of property in this state that limits an interest in the property to a particular person or to a class such as the heirs, heirs of the body, issue, or next of kin of the conveyor or of a person to whom a particular interest in the same property is limited is effective according to the intent of the conveyor.

(c) Status as an heir or next of kin of a conveyor or the failure of a conveyor to describe a person in a conveyance other than as a member of a class does not affect a person's right to take or share in an interest as a conveyee.

(d) Subject to the intention of a conveyor, which controls unless limited by law, the membership of a class described in this section and the participation of a member in a property interest conveyed to the class are determined under this state's laws of descent and distribution.

(e) This section does not apply to a conveyance taking effect before January 1, 1964.

Amended by Acts 1999, 76th Leg., ch. 1510, § 5, eff. Sept. 1, 1999.

Statutes in Context

Article I, § 26 of the Texas Constitution adopts the common law version of the Rule Against Perpetuities, that is, "a future interest not destructible by the owner of a prior interest cannot be valid unless it becomes vested at a date not more remote than twenty-one years after lives in being at the creation of such interest, plus the period of gestation. Any future interest so limited that it retains its indestructible and contingent character until a more remote time is invalid." Interpretive Commentary to Article I, § 21. The court must, however, reform or construe transfers that violate the Rule under § 5.043 to carry out the general intent and specific directives of the grantor to the extent possible without violating the Rule. The court may apply the equitable doctrine of cy pres in this process. *See also* Property Code § 112.036 (indicating that the Rule does not apply to charitable trusts).

§ 5.043. Reformation of Interests Violating Rule Against Perpetuities

(a) Within the limits of the rule against perpetuities, a court shall reform or construe an interest in real or personal property that violates the rule to effect the ascertainable general intent of the creator of the interest. A court shall liberally construe and apply this provision to validate an interest to the fullest extent consistent with the creator's intent.

(b) The court may reform or construe an interest under Subsection (a) of this section according to the doctrine of cy pres by giving effect to the general intent and specific directives of the creator within the limits of the rule against perpetuities.

(c) If an instrument that violates the rule against perpetuities may be reformed or construed under this section, a court shall enforce the provisions of the instrument that do not violate the rule and shall reform or construe under this section a provision that violates or might violate the rule.

(d) This section applies to legal and equitable interests, including noncharitable gifts and trusts, conveyed by an inter vivos instrument or a will that takes effect on or after September 1, 1969, and this section applies to an appointment made on or after that date regardless of when the power was created.

Amended by Acts 1991, 72nd Leg., ch. 895, § 16, eff. Sept. 1, 1991.

Title 4. Actions and Remedies

Chapter 26. Use of a Deceased Individual's Name, Voice, Signature, Photograph, or Likeness

Statutes in Context

Chapter 26 establishes that an individual has a property right in the use of the individual's name, voice, signature, photograph, or likeness after the individual's death. Chapter 26 further explains how that right may be transferred, who owns the right after the person's death, and who may exercise the right.

§ 26.001. Definitions

In this chapter:

(1) "Photograph" means a photograph or photographic reproduction, still or moving, videotape, or live television transmission of an individual in a manner that allows a person viewing the photograph with the naked eye to reasonably determine the identity of the individual.

(2) "Property right" means the property right created by this chapter.

(3) "Name" means the actual or assumed name used by an individual which, when used in conjunction with other information, is intended to identify a particular person.

(4) "Media enterprise" means a newspaper, magazine, radio station or network, television station or network, or cable television system.

Added by Acts 1987, 70th Leg., ch. 152, § 1, eff. Sept. 1, 1987.

§ 26.002. Property Right Established

An individual has a property right in the use of the individual's name, voice, signature, photograph, or likeness after the death of the individual.

Added by Acts 1987, 70th Leg., ch. 152, § 1, eff. Sept. 1, 1987.

§ 26.003. Applicability

This chapter applies to an individual:

(1) alive on or after September 1, 1987, or who died before September 1, 1987, but on or after January 1, 1937; and

(2) whose name, voice, signature, photograph, or likeness has commercial value at the time of his or her death or comes to have commercial value after that time.

Added by Acts 1987, 70th Leg., ch. 152, § 1, eff. Sept. 1, 1987.

§ 26.004. Transferability

(a) The property right is freely transferable, in whole or in part, by contract or by means of trust or testamentary documents.

(b) The property right may be transferred before or after the death of the individual.

Added by Acts 1987, 70th Leg., ch. 152, § 1, eff. Sept. 1, 1987.

§ 26.005. Ownership After Death of Individual

(a) If the ownership of the property right of an individual has not been transferred at or before the death of the individual, the property right vests as follows:

(1) if there is a surviving spouse but there are no surviving children or grandchildren, the entire interest vests in the surviving spouse;

(2) if there is a surviving spouse and surviving children or grandchildren, one-half the interest vests in the surviving spouse and one-half the interest vests in the surviving children or grandchildren;

(3) if there is no surviving spouse, the entire interest vests in the surviving children of the deceased individual and the surviving children of any deceased children of the deceased individual; or

(4) if there is no surviving spouse, children, or grandchildren, the entire interest vests in the surviving parents of the deceased individual.

(b) The interests of the deceased individual's children and grandchildren are divided among them and exercisable on a per stirpes basis in the manner provided by Section 43, Texas Probate Code, according to the number of the deceased individual's children represented. If there is more than one child of a deceased child of the deceased individual, the share of a child of a deceased child may only be exercised by a majority of the children of the deceased child.

(c) If the property right is split among more than one person, those persons who own more than a one-half interest in the aggregate may exercise the right on behalf of all persons who own the right.

Added by Acts 1987, 70th Leg., ch. 152, § 1, eff. Sept. 1, 1987.

§ 26.006. Registration of Claim

(a) A person who claims to own a property right may register that claim with the secretary of state.

(b) The secretary of state shall provide a form for registration of a claim under this section. The form must be verified and must include:

(1) the name and date of death of the deceased individual;

(2) the name and address of the claimant;

(3) a statement of the basis of the claim; and

(4) a statement of the right claimed.

(c) The secretary of state may microfilm or reproduce by another technique a document filed under this section and destroy the original document.

(d) A document or a reproduction of a document filed under this section is admissible in evidence.

(e) The secretary of state may destroy all documents filed under this section after the 50th anniversary of the date of death of the individual whose property right they concern.

(f) The fee for filing a claim is $25.

(g) A document filed under this section is a public record.

Added by Acts 1987, 70th Leg., ch. 152, § 1, eff. Sept. 1, 1987.

§ 26.007. Effect of Registration

(a) Registration of a claim is prima facie evidence of a valid claim to a property right.

(b) A registered claim is superior to a conflicting, unregistered claim unless a court invalidates the registered claim.

Added by Acts 1987, 70th Leg., ch. 152, § 1, eff. Sept. 1, 1987.

§ 26.008. Exercise of Ownership for First Year Following Death of Individual

(a) Except as provided by Subsection (b), for the first year following the death of the individual a property right may be exercised, if authorized by law or an appointing court, by the following persons who may be appointed by a court for the benefit of the estate of the deceased individual:

(1) an independent executor;

(2) an executor;

(3) an independent administrator;

(4) a temporary or permanent administrator; or

(5) a temporary or permanent guardian.

(b) For the first year following the death of the individual, an owner of a property right may exercise that right only if the owner registers a valid claim as provided by Section 26.006.

Added by Acts 1987, 70th Leg., ch. 152, § 1, eff. Sept. 1, 1987.

§ 26.009. Exercise of Ownership After First Year Following Death of Individual

After the first year following the death of the individual, an owner of a property right may exercise that right whether or not the owner has registered a claim as provided by Section 26.006.

Added by Acts 1987, 70th Leg., ch. 152, § 1, eff. Sept. 1, 1987.

§ 26.010. Termination

A property right expires on the first anniversary of the date of death of the individual if:

(1) the individual has not transferred the right; and

(2) a surviving person under Section 26.005 does not exist.

Added by Acts 1987, 70th Leg., ch. 152, § 1, eff. Sept. 1, 1987.

§ 26.011. Unauthorized Uses

Except as provided by Section 26.012, a person may not use, without the written consent of a person who may exercise the property right, a deceased individual's name, voice, signature, photograph, or likeness in any manner, including:

(1) in connection with products, merchandise, or goods; or

(2) for the purpose of advertising, selling, or soliciting the purchase of products, merchandise, goods, or services.

Added by Acts 1987, 70th Leg., ch. 152, § 1, eff. Sept. 1, 1987.

§ 26.012. Permitted Uses

(a) A person may use a deceased individual's name, voice, signature, photograph, or likeness in:

(1) a play, book, film, radio program, or television program;

(2) a magazine or newspaper article;

(3) material that is primarily of political or newsworthy value;

(4) single and original works of fine art; or

(5) an advertisement or commercial announcement concerning a use under this subsection.

(b) A media enterprise may use a deceased individual's name, voice, signature, photograph, or likeness in connection with the coverage of news, public affairs, a sporting event, or a political campaign without consent. Any use other than the above by a media enterprise of a deceased individual's name, voice, signature, photograph, or likeness shall require consent if the material constituting the use is integrally and directly connected with commercial sponsorship or paid advertising. No consent shall be required for the use of the deceased individual's name, voice, signature, photograph, or likeness by a media enterprise if the broadcast or article is not commercially sponsored or does not contain paid advertising.

(c) A person who is an owner or employee of a media enterprise, including a newspaper, magazine, radio station or network, television station or network, cable television system, billboard, or transit ad, that is used for advertising a deceased individual's name, voice, signature, photograph, or likeness in a manner not authorized by this section is not liable for damages as provided by this section unless the person:

(1) knew that the use was not authorized by this section; or

(2) used the deceased individual's name, voice, signature, photograph, or likeness in a manner primarily intended to advertise or promote the media enterprise itself.

(d) A person may use a deceased individual's name, voice, signature, photograph, or likeness in any manner after the 50th anniversary of the date of the individual's death.

Added by Acts 1987, 70th Leg., ch. 152, § 1, eff. Sept. 1, 1987.

§ 26.013. Liability for Unauthorized Use

(a) A person who uses a deceased individual's name, voice, signature, photograph, or likeness in a manner not authorized by this chapter is liable to the person who owns the property right for:

(1) the amount of any damages sustained, as a result of the unauthorized use, by the person who owns the property right or $2,500, whichever is greater;

(2) the amount of any profits from the unauthorized use that are attributable to that use;

(3) the amount of any exemplary damages that may be awarded; and

(4) reasonable attorney's fees and expenses and court costs incurred in recovering the damages and profits established by this section.

(b) The amount of profits under Subsection (a)(2) may be established by a showing of the gross revenue attributable to the unauthorized use minus any expenses that the person who committed the unauthorized use may prove.

Added by Acts 1987, 70th Leg., ch. 152, § 1, eff. Sept. 1, 1987.

§ 26.014. Other Rights Not Affected

This chapter does not affect a right an individual may have in the use of the individual's name, voice, signature, photograph, or likeness before the death of the individual.

Added by Acts 1987, 70th Leg., ch. 152, § 1, eff. Sept. 1, 1987.

§ 26.015. Defenses to Liability

A person shall not be liable for damages under this chapter if he has acted in reliance on the results of a probate proceeding governing the estate of the deceased personality in question.

Added by Acts 1987, 70th Leg., ch. 152, § 1, eff. Sept. 1, 1987.

Title 5. Exempt Property and Liens

Subtitle A. Property Exempt from Creditors' Claims

Chapter 41. Interests in Land

Subchapter A. Exemptions in Land Defined

Statutes in Context

The source of the tremendous protection granted to Texas homesteads is Article XVI, § 50 of the Texas

Constitution. *See Statutes in Context* to Article XVI, § 50 for additional information.

Section 41.001(c) provides that after a homestead is sold, the proceeds remain protected for 6 months. In other words, a person who sells a homestead has 6 months to reinvest the proceeds in a new homestead.

§ 41.001. Interests in Land Exempt from Seizure

(a) A homestead and one or more lots used for a place of burial of the dead are exempt from seizure for the claims of creditors except for encumbrances properly fixed on homestead property.

(b) Encumbrances may be properly fixed on homestead property for:

(1) purchase money;

(2) taxes on the property;

(3) work and material used in constructing improvements on the property if contracted for in writing as provided by Sections 53.254(a), (b), and (c);

(4) an owelty of partition imposed against the entirety of the property by a court order or by a written agreement of the parties to the partition, including a debt of one spouse in favor of the other spouse resulting from a division or an award of a family homestead in a divorce proceeding;

(5) the refinance of a lien against a homestead, including a federal tax lien resulting from the tax debt of both spouses, if the homestead is a family homestead, or from the tax debt of the owner;

(6) an extension of credit that meets the requirements of Section 50(a)(6), Article XVI, Texas Constitution; or

(7) a reverse mortgage that meets the requirements of Sections 50(k) — (p), Article XVI, Texas Constitution.

(c) The homestead claimant's proceeds of a sale of a homestead are not subject to seizure for a creditor's claim for six months after the date of sale.

Amended by Acts 1984, 68th Leg., 2nd C.S., p. 216, ch. 18, § 2(b), eff. Oct. 2, 1984. Amended by Acts 1985, 69th Leg., ch. 840, § 1, eff. June 15, 1985; Acts 1993, 73rd Leg., ch. 48, § 2, eff. Sept. 1, 1993; Acts 1995, 74th Leg., ch. 121, § 1.01, eff. May 17, 1995; Acts 1995, 74th Leg., ch. 121, § 2.01; Acts 1997, 75th Leg., ch. 526, § 1, eff. Sept. 1, 1997; Acts 2001, 77th Leg., ch. 516, § 1, eff. Sept. 1, 2001.

Statutes in Context

Homesteads are classified by property type as either rural or urban. The size of the exemption depends on this classification and is set forth in Article XVI, § 51 of the Texas Constitution. *See Statutes in Context* to Article XVI, § 51.

Note that § 41.002(b) attempts to reduce the size of a rural homestead for a single adult to 100 acres. It is unclear whether the Property Code may cut back the constitutionally provided 200-acre rural homestead.

§ 41.002. Definition of Homestead

(a) If used for the purposes of an urban home or as both an urban home and a place to exercise a calling or business, the homestead of a family or a single, adult person, not otherwise entitled to a homestead, shall consist of not more than 10 acres of land which may be in one or more contiguous lots, together with any improvements thereon.

(b) If used for the purposes of a rural home, the homestead shall consist of:

(1) for a family, not more than 200 acres, which may be in one or more parcels, with the improvements thereon; or

(2) for a single, adult person, not otherwise entitled to a homestead, not more than 100 acres, which may be in one or more parcels, with the improvements thereon.

(c) A homestead is considered to be urban if, at the time the designation is made, the property is:

(1) located within the limits of a municipality or its extraterritorial jurisdiction or a platted subdivision; and

(2) served by police protection, paid or volunteer fire protection, and at least three of the following services provided by a municipality or under contract to a municipality:

(A) electric;

(B) natural gas;

(C) sewer;

(D) storm sewer; and

(E) water.

(d) The definition of a homestead as provided in this section applies to all homesteads in this state whenever created.

Amended by Acts 1985, 69th Leg., ch. 840, § 1, eff. June 15, 1985; Acts 1989, 71st Leg., ch. 391, § 2, eff. Aug. 28, 1989; Acts 1999, 76th Leg., ch. 1510, § 1, eff. Jan. 1, 2000; Acts 1999, 76th Leg., ch. 1510, § 2, eff. Sept. 1, 1999.

§ 41.003. Temporary Renting of a Homestead

Temporary renting of a homestead does not change its homestead character if the homestead claimant has not acquired another homestead.

Amended by Acts 1985, 69th Leg., ch. 840, § 1, eff. June 15, 1985.

§ 41.004. Abandonment of a Homestead

If a homestead claimant is married, a homestead cannot be abandoned without the consent of the claimant's spouse.

Added by Acts 1985, 69th Leg., ch. 840, § 1, eff. June 15, 1985.

§ 41.005. Voluntary Designation of Homestead

(a) If a rural homestead of a family is part of one or more parcels containing a total of more than 200 acres, the head of the family and, if married, that person's spouse may voluntarily designate not more than 200 acres of the property as the homestead. If a rural homestead of a single adult person, not otherwise entitled to a homestead, is part of one or more parcels containing a total of more than 100 acres, the person may voluntarily designate not more than 100 acres of the property as the homestead.

(b) If an urban homestead of a family, or an urban homestead of a single adult person not otherwise entitled to a homestead, is part of one or more contiguous lots containing a total of more than ten acres, the head of the family and, if married, that person's spouse or the single adult person, as applicable, may voluntarily designate not more than 10 acres of the property as the homestead.

(c) Except as provided by Subsection (e) or Subchapter B, to designate property as a homestead, a person or persons, as applicable, must make the designation in an instrument that is signed and acknowledged or proved in the manner required for the recording of other instruments. The person or persons must file the designation with the county clerk of the county in which all or part of the property is located. The clerk shall record the designation in the county deed records. The designation must contain:

(1) a description sufficient to identify the property designated;

(2) a statement by the person or persons who executed the instrument that the property is designated as the homestead of the person's family or as the homestead of a single adult person not otherwise entitled to a homestead;

(3) the name of the current record title holder of the property; and

(4) for a rural homestead, the number of acres designated and, if there is more than one survey, the number of acres in each.

(d) A person or persons, as applicable, may change the boundaries of a homestead designated under Subsection (c) by executing and recording an instrument in the manner required for a voluntary designation under that subsection. A change under this subsection does not impair rights acquired by a party before the change.

(e) Except as otherwise provided by this subsection, property on which a person receives an exemption from taxation under Section 11.43, Tax Code, is considered to have been designated as the person's homestead for purposes of this subchapter if the property is listed as the person's residence homestead on the most recent appraisal roll for the appraisal district established for the county in which the property is located. If a person designates property as a homestead under Subsection (c) or Subchapter B and a different property is considered to have been designated as the person's homestead under this subsection, the designation under Subsection (c) or Subchapter B, as applicable, prevails for purposes of this chapter.

(f) If a person or persons, as applicable, have not made a voluntary designation of a homestead under this section as of the time a writ of execution is issued against the person, any designation of the person's or persons' homestead must be made in accordance with Subchapter B.

(g) An instrument that made a voluntary designation of a homestead in accordance with prior law and that is on file with the county clerk on September 1, 1987, is considered a voluntary designation of a homestead under this section.

Added by Acts 1987, 70th Leg., ch. 727, § 1, eff. Aug. 31, 1987. Amended by Acts 1993, 73rd Leg., ch. 48, § 3, eff. Sept. 1, 1993; Acts 1993, 73rd Leg., ch. 297, § 1, eff. Aug. 1, 1993; Acts 1997, 75th Leg., ch. 846, § 1, eff. Sept. 1, 1997; Acts 1999, 76th Leg., ch. 1510, § 3, eff. Jan. 1, 2000.

§ 41.0051. Disclaimer and Disclosure Required

(a) A person may not deliver a written advertisement offering, for a fee, to designate property as a homestead as provided by Section 41.005 unless there is a disclaimer on the advertisement that is conspicuous and printed in 14-point boldface type or 14-point uppercase typewritten letters that makes the following statement or a substantially similar statement:

THIS DOCUMENT IS AN ADVERTISEMENT OF SERVICES. IT IS NOT AN OFFICIAL DOCUMENT OF THE STATE OF TEXAS.

(b) A person who solicits solely by mail or by telephone a homeowner to pay a fee for the service of applying for a property tax refund from a tax appraisal district or other governmental body on behalf of the homeowner shall, before accepting money from the homeowner or signing a contract with the homeowner for the person's services, disclose to the homeowner the name of the tax appraisal district or other governmental body that owes the homeowner a refund.

(c) A person's failure to provide a disclaimer on an advertisement as required by Subsection (a) or to provide the disclosure required by Subsection (b) is considered a false, misleading, or deceptive act or practice for purposes of Section 17.46(a), Business and Commerce Code, and is subject to action by the consumer protection division of the attorney general's office as provided by Section 17.46(a), Business and Commerce Code.

Added by Acts 2001, 77th Leg., ch. 341, § 1, eff. Sept. 1, 2001. Amended by Acts 2003, 78th Leg., ch. 1191, §§ 1 & 2, eff. Sept, 1, 2003.

§ 41.006. Certain Sales of Homestead

(a) Except as provided by Subsection (c), any sale or purported sale in whole or in part of a homestead at a fixed purchase price that is less than the appraised fair market value of the property at the time of the sale or purported sale, and in connection with which the buyer of the property executes a lease of the property to the seller at lease payments that exceed the fair rental value of the property, is considered to be a loan with all payments made from the seller to the buyer in excess of the sales price considered to be interest subject to Title 4, Finance Code.

(b) The taking of any deed in connection with a transaction described by this section is a deceptive trade practice under Subchapter E, Chapter 17, Business & Commerce Code,[1] and the deed is void and no lien attaches to the homestead property as a result of the purported sale.

(c) This section does not apply to the sale of a family homestead to a parent, stepparent, grandparent, child, stepchild, brother, half brother, sister, half sister, or grandchild of an adult member of the family.

Added by Acts 1987, 70th Leg., ch. 1130, § 1, eff. Sept. 1, 1987. Amended by Acts 1999, 76th Leg., ch. 62, § 7.84, eff. Sept. 1, 1999.

§ 41.007. Home Improvement Contract

(a) A contract described by Section 41.001(b)(3) must contain the following warning conspicuously printed, stamped, or typed in a size equal to at least 10-point bold type or computer equivalent, next to the owner's signature line on the contract:

"IMPORTANT NOTICE: You and your contractor are responsible for meeting the terms and conditions of this contract. If you sign this contract and you fail to meet the terms and conditions of this contract, you may lose your legal ownership rights in your home. KNOW YOUR RIGHTS AND DUTIES UNDER THE LAW."

(b) A violation of Subsection (a) of this section is a false, misleading, or deceptive act or practice within the meaning of Section 17.46, Business & Commerce Code, and is actionable in a public or private suit brought under the provisions of the Deceptive Trade Practices-Consumer Protection Act (Subchapter E, Chapter 17, Business & Commerce Code).[1]

Added by Acts 1987, 70th Leg., ch. 116, § 1, eff. Sept. 1, 1987. Renumbered from § 41.005 by Acts 1989, 71st Leg., ch. 2, § 16.01(30), eff. Aug. 28, 1989. Amended by Acts 1993, 73rd Leg., ch. 48, § 4, eff. Sept. 1, 1993.

§ 41.008. Conflict With Federal Law

To the extent of any conflict between this subchapter and any federal law that imposes an upper limit on the amount, including the monetary amount or acreage amount, of homestead property a person may exempt from seizure, this subchapter prevails to the extent allowed under federal law.

Added by Acts 1999, 76th Leg., ch. 1510, § 4.

Subchapter B. Designation of a Homestead in Aid of Enforcement of a Judgment Debt

§ 41.021. Notice to Designate

If an execution is issued against a holder of an interest in land of which a homestead may be a part and the judgment debtor has not made a voluntary designation of a homestead under Section 41.005, the judgment creditor may give the judgment debtor notice to designate the homestead as defined in Section 41.002. The notice shall state that if the judgment debtor fails to designate the homestead within the time allowed by Section 41.022, the court will appoint a commissioner to make the designation at the expense of the judgment debtor.

Amended by Acts 1985, 69th Leg., ch. 840, § 1, eff. June 15, 1985; Acts 1987, 70th Leg., ch. 727, § 2, eff. Aug. 31, 1987.

§ 41.022. Designation by Homestead Claimant

At any time before 10 a.m. on the Monday next after the expiration of 20 days after the date of service of the notice to designate, the judgment debtor may designate the homestead as defined in Section 41.002 by filing a written designation, signed by the judgment debtor, with the justice or clerk of the court from which the writ of execution was issued, together with a plat of the area designated.

Amended by Acts 1985, 69th Leg., ch. 840, § 1, eff. June 15, 1985.

§ 41.023. Designation by Commissioner

(a) If a judgment debtor who has not made a voluntary designation of a homestead under Section 41.005 does not designate a homestead as provided in Section 41.022, on motion of the judgment creditor, filed within 90 days after the issuance of the writ of execution, the court from which the writ of execution issued shall appoint a commissioner to designate the judgment debtor's homestead. The court may appoint a surveyor and others as may be necessary to assist the commissioner. The commissioner shall file his designation of the judgment debtor's homestead in a written report, together with a plat of the area designated, with the justice or clerk of the court not more than 60 days after the order of appointment is signed or within such time as the court may allow.

(b) Within 10 days after the commissioner's report is filed, the judgment debtor or the judgment creditor may request a hearing on the issue of whether the report should be confirmed, rejected, or modified as may be deemed appropriate in the particular circumstances of the case. The commissioner's report may be contradicted by evidence from either party, when exceptions to it or any item thereof have been filed before the hearing, but not otherwise. After the hearing, or if there is no hearing requested, the court shall designate the homestead as deemed appropriate and order sale of the excess.

(c) The commissioner, a surveyor, and others appointed to assist the commissioner are entitled to such fees and expenses as are deemed reasonable by the court. The court shall tax these fees and expenses against the judgment debtor as part of the costs of execution.

[1] V.T.C.A., Bus. & C. § 17.41 et seq.

[1] V.T.C.A., Bus. & C. § 17.41 et seq.

Amended by Acts 1985, 69th Leg., ch. 840, § 1, eff. June 15, 1985; Acts 1987, 70th Leg., ch. 727, § 3, eff. Aug. 31, 1987.

§ 41.024. Sale of Excess

An officer holding an execution sale of property of a judgment debtor whose homestead has been designated under this chapter may sell the excess of the judgment debtor's interest in land not included in the homestead.

Amended by Acts 1985, 69th Leg., ch. 840, § 1, eff. June 15, 1985; Acts 1987, 70th Leg., ch. 727, § 4, eff. Aug. 31, 1987.

Chapter 42. Personal Property

Statutes in Context

Chapter 42 provides that certain personal property is exempt from the claims of most creditors. This protection may continue after death as detailed in Probate Code § 281.

§ 42.001. Personal Property Exemption

(a) Personal property, as described in Section 42.002, is exempt from garnishment, attachment, execution, or other seizure if:

(1) the property is provided for a family and has an aggregate fair market value of not more than $60,000, exclusive of the amount of any liens, security interests, or other charges encumbering the property; or

(2) the property is owned by a single adult, who is not a member of a family, and has an aggregate fair market value of not more than $30,000, exclusive of the amount of any liens, security interests, or other charges encumbering the property.

(b) The following personal property is exempt from seizure and is not included in the aggregate limitations prescribed by Subsection (a):

(1) current wages for personal services, except for the enforcement of court-ordered child support payments;

(2) professionally prescribed health aids of a debtor or a dependent of a debtor; and

(3) alimony, support, or separate maintenance received or to be received by the debtor for the support of the debtor or a dependent of the debtor.

(c) This section does not prevent seizure by a secured creditor with a contractual landlord's lien or other security in the property to be seized.

(d) Unpaid commissions for personal services not to exceed 25 percent of the aggregate limitations prescribed by Subsection (a) are exempt from seizure and are included in the aggregate.

Amended by Acts 1991, 72nd Leg., ch. 175, § 1, eff. May 24, 1991; Acts 1997, 75th Leg., ch. 1046, § 1, eff. Sept. 1, 1997.

§ 42.002. Personal Property

(a) The following personal property is exempt under Section 42.001(a):

(1) home furnishings, including family heirlooms;

(2) provisions for consumption;

(3) farming or ranching vehicles and implements;

(4) tools, equipment, books, and apparatus, including boats and motor vehicles used in a trade or profession;

(5) wearing apparel;

(6) jewelry not to exceed 25 percent of the aggregate limitations prescribed by Section 42.001(a);

(7) two firearms;

(8) athletic and sporting equipment, including bicycles;

(9) a two-wheeled, three-wheeled, or four-wheeled motor vehicle for each member of a family or single adult who holds a driver's license or who does not hold a driver's license but who relies on another person to operate the vehicle for the benefit of the nonlicensed person;

(10) the following animals and forage on hand for their consumption:

(A) two horses, mules, or donkeys and a saddle, blanket, and bridle for each;

(B) 12 head of cattle;

(C) 60 head of other types of livestock; and

(D) 120 fowl; and

(11) household pets.

(b) Personal property, unless precluded from being encumbered by other law, may be encumbered by a security interest under Subchapter B, Chapter 9, Business & Commerce Code, or Subchapter F, Chapter 501, Transportation Code, or by a lien fixed by other law, and the security interest or lien may not be avoided on the ground that the property is exempt under this chapter.

Amended by Acts 1991, 72nd Leg., ch. 175, § 1, eff. May 24, 1991; Acts 1993, 73rd Leg., ch. 216, § 1, eff. May, 17, 1993; Acts 1997, 75th Leg., ch. 165, § 30.245, eff. Sept. 1, 1997; Acts 1999, 76th Leg., ch. 414, § 2.36, eff. July 1, 2001; Acts 1999, 76th Leg., ch. 846, § 1, eff. Aug. 30, 1999.

§ 42.0021. Additional Exemption for Retirement Plan

(a) In addition to the exemption prescribed by Section 42.001, a person's right to the assets held in or to receive payments, whether vested or not, under any stock bonus, pension, profit-sharing, or similar plan, including a retirement plan for self-employed individuals, and under any annuity or similar contract purchased with assets distributed from that type of plan, and under any retirement annuity or account described by Section 403(b) or 408A of the Internal Revenue Code of 1986,[1] and under any individual re-

[1] 26 U.S.C.A. § 403(b) or 408A.

tirement account or any individual retirement annuity, including a simplified employee pension plan, is exempt from attachment, execution, and seizure for the satisfaction of debts unless the plan, contract, or account does not qualify under the applicable provisions of the Internal Revenue Code of 1986.[2] A person's light to the assets held in or to receive payments, whether vested or not, under a government or church plan or contract is also exempt unless the plan or contract does not qualify under the definition of a government or church plan under the applicable provisions of the federal Employee Retirement Income Security Act of 1974.[3] If this subsection is held invalid or preempted by federal law in whole or in part or in certain circumstances, the subsection remains in effect in all other respects to the maximum extent permitted by law.

(b) Contributions to an individual retirement account, other than contributions to a Roth IRA described in Section 408A, Internal Revenue Code of 1986, or annuity that exceed the amounts deductible under the applicable provisions of the Internal Revenue Code of 1986 and any accrued earnings on such contributions are not exempt under this section unless otherwise exempt by law. Amounts qualifying as nontaxable rollover contributions under Section 402(a)(5), 403(a)(4), 403(b)(8), or 408(d)(3) of the Internal Revenue Code of 1986[4] before January 1, 1993, are treated as exempt amounts under Subsection (a). Amounts treated as qualified rollover contributions under Section 408A, Internal Revenue Code of 1986, are treated as exempt amounts under Subsection (a). In addition, amounts qualifying as nontaxable rollover contributions under Section 402(c), 402(e)(6), 402(f), 403(a)(4), 403(a)(5), 403(b)(8), 403(b)(10), 408(d)(3), or 408A of the Internal Revenue Code of 1986 on or after January 1, 1993, are treated as exempt amounts under Subsection (a).

(c) Amounts distributed from a plan or contract entitled to the exemption under Subsection (a) are not subject to seizure for a creditor's claim for 60 days after the date of distribution if the amounts qualify as a nontaxable rollover contribution under Subsection (b).

(d) A participant or beneficiary of a stock bonus, pension, profit-sharing, retirement plan, or government plan is not prohibited from granting a valid and enforceable security interest in the participant's or beneficiary's light to the assets held in or to receive payments under the plan to secure a loan to the participant or beneficiary from the plan, and the right to the assets held in or to receive payments from the plan is subject to attachment, execution, and seizure for the satisfaction of the security interest or lien granted by the participant or beneficiary to secure the loan.

(e) If Subsection (a) is declared invalid or preempted by federal law, in whole or in part or in certain circumstances, as applied to a person who has not brought a proceeding under Title 11, United States Code, the subsection remains in effect, to the maximum extent permitted by law, as to any person who has filed that type of proceeding.

(f) A reference in this section to a specific provision of the Internal Revenue Code of 1986 includes a subsequent amendment of the substance of that provision.

Added by Acts 1987, 70th Leg., ch. 376, § 1, eff. Sept. 1, 1987. Amended by Acts 1989, 71st Leg., ch. 1122, § 1, eff. Sept. 1, 1989; Acts 1995, 74th Leg., ch. 963, § 1, eff. Aug. 28, 1995; Acts 1999, 76th Leg., ch. 106, § 1, eff. Sept. 1, 1999.

§ 42.0022. Exemption for College Savings Plans

(a) In addition to the exemption prescribed by Section 42.001, a person's right to the assets held in or to receive payments or benefits under any of the following is exempt from attachment, execution, and seizure for the satisfaction of debts:

(1) any fund or plan established under Subchapter F, Chapter 54, Education Code, including the person's interest in a prepaid tuition contract;

(2) any fund or plan established under Subchapter G, Chapter 54, Education Code, including the person's interest in a savings trust account; or

(3) any qualified tuition program of any state that meets the requirements of Section 529, Internal Revenue Code of 1986, as amended.

(b) If any portion of this section is held to be invalid or preempted by federal law in whole or in part or in certain circumstances, this section remains in effect in all other respects to the maximum extent permitted by law.

Added by Acts 2003, 78th Leg., ch. 113, § 1, eff. Sept. 1, 2003.

§ 42.003. Designation of Exempt Property

(a) If the number or amount of a type of personal property owned by a debtor exceeds the exemption allowed by Section 42.002 and the debtor can be found in the county where the property is located, the officer making a levy on the property shall ask the debtor to designate the personal property to be levied on. If the debtor cannot be found in the county or the debtor fails to make a designation within a reasonable time after the officer's request, the officer shall make the designation.

(b) If the aggregate value of a debtor's personal property exceeds the amount exempt from seizure under Section 42.001(a), the debtor may designate the portion of the property to be levied on. If, after a court's request, the debtor fails to make a designation within a reasonable time or if for any reason a creditor

[2] 26 U.S.C.A. § 1 et seq.

[3] 26 U.S.C.A. § 1001 et seq.

[4] 26 U.S.C.A. §§ 402(a)(5), 403(a)(4), 403(b)(8) or 408(d)(3).

contests that the property is exempt, the court shall make the designation.
Acts 1983, 68th Leg., p. 3524, ch. 576, § 1, eff. Jan. 1, 1984. Amended by Acts 1991, 72nd Leg., ch. 175, § 1, eff. May 24, 1991.

§ 42.004. Transfer of Nonexempt Property

(a) If a person uses the property not exempt under this chapter to acquire, obtain an interest in, make improvement to, or pay an indebtedness on personal property which would be exempt under this chapter with the intent to defraud, delay, or hinder an interested person from obtaining that to which the interested person is or may be entitled, the property, interest, or improvement acquired is not exempt from seizure for the satisfaction of liabilities. If the property, interest, or improvement is acquired by discharging an encumbrance held by a third person, a person defrauded, delayed, or hindered is subrogated to the rights of the third person.

(b) A creditor may not assert a claim under this section more than two years after the transaction from which the claim arises. A person with a claim that is unliquidated or contingent at the time of the transaction may not assert a claim under this section more than one year after the claim is reduced to judgment.

(c) It is a defense to a claim under this section that the transfer was made in the ordinary course of business by the person making the transfer.
Acts 1983, 68th Leg., p. 3524, ch. 576, § 1, eff. Jan. 1, 1984. Amended by Acts 1991, 72nd Leg., ch. 175, § 1, eff. May 24, 1991.

Statutes in Context

In *Dryden v. Dryden*, 97 S.W.3d 863 (Tex. App. — Corpus Christi 2003, pet. denied), a parent ordered to pay child support claimed that § 42.005 violated Texas Constitution art. XVI, § 49, because it excepts individuals who owe child support from the protections afforded to debtors in other sections of the Property Code. The court determined that the parent's obligation for child support is not a true debt but actually a natural and legal duty. Accordingly, the court held that § 42.005 was constitutional.

§ 42.005. Child Support Liens

Sections 42.001, 42.002, and 42.0021 of this code do not apply to a child support lien established under Subchapter G, Chapter 157, Family Code.[1]
Added by Acts 1991, 72nd Leg., 1st C.S., ch. 15, § 4.07, eff. Sept. 1, 1991. Amended by Acts 1997, 75th Leg., ch. 165, § 7.56, eff. Sept. 1, 1997.

[1] V.T.C.A., Family Code § 157.311 et seq.

Title 6. Unclaimed Property

Chapter 71. Escheat of Property

Subchapter A. General Provisions

Statutes in Context

Section 71.001 provides that the property of an intestate who dies without an heir (*see* Probate Code §§ 38 and 45) escheats to the state.

§ 71.001. Escheat

(a) If an individual dies intestate and without heirs, the real and personal property of that individual is subject to escheat.

(b) "Escheat" means the vesting of title to property in the state in an escheat proceeding under Subchapter B.[1]
Acts 1983, 68th Leg., p. 3585, ch. 576, § 1, eff. Jan. 1, 1984. Amended by Acts 1985, 69th Leg., ch. 230, § 2, eff. Sept. 1, 1985.

Statutes in Context

With regard to the presumption of death, *see* Probate Code § 72.

§ 71.002. Presumption of Death

An individual is presumed dead for the purpose of determining if the individual's real or personal property is subject to escheat if the individual:

(1) is absent from the individual's place of residence for seven years or longer; and

(2) is not known to exist.

Acts 1983, 68th Leg., p. 3585, ch. 576, § 1, eff. Jan. 1, 1984. Amended by Acts 1985, 69th Leg., ch. 230, § 3, eff. Sept. 1, 1985.

Statutes in Context

Section 71.003 provides that a person is presumed to die intestate after 7 years if no will is recorded or probated.

§ 71.003. Presumption of Intestacy

An individual is presumed to have died intestate if, on or before the seventh anniversary of the date of the individual's death, the individual's will has not been recorded or probated in the county where the individual's property is located.
Acts 1983, 68th Leg., p. 3585, ch. 576, § 1, eff. Jan. 1, 1984.

§ 71.004. Presumption of Death Without Heirs

An individual is presumed to have died leaving no heirs if for the seven-year period preceding the court's determination:

[1] V.T.C.A., Property Code § 71.101 et seq.

(1) a lawful claim to the individual's property has not been asserted; and

(2) a lawful act of ownership of the individual's property has not been exercised.

Acts 1983, 68th Leg., p. 3585, ch. 576, § 1, eff. Jan. 1, 1984.

§ 71.005. Act of Ownership

For the purposes of this chapter, an individual exercises a lawful act of ownership in property by, personally or through an agent, paying taxes to this state on the property.

Acts 1983, 68th Leg., p. 3585, ch. 576, § 1, eff. Jan. 1, 1984.

§ 71.006. Review of Probate Decree

(a) If the state claims that an estate that has been administered in probate court in this state is subject to escheat, the state may have the judgment of the probate court reviewed by filing a petition in district court alleging that the administration of the estate was obtained by fraud or mistake of fact.

(b) The case shall be tried in accordance with the law for the revision and correction of a decree of the probate court.

Acts 1983, 68th Leg., p. 3585, ch. 576, § 1, eff. Jan. 1, 1984.

§ 71.007. Identification of Real Property Subject to Escheat

The tax assessor-collector of each county shall:

(1) take all steps necessary to identify real property that may be subject to escheat; and

(2) notify the commissioner of the General Land Office and the attorney general so that they may take appropriate action.

Added by Acts 2003, 78th Leg., ch. 1276, § 13.002, eff. Sept, 1, 2003.

Subchapter B. Escheat Proceedings

§ 71.101. Petition for Escheat

(a) If any person, including the attorney general, the comptroller, or a district attorney, criminal district attorney, county attorney, county clerk, district clerk, or attorney ad litem is informed or has reason to believe that real or personal property is subject to escheat under this chapter, the person may file a sworn petition requesting the escheat of the property and requesting a writ of possession for the property.

(b) The petition must contain:

(1) a description of the property;

(2) the name of the deceased owner of the property;

(3) the name of the tenants or persons claiming the estate, if known; and

(4) the facts supporting the escheat of the estate.

(c) If the petition is filed by a person other than the attorney general, the person shall send to the attorney general written notice of the filing and a copy of the petition to permit the attorney general to elect to participate on behalf of the state.

(d) An action brought under this section is governed by the procedure relating to class actions provided by the Texas Rules of Civil Procedure.

(e) A petition filed under this section is not subject to an objection relating to misjoinder of parties or causes of action.

Acts 1983, 68th Leg., p. 3586, ch. 576, § 1, eff. Jan. 1, 1984. Amended by Acts 1985, 69th Leg., ch. 230, § 4, eff. Sept. 1, 1985; Acts 1991, 72nd Leg., ch. 153, § 1, eff. Sept. 1, 1991. Amended by Acts 1997, 75th Leg., ch. 1037, § 4, eff. Sept. 1, 1997; Acts 1997, 75th Leg., ch. 1423, § 16.01, eff. Sept. 1, 1997.

§ 71.102. Citation

(a) If a petition is filed under this subchapter, the district clerk shall issue citation as in other civil suits to:

(1) each defendant alleged by the petition to possess or claim the property that is the subject of the petition;

(2) any person required by this chapter to be cited; and

(3) persons interested in the estate, including lienholders of record.

(b) The citation required by Subdivision (3) of Subsection (a) must be published as required for other civil suits and must:

(1) briefly state the contents of the petition; and

(2) request all persons interested in the estate to appear and answer at the next term of the court.

Acts 1983, 68th Leg., p. 3587, ch. 576, § 1, eff. Jan. 1, 1984. Amended by Acts 1985, 69th Leg., ch. 923, § 21, eff. Aug. 26, 1985.

§ 71.103. Party to Proceeding

(a) A person who exercises a lawful act of ownership in property that is the subject of an escheat proceeding must be made a party to the proceeding by:

(1) personal service of citation if the person is a resident of this state and the person's address can be obtained by reasonable diligence; or

(2) service of citation on a person's agent if the person is a nonresident or a resident who cannot be found and the agent can be found by the use of reasonable diligence.

(b) For the purposes of this section, reasonable diligence includes an inquiry and investigation of the records of the office of the tax assessor-collector of the county in which the property sought to be escheated is located.

(c) The comptroller is an indispensable party to any judicial or administrative proceeding concerning the disposition and handling of property that is the subject of an escheat proceeding and must be made a party to the proceeding by personal service of citation.

Acts 1983, 68th Leg., p. 3587, ch. 576, § 1, eff. Jan. 1, 1984. Amended by Acts 1991, 72nd Leg., ch. 153, § 2, eff. Sept. 1, 1991. Amended by Acts 1997, 75th Leg., ch. 1037, § 5, eff. Sept. 1, 1997; Acts 1997, 75th Leg., ch. 1423, § 16.02, eff. Sept. 1, 1997.

§ 71.104. Appearance of Claimants

Any person, whether named in the escheat petition or not, who claims an interest in property that is the subject of an escheat proceeding may appear, enter a pleading, and oppose the facts stated in the petition.
Acts 1983, 68th Leg., p. 3588, ch. 576, § 1, eff. Jan. 1, 1984.

§ 71.105. Trial

(a) If a person appears and denies the state's right to the property or opposes a material fact of the petition, the court shall try the issue as any other issue of fact.

(b) The court may order a survey as in other cases in which the title or the boundary of the land is in question.
Acts 1983, 68th Leg., p. 3588, ch. 576, § 1, eff. Jan. 1, 1984.

§ 71.106. Default Judgment

If citation is issued in accordance with Section 71.102 and no person answers within the period provided by the Texas Rules of Civil Procedure, the court shall render a default judgment in favor of the state.
Acts 1983, 68th Leg., p. 3588, ch. 576, § 1, eff. Jan. 1, 1984.

§ 71.107. Judgment for State

(a) If the court renders a judgment for the state finding that an intestate died without heirs, the property escheats to the state and title to the property is considered to pass to the state on the date of death of the owner as established by the escheat proceeding. The court may award court costs to the state.

(b) If the judgment involves real property, the state may sell the property under the general laws governing the sale of Permanent School Fund lands, and, after the second anniversary of the date of the final judgment, the court shall issue a writ of possession for the property.

(c) If the judgment involves personal property, the court shall issue a writ of possession that contains an adequate description of the property as in other cases for recovery of personal property.

(d) When the record of an escheat proceeding reflects that a lienholder or his predecessor received actual or constructive notice of the escheat proceeding, the entry of the judgment in the escheat proceeding will either satisfy or extinguish any lien which the lienholder or his predecessor claimed or could have claimed on the escheated property at the escheat proceeding.

(e) The sheriff, constable, court clerk, or other officer appointed by the judge in an escheat proceeding shall execute a writ of possession by filing the writ with the deed or map records of the county when the escheated property relates to realty and by serving the writ on any holder, tenant, or occupant of any escheated property. Additionally, the person who executes a writ of possession shall either:

(1) post the writ for at least three consecutive weeks on the door or posting board of the county courthouse in the county where the proceeding was conducted or in the county where the property is located; or

(2) in the case of real property, post the writ for at least two consecutive weeks at a reasonably conspicuous place on the realty; or

(3) publicize the writ in any other fashion ordered by the court.

(f) After validly executing a writ of possession, the sheriff, constable, court clerk, or other appointed officer shall note the method of the execution of the writ on the writ return and shall return the writ to the clerk to be filed in the court records of the escheat proceeding.
Acts 1983, 68th Leg., p. 3588, ch. 576, § 1, eff. Jan. 1, 1984. Amended by Acts 1985, 69th Leg., ch. 230, § 5, eff. Sept. 1, 1985; Acts 1985, 69th Leg., ch. 923, § 22, eff. Aug. 26, 1985.

§ 71.108. Costs Paid by State

If the property does not escheat, the state shall pay court costs. The clerk of the court shall certify the amount of the costs, and when the certificate is filed in the office of the comptroller of public accounts, the comptroller shall issue a warrant for the amount of the costs.
Acts 1983, 68th Leg., p. 3588, ch. 576, § 1, eff. Jan. 1, 1984.

§ 71.109. Appeal; Writ of Error

A party who appeared at an escheat proceeding may appeal the judgment rendered or may file an application for a writ of error on the judgment. The attorney general or the other person acting on behalf of the state in the escheat proceeding may make an appeal or file the writ.
Acts 1983, 68th Leg., p. 3589, ch. 576, § 1, eff. Jan. 1, 1984.

Subchapter C. Disposition of Escheated Property

§ 71.201. Seizure and Sale of Personal Property

(a) If personal property escheated to the state, the court shall issue to the sheriff a writ that commands the sheriff to seize the escheated property.

(b) The sheriff shall:

(1) dispose of the personal property at public auction in accordance with the law regarding the sale of personal property under execution; and

(2) deposit into the State Treasury the proceeds of the sale, less court costs.
Acts 1983, 68th Leg., p. 3589, ch. 576, § 1, eff. Jan. 1, 1984.

§ 71.202. Disposition of Real Property

(a) Real property that escheats to the state under this title before January 1, 1985, becomes a part of the permanent school fund. Real property that escheats to the state on or after January 1, 1985, is held in trust by the Commissioner of the General Land Office for the use and benefit of the foundation school fund. The revenue from all leases, sales, and use of land held for the foundation school fund shall be deposited to the credit of the foundation school fund.

(b) Before the 91st day after the day on which a judgment that provides for the recovery of real property is rendered, the clerk of the district court rendering the judgment shall send to the Commissioner of the General Land Office:

(1) a certified copy of the judgment; and

(2) notice of any appeal of that judgment.

(c) The commissioner shall list real property as escheated foundation school fund land or permanent school land as appropriate when the commissioner receives:

(1) a certified copy of a judgment under which the property escheats to the state and from which appeal is not taken; or

(2) a certified copy of notice of the affirmance on appeal of a judgment under which the property escheats to the state.

Acts 1983, 68th Leg., p. 3589, ch. 576, § 1, eff. Jan. 1, 1984. Amended by Acts 1984, 68th Leg., 2nd C.S., ch. 28, art. II, part B, § 13, eff. Sept. 1, 1984.

§ 71.203. Account of Escheated Property

The comptroller shall keep an account of the money paid to and real property vested in this state under this chapter.

Acts 1983, 68th Leg., p. 3590, ch. 576, § 1, eff. Jan. 1, 1984.

Subchapter D. Recovery of Escheated Property

§ 71.301. Suit for Escheated Personal Property

(a) If personal property of a deceased owner escheats to the state under this chapter and is delivered to the state, a person who claims the property as an heir, devisee, or legatee of the deceased may file suit against the state in a district court of Travis County, Texas. The suit must be filed on or before the fourth anniversary of the date of the final judgment of the escheat proceeding.

(b) The petition must state the nature of the claim and request that the money be paid to the claimant.

(c) A copy of the petition shall be served on the comptroller, who shall represent the interests of the state. As the comptroller elects and with the approval of the attorney general, the attorney general, the county attorney or criminal district attorney for the county, or the district attorney for the district shall represent the comptroller.

Acts 1983, 68th Leg., p. 3590, ch. 576, § 1, eff. Jan. 1, 1984. Amended by Acts 1991, 72nd Leg., ch. 153, § 3, eff. Sept. 1, 1991. Amended by Acts 1997, 75th Leg., ch. 1037, § 6, eff. Sept. 1, 1997; Acts 1997, 75th Leg., ch. 1423, § 16.03, eff. Sept. 1, 1997.

§ 71.302. Recovery of Personal Property

(a) If in a suit filed under Section 71.301 the court finds that a claimant is entitled to recover personal property, the court shall order the comptroller to issue a warrant for payment of the claim without interest or costs.

(b) A copy of the order under seal of the court is sufficient voucher for issuing the warrant.

Acts 1983, 68th Leg., p. 3590, ch. 576, § 1, eff. Jan. 1, 1984.

§ 71.303. Suit for Escheated Real Property

(a) If real property escheats to the state under this chapter, a person who was not personally served with citation in the escheat proceedings may file suit in the district court of Travis County for all or a part of the property. The suit must be filed not later than the second anniversary of the date of the final judgment in the escheat proceedings.

(b) A copy of the petition must be served on the attorney general, who shall represent the interests of the state.

(c) To the extent the claimant is adjudged to be the owner of all or a part of the property, the state is divested of the property.

Acts 1983, 68th Leg., p. 3590, ch. 576, § 1, eff. Jan. 1, 1984. Amended by Acts 1991, 72nd Leg., ch. 153, § 4, eff. Sept. 1, 1991.

§ 71.304. State as Party in Suit for Assets

(a) A suit brought for the collection of personal property delivered to the comptroller under this chapter must be brought in the name of this state.

(b) A suit brought for the possession of real property held in trust by the Commissioner of the General Land Office under this chapter must be brought in the name of this state.

Acts 1983, 68th Leg., p. 3591, ch. 576, § 1, eff. Jan. 1, 1984. Amended by Acts 1991, 72nd Leg., ch. 153, § 4, eff. Sept. 1, 1991. Amended by Acts 1997, 75th Leg., ch. 1037, § 7, eff. Sept. 1, 1997; Acts 1997, 75th Leg., ch. 1423, § 16.04, eff. Sept. 1, 1997.

Chapter 72. Abandonment of Personal Property

Subchapter A. General Provisions

§ 72.001. Application of Chapter

(a) Tangible or intangible personal property is subject to this chapter if it is covered by Section 72.101 and:

(1) the last known address of the apparent owner, as shown on the records of the holder, is in this state

(2) the records of the holder do not disclose the identity of the person entitled to the property, and it is established that the last known address of the person entitled to the property is in this state;

(3) the records of the holder do not disclose the last known address of the apparent owner, and it is established that:

(A) the last known address of the person entitled to the property is in this state; or

(B) the holder is a domiciliary or a government or governmental subdivision or agency of this state and has not previously paid or delivered the property to the state of the last known address of the apparent owner or other person entitled to the property;

(4) the last known address of the apparent owner, as shown on the records of the holder, is in a state that does not provide by law for the escheat or custodial taking of the property or is in a state in which the state's escheat or unclaimed property law is not applicable to the property, and the holder is a domiciliary or a government or governmental subdivision or agency of this state;

(5) the last known address of the apparent owner, as shown on the records of the holder, is in a foreign nation and the holder is a domiciliary or a government or governmental subdivision or agency of this state; or

(6) the transaction out of which the property arose occurred in this state and:

(A) the last known address of the apparent owner or other person entitled to the property is:

(i) unknown; or

(ii) in a state that does not provide by law for the escheat or custodial taking of the property or in a state in which the state's escheat or unclaimed property law is not applicable to the property; and

(B) the holder is a domiciliary of a state that does not provide by law for the escheat or custodial taking of the property or a state in which the state's escheat or unclaimed property law is not applicable to the property.

(b) This chapter supplements other chapters in this title, and each chapter shall be followed to the extent applicable.

Text of subsec. (c) effective until June 1, 2003

(c) This chapter applies to property held by life insurance companies with the exception of unclaimed funds, as defined by Section 3, Article 4.08, Insurance Code, held by those companies that are subject to Article 4.08, Insurance Code.

Text of subsec. (c) effective June 1, 2003

(c) This chapter applies to property held by life insurance companies with the exception of unclaimed proceeds to which Chapter 1109, Insurance Code, applies and that are held by those companies that are subject to Chapter 1109, Insurance Code.

(d) A holder of property presumed abandoned under this chapter is subject to the procedures of Chapter 74.

(e) In this chapter, a holder is a person, wherever organized or domiciled, who is:

(1) in possession of property that belongs to another;

(2) a trustee; or

(3) indebted to another on an obligation.

(f) In this chapter, a corporation shall be deemed to be a domiciliary of the state of its incorporation.

Acts 1983, 68th Leg., p. 3592, ch. 576, § 1, eff. Jan. 1, 1984. Amended by Acts 1985, 69th Leg., ch. 230, § 7, eff. Sept. 1, 1985; Acts 1987, 70th Leg., ch. 426, § 2, eff. Sept. 1, 1987; Acts 1991, 72nd Leg., ch. 153, § 5, eff. Sept. 1, 1991; Acts 2001, 77th Leg., ch. 1419, § 30, eff. June 1, 2003.

Subchapter B. Presumption of Abandonment

Statutes in Context

Section 72.101 sets forth the circumstances under which personal property is presumed abandoned.

§ 72.101. Personal Property Presumed Abandoned

(a) Except as provided by this section and Section 72.102, personal property is presumed abandoned if, for longer than three years:

(1) the existence and location of the owner of the property is unknown to the holder of the property; and

(2) according to the knowledge and records of the holder of the property, a claim to the property has not been asserted or an act of ownership of the property has not been exercised.

(b)(1) The three-year period leading to a presumption of abandonment of stock or another intangible ownership interest in a business association, the existence of which is evidenced by records available to the association, commences on the first date that either a sum payable as a result of the ownership interest is unclaimed by the owner or a communication to the owner is returned undelivered by the United States Postal Service.

(2) The running of the three-year period of abandonment ceases immediately on the exercise of an act of ownership interest or sum payable or a communication with the association as evidenced by a memorandum or other record on file with the association or its agents.

(3) At the time an ownership is presumed abandoned under this section, any sum then held for interest or owing to the owner as a result of the interest and not previously presumed abandoned is presumed abandoned.

(4) Any stock or other intangible ownership interest enrolled in a plan that provides for the automatic reinvestment of dividends, distributions, or other sums payable as a result of the ownership interest is subject to the presumption of abandonment as provided by this section.

Acts 1983, 68th Leg., p. 3593, ch. 576, § 1, eff. Jan. 1, 1984. Amended by Acts 1985, 69th Leg., ch. 230, § 9, eff. Sept. 1, 1985; Acts 1987, 70th Leg., ch. 426, § 3, eff. Sept. 1, 1987; Acts 1991, 72nd Leg., ch. 153, § 6, eff. Sept. 1, 1991; Acts 1993, 73rd Leg., ch. 36, § 3.01, eff. Sept. 1, 1993.

§ 72.102. Traveler's Check and Money Order

(a) A traveler's check or money order is not presumed to be abandoned under this chapter unless:

(1) the records of the issuer of the check or money order indicate that it was purchased in this state;

(2) the issuer's principal place of business is in this state and the issuer's records do not indicate the state in which the check or money order was purchased; or

(3) the issuer's principal place of business is in this state, the issuer's records indicate that the check or money order was purchased in another state, and the laws of that state do not provide for the escheat or custodial taking of the check or money order.

(b) A traveler's check to which Subsection (a) applies is presumed to be abandoned on the latest of:

(1) the 15th anniversary of the date on which the check was issued;

(2) the 15th anniversary of the date on which the issuer of the check last received from the owner of the check communication concerning the check; or

(3) the 15th anniversary of the date of the last writing, on file with the issuer, that indicates the owner's interest in the check.

Text of subsec. (c) effective until June 1, 2004

(c) A money order to which Subsection (a) applies is presumed to be abandoned on the latest of:

(1) the fifth anniversary of the date on which the money order was issued;

(2) the fifth anniversary of the date on which the issuer of the money order last received from the owner of the money order communication concerning the money order; or

(3) the fifth anniversary of the date of the last writing, on file with the issuer, that indicates the owner's interest in the money order.

Text of subsec. (c) effective June 1, 2004

(c) A money order to which Subsection (a) applies is presumed to be abandoned on the latest of:

(1) the seventh anniversary of the date on which the money order was issued;

(2) the seventh anniversary of the date on which the issuer of the money order last received from the owner of the money order communication concerning the money order; or

(3) the seventh anniversary of the date of the last writing, on file with the issuer, that indicates the owner's interest in the money order.

Amended by Acts 1997, 75th Leg., ch. 1037, § 8, eff. Sept. 1, 1997; Acts 2001, 77th Leg., ch. 179, § 1, eff. June 1, 2004.

§ 72.103. Preservation of Property

Notwithstanding any other provision of this title except a provision of this section relating to a money order, a holder of abandoned property shall preserve the property and may not at any time, by any procedure, including a deduction for service, maintenance, or other charge, transfer or convert to the profits or assets of the holder or otherwise reduce the value of the property. For purposes of this section, value is determined as of the date of the last transaction or contact concerning the property, except that in the case of a money order, value is determined as of the date the property is presumed abandoned under Section 72.102(c). If a holder imposes service, maintenance, or other charges on a money order prior to the time of presumed abandonment, such charges may not exceed the amount of 50 cents per month for each month the money order remains uncashed prior to the month in which the money order is presumed abandoned.

Amended by Acts 1997, 75th Leg., ch. 1037, § 9, eff. Sept. 1, 1997: Acts 2001, 77th Leg., ch. 179, § 2, eff. June 1, 2002.

Chapter 73. Property Held by Financial Institutions

Subchapter A. General Provisions

§ 73.001. Definitions and Application of Chapter

(a) In this chapter:

(1) "Account" means funds deposited with a depository in an interest-bearing account, a checking or savings account.

(2) "Depositor" means a person who has an ownership interest in an account.

(3) "Owner" means a person who has an ownership interest in a safe deposit box.

(4) "Holder" means a depository.

(5) "Check" includes a draft, cashier's check, certified check, registered check, or similar instrument.

(b) This chapter supplements other chapters in this title, and each chapter shall be followed to the extent applicable.

(c) Any property, other than an account, check, or safe deposit box, held by a depository is subject to the abandonment provisions of Chapter 72.

(d) A holder of accounts, checks, or safe deposit boxes presumed abandoned under this chapter is subject to the procedures of Chapter 74.

Acts 1983, 68th Leg., p. 3607, ch. 576, § 1, eff. Jan. 1, 1984. Amended by Acts 1985, 69th Leg., ch. 230, § 13, eff. Sept. 1, 1985; Acts 1991, 72nd Leg., ch. 153, §§ 7, 8, eff. Sept. 1, 1991. Amended by Acts 1997, 75th Leg., ch. 1037, §§ 11, 12, eff. Sept. 1, 1997.

§ 73.002. Depository

For the purposes of this chapter, a depository is a bank, savings and loan association, credit union, or other banking organization that:

(1) receives and holds a deposit of money or the equivalent of money in banking practice or other personal property in this state; or

(2) receives and holds such a deposit or other personal property in another state for a person whose last known residence is in this state.

Acts 1983, 68th Leg., p. 3607, ch. 576, § 1, eff. Jan. 1, 1984. Amended by Acts 1997, 75th Leg., ch. 1037, § 13, eff. Sept. 1, 1997.

§ 73.003. Preservation of Inactive Account or Safe Deposit Box

(a) A depository shall preserve an account that is inactive and the contents of a safe deposit box that is inactive. The depository may not, at any time, by any procedure, including the imposition of a service charge, transfer or convert to the profits or assets of the depository or otherwise reduce the value of the account or the contents of such a box. For purposes of this subsection, value is determined as of the date the account or safe deposit box becomes inactive.

(b) An account is inactive if for more than one year there has not been a debit or credit to the account because of an act by the depositor or an agent of the depositor, other than the depository, and the depositor has not communicated with the depository. A safe deposit box is inactive if the rental on the box is delinquent.

(c) This section does not affect the provisions of Subchapter B, Chapter 59, Finance Code.

Acts 1983, 68th Leg., p. 3607, ch. 576, § 1, eff. Jan. 1, 1984. Amended by Acts 1984, 68th Leg., 2nd C.S., ch. 18, § 8(b), eff. Oct. 2, 1984; Acts 1985, 69th Leg., ch. 230, § 14, eff. Sept. 1, 1985; Acts 1991, 72nd Leg., ch. 153, § 9, eff. Sept. 1, 1991; Acts 1993, 73rd Leg., ch. 36, § 3.02, eff. Sept. 1, 1993. Amended by Acts 1995, 74th Leg., ch. 914, § 11, eff. Sept. 1, 1995; Acts 1997, 75th Leg., ch. 1037, § 13, eff. Sept. 1, 1997; Acts 1999, 76th Leg., ch. 62, § 7.85, eff. Sept. 1, 1999.

Subchapter B. Presumption of Abandonment

§ 73.101. Inactive Account or Safe Deposit Box Presumed Abandoned

(a) An account or safe deposit box is presumed abandoned if:

(1) the account or safe deposit box has been inactive for at least five years as determined under Subsection (b);

(2) the location of the depositor of the account or owner of the safe deposit box is unknown to the depository; and

(3) the amount of the account or the contents of the box have not been delivered to the comptroller in accordance with Chapter 74.

(b) For purposes of Subsection (a)(1):

(1) an account becomes inactive beginning on the date of the depositor's last transaction or correspondence concerning the account; and

(2) a safe deposit box becomes inactive beginning on the date a rental was due but not paid.

Acts 1983, 68th Leg., p. 3607, ch. 576, § 1, eff. Jan. 1, 1984. Amended by Acts 1984, 68th Leg., 2nd C.S., ch. 18, § 8(d), eff. Oct. 2, 1984; Acts 1985, 69th Leg., ch. 230, § 16, eff. Sept. 1, 1985; Acts 1991, 72nd Leg., ch. 153, §§ 11, 12, eff. Sept. 1, 1991. Amended by Acts 1997, 75th Leg., ch. 1037, § 14, eff. Sept. 1, 1997; Acts 1997, 75th Leg., ch. 1423, § 16.05, eff. Sept. 1, 1997.

§ 73.102. Checks

A check is presumed to be abandoned on the latest of:

(1) the third anniversary of the date the check was payable;

(2) the third anniversary of the date the issuer or payor of the check last received documented communication from the payee of the check; or

(3) the third anniversary of the date the check was issued if, according to the knowledge and records of the issuer or payor of the check, during that period, a claim to the check has not been asserted or an act of ownership by the payee has not been exercised.

Added by Acts 1997, 75th Leg., ch. 1037, § 15, eff. Sept. 1, 1997.

Title 9. Trusts

Subtitle A. Provisions Generally Applicable to Trusts

Chapter 101. Provisions Generally Applicable to Trusts

Statutes in Context

Under the common law, a person became a bona fide purchaser (BFP) of trust property by (1) paying value for the property and (2) being without actual or constructive notice of the existence of the trust and the concomitant equitable interest of the beneficiary. A BFP takes free of the beneficiary's interest and may retain and transfer the property without subsequent question by the beneficiary or someone claiming through the beneficiary. Because BFP status was denied to purchasers who knew they were buying trust property or were dealing with a trustee, purchasers were prone to pay less than fair market value for trust property because of the increased risk associated with the purchase.

To alleviate this problem, § 101.001 and its counterpart § 114.082, modify the common law rule and permit a purchaser, as well as donees, to achieve protected status even if the grantee is on notice that the grantee is dealing with a trustee or buying trust property (e.g., the conveyance to the trustee reads "Tom Smith, trustee"). This modern approach permits people to deal with trustees with relative safety and permits trustees to negotiate for higher sale prices. However, the purchaser or donee will not be protected under this section if the conveyance to the trustee either (1) identifies the trust (e.g., "to Tom Smith, trustee of the Windfall Trust"), or (2) discloses the name of any beneficiary "(e.g., "to Tom Smith, trustee for Benny Fishery"). The transferee, however may still be protected by § 114.081.

Section 101.001 is not actually in the Trust Code which begins with § 111.001. The reason for this section to be outside of the Trust Code which has a virtually identical provision (§ 114.082) is that § 101.001 applies even if there is no actual trust but rather just a designation of a person as trustee (a possible resulting trust). Section 101.001 applies when the conveyance is "to a person *designated* as a trustee" (emphasis added) while § 114.082 applies when the conveyance is "to a trustee."

---

§ 101.001. Conveyance by Person Designated as Trustee

If property is conveyed or transferred to a person designated as a trustee but the conveyance or transfer does not identify a trust or disclose the name of any beneficiary, the person designated as trustee may convey, transfer, or encumber the title of the property without subsequent question by a person who claims to be a beneficiary under a trust or who claims by, through, or under any undisclosed beneficiary or by, through, or under the person designated as trustee in that person's individual capacity.

Acts 1983, 68th Leg., p. 3654, ch. 576, § 1, eff. Jan. 1, 1984. Amended by Acts 1987, 70th Leg., ch. 683, § 3, eff. Aug. 31, 1987.

Statutes in Context

The trustee should *earmark* the trust property, that is, label the property as belonging to the trust. Earmarking prevents trust property from being confused with the trustee's own property so that the trustee's personal creditors, heirs, beneficiaries, and other claimants do not take trust property under the mistaken belief that it belongs to the trustee. Section 101.002 and its Trust Code counterpart § 114.0821, provide that failure to earmark does not cause the unearmarked trust property to be liable for the trustee's personal obligations.

---

§ 101.002. Liability of Trust Property

Although trust property is held by the trustee without identifying the trust or its beneficiaries, the trust property is not liable to satisfy the personal obligations of the trustee.

Acts 1983, 68th Leg., p. 3654, ch. 576, § 1, eff. Jan. 1, 1984. Renumbered from § 101.001(b) by Acts 1987, 70th Leg., ch. 683, § 3, eff. Aug. 31, 1987.

Subtitle B. Texas Trust Code: Creation, Operation, and Termination of Trusts

---

Statutes in Context

The owner of property may create a trust by transferring that property in a unique fashion. First, the owner must divide the title to the property into legal and equitable interests and, second, the owner must impose fiduciary duties on the holder of the legal title to deal with the property for the benefit of the holder of the equitable title. Once the owner transfers property in this manner, the property is usually referred to as the trust *principal, corpus, estate,* or *res.*

In general, a trust scenario arises when a property owner wants to bestow benefits on a worthy individual or charity but does not want to make an unrestricted outright gift. Thus, the owner transfers legal title to a reliable individual or financial institution and equitable title to the individual or charity deserving the windfall. The holder of legal title manages that property following state law requirements and the original owner's instructions as specified in the trust instrument. The trustee then makes payments to or for the benefit of the individual or charity according to the original owner's instructions. When the property is exhausted or the instructions are completed, the trust ends and, once again, title to any remaining property is unified in the hands of the individual or charity the property owner specified.

The person who creates a trust by splitting title and imposing fiduciary duties is called the *settlor*. You may see the settlor referred to by other terms. In old cases and statutes, the settlor may be dubbed by the archaic term, *trustor*. In tax-related discussions, the settlor is frequently designated as the *grantor* because the settlor is making a grant of the property by splitting the title. The settlor may also be called a *donor* because most transfers of beneficial title are actually gifts.

The person who holds the legal interest to the property is the *trustee*. The trustee has all of the duties, responsibilities, and liabilities associated with property ownership but the trustee receives none of the benefits of that ownership. The best the trustee can hope for is a fee for serving as the trustee. Thus, if I told you I am giving you legal title to $1 million, you would not be very happy. In fact, you would be quite upset unless you were going to get paid because I would have imposed upon you all the burdens of owning $1 million. And, it actually gets worse because you would be holding that legal title as a fiduciary. This means that you would be required to manage the property with reasonable care, avoid any type of self-dealing with the property, and be certain not to be in a position where your own personal interests could be in conflict with those of the beneficiaries. If your conduct would ever fall beneath these standards, even if the lapse were merely negligent, you could be personally responsible in a civil action for damages and could even face a criminal prosecution.

The equitable title to the trust property is held by the *beneficiary*. The beneficiary is entitled to enjoy the trust property but, unlike the donee of an outright gift, not in an unrestricted manner. The beneficiary may receive only the benefits from the property as the settlor specified in the trust instrument. Typically, the beneficiary has no control over the trustee or how the trustee manages the legal title to the property. However, the beneficiary has the right to sue the trustee if the trustee's conduct breaches the fiduciary duties or if the trustee does not follow the settlor's instructions as set forth in the trust instrument. You may see the beneficiary referred to by other terms. The French term *cestui que trust* is often used in older cases. When the emphasis is on the tax consequences of equitable title ownership, the beneficiary is typically called the *grantee* and when the gift element of the transfer is most important, the term *donee* may be used.

Trusts are an extremely powerful, useful, and advantageous estate planning technique. Some of the reasons a property owner may want to convey property in trust are summarized below.

1. **Provide For and Protect Beneficiaries.** The settlor's desire to provide for and protect someone is probably the most common reason for creating a trust. Although a donor could make a quick, convenient, and uncomplicated outright gift, there are many situations in which such outright gifts would not effectuate the donor's true intent.

   (a) Minors. Minors lack legal capacity to manage property and usually have insufficient maturity to do so as well. A trust permits the settlor to make a gift for the benefit of a minor without giving the minor control over the property or triggering the necessity for the minor to have a court-appointed guardian to manage that property. A trust is also more flexible and allows a settlor to have greater control over how the property is used when contrasted with other methods such as a transfer to a guardian or conservator of the minor's estate or to a custodian under the Texas Uniform Transfers to Minors Act (see Property Code Chapter 141).

   (b) Individuals Who Lack Management Skills. An individual may lack the skills necessary to properly manage the trust property. This deficiency could be the result of mental or physical incompetence or a lack of experience in the rigors of making prudent investment decisions. For example, persons who suddenly obtain large amounts of money, such as performers, professional athletes, lottery winners, or personal injury plaintiffs, tend to deplete these windfalls rapidly because they have never learned how to manage their money wisely. By putting the money under the control of a trustee with investment experience, the settlor increases the likelihood that the beneficiary's interests are served for a longer period of time.

   (c) Spendthrifts. Some individuals may be competent to manage property but are prone to use it in an excessive or frivolous manner. By using a carefully drafted trust, a settlor may protect the trust property from the beneficiary's own excesses as well as the beneficiary's creditors. See § 112.035 (spendthrift provisions).

   (d) Persons Susceptible to Influence. When a person suddenly acquires a significant amount of property, that person may be under pressure from family, friends, charities, investment advisers, and opportunistic scam artists who wish to share in the windfall. A trust can make it virtually impossible for the beneficiary to transfer trust property to these people.

2. **Flexible Distribution of Assets.** An outright gift, either inter vivos or testamentary, gives the donee total control over the way the property is used. With a trust, the settlor can restrict the beneficiary's control over the property in any manner the settlor desires as long as the restrictions are not illegal or in violation of public policy. This flexibility allows the settlor to determine how the trustee distributes trust benefits, such as by spreading the benefits over time, giving the trustee discretion to select who receives distributions and in what amounts, requiring the beneficiary to meet certain criteria to receive or continue receiving benefits, or limiting the purposes for which trust property may be used such as health care or education.

3. **Protection Against Settlor's Incompetence.** Once an individual is incompetent due to illness, injury, or other cause, the person cannot manage the person's own property. The court then needs to appoint a guardian of the estate or a conservator to manage the property. The process of judicially determining a person's incompetency may cause the person considerable private and public embarrassment and there is no guarantee the incompetent person will be happy with the guardian's decisions. Guardianships are also inconvenient and costly because guardians act under court supervision and are required to submit detailed reports on a regular basis.

   A trust may be used to avoid this need for a guardian. The settlor may create a trust and maintain considerable control over the trust property by, for example, serving as the trustee, retaining the power to revoke the trust, and keeping a beneficial life interest. However, upon incompetency, the settlor's designated successor trustee would take over the administration of the trust property in accordance with the directions the settlor expressed in the trust instrument. This type of arrangement is often called a *stand-by trust*.

   An alternative method to protect property and avoid the need for a guardian in the event of incompetency is to have the client execute a durable power of attorney for property management. *See* Probate Code §§ 481-506.

4. **Professional Management of Property.** The settlor may create a trust to obtain the services of a professional asset manager, either for the benefit of third-party beneficiaries or for the settlor as the beneficiary. Professional trustees, such as banks and trust companies, have more expertise and ex-

perience with various types of investments than most individuals. Assume that you have just inherited a wheat farm located in Kansas, an office building in New York City, an apartment building in San Francisco, U.S. Government savings bonds, corporate stock in a dozen domestic corporations, oil and gas property in Texas, and an import-export business in Italy. Would you have the skill to handle all of these different types of assets? If not, placing the assets in trust would be one way of obtaining professional management. And, there is another advantage to making a trust conveyance. If you negligently manage your own property and suffer financially as a result, there is not much you can do about it; you cannot successfully bring a law suit against yourself. However, if a trustee is negligent, you can bring suit for breach of fiduciary duties and, if successful, have a strong chance of recovery because most financial institutions and trust companies have money or other assets which can be reached to satisfy a damage award.

Professional trustees also have greater investment opportunities. For example, a bank may combine funds from several trusts into one common trust fund to take advantage of opportunities that require a large investment and to diversify, thus reducing the damage to the value of the trust when one investment turns sour.

5. **Probate Avoidance.** Property in a trust created during the settlor's lifetime is not part of the probate estate upon the settlor's death. The property remaining in the trust when the settlor dies is administered and distributed according to the terms of the trust; it does not pass under the settlor's will or by intestate succession. Advantages to avoiding probate include getting the property into the hands of the beneficiaries quickly, avoiding gaps in management, and evading probate publicity. These advantages, however, do not apply to a trust created in the settlor's will because the property must first pass through the probate process.
6. **Tax Benefits.** Another popular reason for using trusts is tax avoidance. Income taxes may be saved by transferring income-producing property to a trust which has a beneficiary who is in a lower tax bracket than the settlor. Additionally, gift taxes may be avoided by structuring the transfers to a trust to fall within the annual exclusion from the federal gift tax which, as of 2003, is $11,000 per year per donee. Likewise, if a trust is properly constructed, the trust property will not be included in the settlor's taxable estate.
7. **Avoid Conflicts of Interest.** A person may be unable to own certain assets outright if ownership would cause impermissible conflicts of interest. For example, the President, a governor, a mayor, or other political figure may own stocks, bonds, real property, and other investments. While carrying out the official's duties, there would be a tremendous likelihood that conflicts of interest would arise between the person's investments and political decisions. Likewise, a corporate officer may also be placed in similar conflict of interest situations. To eliminate these conflicts, the person places the assets in trust, names an independent third party as trustee, and indicates that the person has no control over the management of the assets and no authority to inquire about the exact nature of the trust investments while the person remains in office. This type of arrangement is often called a *blind trust*.

Chapter 111. General Provisions

Statutes in Context

There are three main time periods of Texas trust legislation.

Prior to 1943. Only sparse codification of trust law existed prior to 1943.

Texas Trust Act. The Texas Trust Act took effect on April 19, 1943 and, as amended, remained the cornerstone of trust law in Texas for over 40 years. The Texas Trust Act was very innovative in its extensive codification of the law relating to the creation, administration, and enforcement of trusts.

Texas Trust Code. The Texas Trust Code took effect on January 1, 1984. The Code modernized and expanded the Act while retaining most of its key features. For the applicability of the Code to old trusts, *see* § 111.006. The Texas Trust Code was one of the major foundations for the Uniform Trust Code approved in 2000 by the National Conference of Commissioners on Uniform States Laws.

§ 111.001. Short Title

This subtitle may be cited as the Texas Trust Code.

Amended by Acts 1983, 68th Leg., p. 3332, ch. 567, art. 2, § 2, eff. Jan. 1, 1984.

Statutes in Context

The settlor is, for the most part, the master of the trust and thus may provide for things to be handled differently than the Trust Code indicates. The terms of the trust trump the Trust Code except that certain self-dealing duties of corporate trustees may not be waived. *See also* § 113.059.

The Code and the Act are treated as one continuous statute. Thus, if a trust refers to the Texas Trust Act, the Code is considered as an amendment to the Act.

§ 111.002. Construction of Subtitle

(a) If the provisions of this subtitle and the terms of a trust conflict, the terms of the trust control except the settlor may not relieve a corporate trustee from the duties, restrictions, and liabilities under Section 113.052 or 113.053.

(b) This subtitle and the Texas Trust Act, as amended (Articles 7425b-1 through 7425b-48, Vernon's Texas Civil Statutes),[1] shall be considered one continuous statute, and for the purposes of any statute or of any instrument creating a trust that refers to the Texas Trust Act, this subtitle shall be considered an amendment of the Texas Trust Act.

Amended by Acts 1983, 68th Leg., p. 3332, ch. 567, art. 2, § 2, eff. Jan. 1, 1984.

Statutes in Context

The Code applies only to express trusts. Other trust-like or trust-nominated relationships are not covered.

§ 111.003. Trusts Subject to this Subtitle

For the purposes of this subtitle, a "trust" is an express trust only and does not include:

(1) a resulting trust;

(2) a constructive trust;

(3) a business trust; or

(4) a security instrument such as a deed of trust, mortgage, or security interest as defined by the Business & Commerce Code.

Amended by Acts 1983, 68th Leg., p. 3332, ch. 567, art. 2, § 2, eff. Jan. 1, 1984.

Statutes in Context

Section 111.004 contains definitions of terms used throughout the Code.

§ 111.004. Definitions

In this subtitle:

(1) "Affiliate" includes:

(A) a person who directly or indirectly, through one or more intermediaries, controls, is controlled by, or is under common control with another person; or

(B) any officer, director, partner, employee, or relative of a person, and any corporation or partnership of which a person is an officer, director, or partner.

(2) "Beneficiary" means a person for whose benefit property is held in trust, regardless of the nature of the interest.

(3) "Court" means a court of appropriate jurisdiction.

(4) "Express trust" means a fiduciary relationship with respect to property which arises as a manifestation by the settlor of an intention to create the relationship and which subjects the person holding title to the property to equitable duties to deal with the property for the benefit of another person.

(5) "Income" is defined in Section 116.002.

(6) "Interest" means any interest, whether legal or equitable or both, present or future, vested or contingent, defeasible or indefeasible.

(7) "Interested person" means a trustee, beneficiary, or any other person having an interest in or a claim against the trust or any person who is affected by the administration of the trust. Whether a person, excluding a trustee or named beneficiary, is an interested person may vary from time to time and must be determined according to the particular purposes of and matter involved in any proceeding.

(8) "Internal Revenue Code" means the Internal Revenue Code of 1954, as amended,[1] or any corresponding statute subsequently in effect.

(9) "Inventory value" means the cost of property purchased by a trustee, the market value of property at the time it became subject to the trust, or, in the case of a testamentary trust, any value used by the trustee that is finally determined for the purposes of an estate or inheritance tax.

(10) "Person" means an individual, a corporation, a partnership, an association, a joint-stock company, a business trust, an unincorporated organization, or two or more persons having a joint or common interest, including an individual or a corporation acting as a personal representative or in any other fiduciary capacity.

(11) "Principal" is defined in Section 116.002

(12) "Property" means any type of property, whether real, tangible or intangible, legal, or equitable. The term also includes choses in action, claims, and contract rights, including a contractual right to receive death benefits as designated beneficiary under a policy of insurance, contract, employees' trust, retirement account, or other arrangement.

(13) "Relative" means a spouse or, whether by blood or adoption, an ancestor, descendant, brother, sister, or spouse of any of them.

(14) "Settlor" means the person who creates the trust. The terms "grantor" and "trustor" mean the same as "settlor."

(15) "Terms of the trust" means the manifestation of intention of the settlor with respect to the trust expressed in a manner that admits of its proof in judicial proceedings.

(16) "Transaction" means any act performed by a settlor, trustee, or beneficiary in relation to a trust, including the creation or termination of a trust, the investment of trust property, a breach of duty, the receipt of trust property, the receipt of income or the incurring of expense, a distribution of trust property, an entry in the books and records of the trust, and an accounting by a trustee to any person entitled to receive an accounting.

---

[1] Repealed; see, now, V.T.C.A., Property Code § 111.001 et seq.

[1] 26 U.S.C.A. § 1 et seq.

(17) "Trust property" means property placed in trust by one of the methods specified in Section 112.001 or property otherwise transferred to or acquired or retained by the trustee for the trust.

(18) "Trustee" means the person holding the property in trust.

(19) "Employees' trust" means:

(A) a trust that forms a part of a stock-bonus, pension, or profit-sharing plan under Section 401, Internal Revenue Code of 1954 (26 U.S.C.A. Sec. 401 (1986));

(B) a pension trust under Chapter 111; and

(C) an employer-sponsored benefit plan or program, or any other retirement savings arrangement, including a pension plan created under Section 3, Employee Retirement Income Security Act of 1974 (29 U.S.C.A. Sec. 1002 (1986)), regardless of whether the plan, program, or arrangement is funded through a trust.

(20) "Individual retirement account" means a trust, custodial arrangement, or annuity under Section 408(a) or (b), Internal Revenue Code of 1954 (26 U.S.C.A. Sec. 408 (1986)).

(21) "Retirement account" means a retirement-annuity contract, an individual retirement account, a simplified employee pension, or any other retirement savings arrangement.

(22) "Retirement-annuity contract" means an annuity contract under Section 403, Internal Revenue Code of 1954 (26 U.S.C.A. Sec. 403 (1986)).

(23) "Simplified employee pension" means a trust, custodial arrangement, or annuity under Section 408, Internal Revenue Code of 1954 (26 U.S.C.A. Sec. 408 (1986)).

(24) "Environmental law" means any federal, state, or local law, rule, regulation, or ordinance relating to protection of the environment.

Amended by Acts 1983, 68th Leg., p. 3332, ch. 567, art. 2, § 2, eff. Jan. 1, 1984; Acts 1987, 70th Leg., ch. 741, §§ 1, 2, eff. Aug. 31, 1987; Acts 1993, 73rd Leg., ch. 846, § 28, eff. Sept. 1, 1993. Amended by Acts 1995, 74th Leg., ch. 642, § 14, eff. Sept. 1, 1995. Amended by Acts 2003, 78th Leg., ch. 659, § 2, eff. Jan. 1, 2004; Acts 2003, 78th Leg., ch. 1103, § 2, eff. Jan. 1, 2004.

§ 111.005. Reenactment of Common Law

If the law codified in this subtitle repealed a statute that abrogated or restated a common law rule, that common law rule is reestablished, except as the contents of the rule are changed by this subtitle.

Added by Acts 1983, 68th Leg., p. 3332, ch. 567, art. 2, § 2, eff. Jan. 1, 1984.

Statutes in Context

The Code applies to (1) all trusts created after January 1, 1984 and (2) all transactions after January 1, 1984 involving trusts even if the trust was created before January 1, 1984.

§ 111.006. Application

This subtitle applies:

(1) to all trusts created on or after January 1, 1984, and to all transactions relating to such trusts; and

(2) to all transactions occurring on or after January 1, 1984, relating to trusts created before January 1, 1984; provided that transactions entered into before January 1, 1984, and which were subject to the Texas Trust Act, as amended (Articles 7425b-1 through 7425b-48, Vernon's Texas Civil Statutes),[1] and the rights, duties, and interests flowing from such transactions remain valid on and after January 1, 1984, and must be terminated, consummated, or enforced as required or permitted by this subtitle.

Added by Acts 1983, 68th Leg., p. 3332, ch. 567, art. 2, § 2, eff. Jan. 1, 1984.

Chapter 112. Creation, Validity, Modification, and Termination of Trusts

Subchapter A. Creation

Statutes in Context

Section 112.001 lists the methods which a settlor may use to create a trust. The most commonly used of these methods are discussed below.

Inter Vivos or Living Trust. A trust which the settlor creates to take effect while the settlor is still alive is referred to as an *inter vivos trust* or a *living trust*. The two basic methods a settlor may use to create an inter vivos trust are distinguished by the identity of the person who holds legal title to the trust property.

In a *declaration* (or *self-declaration*) of trust, the settlor declares him- or herself to be the trustee of specific property and then transfers some or all of that property's equitable title to one or more beneficiaries. The settlor retains the legal title and is subject to self-imposed fiduciary duties. *See* § 112.001(1).

In a *transfer* or *conveyance* in trust, the settlor transfers legal title to another person as trustee and imposes fiduciary duties on that person. The settlor may retain some or all of the equitable title or transfer all of the equitable title to other persons. *See* § 112.001(2).

Testamentary Trust. A settlor can create a trust to take effect upon the settlor's death by including a gift in trust in the settlor's will. *See* § 112.001(3). The split of title and the imposition of duties does not occur until the settlor dies. This type of trust is called a *testamentary trust*. A precondition to the validity of a testamentary trust is for the will itself to be valid. If the will fails, any testamentary trust contained in that will is also ineffective. After the will is established, the trust is examined to determine its validity. The trust is not automatically valid just because the will is valid.

[1] Repealed; *see* now, V.T.C.A., Property Code § 111.001 et seq.

§ 112.001. Methods of Creating Trust

A trust may be created by:

(1) a property owner's declaration that the owner holds the property as trustee for another person;

(2) a property owner's inter vivos transfer of the property to another person as trustee for the transferor or a third person;

(3) a property owner's testamentary transfer to another person as trustee for a third person;

(4) an appointment under a power of appointment to another person as trustee for the donee of the power or for a third person; or

(5) a promise to another person whose rights under the promise are to be held in trust for a third person.

Amended by Acts 1983, 68th Leg., p. 3332, ch. 567, art. 2, § 2, eff. Jan. 1, 1984.

Statutes in Context

Trust intent is the threshold factor in determining whether or not a conveyance of property is sufficient to create an express trust. If the transferor does not manifest trust intent, no trust is created and the court will not intervene to create a trust.

A transferor of property has trust intent if the transferor (1) divides title to the property into legal and equitable components, and (2) imposes enforceable fiduciary duties on the holder of legal title to deal with the property for the benefit of the equitable title holder. *See* § 111.004(4) (defining "express trust").

No particular words or conduct is necessary to establish trust intent. Likewise, the mere use of trust terminology alone is insufficient to show trust intent.

---

§ 112.002. Intention to Create Trust

A trust is created only if the settlor manifests an intention to create a trust.

Amended by Acts 1983, 68th Leg., p. 3332, ch. 567, art. 2, § 2, eff. Jan. 1, 1984.

Statutes in Context

Because a trust is a type of gratuitous property transfer, rather than a contractual arrangement, the beneficiary does not need to give consideration to the settlor for the transfer. Do not be confused when a written document creating a trust is carelessly referred to as a "trust agreement" rather than a "trust instrument." The term "agreement" in this context does not connote an agreement of any kind, contractual or otherwise, between the settlor and the beneficiary.

A promise to create a trust in the future, just like any other promise to make a gift, is not enforceable unless the promise qualifies as a contract.

---

§ 112.003. Consideration

Consideration is not required for the creation of a trust. A promise to create a trust in the future is enforceable only if the requirements for an enforceable contract are present.

Amended by Acts 1983, 68th Leg., p. 3332, ch. 567, art. 2, § 2, eff. Jan. 1, 1984.

Statutes in Context

Generally, a trust must be in writing to be enforceable. The policy underlying the requirement that certain trusts be evidenced by a writing is to protect a transferee who actually received an outright conveyance from having those rights infringed upon by someone claiming that the transfer was actually one in trust. Thus, an alleged trustee will use the lack of a writing to raise the Statute of Frauds as a defense to a plaintiff who is trying to deprive the alleged trustee of that person's rights as the donee of an outright gift.

The writing must contain (1) evidence of the terms of the trust (e.g., identity of the beneficiaries, the property, and how that property is to be used) and (2) the signature of the settlor or the settlor's authorized agent (*see* Government Code § 311.005(6) defining "signed").

The normal requirements are relaxed in some situations for trusts containing *personal* property. Subsection (1) explains when an oral trust may be enforceable and subsection (2) provides when a writing which does not meet the standard requirements may be sufficient.

Courts may enforce an oral trust of real property if the trustee partially performs. In other words, if the alleged trustee acts, at least temporarily, as if a trust exists, the trustee may be estopped from denying the existence of a trust at a later time and claiming the property as the donee of an outright gift. For example, if the trustee permits the beneficiary to possess the land or make valuable improvements to that land, the trustee may be prohibited from later asserting that a trust did not exist.

Violating the Statute of Frauds merely makes the trust unenforceable (voidable) rather than void. Accordingly, the trustee may carry out the terms of a trust which does not comply with the statute of frauds although no one could have forced the trustee to do so.

See also § 112.051(c) which requires a trust revocation, modification, or amendment to be in writing if the settlor created the trust in writing.

---

§ 112.004. Statute of Frauds

A trust in either real or personal property is enforceable only if there is written evidence of the trust's terms bearing the signature of the settlor or the settlor's authorized agent. A trust consisting of personal property, however, is enforceable if created by:

(1) a transfer of the trust property to a trustee who is neither settlor nor beneficiary if the transferor expresses simultaneously with or prior to the transfer the intention to create a trust; or

(2) a declaration in writing by the owner of property that the owner holds the property as trustee for another person or for the owner and another person as a beneficiary.

Added by Acts 1983, 68th Leg., p. 3332, ch. 567, art. 2, § 2, eff. Jan. 1, 1984.

Statutes in Context

A trust is a method of holding title to property. Consequently, the existence of property is essential for the initial creation and continued existence of a trust. No trust exists until it has property and a trust terminates when no property remains.

Any type of property (e.g., real, personal, tangible, intangible, legal, equitable, chose in action, claim, contract right, etc.) may be held in trust. *See* § 111.004(12) (defining "property") and § 111.004(17) (defining "trust property").

If a person cannot transfer the property, such as property belonging to another person, property that has valid restrictions on its transfer, or the expectancy to inherit from someone who is still alive, then that property cannot support a trust.

Legal title to the trust property must reach the hands of the trustee. It is not enough for the settlor to sign a trust instrument, own assets that would make good trust property, and intend for that property to be in the trust. The settlor must consummate this intent by actually transferring or delivering the property.

§ 112.005. Trust Property

A trust cannot be created unless there is trust property.

Added by Acts 1983, 68th Leg., p. 3332, ch. 567, art. 2, § 2, eff. Jan. 1, 1984.

Statutes in Context

Generally, property may be added to an existing trust. However, additions are not permitted if either (1) the terms of the trust prohibit the addition or (2) the property is unacceptable to the trustee (the trustee's duties may not be enlarged without the trustee's consent).

§ 112.006. Additions to Trust Property

Property may be added to an existing trust from any source in any manner unless the addition is prohibited by the terms of the trust or the property is unacceptable to the trustee.

Added by Acts 1983, 68th Leg., p. 3332, ch. 567, art. 2, § 2, eff. Jan. 1, 1984.

Statutes in Context

The settlor must have the capacity to convey property to create a trust. This requirement does not impose any different standard on the settlor as the settlor would face in an outright, non-trust, transfer of the same property. If the settlor can convey property, the settlor may elect to convey that property by splitting the legal and equitable title and creating a trust. Thus, the capacity required to create an inter vivos trust is usually the same as the capacity to make an outright gift and the capacity necessary to create a testamentary trust is the same as the capacity to execute a will (*see* Probate Code § 57).

§ 112.007. Capacity of Settlor

A person has the same capacity to create a trust by declaration, inter vivos or testamentary transfer, or appointment that the person has to transfer, will, or appoint free of trust.

Added by Acts 1983, 68th Leg., p. 3332, ch. 567, art. 2, § 2, eff. Jan. 1, 1984.

Statutes in Context

The trustee must have the ability to take, hold, and transfer title to the trust property, that is, (a) an individual trustee must be of legal age (or have had the disabilities of minority removed) and competent and (b) a corporate trustee must have the power to act as a trustee in Texas. Although the trustee may be a person unconnected with the rest of the trust arrangement, such detachment is not necessary. A trustee may also be the settlor or a beneficiary of the same trust as long as the sole trustee is not also the sole beneficiary. *See* § 112.034 (merger).

§ 112.008. Capacity of Trustee

(a) The trustee must have the legal capacity to take, hold, and transfer the trust property. If the trustee is a corporation, it must have the power to act as a trustee in this state.

(b) Except as provided by Section 112.034, the fact that the person named as trustee is also a beneficiary does not disqualify the person from acting as trustee if he is otherwise qualified.

(c) The settlor of a trust may be the trustee of the trust.

Added by Acts 1983, 68th Leg., p. 3332, ch. 567, art. 2, § 2, eff. Jan. 1, 1984.

Statutes in Context

A person does not become a trustee merely because the settlor names that person as the trustee of a trust. The settlor cannot force legal title and the accompanying fiduciary duties on an unwilling person. Thus, a person must take some affirmative step to accept the position. Once acceptance occurs, the person is responsible for complying with the terms of the trust as well as applicable law.

The trustee's acceptance of the trust may be established in two main ways. First, the trustee may sign the trust instrument or a separate acceptance document. When creating an inter vivos trust, it is common practice for attorneys to have the trustee sign the trust instrument at the same time as the settlor. The signature of the trustee is conclusive evidence of acceptance. Second, the trustee's acceptance may be

implied from the fact that the trustee has started to act like a trustee by exercising trust powers or performing trust duties.

If the named trustee does not accept, the trust instrument is consulted to see if the settlor named an alternate or specified a method for selecting a replacement. If this does not result in a trustee who accepts the trust, the court will appoint a trustee upon petition of an interested person. *See* § 111.004(7) (defining "interested person").

---

§ 112.009. Acceptance by Trustee

(a) The signature of the person named as trustee on the writing evidencing the trust or on a separate written acceptance is conclusive evidence that the person accepted the trust. A person named as trustee who exercises power or performs duties under the trust is presumed to have accepted the trust.

(b) A person named as trustee who does not accept the trust incurs no liability with respect to the trust.

(c) If the person named as the original trustee does not accept the trust or if the person is dead or does not have capacity to act as trustee, the person named as the alternate trustee under the terms of the trust or the person selected as alternate trustee according to a method prescribed in the terms of the trust may accept the trust. If a trustee is not named or if there is no alternate trustee designated or selected in the manner prescribed in the terms of the trust, the court shall appoint a trustee on a petition of any interested person.

Added by Acts 1983, 68th Leg., p. 3332, ch. 567, art. 2, § 2, eff. Jan. 1, 1984.

Statutes in Context

Just as heirs may disclaim inheritances and beneficiaries may disclaim testamentary gifts, potential trust beneficiaries are not required to accept the proffered equitable title. The reasons a beneficiary may decide to disclaim and the requirements of the disclaimer are fundamentally the same as for an heir or beneficiary who disclaims. See *Statutes in Context* to Probate Code § 37A. Note that the Probate Code section applies to testamentary trusts while § 112.010 applies to inter vivos trusts. If the beneficiary properly disclaims, the disclaimed property passes under the terms of the trust as if the beneficiary had predeceased the settlor.

---

§ 112.010. Acceptance or Disclaimer by or on Behalf of Beneficiary

(a) Acceptance by a beneficiary of an interest in a trust is presumed.

(b) If a trust is created by will, a beneficiary may disclaim an interest in the manner and with the effect for which provision is made in the applicable probate law.

(c) Except as provided by Subsection (c-1) of this section, the following persons may disclaim an interest in a trust created in any manner other than by will:

(1) a beneficiary, including a beneficiary of a spendthrift trust;

(2) the personal representative of an incompetent, deceased, unborn or unascertained, or minor beneficiary, with court approval by the court having jurisdiction over the personal representative; and

(3) the independent executor of a deceased beneficiary, without court approval.

(c-1) A person authorized to disclaim an interest in a trust under Subsection (c) of this section may not disclaim the interest if the person in his capacity as beneficiary, personal representative, or independent executor has either exercised dominion and control over the interest or accepted any benefits from the trust.

(c-2) A person authorized to disclaim an interest in a trust under Subsection (c) of this section may disclaim an interest in whole or in part by:

(1) evidencing his irrevocable and unqualified refusal to accept the interest by written memorandum, acknowledged before a notary public or other person authorized to take acknowledgments of conveyances of real estate; and

(2) delivering the memorandum to the trustee or, if there is not a trustee, to the transferor of the interest or his legal representative not later than the date that is nine months after the later of:

(A) the day on which the transfer creating the interest in the beneficiary is made;

(B) the day on which the beneficiary attains age 21; or

(C) in the case of a future interest, the date of the event that causes the taker of the interest to be finally ascertained and the interest to be indefeasibly vested.

(d) A disclaimer under this section is effective as of the date of the transfer of the interest involved and relates back for all purposes to the date of the transfer and is not subject to the claims of any creditor of the disclaimant. Unless the terms of the trust provide otherwise, the interest that is the subject of the disclaimer passes as if the person disclaiming had predeceased the transfer and a future interest that would otherwise take effect in possession or enjoyment after the termination of the estate or interest that is disclaimed takes effect as if the disclaiming beneficiary had predeceased the transfer. A disclaimer under this section is irrevocable.

(e) Failure to comply with this section makes a disclaimer ineffective except as an assignment of the interest to those who would have received the interest being disclaimed had the person attempting the disclaimer died prior to the transferor of the interest.

Added by Acts 1983, 68th Leg., p. 3332, ch. 567, art. 2, § 2, eff. Jan. 1, 1984. Amended by Acts 1987, 70th Leg., ch. 467, § 3, eff. Sept. 1, 1987; Acts 1993, 73rd Leg., ch. 846, § 3, eff. Sept. 1, 1993.

Subchapter B. Validity

Statutes in Context

The settlor may create a trust for any purpose as long as that purpose is not illegal. In addition, the terms of the trust may not require the trustee to commit an act that is criminal, tortious, or contrary to public policy.

Courts have used two main approaches in evaluating the legality of a trust purpose. The first analysis concentrates on the settlor's intent and the effect of the trust's existence on the behavior of other persons. Under the *intent* approach, a trust is illegal if the existence of the trust could induce another person to commit a crime even if the trustee does not have to perform an illegal act. This is the majority approach in the United States and appears to be the one adopted by § 112.031 by its use of the word "purpose." The second approach focuses on how the trust property is actually *used*, rather than on the motives of the settlor.

§ 112.031. Trust Purposes

A trust may be created for any purpose that is not illegal. The terms of the trust may not require the trustee to commit a criminal or tortious act or an act that is contrary to public policy.

Amended by Acts 1983, 68th Leg., p. 3332, ch. 567, art. 2, § 2, eff. Jan. 1, 1984.

Statutes in Context

The historical origin of the two components of trust intent, the split of title and the imposition of duties, is derived from the common law history of trusts. The common law precursor to a trust was called a *use*. Before the fifteenth century, uses were not enforceable and thus a "beneficiary" had no rights and had to hope that the "trustee" would fulfill a merely honorary obligation. This situation changed in the 1400s as uses started to be enforceable as equitable estates in property. By the 1500s, uses were common and were, from the government's point of view, often abused. Property owners were employing uses to avoid their duties of property ownership under the feudal land ownership system, especially financial obligations such as paying money (today called taxes) to the monarch (now the Internal Revenue Service), to hinder creditors and others with claims against the property, and to provide benefits for various religious organizations contrary to the Crown's wishes.

The English Parliament enacted the Statute of Uses in 1536 to end these abuses. The statute *executed the use* which meant that the beneficiary's equitable interest in real property was turned into a legal interest as well. Because this had the effect of eliminating the legal interest which the trustee formerly held, the beneficiary was now the owner of all title, both legal and equitable, and was fully responsible for all of the burdens of property ownership. Had the Statute of Uses been carried out exactly as written, trusts as we know them would not exist.

An important exception to the Statute of Uses developed for the *active trust* and is reflected in § 112.032. An active trust is an arrangement where the trustee's holding of property is not merely nominal in an attempt to gain some untoward benefit, but where the trustee actually needs legal title to the property to perform a power or duty relating to the property for the beneficiary's benefit.

Although the Texas Statute of Uses applies only to real property, a similar result would be reached for personal property because without a true split of title and imposition of duties, the definition of an express trust in § 111.004(4) would not be satisfied.

§ 112.032. Active and Passive Trusts; Statute of Uses

(a) Except as provided by Subsection (b), title to real property held in trust vests directly in the beneficiary if the trustee has neither a power nor a duty related to the administration of the trust.

(b) The title of a trustee in real property is not divested if the trustee's title is not merely nominal but is subject to a power or duty in relation to the property.

Amended by Acts 1983, 68th Leg., p. 3332, ch. 567, art. 2, § 2, eff. Jan. 1, 1984.

Statutes in Context

The settlor may wish to create a trust but may also desire to retain considerable interests in and powers over the trust property. May a settlor do so and still create a valid trust? If the settlor conveys the property in trust so that the settlor and trustee are different persons, there is a clear split of title and imposition of duties. However, if the settlor makes a declaration of trust so the settlor is also the trustee, the reality of the split of title and duty imposition is less clear.

Section 112.033 which codified the result in *Westerfeld v. Huckaby*, 474 S.W.2d 189 (Tex. 1972), takes a very liberal approach by providing that the settlor may retain virtually all interests over the trust property provided there is some beneficial interest created in another person. This interest may be quite "weak" because it is contingent on some future event or is subject to revocation.

§ 112.033. Reservation of Interests and Powers by Settlor

If during the life of the settlor an interest in a trust or the trust property is created in a beneficiary other than the settlor, the disposition is not invalid as an attempted testamentary disposition merely because the settlor reserves or retains, either in himself or another person who is not the trustee, any or all of the other interests in or powers over the trust or trust property, such as:

(1) a beneficial life interest for himself;

(2) the power to revoke, modify, or terminate the trust in whole or in part;

(3) the power to designate the person to whom or on whose behalf the income or principal is to be paid or applied;

(4) the power to control the administration of the trust in whole or in part;

(5) the right to exercise a power or option over property in the trust or over interests made payable to the trust under an employee benefit plan, life insurance policy, or otherwise; or

(6) the power to add property or cause additional employee benefits, life insurance, or other interests to be made payable to the trust at any time.

Amended by Acts 1983, 68th Leg., p. 3332, ch. 567, art. 2, § 2, eff. Jan. 1, 1984.

Statutes in Context

Any separation of legal and equitable title coupled with the imposition of fiduciary duties on the holder of the legal title is sufficient to satisfy the split of title requirement for a valid trust. Only if all legal and all equitable title are in the same person is a trust not created.

If all legal and equitable title becomes reunited in one person after originally being separated, *merger* occurs and the trust will cease to exist. In the normal course of events, this is what happens when the trust terminates and the trustee distributes the property to the remainder beneficiaries. However, merger could occur earlier either because of circumstances the settlor did not anticipate or because the trustee and beneficiary are working together to terminate the trust. A trust containing a spendthrift provision (see § 112.035) will not end via merger unless the settlor is also the beneficiary. Instead, the court will appoint a trustee to keep title split. This rule prevents the trustee and beneficiary from circumventing the settlor's intent by triggering a merger.

---

§ 112.034. Merger

(a) If a settlor transfers both the legal title and all equitable interests in property to the same person or retains both the legal title and all equitable interests in property in himself as both the sole trustee and the sole beneficiary, a trust is not created and the transferee holds the property as his own. This subtitle does not invalidate a trust account validly created and in effect under Chapter XI, Texas Probate Code.[1]

(b) Except as provided by Subsection (c) of this section, a trust terminates if the legal title to the trust property and all equitable interests in the trust become united in one person.

(c) The title to trust property and all equitable interests in the trust property may not become united in a beneficiary, other than the settlor, whose interest is protected under a spendthrift trust, and in that case the court shall appoint a new trustee or cotrustee to administer the trust for the benefit of the beneficiary.

Added by Acts 1983, 68th Leg., p. 3332, ch. 567, art. 2, § 2, eff. Jan. 1, 1984.

Statutes in Context

A *spendthrift clause* is a provision of a trust which does two things. First, it prohibits the beneficiary from selling, giving away, or otherwise transferring the beneficiary's interest. Second, a spendthrift clause prevents the beneficiary's creditors from reaching the beneficiary's interest in the trust. The provision permits the settlor to carry out the settlor's intent of benefiting the designated beneficiary but not the beneficiary's assignees or creditors. Settlors include spendthrift restrictions in practically every trust because they protect beneficiaries from their own improvidence and their personal creditors. Note, however, that neither the settlor nor the beneficiary must show that a beneficiary is actually incapable of prudently managing property to obtain spendthrift protection.

Spendthrift restrictions are easy to create. The settlor does not need to use any particular language as long as the settlor's intent is clear. In fact, § 112.035(b) provides that it is adequate for the settlor to simply write, "This is a spendthrift trust."

A spendthrift provision has no effect once the trustee delivers a trust distribution to the beneficiary.

Under several circumstances, courts will not enforce spendthrift provisions for public policy reasons. The following is a nonexclusive list: (1) A creditor may still reach trust property if the settlor is also the beneficiary under § 112.035(d). Note, however, that some states, such as Alaska, enforce spendthrift provisions even if the trust is self-settled. (2) The court may order the trustees of a spendthrift trust to make payments for the support of the beneficiary's child. See *Statutes in Context* to Family Code § 154.005. (3) Property in a spendthrift trust will not be protected from the beneficiary's federal tax obligations. *See United States v. Dallas Nat'l Bank*, 152 F.2d 582 (5th Cir. 1945).

Subsection (e) prevents the beneficiary of a *Crummey* trust from being deemed a settlor and thereby losing spendthrift protection if the beneficiary elects not to exercise the withdrawal right.

---

§ 112.035. Spendthrift Trusts

(a) A settlor may provide in the terms of the trust that the interest of a beneficiary in the income or in the principal or in both may not be voluntarily or involuntarily transferred before payment or delivery of the interest to the beneficiary by the trustee.

(b) A declaration in a trust instrument that the interest of a beneficiary shall be held subject to a "spendthrift trust" is sufficient to restrain voluntary

[1] V.A.T.S. Probate Code, § 436 et seq.

or involuntary alienation of the interest by a beneficiary to the maximum extent permitted by this subtitle.

(c) A trust containing terms authorized under Subsection (a) or (b) of this section may be referred to as a spendthrift trust.

(d) If the settlor is also a beneficiary of the trust, a provision restraining the voluntary or involuntary transfer of his beneficial interest does not prevent his creditors from satisfying claims from his interest in the trust estate.

(e) A beneficiary of the trust may not be considered a settlor merely because of a lapse, waiver, or release of the beneficiary's right to withdraw a part of the trust property if the value of the property that could have been withdrawn by exercising the right of withdrawal in any calendar year does not exceed at the time of the lapse, waiver, or release the greater of the amount specified in:

(1) Section 2041(b)(2) or 2514(e), Internal Revenue Code of 1986; or

(2) Section 2503(b), Internal Revenue Code of 1986.

Added by Acts 1983, 68th Leg., p. 3332, ch. 567, art. 2, § 2, eff. Jan. 1, 1984. Amended by Acts 1997, 75th Leg., ch. 109, § 1, eff. Sept. 1, 1997.

Statutes in Context

Article I, § 26 of the Texas Constitution adopts the common law version of the Rule Against Perpetuities, that is, "a future interest not destructible by the owner of a prior interest cannot be valid unless it becomes vested at a date not more remote than twenty-one years after lives in being at the creation of such interest, plus the period of gestation. Any future interest so limited that it retains its indestructible and contingent character until a more remote time is invalid." Interpretive Commentary to Article I, § 21.

Section 112.036 makes it clear that this rule applies to all noncharitable trusts. However, the court must reform or construe transfers that violate the Rule under Property Code § 5.043 to carry out the general intent and specific directives of the grantor to the extent possible without violating the Rule. The court may apply the equitable doctrine of cy pres in this process.

§ 112.036. Rule Against Perpetuities

The rule against perpetuities applies to trusts other than charitable trusts. Accordingly, an interest is not good unless it must vest, if at all, not later than 21 years after some life in being at the time of the creation of the interest, plus a period of gestation. Any interest in a trust may, however, be reformed or construed to the extent and as provided by Section 5.043.

Added by Acts 1983, 68th Leg., p. 3332, ch. 567, art. 2, § 2, eff. Jan. 1, 1984. Amended by Acts 1984, 68th Leg., 2nd C.S., ch. 18, § 10, eff. Oct. 2, 1984.

Subchapter C. Revocation, Modification, and Termination of Trusts

Statutes in Context

Unlike under the law of most states, trusts are presumed revocable in Texas. A trust may, of course, be made irrevocable by its express terms.

The settlor may not enlarge the duties of the trustee without obtaining the trustee's express consent.

Subsection (c) augments § 112.004, the Statute of Frauds provision, by requiring a written trust to be revoked, modified, or amended in writing even if the trust originally would not have had to be in writing (e.g., an oral trust of personal property).

§ 112.051. Revocation, Modification, or Amendment by Settlor

(a) A settlor may revoke the trust unless it is irrevocable by the express terms of the instrument creating it or of an instrument modifying it.

(b) The settlor may modify or amend a trust that is revocable, but the settlor may not enlarge the duties of the trustee without the trustee's express consent.

(c) If the trust was created by a written instrument, a revocation, modification, or amendment of the trust must be in writing.

Amended by Acts 1983, 68th Leg., p. 3332, ch. 567, art. 2, § 2, eff. Jan. 1, 1984.

Statutes in Context

Trusts eventually terminate unless they are charitable. Upon termination, all legal and equitable title to any remaining trust property becomes reunited in the hands of the remainder beneficiaries.

The trustee's powers do not end immediately upon trust termination. Section 112.052 permits the trustee to continue to exercise trust powers for the reasonable period of time necessary to wind up the affairs of the trust. The length of this period depends on the circumstances of each case and the type of property involved. More sophisticated investments and businesses may take longer to wrap up and transfer to the beneficiary than other assets which need a mere change in registration or physical delivery.

§ 112.052. Termination

A trust terminates if by its terms the trust is to continue only until the expiration of a certain period or until the happening of a certain event and the period of time has elapsed or the event has occurred. If an event of termination occurs, the trustee may continue to exercise the powers of the trustee for the reasonable period of time required to wind up the affairs of the trust and to make distribution of its assets to the appropriate beneficiaries. The continued exercise of the trustee's powers after an event of termination does

not affect the vested rights of beneficiaries of the trust.
Amended by Acts 1983, 68th Leg., p. 3332, ch. 567, art. 2, § 2, eff. Jan. 1, 1984.

Statutes in Context

The settlor may provide for the disposition of trust property when the trust fails, terminates, or is revoked. Note that the settlor may also use a *negative* provision stating how trust property may not be distributed. If the settlor does not provide for the disposition of trust property, a resulting trust will arise for the benefit of the settlor, or if the settlor is deceased, the settlor's successors in interest (heirs or beneficiaries). See *Roberts v. Squyres*, 4 S.W.3d 485 (Tex. App. — Beaumont 1999, *pet. denied*).

§ 112.053. Disposition of Trust Property on Failure of Trust

The settlor may provide in the trust instrument how property may or may not be disposed of in the event of failure, termination, or revocation of the trust.
Added by Acts 1983, 68th Leg., p. 3332, ch. 567, art. 2, § 2, eff. Jan. 1, 1984. Amended by Acts 1991, 72nd Leg., ch. 895, § 17, eff. Sept. 1, 1991.

Statutes in Context

A court may be willing to permit the trustee to deviate from the settlor's instructions as contained in the trust instrument if the court is convinced that the settlor would have consented to the change had the settlor anticipated the current situation. Deviation typically occurs if (1) the purposes of the trust have been fulfilled, (2) the purposes of the trust have become illegal, (3) the purposes of the trust are now impossible to fulfill, or (4) because of circumstances not known to or anticipated by the settlor, compliance with the terms of the trust would defeat or substantially impair the trustee's ability to accomplish the purposes of the trust. This latter situation is the most often asserted ground for a deviation.

Using its deviation powers, the court may authorize a wide array of administrative revisions such as (1) changing the trustee, (2) permitting the trustee to perform acts that are not authorized or are forbidden by the trust instrument, (3) prohibiting the trustee from performing acts that the settlor mandated in the trust instrument, (4) modifying the terms of the trust, and (5) terminating the trust.

Although the trustee and the beneficiaries have standing to request deviation, the settlor lacks standing to do so.

§ 112.054. Judicial Modification or Termination of Trusts

(a) On the petition of a trustee or a beneficiary, a court may order that the trustee be changed, that the terms of the trust be modified, that the trustee be directed or permitted to do acts that are not authorized or that are forbidden by the terms of the trust, that the trustee be prohibited from performing acts required by the terms of the trust, or that the trust be terminated in whole or in part, if:

(1) the purposes of the trust have been fulfilled or have become illegal or impossible to fulfill; or

(2) because of circumstances not known to or anticipated by the settlor, compliance with the terms of the trust would defeat or substantially impair the accomplishment of the purposes of the trust.

(b) The court shall exercise its discretion to order a modification or termination under Subsection (a) in the manner that conforms as nearly as possible to the intention of the settlor. The court shall consider spendthrift provisions as a factor in making its decision whether to modify or terminate, but the court is not precluded from exercising its discretion to modify or terminate solely because the trust is a spendthrift trust.
Added by Acts 1983, 68th Leg., p. 3332, ch. 567, art. 2, § 2, eff. Jan. 1, 1984. Amended by Acts 1985, 69th Leg., ch. 149, § 1, eff. May 24, 1985.

Statutes in Context

Section 112.055 provides that certain charitable trusts automatically have enumerated terms statutorily provided to assist these trusts in qualifying for favorable federal tax treatment. *See also* § 112.056.

§ 112.055. Amendment of Charitable Trusts by Operation of Law

(a) Except as provided by Section 112.056 and Subsection (b) of this section, the governing instrument of a trust that is a private foundation under Section 509, Internal Revenue Code, as amended,[1] a nonexempt charitable trust that is treated as a private foundation under Section 4947(a)(1), Internal Revenue Code, as amended,[2] or, to the extent that Section 508(e), Internal Revenue Code,[3] is applicable to it, a nonexempt split-interest trust under Section 4947(a)(2), Internal Revenue Code, as amended,[4] is considered to contain provisions stating that the trust:

(1) shall make distributions at times and in a manner as not to subject the trust to tax under Section 4942, Internal Revenue Code;[5]

(2) may not engage in an act of self-dealing that would be subject to tax under Section 4941, Internal Revenue Code;[6]

(3) may not retain excess business holdings that would subject it to tax under Section 4943, Internal Revenue Code;[7]

[1] 26 U.S.C.A. § 509.
[2] 26 U.S.C.A. § 4947(a)(1).
[3] 26 U.S.C.A. § 508(e).
[4] 26 U.S.C.A. § 4947(a)(2).
[5] 26 U.S.C.A. § 4942.
[6] 26 U.S.C.A. § 4941.
[7] 26 U.S.C.A. § 4943.

(4) may not make an investment that would subject it to tax under Section 4944, Internal Revenue Code;[8] and

(5) may not make a taxable expenditure that would subject it to tax under Section 4945, Internal Revenue Code.[9]

(b) If a trust was created before January 1, 1970, this section applies to it only for its taxable years that begin on or after January 1, 1972.

(c) This section applies regardless of any provision in a trust's governing instrument and regardless of any other law of this state, including the provisions of this title.

Added by Acts 1983, 68th Leg., p. 3332, ch. 567, art. 2, § 2, eff. Jan. 1, 1984.

§ 112.056. Permissive Amendment by Trustee of Charitable Trust

(a) If the settlor of a trust that is described under Subsection (a) of Section 112.055 is living and competent and consents, the trustee may, without judicial proceedings, amend the trust to expressly include or exclude the provisions required by Subsection (a) of Section 112.055.

(b) The amendment must be in writing, and it is effective when a duplicate original is filed with the attorney general's office.

Added by Acts 1983, 68th Leg., p. 3332, ch. 567, art. 2, § 2, eff. Jan. 1, 1984.

Statutes in Context

Section 112.057 allows trustees to divide or merge trusts with identical terms to achieve significant tax savings.

---

§ 112.057. Division of Trusts

(a) The trustee may, unless expressly prohibited by the terms of the instrument establishing the trust, divide a trust into two or more separate trusts without a judicial proceeding if the trustee reasonably determines that the division of the trust could result in a significant decrease in current or future federal income, gift, estate, generation-skipping transfer taxes, or any other tax imposed on trust property. If the trustee divides the trust, the terms of the separate trusts must be identical to the terms of the original trust, but differing tax elections may be made for the separate trusts. The trustee may make a division under this subsection by:

(1) giving written notice of the division, not later than the 30th day before the date of a division under this subsection, to each beneficiary who might then be entitled to receive distributions from the trust or may be entitled to receive distributions from the trust once it is funded; and

(2) executing a written instrument, acknowledged before a notary public or other person authorized to take acknowledgements of conveyances of real estate stating that the trust has been divided pursuant to this section and that the notice requirements of this subsection have been satisfied.

(b) A trustee, in the written instrument dividing a trust, shall allocate trust property among the separate trusts on a fractional basis, by identifying the assets and liabilities passing to each separate trust, or in any other reasonable manner. The trustee shall allocate undesignated trust property received after the trustee has divided the trust into separate trusts in the manner provided by the written instrument dividing the trust or, in the absence of a provision in the written instrument, in a manner determined by the trustee.

(c) The trustee may, unless expressly prohibited by the terms of the instrument establishing the trust, merge two or more trusts having identical terms into a single trust if the trustee reasonably determines that merging the trusts could result in a significant decrease in current or future federal income, gift, estate, generation-skipping transfer taxes, or any other tax imposed on trust property. The trustee shall complete the trust merger by:

(1) giving a written notice of the merger, not later than the 30th day before the effective date of the merger, to each beneficiary who might then be entitled to receive distributions from the separate trusts being merged or to each beneficiary who might be entitled to receive distributions from the separate trusts once the trusts are funded; and

(2) executing a written instrument, acknowledged before a notary public or other person authorized to take acknowledgments of conveyances of real estate stating that the trust has been merged pursuant to this section and that the notice requirements of this subsection have been satisfied.

(d) The trustee may divide or merge a testamentary trust after the will establishing the trust has been admitted to probate, even if the trust will not be funded until a later date. The trustee may divide or merge any other trust before it is funded if the instrument establishing the trust is not revocable at the time of the division or merger.

Added by Acts 1991, 72nd Leg., ch. 895, § 18, eff. Sept. 1, 1991.

§ 112.058. Conversion of Community Trust to Nonprofit Corporation

(a) In this section:

(1) "Assets" means the assets of the component trust funds of a community trust.

(2) "Community trust" means a community trust as described by 26 CFR § 1.170A-9(e)(11) (1999), including subsequent amendments.

(b) A community trust with court approval may transfer the assets of the trust to a nonprofit corporation and terminate the trust as provided by this section.

---

[8] 26 U.S.C.A. § 4944.

[9] 26 U.S.C.A. § 4945.

(c) The community trust may transfer assets of the trust to a nonprofit corporation only if the nonprofit corporation is organized under the Texas Non-Profit Corporation Act (Article 1396-1.01 et seq., Vernon's Texas Civil Statutes) and organized for the same purpose as the community trust. The charter of the nonprofit corporation must describe the purpose of the corporation and the proposed use of the assets transferred using language substantially similar to the language used in the instrument creating the community trust.

(d) To transfer the assets of and terminate a community trust under this section, the governing body of the community trust must:

(1) file a petition in a probate court, county court, or district court requesting:

(A) the transfer of the assets of the trust to a nonprofit corporation established for the purpose of receiving and administering the assets of the trust; and

(B) the termination of the trust;

(2) send by first class mail to each trust settlor and each trustee of each component trust of the community trust who can be located by the exercise of reasonable diligence a copy of the governing body's petition and a notice specifying the time and place of the court-scheduled hearing on the petition; and

(3) publish once in a newspaper of general circulation in the county in which the proceeding is pending a notice that reads substantially similar to the following:

TO ALL INTERESTED PERSONS:

(NAME OF COMMUNITY TRUST) HAS FILED A PETITION IN (NAME OF COURT) OF (NAME OF COUNTY), TEXAS, REQUESTING PERMISSION TO CONVERT TO A NONPROFIT CORPORATION. IF PERMITTED TO CONVERT:

(1) THE (NAME OF COMMUNITY TRUST) WILL BE TERMINATED; AND

(2) THE ASSETS OF THE TRUST WILL BE:

(A) TRANSFERRED TO A NONPROFIT CORPORATION WITH THE SAME NAME AND CREATED FOR THE SAME PURPOSE AS THE (NAME OF COMMUNITY TRUST); AND

(B) HELD AND ADMINISTERED BY THE CORPORATION AS PROVIDED BY THE TEXAS NON-PROFIT CORPORATION ACT (ARTICLE 1396-1.01 ET SEQ., VERNON'S TEXAS CIVIL STATUTES).

(1) THE (NAME OF COMMUNITY TRUST) WILL BE TERMINATED; AND

(2) THE ASSETS OF THE TRUST WILL BE:

(A) TRANSFERRED TO A NONPROFIT CORPORATION WITH THE SAME NAME AND CREATED FOR THE SAME PURPOSE AS THE (NAME OF COMMUNITY TRUST); AND

(B) HELD AND ADMINISTERED BY THE CORPORATION AS PROVIDED BY THE TEXAS NON-PROFIT CORPORATION ACT (ARTICLE 1396-1.01 ET SEQ., VERNON'S TEXAS CIVIL STATUTES).

THE PURPOSE OF THE CONVERSION IS TO ACHIEVE SAVINGS AND USE THE MONEY SAVED TO FURTHER THE PURPOSES FOR WHICH THE (NAME OF COMMUNITY TRUST) WAS CREATED.

A HEARING ON THE PETITION IS SCHEDULED ON (DATE AND TIME) AT (LOCATION OF COURT).

FOR ADDITIONAL INFORMATION, YOU MAY CONTACT THE GOVERNING BODY OF THE (NAME OF COMMUNITY TRUST) AT (ADDRESS AND TELEPHONE NUMBER) OR THE COURT.

(e) The court shall schedule a hearing on the petition to be held after the 10th day after the date the notices required by Subsection (d)(2) are deposited in the mail or the date the notice required by Subsection (d)(3) is published, whichever is later. The hearing must be held at the time and place stated in the notices unless the court, for good cause, postpones the hearing. If the hearing is postponed, a notice of the rescheduled hearing date and time must be posted at the courthouse of the county in which the proceeding is pending or at the place in or near the courthouse where public notices are customarily posted.

(f) The court, on a request from the governing body of the community trust, may by order require approval from the Internal Revenue Service for an asset transfer under this section. If the court orders approval from the Internal Revenue Service, the asset transfer may occur on the date the governing body of the community trust files a notice with the court indicating that the Internal Revenue Service has approved the asset transfer. The notice required by this subsection must be filed on or before the first anniversary of the date the court's order approving the asset transfer is signed. If the notice is not filed within the period prescribed by this subsection, the court's order is dissolved.

(g) A court order transferring the assets of and terminating a community trust must provide that the duties of each trustee of each component trust fund of the community trust are terminated on the date the assets are transferred. This subsection does not affect the liability of a trustee for acts or omissions that occurred before the duties of the trustee are terminated.

Added by Acts 1999, 76th Leg., ch. 1035, § 1, eff. Sept. 1, 1999.

Chapter 113. Administration

Subchapter A. Powers of Trustee

Statutes in Context

Sections 113.002-113.026 provide an extensive list of powers which trustees automatically receive. These provisions permit settlors to draft relatively short trust instruments because they do not need to enumerate

all of the powers they wish the trustees to have. Section 113.001 provides that terms of a trust instrument granting additional powers or limiting powers will trump the statutorily provided powers.

§ 113.001. Limitation of Powers

A power given to a trustee by this subchapter does not apply to a trust to the extent that the instrument creating the trust, a subsequent court order, or another provision of this subtitle conflicts with or limits the power.

Amended by Acts 1983, 68th Leg., p. 3332, ch. 567, art. 2, § 2, eff. Jan. 1, 1984.

Statutes in Context

Section 113.002 along with § 113.024 codify the principle of *implied powers*, that is, a trustee is deemed to have whatever powers which the settlor must have intended the trustee to have to achieve the objectives set out in the trust instrument.

§ 113.002. General Powers

Except as provided by Section 113.001, a trustee may exercise any powers in addition to the powers authorized by this subchapter that are necessary or appropriate to carry out the purposes of the trust.

Amended by Acts 1983, 68th Leg., p. 3332, ch. 567, art. 2, § 2, eff. Jan. 1, 1984.

§ 113.004. Additions to Trust Assets

A trustee may receive from any source additions to the assets of the trust.

Amended by Acts 1983, 68th Leg., p. 3332, ch. 567, art. 2, § 2, eff. Jan. 1, 1984.

§ 113.005. Acquisition of Undivided Interests

A trustee may acquire all or a portion of the remaining undivided interest in property in which the trust holds an undivided interest.

Amended by Acts 1983, 68th Leg., p. 3332, ch. 567, art. 2, § 2, eff. Jan. 1, 1984.

§ 113.006. General Authority to Manage and Invest Trust Property

Subject to the requirements of Chapter 117, a trustee may manage the trust property and invest and reinvest in property of any character on the conditions and for the lengths of time as the trustee considers proper, notwithstanding that the time may extend beyond the term of the trust.

Amended by Acts 1983, 68th Leg., p. 3332, ch. 567, art. 2, § 2, eff. Jan. 1, 1984. Amended by Acts 2003, 78th Leg., ch. 1103, § 3, eff. Sept. 1, 2003.

§ 113.007. Temporary Deposits of Funds

A trustee may deposit trust funds that are being held pending investment, distribution, or the payment of debts in a bank that is subject to supervision by state or federal authorities. However, a corporate trustee depositing funds with itself is subject to the requirements of Section 113.057 of this code.

Amended by Acts 1983, 68th Leg., p. 3332, ch. 567, art. 2, § 2, eff. Jan. 1, 1984; Acts 1984, 68th Leg., 2nd C.S., ch. 18, § 11, eff. Oct. 2, 1984.

§ 113.008. Business Entities

A trustee may invest in, continue, or participate in the operation of any business or other investment enterprise in any form, including a sole proprietorship, partnership, limited partnership, corporation, or association, and the trustee may effect any change in the organization of the business or enterprise.

Amended by Acts 1983, 68th Leg., p. 3332, ch. 567, art. 2, § 2, eff. Jan. 1, 1984.

§ 113.009. Real Property Management

A trustee may:

(1) exchange, subdivide, develop, improve, or partition real property;

(2) make or vacate public plats;

(3) adjust boundaries;

(4) adjust differences in valuation by giving or receiving value;

(5) dedicate real property to public use or, if the trustee considers it in the best interest of the trust, dedicate easements to public use without consideration;

(6) raze existing walls or buildings;

(7) erect new party walls or buildings alone or jointly with an owner of adjacent property;

(8) make repairs; and

(9) make extraordinary alterations or additions in structures as necessary to make property more productive.

Amended by Acts 1983, 68th Leg., p. 3332, ch. 567, art. 2, § 2, eff. Jan. 1, 1984.

§ 113.010. Sale of Property

A trustee may contract to sell, sell and convey, or grant an option to sell real or personal property at public auction or private sale for cash or for credit or for part cash and part credit, with or without security.

Amended by Acts 1983, 68th Leg., p. 3332, ch. 567, art. 2, § 2, eff. Jan. 1, 1984.

Statutes in Context

Section 113.011(b) authorizes the trustee to enter into a *long-term lease*, that is, a lease which lasts beyond the term of the trust. Long-term leases restrict the ability of the remainder beneficiary to enjoy the property because it is encumbered by the lease. On the other hand, long-term leases may permit the trustee to earn more income from the property. For example, a company may not be willing to construct a large building on the property unless the company is assured of being able to use it for a long time.

§ 113.011. Leases

(a) A trustee may grant or take a lease of real or personal property for any term, with or without options to purchase and with or without covenants relating to erection of buildings or renewals, including the lease of a right or privilege above or below the surface of real property.

(b) A trustee may execute a lease containing terms or options that extend beyond the duration of the trust.

Amended by Acts 1983, 68th Leg., p. 3332, ch. 567, art. 2, § 2, eff. Jan. 1, 1984.

§ 113.012. Minerals

(a) A trustee may enter into mineral transactions, including:

(1) negotiating and making oil, gas, and other mineral leases covering any land, mineral, or royalty interest at any time forming a part of a trust;

(2) pooling and unitizing part or all of the land, mineral leasehold, mineral, royalty, or other interest of a trust estate with land, mineral leasehold, mineral, royalty, or other interest of one or more persons or entities for the purpose of developing and producing oil, gas, or other minerals, and making leases or assignments granting the right to pool and unitize;

(3) entering into contracts and agreements concerning the installation and operation of plans or other facilities for the cycling, repressuring, processing, or other treating or handling of oil, gas, or other minerals;

(4) conducting or contracting for the conducting of seismic evaluation operations;

(5) drilling or contracting for the drilling of wells for oil, gas, or other minerals;

(6) contracting for and making "dry hole" and "bottom hole" contributions of cash, leasehold interests, or other interests towards the drilling of wells;

(7) using or contracting for the use of any method of secondary or tertiary recovery of any mineral, including the injection of water, gas, air, or other substances;

(8) purchasing oil, gas, or other mineral leases, leasehold interests, or other interests for any type of consideration, including farmout agreements requiring the drilling or reworking of wells or participation therein;

(9) entering into farmout contracts or agreements committing a trust estate to assign oil, gas, or other mineral leases or interests in consideration for the drilling of wells or other oil, gas, or mineral operations;

(10) negotiating the transfer of and transferring oil, gas, or other mineral leases or interests for any consideration, such as retained overriding royalty interests of any nature, drilling or reworking commitments, or production interests; and

(11) executing and entering into contracts, conveyances, and other agreements or transfers considered necessary or desirable to carry out the powers granted in this section, whether or not the action is now or subsequently recognized or considered as a common or proper practice by those engaged in the business of prospecting for, developing, producing, processing, transporting, or marketing minerals, including entering into and executing division orders, oil, gas, or other mineral sales contracts, exploration agreements, processing agreements, and other contracts relating to the processing, handling, treating, transporting, and marketing of oil, gas, or other mineral production from or accruing to a trust and receiving and receipting for the proceeds thereof on behalf of a trust.

(b) A trustee may enter into mineral transactions that extend beyond the term of the trust.

Amended by Acts 1983, 68th Leg., p. 3332, ch. 567, art. 2, § 2, eff. Jan. 1, 1984.

Statutes in Context

The trustee may purchase insurance not only to protect the trust but also to protect the trustee.

---

§ 113.013. Insurance

A trustee may purchase insurance of any nature, form, or amount to protect the trust property and the trustee.

Amended by Acts 1983, 68th Leg., p. 3332, ch. 567, art. 2, § 2, eff. Jan. 1, 1984.

§ 113.014. Payment of Taxes

A trustee may pay taxes and assessments levied or assessed against the trust estate or the trustee by governmental taxing or assessing authorities.

Amended by Acts 1983, 68th Leg., p. 3332, ch. 567, art. 2, § 2, eff. Jan. 1, 1984.

§ 113.015. Authority to Borrow

A trustee may borrow money from any source, including a trustee, purchase property on credit, and mortgage, pledge, or in any other manner encumber all or any part of the assets of the trust as is advisable in the judgment of the trustee for the advantageous administration of the trust.

Amended by Acts 1983, 68th Leg., p. 3332, ch. 567, art. 2, § 2, eff. Jan. 1, 1984.

§ 113.016. Management of Securities

A trustee may:

(1) pay calls, assessments, or other charges against or because of securities or other investments held by the trust;

(2) sell or exercise stock subscription or conversion rights;

(3) vote corporate stock, general or limited partnership interests, or other securities in person or by general or limited proxy;

(4) consent directly or through a committee or other agent to the reorganization, consolidation,

merger, dissolution, or liquidation of a corporation or other business enterprise; and

(5) participate in voting trusts and deposit stocks, bonds, or other securities with any protective or other committee formed by or at the instance of persons holding similar securities, under such terms and conditions respecting the deposit thereof as the trustee may approve; sell any stock or other securities obtained by conversion, reorganization, consolidation, merger, liquidation, or the exercise of subscription rights free of any restrictions upon sale otherwise contained in the trust instrument relative to the securities originally held; assent to corporate sales, leases, encumbrances, and other transactions.

Amended by Acts 1983, 68th Leg., p. 3332, ch. 567, art. 2, § 2, eff. Jan. 1, 1984.

Statutes in Context

Normally, a trustee has a duty to earmark trust property as belonging to the trust. Section 113.017 permits a trustee to hold corporate stock and other securities in the name of a nominee. Note that § 16 of the Texas Trust Act permitted any property to be held in nominee form if certain requirements were satisfied.

§ 113.017. Corporate Stock or Other Securities Held in Name of Nominee

A trustee may:

(1) hold corporate stock or other securities in the name of a nominee;

(2) under Subchapter B, Chapter 161,[1] or other law, employ a bank incorporated in this state or a national bank located in this state as custodian of any corporate stock or other securities held in trust; and

(3) under Subchapter C, Chapter 161,[2] or other law, deposit or arrange for the deposit of securities with a Federal Reserve Bank or in a clearing corporation.

Amended by Acts 1983, 68th Leg., p. 3332, ch. 567, art. 2, § 2, eff. Jan. 1, 1984.

Statutes in Context

A settlor expects the trustee to administer the trust. The settlor selected the trustee because the settlor had confidence in that person's judgment and ability to carry out the settlor's instructions. The settlor did not want someone else to be managing the trust property. However, it would be too burdensome to force a trustee to personally perform all acts necessary in the administration of the trust.

The traditional rule regarding delegation of powers was that the trustee may delegate mere ministerial duties but may not delegate discretionary acts. Although easy to state, the application of the rule was not always easy. The extreme situations were relatively clear. The trustee could delegate ministerial acts such as secretarial and janitorial duties, record keeping, and the collection of income. But, discretionary acts such as selecting investments, deciding which beneficiary of a discretionary trust to pay and how much, and settling claims against the trust could not be delegated.

Section 113.018 adopts a different approach, that is, delegation is permissible if it is "reasonably necessary." Accordingly, the trustee may delegate responsibilities to agents if a reasonably prudent owner of that type of property holding that property for similar reasons as those of the trust, would employ outside assistance.

See also § 117.011 which permits the delegation of investment and management decisions under specified circumstances.

§ 113.018. Employment of Agents

A trustee may employ attorneys, accountants, agents, including investment agents, and brokers reasonably necessary in the administration of the trust estate.

Amended by Acts 1999, 76th Leg., ch. 794, § 1, eff. Sept. 1, 1999.

§ 113.019. Claims

A trustee may compromise, contest, arbitrate, or settle claims of or against the trust estate or the trustee.

Added by Acts 1983, 68th Leg., p. 3332, ch. 567, art. 2, § 2, eff. Jan. 1, 1984.

§ 113.020. Burdensome or Worthless Property

A trustee may abandon property the trustee considers burdensome or worthless.

Added by Acts 1983, 68th Leg., p. 3332, ch. 567, art. 2, § 2, eff. Jan. 1, 1984.

Statutes in Context

The trustee should make trust distributions directly to the beneficiary if the beneficiary is a competent adult unless the settlor requires or authorizes the trustee in the trust instrument to make distributions in another manner. For example, the trust may permit the trustee to pay the beneficiary's college tuition by sending payments directly to the school.

If the beneficiary is a minor or is incapacitated and the trust does not provide distribution instructions, § 113.021(a) supplies the trustee with a variety of distribution options. Note that the trustee determines whether a beneficiary is incapacitated; neither a court nor medical determination of incapacity is necessary.

§ 113.021. Distribution to Minor or Incapacitated Beneficiary

(a) A trustee may make a distribution required or permitted to be made to any beneficiary in any of the

[1] V.T.C.A., Property Code § 161.021 et seq.

[2] V.T.C.A., Property Code § 161.051 et seq.

following ways when the beneficiary is a minor or a person who in the judgment of the trustee is incapacitated by reason of legal incapacity or physical or mental illness or infirmity:

(1) to the beneficiary directly;

(2) to the guardian of the beneficiary's person or estate;

(3) by utilizing the distribution, without the interposition of a guardian, for the health, support, maintenance, or education of the beneficiary;

(4) to a custodian for the minor beneficiary under the Texas Uniform Gifts to Minors Act (Chapter 141) or a uniform gifts to minors act of another state; or

(5) by reimbursing the person who is actually taking care of the beneficiary, even though the person is not the legal guardian, for expenditures made by the person for the benefit of the beneficiary.

(b) The written receipts of persons receiving distributions under Subsection (a) of this section are full and complete acquittances to the trustee.

Added by Acts 1983, 68th Leg., p. 3332, ch. 567, art. 2, § 2, eff. Jan. 1, 1984.

Statutes in Context

The 2003 Texas Legislature enacted § 113.0211 which establishes a procedure for the trustee of a charitable trust to make adjustments between principal and income within certain parameters. The Legislature did not, however, correlate this section with the passage of the Uniform Principal and Income Act which also contains a procedure for making adjustments between principal and income. *See* Property Code § 116.005. Accordingly, it is unclear whether charitable trustees are restricted to § 113.0211 or whether they may use the Uniform Act procedure as well.

---

§ 113.0211. Adjustment of Charitable Trust

(a) In this section:

(1) "Charitable entity" has the meaning assigned by Section 123.001(1).

(2) "Charitable trust" means a trust:

(A) the stated purpose of which is to benefit only one or more charitable entities; and

(B) that qualifies as a charitable entity.

(b) The trustee of a charitable trust may acquire, exchange, sell, supervise, manage, or retain any type of investment, subject to restrictions and procedures established by the trustee and in an amount considered appropriate by the trustee, that a prudent investor, exercising reasonable skill, care, and caution, would acquire or retain in light of the purposes, terms, distribution requirements, and other circumstances of the trust. The prudence of a trustee's actions under this subsection is judged with reference to the investment of all of the trust assets rather than with reference to a single trust investment.

(c) The trustee of a charitable trust may make one or more adjustments between the principal and the income portions of a trust to the extent that the trustee considers the adjustments necessary:

(1) to comply with the terms of the trust, if any, that describe the amount that may or must be distributed to a charitable entity beneficiary by referring to the income portion of the trust; and

(2) to administer the trust in order to carry out the purposes of the charitable trust.

(d) The authority to make adjustments under Subsection (c) includes the authority to allocate all or part of a capital gain to trust income.

(e) In making adjustments under Subsection (c), the trustee shall consider:

(1) except to the extent that the terms of the trust clearly manifest an intention that the trustee shall or may favor one or more charitable entity beneficiaries, the needs of a charitable entity beneficiary, based on what is fair and reasonable to all other charitable entity beneficiaries of the trust, if any; and

(2) the need of the trust to maintain the purchasing power of the trust's investments over time.

Added by Acts 2003, 78th Leg., ch. 550, § 1, eff. Sept. 1, 2003.

§ 113.022. Power to Provide Residence and Pay Funeral Expenses

A trustee of a trust that is not a charitable remainder unitrust, annuity trust, or pooled income fund that is intended to qualify for a federal tax deduction under Section 664, Internal Revenue Code,[1] after giving consideration to the probable intention of the settlor and finding that the trustee's action would be consistent with that probable intention, may:

(1) permit real estate held in trust to be occupied by a beneficiary who is currently eligible to receive distributions from the trust estate;

(2) if reasonably necessary for the maintenance of a beneficiary who is currently eligible to receive distributions from the trust estate, invest trust funds in real property to be used for a home by the beneficiary; and

(3) in the trustee's discretion, pay funeral expenses of a beneficiary who at the time of the beneficiary's death was eligible to receive distributions from the trust estate.

Added by Acts 1983, 68th Leg., p. 3332, ch. 567, art. 2, § 2, eff. Jan. 1, 1984. Amended by Acts 1985, 69th Leg., ch. 149, § 2, eff. May 24, 1985.

§ 113.023. Ancillary Trustee

(a) If trust property is situated outside this state, a Texas trustee may name in writing an individual or corporation qualified to act in the foreign jurisdiction in connection with trust property as ancillary trustee.

(b) Within the limits of the authority of the Texas trustee, the ancillary trustee has the rights, powers, dis-

---

[1] 26 U.S.C.A. § 664.

cretions, and duties the Texas trustee delegates, subject to the limitations and directions of the Texas trustee specified in the instrument evidencing the appointment of the ancillary trustee.

(c) The Texas trustee may remove an ancillary trustee and appoint a successor at any time as to all or part of the trust assets.

(d) The Texas trustee may require security of the ancillary trustee, who is answerable to the Texas trustee for all trust property entrusted to or received by the ancillary trustee in connection with the administration of the trust.

(e) If the law of the foreign jurisdiction requires a certain procedure or a judicial order for the appointment of an ancillary trustee or to authorize an ancillary trustee to act, the Texas trustee and the ancillary trustee must satisfy the requirements.

Added by Acts 1983, 68th Leg., p. 3332, ch. 567, art. 2, § 2, eff. Jan. 1, 1984.

Statutes in Context

See *Statutes in Context* to § 113.002.

§ 113.024. Implied Powers

The powers, duties, and responsibilities under this subtitle do not exclude other implied powers, duties, or responsibilities that are not inconsistent with this subtitle.

Added by Acts 1983, 68th Leg., p. 3332, ch. 567, art. 2, § 2, eff. Jan. 1, 1984.

Statutes in Context

Section 113.025 permits the trustee to investigate trust property for potential environmental liability concerns even before accepting the trust property. This is helpful in protecting the trust and the trustee from liability under the Comprehensive Environmental Response, Compensation, and Liability Act. *See* 42 U.S.C. §§9601 et seq.

§ 113.025. Powers of Trustee Regarding Environmental Laws

(a) A trustee or a potential trustee may inspect, investigate, cause to be inspected, or cause to be investigated trust property, property that the trustee or potential trustee has been asked to hold, or property owned or operated by an entity in which the trustee or potential trustee holds or has been asked to hold any interest or for the purpose of determining the potential application of environmental law with respect to the property. This subsection does not grant any person the right of access to any property. The taking of any action under this subsection with respect to a trust or an addition to a trust is not evidence that a person has accepted the trust or the addition to the trust.

(b) A trustee may take on behalf of the trust any action before or after the initiation of an enforcement action or other legal proceeding that the trustee reasonably believes will help to prevent, abate, or otherwise remedy any actual or potential violation of any environmental law affecting property held directly or indirectly by the trustee.

Added by Acts 1993, 73rd Leg., ch. 846, § 29, eff. Sept. 1, 1993.

Statutes in Context

Section 113.026 permits the trustee, under specified circumstances, to exercise cy pres to replace a charitable beneficiary without the necessity of obtaining a court order if the charity (1) did not exist when the interested vested, (2) ceases to exist, or (3) ceases to be charitable in nature.

§ 113.026. Authority to Designate New Charitable Beneficiary

(a) In this section:

(1) "Charitable entity" has the meaning assigned by Section 123.001.

(2) "Failed charitable beneficiary" means a charitable entity that is named as a beneficiary of a trust and that:

(A) does not exist at the time the charitable entity's interest in the trust becomes vested;

(B) ceases to exist during the term of the trust; or

(C) ceases to be a charitable entity during the term of the trust.

(b) This section applies only to an express written trust created by an individual with a charitable entity as a beneficiary. If the trust instrument provides a means for replacing a failed charitable beneficiary, the trust instrument governs the replacement of a failed charitable beneficiary, and this section does not apply.

(c) The trustee of a trust may select one or more replacement charitable beneficiaries for a failed charitable beneficiary in accordance with this section.

(d) Each replacement charitable beneficiary selected under this section by any person must:

(1) be a charitable entity and an entity described under Sections 170(b)(1)(A), 170(c), 2055(a), and 2522(a) of the Internal Revenue Code of 1986, as amended; and

(2) have the same or similar charitable purpose as the failed charitable beneficiary.

(e) If the settlor of the trust is living and not incapacitated at the time a trustee is selecting a replacement charitable beneficiary, the trustee shall consult with the settlor concerning the selection of one or more replacement charitable beneficiaries.

(f) If the trustee and the settlor agree on the selection of one or more replacement charitable beneficiaries, the trustee shall send notice of the selection to the attorney general. If the attorney general determines that one or more replacement charitable beneficiaries do not have the same or similar charitable purpose as the failed charitable beneficiary, not later than the 21st day after the date the attorney general receives notice of the selection, the attorney general shall request in writing that a district court in the county in which the trust was created review the selection. If the court agrees with the attorney general's determination, any remaining replacement charitable beneficiary agreed on by the trustee and the settlor is the replacement charitable beneficiary. If there is not a remaining replacement charitable beneficiary agreed on by the trustee and the settlor, the court shall select one or more replacement charitable beneficiaries. If the court finds that the attorney general's request for a review is unreasonable, the replacement charitable beneficiary is the charitable beneficiary agreed on by the trustee and the settlor, and the court may require the attorney general to pay all court costs of the parties involved. Not later than the 30th day after the date the selection is final, the trustee shall provide to each replacement charitable beneficiary selected notice of the selection by certified mail, return receipt requested.

(g) If the trustee and the settlor cannot agree on the selection of a replacement charitable beneficiary, the trustee shall send notice of that fact to the attorney general not later than the 21st day after the date the trustee determines that an agreement cannot be reached. The attorney general shall refer the matter to a district court in the county in which the trust was created. The trustee and the settlor may each recommend to the court one or more replacement charitable beneficiaries. The court shall select a replacement charitable beneficiary and, not later than the 30th day after the date of the selection, provide to each charitable beneficiary selected notice of the selection by certified mail, return receipt requested.

Added by Acts 1999, 76th Leg., ch. 63, § 1, eff. Aug. 30, 1999.

Subchapter B. Duties of Trustee

Statutes in Context

If the trust instrument and the Trust Code are both silent about a particular issue regarding trust administration, the common law rules still apply.

§ 113.051. General Duty

The trustee shall administer the trust according to its terms and this subtitle. In the absence of any contrary terms in the trust instrument or contrary provisions of this subtitle, in administering the trust the trustee shall perform all of the duties imposed on trustees by the common law.

Amended by Acts 1983, 68th Leg., p. 3332, ch. 567, art. 2, § 2, eff. Jan. 1, 1984.

Statutes in Context

A trustee may not self-deal by borrowing property from the trust either for the trustee's personal use or for the use of closely related or connected persons. However, the settlor may expressly authorize these loans in the trust instrument. For example, Grandparent may establish a trust for Grandchildren naming Child as the trustee and permit Child to make educational loans to Grandchildren from trust property.

***See* § 111.004(1) (defining "affiliate") and § 111.004(13) (defining "relative" in a narrow fashion which excludes many close relatives, such as uncles, aunts, nephews, and nieces).**

Corporate trustees are allowed to deposit trust funds with itself (that is, loan trust funds to itself) under the circumstances set forth in § 113.057.

This duty may not be waived by the settlor or the beneficiaries for corporate trustees. *See* §§ 111.002(a), 113.059(b), and 114.005(a). It may be waived for individual trustees.

§ 113.052. Loan of Trust Funds to Trustee

(a) Except as provided by Subsection (b) of this section, a trustee may not lend trust funds to:

(1) the trustee or an affiliate;

(2) a director, officer, or employee of the trustee or an affiliate;

(3) a relative of the trustee; or

(4) the trustee's employer, employee, partner, or other business associate.

(b) This section does not prohibit:

(1) a loan by a trustee to a beneficiary of the trust if the loan is expressly authorized or directed by the instrument or transaction establishing the trust; or

(2) a deposit by a corporate trustee with itself under Section 113.057.

Amended by Acts 1983, 68th Leg., p. 3332, ch. 567, art. 2, § 2, eff. Jan. 1, 1984.

Statutes in Context

A trustee may not purchase trust assets for the trustee's personal use. Likewise, a trustee cannot sell the trustee's personal assets to the trust. A trustee cannot be expected to act fairly in these situations because as a purchaser, the trustee wants to pay as little as possible and as a seller, the trustee wants to receive a favorable price. The prohibition also applies to closely related or connected persons.

***See* § 111.004(1) (defining "affiliate") and § 111.004(13) (defining "relative" in a narrow fashion which excludes many close relatives, such as uncles, aunts, nephews, and nieces). Subsections (b)-(g) provide limited exceptions to the prohibition.**

This duty may not be waived by the settlor or the beneficiaries for corporate trustees. *See* §§ 111.002(a), 113.059(b), and 114.005(a). It may be waived for individual trustees.

§ 113.053. Purchase or Sale of Trust Property by Trustee

(a) Except as provided by Subsections (b), (c), (d), (e), (f), and (g), a trustee shall not directly or indirectly buy or sell trust property from or to:

(1) the trustee or an affiliate;

(2) a director, officer, or employee of the trustee or an affiliate;

(3) a relative of the trustee; or

(4) the trustee's employer, partner, or other business associate.

(b) A national banking association or a state-chartered corporation with the right to exercise trust powers that is serving as executor, administrator, guardian, trustee, or receiver may sell shares of its own capital stock held by it for an estate to one or more of its officers or directors if a court:

(1) finds that the sale is in the best interest of the estate that owns the shares;

(2) fixes or approves the sales price of the shares and the other terms of the sale; and

(3) enters an order authorizing and directing the sale.

(c) If a corporate trustee, executor, administrator, or guardian is legally authorized to retain its own capital stock in trust, the trustee may exercise rights to purchase its own stock if increases in the stock are offered pro rata to shareholders.

(d) If the exercise of rights or the receipt of a stock dividend results in a fractional share holding and the acquisition meets the investment standard required by this subchapter, the trustee may purchase additional fractional shares to round out the holding to a full share.

(e) A trustee may:

(1) comply with the terms of a written executory contract signed by the settlor, including a contract for deed, earnest money contract, buy/sell agreement, or stock purchase or redemption agreement; and

(2) sell the stock, bonds, obligations, or other securities of a corporation to the issuing corporation or to its corporate affiliate if the sale is made under an agreement described in Subdivision (1) or complies with the duties imposed by Chapter 117.

(f) A national banking association, a state-chartered corporation, including a state-chartered bank or trust company, a state or federal savings and loan association that has the right to exercise trust powers and that is serving as trustee, or such an institution that is serving as custodian with respect to an individual retirement account, as defined by Section 408, Internal Revenue Code,[1] or an employee benefit plan, as defined by Section 3(3), Employee Retirement Income Security Act of 1974 (29 U.S.C. § 1002(3)), regardless of whether the custodial account is, or would otherwise be, considered a trust for purposes of this subtitle, may:

(1) employ an affiliate or division within a financial institution to provide brokerage, investment, administrative, custodial, or other account services for the trust or custodial account and charge the trust or custodial account for the services, provided, however, nothing in this section shall allow an affiliate or division to engage in the sale or business of insurance if not otherwise permitted to do so; and

(2) receive compensation, directly or indirectly, on account of the services performed by the affiliate or division within the financial institution, whether in the form of shared commissions, fees, or otherwise, provided that any amount charged by the affiliate or division for the services is disclosed and does not exceed the customary or prevailing amount that is charged by the affiliate or division, or a comparable entity, for comparable services rendered to a person other than the trust.

(g) In addition to other investments authorized by law for the investment of funds held by a fiduciary or by the instrument governing the fiduciary relationship, and notwithstanding any other provision of law and subject to the standard contained in Chapter 117, a bank or trust company acting as a fiduciary, agent, or otherwise, in the exercise of its investment discretion or at the direction of another person authorized to direct the investment of funds held by the bank or trust company as fiduciary, may invest and reinvest in the securities of an open-end or closed-end management investment company or investment trust registered under the Investment Company Act of 1940 (15 U.S.C. § 80a-1 et seq.) if the portfolio of the investment company or investment trust consists substantially of investments that are not prohibited by the governing instrument. The fact that the bank or trust company or an affiliate of the bank or trust company provides services to the investment company or investment trust, such as those of an investment advisor, custodian, transfer agent, registrar, sponsor, distributor, manager, or otherwise, and receives compensation for those services does not preclude the bank or trust company from investing or reinvesting in the securities if the compensation is disclosed by prospectus, account statement, or otherwise. An executor or administrator of an estate under a dependent administration or a guardian of an estate shall not so invest or reinvest unless specifically authorized by the court in which such estate or guardianship is pending.

Amended by Acts 1983, 68th Leg., p. 3332, ch. 567, art. 2, § 2, eff. Jan. 1, 1984; Acts 1985, 69th Leg., ch. 974, §§ 1, 2, eff. Aug. 26, 1985; Acts 1989, 71st Leg., ch. 341, § 1, eff. Aug. 28, 1989; Acts 1993, 73rd Leg., ch. 933, § 1, eff. Aug. 30, 1993. Amended by Acts 2003, 78th Leg., ch. 1103, § 4, eff. Jan. 1, 2004.

Statutes in Context

A trustee may not sell property to another trust for which the trustee is also serving as the trustee. A conflict of interest arises because as the trustee of the selling trust, the trustee has a duty to get the highest price possible for the asset. However, as the trustee of the purchasing trust, the trustee has the duty to secure the most economical price. Section 113.054 provides an exception for the transfer of obligations issued or fully guaranteed by the federal government and which are sold at their current market price.

This duty may be waived by the settlor or the beneficiaries for all types of trustees. See §§ 111.002(a), 113.059(b), & 114.005(a).

[1] 26 U.S.C.A. § 408.

§ 113.054. Sales from One Trust to Another

A trustee of one trust may not sell property to another trust of which it is also trustee unless the property is:

(1) a bond, note, bill, or other obligation issued or fully guaranteed as to principal and interest by the United States; and

(2) sold for its current market price.

Amended by Acts 1983, 68th Leg., p. 3332, ch. 567, art. 2, § 2, eff. Jan. 1, 1984.

Statutes in Context

A conflict of interest arises if a trustee invests in the same securities as both a trustee and an individual. This would place the trustee in a position of making decisions for both the trustee as an individual and the trust. The best choice for the trustee may not be the best option for the beneficiaries of the trust. Accordingly, § 113.055 prohibits a trustee from being in this conflict of interest situation. Note that although a trustee may not purchase for the trust stock in corporations in which the trustee individually holds shares, a trustee may retain stock in the trust which the trust already owns when the trustee becomes the trustee as long as it is prudent to do so.

This duty may be waived by the settlor or the beneficiaries for all types of trustees. *See* §§ 111.002(a), 113.059(b), and 114.005(a).

---

§ 113.055. Purchase of Trustee's Securities

(a) Except as provided by Subsection (b) of this section, a corporate trustee may not purchase for the trust the stock, bonds, obligations, or other securities of the trustee or an affiliate, and a noncorporate trustee may not purchase for the trust the stock, bonds, obligations, or other securities of a corporation with which the trustee is connected as director, owner, manager, or any other executive capacity.

(b) A trustee may:

(1) retain stock already owned by the trust unless the retention does not satisfy the requirements prescribed by Chapter 117; and

(2) exercise stock rights or purchase fractional shares under Section 113.053.

Amended by Acts 1983, 68th Leg., p. 3332, ch. 567, art. 2, § 2, eff. Jan. 1, 1984. Amended by Acts 2003, 78th Leg., ch. 1103, § 5, eff. Jan. 1, 2004.

§ 113.056. Authorization to Make Certain Investments

(a) Unless the terms of the trust instrument provide otherwise, and subject to the investment standards provided by this subtitle and any investment standards provided by the trust instrument, the trustee may invest all or part of the trust assets in an investment vehicle authorized for the collective investment of trust funds pursuant to Part 9, Title 12, of the Code of Federal Regulations.

(b) (Repealed)

(c) (Repealed)

(d) Subject to any investment standards provided by this chapter, Chapter 117, or the trust instrument, whenever the instrument directs, requires, authorizes, or permits investment in obligations of the United States government, the trustee may invest in and hold such obligations either directly or in the form of interests in an open-end management type investment company or investment trust registered under the Investment Company Act of 1940, 15 U.S.C. § 80a-1 et seq., or in an investment vehicle authorized for the collective investment of trust funds pursuant to Part 9, Title 12 of the Code of Federal Regulations, so long as the portfolio of such investment company, investment trust, or collective investment vehicle is limited to such obligations and to repurchase agreements fully collateralized by such obligations.

Amended by Acts 1983, 68th Leg., p. 3332, ch. 567, art. 2, § 2, eff. Jan. 1, 1984; Acts 1985, 69th Leg., ch. 341, § 1, eff. June 10, 1985; Acts 1991, 72nd Leg., ch. 876, § 1, eff. June 16, 1991. Amended by Acts 2003, 78th Leg., ch. 1103, §§ 6, 7 & 17, eff. Jan. 1, 2004.

Statutes in Context

The operation of § 113.057 is demonstrated by the following example. Assume that Octopus National Bank (ONB) is serving as the trustee of a trust. ONB keeps $80,000 in one of its certificates of deposit which is earning a competitive rate of interest. In addition, ONB maintains a checking account for the trust which it uses to pay expenses and make distributions to beneficiaries. Both accounts are fully insured by the federal government.

Technically, both of these accounts violate ONB's duty of loyalty. In ONB's capacity as a trustee, it is a lender, while in its capacity as a bank, it is a borrower. Thus, ONB has actually lent funds to itself. (*See* § 113.052.) Because it would be inefficient to force ONB to use another financial institution for banking services, § 113.057 permits certain self-deposits. The certificate of deposit is a long-term investment and thus the transaction has a significant self-dealing aspect and it would not be a great burden on ONB to search elsewhere for this type of investment. However, if the settlor authorized this type of investment, ONB may properly open the CD. (If the trust was created before January 1, 1988, a beneficiary may provide the necessary consent.) With regard to the checking account, the benefit to the trust of having fast and convenient access to trust funds outweighs the self-dealing nature of the deposit. Accordingly, § 113.057 permits self-deposits pending investment, distribution, or payment of debts under the statutorily mandated conditions.

---

§ 113.057. Deposits by Corporate Trustee With Itself

(a) A corporate trustee may deposit trust funds with itself as a permanent investment if authorized by the settlor in the instrument creating the trust or if authorized in a writing delivered to the trustee by a beneficiary currently eligible to receive distributions from a trust created before January 1, 1988.

(b) A corporate trustee may deposit with itself trust funds that are being held pending investment, distribution, or payment of debts if, except as provided by Subsection (d) of this section:

(1) it maintains under control of its trust department as security for the deposit a separate fund of securities legal for trust investments;

(2) the total market value of the security is at all times at least equal to the amount of the deposit; and

(3) the separate fund is marked as such.

(c) The trustee may make periodic withdrawals from or additions to the securities fund required by Subsection (b) of this section as long as the required value is maintained. Income from securities in the fund belongs to the trustee.

(d) Security for a deposit under this section is not required for a deposit under Subsection (a) or under Subsection (b) of this section to the extent the deposit is insured or otherwise secured under state or federal law.

Added by Acts 1983, 68th Leg., p. 3332, ch. 567, art. 2, § 2, eff. Jan. 1, 1984. Amended by Acts 1985, 69th Leg., ch. 149, § 3, eff. May 24, 1985.

Statutes in Context

The trustee may need to post bond conditioned on the faithful performance of the trustee's duties. The court sets the amount of the bond based on the value of the trust property. The trustee may deliver that amount in cash to the court. However, the trustee typically obtains the bond from a surety company. In exchange for the payment of premiums, the surety company agrees to pay the amount of the bond to the beneficiaries if the trustee breaches the applicable fiduciary duties. Of course, if the surety is required to pay, the surety will seek reimbursement from the trustee.

Section 113.058 exempts the trustee from the bond requirement if either (1) the settlor waived bond in the trust instrument or (2) the trustee is a corporation.

§ 113.058. Bond

(a) A corporate trustee is not required to provide a bond to secure performance of its duties as trustee.

(b) Unless the instrument creating the trust provides otherwise, a noncorporate trustee must give bond:

(1) payable to each person interested in the trust, as their interests may appear; and

(2) conditioned on the faithful performance of the trustee's duties.

(c) The bond must be in an amount and with the sureties required by order of a court in a proceeding brought for this determination.

(d) Any interested person may bring an action to increase or decrease the amount of a bond or to substitute or add sureties.

(e) The trustee shall deposit the bond with the clerk of the court that issued the order requiring the bond. A suit on the bond may be maintained on a certified copy. Appropriate proof of a recovery on a bond reduces the liability of the sureties pro tanto.

(f) Failure to comply with this section does not make void or voidable or otherwise affect an act or transaction of a trustee with any third person.

Added by Acts 1983, 68th Leg., p. 3332, ch. 567, art. 2, § 2, eff. Jan. 1, 1984.

Statutes in Context

The settlor is, for the most part, the master of the trust and thus may provide for things to be handled differently than the Trust Code indicates. The terms of the trust trump the Trust Code except that certain self-dealing duties of corporate trustees may not be waived. *See also* § 111.002(a). The settlor may include an exculpatory clause to lower the standard of care or to permit transactions that would otherwise be self-dealing or create a conflict of interest.

The settlor may include an exculpatory clause to lower the standard of care to permit transactions that would otherwise be self-dealing or create a conflict of interest. The 2003 Texas Legislature codified rules regarding the enforceability of exculpatory clauses in trusts. A settlor is prohibited from relieving a trustee of liability for a breach of trust committed (1) in bad faith, (2) intentionally, or (3) with reckless indifference to the interest of the beneficiary. In addition, the settlor may not permit the trustee to retain any profit derived from a breach of trust. *See* § 113.059(c). An exculpatory clause is ineffective to the extent the provision was included in the trust because of an abuse by the trustee of a fiduciary duty to or confidential relationship with the settlor. *See* § 113.059(d).

Note, however, that exculpatory provisions in Chapter 142 management trusts (Property Code §§ 142.001 - 142.009) and Section 867 trusts (Probate Code 867) will be enforceable only if the following two requirements are satisfied.

(1) The exculpatory provision is limited to specific facts and circumstances unique to the property of that trust and is not applicable generally to the trust.

(2) The court creating or modifying the trust makes a specific finding that there is clear and convincing evidence that the exculpatory provision is in the best interests of the beneficiary of the trust.

This new requirement for Chapter 142 and Section 867 trusts is a reaction to the Texas Supreme Court opinion in *Texas Commerce Bank, N.A. v. Grizzle*, 96 S.W.3d 240 (Tex. 2002), in which the court enforced a boilerplate exculpatory clause in a Chapter 142 trust.

§ 113.059. Power of Settlor to Alter Trustee's Responsibilities

(a) Except as provided by this section, the settlor by provision in an instrument creating, modifying, amending, or revoking the trust may relieve the trustee from a duty, liability, or restriction imposed by this subtitle.

(b) A settlor may not relieve a corporate trustee from the duties, restrictions, or liabilities of Section 113.052 or 113.053 of this Act.

(c) A settlor may not relieve the trustee of liability for:

(1) a breach of trust committed:

(A) in bad faith;

(B) intentionally; or

(C) with reckless indifference to the interest of the beneficiary; or

(2) any profit derived by the trustee from a breach of trust.

(d) A provision in a trust instrument relieving the trustee of liability for a breach of trust is ineffective to the extent that the provision is inserted in the trust instrument as a result of an abuse by the trustee of a fiduciary duty to or confidential relationship with the settlor.

Added by Acts 1983, 68th Leg., p. 3332, ch. 567, art. 2, § 2, eff. Jan. 1, 1984. Amended by Acts 1984, 68th Leg., 2nd C.S., ch. 18, § 12, eff. Oct. 2, 1984. Amended by Acts 2003, 78th Leg., ch. 1154, §§ 1 & 2, eff. Sept. 1, 2003.

Subchapter C. Resignation or Removal of Trustee, and Authority of Multiple and Successor Trustees

Statutes in Context

A trustee is not stuck with serving as a trustee until the trust ends or the trustee dies. The trustee may resign either by (1) following the terms of the trust or (2) petitioning the court for permission to resign. The trustee cannot just "walk away" from the job.

§ 113.081. Resignation of Trustee

(a) A trustee may resign in accordance with the terms of the trust instrument, or a trustee may petition a court for permission to resign as trustee.

(b) The court may accept a trustee's resignation and discharge the trustee from the trust on the terms and conditions necessary to protect the rights of other interested persons.

Amended by Acts 1983, 68th Leg., p. 3332, ch. 567, art. 2, § 2, eff. Jan. 1, 1984.

Statutes in Context

Section 113.082 explains the circumstances under which a trustee may be removed from office. Despite the use of the word "may," Texas courts have held that they *must* remove a trustee for the specific reasons enumerated in the statute such as for materially violating the trust or becoming insolvent. *See Akin v. Dahl*, 661 S.W.2d 911 (Tex. 1983). The 2003 Texas Legislature changed the statute by adding the phrase "in its discretion" after the term "may" to make it clear that whether or not to remove a trustee is always a discretionary decision of the court.

The court has broad discretion to remove a trustee "for other cause." However, courts are reluctant to remove a trustee because of dissent between the trustee and the beneficiaries, especially when the settlor appointed the trustee (as compared to a court-appointed trustee). For example, the settlor may have anticipated the beneficiaries' greed and wanted the trustee to stand firm against their demands.

§ 113.082. Removal of Trustee

(a) A trustee may be removed in accordance with the terms of the trust instrument, or, on the petition of an interested person and after hearing, a court may, in its discretion, remove a trustee and deny part or all of the trustee's compensation if:

(1) the trustee materially violated or attempted to violate the terms of the trust and the violation or attempted violation results in a material financial loss to the trust;

(2) the trustee becomes incompetent or insolvent;

(3) the trustee fails to make an accounting that is required by law or by the terms of the trust; or

(4) in the discretion of the court, for other cause.

(b) A beneficiary, cotrustee, or successor trustee may treat a violation resulting in removal as a breach of trust.

(c) A trustee of a charitable trust may not be removed solely on the grounds that the trustee exercised the trustee's power to adjust between principal and income under Section 113.0211.

Added by Acts 1983, 68th Leg., p. 3332, ch. 567, art. 2, § 2, eff. Jan. 1, 1984. Amended by Acts 2003, 78th Leg., ch. 550, § 2, eff. Sept. 1, 2003.

Statutes in Context

If no trustee remains (e.g., the sole or surviving trustee dies), a replacement trustee is selected by (1) the method specified in the trust instrument, (2) the court on its own motion, or (3) the court upon petition of an interested party. If at least one trustee remains, however, the court will not fill a vacancy. However, the majority of the trustees of a charitable (not private) trust may by majority vote to fill the vacancy if they so desire.

***See also* Finance Code §§ 274.001-274.203 (the Substitute Fiduciary Act).**

§ 113.083. Appointment of Successor Trustee

(a) On the death, resignation, incapacity, or removal of a sole or surviving trustee, a successor trustee shall be selected according to the method, if any, prescribed in the trust instrument. If for any reason a successor is not selected under the terms of the trust instrument, a court may and on petition of any interested person shall appoint a successor in whom the trust shall vest.

(b) If a vacancy occurs in the number of trustees originally appointed under a valid charitable trust agreement and the trust agreement does not provide for filling the vacancy, the remaining trustees may fill the vacancy by majority vote.

Added by Acts 1983, 68th Leg., p. 3332, ch. 567, art. 2, § 2, eff. Jan. 1, 1984.

§ 113.084. Powers of Successor Trustee

Unless otherwise provided in the trust instrument or by order of the court appointing a successor trustee, the successor trustee has the rights, powers, authority, discretion, and title to trust property conferred on the trustee.

Added by Acts 1983, 68th Leg., p. 3332, ch. 567, art. 2, § 2, eff. Jan. 1, 1984.

Statutes in Context

The settlor may appoint more than one person to serve as co-trustees. The traditional rule requires all trustees to consent before taking any action with respect to the trust unless the settlor expressly provided otherwise in the trust. Texas rejects the unanimity rule in § 113.085 and permits a majority of the trustees to make decisions regarding the trust. Co-trustees also have a duty to prevent breaches of trust by another co-trustee and, if a breach is discovered, to compel a redress for that breach.

---

§ 113.085. Exercise of Powers by Multiple Trustees

Except as otherwise provided by the trust instrument or by court order:

(1) a power vested in three or more trustees may be exercised by a majority of the trustees; and

(2) if two or more trustees are appointed by a trust instrument and one or more of the trustees die, resign, or are removed, the survivor or survivors may administer the trust and exercise the discretionary powers given to the trustees jointly.

Added by Acts 1983, 68th Leg., p. 3332, ch. 567, art. 2, § 2, eff. Jan. 1, 1984.

Subchapter E. Accounting By Trustee

Statutes in Context

The trustee has a duty to keep accurate records of all transactions involving trust property and to provide accountings to the beneficiaries. This information helps the beneficiaries to determine whether the trustee is doing an acceptable job of administering the trust. Unlike some states, Texas does not require the trustee to render periodic accountings. Instead, § 113.151 provides that a trustee must account only if (1) a beneficiary makes a written demand, or (2) an interested party obtains a court order. The settlor may not waive the trustee's responsibility to provide these accountings. *See Hollenbeck v. Hanna*, 802 S.W.2d 412 (Tex. App. — San Antonio 1991, *no writ*).

The trustee must provide the accounting on or before the 90th day after the trustee receives the demand unless a court order provides for a longer period.

If the beneficiary is successful in a suit to compel an accounting, the court has the discretion to award all or part of the court costs and all the beneficiary's reasonable and necessary attorney's fees against the trustee in either the trustee's individual or representative capacity. Note that the section does not seem to permit the court to award only a part of the attorney's fees; it appears to be an "all or nothing" situation unlike with regard to court costs where the court has the discretion to award "all or part."

Many good reasons exist for a trustee to render an annual accounting even though not required to do so by law or under the trust. The trustee will have an easier time preparing the accounting when the transactions are fresh in the trustee's mind. The trustee may have a difficult time recalling trust events years or decades later. Accountings also have a good psychological impact on the beneficiaries. Beneficiaries like to know what is going on and voluntarily submitted annual accountings may reflect highly on the trustee's conscientiousness and candor.

---

§ 113.151. Demand for Accounting

(a) A beneficiary by written demand may request the trustee to deliver to each beneficiary of the trust a written statement of accounts covering all transactions since the last accounting or since the creation of the trust, whichever is later. If the trustee fails or refuses to deliver the statement on or before the 90th day after the date the trustee receives the demand or after a longer period ordered by a court, any beneficiary of the trust may file suit to compel the trustee to deliver the statement to all beneficiaries of the trust. The court may require the trustee to deliver a written statement of account to all beneficiaries on finding that the nature of the beneficiary's interest in the trust or the effect of the administration of the trust on the beneficiary's interest is sufficient to require an accounting by the trustee. However, the trustee is not obligated or required to account to the beneficiaries of a trust more frequently than once every 12 months unless a more frequent accounting is required by the court. If a beneficiary is successful in the suit to compel a statement under this section, the court may, in its discretion, award all or part of the costs of the court and all of the suing beneficiary's reasonable and necessary attorney's fees and costs against the trustee in the trustee's individual capacity or in the trustee's capacity as trustee.

(b) An interested person may file suit to compel the trustee to account to the interested person. The court may require the trustee to deliver a written statement of account to the interested person on finding that the nature of the interest in the trust of, the claim against the trust by, or the effect of the administration of the trust on the interested person is sufficient to require an accounting by the trustee.

Added by Acts 1983, 68th Leg., p. 3332, ch. 567, art. 2, § 2, eff. Jan. 1, 1984. Amended by Acts 2003, 78th Leg., ch. 550, § 3, eff. Sept. 1, 2003.

Statutes in Context

Section 113.152 enumerates the items required in a trustee's accounting. A trustee may find it convenient to keep records in this format from the beginning to make it a relatively easy task to render an accounting.

§ 113.152. Contents of Accounting

A written statement of accounts shall show:

(1) all trust property that has come to the trustee's knowledge or into the trustee's possession and that has not been previously listed or inventoried as property of the trust;

(2) a complete account of receipts, disbursements, and other transactions regarding the trust property for the period covered by the account, including their source and nature, with receipts of principal and income shown separately;

(3) a listing of all property being administered, with an adequate description of each asset;

(4) the cash balance on hand and the name and location of the depository where the balance is kept; and

(5) all known liabilities owed by the trust.

Added by Acts 1983, 68th Leg., p. 3332, ch. 567, art. 2, § 2, eff. Jan. 1, 1984.

Subchapter F. Common Trust Funds

Statutes in Context

Sections 113.171 and 113.172 permit corporate trustees to commingle the property from several trusts into *common trust funds*. These funds permit trustees to diversify, lower transaction costs, and better leverage the trust property. Individual trustees do not have the option of commingling the property of different trusts. However, they can secure the same benefits by investing in regular commercial mutual funds.

§ 113.171. Common Trust Funds

(a) A bank or trust company qualified to act as a fiduciary in this state may establish common trust funds to provide investments to itself as a fiduciary, including as a custodian under the Texas Uniform Gifts to Minors Act (Chapter 141) or a uniform gifts to minors act of another state or to itself and others as cofiduciaries.

(b) The fiduciary or cofiduciary may place investment funds in interests in common trust funds if:

(1) the investment is not prohibited by the instrument or order creating the fiduciary relationship; and

(2) if there are cofiduciaries, the cofiduciaries consent to the investment.

(c) A common trust fund includes a fund:

(1) qualified for exemption from federal income taxation as a common trust fund and maintained exclusively for eligible fiduciary accounts; and

(2) consisting solely of assets of retirement, pension, profit sharing, stock bonus, or other employees' trusts that are exempt from federal income taxation.

Added by Acts 1983, 68th Leg., p. 3332, ch. 567, art. 2, § 2, eff. Jan. 1, 1984.

§ 113.172. Affiliated Institutions

A bank or trust company that is a member of an affiliated group under Section 1504, Internal Revenue Code of 1954 (26 U.S.C. § 1504), with a bank or trust company maintaining common trust funds may participate in one or more of the funds.

Added by Acts 1983, 68th Leg., p. 3332, ch. 567, art. 2, § 2, eff. Jan. 1, 1984.

Chapter 114. Liabilities, Rights, and Remedies of Trustees, Beneficiaries, and Third Persons

Subchapter A. Liability of Trustee

Statutes in Context

A trustee is accountable for any profit made by the trustee through or arising out of the administration of the trust even though the profit does not result from a breach of trust. *See* § 114.001(a). For example, if the trustee obtains knowledge of a good investment while working for the trust and then makes the investment for the trustee individually, the trustee will be responsible for any profit the trustee makes. In all other cases, however, the trustee must breach the trust before liability attaches. *See* § 114.001(b). The available remedies include:

1. **Lost Value.** The court may award the loss or depreciation in value to the trust property caused by the breach. The plaintiff must be able to demonstrate that the trustee's breach caused the loss but does not need to show that the trustee personally benefited from the breach. *See* § 114.001(c)(1).
2. **Profit Made by Trustee.** The trustee is responsible for any profit the trustee gained by being a trustee, except for the trustee's compensation. The trustee is liable for the profit even if the trust did not suffer a loss because of the breach. *See* § 114.001(c)(2).
3. **Lost Profits.** The court may hold the trustee liable for the profits the trust would have earned had the trustee not breached the trustee's fiduciary duties. These damages are more difficult to prove because of their speculative nature. *See* § 114.001(c)(3).
4. **Punitive Damages.** An intentional breach of duty by the trustee is considered a tort. Consequently, the court may be able to justify an award of punitive damages. *See Interfirst Bank Dallas, N.A. v. Risser*, 739 S.W.2d 882 (Tex. App. – Texarkana 1987, *no writ*).

The statute of limitations does not begin to run against the beneficiary until the beneficiary has notice that the trustee has repudiated the trust. The beneficiary does not have a duty to investigate until the beneficiary has knowledge of facts which are sufficient to trigger a reasonable person to inquire. In other words, the statute of limitations does not run from the date of the trustee's breach but rather from when that breach is, or should have been, discovered. *See Courseview, Inc. v. Phillips Petroleum Co.*, 312 S.W.2d 197 (Tex. 1957).

§ 114.001. Liability of Trustee to Beneficiary

(a) The trustee is accountable to a beneficiary for the trust property and for any profit made by the trustee through or arising out of the administration of the trust, even though the profit does not result from a breach of trust; provided, however, that the trustee is not required to return to a beneficiary the trustee's compensation as provided by this subtitle, by the terms of the trust instrument, or by a writing delivered to the trustee and signed by all beneficiaries of the trust who have full legal capacity.

(b) The trustee is not liable to the beneficiary for a loss or depreciation in value of the trust property or for a failure to make a profit that does not result from a failure to perform the duties set forth in this subtitle or from any other breach of trust.

(c) A trustee who commits a breach of trust is chargeable with any damages resulting from such breach of trust, including but not limited to:

(1) any loss or depreciation in value of the trust estate as a result of the breach of trust;

(2) any profit made by the trustee through the breach of trust; or

(3) any profit that would have accrued to the trust estate if there had been no breach of trust;

(d) The trustee is not liable to the beneficiary for a loss or depreciation in value of the trust property or for acting or failing to act under Section 113.025 or under any other provision of this subtitle if the action or failure to act relates to compliance with an environmental law and if there is no gross negligence or bad faith on the part of the trustee. The provision of any instrument governing trustee liability does not increase the liability of the trustee as provided by this section unless the settlor expressly makes reference to this subsection.

(e) The trustee has the same protection from liability provided for a fiduciary under 42 U.S.C. § 9607(n).

Amended by Acts 1983, 68th Leg., p. 3332, ch. 567, art. 2, § 2, eff. Jan. 1, 1984; Acts 1984, 68th Leg., 2nd C.S., ch. 18, § 13, eff. Oct. 2, 1984; Acts 1989, 71st Leg., ch. 341, § 2, eff. Aug. 28, 1989; Acts 1993, 73rd Leg., ch. 846, § 30, eff. Sept. 1, 1993. Amended by Acts 1997, 75th Leg., ch. 263, § 1, eff. Sept. 1, 1997. Amended by Acts 2003, 78th Leg., ch. 1103, § 8, eff. Jan. 1, 2004.

Statutes in Context

A successor trustee is liable for a breach of a predecessor trustee under the circumstances set forth in § 114.002.

§ 114.002. Liability of Successor Trustee for Breach of Trust by Predecessor

A successor trustee is liable for a breach of trust of a predecessor only if he knows or should know of a situation constituting a breach of trust committed by the predecessor and the successor trustee:

(1) improperly permits it to continue;

(2) fails to make a reasonable effort to compel the predecessor trustee to deliver the trust property; or

(3) fails to make a reasonable effort to compel a redress of a breach of trust committed by the predecessor trustee.

Amended by Acts 1983, 68th Leg., p. 3332, ch. 567, art. 2, § 2, eff. Jan. 1, 1984.

Statutes in Context

A *directory provision* requires the trustee to exercise certain trust powers, especially those relating to investments, as directed by another person or group. For example, the settlor may require the trustee to follow the advice of the settlor's stockbroker in making securities trades and of an investment committee in making other investments. A settlor may find this preferable to naming a professional investor as the trustee to the exclusion of the settlor's spouse or children. Section 114.003 restricts the liability of the trustee for complying with instructions given by people whose directions the trustee is required to follow.

§ 114.003. Person Other Than Trustee in Control

If a trust instrument reserves or vests authority in any person to the exclusion of the trustee, including the settlor, an advisory or investment committee, or one or more cotrustees, to direct the making or retention of an investment or to perform any other act in the management or administration of the trust, the excluded trustee or cotrustee is not liable for a loss resulting from the exercise of the authority in regard to the investments, management, or administration of the trust.

Amended by Acts 1983, 68th Leg., p. 3332, ch. 567, art. 2, § 2, eff. Jan. 1, 1984.

Statutes in Context

Trustees are generally under an absolute and unqualified duty to make trust distributions to the correct persons. A trustee who makes an improper distribution is liable even though the trustee exercised reasonable care and made the mistake in good faith. This duty is stricter than the standard applicable to other aspects of trust management because the beneficiary is the owner of the equitable title and is thus entitled to the trust distributions according to the terms of the trust.

Section 114.004, however, provides protection for a trustee who makes a distribution without actual knowledge or written notice of a fact impacting distribution such as the beneficiary's marriage, divorce,

attainment of a certain age, or the performance of educational requirements. The trustee still has a duty to seek recovery of the mistaken payment and the beneficiary who received the mistaken payment has a duty to repay it. *See* § 114.031.

§ 114.004. Actions Taken Prior to Knowledge or Notice of Facts

A trustee is not liable for a mistake of fact made before the trustee has actual knowledge or receives written notice of the happening of any event that determines or affects the distribution of the income or principal of the trust, including marriage, divorce, attainment of a certain age, performance of education requirements, or death.

Amended by Acts 1983, 68th Leg., p. 3332, ch. 567, art. 2, § 2, eff. Jan. 1, 1984.

Statutes in Context

A beneficiary may give prior approval to the trustee for actions that would otherwise be in breach of trust. Likewise, the beneficiary may ratify breaches of trust which have already occurred. Section 114.005 provides the requirements for a release.

Note that a beneficiary may not relieve a corporate trustee from the self-dealing prohibitions of §§ 113.052 and 113.053.

§ 114.005. Release of Liability by Beneficiary

(a) A beneficiary who has full legal capacity and is acting on full information may relieve a trustee from any duty, responsibility, restriction, or liability as to the beneficiary that would otherwise be imposed on the trustee by this subtitle, including liability for past violations, except as to the duties, restrictions, and liabilities imposed on corporate trustees by Section 113.052 or 113.053 of this subtitle.

(b) The release must be in writing and delivered to the trustee.

Amended by Acts 1983, 68th Leg., p. 3332, ch. 567, art. 2, § 2, eff. Jan. 1, 1984.

Statutes in Context

Generally, co-trustees are jointly and severally liable to the beneficiaries. Section 114.006 explains how a dissenting trustee may attempt to be protected from liability for the acts of the majority.

§ 114.006. Power Exercised by Majority

(a) A trustee who does not join in exercising a power held by three or more cotrustees is not liable to a beneficiary of the trust or to others for the consequences of the exercise nor is a dissenting trustee liable for the consequences of an act in which the trustee joins at the direction of the majority trustees if the trustee expressed the dissent in writing to any of the cotrustees at or before the time of joinder.

(b) This section does not excuse a cotrustee from liability for failure to discharge the cotrustee's duties as a trustee.

Amended by Acts 1983, 68th Leg., p. 3332, ch. 567, art. 2, § 2, eff. Jan. 1, 1984.

Subchapter B. Liability of Beneficiary

Statutes in Context

A beneficiary is generally not in a position to breach the trust and is not liable for breaches of trust committed by the trustee. Under the circumstances listed in § 114.031, however, a beneficiary may be liable to the trust.

§ 114.031. Liability of Beneficiary to Trustee

(a) A beneficiary is liable for loss to the trust if the beneficiary has:

(1) misappropriated or otherwise wrongfully dealt with the trust property;

(2) expressly consented to, participated in, or agreed with the trustee to be liable for a breach of trust committed by the trustee;

(3) failed to repay an advance or loan of trust funds;

(4) failed to repay a distribution or disbursement from the trust in excess of that to which the beneficiary is entitled; or

(5) breached a contract to pay money or deliver property to the trustee to be held by the trustee as part of the trust.

(b) Unless the terms of the trust provide otherwise, the trustee is authorized to offset a liability of the beneficiary to the trust estate against the beneficiary's interest in the trust estate, regardless of a spendthrift provision in the trust.

Added by Acts 1983, 68th Leg., p. 3332, ch. 567, art. 2, § 2, eff. Jan. 1, 1984.

Statutes in Context

Section 114.032 provides for limited virtual representation so that a release may bind beneficiaries who did not actually agree because, for example, they are minors, unborn, or unascertained. Note that this provision may not be used to modify or terminate the trust. *See* § 115.013 (judicial virtual representation).

§ 114.032. Liability for Written Agreements

(a) A written agreement between a trustee and a beneficiary, including a release, consent, or other agreement relating to a trustee's duty, power, responsibility, restriction, or liability, is final and binding on the beneficiary and any person represented by a beneficiary as provided by this section if:

(1) the instrument is signed by the beneficiary;

(2) the beneficiary has legal capacity to sign the instrument; and

(3) the beneficiary has full knowledge of the circumstances surrounding the agreement.

(b) A written agreement signed by a beneficiary who has the power to revoke the trust or the power to appoint, including the power to appoint through a power of amendment, the income or principal of the trust to or for the benefit of the beneficiary, the beneficiary's creditors, the beneficiary's estate, or the creditors of the beneficiary's estate is final and binding on any person who takes under the power of appointment or who takes in default if the power of appointment is not executed.

(c) A written instrument is final and binding on a beneficiary who is a minor if:

(1) the minor's parent, including a parent who is also a trust beneficiary, signs the instrument on behalf of the minor;

(2) no conflict of interest exists; and

(3) no guardian, including a guardian ad litem, has been appointed to act on behalf of the minor.

(d) A written instrument is final and binding on an unborn or unascertained beneficiary if a beneficiary who has an interest substantially identical to the interest of the unborn or unascertained beneficiary signs the instrument. For purposes of this subsection, an unborn or unascertained beneficiary has a substantially identical interest only with a trust beneficiary from whom the unborn or unascertained beneficiary descends.

(e) This section does not apply to a written instrument that modifies or terminates a trust in whole or in part unless the instrument is otherwise permitted by law.

Added by Acts 1999, 76th Leg., ch. 794, § 3, eff. Sept. 1, 1999.

Subchapter C. Rights of Trustee

Statutes in Context

At common law, a trustee was presumed to serve without compensation unless the trust instrument expressly provided otherwise. The policy behind this rule was that a trustee should not earn a profit by serving in a fiduciary capacity. Otherwise, the trustee might take certain actions which were not necessary or not in the best interest of the trust merely to increase the compensation.

Section 114.061 provides that a trustee is entitled to *reasonable* compensation unless the trust expressly provides that the trustee is not to be paid or provides a method for determining compensation. The following factors may be considered in determining the amount of compensation which is reasonable: (1) The amount of time the trustee spent working on trust matters; (2) the gross income of the trust; (3) the appreciation in value of trust property; (4) the trustee's unusual or special skills or experience (e.g., being an attorney or accountant); (5) the trustee's degree of fidelity or disloyalty to the trust; (6) the amount of risk and responsibility the trustee assumed; (7) the fees charged by other trustees in the local community for similar services; (8) the character of the trustee's work, that is, did it involve skill and judgment or was it merely routine or ministerial; and (9) the trustee's own estimate of the value of the services.

The trustee may then take this amount from the trust without court approval. If a beneficiary or co-trustee believes the fee is excessive, that person may seek judicial review. *See* § 115.001(a)(9). The court may deny compensation to a trustee who commits a breach of trust. *See* § 114.061(b).

§ 114.061. Compensation

(a) Unless the terms of the trust provide otherwise and except as provided in Subsection (b) of this section, the trustee is entitled to reasonable compensation from the trust for acting as trustee.

(b) If the trustee commits a breach of trust, the court may in its discretion deny him all or part of his compensation.

Added by Acts 1983, 68th Leg., p. 3332, ch. 567, art. 2, § 2, eff. Jan. 1, 1984.

Statutes in Context

See *Statutes in Context* to § 114.083.

§ 114.062. Exoneration or Reimbursement for Tort

(a) Except as provided in Subsection (b) of this section, a trustee who incurs personal liability for a tort committed in the administration of the trust is entitled to exoneration from the trust property if the trustee has not paid the claim or to reimbursement from the trust property if the trustee has paid the claim, if:

(1) the trustee was properly engaged in a business activity for the trust and the tort is a common incident of that kind of activity;

(2) the trustee was properly engaged in a business activity for the trust and neither the trustee nor an officer or employee of the trustee is guilty of actionable negligence or intentional misconduct in incurring the liability; or

(3) the tort increased the value of the trust property.

(b) A trustee who is entitled to exoneration or reimbursement under Subdivision (3) of Subsection (a) is entitled to exoneration or reimbursement only to the extent of the increase in the value of the trust property.

Added by Acts 1983, 68th Leg., p. 3332, ch. 567, art. 2, § 2, eff. Jan. 1, 1984.

Statutes in Context

Section 114.063 codifies the trustee's reimbursement rights.

§ 114.063. General Right to Reimbursement

(a) A trustee may discharge or reimburse himself from trust principal or income or partly from both for:

(1) advances made for the convenience, benefit, or protection of the trust or its property;

(2) expenses incurred while administering or protecting the trust or because of the trustee's holding or owning any of the trust property; and

(3) expenses incurred for any action taken under Section 113.025.

(b) The trustee has a lien against trust property to secure reimbursement under Subsection (a).

(c) A potential trustee is entitled to reimbursement from trust principal or income or partly from both for reasonable expenses incurred for any action taken under Section 113.025(a) if:

(1) a court orders reimbursement or the potential trustee has entered into a written agreement providing for reimbursement with the personal representative of the estate, the trustee of the trust, the settlor, the settlor's attorney-in-fact, the settlor's personal representative, or the person or entity designated in the trust instrument or will to appoint a trustee; and

(2) the potential trustee has been appointed trustee under the terms of the trust instrument or will or has received a written request to accept the trust from the settlor, the settlor's attorney-in-fact, the settlor's personal representative, or the person or entity designated in the trust instrument or will to appoint a trustee.

Added by Acts 1983, 68th Leg., p. 3332, ch. 567, art. 2, § 2, eff. Jan. 1, 1984. Amended by Acts 1993, 73rd Leg., ch. 846, § 31, eff. Sept. 1, 1993.

Statutes in Context

The court may award costs and attorneys' fees to any party in a trust action. Thus, all parties should request fees so the court may make an equitable and just award.

§ 114.064. Costs

(a)[1] In any proceeding under this code the court may make such award of costs and reasonable and necessary attorney's fees as may seem equitable and just.

Added by Acts 1985, 69th Leg., ch. 149, § 4, eff. May 24, 1985.

Subchapter D. Third Persons

Statutes in Context

Section 114.081, along with § 114.082, explains when a person who deals with a trustee may obtain protection akin to that of a bona fide purchaser. This section protects not only purchasers but anyone who pays money to a trustee provided the payment is (1) in good faith and (2) made to a trustee who is authorized to receive the money. If these two requirements are met, the payor is not responsible for how the trustee uses the money and any title or right the payor receives may not be challenged if the trustee misapplies the money.

§ 114.081. Payment of Money to Trustee

(a) A person who actually and in good faith pays to a trustee money that the trustee is authorized to receive is not responsible for the proper application of the money according to the trust.

(b) A right or title derived from the trustee in consideration of the monetary payment under Subsection (a) of this section may not be impeached or questioned because of the trustee's misapplication of the money.

Added by Acts 1983, 68th Leg., p. 3332, ch. 567, art. 2, § 2, eff. Jan. 1, 1984.

Statutes in Context

See *Statutes in Context* to § 101.001.

§ 114.082. Conveyance by Trustee

If property is conveyed or transferred to a trustee in trust but the conveyance or transfer does not identify the trust or disclose the names of the beneficiaries, the trustee may convey, transfer, or encumber the title of the property without subsequent question by a person who claims to be a beneficiary under the trust or who claims by, through, or under an undisclosed beneficiary.

Added by Acts 1983, 68th Leg., p. 3332, ch. 567, art. 2, § 2, eff. Jan. 1, 1984. Amended by Acts 1987, 70th Leg., ch. 683, § 4, eff. Aug. 31, 1987.

Statutes in Context

See *Statutes in Context* to § 101.002.

§ 114.0821. Liability of Trust Property

Although trust property is held by the trustee without identifying the trust or its beneficiaries, the trust property is not liable to satisfy the personal obligations of the trustee.

Added by Acts 1983, 68th Leg., p. 3332, ch. 567, art. 2, § 2, eff. Jan. 1, 1984. Renumbered from § 114.082(b) by Acts 1987, 70th Leg., ch. 683, § 4, eff. Aug. 31, 1987.

Statutes in Context

A trustee may commit a tort during the administration of the trust. For example, the trustee may negligently injure someone or may convert the property of another believing it belongs to the trust. The trustee also may be liable for the tortious acts of the trustee's employees and agents which are committed in the scope of their work for the trust under normal respondeat su-

[1] As in enrolled bill; there is no (b).

perior rules. At common law, a tort plaintiff was required to sue the trustee personally and could not reach the trust property directly by suing the trustee in the trustee's representative capacity. The trustee could seek indemnification or reimbursement from the trust only if the trustee had not engaged in willful misconduct. If the trust property was inadequate, the trustee was stuck with the loss. Courts justified this strict rule on the grounds that it encouraged trustees to exercise a high level of care for fear of being personally liable and protected trust property from tort claimants.

The trustee is still personally liable for torts committed by the trustee or the trustee's agents/employees. *See* § 114.083(c). However, § 114.083(a) permits plaintiffs to sue the trustee in the trustee's representative capacity and to recover directly against trust property in three situations: (1) the tort is a common incident of the business activity in which the trust was properly engaged (e.g., the trust owns a grocery store in which a customer slips, falls, and is injured because an employee negligently failed to clean up a spill); (2) the trustee is not personally at fault because the tort is based on strict liability; and (3) the tort actually increased the value of trust property, such as conversion. In these same three situations, the trustee is entitled to exoneration or reimbursement from trust property under § 114.062. Because the trustee remains personally liable for amounts the trust cannot reimburse or exonerate, the trustee should purchase insurance. *See* § 113.013.

---

§ 114.083. Rights and Liabilities for Committing Torts

(a) A personal liability of a trustee or a predecessor trustee for a tort committed in the course of the administration of the trust may be collected from the trust property if the trustee is sued in a representative capacity and the court finds that:

(1) the trustee was properly engaged in a business activity for the trust and the tort is a common incident of that kind of activity;

(2) the trustee was properly engaged in a business activity for the trust and neither the trustee nor an officer or employee of the trustee is guilty of actionable negligence or intentional misconduct in incurring the liability; or

(3) the tort increased the value of the trust property.

(b) A trust that is liable for the trustee's tort under Subdivision (3) of Subsection (a) is liable only to the extent of the permanent increase in value of the trust property.

(c) A plaintiff in an action against the trustee as the representative of the trust does not have to prove that the trustee could have been reimbursed by the trust if the trustee had paid the claim.

(d) Subject to the rights of exoneration or reimbursement under Section 114.062, the trustee is personally liable for a tort committed by the trustee or by the trustee's agents or employees in the course of their employment.

Added by Acts 1983, 68th Leg., p. 3332, ch. 567, art. 2, § 2, eff. Jan. 1, 1984.

Statutes in Context

A trustee frequently enters into contracts in the performance of the trustee's investment and managerial duties. For example, the trustee may contract with an attorney to provide legal services or with a janitorial service to maintain an office building that is part of the trust corpus. Unless the trustee takes special steps to avoid liability, the trustee is personally liable for any breach of contract. *See* § 114.084(a). To recoup damages paid to a contract claimant, the trustee must prove that the trustee properly entered into the contract for the benefit of the trust and then seek reimbursement from the trust property. *See* § 114.063. The trustee would be stuck with any loss that results if the trust does not have adequate property to make a complete reimbursement.

At common law, a contract plaintiff could not sue the trustee in the trustee's representative capacity and could not recover directly against trust property. The common law courts did not take notice of the trust relationship and thus did not recognize the trustee as an individual as being a separate entity from the trustee in a representative capacity. Section 114.063, however, permits contract plaintiffs to reach the trust property directly by proceeding against the trustee in the trustee's fiduciary capacity.

A trustee will usually want to take steps to prevent the trustee's exposure to personal liability on contracts entered into for the benefit of the trust. The trustee should include a provision in the contract which expressly excludes the trustee's personal liability. *See* § 114.084(a). Instead, if the trustee only signs in a representative capacity (e.g., "as trustee"), the trustee may still be personally liable but the signature acts as prima facie evidence of an intent to exclude the trustee from personal liability. *See* § 114.084(b).

---

§ 114.084. Contracts of Trustee

(a) If a trustee or a predecessor trustee makes a contract that is within his power as trustee and a cause of action arises on the contract, the plaintiff may sue the trustee in his representative capacity, and a judgment rendered in favor of the plaintiff is collectible by execution against the trust property. The plaintiff may sue the trustee individually if the trustee made the contract and the contract does not exclude the trustee's personal liability.

(b) The addition of "trustee" or "as trustee" after the signature of a trustee who is party to a contract is prima facie evidence of an intent to exclude the trustee from personal liability.

(c) In an action on a contract against a trustee in the trustee's representative capacity the plaintiff does

not have to prove that the trustee could have been reimbursed by the trust if the trustee had paid the claim.
Added by Acts 1983, 68th Leg., p. 3332, ch. 567, art. 2, § 2, eff. Jan. 1, 1984.

§ 114.085. Partnerships

(a) To the extent allowed by law, a trustee who takes the place of a deceased partner in a general partnership in accordance with the articles of partnership is liable to third persons only to the extent of the:

(1) deceased partner's capital in the partnership; and

(2) trust funds held by the trustee.

(b) A trustee who contracts to enter a general partnership in its capacity as trustee shall limit, to the extent allowed by law, the trust's liability to:

(1) the trust assets contributed to the partnership; and

(2) other assets of the trust under the management of the contracting trustee.

(c) If another provision of this subtitle conflicts with this section, this section controls. This section does not exonerate a trustee from liability for negligence.
Added by Acts 1983, 68th Leg., p. 3332, ch. 567, art. 2, § 2, eff. Jan. 1, 1984.

Chapter 115. Jurisdiction, Venue, and Proceedings

Subchapter A. Jurisdiction and Venue

Statutes in Context

Jurisdiction over trust matters is typically in the district court. *See* § 115.001(a). However, if the county also has a statutory probate court, the statutory probate court also has jurisdiction. *See* § 115.001(d). See *Statutes in Context* to Probate Code § 5. If the trust is inter vivos, there is no statutory indication in which of these two courts the trust action should be brought. However, if the trust is testamentary, Probate Code § 5A(b) provides that the action should be brought in the statutory probate court.

Section 115.001(a) provides an extensive list of actions over which the court has jurisdiction. It would be difficult to come up with a trust issue that would not fit into one of the statutory categories.

Of particular importance is § 115.001(a)(8), the ultimate escape clause. The court has the ability to relieve a trustee from any duty, limitation, or restriction which is imposed by the trust instrument or the Trust Code. Thus, a trustee in breach of trust who has an equitable argument that the breach should be forgiven, may "beg" the court for "mercy."

Subsection (b) provides that the court has all of the powers of a court of equity such as the ability to apply cy pres, issue injunctions, and appoint receivers.

The court does not have continuing supervision over the trust unless the court order expressly so provides. *See* § 115.001(c).

§ 115.001. Jurisdiction

(a) Except as provided by Subsection (d) of this section, a district court has original and exclusive jurisdiction over all proceedings concerning trusts, including proceedings to:

(1) construe a trust instrument;

(2) determine the law applicable to a trust instrument;

(3) appoint or remove a trustee;

(4) determine the powers, responsibilities, duties, and liability of a trustee;

(5) ascertain beneficiaries;

(6) make determinations of fact affecting the administration, distribution, or duration of a trust;

(7) determine a question arising in the administration or distribution of a trust;

(8) relieve a trustee from any or all of the duties, limitations, and restrictions otherwise existing under the terms of the trust instrument or of this subtitle;

(9) require an accounting by a trustee, review trustee fees, and settle interim or final accounts; and

(10) surcharge a trustee.

(b) The district court may exercise the powers of a court of equity in matters pertaining to trusts.

(c) Unless specifically directed by a written order of the court, a proceeding does not result in continuing supervision by the court over the administration of the trust.

(d) The jurisdiction of the district court over proceedings concerning trusts is exclusive except for jurisdiction conferred by law on a statutory probate court or a court that creates a trust under Section 867, Texas Probate Code.
Amended by Acts 1983, 68th Leg., p. 3332, ch. 567, art. 2, § 2, eff. Jan. 1, 1984. Amended by Acts 1997, 75th Leg., ch. 1375, § 5, eff. Sept. 1, 1997.

Statutes in Context

Proper venue for a trust action is determined by § 115.002. Different rules apply if there is (1) a single noncorporate trust or (2) multiple individual trustees or if any trustee is a corporation.

§ 115.002. Venue

(a) The venue of an action under Section 115.001 is determined according to this section.

(b) If there is a single, noncorporate trustee, an action shall be brought in the county in which:

(1) the trustee resides or has resided at any time during the four-year period preceding the date the action is filed; or

(2) the situs of administration of the trust is maintained or has been maintained at any time during the four-year period preceding the date the action is filed.

(c) If there are multiple trustees or a corporate trustee, an action shall be brought in the county in which the situs of administration of the trust is maintained or has been maintained at any time during the four-year period preceding the date the action is filed, provided that an action against a corporate trustee as defendant may be brought in the county in which the corporate trustee maintains its principal office in this state.

(d) For just and reasonable cause, including the location of the records and the convenience of the parties and witnesses, the court may transfer an action from a county of proper venue under this section to another county of proper venue:

(1) on motion of a defendant or joined party, filed concurrently with or before the filing of the answer or other initial responsive pleading, and served in accordance with law; or

(2) on motion of an intervening party, filed not later than the 20th day after the court signs the order allowing the intervention, and served in accordance with law.

(e) Notwithstanding any other provision of this section, on agreement by all parties the court may transfer an action from a county of proper venue under this section to any other county.

(f) For the purposes of this section:

(1) "Corporate trustee" means an entity organized as a financial institution or a corporation with the authority to act in a fiduciary capacity.

(2) "Principal office" means an office of a corporate trustee in this state where the decision makers for the corporate trustee within this state conduct the daily affairs of the corporate trustee. The mere presence of an agent or representative of the corporate trustee does not establish a principal office. The principal office of the corporate trustee may also be but is not necessarily the same as the situs of administration of the trust.

(3) "Situs of administration" means the location in this state where the trustee maintains the office that is primarily responsible for dealing with the settlor and beneficiaries of the trust. The situs of administration may also be but is not necessarily the same as the principal office of a corporate trustee.

Amended by Acts 1983, 68th Leg., p. 3332, ch. 567, art. 2, § 2, eff. Jan. 1, 1984; Amended by Acts 1999, 76th Leg., ch. 344, § 4.026, eff. Sept. 1, 1999; Acts 1999, 76th Leg., ch. 933, § 1, eff. Sept. 1, 1999.

Subchapter B. Parties, Procedure, and Judgments

Statutes in Context

An interested person has standing to bring a trust action. *See* § 111.004(7) (defining "interested person").

Section 115.011(b) enumerates the parties who are necessary to a trust action.

Subsection (c) references the requirement that the attorney general be notified of any action involving a charitable trust. See *Statutes in Context* to § 123.001.

A trust beneficiary has the right to intervene in an action against a trustee in contract or tort. *See* § 115.015 (requiring tort and contract plaintiffs to give notice to beneficiaries).

§ 115.011. Parties

(a) Any interested person may bring an action under Section 115.001.

(b) Contingent beneficiaries designated as a class are not necessary parties to an action under Section 115.001. The only necessary parties to such an action are:

(1) a beneficiary on whose act or obligation the action is predicated;

(2) a person designated by name in the instrument creating the trust; and

(3) a person who is actually receiving distributions from the trust estate at the time the action is filed.

(c) The attorney general shall be given notice of any proceeding involving a charitable trust as provided by Chapter 123 of this code.

(d) A beneficiary of a trust may intervene and contest the right of the plaintiff to recover in an action against the trustee as representative of the trust for a tort committed in the course of the trustee's administration or on a contract executed by the trustee.

Amended by Acts 1983, 68th Leg., p. 3332, ch. 567, art. 2, § 2, eff. Jan. 1, 1984. Amended by Acts 1995, 74th Leg., ch. 172, § 1, eff. Sept. 1, 1995.

§ 115.012. Rules of Procedure

Except as otherwise provided, all actions instituted under this subtitle are governed by the Texas Rules of Civil Procedure and the other statutes and rules that are applicable to civil actions generally.

Amended by Acts 1983, 68th Leg., p. 3332, ch. 567, art. 2, § 2, eff. Jan. 1, 1984.

Statutes in Context

Section 115.013 provides for virtual representation under specified circumstances so that a court order may bind beneficiaries who did not actually agree because, for example, they are minors, unborn, or unascertained. *See* § 114.013 (limited nonjudicial virtual representation).

§ 115.013. Pleadings and Judgments

(a) Actions and proceedings involving trusts are governed by this section.

(b) An affected interest shall be described in pleadings that give reasonable information to an owner by name or class, by reference to the instrument creating the interest, or in other appropriate manner.

(c) A person is bound by an order binding another in the following cases:

(1) an order binding the sole holder or all coholders of a power of revocation or a presently exercisable general power of appointment, including one in the form of a power of amendment, binds

other persons to the extent their interests, as objects, takers in default, or otherwise are subject to the power;

(2) to the extent there is no conflict of interest between them or among persons represented:

(A) an order binding a guardian of the estate or a guardian ad litem binds the ward; and

(B) an order binding a trustee binds beneficiaries of the trust in proceedings to review the acts or accounts of a prior fiduciary and in proceedings involving creditors or other third parties;

(3) if there is no conflict of interest and no guardian of the estate or guardian ad litem has been appointed, a parent may represent his minor child as guardian ad litem or as next friend; and

(4) an unborn or unascertained person who is not otherwise represented is bound by an order to the extent his interest is adequately represented by another party having a substantially identical interest in the proceeding.

(d) Notice under Section 115.014 shall be given either to a person who will be bound by the judgment or to one who can bind that person under this section, and notice may be given to both. Notice may be given to unborn or unascertained persons who are not represented under Subdivision (1) or (2) of Subsection (c) by giving notice to all known persons whose interests in the proceedings are substantially identical to those of the unborn or unascertained persons.

Amended by Acts 1983, 68th Leg., p. 3332, ch. 567, art. 2, § 2, eff. Jan. 1, 1984.

Statutes in Context

The court *may* appoint a guardian ad litem to represent the interest of a minor, incapacitated, unborn, unascertained, etc., beneficiary. *See* § 115.014(a). If the trust is sued by a tort plaintiff, the court *must* appoint a guardian ad litem for a minor or incompetent beneficiary. *See* § 115.014(b).

§ 115.014. Guardian Ad Litem

(a) At any point in a proceeding a court may appoint a guardian ad litem to represent the interest of a minor, an incapacitated, unborn, or unascertained person, or person whose identity or address is unknown, if the court determines that representation of the interest otherwise would be inadequate. If there is not a conflict of interests, a guardian ad litem may be appointed to represent several persons or interests.

(b) A court shall appoint a guardian ad litem to defend an action under Section 114.083 for a beneficiary of the trust who is a minor or who has been adjudged incompetent.

Amended by Acts 1983, 68th Leg., p. 3332, ch. 567, art. 2, § 2, eff. Jan. 1, 1984.

Statutes in Context

Contract and tort plaintiffs have an obligation to notify the beneficiary before being entitled to a judgment against the trustee. Section 115.015 explains the timing of the notice and how the plaintiff may obtain a list of beneficiaries and their addresses from the trustee. The purpose of the notice is to alert the beneficiary that something may be "wrong" with the trust administration. Once notified, the beneficiary may decide to exercise the right to intervene under § 115.011(d).

Note that § 115.015(a)(2) requires that the attorney general be given notice only in contract cases, not tort cases. This anomaly is traceable to Texas Trust Act § 21 which was written before Texas abolished charitable immunity. *See Howle v. Camp Amon Carter*, 470 S.W.2d 629 (Tex. 1971) (abolishing charitable immunity as of March 9, 1966); *but see* Charitable Immunity and Liability Act, Civil Practice & Remedies Code, ch. 84. The attorney general may nonetheless be entitled to notice under Property Code ch. 123.

§ 115.015. Notice to Beneficiaries of Tort or Contract Proceeding

(a) A court may not render judgment in favor of a plaintiff in an action on a contract executed by the trustee or in an action against the trustee as representative of the trust for a tort committed in the course of the trustee's administration unless the plaintiff proves that before the 31st day after the date the action began or within any other period fixed by the court that is more than 30 days before the date of the judgment, the plaintiff gave notice of the existence and nature of the action to:

(1) each beneficiary known to the trustee who then had a present or contingent interest; or

(2) in an action on a contract involving a charitable trust, the attorney general and any corporation that is a beneficiary or agency in the performance of the trust.

(b) The plaintiff shall give the notice required by Subsection (a) of this section by registered mail or by certified mail, return receipt requested, addressed to the party to be notified at the party's last known address. The trustee shall give the plaintiff a list of the beneficiaries or persons having an interest in the trust estate and their addresses, if known to the trustee, before the 11th day after the date the plaintiff makes a written request for the information.

(c) The plaintiff satisfies the notice requirements of this section by notifying the persons on the list provided by the trustee.

Amended by Acts 1983, 68th Leg., p. 3332, ch. 567, art. 2, § 2, eff. Jan. 1, 1984.

§ 115.016. Notice

(a) If notice of hearing on a motion or other proceeding is required, the notice may be given in the manner prescribed by law or the Texas Rules of Civil Procedure, or, alternatively, notice may be given to any party or to his attorney if the party has appeared by attorney or requested that notice be sent to his attorney.

(b) If the address or identity of a party is not known and cannot be ascertained with reasonable diligence, on order of the court notice may be given by publish-

ing a copy of the notice at least three times in a newspaper having general circulation in the county where the hearing is to be held. The first publication of the notice must be at least 10 days before the time set for the hearing. If there is no newspaper of general circulation in the county where the hearing is to be held, the publication shall be made in a newspaper of general circulation in an adjoining county.
Added by Acts 1983, 68th Leg., p. 3332, ch. 567, art. 2, § 2, eff. Jan. 1, 1984.

§ 115.017. Waiver of Notice

A person, including a guardian of the estate, a guardian ad litem, or other fiduciary, may waive notice by a writing signed by the person or his attorney and filed in the proceedings.
Added by Acts 1983, 68th Leg., p. 3332, ch. 567, art. 2, § 2, eff. Jan. 1, 1984.

Chapter 116. Uniform Principal and Income Act

Statutes in Context

The settlor may grant certain beneficiaries the right to trust income (income beneficiaries) and other beneficiaries the right to the principal when the trust terminates (remainder beneficiaries). This arrangement places these two types of beneficiaries in conflict. The income beneficiaries want the trust corpus invested in property which generates high rates of return such as corporate bonds and mutual funds. On the other hand, remainder beneficiaries want the trustee to invest in property which appreciates in value such as real property and growth stocks. Many investments that are good for one type of beneficiary will not benefit another. For example, assume that the trustee invested in a government insured certificate of deposit earning 7 percent interest. The income beneficiaries will be elated because the rate of return is relatively high and the investment is extremely safe. However, the remainder beneficiaries will be furious. The CD will not grow in value because the trustee will get back the same amount the trustee invested when the CD matures. In addition, because of inflation, the buying power of the proceeds will shrink to less than the amount invested so the remainder beneficiaries will actually incur a loss. To resolve this problem, a trustee either selects investments that earn both income and appreciate in value, such as rental real property and certain types of stock, or diversifies trust investments to balance investments that earn income and investments which increase in value.

A trustee also needs to know how to categorize property received from the trust assets to carry out the trustee's duty to be fair and impartial to both the income and remainder beneficiaries. Likewise, the trustee must determine whether to reduce income or principal when the trustee pays trust expenses. The trustee has three ways to determine how to allocate receipts and expenses between income and principal. First, the settlor may have provided instructions in the trust instrument. These instructions may state specific allocation rules or may merely give the trustee discretion to make the allocation. *See* § 116.004(a)(1)-(2). Second, if the instrument is silent, the trustee must follow the rules in Chapter 116 which is the Texas adoption of the 1997 version of the Uniform Principal and Income Act. *See* § 116.004(a)(3). Third, if neither the instrument nor the statute specifies the proper method of allocation, the trustee must allocate to prinicpal. *See* § 116.004(a)(4).

The Texas adoption of the 1997 UPIA took effect on January 1, 2004. Prior to this time, Texas followed the 1962 version. Many of the provisions of the 1997 version are significantly different from prior law. Perhaps the most controversial change is the trustee's ability to adjust between principal and income under § 116.005.

Subchapter A. Definitions, Fiduciary Duties, and Other Miscellaneous Provisions

§ 116.001. Short Title

This chapter may be cited as the Uniform Principal and Income Act.
Added by Acts 2003, 78th Leg., ch. 659, § 1, eff. Jan. 1, 2004.

Statutes in Context

Section 116.002 provides definitions used throughout Chapter 116. Note that these definitions do not apply to other Trust Code chapters.

§ 116.002. Definitions

In this chapter:

(1) "Accounting period" means a calendar year unless another 12-month period is selected by a fiduciary. The term includes a portion of a calendar year or other 12-month period that begins when an income interest begins or ends when an income interest ends.

(2) "Beneficiary" includes, in the case of a decedent's estate, an heir, legatee, and devisee and, in the case of a trust, an income beneficiary and a remainder beneficiary.

(3) "Fiduciary" means a personal representative or a trustee. The term includes an executor, administrator, successor personal representative, special administrator, and a person performing substantially the same function.

(4) "Income" means money or property that a fiduciary receives as current return from a principal asset. The term includes a portion of receipts from a sale, exchange, or liquidation of a principal asset, to the extent provided in Subchapter D.

(5) "Income beneficiary" means a person to whom net income of a trust is or may be payable.

(6) "Income interest" means the right of an income beneficiary to receive all or part of net income, whether the terms of the trust require it to be distributed or authorize it to be distributed in the trustee's discretion.

(7) "Mandatory income interest" means the right of an income beneficiary to receive net income that the terms of the trust require the fiduciary to distribute.

(8) "Net income" means the total receipts allocated to income during an accounting period minus the disbursements made from income during the period, plus or minus transfers under this chapter to or from income during the period.

(9) "Person" means an individual, corporation, business trust, estate, trust, partnership, limited liability company, association, joint venture, government; governmental subdivision, agency, or instrumentality; public corporation, or any other legal or commercial entity.

(10) "Principal" means property held in trust for distribution to a remainder beneficiary when the trust terminates.

(11) "Remainder beneficiary" means a person entitled to receive principal when an income interest ends.

(12) "Terms of a trust" means the manifestation of the intent of a settlor or decedent with respect to the trust, expressed in a manner that admits of its proof in a judicial proceeding, whether by written or spoken words or by conduct.

(13) "Trustee" includes an original, additional, or successor trustee, whether or not appointed or confirmed by a court.

Added by Acts 2003, 78th Leg., ch. 659, § 1, eff. Jan. 1, 2004.

§ 116.003 Uniformity of Application and Construction

In applying and construing this Uniform Act, consideration must be given to the need to promote uniformity of the law with respect to its subject matter among states that enact it.

Added by Acts 2003, 78th Leg., ch. 659, § 1, eff. Jan. 1, 2004.

Statutes in Context

The trustee has three ways to determine how to allocate receipts and expenses between income and principal. First, the settlor may have provided instructions in the trust instrument. These instructions may state specific allocation rules or may merely give the trustee discretion to make the allocation. *See* § 116.004(a)(1)-(2). Second, if the instrument is silent, the trustee must apply the rules in Chapter 116. *See* § 116.004(a)(3). Third, if neither the instrument nor the statute specifies the proper method of allocation, the trustee must allocate to principal. *See* § 116.004(a)(4). Note that this last rule is a significant departure from prior law which provided that the trustee must allocate in a "reasonable and equitable" manner if both the instrument and statute were silent.

An allocation in accordance with the UPIA's rules by a trustee who has discretionary authority is presumed to be fair and reasonable to all beneficiaries. *See* § 116.004(b).

§ 116.004. Fiduciary Duties; General Principles

(a) In allocating receipts and disbursements to or between principal and income, and with respect to any matter within the scope of Subchapters B and C, a fiduciary:

(1) shall administer a trust or estate in accordance with the terms of the trust or the will, even if there is a different provision in this chapter;

(2) may administer a trust or estate by the exercise of a discretionary power of administration given to the fiduciary by the terms of the trust or the will, even if the exercise of the power produces a result different from a result required or permitted by this chapter;

(3) shall administer a trust or estate in accordance with this chapter if the terms of the trust or the will do not contain a different provision or do not give the fiduciary a discretionary power of administration; and

(4) shall add a receipt or charge a disbursement to principal to the extent that the terms of the trust and this chapter do not provide a rule for allocating the receipt or disbursement to or between principal and income.

(b) In exercising the power to adjust under Section 116.005(a) or a discretionary power of administration regarding a matter within the scope of this chapter, whether granted by the terms of a trust, a will, or this chapter, a fiduciary shall administer a trust or estate impartially, based on what is fair and reasonable to all of the beneficiaries, except to the extent that the terms of the trust or the will clearly manifest an intention that the fiduciary shall or may favor one or more of the beneficiaries. A determination in accordance with this chapter is presumed to be fair and reasonable to all of the beneficiaries.

Added by Acts 2003, 78th Leg., ch. 659, § 1, eff. Jan. 1, 2004.

Statutes in Context

Section 116.005 is the most innovative provision of the 1997 UPIA. Consider the following example: Settlor created a testamentary trust requiring trust income to be paid to Daughter for life with the remainder to Granddaughter. The trust corpus consists primarily of real estate which is appreciating in value at about 15 percent per year due to its proximity to the edge of a growing city. The land is still subject to a multiple-year lease

which Settlor signed with Tenant many years ago. The rent Tenant pays is significantly below market value and is insufficient to support Daughter as Settlor intended. May Trustee sell part of the land and allocate a portion of the profits to income?

Under traditional trust rules, Trustee could not allocate any of the profits from the sale of the real estate to income. Granddaughter has a right to the principal and appreciation belongs to the principal. However, § 116.005 grants the trustee the power to adjust between principal and income under specified circumstances. The adjustment power section is quite lengthy and requires Trustee to consider a variety of factors such as the settlor's intent and the identity and circumstances of the beneficiaries. In this example, it appears that Settlor established the trust to provide for Daughter and Settlor's intent would be frustrated if Trustee did not allocate some of the profits to income to provide Daughter with an appropriate level of support.

The adjustment power has proven to be an extremely controversial aspect of the 1997 Act because of its tremendous departure from traditional law, the fear that trustees may abuse the power, and the potential of a beneficiary suing a trustee if the trustee does not exercise the adjustment power in the beneficiary's favor. Accordingly, many of the states enacting the 1997 version of the Act have omitted the adjustment provisions or have altered or restricted them in some way.

---

§ 116.005. Trustee's Power to Adjust

(a) A trustee may adjust between principal and income to the extent the trustee considers necessary if the trustee invests and manages trust assets as a prudent investor, the terms of the trust describe the amount that may or must be distributed to a beneficiary by referring to the trust's income, and the trustee determines, after applying the rules in Section 116.004(a), that the trustee is unable to comply with Section 116.004(b). The power to adjust conferred by this subsection includes the power to allocate all or part of a capital gain to trust income.

(b) In deciding whether and to what extent to exercise the power conferred by Subsection (a), a trustee shall consider all factors relevant to the trust and its beneficiaries, including the following factors to the extent they are relevant:

(1) the nature, purpose, and expected duration of the trust;

(2) the intent of the settlor;

(3) the identity and circumstances of the beneficiaries;

(4) the needs for liquidity, regularity of income, and preservation and appreciation of capital;

(5) the assets held in the trust; the extent to which they consist of financial assets, interests in closely held enterprises, tangible and intangible personal property, or real property; the extent to which an asset is used by a beneficiary; and whether an asset was purchased by the trustee or received from the settlor;

(6) the net amount allocated to income under the other sections of this chapter and the increase or decrease in the value of the principal assets, which the trustee may estimate as to assets for which market values are not readily available;

(7) whether and to what extent the terms of the trust give the trustee the power to invade principal or accumulate income or prohibit the trustee from invading principal or accumulating income, and the extent to which the trustee has exercised a power from time to time to invade principal or accumulate income;

(8) the actual and anticipated effect of economic conditions on principal and income and effects of inflation and deflation; and

(9) the anticipated tax consequences of an adjustment.

(c) A trustee may not make an adjustment:

(1) that diminishes the income interest in a trust that requires all of the income to be paid at least annually to a spouse and for which an estate tax or gift tax marital deduction would be allowed, in whole or in part, if the trustee did not have the power to make the adjustment;

(2) that reduces the actuarial value of the income interest in a trust to which a person transfers property with the intent to qualify for a gift tax exclusion;

(3) that changes the amount payable to a beneficiary as a fixed annuity or a fixed fraction of the value of the trust assets;

(4) from any amount that is permanently set aside for charitable purposes under a will or the terms of a trust unless both income and principal are so set aside;

(5) if possessing or exercising the power to make an adjustment causes an individual to be treated as the owner of all or part of the trust for income tax purposes, and the individual would not be treated as the owner if the trustee did not possess the power to make an adjustment;

(6) if possessing or exercising the power to make an adjustment causes all or part of the trust assets to be included for estate tax purposes in the estate of an individual who has the power to remove a trustee or appoint a trustee, or both, and the assets would not be included in the estate of the individual if the trustee did not possess the power to make an adjustment;

(7) if the trustee is a beneficiary of the trust; or

(8) if the trustee is not a beneficiary, but the adjustment would benefit the trustee directly or indirectly.

(d) If Subsection (c)(5), (6), (7), or (8) applies to a trustee and there is more than one trustee, a cotrustee to whom the provision does not apply may make the adjustment unless the exercise of the power by the remaining trustee or trustees is not permitted by the terms of the trust.

(e) A trustee may release the entire power conferred by Subsection (a) or may release only the power to adjust from income to principal or the power to adjust from principal to income if the trustee is uncertain about whether possessing or exercising the power will cause a result described in Subsection (c)(1)-(6) or (c)(8) or if the trustee determines that possessing or exercising the power will or may deprive the trust of a tax benefit or impose a tax burden not described in Subsection (c). The release may be permanent or for a specified period, including a period measured by the life of an individual.

(f) Terms of a trust that limit the power of a trustee to make an adjustment between principal and income do not affect the application of this section unless it is clear from the terms of the trust that the terms are intended to deny the trustee the power of adjustment conferred by Subsection (a).

Added by Acts 2003, 78th Leg., ch. 659, § 1, eff. Jan. 1, 2004.

Statutes in Context

Section 116.006 provides the trustee with the option of seeking court approval of an adjustment between principal and income under § 116.005. The Texas version of this section differs from the uniform version in that it includes additional protections for the beneficiaries.

§ 116.006. Judicial Control of Discretionary Power

(a) The court may not order a trustee to change a decision to exercise or not to exercise a discretionary power conferred by Section 116.005 of this chapter unless the court determines that the decision was an abuse of the trustee's discretion. A trustee's decision is not an abuse of discretion merely because the court would have exercised the power in a different manner or would not have exercised the power.

(b) The decisions to which Subsection (a) applies include:

(1) a decision under Section 116.005(a) as to whether and to what extent an amount should be transferred from principal to income or from income to principal; and

(2) a decision regarding the factors that are relevant to the trust and its beneficiaries, the extent to which the factors are relevant, and the weight, if any, to be given to those factors in deciding whether and to what extent to exercise the discretionary power conferred by Section 116.005(a).

(c) If the court determines that a trustee has abused the trustee's discretion, the court may place the income and remainder beneficiaries in the positions they would have occupied if the discretion had not been abused, according to the following rules:

(1) to the extent that the abuse of discretion has resulted in no distribution to a beneficiary or in a distribution that is too small, the court shall order the trustee to distribute from the trust to the beneficiary an amount that the court determines will restore the beneficiary, in whole or in part, to the beneficiary's appropriate position;

(2) to the extent that the abuse of discretion has resulted in a distribution to a beneficiary which is too large, the court shall place the beneficiaries, the trust, or both, in whole or in part, in their appropriate positions by ordering the trustee to withhold an amount from one or more future distributions to the beneficiary who received the distribution that was too large or ordering that beneficiary to return some or all of the distribution to the trust; and

(3) to the extent that the court is unable, after applying Subdivisions (1) and (2), to place the beneficiaries, the trust, or both, in the positions they would have occupied if the discretion had not been abused, the court may order the trustee to pay an appropriate amount from its own funds to one or more of the beneficiaries or the trust or both.

(d) If the trustee of a trust reasonably believes that one or more beneficiaries of such trust will object to the manner in which the trustee intends to exercise or not exercise a discretionary power conferred by Section 116.005 of this chapter, the trustee may petition the court having jurisdiction over the trust, and the court shall determine whether the proposed exercise or nonexercise by the trustee of such discretionary power will result in an abuse of the trustee's discretion. The trustee shall state in such petition the basis for its belief that a beneficiary would object. The failure or refusal of a beneficiary to sign a waiver or release is not reasonable grounds for a trustee to believe the beneficiary will object. The court may appoint one or more guardians ad litem pursuant to Section 115.014 of this subtitle. If the petition describes the proposed exercise or nonexercise of the power and contains sufficient information to inform the beneficiaries of the reasons for the proposal, the facts upon which the trustee relies, and an explanation of how the income and remainder beneficiaries will be affected by the proposed exercise or nonexercise of the power, a beneficiary who challenges the proposed exercise or nonexercise has the burden of establishing that it will result in an abuse of discretion. The trustee shall advance from the trust principal all costs incident to the judicial determination, including the reasonable attorney's fees and costs of the trustee, any beneficiary or beneficiaries who are parties to the action and who retain counsel, and any guardian ad litem. At the conclusion of the proceeding, the court may award costs and reasonable and necessary attorney's fees as provided in Section 114.064 of this subtitle, including, if the court considers it appropriate, awarding part or all of such costs against the trust principal or income, awarding part or all of such costs against one or more beneficiaries or such beneficiary's or beneficiaries' share of the trust, or awarding part or all of such costs against the trustee in the trustee's individual capacity, if the court determines that the trustee's exercise or nonexercise of discretionary power would have resulted in an abuse of discretion or that the trustee did not have reasonable grounds for believing one or more beneficiaries would object to the proposed exercise or nonexercise of the discretionary power.

Added by Acts 2003, 78th Leg., ch. 659, § 1, eff. Jan. 1, 2004.

Statutes in Context

To avoid the accounting hassle of allocating receipts and expenses between the income and remainder interests, as well as to reduce the inherent conflict of interest between current and future beneficiaries, some settlors adopt a *unitrust* or *total return* approach. The current beneficiary of a unitrust is entitled to receive a fixed percentage of the value of the trust property annually. The current beneficiary may or may not also be entitled to additional distributions. For example, the trust could provide: "Trustee shall distribute 5 percent of the value of the trust property to Current Beneficiary on January 10 of every year. Trustee has the discretion to make additional distributions to Current Beneficiary for Current Beneficiary's health, education, and support. Upon Current Beneficiary's death, Trustee shall deliver all remaining trust property to Remainder Beneficiary."

Under a unitrust, both beneficiaries have the same goal — they want the value of the property in the trust to increase. It does not matter to them whether the increase in value is due to receipts traditionally nominated income (e.g., interest or rent) or principal (i.e., appreciation). All increases inure to the benefit of all beneficiaries. Likewise, all beneficiaries share in the expenses regardless of their usual characterization.

Because of the enhanced ability of trustees to make productive investments when they are concerned only about total return rather than balancing the interests of income and principal beneficiaries, the use of unitrusts is seen by courts and legislatures as desirable. Section 116.007 applies only to noncharitable unitrusts and is included primarily for tax purposes. The UPIA does not contain an equivalent provision.

---

§ 116.007. Provisions Regarding Noncharitable Unitrusts

(a) This section does not apply to a charitable remainder unitrust as defined by Section 664(d), Internal Revenue Code of 1986 (26 U.S.C. Section 664), as amended.

(b) In this section:

(1) "Unitrust" means a trust the terms of which require distribution of a unitrust amount.

(2) "Unitrust amount" means a distribution mandated by the terms of a trust in an amount equal to a fixed percentage of not less than three or more than five percent per year of the net fair market value of the trust's assets, valued at least annually. The unitrust amount may be determined by reference to the net fair market value of the trust's assets in one year or more than one year.

(c) Distribution of the unitrust amount is considered a distribution of all of the income of the unitrust and shall not be considered a fundamental departure from applicable state law. A distribution of the unitrust amount reasonably apportions the total return of a unitrust.

(d) Unless the terms of the trust specifically provide otherwise, a distribution of the unitrust amount shall be treated as first being made from the following sources in order of priority:

(1) from net accounting income determined as if the trust were not a unitrust;

(2) from ordinary accounting income not allocable to net accounting income;

(3) from net realized short-term capital gains;

(4) from net realized long-term capital gains; and

(5) from the principal of the trust estate.

Added by Acts 2003, 78th Leg., ch. 659, § 1, eff. Jan. 1, 2004.

[Sections 116.008-116.050 reserved for expansion]

Subchapter B. Decedent's Estate or Terminating Income Interest

---

Statutes in Context

Section 116.051 provides guidance to the trustee for determining and distributing net income after (1) a decedent dies or (2) an income interest in a trust ends. In a significant departure from prior law, unpaid pecuniary gifts in a will (either outright or in trust) begin to earn interest one year after the decedent dies rather than one year after the court grants letters testamentary. In another change, the trustee may now allocate interest on estate taxes to either principal or income rather than only against principal.

---

§ 116.051. Determination and Distribution of Net Income

After a decedent dies, in the case of an estate, or after an income interest in a trust ends, the following rules apply:

(1) A fiduciary of an estate or of a terminating income interest shall determine the amount of net income and net principal receipts received from property specifically given to a beneficiary under the rules in Subchapters C, D, and E which apply to trustees and the rules in Subdivision (5). The fiduciary shall distribute the net income and net principal receipts to the beneficiary who is to receive the specific property.

(2) A fiduciary shall determine the remaining net income of a decedent's estate or a terminating income interest under the rules in Subchapters C, D, and E which apply to trustees and by:

(A) including in net income all income from property used to discharge liabilities;

(B) paying from income or principal, in the fiduciary's discretion, fees of attorneys, accountants, and fiduciaries; court costs and other expenses of administration; and interest on death taxes, but the fiduciary may pay those expenses from income of property passing to a trust for which the fiduciary claims an estate tax marital or charitable deduction only to the extent that the payment of those expenses from income will not cause the reduction or loss of the deduction; and

(C) paying from principal all other disbursements made or incurred in connection with the settlement of a decedent's estate or the winding up of a terminating income interest, including debts, funeral expenses, disposition of remains, family allowances, and death taxes and related penalties that are apportioned to the estate or terminating income interest by the will, the terms of the trust, or applicable law.

(3) A fiduciary shall distribute to a beneficiary who receives a pecuniary amount outright the interest or any other amount provided by the will, the terms of the trust, or applicable law from net income determined under Subdivision (2) or from principal to the extent that net income is insufficient. If a beneficiary is to receive a pecuniary amount outright from a trust after an income interest ends and no interest or other amount is provided for by the terms of the trust or applicable law, the fiduciary shall distribute the interest or other amount to which the beneficiary would be entitled under applicable law if the pecuniary amount were required to be paid under a will. Unless otherwise provided by the will or the terms of the trust, a beneficiary who receives a pecuniary amount, regardless of whether in trust, shall be paid interest on the pecuniary amount at the legal rate of interest as provided by Section 302.002, Finance Code. Interest on the pecuniary amount is payable:

(A) under a will, beginning on the first anniversary of the date of the decedent's death; or

(B) under a trust, beginning on the first anniversary of the date on which an income interest ends.

(4) A fiduciary shall distribute the net income remaining after distributions required by Subdivision (3) in the manner described in Section 116.052 to all other beneficiaries even if the beneficiary holds an unqualified power to withdraw assets from the trust or other presently exercisable general power of appointment over the trust.

(5) A fiduciary may not reduce principal or income receipts from property described in Subdivision (1) because of a payment described in Section 116.201 or 116.202 to the extent that the will, the terms of the trust, or applicable law requires the fiduciary to make the payment from assets other than the property or to the extent that the fiduciary recovers or expects to recover the payment from a third party. The net income and principal receipts from the property are determined by including all of the amounts the fiduciary receives or pays with respect to the property, whether those amounts accrued or became due before, on, or after the date of a decedent's death or an income interest's terminating event, and by making a reasonable provision for amounts that the fiduciary believes the estate or terminating income interest may become obligated to pay after the property is distributed.

(6) A fiduciary, without reduction for taxes, shall pay to a charitable organization that is entitled to receive income under Subdivision (4) any amount allowed as a tax deduction to the estate or trust for income payable to the charitable organization.

Added by Acts 2003, 78th Leg., ch. 659, § 1, eff. Jan. 1, 2004.

Statutes in Context

Section 116.052 explains how a trustee is to determine the appropriate amount of trust income to distribute to the residuary and remainder beneficiaries once the income interest ends.

---

§ 116.052. Distribution to Residuary and Remainder Beneficiaries

(a) Each beneficiary described in Section 116.051(4) is entitled to receive a portion of the net income equal to the beneficiary's fractional interest in undistributed principal assets, using values as of the distribution date. If a fiduciary makes more than one distribution of assets to beneficiaries to whom this section applies, each beneficiary, including one who does not receive part of the distribution, is entitled, as of each distribution date, to the net income the fiduciary has received after the date of death or terminating event or earlier distribution date but has not distributed as of the current distribution date.

(b) In determining a beneficiary's share of net income, the following rules apply:

(1) The beneficiary is entitled to receive a portion of the net income equal to the beneficiary's fractional interest in the undistributed principal assets immediately before the distribution date, including assets that later may be sold to meet principal obligations.

(2) The beneficiary's fractional interest in the undistributed principal assets must be calculated without regard to property specifically given to a beneficiary and property required to pay pecuniary amounts not in trust.

(3) The beneficiary's fractional interest in the undistributed principal assets must be calculated on the basis of the aggregate value of those assets as of the distribution date without reducing the value by any unpaid principal obligation.

(4) The distribution date for purposes of this section may be the date as of which the fiduciary calculates the value of the assets if that date is reasonably near the date on which assets are actually distributed.

(c) If a fiduciary does not distribute all of the collected but undistributed net income to each person as of a distribution date, the fiduciary shall maintain appropriate records showing the interest of each beneficiary in that net income.

(d) A fiduciary may apply the rules in this section, to the extent that the fiduciary considers it appropriate, to net gain or loss realized after the date of death or terminating event or earlier distribution date from the disposition of a principal asset if this section applies to the income from the asset.

Added by Acts 2003, 78th Leg., ch. 659, § 1, eff. Jan. 1, 2004.

[Sections 116.053-116.100 reserved for expansion]

Subchapter C. Apportionment at Beginning and End of Income Interest

Statutes in Context

Subchapter C explains the amounts to which an income beneficiary is entitled both when the trust begins and when the trust terminates. Note that inter vivos and testamentary trusts have different rules. In addition, the applicable rule may depend on the precise type of asset involved (e.g., a periodic payment such as rent or interest, a corporate distribution, etc.).

§ 116.101. When Right to Income Begins and Ends

(a) An income beneficiary is entitled to net income from the date on which the income interest begins. An income interest begins on the date specified in the terms of the trust or, if no date is specified, on the date an asset becomes subject to a trust or successive income interest.

(b) An asset becomes subject to a trust:

(1) on the date it is transferred to the trust in the case of an asset that is transferred to a trust during the transferor's life;

(2) on the date of a testator's death in the case of an asset that becomes subject to a trust by reason of a will, even if there is an intervening period of administration of the testator's estate; or

(3) on the date of an individual's death in the case of an asset that is transferred to a fiduciary by a third party because of the individual's death.

(c) An asset becomes subject to a successive income interest on the day after the preceding income interest ends, as determined under Subsection (d), even if there is an intervening period of administration to wind up the preceding income interest.

(d) An income interest ends on the day before an income beneficiary dies or another terminating event occurs, or on the last day of a period during which there is no beneficiary to whom a trustee may distribute income.

Added by Acts 2003, 78th Leg., ch. 659, § 1, eff. Jan. 1, 2004.

§ 116.102. Apportionment of Receipts and Disbursements When Decedent Dies or Income Interest Begins

(a) A trustee shall allocate an income receipt or disbursement other than one to which Section 116.051(1) applies to principal if its due date occurs before a decedent dies in the case of an estate or before an income interest begins in the case of a trust or successive income interest.

(b) A trustee shall allocate an income receipt or disbursement to income if its due date occurs on or after the date on which a decedent dies or an income interest begins and it is a periodic due date. An income receipt or disbursement must be treated as accruing from day to day if its due date is not periodic or it has no due date. The portion of the receipt or disbursement accruing before the date on which a decedent dies or an income interest begins must be allocated to principal and the balance must be allocated to income.

(c) An item of income or an obligation is due on the date the payer is required to make a payment. If a payment date is not stated, there is no due date for the purposes of this chapter. Distributions to shareholders or other owners from an entity to which Section 116.151 applies are deemed to be due on the date fixed by the entity for determining who is entitled to receive the distribution or, if no date is fixed, on the declaration date for the distribution. A due date is periodic for receipts or disbursements that must be paid at regular intervals under a lease or an obligation to pay interest or if an entity customarily makes distributions at regular intervals.

Added by Acts 2003, 78th Leg., ch. 659, § 1, eff. Jan. 1, 2004.

§ 116.103. Apportionment When Income Interest Ends

(a) In this section, "undistributed income" means net income received before the date on which an income interest ends. The term does not include an item of income or expense that is due or accrued or net income that has been added or is required to be added to principal under the terms of the trust.

(b) When a mandatory income interest ends, the trustee shall pay to a mandatory income beneficiary who survives that date, or the estate of a deceased mandatory income beneficiary whose death causes the interest to end, the beneficiary's share of the undistributed income that is not disposed of under the terms of the trust unless the beneficiary has an unqualified power to revoke more than five percent of the trust immediately before the income interest ends. In the latter case, the undistributed income from the portion of the trust that may be revoked must be added to principal.

(c) When a trustee's obligation to pay a fixed annuity or a fixed fraction of the value of the trust's assets ends, the trustee shall prorate the final payment if and to the extent required by applicable law to accomplish a purpose of the trust or its settlor relating to income, gift, estate, or other tax requirements.

Added by Acts 2003, 78th Leg., ch. 659, § 1, eff. Jan. 1, 2004.

[Sections 116.104-116.150 reserved for expansion]

Subchapter D. Allocation of Receipts During Administration of Trust

Part 1. Receipts from Entities

Statutes in Context

Section 116.151 explains the allocation of distributions from corporations, partnerships, and other entities. Generally, cash dividends belong to income while stock dividends go to principal. The logic behind the latter rule is that the trust owns the same proportion of the corporation both before and after the stock dividend. The trust may own a greater number of shares but because all other stock holders also own proportionately the same number of additional shares, the stock dividend did not improve the trust's position. Consequently, it would be unfair to allocate stock dividends to income.

§ 116.151. Character of Receipts

(a) In this section, "entity" means a corporation, partnership, limited liability company, regulated investment company, real estate investment trust, common trust fund, or any other organization in which a trustee has an interest other than a trust or estate to which Section 116.152 applies, a business or activity to which Section 116.153 applies, or an asset-backed security to which Section 116.178 applies.

(b) Except as otherwise provided in this section, a trustee shall allocate to income money received from an entity.

(c) A trustee shall allocate the following receipts from an entity to principal:

(1) property other than money;

(2) money received in one distribution or a series of related distributions in exchange for part or all of a trust's interest in the entity;

(3) money received in total or partial liquidation of the entity; and

(4) money received from an entity that is a regulated investment company or a real estate investment trust if the money distributed is a capital gain dividend for federal income tax purposes.

(d) Money is received in partial liquidation:

(1) to the extent that the entity, at or near the time of a distribution, indicates that it is a distribution in partial liquidation; or

(2) if the total amount of money and property received in a distribution or series of related distributions is greater than 20 percent of the entity's gross assets, as shown by the entity's year-end financial statements immediately preceding the initial receipt.

(e) Money is not received in partial liquidation, nor may it be taken into account under Subsection (d)(2), to the extent that it does not exceed the amount of income tax that a trustee or beneficiary must pay on taxable income of the entity that distributes the money.

(f) A trustee may rely upon a statement made by an entity about the source or character of a distribution if the statement is made at or near the time of distribution by the entity's board of directors or other person or group of persons authorized to exercise powers to pay money or transfer property comparable to those of a corporation's board of directors.

Added by Acts 2003, 78th Leg., ch. 659, § 1, eff. Jan. 1, 2004.

§ 116.152. Distribution from Trust or Estate

A trustee shall allocate to income an amount received as a distribution of income from a trust or an estate in which the trust has an interest other than a purchased interest, and shall allocate to principal an amount received as a distribution of principal from such a trust or estate. If a trustee purchases an interest in a trust that is an investment entity, or a decedent or donor transfers an interest in such a trust to a trustee, Section 116.151 or 116.178 applies to a receipt from the trust.

Added by Acts 2003, 78th Leg., ch. 659, § 1, eff. Jan. 1, 2004.

Statutes in Context

A trustee may maintain separate accounting records to determine the income of trust property which is held as a business or farm under § 116.153. Instead of using the UPIA rules, the trustee computes income in accordance with *generally accepted accounting principles (GAAP)*. The trustee may wish to hire an accountant or CPA to assist in this process. *See* § 113.018.

§ 116.153. Business and Other Activities Conducted by Trustee

(a) If a trustee who conducts a business or other activity determines that it is in the best interest of all the beneficiaries to account separately for the business or activity instead of accounting for it as part of the trust's general accounting records, the trustee may maintain separate accounting records for its transactions, whether or not its assets are segregated from other trust assets.

(b) A trustee who accounts separately for a business or other activity may determine the extent to which its net cash receipts must be retained for working capital, the acquisition or replacement of fixed assets, and other reasonably foreseeable needs of the business or activity, and the extent to which the remaining net cash receipts are accounted for as principal or income in the trust's general accounting records. If a trustee sells assets of the business or other activity, other than in the ordinary course of the business or activity, the trustee shall account for the net amount received as principal in the trust's general accounting records to the extent the trustee determines that the amount received is no longer required in the conduct of the business.

(c) Activities for which a trustee may maintain separate accounting records include:

(1) retail, manufacturing, service, and other traditional business activities;

(2) farming;

(3) raising and selling livestock and other animals;

(4) management of rental properties;

(5) extraction of minerals and other natural resources;

(6) timber operations; and

(7) activities to which Section 116.177 applies.

Added by Acts 2003, 78th Leg., ch. 659, § 1, eff. Jan. 1, 2004.

[Sections 116.154-116.160 reserved for expansion]

Part 2. Receipts Not Normally Apportioned

Statutes in Context

Section 116.161 enumerates the receipts which are considered principal. Note that when the trustee sells an asset, both the return of the investment and the profit (capital gain) are allocated to principal. *See* § 116.161(2).

§ 116.161. Principal Receipts

A trustee shall allocate to principal:

(1) to the extent not allocated to income under this chapter, assets received from a transferor during the transferor's lifetime, a decedent's estate, a trust with a terminating income interest, or a payer under a contract naming the trust or its trustee as beneficiary;

(2) money or other property received from the sale, exchange, liquidation, or change in form of a principal asset, including realized profit, subject to this subchapter;

(3) amounts recovered from third parties to reimburse the trust because of disbursements described in Section 116.202(a)(7) or for other reasons to the extent not based on the loss of income;

(4) proceeds of property taken by eminent domain, but a separate award made for the loss of income with respect to an accounting period during which a current income beneficiary had a mandatory income interest is income;

(5) net income received in an accounting period during which there is no beneficiary to whom a trustee may or must distribute income; and

(6) other receipts as provided in Part 3.

Added by Acts 2003, 78th Leg., ch. 659, § 1, eff. Jan. 1, 2004.

Statutes in Context

Generally, receipts from rental real or personal property are income under § 116.162. The section also explains that certain receipts are principal, such as a refundable security deposit.

§ 116.162. Rental Property

To the extent that a trustee accounts for receipts from rental property pursuant to this section, the trustee shall allocate to income an amount received as rent of real or personal property, including an amount received for cancellation or renewal of a lease. An amount received as a refundable deposit, including a security deposit or a deposit that is to be applied as rent for future periods, must be added to principal and held subject to the terms of the lease and is not available for distribution to a beneficiary until the trustee's contractual obligations have been satisfied with respect to that amount.

Added by Acts 2003, 78th Leg., ch. 659, § 1, eff. Jan. 1, 2004.

Statutes in Context

The trustee should allocate interest received on money lent (e.g., a certificate of deposit) to income under § 116.163. In a change from prior law, a trustee no longer may allot to income the increase in value of a bond which pays no interest but appreciates in value (e.g., U.S. Series E savings bonds and other zero-coupon bonds) unless its maturity date is within one year after acquisition.

§ 116.163. Obligation to Pay Money

(a) An amount received as interest, whether determined at a fixed, variable, or floating rate, on an obligation to pay money to the trustee, including an amount received as consideration for prepaying principal, must be allocated to income without any provision for amortization of premium.

(b) A trustee shall allocate to principal an amount received from the sale, redemption, or other disposition of an obligation to pay money to the trustee more than one year after it is purchased or acquired by the trustee, including an obligation whose purchase price or value when it is acquired is less than its value at maturity. If the obligation matures within one year after it is purchased or acquired by the trustee, an amount received in excess of its purchase price or its value when acquired by the trust must be allocated to income.

(c) This section does not apply to an obligation to which Section 116.172, 116.173, 116.174, 116.175, 116.177, or 116.178 applies.

Added by Acts 2003, 78th Leg., ch. 659, § 1, eff. Jan. 1, 2004.

Statutes in Context

Section 116.164 provides that life insurance proceeds are generally allocated to principal.

§ 116.164. Insurance Policies and Similar Contracts

(a) Except as otherwise provided in Subsection (b), a trustee shall allocate to principal the proceeds of a life insurance policy or other contract in which the trust or its trustee is named as beneficiary, including a contract that insures the trust or its trustee to a trust asset. The trustee shall allocate dividends on an insurance policy to income if the premiums on the policy are paid from income, and to principal if the premiums are paid from principal.

(b) A trustee shall allocate to income proceeds of a contract that insures the trustee against loss of occupancy or other use by an income beneficiary, loss of income, or, subject to Section 116.153, loss of profits from a business.

(c) This section does not apply to a contract to which Section 116.172 applies.

Added by Acts 2003, 78th Leg., ch. 659, § 1, eff. Jan. 1, 2004.

[Sections 116.165-116.170 reserved for expansion]

Part 3. Receipts Normally Apportioned

Statutes in Context

Under many circumstances, § 116.171 frees the trustee from the obligation of allocating insubstantial amounts. Instead, the entire amount is allocated to principal. The section, however, does not define "insubstantial." Thus, a $1,000 receipt could be substantial for some trusts but insubstantial for others depending on the size of the trust corpus.

§ 116.171. Insubstantial Allocations Not Required

If a trustee determines that an allocation between principal and income required by Section 116.172, 116.173, 116.174, 116.175, or 116.178 is insubstantial, the trustee may allocate the entire amount to principal unless one of the circumstances described in Section 116.005(c) applies to the allocation. This power may be exercised by a cotrustee in the circumstances described in Section 116.005(d) and may be released for the reasons and in the manner described in Section 116.005(e).

Added by Acts 2003, 78th Leg., ch. 659, § 1, eff. Jan. 1, 2004.

Statutes in Context

Section 116.172 provides guidance for a trustee when allocating receipts from deferred compensation plans, annuities, and similar arrangements such as IRAs. Generally, each year, receipts are allocated to income until they total 4 percent of the asset's fair market value. Amounts in excess of 4 percent are allocated to principal. The Texas version of this section deviates significantly from the UPIA which provides that 10 percent of each distribution is income with the remaining 90 percent passing to principal.

§ 116.172. Deferred Compensation, Annuities, and Similar Payments

(a) In this section:

(1) "Future payment asset" means the asset from which a payment is derived.

(2) "Payment" means a payment that a trustee may receive over a fixed number of years or during the life of one or more individuals because of services rendered or property transferred to the payer in exchange for future payments. The term includes a payment made in money or property from the payer's general assets or from a separate fund created by the payer, including a private or commercial annuity, an individual retirement account, and a pension, profit-sharing, stock-bonus, or stock-ownership plan.

(b) To the extent that the payer characterizes a payment as interest or a dividend or a payment made in lieu of interest or a dividend, a trustee shall allocate it to income. The trustee shall allocate to principal the balance of the payment and any other payment received in the same accounting period that is not characterized as interest, a dividend, or an equivalent payment.

(c) If no part of a payment is characterized as interest, a dividend, or an equivalent payment, and all or part of the payment is required to be made, a trustee shall allocate to income the part of the payment that does not exceed an amount equal to:

(1) four percent of the fair market value of the future payment asset as determined under Subsection (d); less

(2) the total amount that the trustee has allocated to income for a previous payment received from the future payment asset during the accounting period prescribed by Subsection (d).

(d) For purposes of Subsection (c)(1), the determination of a future payment asset is made on the later of:

(1) the date on which the future payment right first becomes subject to the trust; or

(2) the first day of the trust's accounting period during which the future payment asset is received.

(e) For each year a future payment asset is made, the amount determined under Subsection (c) must be prorated on a daily basis unless the determination of a future payment asset is made under Subsection (d)(2) and is for an accounting period of 365 days or more.

(f) A trustee shall allocate to principal the part of the payment described by Subsection (c) that is not allocated to income.

(g) If no part of a payment is required to be made or the payment received is the entire amount to which the trustee is entitled, the trustee shall allocate the entire payment to principal. For purposes of Subsection (c) and this subsection, a payment is not "required to be made" to the extent that it is made only because the trustee exercises a right of withdrawal.

(h) If, to obtain an estate tax marital deduction for a trust, a trustee must allocate more of a payment to income than provided for by this section, the trustee shall allocate to income the additional amount necessary to obtain the marital deduction.

Added by Acts 2003, 78th Leg., ch. 659, § 1, eff. Jan. 1, 2004.

Statutes in Context

A *liquidating* or *wasting asset* is one which goes down in value as it is used to produce income beyond what would be considered mere depreciation from normal use and age. For example, the patent on the 8-track tape was very valuable in the 1970s but has little value today. Likewise, a royalty interest in today's blockbuster motion picture may have little value 50 years from now. The trustee needs to allocate a portion of the proceeds from liquidating assets to principal to compensate for the depletion of the principal which occurs as the proceeds are generated. Section 116.173 governs assets such as leaseholds, patents, copyrights, and royalties. The trustee must allocate 10 percent of each receipt to income and the remaining 90 percent to principal. This allocation is significantly different from prior Texas law which provided that receipts up to 5 percent of the asset's value each year were income with any excess being principal.

§ 116.173. Liquidating Asset

(a) In this section, "liquidating asset" means an asset whose value will diminish or terminate because the asset is expected to produce receipts for a period of limited duration. The term includes a leasehold, patent, copyright, royalty right, and right to receive payments during a period of more than one year under an arrangement that does not provide for the payment of interest on the unpaid balance. The term does not include a payment subject to Section 116.172, resources subject to Section 116.174, timber subject to Section 116.175, an activity subject to Section 116.177, an asset subject to Section 116.178, or any asset for which the trustee establishes a reserve for depreciation under Section 116.203.

(b) A trustee shall allocate to income 10 percent of the receipts from a liquidating asset and the balance to principal.

(c) The trustee may allocate a receipt from any interest in a liquidating asset the trust owns on January 1, 2004, in the manner provided by this chapter or in any lawful manner used by the trustee before January 1, 2004, to make the same allocation.

Added by Acts 2003, 78th Leg., ch. 659, § 1, eff. Jan. 1, 2004.

Statutes in Context

Traditionally under Texas law, oil and gas royalties were allocated 72.5 percent to income and 27.5 percent to principal. These percentages were based on former federal income tax rules which used these percentages for depletion allowances. The UPIA gives only 10 percent to income with the remaining 90 percent to principal. (Note how unfair this would be to a beneficiary who is receiving 72.5 percent and then discovers that the new law cuts the percentage way down to 10 percent.) Texas deviates from the UPIA in § 116.174 by requiring the trustee to allocate these receipts "equitably." In addition, the trustee may use the prior allocation percentages if the trust owned the natural resource on January 1, 2004.

It is irrelevant whether or not any natural resources were being taken from the land at the time the property was placed in trust. In other words, the *open mine doctrine* is not followed in a trust context. *See* § 116.174(c).

§ 116.174. Minerals, Water, and Other Natural Resources

(a) To the extent that a trustee accounts for receipts from an interest in minerals or other natural resources pursuant to this section, the trustee shall allocate them as follows:

(1) If received as nominal delay rental or nominal annual rent on a lease, a receipt must be allocated to income.

(2) If received from a production payment, a receipt must be allocated to income if and to the extent that the agreement creating the production payment provides a factor for interest or its equivalent. The balance must be allocated to principal.

(3) If an amount received as a royalty, shut-in-well payment, take-or-pay payment, bonus, or delay rental is more than nominal, the trustee shall allocate the receipt equitably.

(4) If an amount is received from a working interest or any other interest not provided for in Subdivision (1), (2), or (3), the trustee must allocate the receipt equitably.

(b) An amount received on account of an interest in water that is renewable must be allocated to income. If the water is not renewable, the trustee must allocate the receipt equitably.

(c) This chapter applies whether or not a decedent or donor was extracting minerals, water, or other natural resources before the interest became subject to the trust.

(d) The trustee may allocate a receipt from any interest in minerals, water, or other natural resources the trust owns on January 1, 2004, in the manner provided by this chapter or in any lawful manner used by the trustee before January 1, 2004, to make the same allocation. The trustee shall allocate a receipt from any interest in minerals, water, or other natural resources acquired by the trust after January 1, 2004, in the manner provided by this chapter.

(e) An allocation of a receipt under this section is presumed to be equitable if the amount allocated to principal is equal to the amount allowed by the Internal Revenue Code of 1986 as a deduction for depletion of the interest.

Added by Acts 2003, 78th Leg., ch. 659, § 1, eff. Jan. 1, 2004.

Statutes in Context

Timber is unlike other natural resources because it is renewable; the trees will grow back. The time it will

take the trees to regrow, however, depends on the type of trees. For example, some varieties of pine trees may be ready to harvest in 20 years while other trees such as redwoods may take over a century. Consequently, it is difficult to create a precise allocation rule. Section 116.175 explains that receipts are income if the timber removed does not exceed the rate of new growth but receipts become principal if they are from timber in excess of the regrowth rate. This provision provides more guidance than prior law which merely instructed the trustee to do what was reasonable and equitable.

§ 116.175. Timber

(a) To the extent that a trustee accounts for receipts from the sale of timber and related products pursuant to this section, the trustee shall allocate the net receipts:

(1) to income to the extent that the amount of timber removed from the land does not exceed the rate of growth of the timber during the accounting periods in which a beneficiary has a mandatory income interest;

(2) to principal to the extent that the amount of timber removed from the land exceeds the rate of growth of the timber or the net receipts are from the sale of standing timber;

(3) to or between income and principal if the net receipts are from the lease of timberland or from a contract to cut timber from land owned by a trust, by determining the amount of timber removed from the land under the lease or contract and applying the rules in Subdivisions (1) and (2); or

(4) to principal to the extent that advance payments, bonuses, and other payments are not allocated pursuant to Subdivision (1), (2), or (3).

(b) In determining net receipts to be allocated pursuant to Subsection (a), a trustee shall deduct and transfer to principal a reasonable amount for depletion.

(c) This chapter applies whether or not a decedent or transferor was harvesting timber from the property before it became subject to the trust.

(d) If a trust owns an interest in timberland on January 1, 2004, the trustee may allocate a net receipt from the sale of timber and related products in the manner provided by this chapter or in any lawful manner used by the trustee before January 1, 2004, to make the same allocation. If the trust acquires an interest in timberland after January 1, 2004, the trustee shall allocate net receipts from the sale of timber and related products in the manner provided by this chapter.

Added by Acts 2003, 78th Leg., ch. 659, § 1, eff. Jan. 1, 2004.

Statutes in Context

The trustee should not retain property that does not earn income absent express permission in the trust instrument unless it is prudent to retain it under Chapter 117. Although some nonproductive assets, such as collectible items and unleased land, may have the potential of significantly appreciating in value, the retention of nonproductive property usually would violate the trustee's duty of fairness to the income beneficiaries. Under prior law, the trustee was required to promptly sell underproductive property which meant property that did not earn at least 1 percent of its value per year, assuming the trustee was under a duty to sell either according to the terms of the trust or because it was imprudent to retain the property. Once the trustee sold the underproductive property, the trustee was often required to allocate a portion of the sale proceeds to income as *delayed income* to make up for the income the trust should have earned had this portion of the trust been placed in income-producing investments.

Section 116.176(b) dispenses with the allocation of *delayed income*. Now, the proceeds from the sale or other disposition of a trust asset are principal without regard to the amount of income the asset produced. However, § 116.176(a) does retain the duty to make property productive for marital deduction trusts to make certain they continue to qualify for favored tax treatment.

§ 116.176. Property Not Productive of Income

(a) If a marital deduction is allowed for all or part of a trust whose assets consist substantially of property that does not provide the spouse with sufficient income from or use of the trust assets, and if the amounts that the trustee transfers from principal to income under Section 116.005 and distributes to the spouse from principal pursuant to the terms of the trust are insufficient to provide the spouse with the beneficial enjoyment required to obtain the marital deduction, the spouse may require the trustee to make property productive of income, convert property within a reasonable time, or exercise the power conferred by Section 116.005(a). The trustee may decide which action or combination of actions to take.

(b) In cases not governed by Subsection (a), proceeds from the sale or other disposition of an asset are principal without regard to the amount of income the asset produces during any accounting period.

Added by Acts 2003, 78th Leg., ch. 659, § 1, eff. Jan. 1, 2004.

§ 116.177. Derivatives and Options

(a) In this section, "derivative" means a contract or financial instrument or a combination of contracts and financial instruments which gives a trust the right or obligation to participate in some or all changes in the price of a tangible or intangible asset or group of assets, or changes in a rate, an index of prices or rates, or other market indicator for an asset or a group of assets.

(b) To the extent that a trustee does not account under Section 116.153 for transactions in derivatives, the trustee shall allocate to principal receipts from and disbursements made in connection with those transactions.

(c) If a trustee grants an option to buy property from the trust, whether or not the trust owns the property

when the option is granted, grants an option that permits another person to sell property to the trust, or acquires an option to buy property for the trust or an option to sell an asset owned by the trust, and the trustee or other owner of the asset is required to deliver the asset if the option is exercised, an amount received for granting the option must be allocated to principal. An amount paid to acquire the option must be paid from principal. A gain or loss realized upon the exercise of an option, including an option granted to a settlor of the trust for services rendered, must be allocated to principal.
Added by Acts 2003, 78th Leg., ch. 659, § 1, eff. Jan. 1, 2004.

§ 116.178. Asset-Backed Securities

(a) In this section, "asset-backed security" means an asset whose value is based upon the right it gives the owner to receive distributions from the proceeds of financial assets that provide collateral for the security. The term includes an asset that gives the owner the right to receive from the collateral financial assets only the interest or other current return or only the proceeds other than interest or current return. The term does not include an asset to which Section 116.151 or 116.172 applies.

(b) If a trust receives a payment from interest or other current return and from other proceeds of the collateral financial assets, the trustee shall allocate to income the portion of the payment which the payer identifies as being from interest or other current return and shall allocate the balance of the payment to principal.

(c) If a trust receives one or more payments in exchange for the trust's entire interest in an asset-backed security in one accounting period, the trustee shall allocate the payments to principal. If a payment is one of a series of payments that will result in the liquidation of the trust's interest in the security over more than one accounting period, the trustee shall allocate 10 percent of the payment to income and the balance to principal.
Added by Acts 2003, 78th Leg., ch. 659, § 1, eff. Jan. 1, 2004.

[Sections 116.179-116.200 reserved for expansion]

Subchapter E. Allocation of Disbursements During Administration of Trust

Statutes in Context

Section 116.201 enumerates disbursements which are deducted from income. This section makes two significant changes from prior law. First, trustee compensation is now apportioned one-half against principal and one-half income while former law permitted the trustee to allocate compensation on a just and equitable basis. Second, expenses from accountings and judicial proceeds are also allocated equally while under prior law, all these expenses were charged against income.

§ 116.201. Disbursements From Income

A trustee shall make the following disbursements from income to the extent that they are not disbursements to which Section 116.051(2)(B) or (C) applies:

(1) one-half of the regular compensation of the trustee and of any person providing investment advisory or custodial services to the trustee;

(2) one-half of all expenses for accountings, judicial proceedings, or other matters that involve both the income and remainder interests;

(3) all of the other ordinary expenses incurred in connection with the administration, management, or preservation of trust property and the distribution of income, including interest, ordinary repairs, regularly recurring taxes assessed against principal, and expenses of a proceeding or other matter that concerns primarily the income interest; and

(4) recurring premiums on insurance covering the loss of a principal asset or the loss of income from or use of the asset.
Added by Acts 2003, 78th Leg., ch. 659, § 1, eff. Jan. 1, 2004.

Statutes in Context

Section 116.202 enumerates the expenditures which the trustee must charge against the principal of the trust.

§ 116.202. Disbursements From Principal

(a) A trustee shall make the following disbursements from principal:

(1) the remaining one-half of the disbursements described in Sections 116.201(1) and (2);

(2) all of the trustee's compensation calculated on principal as a fee for acceptance, distribution, or termination, and disbursements made to prepare property for sale;

(3) payments on the principal of a trust debt;

(4) expenses of a proceeding that concerns primarily principal, including a proceeding to construe the trust or to protect the trust or its property;

(5) premiums paid on a policy of insurance not described in Section 116.201(4) of which the trust is the owner and beneficiary;

(6) estate, inheritance, and other transfer taxes, including penalties, apportioned to the trust; and

(7) disbursements related to environmental matters, including reclamation, assessing environmental conditions, remedying and removing environmental contamination, monitoring remedial activities and the release of substances, preventing future releases of substances, collecting amounts from persons liable or potentially liable for the costs of those activities, penalties imposed under environmental laws or regulations and other payments

made to comply with those laws or regulations, statutory or common law claims by third parties, and defending claims based on environmental matters.

(b) If a principal asset is encumbered with an obligation that requires income from that asset to be paid directly to the creditor, the trustee shall transfer from principal to income an amount equal to the income paid to the creditor in reduction of the principal balance of the obligation.

Added by Acts 2003, 78th Leg., ch. 659, § 1, eff. Jan. 1, 2004.

Statutes in Context

A trustee may make transfers from income to principal to compensate for the depreciation of the principal. Under prior law, however, a trustee was required to make a reasonable allowance for depreciation.

---

§ 116.203. Transfers From Income to Principal for Depreciation

(a) In this section, "depreciation" means a reduction in value due to wear, tear, decay, corrosion, or gradual obsolescence of a fixed asset having a useful life of more than one year.

(b) A trustee may transfer to principal a reasonable amount of the net cash receipts from a principal asset that is subject to depreciation, but may not transfer any amount for depreciation:

(1) of that portion of real property used or available for use by a beneficiary as a residence or of tangible personal property held or made available for the personal use or enjoyment of a beneficiary;

(2) during the administration of a decedent's estate; or

(3) under this section if the trustee is accounting under Section 116.153 for the business or activity in which the asset is used.

(c) An amount transferred to principal need not be held as a separate fund.

Added by Acts 2003, 78th Leg., ch. 659, § 1, eff. Jan. 1, 2004.

§ 116.204. Transfers From Income to Reimburse Principal

(a) If a trustee makes or expects to make a principal disbursement described in this section, the trustee may transfer an appropriate amount from income to principal in one or more accounting periods to reimburse principal or to provide a reserve for future principal disbursements.

(b) Principal disbursements to which Subsection (a) applies include the following, but only to the extent that the trustee has not been and does not expect to be reimbursed by a third party:

(1) an amount chargeable to income but paid from principal because it is unusually large, including extraordinary repairs;

(2) a capital improvement to a principal asset, whether in the form of changes to an existing asset or the construction of a new asset, including special assessments;

(3) disbursements made to prepare property for rental, including tenant allowances, leasehold improvements, and broker's commissions;

(4) periodic payments on an obligation secured by a principal asset to the extent that the amount transferred from income to principal for depreciation is less than the periodic payments; and

(5) disbursements described in Section 116.202(a)(7).

(c) If the asset whose ownership gives rise to the disbursements becomes subject to a successive income interest after an income interest ends, a trustee may continue to transfer amounts from income to principal as provided in Subsection (a).

Added by Acts 2003, 78th Leg., ch. 659, § 1, eff. Jan. 1, 2004.

Statutes in Context

Section 116.205 governs whether taxes are paid by income or principal. For example, regular income taxes are charged against income while a capital gains tax, although called an income tax, is charged against principal.

---

§ 116.205. Income Taxes

(a) A tax required to be paid by a trustee based on receipts allocated to income must be paid from income.

(b) A tax required to be paid by a trustee based on receipts allocated to principal must be paid from principal, even if the tax is called an income tax by the taxing authority.

(c) A tax required to be paid by a trustee on the trust's share of an entity's taxable income must be paid proportionately:

(1) from income to the extent that receipts from the entity are allocated to income; and

(2) from principal to the extent that:

(A) receipts from the entity are allocated to principal; and

(B) the trust's share of the entity's taxable income exceeds the total receipts described in Subdivisions (1) and (2)(A).

(d) For purposes of this section, receipts allocated to principal or income must be reduced by the amount distributed to a beneficiary from principal or income for which the trust receives a deduction in calculating the tax.

Added by Acts 2003, 78th Leg., ch. 659, § 1, eff. Jan. 1, 2004.

Statutes in Context

Section 116.206 provides for equitable adjustments between principal and income because of taxes under enumerated circumstances.

---

§ 116.206. Adjustments Between Principal and Income Because of Taxes

(a) A fiduciary may make adjustments between principal and income to offset the shifting of economic interests or tax benefits between income beneficiaries and remainder beneficiaries which arise from:

(1) elections and decisions, other than those described in Subsection (b), that the fiduciary makes from time to time regarding tax matters;

(2) an income tax or any other tax that is imposed upon the fiduciary or a beneficiary as a result of a transaction involving or a distribution from the estate or trust; or

(3) the ownership by an estate or trust of an interest in an entity whose taxable income, whether or not distributed, is includable in the taxable income of the estate, trust, or a beneficiary.

(b) If the amount of an estate tax marital deduction or charitable contribution deduction is reduced because a fiduciary deducts an amount paid from principal for income tax purposes instead of deducting it for estate tax purposes, and as a result estate taxes paid from principal are increased and income taxes paid by an estate, trust, or beneficiary are decreased, each estate, trust, or beneficiary that benefits from the decrease in income tax shall reimburse the principal from which the increase in estate tax is paid. The total reimbursement must equal the increase in the estate tax to the extent that the principal used to pay the increase would have qualified for a marital deduction or charitable contribution deduction but for the payment. The proportionate share of the reimbursement for each estate, trust, or beneficiary whose income taxes are reduced must be the same as its proportionate share of the total decrease in income tax. An estate or trust shall reimburse principal from income.

Added by Acts 2003, 78th Leg., ch. 659, § 1, eff. Jan. 1, 2004.

Chapter 117. Uniform Prudent Investor Act

The trustee is responsible for investing trust property to make it productive while simultaneously protecting that property from undue risk. A trustee is not an insurer of the trust's success and consequently is personally liable for losses only if the trustee's conduct falls beneath the applicable standard of care.

Until January 1, 2004, the propriety of the trustee's investments were judged according to the prudent person standard. A trustee was required to exercise the degree of care and level of skill that a person of ordinary prudence would exercise in dealing with that person's own property. The trustee was required to consider three main factors in selecting an investment. First, the trustee examined the safety of the investment. Risky or speculative investments were not allowed. Second, the trustee determined the investment's potential to appreciate in value. Third, the trustee evaluated the income which the investment was expected to generate. Prior law also contained a portfolio-type provision in that the determination of whether a trustee acted prudently was based on a consideration of how all the assets of the trust were invested collectively rather than by examining each investment individually.

The Texas version of the Uniform Prudent Investor Act took effect on January 1, 2004. Under this "total asset management" approach, the appropriateness of investments is based on the performance of the entire trust portfolio. A prudent investor could decide that the best investment strategy is to select some assets that appreciate and others that earn income, as well as some investments that are rock-solid balanced with some that have a reasonable degree of risk. In selecting investments, the trustee should incorporate risk and return objectives that are reasonably suited to the trust. Different trusts may call for different investment approaches depending on the trustee's abilities, the trust's purposes, the beneficiary's needs, and other circumstances. *See* § 117.004.

§ 117.001. Short Title

This chapter may be cited as the "Uniform Prudent Investor Act."

Added by Acts 2003, 78th Leg., ch. 1103, § 1, eff. Jan. 1, 2004.

§ 117.002. Uniformity of Application and Construction

This chapter shall be applied and construed to effectuate its general purpose to make uniform the law with respect to the subject of this chapter among the states enacting it.

Added by Acts 2003, 78th Leg., ch. 1103, § 1, eff. Jan. 1, 2004.

Statutes in Context

The prudent investor rule is the default standard of care for trustees under § 117.003(a). However, § 117.003(b) authorizes the settlor to provide for a higher or lower standard of care.

§ 117.003. Prudent Investor Rule

(a) Except as otherwise provided in Subsection (b), a trustee who invests and manages trust assets owes a duty to the beneficiaries of the trust to comply with the prudent investor rule set forth in this chapter.

(b) The prudent investor rule, a default rule, may be expanded, restricted, eliminated, or otherwise altered by the provisions of a trust. A trustee is not liable to a beneficiary to the extent that the trustee acted in reasonable reliance on the provisions of the trust.

Added by Acts 2003, 78th Leg., ch. 1103, § 1, eff. Jan. 1, 2004.

Statutes in Context

Section 117.004 is the key provision which explains how the prudent investor rule operates. Subsection

(c) enumerates the factors a trustee must consider when making investment and management decisions. Note that no particular type of property is categorically improper and that some risk or speculation may be prudent. *See* § 117.004(e). A trustee who has or represents as having more skill than a prudent investor has a duty to exercise those additional skills. *See* § 117.004(f).

§ 117.004. Standard of Care; Portfolio Strategy; Risk and Return Objectives

(a) A trustee shall invest and manage trust assets as a prudent investor would, by considering the purposes, terms, distribution requirements, and other circumstances of the trust. In satisfying this standard, the trustee shall exercise reasonable care, skill, and caution.

(b) A trustee's investment and management decisions respecting individual assets must be evaluated not in isolation but in the context of the trust portfolio as a whole and as a part of an overall investment strategy having risk and return objectives reasonably suited to the trust.

(c) Among circumstances that a trustee shall consider in investing and managing trust assets are such of the following as are relevant to the trust or its beneficiaries:

(1) general economic conditions;

(2) the possible effect of inflation or deflation;

(3) the expected tax consequences of investment decisions or strategies;

(4) the role that each investment or course of action plays within the overall trust portfolio, which may include financial assets, interests in closely held enterprises, tangible and intangible personal property, and real property;

(5) the expected total return from income and the appreciation of capital;

(6) other resources of the beneficiaries;

(7) needs for liquidity, regularity of income, and preservation or appreciation of capital; and

(8) an asset's special relationship or special value, if any, to the purposes of the trust or to one or more of the beneficiaries.

(d) A trustee shall make a reasonable effort to verify facts relevant to the investment and management of trust assets.

(e) Except as otherwise provided by and subject to this subtitle, a trustee may invest in any kind of property or type of investment consistent with the standards of this chapter.

(f) A trustee who has special skills or expertise, or is named trustee in reliance upon the trustee's representation that the trustee has special skills or expertise, has a duty to use those special skills or expertise.

Added by Acts 2003, 78th Leg., ch. 1103, § 1, eff. Jan. 1, 2004.

Statutes in Context

Section 117.005 codifies the trustee's duty to diversify to spread the risk so that if one investment goes bad, the entire trust does not suffer. However, the trustee is not required to diversify if the circumstances demonstrate that the purposes of the trust would be better served without diversifying. For example, assume that Settlor created a trust containing Settlor's heirloom jewelry and a 20,000 acre farm that has been in Settlor's family for almost 200 years. At the termination of the trust, all remaining trust property passes to Settlor's children. Should Trustee sell some of this property to create a balanced portfolio of investments? Retaining all trust property in two assets of this type is certainly not a proper diversification. On the other hand, it is reasonable to conclude that Settlor wanted the heirloom jewelry and the farm to remain in the trust so they would pass to Settlor's children and thus Trustee may retain the assets without diversification.

§ 117.005. Diversification

A trustee shall diversify the investments of the trust unless the trustee reasonably determines that, because of special circumstances, the purposes of the trust are better served without diversifying.

Added by Acts 2003, 78th Leg., ch. 1103, § 1, eff. Jan. 1, 2004.

Statutes in Context

The trustee must review trust assets within a reasonable time after accepting the trust or receiving trust property under § 117.006. The trustee must then bring the trust property into compliance with the prudent investor rule. This is a significant change from prior Texas law which permitted the trustee to retain the initial trust property without diversification and without liability for loss or depreciation.

§ 117.006. Duties at Inception of Trusteeship

Within a reasonable time after accepting a trusteeship or receiving trust assets, a trustee shall review the trust assets and make and implement decisions concerning the retention and disposition of assets, in order to bring the trust portfolio into compliance with the purposes, terms, distribution requirements, and other circumstances of the trust, and with the requirements of this chapter.

Added by Acts 2003, 78th Leg., ch. 1103, § 1, eff. Jan. 1, 2004.

Statutes in Context

Section 117.007 codifies the principle that the trustee's loyalty is to the beneficiaries. Accordingly, *social investing* may be problematic, especially if the returns from a "politically correct" investment are lower than from other investments. Social investment refers to the consideration of factors other than the monetary safety of the investments and their potential to earn income and appreciate. Examples of these types of factors include a company's handling of environmental matters, whether a company does business with coun-

tries with policies that do not protect human rights, whether a company employs and pays substandard wages to workers in foreign countries, and the political party affiliation of the company's leadership.

§ 117.007. Loyalty

A trustee shall invest and manage the trust assets solely in the interest of the beneficiaries.

Added by Acts 2003, 78th Leg., ch. 1103, § 1, eff. Jan. 1, 2004.

Statutes in Context

The trustee must act impartially and not favor one beneficiary over another under § 117.008. This is especially important in the context of income and principal allocations under Chapter 116.

§ 117.008. Impartiality

If a trust has two or more beneficiaries, the trustee shall act impartially in investing and managing the trust assets, taking into account any differing interests of the beneficiaries.

Added by Acts 2003, 78th Leg., ch. 1103, § 1, eff. Jan. 1, 2004.

Statutes in Context

The trustee must minimize investment costs under § 117.009.

§ 117.009. Investment Costs

In investing and managing trust assets, a trustee may only incur costs that are appropriate and reasonable in relation to the assets, the purposes of the trust, and the skills of the trustee.

Added by Acts 2003, 78th Leg., ch. 1103, § 1, eff. Jan. 1, 2004.

Statutes in Context

A trustee's compliance with the prudent investor rule is measured by the facts and circumstances existing at the time of the trustee's action under § 117.010. In other words, a trustee's conduct is not judged with the benefit of hindsight (no "Monday morning quarterbacking").

§ 117.010. Reviewing Compliance

Compliance with the prudent investor rule is determined in light of the facts and circumstances existing at the time of a trustee's decision or action and not by hindsight.

Added by Acts 2003, 78th Leg., ch. 1103, § 1, eff. Jan. 1, 2004.

Statutes in Context

The traditional rule regarding delegation of powers is that the trustee may delegate mere ministerial duties but may not delegate discretionary acts. Investment of trust property was deemed a discretionary act and thus was not subject to delegation.

In 1999, Texas altered this rule and allowed the trustee to delegate investment decisions to an investment agent. The statute required the trustee to send written notice to the beneficiaries at least 30 days before entering into an agreement to delegate investment decisions to an investment agent. Generally, the trustee remained responsible for the agent's investment decisions. However, the trustee could have avoided liability for the investment agent's decisions if all of the relatively strenuous criteria specified in the statute were satisfied.

Section 117.011 takes a very different approach. The trustee may delegate any investment or management decision provided a prudent trustee of similar skills could properly delegate under the same circumstances. Of course, the trustee must exercise reasonable care, skill, and caution in selecting and reviewing the agent's actions. In the usual case, the trustee is not liable to the beneficiaries or the trust for the decisions or actions of the agent. *See* § 117.011(c).

§ 117.011. Delegation of Investment and Management Functions

(a) A trustee may delegate investment and management functions that a prudent trustee of comparable skills could properly delegate under the circumstances. The trustee shall exercise reasonable care, skill, and caution in:

(1) selecting an agent;

(2) establishing the scope and terms of the delegation, consistent with the purposes and terms of the trust; and

(3) periodically reviewing the agent's actions in order to monitor the agent's performance and compliance with the terms of the delegation.

(b) In performing a delegated function, an agent owes a duty to the trust to exercise reasonable care to comply with the terms of the delegation.

(c) A trustee who complies with the requirements of Subsection (a) is not liable to the beneficiaries or to the trust for the decisions or actions of the agent to whom the function was delegated, unless:

(1) the agent is an affiliate of the trustee; or

(2) under the terms of the delegation:

(A) the trustee or a beneficiary of the trust is required to arbitrate disputes with the agent; or

(B) the period for bringing an action by the trustee or a beneficiary of the trust with respect to an agent's actions is shortened from that which is applicable to trustees under the law of this state.

(d) By accepting the delegation of a trust function from the trustee of a trust that is subject to the law of this state, an agent submits to the jurisdiction of the courts of this state.

Added by Acts 2003, 78th Leg., ch. 1103, § 1, eff. Jan. 1, 2004.

Statutes in Context

Section 117.012 indicates that certain phrases in trust instruments are deemed to trigger the prudent investor standard. Note that some of these phrases which invoke the prudent investor standard clearly appear to invoke a much different standard (e.g., "prudent person rule").

§ 117.012. Language Invoking Standard of Chapter

The following terms or comparable language in the provisions of a trust, unless otherwise limited or modified, authorizes any investment or strategy permitted under this chapter: "investments permissible by law for investment of trust funds," "legal investments," "authorized investments," "using the judgment and care under the circumstances then prevailing that persons of prudence, discretion, and intelligence exercise in the management of their own affairs, not in regard to speculation but in regard to the permanent disposition of their funds, considering the probable income as well as the probable safety of their capital," "prudent man rule," "prudent trustee rule," "prudent person rule," and "prudent investor rule."

Added by Acts 2003, 78th Leg., ch. 1103, § 1, eff. Jan. 1, 2004.

Subtitle C. Miscellaneous Trusts

Chapter 121. Employees' Trusts

Statutes in Context

Chapter 121 sets forth the special rules which govern pension trusts and death benefits payable under employees' trusts.

Subchapter A. Pension Trusts

§ 121.001. Pension Trusts

(a) For the purposes of this subchapter, a pension trust is an express trust:

(1) containing or relating to property;

(2) created by an employer as part of a stock-bonus plan, pension plan, disability or death benefit plan, or profit-sharing plan for the benefit of some or all of the employer's employees;

(3) to which contributions are made by the employer, by some or all of the employees, or by both; and

(4) created for the principal purpose of distributing to the employees, or the successor to their beneficial interest in the trust, the principal or income, or both, of the property held in trust.

(b) This subchapter applies to a pension trust regardless of when the trust was created.

Acts 1983, 68th Leg., p. 3691, ch. 576, § 1, eff. Jan. 1, 1984.

§ 121.002. Employees of Controlled Corporations

For the purposes of this subchapter, the relationship of employer and employee exists between a corporation and its own employees, and between a corporation and the employees of each other corporation that it controls, by which it is controlled, or with which it is under common control through the exercise by one or more persons of a majority of voting rights in one or more corporations.

Acts 1983, 68th Leg., p. 3691, ch. 576, § 1, eff. Jan. 1, 1984.

§ 121.003. Application of Texas Trust Act

The Texas Trust Act (Chapters 111 through 115) applies to a pension trust.

Acts 1983, 68th Leg., p. 3691, ch. 576, § 1, eff. Jan. 1, 1984.

§ 121.004. Rule Against Perpetuities

A pension trust may continue for as long as is necessary to accomplish the purposes of the trust and is not invalid under the rule against perpetuities or any other law restricting or limiting the duration of a trust.

Acts 1983, 68th Leg., p. 3691, ch. 576, § 1, eff. Jan. 1, 1984.

§ 121.005. Accumulation of Income

Notwithstanding any law limiting the time during which trust income may be accumulated, the income of a pension trust may be accumulated under the terms of the trust for as long as is necessary to accomplish the purposes of the trust.

Acts 1983, 68th Leg., p. 3692, ch. 576, § 1, eff. Jan. 1, 1984.

Subchapter B. Death Benefits Under Employees' Trusts

§ 121.051. Definitions

(a) In this subchapter:

(1) "Death benefit" means a benefit of any kind, including the proceeds of a life insurance policy or any other payment, in cash or property, under an employees' trust or a retirement account, a contract purchased by an employees' trust or a retirement account, or a retirement-annuity contract that is payable because of an employee's, participant's, or beneficiary's death to or for the benefit of the employee's, participant's, or beneficiary's beneficiary.

(2) "Employee" means a person covered by an employees' trust or a retirement account that provides a death benefit or a person whose interest in an employees' trust or a retirement account has not been fully distributed.

(3) "Employees' trust" means:

(A) a trust forming a part of a stock-bonus, pension, or profit-sharing plan under Section 401, Internal Revenue Code of 1954 (26 U.S.C.A. Sec. 401 (1986));

(B) a pension trust under Chapter 111; and

(C) an employer-sponsored benefit plan or program, or any other retirement savings arrangement, including a pension plan created under Section 3, Employee Retirement Income Security Act of 1974 (29 U.S.C.A. Sec. 1002 (1986)), regardless of whether the plan, program, or arrangement is funded through a trust.

(4) "Individual retirement account" means a trust, custodial arrangement, or annuity under Section 408(a) or (b), Internal Revenue Code of 1954 (26 U.S.C.A. Sec. 408 (1986)).

(5) "Participant" means a person covered by an employees' trust or a retirement account that provides a death benefit or a person whose interest in an employees' trust or a retirement account has not been fully distributed.

(6) "Retirement account" means a retirement-annuity contract, an individual retirement account, a simplified employee pension, or any other retirement savings arrangement.

(7) "Retirement-annuity contract" means an annuity contract under Section 403, Internal Revenue Code of 1954 (26 U.S.C.A. Sec. 403 (1986)).

(8) "Simplified employee pension" means a trust, custodial arrangement, or annuity under Section 408, Internal Revenue Code of 1954 (26 U.S.C.A. Sec. 408 (1986)).

(9) "Trust" and "trustee" have the meanings assigned by the Texas Trust Code (Chapters 111 through 115), except that "trust" includes any trust, regardless of when it is created.

(b) References to specific provisions of the Internal Revenue Code of 1954 (26 U.S.C.A.) include corresponding provisions of any subsequent federal tax laws.

Acts 1983, 68th Leg., p. 3692, ch. 576, § 1, eff. Jan. 1, 1984. Amended by Acts 1987, 70th Leg., ch. 741, § 3, eff. Aug. 31, 1987.

Statutes in Context

Section 121.052 permits the employee to pour over the death benefits to a trust. The result is similar to a pour-over will provision under Probate Code § 58a although there are some significant differences. For example, the benefits are governed by the terms of the trust as they exist on the date of the employee's death while testamentary pour-overs are governed by the terms of the trust including amendments made after the testator's death.

§ 121.052. Payment of Death Benefit to Trustee

(a) A death benefit is payable to a trustee of a trust evidenced by a written instrument or declaration existing on the date of an employee's or participant's death, or to a trustee named or to be named as trustee of a trust created under an employee's or participant's will, if the trustee is designated as beneficiary under the plan containing the employees' trust or under the retirement account.

(b) A trustee of a testamentary trust may be designated under Subsection (a) prior to the execution of the will.

(c) A death benefit under a will is not payable until the will is probated.

(d) The trustee shall hold, administer, and dispose of a death benefit payable under this section in accordance with the terms of the trust on the date of the employee's death.

(e) A death benefit is payable to a trustee of a trust created by the will of a person other than the employee if:

(1) the will has been probated at the time of the employee's death; and

(2) the death benefit is payable to the trustee to be held, administered, and disposed of in accordance with the terms of the testamentary trust.

Acts 1983, 68th Leg., p. 3693, ch. 576, § 1, eff. Jan. 1, 1984. Amended by Acts 1987, 70th Leg., ch. 741, § 4, eff. Aug. 31, 1987.

§ 121.053. Validity of Trust Declaration

The validity of a trust agreement or declaration is not affected by:

(1) the absence of a corpus other than the right of the trustee to receive a death benefit as beneficiary;

(2) the employee's reservation of the right to designate another beneficiary of the death benefit; or

(3) the existence of authority to amend, modify, revoke, or terminate the agreement or declaration.

Acts 1983, 68th Leg., p. 3693, ch. 576, § 1, eff. Jan. 1, 1984.

§ 121.054. Unclaimed Benefits

If a trustee does not claim a death benefit on or before the first anniversary of the employee's or participant's death or if satisfactory evidence is provided to a trustee, custodian, other fiduciary, or other obligor of the employees' trust, contract purchased by the employees' trust, or the retirement account before the first anniversary of the employee's or participant's death that there is or will be no trustee to receive the death benefit, the death benefit shall be paid:

(1) according to the beneficiary designation under the plan, trust, contract, or arrangement providing the death benefit under the employees' trust or retirement account; or

(2) if there is no designation in the employees' trust or retirement account, to the personal representative of the deceased employee's or participant's estate.

Acts 1983, 68th Leg., p. 3693, ch. 576, § 1, eff. Jan. 1, 1984. Amended by Acts 1987, 70th Leg., ch. 741, § 5, eff. Aug. 31, 1987.

§ 121.055. Exemption from Taxes and Debts

Unless the trust agreement, declaration of trust, or will provides otherwise, a death benefit payable to a trustee under this subchapter is not:

(1) part of the deceased employee's estate;

(2) subject to the debts of the deceased employee or the employee's estate, or to other charges enforceable against the estate; or

(3) subject to the payment of taxes enforceable against the deceased employee's estate to a greater extent than if the death benefit is payable, free of trust, to a beneficiary other than the executor or administrator of the estate of the employee.

Acts 1983, 68th Leg., p. 3694, ch. 576, § 1, eff. Jan. 1, 1984.

§ 121.056. Commingling of Assets

A trustee who receives a death benefit under this subchapter may commingle the property with other assets accepted by the trustee and held in trust, either before or after the death benefit is received.

Acts 1983, 68th Leg., p. 3694, ch. 576, § 1, eff. Jan. 1, 1984.

§ 121.057. Prior Designations Not Affected

This subchapter does not affect the validity of a beneficiary designation made by an employee before April 3, 1975, that names a trustee as beneficiary of a death benefit.

Acts 1983, 68th Leg., p. 3694, ch. 576, § 1, eff. Jan. 1, 1984.

§ 121.058. Construction

(a) This subchapter is intended to be declaratory of the common law of this state.

(b) A court shall liberally construe this subchapter to effect the intent that a death benefit received by a trustee under this subchapter is not subject to the obligations of the employee or the employee's estate unless the trust receiving the benefit expressly provides otherwise.

(c) A death benefit shall not be included in property administered as part of a testator's estate or in an inventory filed with the county court because of a reference in a will to the death benefit or because of the naming of the trustee of a testamentary trust.

Acts 1983, 68th Leg., p. 3694, ch. 576, § 1, eff. Jan. 1, 1984.

Chapter 123. Attorney General Participation in Proceedings Involving Charitable Trusts

Statutes in Context

The attorney general of Texas has standing to enforce charitable trusts. To increase the likelihood that the attorney general is aware of lawsuits involving charitable trusts, Chapter 123 requires that the party initiating the action give notice to the attorney general. This notice is by certified or registered mail within 30 days of filing but not less than 10 days before a hearing and must include a copy of the petition. *See* § 123.003. Section 123.001(3) provides an extensive list of proceedings to which the attorney general is entitled to notice.

If the attorney general does not receive notice, any judgment or settlement is voidable. In other words, the attorney general may set aside any judgment or settlement at any time. No grounds are required other than the fact that the attorney general did not receive notice. *See* § 123.004.

It is significant to note the broad definition given to the term "charitable trust" in § 123.001(2). The term encompasses any inter vivos or testamentary gift to a charitable entity in addition to traditional charitable trusts. An attorney perusing the statutes might read the caption to Chapter 123 which contains the term "charitable trusts" and not realize that the chapter applies to *all* charitable gifts, whether they be in trust or outright. Likewise, the term "charitable trusts" includes any charitable entity, even if not run as a trust.

§ 123.001. Definitions

In this chapter:

(1) "Charitable entity" means a corporation, trust, community chest, fund, foundation, or other entity organized for scientific, educational, philanthropic, or environmental purposes, social welfare, the arts and humanities, or another civic or public purpose described by Section 501(c)(3) of the Internal Revenue Code of 1986 (26 U.S.C. § 501(c)(3)).

(2) "Charitable trust" means a charitable entity, a trust the stated purpose of which is to benefit a charitable entity, or an inter vivos or testamentary gift to a charitable entity.

(3) "Proceeding involving a charitable trust" means a suit or other judicial proceeding the object of which is to:

(A) terminate a charitable trust or distribute its assets to other than charitable donees;

(B) depart from the objects of the charitable trust stated in the instrument creating the trust, including a proceeding in which the doctrine of cy-pres is invoked;

(C) construe, nullify, or impair the provisions of a testamentary or other instrument creating or affecting a charitable trust;

(D) contest or set aside the probate of an alleged will under which money, property, or another thing of value is given for charitable purposes;

(E) allow a charitable trust to contest or set aside the probate of an alleged will;

(F) determine matters relating to the probate and administration of an estate involving a charitable trust; or

(G) obtain a declaratory judgment involving a charitable trust.

(4) "Fiduciary or managerial agent" means an individual, corporation, or other entity acting either as a trustee, a member of the board of directors, an officer, an executor, or an administrator for a charitable trust.

Added by Acts 1987, 70th Leg., ch. 147, § 4, eff. Sept. 1, 1987. Amended by Acts 1995, 74th Leg., ch. 172, § 2, eff. Sept. 1, 1995.

§ 123.002. Attorney General's Participation

For and on behalf of the interest of the general public of this state in charitable trusts, the attorney general is a proper party and may intervene in a proceeding

involving a charitable trust. The attorney general may join and enter into a compromise, settlement agreement, contract, or judgment relating to a proceeding involving a charitable trust.
Added by Acts 1987, 70th Leg., ch. 147, § 4, eff. Sept. 1, 1987.

§ 123.003. Notice

(a) Any party initiating a proceeding involving a charitable trust shall give notice of the proceeding to the attorney general by sending to the attorney general, by registered or certified mail, a true copy of the petition or other instrument initiating the proceeding involving a charitable trust within 30 days of the filing of such petition or other instrument, but no less than 10 days prior to a hearing in such a proceeding.

(b) Notice shall be given to the attorney general of any pleading which adds new causes of action or additional parties to a proceeding involving a charitable trust in which the attorney general has previously waived participation or in which the attorney general has otherwise failed to intervene. Notice shall be given by sending to the attorney general by registered or certified mail a true copy of the pleading within 30 days of the filing of the pleading, but no less than 10 days prior to a hearing in the proceeding.

(c) The party or the party's attorney shall execute and file in the proceeding an affidavit stating the facts of the notice and shall attach to the affidavit the customary postal receipts signed by the attorney general or an assistant attorney general.
Added by Acts 1987, 70th Leg., ch. 147, § 4, eff. Sept. 1, 1987. Amended by Acts 1995, 74th Leg., ch. 172, § 3, eff. Sept. 1, 1995.

§ 123.004. Voidable Judgment or Agreement

(a) A judgment in a proceeding involving a charitable trust is voidable if the attorney general is not given notice of the proceeding as required by this chapter. On motion of the attorney general after the judgment is rendered, the judgment shall be set aside.

(b) A compromise, settlement agreement, contract, or judgment relating to a proceeding involving a charitable trust is voidable on motion of the attorney general if the attorney general is not given notice as required by this chapter unless the attorney general has:

(1) declined in writing to be a party to the proceeding; or

(2) approved and joined in the compromise, settlement agreement, contract, or judgment.

Added by Acts 1987, 70th Leg., ch. 147, § 4, eff. Sept. 1, 1987.

§ 123.005. Breach of Fiduciary Duty

(a) Venue in a proceeding brought by the attorney general alleging breach of a fiduciary duty by a fiduciary or managerial agent of a charitable trust shall be a court of competent jurisdiction in Travis County or in the county where the defendant resides or has its principal office.

(b) The attorney general, if successful in the proceeding, is entitled to recover from a fiduciary or managerial agent of a charitable trust actual costs incurred in bringing the suit and may recover reasonable attorney's fees.
Added by Acts 1987, 70th Leg., ch. 147, § 4, eff. Sept. 1, 1987. Amended by Acts 1995, 74th Leg., ch. 172, § 4, eff. Sept. 1, 1995.

Title 10. Miscellaneous Beneficial Property Interests

Subtitle A. Persons Under Disability

Chapter 141. Transfers to Minors

Statutes in Context

Individuals who wish to make gifts or other transfers to minors need to select the method used to transfer the property. Transferors have several techniques available to them. First, the transferor could simply make the transfer directly to the minor. In many circumstances, direct transfers will necessitate the appointment of a guardian of the minor's estate. An estate guardianship requires extensive court involvement and thus is costly and time-consuming. In addition, the minor will receive the property outright at age 18, possibly before the young adult has acquired the maturity to handle the property prudently. Second, the transfer could be placed in trust for the benefit of the minor. A trust will avoid the necessity of a guardianship and will give the transferor the ability to designate how the property is to be managed and distributed. Significant transaction costs may be incurred, however, such as attorneys' fees to draft the trust and trustees' fees to manage the trust. In addition, certain transferors, such as creditors, are not able to take advantage of this technique. Third, the transferor may transfer the property to a custodian for the minor. Although not achieving all the benefits of a trust, transfers to a custodian are cost-effective, relatively simple to make, and are available to a wide range of transferors.

Until September 1, 1995, transfers to a custodian for a minor were governed by the Texas Uniform Gifts to Minors Act (TUGMA) and its various amendments. The 1995 Texas Legislature enacted the Texas Uniform Transfers to Minors Act (TUTMA) as a replacement for the outdated TUGMA.

§ 141.001. Short Title

This chapter may be cited as the Texas Uniform Transfers to Minors Act.
Acts 1983, 68th Leg., p. 3698, ch. 576, § 1, eff. Jan. 1, 1984. Amended by Acts 1995, 74th Leg., ch. 1043, § 1, eff. Sept. 1, 1995. Renumbered from V.T.C.A., Property Code § 1 by Acts 1997, 75th Leg., ch. 165, § 31.01(72), eff. Sept. 1, 1997.

Statutes in Context

The transferee must be a minor at the time of the transfer. The age at which minority status is lost is 21, not 18 as under the TUGMA. *See* § 141.002(11). There is no requirement that the minor and the transferor be related.

§ 141.002. Definitions

In this chapter:

(1) "Adult" means an individual who is at least 21 years of age.

(2) "Benefit plan" means an employer's plan for the benefit of an employee or partner or an individual retirement account.

(3) "Broker" means a person lawfully engaged in the business of effecting transactions in securities or commodities for the person's own account or for the account of another.

(4) "Court" means a court with original probate jurisdiction.

(5) "Custodial property" means:

(A) any interest in property transferred to a custodian under this chapter; and

(B) the income from and proceeds of that interest in property.

(6) "Custodian" means a person designated as a custodian under Section 10[1] or a successor or substitute custodian designated under Section 19.[2]

(7) "Financial institution" means a bank, trust company, savings institution, or credit union chartered and supervised under state or federal law.

(8) "Guardian" means a person appointed or qualified by a court to act as general, limited, or temporary guardian of a minor's property or a person legally authorized to perform substantially the same functions.

(9) "Legal representative" means an executor, independent executor, administrator or independent administrator of a decedent's estate, an obligor under a benefit plan or other governing instrument, a successor legal representative, or a person legally authorized to perform substantially the same functions.

(10) "Member of the minor's family" means the minor's parent, stepparent, spouse, grandparent, brother, sister, uncle, or aunt, whether of whole or half blood or by adoption.

(11) "Minor" means an individual who is younger than 21 years of age.

(12) "Transfer" means a transaction that creates custodial property under Section 10.[1]

(13) "Transferor" means a person who makes a transfer under this chapter.

(14) "Trust company" means a financial institution, corporation, or other legal entity authorized to exercise general trust powers.

Acts 1983, 68th Leg., p. 3698, ch. 576, § 1, eff. Jan. 1, 1984. Amended by Acts 1995, 74th Leg., ch. 1043, § 1, eff. Sept. 1, 1995. Renumbered from V.T.C.A., Property Code § 2 by Acts 1997, 75th Leg., ch. 165, § 31.01(72), eff. Sept. 1, 1997.

[1] See V.T.C.A., Property Code § 141.010.
[2] See V.T.C.A., Property Code § 141.019.
[1] See V.T.C.A., Property Code § 141.010.

§ 141.003. Scope and Jurisdiction

(a) This chapter applies to a transfer that refers to the Texas Uniform Transfers to Minors Act in the designation under Section 10(a)[1] by which the transfer is made if at the time of the transfer, the transferor, the minor, or the custodian is a resident of this state or the custodial property is located in this state. The custodianship created under Section 10[2] remains subject to this chapter despite a subsequent change in residence of a transferor, the minor, or the custodian or the removal of custodial property from this state.

(b) A person designated as custodian under this chapter is subject to personal jurisdiction in this state with respect to any matter relating to the custodianship.

(c) A transfer that purports to be made and that is valid under the Uniform Transfers to Minors Act, the Uniform Gifts to Minors Act, or a substantially similar act of another state is governed by the law of the designated state and may be executed and is enforceable in this state if at the time of the transfer, the transferor, the minor, or the custodian is a resident of the designated state or the custodial property is located in the designated state.

Acts 1983, 68th Leg., p. 3700, ch. 576, § 1, eff. Jan. 1, 1984. Amended by Acts 1995, 74th Leg., ch. 1043, § 1, eff. Sept. 1, 1995. Renumbered from V.T.C.A., Property Code § 3 by Acts 1997, 75th Leg., ch. 165, § 31.01(72), eff. Sept. 1, 1997.

Statutes in Context

A person who has the right to designate the recipient of property which is transferable when a future event occurs (e.g., the death of the person) may revocably nominate a custodian to receive the property for a minor beneficiary upon the occurrence of that event. Examples of prospective transfer arrangements included in the scope of this section are wills, trusts, deeds, life insurance policies, annuity contracts, retirement plans, trust accounts, and P.O.D. accounts. This type of designation does not actually create a custodianship relationship until the nominating instrument becomes irrevocable or the transfer to the nominated custodian occurs.

§ 141.004. Nomination of Custodian

(a) A person having the right to designate the recipient of property transferable on the occurrence of a future event may revocably nominate a custodian to receive the property for a minor beneficiary on the occurrence of that event by naming the custodian fol-

[1] See V.T.C.A., Property Code § 141.010(a).
[2] See V.T.C.A., Property Code § 141.010.

lowed in substance by the words: "as custodian for (name of minor) under the Texas Uniform Transfers to Minors Act." The nomination may name one or more persons as substitute custodians to whom the property must be transferred, in the order named, if the first nominated custodian dies before the transfer or is unable, declines, or is ineligible to serve. The nomination may be made in a will, a trust, a deed, an instrument exercising a power of appointment, or in a writing designating a beneficiary of contractual rights that is registered with or delivered to the payor, issuer, or other obligor of the contractual rights.

(b) A custodian nominated under this section must be a person to whom a transfer of property of that kind may be made under Section 10(a).[1]

(c) The nomination of a custodian under this section does not create custodial property until the nominating instrument becomes irrevocable or a transfer to the nominated custodian is completed under Section 10.[2] Unless the nomination of a custodian has been revoked, the custodianship becomes effective on the occurrence of the future event, and the custodian shall enforce a transfer of the custodial property under Section 10.

Acts 1983, 68th Leg., p. 3702, ch. 576, § 1, eff. Jan. 1, 1984. Amended by Acts 1995, 74th Leg., ch. 1043, § 1, eff. Sept. 1, 1995. Renumbered from V.T.C.A., Property Code § 4 by Acts 1997, 75th Leg., ch. 165, § 31.01(72), eff. Sept. 1, 1997.

Statutes in Context

The donor of an outright irrevocable inter vivos gift may transfer the gifted property to a custodian for a minor donee. The donee of a power of appointment may exercise it irrevocably in favor of a custodian for the benefit of a minor appointee.

§ 141.005. Transfer by Gift or Exercise of Power of Appointment

A person may make a transfer by irrevocable gift to, or the irrevocable exercise of a power of appointment in favor of, a custodian for the benefit of a minor under Section 10.[1]

Acts 1983, 68th Leg., p. 3704, ch. 576, § 1, eff. Jan. 1, 1984. Amended by Acts 1995, 74th Leg., ch. 1043, § 1, eff. Sept. 1, 1995. Renumbered from V.T.C.A., Property Code § 5 by Acts 1997, 75th Leg., ch. 165, § 31.01(72), eff. Sept. 1, 1997.

Statutes in Context

A will may authorize the personal representative to make distributions to a custodian for a minor beneficiary. Likewise, a trust may authorize the trustee to distribute to a minor's custodian.

[1] See V.T.C.A., Property Code § 141.010(a).
[2] See V.T.C.A., Property Code § 141.010.
[1] See V.T.C.A., Property Code § 141.010.

§ 141.006. Transfer Authorized by Will or Trust

(a) A legal representative or trustee may make an irrevocable transfer under Section 10[1] to a custodian for a minor's benefit as authorized in the governing will or trust.

(b) If the testator or settlor has nominated a custodian under Section 4[2] to receive the custodial property, the transfer must be made to that person.

(c) If the testator or settlor has not nominated a custodian under Section 4, or all persons nominated as custodian die before the transfer or are unable, decline, or are ineligible to serve, the legal representative or the trustee shall designate the custodian from among those persons eligible to serve as custodian for property of that kind under Section 10(a).[3]

Acts 1983, 68th Leg., p. 3704, ch. 576, § 1, eff. Jan. 1, 1984. Amended by Acts 1985, 69th Leg., ch. 149, § 5, eff. May 24, 1985. Amended by Acts 1995, 74th Leg., ch. 1043, § 1, eff. Sept. 1, 1995. Renumbered from V.T.C.A., Property Code § 6 by Acts 1997, 75th Leg., ch. 165, § 31.01(72), eff. Sept. 1, 1997.

Statutes in Context

Under certain circumstances, fiduciaries may make transfers to a custodian for a minor's benefit even without express authorization from the original owner of the property. These fiduciaries include the administrator of an intestate, the executor of a will, the trustee of a trust, and the guardian of a ward. *See also* § 113.021(a)(4).

§ 141.007. Other Transfer by Fiduciary

(a) Subject to Subsections (b) and (c), a guardian, legal representative, or trustee may make an irrevocable transfer to another adult or trust company as custodian for a minor's benefit under Section 10[1] in the absence of a will or under a will or trust that does not contain an authorization to do so.

(b) With the approval of the court supervising the guardianship, a guardian may make an irrevocable transfer to another adult or trust company as custodian for the minor's benefit under Section 10.[2]

(c) A transfer under Subsection (a) or (b) may be made only if:

(1) the legal representative or trustee considers the transfer to be in the best interest of the minor;

(2) the transfer is not prohibited by or inconsistent with provisions of the applicable will, trust agreement, or other governing instrument; and

(3) the transfer is authorized by the court if it exceeds $10,000 in value.

[1] See V.T.C.A., Property Code § 141.010.
[2] See V.T.C.A., Property Code § 141.004.
[3] See V.T.C.A., Property Code § 141.010(a).
[1] See V.T.C.A., Property Code § 141.010.
[2] See V.T.C.A., Property Code § 141.010.

Acts 1983, 68th Leg., p. 3706, ch. 576, § 1, eff. Jan. 1, 1984. Amended by Acts 1995, 74th Leg., ch. 1043, § 1, eff. Sept. 1, 1995. Renumbered from V.T.C.A., Property Code § 7 by Acts 1997, 75th Leg., ch. 165, § 31.01(72), eff. Sept. 1, 1997.

Statutes in Context

A person who either holds property of or owes a liquidated debt to a minor who does not have a guardian may transfer the property to a custodian for the minor's benefit. Examples of these type of transferors include a tort judgment debtor, a bank holding a joint account on which the minor has the right of survivorship, and a life insurance company holding proceeds due a minor beneficiary.

---

§ 141.008. Transfer by Obligor

(a) Subject to Subsections (b) and (c), a person who is not subject to Section 6[1] or 7[2] and who holds property of or owes a liquidated debt to a minor who does not have a guardian may make an irrevocable transfer to a custodian for the benefit of the minor under Section 10.[3]

(b) If a person who has the right to nominate a custodian under Section 4[4] has nominated a custodian under that section to receive the custodial property, the transfer must be made to that person.

(c) If a custodian has not been nominated under Section 4, or all persons nominated as custodian die before the transfer or are unable, decline, or are ineligible to serve, a transfer under this section may be made to an adult member of the minor's family or to a trust company unless the property exceeds $10,000 in value.

Acts 1983, 68th Leg., p. 3707, ch. 576, § 1, eff. Jan. 1, 1984. Amended by Acts 1995, 74th Leg., ch. 1043, § 1, eff. Sept. 1, 1995. Renumbered from V.T.C.A., Property Code § 8 by Acts 1997, 75th Leg., ch. 165, § 31.01(72), eff. Sept. 1, 1997.

§ 141.009. Receipt for Custodial Property

A written acknowledgment of delivery by a custodian constitutes a sufficient receipt and discharge for custodial property transferred to the custodian under this chapter.

Acts 1983, 68th Leg., p. 3708, ch. 576, § 1, eff. Jan. 1, 1984. Amended by Acts 1995, 74th Leg., ch. 1043, § 1, eff. Sept. 1, 1995. Renumbered from V.T.C.A., Property Code § 9 by Acts 1997, 75th Leg., ch. 165, § 31.01(72), eff. Sept. 1, 1997.

§ 141.010. Manner of Creating Custodial Property and Effecting Transfer; Designation of Initial Custodian; Control

(a) Custodial property is created and a transfer is made when:

(1) an uncertificated security or a certificated security in registered form is:

(A) registered in the name of the transferor, an adult other than the transferor, or a trust company, followed in substance by the words: "as custodian for (name of minor) under the Texas Uniform Transfers to Minors Act"; or

(B) delivered if in certificated form, or any document necessary for the transfer of an uncertificated security is delivered, with any necessary endorsement to an adult other than the transferor or to a trust company as custodian, accompanied by an instrument in substantially the form set forth in Subsection (b);

(2) money is paid or delivered, or a security held in the name of a broker, financial institution, or its nominee is transferred, to a broker or financial institution for credit to an account in the name of the transferor, an adult other than the transferor, or a trust company, followed in substance by the words: "as custodian for (name of minor) under the Texas Uniform Transfers to Minors Act";

(3) the ownership of a life or endowment insurance policy or annuity contract is:

(A) registered with the issuer in the name of the transferor, an adult other than the transferor, or a trust company, followed in substance by the words: "as custodian for (name of minor) under the Texas Uniform Transfers to Minors Act"; or

(B) assigned in a writing delivered to an adult other than the transferor or to a trust company whose name in the assignment is followed in substance by the words: "as custodian for (name of minor) under the Texas Uniform Transfers to Minors Act";

(4) an irrevocable exercise of a power of appointment or an irrevocable present right to future payment under a contract is the subject of a written notification delivered to the payor, issuer, or other obligor that the right is transferred to the transferor, an adult other than the transferor, or a trust company, whose name in the notification is followed in substance by the words: "as custodian for (name of minor) under the Texas Uniform Transfers to Minors Act";

(5) an interest in real property is conveyed by instrument recorded in the real property records in the county in which the real property is located to the transferor, an adult other than the transferor, or a trust company, followed in substance by the words: "as custodian for (name of minor) under the Texas Uniform Transfers to Minors Act";

(6) a certificate of title issued by a department or agency of a state or of the United States that evidences title to tangible personal property is:

(A) issued in the name of the transferor, an adult other than the transferor, or a trust company, followed in substance by the words: "as custodian for (name of minor) under the Texas Uniform Transfers to Minors Act"; or

---

[1] See V.T.C.A., Property Code § 141.006.
[2] See V.T.C.A., Property Code § 141.007.
[3] See V.T.C.A., Property Code § 141.010.
[4] See V.T.C.A., Property Code § 141.004.

(B) delivered to an adult other than the transferor or to a trust company, endorsed to that person followed in substance by the words: "as a custodian for (name of minor) under the Texas Uniform Transfers to Minors Act"; or

(7) an interest in any property not described in Subdivisions (1)-(6) is transferred to an adult other than the transferor or to a trust company by a written instrument in substantially the form set forth in Subsection (b).

(b) An instrument in the following form satisfies the requirements of Subsections (a)(1)(B) and (7):

> **TRANSFER UNDER THE TEXAS UNIFORM TRANSFERS TO MINORS ACT**
>
> I, ______________ (name of transferor or name and representative capacity if a fiduciary) hereby transfer to ____________ (name of custodian), as custodian for ____________ (name of minor) under the Texas Uniform Transfers to Minors Act, the following: (insert a description of the custodial property sufficient to identify it).
>
> Dated: ______________
>
> ________________ (Signature)
>
> ________________ (name of custodian) acknowledges receipt of the property described above as custodian for the minor named above under the Texas Uniform Transfers to Minors Act.
>
> Dated: ______________
>
> ________________
>
> ____________ (Signature of Custodian)

(c) A transferor shall place the custodian in control of the custodial property as soon as practicable.

Acts 1983, 68th Leg., p. 3708, ch. 576, § 1, eff. Jan. 1, 1984. Amended by Acts 1995, 74th Leg., ch. 1043, § 1, eff. Sept. 1, 1995. Renumbered from V.T.C.A., Property Code § 10 by Acts 1997, 75th Leg., ch. 165, § 31.01(72), eff. Sept. 1, 1997.

Statutes in Context

Only one person may be named as a transferee or custodian.

§ 141.011. Single Custodianship

A transfer may be made only for one minor, and only one person may be the custodian. All custodial property held under this chapter by the same custodian for the benefit of the same minor constitutes a single custodianship.

Acts 1983, 68th Leg., p. 3709, ch. 576, § 1, eff. Jan. 1, 1984. Amended by Acts 1995, 74th Leg., ch. 1043, § 1, eff. Sept. 1, 1995. Renumbered from V.T.C.A., Property Code § 11 by Acts 1997, 75th Leg., ch. 165, § 31.01(72), eff. Sept. 1, 1997.

§ 141.012. Validity and Effect of Transfer

(a) The validity of a transfer made in a manner prescribed by this chapter is not affected by the:

(1) transferor's failure to comply with Section 10(c)[1] concerning possession and control;

(2) designation of an ineligible custodian, except designation of the transferor in the case of property for which the transferor is ineligible to serve as custodian under Section 10(a);[2] or

(3) death or incapacity of a person nominated under Section 4[3] or designated under Section 10[4] as custodian or the disclaimer of the office by that person.

(b) A transfer made under Section 10[5] is irrevocable, and the custodial property is indefeasibly vested in the minor. The custodian has all the rights, powers, duties, and authority provided in this chapter, and the minor or the minor's legal representative does not have any right, power, duty, or authority with respect to the custodial property except as provided by this chapter.

(c) By making a transfer, the transferor incorporates all the provisions of this chapter in the disposition and grants to the custodian, or to any third person dealing with a person designated as custodian, the respective powers, rights and immunities provided by this chapter.

Acts 1983, 68th Leg., p. 3709, ch. 576, § 1, eff. Jan. 1, 1984. Amended by Acts 1995, 74th Leg., ch. 1043, § 1, eff. Sept. 1, 1995. Renumbered from V.T.C.A., Property Code § 12 by Acts 1997, 75th Leg., ch. 165, § 31.01(72), eff. Sept. 1, 1997.

Statutes in Context

The custodian must "observe the standard of care that would be observed by a prudent person dealing with property of another." The custodian is not limited by any other Texas law which restricts investments by fiduciaries. If a custodian has a special skill or other expertise (e.g., a professional custodian or trust company), the custodian must exercise that skill or expertise. However, the custodian may retain any property received from a transferor without liability for failing to invest that property in a more productive manner or to diversify.

§ 141.013. Care of Custodial Property

(a) A custodian shall:

(1) take control of custodial property;

(2) register or record title to custodial property if appropriate; and

(3) collect, hold, manage, sell, convey, invest, and reinvest custodial property.

(b) In dealing with custodial property, a custodian shall observe the standard of care that would be observed by a prudent person dealing with property of another and is not limited by any other statute restricting investments by fiduciaries. If a custodian has a special skill or expertise, the custodian shall use that skill or expertise. However, a custodian, in the custodian's

[1] See V.T.C.A., Property Code § 141.010(c).

[2] See V.T.C.A., Property Code § 141.010(a).

[3] See V.T.C.A., Property Code § 141.004.

[4] See V.T.C.A., Property Code § 141.010.

[5] See V.T.C.A., Property Code § 141.010.

discretion and without liability to the minor or the minor's estate, may retain any custodial property received from a transferor.

(c) A custodian may invest in or pay premiums on life insurance or endowment policies on the life of:

(1) the minor only if the minor or the minor's estate is the sole beneficiary; or

(2) another person in whom the minor has an insurable interest only to the extent that the minor, the minor's estate, or the custodian in the capacity of the custodian is the irrevocable beneficiary.

(d) A custodian at all times shall keep custodial property separate and distinct from all other property in a manner sufficient to identify it clearly as custodial property of the minor. Custodial property consisting of an undivided interest is so identified if the minor's interest is held as a tenant in common and is fixed. Custodial property subject to recordation is so identified if it is recorded, and custodial property subject to registration is so identified if it is registered, or held in an account designated, in the name of the custodian followed in substance by the words: "as custodian for ______________ (name of minor) under the Texas Uniform Transfers to Minors Act."

(e) A custodian shall keep records of all transactions with respect to custodial property, including information necessary for the preparation of the minor's tax returns, and shall make the records available for inspection at reasonable intervals by a parent or legal representative of the minor or by the minor if the minor is at least 14 years of age.

Acts 1983, 68th Leg., p. 3710, ch. 576, § 1, eff. Jan. 1, 1984. Amended by Acts 1995, 74th Leg., ch. 1043, § 1, eff. Sept. 1, 1995. Renumbered from V.T.C.A., Property Code § 13 by Acts 1997, 75th Leg., ch. 165, § 31.01(72), eff. Sept. 1, 1997.

Statutes in Context

The custodian has all the rights, powers, and authority over the custodial property that an unmarried adult owner has over his or her own property. The custodian may exercise these rights, powers, and authority only in a custodial capacity.

§ 141.014. Powers of Custodian

(a) A custodian, acting in a custodial capacity, has all the rights, powers, and authority over custodial property that unmarried adult owners have over their own property, but a custodian may exercise those rights, powers, and authority in that capacity only.

(b) This section does not relieve a custodian from liability for breach of Section 13.[1]

Acts 1983, 68th Leg., p. 3710, ch. 576, § 1, eff. Jan. 1, 1984. Amended by Acts 1995, 74th Leg., ch. 1043, § 1, eff. Sept. 1, 1995. Renumbered from V.T.C.A., Property Code § 14 by Acts 1997, 75th Leg., ch. 165, § 31.01(72), eff. Sept. 1, 1997.

[1] See V.T.C.A., Property Code § 141.013.

Statutes in Context

The custodian has the power to (1) deliver or pay custodial property directly to the minor and (2) expend custodial property for the minor's benefit. The custodian is not limited by any standard (e.g., support, education, or medical care) in making distributions as long as the distribution is for the use or benefit of the minor. The custodian need not obtain a court order before making distributions. In addition, the custodian may use custodial property for the minor even if (1) the custodian personally has a duty or the ability to support the minor, (2) another person has a duty or the ability to support the minor, and (3) the minor has other income or property which could be used instead.

A minor who is at least 14 years old and any interested person may petition to the court to force the custodian to distribute custodial property. The court may order distribution of as much of the property as the court considers advisable for the use and benefit of the minor.

Distributions of custodial property are in addition to, not in substitution for, and do not affect any obligation which a person may have to support the minor.

§ 141.015. Use of Custodial Property

(a) A custodian may deliver or pay to the minor or expend for the minor's benefit as much of the custodial property as the custodian considers advisable for the use and benefit of the minor, without court order and without regard to:

(1) the duty or ability of the custodian personally or of any other person to support the minor; or

(2) any other income or property of the minor that may be applicable or available for that purpose.

(b) On petition of an interested person or the minor if the minor is at least 14 years of age, the court may order the custodian to deliver or pay to the minor or expend for the minor's benefit as much of the custodial property as the court considers advisable for the use and benefit of the minor.

(c) A delivery, payment, or expenditure under this section is in addition to, not in substitution for, and does not affect any obligation of a person to support the minor.

Added by Acts 1995, 74th Leg., ch. 1043, § 1, eff. Sept. 1, 1995. Renumbered from V.T.C.A., Property Code § 15 by Acts 1997, 75th Leg., ch. 165, § 31.01(72), eff. Sept. 1, 1997.

Statutes in Context

The custodian is normally entitled to charge reasonable compensation for the custodian's services. The custodian must affirmatively elect to receive compensation each year or else the right lapses. A custodian who was the donor of an irrevocable gift or who exercised a power of appointment may not take compensation.

§ 141.016. Custodian's Expenses, Compensation, and Bond

(a) A custodian is entitled to reimbursement from custodial property for reasonable expenses incurred in the performance of the custodian's duties.

(b) Except for one who is a transferor under Section 5,[1] a custodian has a noncumulative election during each calendar year to charge reasonable compensation for services performed by the custodian during that year.

(c) Except as provided by Section 19(f),[2] a custodian is not required to give a bond.

Added by Acts 1995, 74th Leg., ch. 1043, § 1, eff. Sept. 1, 1995. Renumbered from V.T.C.A., Property Code § 16 by Acts 1997, 75th Leg., ch. 165, § 31.01(72), eff. Sept. 1, 1997.

§ 141.017. Exemption of Third Person From Liability

A third person, in good faith and without court order, may act on the instructions of or otherwise deal with any person purporting to make a transfer or act in the capacity of a custodian and, in the absence of knowledge, is not responsible for determining the:

(1) validity of the purported custodian's designation;

(2) propriety of, or the authority under this chapter for, any act of the purported custodian;

(3) validity or propriety under this chapter of any instrument or instructions executed or given by the person purporting to make a transfer or by the purported custodian; or

(4) propriety of the application of the minor's property delivered to the purported custodian.

Added by Acts 1995, 74th Leg., ch. 1043, § 1, eff. Sept. 1, 1995. Renumbered from V.T.C.A., Property Code § 17 by Acts 1997, 75th Leg., ch. 165, § 31.01(72), eff. Sept. 1, 1997.

§ 141.018. Liability to Third Person

(a) A claim based on a contract entered into by a custodian acting in a custodial capacity, an obligation arising from the ownership or control of custodial property, or a tort committed during the custodianship may be asserted against the custodial property by proceeding against the custodian in the custodian's custodial capacity, whether or not the custodian or the minor is personally liable for the claim.

(b) A custodian is not personally liable:

(1) on a contract properly entered into in the custodian's custodial capacity unless the custodian fails to reveal that capacity and to identify the custodianship in the contract; or

(2) for an obligation arising from control of custodial property or for a tort committed during the custodianship unless the custodian is personally at fault.

[1] See V.T.C.A., Property Code § 141.005.

[2] See V.T.C.A., Property Code § 141.019(f).

(c) A minor is not personally liable for an obligation arising from ownership of custodial property or for a tort committed during the custodianship unless the minor is personally at fault.

Added by Acts 1995, 74th Leg., ch. 1043, § 1, eff. Sept. 1, 1995. Renumbered from V.T.C.A., Property Code § 18 by Acts 1997, 75th Leg., ch. 165, § 31.01(72), eff. Sept. 1, 1997.

§ 141.019. Renunciation, Resignation, Death, or Removal of Custodian; Designation of Successor Custodian

(a) A person nominated to serve as a custodian under Section 4[1] or designated to serve as a custodian under Section 10[2] may decline to serve as custodian by delivering written notice to the person who made the nomination or to the transferor's legal representative. If the event giving rise to a transfer has not occurred and no substitute custodian who is able, willing, and eligible to serve was nominated under Section 4, the person who made the nomination may nominate a substitute custodian under Section 4; otherwise the transferor or the transferor's legal representative shall designate a substitute custodian at the time of the transfer, in either case from among the persons eligible to serve as custodian for that kind of property under Section 10(a).[3] A substitute custodian designated under this section has the rights of a successor custodian.

(b) A custodian at any time may designate as successor custodian a trust company or an adult other than a transferor under Section 5[4] by executing and dating an instrument of designation before a subscribing witness other than the successor. If the instrument of designation does not contain or is not accompanied by the custodian's resignation, the designation of the successor does not take effect until the custodian resigns, dies, becomes incapacitated, or is removed.

(c) A custodian may resign at any time by delivering:

(1) written notice to the successor custodian and to the minor if the minor is at least 14 years of age; and

(2) the custodial property to the successor custodian.

(d) If a custodian is ineligible, dies, or becomes incapacitated without having effectively designated a successor and the minor is at least 14 years of age, the minor may designate as successor custodian an adult member of the minor's family, a guardian of the minor, or a trust company in the manner prescribed by Subsection (b). If the minor is younger than 14 years of age or fails to act within 60 days after the ineligibility, death, or incapacity of the custodian, the minor's guardian becomes successor custodian. If the minor has no guardian or the minor's guardian declines to act,

[1] See V.T.C.A., Property Code § 141.004.

[2] See V.T.C.A., Property Code § 141.010.

[3] See V.T.C.A., Property Code § 141.010(a).

[4] See V.T.C.A., Property Code § 141.005.

the transferor, the legal representative of the transferor or of the custodian, an adult member of the minor's family, or any other interested person may petition the court to designate a successor custodian.

(e) As soon as practicable, a custodian who declines to serve under Subsection (a) or resigns under Subsection (c), or the legal representative of a deceased or incapacitated custodian, shall put the custodial property and records in the possession and control of the successor custodian. The successor custodian by action may enforce the obligation to deliver custodial property and records and becomes responsible for each item as received.

(f) A transferor, the legal representative of a transferor, an adult member of the minor's family, a guardian of the person of the minor, the guardian of the minor, or the minor if the minor is at least 14 years of age may petition the court to:

(1) remove the custodian for cause and designate a successor custodian other than a transferor under Section 5; or

(2) require the custodian to give appropriate bond.

Added by Acts 1995, 74th Leg., ch. 1043, § 1, eff. Sept. 1, 1995. Renumbered from V.T.C.A., Property Code § 19 by Acts 1997, 75th Leg., ch. 165, § 31.01(72), eff. Sept. 1, 1997.

§ 141.020. Accounting by and Determination of Liability

(a) A minor who is at least 14 years of age, the minor's guardian of the person or legal representative, an adult member of the minor's family, a transferor, or a transferor's legal representative may petition the court for:

(1) an accounting by the custodian or the custodian's legal representative; or

(2) a determination of responsibility, as between the custodial property and the custodian personally, for claims against the custodial property unless the responsibility has been adjudicated in an action under Section 18[1] to which the minor or the minor's legal representative was a party.

(b) A successor custodian may petition the court for an accounting by the predecessor custodian.

(c) The court, in a proceeding under this chapter or in any other proceeding, may require or permit the custodian or the custodian's legal representative to account.

(d) If a custodian is removed under Section 19(f),[2] the court shall require an accounting and order delivery of the custodial property and records to the successor custodian and the execution of all instruments required for transfer of the custodial property.

Added by Acts 1995, 74th Leg., ch. 1043, § 1, eff. Sept. 1, 1995. Renumbered from V.T.C.A., Property Code § 20 by Acts 1997, 75th Leg., ch. 165, § 31.01(72), eff. Sept. 1, 1997.

[1] See V.T.C.A., Property Code § 141.018.
[2] See V.T.C.A., Property Code § 141.019(f).

Statutes in Context

The custodianship terminates and the custodian must transfer the custodial property to the minor or the minor's estate when the first of the following events occurs: (1) the minor reaches age 21, if the property was transferred by gift, exercise of power of appointment, will, or trust (If the custodianship was created before September 1, 1995, it will still terminate when the minor reaches age 18.); (2) the minor reaches age 18, if the property was transferred by a fiduciary or an obligor; or (3) the minor dies.

§ 141.021. Termination of Custodianship

The custodian shall transfer in an appropriate manner the custodial property to the minor or to the minor's estate on the earlier of the date:

(1) the minor attains 21 years of age, with respect to custodial property transferred under Section 5[1] or 6;[2]

(2) the minor attains the age of majority under the laws of this state other than this chapter, with respect to custodial property transferred under Section 7[3] or 8;[4] or

(3) the minor's death.

Added by Acts 1995, 74th Leg., ch. 1043, § 1, eff. Sept. 1, 1995. Renumbered from V.T.C.A., Property Code § 21 by Acts 1997, 75th Leg., ch. 165, § 31.01(72), eff. Sept. 1, 1997.

§ 141.022. Applicability

Except as provided by Section 25,[1] this chapter applies to a transfer within the scope of Section 3[2] made after September 1, 1995, if:

(1) the transfer purports to have been made under the Texas Uniform Gifts to Minors Act; or

(2) the instrument by which the transfer purports to have been made uses in substance the designation "as custodian under the Uniform Gifts to Minors Act" or "as custodian under the Uniform Transfers to Minors Act" of any other state, and the application of this chapter is necessary to validate the transfer.

Added by Acts 1995, 74th Leg., ch. 1043, § 1, eff. Sept. 1, 1995. Amended by Acts 1997, 75th Leg., ch. 221, § 1, eff. Sept. 1, 1997. Renumbered from V.T.C.A., Property Code § 22 by Acts 1997, 75th Leg., ch. 165, § 31.01(72), eff. Sept. 1, 1997.

§ 141.023. Effect on Existing Custodianships

(a) Any transfer of custodial property under this chapter made before September 1, 1995, is validated

[1] See V.T.C.A., Property Code § 141.005.
[2] See V.T.C.A., Property Code § 141.006.
[3] See V.T.C.A., Property Code § 141.007.
[4] See V.T.C.A., Property Code § 141.008.
[1] See V.T.C.A., Property Code § 141.025.
[2] See V.T.C.A., Property Code § 141.003.

notwithstanding that there was no specific authority in this chapter for the coverage of custodial property of that kind or for a transfer from that source at the time the transfer was made.

(b) Sections 2[1] and 21,[2] with respect to the age of a minor for whom custodial property is held under this chapter, do not apply to custodial property held in a custodianship that terminated because the minor attained the age of 18 after August 26, 1973, and before September 1, 1995.

Added by Acts 1995, 74th Leg., ch. 1043, § 1, eff. Sept. 1, 1995. Renumbered from V.T.C.A., Property Code § 23 by Acts 1997, 75th Leg., ch. 165, § 31.01(72), eff. Sept. 1, 1997.

§ 141.024. Uniformity of Application and Construction

This chapter shall be applied and construed to effect its general purpose, to make uniform the law with respect to the subject of this chapter among states enacting that law.

Added by Acts 1995, 74th Leg., ch. 1043, § 1, eff. Sept. 1, 1995. Renumbered from V.T.C.A., Property Code § 23 by Acts 1997, 75th Leg., ch. 165, § 31.01(72), eff. Sept. 1, 1997.

§ 141.025. Additional Transfers to Custodianships in Existence Before Effective Date of Act

(a) This section applies only to a transfer within the scope of Section 141.003 made after September 1, 1995, to a custodian of a custodianship established before September 1, 1995, under the Texas Uniform Gifts to Minors Act.

(b) This chapter does not prevent a person from making additional transfers to a custodianship described by Subsection (a). On the direction of the transferor or custodian, custodial property that is transferred to the custodianship shall be commingled with the custodial property of the custodianship established under the Texas Uniform Gifts to Minors Act. The additional transfers to the custodianship shall be administered and distributed on termination of the custodianship, as prescribed by this chapter, except that for purposes of Section 141.021, the custodian shall transfer the custodial property to:

(1) the beneficiary on the date the beneficiary attains 18 years of age or an earlier date as prescribed by Section 141.021; or

(2) the beneficiary's estate if the individual dies before the date prescribed by Subdivision (1).

Added by Acts 1997, 75th Leg., ch. 221, § 2, eff. Sept. 1, 1997. Amended by Acts 1997, 75th Leg., ch. 165, § 31.01(72), eff. Sept. 1, 1997. Renumbered from V.T.C.A., Property Code § 25 by Acts 1999, 76th Leg., ch. 62, § 19.01(91), eff. Sept. 1, 1999.

[1] See V.T.C.A., Property Code § 141.002.

[2] See V.T.C.A., Property Code § 141.021.

Chapter 142. Management of Property Recovered in Suit by a Next Friend or Guardian Ad Litem

Statutes in Context

Chapter 142 provides for the management of property recovered on behalf of a minor or incapacitated person by a next friend or guardian ad litem. Of particular importance is § 142.005 which allows for the court to create a trust to manage the property.

§ 142.001. Management by Decree

(a) In a suit in which a minor or incapacitated person who has no legal guardian is represented by a next friend or an appointed guardian ad litem, the court, on application and hearing, may provide by decree for the investment of funds accruing to the minor or other person under the judgment in the suit.

(b) If the decree is made during vacation, it must be recorded in the minutes of the succeeding term of the court.

Acts 1983, 68th Leg., p. 3711, ch. 576, § 1, eff. Jan. 1, 1984. Amended by Acts 1984, 68th Leg., 2nd C.S., ch. 18, § 14(b), eff. Oct. 2, 1984; Acts 1999, 76th Leg., ch. 195, § 2, eff. Sept. 1, 1999.

§ 142.002. Management by Bonded Manager

(a) In a suit in which a minor or incapacitated person who has no legal guardian is represented by a next friend or an appointed guardian ad litem, the court in which a judgment is rendered may by an order entered of record authorize the next friend, the guardian ad litem, or another person to take possession of money or other personal property recovered under the judgment for the minor or other person represented.

(b) The next friend, guardian ad litem, or other person may not take possession of the property until the person has executed a bond as principal that:

(1) is in an amount at least double the value of the property or, if a surety on the bond is a solvent surety company authorized under the law of this state to execute the bond, is in an amount at least equal to the value of the property;

(2) is payable to the county judge; and

(3) is conditioned on the obligation of the next friend, guardian ad litem, or other person to use the property under the direction of the court for the benefit of its owner and to return the property, with interest or other increase, to the person entitled to receive the property when ordered by the court to do so.

Acts 1983, 68th Leg., p. 3711, ch. 576, § 1, eff. Jan. 1, 1984. Amended by Acts 1984, 68th Leg., 2nd C.S., ch. 18, § 14(c), eff. Oct. 2, 1984; Amended by Acts 1999, 76th Leg., ch. 195, § 3, eff. Sept. 1, 1999.

§ 142.003. Compensation and Duties of Managers

(a) A person who manages property under Section 142.001 or 142.002 is entitled to receive compensation as allowed by the court.

(b) The person shall make dispositions of the property as ordered by the court and shall return the property into court on the order of the court.

Acts 1983, 68th Leg., p. 3711, ch. 576, § 1, eff. Jan. 1, 1984.

§ 142.004. Investment of Funds

(a) In a suit in which a minor or incapacitated person who has no legal guardian is represented by a next friend or an appointed guardian ad litem, any money recovered by the plaintiff, if not otherwise managed under this chapter, may be invested:

(1) by the next friend or guardian ad litem in:

(A) the Texas tomorrow fund established by Subchapter F, Chapter 54, Education Code; or

(B) interest-bearing time deposits in a financial institution doing business in this state and insured by the Federal Deposit Insurance Corporation; or

(2) by the clerk of the court, on written order of the court of proper jurisdiction, in:

(A) the Texas tomorrow fund established by Subchapter F, Chapter 54, Education Code;

(B) interest-bearing deposits in a financial institution doing business in this state and insured by the Federal Deposit Insurance Corporation;

(C) United States treasury bills;

(D) an eligible interlocal investment pool that meets the requirements of Sections 2256.016, 2256.017, and 2256.019, Government Code; or

(E) a no-load money market mutual fund, if the fund:

(i) is regulated by the Securities and Exchange Commission;

(ii) has a dollar weighted average stated maturity of 90 days or fewer; and

(iii) includes in its investment objectives the maintenance of a stable net asset value of $1 for each share

(b) If the money invested under this section may not be withdrawn from the financial institution without an order of the court, a next friend or guardian ad litem who makes the investment is not required to execute a bond with respect to the money.

(c) When money invested under this section is withdrawn, the court may:

(1) on a finding that the person entitled to receive the money is no longer under the disability, order the funds turned over to the person; or

(2) order management of the funds under another provision of this chapter.

(d) Interest earned on an account invested by the clerk of the court shall be paid in the same manner as interest earned on an account under Chapter 117, Local Government Code.

(e) If money is invested under Subsection (a)(2)(E), the court may waive any bonding requirement.

Amended by Acts 1997, 75th Leg., ch. 505, § 22, eff. Sept. 1, 1997; Acts 1999, 76th Leg., ch. 94, § 1, eff. May 17, 1999; Acts 1999, 76th Leg., ch. 195, § 4, eff. Sept. 1, 1999; Acts 2001, 77th Leg., ch. 1420, § 17.002, eff. Sept. 1, 2001.

Statutes in Context

Section 142.005 permits the court to create a trust to manage the property of a minor or incapacitated person recovered by a guardian ad litem or next friend. Only a trust company or bank may serve as the trustee. The trust must contain the provisions listed in this section. Note that a trust created on behalf of a minor may continue past age 18 but must end no later than the minor's twenty-fifth birthday. A trust for an incapacitated individual ends when the individual regains capacity.

The court may include provisions to have the trust qualify as a special needs trust under 42 U.S.C. § 1396(d)(4)(A) so the trust will not prevent the beneficiary from qualifying for Medicaid.

The 2003 Texas Legislature added § 142.005(j) to provide that an exculpatory provision in a Chapter 142 management trust will be enforceable only if both of the following two requirements are satisfied:

(1) The exculpatory provision is limited to specific facts and circumstances unique to the property of that trust and is not applicable generally to the trust.

(2) The court creating or modifying the trust makes a specific finding that there is clear and convincing evidence that the exculpatory provision is in the best interests of the beneficiary of the trust.

This new requirement is a reaction to the Texas Supreme Court opinion in *Texas Commerce Bank, N.A. v. Grizzle*, 96 S.W.3d 240 (Tex. 2002), in which the court enforced a boilerplate exculpatory clause in a Chapter 142 trust.

---

§ 142.005. Trust for Property

(a) In a suit in which a minor who has no legal guardian or an incapacitated person is represented by a next friend or an appointed guardian ad litem, the court may, on application by the next friend or the guardian ad litem and on a finding that the creation of a trust would be in the best interests of the minor or incapacitated person, enter a decree in the record directing the clerk to deliver any funds accruing to the minor or incapacitated person under the judgment to a trust company or a state or national bank having trust powers in this state.

(b) The decree shall provide for the creation of a trust for the management of the funds for the benefit of the minor or incapacitated person and for terms, conditions, and limitations of the trust, as determined by the court, that are not in conflict with the following mandatory provisions:

(1) the minor or incapacitated person is the sole beneficiary of the trust;

(2) the trustee may disburse amounts of the trust's principal, income, or both as the trustee in his sole discretion determines to be reasonably necessary for the health, education, support, or maintenance of the beneficiary;

(3) the income of the trust not disbursed under Subdivision (2) is added to the principal of the trust;

(4) if the beneficiary is a minor, the trust terminates on the death of the beneficiary, on the beneficiary's attaining an age stated in the trust, or on the 25th birthday of the beneficiary, whichever occurs first, or if the beneficiary is an incapacitated person, the trust terminates on the death of the beneficiary or when the beneficiary regains capacity;

(5) the trustee serves without bond; and

(6) the trustee receives reasonable compensation paid from trust's income, principal, or both on application to and approval of the court.

(c) A trust established under this section may provide that:

(1) distributions of the trust principal before the termination of the trust may be made from time to time as the beneficiary attains designated ages and at designated percentages of the principal; and

(2) distributions, payments, uses, and applications of all trust funds may be made to the legal or natural guardian of the beneficiary or to the person having custody of the beneficiary or may be made directly to or expended for the benefit, support, or maintenance of the beneficiary without the intervention of any legal guardian or other legal representative of the beneficiary.

(d) A trust created under this section may be amended, modified, or revoked by the court at any time before its termination, but is not subject to revocation by the beneficiary or a guardian of the beneficiary's estate. If the trust is revoked by the court before the beneficiary is 18 years old, the court may provide for the management of the trust principal and any undistributed income as authorized by this chapter. If the trust is revoked by the court after the beneficiary is 18 years old, the trust principal and any undistributed income shall be delivered to the beneficiary after the payment of all proper and necessary expenses.

(e) On the termination of the trust under its terms or on the death of the beneficiary, the trust principal and any undistributed income shall be paid to the beneficiary or to the representative of the estate of the deceased beneficiary.

(f) A trust established under this section prevails over any other law concerning minors, incapacitated persons, or their property, and the trust continues in force and effect until terminated or revoked, notwithstanding the appointment of a guardian of the estate of the minor or incapacitated person, or the attainment of the age of majority by the minor.

(g) Notwithstanding any other provision of this chapter, if the court finds that it would be in the best interests of the minor or incapacitated person for whom a trust is created under this section, the trust may contain provisions determined by the court to be necessary to establish a special needs trust as specified under 42 U.S.C. § 1396p(d)(4)(A).

(h) A trust created under this section is subject to Subtitle B, Title 9.

(i) Notwithstanding Subsection (h), this section prevails over a provision in Subtitle B, Title 9, that is in conflict or inconsistent with this section.

(j) A provision in a trust created under this section that relieves a trustee from a duty, responsibility, or liability imposed by this section or Subtitle B, Title 9, is enforceable only if:

(1) the provision is limited to specific facts and circumstances unique to the property of that trust and is not applicable generally to the trust; and

(2) the court creating or modifying the trust makes a specific finding that there is clear and convincing evidence that the inclusion of the provision is in the best interests of the beneficiary of the trust.

Acts 1983, 68th Leg., p. 3712, ch. 576, § 1, eff. Jan. 1, 1984. Amended by Acts 1984, 68th Leg., 2nd C.S., ch. 18, § 14(e), (f), eff. Oct. 2, 1984. Amended by Acts 1997, 75th Leg., ch. 128, § 1, eff. Sept. 1, 1997. Amended by Acts 2003, 78th Leg., ch. 1154, § 3, eff. Sept. 1, 2003.

§ 142.006. Claims Against Property

If any person claims an interest in property subject to management under this chapter, the court having authority over the property may hear evidence on the interest and may order the claim or the portion of the claim found to be just to be paid to the person entitled to receive it.

Acts 1983, 68th Leg., p. 3714, ch. 576, § 1, eff. Jan. 1, 1984.

§ 142.007. Incapacitated Person

For the purposes of this chapter, "incapacitated person" means a person who is impaired because of mental illness, mental deficiency, physical illness or disability, advanced age, chronic use of drugs, chronic intoxication, or any other cause except status as a minor to the extent that the person lacks sufficient understanding or capacity to make or communicate responsible decisions concerning his person.

Added by Acts 1984, 68th Leg., 2nd C.S., ch. 18, § 14(g), eff. Oct. 2, 1984.

§ 142.008. Structured Settlement

(a) In a suit in which a minor or incapacitated person who has no legal guardian is represented by a next friend or an appointed guardian ad litem, the court, on a motion from the parties, may provide for a structured settlement that:

(1) provides for periodic payments; and

(2) is funded by:

(A) an obligation guaranteed by the United States government; or

(B) an annuity contract that meets the requirements of Section 142.009.

(b) The person obligated to fund a structured settlement shall provide to the court:

(1) a copy of the instrument that provides funding for the structured settlement; or

(2) an affidavit from an independent financial consultant that specifies the present value of the structured settlement and the method by which the value is calculated.

(c) A structured settlement provided for under this section is solely for the benefit of the beneficiary of the structured settlement and is not subject to the interest payment calculations contained in Section 117.054, Local Government Code.

Added by Acts 1999, 76th Leg., ch. 195, § 5, eff. Sept. 1, 1999.

§ 142.009. Annuity Contract Requirements for Structured Settlement

(a) An insurance company providing an annuity contract for a structured settlement as provided by Section 142.008 must:

(1) be licensed to write annuity contracts in this state;

(2) have a minimum of $1 million of capital and surplus; and

(3) be approved by the court and comply with any requirements imposed by the court to ensure funding to satisfy periodic settlement payments.

(b) In approving an insurance company under Subsection (a)(3), the court may consider whether the company:

(1) holds a industry rating equivalent to at least two of the following rating organizations:

(A) A.M. Best Company: A + + or A+;

(B) Duff & Phelps Credit Rating Company Insurance Company Claims Paying Ability Rating: AA-, AA, AA+, or AAA;

(C) Moody's Investors Service Claims Paying Ability Rating: Aa3, Aa2, Aa1, or aaa; or

(D) Standard & Poor's Corporation Insurer Claims-Paying Ability Rating: AA-, AA, AA+, or AAA;

(2) is an affiliate, as that term is defined by Article 21.49-1, Insurance Code, of a liability insurance carrier involved in the suit for which the structured settlement is created; or

(3) is connected in any way to person obligated to fund the structured settlement.

Added by Acts 1999, 76th Leg., ch. 195, § 5, eff. Sept. 1, 1999. Amended by Acts 2001, 77th Leg., ch. 96, § 2, eff. Sept. 1, 2001.

Subtitle C. Powers of Appointment

Chapter 181. Powers of Appointment

Statutes in Context

A power of appointment is the right to designate the new owner of property. You have this power with respect to the property you own because you may give anything you own to another person. The power to name a new owner of your property is one of the things you take for granted as accompanying property ownership.

You may sever this power of appointment from the ownership of the property itself. When this happens, the following relationships are created. The owner of property (the person who is severing) is the *donor* of the power, the person with the power to appoint the property is the *donee*, and the prospective new owners are the *objects of the power*. When the donee actually exercises the power, the new owners are called the *appointees*. If the donee fails to exercise the power, the property passes to the *default takers*. If the donor failed to name default takers, the property reverts to the donor or the donor's estate.

The donor can create a power of appointment in an inter vivos document, such as a deed or trust, or in a separate power of appointment instrument. The donor can also create a power of appointment by will.

Powers of appointment are generally categorized in one of two ways. First, the power of appointment may be *general*, meaning that there are no restrictions or conditions on the donee's exercise of the power. Thus, the donee could even appoint the donee's own self as the new owner. In many aspects, the donee of a general power of appointment is like the actual owner of the property. Second, the power may be *specific, special,* or *limited*, i.e., the donor may specify certain individuals or groups as the objects of the power which do not include the donee, the donee's creditors, the donee's estate, or the creditors of the donee's estate. In addition, the donor may make the donee's exercise of the power conditional on whatever factors, within legal bounds, the donor desires, for example, only for the appointees' health-related and educational expenses.

The donee of a power of appointment does not have title, either legal or equitable, to the subject property. Instead, the donee only has a power to appoint. The appointees take title from the donor, not the donee.

The donee has no duty to exercise the power of appointment in favor of the hopeful appointees. Unlike a trustee, a donee is not a fiduciary and has no duty to manage the property or to distribute the property. A power of appointment is also not an agency relationship; the donee is not the donor's agent.

The donor may dictate the method the donee must use to exercise the power of appointment. For example, the power may be an *inter vivos power* indicating that the donee must exercise it while alive. Alternatively, it may be a *testamentary power* which the donee may only exercise by will. The donor also may permit the donee to exercise the power in both ways.

Although the donor may create a power of appointment in anyone, powers of appointment are typically used with trusts. Trustees often have the power to decide which beneficiaries will receive distributions and in what amounts. Settlors of trusts also may give powers of appointment over trust property to the beneficiaries.

Subchapter A. General Provisions

§ 181.001. Definitions

In this chapter:

(1) "Donee" means a person, whether or not a resident of this state, who, either alone or in conjunction with others, may exercise a power.

(1-a) "Object of the power of appointment" means a person to whom the donee is given the power to appoint.

(2) "Power" means the authority to appoint or designate the recipient of property, to invade or consume property, to alter, amend, or revoke an instrument under which an estate or trust is created or held, and to terminate a right or interest under an estate or trust, and any authority remaining after a partial release of a power.

(3) "Property" means all property and interests in property, real or personal, including parts of property, partial interests, and all or any part of the income from property.

(4) "Release" means a renunciation, relinquishment, surrender, refusal to accept, extinguishment, and any other form of release, including a covenant not to exercise all or part of a power.

Acts 1983, 68th Leg., p. 3723, ch. 576, § 1, eff. Jan. 1, 1984. Amended by Acts 2003, 78th Leg., ch. 551, § 1, eff. Sept. 1, 2003.

§ 181.002. Application

(a) Except as provided by Subsection (b), this chapter applies:

(1) to a power or a release of a power, regardless of the date the power is created;

(2) to a vested, contingent, or conditional power; and

(3) to a power classified as a power in gross, a power appurtenant, a power appendant, a collateral power, a general, limited, or special power, an exclusive or nonexclusive power, or any other power.

(b) This chapter applies regardless of the time or manner a power is created or reserved or the release is made and regardless of the time, manner, or in whose favor a power may be exercised.

(c) This chapter does not apply to a power in trust that is imperative.

Acts 1983, 68th Leg., p. 3723, ch. 576, § 1, eff. Jan. 1, 1984.

§ 181.003. Chapter Not Exclusive

The provisions of this chapter concerning the release of a power are not exclusive.

Acts 1983, 68th Leg., p. 3724, ch. 576, § 1, eff. Jan. 1, 1984.

§ 181.004. Construction

This chapter is intended to be declarative of the common law of this state, and it shall be liberally construed to make all powers, except imperative powers in trust, releasable unless the instrument creating the trust expressly provides otherwise.

Acts 1983, 68th Leg., p. 3724, ch. 576, § 1, eff. Jan. 1, 1984.

Subchapter B. Release of Powers of Appointment

§ 181.051. Authority of Donee to Release Power

Unless the instrument creating the power specifically provides to the contrary, a donee may at any time:

(1) completely release the power;

(2) release the power as to any property subject to the power;

(3) release the power as to a person in whose favor a power may be exercised; or

(4) limit in any respect the extent to which the power may be exercised.

Acts 1983, 68th Leg., p. 3724, ch. 576, § 1, eff. Jan. 1, 1984.

§ 181.052. Requisites of Release

(a) A partial or complete release of a power, with or without consideration, is valid if the donee executes and acknowledges, in the manner required by law for the execution and recordation of deeds, an instrument evidencing an intent to make the release, and the instrument is delivered:

(1) to the person or in the manner specified in the instrument creating the power;

(2) to an adult, other than the donee releasing the power, who may take any of the property subject to the power if the power is not exercised or in whose favor it may be exercised after the partial release;

(3) to a trustee or cotrustee of the property subject to the power; or

(4) to an appropriate county clerk for recording.

(b) An instrument releasing a power may be recorded in a county in this state in which:

(1) property subject to the power is located;

(2) a donee in control of the property resides;

(3) a trustee in control of the property resides;

(4) a corporate trustee in control of the property has its principal office; or

(5) the instrument creating the power is probated or recorded.

Acts 1983, 68th Leg., p. 3724, ch. 576, § 1, eff. Jan. 1, 1984.

§ 181.053. Release by Guardian

If a person under a disability holds a power, the guardian of the person's estate may release the power in the manner provided in this chapter on the order of the

court in this state in which the guardian was appointed or in which the guardianship proceeding is pending.
Acts 1983, 68th Leg., p. 3725, ch. 576, § 1, eff. Jan. 1, 1984.

§ 181.054. Effect of Release on Multiple Donees

Unless the instrument creating a power provides otherwise, the complete or partial release by one or more donees of a power that may be exercised by two or more donees, either as an individual or a fiduciary, together or successively, does not prevent or limit the exercise or participation in the exercise of the power by the other donee or donees.
Acts 1983, 68th Leg., p. 3725, ch. 576, § 1, eff. Jan. 1, 1984.

§ 181.055. Notice of Release

(a) A fiduciary or other person in possession or control of property subject to a power, other than the donee, does not have notice of a release of the power until the original release or a copy is delivered to the fiduciary or other person.

(b) A purchaser, lessee, or mortgagee of real property subject to a power who has paid a valuable consideration and who is without actual notice does not have notice of a release of the power until the instrument releasing the power is filed for record with the county clerk of the county in which the real property is located.
Acts 1983, 68th Leg., p. 3725, ch. 576, § 1, eff. Jan. 1, 1984.

§ 181.056. Recording

(a) A county clerk shall record a release of a power in the county deed records, and the clerk shall index the release, with the name of the donee entered in the grantor index.

(b) The county clerk shall charge the same fee for recording the release of a power as the clerk is authorized to charge for recording a deed.
Acts 1983, 68th Leg., p. 3725, ch. 576, § 1, eff. Jan. 1, 1984.

§ 181.057. Effect of Failure to Deliver or File

Failure to deliver or file an instrument releasing a power under Sections 181.052 and 181.055 does not affect the validity of the release as to the donee, the person in whose favor the power may be exercised, or any other person except those expressly protected by Sections 181.052 and 181.055.
Acts 1983, 68th Leg., p. 3726, ch. 576, § 1, eff. Jan. 1, 1984.

§ 181.058. Restraints on Alienation or Anticipation

The release of a power that otherwise may be released is not prevented merely by provisions of the instrument creating the power that restrain alienation or anticipation.
Acts 1983, 68th Leg., p. 3726, ch. 576, § 1, eff. Jan. 1, 1984.

Statutes in Context

The 2003 Legislature codified various aspects of the law governing the exercise of powers of appointment when it added Subchapter C. Unless the power of appointment expressly provides otherwise, the donee of a power of appointment may do the following things when exercising the power:

(1) Appoint present, future, or both present and future interests.

(2) Impose conditions and limitations on the appointment.

(3) Impose restraints on alienation.

(4) Appoint interests to a trustee for the benefit of one or more objects of the power.

(5) Create any right existing under the common law.

(6) Grant the objects of the power of appointment the power to appoint the property provided that these powers of appointment must be exercisable only in favor of the objects of the power who would have been permissible objects under the original donee's power.

(7) If the donee has the power to appoint outright to the object of the power, exercise the power to give a power of appointment to the object of the original power. The donee of the original power becomes the donor of the second-generation power. There are no restrictions on the identity of the objects of the second-generation power; in other words, these objects do not have to be permissible objects of the original power of appointment.

Subchapter C. Exercise of Powers of Appointment

§ 181.081. Extent of Power

Unless an instrument creating a power expressly provides to the contrary, a donee may exercise a power in any manner consistent with this subchapter.
Added by Acts 2003, 78th Leg., ch. 551, § 2, eff. Sept. 1, 2003.

§ 181.082. General Exercise

In exercising a power, a donee may make an appointment:

(1) of present, future, or present and future interests;

(2) with conditions and limitations;

(3) with restraints on alienation;

(4) of interests to a trustee for the benefit of one or more objects of the power; and

(5) that creates any right existing under common law.

Added by Acts 2003, 78th Leg., ch. 551, § 2, eff. Sept. 1, 2003.

§ 181.083. Creating Additional Powers

(a) In exercising a power, a donee may make appointments that create in the objects of the power additional powers of appointment. The additional powers of appointment must be exercisable in favor of objects of the power who would have been permissible objects under the original donee's power.

(b) In exercising a power, a donee who may appoint outright to an object of the power may make appointments that create in the object of the power powers exercisable in favor of persons that the original donee may direct, even though the objects of the secondary power of appointment may not have been permissible objects of the original donee's power.

Added by Acts 2003, 78th Leg., ch. 551, § 2, eff. Sept. 1, 2003.

XIV.
TAX CODE

Title 1. Property Tax Code

Subtitle C. Taxable Property and Exemptions

Chapter 11. Taxable Property and Exemptions

Subchapter B. Exemptions

Statutes in Context

Section 11.13 provides a tax exemption for homesteads. Note that § 11.13(j) permits the settlor of a trust in which the settlor placed the settlor's homestead to claim the exemption for tax purposes under certain circumstances.

§ 11.13. Residence Homestead

(a) A family or single adult is entitled to an exemption from taxation for the county purposes authorized in Article VIII, Section 1-a, of the Texas Constitution of $3,000 of the assessed value of his residence homestead.

(b) An adult is entitled to exemption from taxation by a school district of $15,000 of the appraised value of the adult's residence homestead, except that $10,000 of the exemption does not apply to an entity operating under former Chapter 17, 18, 25, 26, 27, or 28, Education Code, as those chapters existed on May 1, 1995, as permitted by Section 11.301, Education Code.

(c) In addition to the exemption provided by Subsection (b) of this section, an adult who is disabled or is 65 or older is entitled to an exemption from taxation by a school district of $10,000 of the appraised value of his residence homestead.

(d) In addition to the exemptions provided by Subsections (b) and (c) of this section, an individual who is disabled or is 65 or older is entitled to an exemption from taxation by a taxing unit of a portion (the amount of which is fixed as provided by Subsection (e) of this section) of the appraised value of his residence homestead if the exemption is adopted either:

(1) by the governing body of the taxing unit; or

(2) by a favorable vote of a majority of the qualified voters of the taxing unit at an election called by the governing body of a taxing unit, and the governing body shall call the election on the petition of at least 20 percent of the number of qualified voters who voted in the preceding election of the taxing unit.

(e) The amount of an exemption adopted as provided by Subsection (d) of this section is $3,000 of the appraised value of the residence homestead unless a larger amount is specified by:

(1) the governing body authorizing the exemption if the exemption is authorized as provided by Subdivision (1) of Subsection (d) of this section; or

(2) the petition for the election if the exemption is authorized as provided by Subdivision (2) of Subsection (d) of this section.

(f) Once authorized, an exemption adopted as provided by Subsection (d) of this section may be repealed or decreased or increased in amount by the governing body of the taxing unit or by the procedure authorized by Subdivision (2) of Subsection (d) of this section. In the case of a decrease, the amount of the exemption may not be reduced to less than $3,000 of the market value.

(g) If the residence homestead exemption provided by Subsection (d) of this section is adopted by a county that levies a tax for the county purposes authorized by Article VIII, Section 1-a, of the Texas Constitution, the residence homestead exemptions provided by Subsections (a) and (d) of this section may not be aggregated for the county tax purposes. An individual who is eligible for both exemptions is entitled to take only the exemption authorized as provided by Subsection (d) of this section for purposes of that county tax.

(h) Joint, community, or successive owners may not each receive the same exemption provided by or pursuant to this section for the same residence homestead in the same year. An eligible disabled person who is 65 or older may not receive both a disabled and an elderly residence homestead exemption but may choose either. A person may not receive an exemption under this section for more than one residence homestead in the same year.

(i) The assessor and collector for a taxing unit may disregard the exemptions authorized by Subsection (b), (c), (d), or (n) of this section and assess and collect a tax pledged for payment of debt without deducting the amount of the exemption if:

(1) prior to adoption of the exemption, the unit pledged the taxes for the payment of a debt; and

(2) granting the exemption would impair the obligation of the contract creating the debt.

(j) For purposes of this section:

(1) "Residence homestead" means a structure (including a mobile home) or a separately secured and occupied portion of a structure (together with the land, not to exceed 20 acres, and improvements used in the residential occupancy of the structure, if the structure and the land and improvements have identical ownership) that:

(A) is owned by one or more individuals, either directly or through a beneficial interest in a qualifying trust;

(B) is designed or adapted for human residence;

(C) is used as a residence; and

(D) is occupied as his principal residence by an owner or, for property owned through a beneficial interest in a qualifying trust, by a trustor of the trust who qualifies for the exemption.

(2) "Trustor" means a person who transfers an interest in residential property to a qualifying trust, whether by deed or by will, or the person's spouse.

(3) "Qualifying trust" means a trust:

(A) in which the agreement or will creating the trust provides that the trustor of the trust has the right to use and occupy as the trustor's principal residence residential property rent free and without charge except for taxes and other costs and expenses specified in the instrument:

(i) for life;

(ii) for the lesser of life or a term of years; or

(iii) until the date the trust is revoked or terminated by an instrument that describes the property with sufficient certainty to identify it and is recorded in the real property records of the county in which the property is located; and

(B) that acquires the property in an instrument of title that:

(i) describes the property with sufficient certainty to identify it and the interest acquired;

(ii) is recorded in the real property records of the county in which the property is located; and

(iii) is executed by the trustor or the personal representative of the trustor.

(k) A qualified residential structure does not lose its character as a residence homestead if a portion of the structure is rented to another or is used primarily for other purposes that are incompatible with the owner's residential use of the structure. However, the amount of any residence homestead exemption does not apply to the value of that portion of the structure that is used primarily for purposes that are incompatible with the owner's residential use.

(l) A qualified residential structure does not lose its character as a residence homestead when the owner who qualifies for the exemption temporarily stops occupying it as a principal residence if that owner does not establish a different principal residence and the absence is:

(1) for a period of less than two years and the owner intends to return and occupy the structure as the owner's principal residence; or

(2) caused by the owner's:

(A) military service outside of the United States as a member of the armed forces of the United States or of this state; or

(B) residency in a facility that provides services related to health, infirmity, or aging.

(m) In this section:

(1) "Disabled" means under a disability for purposes of payment of disability insurance benefits under Federal Old-Age, Survivors, and Disability Insurance.

(2) "School district" means a political subdivision organized to provide general elementary and secondary public education. "School district" does not include a junior college district or a political subdivision organized to provide special education services.

(n) In addition to any other exemptions provided by this section, an individual is entitled to an exemption from taxation by a taxing unit of a percentage of the appraised value of his residence homestead if the exemption is adopted by the governing body of the taxing unit before July 1 in the manner provided by law for official action by the body. If the percentage set by the taxing unit produces an exemption in a tax year of less than $5,000 when applied to a particular residence homestead, the individual is entitled to an exemption of $5,000 of the appraised value. The percentage adopted by the taxing unit may not exceed 20 percent.

(o) For purposes of this section, a residence homestead also may consist of an interest in real property created through ownership of stock in a corporation incorporated under the Cooperative Association Act (Article 1396-50.01, Vernon's Texas Civil Statutes) to provide dwelling places to its stockholders if:

(1) the interests of the stockholders of the corporation are appraised separately as provided by Section 23.19 of this code in the tax year to which the exemption applies;

(2) ownership of the stock entitles the owner to occupy a dwelling place owned by the corporation;

(3) the dwelling place is a structure or a separately secured and occupied portion of a structure; and

(4) the dwelling place is occupied as his principal residence by a stockholder who qualifies for the exemption.

(p) Exemption under this section for a homestead described by Subsection (o) of this section extends only to the dwelling place occupied as a residence homestead and to a portion of the total common area used in the residential occupancy that is equal to the percentage of the total amount of the stock issued by the corporation that is owned by the homestead claimant. The size of a residence homestead under Subsection (o) of this section, including any relevant portion of common area, may not exceed 20 acres.

(q) The surviving spouse of an individual who qualifies for an exemption under Subsection (d) for the residence homestead of a person 65 or older is entitled to an exemption for the same property from the same taxing unit in an amount equal to that of the exemption for which the deceased spouse qualified if:

(1) the deceased spouse died in a year in which the deceased spouse qualified for the exemption;

(2) the surviving spouse was 55 or older when the deceased spouse died; and

(3) the property was the residence homestead of the surviving spouse when the deceased spouse died and remains the residence homestead of the surviving spouse.

(r) An individual who receives an exemption under Subsection (d) is not entitled to an exemption under Subsection (q).

(s) Expired.

Acts 1979, 66th Leg., p. 2234, ch. 841, § 1, eff. Jan. 1, 1980. Amended by Acts 1981, 67th Leg., 1st C.S., p. 127, ch. 13, § 31, eff. Jan. 1, 1982; Acts 1983, 68th Leg., p. 4822, ch. 851, § 6, eff. Aug. 29, 1983; Acts 1985, 69th Leg., ch. 301, § 1, eff. June 7, 1985; Acts 1987, 70th Leg., ch. 547, § 1, eff. Jan. 1, 1988; Acts 1991, 72nd Leg., ch. 20, § 18, eff. Aug. 26, 1991; Acts 1991, 72nd Leg., ch. 20, § 19(a), eff. Jan. 1, 1992; Acts 1991, 72nd Leg., ch. 391, § 14; Acts 1993, 73rd Leg., ch. 347, § 4.08, eff. May 31, 1993; Acts 1993, 73rd Leg., ch. 854, § 1, eff. Jan. 1, 1994; Acts 1995, 74th Leg., ch. 76, § 15.01, eff. Sept. 1, 1995; Acts 1995, 74th Leg., ch. 610, § 1, eff. Jan. 1, 1996; Acts 1997, 75th Leg., ch. 194, § 1, eff. Jan. 1, 1998; Acts 1997, 75th Leg., ch. 592, § 2.01; Acts 1997, 75th Leg., ch. 1039, § 6, eff. Jan. 1, 1998; Acts 1997, 75th Leg., ch. 1059, § 2, eff. June 19, 1997; Acts 1997, 75th Leg., ch. 1071, § 28, eff. Sept. 1, 1997; Acts 1999, 76th Leg., ch. 1199, § 1, eff. June 18, 1999; Acts 1999, 76th Leg., ch. 1481, § 1, eff. Jan. 1, 2000; Acts 2003, 78th Leg., ch. 240, § 1, eff. June 18, 2003.

Title 2. State Taxation

Subtitle J. Inheritance Tax

Chapter 211. Inheritance Taxes

Subchapter B. Inheritance Taxes: Federal Estate Tax Credit and Generation- Skipping Transfer Tax Credit

Statutes in Context

Almost all states impose a tax on at-death transfers. These taxes fall into three main categories. The most common type of death tax imposed by over 35 states including Texas in §§ 211.051 - 211.055 is the *pick-up* tax, also called the *sponge, sop,* or *soak-up* tax. Under this type of tax, the state estate tax is set at the maximum amount of credit which the decedent's estate could claim for paying state death taxes. A pick-up tax is a cost-free tax. The amount of the state death tax is the same as the amount of the federal credit; if the state did not impose the tax, the decedent's estate would owe more tax to the federal government. The decedent's personal representative simply sends two checks, one to the I.R.S. and one to the state government, totaling the same amount that would be owed to the I.R.S. alone if the state did not have an estate tax.

The amount of the federal death tax credit is decreasing rapidly and it will no longer exist as of 2005 (instead, there will be a deduction for state death taxes). The reduction and elimination of the credit will cause a decrease in revenue for pick-up tax states such as Texas.

States may impose two other types of taxes on at-death transfers which may be in place of or in addition to the pick-up tax. The first of these is an estate tax imposed on the privilege of transferring property at death. State estate taxes operate in a similar fashion to the federal estate tax although the property included in the gross estate and the types and amounts of deductions and credits may differ significantly. The second type is an inheritance tax imposed on the heir's or beneficiary's privilege of receiving property. Typically, the closer that the heir or beneficiary is related to the decedent, the lower the rate of tax and the greater the number and size of exemptions.

§ 211.051. Tax on Property of Resident

(a) A tax equal to the amount of the federal credit is imposed on the transfer at death of the property of every resident.

(b) If the estate of a resident is subject to a death tax imposed by another state or states for which the federal credit is allowable, the amount of the tax due under this section is reduced by the lesser of:

(1) the amount of the death tax paid the other state or states and that is allowable as the federal credit; or

(2) an amount determined by multiplying the federal credit by a fraction, the numerator of which is the value of the resident's gross estate less the value of the property of a resident, as defined by Section (c) of this section, that is included in the gross estate and the denominator of which is the value of the resident's gross estate.

(c) Property of a resident includes real property having an actual situs in this state whether or not held in trust; tangible personal property having an actual situs in this state; and all intangible personal property, wherever the notes, bonds, stock certificates, or other evidence, if any, of the intangible personal property may be physically located or wherever the banks or other debtors of the decedent may be located or domiciled; except that real property in a personal trust is not

taxed if the real property has an actual situs outside this state.
Amended by Acts 1981, 67th Leg., p. 2759, ch. 752, § 6(a), eff. Jan. 1, 1982.

§ 211.052. Tax on Property of Nonresident

(a) A tax is imposed on the transfer at death of the property located in Texas of every nonresident.

(b) The tax is an amount determined by multiplying the federal credit by a fraction, the numerator of which is the value of the property located in Texas that is included in the gross estate and the denominator of which is the value of the nonresident's gross estate.

(c) Property located in Texas of a nonresident includes real property having an actual situs in this state whether or not held in trust and tangible personal property having an actual situs in this state, but intangibles that have acquired an actual situs in this state are not taxable.
Amended by Acts 1981, 67th Leg., p. 2759, ch. 752, § (a), eff. Jan. 1, 1982.

§ 211.053. Tax on Property of Alien

(a) A tax is imposed on the transfer at death of the property located in Texas of every alien.

(b) The tax is an amount determined by multiplying the federal credit by a fraction, the numerator of which is the value of the property located in Texas that is included in the gross estate and the denominator of which is the value of the alien's gross estate.

(c) Property located in Texas of an alien includes real property having an actual situs in this state whether or not held in trust; tangible personal property having an actual situs in this state; and intangible personal property if the physical evidence of the property is located within this state or if the property is directly or indirectly subject to protection, preservation, or regulation under the law of this state, to the extent that the property is included in the decedent's gross estate.
Amended by Acts 1981, 67th Leg., p. 2759, ch. 752, § 6(a), eff. Jan. 1, 1982.

§ 211.054. Tax on Property Included in Generation-Skipping Transfer

(a) A tax is imposed on every generation-skipping transfer.

(b) The tax is an amount determined by multiplying the generation-skipping transfer tax credit by a fraction, the numerator of which is the value of the property located in Texas included in the generation-skipping transfer and the denominator of which is the value of all property included in the generation-skipping transfer.

(c) Property located in Texas includes real property having an actual situs in this state whether or not held in trust; tangible personal property having an actual situs in this state; and tangible personal property owned by a trust having its principal place of administration in this state at the time of the generation-skipping transfer.
Amended by Acts 1981, 67th Leg., p. 2759, ch. 752, § 6(a), eff. Jan. 1, 1982.

§ 211.055. Maximum Tax

The amount of tax imposed by this chapter may not exceed the amount of the imposed under Section 2001, Internal Revenue Code, reduced by the unified credit provided under Section 2010, Internal Revenue Code.
Amended by Acts 1981, 67th Leg., p. 2759, ch. 752, § 6(a), eff. Jan. 1, 1982; Acts 2001, 77th Leg., ch. 1263, § 73, eff. Sept. 1, 2001.

XV.
TRANSPORTATION CODE

Title 7. Vehicles And Traffic

Subtitle A. Certificates of Title and Registration of Vehicles

Chapter 501. Certificate of Title Act

Subchapter B. Certificate of Title Requirements

Statutes in Context

Section 501.031 requires certificates of title for motor vehicles to contain a right of survivorship agreement. The inclusion of this language makes it easier for individuals, especially spouses, to hold a motor vehicle in survivorship form. The vehicle will then pass directly to the survivor rather than to will beneficiaries or intestate heirs. The vehicle is a nonprobate asset and would not be listed on the estate inventory.

§ 501.031. Rights of Survivorship Agreement

(a) The department shall include on each certificate of title a rights of survivorship agreement form. The form must:

(1) provide that if the agreement is signed by two or more eligible persons, the motor vehicle is held jointly by those persons with the interest of a person who dies to survive to the surviving person or persons; and

(2) provide blanks for the signatures of the persons.

(b) If the vehicle is registered in the name of one or more of the persons who signed the agreement, the certificate of title may contain a:

(1) rights of survivorship agreement signed by all the persons; or

(2) remark if a rights of survivorship agreement is surrendered with the application for certificate of title or otherwise on file with the department.

(c) Except as provided in Subsection (g), ownership of the vehicle may be transferred only:

(1) by all the persons acting jointly, if all the persons are alive; and

(2) on the death of one of the persons by the surviving person or persons by transferring the certificate of title, in the manner otherwise required by law for transfer of ownership of the vehicle, with a copy of the death certificate of the deceased person attached to the certificate of title application.

(d) A rights of survivorship agreement under this section may be revoked only by surrender of the certificate of title to the department and joint application by the persons who signed the agreement for a new title in the name of the person or persons designated in the application.

(e) A person is eligible to sign a rights of survivorship agreement under this section if the person:

(1) is married and the spouse of the signing person is the only other party to the agreement;

(2) is unmarried and attests to that unmarried status by affidavit; or

(3) is married and provides the department with an affidavit from the signing person's spouse that attests that the signing person's interest in the vehicle is the signing person's separate property.

(f) If the title is being issued in connection with the sale of the vehicle, the seller is not eligible to sign a rights of survivorship agreement under this section unless the seller is the child, grandchild, parent, grandparent, brother, or sister of each other person signing the agreement. A family relationship required by this subsection may be a relationship established by adoption.

(g) If an agreement, other than the agreement provided for in Subsection (a), providing for right of survivorship is signed by two or more persons, the department shall issue a new certificate of title to the surviving person or persons upon application accompanied by a copy of the death certificate of the deceased person. The department may develop for public use under this subsection an optional rights of survivorship agreement form.

Acts 1995, 74th Leg., ch. 165, § 1, eff. Sept. 1, 1995. Amended by Acts 1997, 75th Leg., ch. 165, § 30.39(a), eff. Sept. 1, 1997. Amended by Acts 1999, 76th Leg., ch. 62, § 17.05, eff. Sept. 1, 1999; Acts 1999, 76th Leg., ch. 241, § 1, eff. Sept. 1, 1999.

Title 8. Death and Disposition of The Body

Subtitle B. Disposition of the Body

Chapter 692. Texas Anatomical Gift Act

Statutes in Context

Sections 521.401 - 521.405 explain the interrelationship between anatomical gifts and driver's license designations. Effective September 1, 1997, a driver's license designation is no longer a proper method of making anatomical gifts.

§ 521.401. Statement of Gift

(a) A person who wishes to be an eye, tissue, or organ donor may execute a statement of gift.

(b) The statement of gift may be shown by a card designed to be carried by the donor to evidence the donor's intentions with respect to organ, tissue, and eye donation. A donor card signed by the donor shall be given effect as if executed pursuant to Section 692.003(d), Health and Safety Code.

(c) Donor cards shall be provided to the department by qualified organ or tissue procurement organizations or eye banks, as those terms are defined in Section 692.002, Health and Safety Code. The department shall provide a means to distribute donor cards to interested individuals in each office authorized to issue driver's licenses or personal identification certificates. The department and other appropriate state agencies, in cooperation with qualified organ, tissue, and eye bank organizations shall pursue the development of a combined statewide database of donors.

(d) Effective September 1, 1997, a statement of gift on driver's licenses or personal identification certificates shall have no force and effect, provided, however, that an affirmative statement of gift on a person's driver's license or personal identification certificate executed prior to September 1, 1997, shall be conclusive evidence of a decedent's status as a donor and serve as consent for organ, tissue, and eye removal.

Acts 1995, 74th Leg., ch. 165, § 1, eff. Sept. 1, 1995. Amended by Acts 1997, 75th Leg., ch. 225, § 1, eff. Sept. 1, 1997.

§ 521.402. Revocation of Statement of Gift

(a) To revoke an affirmative statement of gift on a person's driver's license or personal identification certificate made prior to September 1, 1997, a person must apply to the department for an amendment to the license or certificate.

(b) The fee for an amendment is the same as the fee for a duplicate license.

Acts 1995, 74th Leg., ch. 165, § 1, eff. Sept. 1, 1995. Amended by Acts 1997, 75th Leg., ch. 225, § 1, eff. Sept. 1, 1997.

XVI. UNITED STATES CODE

Title 10. Armed Forces

Subtitle A. General Military Law

Part II. Personnel

Chapter 53. Miscellaneous Rights And Benefits

Statutes in Context

Section 551 of the Floyd D. Spence National Defense Authorization Act for Fiscal Year 2001 (codified as 10 U.S.C. § 1044d) provides that a *military testamentary instrument* is exempt from all state law formalities and has the same legal effect as a will prepared and executed under local state law. The statute sets forth the requirements for military testamentary instruments and how to make them self-proved. The motivating factor behind this legislation is that the military lawyers should not be required to learn the law of 50 states to prepare wills for military personnel. With this new legislation, all military lawyers may follow the same procedure without regard to the domicile of their clients. This is especially important when many wills have to be prepared quickly during major military operations.

This legislation could be challenged on tenth Amendment grounds because succession matters were not delegated to the United States by the Constitution and thus are reserved to the states. On the other hand, matters regarding the wills of service personnel are tightly connected with the federal government's right to maintain the military. The case to watch for is one in which the will is valid under the federal law but not under state law and the heirs contest the will.

§ 1044d. Military testamentary instruments: requirement for recognition by States

(a) Testamentary Instruments To Be Given Legal Effect. — A military testamentary instrument —

(1) is exempt from any requirement of form, formality, or recording before probate that is provided for testamentary instruments under the laws of a State; and

(2) has the same legal effect as a testamentary instrument prepared and executed in accordance with the laws of the State in which it is presented for probate.

(b) Military Testamentary Instruments. — For purposes of this section, a military testamentary instrument is an instrument that is prepared with testamentary intent in accordance with regulations prescribed under this section and that —

(1) is executed in accordance with subsection (c) by (or on behalf of) a person, as a testator, who is eligible for military legal assistance;

(2) makes a disposition of property of the testator; and

(3) takes effect upon the death of the testator.

(c) Requirements for Execution of Military Testamentary Instruments. — An instrument is valid as a military testamentary instrument only if —

(1) the instrument is executed by the testator (or, if the testator is unable to execute the instrument personally, the instrument is executed in the presence of, by the direction of, and on behalf of the testator);

(2) the instrument is executed in the presence of a military legal assistance counsel acting as presiding attorney;

(3) the instrument is executed in the presence of at least two disinterested witnesses (in addition to the presiding attorney), each of whom attests to witnessing the testator's execution of the instrument by signing it; and

(4) the instrument is executed in accordance with such additional requirements as may be provided in regulations prescribed under this section.

(d) Self-Proving Military Testamentary Instruments. — (1) If the document setting forth a military testamentary instrument meets the requirements of paragraph (2), then the signature of a person on the document as the testator, an attesting witness, a notary, or the presiding attorney, together with a written representation of the person's status as such and the person's military grade (if any) or other title, is prima facie evidence of the following:

(A) That the signature is genuine.

(B) That the signatory had the represented status and title at the time of the execution of the will.

(C) That the signature was executed in compliance with the procedures required under the regulations prescribed under subsection (f).

(2) A document setting forth a military testamentary instrument meets the requirements of this paragraph if it includes (or has attached to it), in a

form and content required under the regulations prescribed under subsection (f), each of the following:

(A) A certificate, executed by the testator, that includes the testator's acknowledgment of the testamentary instrument.

(B) An affidavit, executed by each witness signing the testamentary instrument, that attests to the circumstances under which the testamentary instrument was executed.

(C) A notarization, including a certificate of any administration of an oath required under the regulations, that is signed by the notary or other official administering the oath.

(e) Statement To Be Included. — (1) Under regulations prescribed under this section, each military testamentary instrument shall contain a statement that sets forth the provisions of subsection (a).

(2) Paragraph (1) shall not be construed to make inapplicable the provisions of subsection (a) to a testamentary instrument that does not include a statement described in that paragraph.

(f) Regulations. — Regulations for the purposes of this section shall be prescribed jointly by the Secretary of Defense and by the Secretary of Homeland Security with respect to the Coast Guard when it is not operating as a service in the Department of the Navy.

(g) Definitions. — In this section:

(1) The term "person eligible for military legal assistance" means a person who is eligible for legal assistance under section 1044 of this title.

(2) The term "military legal assistance counsel" means —

(A) a judge advocate (as defined in section 801(13) of this title); or

(B) a civilian attorney serving as a legal assistance officer under the provisions of section 1044 of this title.

(3) The term "State" includes the District of Columbia, the Commonwealth of Puerto Rico, the Commonwealth of the Northern Mariana Islands, and each possession of the United States.

(Added Pub.L. 106-398, Sec. 1 ((div. A), title V, Sec. 551(a)), Oct. 30, 2000, 114 Stat. 1654, 1654A-123; amended by Pub.L. 107-296, Sec. 1704(b)(1), Nov. 25, 2002, 116 Stat. 2314.)

Title 26. Internal Revenue Code

Subtitle B. Estate and Gift Taxes

Chapter 11. Estate Tax

Subchapter C. Miscellaneous

Statutes in Context

Federal law mandates that life insurance beneficiaries and recipients of property under powers of appointment shoulder their fair share of transfer taxes. See I.R.C. §§ 2206 and 2207. These apportionment statutes are designed to carry out the decedent's presumed intent. Congress believes that most decedents would want the recipients of these transfers to be responsible for their share of the tax rather than for the heirs or the residuary beneficiaries to bear the entire tax burden. If the testator does not agree, the testator may provide otherwise in the will and those instructions will prevail over the apportionment statutes. *See also* Probate Code § 322A.

§ 2206. Liability of life insurance beneficiaries

Unless the decedent directs otherwise in his will, if any part of the gross estate on which tax has been paid consists of proceeds of policies of insurance on the life of the decedent receivable by a beneficiary other than the executor, the executor shall be entitled to recover from such beneficiary such portion of the total tax paid as the proceeds of such policies bear to the taxable estate. If there is more than one such beneficiary, the executor shall be entitled to recover from such beneficiaries in the same ratio. In the case of such proceeds receivable by the surviving spouse of the decedent for which a deduction is allowed under section 2056 (relating to marital deduction), this section shall not apply to such proceeds except as to the amount thereof in excess of the aggregate amount of the marital deductions allowed under such section.

(Aug. 16, 1954, ch. 736, 68A Stat. 402; Oct. 4, 1976, Pub.L. 94-455, title XX, Sec. 2001(c)(1)(H), 90 Stat. 1852.)

§ 2207. Liability of recipient of property over which decedent had power of appointment

Unless the decedent directs otherwise in his will, if any part of the gross estate on which the tax has been paid consists of the value of property included in the gross estate under section 2041, the executor shall be entitled to recover from the person receiving such property by reason of the exercise, nonexercise, or release of a power of appointment such portion of the total tax paid as the value of such property bears to the taxable estate. If there is more than one such person, the executor shall be entitled to recover from such persons in the same ratio. In the case of such property received by the surviving spouse of the decedent for which a deduction is allowed under section 2056 (relating to marital deduction), this section shall not apply to such property except as to the value thereof reduced by an amount equal to the excess of the aggregate amount of the marital deductions allowed under section 2056 over the amount of proceeds of insurance upon the life of the decedent receivable by the surviving spouse for which proceeds a marital deduction is allowed under such section.

(Aug. 16, 1954, ch. 736, 68A Stat. 402; Oct. 4, 1976, Pub.L. 94-455, title XX, Sec. 2001(c)(1)(I), 90 Stat. 1852.)

Statutes in Context

The following example demonstrates the application of I.R.C. § 2207A. Assume that Husband's will provided

that property valued at $300,000 was to be placed in trust with all the income payable to Wife annually. Upon Wife's death, the corpus of the trust was to be distributed to Husband's children from other partners. Husband's estate elected to take the marital deduction treating the entire $300,000 as qualified-terminable interest property (Q-TIP). Wife has just died and the value of the trust property is $1,000,000. Wife's gross estate will include the trust property at its date of death value of $1,000,000. However, the personal representative is entitled to charge this property with the estate tax triggered by the inclusion of the property in Wife's gross estate at the highest marginal rate. This prevents the beneficiaries of the surviving spouse's estate from shouldering the burden of the taxes on the Q-TIP property.

§ 2207A. Right of recovery in the case of certain marital deduction property

(a) Recovery with respect to estate tax

(1) In general - If any part of the gross estate consists of property the value of which is includible in the gross estate by reason of section 2044 (relating to certain property for which marital deduction was previously allowed), the decedent's estate shall be entitled to recover from the person receiving the property the amount by which -

(A) the total tax under this chapter which has been paid, exceeds

(B) the total tax under this chapter which would have been payable if the value of such property had not been included in the gross estate.

(2) Decedent may otherwise direct - Paragraph (1) shall not apply with respect to any property to the extent that the decedent in his will (or a revocable trust) specifically indicates an intent to waive any right of recovery under this subchapter with respect to such property.

(b) Recovery with respect to gift tax - If for any calendar year tax is paid under chapter 12 with respect to any person by reason of property treated as transferred by such person under section 2519, such person shall be entitled to recover from the person receiving the property the amount by which -

(1) the total tax for such year under chapter 12, exceeds

(2) the total tax which would have been payable under such chapter for such year if the value of such property had not been taken into account for purposes of chapter 12.

(c) More than one recipient of property - For purposes of this section, if there is more than one person receiving the property, the right of recovery shall be against each such person.

(d) Taxes and interest - In the case of penalties and interest attributable to additional taxes described in subsections (a) and (b), rules similar to subsections (a), (b), and (c) shall apply.

(Added Pub.L. 97-34, title IV, Sec. 403(d)(4)(A), Aug. 13, 1981, 95 Stat. 304; amended Pub.L. 105-34, title XIII, Sec. 1302(a), Aug. 5, 1997, 111 Stat. 1039.)

Chapter 12. Gift Tax

Subchapter B. Transfers

Statutes in Context

An heir or beneficiary may disclaim property to reduce the person's transfer tax burden. If a disclaimer meets the requirements of a *qualified disclaimer* under I.R.C. § 2518, then the heir/beneficiary is treated as if the person never owned the property. Thus, the heir/beneficiary is not considered to have made a gift when the property passes to another person and the property is not part of the heir or beneficiary's estate.

Compare Probate Code § 37A (disclaimers under intestacy, will, or survivorship agreement) and Property Code § 112.010 (disclaimers of beneficial interests under inter vivos trusts).

§ 2518. Disclaimers

(a) General rule - For purposes of this subtitle, if a person makes a qualified disclaimer with respect to any interest in property, this subtitle shall apply with respect to such interest as if the interest had never been transferred to such person.

(b) Qualified disclaimer defined - For purposes of subsection (a), the term "qualified disclaimer" means an irrevocable and unqualified refusal by a person to accept an interest in property but only if -

(1) such refusal is in writing,

(2) such writing is received by the transferor of the interest, his legal representative, or the holder of the legal title to the property to which the interest relates not later than the date which is 9 months after the later of -

(A) the day on which the transfer creating the interest in such person is made, or

(B) the day on which such person attains age 21,

(3) such person has not accepted the interest or any of its benefits, and

(4) as a result of such refusal, the interest passes without any direction on the part of the person making the disclaimer and passes either -

(A) to the spouse of the decedent, or

(B) to a person other than the person making the disclaimer.

(c) Other rules - For purposes of subsection (a) -

(1) Disclaimer of undivided portion of interest - A disclaimer with respect to an undivided portion of an interest which meets the requirements of the preceding sentence shall be treated as a qualified disclaimer of such portion of the interest.

(2) Powers - A power with respect to property shall be treated as an interest in such property.

(3) Certain transfers treated as disclaimers - A written transfer of the transferor's entire interest in the property -

(A) which meets requirements similar to the requirements of paragraphs (2) and (3) of subsection (b), and

(B) which is to a person or persons who would have received the property had the transferor made a qualified disclaimer (within the meaning of subsection (b)), shall be treated as a qualified disclaimer.

(Added Pub.L. 94-455, title XX, Sec. 2009(b)(1), Oct. 4, 1976, 90 Stat. 1893; amended Pub.L. 95-600, title VII, Sec. 702(m)(1), Nov. 6, 1978, 92 Stat. 2935; Pub.L. 97-34, title IV, Sec. 426(a), Aug. 13, 1981, 95 Stat. 318; Pub.L. 97-448, title I, Sec. 104(e), Jan. 12, 1983, 96 Stat. 2384.)

Title 31. Money and Finance

Subtitle III. Financial Management

Chapter 37. Claims

Subchapter II. Claims of the United States Government

Statutes in Context

See Statutes in Context for Probate Code § 320.

§ 3713. Priority of Government Claims

(a)(1) A claim of the United States Government shall be paid first when —

(A) a person indebted to the Government is insolvent and —

(i) the debtor without enough property to pay all debts makes a voluntary assignment of property;

(ii) property of the debtor, if absent, is attached; or

(iii) an act of bankruptcy is committed; or

(B) the estate of a deceased debtor, in the custody of the executor or administrator, is not enough to pay all debts of the debtor.

(2) This subsection does not apply to a case under title 11.

(b) A representative of a person or an estate (except a trustee acting under title 11) paying any part of a debt of the person or estate before paying a claim of the Government is liable to the extent of the payment for unpaid claims of the Government.

(Pub.L. 97-258, Sept. 13, 1982, 96 Stat. 972.)

TABLE OF CASES

INDEX

Abbreviations

I.R.C.	Internal Revenue Code
TEX. BUS. & COM.	Texas Business and Commerce Code
TEX. CIV. PRAC. & REM.	Texas Civil Practice and Remedies Code
TEX. CONST.	Texas Constitution
TEX. CRIM. PROC.	Texas Code of Criminal Procedure
TEX. DISC. R. PROF. COND.	Texas Disciplinary Rules of Professional Conduct
TEX. FAM.	Texas Family Code
TEX. FIN.	Texas Finance Code
TEX. GOV'T.	Texas Government Code
TEX. HEALTH & SAFETY	Texas Health and Safety Code
TEX. INS.	Texas Insurance Code
TEX. PENAL	Texas Penal Code
TEX. PROB.	Texas Probate Code
TEX. PROP.	Texas Property Code
TEX. R. EVID.	Texas Rules of Evidence
TEX. TAX	Texas Tax Code
TEX. TRANS.	Texas Transportation Code
U.S.C.	United States Code

References are to code sections, rules, and pages. Page references are in *italics*.

SETTLEMENT (*cont.*)
closing administration of estate, TEX. PROB. § 404, *272, 273*
delivery of property, TEX. PROB. § 405A, *273*
ward, TEX. PROB. § 405A, *273*
failure of personal representative to deliver estate, TEX. PROB. § 414, *274*
failure to file final account, TEX. PROB. § 406, *273*
final settlement and accounting, TEX. PROB. § 405, *273*
inheritance taxes, payment of required, TEX. PROB. § 410, *274*
money becoming due pending final discharge, TEX. PROB. § 409, *274*
offsets, credits, and bad debts, TEX. PROB. § 412, *274*

SETTLORS. *See* **TRUST CODE**

SIGNATURES
deceased individual, property rights. *See* **PROPERTY INTERESTS**
disabled individual, notary may sign for, TEX. GOV'T. § 406.0165, *98*

SLANDER
statute of limitations, TEX. CIV. PRAC. & REM. § 16.002, *8*

SMALL ESTATES
application for order of no administration, TEX. PROB. § 139, *209*
collection of upon affidavit, TEX. PROB. § 137, *208*
effect of affidavit, TEX. PROB. § 138, *208, 209*
effect of order, TEX. PROB. § 141, *209*
hearing and order on application, TEX. PROB. § 140, *209*
proceeding to revoke order, TEX. PROB. § 142, *209*
summary proceedings after personal representative appointed, TEX. PROB. § 143, *210*

SPECIFIC PERFORMANCE
statute of limitations, TEX. CIV. PRAC. & REM. § 16.004, *8*

SPENDTHRIFT TRUSTS
provisions for, TEX. PROP. CODE § 112.035, *404, 405*

SPOUSES. *See also* **MARRIAGE**
duty to support, TEX. FAM. § 2.501, *44*
gifts between spouses, TEX. FAM. § 3.005, *45*
incapacitated, guardianship for
accounting, inventory, and appraisement by community administrator, TEX. PROB. § 883B, *371, 372*
attorney ad litem, appointment of, TEX. PROB. § 883D, *372*
community administration, TEX. PROB. § 883, *370, 371*
guardian must deliver community property to community administrator, TEX. PROB. § 884, *372*
notice to court of lawsuits by community administrator, TEX. PROB. § 884A, *372*
recovery of capacity, TEX. PROB. § 883A, *371*
removal of community administrator, TEX. PROB. § 883C, *372*
missing, abandoned, or separated spouse
attorney, appointment of, TEX. FAM. § 3.303, *46, 47*
citation by publication, TEX. FAM. § 3.305, *47*
continuing jurisdiction, TEX. FAM. § 3.307, *47*
court order, TEX. FAM. § 3.306, *47*
homestead, sale of, TEX. FAM. §§ 5.101, 5.102, *54*
management and control of property, TEX. FAM. § 3.301, *46, 47*
notice of hearing, TEX. FAM. § 3.304, *47*
recording order, TEX. FAM. § 3.308, *48*
remedies cumulative, TEX. FAM. § 3.309, *48*
spouse missing on public service, TEX. FAM. § 3.302, *47*
vacating order, TEX. FAM. § 3.307, *47*
right to control deceased's burial or cremation, limitation on, TEX. PROB. § 115, *204*
spousal liability, TEX. FAM. § 3.201, *46*
surviving spouse
allowance in lieu of exempt property, TEX. PROB. §§ 273-277, *241*
family allowance. *See* **FAMILY ALLOWANCE**
homestead property, *38*
delivery of property, TEX. PROB. § 272, *240*
order to set aside, TEX. PROB. § 271, *240*
rights of surviving spouse, TEX. PROB. § 283, *242*

STANDING
guardianships, standing to commence or contest proceeding, TEX. PROB. § 642, *306*
parent-child relationship, adjudication proceedings, TEX. FAM. § 160.602, *70, 71*
Trust Code, TEX. PROP. CODE § 155.011, *427*
will contests, TEX. PROB. § 10, *156*
wrongful death actions, TEX. CIV. PRAC. & REM. § 71.004, *17*

STATE GOVERNMENT
actions against state or political subdivision of, statutes of limitations, TEX. CIV. PRAC. & REM. § 16.061, *13*

STATUTE OF FRAUDS
creation of trust, TEX. PROP. CODE § 112.004, *400*

STATUTE OF USES
validity of trust, TEX. PROP. CODE § 112.032, *403*

STATUTES OF LIMITATIONS
absence from state, effect of, TEX. CIV. PRAC. & REM. § 16.063, *13*
acknowledgment of claim, effect of, TEX. CIV. PRAC. & REM. § 16.065, *14*
actions against state or political subdivision of the state, TEX. CIV. PRAC. & REM. § 16.061, *13*
architects, engineers, interior designers, and landscape architects, suits against, TEX. CIV. PRAC. & REM. § 16.008, *9*
carriers of property, actions against, TEX. CIV. PRAC. & REM. § 16.006, *8, 9*
claim incurred prior to arrival in state, TEX. CIV. PRAC. & REM. § 16.067, *14*
claims, presentment and payment of
barring of untimely claims, TEX. PROB. § 298(b), *245*
time for presentation of, TEX. PROB. § 298(a), *245*
tolling of statute, TEX. PROB. § 299, *245*
closing street or road, actions for relief, TEX. CIV. PRAC. & REM. § 16.005, *8*
complaint naming John or Jane Doe, TEX. CIV. PRAC. & REM. § 16.0045, *8*
construction or repair, suits against persons furnishing, TEX. CIV. PRAC. & REM. § 16.009, *9*
contractual limitations period, TEX. CIV. PRAC. & REM. § 16.070, *14*
and counterclaims and cross-claims, TEX. CIV. PRAC. & REM. § 16.069, *14*
criminal acts, TEX. CRIM. PROC. § art. 12.01. [177-180] [225-228] [215-218], *39*
death, effect of, TEX. CIV. PRAC. & REM. § 16.062, *13*
disability, effect of, TEX. CIV. PRAC. & REM. § 16.001, *7*
failure to return execution, suit against sheriff, TEX. CIV. PRAC. & REM. § 16.007, *9*
five-year period, TEX. CIV. PRAC. & REM. § 16.0045, *8*
foreign judgment, action on, TEX. CIV. PRAC. & REM. § 16.066, *14*
four-year period, TEX. CIV. PRAC. & REM. § 16.004, *8*
guardianship claims procedures, tolling of general statutes of limitations, TEX. PROB. § 787, *346*
jurisdiction, effect of lack of, TEX. CIV. PRAC. & REM. § 16.064, *14*
misappropriation of trade secrets, actions for, TEX. CIV. PRAC. & REM. § 16.010, *9*
notice requirements, TEX. CIV. PRAC. & REM. § 16.071, *14, 15*

TRUSTS (*cont.*)
declaratory judgments, TEX. CIV. PRAC. & REM. § 37.005, *15, 16*
durable power attorney, construction of power
  estate, trust, and other beneficiary transactions, TEX. PROB. § 499, *292, 293*
earmarking trust property, *395*
employees' trusts. *See* **EMPLOYEES' TRUSTS**
as estate planning tool, *396, 397*
fraudulent destruction, removal, or concealment of writing, TEX. PENAL § 32.47, *148*
generally, *395, 396*
inter vivos trusts
  pour-over provisions in wills, *181, 182*
  trustee, devises or bequest to, TEX. PROB. § 58a, *182*
legislation, history of, *397*
liability of trust property, TEX. PROP. CODE § 101.002, *395*
pension trusts, TEX. PROP. CODE § 121.001, *446*
spendthrift trusts and child support payments, TEX. FAM. § 154.005, *61*
Texas Trust Code. *See* **TRUST CODE**
trustees. *See* **TRUSTEES**
Uniform Principal and Income Act. *See* **UNIFORM PRINCIPAL AND INCOME ACT**
Uniform Prudent Investor Act. *See* **UNIFORM PRUDENT INVESTOR ACT**
uses of, *395, 396, 397*

UNCLAIMED PROPERTY
acts of ownership, TEX. PROP. CODE § 71.005, *389*
escheat. *See* **ESCHEAT**
estate funds
  comptroller as indispensable party, TEX. PROB. § 428, *275*
  damages, payment of, TEX. PROB. § 432, *275*
  enforcement of payment by comptroller, TEX. PROB. § 432, *275*
  failure to make payments to comptroller, penalty for, TEX. PROB. § 431, *275*
  failure to notify comptroller, penalty for, TEX. PROB. § 429, *275*
  order to pay funds into state treasury, TEX. PROB. § 427, *274, 275*
  receipt for funds paid to comptroller, TEX. PROB. § 430, *275*
  suit for recovery of funds paid to comptroller, TEX. PROB. § 433, *275, 276*

UNIFORM ANATOMICAL GIFT ACT, *129*. *See also* **ANATOMICAL GIFT ACT**

UNIFORM DECLARATORY JUDGMENTS ACT
construction and interpretation, TEX. CIV. PRAC. & REM. § 37.002, *15*
construction or validity of deed, will, contract or other writing, TEX. CIV. PRAC. & REM. § 37.004, *15*
costs and attorney's fees, TEX. CIV. PRAC. & REM. § 37.009, *16*
judicial review, TEX. CIV. PRAC. & REM. § 37.010, *16*
jurisdiction and power of court, TEX. CIV. PRAC. & REM. § 37.003, *15*
jury trials, TEX. CIV. PRAC. & REM. § 37.007, *16*
parties, TEX. CIV. PRAC. & REM. § 37.006, *16*
person defined, TEX. CIV. PRAC. & REM. § 37.001, *15*
refusal to render, TEX. CIV. PRAC. & REM. § 37.008, *16*
subject matter of relief, TEX. CIV. PRAC. & REM. § 37.004, *15*
supplemental relief, TEX. CIV. PRAC. & REM. § 37.011, *16*
title of act, TEX. CIV. PRAC. & REM. § 37.002, *15*
trusts and estates, declarations relating to, TEX. CIV. PRAC. & REM. § 37.005, *15, 16*

UNIFORM FRAUDULENT TRANSFER ACT
application and construction, uniformity of, TEX. BUS. & COM. § 24.012, *5*
cause of action, extinguishment of, TEX. BUS. & COM. § 24.010, *4, 5*
costs and attorney's fees, award of, TEX. BUS. & COM. § 24.013, *5*
creditors, remedies of, TEX. BUS. & COM. § 24.008, *3, 4*
definitions, TEX. BUS. & COM. § 24.002, *1, 2*
equity principles, TEX. BUS. & COM. § 24.011, *5*
insolvency, TEX. BUS. & COM. § 24.003, *2*
obligation, when incurred, TEX. BUS. & COM. § 24.007, *3*
present and future creditors, TEX. BUS. & COM. § 24.005, *2, 3*
present creditors, TEX. BUS. & COM. § 24.006, *3*
supplementary provisions, TEX. BUS. & COM. § 24.011, *5*
title of act, TEX. BUS. & COM. § 24.001, *1*
transfer, when made, TEX. BUS. & COM. § 24.007, *3*
transferee, defenses, liability, and protection of, TEX. BUS. & COM. § 24.009, *4*
value for transfer or obligation, TEX. BUS. & COM. § 24.004, *2*

UNIFORM PARENTAGE ACT
application and construction, TEX. FAM. § 160.001, *62*
assisted reproduction. *See* **ASSISTED REPRODUCTION**
choice of law, TEX. FAM. § 160.103, *63*
confidentiality, TEX. FAM. § 160.105, *63*
conflict between provisions, TEX. FAM. § 160.002, *62*
definitions, TEX. FAM. § 160.102, *62, 63*
effect of establishment of parentage, TEX. FAM. § 160.203, *63*
genetic testing
  additional testing, TEX. FAM. § 160.507, *70*
  applicability of law, TEX. FAM. § 160.501, *68*
  costs of, TEX. FAM. § 160.506, *69, 70*
  deceased individual, TEX. FAM. § 160.509, *70*
  identical brothers, TEX. FAM. § 160.510, *70*
  order for testing, TEX. FAM. § 160.502, *68*
  rebuttal, TEX. FAM. § 160.505, *69*
  report of, TEX. FAM. § 160.504, *69*
  requirements for, TEX. FAM. § 160.503, *69*
  results, TEX. FAM. § 160.505, *69*
  unauthorized release of specimen, TEX. FAM. § 160.511, *70*
  unavailability of all individuals, TEX. FAM. § 160.508, *70*
gestational agreements. *See* **GESTATIONAL AGREEMENTS**
jurisdiction, authorized courts, TEX. FAM. § 160.104, *63*
marital status of parents, TEX. FAM. § 160.202, *63*
maternity determination, TEX. FAM. § 160.106, *63*
parent-child relationship, establishment of, TEX. FAM. § 160.201, *63*
paternity
  acknowledgment of
    challenge after expiration of period for rescission, TEX. FAM. § 160.308, *65*
    collection and transfer of information concerning, TEX. FAM. § 160.315, *66*
    effect of, TEX. FAM. § 160.305, *65*
    filing fees not required, TEX. FAM. § 160.306, *65*
    forms for, TEX. FAM. § 160.312, *66*
    full faith and credit, TEX. FAM. § 160.311, *66*
    procedure for rescission or challenge, TEX. FAM. § 160.309, *65*
    provision for, TEX. FAM. § 160.301, *64*
    ratification barred, TEX. FAM. § 160.310, *66*
    release of information, TEX. FAM. § 160.313, *66*
    rescission proceeding, TEX. FAM. § 160.307, *65*
    rules for, TEX. FAM. § 160.304, *65*
  denial of
    challenge after expiration of period for rescission, TEX. FAM. § 160.308, *65*